THE BUILDINGS OF ENGLAND

FOUNDING EDITOR: NIKOLAUS PEVSNER
ADVISORY EDITOR: JOHN NEWMAN
EDITOR: BRIDGET CHERRY

NORFOLK 2:
NORTH-WEST AND SOUTH

NIKOLAUS PEVSNER AND BILL WILSON

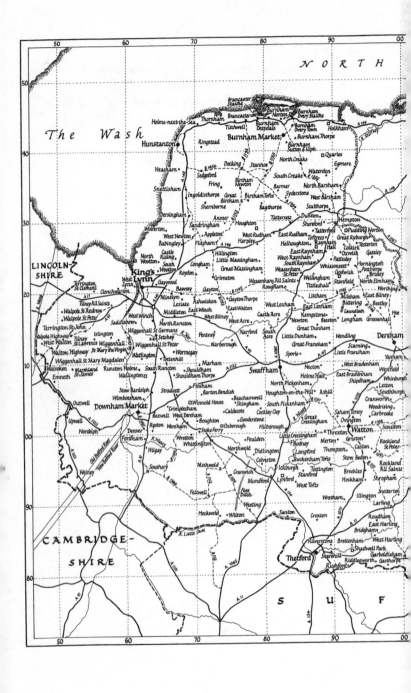

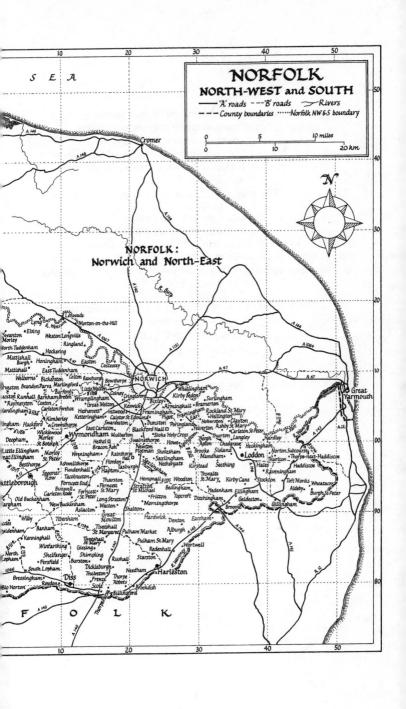

NORFOLK
NORTH-WEST and SOUTH

— 'A' roads   --- 'B' roads   Rivers
--- County boundaries   ···· Norfolk NW&S boundary

0   5   10 miles
0   10   20 km

SEA

Cromer

NORFOLK:
Norwich and North-East

NORWICH

Great Yarmouth

Wymondham

Loddon

Diss   Harleston

FOLK

THE BUILDINGS BOOKS TRUST

is a registered charity established 1994.
It promotes the appreciation and understanding
of architecture by supporting and financing
the research needed to sustain new and revised volumes of
The Buildings of England, Ireland, Scotland and Wales

The trust gratefully acknowledges:

the generous contribution of
THE SAINSBURY FAMILY CHARITABLE TRUSTS
which makes possible the work of revision,
the extension of the series to all the countries of the British Isles,
and the effort to bring appreciation of our architectural heritage
to a wider public

Grants towards the costs of research, writing and illustrations
for this volume from:
THE AMBERSTONE TRUST

THE BRITISH ACADEMY

THE MARC FITCH FUND

THE REEKIE TRUST

Assistance with photographs from
THE ROYAL COMMISSION ON HISTORICAL
MONUMENTS OF ENGLAND

Norfolk 2

NORTH-WEST AND SOUTH

BY

NIKOLAUS PEVSNER

AND

BILL WILSON

THE BUILDINGS OF ENGLAND

PENGUIN BOOKS

PENGUIN BOOKS

Published by the Penguin Group
27 Wrights Lane, London w8 5tz, England
Penguin Putnam Inc., 375 Hudson Street, New York, New York 10014, USA
Penguin Books Australia Ltd, Ringwood, Victoria, Australia
Penguin Books Canada Ltd, 10 Alcorn Avenue, Toronto, Ontario, Canada m4v 3b2
Penguin Books (NZ) Ltd, Private Bag 102902, NSMC, Auckland, New Zealand

Penguin Books Ltd, Registered Offices: Harmondsworth, Middlesex, England

First published 1962
Reprinted 1970, 1973, 1977, 1984, 1990
Second edition 1999
Reprinted with corrections 2000

ISBN 0 14 071060 4

Made and printed in Great Britain
by Butler & Tanner Ltd, Frome and London
Set in 9/10pt Monotype Plantin

FIRST EDITION 'FOR MARK'

SECOND EDITION 'FOR MY FATHER'

CONTENTS

8   CONTENTS

LIST OF TEXT FIGURES AND MAPS

PHOTOGRAPHIC ACKNOWLEDGEMENTS

We are grateful to the following for permission to reproduce photographs:

© Crown copyright RCHME: All photographs except those listed below:

James Austin: 127
Country Life: 112
Martin Charles: 131
A. F. Kersting: 3, 4, 5, 7, 11, 12, 13, 20, 21, 23, 24, 27, 28, 29, 31, 37, 38, 42, 44, 45, 54, 71, 74, 76, 77, 79, 80, 81, 87, 88, 89, 96, 98, 99, 101, 102, 103, 119, 120
Edwin Smith: 1
University of East Anglia: 69, 113

The photographs are indexed in the index of artists, and references to them are given by numbers in the margin of the text.

NOTE: Illustration numbers in the margin of the Introduction refer to either *Norfolk* volume 1 or the present volume, and are therefore indicated as 1/000 or 2/000; in the Gazetteer section the numbers refer only to this volume.

MAP REFERENCES

The numbers printed in italic type in the margin against the place names in the gazetteer of the book indicate the position of the place in question on the index map (pp. 2–3), which is divided into sections by the 10-kilometre reference lines of the National Grid. The reference given here omits the two initial letters (formerly numbers) which in a full grid reference refer to the 100-kilometre squares into which the county is divided. The first two numbers indicate the *western* boundary, and the last two the *southern* boundary, of the 10-kilometre square in which the place in question is situated. For example, Fring (reference 7030) will be found in the 10-kilometre square bounded by grid lines 70 (on the *west*) and 80, and 30 (on the *south*) and 40; Saham Toney (reference 9000) in the square bounded by the grid lines 90 (on the *west*) and 00, and 00 (on the *south*) and 10.

The map contains all those places, whether towns, villages, or isolated buildings, which are the subject of separate entries in the text.

FOREWORD

Norfolk *had to be divided into two volumes as did Sir Nikolaus Pevsner's first edition, and the question of how best to split them caused some debate. But once an alphabetical division was rejected as too frustrating for the reader, the only practical course was to adopt the geographical boundary already established. That boundary follows the* B1105 *from Wells to Fakenham then picks up the river Wensum and trails it to Norwich, and from there by way of the river Yare to Yarmouth. All places which fall on the boundary are taken into the first volume, including Gorleston-on-Sea. In common with other revisions of the* Buildings of England, *the gazetteer describes only that part of the county which existed before local government reorganization in 1974, so for the five parishes* W *and* S *of Gorleston the revised* Suffolk *must be consulted.* * *The introduction that follows is common to both volumes.*

The first edition was one of the more comprehensive of the original volumes, but that alone does not explain the gap of thirty-four years: such is the size of the county that the revision has taken eight years to complete. Indeed, if the reader manages to visit all the buildings described in the text and does nothing else it will account for three years of his or her life. One of the reasons is that the enormous amount of research into vernacular buildings has raised this subject from the byway it was in the late 1950s to a recognized branch of architectural history, with its own journals and institutions. So there is much in the gazetteer concerning small rural houses, farm buildings, windmills and wind-pumps, and, on occasion, tumbledown ruins of clay or timber cottages. Research has also focused on the other end of the scale, so few descriptions of the churches, castles and major country houses have been left unaltered. An attempt at comprehensive coverage has been made for the four major towns – Norwich, Great Yarmouth, King's Lynn and Thetford – but of course it was impossible to achieve. Some buildings I will have missed completely, some seen but not appreciated their significance; there are some to which access was not possible, and some no doubt which did not appeal to me, but which would to others.

Nevertheless, the volumes do include certain buildings as a matter of right: Anglican and Roman Catholic churches before 1900 are all included, as are most built since; Nonconformist chapels generally find a place only if older than 1840, but there is a selection of those built later. Country houses and castles are all included, as are town houses and rural houses of more than very local interest. Of other secular

---

* The parishes are: Belton, Bradwell, Burgh Castle, Fritton and St Olaves, and Hopton.

buildings constraints of space allow only rare mention of the remains of
brick and lime kilns, and similarly railway stations, or former stations,
on branch lines unless they have some other significance. Windmills
and windpumps, as has been implied, receive better attention because
they have such an association with Norfolk. Most church furnishings
are included from before 1900 (except plate, chairs, bells and movable
objects), but furnishings in secular buildings are omitted unless they
form part of a decorative scheme. Buildings demolished since the first
edition are generally mentioned. The few entries in parentheses concern
buildings or interiors unseen by me or other contributors; descriptions
come from sources such as the lists of the Department of Culture, Media
and Sport (DCMS) – formerly Department of National Heritage
(DNH) – or from information provided by correspondents or owners.

Buildings outside towns are described under civil rather than ecclesiastical parishes, though some major buildings (especially country
houses) set away from a village have their own entry. In fairness to all
those owners who showed me round their houses it must be pointed out
that inclusion in the book does not imply that the house is open to the
public. The vast majority are not. Churches are almost invariably
locked, and while it is usually possible to find a keyholder nearby, the
reader must be warned that in a number of cases locating the key
required days of detective work. Some churches are set within the
Stanford Battle Zone, so access even to the land, including the five-
mile-deep cordon sanitaire round the impact zones, requires permits
from the Ministry of Defence. The reason is obvious, and also obvious
is the absence of discussion of military buildings in use as such.

Given that the gestation period of the revision has been so long it is
probably inevitable that the reader will find an occasional description
of a demolished building, so tolerance is requested. As it is, thirty-eight
descriptions have been completely removed or replaced with a footnote
because they were demolished after I visited, and many more were
already unoccupied and in a fragile state, so some must have fallen.
Comments on errors and omissions will, as always, be welcome: the
four boxes of readers' submissions which accumulated after original
publication were a valuable source on their own.

The first acknowledgement to be made is, of course, to Sir Nikolaus
Pevsner. The further the revision progressed, the greater was my admi-
ration for his perception and stamina, and the tone of many of the
gazetteer entries comes from him. Perceptive also is Bridget Cherry,
who as editor read every word and astonished me with her immediate
critical response, often accompanied by sketches of buildings which
revealed some embarrassing deficiencies in the draft descriptions. The
fact that the volumes are not longer than they are is mainly due to her
suggestions for condensing and organization, particularly the Introduction. I am also grateful to John Newman who read and commented
on substantial parts of the text, combining with Bridget Cherry to point
me in the right direction, especially over country houses, churches and
monuments. Of other direct contributors special thanks are due to
Stephen Heywood for his entries on Norwich cathedral, Conventual
Buildings, Bishop's Palace and the Deanery; to John Wymer (JW),
David Gurney (DG) and Andrew Rogerson (AR), all of the Norfolk
Archaeological Unit, for their respective essays on matters ancient and

archaeological in the Introduction, and revision of the gazetteer entries. David Park (DP) revisited Norfolk especially before giving his advice and comments on wall paintings, and Geoffrey Fisher contributed attributions for some C17 and C18 church monuments. Brian Ayres read the introduction to Norwich, long ago when it was three times its length. Where these authorities have contributed to the gazetteer their initials are appended, but any errors are my responsibility.

That the revision would still be in progress without the professionalism and patience of the staff at the Buildings of England office is undeniable, especially Stephany Ungless, her predecessor Kathryn Penn-Simkins, and Elizabeth Williamson. For the illustrations, thanks are due to Susan Rose-Smith for picture research, organization and suggestions, and to the efforts of Steven Cole of the Royal Commission for taking the new photographs themselves. Alan Fagan drew the plans and line drawings, Reg and Marjorie Piggott the maps, but again any mistakes are mine. Elisabeth Ingles was the text editor and Judith Wardman compiled the indexes, both arduous tasks perfectly performed.

Countless other individuals, and staff of many institutions in the county have answered questions or provided material from their own research, so it seems invidious to single some out. Nevertheless, particular thanks are due to Charles Lewis and Damian Eaton (both of Great Yarmouth Museums) for information on Yarmouth, Edwin Rose (sites and monuments officer, Norfolk Landscape Archaeology), the late Alan Canter on the Norwich Survey, Michael Sayer on vicarages, rectories and genealogy, and Birkin Haward for information on stained glass. Thanks must also go to A. Hassell Smith and Richard Wilson, the last two directors of the Centre of East Anglian Studies at the University of East Anglia (U.E.A.), David Lloyd, Mike Brackenbury for maps and information on North Norfolk District, Chris Pearce at West Norfolk, Paul White at Broadland, Stephen Earl at Yarmouth, and Caroline Davison for maps and general information at County Hall. Then there are those whose contributions came by way of general discussion, chief of which in Norfolk is Stephen Heywood, but also Andrea Kirkham on wall paintings, Alastair Ward, Paul Edwards and Colin Jeffries (English Heritage), John Denny, Stefan Muthesius, Rosemary Salt, John Maddison, and Dominika Gaberdiel on medieval patronage in King's Lynn.

Librarians and curators have been cheerful and efficient beyond the call of duty, especially the staff at Norwich (C. Wilkins-Jones and Jean Kennedy); equally helpful have been David Baker and his staff at U.E.A., Alison Gifford, formerly of King's Lynn library, Ron Peabody (archives at Aylsham), David Jones of the Norwich Bridewell Museum and Barbara Green, formerly at the Castle Museum.

Owners of buildings have constantly surprised me by their willingness to give up their time to show me round, and by their appreciation of nice architectural points. That is to be expected (and was found) of Chris Appleton and David Adshead, both of the National Trust, David Holmes of How Hill, Paul Cattermole of Norwich School and Carnary College and Peter Yorke of U.E.A. Private owners who were particularly helpful were J.J.C. Blofeld of Hoveton House, Maggie Whitman at Melton Constable, Sir Ronald Preston of Beeston Hall, S.J. Stearn of Stanfield Hall, Mr and Mrs R.C. Buxton of Kimberley

Hall, Mr and Mrs Sprake of Lodge Farm, Denton, Mrs Margaret
Kelly of King Street, King's Lynn, Mr and Mrs Sproat of Snore Hall,
and Mr and Mrs Fenwick of Geldeston Hall. Firms of architects were
particularly assiduous in finding answers, especially Michael Innes of
Lambert, Scott & Innes, David Luckhurst of Feilden & Mawson,
Chris Ling of J. Owen Bond & Sons, Terry Norton of Wearing,
Hastings & Norton, Dickie Waite, Robert Freakley and Colin Shew-
ring of King's Lynn, Alan Wright of Norwich City Architects,
J. F. Tucker, the County Architect, especially on schools, and Alastair
Brown of Strutt & Parker.

Of those who commented on the first edition and have not already
been acknowledged I should add Michael Riviere; and A. Paget Baggs
and D. M. Young who were also mentioned in the preface to the first
edition. The first edition, and hence this book, was indebted to many
others, in particular the library staff at Norwich (P. Hepworth and
M. Alexander), Great Yarmouth (A. A. C. Hedges) and King's Lynn
(C. H. Senior), I. Cresswell (Norfolk & Norwich Archaeological
Society), G. Rainbird Clarke (Castle Museum, Norwich), R. W
Ketton-Cremer, A. B. Whittingham, A. Stephenson, Rev. C. L. S.
Linnell, B. Cozens-Hardy and Lady Cholmondeley of Houghton.

INTRODUCTION

TOPOGRAPHY

In size, Norfolk is the fourth of the historic counties of England at 1,324,160 acres, but twenty-first in order of population (774,000); that is, it is not an industrialized county. Industry has in fact declined in the last thirty years, but tourism continues to rise in its place, and the shift of population from the country to the towns has been continuous if sporadic since the C19. There are no motorways to Norfolk or within it, for the county is a destination, not a place *en route* to somewhere else. In extent Norfolk is 68 miles E to W and 41 miles N to S. In 1961 the Norwich population was 120,000; in 1991 it was 125,000, hardly more than double its level of a hundred years before, but the satellite towns of Sprowston, Hellesdon, Thorpe St Andrew, Costessey, Taverham and Old Catton have seen huge rises in their population, and in 1991 between them housed 58,000 people. Over a quarter of the population lives within eight miles of Norwich castle; this means that parts of the county are so remote and under-populated that in places it is a wonder that one is less than a hundred miles from London. After Norwich are Great Yarmouth with 47,000, King's Lynn with 35,000 and Thetford with 19,900. A further five towns have populations over 10,000, fourteen between 5,000 and 10,000, seven over 4,000, seven over 3,000 and eighty-six villages and small towns with over 1,000.

It is obvious as one drives through Norfolk that the primary concern is agriculture, but what is less obvious is that it is still a county of landed gentry and estates, for the big houses are usually tucked away out of sight. There are still eight estates with over 10,000 acres and a further fifty-six with over 1,000, and there are countless large consolidated farms with hardly a village or hamlet within their boundaries. It is common in Norfolk to see a big medieval church standing isolated with only a single farmhouse for company, and in places not even that. The churches, as well as the numerous big villages, are one of the signs of the great riches of Norfolk's past, and there are a prodigious number of them: 659, according to Cautley, of before 1700, and that does not include nearly a hundred ruined ones or any of the fifty or so monastic houses which have either completely disappeared or survive only as ruins. No other county in England can compete with these figures.

The SCENERY of Norfolk is certainly varied and not as flat as strangers to the county seem to think. Gas Hill in Norwich is as

steep as Steep Hill in Lincoln, and the Cromer ridge behind
Sheringham rises to 300 ft, sharply descending N to the sea, more
gently to the S. The western chalk escarpment running N–S from
Holme-next-the-Sea to Thetford in the SW is just as high, but in
the main Norfolk has a gently rolling green landscape. There are
four completely distinct and celebrated regions within the county,
all of them to one degree or another man-made, or at least the
combination of glaciation and human effort. An entirely man-
1/1 made element is the Broads, which began as a series of about fifty
shallow pits dug from the C10 to the late C13 in order to exploit
the peat deposits (see p. 37). The low-lying landscape under the
tremendous East Anglian sky is well provided with rivers – the
1/2 Bure, Yare, Chet, Waveney, Ant and Thurne among them – and
it is still a mystery how the pits were kept drained. In the end the
decline in peat-burning, the rise in coal imports and the change
in climate which affected NW Europe after 1250 brought higher
sea-levels and the end of the pits. In 1287 there was a major flood,
and it seems likely that by the first half of the C14 those pits which
remained were deliberately flooded to create fisheries. So today
the visitor to the Broads can be startled by the sight of sails
apparently gliding through the reed beds in a landscape where
the water is not immediately visible.

   The Wash is a product of glaciation, and until the C17 extended
much further inland than today, but great drainage schemes
reclaimed a huge area and created the Marshland S and E of
King's Lynn and the Fens round Downham Market, Wisbech
and a corner of Cambridgeshire. The Marshland is basically a
reclaimed salt-water estuary, to the extent that in the Terrington
marshes the division between land, marsh, sands and finally the
open water of the Wash is difficult to define and stretches for
six miles or more. Human presence is represented by scattered
farmsteads, but there is no lack of competition for these holdings
because the silts and clays are the most agriculturally productive
in Britain. The Fens, of course, also have their origins in glaciation, but the drainage had a different result, for this is a second
peat region. Once drained, the peat, it seems, began to dry and
in drying shrank by as much as ten feet. So the land is today not
only below sea-level but below the level of the rivers which flow
through it; the landscape is one of dykes.

   Breckland could hardly be more different, but it too owes its
present appearance to human activity. It is a large expanse of
2/1 heathland in SW Norfolk and NW Suffolk consisting of chalk beds
overlaid with glacial sands and gravels. It was heavily wooded,
but in the Iron Age clearance began to create open pasture for
sheep, and resulted in erosion of the light sands to produce heath.
Farmers always struggled on this land and during the agricultural
depression of the late C19 many farms were abandoned and large
areas reverted to scrub. Through this process Breckland has
become one of the most important lowland heaths in Britain and
is one of the dwindling habitats of the sand lizard. The best parts
of the heath are, not surprisingly, in the Stanford Battle Zone. In
1922 the hand of man again altered the appearance of large parts
of Breckland, this time when the Forestry Commission created

the largest lowland coniferous forests in the country, the biggest portion bounded by Thetford in the SE, Mundford in the NE, Brandon in the W and Elveden in the S (both the last in Suffolk). The landscape here looks like some parts of North Germany, and provides a foothold for the red squirrel.

GEOLOGY

The solid geology of Norfolk has as its base a platform of ancient Precambrian and Palaeozoic rocks which incline downwards from a depth of 650 ft in the W to 3,200 ft below sea-level in the E.

Of more immediate interest are the later sedimentary layers, mostly of the Cretaceous Period (70–140 million years ago), which form the chalk foundation of the county as we see it today. The oldest of these rocks and deposits are in the W, but they were continually formed in sheets extending across the centre and eastern parts of Norfolk. However, comparatively little of the countryside resembles the familiar south-eastern English downland, although the general line of the Chilterns and the Cambridgeshire Gog Magog Hills continues into the western chalk escarpment, which has older rocks immediately W forming a buffer between the higher ground and the low muds and silts of the Fens.

To go into more detail, there are several distinct geological formations which can be separated into sometimes narrow, sometimes wide N–S bands. The first band is of the Jurassic Period, underlying the Fens and covered by subsequent layers of sedimentary material scoured out by prehistoric ice sheets to form the Wash and the Fens themselves. The Oolitic and Liassic limestones provided by these layers are accessible near the surface only about forty miles further W, and play no part in the visible geology of Norfolk. Working E are two narrow belts of Cretaceous sandstone sandwiched between the Fens and the E coast of the Wash on the one hand and the chalk escarpment on the other, overlying so that on the coast they appear one above the other. The dividing line runs from Hunstanton to Hockwold but neither deposit is more than ten miles wide, and in places as narrow as one. The W band is made up of Lower Cretaceous sands, here cemented by iron oxides to produce carstone, one of the three building stones in Norfolk. It has a coarse gritty texture, is in a range of dark chocolate-brown colours from the oxides with which it is bound, and is prone to fracturing and weathering.

Hunstanton cliffs, the top geological sight of Norfolk, marks 2/2 the dividing line between the carstone to the W and the band of later upper Cretaceous chalk which extends five miles along the coast to Titchwell. This layer provided clunch, an easily quarried white chalk which, after drying, provides soapy uniform blocks of moderate durability for building, and has excellent qualities for carving. The Hunstanton cliffs also reveal another layer, separating the two described, of red chalk in a seam only 3–4 ft thick.

This has occasionally been used in local buildings. The clunch layer has its E boundary at the ridge of the chalk escarpment which falls gently away over central and eastern Norfolk. No longer is the chalk which covers the remaining three-quarters of the county the hard Cretaceous material suitable for building, but instead it consists of comparatively soft flint-bearing deposits. From it are extracted the nodules of flint which form the most widespread building stone, indeed building material, in the county.

The wide chalk plain forming Norfolk E of a line from Titchwell to Thetford has been covered by glacial clay and gravel; on the Breckland Heath by sand and gravel; and E of Norwich by marine silt deposited by the receding North Sea. The glaciers brought Kimmeridge clay and more friable chalk from the Midlands, dark Cromer Till from Scandinavia to the NE of the county, and later Norwich brick-earth inland. So it is only in the valley floors about Norwich and again at the coast at Sheringham and Trimingham that the great chalk sheets can be seen, but the overlying clays proved as important after the C17 for the buildings of the county as did flint, and more so than carstone or clunch, for most of them proved ideal for brick production.

BUILDING MATERIALS

FLINT is the ubiquitous building stone in the county. Nodules are, or were, found lying in the fields everywhere E of the western chalk escarpment, washed out by the rivers in valleys or piled up on the seashore where the action of waves has weathered out the less durable chalk beds which contain them. White-encrusted flint nodules come in every size, from that of a cricket ball to 3–4 ft across, and are capable of being split into even shapes revealing the hard black or grey-black interior silica. As a building material it has two advantages: it is exceptionally durable and readily available, to the extent that enough can be gathered by hand at, say, East Runton beach to keep pace with the construction of a house. Beach pebbles along the N and E coast are an analogous material, but rounded to uniform size and shape by the action of the sea. They are used along the Norfolk coast in the walls of houses and cottages, just as on the coast of Sussex. But Norfolk is the county *par excellence* for flint building.

Prehistoric man used flint for tools and weapons, but for building it had to wait for the Romans and the introduction of mortar, so the earliest flint buildings in Norfolk are at the C3 fort at Caister-on-Sea and the C3 and C4 fortified town of Caistor St Edmund. The walls of both were built of whole or roughly-cut flints bedded in mortar several feet thick. Each layer of 3–4 ft was allowed to harden before the next was applied, separated at Caister by bands of tiles for added strength. This basic technique, usually without lacing bands, remained the same in subsequent

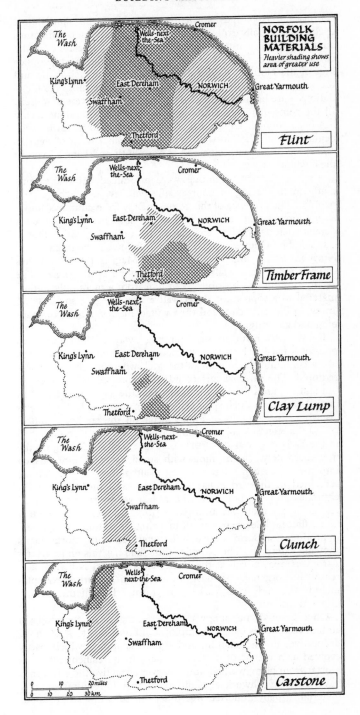

NORFOLK
BUILDING
MATERIALS
*Heavier shading shows
area of greater use*

Flint

Timber Frame

Clay Lump

Clunch

Carstone

centuries. Saxon and Norman churches rely on flint almost
exclusively, usually exposed and laid in rough courses, sometimes
augmented by a little carstone or imported freestone at the
corners, such as at St Mary, Roughton. Even the prestige buildings of the Norman period – the cathedral, Norwich castle and
the castles of the Norman magnates, and all the monastic foundations – are built of coursed flint bedded in fat layers of mortar.
In the ruins this is evident where the covering limestone facing
has been robbed. Unfaced flint was always used in town walls,
beginning with the Norwich cathedral precinct walls of the C11
and those of Norwich city, and at Yarmouth and King's Lynn in
the C13 and C14.

A number of new techniques were introduced, and refinements
made in the laying of courses of small, even, beach or field
pebbles. The evidence of this comes mainly from churches, and it
is in churches that one first notices the use of brick or stone for
details such as window and door surrounds, for which flint is
less suitable. Domestic buildings soon followed: the fragmentary
Norman house under the Norwich Magistrates' Court has
coursed whole flint walls dressed with stone at the angles. The
desire to refine the possibilities of flint from a mere bulk walling
material to a sophisticated decorative agent began, so far as we
know, in the early C14, and the two techniques used were knapping and galleting.

KNAPPING involved the chipping away of flint lumps to
present a flat black surface at one end, the lump tapering away
like a cone into the interior of the wall, where much mortar was
required. The external surface was therefore smooth and glassy,
but still required plenty of mortar to fill the gaps. The early C14
chapel of St James's Hospital, Horning, is an example, but here as
elsewhere the amount of infill mortar on the surface compromised the effect. A solution, employed at the Norwich Guildhall
in the early C15, was GALLETING. This involved making up the
interstices between the flints with small flakes of flint pushed
into the exposed mortar, masking it altogether. The technique
remained in the vernacular vocabulary until the C19, but for
churches and the houses of the rich a yet more sophisticated
and costly solution was invented, SQUARED KNAPPING. Slightly
larger flint nodules were not left in a circular section but squared,
to produce a uniform surface of flint with few or no mortar joints
showing externally. The Norwich Guildhall has this on its rebuilt
S front as does a wall at the Bridewell Museum, Norwich, also
rebuilt but originally dating from the late C14. Earlier examples
include the early C14 work at the former Benedictine Priory,
Great Yarmouth.

Once squared knapping was mastered the most spectacular of
all flint techniques could be employed, FLUSHWORK. It is wholly
decorative, unlike galleting and square knapping which partly
evolved as a means of protecting the soft, unresilient medieval
mortar from being washed out, however attractive the effect may
have been. Flushwork also differs in that it requires another
material, usually imported freestone, but sometimes indigenous

carstone. Panels of ashlar about 2 in. thick were cut to shape and
cemented to the flint of the bare walls, and the cut-out shapes
filled with finely squared knapped flints, providing an effective
and occasionally dramatic play between the dark flint and the
lighter stone. The earliest known flushwork occurs simultaneously
at three sites. Probably the earliest is at the Friary gatehouse,
Burnham Norton, in about 1320. Here are blind Dec windows
and intersecting designs laid with flint and limestone, but the two
elements are not yet flush. A more accomplished example is St
Ethelbert's Gate, Norwich, c. 1316–20, which has intersecting
patterns on the inner face, while Butley Priory gatehouse, Suffolk,
has full-blown Curvilinear designs in addition to chequerwork
patterns.*

The finest example in Norfolk is at St Michael Coslany, 1/60
Norwich, which received in the early C16 elaborate tracery patterns on the S aisle and chancel, but equally instructive is the
flushwork on the E end, which is of the 1880s and a reminder that
it was the C19 which brought the technique to its height. Although
coursed and rubble flint was used for vernacular building right
into the C20, the Gothic Revival resuscitated the technique for
polite buildings. Squared and knapped grey flint is the material
for St Margaret, Thorpe Market, paid for by Lord Suffield in
1796, and similar flintwork covers nearly the entire surface of
Beeston Hall, Beeston St Lawrence, of the 1780s.

The Saxons favoured CARSTONE for church quoins, as did the
Normans where imported freestone was unavailable, but, apart
from isolated places such as Bessingham and Wickmere, large-
scale use from the C13 contracted to its mined area, as at the
Wiggenhalls and Denver. In the later Middle Ages the material
continued to lose favour, being found in only about twenty churches
after 1300, finally appearing in 1476 at Fincham. Although the
geographical constraint applies also to secular buildings, the
chronology was rather different, though meaningful discussion of
its use before the C16 is hampered by lack of surviving buildings.
It is used in Norwich castle and in the late C14 gatehouse at
Pentney Priory, and in the mid C15 at the Tudor Rose Hotel in
King's Lynn, but it is the C17 which sees the start of a minor
fashion, usually combined with brick dressings (Old Hall,
Snettisham; Church Cottage, North Wootton) or with brick in
equal proportions (West Hall, Sedgeford; Trinity Hospital,
Castle Rising). C18 owners in the carstone belt made use of the
material, especially in stables (Houghton Hall), outbuildings,
barns (Church Farm, Grimston) and mills (Narborough and
Snettisham). In the C19 it extended to lodges, almshouses, estate
houses and schools. It was again used for major buildings when the
various forms of vernacular revival came in, such as at Hunstanton
Convalescent Home of 1872–4, and indeed in great parts of the
New Hunstanton development after 1861. Downham Market also
has many C19 carstone buildings, and the villages around likewise.

* Butley Priory is usually dated to c. 1320–5 on the basis of heraldry, but the
Curvilinear tracery patterns cannot be earlier than the 1330s, suggesting that the
most spectacular of the flushwork is a later addition.

E. S. Prior thought it suitable for Home Place (Thornfield Residential Home) near Holt in his Arts and Crafts vision of 1903–5,
forgetting that this was an imported material, even if imported
from the Snettisham quarries only thirty miles away. After the
First World War carstone use virtually ceased.

Some flint techniques were applied to carstone: at Wallington
Hall, of *c.* 1525, is chequered brick and carstone; at Hunstanton
Hall in *c.* 1625–40 *William Edge* provided carstone and flint
chequerwork; at Cliff Farmhouse, Hunstanton, the carstone is
chequered with clunch. Coursed carstone must have been an
early feature, so obvious is the technique, but circumstances
conspire to give us a first example at the Octagon at Hunstanton
Hall in *c.* 1640, then in 1643 at the Old Rectory, Ringstead.
Thereafter, regular courses were normal. Galleting was introduced to carstone walls in the C18 (stables at Ryston Hall; Hall
Farmhouse, East Winch) but most used, it seems, around 1800.
Then there are the curious carstone SLIPS, which appear at about
the time that galleting passed out of fashion. These are the same
size and shape as fat plaintiles and are laid just like brick, as at
School House, Grimston, in 1830 or the Club, West Newton, in
1873. They were popular on the Sandringham estate.

The story of CLUNCH is simpler. The clunch deposits broadly
share the same W boundary as carstone but extend further E and
S, through Swaffham to Thetford. There was only one way to lay
it, in courses like blocks of ashlar, and in this clunch was a
direct substitute, though nowhere near as durable. It was used in
monastic houses from where it was robbed, especially in Thetford,
but surprisingly is unknown in parish churches. The Chantry
House, Oxborough, of 1483 has it, but there is very little from the
C16. A slight revival occurred in the C17 and C18, mainly in
boundary walls in Thetford, barns (Dersingham barn, 1671; the
barn at Old Severall's Road, Methwold, 1697) and some farmhouses (Town Farmhouse, Brancaster, late C17; Barrett Ringstead
Farmhouse, Ringstead, 1714). Grady's Hotel in Swaffham has
a groin-vaulted clunch cellar dated 1765, and in the C19 the
material is represented at Grove Farmhouse, Marham, and at
Castle House, Thetford, in combination with brick. But it was
brick which won the day.

So it is time to gather together the first specimens of BRICK in
Norfolk. Until about 1370 brick, probably always locally made,
was confined to a minor role.* There is some of the late C11
in the Norwich precinct walls and at Hickling Priory are three
doorways with C13 brick arches. In the S range of Hampton
Court, King's Lynn, brick is left visible in the early C14, but early
use was in the main confined to undercroft vaults, such as at
Strangers' Hall, Norwich, and the Norwich Guildhall undercroft,
or, more extensively, at Nos. 3–4 Market Place, Thetford. Clench-
warton church, W of King's Lynn, was provided with a C14

---

* Brick may have been occasionally imported from the Low Countries, but it was
much cheaper to make on site, even if a foreign brickmaker was required to show
how it was done, but it is not a difficult technique once discovered. From the early
C14 Hull could provide brickmakers in plenty.

brick tower, the Greyfriars' tower at Lynn is of brick with stone
dressings possibly of 1364, and, staying with church architecture,
there are brick Perp porches (Feltwell, East Winch, Hardwick),
and piers (St Swithin and St Augustine, both Norwich, and at
Honing), not to mention clerestories and numerous top stages of
towers. When brick is the principal material for main walls as at
the two Wiggenhall St Marys or St Nicholas, King's Lynn, of
before 1419, or for more towers (Walpole St Andrew), then the
material may be said to have arrived. In the 1490s Shelton church
was built entirely of brick. Secular buildings kept pace. The
Norwich Bridewell undercrofts of c. 1370 embrace brick enthusiastically, and brick is laid over a flint core in the Cow Tower,
Norwich, of 1389–90. At about the same date is the stone and
brick hall at Nos. 7–9 King Street, King's Lynn, and of 1410–20 2/52
at St George's Guildhall in Lynn, and then a whole series of major 1/47
C15 brick houses starting with Drayton Lodge and Caister Castle,
West Caister, of the 1430s to Oxburgh Hall, Oxborough, in the
1480s. In the C16 are the brick manor houses at Great Snoring,
East Barsham and Great Cressingham which employ TER- 2/69
RACOTTA as part of their decorative schemes (typically a finer
stuff with a higher proportion of sand, moulded into a decorative
pattern and fired at higher temperatures).

Once brick had become accepted in the C15 for major houses
it filtered into vernacular buildings of all types, although until
c. 1550 it was used mainly for visible enrichment rather than as the
principal material. The E range of Hampton Court, King's Lynn,
has brick NOGGING between the timber studs of c. 1480;
there are remains of nogging a decade later at the Ancient House
Museum, Thetford, at the C15 Telephone Museum, St Andrew's
Street, Norwich, and at the early C16 Martyr's Cottage, East
Bilney. Herringbone nogging appears by the C16 (No. 20 Princes
Street, Norwich). Brick used as a dressing to the corners and
openings of flint buildings began early (remains of a late C14
house at Nos. 221–222 Northgate Street, Yarmouth; Warren 2/74
Lodge, Thetford, early C15) but is represented more fully in
the C16, e.g. Manor House, Brundall; Dove House Farmhouse,
Potter Heigham; Sharrington Hall (alterations); Abbey House,
Binham. At Geofferey the Dyer House, Worstead, the flint is laid
in courses with brick.

A favourite Norfolk strategy was to sandwich a timber-framed
building between brick gable-ends, or to add gables to older
houses. The most spectacular specimen is at The Old Vicarage, 2/57
Methwold, early C16, but more typical are Old Boyland Hall and
Grange Farmhouse, both in Bressingham, all with stepped gables.
Numerous other examples could be cited, for stepped gables are
a hallmark of C16 and C17 houses in the county. The earliest are
late C15: Nos. 20–22 Damgate, Wymondham. For chimneystacks
brick was the only practical material in a county with little stone.
Once accepted for gable-ends to timber buildings, brick extended
its scope to ground floors, particularly in towns where fire was a
risk, and usually mixed with flint. Norwich is the place for that
(see Introduction to Norwich, p. 183), but Hampton Court in

King's Lynn was built this way in the early C14, and in the early C16 are three houses in Common Place, Little Walsingham; there is also the Manor House, Great Walsingham. Yarmouth has none for it is outside the timber-framed zone (although it has one timber house, and so has neighbouring Gorleston-on-Sea).

Until the railways revolutionized transport, brick kilns were set up where they were needed by itinerant brickmakers, who were probably also bricklayers, only to be dismantled when the job was complete. These were temporary clamps, but from the C17 permanent kilns were built near towns that provided continuous demand. There are none of the former remaining in Norfolk and few of the latter, though in the early C19 the county mustered around 200 brickyards, distributed very evenly. After the Second World War the industry virtually ceased. In Tharston, s of Norwich, in the 1840s two million bricks were burnt to construct the railway from Diss to Norwich, and as late as *c.* 1890 a kiln was built at Mundesley to provide bricks for the proposed Cliftonville Estate, but only because the railway had yet to reach the town.

The premier maker of MOULDED AND DECORATIVE BRICK tiles and parts for stacks, windows and so forth was *George Gunton*, who founded his works at Costessey between 1836 and 1845 initially to supply Costessey Hall (completed in 1855). However, he soon looked for wider outlets for the product, COSSEYWARE, advertising in the *Norwich Mercury* on 5 April 1851: 'George Gunton returns his sincere thanks for past favours, and respect-fully begs to announce that he has on hand a large assortment of ornamental chimneys, Norman and Elizabethan window frames, cornices and copings, and every description of moulded bricks, at reasonable prices'. The ornaments were a particular favourite with local Edwardian architects (e.g. Britannia Chambers on Thorpe Road, Norwich) and had a small market elsewhere. The Costessey works closed after the First World War, but *William Gunton* had in 1896 bought the brickworks at Barney, in 1902 those at Little Plumstead and in 1904 the East Runton yard, so production continued until all works ceased in 1939. Nationally, the most celebrated producer of ARTIFICIAL STONE was the firm of *Coade & Sealy*, founded in Lambeth in 1769. Apart from some church monuments COADE STONE is used by *Samuel Wyatt* in *c.* 1782 at the Orangery at Blickling (plaques of interlacing circles), plaques in Adam's style were applied to the Chedgrave Lodges at Langley Park in 1790 by *Soane*, and a plaque designed by *Berna-sconi* decorates the pediment of East Lodge, Holkham Park, of 1799. *Soane* used pre-cast Ionic capitals for the façade at Shotes-ham Park begun in 1784, there is a statue of Justice of 1799 at Thetford Guildhall and the figures at the top of Nelson's Column in Yarmouth of 1817–19 were originally of this material.

The most obvious building material in a rural county is TIMBER, but the ancient woodlands of Norfolk had, even by the time of Domesday, been so eroded that serious stands of timber existed only in the s. On the Breckland Heath and in the western Fens or the eastern Broads there was hardly any at all, and timber for building was expensive. The corporation at Lynn in the 1650s, for instance, was paying 14d. a foot for oak trees, before any of the expenses of carriage and sawing, but in the same years 13s. a thousand for bricks. This partly explains the precocious rise of brick and the extensive use of flint. When timber-framed buildings were dismantled or collapsed it was the normal thing to recycle, so many buildings have moulded bridging beams sometimes a century older than the rest of the building: it makes dating difficult and is a nightmare for those relying on dendrochronological techniques. Hardwick Hall, for example, has been dated to *c.* 1540 on the evidence of the timbers of the jettied s gable-end, but is in reality C17, and when the open hall at Beech Farmhouse, Shipdham, was floored in the C17, C16 bridging beams were inserted. Many examples will be noted in the gazetteer. Although there is no direct evidence, it is likely that some new houses were specifically designed to accommodate available second-hand timbers. Such was the shortage of timber that from the C15 one of the chief bulk imports through King's Lynn was Baltic fir and deal for distribution inland. Vanessa Parker reports a house on Common Staithe, King's Lynn, built in 1612 using only Baltic fir, deal and even imported oak.

There are no cruck-framed buildings in Norfolk; here all is box framing, that is, the trusses consist of a series of vertical studs linked by a tie-beam and support a pair of rafters meeting at the apex of the roof. Arched or straight braces may be provided to support the tie-beams, and there can be any amount of variations to the roof structure itself. The different parts of each truss were typically made in the carpenter's workshop and assembled on the ground in accordance with a numbering sequence, then raised to the vertical and linked to each other with a longitudinal wall-plate at tie-beam level. Into this skeleton went the remaining structural elements, all jointed into the next and fixed with wooden pegs, some joints requiring considerable ingenuity. In Norwich timber as the principal walling material began to wane after about 1500, particularly after the 1507 fire; in King's Lynn the last major timber house was the Greenland Fishery of 1605; Thetford is close to the timber-framed area, but this material was eschewed in favour of flint (the huge forests round Thetford are C20 plantations); at Wymondham timber remained a major material into the C18. In the main timber-framed region indicated on the distribution map construction carried on until the C19.

External CLADDING to timber-framed buildings was by means of wattle-and-daub panels, which remain in fragmentary condition in some houses of before 1500 (The Bell Hotel, Thetford), but the majority have had so many additions, alterations and refrontings that the frame, let alone the cladding, may be difficult to determine. In the early C19 it was common for worn-out wattle panels to be replaced with clay lump.

For buildings constructed of unbaked earths s Norfolk contributes CLAY LUMP. Suitable clay is pounded by a horse or cow in a shallow pit in order to mix a binding agent such as horsehair or straw, then pushed into bats or moulds about 12 x 9 x 6 in. in size and dried in the air. The resulting blocks were cemented together using a clay slip. It was essential that clay lump, like all clay buildings, had a solid flint or brick plinth, was protected at the top and was either limewashed or tarred. Tar was usual on farm buildings. The timber-frame and clay-lump regions of Norfolk mostly coincide, and it seems that from the C15 clay lump was used as an infill in external walls, but on its own in internal partitions. However, the first surviving houses are early C17 (Valley Farmhouse, Bressingham, and a barn at Great Ellingham Old Hall), the method becoming more common later in the century, such as at The Hassocks in Merton of c. 1650 or at All Hallows Farmhouse, Ditchingham, before 1688. The C18 has many examples, but it was not until the second half of the C18 that buildings other than outshuts or small farm outbuildings were constructed entirely of clay lump. Thompson, Carbrooke, Garboldisham and Blo Norton are all villages with considerable C18 survivals, usually of one storey and attic. It is obvious that clay lump was employed mainly in houses low on the social scale, and it must be the case that even in a wooded portion of the county a great many more dwellings were of clay than have survived to the present day. A decline began in the C19, although the material had a certain cachet for richer clients. Pheasantry Cottage at Starston, built in c. 1840, is of clay lump, and there is some also in Majority Cottage at East Carleton, remodelled in 1848 for Sir John Boileau's son. But its use by *Skipper* in 1919 for council houses in Garboldisham and East Harling was a revival, not a survival of the technique.

The picture of ROOFING MATERIALS in Norfolk was, until the railways brought Welsh slate to the towns, one of plaintiles, pantiles and thatch. PLAINTILES are as old as brick, and were fired in the same kilns, and in fact tiles and brick might have been considered together. Such was the extent of the distribution of plaintiles in the S and E of England that an attempt was made in 1477 to standardize their dimensions to $10\frac{1}{2}$ x $6\frac{1}{4}$ x $\frac{5}{8}$ in. They were used, as was brick, first in the better houses, later in vernacular buildings. PANTILES are completely different, not just for their shallow serpentine form and greater size (since the early C18 $13\frac{1}{2}$ x $9\frac{1}{2}$ x $\frac{1}{2}$ in.) but also in their origins, for they are a Dutch invention. The first imports were C17, but even in the ports the chances of viewing pantiles of that date are slim, for they were probably all replaced in the C18 and C19 by indigenous tiles (there are some C17 Dutch pantiles at Hull; *see Yorkshire: York and the East Riding*). English production on any scale began only in c. 1710. In Norfolk the earliest use is around 1740 (The Gables, Brundall, and on a barn at Booton Hall), though the earliest datable building which has a claim to having been pantiled from the start is the Old Meeting House in Norwich of 1693, which has Flemish connections. A refinement from the mid C18 was to glaze pantiles, in Norfolk almost always black, which has a very attractive appearance, e.g. at the Red House at Thornham, c. 1750, and the United Reformed Church at Thetford of 1817. The fullest use of black-glazed pantiles is, however, in the towns after 1860; Norwich possesses rows of terraces of the last half of the C19 boasting black-glazed tiles to the street elevation, but plain red pantiles to the rear. Generally pantiles replaced thatch from the middle of the c18.

The history of THATCH is troublesome because continual replacement means that there are hardly even c19 examples, but there are plenty of documentary references indicating that it was already standard before the Conquest. Of all counties Norfolk is the place to see thatch, not just wheat or other field straw gathered after harvest but also true Norfolk reed from the Broads. This is the best of all thatching materials, though expensive and laborious to cut and transport. Even so there is still a minor industry. Thatch has two advantages: field straw was cheap and, because it was the lightest of all traditional roof coverings, roof structures could be positively flimsy. So it appealed to the poor, not to the wealthy, since its use advertised poverty, if less so than turves of grass (no dwellings with turf roofs survive). Thatch suits flint or clay-lump buildings very well. It appealed strongly to believers in the Romantic movement of the late c18 and early c19, to the extent that pattern books, such as J.B. Papworth's *Rural Residences* of 1818, strongly advocate it, despite the fact that the lower classes, innocent of stylistic movements, were then tearing it off in favour of pantiles. *Cottages ornés* and gate lodges to estates are often thatched. Thatch had always been used for churches, there being 270 with thatched roofs in 1840, and there remain more thatched churches in Norfolk than in all other counties put together. Another impetus came with the Arts and Crafts decade at the turn of the c20. Norfolk is a good county for Arts and Crafts and, given *Detmar Blow*'s and *Boardman*'s love of vernacular materials, Norfolk reed was irresistible (Happisburgh Manor of 1900 and How Hill House, Ludham, from 1903 respectively). From that moment the English thatched cottage set about with honeysuckle entered the nation's spirit.

PRE- AND PROTOHISTORY

BY JOHN WYMER

The evidence for human activity in East Anglia before the coming of the great ice sheet which covered Britain as far s as the Thames Valley is restricted to flint tools in lake sediments or river gravels. This was about half a million years ago. Few sites are known but at one near Mildenhall, Suffolk, such flints come from a great raft of interglacial lake muds actually distorted and moved bodily by the ice. Prior to the coming of this ice sheet, it appears too that a major river flowed from the Midlands across what is now the Fens to join the ancestral Thames near Bury St Edmunds. It passed across part of w Norfolk and the same gravels it deposited in Suffolk have yielded many pointed or ovate flint tools known as hand-axes. Little if anything earlier is known in Britain. The Cromer forest bed, often well exposed at the base of the cliffs on the beach at West Runton, dates to about this time, but no flints fashioned by humans have ever been found in it. Claims for these have been made in the past but are no longer accepted. However, the beds contain a rich mammalian fauna including elephants and hippopotamuses, and give a vivid indication of how this once swampy part of Norfolk would have looked.

It is not certain whether ice ever covered East Anglia again, though the last ice sheet certainly reached as far as the N Norfolk coast about 18,000 years ago, where it was stopped by the great Cromer Ridge, a moraine left by the much earlier ice sheet. Between these two glacial maxima, spanning some 400,000 years, there were fluctuations of climate from very cold periglacial conditions to interglacial periods when it was sometimes warmer than at present. The landscape and drainage pattern gradually assumed its present form. PALAEOLITHIC hand-axes occur in many of the old river gravels, testifying to intermittent human occupation, though probably by the ancestors of 'Neanderthal Man' and not ourselves. They hunted, scavenged and gathered foodstuffs and seem to have found the cooler periods and open landscapes more suitable for the primitive economy they practised. No traces of any dwellings have been found. It is unlikely that the slender traces of such things as stake-holes or temporary hearths would survive, even in the rare instances when buried land-surfaces of the period are found, but some form of protection from the elements they must have had. There are particularly rich sites at Whitlingham and Keswick, which suggest human activity along the river banks.

There is nothing in Norfolk to represent the dramatic change in human society in NW Europe from about 35,000 years ago, when modern humans arrived with an elaborate, sophisticated hunting-gathering mode of life, and little else in the rest of East Anglia apart from a few distinctive flint leaf-points. However, when the last ice sheet melted and the weather ameliorated, rather suddenly it would seem, within centuries rather than millennia, the descendants of these people began to exploit the river valleys and relatively open landscape of this Late Glacial–Early Post-Glacial period. Some may have been indigenous inhabitants, whereas others came across from the Low Countries or Denmark, for the sea-level was so low at this time that a land bridge existed. In the Norwich Castle Museum is a barbed point made of deer antler that was dredged from the North Sea some 25 miles off the coast from this submerged land surface. It has been radiocarbon-dated to about 9800 B.C.

The people who occupied Norfolk in the MESOLITHIC PERIOD, prior to the introduction of food-producing farmers, left behind them a litter of their distinctive flints: diminutive microliths for tipping spears and arrows, axes for felling trees and fashioning the timber, and the usual domestic knives and scrapers. Rich scatters of such flintwork have been found at Kelling and many other places, especially along the Fen edge and Breckland. Otherwise, they have left no visible trace on the landscape. The rising sea-level eventually isolated East Anglia from the Continent, as well as from the rest of Britain.

Arable farming and stock farming were practised from about 4000 B.C. and it would seem that the Mesolithic people adapted their life-style to it. Newcomers there must have been, but the archaeological record of the transition is hazy, though a range of new equipment soon ousted the old. Pottery was introduced and finds of new-style polished axes emphasize the clearance of the forest on a larger scale. Dwellings remain only as a few rare discoveries of post-holes and pits, but this Neolithic period has left us the first visible standing monuments. In Norfolk there are four long mounds or BARROWS used for the ritual disposal of the dead, at West Rudham, Harpley, Ditchingham and Felthorpe. The West Rudham long barrow is impressive, being 217 ft long and 62 ft wide. Cremations were found at the S end, placed on a gravel platform beneath the earthen mound. The Ditchingham long barrow is close to a C-shaped, low, earthen enclosure associated with domestic rubbish. None of the causeway enclosures of this period which occur in much of southern England are known in Norfolk, although crop marks at Roughton and Hainford may indicate ploughed-out examples. Nor are there any visible so-called Cursus Earthworks: straight, parallel banks and ditches running like avenues for considerable distances. However, a crop-mark at Beachamwell has recently been discovered which appears to be such a cursus. Perhaps the most spectacular of Norfolk's Neolithic monuments is the multitude of pits and hollows left by the flint miners at Grimes Graves, Weeting. Fine-quality black flint was obtained with enormous labour from radiating horizontal galleries at the base of wide shafts. It would now seem that this industry did not start here until the later Neolithic period, towards the end of the third millennium B.C., and not so much to satisfy a demand for material to make into functional tools as to make prestige objects possibly as part of a complex social pattern involving the exchange of gifts between different groups. Also dating to this time is the Arminghall henge monument with its horseshoe of vast, vertical timbers within circular banks and ditches, still faintly visible. This was probably the focal point of an extensive burial-cum-ritual area which continued into the Bronze Age.

Pottery styles changed in the later Neolithic period with coarse bag-shaped vessels with thick rims and shoulders, often lavishly decorated with impressions from small bones, fingernails or pieces of wood. This so-called Peterborough Ware occurs particularly in the Breckland and 'good sand' and 'loam' regions of N Norfolk. An excavated hollow at Edingthorpe may have been part of a dwelling.

About 2500 B.C. or a little later a final Neolithic group arrived from the Low Countries and the Middle Rhine, their wares typified by distinctive pottery beakers, barbed and tanged arrowheads, archers' wrist guards and the first copper or bronze objects found in Britain. They were mainly pastoralists and were concentrated in Breckland and W Norfolk. At this time, communal burial had given way to individual burial beneath round earthen mounds (barrows). The occurrence of a small round barrow over such an inhumation at Cley-next-the-Sea suggests the influence of a more war-like NE barrow-using group. As can be seen from a typical battle-axe found at Langley and made of stone indigenous to Schleswig-Holstein, these barrow-using people also made the journey across the North Sea. To a small degree this group may also have been responsible for a British variant form, the necked beaker, likewise concentrated in Breckland. They were also predominantly pastoralists, and no settlement structures have been found. At Trowse Newton, amongst a number of mounds was a double-ditched round barrow with necked-beaker inhumations near the Arminghall henge monument already mentioned.

This brings us to about 2000 B.C. and the beginning of a BRONZE-USING AGE. Contemporary with the latest evidence of the Beaker Folk, a northern culture characterized by the so-called food vessel, whose form suggests an ancestry in Peterborough Ware, filtered into Breckland. Besides finds at Needham, Swannington and Wereham, the inhumation of a young girl with a copper and jet bead necklace found at Methwold probably belongs to this group. Other skeletons found in the same area of the Fens have recently been dated to this time, which seems to have been the peak of local occupation.

The early to middle Bronze Age was a period of barrow burial and these mounds are the most numerous of the prehistoric visible monuments in Norfolk. At least 250 survive and probably three or four times that number have been levelled by centuries of ploughing or intentional destruction. Many form impressive groups, as at Weasenham All Saints, West Rudham, Harpley and Little Cressingham. Only the most important groups or very well preserved barrows are noted in the gazetteer. Some of the 'fancy barrows' or bell and disc types are similar to those found in Wessex. At Little Cressingham a contracted male burial was found with two daggers, a necklace of Baltic amber beads and gold work which point to the same early date as the Rush Barrow Founder's burial of the Normanton group to the W of Stonehenge. On the other hand a barrow at Reffley, King's Lynn, contained a number of urns filled with cremated bone and, in one case, a ring and a segmented bead of faience paste imported from the E. Mediterranean some time in the second millennium B.C.

At this time the urn with cremation as the common rite was general. The urns often had a collared or overhanging rim; they are, like the food vessels, of secondary Neolithic descent. Sometimes these cremations were merely insertions in earlier burial mounds, although Norfolk has some dozen or so sizeable barrow groups which may belong to this period. Towards the latter part of the Bronze Age, from around 1000 B.C., itinerant smiths cast and traded tools, weapons and ornaments in bronze and occasionally gold. They frequently buried their stock-in-trade, presumably for safety but perhaps also as ritual offerings. Norfolk is very rich in such hoards and a distinctly regional tradition of metal-working can be recognized. Flat cremation cemeteries constitute the normal method of disposing of the dead at this time, but occur rarely in strong contrast with the large urnfields of s East Anglia; at Salthouse Heath, for example, a number of tiny mounds was added to the earlier barrows constructed from Beaker times. The most spectacular evidence for structures belongs, alas, to the days before scientific excavation. In Breckland, as at Mickle Mere, ARTIFICIAL ISLANDS, a sort of poor man's version of the famous Somerset lake villages, were found with their attendant domestic rubbish. After 1000 B.C. new bronze types, such as leaf-shaped swords (e.g. at Caistor St Edmund), gold dress-fasteners of Irish origin from Caister-on-Sea, and a group of objects of w European manufacture suggest a re-awakening of foreign contacts, although for much of the Bronze Age Norfolk seems to have been a cultural backwater.

About 500 B.C. or earlier, there may have been some migration from the region of the Low Countries. One group, connected with others in Cambridgeshire and Northamptonshire, settled in Breckland, avoiding the Fens, which had again been rendered uninhabitable by a rise in sea-level. At this time, the dawn of the Iron Age, there was a certain amount of new coastal occupation, e.g. at Stiffkey where there is a single possibly Iron Age barrow. Evidence from Snettisham and elsewhere indicates coexistence with the late Bronze Age inhabitants, but remains are again slight, except for the range of coarse pottery types.

There is only one EARLY IRON AGE site in Norfolk whose complete plan has been recorded. This is Micklemoor Hill, West Harling (excavated between 1932 and 1953), overlooking the river Thet. It consisted of three enclosures, two with circular houses (one of these with a central open area and external ditch) and one with a rectangular building which is closer in plan to the simple type of farmhouse of contemporary northern Europe. Otherwise, evidence for settlement is restricted to pits and post-holes revealed by excavation at such sites as Redgate Hill, Hunstanton. By 300 B.C. a slight smoothing off in the profile of local pottery indicates a general evolution of local craftsmanship which was to remain more or less unchanged until well into the Roman occupation.

The latter part of the Iron Age was a period of unrest and disturbance. A tribal aristocracy was emerging with inevitable warfare or the ever-present danger of it. The defended enclosures of Narborough, Holkham and South Creake may have been constructed at this time. The extended burial at Shouldham of a man with an iron sword is a typical grave.

THE IRON AGE AND THE ROMAN PERIOD

BY DAVID GURNEY

The time at which Norfolk's Iron Age or Celtic inhabitants, the ICENI, first became a discernible tribe is unknown, but one of the tribes who followed the lead of the Trinovantes, who had submitted to Caesar in Gaul in 54 B.C. (*De Bello Gallico* v, 21), were the *Ceni Magni*, who may be equated with the Iceni tribe.

Much of their history must be deduced from coinage, commencing with gold staters of the late CI B.C. Silver coins soon replaced these, some inscribed with the name of Antedios (tribal leader *c.* A.D. 30) and coins inscribed ECEN or ECE, most probably the tribal name, which may have been Eceni rather than the Romanized Iceni.

Relatively little is known about local pottery, though far more about Icenian metalwork, of which the Snettisham torcs are the most familiar. These are penannular twisted bars or wires with decorated terminals, worn around the neck and made from a gold and silver alloy called electrum. A bronze hoard of decorated horse harnesses was found at Ringstead. There are many other finds of Iceni weaponry, harnesses and personal adornment in the county. Iron working took place locally around Middleton and Snettisham.

The Icenian area consisted of Norfolk, N Suffolk, and W into the Cambridgeshire Fens at least as far as March and Stonea, then an island. The distribution of different coin-types suggests at least four possible tribal centres, at or near Caistor St Edmund, Snettisham, Thetford/Bury St Edmunds and March/Stonea, each centre probably that of a sub-tribe or pagi. Central Norfolk, then afforested, seems not to have been intensively occupied. The impression is gained of a relatively insular tribe, with little trade across its borders.

Few SETTLEMENTS of the period have been excavated, but most were probably small farmsteads with timber round-houses, with associated fields and enclosures. DEFENDED SITES or earthwork hillforts are known at Holkham, Narborough, Thetford, South Creake and Warham. The last is the best preserved, with impressive circular ramparts and ditches.

At the Claudian invasion of A.D. 43, the Iceni were pro-Roman, and were not therefore subdued by the force of Roman arms. Two early MILITARY ROUTES into Norfolk were probably the Colchester–Scole–Caistor St Edmund–Brampton road (the Pye Road, on the line of the present A140) and the Colchester–Ixworth–Saham Toney–the Wash (near Hunstanton) road, the Peddars Way. At Saham Toney/Little Cressingham, finds of Neronian-Claudian metalwork indicate the site of an early fort. Another major road was the Fen Causeway, running from Durobrivae near Peterborough across the Fens to Denver, where it divides into two routes, one to the N through Fincham, Kempstone, Billingford to Brampton, and the other due E through Saham Toney and Crownthorpe to Caistor St Edmund.

Problems in Wales in A.D. 47 led to troop withdrawals from East Anglia; to safeguard the rear, a law was enforced disarming the area. This was resisted by some of the Iceni, who staged an unsuccessful small-scale rebellion quashed after a battle at a defended site, possibly Stonea (Cambridgeshire) or Holkham. The tribe then seems to have become a client kingdom, recognizing Roman rule but retaining considerable independence under the rule of the tribal king, Prasutagus. At Thetford, excavations in 1980–2 examined enclosures belonging to this period, apparently an Icenian site of high status, albeit of uncertain function. This situation continued until Prasutagus's death, when he unwisely attempted to leave half his kingdom to his family, rather than the whole to Emperor Nero. Officials were sent to seize the estate, and in the course of this Prasutagus's widow Boudicca and her daughters were beaten and raped. The rebellion led by Boudicca which followed in A.D. 60–1 saw the sack of the new towns of Colchester, London and Verulamium, before the final battle and Roman victory in the Midlands. Peace returned to Icenian territory, no doubt under close military surveillance for several years.

The Roman military capital of Norfolk was established at Caistor St Edmund (Venta Icenorum, meaning 'market place of the Iceni'), which had a planned street grid from *c*. A.D. 70. Its population may have numbered several thousand, out of a total population of more than two hundred thousand in Norfolk during the Roman period. Approximately half of the town was later enclosed by a defensive rampart, wall and ditch, in the C3 or C4, and these can still be seen. The town contained private residences, a glassworks, and public buildings including the forum, baths and two temples.

At Brampton, a small town was defended by a deep ditch. Within the town there is much evidence for metalworking, while to the W was an area of large-scale pottery production with at least 141 kilns, mainly of C2 date. In the C3 and C4, another pottery industry developed in W Norfolk, at Shouldham and Pentney, providing vessels for local use. Many other small kiln sites are known.

The Roman road network developed to cover most of Norfolk, with small towns or villages at road junctions or river fords. These included settlements at Scole (possibly the *Villa Faustini* of the Antonine Itinerary), Long Stratton, Ditchingham, Crownthorpe, Saham Toney, Denver, Fincham, Kempstone, Billingford (Vol. I) and Toftrees. The countryside was dotted with small settlements or farmsteads, but it is only in the W of the county, along the Icknield Way running along the edge of the chalk upland, that masonry VILLAS occur in any number. Here, every few miles from Hunstanton and Narborough, there was a villa, with evidence of Romanized life-style in hypocausts for heating and baths, mosaics and painted wall plaster. To the W, the Fens were dry enough for settlement by the early C2, and this new and fertile land appears to have been an Imperial estate devoted mainly to animal husbandry and salt production. The Fen edge, always an attractive area for settlement, was very densely occupied, but the humble settlements here included temples with links to elaborate eastern cults. Probably in the C3, an episode of freshwater flooding affected much of the Fenland, and this caused considerable disruption to occupation in the area. Many sites never recovered.

From the c3, the Norfolk coastline was attacked by barbarians from across the North Sea. The Roman response to this was to construct a system of FORTS, at Brancaster, Caister-on-Sea and Burgh Castle (Suffolk), with a fourth perhaps near Cromer where coastal erosion has been severe. These forts belonged to the defences under the command of the Count of the Saxon Shore, which stretched from Norfolk to Hampshire on this side of the Channel. The first two forts were sited on each side of a large estuary, at the mouth of which Great Yarmouth now stands. Visible remains can be seen at Caister-on-Sea, while the walls of Burgh Castle are preserved to a considerable height.

The late c4 saw the breakdown of central Roman authority under pressure from barbarian incursions. Military units were withdrawn from Britain, and after A.D. 410, when the link with Rome was finally severed, Saxon raids led to the collapse of Romano-British order and administration. The concealment of an early Germanic sword in the decaying Roman bath-house at Feltwell most probably belongs to the time when Roman Norfolk became Anglo-Saxon Norfolk.

SAXON AND EARLY MEDIEVAL ARCHAEOLOGY

BY ANDREW ROGERSON

Evidence for early ANGLO-SAXON settlement is rarely visible in the landscape and is limited to excavated sites as well as finds collected from the surface of ploughed fields. CEMETERIES are the main source of excavated information. These must have contained the remains of both the Germanic invaders and of that portion, however big or small, of the sub-Roman British population who had remained in the county. From the beginnings of large-scale migration in the mid c5 cremation was the dominant rite, and sites such as Spong Hill in North Elmham and Caistor St Edmund have produced burials in their thousands, most in decorated ceramic urns. Many of these pots carry motifs and designs that show close links with the homelands of the Angles and Saxons in northern Germany and southern Scandinavia. From the late c5 inhumation was also practised. Cemeteries such as one at Morningthorpe contained hundreds of interments, many accompanied by grave goods, but no site has been entirely excavated. Cemeteries were still flat, with only a few graves under small barrows, now all long since ploughed flat. No certainly Anglo-Saxon upstanding barrows are known in Norfolk, but Anglo-Saxon burials inserted into Bronze Age barrows are not uncommon. Burial sites become much rarer or at least more difficult to recognize in the c7, and by c. 700 the influence of Christianity and changing fashion led to the end of accompanied burial and the start of burial in churchyards.

A small but growing body of excavated evidence shows that

rectangular timber buildings supported by earth-fast posts were the norm for rural SETTLEMENTS throughout the Anglo-Saxon period. This evidence survives almost exclusively as stains in the soil, but is full enough to indicate that the Anglo-Saxons' building tradition, which may have owed as much to British influences as to those of their Continental homeland, was fairly sophisticated and far from squalid. The most common building type in the early part of the period is the *grubenhaus* or sunken featured building, in which a flat-based pit forms the major element in the surviving evidence. There is a divergence of interpretation concerning how these buildings were used and as a result how they should be reconstructed: either the pit was covered by a plank floor and used for storage, or living took place on the base of the pit. Alternative reconstructions can be viewed at West Stow near Bury St Edmunds (Suffolk).

Only two FIELD MONUMENTS attributable to the early part of the Anglo-Saxon period are visible today, the Foss Ditch and the Devil's Dyke, both linear earthworks and probably major political boundaries, in the W of the county. For the MIDDLE SAXON period, between *c.* 650 and *c.* 850, there are no known visible remains. For the remainder of Saxon times, despite the Scandinavian invasions in the later C9 and at the end of the C10 and beginning of the C11, there is a similar dearth of field monuments. Only the DEFENDED ENCLOSURE at Tasburgh has any claim for inclusion, and even here the Anglo-Saxon or Viking contribution may have been limited to a refurbishment of the rampart. This paucity of visible Anglo-Saxon sites belies a population of considerable wealth based almost exclusively on an agriculture favoured by climate and soil. Despite the disruptions caused by Viking invasions this population continued to increase and was the largest in England by the C11.

There is as yet no evidence for the re-emergence of TOWNS in Norfolk before *c.* 900. Some places may have been more than normal rural settlements in the C7–C9 and small trading centres probably grew up on or near the coast at places such as Burnham. However, Ipswich remained East Anglia's only truly urban place until the aftermath of the Viking invasions of the later C9, when Thetford and Norwich appeared rather suddenly and grew with great rapidity into major Anglo-Scandinavian towns.

Norfolk's later Anglo-Saxons had great need for fuel for domestic and industrial uses. Much of this demand, particularly in the E of the county, was met by the deep deposits of peat in the valleys of the various rivers which flow into the North Sea at Great Yarmouth. The peat resource was exploited apace for *c.* 350 years until the extraction pits were disastrously flooded in the late C13. This complex of rivers and pits is now known as the NORFOLK BROADS. No other archaeological feature of late *i/i* Anglo-Saxon origin has become such a major modern leisure facility. The Broads are very difficult to view from dry land, and are best appreciated from the water with the help of maps. For this reason individual Broads are not listed in this work, and the interested reader is left to his or her own devices.

Remarkably few examples of medieval SETTLEMENT EARTH-
WORKS have survived in the county, despite Norfolk's large and
wealthy population. The dramatic contraction in the size of the
population which began in *c.* 1300 and was made greater by the
Black Death and later plagues has left evidence in the form of
grass-covered earthworks for deserted and shrunken settlements
throughout the county. Changes in the agricultural economy, in
particular piecemeal enclosures for stock farming and then
emparking, led to further desertions as well as relocations of
settlements between the C15 and C18. These earthworks, usually
slight and never dramatic, consist of the remains of TOFTS which
are the sites of houses, outbuildings and yards normally surrounded by a rectangular arrangement of ditches and/or banks;
streets and roads, often sunken through use below the level of the
surrounding land; small clay, sand and gravel pits; the edges of
commons and greens often demarcated by ditches. In addition
vanished or moved settlements may be suggested by both the
more substantial remains of moats which once surrounded manor
houses and larger homesteads, and by the lonely parish church,
often long since ruined. Many isolated churches, though, are the
product of a dispersed settlement pattern rather than of settlement
desertion or movement.

Many villages were not nucleated in plan, that is, they did not
consist of tightly grouped houses. Over much of Norfolk medieval
settlements were dispersed, often comprising many individual
houses well spaced along the edges of common pastures or greens.
This dispersal has not contributed to the survival of settlement
earthworks because the remains of individual tofts are more easily
destroyed as a result of land-use changes than are the larger
areas of earthworks which mark the sites of deserted nuclear
settlements. In DISPERSED PARISHES, those within which no
main village is identifiable, there are often many individual houses
as well as hamlets with names containing such elements as 'End',
'Green', 'Row' and 'Street', where the traveller must cherish his
Ordnance Survey map, and where in the finding of farmhouses
and cottages great patience is required. In common with that of
many other counties, particularly in the E of England, Norfolk's
old grassland, which contained many well-preserved archaeological sites, has suffered badly in the latter part of this century.
The sites of many deserted hamlets and individual farms and even
of some deserted villages have been flattened by the bulldozer
and the plough, especially since the Second World War. However,
good examples of deserted settlements do survive, particularly in
the W of the county, at places such as Pudding Norton, Roudham,
Godwick and Houghton Park.

MEDIEVAL CHURCHES

Monastic Architecture

The first Christian king of East Anglia was Sigeberht, who had been converted in France and came to the region in *c.* 630, paving the way for St Felix to land in Norfolk in 636, possibly at Babingley on the then E coast of the Wash (or inland at Flitcham). We know very little of the early history of the Church and what we do know is confusing. There were two East Anglian sees by 673, and there are a number of candidates for their sites, although in *c.* 800 one was almost certainly at North Elmham in Norfolk, and the other was very probably at Hoxne in Suffolk. The bishop's church at North Elmham appears from excavated post-holes to have been of timber. The see must have been consolidated by 1071 when it was transferred to Thetford (to St Mary the Greater), then one of the six biggest towns in England, only finally settling at Norwich in 1094. It appears that at North Elmham Bishop Losinga built himself a private chapel of flint and stone over the site of the earlier structure, in turn partly absorbed into a C14 manor house belonging to Bishop Despenser. Of the Saxon period nothing remains above ground at all, and the story of the remains belongs to the Norman period; they are not those of a Saxon cathedral, as used to be thought. By far the oldest monastic order is that of the Benedictines, who came to England in 598 and settled at Canterbury. St Benet's Abbey, Horning, represents their oldest Norfolk presence, and is surprisingly the only pre-Conquest foundation in the county, other than Dereham.

Norwich cathedral is of course the centre of NORMAN ARCHI-
TECTURE in Norfolk, and is one of the monastic cathedrals of England, deliberately established in Norwich as an expression of 1/3 Norman power. There were originally six other major ABBEY or PRIORY CHURCHES, and their foundation by the most important Norman magnates carried a similar stamp of authority. Apart from St Benet's Abbey, there was Castle Acre, founded in 1090 by William de Warenne, Binham in *c.* 1091 (Peter de Valoines), 1/5 Norwich itself in 1094, though preparations had already been made (Herbert de Losinga), Thetford in 1103 (Roger Bigod), Wymondham in 1107 (William d'Albini), and Broomholm at 2/13 Bacton in 1113 (founded from Castle Acre). Of these Castle Acre, Thetford and Broomholm belonged to the Cluniac order (*see* below). They were all large, and at Norwich nearly all is preserved, at Wymondham and Binham mostly the naves, at Thetford and 2/12 Castle Acre eloquent and substantial ruins, but at St Benet's Abbey and Broomholm only gatehouses remain, neither of which is Norman. It is probable that Norwich was begun, or the plan laid out, as early as *c.* 1091; by 1119 it seems that building had progressed to the crossing, and by 1145 it was virtually complete. 1/4 This is very fast, but not as fast as at Castle Acre, built up to the 2/7 E crossing piers by *c.* 1110 and completed by about 1130. Thetford was begun in 1107, the E end was in usable condition by 1114,

and the W end reached by about 1140. Wymondham followed
by the mid century. So Norwich, although the most important
foundation, was not necessarily the first to be completed. The E
end of Binham was probably contemporary with these but built
more slowly, for the details of the nave point to c. 1130–70. Of
Norman work at St Benet's Abbey and Broomholm we can say
little.

Leaving aside the last two, the original plans of the buildings
represent the two principal types of Romanesque planning: the
type with an ambulatory from which chapels radiate, and the
Benedictine or Cluniac (i.e. Cluny II) plan. Only Norwich fits
1/6 the first category, with a typical Anglo-Norman deviation in that
the NE and SE chapels off the ambulatory are not allowed to point
in those directions, but are contrived to face E like the terminating
E apse (replaced by the mid-C13 Lady Chapel). Such oddly-
shaped E chapels occurred also at Canterbury, Winchester and
Worcester. In addition Norwich had an E apsidal chapel to the
aisleless N and S transepts. The other plan type consists of a
chancel with an apse, projecting between apsed chancel aisles,
and apsidal chapels off the transepts, all staggered. Examples
were nearly all replaced in England in the middle of the C12 by
straight E ends. As far as the elevation is concerned, Norwich,
Binham, Castle Acre and Wymondham had a big gallery with
entirely unsubdivided openings, the system of St Étienne in Caen
and Old St Paul's in London, and wall passages at clerestory level.
1/5 At Binham and in the transepts at Norwich these are elaborated by
a tripartite arrangement of one large arch flanked by two smaller
ones.

Thetford, Wymondham and Castle Acre had crossing towers
and two W towers, St Benet's Abbey one W tower and a crossing
tower, Binham and Norwich just crossing towers.* Of all these
the Norwich tower has the most swagger, built in three phases and
completed c. 1140. The idiosyncratic decoration of geometrical
motifs, chiefly circles, lozenges and bull's eyes, is unique, and
easily remembered. Otherwise Norwich cathedral is remarkably
adverse to ornament apart from the piers of the two bays W of
the screen, where the circular piers have the spiral grooving
best known at Durham. These may be part of the original plan,
emphasizing the importance of the nave altar, in the same way
that, slightly earlier, Castle Acre had introduced diagonal grooving in the SW bay of the nave. The rest of the nave piers at
Norwich follow an alternating system based on elaborated drum
and square piers; at Castle Acre the nave piers had a variety of
compound sections but are circular in the earlier E arm. Wymond-
2/12 ham nave piers have been tampered with but may have had coupled
shafts rising to the roof, as at Binham, while the piers between
the chancel and its aisles at Thetford display shafts towards the
central space but segmental projections to the aisles.

Only at St Benet's Abbey do we find an aisleless nave. Doubtless

* One might add that St Margaret, King's Lynn, has two W towers begun in the
mid C12, that to the SW with blind arcading. The foundation of the church had
strong connections with Bishop Losinga.

it was unvaulted, as was the case with Norman Norwich, but groin vaults appear in the aisles of the other churches, and in Castle Acre is some evidence of high vaults in the transepts, which is remarkable for a date of c. 1120–30. Some mention has already been made of DECORATION, but nowhere is there a more ambitious display of blind arcading than on the W front at Castle 2/7 Acre, both inside and out, matched only by Norwich castle. Thetford has similar but less enthusiastic arcading at the W end, repeated on the transept chapels, while Norwich has a continuous run of arcading round the outside of the E arm. Blind arcading was a favourite indeed with the Normans. Castle Acre has its W front further enriched by diaper, rope, zigzag and bobbin motifs on the main portal, and at Wymondham on the S arcade is zigzag, cable and meander, the last indicating a date after about 1150.

Norfolk is astoundingly rich in monastic foundations, though no others are as well preserved as those discussed above. The C12 was the peak century for NEW MONASTERIES, and the Benedictine order wasted no time in Norfolk. In addition to St Benet's, Norwich and Binham, a small priory was founded by Bishop Losinga in 1100 as a cell of Norwich S of St Margaret in King's Lynn, of which some later domestic buildings remain, heavily disguised. At Great Yarmouth the priory established in 1101 by Losinga goes with the parish church of St Nicholas, but of this only the C14 great hall survives (see below, Unfortified Domestic Buildings). Then came the Priory of St Faith at Horsham St Faith, not founded by Losinga but by Robert of Caen as a cell of Conques in 1105-6. Although it was converted at the Dissolution some fragments remain, chiefly the Late Norman chapter-house doorway with four good capitals with interlace and figure carving, and the amazing series of C13 wall paintings. Next was Blackborough (Middleton), which has little to show (c. 1135), then Carrow Priory (called Abbey), founded in 1146 at Norwich but outside the walls. Carrow is intriguing, for the church is one of the largest Norman buildings in the county (195 ft), and it has, and always had, a straight E end, like the nunnery church at Romsey (Hants). Carrow was for nuns, and of their house parts of the E end and the N cloister range are identifiable. Of c. 1160 is the aisleless nunnery at Thetford (St George), still with the S transept with its grand arch, part of the chancel, fragments of the chapter house and two gateways into the precinct. Finally Winnold, founded before 1199, was converted at the Dissolution and is in its remains as halting as Blackborough.

The Cluniac order, from Cluny in Burgundy, was founded in the early C10, and had stricter control of its daughter houses. The Cluniacs came to England at Lewes in 1077 and in Norfolk had only three houses, but three of the biggest: Castle Acre and Thetford were both founded from Lewes and Broomholm (Bacton) founded from Castle Acre, only to be taken under the direct control of Cluny in c. 1195.

Next came the Augustinian canons, who had more houses in Norfolk than any other. West Acre Priory, founded in c. 1100, was as large as Castle Acre and although the remains carry various dates it seems that there was a screen W front, wider than the nave and aisles, and an apsed Norman chapter house. Of Pentney Priory, a medium-sized establishment founded before 1135, only the gatehouse has survived; at Hempton (founded 1135) are bits of wall, and at Coxford (Tattersett) only one C13 arch after its translation from East Rudham in 1215 (originally founded in the mid C12). Although it was founded in 1095 nothing was done at Little Walsingham until 1153, but the priory grew into one of the most important pilgrimage centres in England. A dramatic fragment of the C15 E wall remains. The church had a straight E end, aisles to both the nave and chancel and a central and a W tower. Also standing are parts of the C13 refectory and the C14 dormitory undercroft.*

Of the Cistercians (founded at Cîteaux, Burgundy, in 1098) there is only a fine C13 S wall of the church of the nunnery at Marham, founded before 1249. The Premonstratensians were founded at Prémontreé (near Laon) in 1120, came to England at Newsham (Brocklesby, Lincs) in 1143 and founded West Dereham Abbey in Norfolk in 1188. Of this and their other two houses at Langley (1195) and Wendling (1267) there are serious remains only at Langley. It had an early C13 church, square-ended, with the aisles flush with the E wall, and various domestic buildings such as the cellarium (C13, quadripartite rib vaults), the chapter house (six by three bays with quadripartite vaults and blank arcading), the infirmary (Perp) and the C14 gatehouse. Of the wholly English double order (i.e. nuns and canons) of the Gilbertines, founded at Sempringham (Lincs) in the 1130s, Norfolk had one example, at Shouldham, of which nothing remains. It was founded about 1190. The Trinitarians were founded in 1198 and the mother house in England was at Ingham, founded in 1360 within an existing church. Lastly there was one house of the Hospitallers, at Carbrooke, founded in c. 1193, but nothing remains.

The FRIARS belonged to preaching orders which tended the sick and needy in the growing towns of Europe. Their apparent spiritualism caused a religious revival; they were extremely successful, and their emphasis on preaching led to a new style of architecture based on wide, open naves as preaching boxes, which was an instrumental force in the design of the later Dec and Perp parish churches of England.‡ The Dominicans (Blackfriars) were the first to arrive in England, in 1221, setting up a house in Norwich in 1226. This was moved to the present site when the house of the Friars Penitential was suppressed in 1307. They finished their church in the 1340s, complete with cloisters and the usual monastic arrangements, but it burnt in 1413 and the 1/46 replacement went up in 1440–70, probably on exactly the same

---

* Other Augustinian foundations with remains of mixed extent are Hickling (founded 1185), Peterstone (before 1200), Bromehill (c. 1200), Weybourne (after 1200), Beeston Regis (c. 1216), North Creake (1227), Great Massingham (before 1260), Flitcham (1271), Weybridge and Crabhouse Priory at Wiggenhall St Mary Magdalen.

‡ For more details see Norwich Blackfriars, p. 265.

plan, for the mendicant orders kept to a successful formula. A peculiarity with English mendicants is the narrow passage under the tower between the nave and chancel. The tower at Norwich does not survive, and many of the conventual buildings are lost, but the church remains the most complete of all the mendicant churches of England. The Dominicans had houses also at Great Yarmouth (1271), King's Lynn (1272) and Thetford (1335), but of these only the s crossing arch of the Thetford church survives, embedded in later buildings of the grammar school.

The Franciscans (Greyfriars) came in 1224, and began their Norwich community in 1226, of which we have nothing; shortly afterwards they settled in Great Yarmouth, where the early C14 w walk of the cloisters remains and also some details of the s wall of the church. At King's Lynn (founded c. 1264) the unusual later C14 hexagonal brick tower survives, and at Little Walsingham (founded in 1347) are quite substantial fragments of the guest house, kitchen, little cloister and great cloister, all mixed up with a private house. The Carmelite order (Whitefriars) had been founded in Palestine about 1154, had their first English house in c. 1240 and went to Burnham Norton in 1242–7, where the C14 gatehouse and part of the remodelled church remain. Of the Norwich house (1256) there are later C14 arches and an undercroft of c. 1300, at King's Lynn (c. 1260) only the N precinct gateway, and at Blakeney (1296) only one stretch of the early C16 precinct walls. Of the house at Yarmouth little is known. The Austin Friars, who followed the Augustinian rule, established themselves in England in 1248, arriving at Norwich in 1290, King's Lynn in 1293, Gorleston-on-Sea in 1311 and Thetford in 1387. Only parts of walls and at Lynn the remains of two precinct gateways survive.

This annotated list of monastic foundations has taken us far beyond the Norman style, and we must return to the C12 to examine what is notable of early medieval parish churches.

Early Medieval Parish Churches

Two aspects of ANGLO-SAXON CHURCH ARCHITECTURE in Norfolk require special attention: the problem of Norfolk's round towers, and the extent to which there is any difference between the Saxon and Norman periods.

There are 179 standing ROUND TOWERS in England, of which Norfolk possesses or possessed 140,* Suffolk 42, and other eastern counties 13. The Norfolk and Suffolk examples are concentrated in the E, either side of the Waveney valley, although there is a respectable distribution in the remainder of the county. The antiquarians explained this concentration, especially in SE Norfolk, as a consequence of the lack of good building stone for quoins, forgetting that one can turn a corner with flint just as well as with ashlar or carstone. About seventeen round towers fall within the carstone areas of w Norfolk, and at e.g. Bessingham in the NE the possibly Saxon round tower is entirely of this

* These are the figures for the pre-1974 boundaries.

material, which had to be brought by sea. A square plan would
have been easier. Square towers indeed existed in pre-Conquest
Norfolk, such as the central tower at Weybourne, or the w tower
at Hethel. Carstone for quoins at the corners of naves and chancels
was considered perfectly suitable long into the C13, and at Framingham Earl the Normans were content with large flint nodules
for quoins. Quoins were not a problem, but building in the round
was, for the shuttering of a circular flint tower is considerably
more difficult than for a square one, and leads to problems at the
junction with a flat nave w wall. A round tower demands painfully
acute external angles, one plane of which is curved, and a further
dilemma inside, where the doorway into the nave must on one
side be in a flat wall, on the other a concave one.

The local fancy for round towers must therefore be driven by
considerations of style, and for parallels one must look to the
Continent. A pair of detached round towers is known from the
famous plan of c. 825 for the monastery of St Gall, and from
c. 1000 cathedrals in the Empire favouring twin round towers (e.g.
Augsburg and Gernrode). Round stair towers, at least on major
buildings, had been used since the C9, and single round w towers
in the Schleswig-Holstein region of Germany occur on minor
churches from the C10. There is a round tower at St Magnus on
the island of Egilsay in the Orkneys and there were others no
doubt in C10 Norfolk. The evidence points to a common cultural
pattern round the North Sea.

In Norfolk a case may be made for a pre-Conquest date in
about twenty-two examples, and in these the distribution is much
more widespread, nearly half falling in the w of the county, and
with a cluster around and s of Norwich. However, the majority
are Norman, and they continued late, only universally superseded
in the C13. Little Plumstead has a mid-C12 round tower, Barmer's
is probably late C12, and those at Shimpling, Sustead and Thorpe
Abbots are all C13.

The problem with dating not only the towers but also the
church as a whole is that traditionally an Anglo-Saxon label is
attached to buildings without Norman features, pre-supposing a
stylistic division between the two, and assuming that 'Norman'
features have not subsequently been removed or altered. These
are very great assumptions indeed, and may be mistaken. The
date 1066 marked a sudden political change, but the workmen
and masons did not change because the rulers did, and parish
church building changed only slowly. Norman motifs were gradually introduced into indigenous architecture, here more quickly
than there, and for parish churches up to c. 1150 one must dispense
with the terms 'Anglo-Saxon' and 'Norman' in the study of
English Romanesque architecture: such a division existed in
society but not in church building.

There are a number of features typical of pre-Conquest
architecture which continue into the Norman period. DOUBLE-
SPLAYED WINDOWS, some of which are CIRCULAR, are
traditionally Anglo-Saxon. They appear at Breckles (possibly
early C11, blocked circular tower windows), and Witton, near

North Walsham (three double-splayed nave windows). At Forncett St Peter is a complete pre-Conquest tower with rings of 2/3
circular windows, and other features. However, the obviously
Norman w range of the Norwich cloisters begun in the 1090s
also had double-splayed windows. At Bexwell a double-splayed
window survives in the Norman nave. Gradually the double
splay gave way to the single splay, but the moment is likely to
be the mid C12.

TRIANGULAR-HEADED OPENINGS are also both pre- and
post-Conquest. The twin bell-openings at Bessingham have a
deeply recessed carstone dividing shaft, and there is a high triangular-headed doorway into the nave, none of which have
Norman decoration. Haddiscoe's bell-openings are essentially the
same, but marked as Norman on account of their billet moulding
and scalloped capitals. Triangular heads appear in many other
places (both triangular and rounded at e.g. Beachamwell).
STRIPWORK seems pre-Conquest at e.g. Kirby Cane and
Weybourne, but post-Conquest at Haddiscoe. LONG-AND-
SHORT WORK again is pre-Conquest (at East Lexham, w quoins;
Beachamwell, NW quoins; Aslacton, chancel NE quoins), but is
used in the late C11 at Hempnall and Great Dunham; at Bawsey
it is undoubtedly Norman, as it is at Earlham and Merton. BLANK
ARCADING, which decorates some round towers (Weybourne,
Thorpe-next-Haddiscoe, Kirby Cane, Tasburgh) is a technique
more common after 1066. HERRINGBONE MASONRY and the
use of carstone, sometimes together, are even less reliable as an
indicator of pre-Conquest work than long-and-short quoining:
only in the chancel of Forncett St Peter and in the tower and
nave of Roughton can one tentatively assert a Saxon date; most
examples are Norman, and at the ruined church at Edgefield its
use in the tower is in C14.

Nothing has so far been said of the PLANS OF PRE-CONQUEST
CHURCHES. Essentially there were only two types, distinguished
by the position of their towers. The majority had w towers followed by an aisleless nave and chancel, often with an apsed E end
as at (excavated) Framingham Earl and Stanford. Bessingham
had a continuous nave and chancel. The other, more elaborate
type boasted a central tower, but neither aisles nor transepts. Of
these few the best is at Weybourne, and we know of one at West
Barsham. The rest are all post-Conquest but owe as much to the
Saxons as to external influence.

Of SAXON DECORATION we have very little. The cross under
the tower of the King's Lynn Greyfriars may be either Saxon or
early Norman, with a figure of the seated Christ. At Breckles the
round tower ought to be early C11 to judge by the interlaced knots
on one impost of the tower arch and snakes on the other. Other
examples of interlace are parts of Anglo-Saxon crosses at Whis-
sonsett and Little Dunham, a coffin-lid at Rockland All Saints,
and fragments at Bodney and Cringleford.

NORMAN PARISH CHURCHES are met far more frequently,
although few are complete. Exactly the same forms continue for a
few decades after as before the Conquest, with details becoming

more recognizably Norman as the C12 progresses. Of plans we sometimes find aisles and transepts and thus a third plan form – the cruciform church – can be added to the repertoire established by the Saxons. Inevitably, though, echoes of the Saxons faded as the influence of the new major churches made itself felt, an influence which injected a much more cosmopolitan vocabulary: at Quidenham a doorway with volute capitals to a single order, carstone quoins at Sustead. Gissing has a two-light Norman window with a zigzag surround, and two-light bell-openings with a scalloped capital to the dividing shafts. Zigzag again occurs in the tower arch, and on the S doorway, where scallops recur. Hales and Heckingham may be cited as perfect Norman village churches. Both have round W towers, naves and chancels with apses. In addition there are flat buttresses and single-splayed 2/17 lancets, and, at Hales, external blank arcading to the apse windows. Of the late C11 is Great Dunham, a church with a central tower, nave and a chancel with (formerly) an apse. The W door has billet decoration, i.e. decidedly Norman, but the nave and tower have long-and-short work. The tower has both two-light openings and circular windows. Inside is a motif which was to become a favourite: blind arcading to the nave walls. The two tower arches cannot decide between Saxon and Norman. The late C11 Guestwick had a similar plan and mixture of detail. Of parish churches a further eight have or had the central tower arrangement, of which the best relics are at Gillingham, South Lopham and Fundenhall.

Six ambitious parish churches are cruciform and owed stylistic allegiance to major monastic houses. Aldeby was actually dependent on Norwich; Burnham Overy Town began without aisles; at Syderstone, where the S aisle is probably part of the original plan, are typical short round piers supporting round arches; grandest of all is Attleborough, where the crossing piers were provided with shafting, scalloped capitals and a little pre-waterleaf. The others are Flitcham and Bedingham.

2/4   Of the square central TOWERS of parish churches, South Lopham is the king, and may be dated to no later than c. 1120. For such a tower it is surprising that transepts were not apparently intended. The four storeys rely on simple blind arcading for their decoration, more below than above, the second stage with scalloped capitals. At the corners are clasping buttresses diminishing in scale as each stage reduces in size. This decoration undoubtedly comes from Norwich. At Gillingham arcading is much restricted, but it recurs at Flitcham in the form of three large arches to each side of the second stage.

So to details. Norman PIERS are usually round, with square abaci and round arches, as at Burnham Overy Town and Syderstone. By far the majority of TOWER and CHANCEL ARCHES were undecorated. Exceptions are Bawsey, with a shafted and double-shafted W tower arch with zigzag, and the square piers with only minor impost decoration of Gillingham. The best chancel arches are at Tottenhill, which has colonnettes to the jambs ending in scalloped capitals, and zigzag in the arch; and at

Langford where there are three orders with cushion capitals, and an arch with roll mouldings and bobbins.

Most Norman WINDOWS survive in towers, where the dominating forms are circular windows (Kilverstone, Stockton, Holme Hale, Brooke etc.), and twin bell-openings divided by a central shaft (Kilverstone, Gayton Thorpe, Merton, and Titchwell, where the central shaft is polygonal). Both these forms are familiar from the Anglo-Saxon period. Round-headed lancets appear in the early C12 at Bexwell in a ring of ten to the ringing chamber, in the mid century at Little Plumstead, and elsewhere (e.g. Burnham Norton, Repps, Runhall, Seething). The lancets are generally single-splayed. In the body of the church, survivals tell the same story (e.g. Hunworth, Runcton Holme, West Somerton). The positioning of nave or chancel windows very high in the wall appears to be characteristic, but there are no instances of clerestories in Norman parish churches until the 1190s, and by then the Transitional phase is reached.

There is plenty of other decoration, mainly on DOORWAYS. At Haddiscoe is the earliest doorway, c. 1100, and most interesting 2/15 on account of the figure in a niche above and the nature of the decoration current at that time: chip carving, zigzag and scallops. At the end of the century is Barton Bendish, and by this time the motifs used include double roll-mouldings, billet and waterleaf, but the pointed arch tells us that the E.E. style is imminent. Between these two dates are about seventy doorways but only a handful are of national interest. Multi-order portals appear from the mid C12, perhaps following the precedent at Castle Acre. The biggest – seven orders in the arch – is the glorious doorway at Wroxham, with three orders of decorated shafts and in the arch a riot of zigzags, roll-mouldings, chain and a beaded band. Next in size comes the N doorway at Hales (six orders), again with zigzag, and chip carving and wheels in the hood. Foliage capitals encroach on the side walls as well. The five-order S doorway favours scalloped capitals. Then come Ashby (five orders) and Heckingham (four orders), the brother of Hales's N doorway and 2/16 probably by the same craftsmen. Larling is much smaller but makes up for that by having two orders of polygonal shafts with spiral and chevron decoration, and big roll-mouldings in the arch.

Transitional and Early English Churches

There are three major Late Norman parish churches yet to be mentioned. The first, Castle Rising, is still firmly of the Norman model, but the other two, Walsoken and Tilney All Saints, both in their size and in their details herald the coming of the Gothic style. Castle Rising was probably begun in the mid C12 and has 2/8 rib vaulting under the central tower, the ribs with zigzag, and a splendid W front. There are complex zigzags to the W door and, above, a tall round-headed W window framed by even more vivacious zigzags and rope-twist forms. To the r. and l. is interlacing blind arcading, and above this simpler blind arcading. Tilney All Saints has five nave bays of wholly round piers with waterleaf and stiff-leaf capitals, and keeled mouldings to the NW respond. Walsoken is very grand, ashlar-faced and with seven-bay arcades alternating between circular and octagonal piers with varieties of scalloped capitals and, at the E nave responds, water-leaf. Crocket capitals appear in the chancel, i.e. E.E., and the chancel arch is pointed, but still heavily decorated with Late Norman forms. The largely demolished Norwich Infirmary begun in 1183 had a sophisticated alternating system of Transitional piers, with volute capitals and water-holding bases.

Crocket capitals exist on otherwise Late Norman doorways (Shereford and St Andrew, Kirby Bedon); waterleaf on the shafted tower arches of Attleborough, on Mundham's S doorway, and at Chedgrave's S doorway in the mid C12. Dogtooth occurs on doorways at Runcton Holme and Bedingham, where the N doorway has stiff-leaf under a roll-moulded and keeled arch. Pointed arches make their debut in the otherwise Norman work at Easton and Kirstead, and pointed slit windows combine with a typical Norman inner splay at Mundesley. Keeled mouldings of c. 1190 may be seen, other than at Tilney and Bedingham, at e.g. Burnham Ulph (chancel arch) and St Nicholas, Great Yarmouth (nave arcades of c. 1190, which also had stiff-leaf capitals). These details did not come from Norwich nor, so far as we know, from the major Norfolk abbeys, but were probably disseminated by Lincoln and Peterborough masons.

Once the E.E. style developed, round arches quickly dis-appeared (the chancel of c. 1210 at Emneth is one of the last examples), but circular PIERS, the mainstay of the Norman style, persisted throughout the C13 and lasted to the early C14 – they were easy to make and being relatively cheap always had a fol-lowing – often accompanied by round moulded capitals 1/14 (Hempnall, Foulsham and Horning, all C13). However, octagonal piers once introduced gained ground. The C13 nave of St Mary, North Elmham, adopted the alternating system of Walsoken coupled with chamfered arches with keeled roll-mouldings. The same system occurs at Reymerston (S arcade) and at Thornham, where double-hollow-chamfered arches introduce us to a new and persistent form. Interestingly the arcade was reused in Perp times, illustrating that if funds did not permit then older forms were perfectly acceptable. Double chamfers to arches without hollows may be a slightly earlier C13 motif: at Burnham Norton, c. 1220, they appear on stubby Norman-looking circular piers on the N side, but their brothers opposite are octagonal. At Weybourne the Augustinians added a S aisle after 1200 with circular piers and abaci under double-chamfered arches, and in the same years water-holding bases appear (Braydeston S aisle, Watton). After about 1240 the quatrefoil pier was introduced, sometimes with shafts as at Northwold, sometimes without as at Great Massingham or Little Dunham, and this pier type too was to remain current long after the text-books would have one believe.

The dating of medieval Gothic features must be approached with caution: once a new feature was introduced, certainly from the Transitional years but particularly from the C13, it persisted long after newer forms were developed, and one must beware of assigning buildings to the earliest possible moment. The styles into which for convenience medieval ecclesiastical architecture is divided all merged imperceptibly with each other. This is as true of plan types, moulding designs and particularly window tracery as it is of pier shapes, and not just in Norfolk. Medieval masons did not recognize periods of architecture as the antiquarians did, which, coupled with the fact that until the C15 dependable construction dates are rare, leaves the sobering thought that we just do not know when any particular feature was introduced. As far as dates for Norfolk churches, or parts of them, are concerned there are (apart from monastic foundation dates) four known dates in the C13, 26 dates for the Decorated period and the C14, 162 dates for the C15 or Perpendicular and 64 reliable dates for C16 Gothic.

There are few complete examples of EARLY ENGLISH CHURCHES, for such was the prosperity of Norfolk in the Perp decades that most buildings were partially or wholly rebuilt. Chancels and towers survive best because they were least affected by the later demand for large preaching spaces. E.E. CHANCELS start with Emneth, a marshland church of c. 1210 with circular piers to the chapels bearing arches still round, but with three stepped pointed E lancets added slightly later. The best example is at Burgh-next-Aylsham, enriched by blind dado arcading with 1/10 stiff-leaf capitals and further arcading round the tall lancet side windows. In addition there is a very fine entrance to a N chapel, all of c. 1220–30. From the mid century is the chancel at Blakeney, 1/9 a splendid piece on account of the rib-vault inside, and at the rather rebuilt chancel at Great Cressingham are massive wall arches. Among ARCADES are those of the nave of West Walton, 2/20 another marshland church, which escaped rebuilding presumably because it was already large enough and is as splendid in the style of c. 1240 as Walsoken was in the style of the late C12. It is one of the glories of E.E. architecture and must be by masons trained at Lincoln. The six-bay nave has round piers each augmented by four detached shafts (eight to the chancel piers), eleven with shaft rings and the most gorgeous stiff-leaf capitals. The pointed arches 2/21 with their many fine mouldings are the epitome of E.E. detailing, and the blind arcading to the clerestory is equally unforgettable. ARCADE ARCHES other than in the major churches tend to be plain chamfered, double-chamfered or with one hollow chamfer; the undercut mouldings to the chancel arch at Toft Monks are exceptional, but this verdict is tempered by the knowledge that very few C13 chancel arches survived Perp rebuilding, so there may have been more. The length of arcades is generally shorter than those of the marshland churches.

BLIND ARCADING or arcading around windows is a motif frequently met, just as it is in the major churches of the C12, e.g. at Ellingham and the monastic churches of North Creake and Broomholm (Bacton), and, open now, in the porch at Great Massingham. Such arcading exists also on the powerful

2/19 DETACHED TOWER at West Walton, where also are an external
wall passage and polygonal corner buttresses, features common to
the prominent E.E. towers at Tilney All Saints and Walsoken.
Detached towers are a feature of fenland and marshland churches
and are found also in Lincolnshire. Other detached towers in
Norfolk of late C13 date were the 'clocher' at Norwich Cathedral,
of which nothing remains, and at Terrington St John, which was
later connected up with the nave and rebuilt. Later came East
Dereham, early C16, and Terrington St Clement, c. 1500–27. To
these should be added the sw tower of St Nicholas, King's Lynn,
2/14 of c. 1225 and the sw tower of St Margaret, King's Lynn, complete
by c. 1260–70.

These examples of E.E. architecture are, however, exceptional.
TOWERS of typical parish churches were almost always unbuttressed, of square plan and at the w like that at Shipdham, though
at e.g. Hardingham is a s porch tower. Some circular towers
continued to be built (e.g. Sustead, Thorpe Abbots, Bawburgh,
St Mary Kirby Bedon, Aylmerton, Horsey, Threxton, Freethorpe
and Poringland), two were octagonal from the ground (Toft
Monks and Old Buckenham*), Heacham has a late C13 central
tower, and West Runton has the springers for a vault. At Heacham
circular bell-openings were still used.

Early C13 WINDOWS were pointed lancets, variously organized.
At Barmer and Eaton they remain with internal splays familiar
from Norman examples, at Bracon Ash and Little Snoring chancel
they have shafts inside. E walls of chancels begin to have lancets
grouped together, usually but not always stepped up to the centre,
a refinement leading towards plate tracery. Mundford and Gooderstone both have three stepped lancets, the latter shafted inside,
at the very elaborate Castle Rising are five lancets enriched with
dogtooth and stiff-leaf, and at Great Massingham the five lancets
are gathered under one arch, a further step towards the development of tracery. In towers two-light bell-openings continued. At
Stradsett is a central twisted shaft reused in the Perp period and
West Runton has Y-tracery on a circular shaft. Y-tracery occurs
elsewhere in the C13, probably late (the s aisle at Harpley; in the
chancel of South Creake combined with its elaborated cousin,
intersecting tracery). But lancets remained in use until the end of
the C13: at Horsey is a trefoiled chancel lancet with a splayed
rere-arch, and at Wramplingham is a run of six lancets on one
side of the chancel and five on the other, coexisting with a Y-
traceried window; the date must be c. 1280. At St Andrew, Gorleston, lancets are used in the lower courses of the late C13 tower.

This takes us nearly up to the C14, but we must now return to
consider the development of TRACERY during the C13. Early
PLATE TRACERY survives in the tower of St Nicholas, King's
Lynn, c. 1225 (still with nailhead decoration), and examples
remain, virtually undatable, in numerous other C13 churches
(Reymerston, Attleborough tower, Middleton chancel, Sporle E

* Old Buckenham has blind arcading to the bell-stage. In the C14 three further
octagonal towers were built, at Billingford (East Dereham), Edgefield and Kettle-
stone.

window, Wimbotsham). BAR TRACERY takes us decidedly into the Geometrical phase of the Dec period. The two-light window by the priest's door at West Walton is graced with shafts with dogtooth and other E.E. embellishments and may be *c.* 1240, earlier than the splendid w front of Binham Priory. Binham has 1/13 fully-formed bar tracery on the grandest scale and dates from before 1244, that is, even before Westminster Abbey.* In its original state there were four subdivided lights carrying minor sexfoiled circles and a central crowning octofoiled circle, all kept clearly separate. There is no better example in Norfolk, although the four-light w window at Little Walsingham refectory comes close. At the cathedral, incidentally, there is little of the C13, although late C13 bar tracery does exist in a minor way at the Deanery.

The master masons in charge at Binham, Walsingham and Norwich are much more likely to be of the first rank than those responsible for the other churches mentioned, although they remain anonymous. Not so the designer of the first surviving Norfolk window to break with the discipline of the Geometrical. This is at Trowse Newton, just south of Norwich, and is of 1/15 1282-3 by *Master Nicholas* of the cathedral. There are three trefoiled lights supporting three unencircled quatrefoils, the larger, centre one placed diagonally, the outer ones tipping inwards slightly in a wilful erosion of the purity of Binham.

We return to the early C13 and a note on E.E. DOORWAYS and their mouldings. These are basically an extension of Norman types, with pointed arches and deeper mouldings, though at East Barsham is a moulded round arch of *c.* 1200. Of similar date is a collection ringing the changes on the same themes: the inner s doorway at Barton Bendish (St Andrew); West Dereham's s doorway; Cranwich; Barney. As the century progressed reliance was placed more on deeply undercut mouldings in many registers (Wiggenhall St Mary Virgin, Watlington), with stiff-leaf capitals and dogtooth decoration relegated to a supporting role (Fakenham). By the late C13 detached shafts made an appearance, or rather provided an encore, as at Heacham, coupled with finely cut mouldings in the arch, and finally Norman or E.E. capital forms gave way to naturalistic foliage, as at Tilney All Saints. In Norfolk, however, this is rare.

Other E.E. DECORATION occurs on the liturgical fittings that became more common in the C13: piscinae, sedilia and Easter Sepulchres. Of the last is the rare early example at Scoulton, of sedilia there are a few late C13 efforts such as Postwick, Harpley and Witton (near North Walsham), but of piscinae quite a number. The earliest is perhaps at Clippesby, *c.* 1200, which has waterleaf capitals and a roll-moulded arch. Later examples are at Brockdish (stiff-leaf and a little dogtooth), Ashill (twin trefoiled arches), Little Snoring and Bittering. Double piscinae include St Cuthbert, Thetford, Gooderstone with its pointed trefoiled

---

* It is almost beyond belief that such a perfect example, the paradigm of Geometrical tracery, did not have precursors in the various lost abbeys of the county.

arches, Hardingham, Eccles with stiff-leaf and Pulham St Mary.
2/18 The last is the best, a perfect E.E. design with a moulded arch
intersected by two half-arches, probably c. 1250. The piscinae at
Baconsthorpe, Postwick, Suffield and Bedingham have Purbeck
marble columns, a favourite material for major E.E. buildings,
but rare in Norfolk.* Of E.E. ROOFS only three require a reference and all are scissor-braced: Ormesby St Michael, Kirby
Cane and Stoke Holy Cross.

Decorated and Perpendicular

By the C14 the basic elements of the Gothic church had been
established. What was to come was their elaboration. To introduce the major themes and to establish the skeleton of a chronology of the fully matured DECORATED STYLE in Norfolk in all
its richness and luxuriance one may look first at the ten major, or
at least famous, buildings of the first half of the C14. First in time
is the cloister of Norwich cathedral, and of that the earliest part
is the three bays opposite the chapter-house doorway, built in
1/19 1297–9; the rest of the walk is of 1299–1314. Here is naturalistic
foliage carving and tracery patterns tentatively introducing the
ogee arch in combination with a pair of spherical triangles
developed out of Y-tracery forms. Within the triangles are further
rounded trefoils. This is a logical extension of the Trowse E
window, breaking with but not wholly abandoning the Geometrical style, unlike the Lincoln cloisters of 1296–c. 1300 which
1/20 remain faithful to the old pattern. The Norwich S walk dates from
1314–30, but the tracery itself, by *John* and *William Ramsey*, must
date to c. 1324–6 and brings something quite new – petal tracery,
a motif which went to the gallery of Ely presbytery after c. 1328,
was developed in the clerestory there (finished c. 1335) where the
foils rotate round a diagonal cross, and returned to Norwich in
1/21 that guise in the W walk in the 1340s. Not only does the S walk
tracery employ fully-fledged ogees but it has the earliest petal
tracery in England, which is one of the most important forms in
Dec Norfolk, and the fifth most frequently met tracery pattern in
Lincolnshire, the county most noted for Curvilinear tracery (the
first Lincolnshire petals are of c. 1335–40 at Heydour). As always,
innovations were made by the most important masons at the most
1/18 significant buildings. The NE portal from the cloisters into the
church must come about 1310, and probably is also the work of
the *Ramseys*. It is the most sumptuous of all Dec doorways in the
county, and is extremely interesting. Essentially it is an E.E.
portal: Purbeck marble shafts, rounded moulded capitals and
bases, pointed arch without an ogee and registers of deeply undercut mouldings. What makes it Dec is the seven ogeed and crocketed niches containing statues grafted on to the moulded arch.

Next is the chancel at Harpley, built between 1294 and 1332.
The various windows have split cusps, ogees and reticulation, the
priest's door a cusped and sub-cusped ogee arch, and a vestry

---

* Purbeck marble is used, other than for fonts and fittings, only for the West
Walton arcades and in the cloister at the cathedral.

door similarly endowed leading to a rib-vaulted chamber. Then comes Elsing, built for Sir Hugh Hastings †1347 and begun about 1330, and all of a piece. One notices first that the nave is the widest of all Norfolk parish churches (40 ft) and is aisleless, an unusual thing probably based on the large preaching-space concept pioneered by the mendicants, and which was to dominate the Perp decades. The tower has flushwork, an early example (*see* Building Materials, p. 22) and reticulated tracery containing further small reticulation units, the nave large petal-traceried windows, and the N doorway a cusped and sub-cusped ogee arch. Fourth is Hingham, built between 1319 and 1359 for the rector Remigius de Hethersett. The tower probably comes at the end of this period and provides us with forms typical of quality work of the 1340s and 50s: quatrefoils, wavy lines, rosettes etc. in the base frieze; fleurons in the arch of the W doorway; set-back buttresses. The chancel seems to be *c.* 1335–40 and links neatly, and directly, with the petal tracery of Ely and Norwich. The nave piers are of quatrefoil section with thin shafts in the diagonals supporting arches with two sunk wave mouldings. Then comes the chancel at Ingham, founded in 1340 and completed by 1344, with a good Curvilinear E window and petal tracery in two of the three side windows separated by a window displaying early Perp motifs. Embryonic Perp is perfectly possible for the early 1340s, if exceptionally rare, and the juxtaposition of Dec and Perp windows was popular later in the century. Sixth is the Slipper Chapel at Houghton St Giles, a highly decorated rectangular box of *c.* 1345–55 dressed up with the same motifs as Hingham and Elsing. Seventh is Attleborough, though the Dec is mixed up with Norman, E.E. and Perp. Of immediate interest is the nave, where petal tracery of *c.* 1340 everywhere prevails, most splendidly in the (rebuilt) W window.

This leaves three buildings. For two, Snettisham and Cley-next-the-Sea, we have no dates; for the third, Carnary College chapel in Norwich, one of the most significant dates of all. Snettisham is the most rousing Dec church in Norfolk, on account of the Dec W front with its six-light window and the (rebuilt) spire, 2/22 175 ft tall, in a county all but devoid of spires, stone or otherwise. In the N transept is Y-tracery and intersecting tracery, so we may say only that it is later than *c.* 1280. The W window rivals the best in Lincolnshire, where one would suggest a date in the 1340s, and is an essay in the use of mouchettes, reticulation units and petal tracery ingeniously fitted together. The clerestory alternates between circular windows containing three spherical triangles and two-light windows. Cley also has such a clerestory, the round 1/34 windows this time containing a cusped cinquefoil, and a ruined S transept or chapel with cusped circles and a cusped spherical square, wilful rather than beautiful. The gable above is crocketed, and the inner S door has a cusped and sub-cusped ogee arch.

Finally the Carnary College chapel, founded in 1316, has long 1/26 been recognized as a precursor of the Perp style, and an off-shoot of the London Court School. It is probably by *John Ramsey I*, influenced by the work of William Ramsey I in London. Not only do we find circular windows in the basement (the original pattern on the N side only), but the main windows, if not quite Perp, then might be termed proto-Perp, and must date from a few years either side of 1330, the very years in which Dec window tracery was reaching maturity. With this model the Early Perp tracery at Ingham can be placed in its context.

These examples provide an outline of major developments, but certain features need further comment. The first is the chronology of windows and window TRACERY. The general rule is that the simpler the motif the longer it lasted. Thus lancets, Y-tracery and intersecting tracery all carried on into the C15, particularly in towers, although in major windows only intersecting varieties retained a hold in Dec churches, e.g. in the six-light E window of Southrepps of c. 1320. Next in origin is reticulated tracery, a form based entirely on the ogee arch and capable, especially when built large, of recreating in its own way the orderly beauty of C13 bar tracery. About fifty Norfolk churches have it. The earliest known examples are from the Wykeham chapel near Weston in Lincolnshire of 1311, but Norfolk masons caught on quickly. The five-light E window at Norton Subcourse is apparently earlier than 1319. The Slipper Chapel, Houghton St Giles, has reticulation units within reticulation units, a refinement found in six more churches including the transepts at Great Ryburgh of c. 1370-80 and, earlier, in the bell-openings of Elsing and Hindringham. Dec lasted long; the C15 nave and chancel of Ashmanhaugh still have reticulation and Y-tracery side by side, if they can be trusted. More certain is the date 1404 for two N chancel windows at Little Fransham, and the last surviving example dates from 1427–38 in the bell-openings at Blofield. Circular clerestory windows, often alternating with two-light windows, occur, apart from at Cley and Snettisham, at fourteen other places dateable right through into the Perp period (the last at Terrington St Clement, Heacham and Ingoldisthorpe). Of petal tracery there are altogether twenty-five churches relying on it to one extent or another, its last appearances confined to sound holes of towers (after 1451 at Bradfield and after 1475 at Northrepps).

TOWERS also deserve a note. Unbuttressed towers continued into the early C14, for instance at Thurne, Rackheath, Westfield 2/23 and Bastwick. East Harling, with big set-back buttresses of about 1300 in its lower stages, represents the new pattern. Flushwork appears in parapets, base courses and buttresses after about 1330, though it is rare before 1360. Then there are a number of oddities: at Beeston the tower is embraced by the aisles; three octagonal towers have already been mentioned, as has the hexagonal central tower of the Greyfriars in King's Lynn. A few have processional ways cut through: Riddlesworth, Diss and Metton; ten have or had offset towers, those at Briningham, Colkirk, St Stephen Norwich, Whinburgh and West Bradenham doubling as porches.

The major C13 themes of PIERS and ARCHES continued, though circular piers faded out late in the century (the late C13 N arcade of Horning and the early C14 W piers at Rollesby are two of the last), as did keeled shafts to quatrefoil piers (West Winch, *c.* 1300). Octagonal piers are the most common C14 type, occasionally with concave sides, as at Narborough and Dersingham, but it is the quatrefoil pier with its variations which epitomizes the Dec style, even though it was an E.E. invention. It continued into the C15 but generally gave way to Perp types around 1380. The variations include fillets to foils rather than keels, thin hollows between the lobes, thin shafts between the lobes (Hingham), foils so prominent as to appear almost detached (e.g. at Cockley Cley, early enough in the C14 to employ keels between the foils), or with polygonal projections after about 1375 at Bracon Ash, or at Swanton Morley. The last however must be classified as Early Perp not Late Dec.

Then there are PORCHES, DOORWAYS and their MOULDINGS. Porches did not concern us in the C13 (with the exception of Great Massingham), but they are a Dec and especially a C15 feature, though Norfolk is not the county to visit for Dec porches. Overwhelmingly they are placed to the N and S, apart from Snettisham and Little Walsingham, and single-storeyed, apart from Thurgarton and Hevingham. In total there are twenty-four Dec examples, nothing compared to the Perp. Both of the two-storeyed porches are plain, though Hevingham is quite large and quite late Dec. Of other porches one might single out North Creake for its quatrefoil side windows and date of *c.* 1300, Thompson for its triple niche above the entrance of *c.* 1330–40 and the inner door with three continuous sunk-quadrant mouldings, Banham for its knapped flint and mouchette and reticulated windows, and Gooderstone, which has circular side windows, each with three trefoils set in. Alderford is of 1374 and more Perp than Dec. Of doorways hardly any are special. Thrigby has seaweed capitals to the single order of shafts and a good moulded arch, i.e. early C14. Of the same date is Halvergate which has the bonus of buttress shafts and an ogeed and crocketed gable, the latter appearing in modified form also at St Mary, Barton Bendish. Ogee hoods serve both sides of Sustead's N door, but the general run of Dec doors contented themselves with plain hoodmoulds sometimes terminating in headstops. At St Mary, Warham, and Trunch the priest's doors have the curious feature of a chancel buttress growing out of them. Arch mouldings also are disappointing, though sunk wave mouldings may be seen at Fring (1327) and Thompson (*c.* 1330-40), and double wave mouldings at Wilby.

Of PISCINAE, SEDILIA and EASTER SEPULCHRES there are quite a number, though nothing as good as in contemporary Lincolnshire and Nottinghamshire. In common with such furnishings elsewhere they picked up those elements of the Dec style suited to them, sometimes but not always ten or twenty years after their introduction. Sedilia and piscinae as a single architectural unit were popular from the early C14, as at Hilborough where there are five cinquefoiled arches, or at Besthorpe with four gables over ogee niches. The piscina at St Andrew, Barton Bendish, of *c.* 1330 manages Curvilinear tracery, which is advanced for its date; at Harpley (chancel) the combination

features diapering on the back wall of before 1332, a motif first
occurring at North Creake in painted form. Generally ogees
feature strongly after about 1330. At Great Snoring there are even
miniature quadripartite rib-vaults, while at Great Barningham a
type of stone inlay is used. Easter Sepulchres tend to be the most
lavish of all, and the sequence begins at North Creake in about
1300. No ogees exist at that date but instead buttresses with
pinnacles, a cusped and sub-cusped arch and openwork tracery.
Much the same elements are disposed in the presumed combined
founder's tomb and sepulchre at Raveningham, while the sepulchre at Ormesby St Margaret has tracery in the spandrels of the
gablet.

C14 ROOFS carry on with the C13 scissor-braced type at Bale
and Burlingham St Edmund, both c. 1300. Caston, Whinburgh,
Wilton and Shelfanger are slightly later and the best scissor braces
are at Thompson, of forty trusses, made about 1330–40. From
the early C14 the first arch-braced roofs survive, such as at Stody,
where in addition is a rib-vault effect to negotiate the crossing,
and in several porches. At West Lynn there are tie-beams on
arched braces.

Altogether it must be clear by now that the notion that there
was a sharp boundary between Dec and Perp – traditionally
around 1350 – must be abandoned, just as one must forget the
ideal dates for E.E. This is true not just of Norfolk. If one takes
piers as an example then Dec lasts from c. 1240 to c. 1450; window
tracery gives us the dates c. 1300 to c. 1470. If the earliest Perp
forms are taken as the start of that style then Perp lasts from
about 1330 to the 1570s, suggesting a zone of overlap between
Dec and Perp in Norfolk longer in time than the entire period
usually assigned to pure Dec. The Norman, E.E., Geometrical,
Dec and Perp all coexisted for at least as long as they individually
held sway, but usually longer, and this has implications for dating
on stylistic grounds alone: just because a tower has, for example,
petal tracery it does not mean it is Dec, only that it is later than
1324 (*see* Bradfield where the tower was begun after 1451 and
finished in 1514). There are plenty of instances where Dec and
Perp forms appear side by side in the same building campaign,
and the practice of sandwiching a Dec window between two Perp
ones in aisles or naves seems to have been fashionable in the C15.*
For dating, reliance instead has to be placed on the totality of
elements and the knowledge of the dates of introduction of each
feature, be it moulding patterns, pier shapes, tracery or plan form.

The most conspicuous fact about PERPENDICULAR parish
churches in Norfolk is their large size, accompanied by large
windows, tall and light arcades, clerestories and wide roofs.
Another familiar local characteristic is the use of knapped flint
and flushwork, which become standard decorative devices from

---

* e.g. St George Tombland, Norwich (mid C15), Tuttington (mid C15) and Trunch.
At Tunstead and Denton Dec windows combine with Perp piers, and at Walcott in
a Perp chancel. One might append the fact that the chancel at Ingoldisthorpe mixes
Dec and Perp in the same windows and that Great Cressingham clerestory is of Dec
mouchette type but is definitely C15.

the later C14, either as decoration to towers, base courses or parapets, or applied to whole walls, as at St Michael Coslany, 1/60 Norwich. Mostly the impetus to rebuild and enlarge first centred on naves, which usually required subsequent or simultaneous reconstruction of W towers. Chancels followed if money permitted and work was needed. The pre-eminence of naves in the Perp style of Norfolk is characteristic and probably reflects mendicant ideals already mentioned. Then, equally important, is the fact that big new naves and towers are expensive, but Norfolk was by the late C14 a wealthy county; naves were the responsibility of the parish but donors could always be found. For this we can be grateful, for the Perp style is the style by which Norfolk is remembered, and, of all things, Perp benefits from being presented big.

There are a handful of churches whose construction spans the earliest to the latest Perp, and for which there are known dates, beginning not with a church but with Norwich cathedral presbytery, where the clerestory was added *c.* 1362–86. Here there are big traceried transoms, but the differing designs of the tracery heads, while certainly Perp, indicate that early Perp tracery grew out of Dec reticulation, by the device of straightening the curved members into vertical lozenges. Outside Norfolk the earliest manifestation of this was in Old St Paul's chapter house and cloister (1332–49), and at the E presbytery window of Wells Cathedral of *c.* 1339. Ingham has already been mentioned for its chancel with one Perp window of 1340–4, but its nave founded in 1360 carries the style further. Not only has it reached Perp proportions but the piers have just turned from Dec to Early Perp. The form is still a basic quatrefoil, but with filleted diagonal shafts between the lobes and polygonal capitals. These carry double wave-moulded arches, the whole system very similar to the Late Dec arcades at Hingham apart from the capitals. It is unfortunately debatable whether one can trust the S aisle windows, which have the straightened reticulation unit pattern.

Swanton Morley was under construction in 1379, by which time pier profiles had altered. Towards the aisles are polygonal projections rising without a break to become the hoodmoulds of the wave-moulded arches. Capitals exist only to the demi-shafts to the E and W, and these are circular, but with polygonal abaci. The window tracery at Swanton Morley is equally arresting. The aisle E windows are a variant on the Norwich presbytery style, while the three-light side windows not only repeat the quatrefoiled embattled transom but introduce panel tracery. Moreover the window heads are square, and this fact, the use of panel tracery and the novelty of having pier profiles not radially symmetrical allow us to state that mature Perp was established by the 1380s in Norfolk. A notable feature of the plan is that apart from the diminutive chancel the church is rectangular, even the tower being embraced by the aisles. The impression in the nave is of a unified preaching space, a trend which was influential for the later major Perp parish churches.

At St Nicholas, King's Lynn, everything apart from the offset E.E. tower was begun about 1405 and finished in 1419 and it

is a rich study. This remarkable building, part stone, part brick, has the latest medieval plan and the latest Perp details before their time. It is 203 by 82 ft and, apart from the s porch, a perfect rectangle, remarkable for a church which was only a
2/28 chapel-of-ease. Inside, it is an aisled preaching box, exactly in the manner of the friars' churches, with no structural division between nave and chancel. The piers have a lozenge plan presenting a much wider plane of mouldings to the arches than to the aisles, with vestigial capitals. The windows, which include the tremendous nine-light E and eleven-light w, have tracery with principal mullions (or supermullions) continued right through to the arch.

In other early C15 churches Perp and Dec details appear together. At Salle, where the nave of a major new church was probably complete by 1411, the piers have a regular Dec quatrefoil section but Perp panel tracery is ubiquitous. In the nave of the 1450s–60s at Cawston the mason or the patron favoured the economical option of octagonal piers and double-chamfered arches, though in the chancel chapel is a pier of the Swanton Morley type.

2/35   Finally, at Shelton, the almost complete church of the 1490s and a little later represents the final stage of Perp design. The new work is of brick and consists of a nave and chancel in one,
2/36 with the arcade of moulded lozenge piers under four-centred arches running up to the E end. The aisle windows are set in wall arches, the clerestory windows are double the number of the arcade bays, and the clerestory picks up the early Perp trick of having its mullions extending down over the bare wall to meet the arcade arches, not a common feature in Norfolk. The chancel is represented only by an E sacristy, an indication of the final dominance of naves in the Perp plan. Fewer than twenty-five new chancels were started after about 1360 unless they were part of a complete new church. In Norwich, St Gregory has a chancel of 1394 of only one bay; St Swithin's chancel is even smaller and is no longer divided from the nave; finally, in the premier city parish
1/59 churches, St Peter Mancroft and St Stephen, structural division is given up.

Now some particular remarks developing these themes, first TRACERY. The overwhelming majority of Perp windows are content with ordinary panel tracery set within two-centred arches. Four-centred arches tend to appear after the 1430s (All Saints Norwich, Guist belfry, Poringland clerestory, Martham aisles, Ringland clerestory) but never replaced the earlier type. Windows with stepped transoms, sometimes embattled, were a popular C15 variant, e.g. Great Cressingham E window, Cley-next-the-Sea porch, Fincham s aisle and chancel. Supermullions feature at St Nicholas, King's Lynn, before 1419, in 1437 at Wiveton, a little
2/25 later at East Harling and at Walpole St Peter in conjunction with stepless transoms. From about 1450 they are the normal type in prestigious work such as at Terrington St Clement and Shelton. These elements aside, what one notices particularly about Perp tracery is the fact that any design can fit any date; once panel

tracery was developed around 1380 later masons were content with minor variations.

Norfolk CLERESTORIES with circular windows or with windows alternating between circular and normal shape continued into the C15. Heacham, Brisley and Weston Longville have quatrefoils, the last in a square surround, while Stalham has quatrefoil openings alternating with blind two-light windows done in flushwork. This was fairly common. South Lopham has lettering in flushwork of c. 1470 between the windows; blind windows and an inscription feature at Northwold, while at Tunstead all the clerestory windows are blind. In some cases the clerestory, often a later raising of the height of the church, is so much higher than the chancel that an E window becomes possible. One of the chief thrills of the great Perp churches in Norfolk and the whole of East Anglia is the double clerestory. These ranks of very closely set windows, double the number of the arcade bays below, are as impressive from the outside as they are from the inside, especially in conjunction with the spectacular roofs that were installed at the same time (for which *see* below). The window score is as follows, the larger numbers relating to Late Perp churches without a separate chancel: St Peter Mancroft 17 (1431), St Stephen 16 (1540) (both Norwich), Loddon 15; in naves only at Terrington St Clement 14, Sparham 14, Swaffham 13. The 2/27 earliest remaining example of a double clerestory is at Banningham of c. 1360–70 or possibly St Gregory, Norwich, where Dec tracery was still used.

But before even double clerestories are noticed the visitor is struck by the number and scale of Perp TOWERS in the county. There are only eighteen pre-C19 spires (the best are at the cathedral, Snettisham, Methwold and Wilton),* and a number of pretty spirelets such as at Shipdham and East Harling. Numerous belfry stages were added to earlier towers in the Perp decades, just as they had been in the Dec years. Octagonal was the rule, a shape practically obligatory over a round tower, but a square was required for the heightening of the already very tall tower at Winterton after 1387. It has parapet figures as well as pinnacles, a common feature of Perp upper stages. A few other exceptional towers should be singled out. The crossing tower at Wymondham, of 1390–1409, has its two upper storeys built octagonal from the start. In addition, Wymondham has a massive W tower, attributed to *James Woderofe*, in building from 1447 to 1498. Its principal features are the shafted polygonal buttresses and the large decorated W doorway. The amazingly busy tower of St Peter Mancroft, 1/45 Norwich, probably commenced in the 1430s, has a N–S processional way, with an open vaulted space between four arches, and strong angle buttresses rising to the parapet, with niches. The

* The others are Banham, Beeston, Cranworth, Croxton (Thetford), Downham Market, Earsham, Great Ellingham, Hethersett, Little Walsingham, Quidenham, Seckton, Tilney All Saints, Walsoken and Wilton. Demolished or fallen ones were in Oxborough, East Ruston, Holt, St Gregory Norwich, Denver, St Margaret King's Lynn, Tilney St Lawrence, Watton and West Harling. There will have been more of which we know nothing.

normally flat side walls are covered in tiers of arcading, sometimes
enriched with flushwork. This is the only Perp tower in Norfolk
to have such indiscriminate decoration. Flushwork panelling and
polygonal buttresses are also found at Redenhall.

The more usual Norfolk tower has flushwork panelling, base
friezes, a big W doorway with carved spandrels, angle buttresses
or less frequently diagonal buttresses, and panel tracery in the
openings. At Poringland the C14 octagonal top has alternating
blind windows, as does the Perp top to the Saxon tower at St
Mary, Beachamwell. Apart from its unusually tall belfry stage
1/48 Salle is a typical example, begun in c. 1405–20 but not finished
until 1511. Other datable examples are at Cawston, 1412–21, and
2/26 Great Cressingham, where the tower must have been complete by
1451 if the attribution to *James Woderofe* is correct. The majority
of Norfolk towers are dated in the gazetteer only as Perp or C15,
or even C16, but there are eighty-four towers later than 1400 for
which we know the commencement date and twenty-three top-
stage additions to existing towers.*

PORCHES were very frequently the subject of Perp bequests,
and their attraction to patrons is obvious: they allow the display
of family crests, they are small but capable of almost infinite
decoration and refinement, can show off technical displays in
vaults and above all can be completed within a short space of
time at reasonable cost. Such, mostly two-storeyed, porches are
often the best part of the church.‡ Their decorative potential is
2/29 at once appreciated at St Nicholas, King's Lynn, c. 1410, where
the tall two-storeyed porch has a lavish S front of ogeed niches
and panelling in tiers, and inside is a lierne vault with bosses. At
Great Cressingham the 1439 porch is single-storeyed but still
manages a flushwork base frieze and a niche over the entrance
with a figure. Instead of a vault inside are shafts for wall arches.
Knapped flint was by the middle of the C15 common for porches
(even the floor at Beeston Regis has it), but tiers of flushwork
were rarer, such as those on the S porch at East Harling (between
c. 1440 and 1480), Ludham N porch, South Walsham in 1454 or
at Pulham St Mary where the porch steals the show: carving,
niches, rows of angels, windows all in lavish abandon.

The extravagant Lyhart Porch at Carnary College, Norwich,
of the 1480s is very small but has a rib vault over the staircase.
At Ingham a three-storey porch – unique in Norfolk – was in
construction in 1440, and at Aylsham a two-storeyed porch
1/58 went up in 1488: all knapped flint and flushwork panelling and
a bigger show than normal made of the parvis windows.
Shelton's prominent porch has a tall niche to the first floor

* The decades have the following totals, the addition work in brackets, based on
documented cases. 1400–10: 2 (1); 1411–20: 3; 1421–30: 5; 1431–40: 11 (2); 1441–50:
8 (1); 1451–60: 12 (3); 1461–70: 4; 1471–80: 13 (4); 1481–90: 9 (2); 1491–1500:
4 (2); 1501–10: 9 (2); 1511–20: 2; 1521–30: 2 (4); after 1531: (2). These figures are
surprising only for the late date of some towers.
‡ The statistics out of a total of 133 porches for which dates are known are as follows. 1400–10: 1; 1411–20: 1; 1421–30: 1; 1431–40: 7; 1441–50: 8; 1451–60: 8;
1461–70: 6; 1471–80: 8; 1481–90: 3; 1491–1500: 8; 1501–10: 7. There are in addition
61 for which closer dating than C15 Perp is impossible, and 14 definitely C16.

with windows r. and l., and was obviously intended to have a fan vault. The most common porch vault was a standard tierceron vault (Cawston, Hemsby, St John Maddermarket, Norwich, Cley-next-the-Sea, St Mary Coslany, Norwich, in 1466 etc., and Walpole St Peter in 1435, of two bays and with scenes in bosses), but lierne vaults appeared after 1450 (St Laurence, Norwich) and fan vaults at Shelton and St Giles, Norwich. Of barrel vaults one need mention only those of Terrington St John, Wiggenhall St Mary the Virgin, Beeston Regis and the wooden vault at Happisburgh. There are three timber porches, two C16, at Blo Norton and Shelfanger and a rebuilt porch at Shimpling. Mention of materials introduces brick, of which – at least visible brick – patrons were much less shy in connection with porches than with other parts of a church. The brick porch at Needham with its polygonal angle shafts looks as if it should be early C16 but there are bequests from 1469 and 1470. A larger number of brick porches survive from the 1480s, mixed with flint at Heckingham, without flint at Shelton, and after 1500 of brick alone (e.g. Wiggenhall St Germans).

Concerning PIERS and ARCADES, we have already noted that the pier with polygonal projections and a section not radially symmetrical appeared by 1379, and the lozenge pier was in use before 1419. A typical lozenge has in addition to a longer N–S axis hollows in the diagonals, sometimes with shafts, as at Wiveton (after 1437), or with hollows and wave mouldings in the diagonals (St Martin-at-Oak, Norwich). The general trend throughout the C15 was for piers to become slenderer.

Major stone VAULTS are exceptional. The most important are the lierne vault of Norwich cathedral nave begun in 1463 and continued in the presbytery in c. 1480–90, and the vault in the chapel at the Great Hospital, Norwich, of c. 1470–1. A fan vault 1/43 was intended under the tower at Swaffham from 1485 and the Red Mount, King's Lynn, is a rich specimen of 1505–6. Timber 2/34 ROOFS are another matter, for Norfolk is among the counties richest in, and most ingenious at, church roofs. There are great gaps in our knowledge of their development until the C15. As we have seen, Dec roofs only survive to indicate a continuation of the yet earlier scissor-braced formula, but from the late C14 other types survive. The earliest Perp roofs appear to have been either based on tie-beams or on arched braces supporting the principal rafters, or a combination of both as at St Gregory, Norwich. At Earsham, Hardwick and St Clement, Norwich, are C15 arch-braced roofs with the addition of longitudinal braces, at Sparham the braces rise to the collars, at Swafield right up to the ridge. The most spectacular roof type is of course the HAMMERBEAM roof, usually put in with brave new clerestories in the second half of the C15. There are in Norfolk seven variants on this type, but very few of them were needed for their structural function, i.e. to span a nave too wide for conventional roofs. Perhaps the earliest in Norfolk is the late C14 roof at St Giles, Norwich, which has 1/36 continuous arched braces rising through the tie-beams. At Great

Cressingham (before 1451) hammerbeams are tentatively introduced with alternating arched braces demonstrating that show not
stability was the motive. At West Walton the primitive-looking
late C15 nave roof has two hammerbeams to each tie-beam. But at
St Peter Mancroft, Norwich, a full hammerbeam roof was
conceived in about 1431, the hammerbeams concealed by coving.
Similar coving occurs at Ringland. After St Peter Mancroft hammerbeams gained in popularity, being installed at Blakeney,
1/44 Aslacton and Cawston. The Cawston roof of c. 1460 is particularly
fine: shields in cresting to the hammerbeams, open tracery behind
the posts, figures in front of them, braces to the principals, two
tiers of purlins and at the junction of the principals and ridge
piece dropped braces to figured bosses. Other notable roofs are
1/38 at Wymondham, Worstead ('new' in 1480), Trunch ('new' in
1486), Fincham (1488 with alternating hammerbeams in two
sizes), Necton (c. 1490), Poringland (1495) and St Stephen,
Norwich, finished only after 1540. Of double hammerbeam roofs
the most famous is at Gissing but the best is at Knapton, made
in 1504. It has a total of 160 angels as decoration. The type was
2/37 also deployed at Tilney All Saints and Swaffham, but at those
two the upper register of hammerbeams is purely decorative. Of
other roof types are queenposts at Hockwold, Wiggenhall St
Germans and Wiggenhall St Mary Magdalen, and a crown-post
construction at Swardeston, but the majority are simple arch-
braced roofs with principals and purlins.

There are only about nine EASTER SEPULCHRES of quality in
Perp Norfolk. Two at least – East Raynham and Hunstanton –
were from the start intended as monuments as well, a fashion also
popular in the London area from the later C15, following the early
C14 precedent at Raveningham. At Raynham (after 1499) is a
panelled tomb chest, a superstructure with a four-centred arch
and stepped niches for statues against the back wall. Hunstanton
has the same basic ingredients. At Northwold are four sleeping
soldiers against the tomb chest, which is the closest Norfolk
examples come to Dec work in Lincolnshire and Nottinghamshire, and star- and fan-vaults. Other sepulchres are at Kelling,
Baconsthorpe, Plumstead, Harpley and New Buckenham. The
C15 is not a century of PISCINAE and SEDILIA: one must go
back to the C13 and C14 for that. Brisley has both, partly Dec
and partly Perp; the piscina has ballflower decoration, extremely
rare in Norfolk. Early Perp is represented by the elaborate combined
1/39 piece at Tunstead, which has similar Perp shafting to Beeston
Regis, vaulting at St Nicholas, King's Lynn, and a four-centred
arch at Great Massingham. The Late Perp fittings at Gressenhall
have odd Geometrical ornament on the back wall, and there is
tracery also at Oxborough. Rib-vaulting and demi-figures of
angels occur also at Oxborough, vaulting and panel tracery at
Shropham.

CHURCH FURNISHINGS TO 1550

For church furnishings the natural start is not wood but stone. The beginning is the C7 or C8 fragments of the bishop's throne of the former see (*see* above) incorporated in the E arm of Norwich cathedral *c.* 1121, with flanking interlaced screens. The cathedral also has a choir screen built after the 1463 fire, of which again only parts are original. One is reminded by the remains of part of a screen at Ingham that monastic or friary churches probably also had stone screens. The rest of the story of stone furnishings belongs to FONTS (with the exception of the circular C13 lead font at Brundall and the C15 octagonal brick font at Potter Heigham), which range through the whole Middle Ages commencing with the Normans. Of NORMAN FONTS the majority are square and some are very elaborate. Fincham has three little figures under 2/6 arcading to each side, combining to form Biblical scenes. At Burnham Deepdale we have the Labours of the Months as at 2/5 Brookland in Kent and on one of the fonts at Warham All Saints, recut into an octagon. Breckles has, on different faces, four figures under arches like Fincham, intersecting arches and two Green Men. Interlaced circles decorate the Bagthorpe font, interlace and intersecting arches at Ingoldisthorpe (also recut into an octagon), while Castle Rising has animal heads at the corners looking up. There is a group of four in NW Norfolk which are related by the fact that they have elaborated projecting rims to the bowls, at the corners of which are columns or piers, and which are carried on various numbers of carved and decorated supports. They are at Sculthorpe, Shernborne, South Wootton and Toftrees and Francis Bond called them 'a group of fonts unsurpassed in Europe'. The best of the carving is at Shernborne, but the rest hold their own and include animal heads, interlace and, at Sculthorpe, five figures under an interlaced arcade.

A handful of Norman fonts are of the cauldron (Belaugh and Spixworth) or tub shape (Bridgham and Thuxton). Among circular fonts Shereford has four shafts against the central stem and scallops under the bowl; Little Snoring has foliage in medallions. There are three square Norman fonts of Purbeck marble at Coltishall, Horsford and Thorpe-next-Haddiscoe, all with four shallow blank arches to each side. This motif also occurs, though usually with only two arches, on the C13 PURBECK MARBLE FONTS which were made on the Dorset coast and transported by sea to southern England and East Anglia. There are forty-two in Norfolk, all octagonal, which was in a general way a C13 change from Norman. They vary very little; one of the biggest is at Little Melton, with eight columns round the stem. Of other shapes the Norman square is still represented at Little Fransham early in the C13 and later at Scarning, and cup-shaped fonts exist at Heydon and Holt.

The majority of DEC and PERP FONTS were plain octagons with quatrefoils or shields on the bowl, but a more interesting group has tracery patterns, beginning in the early C14 and extending to the C15. Early examples are Geometrical (Hilborough and Hockham), and late C13 styles predominate until the middle of the C14 (Bressingham, Frenze and Threxton); at Neatishead and Sea Palling are reticulated and early Perp designs, as there are at Shelfanger which may be of the 1360s. Witton (near Norwich) has a mixture of patterns; Great Ellingham even has Kentish tracery; Stoke Ferry has a Perp font with Flamboyant tracery. As a rule one may have to add twenty or thirty years to the date the tracery would suggest in windows.

The so-called EAST ANGLIAN FONT emerged in the later C14, and this type saw the Middle Ages out. It has a number of features, not always present in all examples: a single stem with four seated lions against it or four lions and four wild men; under the octagonal bowl angels or demi-figures of angels sometimes with spread wings; on the bowl carved representations of the signs of the four Evangelists and four angels, often with shields, or the Instruments of the Passion, or any other combination. The earliest may be at Upton, which looks decidedly Dec not Perp. Acle dates from 1410. Among the variations are musical angels (Happisburgh) and angels with shields on which are the emblems of the Trinity (Caistor St Edmund, Saxlingham Nethergate, Shelton). There are in Norfolk about sixty-five such fonts, fewer than the hundred or so Suffolk can muster. The more elaborate version is the SEVEN SACRAMENTS FONT, of which Norfolk has thirty and Suffolk only fourteen. These scenes are played out on the bowl.* The eighth scene varies between the Baptism of Christ (Sloley; Seething, c. 1480), the Trinity (Binham), Last Judgment (Gorleston-on-Sea, late C14; Marsham), the Crucifixion (Salle, 1437; Brooke, 1468; Alderford, 1518) or even a seated Virgin at Gayton Thorpe. The best is probably the C15 font at Little Walsingham, which in common with a number of others is raised on three steps decorated with tracery, as if the fonts were not elaborate enough. The top step at Walsingham and elsewhere is shaped like a Maltese cross. Miniature vaults appear here and there, as at East Dereham in 1468, Loddon in 1487 and as late as 1544 at Walsoken.

After the mason's craft we turn to the carpenter's and FONT COVERS. Norfolk has no example as spectacular as some in Suffolk, and what there are fall generally into the C17. Of Perp covers the earliest is probably at Kenninghall, which may be late C14, and sets the tone in being a drum with radiating buttresses. The cover at Worstead, datable to 1461, has been greatly restored but remains as one of the elegant openwork types with radial fins reducing in stages to the top finial. Castle Acre and Salle are similar, the latter with its original pulley on its bracket. At North Walsham the very tall cover is a series of open drums, at Dersingham just one fat drum with applied gablets and tracery. The Perp cover at Elsing is the most architectural, with (renewed)

---

* The Sacraments of the Roman Canon are: Baptism, Confirmation, Ordination, Confession, Matrimony, Mass and Extreme Unction.

figures in niches, diagonal pierced vanes, rich crocketing and a spire for a top. In the C16 the type simplified into shorter, more solid constructions with narrow buttress fins at the angles as at South Acre, c. 1534, or with crockets up the edges as at Beeston, before 1536. Of FONT CANOPIES, that is, a free-standing baldacchino on piers enclosing the font, Norfolk has two of the four medieval examples in England, at St Peter Mancroft (Norwich) and at Trunch. The Norwich canopy has four piers supporting an octagonal cornice; Trunch has six supports to the cornice 1/40 under which is a fan-vault and above which is a drum encrusted with hanging canopies on all sides.

The supreme example of STALLS with MISERICORDS is the set of over sixty at Norwich cathedral dating from c. 1420 and 1/56 c. 1480. The C14 stalls at Hevingham have blind tracery and mouchette wheels, and broad surfaces for books (they may have been used in the schoolroom over the porch). Of c. 1370–80 are those in St Margaret, King's Lynn: panelled fronts, animal carvings and misericords. The feature most remembered about East Anglian stalls and benches is POPPYHEAD ENDS, which become ubiquitous in the C15 often in conjunction with carved animal heads or figures, e.g. at Salle, where there are misericords too. Tracery is used at Trunch in the C16, and misericords with demi-figures of angels, and one might mention also Castle Acre and East Harling. For sheer delight in figure carving two examples are the early C16 scenes on the stalls at Swaffham showing a woman at work in her shop, and the S transept stall ends of c. 1520 1/55 at the Great Hospital, Norwich. Of the C13 there is only the wonderful stall end at Irstead, the most gorgeous split stiff-leaf 1/17 rising out of a head. As far as BENCHES are concerned the C14 yields only two at Aylmerton with reused poppyheads. At Rockland St Peter are a set of twenty with traceried ends, poppyheads and animals on the arm rests. This is the established pattern, growing ever more elaborate throughout the C15: complete or nearly complete sets survive at Great Walsingham (late C15), Feltwell (perhaps 1494), Hockham (C15) and at Wiggenhall St Germans and Wiggenhall St Mary the Virgin (early C15 to 2/48 early C16). 2/49

But the best of the wood carver's art is to be seen in SCREENS, just as it is in Suffolk, and the later the date the better the quality. They are the most familiar wooden ornament of East Anglian churches and, while they cannot compete with Devon in richness of decoration, they are in their greater restraint just as impressive. There are in all 153 screens more or less complete.* The early screens are characterized by shafts instead of mullions and sometimes elaborate Dec tracery as at Merton, Edingthorpe and Fak- 2/24 enham. At Hempstead (near Lessingham) the tracery forms a complete net; generally, reticulated tracery, mouchette wheels

---

* Minus their roods of course. The dates assigned in the gazetteer suggest that 20 are C14 (most only fragments), 98 are C15, mostly late C15, of which 45 have painted figures or scenes, and 35 lie between 1500 and 1536, of which 16 have paintings. All screens were originally coloured. In addition there are 42 fragments and 11 C15 or C16 dados.

and spherical triangles are the favoured motifs. Cusped ogee arches were the rule for the central opening and two-light divisions r. and l. are more usual than single lights (of the latter e.g. Griston, Harpley and Mattishall); a screen at St Margaret, King's Lynn, has three-light divisions and tracery of reticulation units inside others. Of screens datable to 1400–50 one can count only seven in a satisfactory state. One is at Sheringham and has two-light divisions and panel tracery and even the rood beam carried on solid arched braces with carved dragons, and the rood parapet. A rood beam may also be seen at Costessey. Doors survive in several screens, for instance at Thompson, c. 1330–40, South Walsham, after 1437, and at Cawston in 1460, and evidence of vaulting at Happisburgh, coving at Worstead on the parclose screens, East Harling, Fundenhall and Emneth (where it is ribbed). At Barton Turf is even a skeleton vault under the w coving. Side altars were once apparently a feature, of which bits only remain at Strumpshaw, East Ruston (inner posts) and Costessey.

All of these features may be taken together in the two Norfolk screens which would win a screen competition: Ranworth and Attleborough, probably of the 1480s. Ranworth has cusping in two layers and ribbed coving, and at either side painted partitions defining side altars. Attleborough, however, is the more spectacular because it spans the whole width of nave and aisles, no less than 52 ft, with coving to both sides, but with one-light divisions just cusped, not traceried, and marks only of the position 1/49 of side altars. Both Ranworth and Attleborough put on displays of PAINTED PANELS, and altogether Norfolk and Suffolk are pre-eminent in the painting of their screens, even if only the minority are of high quality. The reader must beware, for paintings were very often applied some time after the screen was made, as at Buxton and Cawston. At Tunstead, Filby, Horsford and elsewhere we know too that painting came later: it was a favourite subject for bequests after the middle of the c15. Of c14 paintings one may single out Edingthorpe's stencilling with early c15 painted Saints on red and green grounds. The Saints at Dersingham are c14, but on the whole c14 screens did not have paintings other than colouring or, at best, vine trails etc. Even the South Walsham and Strumpshaw screens only managed ornamental painting well into the c15. Of c. 1400, however, is Castle Acre (twelve good Saints), after 1433 Swanton Abbot (Saints) and in 1436 Litcham (twenty-two Saints). After this there is a glut of Saints, usually the Apostles, and some other figures. Among these are donors (Aylsham, Edgefield s aisle 1526, and Fritton 1/51 c. 1520); the Heavenly Hierarchies (Barton Turf, Ranworth and Yelverton c. 1505); the Annunciation and Temptation of St Anthony at Tacolneston c. 1515–20; St John Schorn at Cawston, between c. 1490 and 1510, and Gateley, where he conjures the Devil into a boot; the Dance of Death at Sparham; the Life of Christ at Loddon c. 1520–30; the Virgin at North Walsham c. 1470 and with the Child at Great Snoring early c15. In addition Kings, miscellaneous Saints favoured by donors, Evangelists and the Four Doctors crop up now and again.

Of schools of painters we know very little. There were at least two hands responsible for the Aylsham paintings, two for Ludham (after 1493) and North Elmham (*c.* 1505), three at Cawston. The Horsham St Faith artist may have gone to Burlingham St Andrew in 1536 (which is incidentally the latest dated screen in the county), and there was one particularly successful painter or group whose work developed at Southwold in Suffolk after 1470 and may be seen at Ranworth in the later 1470s, and at other places.* Three screens have paintings made on parchment and stuck on, so the studio could have been anywhere. Two are already linked – the second artist at Aylsham and the third at Cawston – and the third, Gateley, joins the group by virtue of the subject, the rare figure of John Schorn. Of other PANEL PAINTINGS one need see only the Norwich cathedral retables, one of *c.* 1380, the other *c.* 1430–40, which are as good as anything in England, and lastly there is the Antwerp retable of *c.* 1530–5 at the Catholic chapel at Oxburgh Hall.

Norfolk is richer than any other county in medieval WALL PAINTING,‡ much of it only discovered since 1962. The one period in which the county is deficient in surviving examples is the Romanesque, though an immensely important scheme has been discovered in 1996 at Houghton-on-the-Hill, which at the time of writing has been only partly exposed. It includes the Trinity, busts holding scrolls, and the Resurrection of the Dead, and may well date from as early as *c.* 1090; an Anglo-Saxon survival is the quatrefoil motif on the draperies covering God's knee. Dating from about a century later, and from the very end of the Romanesque period, are the small-scale but exquisite paintings in the nave s aisle of Norwich cathedral, including unique scenes of the cathedral's foundation by Bishop Losinga.

From the early Gothic period, the star item is undoubtedly the scheme of *c.* 1250 in Horsham St Faith Priory, with its immense Crucifixion and superbly preserved over-life-size figure of a female Saint, and once again a series of small scenes (repainted in the C15) illustrating the foundation legend of the monastery. Other 1/16 important C13 paintings include the exquisite Adoration scene at Shelfanger, the decorative scheme of fictive draperies and pierced roundels at West Walton (partly overpainted in the C18), and the decoration of the east end of the cathedral following the 1272 fire. Also in the cathedral, the Ante-Reliquary Chapel retains fragments of a figural scheme of *c.* 1250–60, and a much more extensive programme of Apostles and other Saints dating from *c.* 1300, in an elegant and mannered style deriving from slightly earlier French-influenced painting at Westminster.

But it is chiefly the explosion of painting in the middle and second half of the C14 which makes Norfolk so memorable for wall painting. Many schemes of this period survive, often of excellent quality, and typically including moralizing subjects such as the Three Living and the Three Dead, the Warning against

* Filby in 1503; North Elmham *c.* 1505; Hunstanton; St Mary Magdalen, 1505, in Norwich.
‡ This wall-painting section by David Park.

Idle Gossip, the Works of Mercy and the Deadly Sins. Among the best paintings of this period are those at Catfield, Crostwick, Heydon, Little Witchingham, Moulton St Mary, Paston, Potter Heigham, West Somerton, Weston Longville and Wickhampton. Continental influences are evident in a number of these schemes, in their elaborate architectural canopies shown in primitive perspective. Much more in the European mainstream, however, and closely paralleled by contemporary painting in north Germany and elsewhere, is the Despenser retable in the cathedral, dating from the end of the century, and very similar in style and technique to two other panels now displayed there but originally from St Michael-at-Plea in Norwich.

Surprisingly, perhaps, in a county so dominated by Perp churches, late medieval wall painting forms something of an anti-climax, though important c15 paintings do survive at Attleborough, Cawston, Hemblington, Sporle and elsewhere. The paintings in 1/50 St Gregory's, Norwich – especially the huge scene of St George and the dragon in the N aisle – are perhaps the finest late medieval wall paintings in England apart from those of Eton College Chapel. One of the very few secular wall paintings in the county is the hunting scene of *c.* 1500 discovered in 1994 in a house at Little Walsingham.

PULPITS are the province of later centuries but a few need mention here. The oldest of the seventeen pre-Reformation pulpits resemble screens in having painted panels and for this purpose are generally hexagonal, a shape that stuck. There are three: Castle Acre *c.* 1400 and Burnham Norton of 1450 both have appropriately the Four Latin Fathers of the Church, while Saints were the theme at Horsham St Faith in 1480. Then paintings gave way to tracery panels: of the late c15 for example at West Somerton, Brisley and Foulden, and the early c16 at Filby. Linenfold panelling appears after *c.* 1520: Irstead, Neatishead, Easton (with tracery also) and in 1537 at Old Catton. Can the Catton pulpit be termed pre-Reformation? Apart from the date there are early Renaissance arabesques, and Renaissance influence is also apparent at Salhouse.

LECTERNS include two memorable wooden ones, at Shelton 1/52 and Shipdham, and a cantor's desk at Ranworth. The Ranworth desk is double-sided and has an eagle painted on one side and a versicle on the other with music. The Shelton lectern is a made- 2/43 up item, but at Shipdham is a splendid piece with pierced tracery wheels. The only READER'S DESK of the period is at Paston which is no more than a couple of elaborate bench-ends linked by the book rest. All of these date to *c.* 1490–1500, which is broadly also the date of introduction of the familiar EAGLE LECTERNS of latten or brass.* Norfolk has fourteen pre-Reformation ones, out of forty-two remaining in England, and these may have been made in Norfolk and exported. The latten lectern type at East

---

* Latten consists of two-parts of copper to one of zinc with traces of lead and tin, and was mainly made in Cologne from where it reached the E coast ports. Its disadvantage was that it had to be hammered, which was less trouble when it was used in monumental 'brasses'. Latten was superseded by brass *c.* 1500.

Dereham of 1482 is found, for instance, at Snettisham and Walpole St Peter, and also Exeter cathedral. A different design is at Outwell. Brass lecterns include St Gregory, Norwich (in the Castle Museum), of 1496, Oxborough c. 1489, the double eagle at Redenhall c. 1500, and at Wiggenhall St Mary the Virgin of 2/44 1518. Earlier than all these is the unusual C15 pelican lectern in Norwich cathedral, possibly made in Flanders on account of the date.

This is perhaps the place to mention DOORS and IRONWORK on doors. Early ironwork begins with the restored Haddiscoe s door of c. 1100, a luscious display of barbed and cusped metal plates, and one of similar date at Raveningham, where are three foliated crosses and strap hinges. Of the mid C12 are pieces at Kirby Bedon, Kirby Cane and Runhall. The C13 is represented at Bradfield and Wroxham (knocker plates) and Swanton Abbot (plate and knocker), the C14 at Alderford (hinges, lock, ring plate with fleur-de-lys decoration), Edingthorpe (knocker), Filby (N door) and Irstead (foliated crosses). At Northrepps is the ring plate. The best C14 work is at Carnary College chapel in Norwich 1/27 where the hinges are so elaborated that the bifurcating tendrils spread like weeds right over the contemporary woodwork. At Tunstead is an amazingly intricate cross round the ring plate, 1/24 about 4 ft in diameter, and the door knocker from St Gregory, 1/25 Norwich, is outstanding. C15 ironwork is less elaborate and less common, for fashion shifted from applied decoration to tracery patterns on the doors themselves. This had happened already in the C14 (Horstead has intersecting tracery), but reached its apogee later. Attleborough has early C15 tracery on the N porch staircase, 2/46 Barton Turf a good W double-leaf door with Perp lozenge tracery, and other W doors possess framing bands of quatrefoils, such as Little Walsingham, Great Snoring and St Michael-at-Plea, Norwich. There are a dozen or so other C15 doors of similar quality. The C16 introduces linenfold panelling, first in an embryonic state at Seething and fully formed at Forncett St Mary.

From metal to STAINED GLASS. Norwich in the C15 had one of the most flourishing schools of glass-painting in England, but the earliest panels are not from Norwich nor are they of the C15, but are the C13 seated figures in trefoils at Carleton Rode, and four Saints in medallions at Saxlingham Nethergate. Of C14 glass there are plenty of reassembled fragments including a French roundel and an English St John the Baptist in the Catholic chapel at Oxburgh Hall, a small St Christopher at Halvergate and some good C14 canopies at Mautby with, in the chancel s windows, grisaille glass. Grisaille glass is found also at Hellington and South Acre. There are complete C14 scenes in the W window at Attleborough, a kneeling donor of c. 1300 at Dunston, a Virgin at North Elmham and a Christ at Pulham St Mary. The most complete C14 glass is at Mileham c. 1350 and Elsing c. 1375. From 2/47 the C15 more of course survives because more was made, usually as isolated pieces, but with one or two better schemes. Colby E window has seven panels of fragments; there are delightful angels at Great Snoring; fragments of Norwich School work at Guest-

wick and Bale. At East Harling are twenty Norwich School panels
of *c.* 1480 and at Shimpling are angels with musical instruments.
The E window of St Peter Mancroft, Norwich, is the best of all,
with forty-two panels of 1445, even though damaged and reset.
The stories are of Christ, the Virgin and various Saints. At Salle
is a splendid E window of 1436–41, splendid at least when it was
intact: nine Orders of Angels and the Fall of the Rebel Angel.
More glass in the s transept of 1444 and *c.* 1470. At North Tuddenham is the life of St Margaret, 1467, at Ringland whole figures
of Saints and donors in the clerestory of *c.* 1460–70, and at Shelton
most of the original glass from the years around 1500.

There is a great deal of interesting foreign glass in Norfolk
churches, thanks partly to the activities of a Norwich merchant,
J. C. Hampp, who in 1802 bought glass at Rouen, the Rhineland,
Nuremberg and the Netherlands. A lot of it he sold on to Lady
Beauchamp Proctor of Langley Park who had it installed in local
churches, usually by *S. C. Yarington.* One might mention
Chedgrave (C16–C17 glass from Rouen), Earsham (particularly
four large early C16 panels), Langley (C15) and Thurton (C16–
C18). Also due to Hampp is the entire E window at Hingham,
German glass of *c.* 1535 bought by Lord Wodehouse in 1813, and
1/54 other glass at Warham St Mary. Of Continental glass from other
sources the best is at St Stephen, Norwich, of 1511 from Maria-
wald, Germany, a late C15 French Baptism at Long Stratton, and
the Adoration of the Magi at Stradsett, from Augsburg and dated
1540.

This brings us to CHURCH MONUMENTS, and first to be
considered are BRASSES. In the main they are of Cologne latten
and so congregate in the E counties, some of Flemish workmanship and some English. The difference is that the Flemings
engraved their brasses while English craftsmen cut the figures out
and laid them in stone. The earliest in England are of the early
C13 but in Norfolk the first is to a member of the Bacon family of
c. 1320 at Gorleston-on-Sea (St Andrew), with his legs crossed.
Then Sir Hugh Hastings at Elsing †1347, the most glorious as
well as the largest of all English brasses. Then at St Margaret,
King's Lynn, are two giant Flemish brasses commemorating
Adam de Walsokne †1349 and Robert Braunche †1364, both of
exceptional quality. Like the Hastings brass there are tiers of
figures and in addition little scenes, for the engraved technique
allowed far more copious detail, including horsemen and a post
windmill on Walsokne's brass and at the foot of the Braunche
brass the Peacock Feast given to Edward III in 1349. A good
series of four figures at Felbrigg was probably made shortly after
1380, all linked by an inscription in Norman French. At South
Acre is the brass to Sir John Harsyck †1384 and wife, both 5 ft
figures, at Reepham Sir William Kerdiston †1391 and wife. It is
the first half of the C15 which provides the best brasses in England
(Blickling †1401, Great Fransham †1414), particularly figures in
military dress (Erpingham *c.* 1415, Burnham Thorpe †1420).
Thereafter they increased in popularity down the social scale and
declined in quality as well as reducing in size. Children were

introduced after about 1450, figures became three-quarters (Frenze †1521) or half-length, figures or even skeletons in shrouds came into fashion, as did the cheapest forms – heart brasses and chalice brasses for priests. Chalice brasses are mainly a Norfolk phenomenon, there being nineteen between 1499 and 1540, two in Suffolk and five in other counties.

Curiously Norfolk is not so rich in STANDING MEDIEVAL MONUMENTS as the wealth of the county would imply, though the highlights are bright indeed. There are a number of coffin-lids from Saxon times (Rockland All Saints) through the C13 (Carbrooke, Hickling, Norwich cathedral) to the C14 (Great Melton). The earliest carved figure, of c. 1100, formerly on the outside of the cathedral, has been interpreted as a retrospective 1/8 depiction of the founder of the see, St Felix. At West Walton is a mid-C13 priest of Purbeck marble like the contemporary monuments to Bishops Northwold and Kilkenny at Ely; his head lies under a flat trefoiled canopy. The C14 priest at Bircham Newton is stone and has an ogeed raised canopy for his head. At Wickhampton are two effigies of c. 1270–80 set within good architectural niches; at East Tuddenham is a knight of c. 1300 obstinately still not taking up the crossed-leg posture popular elsewhere in England and at Necton a C14 lady on a table tomb in the churchyard. Apart from Wickhampton these monuments are carved in the low relief generally given up in the mid C13. Also early C14 are two fine effigies at Banham and Fersfield and the remains of one at South Acre, all of oak and originally covered in gesso. Banham's knight has crossed legs, Fersfield's knight has not. The first highlight is the monument to either Sir Roger (†1337) or William de Kerdiston †1361 at Reepham. A tense 1/28 figure reclines on pebbles with his arms crossed over, set upon a tomb chest with eight weepers beneath cinquefoiled arches. Over it is a choice canopy of two cusped and sub-cusped arches within ogeed gables and a broad frieze of Perp panelling. Just as good and very similar is the monument at Ingham †1344; another is at Burrough Green, Cambridgeshire.

Then a peculiar circumstance: not only is there nothing to single out until 1417 (unless as is likely the Kerdiston monument is to William) but there is practically nothing at all, though the Purbeck marble knight at Mautby with crossed legs might fall into this period, and so too might the Berney monument at Hethersett. Nevertheless, for over seventy years Norfolk squires and knights were indifferent to anything other than the brass engraver's art. But 1417 brings alabaster and the two effigies at Ashwellthorpe done in the detail that the material allowed. Alabaster was first used for monuments in England in the early C14, and once established in Norfolk it stayed until the C18 and beyond. Stone C15 monuments include that to Bishop Goldwell †1499 in the cathedral, but one of the best in England is unquestionably the Morley Monument at Hingham, probably made in 2/30 the 1440s. In general it resembles a miniature Erpingham Gate – but not too miniature, for it reaches right up to the chancel roof. It contains a large number of statuettes up the buttresses, on the top cresting and against the back wall of the recess, which also has, to hark back to a point long since made, intersecting tracery, apparently quite in vogue in the 1440s. There were no effigies but instead brasses on the tomb chest, a London tradition. At East Harling is the canopied tomb of Sir Robert Harling †1435, both he and his wife carved in alabaster, and in the same church Sir William Chamberlain †1462 has a big freestanding monument with vaulting under the canopy, statuary niches, diagonal buttresses and ogee arches on pendants.

The next impetus came only in the early c16, with a group of terracotta monuments of national importance displaying very clear references to the antique and thus the coming of the Renaissance. They are not entirely confined to Norfolk: the Marney monuments at Layer Marney in Essex of 1523 and 1525 are closely connected with them, and so are terracotta details in various Suffolk and Norfolk buildings. Of the Norfolk examples only that to Robert Jannys in St George, Colegate, Norwich, is precisely dateable to 1533–4, but the others seem to be of c. 1525: Bracon 2/31 Ash, the Bedingfeld monuments at Oxborough and the Ferrers 2/32 monument at Wymondham. The monuments all have pilasters with applied balusters, foliage in the panels, cornices, shallow four-centred arches and segmental or straight pediments with putti. This is Italy applied to English wall-monuments and the result is utterly superb and enjoyable, even if, or because, the Classical is not correct Classical. To achieve that the Renaissance has to be assimilated into plans and elevations, not just decorative motifs, and in England events of the 1530s decreed that that should be a matter for secular buildings.

MAJOR SECULAR BUILDINGS
CONQUEST TO 1550

Castles

Norfolk is not a county of castles. By the time of the Conquest there was no realistic fear of further invasions from Scandinavia, and, being isolated on a spur of land jutting into the North Sea, the county commanded no strategic routes other than those of purely local importance. Unless there was fighting to be done on Norfolk soil there was little need for military construction and 1/7 William contented himself with just one, at Norwich itself. The castle, like most early Norman castles, began as a timber structure on a motte shortly after 1066, but was formidable enough to resist a siege in 1075 by Lanfranc against the rebel Earl Ralph, which indicated early enough that in East Anglia generally the threat was to be from local malcontents rather than from organized attack at the outposts of Norman influence. The Norwich motte was strengthened from c. 1100, the outer baileys constructed and the new stone keep raised up from c. 1120. The keep is of a type known as a hall keep, i.e. one longer than it is high, and derives its plan from the earlier royal keeps at London and Colchester. The interior was gutted in the C19, but fortunately we have a copy.

William d'Albini II, a nobleman of more than usual self-importance, married the widow of Henry I in 1138, received various additional titles and immediately built himself a sumptuous stone castle at Castle Rising a few miles NE of King's Lynn. As a model he relied on Norwich keep, and these two may be 2/11 considered together. They are among the mightiest of early English castles and are characterized by an internal division forming two main rooms on each principal floor. The ground floor was for storage and for safety's sake had no external access; internally it was reached from winder staircases within the thickness of the corners of the walls. The main access was at first-floor level, reached by a forebuilding containing a wide stone staircase, with a principal entrance into the upper hall or chamber. The doorway was the place for elaborate decoration, Norwich more so than Castle Rising, and the forebuilding itself was provided with various defensive features. The Norwich forebuilding has vanished, but that at Castle Rising remains one of the most interesting features of the keep, and is the best preserved of all Norman examples. Both keeps had vaulted chapels and private chambers, and both were protected by enormous earthworks. At Norwich only the motte itself, partly natural but mainly artificial, survives today, but at Castle Rising the earthworks are spectacular, covering some 12 acres. The keep sits in a shallow bowl 30 ft deep, surrounded by the main ditch, the floor of which is 58 ft below the rim of the rampart.

These two keeps are completely exceptional among the Norman castles of England, and indeed the Romanesque castles of France, in applying such extensive external decoration in the form of blind arcading to what is after all a severely functional building. Each face of Norwich is covered with arcading in various forms (refaced in the 1830s), a refinement taken up at Castle Rising in the forebuilding.

Other Norman magnates were castle-building at the same time. William de Warenne, one of the king's lieutenants at Hastings, held the manor of Castle Acre, and here excavations have revealed that in the 1070s he began not a fortified castle keep, but a purely domestic building, protected by a ditch and bank with a timber palisade. The rectangular stone house had a basement and living accommodation on the first floor, both levels split by an internal wall, and thus similar to the later keeps just described. The difference is that the basement had external access and the upper chamber wide round-arched windows. That it was susceptible to attack is beyond question, and the fact persuasively records the confidence of the Normans in their superiority even a decade or so after the Conquest. That changed during the civil wars of the Anarchy (1136–54), an event that prompted a rash of castle-building throughout the country, and at Castle Acre William Warenne, the third earl (of Surrey), quickly rebuilt and fortified his house and raised his own tremendous 15-acre earthworks.

These earthworks remain perhaps the most spectacular of all Norman defences, though not much else survives.

Of the early castles one must mention those in the three major towns outside Norwich. Thetford appeared immediately after the Conquest as the candidate for supremacy, so before the Bishopric 2/10 was transferred to Norwich in 1091 an exceptionally tall motte was built, with a timber structure on top, no doubt similar to the first Norwich castle. But a stone keep was never made and the fortifications were demolished in the 1170s. Great Yarmouth and King's Lynn both received fortifications, but of the former we know little and of the latter only a motte and bailey castle can be determined at the site of the Red Mount.

There were other castles, all smaller and all of the MOTTE AND BAILEY type. At Old Buckenham William d'Albini was in possession of a castle within an enclosure of an unusual oblong shape surrounded by a moat, then a novel defensive feature. The keep was presumably of stone, for in 1146 he gave it to the Augustinians to build a priory out of its materials. D'Albini had yet another castle in neighbouring New Buckenham, begun in the 1140s, and historically notable for its circular keep 68 ft in diameter, the earliest in England, sitting on a mound in a circular inner bailey, augmented by two outer baileys. His keep has an internal cross wall and though featureless makes a fine show in its site, strangely isolated from the planned town which grew up to its E in the C12.

Numbers of other small motte and bailey castles depending on earthwork defences were scattered thinly around the county in the late C11 and C12, encouraged by the Anarchy, but for the majority we have only heaps and mounds to examine; others have disappeared without trace. Once again it was the great families who led the way. Denton Castle, another d'Albini effort of c. 1100, had timber buildings and a banked enclosure of uncertain purpose, but at Horsford Walter de Cadomo substituted stone for timber in the C12, although he retained the late C11 motte and circular bailey. Mileham had a square stone keep from c. 1100 (for the FitzAlans), the stub of which juts from a low motte also set within a circular bailey. Wormegay, overlooking the Fens in the W, has a large bailey containing a low motte but no surviving buildings, and at Middleton a particularly impressive motte survives from a conventional site inhabited at least from the early C12.

During the reign of Henry II (1154–89) castle-building declined, at least of castles with the primary purpose of defence. The big three – Norwich, Castle Rising and Castle Acre – continued to develop their defences, for instance with flint-built curtain walls on the ramparts, but even Castle Acre was partially abandoned by the end of the century. Flint replaced timber, moats replaced earthworks and home comforts increased. This transition may be followed at Weeting, for here is the first surviving attempt at a Norman house with minimal defences since the hastily modified experiment at Castle Acre, and it took a century before the barons, here Sir Ralph de Plais, felt themselves secure. Set within a moat are the remains of an aisled hall and a three-storey tower with a first-floor chamber. The narrowness of the windows, thickness of the walls and the provision of an upper hall might mark a hesitancy to reject all safety measures. The date is *c*. 1180.

The C13 was a quiet century, and the castles of the later Middle Ages continually develop the themes which Weeting re-established, to the extent that at the end of the period the division between castles and fortified manor houses blurs considerably. We cannot be sure how Claxton Castle looked when the licence to crenellate was granted in 1333 to Lord Kerdeston, for it was rebuilt in the C15. Gresham Castle was a foundation of Sir Edmund Bacon (licence 1319) and although only fragmentary remains survive it seems to have been an establishment of some size, on a quadrangular plan, with corner towers and a moat. It was not strong enough to survive looting in 1450. In the same year, 1450, Baconsthorpe Castle, three miles w, was begun for John Heydon, also on a quadrangular plan. There were originally two courtyards contained within the moat and curtain walls of flint and brick, and in the spaces so enclosed a considerable retinue must have lived. The same can be said for Caister Castle, West Caister, the spectacular moated twin quadrangle of 1432–5 for Sir John Fastolph. Being of brick Caister has already been mentioned (*see* Building Materials, p. 25). The curtain walls and the moat were enough to defy the Duke of Norfolk in 1469, so practical defensive purpose can be accepted for those if not for the tremendous six-storey solar tower in the NW corner abutting 1/47 the equally lavish three-storey hall range. There is even a small dais window overlooking the moat to the w. Defence and comfort were equally important to Fastolph, which takes us away from true castles into the realm of moated manor houses.

Town and Precinct Walls

Before we turn in that direction a few words are necessary on TOWN WALLS. Some form of Saxon or Anglo-Scandinavian ditch and bank system existed at Thetford and Norwich, but for town walls one must visit only Norwich, Great Yarmouth and King's Lynn. Norwich was provided with flint walls between 1294 and 1/32 1334; forty circular or semi-circular towers were completed by *c*. 1350 and the eleven gateways somewhat later. Cow Tower by the Wensum was rebuilt in 1389–90, of brick over a flint core – a notably early use of brick for anything other than dressings. The area enclosed by the walls is larger than that of the City of London, a reminder that Norwich was one of the three or four largest towns in England. The surviving walls are extensive, which is no surprise, but the extent of the survival of Yarmouth's walls is, so 1/33 much are visitors preoccupied with the pleasures of the sea-front. The surviving walls are higher and the towers more spectacular than those of Norwich. The material is the same, the eighteen towers semi-circular or D-shaped (eleven survive), as at Norwich. None of the ten gates remain. The walls were started in 1285 but construction was slower, so the C14 closed before they were complete.

The walls of King's Lynn are still less known, but with more reason. There were four C13 wooden towers at the points of entry, replaced with brick and flint walls in 1294–1339, extending ludicrously far E and enclosing an area impossible for the town to expand into: they follow the line of a higher, older sea bank. Only a few fragments are comprehensible, but there are three GATES. Guanock Gate to the E appears to us as an C18 folly, so much has it been rebuilt; St Anne's Gate to the N has also been changed from its C15 appearance and today brightens up a bit of dank wall, but the three-storey South Gate survives. The stone S side is largely of 1437, the remainder rebuilt in brick and stone in 1520. There is a first-floor chamber with a fireplace and gunports in the corner turrets.

2/55

The gateways to Norwich and Yarmouth were unfortunately pulled down in the C18 and C19, but other gates and indeed other walls remain which tell us something about the relations between the townspeople and the MONASTIC HOUSES. Chief of these is the wall to Norwich cathedral Close. The Norman flint structure remains in part, but the walls were continually kept in good repair and saw regular service in repelling rioting townsfolk. Two celebrated GATEWAYS face Tombland – St Ethelbert's Gate of the early C14 with its early flushwork and Court School overtones, and Erpingham Gate of 1416–25, an extravagant archway with statuettes in tiers. To the N is the Bishop's Gate controlling entry to the Bishop's Palace, much simpler and completed by 1436; to the E is the Water Gate, an interesting C15 defence of the canal leading from the river into the Close.

1/57

The religious houses in King's Lynn, and here one is referring to the friars, also had walls and gates, but the walls of monastic foundations everywhere must have been the first casualties of the Reformation. Whitefriars' Gate, a small C15 brick and stone archway, remains, as do the NW and NE gates of the Austin Friars, both consolidated and rebuilt. Of the walls which linked the various gates only fragments survive. Thetford, rich in monastic foundations, also has gates: one freestanding but rebuilt in brick and one built into Nunnery Cottages (early C16, flint, clunch and brick) at the Benedictine house of St George; a three-storey fully inhabited C14 defensive gatehouse with windows and fireplaces stands isolated and little-known NW of the Cluniac Priory ruins; in Walsingham a gatehouse was built in the mid C15 into the precinct walls facing the main street and directly W of the W end of the church, just like Erpingham Gate in Norwich. The N stretch of the wall remains particularly high, with another gate. The more important RURAL MONASTERIES often had walls and gatehouses. Broomholm Priory at Bacton has reasonably substantial remains of the C15 walls abutting the gatehouse, which is two bays deep, with side chambers and towards the priory knapped flint and flushwork. Binham still has its gatehouse with pedestrian and carriage entrances; the Carmelite house at Blakeney has parts at least of the early C16 precinct walls. At St Benet's Abbey, Horning,

is a splendid Dec gatehouse fitting the importance of the foun- 1/29
dation, even if the windmill within it spoils the effect, and one can
still trace the precinct walls enclosing a huge rectangular area,
licensed in 1327. The Carmelite friary at Burnham Norton has a
Dec gatehouse, already mentioned in the context of flushwork,
and parts of the walls. Pentney Priory retains its late C14 gatehouse, one of the most imposing of them all, three storeys high
with heated rooms served by winder staircases behind the polygonal battlemented corner towers. Castle Acre has in addition to
everything else part of its precinct walls and gatehouse, the latter
of c. 1500, and looking very comfortable with its mullioned
window and first-floor chamber.

Moated Sites and Fortified Manor Houses*

The most obvious manifestation of the existence of large numbers
of fortified manor houses lower in status than the castles lies in
the large number of MOATED SITES in Norfolk. There are over
400 of them, which is probably no more than half the total ever
built, the rest succumbing to the plough or to later development.‡
Defence was only part of their function, merely intended to make
it difficult for marauding bands to sack the house as well as
the barns and other ancillary farmbuildings which usually stood
outside. Almost anyone could have waded most moats other than
the largest, except when the island was raised very high, presenting
a bank as a substitute for curtain walls, but the only known
Norfolk example is at Antingham, and we have no date for it.
Fashion and status probably played an equal part; it certainly did
for the great C15 brick houses such as Middleton Tower, derived
directly from the late medieval castles, and it is likely that local
landowners were infected by the same desire. Another factor was
land drainage, especially in the boulder clay area of central and s
Norfolk, to provide a dry island for building. More than 70 per
cent of moated sites fall within the boulder clay region and most
of the rest are in river valleys.

Moats as opposed to dry earthwork ditches were first made in
England in the late C12, and these are usually of circular form
(there are eight in Norfolk), but most of them date from the C13
and early C14, a period when castle-building in Norfolk was in
decline. Thereafter moats become rarer, turn rectangular, and
fade out of fashion in the early C16. It is a problem in Norfolk –
with a few notable exceptions – to find a house contemporary with
its moat. Some houses have simply disappeared: at Horningtoft is
a dry circular moat complete with a ditched enclosure formerly
containing a manor house; the manor at Tittleshall had disappeared by 1596; so has the royal manor in its circular moat at
Burgh-next-Aylsham held by Queen Eleanor from 1281; at
Dersingham is a large moat with a causeway and at Hilgay stands
a rectangular moat with earthworks and two ditched enclosures.

* The following paragraphs on moated sites have been jointly written with Andrew
Rogerson.
‡ Essex has the most, over 770, and Suffolk about 740.

These examples probably once contained houses of importance.

Ruins or buildings known through excavation are more numerous. At Hautbois are stumps of flint probably belonging to a house licensed in 1313 on a rectangular island; Bishop Despenser's Manor at North Elmham stood in a late C14 moat within an even larger one. At Warham are the remains of a C15 brick building, at Wighton flint remains of a late medieval manor house; Hales Hall stood on one moat and its gatehouse, barns and associated outbuildings on another to the E. Surviving buildings almost always represent a rebuilding of an older house, sometimes with remains of the original. Remains at least are at Mayton Hall, a late C15 timber-framed building, and at Attleborough Hall, where parts of the C16 house are protected by the most impressive brick-lined moat in the county associated with a minor manor house. Stanfield Hall, Wymondham, might be cited as a similar C16 example. A number of houses have better claim to be as old as their moats: Old Boyland Hall, Bressingham (C16), Brisley Hall (C15) and Elsing Hall (c. 1460–70) among them. Hindringham Hall is a direct replacement in 1562 of an earlier mansion, and so is Blickling Hall, which is the descendant of a late C14 moated house.

In many cases a moated site fell into disuse because a new house was built in the C16 or C17 on virgin ground. Kimberley Hall was built from c. 1700 on a hilltop position, leaving only fragments of the pre-1402 moated house. East Hall, Kenninghall, has the largest double moat in the county, but was demolished in 1520 to be replaced by Kenninghall Place, again on higher ground.

Many moated sites are marked on Ordnance Survey maps, and so merely a selection of the best and most representative are listed in the gazetteer.

Unfortified Domestic Buildings

The fragmentary remains of Norman domestic architecture fall into two categories: town houses and dwellings associated with monastic establishments; there are no rural buildings other than the castles already dealt with.

The two earliest surviving TOWN HOUSES in the county are in Norwich, one being the remains of a house underneath the Magistrates' Court, dateable to c. 1140–70. The remains are only about 6 ft high and represent the lower courses of a rectangular structure of 56 ft by 30 ft built of coursed flint with stone dressings; it appears to have been a FIRST-FLOOR HALL. Wensum Lodge, King Street, is probably slightly earlier, but is far more difficult to interpret because of the later additions. However, the two buildings have three elements in common – the building materials, the plan of a rectangular range at r. angles to the street, and the provision of the main living area at the first floor. This arrangement is familiar from Norman houses elsewhere, e.g. the Jew's House, Lincoln, and Boothby Pagnell, Lincolnshire, and is a formula carried on in the few other houses of the period. An alternative to the first-floor hall system was an open AISLED

HALL, but the only Norfolk example is the range added to Wensum Lodge in c. 1175 parallel to the street.

From the mid C12 we have the Tolhouse, Great Yarmouth, 1/11 built as a private house. The earliest part, parallel to the street, has a wide Norman arch, probably once open to the street, supporting the hall above. Contemporary with the second phase of Wensum Lodge is the remarkable stone house at Nos. 28–32 2/9 King Street, King's Lynn, with two pairs of Norman arches on each floor. The upper hall might have run parallel to the street, then still possible in Lynn, but subsequent alterations, interesting 2/51 in themselves, make this difficult to prove. Another Lynn house with Norman arches stood on Queen Street, but has been demolished. The last evidence for a domestic Norman town house lies in the undercroft of Nos. 50–56 Howard Street South, Yarmouth, where there is a C12 barrel-vaulted chamber (and extensive C15 brick cellars), this time at r. angles to the street. The Lazar House, outer Norwich, which was founded by Bishop Losinga before 1119 as a hospital on open land ½m. N of the later city walls, is a hybrid between a chapel and a ground-floor hall, the plan probably owing more to the former than the latter.

In order to proceed with a survey of domestic architecture we must look at DOMESTIC HALLS OF RELIGIOUS FOUNDATIONS. There is no such thing as a monastic hall, but there are a few frustratingly ruinous lodgings, guest houses and halls, from which we may at least sketch a broad outline of the plan and internal arrangements. For Norman work we are confined to Losinga's palace originally attached by a covered passageway to the N of the cathedral. The main block appears to have been a keep-like tower rather like that at Weeting Castle, but it has been greatly interfered with, although we can say that the main accommodation was at the first floor under an open roof. There are remains of chimney flues in the w wall at both storeys, which is the first confirmation that domestic buildings in Norfolk were heated from fireplaces against the wall, as were the castle keeps at Castle Rising and Norwich. The palace was extended at r. angles in the mid C12 for Bishop Turbe, and there were important extensions and alterations in the C14. At Castle Acre the C12 prior's lodging consisted of a first-floor hall raised above a six-bay, two-aisled vaulted undercroft. But this too was altered in the mid C14 so that the prior's apartments projected from the w front of the church, which was a typical position for guest houses and the like. At Binham the guest house projected in a similar manner, and in 1234 the guest hall at Little Walsingham priory was in construction, though of these we can say little. The same applies to the greatly altered C13 prior's lodging at Norwich (now the Deanery).

At Abbey Farm, Thetford, is a C13 aisled hall (the earliest known after Wensum Lodge). This timber-framed building with a queenpost roof is embedded in a decrepit collection of barn and house conversions w of the priory gatehouse, and must have been one of a series of important C13 and C14 timber aisled halls of which other examples are mentioned below (see p. 86).

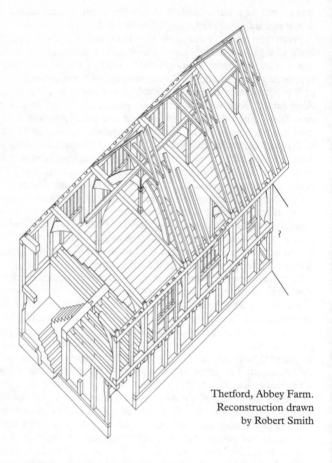

Thetford, Abbey Farm.
Reconstruction drawn
by Robert Smith

In the C14 the tradition of first-floor halls continued. The lodging at Thetford, only a few hundred yards from the last example, reverts to flint and stone construction. Unlike Castle Acre it was freestanding, 60 yds w of the w front of the church, the domestic apartment raised over a vaulted undercroft. Later in the century it was extended E to link up with the outer parlour at the N end of the cloister W walk. At Nos. 17–18 Church Street, King's Lynn, in the domain of the Benedictine priory, is a domestic range with a crown-post roof over the upper hall (remodelled *c.* 1470). Round the corner is Nos. 12–20 Priory Lane, a C14 open hall house also with a crown-post roof, much altered and converted in the mid C15 to a storeyed house by the insertion of a floor, the first known instance of a modification which became universal in the C17. But the earliest open hall associated with the Norfolk Benedictines is at Yarmouth, where it forms another kind of hall, that of St Nicholas School estab-lished in the surviving buildings in the middle of the C19.

OPEN HALL HOUSES were destined to dominate the later medieval centuries in lowland England in both major and minor buildings, so a fuller explanation of their function and plan may be permitted. The basic plan was of a hall range open to an elaborate roof with a one- or two-storey service wing at one end sometimes built at r. angles. Between them was a passage, the screens passage, entered from either end, with usually two doors opening into service rooms. The hall was shielded from the draughty passage by a screen, almost always of timber, and at the opposite end (the high end) was the raised dais lit by a large dais window. This was an area reserved for the owner, and from it an internal ladder or staircase rose to a private first-floor solar in a second block. Heating came either from a fire burning in the middle of the floor or, in very special cases, from a proper flued fireplace set in a side wall (probably some monastic lodgings had this; clerics were likely to relish the better provisions of a first-floor hall long enjoyed by castle owners or those in gatehouses, e.g. Losinga's palace and Thetford priory gatehouse).

The hall at Yarmouth still has its open roof, with the hall carrying on through both floors, even if the roof is of 1853. There are large C19 windows set in the original surrounds and a screens passage at the low end of the hall out of which opened five doorways; the screen itself disappeared only in this century. Whether a solar staircase originally led from one of these doors or from the door in the S wall at the high end is impossible to say. The kitchens are all C19, but are in the right place, reached through the service doors. Peterstone priory had a C14 hall house now incorporated into a barn, and in the two secular colleges which remain in Norfolk are further open halls in one wing of a courtyard plan. These are Rushford College and College Farmhouse, Thompson, founded in 1342 and 1349 respectively. The first has service doors, the second part of the passage and the dais window; both were suppressed at the Dissolution, the halls floored and converted to private houses.

First-floor halls continued to be built, but in decreasing numbers. An early C15 timber-framed one stands immediately W of the aisled hall already mentioned at Abbey Farm, Thetford. The survey of halls associated with religious foundations can close, however, with the mention of the master's lodging at the Great Hospital, Norwich, of c. 1450 and the prioress's Lodging at Carrow (see Outer Norwich), both with plenty of evidence of the developed open hall house.

The Gatehouse in the Later Middle Ages

The later monastic gatehouses, such as Pentney and Castle Acre, were so wedded to domestic culture that at the Reformation many escaped demolition. The presumption that it was the first floor which was the proper site for the main room, underlined by such a disposition in castle architecture, allowed the gatehouse form to pass into the realm of purely domestic architecture. If Norfolk examples could not show the way then others could, e.g. the

tremendous and unashamedly domestic gatehouse at Thornton
Abbey, Lincolnshire, of the later C14.

Among SECULAR GATEHOUSES is the inner gatehouse at
Baconsthorpe Castle of 1450–86, thoroughly domestic, with
comfortable suites of rooms to the upper floors and large windows.
Brick is used extensively in the details, particularly in the interior,
but for the exterior elevations knapped flint was favoured. The
move from flint to brick on a large scale first occurs at Caister
Castle in the work of 1432–5 when 1.7 million pink and yellow
bricks were made on the site and assembled into a hall and solar
range so elaborate that the normal hall-house plan is difficult
to appreciate. Middleton Tower, probably complete by 1460,
continues the gatehouse tradition, three storeys high and again of
brick, with oriels to the first floor and the usual signs of opulence
in the interior fittings. Elsewhere in England brick was being used
on the same lavish scale in the same years, especially in counties
bordering the North Sea and thus open to influence from the
Netherlands and the Baltic towns, where brick buildings already
existed. Early instances are the brick transepts of Holy Trinity,
Hull, c. 1300–20, and the Hull town walls begun in 1321, but of
more relevance are later examples: the North Bar at Beverley
(Humberside), a gateway built in 1409–10, Faulkbourne in Essex
of before 1440, and in Lincolnshire (apart from Thornton) the
tremendous keep at Tattershall begun in 1434, the mid-century
Hussey Tower in Boston and Wainfleet school of the 1480s.

In Norfolk there are only the remains of a brick and flint
gatehouse at Elsing Hall, c. 1460–70, and a more complete and
still wholly Perp brick gatehouse at Hunstanton Hall of c. 1487.
Then there are the remains of a brick and stone gatehouse of the
late C15 at Bexwell Hall, arranged probably as an open hall with
an internal solar staircase. But it is Sir Edmund Bedingfeld's
2/68 Oxburgh Hall in the 1480s which claims the position of the
primary C15 brick gatehouse of England. Two seven-storey polygonal towers flank the entrance, elaborated with recessed panels
with brick cusping, moulded machicolations, brick internal staircases with inset handrails (like Tattershall and Caister) and brick
vaults to the tower rooms. These details tell us that brick had
become established as a fashionable not merely utilitarian
material.

C15 and Early C16 Brick Houses

The brick gatehouse and sub-castle architecture just described
were not the only standard-bearers of the new fashion for brick.

The ruinous Drayton Lodge appears to use bricks from the
kilns at Caister Castle (Sir John Fastolph held the manor) and is
presumably of the 1430s, but of details of the plan one notices
only that it was a rectangular range with a fireplace in the ground
floor, and round corner towers to the angles. The brick is laid in
English bond. Decoration of Oxburgh type appears in the late
C15 extensions to Welle Manor Hall, Upwell (trefoil brick friezes
and polygonal stair turrets), with an early example of stepped

gables, a favourite motif in Norfolk into the c18. Snore Hall, Fordham, remains only as a puzzling house belonging to the Skipwiths, for it appears to be a brick solar extension of the 1470s 2/56 to an earlier timber-framed building now lost. It has minor brick decoration to the W gable and the porch attached to it, and the principal room is on the first floor. Just as puzzling because there is little evidence is the giant twin-moated Hales Hall put up for Sir James Hobart, Henry VII's Attorney-General. The house had octagonal corner turrets; other ranges including the barn are of red brick with blue brick diaper, which is another adornment with which the reader will become familiar.

The Priory, Wiggenhall St Mary Magdalen, is of considerable interest, for not only is the inserted floor in the hall a very early instance, but the use of terracotta is a minor but significant step. The timber-framed hall house of c. 1500 remains substantially intact, but the inserted floor with fine ribbon-moulded bridging beams with vine trail cannot be much after 1530, providing a very neat illustration of the date of the change from feudal to modern planning. A new brick skin, and a porch and cellar both with terracotta rib-vaults, complete the transformation from old-fashioned to ultra-modern in the space of a quarter of a century. Terracotta and stepped gables recur more splendidly at Wallington Hall, c. 1525, with chequerwork in brick and carstone to the E gable. The hall from the start had a side stack and a bay window and parts at least of the solar staircase remain. Next to be recorded is the E gable of Denver Hall, c. 1520. The gable is stepped, has round decorated pinnacles and chimneyshafts, and terracotta panels with initials and other motifs, one of which is a half-hearted pediment. Lammas Manor confirms the date of its diapered brick by its datestone: 1525; it has octagonal moulded chimney flues and a stair turret. Diapering, polygonal angle-shafts, arched brick windows with intersecting tracery, and a stepped gable all appear in the former service block of the Duke of Norfolk's mansion at Kenninghall Place. These various elements from these few buildings (except intersecting tracery which was an archaism and terracotta which was a short-lived fashion) form the essential vocabulary of more minor buildings in the two centuries to follow. Once Rainthorpe Hall, a less complete but nevertheless still recognizable early c16 brick hall house with some timber framing to the upper floor, and Swannington Hall, also with a hall fireplace, have been mentioned, we may leave this group of brick buildings to consider the premier league.

Oxburgh Hall in the 1480s was a courtyard house and had, it must be remembered, a conventional open hall in the S wing (demolished 1778), though there was nothing conventional about its size and appointments. It is joined at the pinnacle of Norfolk's brick houses by Thorpland Hall, the Old Rectory at Great Snoring, Manor House at East Barsham, and the Manor House at Great Cressingham. The first three are close together E of a line between Walsingham and Fakenham; Great Cressingham lies 21m. S. The earliest is Great Snoring, but dateable only to c. 1500–25, for either Sir Ralph Shelton or his son. Only one façade of a polygonal courtyard house has survived, but it has two bays of three- and four-light windows under hoodmoulds, and two bands of terracotta. One has initials but the other has balusters separating profile heads in square panels, a decidedly Renaissance innovation. The best of the group is East Barsham, built for Sir Henry Fermor *c.* 1520–30, though one has to be cautious for there was considerable reconstruction in the early C20. Despite this the house and its gatehouse are the exemplar of the great Tudor manor house. The gatehouse has polygonal corner turrets, battlements, fine entrance arches still rather Perp, and a profusion of carved and moulded brick ornament of the highest quality. The house has a two-storeyed porch, a hall to the l., and more display of moulded and carved brick including friezes with arms, tracery and, Renaissance again, heads. The last probably is derived partly from Layer Marney, Essex, and Sutton Place, Surrey, to which these four houses are related. Great Cressingham of *c.* 1545 has no such Renaissance hints, but instead an extraordinarily bold treatment of the upper floor covered in terracotta tracery panels. Thorpland Hall is less dateable than Great Snoring, and is once more only one range of a larger house. There are polygonal angle buttresses and – Thorpland's particular contribution – a tremendous display of decorated round chimneyshafts with star tops.

1/61

2/69

Guildhalls

Medieval guilds were in the main associations of merchants, some of which were wealthy enough to build their own halls, and most of which made periodic donations to the fabric of parish churches, for town walls and other public works. Of the thirty or so C14 guilds in King's Lynn only three had their own halls in the mid C16, which were available for leasing or rent to the remainder. The association of these private halls with public works and ultimately the recognition as something akin to a town hall came early, for the chief officers of the guilds were almost inevitably also the officers of the town. In 1204 for instance the Trinity Guild of Lynn was regularized by charter, at which point one finds that the guild alderman was also the mayor, and the officers of the town were guild members. They met in their own hall to conduct town business, and the hall in effect became the town hall; when the guilds disappeared after the Reformation, the guildhalls became town halls in fact.

The C15 was the great age of guildhalls in Norfolk, and as their construction was a direct indicator of wealth accumulated through trade, the best are in the main trading centres. The oldest standing building known to have had civic purpose is the Tolhouse at Great Yarmouth, as we have seen a C12 Norman hall taken over by the town in the C13. It was probably the town which added the castle-like forebuilding with its decorated entrance doorway at the first floor in the middle of the following century. Yarmouth it seems had a second guildhall on Hall Quay, of which we have only an enormous late C14 timber truss relocated against a wall in the yard of an inn. Of the major guildhalls the next in date is the Norwich guildhall, built in 1407–13 on the site of a C14 toll house, and provided with a new council chamber at the E end in 1535. Like the Yarmouth Tolhouse the meeting room was on the first floor, following secular practice. The guildhall is picturesque in the extreme, especially happy in its galleted and knapped flint walls even if much of it dates from the C19; it originally had two towers.

St George's Guildhall, King's Lynn, followed in 1410–20, of 2/52 brick and stone, with polygonal corner towers to the street front and buttresses along the sides. It is edge-on to King Street partly because of the constraints of narrow frontages in towns, and partly – and here is a cogent reminder that guildhalls started as the headquarters of commercial concerns – to facilitate the construction of warehousing at the back leading to the quayside. Holy Trinity guild had a hall hard by the N porch of St Margaret's church in Saturday Market, Lynn, but this burnt in 1421, and a new hall went up in 1422–8, which will be remembered for its 2/54 *tour-de-force*, the external chequered flintwork of the original hall and that of the C17 extension to the l. In plan and elevation it is much like St George's, set at r. angles to the street, with an undercroft and a big Perp window lighting the first-floor meeting chamber. It even has polygonal corner turrets.

Then there are minor guilds of which something survives, and buildings with dubious claims to guildhall status. In the first category one thinks of the hall of the Guild of St James, Pulham St Mary, built in 1401 and incorporated in the later Pennoyer's School. A guildhall was necessary in Little Walsingham only after the Dissolution, since before then everything which needed regulating was ordered by the prior, so we have the C16 flint and brick Guild House. Fragments only remain of the Dereham guildhall, but there is nothing of the medieval guildhall in Thetford. In the second category are the guildhall at Blakeney, a mid-C14 vaulted undercroft at r. angles to the quay and probably a warehouse, the Old Vicarage, New Buckenham (C15), and the Old Guildhall, Banham, a late C15 timber-framed building which may have had a long first-floor chamber.

VERNACULAR BUILDINGS
THIRTEENTH CENTURY TO 1550

The first and most pressing question is one of definition. Usually vernacular is taken to mean any building designed and built locally using local materials without reference to factors pertaining elsewhere. There are no good descriptions of early domestic buildings at the bottom of the social pile, but the likelihood is that they were low and mean, of timber or clay, with straw for a roof, and it is equally likely that their life-span was measured in years not decades. Probably too some dwellings were intended to

last only a season. To the occupier of one of those in, say, the
C14, the luxury of some of the hall houses about to be listed must
have seemed, and been, beyond credible ambition. This is the
problem with 'vernacular', for it has social implications. What is
vernacular to one stratum of society is the opposite to another.
The definition loosely followed in the next few pages is one of
innovation: non-vernacular buildings introduced new ideas to
the area, whether in building materials, plan form, elevation or
decoration, and vernacular ones followed suit on a less ambitious
scale anything from thirty to a hundred years after. A medieval
building which survives is likely to have been of considerable
status when it was new, and the constant filter of new ideas from
above meant that quite elaborate buildings of the post-medieval
period adopted archaic plans when measured against superior
older buildings.

Rural Houses

Vernacular houses before 1500 are remarkably consistent in that
the survivors exhibit, or once exhibited, variations on the theme
of HALL HOUSES, and the variations can be traced further back
in major buildings or those belonging to monastic foundations.
The oldest type is represented by just two C14 AISLED HALL
HOUSES, at Manor Farmhouse, Runcton Holme, and Rush Fen
Cottage, Geldeston. The house type consists of a central vessel
open to the roof with either one or two aisles separated by free-
standing posts linked by tie-beams and arcade plates and supporting a roof of twin passing braces. Both Norfolk examples have
octagonal aisle posts, but only at Geldeston are two aisles visible.
There are twenty-five such houses known in N Suffolk.
   RAISED AISLE HALL HOUSES are also a type specific to N
Suffolk, and the two Norfolk examples are part of the Suffolk
group. They are at Lodge Farmhouse, Denton, and at Nos.
16–18 Old Market Place, Harleston. As with the aisled halls
timber was the natural material, but the one type is not the
descendant of the other: aisled halls were built for their ability
to enclose large spaces and with considerations of status; raised
aisles were a consequence of the introduction of a new roof
type, the queenpost roof, of which more below. The raised
aisle hall has a heavy beam spanning the interior above head
height and jointed into the principal studs of the outer walls.
On this are a pair of aisle posts rising to an arcade plate running
longitudinally and linked by a secondary tie-beam. Either a
crown-post or a kingpost completes the truss; in Norfolk both
have the former.
   The rest of the story of hall houses belongs to the OPEN
HALL, with one or two exceptions. The basic plan has already
been described (*see* p. 81), but in vernacular examples the
deviation from it increases: many halls had only one cross wing
with a solar over the service end; some minor late open halls
were tiny (e.g. The End House, Dunston, early C16); some
clung to the tradition of an external solar stair (Brumstead

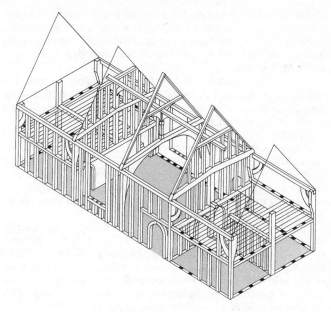

Rushall, Scotland Yard. Isometric by Robert Smith

Hall, C15); some seem to have dispensed with a screen. All of the 300 hall houses described in the gazetteer have been altered and added to as demands for comfort rose, and adapted to other house types when the social basis of the open hall collapsed; this began in Norfolk in the last decade of the C15. The insertion of chimneystacks in the passage, flooring of the halls, reconstruction of service blocks, attachments of outshuts to the rear of the hall and provision of unified brick façades from the C17 disguises most, so details of the plan have to be extrapolated from fragmentary evidence.

There are no surviving C13 halls in rural Norfolk, and only tantalizing bits of them in the towns, but the developed open hall house emerges in a handful of C14 examples, certainly influenced by the halls of the rich. School House, Brooke, has its crown-post roof smoke-blackened from the open fire but otherwise exhibits most of the alterations just described. The Old Rectory, Snetterton, has the remains of two fine trefoiled service doorways; Welle Manor Hall, Upwell, allows the inspection of a complete late C14 screens passage with wave-moulded early C15 service doors. Sharrington Hall, apparently a C16 E-plan house, retains its hall plan and the dais window. One of the most complete outside the towns is the early C15 Scotland Yard, Rushall, and another is Jacques, Garboldisham, from the late C15. There the 2/66 hall with its dais window, screens passage, service end and first-floor solar all remain, even if reorganized, as does the smoke-blackened crown-post roof. The early C16, nearly at the end of the open hall tradition, has most surviving examples, and if compensation for the rate of survival of earlier structures is made, there can hardly have been a parish in the county which did not have at least one and probably several hall houses at some point in the Middle Ages.

Norfolk has examples of two further hall house types, the WEALDEN HOUSE and the FIRST-FLOOR HALL. Wealden houses are a product of the Kentish weald, and the four in Norfolk must be direct imports built for families with Kentish connections (contradicting our definition of vernacular). The best is the late C14 White Cottage, Wacton, where the central recessed hall is apparent under a visible queenpost roof. In the C15 Yew Tree Cottage, Forncett St Mary, the screens passage is more or less complete. From the early C16 is Crawford's, New Buckenham, of which we have only the elevation, and a little more detail survives in The Wooden House, West Acre.

First-floor hall houses represent an extension of the practice for early castles, monastic ranges and buildings with a primary civil purpose, and the few surviving domestic examples must have been built for status, because the type was decidedly old-fashioned by the mid C15. Church Farmhouse, Blo Norton, has a jettied first floor containing an impressive five-bay crown-post roof. A century later, after the Reformation, is Abbey Farmhouse, Old Buckenham, with a five-bay upper hall jettied front and back and lit through a continuous frieze of windows. It was probably modelled on an earlier monastic range belonging to the abbey which stood in the next field. The late C15 No. 20 High Street, Little Walsingham, is a curious hybrid: it has, and always had, a hall on both floors, the lower approached via a screens passage in the open hall tradition, but with an additional upper hall open to the roof and jettied on both sides. It too may have had a monastic origin.

Urban Domestic Buildings

It is only from the C13 that buildings belonging to the merchant classes or the lesser nobility can be identified, and only from the Late Middle Ages any from lower on the social scale. Houses in towns and country hardly varied in the early part of this survey, and when they did it was pressures of space and considerations of commerce that altered the outlook of occupants of the town houses.

It is not the first-floor hall favoured by the Normans which is first identifiable, but two C13 versions of an open hall house. Clifton House, King's Lynn, has the remains of two halls, one C13 and the other C14, both built with their gable-end to the street. Also in King's Lynn is Nos. 4–6 St Anne's Street, this time a hall parallel to the street probably entered from opposing C13 doors, one of which remains at the back. Neither these nor the original C14 hall at Norwich Strangers' Hall tell us of the precise arrangements for kitchens, services or sleeping quarters, but the early C14 S range at Hampton Court, King's Lynn, is more eloquent. The hall is to the r. of the screens passage, which retains three arched doors to the service rooms to the l. The hall is large, 33 by 22 ft and originally open to the roof. To its r. (w) is a further range with independent external access, over which must have been the solar or private chamber reached by an internal stair from the hall. The plan of the C14 hall house at Dragon Hall, Norwich, is the first known example of an L-shaped plan, with the services to the street front and the hall at the back, overlooking a private courtyard. Access to the screens passage is via opposing doorways, so the entrance doorway is off a lane by the side, not from the main thoroughfare. This disposition suits a narrow site, and was probably the most common arrangement for urban hall houses, though survivals are generally confined to King's Lynn, where a formula for the entry had to be contrived in the absence of convenient alleyways down one side.

Nos. 7–9 King Street, King's Lynn, presents a fully-developed L-plan of the late C14. The services to the front take up the entire street frontage, and the hall lies behind and to one side at r. angles, leaving room for a small rear court served by a passage cutting through from the street; in the angle between the two ranges is the screens passage entry. This form remained popular in towns throughout the C15: see e.g. in Lynn, No. 2 St Margaret's Place and several examples in King Street; in Wymondham, No. 18 and Nos. 20–22 Damgate; in Thetford, 19 Guildhall Street.

On bigger, older sites, or on plots where adjacent properties could be bought up, it remained fashionable to build halls parallel to the street. Again most survivors are in Lynn. No. 2 St Anne's Street of c. 1400 is jettied front and rear, as is the contemporary Nos. 30–32 Pilot Street. In Norwich enough property was acquired by a merchant, Robert Toppes, adjacent to Dragon Hall 1/42 in the mid C15 to construct a new parallel hall with a brick and flint ground floor supporting a timber-framed upper floor, one of the earliest instances of this construction. Also innovative are the projecting first-floor windows. Constraints of space also applied to courtyard houses, most of which developed piecemeal, one range being added in successive periods. Hampton Court in Lynn has been mentioned for the C14 s range, but the three other ranges took until about 1600 to complete. Strangers' Hall in Norwich also developed its small yard by a series of encroach-ments and the mid-C15 Bacon's House, Colegate, Norwich, achieved its enclosed court only in the C17. However, No. 9 and Nos. 11–13 Nelson Street, King's Lynn, were probably late C15 courtyard houses from the start, as was Nos. 19–21 Bedford Street, Norwich. All of these courtyard arrangements were for merchants.

Warehouses

Also for the major merchants were WAREHOUSES, but with the exception of the C14 'Guildhall' at Blakeney and the timber buildings known to exist by c. 1050 by the river in Norwich, we can only discuss examples in King's Lynn. But the Lynn buildings are wholly exceptional in profusion and grandeur. C12 warehouses were probably integral with domestic quarters but by the C13, when the river had migrated far enough W, purpose-built warehouses cropped up on the W sides of the main N–S thoroughfares. They were of flint, brick or stone, or a combination of all three, and built at first parallel to the street. Such a warehouse existed behind No. 18 Tuesday Market Place (C14, demolished 1975). Hampton Court acquired its W range facing the river in the mid C15, and to facilitate removal of goods had an open seven-bay brick arcade. This was one of the last parallel warehouses built; the earlier ones were made redundant and the sites redeveloped as the river continued to shift its course. So the design changed to ranges built behind the L-shaped hall houses at r. angles to the river, which could be extended as necessary. No. 2 St Margaret's Place had such a brick warehouse in the C15, rebuilt in the early C16, as does No. 13 Nelson Street. Behind St George's Guildhall is a whole series of warehouses built against their predecessors' gable-ends in the C15. St Margaret's House in St Margaret's Place has two parallel brick ranges with partly timber-framed upper floors erected in 1475 for the Hanseatic Steelyard, one of four in England and the only survivor. Finally Marriotts Warehouse: the early C14 stone ground floor was augmented with a brick upper floor around 1500. The date is remarkable enough but the real curiosity is that we know that in the C14 it must have stood in the river itself, on an island linked to the quay by a causeway or bridge. Its specialized purpose probably was to transfer goods between river craft and sea-going vessels. For further discussion of warehouses *see* Introduction to King's Lynn, Vol. 2.

Shops

The surviving evidence of shops indicates that they were set at the front of otherwise quite normal houses with a passage at one side leading straight through to the hall and courtyard and with a side entry from the passage into the shop. Many of the King's Lynn L-plan houses must have begun like this; Nos. 40–42 King Street still has this C14 plan. It is timber-framed as is the late C14 range tacked on to the Norman house at Nos. 28–32, where slots for a pentice hood over the serving bays and the low windows under the jetty must guide us as to its appearance. Another timber Lynn house at No. 2 St Anne's Street (*c.* 1400) indicates that the unglazed serving bays had internal shutters which hinged up during business hours. As late as *c.* 1540 similar shutters occur at No. 2 Nelson Street, this time protecting three arched serving bays. In the E range of Hampton Court remains the roll-moulded frame of a serving window of *c.* 1480. The very grandest shop-cum-domestic ranges have been demolished, of which the best was probably that belonging to Walter Coney in Saturday Market (late C15). Although it was pulled down in 1816 an illustration shows it to be timber-framed, jettied on all three storeys and with brick nogging between the studs. On the ground floor of at least two sides were open four-centred arcades, and the whole was lavishly carved and appointed.

Norwich has a solitary identifiable shopfront at No. 15 Bedford Street (c16) and evidence of the existence of a few more, and Wymondham likewise. The mid-c15 timber-framed Green 2/65 Dragon pub in Wymondham is the best surviving town house and shop arrangement in the county. As usual it has a front shop range and a rear hall, both jettied. Since an alleyway was available the entry to the hall could be made on the s side, dispensing with the passage through from the front, and the whole ground floor of the front block given over to an arcade of four-centred openings. These examples are from significant buildings which have survived, and are with the exception of Walter Coney's house a variant on town-house themes. That there was a type more recognizable to the c20 eye is proved, however, by Nos. 6–14 St James's Street, King's Lynn, which may be reconstructed as a row of mid-c15 timber-framed shops with a chamber over each, both unheated. It is the only known example of that date in the county, but there must once have been more, possibly e.g. at Bedford Street, Norwich.

Farmbuildings

Farmbuildings which were built as such are understandably rare before the c17: they were usually of more flimsy construction than the farmhouses they served, and of the vast majority we have nothing to say. Those that do survive were generally spectacular testimonies to rural wealth, and take the form of timber-framed AISLED BARNS. First in the sequence is the early c14 barn at Hall Farm, Hemsby. There are eight pairs of aisle posts with 1/30 arched braces to the tie-beams and arcade plates, spurs to the wall posts and passing braces rising through the posts to the tie-beams. The same details appear inside the slightly later barn at Low Farm, Keswick. The c16 aisled barns at the Grange, Langley, and at College Farm, South Runcton, both have five bays and variants of the newly introduced side-purlin roof. Norfolk's three principal unaisled barns compensate for lack of aisles with their double queenpost roofs: Dairy Farm barn, Newton Flotman, at 2/62 the Old Rectory, Great Snoring and at Priory Farm, Aldeby. The first is late c15 and as well built as any rural house, and its roof is the best example to be seen in any Norfolk secular building. The brick barn at Hales Hall has already been mentioned as part of 2/61 another story.

Jetties

The most obvious structural embellishment to timber-framed buildings is the jetty, which had three important functions. By projecting an upper floor a larger room could be contrived than the size of the plot would allow, useful in narrow town plots. Structurally it permitted the use of weaker bridging beams because a beam with internal supports is less liable to internal flexing, although the cost saving was less than the cost of the jetty in the first place. Finally the jetty had a positive decorative and status function. The last two properties explain the spread of the technique to rural areas. The last C14 jettied building which we know was at No. 8 Purfleet Street, King's Lynn (demolished 1966), and this jetty was an internal one, that is, the upper floor of the two-storey street range projected into the open hall at the back. Such has been the rate of destruction and alteration that the first nearly complete examples of the early C15 come down to us fully formed, so that their evolution is obscure. No. 2 St Anne's Street, King's Lynn, is jettied front and rear, and The Briton's Arms, Elm Hill, Norwich, has jetties not only on both floors but continuing round two flanks. This introduces a complication, for a dragon beam is required in this circumstance, jutting out diagonally at the corner to support both overhangs.

Of the thirty-five or so surviving C15 jetties the only ones to appear outside towns are at Church Farmhouse, Blo Norton, at 2/57 Mayton Hall and at the Old Vicarage, Methwold. About eighty C16 jettied buildings are described in the gazetteer, of which twenty-one are outside towns, where space was not a prime factor. In the C17 the figures are thirteen out of forty; the only C18 jetty is at No. 17 Timberhill, Norwich.

Roofs

SCISSOR-BRACED ROOFS are one of the single-framed roof types and consist of pairs of straight braces at high level crossing between the principal rafters. Their mechanical fault is that they provided no horizontal stiffening and were therefore required in large numbers. This fact and their inherent unsuitability to timber-framed buildings (too many principal studs would be required) excluded their use other than in masonry buildings with solid gable walls. They were, however, a prestigious form, appearing in churches of the C13–C15, probably in the castles, though no examples survive, and in secular buildings of significance. The only reported domestic C13 survivor is at the stone hall at Nos. 4–6 St Anne's Street, King's Lynn,* then they appear in the roof of Carnary College, Norwich, and in the early C15 at the two King's Lynn guildhalls. The roof in St George's guildhall is particularly fine, with sixty-one trusses (this is the biggest; the early C14 nave roof at Thompson has forty trusses, Whinburgh nave thirty-two). Other C15 examples include Wensum Lodge and Nos. 19–21 Bedford Street, both in Norwich, but the roof type was by this time virtually redundant, finally appearing in the first years of the C16 in combination with a crown-post at Suckling House, Norwich.

The QUEENPOST truss is much more stable. This type has on the tie-beam two vertical posts rising to meet the principal rafters usually a little higher up than the mid-height of the roof, where

---

* I have not seen this roof myself.

they are trenched into longitudinal purlins. A collar links the tops
of each pair of posts and the posts normally were provided with
arched braces to the purlins and in better examples to the collar
also. The superiority of this type over the scissor-braced roof is
evident: the purlins give a measure of longitudinal stiffening,
the collars lateral bracing, and the secondary rafters between the
principal trusses could be of smaller section and rest on the
purlins. Apart from roofs with passing braces this is the oldest
roof type appropriate to timber framing and makes its debut in
Norfolk in the aisled C13 hall at Thetford Abbey Farm, complete
with arched braces in three directions. In the late C14 a similar
roof was provided at the White Cottage, Wacton, and in the C15
they begin to survive in numbers. At the Great Hall, Norwich
(early C15), they are over a flint and brick open hall, at Hales
Barn (late C15) all brick, but most are associated with timber
frames, e.g. Moat Farmhouse, Bedingham (c. 1470–80); Pykerell's
House, Norwich (late C15). At Ash Farmhouse, Shipdham, one
late C15 truss remains, smoke-blackened from the original open
fire, and at King's Head Cottage, Banham, the late C15 roof has
two pairs of octagonal posts with capitals and bases. There is
incidentally also here the remains of a smoke louvre in the ridge.

All these examples were at the very top of the vernacular

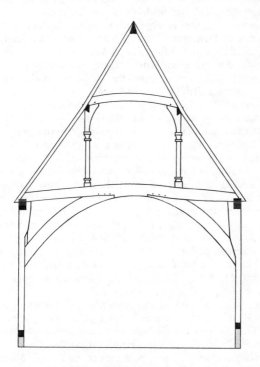

Banham, King's Head Cottage.
Section of roof drawn by Robert Smith

tradition even if some of them, such as King's Head Cottage, were quite small. The most striking variant of the queenpost roof was replication in two registers to provide the rare double queen-post roof. Since the second tier stands on the collar in the same way that the lower stands on the tie-beam only very wide spaces and very high roofs could accommodate it, so, apart from the barns already noted, only at the Black Lion Hotel, Little Walsingham, has a C15 domestic double queenpost roof been identified.

Norfolk seems to have rejected the KINGPOST ROOF other than in some churches (Kenninghall and Shropham naves) and at Mill Farmhouse, Old Buckenham (early C15), in favour of its cousin the CROWN-POST ROOF. The former has a single central post standing on the tie-beam and rising to the ridge piece; the latter is much more picturesque and more stable. This type has a single post on the tie-beam rising only as far as the collar. At the meeting was the crown purlin, a single member running the length of the roof to provide longitudinal stiffening. Usually arched braces, sometimes solid, rose from the post in four directions. Not as robust as the queenpost roof, it represents nevertheless the single most common type for hall houses, and only passed from use in the C16 when open halls themselves disappear. Like the examples already mentioned it was intended to be seen, and the bigger the hall the more elaborate was the roof.

The crown-post roof emerges from a hybrid in the hall truss of the s range of Hampton Court, King's Lynn, in the early C14. This is basically a roof with passing braces, a type presumably as old or older than the scissor truss, augmented at Hampton Court by further straight braces from the tie-beam to the principal rafters, creating a lattice effect, and a plain crown-post. A similar example is at School House, Brooke, and another variant exists in the one truss preserved of the C14 Great Yarmouth Guildhall (*see* also the celebrated example at Edgar's Farmhouse, Stow-market, Suffolk, *c.* 1340, combined with a crown-post). The raised aisled hall at Harleston, already mentioned, is finished with a crown-post standing on the collar, with four solid arched braces, but the first identifiable roof where the crown-post addresses us without help is in the former C14 chapel at Priory Farmhouse, Litcham. Here the post is octagonal. Also octagonal is the post over the early C15 first-floor hall in the later barn at Abbey Farm, Thetford, with moulded bases and capitals, and, exceptionally, arched braces from the tie-beams to the collars. At Church Farm-house, Blo Norton, the four crown-posts are square but make up for it with side fillets. So the pattern continues throughout the C15 and into the C16. Some regional variations can be identified in towns, where enough crown-posts survive in a small enough area. In King's Lynn a common C15 type is to have straight or arched braces from the tie-beam to the crown-post (No. 2 St Margaret's Place; Tudor Rose Hotel, St Nicholas Street; Nos. 17–18 Church Street). The type recurs at the Priory, Wiggenhall St Mary Magdalen, of *c.* 1500, and is found elsewhere, such as in the C14 Merchant Adventurers' Hall, York. A few of the first storeyed houses retained the crown-post type, e.g. the late C15 No. 20 High Street, Little Walsingham, or the range of houses built in 1529 in the Market Place at New Buckenham: in both 2/67 cases the roof was not meant to be seen.

The DECORATION of timber framing in Norfolk cannot compete with that in Suffolk and Essex, but some features require notice. Of carved corner posts to dragon beams the best are at No. 1 Common Place, Little Walsingham, and No. 1 Mere Street, Diss, both late C15. Of the same date is the post at No. 23 St Nicholas Street, Diss, with a carved Annunciation and Nativity; at No. 2 Nelson Street, King's Lynn, there is a carved panel of c. 1540. Double wave mouldings applied to internal timbers can be identified from the C14 at Rushford College, the early C15 at Welle Manor Hall, Upwell, the later C15 at No. 91 King Street, Norwich, and the best example at the Ancient House Museum, Thetford, c. 1490, which can at least stand comparison with any county. The Thetford museum also has fleur-de-lys, punched studs and bridging beams with multiple roll mouldings. Multiple rolls are well preserved in late C15 to mid-C16 houses elsewhere (e.g. Old Vicarage, Methwold, which also has ribbon-moulded timbers, as has Old Manor Farmhouse, Walpole St Peter). Ribbon mouldings laced with vine trail are confined to houses with real prestige, such as The Priory, Wiggenhall St Mary Magdalen, a house in Wright's Court, Norwich, and Church Farmhouse, Earlham. Only a handful of timber SCREENS survive in Norfolk.

Once BRICK had become accepted in the C15 for prestige houses it filtered into vernacular buildings of all types, but until 1550 it was used mainly for visible enrichment and for prominent features rather than as the major material. The E range of Hampton Court, King's Lynn, has brick nogging between the timber studs of c. 1480, there are remains of nogging a decade later at the Ancient House Museum, Thetford, at the C15 Telephone Museum, Norwich, and Martyr's Cottage, East Bilney (early C16). Herringbone nogging appears in the C16 (No. 20 Princes Street, Norwich). Brick used as a dressing to the corners and openings of flint buildings began early (of the late C14 are the remains of a house at Nos. 221–222 Northgate Street, Yarmouth; early C15 at Warren Lodge, Thetford) but is represented more fully in the C16, e.g. Manor House, Brundall, and Dove Farmhouse, Potter Heigham. At Geofferey the Dyer House, Worstead, the flint is laid in courses with brick. The combination of brick with timber framing, stepped gables and the advantages of brick for fire-proofing have already been mentioned under Building Materials (*see* pp. 24–6).

Early Storeyed Houses

Until the Tudor era houses of any pretension were built according to the established open-hall plan, suited to the status of their owners and the use of the hall. In lesser buildings a hall arrangement would hardly have been appropriate, but of these we know nothing, and of buildings important or big enough to have survived the sign of change comes in the towns in the last decade of the C15 (the late C15 hall of the Bishop of London's palace at Fulham is an imposing example). Although the origins of storeyed houses are debated, owners must have found that conducting their business in a communal hall with probably only one private upper chamber did not provide the comfort which their status might have suggested. Moreover, one of the original functions of the open hall was the accommodation of retainers owing some form of seigniorial duty, and that was completely redundant by the late C15, especially in towns. The better hall houses were fitted with side chimneys as the C15 progressed, but the remainder of the building was seldom heated. There was a shortage of rooms, which could be solved by the addition or enlargement of end blocks on unrestricted sites but only with difficulty in towns. The open hall, taking up a substantial volume in the middle of the building, was grand but not practical, and being open to the roof prevented access at first-floor level between chambers over the end blocks. On the vernacular level halls were made smaller, and finally dispensed with altogether, but the new order was not universal until the mid C16 and took even longer in some major buildings, where the interests of status and display lingered on.

The earliest surviving storeyed houses are late C15, timber-framed, and are basically floored hall houses, i.e. two-storeyed throughout and floored from the start. The Ancient House Museum, Thetford, has a hall-screen-services plan with the panelled screen intact, but the elaborate ceiling timbers of the hall are contemporary and allow a commodious chamber above. Both these rooms were heated and the winder staircase was probably in a recess by the stack. No. 20 High Street, Little Walsingham, is similar, and clings to the earlier type in retaining an open crown-post roof, as does Church Farmhouse, Kenninghall. Brick arrives at Old Manor Farmhouse, Walpole St Peter, c. 1500, but it has been so altered that one cannot recover the plan except to say that there were two main rooms on each floor. The same applies to the early C16 examples at Clark's Farmhouse, Martham, and Forge Cottage, Burnham Market. The Tudor Lodgings at Castle Acre was probably built and owned by the priory and represents the most advanced house of its date in the county. It was two houses, each a mirror of the other backing on to a central shared stack with winder staircases in the lobby at one side. There are the remains of one through passage to the w and another of the innovations, a clasped purlin roof.

Mention of a through passage anticipates the later C16, but side purlin roofs are part of the move from the open hall, for in the storeyed house there was neither demand nor space for an elaborate and conspicuous roof. A much simpler roof truss as strong as the crown-post could be made by removing the vertical members of a queenpost roof but retaining the side purlins clasped between the principals and the collar. This type, the CLASPED PURLIN roof, quickly came into use and by the 1520s most of its variants were established. The Shirehall, Little Walsingham, is another monastic range, with an early C16 clasped

purlin roof and curved wind-bracing. In Norwich the Louis Marchesi pub in Tombland survived the 1507 fire and retains its
c. 1480 roof, here with diminished principals (the principal rafters
reduce in section to accommodate the purlin and remain of this
scantling up to the ridge, usually the same section as the common
rafters). No. 55 The Close, Norwich, has arched braces to the
principals (late c15), No. 12 Market Place, Wymondham, has
braces to the tie-beams (early c16). Also early c16 is the w range
of St Margaret's House, King's Lynn, with an upper tier of
clasped purlins and a lower tier of butt purlins, i.e. the purlins
are morticed into the side of the principals, and curved wind-
bracing. Once established the side purlin roof became ubiquitous,
and its success seems to have revived interest in modest queenposts, e.g. at Ducksfoot Farmhouse, Pulham Market, of c. 1550,
which began as an open hall, reminding us of the slow pace of
change in rural areas.

ARCHITECTURE 1550–1700

Major Country Houses

There are no major houses of more than county interest in Norfolk
between the group with terracotta detailing ending with Great
Cressingham c. 1545 and Blickling Hall (begun in 1618), but there
are a number which illustrate the merging of old forms with the
new to create the ELIZABETHAN STYLE. Lovell's Hall, Terrington St Clement, is dated 1543 and is still essentially medieval,
but has a brick upper floor over stone, a half-H-plan, mullioned
windows, some of which have transoms, and, a vital addition, a
two-storeyed porch. Blo Norton Hall was enlarged in the 1580s
and provided with both straight and stepped gables and some
pediments over the windows. The existing timber-framed hall
arrangement was not only kept but provided with a new timber
screen which mixes in a charming way traditional panelling and
Renaissance fluted pilasters of the Ionic order. Enough remains
at Heydon Hall (Saxlingham), begun in 1550, to follow the plan,
again medieval in concept, with a porch leading to the screens
passage and hall lighted through mullioned windows. The internal
arrangements at Little Hautbois Hall (Hautbois) begun after 1553
have been altered but the exterior is interesting enough: three
irregular bays each rising into tall dormers on the wall-plane,
fully formed mullioned and transomed windows, polygonal angle
pinnacles, twin clustered chimneyshafts, straight gables, and a
porch. It is of brick, and from this point onwards brick was the only
material considered unless there were exceptional circumstances.

The first house recognizably of the new order and typical of
the Elizabethan style is Felmingham Hall, dated in a fireplace
1569. Most of the familiar motifs are here: stepped gables, central
porch, brick (but the mullioned and transomed windows replaced
with c19 sashes), and in addition the fact that the w front is

symmetrical and the porch is full-height. There is a principal room in the hall position but no longer an open hall and not the main public room. As the C16 progressed the old halls passed out of fashion and other rooms took on specialized purposes, all or nearly all heated. Diapered brick is often used as decoration. Next is Stiffkey Old Hall, the first of a series built for a new generation of men who rose to prominence through royal service, not from inherited wealth. It was for and it seems by *Sir Nicholas Bacon*, Keeper of the Great Seal, to be given to his son, and is not from the usual Elizabethan mould. For a start it is, not surprisingly in a seaside parish, of flint with brick dressings, secondly it has a U-plan and thirdly it is designed on a mathematical formula based on the ratio 2:1. The date is 1576–81. Another court official,

1/62 Henry Dynne, an Auditor of the Exchequer, built Heydon Hall (Heydon) in 1581–4 as the ultimate manifestation of the style: it is brick, with a rigidly symmetrical five-bay s front on the E-plan, even if the three-storey central porch projects only a little. Mullioned and transomed windows under pediments are set in alternating recessed and projecting bays defined by polygonal angle-shafts terminating in pinnacles. Over the roof are banks of clustered chimneys. The only echo of another age is in the four-centred entrance doorway. Among other examples are the mag-

2/70 nificent if altered Breckles Hall of 1583, Thelveton Hall of the 1590s, Morley Old Hall and Dersingham Hall (both *c.* 1600), the latter with some carstone, and Kirstead Hall of 1614. The last persists with a plan based on the hall-screen formula though the symmetrical exterior of course betrays none of that.

Of all the details enumerated only pediments over windows and symmetrical façades are Renaissance; all others have pre-Reformation origins.* Mullioned and transomed windows feature at the early C16 Gibraltar Gardens pub in Norwich; stepped gables begin in the late C15 e.g. at Hales Hall barn. Polygonal angle-shafts are familiar not only from churches but from the gates in the Norwich precinct walls and the story of the hall and screen arrangement has already been told (*see* above, pp. 86–9). The survival of this last feature even in a reduced single-storey form was a matter of prestige; it is more to do with a grand entry, and occurs only where there is space for it and only in the grandest houses.

Another gable type is the SHAPED GABLE and its close relation the pedimented DUTCH GABLE. Gables in the Low Countries and England were probably derived from common sources, including late C16 publications such as those of *Vredeman de Vries*. The 'Holborn' type of Dutch gable, often with voluted ends, drawn by Smithson in 1619 is connected with Inigo Jones and has a different source, possibly from Italian churches. This type

2/80 occurs at Raynham Hall, but not in the Netherlands until the mid C17. As far as shaped and Dutch gables are concerned the unpedimented type is the more common. There are various

---

* Pediments over windows were established for England at Somerset House in London in 1550.

arrangements of concave or convex stages, or a combination
sometimes with an ogee curve. They all appear in Norfolk and
Suffolk at various moments beginning in 1620 at Merton Hall
gatehouse, in 1624 at the Blickling service wings (with pediment),
and carry on in Norfolk until the 1760s.

Norfolk possesses only one 'prodigy house', Blickling Hall of 1/65
1618–29, for Sir Henry Hobart, the Lord Chief Justice, and his
son, celebrated as the antithesis of the contemporary but Classical
Queen's House at Greenwich. But this is in one respect an unfair
comparison because what is often forgotten is that at Blickling
Robert Lyminge was remodelling a medieval and Tudor building,
not building a new house on a virgin site. The existence of a moat
tells one that. The courtyard plan, and the full-height medieval
hall with a screens passage and whole wings were already established and were just reworked to fit in with Jacobean taste, exemplified at Hatfield, another of Lyminge's houses. Nevertheless
Blickling is more than a cosmetic exercise for, apart from the
tremendous plasterwork and fittings, Lyminge organized a suite
of private rooms unparalleled in the county, including a great
chamber, withdrawing room and long gallery. Entirely new are 1/66
the two projecting front wings dated 1624 and ending in Dutch 1/68
gables, the brick of the E one laid in Flemish bond, a very early
instance of this in England.

Closely associated with Blickling by reason of the craftsmen and location is Felbrigg Hall, also on the site of an older
house but this time completely rebuilt for Thomas Windham in
1621–4. Of this time is the small s range, only one room deep, built 1/69
of brick with Ketton stone dressings, and altogether a restrained
version of Blickling's s front complete with shaped E and W
gables. There is a central full-height porch, then two bays of
mullioned and transomed windows r. and l., then terminating
two-storey canted bay windows. In the parapets of these three
projections are cut-out letters. Inside there is little to see of the
C17 but there appears to have been an old-fashioned asymmetrical
room arrangement behind a symmetrical front incorporating a
screens passage (like the slightly older Kirstead Hall). The private
apartments were on the first floor, but the ground-floor layout
would have been familiar to any C14 or C15 noble, even if the
symmetrical exterior with its Tuscan columns framing the
doorway would puzzle him. In this Felbrigg stands at the end of
a long tradition.

The greatest and most sudden change in all English architecture
was brought about between 1615 and 1623 by Inigo Jones. It was
far deeper than the change of a hundred years earlier, for his
buildings are fully Classical, not just with Classical trimmings
tacked on as at Blickling. Despite the fact that few of Jones's
contemporaries could keep up with him his buildings were influential, and one man who studied them was Sir Roger Townshend
in 1620 in company with his mason *William Edge*. When he
returned to Norfolk he changed the plan of a house he had started
in 1619, and built Raynham Hall in 1622–35, so introducing the
Inigo Jones style to Norfolk. The house is symmetrical on three

fronts, but is also symmetrical on plan, a first for Norfolk, with a
2/80 hall occupying the centre seven bays of the w front and entered
from doorways in the outer bays which led to screened passages,
2/81 one at each end. The garden front has an attached portico which
suggests knowledge of Jones's designs for the Banqueting House
in Whitehall and the King's house at Newmarket. Both the portico
and the four great pedimented 'Holborn' gables at the front
and back may be a Jones invention. They recur at Kirby Hall
(Northants) in the 1638 N front by Nicholas Stone, who was also
influenced by Jones.

Other major houses of the time were Quidenham Hall, a courtyard house of 1606 with stepped gables and pedimented wings,
greatly altered, and Merton Hall of 1613. Merton was entirely in
the E-plan tradition, with stepped gables, but burnt in 1956
leaving only the gatehouse already mentioned. Hunstanton Hall
also has suffered from fires but the inner court by *William Edge*,
added in *c.* 1625–40, carries on from Raynham only an external
symmetry and cross-casement windows. Less exalted houses
tended to ignore Raynham altogether and continued the late
Elizabethan tradition: at Brockdish Hall of 1634 and Wilby Hall
after 1635 we might be discussing the first signs of Renaissance
detail, applied, as was usual, as columns to the porches. The same
applies to Wiveton Hall, which has shaped gables, pediments over
the windows, an H-plan, and the date 1652.

The first really important mansion after Raynham featured
the triple-pile plan within a Classical shell. This is at Melton
1/71 Constable. It is probable that just as at Raynham the house was
put up by its owner, in this instance *Sir Jacob Astley*, between
1664 and 1687 with assistance from a 'master bricklayer' as Roger
North has it (North was a gentleman architect living at Rougham,
though his house does not survive). The influences were not of
Jones tempered with Jacobean playfulness, but Hugh May and
Sir Roger Pratt. The ashlar and brick house aims to be the perfect
late C17 Classical house, set under a hipped roof with a slight
central pedimented projection and regularly placed upright
windows.

One of the few C17 architects who did thoroughly understand
Jones's Classicism was *Sir Roger Pratt*, but the house he built for
himself at Ryston in 1668–72 has been so altered that only the
fact of a double-pile need detain us. In 1675–8 the same move
towards comfortable elegant Classicism had been made at Fel-
1/70 brigg where *William Samwell* added the restrained w wing, all of
very fine brickwork. Felbrigg probably represents a similar but
independent solution to Melton Constable, but a number of other
fine houses owe their origins directly to Melton. Hoveton House
adopts the double-pile plan at the very end of the C17, the façade
again with superior brickwork, a pedimented centre and giant
Corinthian pilasters. Hanworth Hall, very early C18, rejects both
quoins and pilasters, but is another double-pile house, while
Ditchingham Hall of *c.* 1715 continues the type, this time with a
doorcase supporting a segmental pediment. A segmental pediment and rusticated brick quoins are the decoration applied to

Aylsham Old Hall, a minor beauty of 1686 just slightly lower in 1/87 status to a country house and favouring projecting end wings rather than a more or less flat façade crowned with a central pediment. This type represents another stratum of building based on the older H- or half-H-plan, but they all have in common the fact that it is the bricklayer not the mason who is the dominating craftsman, at least externally.

Lesser Rural Houses

Norfolk in the C16 and C17 was a county of landed gentry, few of whom could command country houses on the scale of those just discussed. But what was lacking in size and innovative design is made up for by numbers, even if many MANOR HOUSES were later relegated to farmhouse status because of amalgamation or expansion of larger estates.

The grander manor houses mimicked the seats of their betters, and only a few need mention to drive home the point. They are generally of brick. Hardingham Old Hall (built between 1580 and 1606) has a symmetrical front (but with a later bay added to the r.) with a full-height porch kitted out with polygonal angle-shafts. The windows have pediments and at the back a couple of external stacks and staircase outshuts. External staircases, usually at the back, are a recurring feature of houses of the middle order from the C15 (Welle Manor Hall, Upwell; Pickwick Cottage, New Buckenham), the C16 (Brecklands House, Garboldisham; No. 6 The Close, Norwich; Lammas Manor) and into the C17. Flordon Hall, after 1595, is timber-framed but on the E-plan, with brick gable-ends and a porch again with polygonal angle-shafts opening into the lower end of a hall. Manor Farmhouse, Stokesby, of 1633 has diapered brick and stepped gables; the late C17 Eccles Hall relies on shaped gables; and so too does the otherwise Classical Itteringham Manor Farmhouse of 1707. Their use at Itteringham illustrates that shaped gables; remained a popular feature: the latest date is 1766 on a house in Coltishall, but the type was revived as early as c. 1800 at The Gables at Cley. There are only about a dozen examples in England before Merton Hall and in Norfolk the majority date from c. 1670 to 1730. They are primarily an East Anglian feature, although their use was extensive in the East Riding of Yorkshire. Greengates at Hoveton, after 1708, is a yet more charming version of Itteringham. Erpingham House, early C18, favours a more polite façade, but the same motifs apart from the straight pediment over the door. The small but imposing Gateley Hall of 1726 concurs.

These last houses mix Classical with the vernacular, and again it is the brickwork which provides not only the decoration but the character. This is taken to the extreme in a small group of houses in which the bricklayers assert themselves with unusual gusto in a style usually labelled ARTISAN MANNERIST. The style, if it can be called that, had no major practitioners but originated in London in the 1620s in houses and livery companies apparently designed by the masons and bricklayers who built them.

Advantage was taken of the opportunities they presented for
1/64 virtuoso display of craftsmanship. The best in Norfolk is Stalham
Hall of *c.* 1670 which has a façade with two orders of pilasters, the
upper standing on bulgy bases on a heavy stringcourse. There are
paired pilasters at the corners and pilasters also to the porch. The
main gables are stepped. The S gable of Chestnut Farmhouse,
Hardley, a little earlier, has clasping pilasters to the corners, bulgy
pilasters to the mullioned windows and twin gables side by side
2/79 over them. Scole Inn of 1655 comes closest to London style: blind
panels between the windows and five prominent Dutch gables to
the front, and shaped end gables out of which grow panelled
stacks. A barn at Colton Old Hall dated 1666 has a little of the
same style, as do the gatepiers to Colney Old Hall with their oval
recesses echoed by concave bosses. The Scole Inn design is more
or less repeated on the fancy new brick façades to earlier timber-
framed buildings at Brockdish Grange and Brockdish Grove, both
nearby, and dated 1676 and 1672 respectively. One might also
mention the good brickwork at Bergh Apton Manor, late C17,
and at Bramerton Grange W front of *c.* 1670–80.

Now for the planning of smaller houses. In 1550 the majority
of existing buildings had halls open to the roof, but the type was
already in decline. One way of modernizing a house, as we have
noted, was to floor the hall, which had further implications. At
Danegelts in Geldeston the C16 timber-framed hall house was
floored in the C17, creating a problem of heating since an open
fire was no longer practicable. The solution was to place a chimneystack within the screens passage, allowing a fireplace to the
room on each side and also to the new rooms created on the first
floor. The external doorway remained in the same place, and so
the LOBBY-ENTRANCE plan was created: on entering one is
confronted with a brick wall, with doorways r. and l. into the
former hall and into the former services. Church Cottage, Ket-
2/64 teringham, illustrates the type and the grandeur of the stack
testifies to the prestige that went with it. Sometimes the passage
was retained (e.g. Valhalla, Garvestone) and the stack built
against it, usually in the hall, but this solution meant that a second
stack was needed for the kitchen. Houses altered in this way
often retain their crown-post roofs, e.g. Whittleton's Farmhouse,
East Ruston, floored perhaps in 1602, or the Maid's Head
pub in Newton Flotman, floored early in the C18. The dates
of conversion in the main are C17, several are C16, a couple only
in the C15.

The early storeyed houses already mentioned did not as a rule
adopt the lobby-entrance plan (Clarke's Farmhouse at Martham
is early C16 and may have been a lobby-entrance from the start,
but is exceptional), so it is only from the late C16 that the type
can be appreciated in the majority of parishes. Among the first is
Banham's Farmhouse, Browick (Wymondham), of *c.* 1570, with
reused ribbon-moulded bridging beams, and The Lindens, Horsford, which combines timber framing with brick. Dove House
Farmhouse, Potter Heigham, is an example in flint, with a circular
stairwell. By the early C17 the lobby-entrance plan was a standard

for smaller houses, e.g. Carey's Cottage, Kenninghall, and Islay House, Great Ellingham. A winder staircase was usually provided beside the stack in the corresponding rear lobby. In the C18 the type was ubiquitous.

The THROUGH-PASSAGE plan was a close relative of the hall-house type, but without the open hall, in which a passageway ran right through the house on the shorter axis, but it was never popular in East Anglia. Of the dozen or so examples in Norfolk most are simply the remains of the screens passage which survived after hall conversion (e.g. Brumstead Hall and No. 99 High Road, Needham). New houses with this plan date from the late C16, such as Porch Farmhouse, Poringland, of c. 1590, which has in addition gable-end stacks with staircase outshuts. For larger houses at least three rooms wide and for grander two-roomed houses an alternative to the lobby-entrance prescription was to construct a brick gable-end or ends carrying stacks. These could either be additions to an older house (e.g. Methwold Old 2/57 Vicarage, early C16) or new houses otherwise of timber-framed construction (Old Buckenham Abbey Farmhouse, mid C16; 2/59 The Poplars, Wreningham, 1586). Chimneystacks were until the C17 still a luxury other than in houses at the top of the social scale, and an item to show off, which explains their highly decorative character. Even at Snore Hall, in a particularly 2/56 opulent late C15 brick wing, a central stack was provided only in the 1580s.

Many houses were given NEW BRICK FRONTS applied to older cores, so a great many houses in town and country, even perhaps the majority, do not appear as they really are, for refronting was an ideal way of upgrading a building, especially as neighbours could see that it had been done. Often a simultaneous refurbishment went on inside. The major houses tended to be rebuilt entirely or had a whole new wing applied. Once brick became fashionable, it seems, everyone who could afford to had to display it. The corollary is that timber framing especially went so far out of fashion after about 1700 that it hardly occurs outside the vernacular level. Exposed studwork inside was equally unpopular, especially in hallways or reception rooms, so throughout the C18 and C19 evidence of framing was eliminated. This is why so many timbers have divots made by an axe to provide a key for plaster. There is no difference in chronology between town and country, but a higher proportion of skins was applied to buildings in towns, and the peak period was the first half of the C18.* The earliest might be Gowthorpe Manor, Swardeston, possibly bricked in 1574, though this is difficult to credit, especially as there was then a long gap until the Brockdish buildings, already mentioned, and Marlingford Old Hall which was given a brick skin in 1679 and a new staircase. Sparrow Green Farmhouse, Gressenhall, followed c. 1680, complete with porch, and after 1700 there was a flood of

---

* Of surviving houses which have been given a new front or fronts rather than undergoing complete reconstruction the percentage are as follows: before 1650 2%, after 1650 6%, 1701–1750 32%, 1751–1800 17%, 1801–1850 17%, 1851–1900 23%, after 1900 3%.

symmetrical three-and five-bay fronts with modest doorcases. The better fronts had moulded brick and gauged flat arches over the openings (skewback arches); after about 1720 almost all openings have the latter. Typical are the Manor House, Wereham (façade 1729), West Lodge, Easton (1743), Vicarage, Bacton (c. 1760 of knapped flint), and Church Farmhouse, Stalham (1811 and of gault brick).

In towns it was easier to add a brick skin than to add a new wing to the front, especially if only the front faced the street, so one difference between town and country is that in the towns the earliest refacing was done to superior houses, although the fashion spread quickly. The biggest surge also came in the first half of the C18: c. 1700 at Nos. 56–60 King Street, Norwich; early C18 at Thoresby College, King's Lynn, already no stranger to brick and stone, with a row of five Dutch gables to the street; Clifton House, Queen Street, King's Lynn, received a most swagger Classical front in 1708 for the merchant Samuel Taylor. It has a two-storey, seven-bay elevation, and in the second bay a recessed doorway fronted by a pair of Baroque barley-sugar columns. Sash windows and a hipped roof complete the modernization. Good examples of similar remodelling are at No. 97 King Street, Norwich, in c. 1690, and at Oakleigh House, Swaffham, of the 1730s. Queen Street in King's Lynn, like Magdalen Street in Norwich, appears to be an C18 and C19 creation, but behind practically every brick front is a timber house. High Street, Little Walsingham, South Quay, Yarmouth, and most of Wymondham are the same, to name only a few. With this topic we are already in the realm of town houses.

Town Houses

The two Norwich TOWN HOUSES which approached the size and scale of major country houses have been demolished or altered out of recognition. One was the Duke of Norfolk's palace in Charing Cross, a large courtyard building begun in 1561 and rebuilt in 1602 but abandoned by 1711. The other was Henry Hobart's Chapel Field House, converted out of the remains of the dissolved collegiate buildings, bought by him in 1609 and converted in the 1750s to form the Assembly Rooms. Such was the pressure for land near the centre of town that the Duke had to accept a malodorous site immediately downstream of the dyers' quarter (John Evelyn thought it an 'old wretched building'), and indeed it was space that limited the development of large houses. Before the 1507 Norwich fire the Pastons had been able to find room for a courtyard house at Nos. 41–43 Elm Hill, and Edmund Woode (a mayor) managed to buy enough land at Nos. 11–15 Fye Bridge Street in the 1540s for another. Generally however the courtyard could only be created piecemeal, one range added at a time, as at Gurney Court, Magdalen Street, where two wings went up in the late C16, but the others had to wait until the late C17 and 1730. At Nos. 3–4 South Quay, Great Yarmouth, the merchant

Benjamin Cooper was only able to create his courtyard arrangement over twenty years, starting in the 1590s. There were other
courts in Yarmouth and Norwich, but the C18 saw them all
encroached by tenements which deteriorated in the C19 into
slums. No. 3 Broad Row, Yarmouth, is an early C17 house
built within such a courtyard, and at No. 5 the cellar has steps
leading up to a yard long since built over.

King's Lynn remains the town with the most early courtyard
houses, but they continued to be built for the richer merchants
where possible. Tuesday Market Place still has two, one being
the obvious courtyard plan of the Duke's Head Hotel built for
Sir John Turner in 1683–9 and sporting a pre-Baroque brick
façade.* The other is at Nos. 8–10, not at all obvious, having
been broken up into various properties and generally altered, but
enough remains to date it to the C16. In Norwich the N end of
the Market Place is closed by a brick nine-bay mansion of c. 1700
heavily disguised by shops, but with a courtyard approached
through the central entrance. The L-PLAN remained the favourite
for houses with less pretension in King's Lynn, at least into the
C17, such as No. 29 Queen Street of 1630. Greenland Fishery
House of 1605–8 established the plan of a single range with the
living quarters facing the street and service rooms in the rear
wing. This was taken up and elaborated in 1645 at the Tudor
Rose Hotel, St Nicholas Street, and in other towns, e.g. Wymondham (the Queen's Head in Bridewell Street and the White Hart,
Market Street, both of c. 1616 after the fire). But even in Wymondham the old hall-house town plan combining a shop at the front
was continued at No. 3 Bridewell Street, even if No. 4 opposite
favoured a central entrance.

The LOBBY-ENTRANCE plan came to towns in the early C17;
there is a brick row of them at Nos. 22–28 Nelson Street in King's
Lynn, a timber-framed version clad with C19 brick at McIntyre
House, New Buckenham, and at No. 16 Damgate, Wymondham,
but the lobby-entrance was never a popular choice. This takes us
down the social scale, and for small houses the visitor at first must
look for buildings with their gable-end facing the street to take
advantage of their long narrow sites. This was a common late
medieval arrangement, surviving at No. 1 Chapel Street, New
Buckenham. The gables of almost all timber-framed houses were
jettied. Examples are, in Norwich, at Nos. 3–4 Haymarket (mid
C16) and No. 12 Tombland (C17); in Yarmouth at No. 160 King
Street (late C16); the latest known date is 1720 at No. 102 High
Street, Gorleston-on-Sea.

The bulk of the C16 and C17 population however lived in small
tenements of houses of indistinct plan, often built into courtyards
or converted out of bigger town houses of the previous century.
Almost all were swept away in slum clearances, especially in
Norwich before the Second World War and in Yarmouth after.
In Norwich it appears that a great many were two-storeyed even

* The architect of the Duke's Head might be *Henry Bell*, who probably built the
fourteen-bay Classical house for Charles Turner in 1703 which faced the hotel across
the square (burnt 1768).

in the C16 and that most had brick fireplaces, and in the C17 the trend continued. One curious fashion in Norwich which may be recorded at this point is the device of raising outsized gabled dormers to provide for extensive attic occupation. Many of them are as high as a whole storey of the house below. They appear in the early C16 house at Nos. 12–16 Elm Hill, but may in fact be a late C16 addition. Others of the C16 are at No. 74 Upper St Giles Street and of 1599 gracing the Mischief Tavern on Fye Bridge Street. In the C17 they are found everywhere (Nos. 2–4 Elm Hill, *c.* 1619, Nos. 100–104 Pottergate in 1687), but peter out in the C18. Nos. 2–4 White Lion Street might possess the latest C18 example.

Major Houses: Interior Fittings

For PANELLING and plasterwork a brief summary is all that is required. Linenfold panelling dated 1581 exists at Narborough Hall, and there is earlier linenfold in the Norwich Guildhall but there is not much linenfold in Norfolk other than on church pulpits and occasional doors. By 1679 FIELDED PANELLING had arrived at Marlingford Old Hall and large-framed panelling on the dado of the Aylsham Old Hall staircase, and in other rooms. Thereafter large-framed was the rule where panelling was applied at all. PLASTERWORK is less common than panelling and Norfolk is not the county for it, the subject hardly requiring mention before the C17. There is however some outstanding C17 work in three major houses, and outstanding not just for Norfolk. At 1/66 Blickling in 1620 *Edward Stanyon* produced flower and star shapes 1/73 with little pendants and the tremendous gallery ceiling with figurative scenes and didactic panels, while in 1628 *Lyminge* used strapwork to effect on the ceiling of the former staircase. Stanyon worked also at Felbrigg but what is remembered there is the 1/74 drawing-room ceiling dated 1687 by the same anonymous hand as the plaster at Melton Constable. Both have the inimitable, completely detached fruit and flower garlands of the Grinling Gibbons era and both bear comparison with *Edward Goudge*'s work.

Construction and Fittings of Smaller Houses

The development of STAIRCASES is another matter which merits attention. In smaller houses it is the WINDER STAIR which dominates, usually positioned in an alcove by the chimneystack and dependent for its site on the position of the stack: in the centre in a lobby-entrance house, or against the gable walls in an end-stack house. Exceptionally, staircases were positioned in the space formerly taken by the screens passage (e.g. Fincham Hall). Staircases of the C15 tended to be elaborated ladder stairs often with treads made of solid slabs of timber. At Little Hautbois Hall, Hautbois, they are reused, at the dower house at Flordon Hall of *c.* 1600 they are contemporary, but almost all solid treads have disappeared, especially in grander houses which were able to make a feature of staircases after the mid C16. At Churchgate House in Wymondham a new staircase was created in the angle of two wings around 1560 with turned balusters and a closed string, a formula that remained popular into the C18. A similar staircase of 1579 at Wood Hall, Hilgay, introduces strapwork on the newel post, and moulded handrails occur at Hall Farmhouse, Trunch. At Old Hall, Great Ellingham, the turned balusters sit on square bases and the newels become panelled and receive ball finials. Carved newels and moulded handrails may be seen at the Old Rectory, Stratton St Michael. But it was the early C17 that saw the great expansion of elaborate staircases in minor buildings: flat balusters at Old Hall, Saxlingham Nethergate, and at Old Hall, Knapton, the latter embellishing an open-well staircase. The Black Boys Hotel in Aylsham has a splendid carved closed string, Pilgrim's Farmhouse, Spooner Row, a dog-leg stair with acorn finials and matching dado panelling, the latter a feature which was to become essential for the better off in the later C17 and C18. Tapering balusters crop up at Gable End, Colkirk, and splat balusters at Oakleigh House, Swaffham. The last combines strapwork and elaborate finials. Flat carved balusters remained popular throughout the century (West Hall, Mundford; Hall Farmhouse, East Winch; Wiveton Hall) but vase-turned balusters came a close second (e.g. Manor Farmhouse, Salle) and the habit of siting staircases in their own towers at the back continued (Stonegate Farmhouse, Little Walsingham; Valley Farmhouse, Gunthorpe). In the 1630s openwork panels were used instead of balusters at No. 97 King Street, Norwich, but these were never common. By the 1640s in houses of any pretension appreciation of the staircase as an opportunity of display filtered down from the great houses of one or two generations earlier (e.g. Blickling) and justified separate treatment. So at Kirby Cane Hall in 1642 the stairs occupy a separate room at the back reached by a passage from the door. Stalham Hall of c. 1670 contrives a separation by the old device of a rear staircase tower containing an open-well stair with turned balusters and square newels with ball finials.

The difference between the C17 and C18 is one of construction, from the closed to the open string, one of the first of which is at Aylsham Old Hall of 1686. Aylsham also boasts twisted balusters, which occur at Melton Constable in the 1680s and which were the favourite design in good houses in the early C18, as elsewhere in England. Oxburgh Hall and Dial House, both in Emneth, and the Old Rectory, Kirby Bedon, may be taken as examples, along with the most splendid staircase in Itteringham Manor Farmhouse, of 1707. The Old Rectory has a ramped and wreathed handrail, at Aylsham only ramped. Examples readily visible to the visitor are those in the entrance narthex at St George, Great Yarmouth, of 1714 by the London team of *John Price* and his son. Close in date must be the stair in Nos. 15–16 Tuesday Market Place in King's Lynn, with the added attraction of tiny Corinthian columns as newel posts. Open strings, narrow ramped and wreathed handrails and columns instead of balusters characterize the entire C18 until the introduction of the simple stick baluster around 1760. In Norfolk one of the first is at Hethersett Old Hall School of 1774, but they became immensely popular; they are the most common staircase type in the county, and are still built.

Lesser houses also had PLASTERWORK on the ceilings. In the period *c.* 1590–1610 the same plasterer worked at the Manor House, Oulton Street, Lowestoft (Suffolk), then in Great Yarmouth at Nos. 1–2 and Nos. 3–4 South Quay, and at the house 1/72 in Row 117. He favoured geometrical shapes: concave-sided stars, squares with wavy lines, but also pendants and little figures.

Of the early C17 are single rooms at e.g. Barningham Hall (strapwork), Old Hall, Forncett St Mary (vine trails), a perfect pendant in the form of Noah's Ark and the Hand of God of 1619 at Quidenham Hall, and McIntyre House, New Buckenham, in 1624 (floral trails). Kirstead House Farmhouse, Kirstead, is only a timber-framed lobby-entrance house of the mid C17 but manages a plaster ceiling with garlands and angels. Another small house, Old Rectory Cottage, Caston, has a plaster ceiling which might be early C17 but is undatable. One suspects a great many other houses of manorial or lesser status had plasterwork too.

A great many C17 houses have perfectly plain small-framed PANELLING in principal rooms, such as No. 4 South Quay, Great Yarmouth. Some are more elaborate: at College Farmhouse, Thompson, panelling was added during late C16 alterations, with Ionic pilasters and a palmette frieze; the White Lion pub in Yarmouth combines small-framed panelling with an early C17 chimneypiece; the Duke's Head in the same town has Corinthian pilasters of 1609; Catton Old Hall has arcaded panelling possibly of 1632.

Roofs

By 1550 not only the crown-post roof but all elaborate roof constructions in secular buildings gave way to the utilitarian SIDE PURLIN ROOF. Basically each truss is an A-frame made up of opposing principal rafters meeting at the ridge, sometimes with a longitudinal ridge piece and usually with collars. The collars might or might not be braced to the principals depending on the span covered, but all of them have at least one and commonly two side purlins running between each truss along the length of the roof to provide the necessary stiffening, and they all have tie-beams linking their bases. There are variations to the basic model, each invented to reduce complexity and weight of timber without sacrificing strength, but this is the design of virtually all roofs up to the present day:* it is cheap, strong, uses only one principal rafter to each principal stud in a timber-framed building, is equally at home with brick or flint, and offers an attic space unobstructed by vertical timbers. Another function of the purlins is to provide support for the secondary rafters, set between the principals and

---

* Unless in special building types such as assembly rooms, town halls or, in 1609 at Trinity Hospital, Castle Rising, where queenposts were revived.

of smaller section, to which the battens were nailed for tiles or thatch. Any number of secondaries could be accommodated.

The first side purlin roofs have CLASPED PURLINS, that is, the purlin is clasped into the acute angle at the junction of the collar and principal rafter, in the same way as purlins in queen-post roofs. There was however a drawback in that the secondary rafters all had to be the same thickness as the principals to ensure that all outer faces of the roof members were on the same plane, and this was not only expensive but added weight without compensating strength, exactly what was not wanted. The solution, first found in Norfolk in about 1480 at the Louis Marchesi pub in Norwich, was DIMINISHED PRINCIPALS. The clasped purlin is trenched into the principals, which reduce in section from the collar to the ridge, so that secondary rafters need only be the same thickness as the upper part of the principal. Moreover the joint so created between these three members was much stronger than the earliest queenpost type of purlin. If the roof was big enough to justify a second tier of purlins then these were set lower down and simply trenched into the inner face of the principals.

Arched braces were frugally deployed from the start between collars and principals (Swannington Hall, early C16), or from wall posts to principals (No. 55 The Close, Norwich, late C15), but other features have their own chronology. Arched wind-braces fitted between the principals and purlins were introduced around 1500 and continued in that form until the 1730s. School House, Swaffham, has them in 1736, but from the late C17 arched wind-braces were replaced by straight ones, presumably for reasons of economy. Their purpose was to prevent deflection of the three-way joint between collar, purlin and principal rafter in a clasped-purlin roof, but they were found to be even more desirable for the intrinsically less robust butt-purlin roof.

The BUTT-PURLIN ROOF is a simpler affair and succeeded the clasped purlin type in the late C16, although the two ran side by side for a considerable period, as the early C18 former pub on Bridge Street, King's Lynn, and Nos. 1–2 Prospect Terrace, Attleborough, demonstrate. Instead of clasping purlins with a complicated joint in the angle of a diminished principal, the principals at, for example, Hall Farmhouse, Trunch, have the same section from tie-beam to ridge and have two tiers of purlins fitted to the side faces by means of ordinary mortise and tenon joints. Two tiers were usually needed unless the roof was very low. Arched wind-braces and collars complete the picture. This roof belonged to the C17, the next change being to STAGGERED BUTT-PURLINS around 1700. Erneford House, Holme Hale, is about that date, but examples may be found everywhere into the C19, particularly in barns and minor houses. Ordinary butt-purlins were tenoned in the normal manner, but were alternately staggered up then down between principals in an effort to make one run of timber perform the mechanical function of two proper tiers. They were admittedly a useful device where dormer windows were fitted but it is debatable whether the saving justified the loss of rigidity, and true butt-purlin roofs continued to be built. The final modification introduced the TAPER-TENONED PURLIN in the middle of the C18, again for reasons of cost and mainly in outbuildings, e.g. the barn at Grange Farm, Burgh St Margaret. The tenon was eliminated and the purlin simply cut away to a point, like the point of a chisel, inserted into the mortise and held by the usual dowel: altogether a sloppy type of carpentry.

Two eccentricities call for comment. The first is the habit of carpenters in Wymondham of building clasped-purlin roofs set into UNDIMINISHED PRINCIPALS. The late C16 Nos. 3–5 Town Green are like this but most date from after the fire of 1615 (e.g. No. 3 Bridewell Street, 1616). That they were used elsewhere is obvious from the example of a generation earlier at Nos. 33–34 Bridge Street, King's Lynn, but they are seldom encountered outside Wymondham. The second is the use of what is termed here UPPER CRUCKS, but they are not crucks, merely cranked timbers instead of principals designed to increase the available headroom in the attic. Almost all have been found in buildings dating from c. 1600 to 1620 although the latest known roof of this type is of 1644 at No. 25 South Quay, Great Yarmouth. Yarmouth is in fact the place to find them, there being about twenty-five, half the entire Norfolk total.* They occur more sparingly in Suffolk and Essex.

Barns

Only a handful of barns survive from the C16, but they tend to be as grand as the farmhouses which accompany them, though few set the pace in the use of materials or roof structures. The aisled barns at The Grange, Langley, and at College Farm, South Runcton, are both timber-framed and both have clasped purlins, that at College Farm even with diminished principals. The giant Waxham Great Barn of c. 1570 and its sister at Paston dated 1581 are both in a flint area and flint is indeed the material, augmented with brick. The roofs of these are of a type with tie-beams alternating with hammerbeams, as had occasionally been used in churches a century earlier. It reappears at Godwick Hall barn, probably of 1586 like the farmhouse it once served, but these are the only instances of this roof type yet discovered in secular buildings in the county. Of c. 1590 is the barn at Old Hall Farm, Burlingham St Edmund, timber-framed with brick end gables like a house, and roofed with clasped purlins. A similar date and roof at Brundish Farm, Raveningham, and then at the Old Hall, Great Ellingham, is weatherboarding in two barns, the later C17 one with some clay lump, an early use. In the early C17 aisled barns enjoyed a renaissance at Church Farm, Rollesby, and at Home Farm, Hemsby, but the rest of the story is of utilitarian but well-built structures reflecting in their materials the region in which they are found. At Ivy Farm, Burnham Thorpe, the early C17 barn has the so-called upper crucks (see above), as had a demolished barn at Honing. Exceptionally, barns were attached

* Not all are mentioned in the gazetteer. The totals are only of those so far discovered, a point always to be considered.

to houses (Faxman's Farm, Roughton; Chestnut Tree Farm, Forncett St Peter; and Keeper's Cottage, Ranworth), but this was never an East Anglian fashion. Stepped gables and other fancies sometimes add some sparkle (stepped gables at Manor Farm, East Ruston; Hall's Farm, Moulton St Mary; Gowthorpe Manor, Swardeston; Dersingham Tithe Barn, 1671; Beech Farm, Thurton, 1698; Dutch gables at Aylsham Old Hall, 1686; Manor Farm, Kirby Bedon, 1693; Church Farm, Ridlington, 1698). The late C17 barn at Stanninghall Farm has blank arcading against the plinth and clasping pilasters to one of the porch entrances.

Public Buildings

At various moments of invasion threat or of domestic unrest corporations were reminded of their medieval TOWN WALLS and FORTIFICATIONS. From time to time monarchs reminded them also, but the emphasis from the C16 was on coastal defences: Henry VIII in 1539 ordered an inspection, and there was another during the Armada scare, when repair of the walls and castle of Norwich was ordered. Some fortifications, now lost, were made on the N coast at Cley and Weybourne in 1588. In Norwich further repairs were made to the walls in 1642 and to the castle the following year. At Great Yarmouth various bulwarks were built for cannon on the beach in 1539 and in the 1540s and 1550s repairs were made to the walls, mostly clearing of rubbish and sand dunes. In 1569–70 a Mount was established, for three tiers of guns, and in 1588 a triangular ravelin tower abutting the town walls. The site at least of this can still be made out, but not of the harbour fort erected in 1653 against the Dutch, nor of the batteries pointing inland provided but not used at the time of the Civil War. King's Lynn had a fort at St Anne's in 1570, which was repaired after 1625 to repel pirates, who had recently been a nuisance, but the main military excitement Lynn experienced came in 1643 when the Parliamentarians attacked and seized the place, then went about making the defences rather more secure than before, with a complete enceinte. Nothing of all this survives.

Fortifications are to defend shipping and trade as much as to repel invasion, and trade brings taxes, and taxes CUSTOMS HOUSES. Most customs activity went on in existing civil buildings, and at Cley and Wells-next-the-Sea ordinary houses which were used for the purpose still remain. The customs house *par excellence* however is in King's Lynn and was built as a Merchants' Exchange by *Henry Bell* in 1683. It is one of the most perfect Classical buildings in provincial England. Henry Bell was one of 2/76 the gentlemen-architects who flourished in the C17, as well as being a much-travelled merchant, wit and twice Mayor of Lynn. The Customs House brings us back to the comfortable late C17 domestic architecture on the landed estates, but looks directly to London and Dutch examples, especially with its two super-imposed orders of pilasters.

The only new GUILDHALL in this period is the 1624 extension to the Holy Trinity Guildhall in King's Lynn, because until the

C18 Norfolk towns contented themselves with existing buildings. The oldest surviving MARKET CROSS is of 1600 at North Walsham, replacing a cross burnt out in 1549, and is a remarkable timber octagonal structure with a triple lantern on top and an 2/71 open ground floor. The Wymondham cross of 1617–18 is also octagonal and also open to the ground floor, with a meeting room 2/72 above. At New Buckenham the Market House is rectangular, having been adapted from shops before 1718, but has an upper meeting room as well. The best of the crosses have been demolished. At King's Lynn there was a C15 shelter, superseded by a hexagonal cross with on the ground floor ordinary shops with folding down shutters and a meeting room above. This was replaced in 1707–10 by an ambitious domed octagon by *Henry Bell*, demolished in 1829. The Norwich cross was the most arresting of them all, put up in stone in 1501–3 and nearly 70 ft high. It had an octagonal chapel and a meeting room above and a projecting canopy at first-floor level supported on Perp piers. The windows were also Perp, but the Classical cornice shown on drawings made before demolition in 1732 must be an alteration. 2/73 The cross at Swaffham of 1575 was replaced in 1783, but in the C19 it was not felt necessary to reinstate those at Watton and Thetford.

BRIDGES were generally the responsibility of corporations within towns, but probably of local landowners in the country. The C13 Fye Bridge in Norwich was rebuilt in 1829, but the Bishop's Bridge of *c.* 1340 remains, with as much brick as stone and three segmental arches. Also C14 is the bridge at Potter 1/31 Heigham; the C15 bridges at Wiveton and Newton Flotman may 2/60 be mentioned, and of *c.* 1520 that at Cringleford. At Thetford the oldest remaining is Melford Bridge, built of brick with two circular stone arches in 1697 for the Wodehouse family. Nun's Bridges in Thetford is an ancient site even if the bridges date from the C18. There are many lost bridges, particularly in Great Yarmouth, and of the early C16 bridge at the E gate of Lynn at Gaywood only two ribbed stone arches survive.

In the Middle Ages HOSPITALS for the infirm ranged from the Norman Lazar House in Norwich to the C14 hospital at Horning Hall (founded 1153) and the Great Hospital in Norwich. The last is still in operation as almshouses. Hospitals in the sense of infirmaries disappeared after the Reformation, until the C18, but ALMSHOUSES appealed to the philanthropy of local magnates, many of whom had made fortunes out of the destruction of the monasteries. Fulmerston Almshouses in Thetford is such a case but was not begun until 1610, and the front was reordered in the C19 into a symmetrical single-storey block. Single-storey and of linear plan was a standard C17 type, such as at Stow Bardolph, rebuilt *c.* 1870, but the quadrangle plan was also favoured when there was money to spend. In 1609–14 Henry Howard, Earl of Northampton, paid for the quadrangular Trinity Hospital at Castle Rising complete with a chapel facing the entrance, and at 2/78 Gaywood is a very sedate single-storey quadrangle in brick rebuilt in 1649.

CHURCHES AND CHURCH FURNISHINGS
1550–1700

Between the Reformation and the C18 only one new Anglican church was begun in Norfolk, and that is no more than a small brick chapel of 1624, St Peter, Hoveton. All Saints, Santon, was rebuilt in 1628, St Peter Hungate in Norwich received a new chancel in 1604 and six churches received new porches where there had been no porch before. Essential repairs, especially to towers, of course had to be carried on unless the building was to be abandoned. A few posthumous Perp items were completed. St Stephen in Norwich has already been mentioned (*see* p. 62), and there were a few others. The tower at Griston was completed in 1568, and a two-storey vestry added at Scarning in 1576. There were a few Nonconformist chapels put up from the end of the C17, which will be dealt with below, but to take the survey of ecclesiastical architecture forward one must concentrate on MONUMENTS and FURNISHINGS.

The Renaissance spirit of the grand terracotta tombs at Oxborough, Wymondham and Norwich survived, although the use of terracotta never caught on. Those tombs have no effigies and there is one type of Elizabethan monument which rejects not only effigies but is even shy of any demonstrative ornament. Sir Francis and Sir Thomas Lovell (†1550 and †1567) have identical monuments at East Harling, both dignified pieces, but with neither Early Renaissance nor strapwork decoration. At Shelton are two more identical tomb chests to members of the Shelton family, both content with mere shields, and at Tasburgh there are three shields in cusped fields. Thomas Wodehouse †1571 at Waxham is typical also: a four-centred arch flanked by Corinthian columns and a tomb chest again with shields, that is, Renaissance mixed with Gothic. The monument to Thomas Holdiche (†1579) at Ranworth is virtually a copy. Elizabeth Calthorpe in the cathedral (†1582) and Honor Bacon (†1591) at Ashmanhaugh are similar. Strapwork, a favourite Jacobean ornament, makes a tentative appearance in the 1570s at St Martin-at-Palace, Norwich (Lady Elizabeth Calthorpe †1578), and at St Mary, Feltwell (†1580). Where effigies are admitted they are recumbent, as had been the custom before the Reformation. Such is the case with the monument to Sir Robert Southwell at Woodrising (†1563). The material is alabaster and the effigy is set on a low gadrooned sarcophagus behind four Doric columns.

Much more common is the wall-monument with kneeling effigies, a Renaissance newcomer from France via the Netherlands, though there were medieval precedents both on the Continent and in English brasses. The small C16 monuments typically have two figures facing each other across a prayer desk, and typical too are the files of children squeezed in behind their parents often in uncomfortably cramped attitudes or, more spaciously, ranged along a predella. One of the earliest commemorates

Nicholas and Anne Sotherton in St John Maddermarket, Norwich. He was a mayor †1540, but the monument is a generation later in style, closer to other mayors of Norwich who face their wives across prayer desks, such as Robert Suckling (†1589, St Andrew) and Thomas Pettus (†1597, St Simon and St Jude). The figures generally are set in architectural frames usually with an arched niche. The best include that to Henry Hawe †1592 at Hilgay, and Bridget Coke †1598 at Tittleshall, the arch with beautiful crumpled ribbonwork, and eight children below. The type continues well into the C17, e.g. Sir William Heveningham and wife, Ketteringham, †1678. Another type of wall-monument is represented at Stiffkey, to Nathaniel Bacon, before 1615 (no effigy, but an obelisk and a black marble cloth hanging down). The monument to Mrs Pope at North Barningham †1621 has two Mannerist angels holding open a curtain, the same office as angels perform for Sir Drue Drury at Riddlesworth (†1617). At North Tuddenham a monument of †1629 still uses strapwork but the open pediment is definitely post-Jacobean.

For larger standing monuments, however, the traditional recumbent effigy and the effigy reclining more or less comfortably on one elbow were both popular. A new feature is the reclining figure on a half-rolled-up mat, first introduced to England from the Netherlands in about 1570. Sir Clement Paston at Oxnead †1597 is the first of these in Norfolk and other good ones commemorate Sir Wymond Carye †1612 at Snettisham, and the big monument with a backplate and flanking columns at Besthorpe †1639 (Sir William Drury). This is still of alabaster. Where husband and wife were both represented (as was usual) he is normally placed above and behind her. Sir Clement and Lady Spelman (†1607) at Narborough are splendid, with their heads propped up on their elbows, as in life. Rose Claxton at Rollesby (†1601) is the same, though much stiffer. The Jacobean decades were much more exuberant in their monuments than the C16 had been, full of obelisks, strapwork, coffered arches, achievements and predella panels of children. Typical is the huge monument 1/83 to Sir William Paston made in 1608 by *John Key* and *William Wright* at North Walsham; he props himself up on his elbow on a sarcophagus within a coffered arch liberally decorated on the back wall. Paired Ionic columns either side support a cornice and there is a superstructure above that with three obelisks and a couple of griffins.

There were other classes of monuments, such as four- and six-posters, though Norfolk has none of the latter and only two four-posters, at Little Walsingham (†1632) and at St Peter Parmentergate, Norwich (1623, with recumbent effigies). A frontal bust appears on the monument to Francis Windham †1592 in St Peter Mancroft, Norwich, and busts are fairly common in the C17, e.g. at North Barningham †1639, and in works by *Stone* discussed below. The North Barningham monument is of marble, a material introduced from *c.* 1620 instead of alabaster or painted freestone for smaller monuments, and linked to the change in taste away from polychromy to black and white.

By the C17 we can begin to follow the careers of individual sculptors, but of them all only two, *Martin Morley* and *W. Linton*, are from Norwich workshops. For Norwich men we have to wait for the C18. The best of all sculptors of the first half of the C17 is *Nicholas Stone*, and he, or at least his workshop, has a big Norfolk presence. Sir Thomas Hewer and wife at Emneth and Alderman Anguish in St George Tombland, Norwich, were both made in 1617 and are both typical work of the time, but his monument to Sir Edmund Paston at Paston of 1635 is different. It has a restrained Classicism associated with the innovations of Inigo Jones, with an urn instead of an effigy or tomb chest set within an aedicule consisting of two columns supporting an entablature and a broken segmental pediment. A Classical pediment over a niche had been made earlier, to Bishop Jegon at Aylsham †1617, but Stone displays an understanding of Jones's designs. After this the antique vocabulary becomes more important. *Stone*'s monument to Dame Katherine Paston at Paston of 1629 has her in a typical Jacobean reclining attitude but with her upper body propped up on her arm, not just her head. Lady Katherine Paston at Oxnead †1637, also by *Stone*, is represented as a bust on a pedestal. In the monuments of *c*. 1639 at Holkham *Stone* returns to kneeling figures, though a bust appears within a pediment.

There are four other particularly notable reclining monuments. Thomas Marsham †1638 at Stratton Strawless is shown in middle age (*see* below); Lady Dionys Williamson †1684 at Loddon is depicted in old age reclining on her tomb chest with its deeply gadrooned edge, very much in *Grinling Gibbons*'s style. At North Barningham is the monument to Sir Austin †1639 and Dame Elizabeth Palgrave (with busts), and, one of the highlights of C17 English sculpture, the effigy of Lady Adams at Sprowston in a joint monument with her husband Sir Thomas †1667.

A conceit made popular through *Stone*'s 1631 monument to John Donne in St Paul's Cathedral was the portrayal of the dead person about to rise from that state. The first resurrection monument in Norfolk is to Thomas Marsham †1638 at Stratton Strawless. Marsham is shown in his shroud and there is a ghastly charnel-house scene as well, while Mary Calthorpe's effigy at East Barsham †1640, by *J.* and *M. Christmas*, actually rises out of its coffin in its shroud. Other charnel-house scenes, sometimes of grisly reality, are on the monument to William Peck †1635 at 1/84 Spixworth, the effigies in shrouds, and Sir Edward Barkham and wife †1634 at South Acre with a charnel-house panel on the chest between the sons and daughters.

With monuments as much as with buildings one must beware of the notion that a new idea or style immediately flushed out older ones. A snapshot of the position in the 1640s for example reveals several types of monument. Thomas Richardson at Honingham †1642 is represented by a three-quarter-length figure with a baton and sword in an oval recess – very much in advance of early C18 fashion. But John Mingay †1625 and wife †1642 at St Stephen, Norwich, have a tablet with two kneeling figures either side of a prayer-desk; Sir Edmund Reve and his wife †1647 at

Long Stratton are depicted as recumbent effigies. The process was, however, changing. *Edward Marshall*'s monument to Dame Frances Playters †1659 at Dickleburgh has a frontal demi-figure set in an architectural frame more in the Artisan Mannerist mode than the Classical, and at Caister-on-Sea William Crowe †1668 is shown as a bust between Corinthian columns, and that is almost Georgian. It is attributed to *C. G. Cibber*. Bowed inscription panels appear in the 1660s, at Thursford †1666 by *William Stanton* and †1672 at Burnham Overy Town. At St Nicholas, King's Lynn, the kneeling figures formula was modernized by turning them from profile to nearly frontal in a monument †1675. Henry Marsham †1692, his wife and son at Stratton Strawless all kneel frontally in a space much too small to hold them, so much so that the babe on the r. has to stand up. Then more standing figures begin to appear, notably that depicting Clement Spelman †1679 at Narborough, possibly by *Sir William Wilson*, and originally on a pedestal 8 ft tall. This survey of monuments can end for the moment with that to Sir Thomas Hare †1693, depicted in Roman armour, one of many monuments in the brick mausoleum built in 1624 at Stow Bardolph.

Of BRASSES it need only be recorded that there are thirty-one surviving during the period with which we are presently concerned which are more than mere inscriptions. Familiar habits include armour (Sir Peter Rede at St Peter Mancroft, Norwich, †1568 and Henry Hobart †1561 at Loddon) and contemporary dress (Mary Rust at Necton †1596). Kneeling figures occur at e.g. Narborough †1561 and at Burgh St Margaret †1608, but the day of the monumental brass had passed. The last significant one is of †1660, to Philip Tenison at Bawburgh, in his shroud. Norfolk is not the county for HEADSTONES and the C17 not the century. Where good groups are found they are C18 and in the marshland churches, i.e. closest to the limestone belt. An exception is one of the earliest, †1653 at Stoke Holy Cross, another †1682 at West Walton, then, of the C18, one must go to Emneth, Middleton, Northwold, Terrington St John, Upwell, Walsoken and West Dereham.

The Puritan iconoclasts in the mid C17 caused much damage to CHURCH FURNISHINGS, particularly those which bore images specific to the Roman church, though practically any image would do. Paintings on screens and carvings on fonts were a favourite target, William Dowsing in 1643 recording, for instance, the mutilation of the C14 font at Gorleston-on-Sea. Of the twenty-three new FONTS provided in Norfolk in the two centuries from the Reformation only five can be dated earlier than 1660, and one suspects that the rest are replacements after the Restoration of fonts which so enraged the Parliamentary visitors that they were totally destroyed. The early C17 font at Cockthorpe and the new bowl of 1619 at New Buckenham are basically still Perp, but in 1627 strapwork appeared on the bowl at St Nicholas, King's Lynn, and again at Terrington St John in 1632. Thereafter fonts were plain and octagonal, though the font at Ashwellthorpe of 1660 has the Perp motif of shields in barbed quatrefoils. A few balusters were made, rather coarse at Little Plumstead in the C17, a little better in the four C18 examples: wooden at Croxton (near Thetford), stone at Anmer, Melton Constable and Carleton Rode. The last, daringly, has a fluted stem.

FONT COVERS fared much better (there are forty-one between 1550 and 1704) and are on the whole finer and bolder than other woodwork. The best of the Jacobean ones are at Terrington St 2/45 Clement and Walpole St Peter, both with opening doors. At Terrington the style is Laudian Gothic, at Walpole Gothic tinged with Classical. The majority favour the radial display of fin-like volutes familiar from late medieval covers (Field Dalling) or have a central turned baluster with scrolled openwork attachments (Hales), or even turned balusters supporting an ogeed or domed superstructure (St George Tombland, Norwich; Swardeston; Great Walsingham). At Horsham St Faith is a strapwork obelisk, and obelisks occur elsewhere, for example at St Michael-at-Plea, Norwich, and East Bradenham. The Saxthorpe cover of 1621 has a drum with foliage carving, not strapwork; at Wiggenhall St Mary the Virgin we have an octagonal canopy with a pelican on top (1625), at St Andrew, Norwich, a similar canopy with a ball finial (1637) and at Plumstead in the early C18 distinctly old-fashioned splat balusters.

As far as other C17 WOODEN FURNISHINGS are concerned the places to visit are Wilby, Walpole St Peter, Tibenham and Thompson, in that order. Wilby suffered a fire in 1633 which consumed the medieval fittings and also the nave roof, all of which were replaced in the next five years. The quality is rather uneven. To take the pieces thematically, we shall begin with PULPITS. With a total of eighty-eight they are by far the most frequently met item in these years, and to narrow it further fifty-four of them are from the time of James I.* In essence the story is a direct continuation of the medieval type: they are hexagonal or octagonal, sometimes with a back panel and tester, but usually not. A characteristic Elizabethan and Jacobean motif is the short broad blind arcading familiar from contemporary domestic wood-work, and in addition some arabesque, strapwork or other orna-ment. Beeston pulpit of 1592 has segmental arches on long pilasters, at Salle is a three-decker adapted out of a Perp piece, and three-deckers may be seen also at e.g. Reymerston and Wilby. The Reymerston pulpit has lunette arcading, those at Tacolneston and Woodton arches in perspective. Of the Jacobean ones the best is at Tibenham, where the pulpit has standard arcaded panels but the tester has strapwork, obelisks and pendants, and coffering on the underside. At Loddon is a good strapwork frieze of 1603, at Cley colonnettes at the angles, a rare device repeated in 1614–26 at North Elmham which provides another rarity, one of only a few names for a pre-C19 piece. It is by *Francis Floyd*, a local carver. Walpole St Peter (1620) has a curved staircase, Wiggenhall St Germans decoration of geometric panels rather than blank arches. That was in 1631, but blank arches were never given up:

---

* Thirteen do not permit dating other than to the C17.

Watlington in 1661 has them. In the early C18 at Attleborough is
a good pulpit, perhaps by *Ver Brugen*, complete with a staircase
with the twisted balusters of the time.

Some HOURGLASS STANDS are still attached to pulpits, needed
to keep a watch on the length of sermons. The best are at Braydeston, Catfield and Colby, the latter still with its hourglass.
READER'S DESKS are also often attached to pulpits, at least to
pulpits of the two-or three-decker type (e.g. Merton, Thompson,
Hempstead and Foxley). At Tibenham is an odd four-sided and
four-legged desk, like a library desk. Edingthorpe is dated 1587.
Bressingham has a very odd set of later C16 BENCHES, with
traceried ends and animals or figures and poppyheads, that is,
early C16 in character. But the buttresses towards the nave are
balusters, not very well done. Brisley has pews for squire and
rector with lunettes in friezes, dated 1590, and there are Jacobean
FAMILY PEWS at Frenze near Diss (turned balusters), at Hardwick (with a tester) and at Thompson of *c.* 1630 (panelled). The
elevated family pew of John Buxton at Tibenham was specifically
licensed by Archbishop Laud in 1635 and is most odd. The pew
of 1640 at Little Barningham has Death appearing as a skeleton
in a shroud and a less than cheerful inscription to go with it, and
finally at Melton Constable is the Hastings Pew of 1681, also
slightly elevated. The STALLS at East Bilney are probably a C19
creation out of Jacobean panels. The more ordinary benches of
Bittering, West Rudham and Foxley have poppyheads, but the
Wilby benches of the 1630s have fleur-de-lys ends instead. Of
them all those at Thompson are the best, dated 1625 and 1632,
with poppyheads. For BOX PEWS mention of those at Barton
Bendish (St Andrew), dated 1623, with a whole catalogue of hinge
types will have to suffice.

COMMUNION RAILS as a rule were introduced in the years of
Archbishop Laud, that is *c.* 1635–45, as part of his decree that
altars should be placed at the E end and protected but not
screened. A number are, or were, three-sided (Westfield; West
Dereham) but the majority have just one run. They must parallel
domestic staircases very closely, so it is doubly a pity that dating
can only be stylistic. The dates we do have in Norfolk are these:
Thompson of *c.* 1630 (turned balusters); Wilby of 1633–8 (two
tiers of balusters in the gate); Swannington of *c.* 1660 (six balusters
set in pairs of three); Merton in *c.* 1690 (twisted balusters); St
Margaret, Norwich, in 1707 (dumb-bell balusters reused in the
tower screen). The baluster type is universal with the exception
of West Acre which has pierced fretwork oblongs, and Tilney All
Saints with muntins dividing open arched panels. Occasionally
there are panelled square newels, as at Thurton and Bedingham,
and at West Winch is a curious variation: dumb-bell balusters
with figures bearing attributes against the posts.

SCREENS do not figure much in these years. There are only
eleven, and that includes those at Sidestrand and Congham which
are C19 creations out of Jacobean panels, and the Hardwick
screen, which is Perp but renewed in its top parts in 1661 after
damage by the Puritans. St Margaret, King's Lynn, has a crossing

screen of 1584. At Tibenham there is only a fragment, at Wilby only the base. So the best is the rather domestic early C17 W screen at Walpole St Peter: three pedimented entrances defined by fluted pilasters carrying a balustrade of bobbin-turned balusters. Arcaded panelling exists at Catfield tower screen of 1605; Tilney All Saints rood screen of 1618 has five open arches, balusters and obelisks; and another such is at All Saints, King's Lynn. There are elongated balusters at North Elmham tower screen. Closely associated with screens are a small number of C17 WEST GAL-LERIES at Coltishall, Beetley, East Harling and Walpole St Andrew, all with twisted or turned balusters. Of REREDOSES are minor pieces at Colby (late C17) and Hedenham (*c.*1700), but the best was at St Nicholas, King's Lynn, designed by *Henry Bell* in 1704 but removed. COMMANDMENT BOARDS exist at Shipdham (1630), Terrington St Clement (1635) and at Caister-on-Sea (1688) and POOR BOXES in a number of places, mostly of 1639 and all variants of balusters except for the wooden parson at Watton and the panelled box at Wiggenhall St Mary the Virgin. Of LECTERNS there is even less: a C17 eagle at Hilgay and in about 1700 a baluster at Attlebridge. That leaves ROYAL ARMS, sometimes painted, sometimes carved, sometimes both. Mon-archs represented are James I at Tilney St Lawrence and Hil-borough (both painted), Elizabeth I at Ludham, Kenninghall and Tivetshall St Margaret, the last filling the whole of the chancel arch (all painted), James I at Hilborough, Charles I at Burnham Norton, Charles II at Gorleston and elsewhere, Great Witch-ingham and Stow Bardolph, the last well carved. Carving rather than painting is standard after about 1665, so we have William and Mary at Ingworth and Blo Norton, William III at Shelton, a 2/50 glorious carved piece, Queen Anne at Hanworth and George I at Kilverstone, done in plaster. STAINED GLASS has already been mentioned in the context of C16 and C17 pieces imported from Europe, usually after 1800, but there is one native panel, a mem-orial to William Newce †1610 at Tasburgh, with his two wives and an inscription.

ARCHITECTURE 1700–1830

The type of comfortable Classical house exemplified by Hanworth Hall and Ditchingham Hall reached its developed form by the time Queen Anne ascended to the throne in 1702. Norfolk has three examples, Great Hockham Hall of 1702, Lexham Hall (East Lexham) of *c.*1715 and Cavick House of *c.*1720. Lexham is the finest and better fits the Queen Anne pattern even if it has been altered inside and out. The type is generally square on plan, of two storeys and dormer attic, the dormers fitted into a hipped roof which is truncated to form a flat and which rises from deep eaves typically fitted with modillions. The corners are articulated by rusticated quoins and the stacks are of simple square or rectangular section. Other houses of this type are Tacolneston Hall of *c.* 1700, a reconstruction of an early C16 timber-framed house, and Hope House at Hindolveston of 1715. Two houses possibly by *Henry Bell* should also be mentioned here. At Narford Hall Sir Andrew Fountaine began his new house in 1702, possibly employing *Bell* to provide the seven-bay s front in a mixed Queen Anne-late C17 Classical style. It has a broken segmental pediment over the door, and so too does the double-pile Stanhoe Hall begun the following year, also possibly by *Bell*. The restrained orangery at Felbrigg of 1704–5 reaches back through its reliance on plain but fine brickwork to Samwell's wing.

2/83

The BAROQUE style even in a minor form missed Norfolk almost completely. It was represented only by the demolished West Harling Hall, built after 1725, which had giant rusticated pilasters and a deep attic storey. Certain Baroque-inspired features can be found, such as the barley-sugar columns attached to the doorcase of Clifton House in King's Lynn of 1708, and then there is a range of buildings in town and country in the first half of the C18 which rely on giant pilasters, such as Dial House, Emneth (1730), West Bradenham Hall (before 1753), Shropham Hall (completed 1739) and No. 3A King Street, King's Lynn.

In the years 1715–20 a new fundamental change of fashion took place in English architecture, away from the comfortable domestic houses of the developed Classical to the grand official display of PALLADIANISM. The first volume of Campbell's *Vitruvius Britannicus* (1715) and an English translation of Palladio's *Quattro Libri* (by Giacomo Leoni, 1715–20) were published at just the moment when noblemen were either sending their sons off on the Grand Tour or opening their own minds to Palladio (and much else) by going themselves. One of these was the second Sir Andrew Fountaine who came back from his second tour in 1716 and immediately added the library quadrangle at Narford (in 1716–18) to a design dependent on Campbell's Wanstead House, still under construction but published in *Vitruvius Britannicus*. *Fountaine* himself seems to have joined the list of amateur architects by designing it himself, and, moreover, was a member of the Burlington-Campbell-Benson group who led the break from the old to the new.*

The two exceptional C18 country houses of Norfolk are Houghton Hall, begun in 1722 for Sir Robert Walpole, the Prime Minister of George I and II, and Holkham Hall, begun in 1734 for Thomas Coke, later first Earl of Leicester. Both embody Palladian principles and in both cases the story of the architects involved is complicated. *Thomas Ripley* was executive architect at Houghton in 1720, but there is confusion over the actual attribution. *Campbell* claimed the design in the third volume of *Vitruvius Britannicus* issued in 1725, though undated drawings suggest that *James Gibbs* may have been involved in the early stages and that Campbell may simply have regularized his rival's designs. Gibbs

---

* There is a tantalizing ruin in the grounds of West Dereham Abbey of a house put up for Sir Thomas Dereham, who had been a diplomat in Tuscany. He had an Italian palazzo with a *piano nobile*. The interesting part is the date: 1697.

certainly designed the corner domes, not a Palladian feature, which were under construction in the late 1720s; Campbell's drawings had proposed pedimented end pavilions similar to Wilton House. The splendid interiors by *William Kent* were not ready until 1731. The house is a giant Palladian villa with quadrant 2/87 wings ending in pavilions, faced with Yorkshire sandstone. The main apartments are all on the *piano nobile*, raised over a basement, which is a Palladian standard. Holkham also has a *piano* 2/85 *nobile*, in a rectangular block connected by short straight links to four wings rather than the long quadrants of Houghton. The centre is more severely correct than Houghton, with a detached pedimented portico and raised angle pavilions instead of Gibbs's domes at Houghton. The building material is a locally made faun-coloured brick, thought to resemble antique brick, and is an early example of Palladian use of pale brick. The executive architect of Holkham was *Matthew Brettingham*, a Norfolk man appointed in 1725, but the design, which owes much to Chiswick House, seems to have developed through discussions between Coke and his friends *Lord Burlington* and *William Kent*. *Coke*, who probably promoted designs of his own, had met Kent in Italy, who was then a bad painter and not yet an architect. Building began in 1734 and did not finish until 1761, after Kent's death.

Kent provided lavish interiors at Houghton, especially the double-height stone hall with its doorways and chimneypiece (by 2/88 *Rysbrack*), all heavily carved under a rich plaster ceiling. The saloon has a great coved ceiling and more exuberant treatment of doorcases and chimneypiece, and the open-well staircase is decorated with paintings by Kent himself. The other rooms are equally handsome. Good though Houghton's interiors are, they cannot compete with *Kent*'s at Holkham, but neither can any other English mansion, especially the tremendous apsed staircase 2/84 hall derived from Palladio as a fusion of a Roman basilica and an Egyptian hall. Both houses have 'rustic', or ground-floor, family rooms under the state rooms of the *piano nobile*.

When the architecture of Houghton was finished but before Holkham had been started, *Thomas Ripley* secured the commission of Wolterton Hall from Sir Robert Walpole's brother Horatio. Built in 1727–41, Wolterton manages to bend Palladianism into a shell derived from the tradition of Melton Constable and other late C17 hip-roofed houses. It is a seven-by-three-bay brick block raised over a rusticated Portland stone basement, and has a triple-pile plan. The staircase rises right through the centre of the house to a lantern, the light reaching the rooms through internal windows. *Brettingham* in turn benefited from his association with Holkham to the extent that he was asked by George Proctor, probably in 1742–4, to turn the newly-built but conventional two-storey Langley Park into a reduced version 2/92 of Holkham by means of an attic storey, corner towers with Holkhamesque pyramid roofs and two new satellite wings. But he was unable to create a *piano nobile*. At Kimberley Hall, built 2/91 by *William Talman* for Sir John Wodehouse after 1700, four corner towers were added in 1755–7 by *Thomas Prowse* for Sir Armine.

Either *Matthew* or *Robert Brettingham* put up Nos. 15–17 Cow Hill in Norwich in the mid century, with direct references to Holkham on a minor scale, and indeed called Holkham House. *Matthew Brettingham* had already (in 1742) built Gunton Park for Sir William Harbord, though it has been so remodelled (by *Samuel* and *James Wyatt* in 1780–5, and after 1822) and damaged by fire and again reconstructed, that its Palladian features can only be guessed at. The late C18 Wolferton House, Sporle, has single-storey pavilions in the Palladian manner and Fransham Place, Little Fransham, of *c*. 1800 (formerly the rectory) has miniature equivalents.

2/107

These last two are exceptional for after about 1760 direct Palladian references begin to fade away in larger Norfolk houses, though certain motifs, such as porticoes and Venetian windows, remained popular for a considerable time. Porticoes are found at Sennowe Hall, Guist, in 1774, and Aldborough Hall, early C19; Venetian windows at e.g. The Firs, Old Catton of *c*. 1757–61, Hargham Hall of *c*. 1800, and the lodges at Weston House, Weston Longville, early in the C19. Palladian principles depending simply on proportions and planning affected Georgian buildings more subtly. Mid-C18 Norfolk houses could be elegant without being ostentatious: Honing Hall of 1748 is an example of the well-designed house for a wealthy landowner rather than a great magnate, and is an image of our idea of a polite GEORGIAN COUNTRY HOUSE. It is symmetrical, has a hipped roof, a central decorated pediment, sashes, a pedimented doorcase on Ionic columns and an emphasis on good-quality red brick. Salle Park of 1761 is another case, at seven bays bigger than Honing and benefiting from two principal fronts, but shy of excessive decoration or any plasticity of form.

By the 1740s a new influence made itself felt in country houses, the GOTHIC REVIVAL. In Norfolk the earliest Gothick of all is a 1751 fireplace in Churchman's House, Upper St Giles Street, Norwich, taken from Batty Langley's *Gothic Architecture Improved* of 1742, and then the Felbrigg library in the early 1750s. From the mid 1750s it is expressed mainly by Y-tracery windows in several houses (Miller's House, Ellingham; Red House, Thornham; Westwick Lodges). A Gothick façade was added to Trowse Old Hall, Trowse Newton, in *c*. 1770. It is not an accomplished piece, but an amalgam of pattern-book examples. There are two major and belated C18 examples in Norfolk, both for different branches of the Preston family and both attributed to one of Norfolk's most famous architects, and one who worked more outside the county than within it, *William Wilkins* the elder.

1/89 Beeston Hall, Beeston St Lawrence, was apparently built in 1773–7 then recased in an even more Gothick form in 1785–7, crenellated all round, fitted out with arched windows with intersecting glazing bars and covered with knapped flint. Interestingly the Gothick did not extend to the interior. The other is

2/105 Stanfield Hall near Wymondham, a C16 house remodelled more than once, so one is not prepared for the tremendous full-height,

2/104 fan-vaulted staircase hall of 1792 done in stone. This at least is in advance of national style, for the Gothick is not applied as a plaster skin to a conventional building but is fully understood (by C19 standards), and built in a manner historically correct. By the opening of the C19 the Gothic idiom was fully accepted and the opportunity was everywhere taken to remodel older houses. *Humphry* and *John Adey Repton* did so at Barningham Hall in 1805–7, while *Donthorn* put up Cromer Hall in 1827, and again in 1829 following a fire, in a lavish flint Gothic.

In the early 1780s another new idiom came to Norfolk houses, not a national style but the spare and idiosyncratic NEO-CLASSICISM of Sir John Soane, who built his career on a number of small houses in East Anglia practically devoid of the Classical orders. They greatly influenced other, local, architects. The important ones are Letton Hall of 1783–9, Shotesham Park, begun 2/106 in 1784, Saxlingham Nethergate Rectory of 1784–7 and the Chedgrave and Thurton Lodges to Langley Park, designed in 2/94, 1784. Between 1782 and 1807 *Samuel Wyatt* designed dozens of 95 lodges, outbuildings and farmbuildings at Holkham in a Neo- 2/108 classical style rivalling that of Soane, of which the Great Barn of 2/111 c. 1790 is perhaps the most remarkable: a barn in Neoclassical clothes is rare indeed. It is disappointing that the GREEK TASTE after 1800 does not provide more Norfolk buildings, given that one of the best exponents of it was a Norwich architect, *William Wilkins Jun.* Nevertheless there is the extraordinary screen of five giant Greek Doric columns making up the S portico at Lether-ingsett Hall, added to an existing house in about 1808, and the unforgettable Nelson's column at Yarmouth, the earliest such 1/94 monument, erected in 1817–19 by *William Wilkins Jun.* Sher-ingham hall must be mentioned here, as a collaboration in 1812–18 by the father and son team of *Humphry* and *John Adey Repton*, who created one of the most subtle renderings of Neoclassic Italianate in the county, made especially happy in its setting, for park and house complement each other in a way only the Reptons could manage. Elmham Park, North Elmham (demolished in 1924), was another significant Neoclassical house, redone in about 1825 by *Donthorn*, who could and did turn his hand to any style, here angular and spare, and one must add Thornham Hall built before 1811 for George Hogge, a member of one of the three most important families of King's Lynn merchants, in a Neoclassical tempered with Palladian overtones.

Space does not permit an indication of INTERIOR DECO-RATION other than to direct the reader to the best. Some have already been mentioned. Narford Hall is the best place in England to see painted decoration by *Pellegrini* between 1708 and 1713, but of all the interiors the grandest are the work of *Kent* at Houghton and Holkham. At Raynham *Kent* was called in by the 2/86 second Viscount Townshend in about 1728–9 to remodel the C17 2/89 house, so his schemes there are his earliest in Norfolk. The entrance hall, one and a half storeys in height, has rich plasterwork still in a late C17 style and has walls articulated with Ionic pilasters. Cavick House, Langley Park, Gateley Hall and Churchman's 2/90 House in Norwich all have exuberant Rococo plasterwork. In the light of these works owners of other older houses succumbed to the pressure for an internal face-lift, the chief of which are Blickling and Felbrigg. At Blickling various remodellings took place inside and out in the years 1766–79 by *Thomas, William* and *John Ivory*, members of an important Norwich dynasty. They were done in a sympathetic Jacobean way. It was only in 1767 that 1/67 alterations to the hall and re-siting of the staircase first imposed a Palladian symmetry to the building, but only to a part of it. Felbrigg had a more thorough modernization under *James Paine* in 1751–5. His is the dining room, with a Kentian fireplace and plasterwork by *Rose* and *Green*, and to go with it were a new staircase and a library, the latter a Gothick essay.

Gardens and Grounds

Grander houses were not set in isolation, but were integral with their parks and LANDSCAPED GARDENS. Of FORMAL GARDENS accompanying Jacobean and Stuart mansions there are none in England left in their original state, though at Blickling an impression may be gained in the garden to the E of the house.* Long straight avenues aligned with the house were popular from the 1680s, influenced by French and Dutch formal landscaping, such as exists at Aylsham Old Hall of the 1680s, now agricultural and cut off by the road to Blickling, and at Swanton Abbott Hall in *c.* 1710. That they were still popular in the 1730s is confirmed by *Bridgeman*'s Coronation Avenue at Gunton in *c.* 1730. A great wood was established at Felbrigg, N of the house, in 1673–87. At Narford, Houghton and Raynham the plantings of the early 1720s were still formal, but the first two were accompanied by GARDEN BUILDINGS, a temple and a water tower respectively. *Bridgeman* enlarged the Houghton grounds in *c.* 1725–7, years when he was also at work at Wolterton. The senior park and the biggest in Norfolk is however at Holkham and it is instructive to note that work on the park was begun before the house – parks were not laid out as an afterthought. The early park buildings are *Kent*'s obelisk and temple (1729–30), and it was Kent who first planned the grounds. The temple, like Blickling's, is of the Roman Doric order and has distinct Palladian character. *Capability Brown* improved the park in the 1760s, *William Eames* and *John Webb* did the same for the lake in 1801–3, and there were continual extensions and new buildings right into the C19. *Wyatt*'s farm buildings have already been referred to.‡ At Blickling the second Earl of Buckinghamshire found four avenues of trees, an artificial hill and a small lake when he succeeded in 1756, and he developed them further. Close to the house is the temple and a fountain, both probably of the 1730s, and later came *Stone*'s statue of Hercules and an orangery of *c.* 1782 by *Samuel Wyatt*.

---

* Since the 1970s an increasing number of formal gardens have been recreated along C17 lines, though not in Norfolk.

‡ Many of them will be found in the gazetteer in other parishes: Warham and Wighton in volume 1; Castle Acre, Kempstone, Mileham and South Creake (including the important Leicester Square farm of 1793–1801) in volume 2.

Gunton park was augmented by two lakes in the middle of the
C18 and by a deer park and groups of trees in 1825. *Capability
Brown* worked at Kimberley in 1762 (very open parkland taking
advantage of a surprisingly steep hill), at Melton Constable in
1764–9 (a belated attempt to catch up on fashion), at Langley in
1765, and at Ditchingham Hall at uncertain date. *Richmond* and
Repton between them sorted out Beeston's park and peasants in
the 1770s and 1780s (*see* below), though their contributions are
not well recorded; *Repton* alone worked at Honing Hall in 1792,
and, already more than once referred to, at Sheringham Hall in
1812–18. Finally, Stradsett Hall park was organized by *J. C. Loudon* in 1810–13 as part of general improvements to the house
(Loudon designed a good if small cast-iron bridge over the ha-ha).

Landscaping of parks could also lead to the creation of ESTATE
VILLAGES. Some villages were found to be inconveniently close
to the house and were simply relocated, of which Houghton New
Village is the earliest, begun in 1729. Two rows of five four-bay
houses look generously spacious until one realizes that each house
contains two or three dwellings, and to go with them some farms
and a set of almshouses, all arranged quite formally. Holkham
estate village is a creation of the early C19, the first houses by
Wyatt, but continual additions were made until the end of the
C19. In the main the houses are simple semi-detached or detached
ones, deliberately arranged in a picturesque manner not apparent
at Houghton. At Beeston Hall (Beeston St Lawrence) Jacob
Preston did not bother in the 1780s building a new village to
replace the one cluttering up his view of the church, but just
cleared it away, so today there is no village at all. Wherever a
medieval church is found in an C18 park, one must suspect a
village has been removed (e.g. Felbrigg and Narford).

The Smaller Georgian House in the Country

Apart from the odd Venetian or Diocletian window or Gothick
detail the bulk of quality housing in the country ignored Palladianism and the symbols of the subsequent reaction against it.
There were a great many new houses put up, and as great a
number of older houses given new brick fronts and attendant
internal remodelling. Houses of the first half of the century
developed C17 ideas along lines geared to greater comfort, but
from the mid C18 pattern books encouraged the occasional adoption of motifs such as Gibbs surrounds to doors and windows
(James Gibbs's *Book of Architecture* was published in 1728). At
Gunton Park the *Wyatts* in their alterations of 1780–5 popularized
the full-height bow and cast-iron veranda, the former taken up
by *Soane* at the Old Rectory, Saxlingham Nethergate, from which
it was disseminated into numerous more modest houses of the
1790s to 1830s. Knapton Hall Hotel, a very superior example of
the small Georgian house, has both in the early C19, and the Old
Rectory, Buckenham, in 1827 was embellished by a veranda all
the way round the house. These few details must be a guide to
the type.

Almost all new houses were variations on a simple plan: three or five bays of sash windows, a central door leading to a passage with main ground-floor rooms r. and l., and a staircase at the end. Kitchens and offices were at the back and, usually, two further living rooms. Older houses simply given new façades of course had archaic plans dependent on outshuts for service rooms, but from the front it is difficult to tell the difference, as was intended. Unless situated in a flint or carstone area the material was always brick, or had at least a brick front (Grange Farmhouse, Smallburgh, early c18) and the gabled or hipped roof was always pantiled. Thatch was never used in houses of substance, such was its association with poverty.

Most of these houses are farmhouses, and in c18 Norfolk farming underwent a change which was to have ramifications throughout the country, for Norfolk above all was the county which pioneered new methods and new markets in agriculture. The open field system in Norfolk collapsed in the c16 as either tenants or lowly landowners swapped their strips to create consolidated holdings. By the middle of the c18 this process was virtually complete, so that parliamentary enclosures in the late c18 and early c19 concentrated on common land to the detriment of the very poor and to the benefit of those who had raised themselves above that station. In the c17 winter crops, particularly turnips for fodder, were introduced, removing the need to slaughter livestock at the end of the season, so at a stroke farmers' incomes might double. Between 1720 and 1760, for instance, the rental income of the Holkham estate rose by 44 per cent, reflecting the ability of tenants to pay at a time when prices for produce remained static. The benefits of winter crops and the four-year crop rotation system were publicized by such men as 'Turnip' Townshend of Raynham (the second viscount) in the early c18 and by Thomas William Coke of Holkham at the end of the century, and exploited by the often anonymous farmers who built the smaller Georgian houses out of the proceeds. Thomas Coke is usually credited with perfecting the rotation system, with the result that in 1800 two thirds of all land in the county was under the plough and Norfolk exported more grain to Holland (and hence to wider markets) than all other counties of England put together. That is an extraordinary statistic, and is the reason why practically every parish has a comfortable and polite Georgian farmhouse.

In new houses old motifs continued, e.g. shaped gables at Hill House, Little Snoring, chequered brickwork at Beck Farmhouse, Guist, a moulded platband and rusticated quoins at Manor House, Baconsthorpe (1724). New façades were so desirable that they were added to houses sometimes no more than a few years old: Manor House, Wereham, was bricked in 1729 only seven years after construction, while Ormesby Old Hall, Ormesby St Margaret, is an exemplar of the c17 houses which received a spanking new façade, here of seven bays and added in 1735, with raised and fielded panelling inside and a twisted baluster staircase to go with it. It has one of the earliest Norfolk doorcases taken from Gibbs's 1728 book, and from the mid 1730s Roman Doric doorcases became a standard (Barton Hall, Barton Turf, 1742; Sycamore Farmhouse, Northwold, mid C18; High House, Terrington St Clement, 1753). The Gothick taste finds expression in smaller houses as intersecting tracery to windows, and the Greek style as porches added to façades (the earliest surviving Greek Doric in Norfolk is the shop front at the Sir Garnet Wolseley pub in Norwich, and the doorcase at the East Dereham Guildhall, both late C18). Bowed porches and porches with Greek Doric columns *in antis* were popular in the years 1815–25 (No. 21 Sussex Street, Norwich; Grove House, Marham). By the first decades of the C19 houses could be built in a number of competing styles, indicated by an advertisement placed in the *Norwich Mercury* in February 1813 by William Hinsbey, an architect who needed advertising: he could apparently design in 'the Castellated, Gothic, Grecian, Italian and Fancy Cottage styles'.

Rectories are an interesting type absolutely in step with ordinary domestic architecture, and from the end of the C18 indicate the pattern of the smaller polite house. Langham Hall of *c.* 1820 is only atypical because it was built by the *Rev. Stephen Rippingall* for himself and has pilasters and five instead of three bays. Kempstone Lodge of 1788 and the Old Rectory, Itteringham, of 1789 have the tripartite sashes then coming into fashion, while the early C19 Rectory at Saxlingham (Holt) presents a gault brick front. In 1815 the *Rev. William Gunn* built Sloley Hall, five bays, gault brick and with a Neoclassical porch, and much the same at Smallburgh Hall in 1820.

As far as permanent PEASANT HOUSING is concerned the C18 is the century from which most survivals may be discussed, but a rare early survivor, Cobbler's Cottage, The Street, North Lopham, was built around 1600. It was of one storey, had only one room, no fireplace and is timber-framed and thatched and clad with plastered wattle and daub. The mid C18 brought a brick fireplace attached to the N gable, at which time an upper room was created lit through a dormer window, and later still a further room was added against the N gable and the house divided into two. Such buildings must have been miserable hovels, but it was in such houses that the bulk of the landless population lived. These houses are very difficult to identify. Many were demolished, or have fallen of their own accord, and survivors have been extended and enlarged as the C18 turned into the C19, so that the majority are lost to anything other than complete archaeological investigation. They are without architectural embellishments and so are difficult to date. Mostly houses had one storey and a dormer attic and two ground-floor rooms, but there was no established plan-form. Timber framing (often salvaged from other buildings), clay lump and flint are used in their relevant areas set on a flint and brick plinth. Examples of C18 clay lump may be seen in Merton, Carbrooke and in the Pulhams, slightly more exalted cottages at Sustead (The Thatched Cottage, early C18, one storey and attic) or Nos. 5–11 Clarke's Lane, Thursford (a row of four, each with a door and window), or the pair dated 1710 at Farm

Cottage, Melton Constable. In the middle of the c18 the benefits of improvement in agriculture eventually filtered down to the meanest level of society – so The Thatched Cottage at Buxton has brick corner pilasters and a lobby-entrance plan while The Thatched House at Stokesby had a new brick front added in 1757 and three bays separated by pilasters. It was not then in single occupation. We have already noted that lobby-entrance planning was normal by the c18 for houses which shouldered their way out of the hovel category, but not for reasons of architectural taste. Such a plan was the cheapest means of accommodating a central stack. The majority of surviving cottages, like the Stokesby house, were organized into units of multiple occupation and have been converted only in the c20, work which involved removal of internal partitions, so plans may be impossible to recover.

Town Houses

Norwich was a populous city in the c18 and also a wealthy and civilized city, and this is reflected in its merchant's houses, public buildings and also in a number of excellent local architects.* Celia Fiennes wrote in 1698 that 'the whole Citty lookes like what it is, a rich thriveing industrious place' and she said of houses that 'none of brick except some few beyond the river which are built of some of the rich factors like the London buildings'. In fact quite a number of houses by this time were timber-framed only to the upper first floors, but the ones with which we are presently concerned are all or predominantly of brick, and none of them continued the courtyard planning of earlier times. Most of the houses beyond the river were remodelled in the c18 or rebuilt. Nos. 27–29 Colegate is indeed a c17 timber-framed house raised a storey in the c18; at Colman House on Pottergate is another timber building clad in brick and heightened to three storeys late in the c18. A swish new brick skin was added to the c17 No. 79 King Street early in the c18, and begins an impressive sequence. It is five bays wide, with a Doric pedimented doorcase and a Venetian and a Diocletian window, one in each storey above. Those motifs recur. The rather altered No. 85 is a smaller version of the same thing. Of the same time is the excellent No. 18 Colegate, built for Thomas Harvey, a mayor. This time there are seven bays and a doorcase with engaged Ionic columns, plastered quoins and decorated eaves, and inside a staircase with two twisted balusters to each tread, a good lugged chimneypiece and minor plasterwork. Next door at No. 20 the three centre bays break forward and the front is articulated by giant Ionic pilasters. That is seldom encountered. No. 2 The Close is a classic of its type: seven bays and two-and-a-half storeys raised over a basement and entered through a doorcase with Ionic columns set against rustication. In 1727 Nos. 50–52 St Giles Street adds moulded window surrounds to the repertoire in a street full of worthwhile Georgian façades. Nos. 38–40 Bethel Street of c. 1740

* Individual architects are discussed on p. 155.

has as well as Ionic columns to the doorcase a pulvinated frieze, original sashes and another staircase with two twisted balusters to the tread. There are three twisted balusters a little further along at No. 35 St Giles Street, large-framed panelling, relief plaster ceilings and two good internal doorcases. A prominent Venetian window graces No. 44 Magdalen Street of the 1740s. Much the same as these houses is No. 24 Magdalen Street of the mid C18.

But the very best Georgian house in Norwich is the one built for Alderman Churchman in St Giles Street before 1727 and 1/91 remodelled by his son Sir Thomas in 1751. It was an L-plan house with a three-bay façade set back, but was pushed up to the street line by Sir Thomas and turned into a double-pile, a rare thing on a city plot, but the idea seems to have been to create a modest country house in the town in the same way as *Brettingham* did, probably at the same time, at Holkham House, Cow Hill. The centre three bays break forward under a pediment containing a Diocletian window; there are rusticated quoins to the middle, and at the first floor is a segmental sash with a Gibbs surround. There are three principal rooms downstairs in the front (i.e. N) pile, the centre being a two-storey entrance hall, but the rear pile containing the staircase was remodelled in the 1820s. Nevertheless the interior is a show-case of mid-C18 decoration, especially plasterwork of the Langley Park and Gateley Hall type, and there is a chimneypiece like that in the library at Langley, and two Gothick fireplaces upstairs.

Churchman's House was the last of its type in Norwich, for the subsequent history, with one or two exceptions, is one of speculative building (an exception is *Thomas Ivory*'s demolished house at No. 31 King Street for Sir Edward Astley). In about 1750 probably *Thomas Rawlins* built the five-bay No. 94 Upper St Giles Street, and decorated the façade only to the extent of the obligatory Classical doorcase. *Thomas Ivory* leased land from the Great Hospital in 1752 and built St Helen's House in Bishopgate (altered) for himself, but went on to convert the Assembly Rooms with *Sir James Burrough* in 1754–5. *Ivory* put up Nos. 25–27 Surrey Street about 1770, but they have unfortunately been demolished; surviving is his No. 54 All Saints Green, a superbly elegant five- 1/90 bay block of 1771–2 intended for rent. For decoration he allows himself rustication round the doorcase and a good nine-vaned fanlight, and, over the ground-floor windows only, blank tympana, new then even for London. On the other side of the same street is St Catherine's Close of 1780, which *Ivory* gives a curved porch, more blank tympana and canted bay windows at the back. Others were about the same business, e.g. *Matthew Brettingham* at No. 15 Surrey Street in the 1760s, and *Robert Mylne* at No. 9 Surrey Street. Unidentified architects continued the same type of restrained speculative house into the C19: No. 28 St Giles Street and other houses in Colegate, All Saints Green, Palace Plain and Ber Street.

Before we consider the development of the unified terrace in the county, one must remember that notable and enjoyable town houses exist not only in Great Yarmouth and King's Lynn but in

many of the smaller market towns. Just as in Norwich the early
C18 houses were as often a refacing of an older house as a new
build, while at Lynn they were typically made of the brown brick
from the Wisbech area. Burnham House in Nelson Street is a
case, still fitted with cross casements, while the new front of 1725
applied to part of No. 18 Tuesday Market Place has (renewed)
sashes and a heavy cornice. The N part received its skin only in
1803–4 including a full-height bow, then a feature at the top of
its popularity. There are good interiors of 1725. Then there is the
very cosmopolitan Barclays Bank in the Market Place, built as a
merchant's house in 1768 and refronted in the 1950s, and one
must not forget that perhaps the best of all early C18 town houses
was also in the same square, designed by *Henry Bell* in 1703 but
demolished in 1768. Of 1788 is the very fine No. 15 Nelson Street,
six bays of brown brick quoined at the edges and with a wrought-
iron staircase balustrade and minor plasterwork and panelling. In
Yarmouth the leading houses are the Old Vicarage at Church
Plain of 1718, another extension to an older house, here with a
shell-hood over the door. The merchant John Andrews built
himself a handsome new red brick house with stone dressings at
No. 20 South Quay, and Robert Robins at No. 51 King Street
had a house described as new in 1772, but it looks twenty
years earlier with its rusticated quoins, window surrounds and
platbands.

One of the best streets for Georgian refrontings is High Street
in Little Walsingham, most of them before 1750 and in fact there
are few C18 houses built from scratch. One is Aeldred House in
the Friday Market, a little provincial compared to Norwich but
nevertheless imposing, partly because it has eight bays. The
smaller Elmham House is another case. A selection of the best in
other towns would include, in Wymondham, Nos. 19–21 Market
Place (early C18, with three-light casements), Priory House of
c. 1710 and Caius House of *c.* 1740. The last could hold its own
in any town even if in its deployment of giant pilasters and a
central pediment superimposed on the half-storey attic over a
cornice it is C17 rather than C18 in character. It has a very good
staircase still with three twisted balusters, but otherwise has been
brutally treated in the C20. Smaller towns and even large villages
have their town houses: No. 5 Redenhall Road and Candler's
House, both in Harleston; at Aylsham are several houses relying
on giant pilasters around 1710–20 (e.g. Knoll House); again at
the Old House, Coltishall, in 1727; still the same formula at
Aylsham House, North Walsham, of *c.* 1730–40. Beaconsfield
House in Hingham can be added to these. Palladian echoes are at
the mid-C18 The Limes in Acle, but of big houses with reduced
decoration on the post-1750 Norwich pattern only Montpellier
House in Swaffham, Harvey House in Watton and Stoke Ferry
Hall are significant.

With speculative houses went speculative TERRACES, but the
earliest Norwich and Norfolk example is late by the standards of
most large towns. It is at Nos. 29–35 Surrey Street, put up in
1761–2, and is probably by *Thomas Ivory*. Of all the terraces this

is exceptional, because Surrey Street was already an established
thoroughfare and terraces in the accepted sense of the word are
associated with new roads and with the expansion of towns from
the late C18. The first of these was Southtown Road in Great
Yarmouth, begun in 1775 with nine houses, but totalling seventy-
nine by 1819, not all of which are terraces, but mixed with semi-
detached and detached. In the early C19 two simple two-storey
rows went up in City Road, Norwich, outside the walls, for the
artisan classes (Jubilee Terrace), and a row of back-to-backs at
Nos. 27–33 for workers, while better terraces sprang up in King's
Lynn in and around Valingers Road after 1807. Regent Road in
Yarmouth was built in 1812–13 and lined with three-storey gault-
brick terraces intended for residential use; then in 1821–4 came
Sussex Street, and in 1821–7 The Crescent, Chapelfield, both in
Norwich and both very polite on the intimate scale of provincial
England. In the 1820s the pace accelerates, notably in King's
Lynn with the development of London Road in 1825, all brown
brick but with stucco bands and front railings. Guanock Place 2/120
is one such, now without railings. Nos. 51–57 Bracondale in
Norwich continue the story, less monumental than the terrace of
c. 1830–40 at Nos. 47–69 Newmarket Road. After this the terrace
was standard for all new roads.

Public Buildings

Town architecture is not complete without PUBLIC BUILDINGS,
and we have already noticed that until the C18 towns other than
Norwich, King's Lynn and Thetford settled for existing buildings
for their TOWN HALLS. C15 domestic buildings associated with
the priory at Little Walsingham became the shirehall in the early
C18, but not until 1778 did it receive a new façade and only in
1805 its courtroom fittings. The present council offices in Diss
occupy a respectable early C18 town house, but at Great Yarmouth, the biggest place to be still using its medieval tollhouse
for municipal administration, the situation was rectified in an
emphatic manner. The corporation called in *John Price and Son* of
London in 1715 to provide an elegant Classical town hall
including an assembly room, but this, the most accomplished of
all early Georgian civic buildings in the county, was swept away
for the new town hall in the 1880s. Also completely rebuilt is
the Thetford Guildhall of 1799–1800. At Holt a shirehall was
constructed in the C18, but the late C18 guildhall at East Dereham
is another domestic conversion and the Wymondham town hall
of c. 1820 is certainly purpose-built but looks just like an ordinary
house, and so does that at Swaffham of the same time. Swaffham
did get a shirehall in 1839 by *John Brown*, almost too big, of
stuccoed brick, pilasters and pediment, and at Norwich the new
shirehall was under way in 1822–4 to designs of *William Wilkins
Jun.* (recased in 1913–14).

The last MARKET CROSS to be built in Norfolk was at
Swaffham in 1781–3, a very becoming dome on unfluted Doric
columns by *James Wyatt*. It was for a private client, the third

Earl of Orford. BRIDGES had, by the appointment of Thomas
Dove as County Surveyor (1801–6) and his successor Francis
Stone (1806–35), become the responsibility of civic authorities.
Stone built about fifteen, of which the most notable is the cast-
iron structure at Thetford of 1829, a material pioneered by
James Frost at Coslany Bridge in Norwich, but still designed as
if of masonry. Iron used on its own appeared in *Arthur Browne*'s
Carrow Bridge, Norwich, in 1810 (replaced in the C20) and
then, spectacularly, at Duke's Palace Bridge, Norwich, in 1822
(one whole side re-erected in the Castle Mall car park entrance;
the designer is unknown).

GAOLS in the C18 mainly took the form of holding cells until
the fate of the prisoner could be decided, there being very few
long-term prisoners before the C20: transportation to Australia
after 1787 or hanging at any time was preferred. Conditions slowly
improved after the Acts of Parliament of 1778 and 1782, and new
buildings appeared designed for the purpose. *John Soane*'s new
work at Norwich Castle of 1789 was swept away by the brand-
new radial-plan gaol built on the castle mound by *William Wilkins
Jun.* and *Francis Stone* in the 1820s, in turn redeveloped. At the
Yarmouth Tolhouse the basement was adapted for cells after
1796, with a cunning ventilation system required by the interest
then being taken in deaths in custody by coroners' courts. Treadmills were set up behind, and treadmills and cells also feature at
Little Walsingham (1787, enlarged in 1822). The Thetford Gaol
of 1796 would look like a bleak three-storey town house if it were
not for the carved chains above the two entrances; at Wymondham the gaol and magistrates' courthouse of 1787 is from the
outside exactly like a town house, and so too is the best of all C18
Norfolk gaols, at King's Lynn. Built in 1784 by *William Tuck*, it
occupies a sensitive site next to the Guildhall in Saturday Market
Place, and is exactly the type of two-and-a-half-storey, five-bay
town house familiar from Ivory's Norwich houses, with the crucial
exception of the central rusticated entrance decorated with festoons of shackles beneath a barred lunette window. It is in fact a
house, with cells tucked away in the rear yard.

Almshouses, hospitals and workhouses were all related by their
charitable function, to the extent that in the early C18 the first
two were not distinguished. As far as ALMSHOUSES are concerned
the quadrangular arrangement of single-storey dwellings
remained popular, as at Doughty's Hospital in Norwich of 1687
1/92 (rebuilt) or at the splendid Fishermen's Hospital in Great Yarmouth, put up at public expense in 1702. Framingham's Almshouses in King's Lynn continued the theme in 1704 under private
benefaction, and in 1763 at Church Lane, Heacham, both rebuilt.
At Watton in 1831 is a linear set of almshouses made of clay
lump. Hospitals, and here one thinks of INFIRMARIES, were a
reintroduction of one of the functions of the monasteries, and
in Norwich are important early examples. First was the Bethel
Hospital of 1712–13 probably by *Richard Starling*, the first
purpose-built lunatic asylum in England, and with cells as if it
were a gaol. The Norfolk and Norwich Hospital of 1770–5 by

William Ivory is or was recognizably a hospital in the C20 sense, and is significant as an early development outside the city walls. At Yarmouth the admiralty paid for St Nicholas' Hospital for those wounded in the Napoleonic wars (by *William Pilkington*, 1800–11), a monumental quadrangle with impressive façades to the court but spare interiors and exterior surfaces. The Bethel Hospital was a private venture, but St Andrew's Hospital at Thorpe St Andrew was done by *Francis Stone* as County Surveyor in 1811–14, designed like a country house façade in the tentative way of C18 hospitals. King's Lynn was the last of the big towns to build, and called in a London man, *Samuel Angell*, to work with *John Sugars*, for the perfectly ordinary General Hospital of 1834. 1/93

WORKHOUSES were designed to ameliorate the problem of the very poor, and had existed in Lynn in 1701 and in Norwich in 1711; but it was only after the Workhouse Test Act of 1722 that any appeared in the country and by 1803 there were around 130, mostly very small. Local Acts of Parliament were sought from the third quarter of the C18 to amalgamate hundreds and so to produce the first workhouses with a catchment of several or dozens of parishes: the first was in 1763–4 at Loddon and Clavering, now Hales Hospital. There were four more in the E and S of the county and nine in Suffolk, together an early effort to rationalize provision for the poor. The plan is usually based on an H (Hales, Rollesby, Gressenhall), at Gressenhall more consciously Classical than the others. After this experiment of the 1770s it was natural that the same system should be adapted to the provisions of the Poor Law Amendment Act 1834, and so twelve new union workhouses were built between 1835 and 1838. Until 1851 three local architects split the work between them. *William Thorold* begins in 1836 with the Classical Thetford (demolished), introduces pedimented gables at Pulham Market and the quadripartite radial plan like a model prison, and similarly at Hindringham. Also in 1836 comes *Donthorn*, presenting a bad stripped-down Tudor at Gayton, but a more accomplished Tudor at Aylsham, in 1848–9, with a version of Thorold's octagonal central hall. He repeated it at West Beckham (demolished apart from a ruinous annexe). *John Brown*, the county surveyor from 1835, also favoured Classical at the thirty-six-bay Docking and at the smaller Swainsthorpe, both 1836–8. The same was at Yarmouth, 1838. By the 1850s Tudor and Elizabethan styles had arrived (King's Lynn and Downham Market), and this reminds us that the Georgian era was at an end.

About as far from workhouses as possible were the ASSEMBLY ROOMS fitted up in towns for the entertainment of the local dignitaries, not necessarily the rich. The early provision was in the better INNS, notably at the White Hart at Scole of 1655, where the room was, as was usual, on the first floor. The Black Boys Hotel at Aylsham has another dating from the early C18, and at Great Yarmouth provision was built into the Town Hall in 1715. The best of all is at the Assembly House in Norwich, already mentioned, refitted in 1754–5 by *Thomas Ivory* and *Sir James Burrough*, 2/79 and in emulation of this the market towns of East Dereham (1756) and Swaffham (1776–8) also had purpose-built assembly rooms when they were momentarily fashionable. At Lynn *William Tuck* and *Thomas King* in 1766–8 made a plain assembly room behind the Guildhall in Saturday Market Place, but Thetford, in the doldrums since the Middle Ages, managed only a pump room in 1818, and it did not last long.

Commercial and Manufacturing Buildings in Towns

The most obvious remnants of commercial activity during this period are SHOPS, and in particular SHOP FRONTS, but such is the rate of attrition that there are few representative survivals. It was from the middle of the C18 that shopkeepers perceived the advantage of the modern shop front as a vehicle for increased sales, an early favourite being the bowed front made up of many small panes. In Norfolk the place for these and other early types is, strangely, High Street, Wells-next-the-Sea. The bowed display window at No. 46 is late C18, that at No. 7 is of *c.* 1820, but the best of the late C18 examples is at the Paper Shop in Burnham Market. The style carried on where trade was not good enough to replace it with newer fashions, e.g. in the early C19 at a shop in Long Stratton, No. 30 Market Street, Wymondham, and at three shops in Damgate Street. The type was still used as late as *c.* 1840 at Victoria Stores in Mattishall. However, there were structural disadvantages with the bowed front, especially what to do about the cornice and the junction with the flat wall of the building behind. Greek taste from about 1810 provided the solutions: rectangular in shape, an entablature for a fascia board and a cornice for weather protection. The late C18 No. 14 Market Place, Aylsham, was advanced for the provinces in its fluted Ionic columns under an entablature, as was the shop at No. 6 Hall Quay, Yarmouth, which in *c.* 1810–20 sandwiched a tripartite sash between engaged Ionic columns. Nos. 13–15 Mere Street, Diss, favours the Greek style, while at Nos. 1–3 Staithe Street, Wells, is a screen front of fluted Ionic columns of about 1840. In the early C19 a variation was the double-fronted display window, with a door in the centre, which was used where the front was wide enough (No. 12 High Street, Wells, early C19; Nos. 18–20 Market Street, Wymondham, mid C19). There is in addition one very interesting FACTORY in Norwich, the six-storey New Mill (Jarrold's Printing Works) of 1839 by either *John Brown* or *Richard Parkinson*, both functional and dignified, and one of the best of its date in England. It was built for yarn production.

1/96

Churches, Chapels and Church Furnishings

Demand for new Church of England buildings remained slight. There were enough medieval churches to go round in town and country, and only three new ones were built, though maintenance continued as it had in the previous century. So at St Augustine's in Norwich the tower was cased in brick in 1683–7, and at Hoveton

the w tower was completely rebuilt in 1765, also of brick. The
first new church, at North Runcton, is in fact a rebuilding in
1703–13 by *Henry Bell* derived ultimately from Wren in a com-   2/96
petent Classical style. St George, Yarmouth, is an engaging
Baroque, again with direct precursors in Wren's City churches   1/79
and built by *John Price* and his son in 1714–16 as a chapel of ease.
At Gunton Park the old church was demolished in 1766 and after
1770 *Robert Adam* raised for Sir William Harbord a splendid
Neoclassical replacement, more a garden temple than a church,   1/80
with a tetrastyle portico facing the house. The only other church-
building event of importance, as far as the Church of England
was concerned, is *Matthew Brettingham*'s reconstruction of the
nave of St Margaret, King's Lynn, after the sw spire collapsed in
1741. It is a remarkable effort in the Gothic mode, but a Gothic
which was neither understood nor even appreciated.

If the established Church was quiescent, then the NON-
CONFORMISTS were not. First off the mark were the Congregationalists and the Quakers, and the earliest of all was
Guestwick Congregational Chapel, founded in 1625 and timber-
framed, but unfortunately rebuilt in 1840. Next in date is the
Friends' Meeting House at Yarmouth, but in 1692 they merely
adapted a building which had been occupied by a cell of the
Augustinians (of Gorleston), and the building is more interesting
for its C15 remains. The Congregationalists had a chapel in Yarmouth in 1642, and another in Norwich in 1647, but the Norwich
chapel was replaced in 1693 by the Old Meeting House, and this   1/75
remains the oldest surviving specimen in the county. The fine
five-bay façade has Corinthian pilasters, doorways in the outer
bays, originally cross-casement windows and a hipped roof. Inside
are galleries on three sides and all the fittings. Bigger but faithful 1/76
to the same architectural motifs was the Friends' Meeting House
in Gildencroft, Norwich, but this was rebuilt in 1958. Then there
is a series in the countryside, all much less cosmopolitan in
style, e.g. the Friends' Meeting Houses at Lamas, *c.* 1700, and
Tasburgh, early C18, and the Oulton Congregational Chapel   1/77
of 1731, which has pairs of shaped gables and originally cross-
casement windows. The four-bay façade is entered through doorways in the end bays in the normal C18 manner and the interior   1/78
fitted with galleries. The former Presbyterian chapel at Hapton
still had a timber frame in 1749.

The best of all Nonconformist chapels is the Octagon Chapel   1/81
in Norwich by *Thomas Ivory*, 1754–6. It would be unusual enough
for its shape (which led to similar chapels elsewhere in England),
but is marked out for its interior arrangement of eight Corinthian   1/82
columns carrying timber galleries. The Gibbsian overtones were
amongst the first in the city. After the mid century most of the
market towns had their chapels: Diss in 1745, with a precocious
example of a tight three-bay façade; Dereham and North
Walsham in 1772; Aylsham in 1790 (for the Baptists); Briston in
c. 1780 (Methodist, with the new standard three-bay façade
entered through a central doorway). At Tivetshall St Margaret the
Friends' Meeting House of 1812 looks like a domestic building, as

2/97 does the United Reformed Church at Thetford of 1817. A serious
composition was attempted by *J. T. Patience* at the Friends'
Meeting House in Upper Goat Lane, Norwich, with a portico and
projecting wings and a good interior. After the 1790 Relief Act came
the R.C. church of St John, Norwich. Then the 1826 church
at Thetford (plain exterior) and the Willow Lane chapel, Norwich,
of 1827 (replacing St John), where *J. T. Patience* employed the
Nonconformist composition typical of early Catholic churches.

Monuments

The new spirit represented by Sir Thomas Hare reclining in Stow
Bardolph church in his Roman outfit continued with the standing
figure of Col. Edmund Soame †1706 at West Dereham, by *Robert
Singleton*. As the C18 progressed tomb chests faded from the
picture in favour of wall monuments and tablets far more
restrained than those of the C17. It is more instructive in the C18
to pick up the work of individual sculptors than to attempt a
chronological approach, and we shall begin with major national
figures.

William Stanton (1639–1705) provides a link between the C17
and the C18, but only his monument to Dean Fairfax in Norwich
cathedral †1702 and one of †1704 at Hethersett are C18, and
both have Corinthian columns framing inscription tablets. His
son *Edward Stanton* (1681–1734) produced good cartouches at
Bylaugh †1707 and at Thurlton †1717. His partner *Christopher
Horsnaile* (†1742) returned to the semi-reclining effigy at Langford in a monument made in *c*.1730 to Sir Jacob Garrard who
had died in 1666, but added a contemporary touch with two stern
standing figures in Roman dress (his son and grandson) and an
equally forbidding urn. *Peter Scheemakers* (1691–1781) has but one
2/98 monument in Norfolk, to Susanna Hare †1741 at Stow Bardolph,
and again a semi-reclining figure appears, but the form seldom
occurs after that. *Sir Henry Cheere* (1703–81) made a fine Classical
tablet at St Giles, Norwich, †1742, and possibly a chimneypiece in
Churchman's House, facing the church, after 1751. In 1753 *John
Powley* produced an obelisk at Narford commemorating Sir
Andrew Fountaine as a frame for a bust by *Louis Roubiliac*
(*c*.1705–62), and Roubiliac also provided the busts for the enor-
2/101 mous pedimented monument to Thomas Coke (first Earl of
Leicester) †1759 by *Charles Atkinson* at Tittleshall. The two
tablets to Sir William Browne (†1774) and his wife (†1763) at
Hillington are apparently designed by *Browne* himself, his with a
portrait medallion. *Joseph Wilton* (1722–1803) was the carver, and
to Wilton belongs the last word in Neoclassicism at Horsford
(Mrs Jane Day †1777): an urn on a plinth, a wreath and vases
2/100 either side. Another good bust at West Harling (†1780) is also by
Wilton. William Windham III, Pitt's Secretary of State for War,
also is remembered by a bust by *Joseph Nollekens* (1737–1823)
set into a standing monument at Felbrigg, and at Tittleshall
Nollekens made a good group of figures for Mrs Jane Coke
†1800.

The C19 opens with a simple tablet at Burnham Thorpe †1802 by *John Flaxman* (1755–1826), an even simpler inscription to William Cowper at East Dereham in 1802 and a relief of Harriet Peach †1825 carried up to heaven by two angels at Ketteringham. That was not only a favourite of Flaxman's but had appeared in Nollekens's Tittleshall group. There are three church monuments by *Coade & Sealy*: at Thorpe St Andrew (†1810, tablet with reclining woman), Melton Constable (†1812, similar) and at St Stephen in Norwich (†1812), mixing Gothic with the usual putto and urn. The remaining important pre-1840 monuments in Norfolk belong to various members of the Westmacott dynasty and to John Bacon the younger. *Sir Richard Westmacott* (1775–1856) erected in 1807 a monument at Ketteringham with a mourning woman beneath a broken column and a military still life indicating that Wright Atkyns had been in the Dragoons; a seated mourning woman appears also at Old Catton †1820 and again at Stradsett †1823. Anything made by *John Bacon Jun.* (1777–1859) before he went into partnership with Samuel Manning in 1818 is likely to be competent, afterwards likely to be studio-produced. One of his best is to Lady Wilhelmina Micklethwaite †1805 at Sprowston, which has three scenes representing events immediately after her death in childbirth, i.e. allegorical. He has fine figures at Ryston round an urn †1807, draped sarcophagi at Melton Constable †1808, and in the Gothic mode at Bylaugh †1817. Good monuments by him are also at St George Colegate, Norwich, †1810, Ormesby St Michael †1806, and at Sheringham to Abbot Upcher †1819, which is one of the better of his post-Manning period. *Henry Westmacott* (1784–1861) supplied a Grecian tablet at North Elmham †1820, and *Richard Westmacott* (1799–1872) at Holy Trinity, Marham, †1847, provides a monument depicting two angels kneeling over an altar.

Local sculptors almost always followed national trends, even if two of them were every bit as accomplished as the London masters. *Robert Singleton* (†1740) was from Bury St Edmunds, but had a healthy practice in Norwich: at Norwich cathedral (Thomas Batchelor, 1729, with his partner *George Bottomley*); the semi-reclining figure of a cherub at St George Colegate, Norwich (Thomas Pindar Sen. †1722); and two busts at Hockwold (Jermyn Wyche, 1719).

Robert Page (1707–78) was one of the best sculptors, particularly in his exploitation of the properties of coloured marble, and there are in Norfolk churches about twenty of his monuments. His first known monument, to John Moore †1725 in the cathedral, is architectural, but his simple white tablet commemorating Mary Lubbock †1729 in St George Colegate, Norwich, sets the tone for much of the C18. So does the first of his monuments for the Astleys at Melton Constable (to Sir Philip †1739) where he provided two portrait medallions above a sarcophagus. He used obelisks to effect at Sprowston (Nathaniel Micklethwaite †1757) and, significantly, in his own monument at St John, Timberhill, Norwich. *Thomas Rawlins* (1727–89), the son of a Norwich weaver, was an architect with ambition if not one with a successful practice, but as a sculptor he ranks high. Like Page he was an expert with coloured marbles, and since most of his monuments are after 1750 his style is mournful Rococo to Neoclassical, the change being illustrated in two monuments in St Andrew, Norwich, the first to John Custance (†1752), the second to Richard Dennison and wife (†1767 and 1768). An obelisk with a weeping putto in the same church commemorates Hambleton Custance †1757. An obelisk is also the motif in the cathedral monument by *Rawlins* to William Rolfe †1754, and again in St Giles, Norwich (Sir Thomas Churchman †1781). The last is particularly good, fully Neoclassical, complete with a portrait in an oval medallion. At East Bradenham Gibson Lucas †1758 is remembered by the whole repertoire of Neoclassical accoutrements: an obelisk of course, cherubs' heads, garlands and a cartouche. The apron is of Sienna marble. Several marbles combine at Wymondham (John Drake †1759).

John Ivory (c. 1730–1805) was the nephew of the architect Thomas Ivory and cousin to William Ivory, and the three worked together at Blickling in the 1760s and 70s, though John by reason of his apprenticeship to Robert Page concentrated on sculpture. He was not the equal of Page or Rawlins and in the 1780s often worked in conjunction with *John de Carle*, who was primarily a builder noted for erecting houses designed by John Soane. His best monument is probably that to Charles and Mary Mackerell (†1727 and 1747) in St Stephen, Norwich, a very architectural marble tablet, but most of his monuments rely on the simple later C18 formula of a weeping cherub by a broken column which was in everyone's repertoire (Cyril Wyche †1780 at Hockwold and Sarah Norris †1787 at Barton Turf, both joint commissions with *de Carle*), or the Neoclassical urn in front of an obelisk (Clement Francis †1792) at Aylsham.

Other Furnishings

The C18 was not rich in church furnishings – what was needed had been provided in the C17 – and wooden furnishings of all periods were far more likely to be replaced by improving Victorian vicars. Monuments were different, for country squires were more than pleased to retain documents in stone that publicly expressed their glorious ancestry. By far the largest number of C18 furnishings are PULPITS, but there are only about twenty-five of them and they all follow on from the C17 pattern as the C17 followed the medieval. That in Attleborough has already been mentioned (*see* p. 118), brought from the Broadway Chapel in Westminster, and of very fine pulpits one should add that in St Nicholas, Great Yarmouth, of c. 1715–20, moved from St George's, Yarmouth. It is panelled and has a little leaf decoration and shafts in the angles. Just as good is the pulpit in St Margaret, King's Lynn, also early Georgian and with marquetry inlay on the (relocated) tester. Thurning has *James Burrough*'s three-decker of 1742 originally in Corpus Christi College, Cambridge, and the mid-C18 piece at St George Colegate, Norwich, has a carved panel, but the run of C18 pulpits are plain and polygonal. In 1800–1 St Mary Magdalen, Warham, was restored by the vicar *W. H. Langton* and *William Jary*, setting a pattern of church restorations that characterizes the Victorian decades. The work included all the fittings, including the three-decker pulpit, font, pews, communion rail etc. Other three-deckers are at East Walton (C18), at Ketteringham (1837) and at Bylaugh (1810).

The BOX PEWS and PEWS at Bylaugh were replaced at the same time, and there are C18 examples at St George Colegate Norwich, East Walton, Foulden, Terrington St Clement and at Walpole St Peter. The better ones include the late C18 panelled box pews at Felbrigg, and at Hanworth of 1766, with a canopy and a curious urn. COMMUNION RAILS pick up where they left off in the late C17, usually with twisted balusters and all early C18 except for those at Hempstead near Holt, probably of 1744. The marble rails at Didlington are C18 but came from the Hall after 1852 according to Kelly. Of SCREENS only two require notice: the cast-iron extravaganza running across the nave and aisles at Terrington St Clement installed in 1788, and *John Adey Repton*'s screen at Blickling of *c.* 1830.

VICTORIAN ARCHITECTURE

The VICTORIAN AGE has not left its mark on Norfolk in the way it has elsewhere. But although Norfolk was not industrialized, it had industries, and the towns attracted impoverished agricultural workers. The population of Norwich rose from 37,000 in 1811 to 80,000 in 1871. Most of the newcomers became slum dwellers in divided tenements or in unsanitary houses erected in former gardens within the city walls, so that in 1870 the town was still of manageable size with extramural building concentrated only to the w and s. New churches were built principally in the newly developed areas of towns. In the county as a whole there were plenty of existing churches, although there was scope for restoration and refitting. The *nouveaux riches* families clamouring for super-mansions were scarce; the established ones in their ancestral seats in the main contented themselves with extensions in the fashionable style of the day, often by London rather than local architects.

Churches and their Furnishings 1830 – 1902
In the C19 the Church of England was given new energy by the Oxford Movement, with its emphasis on piety and pastoral care, and influenced by the Ecclesiological Society (founded as the Cambridge Camden Society), which from the 1840s provided guidance on the ideal new church. This was to be Gothic, with

nave and chancel differentiated. Political acceptance of Roman Catholicism and the growth of Nonconformity helped to spur the Church into action. In Norfolk Bishop Edward Stanley (1837–49) discovered that more than half the clergy were not resident in their parishes, indeed had nowhere within them in which to live, so sixty-eight new rectories were built in the first five years of his episcopy alone. Most of the crumbling churches in Norfolk were restored after 1830, and from the period 1830–1902 the county has sixty-five churches either completely new or substantially rebuilt. Very often a local landowner provided the funds. Architecturally, only a few are outstanding.

The first new Anglican churches were in expanding Great Yarmouth: St Mary, Southtown Road (1830–1), and St Peter (now St Spiridon, 1831–3), both by *J. J. Scoles* (who worked more often for the Catholics). St Mary is in a feeble lancet style, St Peter is Perp. The lancet style was particularly popular before the High Victorian age, chiefly because it was the cheapest, but also because of its Ecclesiologist advocates. *John Brown*'s Hainford (1838–40) and Christ Church, New Catton, Norwich (1841–2), illustrate the type. At St Mark, Lakenham, *Brown* tempered the first pointed with a little Perp and provided a w gallery (not a feature approved of by *The Ecclesiologist*). At Walpole Highway is the first attempt at Norman for a completely new building, by *J. C. Buckler* in 1844. At King's Lynn, St John Evangelist was commissioned from *Anthony Salvin* by Daniel Gurney in 1844, in the E.E. style and planted as close to the planned new terraces near the railway as possible.

From the late 1840s architects drew on a wider range of sources: at Welney in 1847–8 is a small church without a tower by *Buckler* (plate tracery); North Wootton, 1850–3, by *Salvin* is E.E. and does have a tower; to serve the district of Thorpe Hamlet E of Norwich *Brown* delved into the Norman style in 1851 and at Brettenham in 1852 *S. S. Teulon* produced a restrained Dec. The first distinguished C19 work comes at Martham, where in 1855–6 *Philip Boyce* restored the church and built a new chancel in an exuberant Curvilinear with an amazing cusped chancel arch and fittings to match. *G. E. Street* built the Norman Roydon (near King's Lynn) in 1857 without any of the brick and polychromy he was by then advocating. At St John in Great Yarmouth *J. H. Hakewill* in 1857–8 put up a small neat church for poor fishermen, and therefore in the poor style – the E.E. – although an expanding population required continual enlargements, spoiling the effect. The Dec reappears in *Kerr*'s competent Framingham Pigot of 1859. One of the glories of Victorian architecture is at Gillingham where *T. Penrice* found a decaying but good quality Norman church, to which he added in 1859–60 a super-Norman aisled nave and chancel, convinced that he knew Norman better than the Normans. In 1864 *Jekyll* returned to a minimal E.E. at Hautbois, and at Thorpe St Andrew in 1866 he introduced brick and built a weird s aisle arcade. The next ten years saw an increasingly blatant use of brick (St James, Yarmouth, by Seddon) and a more eclectic approach (Christ Church,

Mount Pleasant, in Norwich by *J. H. Brown & J. B. Pearce* of
1873–9 for example has Norman, Perp, Dec and E.E. all mixed
up). Then another milestone at Booton, designed by the rector
Whitwell Elwin and built in 1875–91, using any Dec and pre-Dec 1/101
forms he could gather from other churches assembled without
reference to Gothic principles. A hammerbeam roof was included,
even though it was a Perp innovation in Norfolk, while the two
lacy w towers are an English version of c14 Italian style.

High Victorian Dec complete with brick polychromy is represented at Fulmodeston in 1882 by *William Basset Smith*, the
same decade that sees a more sober and scholarly attitude to
historicism. This is apparent at Edgefield where *J. D. Sedding*
mixed up Dec and Perp in 1883–4, but his motive must also have
been to weld together such sources into a new style appropriate
for the c19. Materials, including some windows, were salvaged
from the old church. So were materials for *Habershon & Faulkner*'s
West Beckham of 1890–1, which is odd in having the walls of
pebble inside and out.

Roman Catholic churches were generally much smaller, with
the exception of St Mary Regent Road in Yarmouth, in which
J. J. Scoles achieved a better synthesis of Gothic than in his previous efforts in the town. *Buckler* built a large brick church at
Costessey in 1834–41 without any Roman extravagance for a
Catholic patron, and at Oxburgh Hall, Oxborough, a chapel was
built for the Bedingfelds in 1835–9, not necessarily by A. W. N.
Pugin. This chapel is in the lancet style and of red brick; most
of the interest is in its reused foreign fittings. *A. W. N. Pugin*
remodelled the medieval church at West Tofts after 1845, quite
ambitiously, and with a complete set of fittings, unfortunately
dispersed. Another private chapel is at Lynford of 1877–8 by
Henry Clutton, a simple box. At King's Lynn *Pugin* designed a
church for public use in 1845, which was inadequately replaced in
1897 by *W. Lunn*. That leaves St John in Norwich, which
became the Catholic cathedral in 1976. It does indeed look like a 1/102
cathedral, built between 1884 and 1910 by *George Gilbert Scott
Jun.* and *John Oldrid Scott* for the Duke of Norfolk in the E.E. 1/103
manner, completely overlooking any of the new freedoms brought
about by the Arts and Crafts movement, but instead relying on
historicism and in its own way trying to out-compose c13 masons.
But it certainly works, and is particularly happy in its stained glass
by *John* and *Dunstan Powell*.

Nonconformist churches continued with their standard display
of a three-bay gable-end to the street, especially after 1840, but
the older type of chapel resembling a domestic building persisted,
dressed up with a little Gothic in the windows (East Dereham
Congregational chapel of 1815), but after 1820 more commonly
Classical (Wesleyan Methodist at Methwold, 1831; the demolished Wesleyan Chapel, Lady Lane, Norwich, 1824). *Boardman*'s
Congregational Church, Princes Street, Norwich, of 1869 is still
Classical, but the change to Gothic had already been made.
G. E. Street introduced an Italianate Gothic to Norfolk's Non-
conformists at the Union Chapel, Market Street, King's Lynn, in

1859 (now the museum). It looks like an Anglican church not a Nonconformist chapel, and so does *Thomas Jekyll's* amazing Methodist church at Holt, 1862–3, which provides the best poly-
1/100 chromatic brick display in Norfolk. It is technically in the lancet style and in plan much more Anglican than Methodist, but Jekyll's free application of the E.E. to such a large building is not wholly convincing. Mimicking Anglican churches continued in bigger towns for bigger chapels: Middlegate Congregational church in Great Yarmouth by *J. T. Bottle* (1870, now council offices) is Dec, even with flushwork; the second Congregational church in East Dereham by *Boardman* (1873–4) is in the second pointed style. Italianate Gothic remained popular for chapels which did not embrace Anglican plans and exteriors (the demolished Methodist Temple at Yarmouth of 1875 was one of the most striking), but stripped-down English Gothic was the favourite from the 1860s, especially for small rural chapels, even if Classical came a close
1/107 second. In 1898 *Edwin Lutyens* built the Methodist church at Overstrand, which uniquely in Norfolk owes allegiance to Arts and Crafts, but has a peculiar raised clerestory with lunette windows.

As for CHURCH RESTORATIONS during this period, hardly a medieval church in Norfolk escaped, and, to be fair, many required sometimes extensive work. The restorers' attitudes are interesting. Before the 1850s most architects either recast the church in the style which predominated in the existing building, or introduced a style of their choice, usually E.E. if money was scarce, Perp if not. At South Runcton in 1839 *John Brown* saw Norman so produced Norman, Ketteringham in 1845 went the same way and at Docking in 1838 the young *Ewan Christian* Victorianized the interior. In 1849 Ruskin published *The Seven Lamps of Architecture*, which among other things deplored the practice of completely gutting churches and renewing what could be repaired. The concept of preservation rather than alteration slowly crept in, helped by the antiquarians' increasing grasp of the development of medieval architecture. At East Raynham in 1866–8 *Clark & Holland* copied the original, and at Limpenhoe in 1881–2 *A. S. Hewitt* found that he could reset existing windows. Sedding was infected by the same desire at Edgefield to preserve original materials, likewise *W. E. Nesfield* in his rebuilding of St Giles, Houghton St Giles. A popular action was the removal of plaster ceilings (usually later additions) to reveal medieval roof structures. Few ceilings survived the Victorians (an exception is the ceiling of 1803 at Beeston St Lawrence).

Victorian Church Furnishings

CHURCH FURNISHINGS were of crucial importance to the Eccle-siologists, and this resulted in hundreds of new sets of timber fittings even where medieval and Georgian ones were perfectly sound. The Georgians were not exponents of Gothic, and their box pews and galleries were not considered appropriate for High Church worship. The Oxford Movement was set against the large

MONUMENTS of their predecessors, which glorified man not God, so although there are plenty of tablets there is hardly anything bigger. The figure seated by an urn is still found, e.g. at Ketteringham, 1833 by *Daniel Willson*. At Docking the traditional formula for women who died in childbirth, rising up to heaven, is adopted for Mrs Woolmer Cory †1837, but she wears the flowing garments typical of Victorian figures, and is set in a Gothic surround. At West Tofts *Pugin* provided an E.E. gabled canopy for Jane Sutton in 1846. In the Oxburgh chapel the monument to Geraldine Trafford †1860 also shows her being raised up to heaven, but in the same place there is an alabaster tomb-chest in medieval style (†1862), a theme most notably repeated for the monument by *Sir Joseph Boehm* in Holkham church to Juliana, Countess of Leicester, †1870. A consciously medieval effect was created by *George Frederick Watts* in 1878 at Blickling, with figures in the round, set on a chest by *J. H. Pollen*. 2/103

Of other stone and timber FURNISHINGS there is little to say in Norfolk: the best are in the cathedral, e.g. presbytery altar rails of *c.* 1890 by *Seddon*, and N transept screens. C19 pulpits looked like their precursors (a triple-decker is at Bawdeswell, 1845), as did fonts and benches. But STAINED GLASS is completely different; there is plenty, much of it is good and a much higher proportion of output comes from local men than in the country as a whole. By the late C18 the glass staining and painting craft in England had all but died out and in the first years of the C19 there were no workshops in Norwich at all. What glass there was being installed in the county was N European, usually C16, principally imported by John Hampp after 1812. A good deal of it was fitted by *Samuel Carter Yarington* (1781–1846) who described himself as a glass painter in 1812. His earliest surviving glass in Norfolk is of 1822 at the cathedral, but that is commendably early, for of the forty windows installed in Norfolk between 1800 and 1830 only half had new pieces. After 1840 glass came into real demand as more churches were built or restored, peaking at over 300 new installations in 1860–70, and Yarington eventually turned out to be the second most prolific local glassmaker in the county, after the firm of *J. & J. King* of Norwich. Yarington's best glass is at Aylsham *c.* 1842 and Burnham Thorpe *c.* 1840, derived from the German Renaissance style he must have learned from the glass he installed earlier.

Yarington may have been associated with *Robert Allen* (1745–1835) who came to glass late in life from the Lowestoft Porcelain works, but bringing with him porcelain-decorating techniques crucial to the revival of glass staining. *John Dixon* (1783–1857) of Bethel Street first appears as the restorer of glass at St Peter Mancroft in Norwich, where he made copies of panels that could not be recovered (some of his copies are at Felbrigg Hall). Another associate of Yarington's was *James George Zobel* (1791–1879), but hardly anything of his survives. *Joseph Grant* (1809–*c.* 1875) and his brother *James* (1801–60) of Costessey produced five windows for Buckler's new church of St Wulstan in Costessey in 1841, fairly primitive in character, but Joseph on his own executed much more accomplished work at Long Stratton in 1858 and Banningham in 1862. Another vague figure is *William Culyer* (1818–77), also of Norwich (Old Catton, *c.* 1846, Stoke Ferry, 1848), who appears to have joined *J. & J. King* in 1854. This was the firm that was to dominate a new Norwich school of glass painters, founded by *James King* (1775–1851) in the 1820s, and joined by his sons *James* (1804–65) and *John* (1807–79) in around 1836. The sons formed the firm of *J. & J. King* after 1850, which employed nine men (twenty men in 1861 and six apprentices) producing high-quality glass of conventional design but with strong clear colours. Some of their best glass is at St Gregory, Norwich (various dates), Antingham in 1868, Alburgh in 1872 and Saxthorpe in 1888, and in all seventy-five windows are by them. The firm rose to prominence partly as a result of their willingness to learn from the national firms who were by the 1850s filling Norfolk windows in greater numbers, and partly through the appointment of *Thomas Scott* (1845–1920) as chief designer in the thirty years from *c.* 1865. The firm produced its last windows in the 1890s and wound up in 1927, to be replaced by *George King* (1886–1965), no relation, later *G. King & Son* of Norwich. This firm remains the principal glass restorer in the county and one of the chief in England.

The first outside craftsman with a presence in Norfolk is *Thomas Willement* of London, who has some heraldic panels in the chapel at Oxburgh of 1838, though his best surviving work is at Buxton *c.* 1859. There was until 1912 a window by *Hoadley & Oldfield* of London installed in 1838 at Upwell, then a piece by *de la Roche* of Paris of 1844 at Necton, and in the same year *William Wailes* of Newcastle fitted up a window at Sedgeford (destroyed) and so began an association with the county that lasted until the 1870s. He was a favourite with most of the leading architects of the High Victorian period. *James Powell & Sons* of London appear *c.* 1850 and their artists made some of the best glass of all, especially at Thursford (1862), Banham (1857 and 1878) and Methwold (1866), culminating in the aesthetic movement glass at Gar-boldisham (1880s). *Ward & Nixon* of London are represented from *c.* 1845 (Filby †1849 is their best), and after Nixon retired in 1850 *Ward & Hughes* carried on, and produced more glass in Norfolk than any other company, 119 windows in all. *Adolph Didron* and *Eugene Oudinot* of Paris made an exceptionally fine set of windows at Feltwell in 1859–63, which remains the best contemporary Continental glass in the county. The new style introduced by *Morris & Co.* is represented by some glass by the firm at Sculthorpe (1864 by *Ford Madox Brown* and 1865 by *Burne-Jones*), and at Antingham (*c.* 1865).

2/117

Country Houses

Among the county's new or substantially rebuilt C19 MANSIONS an early example was Costessey Hall near Norwich (now in ruins), an extension to an older house in a free unrestrained medieval-Tudor of *c.* 1826–55 by *J. C. Buckler* for the Catholic Jerningham

family. At the same time Gothic was used by *Donthorn* at Cromer
Hall, and more flamboyantly at Shadwell Park by *S. S. Teulon* 2/112
(1856–60). The best of the super-mansions was *Charles Barry Jun.*
and *Robert Banks*'s Bylaugh Hall of 1849–51 (now ruined), a
limestone-faced Elizabethan pile derived from Wollaton, the elder
Barry's Highclere of 1842 and ground plans produced by *William
Wilkins Jun.* in 1822 for an unbuilt house on the site.

The lead given by Bylaugh was not taken up. Rackheath Hall
of 1852–4 is decidedly post-Georgian rather than fully Victorian,
but Lynford Hall of 1856–61 by *William Burn* is a Victorian image
of the Jacobean revival with direct references to Raynham Hall
and Hatfield.* Lynford is asymmetrical, and so too is Taverham
Hall, where Jacobean is tempered with Tudor (*David Brandon*,
1858–9). After this the Elizabethan rather than Jacobean dominated, first (after Bylaugh) at the overpowering Dunston Hall of 2/114
1859–78 (begun by *J. C. Buckler*, finished by *Edward Boardman*),
then at Holt Hall in *c.* 1860, at Crown Point Hall just s of Norwich
(now Whitlingham Hospital) of 1865 by *H. E. Coe* and at Cawston
College as late as 1896 (by *Sir Ernest George* and *A. B. Yeates*).
Brandon remained doggedly faithful to the Tudor at the demolished and unaccomplished Stow Bardolph Hall in 1873 and
A. J. Humbert retained the Jacobean style at Sandringham in his
remodelling from 1870. The Italianate style, or a style derived
from the Italianate, arrived in Norfolk in a hesitant way in the
early C19, appearing e.g. at Yaxham House of 1820–2 by *Robert
Lugar*. The domestic revival style derived from English C17 architecture was represented by an early example: Garboldisham
Manor of 1869–73 by *George Gilbert Scott Jun.* (now demolished).
Ken Hill, Snettisham, a masterpiece by *J. J. Stevenson* of 1878– 2/115
80, developed the style further. But apart from Lord Suffield at
Langham Lodge in 1885 the style had few Norfolk patrons.

Some older houses received face-lifts. *Pugin* and *Buckler* remodelled Oxburgh Hall after 1835, creating the romantic Tudor
moated house we see today. There were some efforts at authentic
medieval restoration: *Jekyll* restored Elsing Hall to its medieval
form in 1852; and at Middleton Sir Whincop Jarvis restored the
great C15 tower in 1856–64. But more often English architecture
of the C16–C17 was the ideal: *Blore* favoured Tudor at Shadwell
Park (1840–3), Jacobean at Merton Hall (1846). Neo-Elizabethan
was used by the *Bucklers* to transform Wattlefield Hall, Wymondham, and by *James & Turner* at Barton Hall, Barton Bendish (both
1856). The castellated style appears at Salhouse Hall, *c.* 1860–70,
but this remains an exception in Norfolk. Elizabethan continued
popular in the later C19 (Sprowston Hall, 1872–6, Hempstead
Hall, 1877–80, the latter, unusually, using knapped flint). Historicism with a local flavour is reflected by the addition of shaped
gables to older houses (Swannington Manor, before 1855, Bawdeswell Hall, 1861), a trend which gathered strength in the 1880s

---

* Lynford has an amazing set of French-inspired garden railings by *Burn*, and other
memorable iron gates are at Rackheath (by *Cottam & Hallen*), shown at the Great
Exhibition of 1851, and at Sandringham House, by *Thomas Jekyll*, 1861–2.

with the vernacular revival (Pynkney Hall, Tatterford, 1880 by *Ewan Christian*).

Smaller Houses in the Country

As in the late c18, rectories provide an indication of how these styles were received in the smaller house. *Donthorn*'s Rectory at Great Moulton of 1831 is Italianate, but this style was not generally taken up. Neo-Grecian is used at Briningham House, 1838, but petered out in the 1840s in favour of various forms of Gothic (East Bilney, by *Arthur Browne*, 1836; Cedar House, Beighton, *c.* 1850; *Pritchett*'s High Victorian Gothic at Ingoldisthorpe, 1856–8). Then there is a shift to Tudor, and later to Jacobean. *Teulon* put 2/121 up the rectories at Bressingham and North Creake in 1842 and 1845 respectively in Tudor, but at Booton in *c.* 1860 *Thomas Allom* adopted the Jacobean. Other than rectories, the smaller house continued with the simple three- or five-bay façade, usually with a Greek or Roman Doric porch. Tudor or Jacobean influence becomes apparent from the 1840s, e.g. Eastfield House, East Harling (1840s), and Warren Farmhouse, Hilborough, in 1845. In the 1860s Gothic was still in vogue (Green Farmhouse, Kimberley, or at No. 44 Lynn Road, Snettisham, of 1867), plainer styles from the 1870s.

Victorian agricultural workers fared worse than their predecessors. Wages were so low in East Anglia that starvation was still a risk (enlarged workhouses were provided in the 1830s for a good reason). Even those estates with the most conscientious owners rarely provided enough housing for the landless labourers, and when they did so rarely kept them in repair. The model cottages built at Holkham in the early c19 were showpieces confined to the main entrances to the park, as was the model village at Houghton. The *Norfolk News* in articles called 'The Cottage Homes of England' published in 1863–4 was very critical of the position in Norfolk. Typical was a village which had 'little else but thatched roofs, old rotten and shapeless, full of holes and overgrown with weeds, windows sometimes patched with rags and sometimes plastered with clay'. Overcrowding was as bad as the accommodation. Most of these dwellings have been swept away, but the general description remained fair until the end of the century; so the cottages we admire now are either restorations of a group of houses amalgamated into one, or were from the beginning aristocrats of the hovel, often taken from designs printed in pattern books. Ivy Cottage at Snettisham is in Gothick dress of *c.* 1840, and Manor Farm Cottages, Runham, have excellent mullioned windows with lattice glazing set into a two-storey front. At Paston is Heath Cottage, a remarkable mid-c19 brick house which is only one bay wide and has one room on each floor, like a house a child might imagine.

Some quite decent rows of two-storey mid-c19 cottages survive in village streets, such as Nos. 18–20 Church Street, Northrepps, and there are also deliberately elaborate ones designed for estates and prominently located. In 1855 Little Ellingham Hall decorated its approach with a clock tower on a cruciform base containing two cottages. Branthill Cottages in Wighton of 1834 (Holkham Estate) are substantial examples in flint dressed with brick and with cast-iron casements. No. 46 Creake Road, Sculthorpe, of 1859 (Cranmer Hall Estate) is cruciform, one cottage in each arm. Finally are a group of cottages at Egmere built in 1878–80 of shuttered concrete, which is early for Norfolk. Two further concrete pairs on Creake Gate Road, Wighton (also for Holkham), have Holkham's cast-iron windows. In the 1890s Sir Alfred Jodrell built the whole of Glandford model village, all flint and brick and shaped gables. With these and others, such as the estate cottages at Brettenham of the 1870s (for the Shadwell Estate), a good standard of housing was provided for the classes who always looked over their shoulder at the union workhouse.

Interest in agricultural reform led to some MODEL FARMS and FARMBUILDINGS. The complete model farm consisted of a planned arrangement of house and farmyard. Home Farm, Starston, was designed by *Samuel Taylor c.* 1840, with stock sheds sensibly disposed round the cattle yard, though the house itself has been demolished. *Loudon* illustrated the farmyard in his *Encyclopedia* in 1846. At Egmere Farm, Egmere, *G. A. Dean* designed a similar courtyard arrangement for the Holkham Estate in 1851–6, and at Home Farm, Marham, a group built for Henry 2/109 Villebois of Marham House includes the house and two barns framing the entrance to the yard like rustic pavilions. Model farm buildings were also added to older farmhouses as at Hall Farm in Felbrigg Park (1832–55), Hall Farm, Metton (*c.* 1837–40), Hall Farm, Stratton Strawless (1838); and Manor Farm, Crimplesham (1881).

Urban Expansion and Seaside Development

The outward expansion of the major towns which had begun in the later C18 continued through the C19, predominantly by developments of terraces after *c.* 1840, and it is these terraces, especially those erected in the great building booms of the mid 1870s and around 1900, that greet the visitor driving in from the country. Pre-1850 TERRACES favoured various versions of the Classical vocabulary for their decoration, such as Greek Doric porches at Nos. 77–81 Newmarket Road, Norwich, of *c.* 1840–5, or with Ionic columns attached (Nos. 89–90 London Road, King's Lynn). The arrival of the railway, particularly in King's Lynn and Norwich, both in 1844, led to some interesting responses. In Lynn the proud and monumental St John's Terrace was begun immediately, and was followed in 1849 by quality terraces in the new Waterloo and Portland Streets. It seems that civic dignity demanded a development of the railway quarter with houses of London quality: this concern did not last long. In Norwich the immediate effect was different, probably because the town already had its own West End at Bracondale; instead of residences for the middle classes there were railway workers' cottages erected in 1847 by *Grissell & Peto* in Hardy Road and

Cozens Road. Notable examples of later Norwich speculative terraces are those in Unthank Road of 1877 facing Grosvenor Road by *Edward Boardman*, and Carlton Terrace in Surrey Street of 1881. They are solid middle-class houses, but the situation for the poor remained as it had always been, so that before 1900 some 700 back courts and alleys in Norwich were filled with slums. In response 800 new houses were constructed outside the city walls in 1900 alone, but Norwich was not to solve its slum problem until the 1930s.

Although The Walks in King's Lynn had been landscaped in the mid C18, it was not until the middle of the C19 that PUBLIC PARKS appear in the county, first at Norwich in 1852 (re-landscaped in 1877 including a glorious pagoda by *Jekyll*, now gone; the bandstand is of 1880), then at Great Yarmouth in 1866. Public CEMETERIES are another feature of the modern townscape which were all but unknown before urban churchyard burials were prohibited in England. That happened in Norwich in 1856, and Earlham Road Cemetery was laid out to compensate, for the existing Rosary Road Cemetery (1819) could not cope. Other towns followed: East Dereham in 1869, Gorleston in 1879 and Caister-on-Sea in 1899.

With its long coastline Norfolk makes a rich study for the rise of SEASIDE DEVELOPMENTS from an early period, though there were only two resorts before the railways brought tourists in numbers and converted fashionable Cromer and Yarmouth into popular destinations. The most important and earliest resort is Great Yarmouth, which had a bath house as early as 1759, replaced by the Bath Hotel in 1835 at the centre of a seaside strip quite distant and separate from the existing town. That separation allowed a degree of planning, which became more professional once *Alfred Morant* became Borough Engineer in the middle of the century. In the early C19 St George's Road made a connection between the two parts of the town, and further roads began to extend E in the 1850s and 60s. In 1856–64 Marine Parade was built on the seafront and attracted more hotels and other places of recreation, and churches opened in the new terraced streets immediately behind. In 1841 the Victoria Building Company embarked on an ambitious scheme challenging Brighton as the pre-eminent English resort, and at the end of the century were built numerous monuments to pleasure by a handful of local
1/108 architects such as *A. S. Hewitt*, *Bottle & Olley*, *A. J. Lacey* and,
1/109 memorably, *R. S. Cockrill* at the Hippodrome of 1903. The Marine Parade area of Yarmouth continues to develop in the present day, but it is the buildings of immediately before the First World War that mark Yarmouth as special.

The salient facts about other resorts are more easily outlined. Cromer was famous in the early C19, had a bath house in 1814, and two modest hotels (the Albion and the Ship) at about the same time. The railway came in 1877, inconveniently set far to the S, and another more central station in 1887. That began Cromer's heyday, and signalled the construction of *George Skipper*'s three massive hotels between 1891 and 1896 (of which only the Hotel de Paris remains). The Esplanade (1894), the pier (1900–1) and *A. F. Scott & Son*'s Cliftonville Hotel of 1897 followed. Observing the success of Cromer and Yarmouth was Henry Le Strange of Hunstanton Hall, who decided on a completely new resort, New Hunstanton, to the SW of the existing village and an acceptable 1¼m. from the Hall. Le Strange campaigned for a railway link to King's Lynn, which arrived in 1862, and *William Butterfield* planned the town in 1861. The church went up in 1865–9 (by *Preedy*), also the Sandringham Hotel and the Royal Hotel. *J. W. Wilson*'s pier was of 1862, and there are plenty of good streets of terraces and houses of the 1870s and 80s done in the warm local carstone.

In the 1890s the railway began to reach other seaside villages, prompting rashes of building at Sheringham and Mundesley. Mundesley had two hotels of its own, the Hotel Continental (1892) and the Manor Hotel (1900), and there was a scheme to develop the Cliftonville Estate after 1890, but this failed. At Sheringham the legacy of the late Victorian and Edwardian resort is two churches, the former Sheringham Hotel of 1890–1 (*H. J. Green*'s Grand Hotel of 1898 has been demolished) and, unusually good for a post-1914 seaside building in Norfolk, the streamlined but altered terrace at Nos. 1–9 Sea Cliff, by *R. L. Martindale*, 1936. Gorleston began its own resort in the 1880s and 90s. It aimed to secure the genteel visitor whom neighbouring Great Yarmouth no longer courted, the plan masterminded by the Borough architect *J. W. Cockrill*. The Cliff Park Estate of 1883 was intended for select holiday homes, but was only partially successful; Marine Parade followed after 1890, then the buildings provided by the Corporation: *Cockrill*'s eclectic and amusing Pavilion of 1901, the floral garden and bandstand in 1895–6, the Winter Gardens in 1929 (by *A. W. Ecclestone*) and the Floral Hall in 1939 by the then Borough Engineer, *S. P. Thompson*.

Public Buildings

Norfolk has one grand C19 TOWN HALL, not quite as big and self-confident as those of northern industrial towns, at Great Yarmouth, of 1878–82 by *J. B. Pearce*, in a free northern Renaisbsance style complete with a 110 ft tower. The best of the interiors is the Assembly Room on the first floor. At Norwich the Corporation restored the Guildhall, including in 1861 a three-storey porch added by *T. D. Barry*. At King's Lynn in 1895 *Tree & Price* of London so conscientiously modelled their extension to the Guildhall (Holy Trinity) that one might at first take it as C15. Inside, the C17 was favoured for details. The same acknowledgement to the past is evident in *H. J. Green*'s new Thetford Guildhall of 2/119 1902, for it is a straight replacement of its 1799 predecessor. Local centres sometimes aspired to town halls too, but none are memorable: Aylsham in 1856–7; Loddon in 1870 (Jacobean); Downham Market in 1887 (Renaissance, by *J. J. Johnson*); Cromer in 1890 by *George Skipper*; and New Hunstanton in 1896 by *G. J. & F. W. Skipper*. CORN HALLS and EXCHANGES were

more obviously houses of Mammon, and this was reflected in
their occasional rude jollity. All of them were built between 1842
and 1861 (the Yarmouth Corn Exchange of 1842 and *T. D. Barry*'s
Norwich exchange of 1859–61 have been demolished). Harleston
received a crude design dependent on giant Tuscan columns in
1849, by *John Bunn*, and in 1854 three were begun: the exuberant
exchange at King's Lynn by *Cruso & Maberley*; *John Brown*'s
Fakenham; and the most striking of all, the Greek-inspired hall
2/118 at Diss, by a local man, *George Atkins*. The East Dereham and
Swaffham exchanges were built in 1856–7 and 1858 respectively.
The two best purpose-built COURTHOUSES in Norfolk are at
King's Lynn and Downham Market, both of 1861 and both
Italianate, the style then favoured for courthouses.

ALMSHOUSES are usually small and attractive, rarely more
than one storey and attic, and only the largest have a U-plan. The
Tudor Gothic row at East Bilney of 1838, built by Rebecca and
William Pearce, reflects the new model already seen at Watton;
Tibenham in 1846 has a bigger version; Framingham's Almshouses in Lynn by *Sharman* of Spalding are again Tudor and big
enough to have a U-plan. Another U-plan arrangement at Harpley
in 1850 is becoming Jacobean. Completely different is the former
Sailors' Home in Great Yarmouth (now the Maritime Museum),
an elaborate three-storey block of 1858 by *A. W. Morant* in the
Italian style and curiously set up in the middle of the fashionable
resort. Another form of philanthropy is represented by All Hallows
Convent at Ditchingham, a religious House of Mercy built in 1858
by *Henry Woodyer* on a cruciform plan. The existing Fulmerston
Almshouses at Thetford were refurbished and Gothicized *c.* 1860,
Doughty's Hospital in Norwich was rebuilt on the same plan in
1869–70 and new almshouses in three ranges went up in Friars
Street, King's Lynn, in 1866. Almshouses continued to be built
into the 1880s; those at Croxton Road, Thetford, of 1885 for
George and Sarah Tyrrell are still Tudor, while the Ickburgh
almshouses of 1887 have gables with half-timbering, like the better
detached villas of the period in Norwich.

The most interesting HOSPITAL is the Mundesley Hospital of
1898–9, designed and built by the firm of *Boulton & Paul* of
Norwich out of town as a tuberculosis hospital, and architecturally
important as a major prefabricated building. Other hospitals are
less remarkable: in 1879–84 *Edward Boardman* and *T. H. Wyatt*
rebuilt the Norfolk and Norwich Hospital in Jacobean Revival
dress and gave it a *porte-cochère* as if it were a town hall; *Boardman*
extended the Bethel Hospital in Norwich in 1899 and built the
utilitarian Nurses' Home at the Norfolk and Norwich in 1902.

SCHOOLS are a major new category of buildings. Organized
schooling for the mass of the population began when the churches
stepped in immediately after the Napoleonic Wars. The Church
of England was behind the National Schools and the Nonconformists supported the British Schools. Grants were available
for construction from the government after 1840, in 1870 the
Education Act permitted the formation of Board Schools, and
finally in 1876 elementary education became compulsory. In the

period up to 1880 nearly 130 National Schools were built in Norfolk, fewer than ten British Schools, sixty-three Board Schools and a hundred or so privately founded establishments. Most surviving schools are small and were built in the country or in small market towns. Those in the bigger towns were mostly rebuilt in the c20. Gothic was preferred for church schools, and many were built to look as similar to chapels as possible, such as the tiny Welborne school of 1847. At Spooner Row, near Wymondham, *John Buckler's* lancet-style chapel of 1843 was in fact built as the school. At Burnham Market the British School moved into the Congregational Chapel, and at Thorpe Market the 1826 school was modelled on the Gothick church of 1796, both privately funded by Lord Suffield of Gunton Park. For the second pointed style as the High Victorian period interpreted it, the school at Thornham of 1858 is as good as any. Local schools often demonstrate refined use of local building materials, e.g. the Old School at Baconsthorpe is of flint with brick dressings and, as it was built in 1816, it looks not like a chapel but a three-bay house. The School House at Grimston is of carstone slips. The Gothic only relaxed its hold towards the end of the century: the Girls' Grammar School in Thetford built in 1888 by *J. Osborne Smith* to go with the ancient boys' school is of domestic red brick and half-timbering. Tudor made its mark at the new buildings at Gresham's School, Holt, of 1900–3 by *Howard Chatfeild Clarke*.

Industrial and Commercial Buildings

The production of cloth is the oldest and most significant Norfolk industry and was the basis of the county's wealth from the c14 to the c19. Most activity took place around Norwich and in the NE of the county; until the c19 it was a cottage industry, and at Worstead there are still a few buildings which tell its story. Preliminary spinning was done everywhere in the county within practical reach of the Norwich markets, often by women and children. Celia Fiennes' journey in 1698 took her from Norwich to Attleborough: 'thence we went mostly through lanes where you meete the ordinary people knitting 4 or 5 in company under the hedges; to Attleborough ... then over an open down like Salisbery Plaine, still finding the country full of spinners and knitters'. The finished yarn was collected and passed to weavers, and there were in 1800 about 100,000 outworkers serving the Norwich market.

In the c19 there was an attempt in Norwich to revive the cloth trade in the face of competition from northern powered looms by provision of purpose-built mills at Albion Mills and the steam-powered Norwich Yarn Works in 1839. The latter, by *John Brown* 1/96 or *Richard Parkinson*, is functional and dignified, and one of the best of its date in England (now a printing works and offices). Further mills were constructed by the river but after 1850 it was clear that Norwich and Norfolk as a force in the textile trade was a memory, and by 1900 the industry supported only 6,000. In 1845 there were 428 power looms in Norfolk, but there were

31,000 in Yorkshire. Coslany was the industrial quarter of Norwich and it was there that Barnard's set up their IRON WORKS in 1851, though their rivals Boulton & Paul between 1865 and 1891 developed a huge site at Mountergate, most of which has been redeveloped or stands empty. Their Riverside Works s of Thorpe Station were founded to meet war demand after 1916; today the site is a weed-strewn concrete plain. Both Barnard's and Boulton & Paul were companies with international trade, producing everything imaginable that could be made out of iron and steel, from barbed wire to fence Australian sheep stations to agricultural machinery, decorative gates and prefabricated buildings. Burrells of Thetford produced steam traction engines and other agricultural machinery for export and home sales from two factories in Minstergate. The paint shop built in 1846–7 has a tensioned steel frame and a roof of Belfast trusses. Other towns had their foundries, particularly King's Lynn and East Dereham, but it is MALTINGS which survive most frequently as empty or converted shells. Most towns have them. At Millgate in Aylsham are a set of one storey and attic of 1771 (converted to flats), at the Crostwight Hall complex was a mid-c18 maltings, Letheringsett has a maltings of *c.* 1800 to go with an existing brewery, the Wensum Lodge centre in Norwich is converted out of a maltings and brewery set up in 1851, and further examples may be seen in King's Lynn, Diss and Thetford.

By 1870 in Norwich LEATHERWORKING was the most important single industry, again concentrated in the St George's Street and Coslany area, of which the most eloquent building is *Edward Boardman*'s Norvic Shoe Factory in Colegate (now converted to other uses). It is a giant, originally designed for outworking techniques, but the extension of 1894 catered for machines. Of other industries requiring factories Norwich has the Rowntree Mackintosh complex at Chapelfield, originally built by *Boardman* in 1899 as a variant on his Norvic works, but bombed in 1942 and rebuilt. Colman's mustard firm was set up originally at Stoke Holy Cross, s of the city, but relocated to Carrow in 1858 to a site which by 1900 extended over twenty-six acres.

Great Yarmouth was one of the six most important FISHING CENTRES in Britain from the Middle Ages to the c20. The industry peaked in 1921 when 1,149 boats sailed from the port, but over-fishing and competition meant that by the 1960s there were no fishing vessels at all. The legacy of the peak century, the c19, is to be seen in numerous FISH CURING WORKS. The first survivors are from the early c19, but the only one complete enough to be brought back into production is built into the South-east Tower of the walls. It still retains its brine tanks (a mid-c19 refinement to the process) and its smokehouses. It was one of the largest concerns, although nowhere near the size of the Tower Works in nearby Blackfriars Road, built in 1880 and occupying a whole block, with banks of smokehouses deployed along the N front. Just as with brewing, every fishmonger had his own miniature smokehouse (two of which may be seen working at Gorleston, a town also dependent on fish), and here and there in back yards the remains of these tall, square little brick buildings are identifiable by their smoke louvres. To the s of Yarmouth, that is s of St Nicholas' Hospital, is a large industrial area built up in the later C19 and devoted to rope works, boat-builders' yards and fish curing works, now half-derelict. A curiosity at Yarmouth is the survivor of a pair of brick ICEHOUSES on the river bank opposite Hall Quay, built in 1859–62 to provide ice for the fishermen. Domestic icehouses are generally subterranean.

Norfolk is a county of WINDMILLS and WINDPUMPS: these brick towers, usually without sails, used to decorate the Fens in the w and still do in the Broads in the e, and existed once on practically every elevated site. Windmills were as familiar in the Middle Ages as they are today, the first type being the POST MILL. It is impossible to say when they were introduced, but certainly there is one depicted on the Walsokne brass at St Margaret, King's Lynn, †1349. The only remaining one in Norfolk is at Garboldisham, c. 1780, and this is one of the last built, with a round brick buck instead of the supporting timber cants of the Walsokne image. SMOCK MILLS replaced them, timber polygonal structures with a rotating cap at the top carrying the sails and the same machinery as tower mills. The earliest dated example in the county is the Belle Vue Tower at Melton Constable, which began as a smock mill in 1721. There was another at Garboldisham in c. 1788. The brick TOWER MILL is, however, the type which dominates, not just because it was inherently more durable but because it could contain the latest machinery. The earliest date from the C18. Tower mills could be raised in height more easily, from the minimum of three floors to a maximum of seven or more. The mill at Walton Highway was a three-storey tower in c. 1740 but five storeys in 1815. The mill within the gatehouse at St Benet's Abbey (Horning) may be c. 1735, Ludham High Mill 1742. By far the majority, however, are C19, the last of all put up in 1885. WINDPUMPS are analogous to mills, but have different machinery designed to drain the Fens or the Broads or to keep drained areas from flooding. On the Broads especially there are points from which more than a dozen can be seen. Like mills they fell out of use when steam or diesel engines were perfected, but the process took slightly longer. The oldest type extant in Norfolk is the HOLLOW-POST WINDPUMP, of which there is one C17 example at Ludham, restored by *Richard Seago* in 1988, the shaft driving a scoop wheel. At Tunstall Dyke two stages survive of the only C18 SMOCK PUMP, at Horning Ferry is a mid-C19 version converted to a house and also at Horning is Hobbs Mill, a late C19 trestle mill supported on four baulks of timber. Brick TOWER PUMPS are represented by *Robert Martin*'s Wiseman's Mill at Ashby with Oby as early as 1753, and thereafter brick towers were the standard. Thurne Dyke mill of 1820 was raised a storey from two to three and has all of its machinery; the early C19 Commission Mill at Stokesby is by *William Rust*; and there are a number by the millwright *Dan England* in the late C19 and early C20 (Horsey, 1897, West Somerton Marsh, 1900). The best-preserved mills are Stracey Arms, Halvergate, of 1883 and

Berney Arms Mill, Reedham. These are all in the Broads; in the Fens remain only a few stumps and conversions.

WATERMILLS are not as frequently met as in counties with fast-flowing rivers, but a big mill pond could compensate. Often a MILLER'S HOUSE is attached or adjacent, which tends to explain their survival. No mill in Norfolk is particularly old, though at Corpusty there are bits and pieces of 1699 surviving the rebuilding of *c.* 1880. The oldest is the two-storey brick mill of 1737 operated by Thomas Beeston at Burnham Overy Town, raised a storey in about 1814 and given as a companion to a tower windmill. Next in date is Hunworth Mill of *c.* 1760, with a miller's house included. Bacton Wood Mill, Bacton, of *c.* 1780 (brick, three storeys) is one of the places to visit for those interested in machinery, and so too is Hilborough. The other mill at Burnham Overy Town, picturesque but rather damaged, was built in 1790 by *Edmund Savory*, who also had a windmill to hedge his bets. Both Savory and Beeston enjoyed comfortable miller's houses. The exploitation of both wind and water at Burnham was an obvious advantage, but only at Little Cressingham of *c.* 1821 are two pairs of stones driven by water and on the floor above two more by wind. Is it a unique arrangement in England?* There are several other worthwhile watermills, including many in picture-book settings: the weatherboarded Stoke Holy Cross of 1776, enlarged in 1814 for the Colman's mustard business; Buxton of the late C18 is of brick to the lower two storeys but weatherboarded above; and Lenwade, probably early C19, has a house attached.

None of these mills touches the Fens, but the Fens make up for this in the uncommonly interesting history of HYDRAULIC ENGINEERING, designed both to reclaim land (and keep it reclaimed) and to improve river navigation. It was the Dutch who were the acknowledged experts in this area, and they seem to have been a presence from the C16: in Haddiscoe church is a monument to the wife (†1525) of Pier Piers, who maintained dykes; at Great Yarmouth the seventh haven was only possible because further s the Dutchman *Johas Johnson* had in 1560 suc-cessfully cut a permanent harbour entrance, after English experts had failed. But it is in the Fens that really major schemes were needed, and in 1630 *Cornelius Vermuyden* was called in by the fourth Earl of Bedford to advise. He contemplated whole new rivers and a scheme of dykes and sluices, some of which were built, but which could only be completed after 1947 by *Sir Murdoch MacDonald & Partners*, though in *c.* 1825–8 *John Rennie* rebuilt the Denver Sluices, themselves a major undertaking, after earlier ones had flooded.

There are a few other relics of Norfolk's industrial past. At 1/97 Fakenham is a fascinating GAS WORKS of 1846 with its various retorts and tubes, at Carleton Rode a former STEAM MILL of clay lump built in 1856 and at West Walton stands a small mid-C19 brick FURNACE for forging cart tyres. Norwich's chief

---

* Also at Cressingham is an early C19 PUMPHOUSE containing a Bramah three-throw water pump serving Clermont Hall gardens. The pump has its own water-wheel.

monument of C19 public utilities is the sewage PUMPING STATION at New Mills, originally of 1868, but upgraded in 1897 and still with its water-driven compressor.

Among purpose-built COMMERCIAL BUILDINGS are the Tudor SAVINGS BANK in St James' Street, King's Lynn, of 1859–61 by *Medland & Maberley*. Banks in the mid C19 were becoming major concerns, and felt it no longer practicable or desirable to remain in premises built as houses. In the mid C19 *R. M. Phipson* built one of a series of banks at Hall Quay in Great Yarmouth, for Lacon, Youell & Co. (now Lloyds Bank), and in 1854 *Salvin* refronted an existing building for Gurney's Bank on the same quay in a mature Italian Palazzo style. One of the biggest, if short-lived, banks was Sir Robert Harvey's Crown Bank, built in 1866 on a grand new site at Agricultural Hall Plain in Norwich by *P. C. Hardwick*, while the London and Provincial Bank was set up in Regent Street, Yarmouth, in 1901 (by *A. S. Hewitt*). In 1863 came one of the most remarkable of Norwich's commercial buildings, a cast-iron and glass-fronted engineers' SHOWROOM, now 1/99 called Crystal House, on Cattle Market Street. In the 1870s another similar showroom was built in Davey Place (demolished 1960).

NORFOLK ARCHITECTS: EIGHTEENTH TO EARLY TWENTIETH CENTURIES

The starting place for a review of LOCAL ARCHITECTS is not Norwich but King's Lynn and the work of *Henry Bell* (1647–1711). Bell was a merchant-architect who had no need of the work beyond his personal interest, for he inherited his father's trading interests in 1686. Outside Norfolk he was jointly in charge of the reconstruction of Northampton following the fire of 1675; within the county he did the King's Lynn buildings, Stanhoe Hall, and North Runcton church. Had he devoted himself full-time to architecture Bell might today be regarded as a major figure, for he was the first local man to appreciate national late C17 trends. *Matthew Brettingham* (1699–1769) is the chief of the Norwich-based men active in the first half of the C18. He began as a bricklayer apprenticed to his father but gained an immediate foothold in the architectural world when Thomas Coke in 1726 commissioned plans and elevations for Holkham Hall, and was retained as executive architect from 1734 in charge of the building of the house to Kent's designs. It was this association which formed his rather pedestrian if competent Palladian style and gave him his introduction to patrons. Brettingham may have designed the temple at Blickling in the 1730s. He gained experience in the Gothic when he tinkered with the w front of Norwich cathedral from 1739, experience which proved deficient when in 1742–6 he rebuilt the nave of St Margaret, King's Lynn. Throughout the 1740s he had a number of commissions in Norfolk for country houses, some no more than remodellings or additions: Gunton

Park in 1742, Hanworth Hall *c.* 1742–3, Langley Park and Heydon Hall. From the mid 1740s he was employed in London and elsewhere, but was also during the 1740s a surveyor of Norfolk bridges. His principal public work in Norfolk was his Shire Hall and repairs to the adjacent Norwich Gaol in 1747–9, both in conjunction with his brother *Robert* (1696–1768). By the 1760s he was engaged in speculative construction of town houses in Norwich, a business venture also taken up by Thomas Ivory.

Thomas Ivory (1709–79) was the leading Norwich architect in the third quarter of the century, but his architectural ambitions were supplemented by a considerable business as a builder and timber merchant. His first large commission was for Thrigby Hall in 1735 (since rebuilt) when he was a young man and before he purchased the freedom of Norwich in 1745. His appointment as carpenter to the Great Hospital of Norwich in 1751 is a more telling indication of his trade but he nevertheless built some speculative houses on Great Hospital land, including St Helen's House after 1752. In 1754–5 with *Sir James Burrough* he remodelled Chapel Field House (Assembly House) for the Hobarts, and this contact may have led to Ivory, with his son *William* (*c.* 1738–1801) and nephew *John* (the sculptor, *c.* 1730–1805), being employed in remodelling Blickling Hall from the 1760s. Thomas's reputation mainly rests on the Octagon Chapel in Norwich, of 1754–6 for the Presbyterians, an extremely accomplished work with internal details of Gibbsian origins, the H-shaped Norfolk and Norwich Hospital of 1770–5 (altered) and several solid and elegant town houses.

William Wilkins the elder (1751–1815) was a plasterer working with his father, also William, from 1773 to 1783, appearing first in Norfolk at Blickling Hall in the late 1770s supervised by William Ivory. After his father's death in 1783 he advertised himself as an architect, though his works in Norfolk are few and favour the Gothick, a subject in which he took an academic interest. Beeston Hall (Beeston St Lawrence) of 1785–7 is the earliest major Gothick house in Norfolk, and is attributed to Wilkins on account of that fact. At Stanfield Hall in 1792 he created the perfect Perp staircase hall, bending ecclesiastical patterns into a domestic environment. He was engaged at Norwich Castle in 1792, repaired the cathedral in 1806–9 and finally, in the year of his death, restored St Ethelbert's Gate. Wilkins is overshadowed by his son *William Wilkins* the younger (1778–1839), who though born in Norwich set up his first architectural practice in Cambridge in 1804 after returning from a tour of Italy and Greece. He removed to London in 1809 and became one of the leaders of the Greek Revival movement, a style epitomized by his Nelson Monument of 1817–19 at Great Yarmouth. That is his earliest Norfolk work, contemporary with not very extensive alterations made to Keswick Hall. His other Norfolk commissions included designs for Bylaugh Hall in Elizabethan style (1822, not executed), the Tudor Gothic Shirehouse at Norwich (1822–4, rebuilt since) and the New Norwich Gaol (1823), assisted it seems by *Francis Stone*. It was a very interesting radial panopticon; some of it remains.

Humphry Repton (1752–1818) who lived for a time in Norfolk is best known as a landscape gardener with many works in the county. His architecture is confined to small alterations (Honing Hall in 1792) or to larger additions in conjunction with his eldest son *John Adey Repton* (1775–1860). John Adey was an accomplished draughtsman who trained first with the elder Wilkins, then with Nash. In 1818 he settled in Essex, but standing to his credit in Norfolk are the Gothick alterations to Barningham Hall of 1805–7, with his father, some minor work to the staircase at Felbrigg (1813) and Hoveton Hall of 1809–12. Sheringham Hall of 1812–18 is by far his best Neoclassical effort, disguised as a villa. Minor work at Blickling in the 1830s and, perhaps, the Orchards at Aylsham in 1847 completes the picture. Of Humphry's fourth son, the successful *George Stanley Repton* (1786–1858), we have only a couple of references in Norfolk: Burgh Hall, Burgh-next-Aylsham (demolished), and at Wolterton Hall, 1828–9.

William John Donthorn (1799–1859) was born in Swaffham and after training with Jeffry Wyatville set himself up in London and Norfolk producing Greek Revival country houses, few of which survive, and a number of generally Tudor Gothic parsonages. By the mid 1820s he had switched to Gothic at Hillington Hall (1824–8, demolished), and at Felbrigg stables in 1825–31 and Cromer Hall of 1827 and 1829. As early as 1831–2 he attempted the Italian style at the Old Rectory, Great Moulton, and in the 1830s the Tudor (for his workhouses *see* above, p. 133). The Leicester monument at Holkham is a giant Corinthian column of 1845–8 modelled on Nelson's Column in London, and there are a few church restorations. At Stoke Ferry in 1848 he virtually rebuilt the church, as he did at Bagthorpe in 1853–4 in a mixed E.E. and Dec.

Other Norfolk architects owe their local prominence partly to their appointment to official surveyorships in the C19. The first is *Stephen Mear* (*c.*1752–1827), who was surveyor to the Great Hospital, but of his work outside that building, and within it, little survives. His son *William Mear* (1796–1866) enlarged Mousehold House in Norwich in 1821 and made a number of designs for rectories and a very typical small Georgian house at Witton, near Norwich, in 1819 (demolished). *Arthur Browne* (*c.*1757–1840) was more significant than his surviving works suggest, especially as an exponent of the Gothic after *c.*1800, but today we only have Surrey House in Surrey Street, Norwich, and two church monuments. More lasting has been the work of *Joseph Stannard* the elder (1771–1855) and his son *Joseph Stannard* the younger (1795–1850), both contractors as well as architects and two of the more important early C19 figures in Norwich, working in partnership. The younger Stannard was city surveyor in 1840–8. It was the Stannards who carried through Repton's additions at Barningham Hall, and of their own work one may single out some of the official architecture of Joseph Jun.: the refacing of the Guildhall in 1835, the concrete raft placed under the Shire House in 1846 and the Classical front of the Royal Arcade (formerly Royal Hotel) in 1846. The younger Joseph also designed Strumpshaw Hall in

1835–6 (standard Georgian); the elder Joseph dabbled in church restorations: St Mary Reepham and Attleborough.

The 1830s saw the beginning of an energetic series of church restorations and new churches. The Diocesan Surveyors made major contributions, especially *John Brown* (1805–76) and *Richard Makilwaine Phipson* (1827–84). Both were also County Surveyors, Brown in 1835–59, Phipson in the 1860s. Brown built or restored twenty-five Norfolk churches, including work on the cathedral, and in his county capacity was involved in practically every official building from the 1840s to 1860s. He was also involved with the Victoria Building Company's efforts at Yarmouth and had a small if lucrative private practice. Phipson (of Ipswich) had a huge practice restoring churches in East Anglia, twenty-six of which are in Norfolk, and a private client base smaller than Brown's. *Herbert John Green* was also among the major church restorers (seventeen; he was Diocesan Surveyor 1881–98).

Thomas Jekyll (1827–81) of London and Norwich restored Elsing Hall (1852) and several churches (Trimingham, 1855; Eaton, 1860–1; Thorpe St Andrew, 1866), and built a new church at Hautbois in 1864. All of them are slightly odd, though for oddness the E.E. Methodist Chapel in Holt of 1862–3 takes the medal. His designs in ironwork, often for Barnard, Bishop and Barnard's foundry in Norwich, are notable; they include the Norwich Gates at Sandringham and the pagoda formerly in Chapel Field, Norwich. His cast-iron fire grates, made by Barnards, were widely successful in the 1870s and 80s: some are at Mergate Hall, Bracon Ash.

Edward Boardman (1833–1910) succeeded John Brown as the most successful Norwich architect in the second half of the C19. He was born in Norwich but received his training with Lucas Brothers of London, returning to found his own practice in 1860. In 1889 his son Edward Thomas Boardman (1861–1950) joined the firm and virtually took over after 1900. The elder Boardman did much official work, such as the major city improvements of the 1870s, but was not appointed city surveyor or to the new post of city architect. He restored Anglican churches in the 1880s (e.g. St Etheldreda and furnishings in St Edmund Fishergate, both Norwich, and Sprowston) and built new Nonconformist chapels (he was a Congregationalist) such as the Methodist chapel, Chapel Field, in 1880, the still Classical Congregational church in Princes Street in 1869 and the Congregational chapel at East Dereham in 1873–4, in a second pointed Gothic. His civil works in Norwich include rebuilding Ivory's Norfolk and Norwich Hospital in 1879–84, remodelling the castle and gaol as the art gallery in 1887, and building the sumptuous Royal Hotel, in a free Flemish style with plenty of ornate brickwork and Cosseyware, in 1896–7. His style was fluid enough for him to copy anything.

George John Skipper (1856–1948) was Boardman's chief rival, and his work stands out with much greater brilliance. Skipper was born in East Dereham, and after training in London returned there to work in his father's building firm, setting up as an architect in 1879. After some minor competition successes he secured the

Cromer Town Hall job in 1889, and went on to build the Cromer seaside hotels in the 1890s (*see* above). In 1896 he built himself new offices in London Street, Norwich, which have an amazing terracotta front, and in 1899 the Royal Arcade, also in Norwich, 1/98 which stands as a high point in English Arts and Crafts. But it was after 1900 that Skipper realized his potential as an exponent of Edwardian Baroque, to the extent that the Norwich Union 1/110 building in Surrey Street of 1903–4 may with reason be regarded as the best of its kind in the country. In 1908 Skipper remodelled Sennowe Hall, Guist, for Thomas Albert Cook in his familiar Baroque, but did little else outside the towns, except for some clay lump council houses at Garboldisham in 1919–20 (demolished 1988), and others at Harling and in Suffolk (*see* below).

Meanwhile in Yarmouth the appointment of *Alfred Morant* (1828–81) as Borough Engineer in 1856 greatly regulated the rapid expansion of the new town (he came to Norwich in 1865 and went on to Leeds in 1872), but more significant was the long tenure of that office by *John William Cockrill* (1849–1924), borough engineer from 1874 to 1922. In addition to his work at Gorleston he built the cemetery chapel at Caister of 1899, a strange building, with an Arts-and-Crafts Perp window, and the Institute of Art and Design in Yarmouth of 1912, in steel, brick and concrete, sparely decorated. He used concrete widely, for example selecting the material for the replacement figures on Nelson's monument in 1896.

NORWICH OFFICERS C19 AND C20

Surveyors		Architects		Engineers	
John Rooks	1806 – 33				
Samuel Blyth	1833 – 7				
John Athow	1838 – 40				
J. Stannard Jun.	1840 – 8				
John Bunn	1848 – 54				
E. E. Benest	1854 – 9				
T. D. Barry	1859 – 68			Alfred Morant	1865 – 72
James S. Benest	1868 – 78				
W. Walter Lake	1878 – 88				
John Brockbank	1888 – 90	John Brockbank	1888 – 90		
P. P. Marshall	1890 – 8	P. P. Marshall	1890 – 8	P. P. Marshall	1878 – 98
A. E. Collins	1898 – 1925	A. E. Collins	1898 – 1925	A. E. Collins	1898 – 1925
J. S. Bullough	1925 – 43	J. S. Bullough	1925 – 38	J. S. Bullough	1925 – 43
		J. N. Meredith	1938		
		L. G. Hannaford	1939 – 56		
H. C. Rowley	1943 – 66	D. Percival	1956 – 74	H. C. Rowley	1943 – 66
R. K. Binks	1967 – 74*	J. Pogson	1974 – 81	R. K. Binks	1967 – 74
		A. Whitwood	1981 – 93‡	R. M. Alstead	1974 – 82
				D. Hawkes	1982 – 9
				Andrew Cowburn	1989 –

* City Surveyors amalgamated with Engineers in 1974.

‡ City Architects amalgamated with Planning Department from 1993, Chief Architect Paul Mearing.

THE TWENTIETH CENTURY

Edwardian Architecture

Few COUNTRY HOUSES were built after the agricultural depression of the 1870s, which extended to the First World War and eroded the financial base of traditional landed families. Everywhere rent rolls fell, farms lay empty or were let free in order to maintain the condition of the soil, and owners were forced to sell first plots of land, then household collections and finally whole estates. In 1884 Sir Andrew Fountaine of Narford sold his collection of enamels, ceramics and drawings, and in 1909 Lord Amherst disposed of his library at Didlington Hall. By the late 1890s new country houses were being built for a different breed of client and in a different idiom. The clients were men who had made fortunes out of industry and commerce and the style was the ARTS AND CRAFTS.

The architects who believed in its tenets have left some of their most significant work in Norfolk. The first is *Lutyens*'s The Pleasaunce in Overstrand, contrived out of two existing houses in 1897–9 for Cyril Flower, first Lord Battersea, who had married a daughter of Sir Anthony de Rothschild. The house emphasizes the use of local materials, irregular and capricious forms and historic English sources. At nearby Overstrand Hall the client was Charles Mills, a partner in the bank Glyn Mills, and for him in 1899–1901 *Lutyens* produced a tremendous courtyard house mixing every conceivable style. The same reliance on local materials is evident at St Mary's, Happisburgh, put up by *Detmar Blow* for Albemarle Cator in 1900 on the butterfly plan celebrated from Prior's The Barn at Exmouth, and at *Prior*'s own Thornfield Residential Home at Holt (formerly Home Place) in 1903–5, a huge butterfly-planned house, complicated and wilful in its forms. The last of the significant butterfly houses in England is in the same area: Kelling Hall of 1912–13, the first country house by *Edward Maufe*, for the chairman of Royal Dutch Petroleum and Shell. Other Arts and Crafts variants include the Presbytery at Houghton St Giles of 1904 probably by *Thomas Garner*, which uses Gothic sources, and Sutherland House, Cromer, by *Edward May* in 1906, derived from C16 domestic architecture.

The Arts and Crafts had a lasting impact, but other styles remained current. The stable block at Merton Hall of 1898 by *Milne & Hall* carried on the Jacobean of the house. At How Hill (Ludham) in the Broads *Edward Thomas Boardman* began his holiday home in a vernacular revival style in 1903, Beachamwell Hall was rebuilt in 1904–6, after a fire, by *Wimperis & Best*, in exactly the same late C17 manner as it had been before, and the same firm took on Little Massingham House in 1904–5 in the then outmoded Queen Anne style. Weasenham Hall of 1905 is also Neo-Jacobean, but at South Pickenham Hall in 1902–5 *Robert Schultz* changed tack to the Neo-Georgian, albeit with shaped gables, and the same style features at a house in Sprowston of

c. 1913 by *Oswald Milne*. This appreciation of past styles is even
more apparent in Edwardian additions to existing houses, of
which the chief are the estate buildings at Kilverstone Hall by
Boardman in the first decade of the C20, *Somers Clark*'s work at
Raveningham Hall, *Blow* and *Lutyens* at Breckles Hall (1900 and
1908), *Sir Guy Dawber* at Wiveton Hall in 1907–9, and *Skipper* at
the house and park at Sennowe Hall, Guist.

The Arts and Crafts appears in some church furnishings, for
example at Wheatacre, 1904–5 by *Sedding* (font cover), and in
stained glass (1889 at Titchwell, possibly by *Edward Frampton*;
Sustead of *c.* 1897 by *Christopher Whall*; South Walsham in 1907
by *R. O. Pearson*),* but only two commercial buildings deserve a
place in any book on the subject in England: the Royal Arcade, 1/98
Norwich, especially the Back of the Inns front, by *George Skipper*
of 1899, and Fastolff House in Regent Street, Great Yarmouth,
built in 1908 as an office block by *Ralph Scott Cockrill*, with a
tremendous faience façade terminating in a high clerestory.
Yarmouth, especially on Marine Parade, is the place to see pre-
war faience and terracotta.

Another strand of the Edwardian decade was the unashamed
Baroque of public and COMMERCIAL BUILDINGS, though only
the latter category figures in the county, chiefly in Norwich, where
the versatile *George Skipper* became a leading exponent of the
style. His earliest essay is the white and brown terracotta office at
No. 7 St Giles Street of 1900, but he was never better than at the
Norwich Union Offices of 1903–4, though his contemporary
Jarrolds Department Store at the corner of the Market Place
approaches it. *Skipper*'s Telephone House in St Giles Street,
1906, is a smaller version of the Norwich Union building, imitated
further along the street in 1907 at the Masonic Hall by *Albert
Havers*. At Great Yarmouth *A. S. Hewitt* overdid the style in his
1904–5 National Provincial Bank and *Francis Burdett Ward* carried
it still further at the Regent Cinema of 1914, the most extravagant
of its date outside London. Of other commercial buildings the
most remarkable was Roberts Warehouse in Botolph Street,
Norwich (demolished), built in 1903 by *A. F. Scott*, an early
example of European Functionalism diametrically opposed to
Skipper's Baroque. The building provided a bridge to Modern
Architecture, but few in Norfolk went across it. The (now derelict)
former Citroën Garage in St James's Street, King's Lynn, has an
early reinforced concrete frame and curtain walling. That was in
1908, and in 1912 *A. F. Scott* used the same technique but clad
with stone for the Classical Marks & Spencer's in St Stephen's
Street, Norwich, no doubt influenced by the first phase of Self-
ridge's in London completed in 1909.

PUBLIC BUILDINGS of the period are scanty, apart from the
new Thetford Guildhall of 1902 and the refacing of the Shire Hall 2/119
in Norwich in 1913–14. For SCHOOLS, Gothic continued to
be used (e.g. George White Middle School, Norwich, 1903 by
C. J. Brown) but the rebuilt Gresham's School at Holt is Tudor

* Churches themselves are not significant in the Edwardian decades.

2/122 and the best Edwardian school, the Edward VII High School in King's Lynn, is in a Dutch Queen Anne style by *Basil Champneys* in 1903–6. Its plan with classrooms off a central hall, as well as its style, owes much to the London Board schools. The enormous City of Norwich School of 1910 finds *C.J. Brown* in a Baroque mood. Growing concern for public education led also to the provision of public rather than subscription LIBRARIES, but of those funded by the American steel tycoon Andrew Carnegie only one survives of Norfolk's three, at King's Lynn, built in 1904–5 by *H.J. Green*. The others were at Great Yarmouth (bombed 1941) and Gorleston-on-Sea (replaced 1974–7). Of HOSPITALS mention of the West Norwich Hospital of 1908–9 by *Morgan & Buckenham* will suffice.

Norfolk between the Wars

LOCAL AUTHORITY HOUSING made a tentative start before the First World War with two pairs at Edgefield, 1912, and fifty in Bury Road, Thetford, pleasantly and thoughtfully designed by *S.J. Wearing* in 1912–14. The Housing Act of 1919 which required councils to build homes for the working classes was embraced in Norfolk more enthusiastically than in most counties, and in Norwich more than any town. Most local authorities provided uniform ranks of brick semi-detached houses; these are rarely mentioned in the gazetteer. But there are exceptions, beginning with *Wearing*'s Thetford houses, continuing with *Skipper*'s clay lump crescents at Garboldisham and East Harling of 1919–20, deliberately built as 'houses fit for heroes', and reintroducing a traditional building material which had gone out of fashion. In Thetford *Wearing* built seventy-two houses as an estate at Newtown in 1920–3, and a final forty at St Mary's estate in 1938–9. In Norwich between 1918 and 1932 seven big new estates on green-field sites were completed, while in King's Lynn the expansion towards Gaywood, South Wootton and South Lynn came in the 1930s.*

The position of landowners changed radically in the C20. The boom immediately after the First World War led to the sale of a quarter of all estate land in the county between 1917 and 1920, but many small estates did not recover from the depression which followed. Some owners managed some alterations and additions; Oxburgh Hall, Emneth, received two new bays with Dutch gables in 1920, Felthorpe Hall four new bays in 1935, West Bradenham Hall a whole new wing in 1936. A few new houses were built: the Neo-Georgian Stody Lodge for the first Viscount Rothermere,
1/115 1932 by *Walter Sarel*; Templewood, Northrepps, for Lord Temple-
1/116 wood, 1938 by *Seely & Paget* in the guise of a Palladian villa. The MODERN MOVEMENT made little impact in Norfolk. The best
1/121 house, Manor House, Ridlington, of 1935 by *J. Owen Bond*, is poor in comparison with contemporary work at Cambridge, as is *Lacoste*'s house in Hamilton Road, Hunstanton, or even

---

* Further information is given in the respective introductions to towns.

Martindale's streamlined terrace at Sheringham of 1936. Also streamlined is the 1930s Pottergate Tavern in Norwich, but the architect is unknown. The most obvious candidate is *J. Owen Bond*.

Fewer than a dozen new CHURCHES were provided for the new suburbs between 1900 and 1914, and fewer still between the wars. At Lakenham in Norwich *Cecil Upcher*'s new building of 1932–8 is vaguely E.E., and for the Mile Cross estate *A. D. R. Caroé* and *A. P. Robinson* provided St Catherine in 1935. At Recorder Road in Norwich is a Church of Christ Scientist of 1934–5 by *Herbert Ibberson*. But by far the most interesting is the cruciform R.C. church of St Peter the Apostle at Gorleston, 1938–9. It is the only church built by *Eric Gill* and relies on the motif of a stilted arch without piers or capitals, all severely functional.

The most notable PUBLIC BUILDING of this period is Norwich City Hall, one of the most accomplished Swedish-derived public 1/111 buildings in England of the inter-war years, designed by *C. H. James & S. R. Pierce* in 1931, but not constructed until 1937–8. The first of the new buildings was thus *Stanley Livock*'s fire station round the corner in Bethel Street (1932–4). *James & Pierce* laid out the memorial gardens in front of the City Hall in 1938, with *Lutyens*'s War Memorial of 1927. The whole Market Place, especially its contrast of medieval Guildhall and church on two sides and the city hall on another is one of the best examples of municipal town planning in England. The only other municipal offices are in *F. R. B. Haward*'s featureless block behind Great Yarmouth Town Hall, put up in 1938, and the only other public building of note other than in parks is the Crematorium at Horsham St Faith, a brick building in mixed style by *J. P. Chaplin*, 1936. Of PARKS the most notable is Eaton Park in Norwich, laid out by *A. Sandys-Winsch* in 1924–8, with a domed pavilion and a circular colonnade. More intimate is the James Stuart Gardens, Recorder Road, also in Norwich, completed in 1922 by *Edward Boardman & Son* for a private patron.

The principal concern of Norwich in the 1920s and 30s was, however, SLUM CLEARANCE, a programme that went hand-in-hand with the construction of council estates. It began with the wholesale destruction of tenement buildings to the N of the centre which had grown up in previous centuries in courtyards of once fashionable houses. There was a reaction against such demolition, spurred by growing interest in vernacular buildings, and this led to some restorations: the Ancient House Museum in Thetford, restored by the local authority in 1921–4; Suckling House in Norwich, saved by Ethel and Helen Colman in 1923 (work directed by *Edward Boardman*) and presented to the Corporation. These were flagship buildings, but it required the formation of the Norwich Society to prevent the demolition of the slums in Elm Hill. They were restored from 1927 and other restorations followed. By the time the Second World War began to inflict serious damage, interest in historic buildings was of real concern to the authorities. This was poignantly demonstrated at Great Yarmouth, where in 1943 B. H. St John O'Neil hurried round the

Rows recording what could be recorded, often returning to find that the building he had measured the previous day had been flattened.

The remaining architectural activity concerns COMMERCIAL BUILDINGS. At Yarmouth seafront *Olley & Haward* built a good pedestrian shopping arcade in 1925–6, but it was the banks which built most, in a range of Classical styles. At the National Westmin-1/105 ster Bank in London Street, Norwich, of 1924 *F. C. R. Palmer* and *W. F. C. Holden* opted for a Wren church; at Lloyds Bank on Gentleman's Walk *H. Munro Cautley* in 1927–8 reverted to the reduced Baroque of Edwardian days, but at King's Lynn he gave the Lloyds Bank a more Classical air in 1928. Of the same time is the best of all Norfolk banks, Barclays, facing Agricultural Hall Plain in Norwich and taking a whole block to house the basilican interior. It nods more than once in the direction of American Renaissance banking halls. By *E. Boardman & Son* and *Brierley & Rutherford*. Then came the Wall Street crash and the depression and no more new banks.

Norfolk after 1945

The SECOND WORLD WAR caused another cessation of building, to the extent that City College in Norwich, begun in 1937 (by *L. G. Hannaford*), stood until 1949 as an incomplete steel frame. POST-WAR ARCHITECTURE has some interesting trends in Norfolk, not least the rise in importance of the borough surveyors and engineers and the emergence of considered TOWN PLANNING. Norwich and Great Yarmouth faced planning problems as soon as hostilities ceased, Thetford only after 1958, King's Lynn from the 1960s. In Norwich the perceived need was to clear damaged streets, to rebuild a new modern city, especially in the Brigg Street area, and to demolish terraces of C19 houses. A new slum clearance was undertaken, and as in the 1920s scant regard was paid to architectural or historic merit if a building stood in the way, and even less effort was made to integrate new structures into the fabric of the medieval city. The man in charge was *H. C. Rowley*, city engineer and surveyor 1943–66, and planning officer from 1944. The city architect until 1956, *L. G. Hannaford*, was not often consulted. In Yarmouth far more serious bombing took place and the borough engineer, *F. H. Dyson*, took the more radical approach and saved only those Rows which were comparatively undamaged and were well away from the proposed new roads within the town walls (such as Yarmouth Way of 1953). Even so, only Broad Row and Market Row of the 145 pre-war Rows are recognizable.

The provision of HOUSING was by 1945 almost completely a council matter, and at Norwich a further 12,000 houses were built in the ten years after the war, so that in the late 1950s 40 per cent of the city population lived in council houses, the highest percentage of any British town. They were mainly on low-rise estates (West Earlham, begun 1947; Heartsease from 1954); seven tower blocks followed, the first of 1963. At Yarmouth *F. H. Dyson* presided over construction of 3,384 council houses beginning in 1952 with housing at the s end of South Quay, arranged in narrow rows imitating the former actual Rows, then turning to the North Quay area in 1956–7. By the 1960s the deck access system used by Dyson was introduced in Norwich, as for the Barrack Street flats by *David Percival*. Percival was a dynamic city architect appointed in 1956, to whom is owed almost all of the better municipal schemes into the 1970s. In Thetford a completely different revolution took place in council housing, for in 1958 the town was accepted as an overspill town for London and the population quadrupled over the next thirteen years. To hold them the *London County Council Architect's Department* under *Hubert Bennett* constructed three giant estates on virgin ground. The second of them, of 1965–7 (Redcastle Furze Estate), was based on the Radburn principle, separating cars from pedestrians, but otherwise has nothing unusual. The population increase had huge implications for the small town centre. King's Lynn was also marked as a London overspill area, with three new estates on the outskirts begun in 1962, but whereas at Thetford new needs were accommodated within the existing town centre, at Lynn the bulldozer between 1962 and 1971 destroyed a fifth of the town's historic buildings in favour of barren new streets and shopping centres.

But there was another trend in council housing already under way in the countryside. In 1944 the Dudley Report laid down the requirements for new RURAL COUNCIL HOUSING to supersede the uniform suburban semi-detached houses of the inter-war period. These were modified by the Ministry of Health's new 1949 Housing Manual which indicated that relating a house to its setting was desirable. This was already being advocated by *Thomas Sharp* elsewhere in England, but in Norfolk it was achieved by *Herbert Tayler* and *David Green* between 1945 and 1976 for the then Loddon District Council (now part of South 2/127 Norfolk District). The very first of their 739 houses in estates in twenty-six villages, in Thurlton in 1946, were variants on older rural housing, but the variations included colourwashing and a frieze of casement windows under the eaves. Thereafter they produced a series of gentle accommodating houses mixed in groups or in straight or undulating terraces, using a variety of local materials. By composing their buildings into coherent groups they broke completely from the past and were widely influential in the 1950s, so it is a pity that uPVC windows and alterations by owner-occupiers are taking their toll. Windmill Green at Ditchingham (1947–8) was included as a model in the 1949 Housing Manual.

The Alderson Place flats in Finklegate, Norwich (1959–60 by *Percival*), is a rare example of sympathetic council housing, and there was a decline in standard in the 1960s. It was left to Essex County Council to rejuvenate interest. Their *Design Guide for Residential Areas* of 1973 drew on local vernacular buildings for inspiration and sparked off a neo-vernacular revival based on housing fitting into its environment, low rise and with various

gabled roofs set at odd angles. *Tayler & Green* were still doing
this, for example at Loddon, and it was their style coupled with
the Essex *Design Guide* which gave us 'Norfolk Cottage Vernacular'. At its best this style is excellent, especially in the houses
of 1976–7 by *David Summers* at Great Snoring, and *Feilden &*
1/119   *Mawson*'s Friars Quay in Norwich (job architects *David Luckhurst*
and *Ray Thompson*), begun in 1974. It begins to pall, however,
when applied to entire new settlements, as at Bowthorpe New
Villages from 1975.

Friars Quay was a successful attempt to develop a derelict city-
centre industrial site, which was repeated in Norwich at Hopper's
Yard in 1973–4 (by *Percival*, replacing Barnard's factory), at Barnard's Yard, Coslany Street, and at Anchor Quay (converted
brewery) in the 1980s. Such developments were part of a general
realization in the early 1970s that old sub-standard houses in
former industrial areas of the city could be renovated. The programme begun by *Percival* at Pope's Buildings in Calvert Street
in 1972–3 produced a much better solution than demolition and
new building could have done. The new outlook and the reaction
against high-rise housing led to some commendable work in the
county from the mid 1970s. Langham Place in Norwich of 1979
is by *David Percival* after he moved from the city to *Edward
Skipper & Associates*; in 1983 *Chaplin & Farrant* built a successful
open courtyard for the elderly in Recorder Road, Norwich, social
groups having been targeted for housing since the late 1970s.
Feilden & Mawson are responsible for the two-storey deck-access
2/129   system at Suffield Court in Swaffham built in 1985–6, which is
1/122   one of the best blocks of its date. Finally at Silkfields in Norwich
P. Mearing of the City Architect's Department built extensive ranges
of sheltered housing in 1990–2 on the site of yet more redundant
factories, in which the Post-modern reaches back for its details
not to Classicism but to vernacular design.

The new post-war estates required SCHOOLS, but the first
which merits notice is atypical, for the *Smithsons*' Hunstanton
2/123   School of 1950–3 is a ruthlessly perfect and symmetrical steel box.
Light steel frames had been used for schools since the 1920s, but
not internally exposed to such deliberate effect. More typical of
post-war schools (low steel-framed blocks under flat roofs with
windows set in horizontal bands, and classrooms opening off long
corridors) are the estate schools, especially the Heartsease Junior
(1956) and Infant Schools (1960) in Norwich by *Percival*, or his
large and low Hewitt School of 1956–8. Schools continued in this
mould until the Plowden Report of 1967 advocated their breaking
down into small, friendlier units. The first in Norfolk is Cringleford Primary School (1970, by *Tayler & Green*), a series of
several small blocks. The 1970s saw a softening of rectilinear
grids into traditional brick and pitched roofs, sometimes, as at
Hethersett First School, with a radial plan (1972–6 by *B. Johnson*
of the *County Architect's Office*). Other schools of the 1970s are
Norfolk Cottage Vernacular in style (Clover Hill First School,
Bowthorpe, of 1977, by *R. W. Haydon* of the *County Architect's
Office*). Under *J. F. Tucker* as County Architect *Chris Garner*

produced Terrington St Clement High School in 1979–80, each of the pavilions disposed around a central covered way. Rosemary Musker High School in Thetford of 1983 by *J. F. Tucker* not only 2/124 has seven separate pavilions arranged at various angles, but a traditional construction instead of system building. The smaller Hethersett High School is from the same office.

The vernacular themes introduced into housing and the softening of box design in schools in the 1970s had echoes in public and commercial buildings. PUBLIC BUILDINGS immediately after the war were wholly conventional, e.g. Neo-Georgian for police stations (King's Lynn, 1953–5, by the then County Architect *C. H. Thurston*), but hints of vernacular arrived with *David Percival*. As early as 1959–61 the swimming baths on Aylsham Road, Norwich, had flint panelling applied as cladding, and so did the Norwich Central Library of 1960–2 (destroyed by fire 1994). Otherwise these two are ordinary steel-framed buildings, and so is the library at Gorleston of 1974–7 by *F. Jackson* and *Kenneth King*, dressed in pre-cast flint panels as far away from vernacular technique as is possible; the fashion was short-lived. Norfolk County Hall (1966, by *Reginald Uren*) had already rejected it for 1/117 a straightforward steel-framed office block.

A different approach was adopted later for a number of very successful public buildings, beginning in 1978–9 with the South Norfolk District Council Offices at Long Stratton by *Michael* 2/125 *Innes* of *Lambert, Scott & Innes*. Strong brick-clad forms are arranged as two irregular hexagons in close connection but asymmetrical, and inside everything is open-plan and on different levels. Also of 1979 is the Magistrates' Court at King's Lynn by 2/131 *Leonard Manasseh Partnership*, well handled on a sensitive site by the river. For sheer imagination the King's Lynn Crematorium 2/126 of 1979–80 is hard to beat, with a huge paper-dart roof supported on glulam rafters (by *David Grace* of the *District Architect's Office*). Norwich's new Magistrates' Court built by *Robert Goodyear* (of 1/118 the *City Architect's Department*) in 1982–5 resorts to debased Classical, but with so much conviction that the *Property Services Agency* in 1988 could only copy it for the adjoining Crown Courts. Then the District Council Offices at Cromer by *David Gipson* in 1/124 1988–90 took the open-plan concept a stage further with a huge curving internal space under mighty glulam rafters. Altogether municipal architecture in Norfolk after 1975 has been excellent.

COMMERCIAL BUILDINGS immediately after the war started well enough with *J. Owen Bond*'s new Bonds Department store in Norwich of 1946 (the name is not a coincidence) and Norfolk House in Exchange Street of 1950–1 by *Alec Wright*. By the mid 1950s reconstruction of Norwich was in full swing, Debenham's in Rampant Horse Street of 1954–5 by *Eric Scott* of *A. F. Scott & Sons* setting the tone: big, practical, dull and alien in a medieval street. Soon it was small medieval buildings which were alien in the quarter S of the Market Place, especially when contrasted with the early Norwich Union buildings between All Saints Green, Westlegate and St Stephen's Street. The Glass Tower on Westlegate of 1960–1 by *Chaplin & Burgoine* was the first commercial tower block in the city, a commendable attempt to fit a modernist structure into a medieval thoroughfare, succeeding where the block-like 1963 extension to Jarrolds on Exchange Street does not. The giant Sovereign House at St Crispins by *Alan Cooke Associates* contributed in 1966–8 to the carving up of the whole section N of the river by the inner link road (built 1968–75). The Eastern Daily Press offices at the castle end of Rouen Road by *Yates, Cook & Derbyshire*, 1970, picks up the idea of glossing over a functional and bald building with a screen of flint at the front, but that only emphasizes a lack of conviction in what the architects were doing.

In the same years bad office blocks were going up in King's Lynn and Great Yarmouth (among them surprisingly *Tayler & Green*'s Yarmouth House of 1970) and the Market Gates area of Yarmouth was insensitively flattened in 1973–7 for a grisly shopping centre. But in 1970–1 the first good Norwich office block since 1951 was built, unfortunately situated on an industrial estate at Sprowston, where it is seldom seen. It is the British Gas Offices by the *Design Group for Industry*, open-plan and with an exterior consisting of alternating wide and narrow horizontal bands. 1975 brought Elliot House on Ber Street, presenting cantilevered storeys to the street elevation like a jettied vernacular building (*D. Cooper* of *Edward Skipper & Associates*). Good brick detailing appears at St Peter's House on Rouen Road (1975 by *Keith Blowers* of *Elsom Pack & Roberts*) and a whole range of features to the front of *Sir Frederick Snow*'s excellent offices at Nos. 51–59 Rose Lane, built in 1976–7. The new sensitivity continued with the
1/120 Anglia Television Centre of 1982 where *David Luckhurst* of *Feilden & Mawson* applied Norfolk Cottage Vernacular to an office block.

In the 1980s redundant older factories were converted to factory or residential units, and offices refaced to reflect the city's new demand for composed, or at least striking façades. *A. J. Coiley* added bright blue curtain walling to Norvic House in Chapelfield Road in 1988. At the Bank of Scotland, *Lambert, Scott & Innes* applied a timber elevation in the same year, and at Austin House and Cavell House on St Crispins Road, *Chris Garner*, now working with *Feilden & Mawson*, completed in 1994 two very big office blocks coming full circle in their devotion to soft red brick and glancing back to the Victorian warehousing they replaced. The biggest and most delicately situated of all late C20 developments
1/129 is, however, Castle Mall right under the Norman castle, and the
1/130 solution chosen was to bury it underground (opened in 1993, by *Michael Innes* of *Lambert, Scott & Innes*). Engineering plays as much of a role as architecture (consulting engineers: *Ove Arup & Partners*), and results in the best city-centre shopping mall in England of its date.

The University of East Anglia has the most important collection of buildings on a single site in the county, a green-field site free from urban planning constraints. Moreover, it retains a cohesion not always possible with successive phases of construction in older C20 universities (e.g. Exeter) because the two master plans, by

Denys Lasdun in 1962 and *Rick Mather* in 1987, interact successfully. The principal difference is that Mather's buildings to the N of the main teaching wall are intended to stand alone, Lasdun's to be part of an integrated whole. Lasdun's main blocks anticipate the horizontality familiar in his National Theatre (first plans 1961, completed in 1976) at the South Bank in London, though his concrete ziggurats built in 1966–7 break with any- 1/125 thing then to be seen in Britain. The interest in creating a new type of urbanity through stepped-back forms and pedestrian access, however, can be compared to the Brunswick Centre in Bloomsbury (designed in 1960, but not built until 1969). The major addition to the University in the 1970s, *Norman Foster*'s Sainsbury Centre of 1974–8, represents an important strand of 1/127 international Functionalism: a welded tubular frame enclosing an open space with 8ft walls containing all the service machinery. In 1983–5 *Rick Mather* also broke with Lasdun at the School of Education and Information building, introducing an open court- 1/128 yard plan and spectraglaze panels applied to an irregular exterior surface, which provide an entirely different mood from Lasdun's concrete forms. Mather's Climatic Research Unit, built in 1985, has a similar construction, but is circular and full of tricks, and equally tricky and engaging are his residences at Constable Terrace of 1993, designed along 'green' principles. There are 1/126 many other important buildings at U.E.A., for which *see* the gazetteer entry. Reflections of the Sainsbury Centre are at the Bespak factory extension in King's Lynn built in 1978–80 by *Cambridge Design* (job architect *Julian Bland*), at Norwich Airport Terminal of 1988 by *Alan Wardle* of the *City Architect's Department*, and, a distant echo, in Castle Mall.

This leaves the few post-war CHURCHES, of which *Bernard Feilden*'s Presbyterian church on Unthank Road, Norwich, of 1954–6 is the best, in a Swedish Expressionism popular in the middle of the century, while *A. J. Chaplin* built St George Sprowston (R.C.) in 1962 along entirely traditional lines. Then there are the surprisingly scarce PRIVATE DOMESTIC BUILDINGS, of which first COUNTRY HOUSES. Demolitions continued, such as Hillington Hall in 1946 (remains consolidated into a new house by *Marshall Sisson*), but repairs were also done, as at Cley Old Hall in 1948 by *Paul Paget* and *Hubert Blount*, then more memorably at Lexham Hall, East Lexham, in 1948–50 by *James Fletcher-Watson*. Fletcher-Watson had already shown his skill in rebuilds at the Dolphin Inn in Norwich, and in his country house restorations was not afraid to remodel in a manner which the original architects would, one feels, have approved. At Kimberley Hall, for instance, he remodelled the centre of the house in 1951, introducing a two-storey staircase hall. Additions to the more modest Warham House, Warham, followed in 1957–8, and in the 1960s he began to build from scratch, always in a restrained Neo-Georgian: the Bishop's House in Norwich Close, 1959; East Carleton Manor, 1964, and Watlington Hall the following year. *Cecil Smith* kept to Neo-Georgian for Hockering House, built in 1968. Among 2/128 smaller PRIVATE HOUSES, there is little more of note. *Feilden &*

Mawson have a good house at No. 71A The Close, Norwich, of 1955; in 1971 *Spence & Webster* built a Miesian steel box in Hamilton Road, Hunstanton, and in 1976 *James Cornish* designed for himself Boscarne in Stoke Holy Cross, a three-sided block-built house only one storey high reacting against the prevailing Norfolk Cottage Vernacular. Equally imaginative is *Neylan & Ungless*'s Wall House at Garboldisham, built in 1978–81 against two sides of an existing wall. These are isolated examples, for the principal activity on the domestic front from the 1970s has been restorations of existing houses, which become more sympathetic to vernacular architecture every year. This is an encouraging sign in a county that has seen few of the worst excesses of c20 municipal planning and official architecture, and it is a note on which we can happily leave Norfolk.

FURTHER READING

The first volume to consult is *A Bibliography of Norfolk History* by Elizabeth Darroch and Barry Taylor, issued by the Centre for East Anglian Studies in 1975 and followed by a supplement dealing with publications of 1974–88 by Barry Taylor (1991). Occasionally a note of the contents of each work listed is provided. The Victoria County History produced a few volumes in the early c20, but the Royal Commission on Historical Monuments of England has not so far turned in Norfolk's direction. Of the antiquarian books the most useful is Francis Blomefield's *Essay Towards a Topographical History of the County of Norfolk*, published incomplete in 1735–75, and only in its finished form in 1805–10. Blomefield himself only completed two-and-three-quarter volumes on the s part of the county before he died in 1752. Other antiquarian works worth consulting are Tom Martin, *The History of the Town of Thetford etc* of 1779, and Henry Manship's *History of Great Yarmouth*, completed in 1619 and edited by C. J. Palmer in 1854. Palmer himself produced the more scholarly *Perlustration of Great Yarmouth* in 1872.

Of modern general books on the county *An Historical Atlas of Norfolk* edited by Peter Wade-Martins in 1993 is valuable not only for its ninety-three short articles on myriad subjects but for its comprehensive bibliography, while Susanna Wade-Martins' *A History of Norfolk* (1984), D. Dymond's *The Norfolk Landscape* (1985) and David Yaxley's *Portrait of Norfolk* (1977) give a better overview of the county than is possible in this book. The county archaeological journal is *Norfolk Archaeology* (from 1847), which contains many indispensable articles, some of which will be referred to in their place, and there are the publications of *East Anglian Archaeology* (from 1976) and the various bulletins of the *Norfolk Industrial Archaeology Society* (from 1971). In addition of course the reader should refer to the several national journals. For the towns other than Norwich the best study of medieval buildings relates to King's Lynn with Vanessa Parker, *The Making of King's Lynn*, 1971, supplemented with a different perspective in Paul Richards, *King's Lynn*, 1990. The *King's Lynn Preservation Trust*, founded in 1958, has produced a number of trustworthy pamphlets on buildings it has restored. Colin Tooke in *The Rows of Great Yarmouth*, 1987, is useful on that subject if very briefly, and B.H. St J. O'Neil printed the results of his 1943 survey as 'Some Seventeenth Century Houses in Great Yarmouth' in *Archaeologia*, XCV, 1953. Generally, however, Yarmouth literature is deficient. The only comprehensive c20 survey of Thetford is in Alan Crosby's social and economic history, *A History of Thetford*, 1986, and of East Dereham similar treatment is given in Ben Norton, *The Story of East Dereham*, 1994.

For GEOLOGY the reader is referred to the maps produced by the British Geological Survey, *East Anglia*, 1: 250,000 Series of 1985, and to G.P. Larwood and B.M. Funnell, 'The Geology of Norfolk' in *Norwich and its Region*, edited by F. Briers, 1961. H. Godwin, *Fenland: its Ancient Past and Uncertain Future*, 1978, and various authors, *The Making of the Broads*, Royal Geographical Society Research Series No. 3, 1960, shed light on those regions. ARCHAEOLOGY in the county has been reasonably well researched, particularly in the bulletins of *East Anglian Archaeology* already mentioned, but a good start may be made with C. Barringer (ed.), *Aspects of East Anglian Prehistory*, 1984, which covers a number of subjects. One of the contributors to that volume, J.J. Wymer, also has a useful account in *Palaeolithic Sites of East Anglia*, 1984. The pre-Roman period (i.e. the Iron Age) is outlined in a series of accounts in *East Anglian Archaeology*: J.A. Davis and others, 'The Iron Age Forts of Norfolk', 1992 (issue 54); for Thetford see A.K. Gregory and others in issue 53 (1992); for excavations on the N coast and at the Roman town of Caistor St Edmund see A.K. Gregory and D. Gurney in issue 30 (1986). More accessible is a series of four popular but informative little books produced in conjunction with the Norfolk Museums Service entitled *Norfolk Origins*, by various authors, covering the ages between the first hunter-gathering folk and the Norman Conquest, issued between 1981 and 1990. The best volume detailing Norfolk from the Iron Age to the Conquest is however Tom Williamson, *The Origins of Norfolk*, 1993. This has a very full bibliography. For more detailed and particular information the reader is directed to the *Sites and Monuments Record* held by the Norfolk Archaeological Unit at Gressenhall.

This brings the first STANDING BUILDINGS apart from the various Roman remains. Everything of consequence has a description in the *Statutory Lists of Buildings of Historical or Architectural Interest* issued by the Department of the Environment and the Department of National Heritage, especially the lists relating to the 1982–7 resurvey. Some towns have been reviewed since (King's Lynn, Wymondham, Great Yarmouth, Thetford and Swaffham), but the descriptions are brief and there is no comment attached to them. The best general books on architecture remain H.M. and J. Taylor, *Anglo-Saxon Architecture*, 1965, and E. Fernie,

Architecture of the Anglo-Saxons, 1983, but for the question of round towers there is S. R. Heywood, 'The Round Towers of East Anglia', in J. Blair (ed.), *Minsters and Parish Churches, the Local Church in Transition 950–1200*, 1988, and W. J. Goode, *East Anglian Round Towers and their Churches*, 1982. Romanesque church architecture is discussed in B. Cherry, 'Romanesque Architecture in Eastern England', *Journal of the British Archaeological Association*, 131, 1978. There are a number of general books on castle architecture with references to Norfolk beginning with E. S. Armitage, *Early Norman Castles of the British Isles*, 1912, and D. Renn, *Norman Castles in Britain*, 1968, but for a modern introduction see R. Allen Brown, *English Castles*, 1976. The results of the most recent excavations at Castle Acre were published in the *Archaeological Journal* in 1982 and 1987, but the most accessible descriptions are provided in the Department of the Environment (English Heritage) guide books.

For later medieval CHURCH ARCHITECTURE, there is of course an extensive national literature, the principal general volume on the Decorated style being Jean Bony, *The English Decorated Style*, 1979, and for the Perpendicular J. Harvey, *The Perpendicular Style 1330–1485*, 1978, both of which have their own bibliographies. On Norfolk churches specifically one thinks of H. Munro Cautley's *Norfolk Churches* of 1949, rather more brief than was possible for his Suffolk volume, and the nineteen volumes of a systematic survey made by T. H. Bryant, *Norfolk Churches*, 1890–1906. R. Fawcett, *Later Gothic Architecture in Norfolk* (unpublished Ph.D. thesis, University of East Anglia), 1975, is valuable, as is his *The Architecture and Furnishings of Norfolk Churches*, 1974. For wills and their relevance to church fabric in 1370–1550 one has to consult P. Cattermole and S. Cotton, 'Medieval Parish Church Building in Norfolk' in *Norfolk Archaeology*, 38, 1983, and for screens an equivalent list appears in S. Cotton, 'Medieval Rood-screens in Norfolk – their Construction and Painting Dates', *Norfolk Archaeology*, 40, 1987. On brasses is R. Greenwood and M. Norris, *The Brasses of Norfolk Churches*, 1987, and R. Le Strange, *A Complete Descriptive Guide to British Monumental Brasses*, 1972, which has a good section on Norfolk. C. Woodforde's *The Norwich School of Glass-painting in the Fifteenth Century*, 1950, remains valuable.

For C19 churches the best survey is E. Baty, *Victorian Church Buildings and Restoration in the Diocese of Norwich* (unpublished Ph.D. thesis, University of East Anglia), 1987. R. Ladbroke's useful drawings of churches in the 1820s were published in 1843 in five volumes: *Views of the Churches of Norfolk*. Nonconformist chapels and meeting houses were surveyed by the Centre of East Anglian Studies in 1988-93, and the results published as J. Ede, N. Virgoe and T. Williamson, *Halls of Zion*, 1994. Stained glass is thoroughly catalogued in B. Haward, *Nineteenth Century Norfolk Stained Glass*, 1984, with a good introduction on glass painters, and the gazetteer also notes the existence of medieval and imported glass.

COUNTRY HOUSES. G. Winkley, *The Country Houses of*

Norfolk, 1986. M. Sayer gives concise descriptions of country houses and manor houses with information on their owners in the Norfolk section of *Burke's and Savills Guide to Country Houses*, III, East Anglia, 1981. Various *Country Life* articles are as usual invaluable. Major gardens are listed in part 29 of the *Gardens Register* compiled by English Heritage, 1987. For the history of major houses and their owners from the time of the agricultural depression the best account is Pam Barnes, *Norfolk Landowners since 1880*, 1993. The following list includes the most important recent articles on individual country houses. Beeston Hall: R. Haslam, 'Beeston Hall', *C.L.*, 173, 1983. Blickling: C. Stanley-Millson and J. Newman, 'Blickling Hall: the Building of a Jacobean Mansion', *Architectural History*, 29, 1986. Hanworth: R. Haslam, 'Hanworth Hall', *C.L.*, 15 January 1987. Heydon: J. Cornforth, 'Heydon Hall, Norfolk, and its Village', *C.L.*, 172, 1982. Houghton: J. Harris, 'James Gibbs, Eminence Grise at Houghton' in *New Light on English Palladianism*, 1988 (Georgian Group Symposium). Holkham: J.M. Robinson, 'Estate Buildings at Holkham I and II', *C.L.*, 1974. Narford: S. Parissien, J. Harris and H. Colvin, 'Narford Hall, Norfolk', *Georgian Group Report and Journal*, 1987. Shadwell: M. Girouard, in *The Victorian Country House*, 1971 (also Ken Hill, Snettisham). Raynham: M. Airs, 'The Designing of Five East Anglian Country Houses 1595–1637', *Architectural History*, 21, 1978 (also Stiffkey).

There is still a lack of research into VERNACULAR ARCHITECTURE in England, and what there is does not centre on Norfolk. The well-known books, such as E. Mercer, *English Vernacular Houses*, 1975, and R.W. Brunskill, *An Illustrated Handbook of Vernacular Architecture*, second edn 1978, mention the county where necessary but not exclusively. Similarly C. Hewett's books on carpentry, especially *English Historic Carpentry*, 1980. For brick, R. Brunskill and A. Clifton-Taylor condense and bring Nathaniel Lloyd's 1925 book up to date in *English Brickwork*, 1977. Only one systematic survey has been made of Norfolk's farmbuildings, but not for the whole county, published as A. Carter and S. Wade-Martins, *A Year in the Field: the Norfolk Historic Farm Buildings Project*, 1987, and by S. Wade-Martins, *Historic Farm Buildings*, 1991. J. McCann in *Clay and Cob Buildings*, 1983, concisely follows clay lump in Norfolk, but in 'Is Clay Lump a Traditional Building Material?' in *Vernacular Architecture*, 18, 1987, examines the claim that the early C19 is the first time it is used. For medieval houses M. Wood, *The Medieval House*, 1965, remains a useful study though most examples are not vernacular. The most significant source is the periodical *Vernacular Architecture*, published since 1970. Also worth consulting is P. Eden, 'Smaller post-medieval Houses in Eastern England' in L.M. Munby (ed.), *East Anglian Studies*, 1968. The history of shaped gables will be found in R. Ellis, 'Shaped Gables in Norfolk and Suffolk', *Transactions of the Association for the Study and Conservation of Historic Buildings*, 8, 1983. For corn windmills the only good book is H. Apling, *Norfolk Corn Windmills*, 1984.

For INDUSTRIAL ARCHAEOLOGY there are the Reports of the

Norfolk Industrial Archaeological Society from 1984, and on fortifications other than castles P. Kent, *Fortifications of East Anglia*, 1988. A. Reid (ed.), *Cromer and Sheringham: the Growth of the Holiday Trade, 1877–1914*, 1986, studies that subject.

NORWICH is curiously short of early accounts, other than the 1806 edition of Blomefield's *Essay*, but there are three recent general accounts dealing with various periods. Brian Ayres's *Norwich*, 1994, covers the early medieval evolution of the town and summarizes very well the fairly extensive archaeology. J. Pound, *Tudor and Stuart Norwich*, 1988, devotes a chapter to buildings, while S. Muthesius provides an excellent essay on 'Nineteenth Century Housing in Norwich', in C. Barringer (ed.), *Norwich in the Nineteenth Century*, 1984. For Georgian Norwich the best account remains. J. Wearing, *Georgian Norwich: its Builders*, 1926. The archaeological excavations are usually described in the relevant issues of *Norfolk Archaeology*, including the first seven reports of the Norwich Survey, 1972–8, and since then those reports have appeared in *East Anglian Archaeology*. Some offshoots of the Norwich Survey have been issued as e.g. M.W. Atkin and S. Margeson, *Life on a Medieval Street*, 1985 (the Alms Lane excavations of 1976), Brian Ayres, *Digging Under the Doorstep*, 1983 (major excavations of 1979–81), *Digging Deeper*, 1987 (covering a prolific period of work in 1985–7). There are other popular but authoritative publications. A very good introduction to the history of the city through all periods is B. Green and R. Young, *Norwich: the Growth of a City*, 1981, which has its own useful bibliography. Another publication arising from the authors' work for the Norwich Survey is a very important article: R. Smith and A. Carter, *Norwich Houses before 1700*, reprinted from *Vernacular Architecture*, 14, 1983.

Norwich castle is the target for little other than archaeological reports (the best discussion is by P. A. Faulkner, *Report on Norwich Castle Keep*, 1971, but a copy is hard to find), but the cathedral has very recently been the subject of two books: E. Fernie, *An Architectural History of Norwich Cathedral*, 1993, and I. Atherton, E. Fernie, C. Harper-Bill and A. Hassell Smith (eds), *Norwich Cathedral*, 1996 (only parts of which were available before going to press). These two books render further guidance superfluous. On Norwich housing since the first edition see M. Horsey and S. Muthesius, *Provincial Mixed Development; the Design and Construction of Norwich Council Housing under David Percival, 1955-73*, 1986.

ARCHITECTS. For medieval masons there is J. Harvey's *Biographical Dictionary of English Medieval Architects down to 1550*, second edn 1984, and more particular work by R. Fawcett in 'A Group of Churches by the Architect of Great Walsingham' in *Norfolk Archaeology*, 37, 1980, and 'St Mary at Wiveton in Norfolk and a Group of Churches Attributed to its Mason' in *Antiquaries Journal*, 57, 1982. Picking up more or less where Harvey leaves off is H. M. Colvin's indispensable *Biographical Dictionary of British Architects 1600–1840*, third edn 1995. The Victorian period is fully detailed in the *Directory of British Architects 1834–1900* issued by the British Architectural Library in 1993, but from 1840 the reader may also consult C. Brown, B. Haward and R. Kindred, *Dictionary of Architects of Suffolk Buildings 1800–1914*, 1991. This deals with many Norfolk architects by virtue of the fact that the Norwich diocese includes parts of Suffolk, and many C19 Norfolk architects worked in Suffolk. For the Edwardian period there is A. Stuart Gray, *Edwardian Architecture: a Biographical Dictionary*, 1985. The C20 has been only scantily researched, though reference to James Fletcher-Watson's country houses is made in J. Martin Robinson, *The Latest Country Houses*, 1984. For sculptors the best is R. Gunnis, *Dictionary of British Sculptors 1660–1851* (third edn forthcoming).

NORFOLK

ALBURGH

ALL SAINTS. A small church with a remarkably tall tower. The tower has flushwork panelling l. and r. of the W doorway and niches l. and r. of the W window. The buttresses cease below the bell-stage with unfortunate effect on the outline. Money was left for 'ye butrasyng of the stepill' in 1504. Two-stepped battlements with flushwork panelling. Pinnacles with little flying buttresses, which do not appear on Ladbroke's drawing of 1822 and must be due to *R. M. Phipson*'s restoration of 1876 (cost £1,340). Phipson reworked the S side of the chancel, inserting the windows, and added a vestry to the NE. The N and S sides otherwise Perp. C15 nave roof with arched braces. – SCREEN. Richard Tyte left money for the new screen in 1464, of which we have only the dado, with nice tracery (two plus two panels for one upper division) and much remaining colour. – STAINED GLASS. In a chancel S window a Sower and a Harvester, 1872 by *J. & J. King*, to a design by *T. J. Scott*.

C17 timber-framed COTTAGES in plenty. On Church Road ALBURGH HALL is dominant, of four window bays, with a brick Dutch gable to the N and lozenge chimneyshafts to the ridge stack. C19 porch and single bays at each end. On THE STREET first IVY FARMHOUSE with its stables and dairy block, and ASHTREE FARMHOUSE, both C17 and somewhat altered. TUDOR HOUSE has diamond shafts to the chimney. THE WHITE HOUSE represents the early C18 and a jump into brick: two storeys in three bays; sashes and stepped gable-ends. At the back a C17 timber-framed wing. BROCK'S BARN at Piccadilly Corner, ½ m. S, is a C17 lobby-entrance house with brick gable-end walls.

ALDEBY

ST MARY. Established *c.* 1100 as one of five priory churches dependent on Norwich, suppressed in 1538.* Aldeby was the least important, with a prior and four monks whose primary concern was farming. There were 800 acres and a mill in 1275 but by 1514 the church and farm buildings were in a ruinous state. The foundation was both monastic and parochial.

---

* The others were: St Nicholas, Yarmouth; St Margaret, King's Lynn; St Leonard, Norwich; St Edmund, Hoxne, in Suffolk.

Basically a cruciform Norman church over-restored in 1880: see the w doorway, quite an ambitious piece with three orders of colonnettes, decorated capitals (volutes, waterleaf, palmettes and foliage just turning to stiff-leaf), and zigzag and scalloping in the arch. In the nave on the N side a restored Norman lancet. The crossing tower can also be assumed to be Norman, though there is no evidence left. There is much brick in the base. The date 1633 recorded inside refers to a reconstruction, including the brick stair-turret on the s side: 'This stepel was belt 1633'. The bell-openings are c20, but their surrounds look c. 1310–20. Flushwork panelling on the two-stepped battlements. The arches to the w and E are tall and pointed, those to the s and N are of four chamfers dying into the imposts, a motif mostly of the early c14. The N transept arch boarded over. Most of the s transept has disappeared, leaving a blocked semicircular arch into the crossing. In the long N transept is a c13 E recess (in the 1880 restoration found to have a wall painting, which was plastered over), to the w and E splayed c13 lancets. The round-arched niche in the w wall is hardly Norman. The N window of the transept (cusped intersecting tracery) looks c. 1310–20. Similar date for the chancel N Y-tracery windows, for the sedilia and piscina and the shafts inside. Intersecting tracery to the three-light E window and in the s aisle windows. The nave roof is boarded, but the eaves have been raised in red brick, so one assumes a rebuild like the chancel roof. Handsome c14 N porch of knapped flint with flushwork panelling in the base and buttresses; the entrance has fleuron decoration in an inner moulding, an outer moulding, and the hoodmould. In the spandrels of the entrance shields on tracery. – FONT. c15. Octagonal. Eight shafts against the stem, four shields and four flowers in cusped fields against the bowl.

PRIORY FARMHOUSE, St Mary's Road, near the church, has the date 1719 on the N gable. The house probably stands on the site of an earlier monastic building, or farm buildings serving the priory, and reuses masonry from it. E-plan, two storeys and attics. The w front unprepossessing, with render, sashes and four brick buttresses. The doorcase has pilasters. In a wing to the N a stepped external stack and evidence of mullioned windows. The BARN 80 yds E is knocked about, but is timber-framed and has an early c16 double queenpost roof, not as good as e.g. Dairy Farm Barn, Newton Flotman (q.v.), but remarkable notwithstanding.

ST MARY'S ROW, N of the church. By *Tayler & Green*, 1948–53 (*see* Introduction, p. 165). This is a straight terrace of one-storeyed council houses, good in design and colourwashes. The different trellises for climbing plants next to the doors are a nice touch, providing privacy and a wind-break; only one occupier has so employed them at the time of writing. Casement windows remain intact.

WAVENEY COTTAGES, 60 yds w of the last, also by *Tayler & Green*, same date. A two-storey range.

ALDEBY HALL, ½ m. SW. A minor late c18 house of five bays,

the doorcase with fluted pilasters and an open pediment. Sashes.

ALDEBY HOUSE, ½m. NNE. Late C17, red brick, with a later W wing. The N front has cross casements and a large external stack. Shaped end-gables with blocked casements under seg-mental pediments to W, transomed casements to E. S wing with a stepped gable.

To the N of Aldeby House, off the Haddiscoe Road, the early C17 is represented by GRANGE FARMHOUSE, with all the features of that moment: stepped gables, stepped external stacks, pedi-mented and transomed casements, timber-frame construction between the gables. The main entrance has a polite C19 door-case.

ALPINGTON

2000

1 m. NW of Bergh Apton church

ALPINGTON HALL, Church Meadow Lane, declining into a farmhouse. Stepped gables and mullioned windows, of which the five-light window in the W façade is a survivor. C17, but considerably altered. The stack has four lozenge shafts.

OLD HALL, ⅜m. NE of Alpington Hall. Early C18. Three wide bays to the S front in two storeys, the middle bay under a steep pedimental gable with a circular window in it. Big doorway with a pediment on brick Tuscan pilasters. Lower attachments l. and r. of the elevation, lit, like the main block, through C19 case-ments.

For timber-framed HOUSES, one has to look hard. MEADOW COTTAGE is one, with a lobby-entrance and brick fireplaces with quadrant-moulded four-centred arches. C17 rather than C16. Two storeys and attic in four bays. Doorway with moulded surround. The frame of DAIRY FARMHOUSE, Reeder's Lane, has been encased in C20 brick. Ridge stack with a winder beside it, also C17. The best is the early C16 AVENUE FARM COTTAGES, completely bricked-over in the C19 when split into two and out-wardly a four-bay house of that date with two doorways, but the gables are C18. Two square crown-posts in the roof with their crown purlin.

ANMER

7020

ST MARY. In the grounds of Anmer Hall and since 1896 part of the Sandringham estate. Late C13 and early to mid-C14 but very much restored, first the chancel in 1856 by *Frederick Preedy*, then the roofs in 1876, the tower in 1888; in 1906 the seats and the S chapel were re-fitted at the joint expense of Edward VII and Vice-Admiral Sir F.T. Hamilton. E window of four lights with intersecting tracery, restored, but correctly (see Ladbroke's drawing *c.* 1823). Preedy added the corner pilasters and the S windows. The best parts are the S chapel, with Curvilinear tracery in the E window, and cusped Y-tracery in the S window. Also the S porch which has a pointed tunnel vault with chamfered transverse arches, renewed C19. The simple S doorway is late C13. Both these structures belong to the time of Sir Oliver Calthorpe, then lord of the manor. Perp W tower added to the existing nave, which was extended W leaving the N and S doors placed unusually far E of the tower. Apart from the doorway the late C13 origins of the nave are thoroughly obscured, partly by its Perp windows, partly by restorations. – FONTS. One octagonal, with shields, and looking so Victorian that it must be. The other (S chapel) is an C18 baluster. – PAINTINGS. Three in the chancel, by *Sir Noel Paton*, 1883, were removed to Sandringham House after restoration in 1986 (Man of Sorrows, Orate et Vigilate, and the Good Shepherd). – STAINED GLASS. W tower by *Ward & Hughes*, 1889.

ANMER HALL. The Coldham family sold it to the Prince of Wales in 1896. It faces S, away from the church and village. Long, charming, late Georgian brick S façade of thirteen bays in two storeys and attic. Brown brick with fine red brick dressings. In the middle a semicircular porch on fluted columns. The side windows on the ground floor are arched and set in blank arches. On the upper floor the same applies to the three centre windows. Above them a pediment. Five pedimented dormers. The back is of carstone in thin slabs and red brick dressings showing evidence of rebuilding after 1896. The ogee-headed windows with their C18 sashes are slightly earlier than the S façade. Two-storey porch and balancing NE tower are *c.* 1900.

Much of the VILLAGE was rebuilt in the first decade of the C20 for Edward VII. Notable are the METHODIST CHURCH, 1904, and the ANMER CLUB, 1909, built for the spiritual and secular sides of life. The latter has a jettied attic floor and a timber veranda. W gable with three projecting casements.

BARROW. A fine bell barrow E of the village.

SHRUNKEN VILLAGE EARTHWORKS in parkland to the N, W and S of the church.

7020

APPLETON
½ m. SE of West Newton

CHURCH. In ruins. Round tower with a small W lancet and a triangular-headed W bell-opening looking more Anglo-Saxon than Norman. Unmoulded tower arch. S aisle of three bays with octagonal piers. The arch-moulding indicates an early C14 date. The chancel has gone.

APPLETON HALL. On the Sandringham estate. 1863 but replacing a house of 1596 which was burnt in 1707.

ROMANO-BRITISH VILLA. In Denbeck Wood is the site of a C3 and early C4 villa excavated in 1947–8. One building had a fine tessellated mosaic floor beneath which was found the skeleton of a new-born infant. The building was near a walled cobbled yard with three lean-to structures (DG).

DESERTED VILLAGE EARTHWORKS. In a pasture to the S of the church, including a hollow way and several tofts. (AR)

ARMINGHALL

ST MARY. Unbuttressed W tower with a roll-moulded arch to the nave. Nave and chancel in one. The windows, except for the three-light Perp E window, mainly seem to be E.E. lancets, but the church was almost all renewed in *J. P. Seddon*'s restoration of 1876. The S porch was added then. – BENCHES. Eight poppy-heads to the otherwise C19 chancel stalls with the unusual arrangement of a dainty band of foliage or fleurons running along close to the edge. The Victorian benches were designed by Seddon, but the drawing at the RIBA is more ornate than the execution. Seddon's also the boarded roof. – MONUMENT. John Herne †1661, but put up only in 1697 (attributed by Jon Bayliss to *Martin Morley*). Big tablet with long Latin double-column inscription. The surround is of heavy, curly foliage. Carved helmet at the top.

ARMINGHALL HALL. The Elizabethan house was demolished in 1906 when terracotta plaques and other materials were reused at Crown Point Hall, now Whitlingham Hospital. *See* Trowse Newton (Vol. 1).

HENGE MONUMENT. *See* Bixley.

ASHBY ST MARY

ST MARY. W tower, and a low nave and chancel under one roof, with ghastly concrete tiles on the N side. The tower is Perp, two-light bell-openings repaired with brick, three-light restored W window, crenellated parapet. But the church is older. Norman nave, see the SW quoins of carstone, one N window, and the impressive S doorway. This has two orders of colonnettes separated by nook-shafts, and five orders in the arch decorated with zigzag, bobbins, stars and lozenges. The chancel was rebuilt in the C13, see one small N lancet. The C19 restoration replaced the E window with a smaller one, leaving parts of the old jambs visible. Boarded roofs, the nave with moulded C17 coving. – FONT. Octagonal. With its elementary geometrical motifs it could be of the 1660s. – FONT COVER. Jacobean, with simple strapwork. – COMMUNION RAIL. C17, heavy turned balusters and roll-moulded rail. – STAINED GLASS. In the E window one C17 Flemish roundel. – S chancel with Light of the World after *Holman Hunt*, probably 1880s.

ASHBY HALL. Early C19 W front of three bays with a porch on two pairs of unfluted Ionic columns. Sash windows and gault brick. The back however is of red brick, is of double-pile plan and has two shaped gables to the E. Two panelled ridge stacks. Fenestration of mixed sashes and casements, mostly C19. This part can be dated approximately by comparison with the BARN,

30 yds E, which has the same shaped gable to the N and the date 1736 on it – a date rather late for this feature, but not impossible. The same date no doubt again applies to the charming TOWER close to the house on the S, a square three-storeyed structure of chequered brick with rusticated brick quoins and a pyramid roof on which rises a glazed wooden lantern with unfluted columns. The casement windows are under segmental tympana of brick with brick decoration and there is a platband at the first floor. The lantern was added in the C20. Built as a garden house, the tower is now a dwelling.

ASHILL

ST NICHOLAS. Of the C13 are the remains of a blocked N doorway, the shafting inside the chancel E window, and the angle piscina with its twin trefoiled arches. The E window itself is C19 and of Dec forms. Y-tracery side windows. The broad W tower is Dec. W doorway with big ogee arch comprising five orders of mouldings. Above is a three-light window with a reticulation motif inside each reticulation unit. Y-tracery in bell-openings. The tower arch has prominent fillets but already polygonal capitals and a wave-moulded arch. Dec S arcade of six bays with octagonal piers and double-chamfered arches. The capitals differ. Similar chancel arch. Dec also probably the clerestory. All the windows are over-restored. They are Perp and big on the N side, smaller and some with stepped embattled transoms in the S aisle. C15 S porch with a cusped niche above and a window to the parvis. Roof with tie-beams and much tracery over. – SCREEN. Only small parts are old. – STAINED GLASS. Good C15 figures assembled in the N windows. There was a bequest in 1458 for a window in the chapel of St John Baptist. Was that in the N aisle? E window, by *Lavers, Barraud & Westlake*, 1889. Other chancel windows by the same.

THE GLEBE, Swaffham Road, was built as the rectory in 1772. Five-bay brick house, the centre bay on the S side broken forward under a pediment. Single-storey pavilions r. and l. In *c.*1800 another block was added to the E. Rather good stick baluster staircase inside.

ROMANO-BRITISH ENCLOSURE. S of Holme Hale is, or rather was, a twelve-acre enclosure of the Claudian-Neronian period. In the Flavian period, three shafts or wells were dug, probably associated with ritual activities, leaving deposits of complete pottery vessels, knives, wicker baskets and hazel brushwood. Finds of building debris suggest the presence of a structure within the enclosure. (DG)

EARTHWORKS. SW of Panworth Hall are a MOAT and EARTHWORKS including a hollow way and toft boundaries marking the site of the Old Hall and the small deserted settlement of Panworth. (AR)

ASHWELLTHORPE   *1090*

ALL SAINTS. W tower of the late C13, see e.g. the two-light w
   window and the bell-openings with their Y-tracery. The battlements with brick and flint chequerwork are of course later.
   Early C14 chancel, see especially the entertaining E window,
   which has normal cusped intersecting tracery but suddenly, at
   the top, a tiny ogee arch to house the top quatrefoil. Perp the
   very tall nave S windows. Two-storey C15 S porch (niches r. and
   l. of the arch), except for its repaired top which, with its heavy
   segmental gable of brick, looks *c.* 1700. There was a burial in
   the porch in 1420 (the rector, John Quetyl). On 10 May 1398
   John Faudy, a carpenter from Salle, contracted with Sir
   Edmund de Thorpe to make the roofs of the nave and N chapel
   within two years, for 17½ marks (£11.60). The date of the N
   chapel is therefore nicely fixed. The arch towards the chancel is
   Perp, but the N window may well be a Victorian contribution.
   The E window certainly is Late Perp. All this matters, because
   between the chancel and the chapel stands the Thorpe MONU-
   MENT, and this is in all probability to Sir Edmund, who died in
   1417. The architectural evidence fits that date anyway. The
   monument is a very fine piece of the alabasterer's craft. Tomb-
   chest with erect young angels holding shields: two effigies, well
   carved, she (Lady Joan) with angels by her pillow, he with his
   head on his helmet, both with dogs by their feet. – FONT.
   Octagonal, with shields on barbed quatrefoil fields. The carving
   is hard, the date surprising: 1660. – SCREEN. Base only, with
   unusual tracery, repeating the motif of the four-petalled flower
   in the spandrels. – CHEST. Italian; C17. Of pokerwork. With
   soldiers, a tent, a town – a martial piece.
A HOUSE opposite the church has a stepped end-gable and two
   pedimented windows.
ST MARY'S CHAPEL (CHANTRY HOUSE), 1 m. s of Wreningham
   Church on Blacksmith's Lane. This was in fact a chapel of St
   Mary founded in 1311 by Sir John de Thorpe in Ashwell, which
   was a separate settlement until the mid C13. Brick and flint,
   formerly rendered; pantile roof. The building represents the
   chancel only, with fragments of the chancel arch to the w and
   an E window opposite. Various blocked windows and all details
   no earlier than *c.* 1400. The four trusses of an arch-braced roof
   remain, with one tier of purlins. The chapel was suppressed at
   the Dissolution and passed in 1589 to Sir Thomas Knevet, and
   it was presumably for him that it was converted to a house. Of
   this more is apparent, surprisingly for the date with a screens
   passage serving a ground-floor hall to the w and two service
   rooms to the E. The fireplace was inserted against the w wall,
   blocking the former chancel arch, and given a winder staircase
   to its S. An attic storey was reached by an extension of the stairs,
   but this was removed early in the C19 when further extensions
   were made. Restored in 1984.
ASHWELLTHORPE HALL, ½ m. from the church on the N side of
   The Street. Tudor, brick, with stepped gables and appearing all

of 1831 and 1845. In those years Lady Berners added her new ranges to the N and S of the early C17 house, which was greatly altered in the process. The E and W stepped gables have restored mullioned windows under hoods. Octagonal chimney flues with star tops are also of *c*. 1600. C17 GARDEN WALLS to the W, with an octagonal corner GAZEBO. Moulded pediments over windows.

THE STREET runs E–W through the village and is decorated with several C16–C17 timber-framed houses, mostly altered. HALL FARMHOUSE on N side has a late C16 two-storey NE wing fitted with (blocked) diamond-mullioned casements. C17 SW block, altered. PEEL FARMHOUSE, S side of the road, still has some pargeting to the façade, and a stepped brick N gable-end. WOOD FARM COTTAGES are interesting in that they are a mid-C19 pair built of clay lump, but in other respects quite ordinary. THE GRANGE at Toprow is a late C18 brick house of two storeys and attic in five bays. The staircase window and the bow window to the r. have Gothick arched glazing bars to their sashes, as has the central door.

6010 ASHWICKEN

ALL SAINTS. Reached from the E by a chestnut avenue. In 1777 it was described as unfit for use because of lack of repair. Late C13 W tower, with a two-light W window with a quatrefoil vesica. Later C18 repairs seem to have reduced the bell-stage and provided big W buttresses of diaper-patterned brickwork. The pyramid roof is C19. Perp nave with C19 N windows reduced from three to two lights; S windows renewed, three lights, but on the same pattern as shown by Ladbroke *c*. 1824. The S porch has had its S front rebuilt in the C19, perhaps in 1860 when the chancel was partly rebuilt and Gothicized, with a smaller chancel arch. The interior is all Victorian, and not very inspiring. – FONT. *c*. 1850 in Dec style. – STAINED GLASS. Ordinary E window by *Ward & Hughes*, †1878.

1090 ASLACTON

ST MICHAEL. Anglo-Saxon round tower with two-light bell-openings, the lights triangle-headed on a central column. Tower arch on the simplest imposts. Traces of Saxon long-and-short work at the chancel NE corner. Perp S porch with flushwork panelling, traceried spandrels to the entrance, and a niche over. There was a bequest for it in a will of 1438. S arcade and chancel arch Perp. Three-bay arcade with octagonal piers and double-hollow-chamfered arches. The clerestory has two-light windows. Nave and aisle roofs both from the restoration in 1889–90 (£400). – FONT. C15. Octagonal, with shields. – SCULPTURE. The lectern of the pulpit is supported by a shaft with the victorious David, and David and Goliath small

below. Probably Flemish, C16. – STAINED GLASS. †1867, by
J. & J. King; a Crucifixion, the colouring better than the
drawing.

MANOR HOUSE, WSW of the church on World's End Lane.
T-plan house retaining stepped gables to the E and S ranges. In
the N gable-head are remains of C16 or C17 blocked windows
under hoodmoulds. Other windows replaced in the C19. The
late C20 roofing tiles are a pity.

WORLD'S END FARMHOUSE is more rewarding, for the late C16
timber-framed house has jetties to the first floor and to the NW
gable. Two storeys in three bays, the windows renewed. Some
roll-moulded bridging beams in a NW room.

On LOW COMMON, ½ m. NW, is EAGLE FARMHOUSE. C17
timber-framed range of one storey and attic to which has been
added to the W a mid-C19 red brick house. The same story at
BRIDGE FARMHOUSE nearby.

The VILLAGE has several more C17 houses and cottages, notably
LIMETREE HOUSE on The Street, which has a small C18 addition forming the SE wing. Four bays with original sashes set
into exposed boxes. Inside is some large-framed panelling to
hall and drawing room. The hall overmantel has a painting of
Channonz Hall, mostly demolished 1784, which is 1 m. SW. Is
there a connection, or was the painting just salvaged?

WOODROW FARMHOUSE, Woodrow Lane. The C17 timber-
framed house with a late C19 brick skin need not detain us, but
the BARN to the E seems to have started as a late C16 house, for
there are traces of diamond-mullioned windows once closed
with shutters. Externally weatherboarded, it has inside four
bays of principal jowled studs.

WINDMILL. Stump of a tower mill, ½ m. SSE. Early C19, four
storeys.

ATTLEBOROUGH   *0090*

ST MARY. A very stately church in the middle of an uncommonly
featureless little town, and it would be statelier yet if it had not
lost its aisled E arm in 1541. The central tower, however, remains,
and this is Norman, at least in its lower parts. The W, N, S and
E arches are all there, amply and strongly shafted, though part
of the shafting of the E arch is now outside the church. The capitals have, below a scallop, wide fleshy stylized leaves similar in
character to waterleaf. Of windows, two to the W are shafted
and look into the nave, one above the other. To the E the row of
Norman windows is C19. The upper part of the tower is E.E.,
with wide two-light bell-openings with a quatrefoiled circle in
plate tracery. The rest of the church is almost uniformly Dec of
about 1340 apart from the nave arcades, but the dating is complicated. There was a Norman chancel and apse, but this was
replaced by an aisled E arm for the Mortimer family, completed
only in 1405 and given over to a college, which explains its
demolition at the Dissolution. There are a N and a larger S

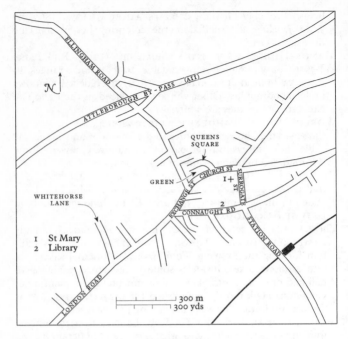

QUEENS
SQUARE

CHURCH ST

GREEN

1 +

WHITEHORSE
LANE

CONNAUGHT RD

1   St Mary
2   Library

300 m
300 yds

Attleborough

transept, all of the same style, though the s transept was founded
by Sir William Mortimer in 1297, the year in which he died, and
the N transept by Thomas Chaunticlere c. 1350. He died in 1379
leaving £20 to, presumably, alter it to accommodate his tomb.
Then the nave was altered between 1405 and 1436 by the provision of five tall bays of Perp piers, leaving the outer aisle walls
and their windows intact, and finally as late as c. 1505 money
was left 'to make cleristories', which probably refers only to a
new roof.

The leitmotif is the four-petalled flower. This occurs everywhere in original and redone windows and culminates in the
proud w window of five lights which must have been reconstructed with the arcades, so high does it reach. The N porch
was built for Sir John Ratcliffe, who died in 1441. It is two-
storeyed and faced with knapped flint. The entrance has fleurons
up one order of jambs and arch, and also shafts with little heads
as capitals. A tierceron star-vault inside. Two-light window
above with niches l., r. and over.

INTERIOR. The five-bay arcade has thin quatrefoil piers
with polygonal capitals and big wave-chamfered arches. In the
aisle walls all the way along are wall arches framing the
windows, which, as we have noted, are c14. The Perp s transept
E window must be re-set and in fact it is supposed to come
from the college E of the tower. Early c16 nave roof, repaired
by *Joseph Stannard* in 1844; it has traceried spandrels to the

cambered tie-beam braces. Stannard also renewed the aisle roofs.

FURNISHINGS. The ROOD SCREEN of Attleborough is prodigious, 52 ft long. It runs through nave and aisles and has its ribbed W coving complete, part of its E coving, and the loft parapet. The doorway has a depressed cusped ogee arch. The other bays have single lights with no tracery, only very fine cusping and subcusping at the tops. But in a number of bays the whole opening is blocked by a panel with a large painted figure. In front of these bays stood lay altars. Their height can be deduced from the height of the lower, blank parts of the painted panels. In the architectural parts also there is plenty of the old colour preserved. All this is of *c.*1480, while the arms of the sees of England and Wales on the loft date from 1615. – FONT. C15, installed in 1975. – PULPIT. Installed here from the Broadway Chapel, Westminster. Early C18 and very good, possibly by *Ver Brugen*, an assistant of Grinling Gibbons. The stair-rail has twisted balusters and carved tread-ends. – STALLS. There are two stalls, in the S aisle, with MISERICORDS with carved heads. – LECTERN. Of 1816. An eagle lectern of the traditional type, but of cast iron and not of brass, and with very untraditional steps. They have handrails l. and r., also of cast iron, and these rest on snakes and have palm-branches at the top. Formerly in St Nicholas, King's Lynn. – DOOR. To the porch staircase, traceried, early C15. – 46 WALL PAINTINGS. Above the low W arch of the crossing tower a large area of painting, most of the figures now silhouetted against the white wall. The date is presumably that of the completion of the screen. Uncovered during the restorations of 1844 –5 and covered again until 1935. The painting originally formed a huge rood composition, with figures of prophets and angels bearing the Instruments of the Passion above the horizontal arm, and feathered censing angels and other figures below. The vertical arm of the cross was destroyed when the two Romanesque windows were reopened in 1845. At the top of the wall are remains which have been interpreted as part of the Annunciation, while small figures in niches survive to the l. of the rood group. Over the S door is a fragmentary St Christopher with a kneeling female figure to the r., while a number of consecration crosses also survive. (DP) – STAINED GLASS. C14 fragments in the W window, with some complete scenes, e.g. Immaculate Conception. The bits were assembled by *J. King* in 1845 and restored. Of the various later windows the best is the E window with scenes by *J. Powell & Sons*, 1853: Nativity, Crucifixion and Ascension.

THE TOWN

Attleborough's position on the Norwich–London road stimulated the foundation of a market before 1226. The first Norfolk turnpike opened in 1695 between Attleborough and Wymondham, and the increase in traffic maintained the market's position at the end of the century, when only thirty-five market towns remained in the county out of a medieval total of 140. By 1851 Attleborough was the thirteenth largest town in Norfolk with a population of 2,300; and in 1991 it was fourteenth (population 7,600). In the early C20 the Christmas turkey market was the largest in England, but the only manufactured product was cider (the plant closed in the 1980s). The same road, which was the source of the town's modest prosperity, caused serious congestion from the 1950s until the opening of the bypass in 1985, which was the signal for rapid expansion. The new housing infill was well managed in the late 1980s, spreading mainly along the road towards Norwich. Over 1,000 new dwellings were visualized in the 1990s but far fewer actually constructed, and at the time of writing the peripheral areas of the town are becoming clogged, and dominated by raw red brick and pantiles; nothing so far built calls for a second glance.

There are two main areas, the large central site dominated by the church and bounded by the one-way roads, and Queens Square, just to the N. The latter is the natural starting-point, the Square forming the N side of a green bounded by Church Street to the S. In the GREEN itself a VILLAGE PUMP, of timber and set up to commemorate the Diamond Jubilee of 1897. At the W end at the beginning of Exchange Street is CYPRUS HOUSE, c. 1700, with stepped gables but a Georgian doorway, and inside a wide early C18 staircase. The petrol station next door is unfortunate. In the SQUARE proper are a row of minor latish Georgian buildings, of which the best is the DORIC RESTAURANT, three bays with giant pilasters terminating the front. Next to it a large gault brick bank of the 1860s which tells more of Victorians' assertiveness than of their sensitivity to the surrounding buildings.

In CHURCH STREET stands the GRIFFIN HOTEL. Mid-C17, timber-framed and with a lot of later alterations in brick. Although some studwork remains inside the best room is over the carriage entrance. This has masons' mitre panelling and is reached by a dog-leg staircase with ball-turned balusters, all of the late C17. Further S on the other side of the road INTERNATIONAL STORES has a respectable tiled shopfront of the early C20. SURROGATE STREET turns S, with THE RECTORY set back. Red, gabled, asymmetrical and dated 1839. Nothing further needs reporting until the junction with Connaught Road. Here is a stone CRIMEAN WAR MEMORIAL with the plinth acting as a milestone, the upper parts inscribed with the names of battles and carrying two wrought-iron lamp brackets. The 1856 mason was 'E. Robins of Windham' (sic), the 1985 restorer H. L. Perfitt of Diss. Mr Perfitt remade the plinth panels.

CONNAUGHT ROAD is disappointing except for the library (see below) and the picturesque THATCHED COTTAGE, a mid-C16 timber-framed T-plan house of local type. The framing is however complete and has a clasped purlin roof structure. Up into EXCHANGE STREET and, opposite Cyprus House, the former CORN HALL, 1863, grey brick, one-storeyed and unassuming. It has the usual sheaf of corn in the central pediment.

Of other houses with polite pretensions one might mention SHERBOURNE HOTEL of *c.* 1700 at the very entrance from Norwich. It has five bays in two storeys, a hipped roof, blue brick with red trim and a simple doorcase below a simpler fanlight. The early C20 extensions to the rear and the later ones to the s gable do not help it. ATTLEBOROUGH LODGE on Ellingham Road ½ m. NW has an applied timber frame and clay panels to its Tudor façade but is really a brick house of about 1840. An overmantel is dated 1843. 30 yds E is a contemporary DOVECOTE, an elongated hexagon in plan and still with its swinging ladder inside.

Nos. 1–2 PROSPECT TERRACE, at the junction of Whitehorse Lane and London Road ½ m. SW of the church. Brick skin of *c.* 1870 applied over a timber frame of *c.* 1710. The clasped purlin roof is one of the last built in Norfolk.

BRANCH LIBRARY, Connaught Road. A very pleasant, fresh little building of 1959. By *G. W. Oak*, architect to the Education Committee. Steel framed, clad in buff brick under a very shallow pitched roof, the two roof slopes of unequal length. Tall metal windows to N and S. Apart from tiny offices at the W end the interior is one big space.

ATTLEBOROUGH HALL, ½ m. N of the church. A moated site: architecturally unimportant now, but with plenty of characteristic local detail of the C16 and C17. The MOAT, about 60 ft wide and very deep, is late C16, of flint and brick supported at intervals by stepped buttresses. Over the S arm is the BRIDGE: arched and with more buttresses. Rather heavily restored. The HOUSE is timber-framed inside, but has outer brick walls of the late C17, again with additions and apart from occasional blocked windows all the details are C19. Inside are four C16 bridging beams (in the kitchen) and a C17 open-well staircase rising through three storeys into the attic: moulded string and the handrail, also moulded, on turned balusters and square newels. In various rooms C18 and C19 panelling.

Of outlying FARMHOUSES the story is of timber-framing with wattle and daub or clay lump infill, mainly C17. The best are BOROUGH FARMHOUSE, 1¼ m. SE, dated 1603 in plaster upstairs, lobby-entrance plan, a four-light diamond-mullioned window in the E wall. WESTMOOR, ¼ m. NNE of the last, is more of a cottage hiding its late C17 timber frame behind a C19 brick skin. POTMERE FARMHOUSE on Haverscroft Street (1⅝ m. SW of the church) is, like Borough Farmhouse, early C17, but more archaic in its through-passage planning. In the late C17 the upper parts of what seems to have been an open hall were floored and the tie-beams cut to allow doorways. An open hall in the early C17 is old-fashioned indeed.

BUNN'S BANK. A fragmentary earthwork with a bank on the N side some 2 m. long runs along the S edge of Attleborough and curves N across Old Buckenham and the edge of Besthorpe parishes. It has not been excavated, and no convincing date for its construction has yet been advanced (AR).

BABINGLEY

6020

St Felix. Said to be the place where St Felix landed about 636 from Burgundy and thus where Christianity entered East Anglia. The present church is not older than the C14. Like so many others in this part of Norfolk, it is ruinous. The walls stand, but the roofs are gone. It was repaired in 1849 but after the mission church was built in 1880 by the main road there was no use for it. w tower with Y-tracery in the bell-openings and mouchette tracery in the two-light w window. s aisle with a w lancet. The two-bay arcade has an octagonal pier and double-chamfered arches. The N aisle had already been done away with when the church was still in use. The E window of the chancel was large; the tracery seems to have been Curvilinear. The chancel arch is blocked and in it is a re-set window with Curvilinear tracery. s porch late C16, of brick, with an arched vault inside.

Babingley Hall. A farmhouse in a moated site refronted c. 1820 but with stepped gables and a core of c. 1610.

Moated site. 350 yds e of Babingley Hall. A much smaller square moated site now unoccupied (AR).

BAGTHORPE

7030

St Mary. Derelict. Rebuilt in 1853–4, by *W. J. Donthorn* but not one of his ambitious efforts. The contractors were the local Syderstone firm of *Harper & Sons*. Nave and short chancel. Bellcote at the E end of the nave. E.E. style with lancets, but Dec the two-light w window and a three-light E window. No chancel side windows. – FONT. Norman. Square, with angle colonnettes. Otherwise plain except for one side with interlaced knot-motif circles. – STAINED GLASS. Goodish E window in style of *C. A. Gibbs*, c. 1850–5, scenes from Life of Christ.

Immediately s of the church a row of four Late Georgian estate COTTAGES, c. 1820. Flint with brick trim. One storey and dormer attic. Pointed windows with Y-tracery.*

BANHAM

0080

St Mary. All of the first two thirds of the C14. Restored in 1863–5 for the Rev. Fardell. The w tower may be first, with Y-tracery in the bell-openings (replaced) and quatrefoiled sound-holes. Pretty recessed lead-covered spire with broaches. Long Dec chancel, unfortunately with a Victorian E window. One low-side lancet, otherwise reticulated tracery of 1865, but probably accurate. Mouchette and reticulated tracery also in the N aisle windows and in the deep s porch, which has an entrance with fleurons on one arch-moulding and ogeed niches in the s buttresses. The porch is of knapped flint. The five-bay arcades look

---

* BAGTHORPE HALL. The Georgian house of two and a half storeys has been demolished.

Late Dec, i.e. they have quatrefoil piers with thin shafts in the diagonals and polygonal capitals. Double-hollow-chamfered arches. The chancel arch is of the same type. The nave roof is impressive. It carries a date 1622, and that explains perhaps the massive barn-like timbers. Tie-beams, kingposts with struts, and queenposts. Most of the tie-beams have the characteristic sunk-quadrant mouldings of the first quarter of the C17. The E truss probably C15. The scissor-braced chancel roof is from 1865. S aisle roof dated 1802, N aisle 1858. – FONT. Plain, octagonal, C14. – FONT COVER, 1864. – SCREEN, 1875. – STAINED GLASS. Virgin and Child, C16, Flemish, put into a N aisle window only in 1962. – E window by *J. R. Clayton*, 1857, while he was with Powell's works. – Chancel N also by *Powell*, to designs by *Holiday*, 1878. – The same combination for the S aisle E window, three lights, Nativity, Baptism and Ascension, 1864. – S aisle two-light window by *Kempe & Co.*, 1914. All this glass is good. – MONUMENT. In NE chapel a Knight of the early C14, widely regarded as a representation of the founder Sir Hugh Bardolph, but since he died in 1203 it is a bit too much of an afterthought. Oak. With crossed legs, wearing a mail coif. Unfortunately painted over. It is set in a recess with an ogee arch and wave mouldings.

BANHAM HALL, ¾ m. NNE. Later C16. Timber-framed with stepped gables over the projecting wings. The wings have pedimented windows. In the recessed middle some pargeting of scroll and diaper patterns extending into the N return. Two five-light timber mullioned first-floor windows. The rear (W) elevation has a stepped gable too, and an external stack gabled back to the roof. Inside there is a timber-framed stairwell with a dog-leg stair.

The GREEN. Immediately E of the church is an uncommonly attractive green, lined with trees. Among the houses the remarkable ones are the late C15 OLD GUILDHALL on the N side, timber-framed with a jettied upper floor and a bricked-in ground floor. Converted to houses, but still with windows added in the C18. Inside is the original crown-post roof, the posts octagonal and with polygonal bases and capitals. CHURCH FARMHOUSE in the NE corner is an interesting house of the early C17, although plain for its date. Two storeys in three bays. Diamond flues to the side stacks. Through-passage plan. Apparently of brick but the brick is deceptive, because its rendered skin hides the fact that it gives way to a timber frame as it rises to the attic. The stairwell is completely timber-framed, and the roof is carried on studs with arched braces. The walls themselves become mud-and-stud. The upper purlins of the roof are clasped; curved wind-bracing. NORFOLK HOUSE at the E end of the S side has two pedimented early C19 shop windows, and then THE PRIORY, W of Norfolk House. It is three separate houses now, of C17 origins with a timber frame skinned in brick in c. 1850. Of the C17 is the chimney-stack to the W which has punched roundels, and of the early C18 the Dutch W gable. The E house (The Priory) has a good timber frame and C17 fireplaces inside.

CROWN STREET is not exciting until on the r. KING'S HEAD
COTTAGE, a late C15 timber-framed house badly restored in
1983. An open hall with the usual flooring and conversion in the
C17, this time to a lobby-entrance plan, with the inserted stack
placed in the former screens passage. What is unusual is the
survival of two pairs of octagonal queenposts in the roof with
capitals and bases. Even better is the central smoke louvre, or at
least the space for it, proving that halls really did have open
fires burning in the middle of the floor.

WASH FARMHOUSE, Wash Lane. An early C17 timber-framed
house cased in brick in the middle of the C19 and added to
(rear wing) c. 1900. A pair of upper crucks remain in the roof,
really no more than cranked timbers. There are hundreds of
these scattered throughout East Anglia dating from the first
quarter of the C17 (*see* e.g. Great Yarmouth, Vol. I).

OUTLYING FARMS. They are typically C17, almost all timber-
framed with wattle-and-daub infill and usually some brick. The
best are HILL FARMHOUSE, Winfarthing Road, and POTASH
FARMHOUSE, Haugh Road. HOME FARMHOUSE, Church
Hill, is an early C16 hall house with a C17 inserted stack placed
outside the hall, not in the passage.

BARFORD

1000

ST BOTOLPH. W tower, nave and chancel. The latter C13, the rest
Perp. There are bequests for building the tower in 1344–99, the
work more of the end than the beginning of this period.
Chancel lit through lancets but with a Perp E window. Perp
windows in the nave. To the l. and r. of the wave-moulded Perp
chancel arch are niches, three on either side, connected with
former side altars. There is a piscina to the s. The rood-loft
stair rises in a N window. C19 restorations renewed windows
and replaced roofs. – FONT. Octagonal, C14, with blind tracery.
– SCREEN. C14. Shafts with shaft-rings instead of mullions.
Ogee arches with two varieties of tracery above them. Part of
the tracery is nearly Flamboyant and would seem C16. The
wooden frieze under the tower with shields and tracery is said to
come from the panelling behind the altar.

CHAPEL STREET has some pleasant minor houses, notably
DALSTRAND and SCHOOL FARMHOUSE. The former C17,
brick over a timber frame and casement windows. The latter
has a date on the stack once read as 1694 but now too weathered
to judge. Two storeys in three bays, blocked windows and C19
casements. The door and stack in the lobby-entrance position,
and the stairs next to the stack.

BARMER

8030

ALL SAINTS. Redundant and surrounded by big trees, with not a
cottage in the immediate neighbourhood. A small church with a

wide round tower opening into the nave through an arch with late C12 responds. The chancel arch could well be Norman, even if the step-chamfering and the pointing prove to be from the 1885 restoration by *Frederick Preedy*. The rest of the chancel, and the N aisle wall, he completely rebuilt for £650. The C13 nave has internally splayed lancets and a simple corbel table. C14 the N arcade with octagonal piers and double-chamfered arches. C14 also the aisle W and E windows. – SOUTH DOOR. C19, of cast iron, with a cast iron tympanum.

BARN at BARMER FARM, dated 1754. Red brick, laid in English bond. Platband to the E side returning into the gable-ends. Honeycomb ventilation panels.*

BARNHAM BROOM   0000

ST PETER AND ST PAUL. Perp W tower with flushwork battlements and the signs of the Evangelists as pinnacles. Bequests for the tower in 1434 and for a new bell in 1440. Nave and chancel, the latter leaded in 1516. All windows are Victorian Perp from the 1850–1 restoration, which gave the church its fittings too, and the chancel roof. Horrible concrete tiles on the nave roof, of 1972. The roof itself is Perp, with the principals carried on arched braces. Angle piscina with bare shields in the bare reveals. – SCREEN. Good, C15. Dado with painted saints, including the Norfolk saints Walstan and Withburga. One-light divisions above with ogee arches and nice, delicate tracery. – MONUMENTS. Brasses to Edmund Brighteve †1467, with 12 in. demi-figure, and to John Dorant †1503 and wife, 18 in. figures (W end, on floor). – Broken coffin-lid with foliated cross (porch). – Nicholas Ganning †1680 and his son †1708. To the l. and r. of the inscription little piles of little books.

ST MICHAEL'S. The former Rectory. The C16 lobby-entrance house was given a new five-bay façade in the C18 and the plan altered. Casement windows. Veranda under a sloping roof. Hipped main roof. There is a rear block also C18 and an early C19 wing attached to the side.

BARNHAM BROOM OLD HALL. A rectangle of red brick. The solid three-storey porch and the part (four bays) of the house to its l. are early C16, built for the Chamberlayne family who came here in the mid C15. The remainder, including works to the interior which converted the house from an open hall, was done for Edward Chamberlayne c. 1614. Sold to Sir Philip Wodehouse of Kimberley in 1644 and declined into a farmhouse before finally falling derelict, but restored in the 1960s. Diapers of blue brick are not burnt but stained blue. The porch entrance has a richly moulded depressed four-centred arch, a three-light window above and a cusped two-light window in the gable, all with rendered brick surrounds. Being stepped the gable must be a C17 alteration. Polygonal angle turrets with little

* BARMER HALL. Demolished 1956.

obelisks on top, like the gable apex. To the l. are the remains of
a large hall window corresponding to the hall bay, originally
taller and with a depressed arch. Between this window and the
porch is a blocked mullioned window partly covered by the
porch. To the l. one four-light window to each floor replaces a
full-height canted bay presumably intended for a staircase, and
l. again an early C19 window to each floor. On the base of the
hall chimneystack a little bit of trefoil brick frieze. The l. end-
gable is also stepped and has an external stack. To the r. of the
porch is a two-bay extension of 1614 with pedimented mullioned and transomed windows. The room above is the great
chamber. The porch shields a splendid timber door with six
linenfold panels opening into the former screens passage with
an open-well staircase set in a turret at the back, no doubt of
1614. The hall is distinguished by early C16 ribbon-moulded
bridging beams. Pleasant four-centred doorway at the head of
the stairs with a hare and hound in one spandrel. This opens
into an inserted passage, and from here to the great chamber.
The fine PLASTERWORK is unexpected; on a part of the extended
cornice with running leaf scrolls the date 1614. The ceiling has
deep, thin ribs in interlace stars etc., with fruit, fleurs-de-lys
and a drop pendant in the middle with little figures and boars'
heads above an open boss. Other smaller pendants mark the
main intersections of the ribs.

To the w of the village is an C18 BRIDGE over the River Yare: segmental arch, brick with stone dressings. Just upstream is the
MILL HOUSE to a former watermill. Early C18 but altered.
Rendered and coloured brick, of two storeys in three bays,
extended one more bay c. 1960. Moulded brick cornice. Sashes.

BARTON BENDISH

A parish originally with three churches. All Saints was demolished
in 1788 and St Mary's declared redundant in 1976.

ST ANDREW. Flint and carstone. Inner s doorway of c. 1200, with
a pointed arch decorated by double roll mouldings, but still
billet on the hoodmould, and still Norman waterleaf capitals to
the supporting shafts. Also of c. 1200 are the N lancets, renewed
in the restoration of 1868. On the s side of the nave one tall
two-light window of the late C13, with Y-tracery and a transom
low down. The other windows Perp. Perp also the w tower with
niches in the w buttresses, the s porch with flushwork decoration, the pretty niche in the nave E wall, and the rood stair close
to it, which is specially well preserved. The chancel of the
church is c. 1330 – see the reticulated side windows, the mouchette
E window and the piscina also with Curvilinear tracery. From
1868 are the nave and chancel roofs. – BOX PEWS. Dated 1623.
Nice and simple, but with arcading to the side panels and knobs
to the gates. All the popular C17 and C18 hinges are here: cockshead, butterfly, H and HL. – TILES. C14 tiles in the sanctuary

floor with floral or geometric patterns. – STAINED GLASS.
Raphaelesque E window, c. 1880. Said to be the work of a *Mrs
Nelson* who also, in 1884, did the paintings to the l. and r. of the
window. Was she with *Heaton, Butler & Bayne* at the time, for
that is the style? – MONUMENTS. Three small tablets to the
Berneys in the nave. The family owned Barton Hall until 1935.
Captain Thomas Berney †1900 in the Boer War, as the inscrip-
tion tells us.

ST MARY. ¼ m. to the w of St Andrew. Nave and chancel only; the
tower collapsed in 1710 taking with it part of the w end of the
nave, and it was not rebuilt during the restorations of 1789,
which cost £80. The ambitious Late Norman w doorway was
transferred from All Saints in that year. It has very odd details.
The outer order of the arch exhibits normal beakheads, but on the
shafts below that are big leaves instead behaving like beakheads.
The inner order in shafts and arch consists of bobbin mouldings. Hoodmoulding with dogtooth. Bellcote erected in 1871,
with a bell of 1691. The two-light w window is from 1858. The
rest of the church has Dec elements, notably the reticulated
chancel windows, the two big two-light windows in the nave N
and s walls (Y-tracery and mouchette design), the small priest's
doorway with a crocketed ogee arch, the doorway from the
chancel into the vestry with a hoodmould on heads. One of the
heads has the typical plaiting of the hair of the later C14. The
sedilia is a simple stone step with a front decorated with quatrefoils. – BOX PEWS. Put in during the 1789 work but reduced in
the 1865 alterations. – WALL PAINTING. Enigmatic painting of
c. 1330 on the nave s wall, of a figure standing within a large
wheel above a bier; presumably a morality subject (DP). –
SCULPTURE. Two wooden reliefs of steep triangular shape,
each with a well-carved angel. What were they the wings of?

BARTON HALL. An Elizabethan brick house of two storeys
remodelled by *James & Turner* of Norwich in 1856. The s front
has three bays with stepped gables to the two dormers and a
stepped gable to the E wing, the latter the only one of the C16.
Fenestration of C19 cross casements. Bold quadruple-flued
ridge stacks.

On Church Road, next to St Andrew's Church, is THE OLD
POST OFFICE, dated 1713, brick, carstone and thatch and a
little too modernized for comfort. Brick tumbling in the w gable-
head, which is early for a cottage of this type.

EARTHWORKS. W of Abbey Farm, earthworks relating to a
sunken way and ditched toft boundaries show that the village
was once much longer in medieval times. (AR)

DEVIL'S DYKE. *See* Narborough.

BARWICK   8030

ST MARY. s of Barwick House, in a field, only overgrown foundations.

BARWICK HOUSE. Of the 1740s when it was owned by Robert

Glover. The brick of the S façade is laid in header bond. Four giant pilasters and a platband. The windows and central porch are C19, which is a shame. Hipped roof with three pedimented dormers. The pair of stacks have pointed blind panels. Various late C19 additions to E and N. To the NE stands a superior BARN, dated 1742. Six bays wide with two cart entrances in transepts and sashes and dormer windows lighting the hay-loft. The dormers have circular windows and Dutch gables. The STABLES further NE are dated 1748, red brick, five bays of carriage doors, three of which are blocked. Platband and moulded cornice.

BAWBURGH

St Mary and St Walstan. The round tower has a conical roof, and a C13 arch to the nave. Chancel E window of three lights with intersecting tracery and lancets in the N and S walls. Two are cinque-cusped. This goes with the date 1309 reported in the *Gent. Mag.* (in 1763) for the rebuilding of the chancel. In 1320 the E window was glazed and the chancel re-roofed, but more work was at least contemplated when money was left in 1492 towards the 'new chancel'. The nave has Perp windows and stepped brick W and E gables. The latter may be connected with repairs and re-roofing done in 1633 (also according to the *Gent. Mag.*). The S porch roof is arch-braced. Inside, on the N side of the nave, the arch to a former N chapel, probably the chapel of St Walstan, a local Norfolk saint, †1016. His Holy Well is placed to the N (*see* Church Farm below). – SCREEN. Only fragments from the C15. – BENCH ENDS. Some, with C15 poppyheads. – POOR BOX. A C17 turned baluster. – STAINED GLASS. Fragments of the C15 in the N and S windows including heads. – BRASSES. (Robert Grote †1500; nave.) Also (chancel floor) Thomas Tyard †1505, in his shroud, 2 ft long. William Rechers †1531, with a chalice. Philip Tenison †1660, also in a shroud; 14 in. long.

Church Farmhouse, NW of the church. Brick. The back has C15 buttresses and two blocked arched windows. Angle buttress at the NW corner. Of the C17 are the window reveals to the façade, now fitted with C19 cross casements. The E gable has a stack rising into three polygonal shafts. Winder staircase with a polygonal newel post. Roof of diminished principals and clasped purlins. St Walstan's Well is in the grounds.

The village. Church Street runs E towards the hamlet. Flint Cottage and Chapel View are both C17 lobby-entrance houses of brick and flint, variously altered. Child's Terrace is a C17 row with some C15 material including a blocked arched window in a gable wall. The restoration of c. 1970 was a bit drastic. Crossing over the River Yare and a little to the W the King's Head on Hart's Lane. The earlier part is the C17 lobby-entrance range edge-on to the street: one storey and dormer attic, re-faced, C19 windows, stepped gable to the S. The fireplaces and the stairs by the stack remain. The street front is an early C19 addition; the brick and weather-boarded squash courts to the w are late C20. 200 yds E to HALL FARM PLACE off NEW ROAD, a small development of new houses where BAWBURGH HALL stood until 1963. It was dated 1634. It had two square two-storey buildings of ashlar known, for no valid reason, as the Slipper House (i.e. the house where pilgrims to St Walstan's Well would deposit their shoes) and the Hermit's House, both now garden buildings of the new housing. There is no evidence that one of the two was a dove-cote. They probably date from the same time as the Hall, but much use is made of materials from a church. HERMIT'S HOUSE has a C14 plinth, a pyramid roof with a figurative pin-nacle and immediately below it a fine leaf frieze and a quatrefoil frieze. There is on each side one oval recess. The smaller SLIPPER HOUSE has two doors with wave mouldings and must have been a summerhouse. It has wooden windows with ovolo-moulded mullions and transoms and four high gables with small round recesses or blind windows in them. There is also a band of circles round the initials L. S. To whom do they refer? No. 4 Hall Farm Place is of brick and flint, with ashlar, proba-bly C16 in origin but converted to a house c. 1980 with the attendant re-fenestration. This also has the initials L. S. in the stone end wall. Re-set in it are hoodmoulds of windows and two big gargoyles.

LODGE FARMHOUSE, a little further E. Early C17 brick house with C19 rear additions. The E front with disturbed brick, the C19 sashes set within C17 frames and under pediments. Stepped end-gables. Good plaster overmantels, one with arms of Wodehouse impaling Yelverton, which seems to suggest 1625–35. Wild men with clubs and cresting of birds, helms etc. A first-floor four-centred fireplace has arms of Charles I in its overmantel.

BARROW. About 1 m. N of the village is a large bowl barrow, diameter 145 ft, height 4 ft 6 in.

BAWSEY

6010

ST JAMES. Ruinous since before 1770. Carstone and stone dress-ings. Prominently placed on an eminence N of Church Farm. Of the Norman central tower only the N and E walls remain to full height. One original N window and remains of shafted two-light upper windows. The W arch was shafted to the W and double-shafted to the E, only one shaft surviving. It has zigzag decoration in the arch. The E arch is unmoulded and shafted only to the W. It is worth mentioning that the surviving quoins of the tower exhibit unmistakable long-and-short work below the Norman bell-stage. The nave has early masonry too, but no features. The chancel S wall stands and seems C15.

ST MICHAEL. See Mintlyn, p. 544.

CHURCH FARMHOUSE. Two storeys in five bays, the r. bay pro-jecting. The two l. bays are a C19 addition to the smaller early C18 house.

MOATED SITE. A fine rectangular moated site in a wood ½ m. SW
of the church. (AR)

7000   BEACHAMWELL

With Caldecote (*see* p. 239) there were here four parish churches
in the Middle Ages distant from one another a mile or less.

ST MARY. Anglo-Saxon round tower. The lights of the two-light
bell-openings have arched (S and E) or triangular (N and W)
heads. The latter have a central baluster with rough capitals, and
on the N a piece of interlace has been reused. The tower arch is
completely unmoulded and has no imposts. Above it, and not
in line with it, a window (or doorway) into the tower. It may be
that the tower arch is a former W door and the tower is itself an
addition. Perp top to the tower, octagonal and with blind flushwork tracery of the same design as the open traceried windows
on each alternate facet. Saxon also the model long-and-short
work at the NW quoin of the nave, which means that part of the
N nave wall at least is Saxon too. The body of the church is
thatched. The low S arcade has two bays with Early Perp piers
(the curved projections still have fillets) and double wave
mouldings in the arches. On the pier at the SW end interesting
GRAFFITI. A demon and, higher up, a record of quantities and
prices of materials supplied to the masons. The two E bays are
of 1832, when the E bay of the S aisle was added 'by' *John Motteux*
(inscription). The exterior of the aisle is of knapped flint.
Sumptuous doorway from the chancel into a former vestry.
Mid C14. Nice brick N porch with a C16 stepped gable. The
inner N doorway is double wave-moulded. – PULPIT. Simple,
Jacobean. – CHEST on legs. Of iron, designed by *John Motteux*
and made by *Joseph Bramah* of London, the famous lock-
makers, in 1835. It has six octagonal shafts and opening sides. –
MONUMENTS. Brass to a priest, late C14; 20 in. figure; another
to John Grymeston †1430 with a demi-figure of 13 in. (both
chancel floor).

ST JOHN, ¾ m. NW. The unbuttressed W tower and three crags of
the N wall stand.

ALL SAINTS, ½ m. SSW. The ruins of the chancel E wall and parts
of the chancel side walls finally collapsed in 1989. In the rubble
was found part of a late Saxon wheel-headed cross.

To the N and NW of St Mary are pairs of identical C19 COTTAGES
of gault brick set about The Green. Built about 1815–20 probably for John Motteux †1843 in old age. The houses have, or
had, two storeys and two doors, with cast-iron casement windows. Nos. 26–27 and Nos. 28–29 are best preserved.

BEACHAMWELL HALL was enlarged for John Motteux *c.* 1800,
but was burnt in 1902 and rebuilt on the same lines in 1904–6
by *Wimperis & Best*. Two storeys and attics, five-bay façade with
the centre bay slightly advanced, rusticated quoins. Big shell
hood over the door. The whole is in the late C17 fashion with

hipped roofs, dormers and strong, plain stacks. The seven-bay garden façade has advanced end bays. The STABLES and OUT-BUILDINGS are of the late C18.

BOWL BARROWS of the village, known as Hangour Hill, is visible from the road in a ploughed field. (JW)

DEVIL'S DYKE. *See* Narborough.

BEAUPRÉ HALL *see* OUTWELL

BEDINGHAM

2090

ST ANDREW. Possibly started as a cruciform C12 church (see the imposts of the N aisle chapel) which received nave aisles and a new chancel in the late C13. One C12 doorway seems to have been re-set in the N aisle and the other in the chancel. Some minor Dec work to the S chapel and finally both chancel and nave given a late Perp clerestory and the S aisle Perp windows. C12 round tower with later octagonal top, C15 bell-openings and battlements. Flushwork tracery patterns on the unwindowed facets. The semicircular arch to the nave has been filled in. The chancel has a fine late C12 priest's doorway with colonnettes, varied mouldings and dogtooth decoration, an E window of four lights with intersecting tracery, a S window with tracery of a triangle above two lights, and inside, a drop-sill sedilia. The piscina is of the angle type with a Purbeck marble column and, oddly enough, there is a matching one without function W of the sedilia. In the late Middle Ages the chancel was given a clerestory. The N aisle has another late C12 door-way: two orders of colonnettes, stiff-leaf capitals, and a roll-and keel-moulded arch. E aisle window of three stepped lancet lights under one arch. The W window has Y-tracery. S aisle with one W lancet and a transeptal E chapel which is a little later than the rest; though it has intersecting tracery in the E window, the S window is reticulated, i.e. Dec. Yet the S arcade seems somewhat earlier than the N arcade. The former has quatrefoil piers, the latter octagonal piers. Both arcades have double-chamfered arches. The chancel arch and the arches into the aisle chapels belong to the type of the S arcade, but the N arch has C12 imposts. Perp the S aisle and the doubled clerestory windows, i.e. six as against three arcade bays. These windows, and the chancel clerestory, may relate to work known to be going on in the early 1520s. Perp S porch. Roofs replaced in the late C19 restoration.

FONT. On two steps, the upper quatrefoiled. Against the stem four lions, against the bowl the signs of the Evangelists, a lion, an angel and a flower. – PULPIT. Later C17, with odd-shaped panels and with garlands down the angles. – SCREEN. C15. Wide one-light divisions, richly crocketed ogee arches, close panel tracery. In the spandrels four-light transomed minia-ture windows. – BENCHES. Some with poppyheads, one with a

man's and one with a woman's head. On one there is a flower as
decoration of the arm. – INSCRIPTION. Ornate inscription on the
back of one bench. Perhaps from the screen. – BOX PEWS. In
the aisles. – COMMUNION RAIL. Early C18, with twisted balusters
and panelled square newels. – SCULPTURE. Three stone bosses
of unknown provenance (N aisle E). – STAINED GLASS. In the N
aisle E window fragments of C14 and C15 glass, restored in 1961.
The roundels come from King's College, Cambridge. – MONU-
MENTS. Tablets to the Stone family, chancel N wall, †1762–
1829, with urns in front of obelisks. Slabs to the same family in
the aisles.*

HALL FARMHOUSE, ½ m. ESE. Of brick. The house of *c.* 1700 has
altogether five shaped gables. A pair of them crowns the S front,
which is of four bays. The windows are cross casements and have
raised brick frames. First-floor platbands. The shaped gable to
the W front is in an advanced central bay and its windows again
have raised brick frames. Brick pilasters. Two lower, and later,
porches r. and l. also with shaped gables.

PRIORY FARMHOUSE. C16. Brick and parts at least of a timber
frame. The E front is only two bays wide with a central C19
doorway. The S gable-head has octagonal finials above kneelers
and a stack with three octagonal shafts. The main range runs
W from here, its S front with an underbuilt timber-framed
porch and, r., a rebuilt doorway with an arched head. Ridge
stack with three octagonal shafts. Too many C20 patches and
windows.

YEOMAN'S COTTAGE, Hall Road, as altered externally as Priory
Farmhouse, has a C19 red brick skin and C20 windows. But
inside is a C16 timber frame complete apart from the roof. Jowled
principal studs carry arched braces to the tie-beams. The first
floor evidently an insertion, so we have a hall house on the
through-passage plan. Various blocked mullioned windows.

OSBORN'S FARMHOUSE, School Road, was a slightly earlier
timber-framed C16 hall house, for the roof has one queenpost
truss to the E, the rest replaced and raised *c.* 1620: clasped
purlins with upper crucks. Over this higher part is a stack with
four diamond shafts. Again there are mullioned windows mixed
with C20 casements.

MOAT FARMHOUSE, on Upgate Street to the S. Another timber-
framed hall house cased in C19 brick, here retaining the screens
passage and even one service doorway to the N. The open
hall was S of this, inevitably given a C17 floor. It still has three
bays of a queenpost roof with arched braces to the collars, of
c. 1470–80.

BEESTON

ST MARY. The best church by far in this strangely obscure and
inaccessible area. Mostly Dec. The aisles embrace the tower.

---

* The Stones had Bedingham Hall, demolished 1829.

This is Dec to the bell-openings, but a new Perp bell-stage was added and a spire, recessed behind battlements (rebuilt in 1873). Inside, however, the tower arch is more C13 than C14. Dec chancel with a proud five-light window with reticulated tracery. Dec N and S windows of the same time but with tracery in the reticulation units (cf. Great Walsingham, Vol. 1). Dec N porch with some chequer flushwork. The Dec clerestory had circular windows, but about 1400 a new clerestory was built, so high that it could be given an E window (three-light Perp tracery under four-centred heads). The date is ascertained by the gift by a guild of eight clerestory windows, i.e. the glass, in 1410. The interior now poses an interesting problem. It is impressive, wide and high, and with its tiled floor and its untreated old oak very moving. The problem is this. The tall and slender piers of the four-bay arcade have a section well within the Dec tradition, but bases and capitals one would call Perp. Cautley in fact believed in a rebuilding of the arcades, which is probably exactly what happened at nearby Great Walsingham, where the arcade arches are of the same type. It seems that there was an ambitious church of about 1350 which, for some reason, had new arcades fifty years later. The arches of the arcade have wave mouldings sloping into short vertical pieces at the start of the arches. The chancel arch is identical in its mouldings with the arcade piers.

The roofs of Beeston Church are a special pleasure. In the nave there are hammerbeams on very tall wall-posts with fine carved figures under nodding ogees. The hammerbeams are connected by shallow longitudinal arched braces. They altern-ate with short horizontal pieces with figures against them, sup-porting principals. These pieces proceed from the apexes of the longitudinal arched braces. The N aisle roof is similar. The chancel roof is domestic-looking C17: arch-braced and with wind-bracing to the purlins.

FURNISHINGS. FONT COVER. Perp, simple, with crockets up the edges. It was here by 1536 because there was a bequest to Wendling in that year to make a font cover like the one at Beeston. The FONT itself is a plain octagonal C14 piece. – PULPIT. Datable to 1592. With segmental arches on unusually long pilasters. – SCREENS. Painted on the rood screen twelve defaced figures. Tall ogee arches. The top framing is missing. – Two PARCLOSE SCREENS, that of the N aisle of superb quality, wide, thickly crocketed ogee arches and close tracery. The S screen is simpler. – BENCHES. Many, with C15 poppyheads. Figures on some of the arms. Some backs pierced with little quatrefoils and arches. The blocks of benches taper off towards the W to leave space for the font. – PAINTING. On the E and W walls of the nave some bold ornamental motifs. Datable to the beginning of the C17. – STAINED GLASS. One Perp canopy left in the E window. Other windows with plain C19 coloured glass.

A well-preserved MOATED SITE borders the churchyard on the S side. (AR)

BEETLEY

St Mary Magdalene. Mainly Dec. Fine mid-C14 w window in
the tower. The crenellated parapet and rebuilding of the belfry
can be fixed by bequests to 1500–31. Y-tracery bell-openings.
The w door with its four-centred arch may also be of this time.
Wave-moulded tower arch. Dec s aisle windows. Good chancel
Dec e window and side windows. The arcade of the former N
aisle seems to have been in the mouldings of its quatrefoil piers
like the chancel arch, and both were Dec too. The aisle was
taken down in the late C18 and wooden Y-tracery windows put
in. Piscina with a cusped ogee arch; of the sedilia only little preserved. – FONT. Octagonal, Perp. Stem with tracery and shields,
bowl with shields in cusped fields. – FONT COVER. Early C17;
turned central baluster. – WEST SCREEN. C17, turned balusters.
BEETLEY HALL, 500 yds N. Two storeys, six bays, with early C18
brickwork but the windows C19. Good C19 iron veranda, its
roof supported on scrolled braces.
OLD HALL, 500 yds NW of the church. C16 timber-framed house
faced with brick and extended N in the C17. Two storeys and
attic. The front has a central full-height porch terminating in a
late C17 shaped gable. Ovolo-moulded arched entrance, mullioned and transomed windows. Main elevation with two C18
mullioned windows surviving, other windows later. In the N
gable a blocked diamond-mullioned window. Inside the gable is
a winder staircase.
MOATED SITE. A rectangular moated site marks the low-lying
position of a former manor house in a meadow e of Spong
Bridge. (AR)

BERGH APTON

Bergh Apton is a scattered place, without a coherent centre, but
with many houses requiring notice.

St Peter and St Paul. Much altered in 1838, when the battlements and the N transept were added and the s transept and
chancel remodelled by *John Brown*, who was the then Diocesan
(and county) surveyor. The chancel still has arched windows.
Those in the transepts have intersecting tracery, the nave
Y-tracery. Late C14 w tower, with chequered brick and flint in
the battlements and a two-light w window. Roofs with arched
braces. – WEST GALLERY, presumably Brown's, has traceried
panels. – FONT. C15. Octagonal. Against the stem four lions and
four statuettes. Against the bowl the signs of the four Evangelists
and four elegant standing angels. – STAINED GLASS. e window
by *Charles Kempe*, *c.* 1910. – A s window of 1885 and a N window
of 1896, both by *Ward & Hughes*. The newer one has a Good
Shepherd in an architectural frame. Interesting but terrible.
BERGH APTON HALL. Of *c.* 1700, brick, the N front of seven bays
and two storeys. Giant pilasters at the angles and at the angles

of the three-bay centre, all with moulded capitals. Windows with wooden crosses (replacements) and raised lintel-stones, that in the centre above the door enriched with a rusticated surround. Hipped roof. The returns have platbands. The staircase has turned balusters and square newels with fielded panels.

BERGH APTON HOUSE, Church Road. An early C19 house, whitewashed and thatched, with intersecting, Gothick, glazing bars to the sashes. The stacks in the Tudor manner.

APTON MANOR (formerly Street Farmhouse), The Street. The back is early C17 with a mullioned window under a gable. The s front has a late C17 porch of two storeys with a shaped gable and an oval window in it. Rusticated brick quoins. Round-headed doorway; window with brick rustication. The casements to the façade are all replacements. Lozenge shafts to the ridge stack. The N front has two full-height projections, each with a stack, separated by an outshut with a door l. and r. (cf. Bramerton Grange). Good chimneys.

THE OLD RECTORY, The Street, opposite the last. Late C18, rendered and whitewashed. Two storeys in five bays, the centre three slightly advanced. Porch on square unfluted columns, stringcourses between the floors, elaborated window surround over the porch. Two bow windows to the rear, of one and two storeys. The COACH HOUSE attached to the NE has three double doors under elliptical arches and a slated veranda on fluted cast-iron columns.

MANOR HOUSE, The Street. Pleasant house of gault brick under a shallow hipped roof. The w front has three wide bays each with two sashes, the centre bay advanced and accommodating the entrance portico: two Doric columns *in antis*. Its flat roof has an iron balustrade. The elevation is closed by corner pilasters. E front has only one sash in the first-floor outer bays.

WASHINGFORD HOUSE, 1 m. N of the church on Cookes Road. The s front has lower courses of brick of *c*. 1600, but the rest is early C19. Very plain, in six bays, two and a half storeys (the central canted bay is C20, reusing a tripartite sash). The tall chimneystack with three octagonal shafts, one of them of decorated brick, goes back to the C16 or early C17. The other stack is C19.

HOLLY LODGE FARMHOUSE, Church Road. The N front has four bays and two porches, one with a C17 stepped gable. Main E gable also stepped. This end is the earlier part, having a tie-beam with sunk quadrant mouldings, i.e. *c*. 1600–25. The remainder remodelled. The COTTAGE 80 yds SW is an early C19 *cottage orné*, of coursed ashlar, which must be reused. Also reused is the C16 four-centred arch over the E door and in a dormer some miniature C14 vaulting.

Nos. 54–55 BUSSEY BRIDGE. A pair of Gothick cottages of *c*. 1810, whitewashed and thatched. Even the dormer windows have intersecting tracery.

CHURCH ROAD. An estate built for the former Loddon District Council by *Tayler & Green* in 1951–6, enlarging a pre-war development of semi-detached pairs. The houses gather round a small triangular tree-studded green, perfectly matched in scale to their rural setting. The architects developed their own attractive and characteristic style after 1950, and provided terraces of one- and two-storeyed cottages contrasting with bungalows arranged on a different axis. Colour changes from red to yellow and blue brick. Even a little bargeboarding occurs to make the group prettier. The rainwater pipes are carried down diagonally from the projecting eaves to the ground close to the house, an arrangement also used for decorative purposes. Those that have been sold sport uPVC windows. The estate anticipated certain aspects of the Essex Design Guide of 1973 and the 'Norfolk Cottage Vernacular' of the 1970s (*see* Introduction, pp. 165–6).

0090
BESTHORPE

ALL SAINTS. A fine, uniform building of the early C14. The W tower has foiled circular sound-holes and Y-tracery in the bell-openings (restored). N and S transepts, the three-light S window of the S transept with mouchette tracery. The chancel may be a little earlier than nave and transepts, as its later-looking feature, the five-light mouchette-traceried E window with ogee motifs, i.e. altogether Curvilinear in style, dates from the restoration of 1876 and is by *J. B. Pearce*. The side windows are of cusped intersecting tracery, more of *c.* 1315. Inside the chancel, however, the sedilia and piscina have ogee arches contained under a row of four gables. The sedilia rise up into the window. The S transept is more lavishly appointed than the chancel. It has a broad niche l. of the E window and a narrower one r. of it, and in addition a big piscina: ogee motifs, steep crocketed gables, buttress shafts. – STAINED GLASS. C15 glass collected in detached frames. – MONUMENT. Sir William Drury †1639, attributed to *John* and *Matthias Christmas* (GF). Alabaster. He rests on his elbow on a half-rolled-up mat in military dress. His wife, l., and children, r., kneel, facing him, outside paired Tuscan columns. Superstructure ending in a semicircular gable. In the predella two reclining babies and a skull. – SCREEN. 1931.
BESTHORPE HALL. Not exciting considering its late C16 origins, and this due to the various alterations. Brick. The main (E) façade is from 1881 and has a tall porch. The S gable remains in English-bond C16 brick with pedimented cross casements to each floor and the attic, the windows themselves replaced. Alterations to the W front in 1965 and a wing added in 1891. Two nice C18 GARDEN PIERS of brick with big pineapples. To the W of the house is a walled area said to be a TILTING GROUND. N and S walls of C16 brick, and parts of an E wall. Polygonal engaged columns mark the entrance to kitchen gardens, and there is a C17 SUMMERHOUSE.
CHURCH HOUSE, at the E end of the village, on Silver Street. Partly timber-framed, skinned in brick in the late C17. Giant pilasters to the edges of the façade and N return, the latter under a shaped gable containing round and oval windows, i.e. late C17.

Sunk-quadrant mouldings to ceiling joists suggest the early C17 for the timber-framed house. Odd that it should have been given a brick skin so early; probably a change of ownership. Also on Silver Street MAYFIELD FARMHOUSE, a C16 timber-framed house with roll and hollow mouldings to the principal spine beam. From the front it is a two-storey, three-bay early C19 brick house given its new skin at the conventional time.

BESTHORPE OLD HALL. The same again. Roll-moulded C16 bridging beams elaborating the timber frame and a dull C18 brick skin. It does have a two-storey C16 porch with a four-centred entrance with colonnettes.

BUNN'S BANK. *See* Attleborough.

BEXWELL 6000

ST MARY. Norman round tower of carstone with a doorway to the ringing chamber and, above, a ring of ten blocked lancets. This is reminiscent of nearby West Dereham and distant Haddiscoe, both of which are early C12. The top of the tower is late medieval and octagonal (money was left for the 'steeple' in 1517). The arch to the nave is large, with imposts that become stringcourses to the w nave wall, an early C12 feature as well. In the nave one Norman N window with a double splay, one blocked s window. Also, facing one another, two very long lancets, but these date from the thorough 1874 restoration as does the stepped lancet E window, which replaced a four-light window with intersecting tracery, according to Ladbroke's drawing. Pretty niche above the C14 s doorway. Stepped chancel sedilia and cinquefoiled piscina, knocked about. – PULPIT. High Victorian (1874?), of stone, by *W. Lawrie* of Downham Market. Marble colonnettes to the sides and an alabaster relief of Christ and the Cross. – FONT. Octagonal, C17. – STAINED GLASS. In the Norman N window one small Perp head of Christ from the C15. – MONUMENT. Francis Bachcroft †1658. Tablet of black and white marble, definitely post-Jacobean in style. Less so is the tablet to Henry Bexwell on the opposite wall, †1654, with a book and an hourglass.

BEXWELL HALL. A stone BARN to the N of the church seems to be a late C15 gatehouse to the former manor of the Bexwells. As much brick as stone in the construction. The E face has a gateway between two polygonal turrets. To its r. and l. are mullioned windows under straight hoods, all blocked. To the w side the gateway is flanked by cusped windows and mullioned windows, again under square heads. Inside, a fireplace can be distinguished, and also a staircase bay to the s.

BICKERSTON 0000
½ m. NE of Barnham Broom

ST ANDREW. Some fragments in a field by the road.

BILLINGFORD
Near Diss

1070

ST LEONARD. N of the windmill up a rising track to the Hall. W
tower cut down to nave level and given a pyramid roof. Three-
light Perp W window. The S nave windows are Perp, all those to
the N side of nave and chancel Dec. The restoration of 1881 left
many marks, particularly the rebuilding of the chancel E wall.
The medieval nave roof is scissor-braced, except that every
so often a beam of bigger scantling is used and supported by
modest arched braces. Embattled wall-plate. – FONT. Octagonal,
Perp. Four lions against the stem, the signs of the Evangelists
and demi-figures of angels with shields against the bowl. –
FONT COVER. C17. – PULPIT. Plain, Jacobean, with a tripartite
back-panel and a small tester with pendants. – SCREEN. C15. Of
broad one-light divisions with ogee arches. – BENCH ENDS.
C15, with a border of fleurons and poppyheads. – DOORS. The
S door has fleurons on the battens, the door to the former upper
storey of the porch has tracery with ogee arches. – WALL
PAINTINGS. Late medieval painting, high up on the S wall. The
subject is unidentified, but includes at top r. a small scene of a
figure confronting three black figures at the entrance to a building (DP). – STAINED GLASS. Bits of late C14 glass in the chancel
and nave windows.

BILLINGFORD HALL, 200 yds N. To the N is a C17 timber-framed
range with a lozenge-shaped stack, but to this was added a late
C18 house facing S. Red brick. Two storeys in three bays, central
reeded doorcase. 70 yds E is an C18 brick DOVECOTE. Square,
with a pyramid thatched roof.

WINDMILL, to SSW of church on the Common, easily seen from
afar. 1860. Tower-mill with cap, four sails and fan; some machinery inside. The first mill to be restored by the Norfolk Windmills
Trust, from 1965, but subject to a bewildering sequence of
repairs (e.g. two sets of stocks since then). The present stocks
by *John Lawn*, 1991. Ceased working by wind only in 1956.
Open to the public in summer.

GROVE FARM COTTAGES, Upper Street, ¾ m. NE. C16 timber-
framed hall house with a wonderful six-light dais window cut in
half internally for the C17 floor. Also of the C17 a new wing to
the SW, still showing two diamond-mullioned windows. Much
else is C20.

CORNER COTTAGE, THE WHITE HOUSE and ORCHARD
COTTAGE at Upper Street are all C17 timber-framed cottages.

BIRCHAM NEWTON

7030

ALL SAINTS. Small, of the C12 and late C13, but much renewed.
Nave and chancel of two bays each. Unbuttressed W tower with
lancets, chancel with Y-tracery and intersecting tracery, i.e. of
c. 1300–10. S door of the same date. Mid C12, but restored, is
the round-headed chancel arch. Trefoil-headed C13 piscina. –

FONT. C12, tapering sides. BOX PEWS, dated 1858, with (revived) poppyheads and a double-decker PULPIT. – MONUMENT. Interesting C14 effigy of a priest. The canopy is a nodding ogee arch. In the spandrels sun and moon, a motif usual in tympana, but unusual in monuments. The priest is carved in a lower relief than one would expect for *c.* 1330.

BIRCHAM TOFTS   7030

ST ANDREW. Ruinous, i.e. roofless since 1952. Much luscious elder outside and inside the church. Simple C13 doorway. W tower and nave. The tower has an early C19 window and brick mullioned bell-openings and a Perp arch towards the nave. The chancel was pulled down a long time ago.

BITTERING   9010

ST PETER. Entirely on its own. Nave and chancel under one roof. Twin ashlar bellcote on the W gable perhaps of the C17. The rest E.E. but altered C15. The E end of the chancel has a group of three stepped lancets. On the other sides of the church lancets and two-light square-headed windows. Double-chamfered N and S doorways. Angle buttresses to E end, with plenty of brick repairs. The chancel has an E angle piscina too. C19 kingpost roof. – SCREEN. Perp, plain. – PULPIT and some BENCHES have Jacobean panels and knobs, and in the pulpit strapwork. – STAINED GLASS. In the chancel E lancets a Crucifixion by *Lydall Armitage, c.* 1925.*

The church was in the Middle Ages part of a manorial group. Between the church and the road was a moated manor house demolished in the early C19 (the moat remains choked with trees) and replaced by Bittering Hall, S of the church, itself demolished in 1981 and the land given to gravel pits.

MANOR FARMHOUSE, ¼ m. N. C17 lobby-entrance house of flint with brick dressings. All brick to W parts, rebuilt late C18. C18 cross casements. Big stack still with multiple octagonal flues.

BITTERING PARVA. To the N of the road the earthworks of the deserted village of Bittering Parva are strung along the S side of a small E–W stream. (AR)

BIXLEY   2000

ST WANDREGESELIUS, a unique dedication in England. He was abbot of Fontanella in Normandy in the C7. The church has an unbuttressed W tower from the early C14 which had repairs, or a partial reconstruction, in the early C16 – money was left in 1526 and 1535. The tower was restored in 1868 and the rest of

* CHAPEL OF ST NICHOLAS. 1⅝ m. E, on the road to East Bilney. Foundations no longer visible.

the church completely rebuilt. Nave and chancel in one, the fenestration a mixture of lancets and Curvilinear tracery, the S transept with a triangular window. The four-part roof over the crossing looks like a Teulon design. – FOUNDATION STONE. Commemorates the rebuilding of the church by William of Dunwich, Bailiff of Norwich, in 1272. – MONUMENTS. Those to the Ward family are the high point of the church. The Wards lived at Bixley Old Hall.* Edward Ward †1583. Kneeling effigies facing one another across a prayer desk, in a field defined by a pair of Ionic pilasters. Their nine children crowd behind them. Four-centred arch but a big pediment. – Sir Edward Ward †1742. A wall monument signed by *Robert Page*. Tablet with two Corinthian columns supporting a broken segmental pediment. Three cherubs' heads at the foot. – Sir Randall Ward †1762. Wall monument with two mourning cherubs and an open pediment. – Susan, Countess Rosebery †1771. Sarcophagus and obelisk.

BIXLEY MILL, Loddon Road. An extraordinary eleven-storey tower mill when built for Charles Clare in 1838. Reduced to seven then five in the C20.

Earthworks of the DESERTED VILLAGE lie in three fields E of the church. Two N–S streets are flanked by five dispersed tofts (AR).

HENGE MONUMENT. 1¼ m. NW of Arminghall is the site of the Neolithic or Early Bronze Age henge monument first discovered from the air in 1929 and excavated in 1935. The monument is visible now as a circular depression marking the single ditch with minor and slight outer banks. It measures 120 ft in diameter, and has an entrance causeway on the SW. Within was a circular setting of stout oak logs. It is radiocarbon dated to about 3200 B.C. and was probably the focal point of a large barrow group now no longer visible extending into the parishes of Trowse Newton and Caistor St Edmund. (JW) The presence of Iron Age material in the ditch silting suggests some later reuse prior to the Roman occupation. For some of the dozens or so barrows in the surrounding area, *see* Trowse Newton, Vol. I.

BLACKBOROUGH PRIORY and
BLACKBOROUGH END *see* MIDDLETON

2000

BLACKFORD HALL
1¼ m. E of Stoke Holy Cross

The HOUSE now is a quite ordinary C18 composition of two storeys and three bays. However the CHAPEL in all probability belonged to a former mansion situated inside the moat. Part of the moat remains to the N. Of *c.* 1300, it was converted to a house in the C16 and partly rebuilt in 1703. Of the first date the

---

* BIXLEY OLD HALL was demolished at the beginning of the C20 but in its latest form was one of the works of *Robert Buxton*, the amateur architect. He designed the house for Sir Edward Ward before 1719.

E window of three lights with intersecting tracery and two lancets on the N side. In the S side, re-set, is a Norman roll-moulded arch with zigzag decoration at r. angles. In the N wall opposite is a C16 timber door in the position of a through-passage door.

BLO NORTON   0070

St ANDREW. Dec w tower of only two stages lit through a timber Y-tracery w window from the restoration of 1876–9 (£700). The tall tower arch inside still looks C13. Nave and chancel in one, also unfortunately so inside. Timber-framed C16 N porch, the four-centred entrance with floriated spandrels. The window shapes in the chancel, pointing to the end of the C13, though renewed, may well be correct. Ladbroke shows only one lancet in the N wall and the E window differing from the present triple lancets, which have glass of 1863. Dec windows and s doorway in the nave, the windows with hollow-chamfered rere-arches inside. – FONT. Octagonal, with blank window designs, shield and quatrefoil motifs, also a six-cornered star. C14, though it may have been re-cut in the C17. – ROYAL ARMS. Painted, under the tower, of William and Mary, but with the arms of James I – a bit of recycling. – STAINED GLASS. E window, 1863, has a Resurrection, Crucifixion and Ascension by *William Wailes*. – MONUMENT. S nave, to Duleep Singh †1926; hideous. – CURIOSUM. Two collecting shoes, i.e. little shovels in the shape of a dustpan. Dated 1610, but made as replicas in 1910.

BLO NORTON HALL. Timber-framed L-shaped house with brick end walls of the mid C16, enlarged and much altered in Queen Elizabeth's time. The only date is 1585, on a terracotta panel on the external kitchen chimneystack to the E front. Immediately N of this the timber frame is exposed, as it is to the W front. The date has the initials EHB, presumably standing for Elizabeth and Henry Brampton, the mother and son who then owned the house. From the first phase is the timber-framing with the close uprights, the position of the hall with the traces of a winder staircase at the exit of the screens passage and the hall fireplace. But the main N front with the shallow bay windows and the pediments over some windows is no doubt Elizabethan, and Elizabethan also must be the stepped gables to the S. The gables to the N are straight.

The through passage runs immediately E of the Elizabethan SCREEN separating it from the hall: seven reeded and fluted 58 pilasters with early Ionic capitals; top rail with consoles and guttae decoration. Formerly two doors through it. The hall fire-place is four-centred, and the NW room has the same thing enriched with a panelled overmantel, and so too does a first-floor room. In the W wing is a later C17 dog-leg staircase with sturdy turned balusters.

The date 1564 on the brick ARCHWAY in the garden is untrustworthy in its lettering, and in any case the archway is said to have been brought by the then tenant – Prince Frederick Duleep Singh – from his other property at Elveden, Suffolk.

CHURCH FARMHOUSE, The Street. T-plan, the stem starting as a
63 C15 first-floor hall, or Great Chamber, altered *c.* 1720. Timber-framed and plastered. The E front has a roll-moulded bressumer to the first-floor jetty and two upper casements of C16 date. To the S is an extension which was for a blacksmith's forge, with the brazier built into the back of the C15 hall stack. Inside, the main ground-floor room has multiple roll-moulded bridging beams and joists. The roof has four square-section crown-posts with side fillets below the four arched braces.

Many late C17 or early C18 timber-framed COTTAGES with wattle and daub infill, especially on The Street, the principal road of this village. Chiefly, BLO NORTON HOUSE, WHITE-HOUSE FARMHOUSE and HAMPTON HOUSE, the last with a good external stack to the N, but less good replacement fenestration.

BODNEY

ST MARY. Nave and chancel in one. No windows original, although they are all Late Perp in appearance. But the Ladbroke drawing corresponds to their present appearance. E window with cusped intersecting tracery. The wave-moulded chancel arch appears mid-C14. W window is a cusped Y. C19 bellcote in place of a tower. – FONT. Octagonal, C14. – PULPIT. C17, polygonal, with a fluted frieze. – BENCHES. Some with pierced, traceried backs and poppyheads. – SCULPTURE. One small piece of Anglo-Saxon interlace in the NE buttress.

Immediately E are humps of foundations. It has been suggested they are of an early church.

BODNEY HALL FARMHOUSE. C16 timber-framed block re-skinned with C18 brick and elongated to the S. Three bays of sashes and a central porch on a pair of Roman Doric columns. Hipped roof. The C16 queenpost roof survives, as do some good moulded bridging beams. Additional wing *c.* 1840.

BOUGHTON

ALL SAINTS. The W tower was according to Blomefield built in 1416, but the reference is to 3s. 4d. left in that year only for 'new work'. There is another reference to the bell-frame in 1530, but the tower must be essentially of *c.* 1300 – the bell-openings and the W window have trefoils. Stair-turret with quatrefoil openings. The body of the church rebuilt by *R. J. Withers* in 1872. The head of the S doorway is original. Withers's windows are intersecting in the nave and intersecting and lancet in the chancel, hardly inspired. The interior is not dramatic either: scissor-braced roofs and a little arcade screen to the E end.

The VILLAGE has a large, square pond, quite an asset. Of HOUSES

little to note. THE POPLARS on Chapel Road is of *c.* 1830; five
bays of windows although recessed strips to the brick façade
give it an appearance of eight bays. Fluted engaged columns to
the doorcase.

BOWTHORPE *see* NORWICH VILLAGES, *1000*
Vol. 1, p. 343

BRACON ASH *1090*

ST NICHOLAS. Nave and chancel. W of the S doorway is a frame
for one bell with a gabled roof over. The N porch has a stepped
gable which may be of the early C19. In the S aisle two Dec windows with mouchettes. The S arcade, of three bays, has piers
with polygonal projections and double-hollow-chamfered
arches. In 1375 money was left for covering an aisle. This is getting late for the windows, early for the piers, but for neither
impossible. The chancel is a fine piece of late C13 work, which
the over-restored windows (Y- and intersecting tracery, including a wooden SE window, 1807) do not betray. But inside the
windows are splayed and shafted, with a continuous hoodmould, and there was a curiously close group of them on the
N side, now blocked by the addition in the mid C18 of the
stone-built Berney mausoleum. This is quite a stately, if ponderous, affair to the outside, quoined and with a pedimented
middle bay flanked by intermittently blocked pilasters. Blocked
circular windows with four heavy keystones. – ROYAL ARMS of
George III in a frame of pilasters and pediment. – MONUMENT.
The door to the Berney Mausoleum is surrounded by the front
of an Early Renaissance monument of terracotta, without doubt
the work of the same craftsman who did the Bedingfeld
monuments at Oxborough and the nearby Wymondham monument (qq.v.). Four bays divided by baluster-pilasters with little
pendant capitals, and delicately detailed panels. The tomb-
chest of course had to be removed when the mausoleum was
made.

BRACON HALL. John Berney bought the estate in the mid C18,
but the Queen Anne house he found was replaced by the present nice three- by three-bay house only in 1833. The centre bay
set back. Two storeys. Hipped roof. Tripartite sashes under
curiously depressed arches. There is a porch on two pairs of
unfluted columns. Also of 1833 the large STABLES with five
bays, pedimented centre, two Diocletian windows and an open
arcade to the ground floor. Some arcade openings blocked.
They declined into farm buildings in the C19, but now have
various uses including a domestic conversion. Angle pavilions.
The previous property is mentioned in Repton's *Theory* of 1803.

MERGATE HALL, ⅝ m. SE, on Mergate Lane. The manor of the
Kemp family. C17, with various additions. The W front of two
storeys and dormer attic arranged in eight bays symmetrically

between two gables. Two-light cross casements. To the N end are a further two bays with an outsized dormer and stepped gables. In front of this is a single-storey extension added late in the C18, also with stepped gables. S front altered early C19, although bits of C17 pediments can be seen. The E front, also altered and enlarged from the early C19, is all stepped gables and crenellations, including a two-storey bow. Plenty of C17 and C18 panelling inside, and bridging beams with sunk quadrant mouldings. The rear additions provide the staircase, with stick balusters, set in an apsed well. There is a collection of cast-iron fire grates made by *Barnard, Bishop and Barnard* to designs of *Thomas Jekyll*. Clasped purlin roof. On two OUT-BUILDINGS the dates 1789 and 1790.

DOWER HOUSE, Mergate Lane. C17, of brick and partly timber-framed, though the timber was re-cased in 1789 according to the tie-plates. Mullioned windows with ovolo mouldings light the lower storey. Stepped gables. Clasped purlin roof with diminished principals.

BRACON LODGE, $\frac{7}{8}$ m. ESE. Of gault brick, five bays and two and a half storeys with a one-bay pediment and a segmental porch supported on two Roman Doric columns and two engaged columns. Door with margin lights and a pretty fanlight. Stick baluster staircase. This is all *c.* 1800, but is only a re-skinning of an C18 house, as the pair of external stacks at the rear show. In the garden a crinkle-crankle WALL.

Other more minor C17 timber-framed HOUSES include MERGATE FARMHOUSE, Hawkes Lane, lobby-entrance, altered C18 and C19. Early C17 upper crucks in the roof. Nos. 65–66 HAWKES LANE, same date. LITTLE POTASH, Potash Lane, is late C16, with brick infill between the studs, and mullioned windows replaced in the C17.

2000   BRAMERTON

ST PETER. The curious thing about the church is that to the l. and r. of the tower the room on its ground floor widens to the width of the nave, and that a traceried squint allows a view of the altar from the S part of this widening. The corresponding N squint is blocked. It is almost like a stunted W transept and is probably connected with works referred to in a will of 1463. The tower seems late C13 to early C14. It has Y-tracery in the belfry openings. Dec nave. A head-bracket above the S doorway. One S window of Early Perp forms. Dec chancel, but with a priest's doorway of early C17 brick. The windows have petal tracery on the S side and a lancet on the N, and a reticulated three-light E window. The N transept is of 1857: false hammerbeam roof. The church was restored, with the usual re-seating, re-roofing etc., in 1866. – FONT. Disused. Octagonal. Against the underside of the bowl a frieze of fleurons with big seaweed-like leaves at the corners. – COMMUNION RAIL. Early C18, tapering reeded square balusters. – STAINED GLASS. Transept

E window has two panels of Christ with Maries, by *Ward & Hughes*, †1875. E window, probably by *Heaton, Butler & Bayne*, 1867.

BRAMERTON HALL, ⅝ m. N on Surlingham Lane. Built for John Blake *c.* 1830, extended to N *c.* 1870. Five wide bays in two storeys. Doorcase with Doric columns.

Bramerton consists almost entirely of THE STREET. S of the church is BRAMERTON GRANGE. The re-faced E front of two storeys is in three bays curiously set back one from the next and under late C18 crenellated parapets. The N return mid-C17, with cross casements (renewed) and a platband. The W front *c.* 1670–80, five bays, doorway with an open pediment set to the r. Brick quoins and brick intermittent rustication l. and r. of the windows. Dentilled platband. Staircase *c.* 1680 also, stout turned balusters, panelled newel posts. GROVE FARM COTTAGES. Timber-framed late C17 houses on the lobby-entrance plan given a brick skin in *c.* 1750. On the E side of the road ORCHARD HOUSE, C17 as well, brick, still in English bond, in four bays. The C20 windows and interior details do no good. One mullioned window survives at rear.

BRANCASTER

7040

ST MARY. The chancel may be the earliest part, see the confused evidence of blocked C12 windows on the S side. Work was carried out, or proposed, in 1405 when money was left for 'building' the chancel. E window C19. Arcades of the C14. Four bays, octagonal piers, double-hollow-chamfered arches. The seats round the piers were absorbed by the raising of the floor. The straight-headed, very long N windows could be contemporary, the S windows are very odd. They have tracery in the spandrels of the hoodmould and might be C17. Perp two-light clerestory windows and a three-light window in nave E gable. A bay added to the W end of N aisle *c.* 1900. C14 S porch with quatrefoil side openings. C15 W tower with flushwork in the battlements. Roofs from the 1832 restoration. – FONT. Perp, octagonal. – FONT COVER. Fine, tall wooden canopy of 1493. – SCULPTURE. A figure from a former wall-post. – LANTERNS. Three lanterns on poles, Italian.

ST MARYS, the former Rectory on London Street, *c.* 1820. Stuccoed, two storeys in five bays and a porch on unfluted Doric columns.

TOWN FARMHOUSE. Late C17 house of clunch blocks and brick dressings raised in height in the early C18. Remains of C17 windows, especially to the N front.

BANODUNUM. The site of the Saxon shore fort, excavated periodically between 1846 and 1935, is on Rack Hill, at the E end of the village. The fort wall enclosed an area of six acres, and the corners had internal turrets. Little is known of the interior, but excavation has examined an extensive planned settlement W of the fort. This has been dated late C2 and C3, pre-dating the fort, which is probably of the second quarter of the C3. Nothing is visible of the fort's structures or defences, although the impression of the fort platform can be discerned. (DG)

BRANCASTER STAITHE

7040

DIAL HOUSE, on the Quay. A long range now divided into four properties, though the E pair, DIAL HOUSE and DIAL COTTAGE, were amalgamated into one and much rebuilt at the back in 1950 and remodelled internally in 1983. This part, which is of *c.* 1700, nevertheless provides the excitement. Flint with brick trim, of two storeys in three bays, with rusticated quoins. There is a two-storey porch, also with rustication and an oddly shapeless 'shaped' gable. The rest of the façade and its windows have been knocked about. The two W houses are early C19.

STAITHE HOUSE. Mid-C18 or slightly later. Of seven bays and two storeys. Three-bay centre under a pediment. Doorway with pediment on fluted Ionic columns. Moulded platband between the floors. Sashes mostly original, a rare thing in the salty, corrosive air. The front is of gault brick. Good chimneypiece in the entrance hall. Staircase with two turned balusters to each tread. W ground-floor room has pedimented doors.

BRANDON PARVA

0000

ALL SAINTS. Unbuttressed W tower with a two-light Perp W window and a Perp top. Some flushwork in the battlements. Nave and chancel also Perp, the windows in the nave renewed 1854–60. The E window also renewed, but in the C18 (Y-tracery). The handsome tower arch has a hoodmould decorated with fleurons and rests on two head corbels. Nice chancel roof with arched braces, a moulded and castellated wall-plate, and bosses. Chancel arch, nave roof and furnishings from the restoration. – MONUMENT. John Warner †1702. Tablet with inscription surrounded by flat carving. The figurework is both funny and engaging; the assortment of bones in a napkin at the foot should also not be missed.

MANOR FARMHOUSE. Much altered C17 brick house. The openings in the W gable have moulded brick hoodmoulds.

BRECKLES

9090

ST MARGARET. Round tower with polygonal top distinguished by chequer brickwork. Below the top stage are small blocked circular sound-holes. The arch towards the nave has very remarkable imposts with a band of ornament, partly interlace, partly of a snaky kind. All this must be pre-Norman, and is probably of the early C11. The chancel arch is mostly of the

restoration of 1970–4, although the main, and 'thorough',
restoration was done by *E. B. Lamb* in 1862. The peculiar
angles to the roof purlins are his. The chancel has an angle
piscina formed of two trefoiled ogees. – FONT. Norman, square.
On one side are two Green Men, on another big leaf motifs, on
the third intersecting arches, on the fourth four upright figures
under arches (cf. Fincham), one of them praying, another with
outstretched arms. – SCREEN. Late C14, with pretty flower
frieze at the top of the dado, but somewhat restored in 1862. –
BENCH ENDS. Some are old. – MONUMENTS. Slab to John
Webb †1658 and, attached to it by a strap and buckle, a small
oval slab to his daughter Ursula Hewyt †1658. The inscription
says *Stat ut vixit erecta*, which refers to the strange fact that she
was buried in an upright position.

BRECKLES HALL. Elizabethan brick house built for Francis
Wodehouse and dated 1583 on the chimneypiece of one completely panelled room on the first floor. The house was extremely
well repaired by *Detmar Blow* shortly after 1900, and added to
and (less well) altered inside by *Lutyens* after 1908. Where they
survive, and there are a lot of them, the Elizabethan windows
have their glass and metal fittings intact. The mullions of the
timber windows are typically hollow-chamfered, those of the
brick windows ovolo-moulded.

The W front, built on the E-plan, is largely a reconstruction,
indeed the porch which turns it from an H-plan to the E is
Blow's: two storeys with polygonal angle-shafts. Wide projecting gables r. and l. leaving only one bay between them and the
porch. The more original S side has two mighty chimney-breasts
gabled back to the roof, both with octagonal flues. C16 door, the
fittings complete, under a pair of overlights. On the E side a
curious arrangement. The l. stepped gable – the only stepped 70
one in a house of straight gables – corresponds to a gable on the
front. But it is followed by a row of seven lower straight gables.
There are four gabled dormers behind these, lighting the long
gallery, which are the only gables shown on a drawing of 1886.
The windows below them have no transoms. It is unusual for
Elizabethan houses to be more than one room deep, but the
small rooms below these gables lie at the back of the hall, etc.,
which are entered from the front. They seem to be an addition,
perhaps by Lutyens. The water hoppers are his, dated 1908.
Much reconstructed N side. Here Lutyens added his service
range in Elizabethan mode. One storey and attic, with five
gabled dormers on the W side, four to the E, mullioned windows
and clustered octagonal stacks.

INTERIOR. The internal arrangements of the house are
altogether very changed. Hall and kitchen quarters have been
knocked into one very large room. Originally the hall extended
to the r. of the porch. In this part of the house, facing S, is the
main staircase, with straight flights. The other big fireplace in
the present hall must be that of the original kitchen. Interesting
genuine priest-hole. The Mrs Wodehouse of c. 1583 was known
as a 'popish seducinge recusant'. Two good wooden overmantels.

Lutyens's interior appointments are plain and disappointing.
Fine front GARDEN with embattled walls and an archway
with two brick rings on top. Perhaps it had obelisks in addition
originally. There are other C16 garden walls, but the present
planting arrangements are late C19 and C20.

0080   BRESSINGHAM

ST JOHN BAPTIST. Late C13 chancel, see the simple sedilia and
one N window with a curiously irregular quatrefoil in the head.
Dec arcades of four bays with octagonal piers and double-
chamfered arches. Dec also the S doorway. The rest is Perp. w
tower with flushwork panelling on base, buttresses and battlements. The w window has clearly carved shields in the spandrels and crowns and fleurons in the arch mouldings. Niches l.
and r. of the w window. In 1480 funds were set aside to 'edify'
the N aisle. Very handsome clerestory consisting of eight closely
set two-light windows with flushwork between. On this an
inscription commemorating Sir Roger Pilkington †1527. The
date is in the inscription. Hammerbeam roof. The braces on the
hammerbeams carry up to the ridge, i.e. there are no collar-
beams. Various bequests for leading run from 1505 to 1515 and
in 1517 there was an appeal for funds to finish the roof. Sanctus
bellcote on the E gable of the nave.
    FURNISHINGS. FONT. Octagonal, with a traceried stem and
on the bowl a number of window patterns of the late C13, as if
taken from a pattern book. Font tracery lagged behind window
tracery in date usually by about thirty years. – PULPIT. Jacobean;
with strapwork. – BENCHES. A very curious set, a mid- or later
C16 variation on the local theme, i.e. the theme of traceried
ends, buttresses l. and r. of the arm-rests, and animals or figures
on them and poppyheads. Many of the motifs carry on the early
C16 types, especially on the ends towards the aisles, but towards
the nave the buttresses are clumsy balusters, the tracery scroll
ends or arabesques including the familiar heads in roundels,
and in one case there is a standing female figure with a sword
instead. – BOX PEWS. – STAINED GLASS. Old bits in the E window. Two windows in N aisle attributed by Birkin Haward to
Heaton, Butler & Bayne, but fitted by *J. & J. King* of Norwich.
One has figures of St Peter and St Paul, †1868, the other with
roundels and heads of St John Baptist and Salvator Mundi, †1865.
– CURIOSUM. Three so-called collecting shoes, i.e. wooden
shovels more or less the shape of a dustpan. They are dated 1631.
BRESSINGHAM LODGE, Diss Road. Built as the Rectory in 1842
121   by *S. S. Teulon*. Gabled, red brick, Tudor. Façade to the W only
three bays wide, the centre bay projecting, the side bays with
gables. Canted bay in centre under a battlemented parapet.
Diamond-flued stacks. In much the same manner are the
STABLES and CART SHEDS E and NE of the house.
The VILLAGE sprawls along the principal roads, and everywhere
are C17 timber-framed houses and cottages. A selection only

can be mentioned. JUBILEE FARMHOUSE on Common Road has a thatched roof and a lobby-entrance plan. Three late C18 casements to the ground floor and in the dormers above. C18 shell-hood cupboard inside. YE OLDE CHEQUERS, Diss Road, late C17, two storeys, casements of two to four lights, thatched roof and a pair of plank doors. More thatched cottages on Fen Street, ½ m. w of the church, see e.g. WAVENEY RISING and WOOD PIGHTLE. On Lady's Lane DEAL FARMHOUSE again demonstrates the C17 lobby-entrance plan-form, and so too does THE SPINNEY, School Road.

The C18 contributes rather less, and the material is brick. ALGAR HOUSE, Algar Lane, 1 m. NNW of the church, is *c.* 1730. Two storeys in five bays; sash windows in exposed boxes.

OLD BOYLAND HALL, Boyland Common, 2 m. NNE. A C16 timber-framed house with a moat. The gable-ends of brick. The first floor jettied, with a bressumer on brackets and, inside, a dragon beam at the SW corner. Windows all changed in the C20. C19 brick wing to N.

GRANGE FARMHOUSE, High Road. Another C16 timber-framed house presenting to the S front three bays fitted with C19 and C20 casements and a diamond-flued ridge stack l. of centre. One-bay gable-ends either side terminate E and W wings. The W wing has a nice brick stepped gable at the N sprouting twin round chimneyshafts in moulded brick. This serves a stone four-centred fireplace in the attic. The roof in this wing has wind-braces. Further four-centred stone fireplaces elsewhere, and moulded bridging beams.

VALLEY FARMHOUSE, ½ m. NNW. Early C17, timber-framed and with clay lump infill, one of the earliest examples of clay lump in Norfolk. Two storeys and attics. The central porch is C19 and the cross casements r. and l. are C18. Diamond flues to the ridge stack. The gable-end of the W wing is of brick, with a stepped parapet, a pair of oval windows and a stack. The staircase has turned balusters.

BRESSINGHAM HALL, Diss Road, SE of the church. A simple late C18 three-bay, two-storey house with a central pediment. Used as part of a museum of steam-driven machines.

BRETTENHAM   9080

ST MARY. Essentially by *S. S. Teulon*, 1852 (cf. Shadwell Park). He was employed by Lady Buxton to remodel and improve the almost ruinous old church. Of this the Norman S doorway was kept, with one order of chevron and twisted shafts, volute capitals, and zigzag in the arch. Also preserved were the base of the W tower and some nave masonry, especially at the SW corner. The new work is Dec and has none of the assertive Teulon style, except perhaps in the octagonal N vestry under its steep roof and in the crossing. The latter is roofed with tri-radial timbers, a theme he was to extend in Shadwell Park. – COMMUNION RAIL and SCREEN base of alabaster. – TOWER SCREEN and

PARCLOSE SCREENS of iron and certainly worth noting. – STAINED GLASS. The original schemes were by *Gibbs, Wilmshurst & Oliphant* and *Ward & Nixon*, but only a rose in the N transept and the two-light W tower window remain: *c.* 1852 by *C. A. Gibbs*. The rest is by *A. L. Moore* of London, 1889–90. The church was re-furnished 1903 by the Musker family; Teulon's fittings presumably removed to Rushford (q.v.).

The HOUSE to the NE and some ESTATE HOUSING of red brick, particularly Nos. 1–3 KILVERSTONE ROAD, are of the 1870s.

LODGE to Shadwell Park, one of several of the same design, thatched with a tree-trunk veranda and modest Gothic windows, probably of *c.* 1830.

BARROWS. To the SE of Great Snarehill Belt are the Seven Hills, originally formed by some eleven barrows running E–W; there are now six. To the E are three bowls and to the W a bell and two bowls. All are over 100 ft in diameter. Nothing is known of their contents.

ROMANO-BRITISH VILLAGE. At the junction of West Harling parish, the crossing point of the Thet by Peddar's Way, extensive finds indicate a posting station on the Roman road and a settlement with buildings and burials around the fording point. (DG)

BRIDGHAM

9080

ST MARY. Nave and chancel. Although there is no record of a W tower, it looks as if one has existed and disappeared. Nave windows (Y-tracery) of *c.* 1300, chancel windows (reticulated tracery) Dec. The chancel has a separate lowside window. N porch with flushwork panelling, the upper parts damaged. Inside the porch is a tunnel vault with transverse ribs. The best thing in the church is the sedilia and double piscina, two separate compositions, the latter looking earlier Dec than the former. – FONTS. Norman font from Roudham, tub-shaped with angle spurs. – Perp FONT on two steps, of which one is quatrefoiled. Against the stem four lions, against the bowl reliefs of the so-called Mercy Seat, the Assumption, two seated figures, and demi-figures of angels with the emblems of the Trinity and other emblems. – SCREEN. The base only, C15, with painted ornamental motifs. – READER'S DESK. Jacobean, not it seems in its original state, and used as a pulpit. – BENCHES. Against one end a commemorative inscription. Others complete but very dilapidated. – PAINTINGS. Moses and Aaron, C18. The Moses looks rather like a rustic version of El Greco. – STAINED GLASS. In two chancel N windows fragments of the original early C14 glass.

The VILLAGE is pleasant enough but with few highlights. THE GROVE sits off the S side of the main street with its stepped W gable in Flemish-bond brick. Is it then an example of mid-C17 stepped gabling like Wilby Hall? The house otherwise is early C17 and timber-framed inside. Lobby-entrance plan. Three-storey tower to the rear.

BRISLEY

St Bartholomew. Strong Perp w tower for which there are donations recorded from 1435 to 1453. The doorway has shields in the spandrels and a row of shields above. Big four-light Perp w window. Below the bell-openings are oblong sound-holes with a grid of panel units. Tall tower-arch. Perp N porch, leaded in 1435. Perp windows, specially pretty those of the clerestory, two to each bay, with quatrefoiled circles in the spandrels and brick and flint relieving arches. Perp five-bay arcades. Octagonal piers, double-chamfered arches. The chancel is uncommonly interesting. It is tall and wide and has on the N side large windows with Curvilinear tracery of mouchette type, on the s and E sides large Perp windows. Yet they are evidently part of the same building campaign, and thus illustrate the fact that to the medieval mason – at least in the C14 – both forms were equally valid. The four-centred chancel arch has wave mouldings. Sedilia and piscina equally good, and equally divided between Dec and Perp. Detached, slender quatrefoil shafts, cusped and crocketed ogee arches, but panel tracery in the spandrels. The piscina has a frame decorated with ballflower (an unusual thing in Norfolk). Nave roof partly old, aisle roofs wholly C15, with roll-moulded beams and wall-plate. – SCREEN. Tall, with a straight top. Very fine tracery and foliage. Restored. – DOOR. N door in the chancel to the crypt is partly C14, partly new, but the iron hinges are c. 1300. – BENCHES. C15, with poppyheads and arm-rests in the form of animals. Two benches have thin pierced traceried backs; one (in the front, N side) has a small book cupboard. – PEWS for squire and rector, with lunettes in the friezes and the date 1590. Door with cockshead hinges. – Three-decker PULPIT of three different centuries. C15 hexagonal stem, C17 panelling to centre section and a C15 hexagonal upper section, with blind tracery in the panels; then an C18 tester, panelled. – WALL PAINTING. Much painting throughout the nave, and more still to be uncovered. Decorative painting on the arcades, and a fine St Christopher of c. 1360 on the s aisle wall, flanked by St Andrew and another figure. A later St Christopher by the N door, and an angel on the cut-away jamb of the E window in the N aisle wall. (DP) – STAINED GLASS. E window of 1855, in the style of *Charles Clutterbuck*. Crucifixion scene. – BRASS. John Athowe, priest, †1531.

Brisley Hall. To the SE off Elmham Road. Moated. A C15 house was incorporated into new work in the C17, extending N. The E and w fronts each has a C17 three-storeyed porch, that to the w with an ovolo-moulded mullioned window in the gablehead under a moulded pediment. The façade originally had four-light mullioned windows under hoods, of which only one survives intact. The C17 hoods otherwise have three-light C19 cross casements under them. The E porch is converted out of a staircase outshut. The windows generally are heavily restored C18 cross casements, though there recurs a four-light mullioned window and C17 hoodmoulds. Chimneystack with five diagonally set shafts. The interior has late C15 roll-moulded bridging beams.

Also on Elmham Road CHURCH BUNGALOWS, a row of three early C19 Gothick houses with traceried doors and Y-tracery arched windows. The veranda looked better, and more of the *cottage orné*, when it had rustic tree-trunk supports.

BROCKDISH

ST PETER AND ST PAUL. In the nave a N window to which is assigned a C12 date. Two suspicious-looking Norman N windows in the chancel, one suspects renewed. In the S aisle, probably re-set, a fine piscina with a cinquefoiled arch, stiff-leafed cusps, and some dogtooth decoration, i.e. *c.* 1230–50. Dec S arcade with odd piers: quatrefoil, set diagonally, with fillet-like projections between the foils. Arch with two sunk hollows. The E respond has been converted into a vaulted canopy for an image. Dec also the exterior of the S aisle. The doorway is medieval, the windows, like most of the exterior of the church, are of Victorian workmanship dating from the restoration by *F. Marrable*, 1864–6, under the close supervision of the antiquarian rector George Francis. Perp nave windows and Perp S porch, both probably entirely Victorian; they look different in Ladbroke. The porch has flushwork panelling. Entrance with shields up jambs and arch. Niches l. and r. Top quatrefoil frieze. The W tower had to be rebuilt in brick in 1713 and subsequently re-cased with a higher stair-turret in 1864 to look medieval, but medieval in the style of Hertfordshire or Kent. The nave roof is early C15 and has tie-beams and arched braces up to the ridge. S aisle roof also C15 but repaired in 1827. Chancel roof 1864.

FURNISHINGS. SCREEN. Only the base is preserved, and this restored by *Marrable*; tracery above is of 1899. – STAINED GLASS. E window by *M. & A. O'Connor*, a good Crucifixion of *c.* 1870. S aisle E window with some C17 foreign roundels. – MONUMENT. In the S aisle against the E wall (re-set for use as an altar) is a Late Perp monument of Purbeck marble. Tomb-chest with shields in cusped lozenges and remains of the recess above. Panelled jambs, quatrefoils against the underside of the top arch. A corbel for an image to the l. of the monument.

RECTORY, Church Lane. A mid-C19 Tudor affair, with an off-centre gabled bay and a gabled porch.

The VILLAGE has examples from all periods. On Common Lane is SHERIFF HOUSE RESTAURANT, a late C16 timber-framed house with a jettied N gable and a cluster of four octagonal chimneyshafts. Three-light cross casements, two with pediments. The range to The Street is C17: mixed fenestration. THE RED HOUSE, Grove Road, of two storeys in five bays, late C18, red brick. Pedimented doorcase. In the early C19 clay lump was used on its own, i.e. not as an infill to a timber frame. KENT

House, Grove Road, is of this type. Nos. 3–4 Grove Road of the same material. On Scole Road more c17 timber-framed houses (White House Farmhouse, Corner Farmhouse) and the same on The Street (Empton House, King's Head public house, with false external framing; also Greyhound Inn).

Brockdish Grange, ½ m. NNW. A fine timber-framed c16 house re-fronted in brick in the mid-c17 style, but dated 1676 in the centre of a field with pilasters and segmental pediment, the only detail which looks more 1676 than 1655. The house is otherwise the Scole Inn's little brother (q.v.) and is probably modelled on it. The façade faces N. Dutch end-gables, and three similar shaped gables over the façade. Timber mullioned and transomed windows (renewed). The central doorcase has a pair of fat Ionic columns under a pulvinated frieze. Square chimneystacks with blank arches. The timber-frame is elusive, but details of wall-plates and the roof (straight wind-braces) indicate that the re-facing was just that, not a rebuilding, so the plan-form remains an earlier type. It comprises a single rectangle, somewhat elongated (*see* e.g. similar types at Aspull Hall, Debenham, and Wattisfield Hall, both Suffolk), with the end bays fitted with spine beams rather than bridging beams. At the W end in the position of the present c17 stack was possibly a smoke bay. The N front has a three-bay centre and slightly projecting end bays. The centre is now a hall but was formerly subdivided and had a passage running along the back (i.e. the S), and very likely service rooms to the E. The S front has a blocked door to the r. forming a lobby-entrance with the E stack, but this can hardly be a c16 feature. One's attention however is directed to the stair-tower to the W end, all of brick and a new build of 1676. The stairs are a direct copy of those in the Scole Inn: dog-leg, closed-string, turned vase balusters, moulded handrail.

The Grove, E of the former. A simpler version of the same type, but with two traditional cross gables and much altered. The windows are renewed cross casements. Doorway tucked away to the l. of the front next to the l. cross gable. Dated on rainwater heads 1672, which relates to the brick re-facing of an earlier c17 timber-framed house. The timber frame can be readily appreciated in the rear wing. The date 1672 fits the dog-leg staircase, with sturdy dumb-bell balusters. Ovolo-moulded bridging beams from *c.* 1620. An odd Ionic arcade at the back of the front range embedded into the wall and visible only from the inside.

Brockdish Hall, E of the former. There is a fine three-storeyed porch to the W, dated 1634, but still in the Elizabethan tradition. Red brick polygonal angle-shafts with pinnacles. Stepped gables. Pedimented mullioned and transomed windows. The three-bay S front is Georgianized but has also polygonal angle-shafts. Rear wing is timber-framed but with a brick skin and good c17 mullioned and transomed casements. Early c17 ovolo-moulded bridging beams inside. The W porch may have formed the centre of an E-shaped façade.

BROOKE

ST PETER. Round tower with a sixteen-sided parapet and some
round C12 windows to the ground stage. There is a distinct
change of flintwork to the second stage and inside remain four
blocked bell-openings. The top stage seems a mid-C15 addition. S doorway of *c*. 1200. One capital (to the W) still with
something like waterleaf, the other with amorphous foliage. The
arch and hoodmould with roll and wide fillet mouldings on
heads. Chancel Dec, if it can be trusted in the light of *John
Brown*'s general restoration of 1849. The windows replaced by
him. Double piscina inside has two pointed arches on a shaft,
very plain and reworked. N aisle and N clerestory with eight
closely placed windows, all renewed. Perp nave, panel-tracery
windows. The aisle arcade is baffling. Two bays are simply cut
through the pre-existing wall with coarse continuous chamfers
and two-centred arches, the other two with an octagonal pier
and many-moulded four-centred arches. The proper bays probably relate to a reference to a new aisle in 1508. The nave roof is
arch-braced. The braces stand on demi-figures of angels bearing shields. Against the clerestory a plaque with the date 1636.
  FONT. Money was left for it in 1466 and 1468. Octagonal,
with eight statuettes against the stem, eight demi-figures of angels
against the underside of the bowl, and the Seven Sacraments
and the Crucifixion against the bowl. Some of the rich polychromy survives. (Also an odd little model of the same font,
made, according to tradition, in Italy in 1850; not on display.) –
HOURGLASS STAND. C17. Of iron, by the pulpit. – SOUTH
DOOR. C15. Six vertical panels of tracery with crocketed ogee
arches and fancy quatrefoils above. – STAINED GLASS. Bits of
original glass in the N aisle. – MONUMENTS. Thomas Seaman
†1740. Pilasters and pediment. Two cherubs' heads below the
pediment. – John Fowle †1786. With a shield against an obelisk.
– WALL PAINTINGS. An unusual C14 series of the Seven Deadly
Sins was discovered in 1849, but limewashed over.
BAPTIST CHAPEL, High Green. 1831. Already Tudor, and with a
stepped gable. Nonconformists in the 1830s usually still built
classically.
PORCH HOUSE, The Street, ½ m. SW. Mid-C17, the brick still in
English bond and the house extraordinarily ornate for its size.
The distinguishing motif is the mullioned window with two
small pediments side by side instead of one big one (cf. Hardley).
In one case they are even segmental. Other windows have
normal pediments. In addition windows and the upper storey of
the porch are framed by plain brick pilasters or alternately
blocked brick pilasters. The door and fanlight of course are C19.
Pilasters to the corners of the house as well. The simultaneous
rear wing has the same motifs. Bridging beams with sunk-
quadrant mouldings.
OLD VICARAGE, a little farther W on the same street. The C17
timber frame rather done away with in the early C19. Two-storey,
three-bay N front, pilastered doorcase and early C19 sashes and

one bow. A mid-c19 wing added behind. Then MERE HOUSE, another small house of the mid c17. This has angle rustication of even width made up in each course of one long and one short block. Also rustication l. and r. of the windows. Stepped gable. The ridge stack has a cluster of five shafts. NORTH LODGE, of c. 1830, and the c18 brick DOVECOTE in DOVECOTE CLOSE are all that remains of BROOKE HALL (the seven-bay Grecian addition was of 1827–30 by *William Wilkins Jun.* for Rev. John Holmes). A fine lake remains. The LODGE has only one storey, in Tudor dress under thatch, and with a timbered gable over the door containing an oriel.

THE STREET has a number of other c17 timber-framed houses, usually added to or altered, e.g. Nos. 26–28 (queen-strut roof), No. 45, Nos. 79–83 (late c18 five-bay front, four-centred fire-places, roof with curved wind-braces and cambered ties).

At HIGH GREEN some more timber-framed houses, notably WATERFIELD COTTAGE, c16, quite small but extended in the c20. Some former ground-floor windows show shutter rebates on the inside, there is a four-centred brick fireplace in an upper room and the roof structure luxuriates in curved wind-braces and clasped purlins. SCHOOL HOUSE (Nos. 2–4). c14 hall house, now of one storey and attic following flooring in the c17 and insertion of stacks. The timber frame almost invisible from outside behind brick and flint walls pierced by c19 and c20 open-ings. Good bolection-moulded fireplace surround in an upstairs room. The roof is smoke-blackened from the original open fire, and has a crown-post arrangement and stud walls made up of intersecting braces such as are found in c14 houses in King's Lynn. THE WARREN (No. 45), early c17 with an c18 brick bay.

OLDHOUSE FARMHOUSE, 1½ m. SW on Woodton Road. Early c17 brick house with a timber-framed S wing skinned in c19 brick. Two storeys and attic in four bays fitted with c19 case-ments. The gable of the S wing to the l. Central chimneystack carrying octagonal shafts. At the back a stair-tower contains a dog-leg staircase with turned balusters. The plan heavily depends on the virtually obsolete hall-house arrangement; the roof has clasped purlins.

ENTRANCE LANE, NW of the church. Council Housing of 1952–3 by *Tayler & Green* (*see* Introduction, p. 165). The group is of fourteen houses only, of one and two storeys. Pleasant varied brickwork, but marred by uPVC windows. An intended enlarge-ment for the elderly, CHURCHILL PLACE, came only in 1966, by the same architects. Groups of two-storeyed houses face the road, with close-knit terraces of single-storey houses behind, well planned, but poorer in detail. More uPVC.

BROOME   3090

ST MICHAEL. Away from the village to the N. The Perp W tower quite ornate. From a donation we know it was in building in 1431. Flushwork-panelled base. The W doorway has tracery and shields in the spandrels. Quatrefoil frieze over. Three-light w window with dainty Perp tracery. A little niche above it. Traceried sound-holes. Crenellated parapet. Tall arch to nave, with mouldings dying into the arch. The tower is strikingly similar to the near-contemporary Wickhampton (q.v. Vol. 1, p. 722). The nave also Perp, see the three-light windows under basket arches. Outwardly Perp chancel, except for the C14 priest's doorway and E and N windows. The E window has cusped Y-tracery and ballflower in the hood. Can this be part of the 1866–7 restoration? The doorway is probably of the same date as the chancel arch, with its polygonal responds and double-chamfered arch. Inside the chancel curious shafting demonstrates a C13 rather than a Perp date. The start close to the s corner is probably for a C13 window with a dropped sill. An arched opening further E has stiff-leaf capitals to its shaft for the same thing. The rest is unexplained. – FONT. Only the step with quatrefoil decoration and the stem with four lions are original. – SOUTH DOOR. C15, with some ironwork. – ORGAN CASE. Mahogany; early C19; Empire style. – MONUMENT. John Fowle †1732. Lively tablet with two putti on the open pediment.

BROOME PLACE. Built c. 1700 by an otherwise unknown architect called *Britten*. Two storeys in seven bays. Considerably altered in 1887 for Edmond Tyrel de Poix, for whom were added the two canted window bays to r. and l. (four in all). In the middle a porch with fluted pilasters. The roof-line has shaped gables, a big centre one and two smaller ones, which are repeated to the N, and could be early C18. The rear has a C19 Perp staircase window. Of 1887 also the wing to the E with its four shaped gables. The library has an early C18 plaster ceiling. The staircase lantern from Mentmore (Bucks).

BROOME HOUSE FARMHOUSE, Bungay Road. A C17 range has many four- and five-light mullioned windows, the mullions ovolo-moulded. Stepped w gable. The stepped s gable belongs to a slightly later timber-framed wing. Sunk-quadrant mouldings to the tie-beams and bridging beams on the upper floor.

ST MICHAEL'S PLACE, Sun Road, 1 m. s of the church. 1955–6. A small terrace of four two-storey houses by *Tayler & Green (see* Introduction, p. 165). Good use of patterned and rough-textured brickwork. First-floor windows form themselves almost into a continuous frieze. Of the diagonal downpipes only a couple remain.

BROOME HEATH. The Neolithic long barrow on the heath is some 160 ft long by 83 ft broad and 6 ft at the highest point. It has not been excavated, but Windmill Hill sherds have been found on its surface.

BROOMSTHORPE see TATTERSETT

BROWICK see WYMONDHAM

BUCKENHAM TOFTS   8090

1½ m. e of Ickburgh, in the Stanford Battle Zone (military training area)

Of the seven- by seven-bay HALL only part of one wing is preserved. The stables, a three-bay pedimented block with a cupola, were demolished in the 1980s. They were part of the alterations done by *Samuel Wyatt* for the tenth Lord Petre in 1803.

BULL'S GREEN *see* TOFT MONKS

BUNN'S BANK *see* ATTLEBOROUGH

BUNWELL   1090

ST MICHAEL. All Perp. w tower with chequerboard flushwork decoration on the buttresses and also sacred initials. The doorway has traceried spandrels and a shield in a foiled field above. A string of bequests for the construction of the tower starts in 1499 and ends in 1508, including one in 1505 'toward the makying up of the stepill of Bonewell every yere when the masons work on it 6s. 8d. ...'. These dates are convincing. The s porch (bequest for leading, 1540) has flushwork panelling all round, looking oddly as if it was intended to rise into a second storey. In the nave as well as the chancel large Perp windows. The nave is remarkably wide and was re-roofed in 1905–7 with tie-beams on arched braces, except for one pair of hammerbeams. Big restoration in 1890, which accounts for most of the fittings. – FONT. Octagonal, Perp, with shields in foiled panels. 12 d. was left to paint it in 1458. – STAINED GLASS. e window, 1914, by *J. Hardman & Co.*

GOWER'S FARMHOUSE, Bridge Road. A late C15 timber-framed hall house floored internally in the C17 in the usual fashion. Two storeys, with a few small mullioned windows and some pargeting. The new C17 stack provided a lobby-entrance. Roof with arched braces supporting tie-beams and wind-braces between principals.

BUNWELL MANOR HOTEL, Rectory Road. Formerly the Rectory. C16, timber-framed augmented with some brick.

On BUNWELL STREET and GREAT GREEN are C17 houses and cottages, mostly timber-framed. Very few have original details. QUAKER'S FARMHOUSE on Hall Road, still with cross casements, and PERSEHALL MANOR (Hall Road) with its clustered octagonal stacks represent the better houses. The latter Georgianized by a brick skin. On LOW COMMON, PARK FARMHOUSE and LION COTTAGE are both early C19 red brick houses of passing interest, while COWGATE FARMHOUSE has a C17 timber frame behind the mid-C19 brick skin. OLD QUEEN'S HEAD, Turnpike Road is what it seems – an C18 brick house of two storeys and five bays with cross casement windows, while BANYARD'S HALL appears to be a C19 brick house, but is again a C17 timber-framed building. Its moat suggests even older origins.

BURFIELD HALL *see* WYMONDHAM

BURGH APTON *see* BERGH APTON

4090

BURGH ST PETER

ST MARY. By the river Waveney, 1¼ m. from the village. The W tower looks like someone's folly of telescoping brick boxes imitating a pyramid. It was intended as a mausoleum for the family of the Rev. Samuel Boycott, who had it built in 1793. Brick vaults in the broad base, which has diaper of flint and red brick probably representing early C16 work. Above that there are four steps, each with pointed windows, ending with a small cube at the top. The buttresses have steps as well. Wooden W window with intersecting tracery. Nave and chancel in one, thatched. The nave doorways early C14 with simple double-chamfered arches, the windows renewed, but those of the S side (Y-tracery) and the lancet on the N side would make sense. The chancel fitted with windows of the early C14, the E intersecting, again all new-looking, but confirmed by what remains of the sedilia and piscina with their cusped heads. The piscina has a shelf. The C15 is represented by the arch-braced nave roof with roll-moulded purlins and wall-posts. C19 chancel roof. – FONT. Octagonal, probably late C14, with eight heads against the underside of the bowl and panels with shields and roses against it.
The remains of another CHURCH, presumably St Peter, to the W of St Mary have disappeared.

8040

BURNHAM DEEPDALE

The Burnhams are a remarkable example of the medieval prosperity of Norfolk and the closeness of village to village and parish church to parish church. From Burnham Market (i.e. Burnham Westgate) church it is ⅜ m. to Burnham Ulph, ⅝ m. NE to Burnham Norton, 1 m. SE to Burnham Sutton, and 1 m. NE to Burnham Overy. The great century for the Burnhams was the C13, based on trade. The river Burn was navigable for seagoing vessels as far as Burnham Thorpe, now nearly three miles inland. By the C15 only Burnham Overy Town had docking facilities, but remorseless silting of the little river in the C16 stopped ships at Burnham Overy Staithe. This combined with the rise of other ports (Cley, Blakeney, Wells and King's Lynn) caused the eight Burnham villages to slumber, a slumber disturbed today only by the summer tourist migration.

ST MARY. Anglo-Saxon round tower, see the triangular head of the upper doorway towards the nave. Round-headed bell-openings. The tower had a w doorway. Nave and chancel all with Victorian fenestration. However, the simple N doorway is of *c.* 1190 and the N arcade (three bays, octagonal piers, double-hollow-chamfered arches) is of the C14. General restoration in 1875–6 by *Frederick Preedy* gives the exterior most of its appearance, e.g. all the windows. C19 roofs. – FONT. A very interesting and rare Norman 5 piece of the early C12, with the Labours of the Months in arcading. January a man with a drinking horn, February a man warming his feet, March a man digging, April a man pruning, May beating the bounds, June weeding, July scything, August binding a sheaf, September threshing, October grinding corn in a quern, November slaughtering, December feasting. On the w side four 'Trees of Life'. Top frieze with big animals and plants. It is rare to find on any English Norman piece so consistent a programme. The piers under the bowl are C19. – STAINED GLASS. Many fragments in the E and W windows of the porch and the vestry E window. The chancel E window has a Crucifixion, the N aisle a Nativity, S aisle a sower, all 1875–6 by *Preedy*, all good. – VESTMENT. A chasuble, given in 1921, said to be Rhenish C15. – SCULPTURE. Figures for the rood by *Sir Walter Tapper*, 1932.

WHITEHILLS FARMHOUSE. Red brick house of the early C18. Two storeys in six bays. The casements are replacements. Platband between the floors.

BURNHAM MARKET

ST MARY. C13 W tower thoroughly overhauled in the C15, when Y-tracery was inserted in the bell-openings, and a richly panelled crenellated parapet added. The parapet contains the arms of a lord of the manor (William Lexham) who died in 1500, and of the Calthorpes, and also figures illustrating the Creation, Fall, Nativity, Crucifixion, Resurrection etc. The donor himself is represented on the N side. Late Dec tower arch (wave and hollow mouldings but still circular responds). In 1740 the tower was described as ruinous and a big brick buttress was put up, and another in 1876, creating an overbearing set-back buttress. Of the C13 only traces of blocked windows in the S face. C14 three-bay arcades. Octagonal piers and double-chamfered arches. Clerestory windows are quatrefoils alternating with trefoils in niches to the N and two-light to the S. Contemporary N chapel extended a further bay E when the whole exterior was over-renewed during *Frederick Preedy*'s restorations of 1878–9. He replaced, e.g., the intersecting tracery of the E window with a Geometrical pattern and put in an elaborate crown-post chancel roof. Nave roof C19 also. The S porch lost its upper storey. – FONT. Octagonal; quatrefoils to bowl panels. – STAINED GLASS. In a S aisle window Faith and Charity by *Henry Holiday* of the firm *J. Powell & Son*, †1869. Another S

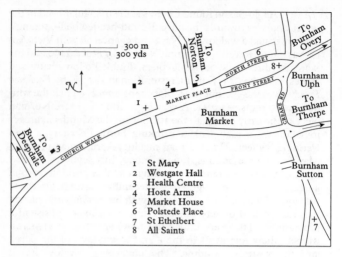

Burnham Market, Sutton and Ulph

aisle window with Suffer Little Children by *Ward & Hughes*, †1870. E window by *A. F. Erridge*, 1953. – BRASS. (chancel, N wall). John Huntely †1523. Wife and children alone are left. Her figure is 17 in. long.

WESTGATE HALL, behind the church to the N. The existing late C18 house was altered by *John de Carle* of Norwich in 1783–5 after a design made by *Soane* for *Thomas Pitt*, later the first Lord Camelford. Pitt (the cousin of William Pitt the younger) was an architect in his own right and the austere exterior must owe more to him than to Soane. Although there is no documentation Soane's bills seem to indicate work to the roof and pediment.* Pitt was important to Soane as an early patron, the two having met in Italy in 1778. Gault brick, five widely spaced bays with a three-bay pediment and two and a half storeys. Two-storeyed, one-bay wings. Two broad simple chimneystacks in Soane's style. The principal rooms are on the first floor, and in the drawing room is a chimneypiece which is definitely Soane's. Cantilevered imperial stone staircase in an apsed space at the back and visible from outside. It has cast-iron balusters. No interiors of distinction. The house came to the County Council in 1932 and was used until bought privately in the early 1990s as an old people's home.

More in Soane's style are the STABLES to the E, 1783, parallel to the house and adapted from an existing building. Gault brick front of seven bays under a pedimented three-bay centre, the round-headed windows with pilasters and recessed panels. Much altered in the 1930s.

LODGE. 1932 by *Sir John Simpson & Partners* for the County Council. Soanian in style.

---

* I am grateful to Ptolemy Dean for information on Soane's contribution.

HEALTH CENTRE, Church Walk, 400 yds W of the church. 1984 by *Ian Steen*, big steeply pitched pantiled roofs, dropping low on to short brick walls. Velux roof lights.

PERAMBULATION

A handsome broad village street, the MARKET PLACE, leads E from the church and Hall. Several minor Georgian houses and not a cottage that does any damage. First to be noted is a red brick three-bay house on the S side, WESTGATE HOUSE, with coursed clunch to the gable walls. Pedimented door with a Greek key motif to the panels and a fanlight. Then, also on the S side, BURNHAM HOUSE, a bigger gault brick five-bay house with a Doric porch and a parapet. The core is of clunch and brick, late C18, façade added *c.* 1800. On the N side a series of C18 and early C19 houses and cottages between the church and the Hoste Arms of perfect scale for the street: brick or flint and brick, with pantile roofs of different pitches. The HOSTE ARMS public house follows: early C18, two storeys and dormer attic in seven bays of C19 sashes; the exterior C19 in character, but some early C18 panelling inside. Immediately E stands FORGE HOUSE (ANNA dressmakers), the most interesting house in Burnham. Outwardly C19, of five bays, two storeys, sashes, with shop display windows and divided into two. The l. part has sumptuous early C16 roll-moulded bridging beams, joists and wall-plates to both ground and first floors, indicating an early storeyed house, i.e. there was never an open hall. The original house was two rooms wide and one room deep.

At this point a stream meanders diagonally across the street, and further on MARKET HOUSE, Burnham's most imposing façade. C17 origins, but with an early C18 red brick skin to the ground, mid-C18 to first floor, the two builds separated by a moulded platband. Five bays of sashes in three storeys with a gabled Roman Doric porch. Back to the S side and VINE HOUSE, of seven irregular bays with a renewed porch set to the r. Further E by the Post Office, the PAPER SHOP, a late C18 four-bay painted brick house and shop with a splendid bowed shop front consisting of two twenty-paned display windows under four-centred arches separated by a (replaced) doorway under a primitive six-vaned fanlight. Interior opened out and altered.

The street splits at the E end. Forking N into NORTH STREET, first on the S a house of *c.* 1770 built of coursed clunch blocks with brick dressings (ANNE HAMILTON ANTIQUES). Then the former CONGREGATIONAL CHAPEL, then British School, now a bank, built in 1842, of flint pebble and gault brick trim, one-storeyed and a rum design; and then a double house (NORTHGATE HOUSE) with two heavy Ionic door surrounds of different widths and a carriageway between. On the other side lies POLSTEDE PLACE. Twelve retirement houses by *Sidney Bernstein Architects* (job architects *Sidney Bernstein* and *Robert Mitchell*), 1990. Two-storeyed terraces with varying roof lines and varying angles and recessed planes set back from the road, blending in with the traditional local styles, but not over-slavishly. The red of the pantiled roofs slightly garish, but they will weather down. The end of North Street brings us to All Saints, Burnham Ulph (q.v.), demonstrating the degree of integration of two parishes which until the early C19 stood aloof. Through the churchyard and once more W along FRONT STREET. This is lined with two-storey flint and brick houses which steadily increase in age as one approaches the Market Place, beginning at the E in the 1830s. OLD CRABBE HALL (s side) has an ovolo-moulded window of the early C17 at the back but the ubiquitous brick façade of c. 1800. HAMILTON HOUSE, adjacent, has C17 bridging beams. HIGH HOUSE (N side) boasts an early C19 Doric doorcase. Next to it No. 1, with a brick gable to the street with rusticated quoins and the date 1791. Three round-arched windows to the W flank. At this point one emerges again in the Market Place.

BARROW. There is a fine barrow in the SW corner of Burnham Westgate, with a Second World War pill-box built into its N side. (JW)

BURNHAM NORTON

ST MARGARET. Round tower with round-headed windows, six to the belfry stage, filled with honeycomb brick. The doorway into it from the nave may well be Anglo-Saxon evidence (cf. Burnham Deepdale). Another (blocked) doorway above it. Fine early C13 five-bay N aisle with short circular piers with circular abaci and double-chamfered pointed arches. The S aisle E parts of two bays are a little later. The E respond has a little stiff-leaf. The arches have hollow chamfers. Then the three W bays with octagonal piers. The nave heightened in the C15 and given a clerestory of four two-light windows under square hoods. Aisle W windows of c. 1300 (Y-tracery), remade in 1962, having been blocked. Nice Early Dec S doorway with worn fleurons in the abaci and shallow arch mouldings. Lancets and Curvilinear tracery in the chancel (E window altered C19). Late Perp aisle side-windows with stepped castellated transoms. Tudor N porch, but a Dec inner doorway comprising two hollow-moulded arches and a hood on headstops. – FONT. Norman, square, big, on five short columns with variously decorated shafts and cushion capitals. On the sides of the bowl simple patterns, e.g. a trellis, blank arches. – SCREENS. The rood screen much damaged and with defaced paintings. Inscription referring to William Groom. Also the date 1458. Restored 1953 by *Howard Brown* when it received new coving. The rood stairs which go with it are of brick. – C19 PARCLOSE SCREENS between nave and aisles and between the W aisle piers. – PULPIT. Outstanding Perp hexagonal piece with excellent paintings of the four Latin Fathers of the Church and of the donor Johannes Goldalle and his wife Katherina, and the date 1450; restored 1973 by *Pauline Plummer* when considerable over-painting was removed. The Doctors are seated on elaborate thrones, and shown writing at desks rather than holding scrolls as on the similar pulpit at Castle Acre. (DP) – Another PULPIT. Assembled in the C19 from Jacobean panels, which is why it is square, not hexagonal. Thin back-board and small tester carved with strapwork. The door has cockshead hinges. – WALL PAINTINGS. Remains of medieval painting above and beside the chancel arch; fragmentary small Crucifixion on E respond of N arcade. – ROYAL ARMS. One of Charles I, another of George IV, which is painted on vellum and signed '*Zech. Fenn* 1826 Painter Walsingham'.

FRIARY, ¼ m. E, on Friar's Lane. Remains of a Carmelite house founded in 1242–7, the first in Norfolk. Licence to enlarge the premises in 1249 and 1353. Dec gatehouse with important flushwork panelling, an early case (cf. Butley, Suffolk, and Ethelbert's Gate, Norwich). The stilted archway decorated with early C14 mouldings. Above is a recess with plinths for three images. These two elements are themselves recessed. Flanking the upper recess is one trefoiled blind window r. and l. with flint infill, one might say a proto-flushwork technique because the flint and stonework are not flush. Above again the remains of Curvilinear tracery in the three-light W window (tracery only lost in the 1960s). Flanking this more of the proto-flushwork, taking the form of two-light blind Dec windows. The blank tracery on the E side is intersecting and cusped. Vault inside the gatehouse. Two bays, diagonal and ridge ribs and two mutilated bosses. The springers rest on engaged colonnettes with circular moulded capitals. The mouldings again look early C14. The design of the blind windows, the vault, the intersecting E tracery and the mouldings fit a date of *c.* 1320, placing the gatehouse at the very beginning of the flushwork tradition. Access to the upper chamber via a doorway high in the N wall.

No more than 15 ft E of the gatehouse stands the W wall of the church, which was quite small, smaller than a parish church. Doorway with two continuous hollow chamfers. Niches l. and r. Blocked W window above. More fragments of walls further E defining the precinct, and running N along the road from the gatehouse. Also in FRIARY COTTAGE to the N an early C14 doorway, a big buttress and other details. A great deal of this flint and clunch building is C19 and C20, although in the SE corner is a winder stair partly of timber in its upper parts which might be C16. Of C14 origins, though, there is no doubt.

BURNHAM OVERY TOWN   *8040*

ST CLEMENT. Not at once a coherent building owing to altera-tions. It is, or was, an aisleless Norman cruciform church, of which the central tower remains, without its top stage. It was taken down at an unknown date to prevent collapse and the tall wide round arches to the four arms blocked to leave low and mean entrances so one walks through the tower from the nave to the present chancel – a bizarre thing. Only to the lost N transept is there a wider but messy opening. However, the ghosts of the original arches, on very simple imposts, may be discerned towards the chancel and former s transept. The roof-lines of transepts are also visible externally. The tower has Norman windows filled with C19 Y-tracery but the missing top stage had circular bell-openings. The transepts were probably added slightly later. On top of the tower a pretty C17 cupola.

The church did not remain in this state for long. The nave received N and s aisles about 1200, the former of three bays, the latter of four, but the N aisle was subsequently removed, leaving pointed wall arches inside and corresponding marks in the flint-work outside. The s aisle has circular piers with circular abaci, and further E a quatrefoil pier. On the capital of this and of the quatrefoil E impost are primitive but engaging heads, and the second pier, i.e. a round one, has a ring of waterleaf as a capital. Double-chamfered pointed arches. Then, a little later in the C13, a remodelling of the chancel took place which included the fine group of three widely spaced single-stepped lancets at the E end, shafted inside, and a s chancel aisle. This is of three bays, circular piers, double-hollow-chamfered arches. In 1835 there was a restoration and the chancel s wall was rebuilt further N, squeezing the aisle into a passageway, which is further narrowed by the alarming outward lean of the piers. The s windows are of this time: chancel aisle has two twin lancets, s nave aisle two- and three-light timber mullioned windows, looking odd in a church. The N nave aisle has a two-light and a three-light window with intersecting tracery and, internally, ogee heads suggesting c. 1310–20. If these are not of 1835 then the N aisle must by then have been demolished. w nave window also 1835. s porch C15, but there is a C14 inner doorway. C15 nave roof with prin-cipals on arched braces. – FONT. C15. Octagonal and re-cut, leaving fragments of a baptism scene and another unidentifiable scene on two of the plain bowl facets. – PAINTING. Small C15 St Christopher with fragmentary inscription, on the N nave wall. Conserved 1984 by the *Perry Lithgow Partnership*. – MONU-MENT. Robert Blyford †1672 (N nave wall). Bowed slate inscrip-tion panel, leaf trail in side volutes, skull and crossed bones below, broken segmental pediment above with achievement. – ORGAN. A small chamber organ of 1823 by *J. King*.

CROSS, c. 100 yds w on an island in the road at the foot of the hill. Base and a short length of late C14 octagonal shaft.

WINDMILL and WATERMILL, 300 yds s. An attached pair. The watermill straddling the River Burn has the date 1737 and was operated by Thomas Beeston who added the windmill in 1814. A good group including the Miller's House to the E. The five-storey tower mill was burnt out in 1935. The watermill is of red brick, of two storeys but raised into three probably in 1814. Usual casement windows. Undershot water wheel. The MILLER'S HOUSE is dated 1744, red brick, two storeys and attic. Seven bays augmented by a wing to the NE. Two porches on Doric columns and pilasters. Various C19 alterations. Good staircase inside, with three turned balusters to each tread.

WINDMILL, ⅜m. NW. A fine piece, even though converted to a house in 1926 by *Henry Cartree Hughes*, a Cambridge architect. Tarred brick, six-storey tower, ogee cap and skeleton fan, the latter put in by *Thompson & Son* during the restoration of 1957, but not following the original. Also by Thompsons were the stocks and sails, but these have been replaced since 1983. No shutters. A low gallery at first-floor level. Machinery remains in the cap only. The tower was built by *Edmund Savory* in 1816 (see tablet over the gallery door) to supplement the operation of his watermill, quite a common arrangement if one had a big enough business. Hughes's domestic extensions are low and modest enough, though the concrete block construction is a pity.

WATERMILL, 200 yds SW of the last. Picturesque group, with the Mill House, cottages and farm buildings of Mill Farm clustered together on a double bend in the road. The River Burn, surprisingly majestic at this point, completes the picture. The watermill is very long, two storeys, red brick and pantiled, but it was not all put up at the same time. The bridge and watermill are of 1790, and were operated by the same Edmund Savory as the windmill. In the middle of the C19 big granary extensions were added to the SW end, extending down Mill Road away from the farm, but a serious fire in 1959 gutted the structure and so the roof and much internal brickwork is of 1960. The floors are concrete. In 1989 the machinery was removed, with the exception of the undershot water wheel and the pitwheel, and the whole SW half turned into an animal shelter. The new granaries were required after the NE bays at the junction with the lane were added in 1820. They housed four pairs of stones driven by steam generated in the adjacent engine house – see the tall panelled stack. The Cornish boiler later served a maltings as well, in the buildings added yet further E down the lane.

The MILL HOUSE started as a double-pile flint building with brick dressings. The date of 1779 appears on the NW stack with the initials I. S., presumably indicating a John or James Savory. A small brick block was added to the SW corner in the 1820s (possibly in 1827 when John Savory took over the house and business from his father Edmund) and the S front, facing the mill, was given a new skin. The timber and wrought-iron loggia came in the 1860s when a proud three-bay, two-storey E wing was added in gault brick under a hipped roof. The panelled clasping pilasters are a nice touch. Too many C20 restorations have left a disappointing interior. The entrance hall has a Greek-key frieze. The stick-baluster staircase is not original.

PETERSTONE FARMHOUSE, 1¼m. E of the church. At the back (i.e. the N side) is a single-chamfered doorway with a hood-mould, and more fragments from Peterstone Priory, a house of Augustinian Canons founded before 1200. Rebuilt *c.*1830 in gault brick to form a row of cottages. The BARN was converted at the same time from a domestic monastic range, only parts of a window in the S gable and a pointed C14 arch at the NW corner showing externally. Inside are remains of three N doorways.

Opposite was the site of the great HOLKHAM ESTATE BRICK-
WORKS which provided brick and tiles for the estate, surround-
ing parishes and the rest of England from 1729 (the Temple,
Holkham Park, q.v.) to the 1950s.

BURNHAM OVERY STAITHE

8040

THE MOORINGS, Tower Road. Former maltings. The maltster's
house is early C19. Gault brick. Two storeys in four bays. The
porch has a pair of Doric columns. STAITHE HOUSE, 50 yds
SW, has C17 evidence in the rustication round the windows and
to the ends of the elevation. Re-worked early C20.

THE GARTH, Wells Road. The coastguard's house when built
c. 1830. Gault brick. Two storeys in three bays with lower attachments r. and l. Ground-floor sashes in recesses.

GUN HILL FARMHOUSE, Wells Road. Of the early C18 is the
shaped W gable. The seven-bay façade has cross casements,
rather altered. Platband.

BURNHAM SUTTON

8040

⅞ m. SE of Burnham Market

ST ETHELBERT. The parish amalgamated with Burnham Ulph in
1422 and the church was demolished in 1771, leaving only fragmentarily preserved lumps.

BURNHAM THORPE

8040

ALL SAINTS. The architectural history of the church starts with
the four-bay arcades. They are of the early C13 and have circular piers, circular capitals, and double-chamfered arches. The
aisle windows are Dec under depressed arches, the W and E
windows look even pre-Dec, i.e. *c.* 1300 (cusped Y-tracery).
Kelly tells us that the S aisle was added during the extensive
restorations of 1892–5, which cost £5,000. The roofs are from
this time. Small Perp clerestory. Dec chancel with characteristic
chancel arch and an excellent E wall with chequered flushwork
decoration. Three-light (restored) window with a flushwork frieze
below, connected with the window by descending mullions.
Three niches, l., r. and above the window. The chancel side-
windows are Perp with straight lines instead of the shanks of
arches. Perp sedilia and piscina with ogee arches and big fleurons
in the spandrels. The sedilia arches rest partly on two demi-
figures of angels. Hoodmould with fleurons. The Perp W tower
has a four-light window and battlements with flushwork panelling and shields. Much of it is a rebuild from 1842, as it fell in
the C18. – FONT. Of Purbeck marble, octagonal, with two shallow pointed arches to each side. C13. – STAINED GLASS. E window probably by *S. C. Yarington, c.* 1840, St Peter and Four

Evangelists, not complete. – MONUMENTS. C15 four-centred
wall arch in N aisle. – BRASS to Sir William Calthorpe †1420
(chancel floor). The figure is 3 ft 6 in. long in military dress.
Thin buttresses carry a top frieze. Inside an ogee gable. – Rev.
Edmund Nelson (Admiral Nelson's father; Nelson was born at
Burnham Thorpe) †1802 by *Flaxman*. Tablet with a simple
urn. – Ann Everard †1841 and William Everard †1847, both by
J. G. Lough, and both of white marble, one with two mourning
women, the other with two standing women l. and r. of the
inscription.

MANOR HOUSE, immediately NW. An C18 house of clunch and
brick. Two storeys in four wide bays. Tripartite ground-floor
sashes of the early C19, upper sashes within rusticated surrounds.
Porch on columns and a platband between the floors. C19 brick
rear wing. The W gable has some C17 flintwork. Hipped roof.

NELSON MEMORIAL HALL, S of the church overlooking the
village playing-field. A nice design of *W. P. Cave*. The date is
1891. The N side has three round brick arches in the flint walls
filled with stepped casements. Cupola on the roof. Additions
1939 and 1951 to the S.

OLD RECTORY, Creake Road. The Rectory in which Admiral
Nelson was born has disappeared, and this one replaced it in
1802. Five bays with two outer bow windows and a porch in the
middle on square piers.

WHITEHALL FARMHOUSE, Walsingham Road. The C17 house
was given a brick E front in the C18, the brick unusually for the
date laid in English bond. Fenestration now C19 and C20. At
the back the material is flint and clunch, dressed in brick.

The main road in the village is THE STREET. The SCHOOL
HOUSE is early C17, with rustication at the corners and a brick
entrance arch. Windows replaced C20. The BARN at Ivy Farm
has to the N side brick openings with rusticated sides. The roof
has upper crucks, so the date is early C17.

BARROW. The barrow excavated N of Leath House in 1862 contained Roman pottery.

BURNHAM ULPH   8040

Burnham Ulph and Burnham Sutton were amalgamated in 1422.
For St Ethelbert of Burnham Sutton *see* Burnham Sutton. The
parish of Burnham Ulph merges imperceptibly with Burnham
Market to the W. Cotman's drawing of 1817 shows the church
with a partly ruinous chancel and with only a distant farm for
company.

ALL SAINTS. Excellent pointed chancel arch of *c.*1190. Keeled
responds with characteristic waterleaf capitals with volutes. The
waterleaf extends on to the plain imposts of the arch. The slots
for a former screen cut into the capitals. One S window of the
same date inside but renewed in the C14 outside. In the chancel
N wall and the nave W wall windows with Y-tracery, i.e. of

c. 1300, but on the N a lancet with some dogtooth. No tower; only a W bellcote which in form at least is medieval. The church was mostly rebuilt in 1879, though quite accurately to judge by Cotman's drawing. Of that date the scissor-braced roofs. Vestry added 1910. – PULPIT. C18, hexagonal, on a C19 stem.

BURSTON

ST MARY. Mostly Victorian in its external appearance, although its origins are C15. Chancel and vestry all C19. The tower collapsed in 1753, which explains the big brick buttresses holding up the nave W wall. Nave with Perp windows, all renewed during the restoration of 1853. – FONT. C15. Round the stem, not in niches, eight figures, quite good.

RECTORY, S of the church. By *Vulliamy*, 1840. Red brick with bargeboarded gables. It was for the Rev. Temple Frere, and was enlarged in 1862.

STRIKE SCHOOL, Church Green. The teachers of the village school supported striking farm workers in the troubles of 1914 and were sacked for their pains. A public subscription in 1917 raised sufficient funds for a new independent school, where they carried on teaching. The result is more interesting for its history than its architecture: a single-storey, three-bay building with a central door and casement windows r. and l.

Burston is in the centre of the timber-framed area of Norfolk, close to the Suffolk border. Nearly all vernacular buildings are of this material, often masked by later brick. Of C16 and C17 houses the best are BRIDGE GREEN FARMHOUSE, Gissing Road: C16, but the timber frame visible only internally, as a red brick skin was applied in the C19. HIGH HOUSE FARMHOUSE, Heywood Road. Late C16, timber-framed, with rebuilt stacks dated 1586. C19 windows. MANOR HOUSE FARMHOUSE, Station Road. Early C17, timber-framed. The plan already a lobby-entrance, with a stack over the door terminating in octagonal flues.

CAISTOR ST EDMUND

VENTA ICENORUM. The walled town and Roman administrative capital of Norfolk lies between the road and the River Tas – the church lies just within the E wall. The walls, running for *c.* 1100 ft N–S and 1400 ft E–W, enclose some thirty-four acres. They are of tiles and brick with a flint coping. The basic plan, still visible from the air, is as usual of blocks or *insulae* divided by lanes with a central forum or basilica. Other public buildings include what were probably the municipal baths. The N wall is particularly well preserved, and the porter's lodge at the W gate has been recovered.

The structural history of the town may be briefly summarized. There are indications that the nucleus of early settlement

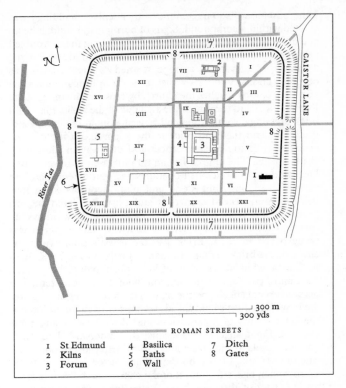

Caistor St Edmund. Plan of Venta Icenorum

I	St Edmund	4	Basilica	7	Ditch
2	Kilns	5	Baths	8	Gates
3	Forum	6	Wall		

lay to the NE of the town, in the grounds of Caistor Hall. Following the Boudiccan revolt in A.D. 70 a number of clay-floored timber huts were built, linked by a network of streets. In the late CI pottery kilns were in use on the N side of the town. In c. A.D. 150, on a site some 200 ft wide, the forum and basilica were constructed but were destroyed by fire c. 200 and rebuilt c. 300 of masonry, with a colonnaded façade looking on to a gravelled street. The baths with their wooden pipelines are contemporary with the first forum. At the beginning of the C3 the wall was built enclosing half the town (thirty-four acres), 11 ft thick, 20 ft high, and of concrete faced with squared flint and brick. Its construction involved truncating some of the street-plan. The rectangular and U-shaped towers and the ditch, 80–100 ft wide, are backed by an earthen rampart. Their date is close to A.D. 200, when two Romano-Celtic temples were erected with central square towers, perhaps originally up to 50 ft high, and surrounding porticoes. At the same time the old wattle-and-daub houses were replaced by masonry-footed and timbered buildings, the baths reconstructed, and a glassworks opened. However, until c. 250 the forum was in some disrepair, as was the S gate. Outside the walls to the NE beside Caistor

Lane a separate square temple with ancillary buildings was erected within a compound. Signs of burning and sudden death and a Saxon settlement beyond the town belong to the troubled period of *c.* 360–400. This settlement lies some 1100 ft SE of the E gateway. Excavations in 1932 seemed to show that it was occupied until A.D. 500; it overlies some C2–4 Roman huts. (DG)

ST EDMUND. One reaches the church by crossing the moat of the Roman town and turning to the SE angle of the walls. Flint with brick dressings, some stone and reused Roman material, especially flint and tiles and brick in the N porch. Of the C11 the evidence is in the blocked lancet and doorway in the S wall, visible inside. The church has an unbuttressed W tower with a Dec window, but brick bell-openings and battlements panelled in brick and flint, not stone and flint. Bequests for a new bell-frame are recorded in 1525 and 1533. Rendered chancel probably of *c.* 1300, nave with Perp panel-tracery windows, an earlier N doorway and a brick S doorway. The N porch was being paved in 1462. Brick also the priest's doorway in the chancel, the brick perhaps Roman. – FONT. Given by Richard de Caistor while he was vicar of St Stephen, Norwich, between 1402 and 1419. Octagonal with four lions against the stem, four demi-figures of angels and the signs of the four Evangelists against the bowl. The angels hold shields with the emblem of the Trinity, the Instruments of the Passion, and three crowns and three chalices. Eight angel heads against the underside. The plinth has quatrefoils to each facet and a black-letter inscription referring to the Guild of St John Baptist at Caistor. – PAINTING. St Christopher, also a St John N of the chancel arch, both faded.

OLD HALL, N of the church on Stoke Road. The house has a three-storey central porch with a shaped gable to the SE front. In the gable one pedimented window. The gable had a date 1647, which is no longer visible, but the entrance with a pretty and lively Jacobean surround comprising another pediment and three low-relief pinnacles is dated 1612. As the house was built for John Pettus who acquired the estate in 1606, the top storey of the porch is therefore an addition. Pettus arms on the doorway. The rest of the façade is of two storeys in three irregular bays. Mullioned and transomed windows in the porch, sashes fitted to the main wall except for the upper r. three-light leaded casement. External gable-end stacks and a pair of compound flues emerging over the roof-line. Stepped gable to a rear wing and plenty of mullioned and leaded windows including a six-light one with a transom and king mullion. Inside is a stair-turret to the rear which has a small closed-string staircase with vertically symmetrical turned balusters carrying on right to the top of the house. Chimneypiece to ground-floor W room with Corinthian columns; that to the E room C17, with a four-centred moulded arch.

CAISTOR HALL, NE of the church, also on Stoke Road. Built for the Dashwood family. Very early C19 three- by five-bay grey brick house, now a country club. To the l. of the main house a four-bay attachment, so the W front appears as of seven bays.

The newer part cannot be much later than *c.* 1820. Both parts have hipped roofs. Handsome porch to the r., a shallow curve on coupled Roman Doric columns. Staircase with a wreathed handrail and cast-iron balusters.

OLD RECTORY, Norwich Road. Four-bay S front. The two l. bays are late C18, the others slightly taller and added in the early C19. Door set to the l. under an open pediment. Sash windows. Two decent, if modest, staircases, both curved, both with stick balusters but one with a pine handrail (w), the other mahogany.

CALDECOTE   7000

1½ m. N of Oxburgh Hall

On a mound the scantiest remains of a former parish church.

CALVELEY HALL *see* REYMERSTON

CARBROOKE   9000

ST PETER AND ST PAUL. The chancel is of the late C13, see the single-chamfered priest's doorway, the two-step sedilia, and above all the splendid E window of five lights, with a quite original composition of the tracery. The lights intersect and are cusped; at the top is a large quatrefoiled circle flanked by two smaller trefoiled circles and two mouchettes. The foils are all separated from each other by barbs. The window is shafted inside. N and S chancel windows of three lights and C15, similar to Litcham. Early C14 ogee-headed S aisle piscina. Late C15 S porch with a late C14 S doorway inside, with a big ogee arch.

The rest is mostly Perp. Tall w tower. Frieze of shields above the doorway. Tall arch towards the nave. Under the tower two caryatid busts to carry the floor of the first stage. Two-storeyed N porch now used as a vestry and the entrance blocked. A niche above the entrance. A tierceron star vault with bosses inside. The porch, the tower and the aisles have a base frieze of flush-work panelling. This is so similar to the base courses at Blickling, Barton Turf and St Giles, Norwich (qq.v., Vol. 1) that the same hand must be at work. Big aisle windows. The tracery in the chancel windows is more intricate than that of the aisles. Interior with Perp arcades of five bays. The piers have wave mouldings and shafts and various fine mouldings between. Triple-chamfered arches, elaborated with wave mouldings. Tall chancel arch and panelling in three tiers to its l. and r., again inviting comparison with St Giles, Norwich. The late C15 roof has wall-posts on figures sticking out and angels also sticking out as false hammer-beams. – FONT. Octagonal, with a variety of C14 tracery patterns. – SCREEN. Of tall one-light divisions with ogee arches. Crockets and simple tracery over. Money was given for work on the rood loft in 1521. Painted dado panels are missing. – MONUMENTS.

Two early C13 coffin-lids with foliated crosses, assigned by Blomefield to the Countess of Clare and one of her sons, which is borne out by their inscriptions. – STAINED GLASS. E window †1910, by *J. Powell & Sons*.

There was a Preceptory of Hospitallers at Carbrooke, founded by Roger de Clare *c.* 1193. In the early C19 foundations were still visible just SE of the church, and there are still substantial earthworks consisting of a moat, banks and fishponds. (AR)

An interesting village for the study of clay lump construction (*see* Introduction, p. 27). Its use can be traced from its combination with timber-framing of the C17 at THE STRIPED COTTAGE, Broadmoor Road, to its C19 application on its own in the mid-C19 cottages WEST COTTAGE and PENDLE COTTAGE at Caudlesprings, ½ m. from the church on the road to Watton. The THATCHED COTTAGE on Church Street has C18 clay lump in combination with flint, dressed with red brick. Of more major buildings, THE MANOR HOUSE ¼ m. N on Shipdham Road: C17, lobby-entrance, with a big offset external S stack and a brick re-facing of the C18. CARBROOKE HALL 1 m. SE on the Watton Road was a five-bay house of *c.* 1780, as can most easily be appreciated from the S, garden, front. The three-bay extension to the W is of 1832, for the Dewing family.

WINDMILL, 1 m. S of the church. In 1856 Richard Dewing bought and replaced the post mill with the present derelict five-storey brick tower mill. It has no cap or sails.

0000

CARLETON FOREHOE

ST MARY. W tower of 1713, flint and red brick, with intersecting wooden windows to the bell-stage. Nave and chancel all C15 with Perp windows, all seemingly restored. Niches l. and r. of the chancel arch. Three restorations: 1839 (pews, organ gallery); 1863 (general); 1876 (more pews). – STAINED GLASS. E window 1885.

CHURCH FARMHOUSE, S of the church, across a field. Brick, with a two-storeyed porch which has a shaped gable and a cinquefoiled circle in it. Probably early C18. C19 windows. Much rebuilding in 1881.

GELHAM LODGE. Another house with a two-storeyed porch and a shaped gable (S of Church Farmhouse on Barnham Broom Road). The porch added *c.* 1700 to a timber-framed house. C20 mullioned windows.

To the SE again is the BRIDGE erected over the River Tiffey in 1815 for the Wodehouses of Kimberley (q.v.). The little river feeds the lake beneath Kimberley Hall.

1090

CARLETON RODE

ALL SAINTS. Remarkably lavish chancel of the late C13, unfavourably restored in 1877–83 after having been given a thin new roof in 1850. Among the windows are two with pointed trefoiled lights and a trefoil over. The E window of four lights with intersecting tracery has thin shafts attached to the mullions. The priest's doorway with shafts and fine arch-mouldings looks late C13 but the capitals are suspiciously like those of the 1850 roof corbels. Late C13 the double piscina, again with pointed trefoiled arches and a cusped pointed quatrefoil above. Hoodmould on leaf corbels. Of the sedilia only the beginning is preserved. Leaf corbels otherwise as well. Of the same date the N aisle doorway, N aisle w window, and the s aisle E window (clumsily rebuilt in the C18). The piscina close to it seems Victorian. Clerestory redone in 1850, with the scissor-braced nave roof. C15 s porch. Arcades of four bays with octagonal piers and double-hollow-chamfered arches. The chancel arch of the same pattern. Very low Dec w tower, repaired in 1717 after a partial collapse, when no doubt the strangely bare flushwork designs were introduced. It was left one storey short. Most of the nave and aisle windows are Perp with stepped embattled transoms (mullions renewed). Above the chancel arch a foiled circular window, probably of 1850. – FONT. C18, with fluted stem. – SCREEN. On the dado twelve C15 painted figures, below average in artistic merit. Restored by *Tristram*, 1937. – WALL PAINTINGS. Many unusual but restored consecration crosses in the chancel (DP). – STAINED GLASS. In each chancel window is a trefoil panel of a seated figure against a dark blue ground, all blackened with age. They must be of the C13 still and help to date the chancel.

BAPTIST CHAPEL, Chapel Road. 1812, brick, three by two bays under a pyramid roof. Doorcase in w front with pilasters. Simple gallery on three sides inside. A little schoolroom to the NW added in 1904.

OLD RECTORY, Church Road. Mid-C18, of red brick. Two storeys and dormer attic in five bays. The sashes set within exposed boxes. The C17 timber-framed rear jostles with C19 extensions.

OLD HALL FARMHOUSE, Old Hall Road, ¾ m. NW. Outwardly of C19 brick, inwardly an early C17 timber-framed house.

THE STEAM MILL, Mill Road. Clay lump, with a chimney bearing the date 1854. The front has three bays of sashes, and there is a further wing to the s. Now a house.

The VILLAGE has three settlements – Carleton, clustered round the church, Flaxlands ¼ m. NW and Uplands Street 1 m. w. On ASH LANE is THE ASHES, an early C18 house completely cased with brick in *c.* 1850, but with a C17 timber-framed rear wing, also bricked over. WHITEHOUSE FARMHOUSE has early C17 details to the timber frame, as does ASH FARMHOUSE, the latter again with a brick skin, but with a winder stair in the lobby by the stack. REEDER'S FARMHOUSE, Old Hall Road, is again early C17 and timber-framed, and has sunk-quadrant mouldings to the bridging beams, typical of the Wymondham style. The pattern of minor C17 timber-framed houses, often with C19 brick skins, is repeated throughout the neighbourhood.

CARLETON ST PETER

St Peter. w tower very late Perp. Donations 1502–25, and in 1537 specifically for the battlements. Flint with much brick trim, e.g. the intersecting w window, the bell-openings, and the stair projection. Nave and chancel under one roof. All windows renewed, except one s lancet of *c.* 1200 with roll mouldings. There is however also in the s wall also a trace of a blocked Norman window. A N lancet looks C14 but has inside also a round head. Chancel piscina of the late C13. In the chancel N wall a plain recess with a long black-letter inscription from the Geneva version of the New Testament, i.e. the version of 1557. – SCREEN. Mostly Victorian, but probably reflecting a genuine C14 screen with the quite typical large roundels above the ogee-shaped entrance arch. One has a six-pointed star, the other a curious shape of two intersecting mouchettes. – BENCHES. Some with C15 poppyheads.

CASTLE ACRE

St James. A large church, situated between the outer walled town to the E and the precinct of the priory. Powerful Perp w tower with a w doorway, four-light w window with embattled transom, small quatrefoil openings in circles higher up, and top battlements with flushwork panelling. Money was left for its construction in 1396. N and s sides Perp, except for the priest's doorway of the later C13 with colonnettes, and three good Dec N windows. Above the priest's doorway is a blocked arched E.E. opening. Two-storey Perp N porch, with shields in the diapered spandrels. N vestry, also two-storeyed, with animals sitting on the corners. Perp clerestory of three-light flat-headed windows. Inside, a curious anomaly in the arcades. Quatrefoil piers of the early C14 (with the four shafts almost detached) were reused in Perp arcades and alternate with similar C15 piers. Five bays, double-hollow-chamfered arches. The chancel arch corresponds to the Perp parts of the arcades. The four-light E window has disappointing plate tracery dating from the restoration of 1875 by *Ewan Christian*. In the chancel, however, the big sedilia seem to go with the priest's doorway. At least the chopped-off decoration of the gable seems of *c.* 1300.

FURNISHINGS. FONT. Tall, octagonal, with rolls curving up the edges from the stem to the bowl. C15. – FONT COVER. Very tall steeple-like affair with arches and spirelets to the Perp canopy, with some of the colouring preserved. – STALLS. Front with reused panels from screens, decorated with ornamental painting. Seats with MISERICORDS: a lion's head, a demi-figure of an angel, an eagle. – SCREENS. The dado of the rood screen has twelve good paintings of the apostles, with St James the Great (dedicatee of the church) paired with St Peter in the centre. Usually dated as early as *c.* 1400 or the early C15 on account of the flowing drapery style, they have recently been more

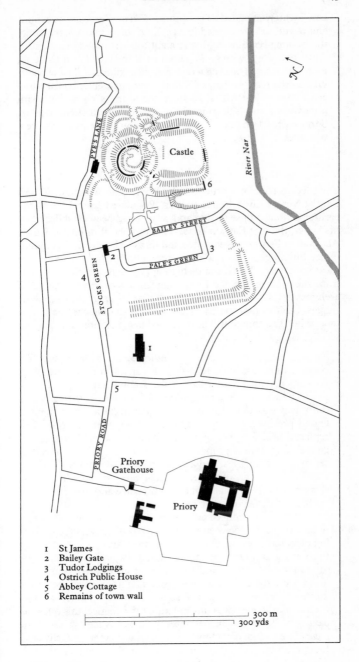

1 St James
2 Bailey Gate
3 Tudor Lodgings
4 Ostrich Public House
5 Abbey Cottage
6 Remains of town wall

300 m
300 yds

Castle Acre

convincingly assigned to *c.* 1440 (a *William Castleacre* 'steynour and peyntour' is recorded in 1445). Of the parclose screen only the framing remains, with a straight top on arched pieces (DP). – PULPIT. Perp, with good paintings of the four Latin Doctors, each with a scroll bearing a text from his writings. Like the paintings on the rood screen, of *c.* 1440, and apparently by the same artist (DP). – BENCHES. Eight in the N and S aisles, low, with poppyheads and little animals on the arms. – STAINED GLASS. Some early C15 fragments on a white ground are in the S aisle E window.

PRIORY

Founded in 1090 or a little later by William de Warenne, second Earl of Surrey, for Cluniac monks. Populated from Lewes, the earliest Cluniac house in England, which had been established by his father, the first Earl, in 1077. The number of monks at Castle Acre varied between twenty-five and thirty. The size and grandeur 7 of the buildings is astounding in the light of this. The ruins are most impressive. Much stands high up, though only the SW tower from the S gives one the impression of a recognizable piece of architecture. Otherwise it is a landscape of crags and fabulous shapes. Built of flint, partly faced with alternating grey or brown sandstone. The church will be described first, the monastic quarters second, the gatehouse last.

CHURCH. The original plan, now indicated on the lawn, was of a chancel with apse, chancel aisles with apses, and transepts with apsidal chapels, i.e. the plan of the second building at Cluny, not of Lewes or of the magnificent Cluny III. In the early C14 the E end was pulled down and replaced by a larger, square-ended presbytery. In the C15 a N chapel, also square-ended, replaced and lengthened the N chancel aisle and N transept chapel. There was a proper crossing with a tower over, a nave of seven bays with aisles, and a W façade with two towers. A doorway in the N wall of the N transept opened into the oblong sacristy, with the remains of a C16 fireplace and oven.

Of the ELEVATION not much can be said. The church was apparently, as was indeed customary, built from E to W, but details remain only near the W end. The two-bay E arm and the E crossing piers must belong to *c.* 1100–10, the transepts *c.* 1110–20, a third phase in *c.* 1120–30 taking us to the W end. The piers were of compound section and the aisles groin-vaulted, and so no doubt were the chancel chapels too. The transept chapels were groin-vaulted also. The transepts show indications of high vaults, but the nave was unvaulted. Of the chancel this question cannot be decided. The best-preserved part is the SW bay of the nave. The rounded respond has diagonal grooving exactly as at Durham (begun 1093) and in the nave at Norwich (*c.* 1115–20). The arch has plenty of zigzag, and so has the large, unsubdivided gallery arch. Wall passage inside the clerestory windows. The aisle has wall-shafts connecting with the piers. The nave

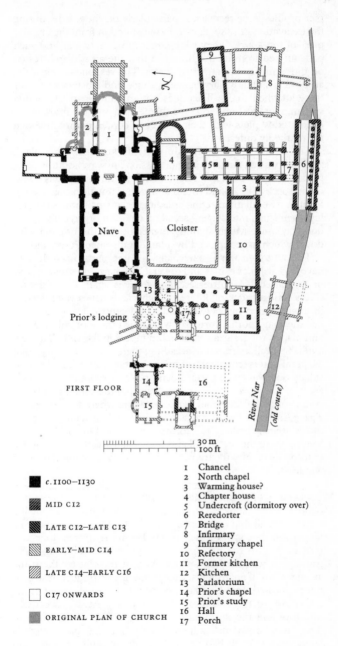

FIRST FLOOR

River Nar (old course)

|————————|————————————————| 30 m
|————————|————————————| 100 ft

■	*c.* 1100–1130	1 Chancel
		2 North chapel
▨	MID C12	3 Warming house?
		4 Chapter house
▨	LATE C12–LATE C13	5 Undercroft (dormitory over)
		6 Reredorter
▨	EARLY–MID C14	7 Bridge
		8 Infirmary
▨	LATE C14–EARLY C16	9 Infirmary chapel
		10 Refectory
□	C17 ONWARDS	11 Former kitchen
		12 Kitchen
▨	ORIGINAL PLAN OF CHURCH	13 Parlatorium
		14 Prior's chapel
		15 Prior's study
		16 Hall
		17 Porch

Castle Acre Priory. Plan

pier profiles were recovered, particularly on the N side, during
the excavation in 1889, and show a distinction from the circular
piers of the E arm. They were larger in the E–W axis and each
pair differed from its neighbour in that the arcade arch rested
on different pairs of attached shafts. The responds against the
aisle walls similarly vary between single and clusters of two or
three attached shafts. This does not amount to an alternating
system, merely a variation on a theme, and only the more richly
decorated W piers with their echoes of contemporary Norwich
are markedly different.

The inside of the W façade is richly arcaded. This blank
arcading was an Anglo-Norman passion anyway, and it is done
to excess at Castle Acre. The doorway in the middle has a segmental arch with a blind round arch above it with zigzag. To the
l. and r. first tall intersecting arcading, then small normal arcading, then small intersecting arcading cut off inorganically by the
doorway arch. Much shafting higher up for the original windows, which were replaced by a large transomed Perp window.

The WEST FRONT is externally in three parts, according to
nave and aisles or gables and towers. The parts are separated by
nook-shafted flat buttresses. The front is again covered with
divers blind arcades, of different heights and shapes, not matched
in their relationship between sides and centre. The centre bay
has the main portal, formerly with four orders of colonnettes,
and diaper, rope, zigzag and bobbin motifs in the arch. To the l.
and r. first tall intersecting arcading, then round arcading, then
again tall intersecting, cut off by the portal. To the l. and r. subsidiary doorways with fewer orders and less decoration, and even
areas of blank wall round them. Above, in the centre of a string
course of corbels, a small tier of arcading where the arches are
zigzag (instead of having zigzag applied to them), and again tall
blank arches flanking the former windows. On the l. and r.,
leading up to the tower, tall and then small arcading, and above
that (on the S side) the transition into E.E. with shafted, pointed
windows.

MONASTIC QUARTERS. The CLOISTER is on the S side of the
church, 30 yds square. The walks must have been remodelled
c. 1500 and all that remains of the C12 cloister is the mark of its
higher roof-line against the church. From the church doorways
lead to it from the first and last bays of the S aisle. In the S
transept W wall the book-niche. Against the cloister the usual
arrangement of apartments, except that the warming house cannot be located. In a Cluniac monastery it is usually sited in the
undercroft of the dormitory. Is it at Castle Acre between the
refectory and the dormitory, in the SE corner of the cloister?
The CHAPTER HOUSE adjoined the S transept, but is slightly
later, say c. 1140. It had originally a tunnel vault, an apse, and
once more plenty of blind arcading, of which only the lower parts
of some shafts survive. Above, on the N side, are some round
wall arches, so high that there must have been tiers of them.
The apse was removed in the C14. To its S the DORMITORY

STAIRS, about 6 ft 6 in. wide, and then the UNDERCROFT of the
S half of the dormitory, two-naved in eight bays and with wall-
piers. Of the DORMITORY the four windows above the cloister
roof still show, with arcading to the w, all altered with brick in
the C15. Of the C14 are the five buttresses added to the E side of
the s bays. In the corner to the s range there was a small garderobe
which could be cleared out on the ground floor. But this can
only have been subsidiary; for, as customary, there was a whole
lavatory building to the s, the REREDORTER, standing at r.
angles to the dormitory, being 91 ft long (compared with the
c. 110 ft of the dormitory) and exceptionally well preserved. All
mid-C12. It was approached from the dormitory by a bridge, i.e.
across some tunnel vaults. The river is tunnelled over, about 9 ft
6 in. in width. To the s the drain and above this the lavatory
cubicles. The seats rested on stone brackets; the floor had considerable slope. To the E of this group the INFIRMARY, two
halls, the N one Norman, the other of the early C14. Late C14
passages connected them with each other, with the dormitory,
and (a long one, 100 ft) with the s chancel chapel. These must
replace earlier timber passages. In the C14 a new passage s to
the river and the infirmary garderobe were added. The infirmary chapel was in the E end of the C12 hall.

Of the REFECTORY no more than the walls are visible. It
occupied more than the entire width of the s cloisters, 118 ft
long. To its w the Norman KITCHEN with four mighty pillars
no doubt put up to support a louvre. To its s a detached later
kitchen of the C15, across the drain.

The WEST RANGE at Castle Acre is specially interesting; for
here the original PRIOR'S LODGING was so progressively
extended and improved that by about 1500 the prior was in
possession of an objectionably lavish and worldly residence. Of
the two-storey C12 apartments running N–S parallel with the w
cloister walk the undercroft survives, six bays, two-naved and
groin vaulted. Its N end was divided off and formed the PARLA-
TORIUM. This was tunnel vaulted and had doorways to the N
and the E. Here also was access to the original prior's lodging,
which lay above. The CHAPEL is above the parlatorium and still
has its shallow late C12 E bay. Arch with thin continuous shafting; tunnel vault. The E window is an early C14 insertion (three
lights, intersecting tracery). Traces of C14 WALL PAINTINGS on
the window jambs and E and s walls: a mitred bishop is apparent, and fragmentary decoration including gilding. The sedilia
is Dec, and the fireplace an indication that the room was secu-
larized in the C16. Ceiling with early C16 roll- and hollow-
moulded tie-beams on knuckle braces, decorated with small
painted roses, under a C15 scissor-braced roof. The chapel now
communicates directly with the prior's study immediately w.
This is part of the mid-C14 extension to the PRIOR'S HOUSE
and consists of one room on each of the two storeys. The lower
room is divided into two by a solid wall, each part vaulted with
two bays of quadripartite rib vaults. Above is the study, formerly
probably the solar, and it, like the chapel to its E, has a C16

inserted fireplace sharing the same stack. Of the C16 also are the two oriels, one to the W on a much-moulded bracket and with quatrefoil friezes, the other to the N, semicircular (which is rare and seems to be later; for the lights of the window are uncusped) and on squinches. The N oriel has inside a four-centred arch on thin shafts. A C16 stepped brick gable to the W. In the C14 too the prior seems to have taken over the whole of the upper floor of the W range as a grand hall, certainly secular in spirit, of which the study block was only the northerly of two added ranges. The other took over the C12 kitchens at the S.

The main entrance to the priory in the C12 was by a spacious two-storeyed PORCH midway down the W range. This is of the ending of the C12. Two-bay rib vault with keeled ribs on corbels. Entrance arch with zigzag, also at r. angles to the wall plane. It is not easy at once to recognize this porch, for it lies now inside the prior's porch, the last of the extensions to the prior's house, of the early C16. The new porch has diagonal buttresses and an entrance with a four-centred arch. Niche to the r. Area of chequer flushwork above. First-floor window of four lights with embattled transom under a four-centred head. The timber-framed gable-head is on a cranked tie-beam.

GATEHOUSE. This lies to the N. The precinct walls are amply preserved. The gatehouse is of *c.* 1500, of cut flint, clunch and copious brick dressings. Two storeys, rectangular plan. Diagonal buttresses with set-offs. Tall carriage entrance under a four-centred arch. Smaller two-centred pedestrian entrance. Brick windows formerly with mullions. Staircase at the SW corner. Fireplace in the spacious porter's lodge to the E. The first floor, now open to the sky, was probably a single chamber.

CASTLE

One of the grandest motte-and-bailey castles in England, and called by E. S. Armitage 'perhaps the finest castle earthworks in England'. The total area is fifteen acres. William de Warenne was awarded Lewes (Sussex), Conisbrough (Yorks), Reigate (Surrey) and Castle Acre (among others) as a reward for his part in the Conquest, his principal residence being Lewes. The castle of the Warennes at Castle Acre is mentioned in 1085 when Gundrada, William's wife, died here, but it probably was begun in the 1070s.

The site involved an upper and lower ward with a barbican to the E, and the town to the W, itself protected by ditches and walls. The traditional bailey is the lower ward, the motte the upper ward, all quite normal. Excavations in the 1970s, however, show that something distinctly unusual was built, in that the earliest stone building in the centre of the UPPER WARD was a purely domestic structure. It was of stone, rectangular (roughly 79 ft square), and is one of the earliest pieces of evidence for the Norman domestic plan: basement as storage with external access, the first floor as living accommodation reached by an external staircase. The first-floor windows were

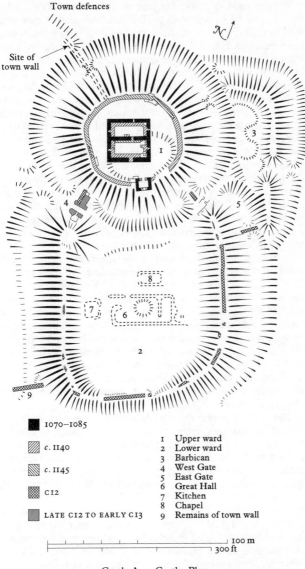

Castle Acre Castle. Plan

■ 1070–1085	
▨ c. 1140	
▨ c. 1145	
▨ C12	
▨ LATE C12 TO EARLY C13	

1 Upper ward
2 Lower ward
3 Barbican
4 West Gate
5 East Gate
6 Great Hall
7 Kitchen
8 Chapel
9 Remains of town wall

100 m
300 ft

wide and round-arched. The two floors were divided internally
by E–W spine walls. The N room had a first-floor fireplace set
into the N wall under a hooded flue. All this must have been in
place by 1085 and has been described as a 'country house'
rather than a fortified castle keep. It was protected only by a
circular ditch and timber palisade entered over a wooden bridge
to the S.

William died in 1088, the year he was created first Earl of
Surrey, and was succeeded by William, the second earl, who
died in 1138. For most of the second earl's life things must have
been peaceful, but in the late 1130s unrest led to the civil wars
of Stephen and Matilda's time, and a rash of unlicensed castle
building. Suddenly the country house must have seemed inadequately defended, and it was probably William, the third
earl, who transformed the upper ward. Around 1140 the house
was gutted and the thickness of the walls doubled on the inside.
The S wall of the keep shows the straight join where this was
done. The windows and doors were blocked up and one of the
two wells (the NE one) was surrounded by a shaft so as to be
accessible from the first floor only. The spine wall remained in
the manner of castle keeps of the time (e.g. Castle Rising and
Norwich). At the same time the ditch was deepened and the
ground level of the upper ward raised, burying the new keep
deeper into the ground. The wooden palisade was replaced with
a flint wall with a crenellated parapet, which is the wall we see
today, enclosing a space 180 ft in diameter.

In c. 1145, before the keep was anywhere near complete, the
half of it S of the spine wall was demolished and the exposed S
face of the wall dressed in flint. What for? Was it just getting too
big and too difficult to build in a reasonable time? The remaining half presumably continued in construction; the curtain wall
certainly did, acquiring greater height to the N. The gatehouse
to the S was also strengthened. The finds of bones, pottery and
coins in the upper ward testify to the fact that it was fully occupied in the C12, but the occupation did not last long. William,
the third earl, died in 1147 while on the Second Crusade, and
the ward seems to have been all but abandoned c. 1200 in favour
of the lower ward.

The LOWER WARD ran S as far as the River Nar, which has
shifted its position further S from its C12 course. The Nar was
then navigable to this point. The lower ward and the barbican
to the E were contemporary with the upper ward in all respects,
both with massive earth ramparts topped first with timber, then
with flint walls. In the NW corner was the WEST GATE, in the
NE corner the EAST GATE. Decent pieces of C12 wall survive to
the curtain walls, particularly to the S and E. The space so
enclosed had a dual purpose – to provide a first line of defence
for the keep itself, and to hold the storehouses, domestic halls
and barracks for the retinue and staff, guest-houses and all the
other buildings obviously necessary for the upkeep of one of
the largest retinues in the country. The outline of three buildings can be determined in the grass, the biggest of which must
be a C13 GREAT HALL. This, it is supposed, is the replacement
accommodation after the upper ward was abandoned. W of it may
be the kitchen, and the marks N have been suggested as a chapel.

The EAST GATE has all but disappeared. It led into an area
of further walling to the E of the upper ward, the BARBICAN,
itself with crenellated walls surmounting earth banks, and its
own E gatehouse. This area is immediately S of the present-day

castle car park. Between the East Gate and the barbican was a heavy wooden BRIDGE, of which enough evidence was found during the excavations for a reasonable reconstruction.

The WEST GATE led into the walled town. It is of early C13 construction in its present form, which was similar to the surviving Bailey Gate, or N town gate. Two round towers faced W. To the s an opening led into a vaulted room and to the N access was provided into a rectangular building with a garderobe. This may have been a guard room.

THE TOWN

When the castle was strengthened during the C12 a PLANNED TOWN was laid out to its W and s defined by a ditch and wall. The Bailey Gate marked the N entry to it. The route of the wall ran NW from the upper ward, followed the present line of Pye's Lane, through the Bailey Gate and along the south part of Stocks Green. Where the two arms of Stocks Green merge into Priory Road the wall and ditch turned sharply s, 55 yds E of the church. The wall then followed a course direct for Chimney Street, turning at r. angles to meet the SW corner of the lower ward of the castle. At this point is the only surviving fragment of wall: flint, formerly with ashlar dressings and battlements, C12. The street pattern was the usual grid, and is clear enough today. The main thoroughfare was Bailey Street, running N–S.

The s gate has disappeared, but the N one, BAILEY GATE, is the only part of the castle-town complex which fully survives. It dates from c. 1200 and has two round towers to the N. Whole flints and ashlar dressings. Unmoulded two-centred arches N and s, both with rere-arches inside. Grooves for the portcullis and hinge pins for the gates.

Perambulation

Castle Acre is a pretty town, or rather a village. Its population in 1991 was 700, though in 1891 it was 1,400. At the crossing of Peddar's Way and the River Nar, it was both a trading route and a stopping place for the pilgrimage to Walsingham. The Reformation caused a decline. BAILEY STREET now is lined with unpretentious C18 and C19 houses and shops, and only Nos. 63–64 on the E side deserves attention. The flint façade with occasional brick and ashlar quoins is late C15, and the N gable displays itself as a façade not always crowded by newer buildings. Towards the bottom of the street one turns r. into PALE'S GREEN and at the bend in this road on the l. is No. 61, TUDOR LODGINGS. An aptly named early C16 pair of monastic lodgings with the advanced internal plan-form typical of this rare type: two houses of mirrored plan, sharing a central stack with winder staircases fitted back-to-back into the s stack embrasure. This plan is the most common on the vernacular level for paired houses right into the C20, but very uncommon in the C16. Converted to a single house in 1969. Knapped and galleted flint with brick dressings, two storeys. The s façade would be symmetrical if it were not for the through-passage at the w end, now with blocked doorways to the N and s. Otherwise the two houses are entered through square-headed doorways with chamfered reveals and each lit through one casement to each floor. The windows are clearly replacements and reduced in size. Both apexes of the gables had moulded finials with star tops, but only the w one remains. Big ridge stack with four flues. Inside there are handsome multiple-roll-moulded bridging beams to the ground and first floors and a clasped purlin roof. In the garden behind is, in the sw corner, a C16 square DOVE-COTE, formerly with diagonal buttresses, and formerly, no doubt, with doves. Fragments of nesting boxes survive. In the opposite s corner a HOUSE, again C16, but lowered by a storey in the C18 to become a single-storey barn. It has superior coursed flint.

The road loops back into Bailey Street, so again under the Gate and l. into STOCKS GREEN, which is a long green with the road passing N and s of it. Like the other greens this one belongs to the Holkham Estate. Nothing earlier than the C18 unless perhaps the five-bay OSTRICH PUBLIC HOUSE on the N side: the end gable has kneelers at first-floor level, indicating a jetty. There are two ranges running back, the E one with a room open to the butt-purlin roof, but this open hall-like arrangement is C20 – see the blocked first-floor windows. WILLOW COTTAGE on the s side is of knapped flints. Two storeys, five two-light casements to the upper floor with elaborated brick surrounds. The w gable dated MJM 1765, but the true date probably thirty years earlier. Continuing w into PRIORY ROAD brings us to ABBEY COTTAGE, NW of the priory church, i.e. at the NE corner of the priory precinct. Small, oblong, with a blocked E window large enough to be the window of a chapel. The gable wall is certainly C15 and has chequered flushwork to the plinth, otherwise coursed ashlar. The rest of the building is mostly a flint-built C19 cottage.

THE OLD FOUNDRY, Newton Road. Rendered C18 façade, now with C20 detailing, but with flint and brick gables from the early C17. The fireplace bressumer against the w gable has the date 1636.

WICKEN HOUSE, 1½ m. N. One of the farms for the Holkham Estate by *Samuel Wyatt*, 1784–97. The house was bought in 1955 by Sir Kenneth Keith, who commissioned a remodelling from *James Fletcher-Watson*, involving a new roof, pediment and doorcase. The house has been extended since. Swimming pool decorated by *David Hicks*, other internal decorations by *Francis Egerton*.

CASTLE RISING

ST LAWRENCE. Late Norman, with a central tower. William
8   d'Albini II began it probably *c.* 1140 (after he had begun the

castle) to replace the existing church, which is today a ruin in the earthworks (*see* below). Various materials – carstone from Sandringham dressed with Barnack stone. The base of the nave has large carstone blocks. The w front is a swagger piece of Norman decoration. The doorway has two orders of colonnettes with complex zigzags in the arch. The wall to the l. and r. is plain, but, above, the window has continuous complex zigzags and rope-twist in the side colonnettes, and to its l. and r. is arcading in two layers, the back layer with chevron, the front layer with intersecting arches with zigzag. Above, simpler blank arcading and a circular window with short shafts inside. The window and arcading do not appear as such in early C19 illustrations and are the invention of *Anthony Salvin* in 1846, based on fragmentary evidence. Salvin's restoration of 1845–9 was quite extensive. Inside, the window arrangement below it shows that the blank arcading replaces a former simpler arrangement of one window to the l. and one to the r. of the middle window. The s and n doorways into the nave are plainer. The other Norman forms on the s side are renewed. The nave windows are Salvin's. s porch in greensand and limestone, 1883, for Mary Howard, who stamped her mark on the church as much as anyone.

Now the central tower. Its saddleback top is Victorian, of 1860 by *G. E. Street*, who conducted a restoration in that year, undoing much of Salvin's earlier work. Street seems to have noticed the similarity of the roof to the forebuilding of the castle. Below, the w arch is a splendid piece, the e arch simpler. The w arch has strong shafts with decorated scrolly capitals. The n arch is new, the s arch of the C13, with five shafts, the middle one keeled, and a finely moulded arch. The arch cuts into a pair of former Norman windows. The stage above has one window on each side. A wall passage runs in front of them and connects them. To the w the passage is open to the outside, i.e. in this case to the nave, and by an arch to the e. It has a triple arcade with strong columns carrying many-scalloped capitals and zigzag arches. The tower is rib-vaulted inside, a bold and rare motif. The ribs are broad and decorated with zigzag. They stand on shafts in the angles. Of the C13 the s transept arch has already been referred to. The present s transept itself is of 1883, of sandstone, and E.E. in manner. A n transept planned in the 1890s was never built. The C13 also altered the Norman chancel. Of the latter only the flat buttresses, remains of two s windows, and parts of a nutmeg frieze on the s and e sides. Due to the C13 is the fine group of stepped and shafted lancets in the e wall (dogtooth inside and stiff-leaf capitals) and perhaps the conversion of the round arch on the e side of the central tower into a pointed one. The chancel was apparently ruinous in the early C19. To the l. of the Norman w arch of the tower a Norman altar niche. To the l. of that, in the n wall of the nave, another bigger Norman recess. To the r. of the w arch an E.E. altar niche with dogtooth ornament and detached shafts. The chapel to the r. of this is recent, but the squint shows that a chapel existed here before. A new nave roof was made in 1749 by *Jacob Foreman*, but replaced in 1849.

FURNISHINGS. FONT. Norman, square, on a fat, short, round stem. The rim of the bowl has a plaited band and at the corners heads (of cats?) looking up. Below are three big scallops, richly decorated on two sides. – BANNER STAFF LOCKER. With ogee head; N of the E window. – SCULPTURE. A Perp panel with angels holding a shield (E.E. altar niche). – PAINTING. Tristram mentions dim traces of a small C13 Crucifixion on the N side of the tower arch. – STAINED GLASS. E window of 1840, possibly by *S. C. Yarington*, taken out in 1975. – Two chancel S windows *c.* 1854 by *A. Lusson* of Paris also removed in 1975. – N chancel lancet. This could be by *E. B. Lamb*, the architect, 1857, Christ in Glory. – W window, possibly by *William Wailes*, *c.* 1860. – MONUMENT. Fulke Greville Howard †1846. Gothic tablet, without effigy. By *C. Raymond Smith*.

To the N of the church the former RECTORY, a pleasant, spacious, three-bay house of gault brick, built in 1810 for the Rev. William Fawssett. Two storeys, broad panelled angle-strips and a pediment over the projecting middle bay. The doorcase with its pediment is C20.

To the W of the church, on the Green, the MARKET CROSS, a big, well-preserved C15 affair of Barnack stone (the last restoration 1974). Octagonal base with clasping polygonal buttress shafts, square upper stage with angle-shafts, then the shaft and the cross. The whole about 20 ft high.

To the E of the church the TRINITY HOSPITAL, founded by Henry Howard, Earl of Northampton (†1614), built 1609–15 for £451. He also endowed almshouses at Greenwich and Clun, Shropshire. Brick and carstone. A quadrangle, one-storeyed, except for the W entrance which has a gable between two small picturesque turrets. The upper room has original panelling. Nine bays in all to the front, with three two-light casements r. and l. of the entrance. Lozenge shafts to the two ridge stacks. In the opposite wall the CHAPEL projects in the centre. It was rebuilt *c.* 1870 with a three-light Perp E window and restored in 1936. CROSS and CANDLESTICK by *Voysey*, 1897. To the r. of the chapel is the HALL, to the l. the Governess's quarters. The internal courtyard has casements and paired doorways, in the usual manner. The rooms of the hospital still contain their Jacobean furniture.

CASTLE FARMHOUSE, SW of the church. Mid-C18. Two storeys in three bays. The walls of galleted carstone with brick dressings. Simple fluted doorcase, casement windows. The two BARNS reuse Barnack stone from the castle. Mid-C18. Both threestead, now under one roof.

CASTLE

The castle was begun by William d'Albini II *c.* 1138, the year he married Alice of Louvain, the widow of Henry I. At once he was created Earl of Lincoln and in 1141 Earl of Sussex and underlined his new importance by adding the castle to the family estates (notably Buckenham Castle in Norfolk and the Snettisham manor). He died in 1176. On the death of William d'Albini V in 1243, young and childless, the castle passed to the Montalts. Robert Montalt, Lord of Rising 1299–1320, is one of the more architecturally significant members of this family, as it is likely that he was responsible for some early C14 alterations to the keep. In 1331 the Crown took it over and until her death in 1358 Isabella, the dowager queen, lived in comfort and the lightest of supervision following her part in the murder of her husband Edward II. It appears that a substantial residential suite was erected s of the keep about the time she took possession. In the C15 the castle decayed, and there were quite a number of surveys of its condition; one in 1482–3 tells us that 'there ys never a howse abyll to kepe owt the reyne water, wynde, nor snowe'. In 1544 it came to Thomas Howard, Duke of Norfolk, but had probably already entered what Professor Allen Brown calls the 'squatter' period, a time of minor demolition and alteration. The castle was not tested in any military action and proved incapable of posing a threat to either side during the Civil War of the following century. In 1822 Fulke Greville Howard began sporadic restorations until his death in 1846, and in 1958 the castle came into the custody of the State, which initiated more excavations in the 1970s. Now a substantial controlled ruin in the care of English Heritage, and open to the public.

The principal surviving part is the keep, and fragments of other 11 buildings, but there still are very mighty EARTHWORKS, covering an area of twelve acres. The main enclosure is roughly oval, and has a circumference of 350 yds. To its E and W are additional, and contemporary, rectangular enclosures. The E one is 90 by 64 yds and has a deep ditch and bank, the w one is rather smaller and turned into a plateau by dumped earth. The main

Castle Rising Castle. Engraving, by Millecent

ditch is spectacular and goes down to a depth of 58 ft from the rampart, which is itself about 30 ft above the level of the inner bailey, giving the appearance of a shallow bowl. This effect rather reduces the dominating impact of the keep which seems to peep over the rampart, and resulted from raising the rampart and digging out the ditch at the end of the C12. The surplus earth probably filled the W outer enclosure.

The BRIDGE across the ditch is Perp and of mixed materials, but replaces an earlier stone bridge, of which ashlar quoins remain. The inner of the pair of arches has now gone and the survivor has been given a brick four-centred arch and saddleback parapet. The GATEHOUSE is Norman and consists of a large simple archway either side of the passage decorated with two plain arches inside. The SE arch is higher and leads to the remains of the staircase to the former battlemented upper storey, still visible in C18 engravings. The gatehouse when built extended further into the bailey and had walls projecting outwards towards the bridge; it was not, as it is today, embedded in the earthworks to the height of the entrance arch. Of former CURTAIN WALLS the evidence is documentary rather than physical. Nathaniel Buck's 1738 engraving shows the existing brick walling abutting the gatehouse to the S, fragmentary remains elsewhere and one of the three towers said to have been constructed equidistant round the rampart. These towers and full, crenellated curtain walls are shown in a 1588 map of Rising Chase. Moreover in 1365 the Black Prince (the then owner under the Crown) authorized £81 for the repair of a 'tower Called Nightegale', and in 1503–6 a survey tells of a 'Nyghtyngall Towre' and the fact that the walls had been badly repaired and were in danger of collapse. At the N side of the rampart there are more foundations of walls, but further excavations are required. Since nothing seems earlier than the late C14 and as the earthworks had to be raised in the late C12 (or early C13) it is unlikely that William d'Albini's castle had them.

Of the OTHER BUILDINGS inside the bailey very little remains. Some walling N of the keep, almost buried in the earthworks and only uncovered in the 1840s, belongs to the parish CHURCH which stood on the slight prominence SW of the village, an encumbrance to William d'Albini on this site; he built the new church in the village centre and probably used the old for storage. Very small (43 ft long), three-celled with possibly a central tower and with an apsidal E end. It had N and S nave doors and was lit through splayed lancets, of which two can be seen in the apse. Its date must be of the last third of the C11. There were in addition in the bailey the GREAT HALL or chamber connected by a covered gallery to a range of lodgings to its W. Running E from the lodgings a CHAPEL, and 50 ft E of them all a large KITCHEN block. A latrine was built at the N end of the lodgings range. Substantial, if partial, foundations of these buildings can be inspected S of the keep, all of them of the mid C14 or a little earlier, and associated with Isabella's occupation.

The KEEP is one of the largest and one of the most decorated in England. It is a companion piece to the yet grander Norwich keep and from it borrows much of the plan. Both are of a type known as hall keeps as against the more usual tower keeps, that is, they are broader than they are high. The measurements of Castle Rising are 78 ft 6 in. E–W by 68 ft 6 in. N–S by a height of only about 50 ft. There were only a basement, inaccessible from outside, and a principal floor, though the latter was in parts again horizontally subdivided. The rubblestone walls faced with Barnack stone are nearly 7 ft thick and strengthened by shallow clasping corner buttresses which have lost their pinnacles. Some of these are given the decorative enrichment of nook-shafts. The W wall is embellished by three big blank arches, the centre one much higher than the others. The double arch to its l. with a missing central shaft is as originally intended, the arches covering the garderobe discharge chutes. The r. arch should be the same, and has the same function. The S and N sides each have three shallow buttresses rising to the stringcourse below the former parapet. The principal enrichment however is lavished on the E wall, or rather the staircase and FOREBUILDING which are set in front of it. The staircase is entered from the S. Its S and much longer E wall have small decorative blank arcading, partly with intersecting arches. To the S also medallions with heads of monsters, these once continuing into the E return. This E wall now has a broken-in flight of steps at the upper level above an intermediate staircase landing, and provided access to a *meurtrière*, or murder-hole. The forebuilding has been called by Hamilton Thompson the best-preserved in England. It was a common feature of C12 castles, its purpose being to protect the first-floor, and only, entrance to the castle while allowing a grand entrance via a staircase. This one has clasping buttresses with nook-shafts to the corners and a narrower, similar, buttress rising between the pair of big arched first-floor windows. These, and the two further windows to the N and one to the S faces, were unglazed after the Norwich pattern, the mullions being insertions of the C16. The upper storey with shouldered windows and the odd steeply pitched roof are of Robert de Montalt's time, *c.* 1300–10.

The STAIRCASE itself is remarkably wide and suitably grand. There is an arched doorway at the foot and another half-way up under the *meurtrière*, this with two orders of shafts, cushion capitals and a roll-moulded arch. Both parts had timber roofs. The staircase is divided from the vestibule on the upper floor of the forebuilding by a third arched doorway, with shafts, but plainer. One should ignore the brick-lined C16 doorway forced into the basement at the foot of the stairs, as it totally negates the defensive function of the forebuilding and staircase landing. The VESTIBULE received its two-bay rib vaulting when Robert de Montalt added the upper floor, and it sits uncomfortably on the C12 wall-shafts. To the W is the main ENTRANCE into the Great Hall of the keep, Norman, with three orders of shafts, cushion capitals and richly decorated arches: chevron and dogtooth separated by roll mouldings. In the 'squatter' period it was blocked to form a fireplace and tiles from a disused kiln near Bawsey inserted below the Norman arch by Fulke Greville Howard's widow.

The keep is divided lengthways (E–W) by a thick wall (cf. Norwich, London and Colchester) and has lost both its floors and roof. Our tour should begin in the BASEMENT which is accessible by a newel staircase in the NE angle of the keep and is entered from the vestibule in the forebuilding. The larger (N) of the two rooms had three heavy piers along its centre. They carried beams for the hall floor, except for the groin-vaulted W quarter, which required greater strength for the kitchen and service area above. Note the deep well. S of the main basement room and connected with it by a Norman doorway is the second basement room. This has a fine arch and groin vaulting at its E end to help carry the rooms above, in this case the chapel and antechapel. No piers were necessary for the floor joists due to the narrower span. In the SW corner is the castle's other newel staircase, serving the Great Chamber.

The staircase into the basement now returns us to the GREAT HALL, straight into a rough passage inside the N wall. It was crudely cut through the deep arched window embrasures in the C16 to give access to the rooms W of the hall after the hall floor had collapsed (in 1506 the keep was still roofed, in the survey of 1542–3 '[the keep] is cleane wasted awaye, except the mayne walles'). The hall has two E windows high up, partially blocked, and N windows screened by the cut passage. Two of these are of two lights, another has a trilobed lintel. Opposite the central two-light window is the deep recess marking the Lord's place and to the r. of this the entrance to the Great Chamber. The figured corbels for the former roof beams are C14, so presumably the hall was re-roofed then. The smaller NW room is entered through the low corner door and is the KITCHEN, vaulted and with a vent placed in the NW angle turret of the keep (cf. Norwich). Wall recesses in the S and E walls and also in the service room to the S of the kitchen. This had its own doorway in the W wall next to the entrance to the great chamber, now much eroded. Also enlarged is the entrance to the passage to the GARDEROBES, discharging into the area below the l. hand of the three outer blank arches mentioned earlier. This passage has been broken through to provide access between the kitchen and the service room in the 'squatter' days. From the SE corner of the hall a passage provides access to the *meurtrière* above the intermediate landing of the main staircase and returns to the antechapel. We reach it via the visitors' walkway.

The ANTECHAPEL is lit only through a splayed lancet to the hall and the door into the actual chapel in the SE corner of the keep. The antechapel is of unknown function, and if indeed with devotional purpose is a very generous provision in a building sparsely furnished with smaller, more intimate retiring rooms. The CHAPEL is divided into three parts and is the most

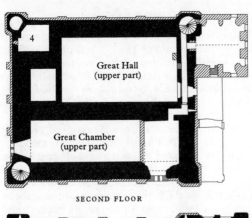

SECOND FLOOR

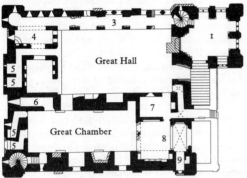

FIRST FLOOR

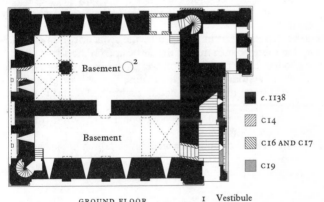

GROUND FLOOR

■ *c.* 1138

▨ C 14

▨ C 16 AND C 17

▨ C 19

1 Vestibule
2 Well
3 Sixteenth-century passage
4 Kitchen
5 Garderobes
6 Closet
7 Antechapel
8 Chapel
9 Vestry

Castle Rising Castle Keep. Plans of ground, first and second floors

sumptuous area of the castle. In the westernmost part or 'nave'
are remains of Norman arcading. The E part is rib-vaulted and
built in the thickness of the outer wall. The ribs meet in the
centre, and a stone with four faces, but not structurally a boss,
marks the meeting. To the S a small barrel-vaulted vestry.
Handsome arch to the W of the vaulted chancel with double
axe-head decoration supported on circular responds with cushion capitals half-elaborated into scallops. There were, probably,
a S and an E window of five and three lancets respectively.
Possibly the 'nave' was vaulted too as it had to support a room
above. The chapel W wall has later apertures looking into the
Great Chamber S of the hall, there being no access originally.

The GREAT CHAMBER fills the remainder of the space on
this side of the keep. Two large S windows, one trilobed, and,
between them, a generous fireplace, later lined with brick. In
the SW corner is the second newel staircase already mentioned.
The two-light window high in the W wall is C19, but the two
rounded doorways at the former floor level lead to GARDE-
ROBES, one with, apparently, a very rare URINAL. These discharge to the r. hand wall arch outside. In the N wall, just l. of
the entrance to the hall, is a large closet.

There was only one room above this level until the C14, and
this was over the chapel, lit now by a two-light C19 window. It
is reached by the NE newel stair and a long mural passage. The
passage also passes the C14 upper storey of the forebuilding.
This has a curiously incomplete, or half-ruined and consolidated, transverse rib vault which explains the steepness of the
forebuilding roof. Inside and l. of the door is a Norman shaft
terminating in a cushion capital: it is the only parapet-height
nook-shaft to the C12 clasping buttresses one can comfortably
examine.

RISING LODGE HOTEL, clasped by the arms of two main roads
by the roundabout 1 m. S of the castle and on the site of a hunting lodge. Early C19 house of two storeys in three bays built of
galleted carstone with brick as trimming. A pair of unfluted
columns supports a bowed porch. Sashes and tripartite sashes.

EARTHWORK, Keeper's Wood, ½ m. E of the castle. A small ringwork, with a central depression, not a barrow, but maybe a
siege-castle. (AR)

BARROW. A bowl barrow with well-defined ditch lies in the wood
E of the hospital.

CASTON

HOLY CROSS. Chancel of c. 1300. The three-light E window has
intersecting tracery, but a cinquefoiled circle at the top and
ogees. Dec W tower, the doorway with a bold ogee head, the
window above it with a small reticulation motif inside each unit
of reticulated tracery (cf. Thompson nearby). Double wave
mouldings to the arch into nave. There was repair work going
on in the later C15, money being given for the tower in 1477 and

1520. Perp nave windows (but one blocked earlier N window) and modest Perp N porch of two storeys, converted to a vestry. The nave roof is scissor-braced, early C14, but boarded with C15 panels and decorated with ribs and bosses. Traces of a painted scheme remain. – PULPIT. Jacobean, simple panelling and with a top rail decorated with incised lunettes. – SCREEN. Only the base is preserved. – BENCHES. 1839. – STALLS. Two with MISERICORDS; heads. – Some few BENCH ENDS with poppyheads. – CHANDELIER. Large, in two tiers of nine branches. Said to have been given to Cheshunt Church, Hertfordshire, by Charles I and originally from Hampton Court. It arrived here in 1871. – STAINED GLASS. In a s nave window many C15 fragments newly arranged, including two whole figures. – In the chancel much from the time of the restoration (1852–4).

CHURCH FARMHOUSE, Church Lane, w of the church. To the N an eminently decorative C16 brick gable with panelling stepped up like an organ-pipe, as if it were the gable of a Hanseatic church. In all there are eleven trefoiled arches in moulded brick. If the steps to the gable-head remained the effect would be richer still. There is nothing else like it in Norfolk. Heavy NE diagonal buttress. The s front has five bays of two-light C19 casements and a central door. A lower mid-C17 wing to the rear (w) has a big shaped w gable.

WINDMILL, The Street. A six-storey brick tower mill of 1864, built for Edward Wyer by the millwright *Robert Hambling* of Dereham. It has a Norfolk boat-shaped cap, and sailframes. Inside, the machinery is intact, and outside, abutting to the s, is the two-storey brick GRANARY, now a house.

FLAXMOOR, a biggish house on The Street, presents an early C19 six-bay façade which alters the house to a double pile. The rear elevation has a full-height stair-tower and in it is a C16 winder staircase. Also of the C16 are the moulded bridging beams of the kitchen located in the cross wing to the l. This was remodelled in the 1880s, no doubt at about the time the ogeed *Boulton & Paul* GREENHOUSE was added to the s wall.

OLD RECTORY COTTAGE, The Street. Early C17 timber-framed house disguised in the early C19 by encasement in fashionable brick. Only a single storey with attic and three-celled in plan. Later in the C17 a s wing was added, which received its brick skin in the C18. The interest lies in the plaster ceiling of the w ground-floor room: two angels with spread wings, four large roundels with fleurs-de-lys and lotus leaves in the corners, and a further sixteen small Tudor-like roses. Its quality is better than local, its date possibly C17, equally possibly C19.

THE THATCHED COTTAGE, also on The Street, is an early C16 hall house, timber-framed, greatly altered save for the frame itself, if we exclude the early C19 roof.

Three houses on The Street, THE VILLA, STANSFIELD and IVAN HOUSE, look like suburban city dwellings. 1911–12 by the builder *Amos Davey* of South London, using second-hand London doors and windows.

CAVICK HOUSE *see* WYMONDHAM

CHANNONZ HALL *see* TIBENHAM

CHEDGRAVE

ALL SAINTS. A very irregular church, set attractively on a slight eminence at the E end of the village above a playground, with a screen of pine trees and a view into the heath. The church is of the mid C12, and what makes it look so irregular is the fact that it has a tower to the N of the short chancel. The chancel is *c.* 1500, and it seems that at that moment a Norman NE chapel or transept was raised up into the tower; a very odd thing. However the tower has genuine W and E lancets to the lower stage, and the nave is also certain to be Norman, by the survival of both doorways. That on the N side is simple but re-assembled (one order of colonnettes with single-scallop capitals), that on the S quite sumptuous. It has two orders of colonnettes with shafts decorated with chevrons and spirals, the capitals with scallops and a kind of pre-waterleaf. In the arch scalloping, a spiral-twisted rope moulding, and two zigzags meeting to form lozenges. The hoodmould has two orders of scallops at r. angles to the wall. The W window of the nave may also be a thoroughly altered Norman window. A drastic restoration took place in 1819, for the Rev. Thomas Beauchamp, much too early to expect sensitivity, as the frightful brick N aisle indicates (one Perp window, one Y-tracery window). But this seems discreet compared with the brick W extension of the N aisle of 1993–4, like a two-storeyed house hitting one in the face as one enters the churchyard. Remains of foundations of a round W tower discovered during construction. Chancel restored again in 1872. S porch added 1880. – FONT. Brought from St Julian, Norwich, C15 but re-cut in 1845. – STAINED GLASS. In the E window much foreign glass of the C16–C17, part of a consignment imported from Rouen by *John Hampp* in 1802 and erected in the Beauchamp churches (cf. Langley and Thurton). The glass here rearranged by *King* of Norwich in 1960. – S and N DOORS. 1819 with iron-work copied from Haddiscoe.

On the way from the church to the crossroads one passes Nos. 7–9 HARDLEY ROAD (formerly Crossways Farmhouse), a house dated 1669. A timber frame sandwiched between shaped brick gables and whitewashed. Three irregular S bays. Gables with platbands, blocked windows and internal stacks.

To the N of the crossroads THE RISE, an estate of houses for the Loddon Rural District Council by *Tayler & Green*, 1951–5. It ends in a close, Hurst Road. The two-storeyed terrace on the road is built on a curve. The linking of gable-ends with screen walls, the length and relation of terraces, and the brick pattern, especially to the gable-ends, ought to be observed, in colour and in relief. Canted porches. Single-storey houses leading up to Hurst Road. Windows and doors mostly uPVC, most regrettable. On Tayler & Green's housing, *see* Introduction, p. 165.

To the s, No. 3 NORWICH ROAD, close to where Chedgrave meets Loddon, on the w side a very handsome late C18 double shopfront. The display windows both bowed, either side of the entrance. This part is an addition to a C16 timber-framed house given a brick skin.

CHEDGRAVE MANOR, Norwich Road, ⅝ m. w of the church. An early C19 gault brick house with hipped slate roofs built for the Gilbert family. The N façade of two storeys in five bays: fluted Doric columns to the portico porch; sashes. Later C19 extensions to the w. w again the contemporary STABLES: central carriage doorway, semicircular windows.

OLD RECTORY, Rectory Lane. Again a timber-framed house with a later brick skin. Four gables arranged in a cross, that to the road with clasping pilasters. An external stack occupies the sw angle. The four-bay N block is late C17 inside, early C19 outside, lobby-entrance plan, the door with an open pediment and Doric pilasters. The staircase has late C17 turned balusters.

CHEDGRAVE MARSHES   4000

In the triangle formed by the confluence of the Rivers Yare and Waveney are three derelict C19 WINDPUMPS, none individually of interest, but together a picturesque group. They are TOFT MONKS, SIX MILE HOUSE and PETTINGELL'S MILL.

CLAXTON   3000

ST ANDREW. Unbuttressed w tower with much brick trim, e.g. the quoins, the windows and the wide surrounds. Originally probably a Dec tower (see the arch towards the nave), reworked in the late C15. Bases for pinnacles at corners of the brick parapet. Late C15, or early C16, brick s porch entered under a four-centred arch. The nave is thatched. It is basically Norman. The N and s doorways seem to be E.E. One s window Perp with straight diagonal lines, where one expects the curves of arches. N aisle demolished and the former N arcade blocked: three bays with octagonal piers and arches with one chamfer and one hollow chamfer. Nave roof with scissor-bracing, somewhat rebuilt. The chancel is of 1867, with Geometric windows. In it is a piscina of c. 1300. – FONT. C15. Octagonal. Four lions against the stem, four shields (emblem of the Trinity, Instruments of the Passion, a lion and St Andrew's Cross, two lions and two flowers). – Some BOX PEWS. – MONUMENT. Sir Henry Gawdy †1620, but erected 1637. Large tablet with nice restrained decoration. No effigy.

Former CHAPTER, ¾ m. ESE. No doubt late C18. The five-bay front has two doorways with typical Late Georgian domestic cases, two large and two small windows.

CLAXTON CASTLE. The remains of a red brick castle with lime-stone dressings. In 1333 William, second Lord Kerdeston, obtained a licence to crenellate but the present remains appear entirely C15. They are mostly one long wall with three round towers. At the E end are traces of a staircase, and more substantial fragments of another in the W tower. Sir Thomas Gawdy's repair work in 1566 may have swept away the earlier portions and no attempt to explain them further seems to have been published.

The castle is in the grounds of CLAXTON MANOR, to the W. Late C17 with a C19 S front in five bays and two storeys: central full-height porch, cross casements in stone surrounds. The C17 part to the N has a shaped E gable and, beneath it, three- and four-light casements with oddly ill-defined pediments. At the NE corner is a large external stack. Nearby a long BARN with the date 1706 in the N gable. Brick and thatched. Two cart entrances to the W side, opposed by two gabled projections on the E, i.e. a fivestead barn. The date could apply to the house as well.

THE WARREN, at the E end of the village, set back from the main street. One of the council estates designed by *Tayler & Green* in 1948–9. A terrace of eight houses, gently stepping up a gradient and each stepped forward from its neighbour. The colour of the houses, introduced in 1955, varies between grey, pink, blue and yellow. The upper windows placed immediately below the projecting eaves are specially characteristic, but only the end houses retain their metal casements (others UPVC), and only some their plank side doors to passageways. Plain porches.

CLENCHWARTON

5020

ST MARGARET. C14 W tower. It is of brick and has three stages. Wave-moulded W doorway, lancets to ringing chamber and cusped ogee belfry windows. A complete C14 brick tower is not common, even in Norfolk. The Perp nave is of carstone and ragstone. C15 windows with panel tracery. Carstone and brick again in the chancel but this is of 1864. Perp S porch, back to brick; barrel-vaulted inside, on four ogeed transverse ribs. Restored 1861. – FONT. Octagonal, 1835. – PULPIT. Elizabethan or Jacobean. Polygonal, with arcaded panels. – MONUMENT. To one of the Forster family †1742 (S chancel). Fluted Ionic columns flank the inscription panel. Obelisk and three urns. Signed by *John Fellowes* of King's Lynn. – STAINED GLASS. E window has an Adoration, Crucifixion and Ascension, probably by *C. A. Gibbs*, †1864. S chancel window looks like *Hardman & Co.*, †1909, N chancel Resurrection etc. by *Ward & Hughes*, †1868.

An octagonal CROSS in the churchyard: C14, octagonal shaft in a square socket stone.

COCKLEY CLEY   7000

ALL SAINTS. *R. M. Phipson*'s restoration of 1866–8 makes the church look all new. The round tower fell on 29 August 1991 (it had an arched lancet above the Dec w window, Y-tracery to the bell-stage, and an octagonal parapet of Phipson's), but it seems to have been rebuilt early in the C14 with the nave w wall on the same plan as its Late Norman predecessor and is characterized by two bands of cut flint at 12 and 24 ft above the ground (cf. Tuttington and Edingthorpe, Vol. 1). The chancel in E.E. style is partly a reproduction of the original state. It has five lancets N and S (three lancets and two Perp windows are shown on the S in Ladbroke's drawing) and three stepped E lancets shafted inside, the shafts to the central light fully detached; cf. Gooderstone nearby. Early C14 S aisle, originally with intersecting tracery to the windows and a lancet in the w wall. The S doorway is untampered-with, of the mid C14 with wave mouldings. Good s arcade of three bays, with quatrefoil piers, the four foils almost detached and with keels between them. Moulded capitals, double-hollow-chamfered arches. Phipson added a N aisle to match and altered the windows to the present Dec forms, the N ones with a cusped cinquefoil vesica or cusped triangles, the s just encircled quatrefoils. C19 roofs, necessary in the nave because Phipson reduced its width and dispensed with a C14 clerestory. – MONUMENT. John Baines †1736, a small, completely asymmetrical cartouche (N aisle wall).*

ST MARY, a former church, to the E of the road to Hillborough, converted to a cottage and converted back to a chapel in recent years, so it is surprising that so much of the original church remains. The date is probably early C12, and it consists of a nave with an apsed chancel leading off, but no tower. The chancel itself is rebuilt but the chancel arch remains, with the block imposts, the high round arch and bits of rolled ornament familiar from Saxon examples. Various tight lancets with deep internal splays, and one, at the SE corner, with a later chamfered rere-arch. The arched S doorway has chevron decoration but no shafting or rebates.

COCKLEY CLEY MUSEUM. Adjacent to St Mary. A C17 house converted in the late C20 to a museum, having had an C18 remodelling. Flint and brick. Two storeys in four bays. Casements. Two doorways. C17 still the ridge stack with its twin lozenge flues. A little of the timber frame at the back shows that in the C18 the house was raised a storey. The E bay is wholly C18.

COCKLEY CLEY HALL, ½ m. NE. The late C17 house was replaced in 1870–1 by *R. M. Phipson* for Theophilus Russell Buckworth. Red brick with ashlar quoins and dressings, in a watered-down Italianate style. Two and a half storeys in seven bays, the centre bay projecting and containing the entrance under a broken segmental arch. Big single-storey bay windows r. and l. Five-bay lower wing to the r., yet in a full three storeys. A fine lake to the s.

---

* I could not find the monument to Richard Dashwood †1738, by *John Fellowes* of Lynn, mentioned in the first edition.

COLKIRK

ST MARY. One of the handful of Norfolk churches with towers
both off-set and acting as porches, here in the normal position
of a s porch. The cusped Y-tracery in the bell-openings, quatrefoil responds to the porch entry and the characteristic mouldings of the inner doorway (without capitals) indicate c. 1330.
Bright brick C20 battlements. The rest is Perp, except for the N
aisle with its four-bay arcade of octagonal piers and double-
chamfered arches, which dates from 1871 and is by *Charles
Moxon*. The former C14 N doorway was re-set in Moxon's new
vestry at the E end of the aisle. The chancel seems to be an
addition, and, indeed, has a late C14 chancel arch of wave mouldings with polygonal capitals to responds. The main restoration
was by *Butterfield*, 1858–62, i.e. before the N aisle, and included
the tiled floor, benches, pulpit, altar rails and probably the arch-
braced roofs. – FONT. Odd. Circular, with coupled colonnettes
in the four diagonals of the bowl. Four short columns as supports
have cushion capitals. It is probably late C12. – SCREEN. 1912.
– STAINED GLASS. A jumble of C15 fragments in a chancel s
window collected in 1870. Three-light E window by *William
Wailes*, 1858. Six panels of the Life of Christ in memory of Rev.
Ralph Tatham †1856. The other s chancel window by *Ward &
Hughes*, signed by *Henry Hughes* himself, 1876, an Adoration of
Shepherds and Baptism of Christ. s nave window †1876, also
Ward & Hughes. – MONUMENT. A cartouche to Samuel Smith
†1663, in N aisle. It has verses based on an anagram of his
name. Moved here from Oxwick in 1946. Alabaster surround
with a coat of arms in the crowning segmental pediment. –
William Timperley †1660 (in vestry behind the organ). Stone,
with a lunette at the top in which are rustic angels bearing
scrolls. – Nicholas Timperley and Ann Barker, his sister, †1664
and †1662 (opposite the last). Black and white marble. Segmental
pediment over inscription panel and scrolled consoles r. and l.
Jon Bayliss attributes both these monuments to *Martin Morley*.
Both are re-set from the chancel.

Everything else requires a walk down HALL LANE. HALL
FARMHOUSE, ½m. NE of the church. Late Elizabethan. Flint
with brick and stone trim, the flint galleted. The two-storeyed
porch has a four-centred arch to the doorway and an upper
window under a moulded brick pediment. Evidence of other
openings or the original extent of horizontal windows mark the
façade and the rear elevation. The rear still with three three-light
mullioned windows, with transoms. W gable retains a garderobe
outshut. The E stack has a winder staircase next to it, a position
to become the norm in smaller houses from the C17 to the C19.
The hall bridging beams are still roll-moulded.

To the E and W of the house are two BARNS, the former dated
1742 in tie irons. Ventilation panels in two tiers. The roof has
two tiers of staggered butt-purlins and two collars to each principal truss. Unstaggered purlins might be expected for the date,
like the roof of Street Farm barn at Horsey, also dated 1742.

The w barn is of C17 origins and has loop ventilation holes, but the roof was replaced in the C19.

COLKIRK HOUSE. 1834. Gault brick. Reduced cruciform plan. Three-bay N front, the centre bay advanced under a pediment and flanked by doubled pilasters. Paired pilasters also to the corners. Things improve inside. Good stone staircase with cast-iron balusters. The hallway has three groin-vaulted cells, and there is decent plasterwork to the principal rooms.

GABLE-END. A small early C17 house of colourwashed coursed flint with brick details. The windows changed to casements, some under C17 hoodmoulds. The C17 staircase has tapering balusters and occupies the middle bay, the balusters taken from the demolished Toftrees Hall c. 1950.*

COLNEY   1000

ST ANDREW. Anglo-Saxon round tower with three blocked double-splayed windows. Flat quadrant pilasters between nave and tower. The rest of the church Dec, or the C19 restorer's idea of Dec. The tall tower arch, with imposts none too elementary, is the restorer's version of Norman. Nice windows in the S nave with the motif of the four-petalled flower. Blocked C16 N door and a C16 brick S porch, the curiously naive tracery brick as well. Chancel arch, roofs etc. from the 1886–7 restoration by *H.J. Green*. – FONT. C15. Octagonal. On a base of Maltese cross shape. Against the stem fleurons in sunk panels. Against the bowl the signs of the Evangelists, the Crucifixion, Baptism, and two flowers. – STAINED GLASS. In a N nave window two good figures by *H. E. Wooldridge* of *J. Powell & Sons*, †1874. – MONUMENTS. Tiny chalice brass to Henry Alikok †1505 (chancel floor). – John Tomson †1575. Tomb-chest with fluted and reeded Ionic pilasters and inscription. Palmette frieze below the top slab (chancel N). – In the porch gable a tablet to John Fox, who was run over by his own team of horses in 1806. The inscription continues with a road-safety message: 'Reader, if thou drivest a team be careful and endanger not the Life of another or thine own'.

BUPA HOSPITAL, 300 yds E of the church. 1983–4 by *Lambert, Scott & Innes* (job architect *Michael Innes*). The wards two storeys high, the diagnostic block with the operating theatres three storeys. Big pantiled roofs dominating it all. Further sixteen-bed unit and operating theatre added 1988–9.

NORWICH RESEARCH PARK. On Colney Lane opposite the church stand a series of laboratories involved with food plant research, begun in the 1960s, collectively named in 1991. The biggest group to the w is the JOHN INNES CENTRE. John Innes (1829–1904) was a plantation owner, rum merchant and property developer who provided in his will for a horticultural institution, later the John Innes Institute. The institute moved here from Bayfordbury, Herts, in 1967 into temporary buildings by

---

* Information from Paul Rutledge.

Skipper & Corless and *Alan Paine*, replaced by the MAIN
BUILDING of 1969–72 by *Feilden & Mawson*. Three storeys, in
a T-shape consisting of a dark brick ground floor and light
concrete and glazed panels to the upper floors. Then came the
SAINSBURY LABORATORY, 1988–9 by *David Luckhurst* of
Feilden & Mawson running S from the E end and a linking block
to the CAMBRIDGE LABORATORY, opened September 1990,
by the same architect. These form three sides of a courtyard,
closed on the N by the LIBRARY (1990, *David Luckhurst*) and
the bowed main entrance (1985–6) opening into the original
wing. The two laboratories, both three storeys high, have horizontal tiers of windows and a steel frame clad in *Trespa* panels,
a smooth Scandinavian compressed board, finished in two tones
of metallic grey. The courtyard elevation of the Cambridge
Laboratory has projecting slatted sun canopies over the windows
of the lower two storeys, and both have the top floor shaded by
the deep overhang of the extraordinarily high roof, which comprises six different planes stepping up like the silhouette of an
Alpine mountain.

To the N of the site three buildings. The very large and tall
block of 1994–5 to the W, monolithic like a power station, by the
Building Design Partnership (*Charles Broughton*; other design work
by the constructors *Amec*), is the JOSEPH CHATT BUILDING
(containing the nitrogen fixation laboratories). Steel-framed,
brick cladding, extruded staircase by the diminutive main entrance,
high roof containing machinery and clad with ribbed steel panels.
Impressive interior atrium open to the glazed roof sloping to the
middle, with windows giving off to rooms at many levels. Down
the centre run two elevated walkways, one above the other, and
to the E and W walls great fat ducting pipes, so that the comparison with a power station is reinforced. LECTURE THEATRE
abutting E, same date, same architects. Entrance under a sail of
an overhang, to r. of a fully glazed staircase. Inside, the main
rooms set within a partly exposed drum bounded by circular
passageways. The RECREATION BUILDING of 1972 closes the
group to the E: nothing unusual or noteworthy.

On the E side are three institutions. To the l. of the common
access is the BRITISH SUGAR TECHNICAL CENTRE. The first
phase by *John Sennitt*, begun while he was with *Feilden &
Mawson*, finished under his own practice, 1967–8: single-storey,
steel-framed and with timber fascias to the long sides, concrete
curtain walling to the E and W ends. Larger two-storey extensions E and SE, by *John Sennitt*, 1987–9. Two-storey horizontal
blocks forming a double-L plan, steel-framed but clad with
versicor, i.e. pressed steel panels with insulation between the
skins. Plain interiors. E again is a long low building of dark brick
and glass, by *David Luckhurst* of *Feilden & Mawson*, 1969, built
as the Coastal Ecology Research Station but now part of the
FOOD SCIENCE LABORATORY, the main block of which is to
the SE. The new building, opened 1990, by *John Aitcheson* of
the *Property Services Agency* for the Ministry of Agriculture.
Three storeys, steel-framed again and clad with powder-coated

sheet steel, the panels set into a grid of rectangles. Bold design
of two three-storey arms connected by a taller canted entrance
bay projecting from the external angle. Horizontal friezes of
direct-glazed windows, but more wall than glass.

To the r. of the main entrance the INSTITUTE OF FOOD
RESEARCH, 1966–8 by *David Luckhurst* of *Feilden & Mawson*.
Large, three- and four-storey rectangular blocks with grooved
pre-cast concrete panels as curtain walling over a reinforced
concrete frame. Horizontal aluminium windows in redwood
frames with projections, like balconies, to the upper floors.
Prominent plant rooms on the flat roof and a forest of ventilation stacks (not part of the original design).

COLNEY HALL, ⅝ m. w, off Watton Road. A house built for Joseph
Scott in 1834, added to later in the C19, drastically reduced in
size and by a storey in 1960 and made pretty in a Neo-Georgian
way. Now two storeys, with balcony and veranda of 1960. Of
the features of 1834 there remain two very handsome Venetian
windows with Corinthian columns inside and some chimneypieces. Attached to the r. an elegant three-bay ORANGERY built
of ashlar blocks. Central pediment and balustraded parapet.
Round-arched windows. Inside it has been made into a grotto,
no doubt in the C19.

THE RECTORY, w of the church. Shaped end-gables, and a shaped
gable to the porch attached to the three-bay façade. Datestone
1715. A curiosity to the rear is a pre-fabricated extension of 1891
made by *Boulton & Paul* of Norwich.

OLD HALL, w of the Rectory. The thick GATEPIERS are typical
mid-C17 Artisan Mannerism. An oval concave recess is answered
by an oval convex boss. Wrought-iron gates with scrolled overthrow. Crenellated walls. The HOUSE has C17 stepped gables,
but very much re-worked in the C19 and *c.* 1980.

COLTON   *1000*

ST ANDREW. All of *c.* 1300–50, but over-restored. Unbuttressed
w tower with flushwork-panelled battlements. The top stage
must be C15 (there was a bequest in 1459 and bells were cast
from 1505). Nave and chancel. One N window has Curvilinear
tracery which seems to be original. The rest all Dec in style too.
The church originally had aisles, but the arcades were removed
at some time to widen the nave. The roof is a C17 type, arch-
braced tie-beams and arch-braced principals, so was this the date?
– FONT. Perp, octagonal, with quatrefoils. – WEST GALLERY.
Very low, Gothic, of 1855. – ORGAN. Elaborate High Victorian
Gothic, also of 1855. – SCREEN. Not tall, with one-light divisions, only partly C15. – BENCH ENDS. Some with C15 poppyheads. – WALL PAINTING. On the w wall. Two seated women
talking to one another. Little devils push them together. The
scene represents the vice of gossiping. Faint. Of the C14. Incised
consecration cross on N wall. – STAINED GLASS. Plenty in chancel by *Lavers & Westlake*, only one dated, 1912. – MONUMENT.

Philip Pooley †1715, with a bust at the top. – Mrs Browne †1741. A single Corinthian column before a back-plate.

OLD HALL, The Street. Brick, dated 1664 in the N gable, which has lost its stepped parapet. Early C19 façade, re-fenestrated in the C20. The big red brick BARN says in large, boldly framed numerals: 1666. It still has stepped gables, though the frames of the numerals with their lugs are typical Artisan Mannerism of the mid C17.

Across the road the former Inn, the OLD HORSE AND GROOM, also with stepped gables. This is dated 1660. The gable is attached to a timber-framed house.

7090   COLVESTON
                    1 m. NE of Cranwich

ST MARY. Only low mounds remain. In 1962 fragments of wall could be seen.

7020   CONGHAM

ST ANDREW. W tower apparently of the early C14, though there was 'emendation' in 1446, or at least money left for it which does not necessarily mean work was done. W doorway and window from the 1873 restoration. Y-tracery bell-openings filled in. Tall arch to nave with double-hollow-chamfered arch. The rest so over-restored that little can be said. Windows of many varieties including a plate-tracery one to the N. The Geometric Dec E window C19. – FONT. C13. Of Purbeck marble, octagonal, and with three shallow blank arches to each side. The base of eight granite columns has the date 1864. – SCREEN. Under the tower. Made up of Perp and Jacobean parts. – REREDOS and PULPIT both c. 1897, from the *Royal Carving Workshop* at Sandringham.

CONGHAM HALL, ½ m. S. Early C19 house with an E façade of two storeys in seven bays. The porch has two Doric columns and two unfluted pilasters. S front with a canted bay in the middle.

CONGHAM LODGE, ½ m. N. An early C19 T-shaped house with the façade to W. Two storeys. Only the r. three bays are C19, with a bowed porch on unfluted columns and pilasters supporting a Doric entablature. The remaining five bays are of 1914. S side has two-storey canted bays either side of the doorway. The staircase has iron balusters.

CONGHAM HOUSE. 1856–9 by *Salvin* for Robert Elwes. Tudor style, demolished.

1010   COSTESSEY

ST EDMUND. NW tower, the brick top with a medievalizing Lombard frieze and lead spire of 1930. Wide and high nave with windows whose intersecting tracery dates from the restoration of 1886–98 by *T. H. B. Heslop*, paid for (in the chancel at least) by the trustees of the Norwich Great Hospital. They had rebuilt the chancel in 1391–7, but most details renewed since then. Many of the windows constructed, not surprisingly, of Cosseyware (for Cosseyware, *see* Introduction, p. 26). The chancel has a Victorian E window, one original Dec S window with petal tracery, and the others Perp of a very idiosyncratic style, with horizontal lines in the tracery heads. The S porch Perp and quite ambitious with its flushwork panelling on the E and W sides as well as the front. Its upper parts rebuilt. – FONT. C15. Octagonal, with shields in cusped fields. – PULPIT. Jacobean, a good, large piece, given by the Rev. Whitwell Elwin when he rebuilt Booton Church. – SCREEN. C15. Good. With one-light divisions and ogee arches. Leaf in the tops of the arches. Panel tracery above. On the l. and r. fragments of projecting wings, no doubt to separate the screen from side altars (cf. Ranworth, Vol. 1). – The ROOD BEAM is preserved above the screen. – STAINED GLASS. E window by *Alex Booker*, †1889.

OUR LADY AND ST WALSTAN. R.C. By *J. C. Buckler* to go with Costessey Hall, for the Catholic Jerningham family. Opened in 1841 after seven years in building (so it is the sixth oldest purpose-built public Catholic church in the East Anglia diocese). The early Catholic churches tended to look to Nonconformist design, and here Buckler provides a large seven-bay preaching nave and a vestigial two-bay chancel. Brick, no aisles or tower, lancet windows, unexciting. Pleasant if plain interior, cheered by the three-bay stone W gallery doubling as an organ chamber. – STAINED GLASS. Good, but becoming weathered. In the chancel, by *James & Joseph Grant, c.* 1841.

ST HELEN. A very simple barn-like church of 1975 by *Andrew Anderson*, using second-hand bricks pierced by ranges of slit windows. Pantiled roof. Interior just as simple.

COSTESSEY HALL (Costessey Park), now in ivy-clad ruins. The manor belonged to the Catholic Jerningham family from the mid C16 to 1925. Original house of 1564, the Gothick chapel of 1809 partly by *Edward Jerningham*, the poet,[*] but the bulk of the house by *J. C. Buckler* of Oxford *c.* 1826–55. The old part of the house was E-shaped with far-projecting wings and polygonal angle buttresses or shafts to the porch and the ends of the wings. The new part rose behind it and to its r. It was large, of red brick, and partly medieval, partly of Tudor details. The climax was a big asymmetrically placed tower with machicolations. The park is now a golf course.

Various OUTBUILDINGS. STABLE BLOCK to the N in a U-shaped complex by *Sir John Soane*, 1784. Of red brick, two storeys, with six bays of C20 windows (but C18 Diocletian windows at the back). Pedimented and with hipped roofs. The round-arched windows are repeated in the BARN.

[*] The chapel, shown in a print of 1810, was a free-standing oblong of eight bays separated by prominent stepped buttresses and with a parapet and a large W window, like a reduced King's College Chapel.

PARK HOUSE. A C17 house remodelled in the C19, presumably a
dower house to the Hall. Stepped gables. Chimney flues of
Cosseyware. Mullioned windows. The cellar barrel-vaulted in
brick.

LODGES. COSTESSEY LODGE on Dereham Road, *c.* 1830, probably by *J. C. Buckler.* A Gothic L-plan house with a polygonal
turret in the inner angle forming the entrance. Cusped mullioned
windows of moulded gault brick. Intricate chimneystacks, pinnacles to the gables and also a triangular oriel window. Barely two
storeys in height, with gabled through-eaves dormers appearing
early here. Partial panelling to principal ground-floor rooms,
mainly C20.

BEEHIVE LODGE, Ringland Lane. An early C19 *cottage orné* on a
circular plan. Y-tracery windows with tree-trunk posts in front
of them, supporting the eaves. Octagonal central stack.

ROUND HOUSE, Dereham Road. Octagonal toll house serving
the Dereham Turnpike, opened in 1770. Not regularly faceted.
C20 windows. Four circular flues to the central stack.

THE STREET is the main road in the village. On it the church and
various C17 HOUSES, altered C19 and C20. On the W, No. 63
has early C17 two-light windows still in the gable-end, but otherwise C19. The bridging beams have small rolls to the corners.
No. 93 is still a through-passage-planned house with decorated
gable-ends, though the front, apart from the C17 door, is late
C19. At the back a mullioned window. The BARN at CHURCH
FARM dated 1688. Timber-framed with a brick gable-end and a
decent queenpost roof. On the E side it is enough to notice No.
80, and No. 88, both with parts of C17 window details. No. 100
is dated 1775, and has a rusticated door surround under a
pediment. No. 104, back to the C17, formerly a pub, with a
timber frame embedded in the brick and flint. Lobby-entrance
plan. The same at No. 120, though here is a stepped gable to go
with the lobby-entrance. Nos. 138–142 was an imposing house
when in one occupation. L-plan, again lobby-entrance. Various
C20 additions.

At WEST END, Nos. 52–58 is a short terrace of 1853 in the Neo-
Norman style. Gault brick. Round-arched openings and roll-
moulded hoods. No. 70, being Gothic, seems much more
modern even though it is of 1849. Square hoods over the windows, elaborate stacks.

COSTON

0000

ST MICHAEL. Redundant. Apart from the chancel E wall, which
must be Georgian, the church seems to be of the late C13 and
unusually complete. There is a stringcourse on the N side taking
in the doorway and the tower. C16 brick and flint S porch. The
W tower is unbuttressed. The belfry stage of course is C14 – see
the Y-tracery windows – and the knapped flint of the crenellated parapet late C14. The arch towards the nave is no more
than a chamfered doorway. The windows are lancets with a sur-

round of two hollow chamfers to the outside and a moulding to
the inside which starts in two little stylized leaves. C13 piscina in
SE nave. The chancel arch is narrow and low. The arch is also
of two hollow chamfers. The inner order rests on capitals which
rest on small twisted corbels. C15 roof, with cambered ties on
arched braces dropping to wall-posts. In the Georgian E wall
three capitals or corbels re-set. This wall rebuilt slightly farther
w than the original. – FONT. Perp, octagonal. – PULPIT.
Jacobean, plain, hexagonal. – MONUMENT. In the churchyard a
headstone to Charles Carr †1883. Of interest only in that it
records that he was tragically hit by a sail of Runhall mill.

COSTON HALL, E of the church. Brick C17 house with big C19
additions. Of the original there remain mullioned and transomed windows in the E gable, under pediments.

COXFORD PRIORY see TATTERSETT

CRANWICH   7090

ST MARY. Thatched roofs. Anglo-Saxon round tower with a
small round w window below a later arched window. Above are
round sound-holes with knot patterns representing the C11 bell-
stage. A new bell-stage above has four crude arched openings
below a crenellated parapet. The arch to the nave has been
lowered. The s doorway is of c. 1200. Round arch with one slight
chamfer, hoodmould with dogtooth. The s porch and windows
C15, though one cusped C14 lancet is apparent. Square-headed
Perp N windows. The chancel style of c. 1300 (windows with
intersecting and Y-tracery) but perhaps of the time in the early
C19 when the interior was redecorated. On the other hand the
piscina looks original work of c. 1300: undercut arch on engaged
colonnettes. – FONT. C14, plain and octagonal.

CRANWORTH   9000

ST MARY. Dec throughout. Unbuttressed w tower. The w window has Y-tracery. Sound-holes circular and quatrefoiled. Bell-
openings with a reticulation unit. Tower arch with head corbels.
Recessed spire. Both aisles have Dec windows. The N doorway
has a hoodmould on big headstops. The arcades (that on the s
side obviously new or renewed) have four bays with quatrefoil
piers with spurs in the diagonals and polygonal capitals to the
foils. s porch rebuilt 1899 during the second C19 restoration
(the other 1852). These works provided the roofs and most of
the fittings. In the chancel reticulated tracery. Lowside window
on the s side, the part below the transom now blocked. – FONT.
C14, octagonal. – MONUMENTS. Several good tablets from
the late C17 to the late C18, mostly commemorating the
Gurdons of Letton Hall. A cartouche to Sir William Cooke

†1708 attributed to *Thomas Cartwright* the Younger. – STOCKS. Outside the churchyard gate.

OLD RECTORY. By *Fuller Coker*, a builder from Shipdham, 1839. Two storeys in five bays, the end bays raised up. Porch with unfluted Doric columns. Staircase with twisted balusters, screen with a pair of Ionic columns in dining room.

CLAY COTTAGE. Two storeys in four bays, the windows all C19 or C20. C17 stack, as is the winder staircase. Lobby-entrance plan.

ROMANO-BRITISH VILLA. Extensive remains discovered in 1947 indicate the site of a building and a gravel metalled courtyard. The pottery is mainly C4. (DG)

6000   CRIMPLESHAM

ST MARY. Of rendered carstone. Broad Perp w tower of *c.* 1400, with the bell-openings filled with brick, possibly a feature of 1816, when work was being done. Note the carstone flushwork on the buttresses. Early C17 brick s porch. Chancel of 1875–7, reusing fragments of original stone in the windows and priest's door. The chancel arch is odd, seemingly with C12 responds but the rest 1877. The nave restored and given a new roof and floor in 1897, which involved rebuilding its E gable; nave furnishings 1872. In the nave a Norman s doorway, quite big, with one order of one-scallop capitals and an arch with rope and billet motifs. Also a similar Norman N doorway (within a C19 vestry) and a Norman N window. These details of mid C12. The C14 and C19 windows are enlargements of lancets. – FONT. C17. – SCREEN. Under the tower, early C16 from St Andrew, North Weald Bassett, Essex (demolished 1969). Linenfold dado panels below an inscription. Upper panels with C17 pendant tracery. E coving taken from a different screen. – N and s DOORS. Late C15, replacing round-headed originals.

MANOR FARM, by the church, has a model set of FARM BUILDINGS of 1881. The C18 HOUSE is of six bays, the centre two advanced under a pediment, but was remodelled in the mid C19.

CRIMPLESHAM HALL. Said by Kelly to be by *Waterhouse* and of 1881, but if involved he can only be responsible for the interior details. It looks *c.* 1850–60 and was for the Bagge family of Stradsett. An asymmetrical composition of gable-ends in gault brick, with brick corbelling of rather a wild kind, a little *à la* Lamb. The interior fittings remain including the top-lit dog-leg staircase approached from the tiled entrance hall. In the gardens a lake and, overlooking it, a FOLLY, 80 yds SW of the house. Early Victorian probably, and of very irregular composition, of stone and gault brick, with a tall, thin tower rising out of a courtyard. The court has medieval fragments, including three C14 doorway arches, one from the C13 and several Early Perp windows. Could they be from one of the adjoining monastic houses, Winnold Priory or West Dereham? The three-stage tower could be better called a campanile. It is entered through another C13 doorway, above which is a C14 cross-legged figure under a canopy. In the first-floor room the floor has a hollow-sided octagonal mosaic pattern as if it were in an C18 grotto. The materials are dark cobbles and horses' teeth.

CRINGLEFORD

Cringleford just retains a separate identity from Eaton and thus Norwich on the other side of the River Yare. Until the C20 it consisted of a few houses clustered round the church with the Hall isolated to the sw, but development along the existing roads from the 1930s produced an urban setting without a recognizable centre. The nearest shops are in Eaton.

St Peter. Unbuttressed w tower with a late C14 w window, restored. Nave and chancel, all C11, see the surviving double-splayed nave and chancel windows. The lowside window in the chancel however is single-splayed. s aisle with its arcade is of 1898, when extensive restorations were carried out. The new aisle reuses material from a former s aisle. The arcade of three bays: octagonal piers and double-chamfered arches. N porch more C15 with basket-arched recesses inside. The chancel arch C15 too. – FONT. Octagonal, C15. On steps the shape of a Maltese cross. Stem with fleurons in sunk panels. Bowl with vine trail like the font at Ketteringham. – SCULPTURE. In the nave w wall several pieces of Saxon interlace. Also a part of a Norman colonnette. – WALL PAINTING. On an original window in the chancel N wall, contemporary decoration in red of counter-changed triangles and pinwheels set out on lines which converge in the centre of the window (DP). – PAINTINGS. Wedding Feast at Cana; *Bassano* workshop. – Virgin and St Francis(?); Florence, C17. – STAINED GLASS. E window, 1898. By *Lavers & Westlake*, the Three Marys at the Tomb. s chancel glass also by *Lavers & Westlake*, same date.

PRIMARY SCHOOL (Church of England), 1970–1 by *Tayler & Green*. Low-key design with multiple small blocks instead of one large one, the earliest example of the pavilion style of school architecture in Norfolk (*see* Introduction, p. 166). Windows consciously all different sizes.

No. 4 FORD END, SE of the church on Newmarket Road. With a shaped gable and oval windows under it, i.e. of *c.* 1700 or a little earlier. The west front is Georgianized and there are three-bay additions of 1929 to the l. and alterations to the rear, including a stair-turret and a wing with its own shaped gable – very anti-quarian for 1929. This continues inside where one finds a stair-case in C17 style and a strapwork chimneypiece in the rear wing, all of 1929. The main roof is a butt-purlin original, *c.* 1700.

CRINGLEFORD HALL, Intwood Road, ⅝ m. sw of the church. So many late Georgian and early Victorian additions that the tim-ber-framed C16 centre block with its jetty and stepped brick gable goes almost unnoticed. The framing itself is hidden behind a rendered brick skin. Grey brick w range of three bays, with a central curved porch on columns facing w. In the angle between this and the C16 work is the bowed s front of the music room which has recesses r. and l. of the marble chimneypiece and mirrors between the windows: all late C18. The staircase is only just C18: closed string and turned balusters still in a late C17 tradition. From 1845 to 1959 it was used as the parsonage.

BRIDGE. Over the river Yare. Of two arches, both four-centred and
60 separated by cutwaters. One assumes the date 1520 on the grounds that it replaced one washed away in 1519. Widened in 1780. The material is limestone, at least in the facings, a rarity in Norfolk other than for churches and bridges. It still carries a lot of traffic despite the Cringleford by-pass to the N.

MILLHOUSE, close to the bridge. Pretty, of three bays in three storeys facing the river. Colourwashed brick, almost all of 1795. Central doorway with timber pedimented doorcase.

ROUND HOUSE, at the w entry to the village on Newmarket Road. Octagonal, not round, of c. 1805 for Sir Roger Kerrison. Red brick, Gothick windows with Y-tracery and, a surprise, of two storeys.

POND FARMHOUSE, Newmarket Road. Timber-framed and turns its back on the road. Brick skin to façade. Five bays in one and a half storeys and with a complicated building sequence as if parts regularly collapsed and were rebuilt. The first bay (from l.) is c. 1800 with its brick gable-end, the next bay is late C17, the next must be early C17, the fourth c. 1500 and the last early C17 again, with its own brick gable-end. Inside, the earliest bay (fourth) turns out to be one and a half bays, timber-framed, with a queenpost roof and arched braces to tie-beams and collars.

Nos. 8–10 Newmarket Road (CRINGLEFORD HOUSE and ROSALIND HOUSE) built as one house c. 1794 on the site of an earlier house, Flotmans, of 1584. Parts of the original reused, e.g. some roof timbers. Brick, five bays, with a pedimented doorway re-set into the late C19 central porch. Later extensions to sides and rear.

CROWNTHORPE

ST JAMES. Redundant and converted into a house in 1988 which saved it from ruination. It was a chapel-of-ease to Wicklewood. Unbuttressed Perp w tower without parapet. The date 1714 must refer to the rebuilding of the belfry stage. Continuous nave and chancel, the latter C13 with lancets and a good double piscina. The nave slightly younger. Former roof-line visible on the tower. The present roof is pierced by roof-lights. The E window is formed of three simple lancets, but this more C19 than C13. A N and a s chapel off the nave were destroyed and the windows re-set, possibly during the restoration of 1844. The Perp arch into the s chapel remains. It has a good Perp window. Another restoration in 1880 provided the hammerbeam roof.

CROXTON

8080

Near Thetford

ALL SAINTS. Round tower with polygonal top stage perhaps of the
C14 and a short slated spire. Chancel with an early C13 priest's
doorway. Slightly pointed, one slight chamfer, hoodmould with
dogtooth. The N and S windows of the chancel and nave point
to c. 1300, but are renewed. Curvilinear E window of three lights
with the double-ogee pattern, c. 1340. One E buttress has flushwork decoration. In fact the chancel was rebuilt, faithfully, it
appears, and reusing some pieces, in 1884. The rest restored
1856. S aisle rebuilt in 1884 also, opening up the C14 three-bay
arcade. Octagonal piers, double-chamfered arches. The chancel
arch goes with the arcade. Early Tudor clerestory faced with
knapped flint. Good hammerbeam roof inside of c. 1500. It has a
crenellated wall plate and hammerbeams, panelled spandrels to
the arched braces and pendants. – FONTS. One is big, octagonal, Perp, and may originally have had reliefs of the Seven
Sacraments (Cautley). The other is a modest wooden C18
baluster, rather rare.

CROXTON PARK, 1 m. NW. Early C18 house with a seven-bay
façade. Centre three bays recessed, leaving the side bays under
shaped gables. Pedimented porch.

Croxton is surrounded by Thetford Forest, which was planted to
leave a huge clearing in which the village is set, and is spread along
the B-road N from Thetford which peters out into the Stanford
Battle Area. There are three FARMHOUSES, serving HALL
FARM, CHAPEL FARM and HILL FARM, all C18, all relying on
flint. Chapel Farmhouse has reused ashlar and although altered
its lobby-entrance plan is evident. The entrance is to the N, but
the S front boasts very positive chequered masonry, also reused.

DENTON

2080

ST MARY. The W tower is a curiosity. It was a flint round tower
which fell in the late C18 leaving part of a curved section stuck
to the nave. To this was added a brick square W part, so the thing
looks now like a letter D. In the early C19 the top stage was
added, only to be heightened under the auspices of Archdeacon
Bouverie in 1868 as part of his general restoration (furnishings
in chancel, re-roofing of nave and aisles). The loss of the nave
roof is a pity since it is known to have been of 1535–8 using
materials from Langley. All windows of the church are renewed.
Long chancel of the late C13 with a fine steep E window of five
lights with intersecting tracery, Y-tracery in the side windows.
Interesting piscina with traceried gable. The sedilia are only
partially preserved. Perp aisles, but the E and W windows Dec,
which does not necessarily signal an earlier date. Arcades of
three bays with octagonal piers and double-chamfered arches.
The clerestory has two square quatrefoiled windows on either
side. Perp N porch of two storeys. Niche between the upper

windows. Tierceron star vault inside, with bosses of the Coronation of the Virgin, the Nativity, the Resurrection and the Ascension. – FONT. Octagonal, with shields in quatrefoils. – CHEST. Twelve panels from the former screen, with painted early C16 figures, including the local St Walstan. – STAINED GLASS. Many bits and pieces in the E window assembled by Archdeacon Postlethwaite and arranged by *Joshua Price* of London in 1716–19. There are English C15 figures as well as Continental C16 and C17 panels and much heraldic glass, up to Price's own time. It is an important early collection, but was rearranged in the C19. – N aisle E window, †1855 by *Ward & Hughes*, Crucifixion, Ascension, Nativity and Christ with Angels, all good. – S aisle E and W also by *Ward & Hughes*, †1860 and †1863 respectively. – MONUMENT. Robert Rogerson †1684. Tablet with, l. and r. of the inscription, piles of books.

UNITED REFORM CHURCH, Chapel Corner. Built for Congregationalists 1821, restored in 1963. Red brick. Three by three bays with a pyramid roof. S front with two doors and one sash between them; three sashes above. The doors have primitive porches with lean columns. Gallery to three sides, on slender cast-iron columns. – PULPIT. Polygonal and panelled and surrounded by baluster railings. – BOX PEWS. The whole set, to the sides as well as against the S wall by the doors.

DENTON HOUSE, ½ m. S of the church. In the gardens a GROTTO, the best in the county. Built by *Stackhouse Thompson*. Of flint with plenty of other materials. It has a tripartite front with pointed entrance and subsidiary arches and the date 1770 in black-letter in the pedimental gable. Inside is a round room with a round skylight and eight round piers in a circle. The room has decoration of all kinds of shells and also mirrors. Close by a RUIN reusing a Perp three-light window from a church. The Tour of Norfolk (1819) tells us of a pagoda in addition. The house was rebuilt in the later C19.

LODGE FARMHOUSE, Middle Road. A brick-skinned and whitewashed house apparently of about 1840. Inside though it was revealed during alterations in 1993 that it is a mid-C14 raised-aisle hall house, a form which was concentrated in N Suffolk, but is very rare in Norfolk (the only other known is in the Old Market Place, Harleston). Dendrochronological dating indicates that the timbers were felled in 1361–2. The type is similar in appearance to a normal aisled hall, but the aisle-posts are raised up on heavy beams at about head height, so giving the interior a two-tiered aspect. The big supporting beams were an invitation to apply flooring when these open halls were converted from the C16. At Lodge Farm one supporting cross beam remains, on solid arched braces decorated with two sunk-quadrant mouldings separating a hollow. The mouldings continue into the cross beam itself, which is morticed into jowled principal studs. In the floor above two pairs of square aisle-posts rise to the roof. At high level the aisle-posts have, or had, arched braces to the arcade plate and to the tie-beam above.

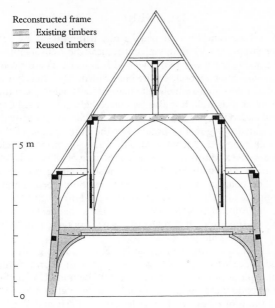

Reconstructed frame
░░░░ Existing timbers
▨▨▨ Reused timbers

⌐5 m

∟0

Denton, Lodge Farm. Orthographic reconstruction. Section

Curious long slots in the posts show that deep spandrel pieces, probably pierced and decorated, were intended for the arcade plate as well, so the whole was richly conceived. One arcade plate remains, with ovolo mouldings, sawn in half and used elsewhere. On top of the tie-beams between the tops of the aisle-posts was a crown-post construction, of which only mortice holes remain following the C19 reorganization. The rear wing and the dormers entirely of 1993.

The predominant vernacular type is a C17 timber-framed HOUSE, of which the best examples are PEAR TREE FARMHOUSE and IVY FARMHOUSE, both on Darrow Green Road and both with some mullioned windows remaining. VALLEY VIEW, Trunch Road, is similar. The C19 practice of casing C17 timber houses in brick is common here as elsewhere. e.g. LOW FARMHOUSE, Wortwell Road, MANOR FARMHOUSE, Manor Farm Road, and the KING'S HEAD public house at Great Green. Of C18 brick houses the biggest is the RECTORY, Earsham Road, but the best is DENTON LODGE, Earsham Road: two storeys in five bays with an open pediment over the doorcase supported on unfluted columns.

MOTTE AND BAILEY CASTLE, 1¼ m. NW of the church at Darrow Green. Hidden in woodland until the C19, this small castle is well preserved although tree-covered. Probably built by the d'Albinis in the late C11 or earlier C12. To the NE a rectangular banked enclosure is of uncertain date and function, although it may be a deer park.

HANGMAN'S HILL, near the castle, is a pit upcast mound. (AR)

St Mary. Of carstone with the usual ashlar trimmings. Late C13 w tower supported by diagonal buttresses, the bell-openings with Y-tracery, the lower two stages with lancets. The top was raised in 1895 after a wooden spire blew down. The church was restored in 1868–70, to which date many details belong. On the s side Y-tracery as well, but also two three-light transomed C15 straight-headed Perp windows. Early C15 chancel arch with concave-sided polygonal responds, but the outer details of the chancel all renewed. Niches l. and r. of the E window. Angle piscina inside a s window. N arcade and N aisle of 1870. Scissor-braced nave roof with fine heraldic cresting along the wall-plates. The boarding from 1870. – STALLS. Some bench ends with poppyheads reused. – STAINED GLASS. Three-light E window has an Adoration by *Ian Pace*, 1884; the s chancel windows probably by *Pace* too. Examples of Pace's work are not common, which is a good thing.

Denver Hall, se of the church on Ely Road. The E gable is a splendid piece of *c.* 1520. Brick, stepped, with round richly decorated pinnacles, round chimneyshafts behind. Under the steps terracotta panels with letters and ornamental motifs. The same at the foot of the wall. The letters are IWE and WEN. They are supposed to refer to the Willoughby family. Four-light cross casement (renewed) on the ground floor under a hood-mould, on the first floor a blocked window under both a hood and a pediment of wavering shape. Between the two an ogeed plaque with coat of arms. w gable has a stepped C16 external stack with twin flues. The main s front is of the mid C18, gault brick, eight bays in two storeys. Inside, the earliest details are mid-C18 and of note only the staircase with its turned balusters.

　　Detached from the house 20 yds to the N a little Elizabethan
75　GATEHOUSE, also brick. Square plan with diagonal corner buttresses, one modified, under a gabled roof. The gatehouse faces N, away from the house, and is entered through a four-centred pedestrian arch below a stone coat of arms. A terracotta colonnette r. and l. The s entrance is under a square hood. The upper floor was probably used as a summer pavilion and lit through a two-light mullioned window in each side. This room reached by an external stone staircase to the w. The little building carries the date 1570. The roof structure would have been interesting, but now is all C20.

Windmill, ¾ m. sw. A corn, not a drainage mill. A fine sight as it rises tall above surrounding buildings. It is a tower mill put up in 1835 for John Porter, and restored at regular intervals throughout the 1970s and 80s by the *Norfolk Windmills Trust*. Six storeys, sails and fan and most of the machinery, none of which is remarkable. Ogee cap. A good set of C19 GRANARY BUILDINGS crouches at its foot.

Denver Sluices. The Salter's Lode and the Old Bedford Sluices were probably built *c.* 1825–8. The Old Denver Sluices are by *John Rennie*, 1834, but were remodelled with steel doors and widened to the W in 1923. A new flood-gate was put in in 1928, only to be replaced in 1963 and again in 1983. Only the core of the structure is therefore now by Rennie. The Denver–Littleport road crosses it. This forms part of the great new drainage installations of the River Ouse instigated by an Act of Parliament in 1949 but described by the great Dutch engineer, Cornelius Vermuyden, in 1642 in almost exactly the terms expanded by *Sir Murdoch MacDonald & Partners* after 1947. A completely new river, called prosaically the Cut Off Channel, has been built. It is 15½ m. long and receives the rivers Lark, Little Ouse, and Wissey. The main river was widened and deepened for 19 m. This work carries water from the S to Denver Sluices. Lower down another new river is complete. This is called the Riley Channel, and to it belong the New Denver Sluices, completed in 1959, and the new tail sluices at King's Lynn (*see* p. 479).

Nos. 10–10A WHIN COMMON ROAD, SSW of the church. Once a farmhouse but converted to two houses in the 1980s. Shaped S gable to the three-bay C17 wing. Brick and slate. On SLUICE ROAD, No. 63 (formerly called Manor House Farmhouse) was originally a C16 carstone and brick house which shows little from that date apart from the chimneystacks, and those to the E gable are rebuilt. Two houses on DOWNHAM ROAD illustrate that carstone can be galleted just like flint, CROW HALL *c.* 1740 and later, and No. 2 (formerly the Rectory) *c.* 1770.

ROMAN ROAD. Just E of the Ouse, a small earthwork may indicate the line of the Fen Causeway, which ran from Peterborough to Brampton, and which emerged from the Fen at this point. (DG)

DEOPHAM   *oooo*

ST ANDREW. A big church with a big Perp W tower. The tower has set-back buttresses connected diagonally across the corner in the manner of nearby Hingham. The SE buttress impinges slightly on the aisle on that side. The buttresses have chequered flushwork right up to the top. Hexagonal turret pinnacles with flushwork panelling. W doorway, W window with stepped embattled transom, blocked window above, and tall bell-openings with steep gables reaching up into the flushwork-panelled battlements. Bells were being hung in 1473. Moreover there is a quatrefoil base frieze and a pretty vine frieze above the doorway level, these features also present at Hingham: so to the C15 mason there was nothing wrong with motifs of a century earlier. The tall tower arch has three orders of double wave mouldings. Dec S aisle and S arcade. The arcade is of five bays and has octagonal piers and double-chamfered arches on low stepped bases. The S doorway has traceried spandrels and a crenellated top, and the windows are clearly Dec. They have cusped mouchettes flanking coarse reticulation units. Only the aisle E window is Perp. The N arcade is Perp too, though the aisle windows favour the Dec style. The arcade piers are odd, consisting of square piers set diagonally with the corners slightly chamfered – i.e. essentially a lozenge plan reduced to the simplest form. High moulded bases. Two-light clerestory windows. Good nave roof of low pitch with cambered tie-beams on arched braces with traceried spandrels. Bosses at intersections of the roll-moulded purlins and ridge-piece. Roll-moulded also the boarded ashlaring. The head-corbels of the former roof below, only on the S side; on the N side they were no doubt removed when the arcade was rebuilt. Dec chancel, but with a restored five-light E window and a hammerbeam roof installed during the 1864 chancel restoration. – FONT. Octagonal, with small punched tracery motifs. – SCREEN. Part of the base in the S aisle at the E end. Painted brocade as decoration of the inner panels of the dado; late C15, the loose paint fixed 1978, by *Anna Hulbert*. Further fragments against the S aisle wall. – DOORS. Fine traceried S door with a pattern of quatrefoils, minor W door arcaded only in the arch. – STAINED GLASS. In the tracery of the N aisle E window assembled fragments. – MONUMENT. Coffin-lid with foliated cross (S aisle).

CROWN FARMHOUSE, ½ m. WNW. T-shaped C16 timber-framed and brick house. The ground floor is brick, but the first floor is jettied – a real mixture, repeated in the N and S gable-ends – in the manner of contemporary Norwich houses. The façade has mullioned and transomed windows below, casements above. Gable stacks, that to S with four octagonal flues. To the rear are some arched braces on studs supporting the jetty bressumer.

Rendered timber-framed HOUSES are the rule here until the C18, see e.g. HALL FARMHOUSE at Low Common and MEADOW COTTAGE, Park Lane, both C17.

DEREHAM

Dereham, formerly known as East Dereham, is the administrative centre for the district of Breckland, and has always been locally important. Its population in 1991 was 13,300, so it is the sixth largest town in the county, a surprise as one surveys the provincial Market Place. Its boom years were in the middle of the C18 and the third quarter of the C19, when the railways turned the place into an important junction.

In A.D. 654 King Anna of the East Angles was killed at the battle of Blythburgh, and his daughter Withburga fled to Dereham to found a nunnery. It was sacked by the Danes in 870 but rebuilt. In 974 the remains of St Withburga were stolen by the Abbot of Ely and of the house nothing, not even its site, is known.*

The Domesday Survey suggests a population of about 250, which rose to about 1,000 in the mid C16. The medieval market, established by the mid C13, was probably located in Church Street, immediately E of the church: the present Market Place may not have developed until the late C16. The early market pros-

---

* In fact it is possible that Withburga was associated with West Dereham (q.v.).

pered, dealing in cloth, leather and agricultural produce, to the extent that in the C17 it dominated a large area in the centre of the county as neighbouring markets at Elsing, Whinburgh, Gressenhall and Shipdham all disappeared. By the end of the C17 the nearest rivals were Hingham (7 m. s) and Foulsham (7 m. NE) but nothing nearer than Castle Acre to the w and Norwich to the E.

A fire of 1581 destroyed nearly 400 timber-framed and thatched houses in the centre, three quarters of the total, and resulted in a major rebuilding which may account for the present-day layout. Another fire in 1679 destroyed 170 houses, valued at £19,000. The earliest surviving domestic buildings in the town therefore date from the late C17 (an exception is Bishop Bonner's Cottage Museum), but the dominating centuries are the C18 and C19 and the material is brick. Prosperity brought a little élan to the town and, like Swaffham a little later, an Assembly House in 1756. Two decent mid-C18 houses remain – Quebec Hall and Hill House – built for local entrepreneurs (the former considerably altered).

In the C19 the population grew from 2,200 in 1811 to 5,500 in 1899, encouraged by the Norwich–Swaffham turnpike (1770) and later by the railways (1846 from Wymondham and 1848 from Swaffham), which brought significant industry. Ironwork, especially for churches, was made here in Gidney's St Nicholas Ironworks, Cowper Road, a boot and shoe factory was set up in Church Street, in 1874 Skipper's leather works s of the railway station employed 100 men and from the 1860s there was a big presence of malthouses near the railway. The Nonconformists arrived in force.

The agricultural market still flourished in the early C20, but the biggest expansion came in the twenty years after 1970. The quiet Toftwood area to the s became a sea of housing, and further estates grew up in all other directions. The trade this brought to retail businesses in the Market Place, High Street and Norwich Street in particular has resulted in the most systematic destruction of interiors seen in any Norfolk town in the drive to provide open sales areas. So although the town still has some good C18 houses, hardly a plan-form of any house or shop in the centre is older than 1975.

ST NICHOLAS. A large church at the w end of the town and connected with the Market Place by the wide Church Street. The church presents itself very proudly, thanks to its mighty detached bell-tower and the grouping of the church itself round its crossing tower. Both towers lack parapets, battlements and pinnacles, which makes them appear somewhat forbidding. The appearance of the central tower apparently is the result of changes in 1539, when it was reduced in height and re-roofed, according to the churchwardens' accounts.

The BELL TOWER lies to the s. Bequests for it (the new 'stepill or clocher') were made between 1501 and 1536 but the first references in wills to actual construction come in 1516. References in 1524 and 1525 to finishing and providing timber for the roof, giving us the date c. 1515–25. It is a sturdy piece, necessary for the immense weight of the ring of eight bells, and has diagonal buttresses and a w doorway. Four stages, square on plan, with a clock taken from West Tofts in 1978 (1902 by *Whitchurch*). Only the three-light belfry windows are not lancets. Plenty of brick used inside, the ground stage re-lined in the C18.

The CHURCH itself is an interesting building with a complicated and worthwhile architectural history. The exterior looks principally Dec and Perp, but the story starts much earlier with the Norman s doorway, and (inside) two spiral-fluted Norman columns. The doorway has two orders of shafts, two roll mouldings, and big trefoils with cusps, the ones at the springing with heads (cf. the Prior's door at Ely). It must be re-set, as we shall see presently. The spiral-fluted columns flank the entry to the chancel or rather, as it is now, the entry to the projecting part of the chancel. The architectural puzzle is the history of the crossing tower. Did the arch with these columns mark the E side of a former crossing, one bay E of the present one, or the apse arch of a church whose crossing lay where it lies now? The latter seems at first more likely, for the crossing tower as we see it is Dec – see the mighty piers, the details of the internal gallery above, and the paired two-light upper windows with thin tracery – and the C14 was not usually the time to start new crossing towers. On the other hand the following arguments must be taken into consideration. The responds to the s chapel are Norman in their lower parts, and a s transept is more probable than a Norman s chapel. The responds to the N chapel are early too, even if early C13 and not Norman. They are keeled and rest on typical twisted little brackets. If the original crossing was E of the present Dec crossing, what then was the reason for the shift?

This brings us to the second phase in the history of the building. It is principally represented by the arcades. They are of five bays but differ considerably from one another. The s arcade is earlier. It has a half-quatrefoil w respond, one octagonal and three circular piers, and a half-octagonal E respond. The N arcade starts in the same way but is continued by slender quatrefoil piers. The s arches are double-chamfered, the N ones double-hollow-chamfered, and all bases are of the water-holding type. It is justifiably assumed that the two w bays of both arcades stand at the end of the operation and represent an enlargement of the church to the w. If this is so, the former w responds of the shorter nave were re-set farther w. The arcades must be C13. The w wall with its big doorway, the wide ogee niches to its l. and r., and the large window above with its cusped intersected tracery can only be of after 1300. The N aisle windows, which are wholly Dec with Curvilinear tracery, might follow here. To reconstruct then the appearance of the church in the C13, one must place a crossing tower one bay to the E of the present crossing and imagine instead a continuation of arcades such as the present E bay. The assumption must be that a Norman crossing tower fell and damaged the E bays of the arcades, and so a sturdier crossing tower was built and the former crossing added to the chancel.

By the later C13 the chancel had its present form. Its C13
E.E. style is represented by the windows with plate tracery and
three more with three stepped lancet lights under one arch (two
replacing Perp windows in 1857), the cinquefoiled circular window above the E window and the surround itself of this now
Perp window. Also C13 are the priest's doorway, the over-renewed
sedilia and piscina (the latter with dogtooth), and the aumbry
niche opposite, complete with lamp-holder. Dec contributions
in addition to the Dec W end and the N aisle windows are the
transepts, although this is now reflected only in their curious
upper windows, and the upper window of the S chapel (altered
1502). Perp are the S aisle windows (added in 1464–6), and the
S porch given by Roger and Margaret Boton in 1500. This has a
decorated base frieze, flushwork decoration of the buttresses,
entrance with the Annunciation in the spandrels and niches to
the l. and r. of the doorway. Also Perp are the E window, the
windows of the transepts and the chancel chapels, and the
proud crenellation of the S chapel. This and the N chapel have
handsome ceilings with bosses and some old colour. In the S
chapel roof are late C15 panels painted with the Lamb in a 38
wreath.

Of later works one must record the insertion of the chancel S
door in 1862 with ironwork by *Gidney's*, major restorations of
1876 and 1885–6, the addition of the vestry in the NW corner of
the chancel and transept in 1922, the blocking of the N nave
door in 1975 and the glass lobby inserted in the S aisle entered
from the S door in the same year.

FURNISHINGS. – FONT. Provided in 1468 for £12 14s. 9d.
On two steps, the upper one quatrefoiled. Against the stem
eight figures under miniature lierne vaults, under the bowl
figures of angels, and against the bowl the Seven Sacraments and
the Crucifixion, the scenes all under tierceron or lierne vaults. –
SCREEN. S transept. Brought from Oxborough in 1949; *c.* 1480.
Painted figures of saints. – ROOD SCREEN. 1921 as a war memor-
ial. – LECTERN. Of latten, East Anglian, of 1482. The same
type as the lecterns at Snettisham, Walpole St Peter and Exeter
Cathedral. – CHEST. N transept. Flemish, early C16, carved 39
Nativity and Sibyls with very Mannerist figures; good. Provided
in 1786 by Samuel Rash, a local brewer, as a plaque recalls. –
ORGAN. Remnants of a *Bernard Smith* instrument of 1785,
reconstructed in 1876 by *Hill* of London and again in 1995 by
Bower & Co. of Wroxham and moved into the N transept. –
STAINED GLASS. Chancel NE and SE by *Wailes*, 1857. – S
transept S of 1847, by *Heaton, Butler & Bayne*. Interesting, with
kneeling figures in three tiers. Strong colours. Much duller is
the same firm's chancel E window of 1904 and their N transept
window of 1905. – REREDOS. 1857, four paintings added 1929.
– MONUMENTS. Small brass demi-figure of Edmund Kelyng
†1479 (chancel S). – Etheldreda Castell †1486, brass figure
17 in. long with a typical butterfly headdress (by the lectern). –
William Cowper, the poet, 1802 by *John Flaxman* in N transept.
Stone block with inscription and above it, in the round, the

Holy Bible, The Task* and a palm-branch. – Many HEAD-
STONES in the churchyard, but few of interest.

In the churchyard also, to the W of the church, ST WITH-
BURGA'S WELL, named after the founder of the nunnery.
Although reconstructed in the early C19 it seems substantially a
partly subterranean C14 structure, with the beginnings of ribs for
two vaulted bays against the E wall.

GUILDHALL. District Council Offices. For the older part on St
Withburga Lane, *see* Perambulation. The irregular courtyard of
rather orange brick and black pantiles to the over-sized gabled
roofs by the *District Council Architect's Department* (job architect
David Everett) was opened in 1992. Two storeys, sometimes
with through-eaves dormers, sometimes full dormers. Spare on
details apart from narrow mannerist semicircular stair-towers
on the gable-ends of the E wings, which do not close the courtyard and do not fall in line with each other. Utilitarian interiors.

ASSEMBLY ROOMS, now the Town Hall, Market Place. Built in
1756 at the time of Dereham's brief cultural ascendancy. Red
brick, with five bays of sashes to the E front, those to the upper
floor arched. The entrance is to the l. of the S return in what
was one of three open arches in the C18, the others blocked
with sashes. The former first-floor ballroom occupying the
entire E front has a wrought-iron balcony to the S and two pedimented doors to the N, otherwise the interior is offices.

CORN HALL, Market Place. 1856–7 by *J. & M.W. Goggs* of
Swaffham, in response to the post-railway fillip to the local
economy. It closed in 1926 and reopened as a cinema, a purpose,
among others, it still performs. Brick, with a stuccoed façade in
the form of a triumphal arch closed to the l. and r. by three
naive Corinthian columns each side with block entablatures
and above by an over-heavy attic. Until struck by lightning in
1950 there was a statue of Coke of Norfolk, the agricultural
reformer, on the parapet. C20 aluminium and glass doors dis-
figure the deep arched entrance portico, and the interior has
been floored for its present purpose.

BAPTIST CHURCH, High Street, set far back on the E side. 1849,
with some reordering and restoration in 1973. The broad front
of three bays with a three-bay pediment is articulated by twin
giant pilasters at the corners and single ones marking the centre
bay. Built of very white and very red brick, stuccoed and
painted cream and ochre in 1973, with arched windows and
doors. Gallery on three sides inside, quite plain, on the usual
cast-iron columns. Panelled pulpit and organ at E end, and
below them the total-immersion font.

COWPER CONGREGATIONAL CHURCH, Market Place. 1873–4
by *Edward Boardman*. Of Kentish rag with Bath stone dressings
over brick; the long N and S flanks all brick. Squashed into its
site in place of a house in which the poet William Cowper died
in 1800. Big five-light bar-tracery window over a gabled porch,

---

* A lengthy poem by Cowper of 1785 on the subject of his sofa, composed in blank
verse. Various moralistic passages. The task was set him by Lady Austin, hence the
name of the volume.

which has foliate capitals to the colonnettes. To the l. is a thin tower with an arched doorway, a tall narrow lancet and twin bell-openings in successive stages. Panelled parapet. It is a wholly medieval design, not at all in the usual chapel style, indeed the five-bay interior is aisled. Double-chamfered arches on circular cast-iron columns. – PULPIT. 1874. Polygonal, of stone, with marble colonnettes to the angles. – STAINED GLASS. In N and S aisles pretty Biblical scenes of the 1880s, the artist unidentified.

COWPER CONGREGATIONAL CHAPEL, London Road. Two red brick oblong blocks, both with hipped roofs. The S part is the older, of c. 1815: four-bay S front with central door and two tiers of sharply arched windows, those to the ground floor with intersecting glazing, those above originally all blind. The flanks of this part have two tiers of similar windows on the E side, but only two long windows to the W, which confirm that the interior was originally single-storeyed. The extension, of c. 1820, has two further long windows on the W side but three windows, on two levels, on the E side copying the existing ones. Two of the S upper windows opened in 1968 when the interior was floored to become a community hall. The chapel was used as a school after the Congregationalists opened their church in the Market Place in 1874.

TRINITY METHODIST CHURCH, Theatre Street. The old chapel of 1824 stood immediately W, but with the population rising to 5,563 in 1881 it was clear to the authorities that Dereham should be the centre of the middle Norfolk circuit, not Swaffham, whose population was declining. *Edward Boardman* was invited in 1880 to provide a more conventional Nonconformist version of the Congregational Church in the Market Place. Exactly the same materials, this time faced with stone all round in crazy paving coursing. Big four-light S window exhibiting Dec detail flanked by set-back buttresses, central arched doorway leading to the narthex, from which a stair rises to the gallery in the SW quadrant. The balancing quadrant is a cupboard. Plainer flanks, with two-light plate tracery. The highlight is Boardman's eccentric queenpost roof, with odd semicircular braces (made by *James Mumford* of Commercial Road).

CEMETERY CHAPELS, Cemetery Road. The cemetery opened in 1869 and two identical E.E. chapels were provided by *John Henry Brown* of Norwich, one for the Anglicans (N), another for the rest, linked by a covered screen walkway with an elaborate trefoiled entrance arch banded with ashlar and blue and red brick. Diminutive apses to the chapel W ends (liturgically the E) made to look much bigger inside by the arch before them. They make the best of the contrast between flint, stone and brick.

PERAMBULATION

The centre of Dereham is the MARKET PLACE. Its W and E sides are not parallel; they taper to the N, and then the open space widens again, into a triangle with the war memorial in the

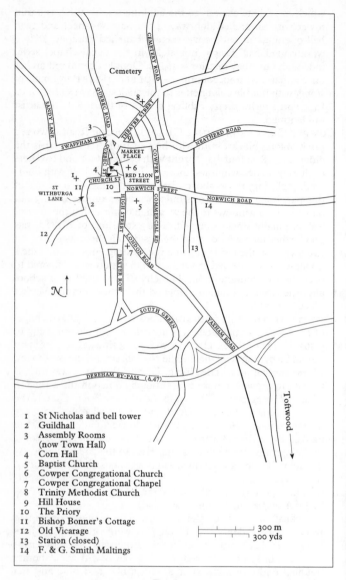

1   St Nicholas and bell tower
2   Guildhall
3   Assembly Rooms
    (now Town Hall)
4   Corn Hall
5   Baptist Church
6   Cowper Congregational Church
7   Cowper Congregational Chapel
8   Trinity Methodist Church
9   Hill House
10 The Priory
11 Bishop Bonner's Cottage
12 Old Vicarage
13 Station (closed)
14 F. & G. Smith Maltings

Dereham

centre. Among the pleasant late Georgian houses of red brick
in these adjoining spaces, only Edward Boardman's Congregational Church (*see* above) of 1874 breaks the continuity of
the frontages. The Corn Hall (*see* above) of 1856–7 lies at the s
end of the w side. These two buildings will act as landmarks.

Next to the Corn Hall and closing the Market Place to the s
is Nos. 3–4, a free-standing six-bay block originally of 1815 but

re-worked in the 1860s and given rusticated quoins to three sides. N of the Corn Hall are two blocks of late C18 and early C19 houses and shops, Nos. 5–8 and Nos. 11–13, separated by a slab-like C20 intrusion where the Post Office used to stand. On the E side the story starts at the S end with No. 41 facing down Church Street, unusual for the early C19 cast-iron entrance to a former carriageway. Further N, WOOLWORTH'S of 1963, a poor replacement for the King's Arms Hotel which had been rebuilt after the 1679 fire and had an early C19 Greek Doric porch. Then LLOYDS BANK, a mid-C18 house re-fronted in 1891: red brick, stone dressings and balustraded parapet. Of the houses N of the Congregational Church at once Nos. 35–36. Of the mid C19, three storeys in five bays divided into two unequal properties by rusticated and vermiculated quoins, repeated at the corners. The three-bay r. part has a first-floor Venetian window. No. 34 follows, the three-storey, four-bay Italianate BARCLAYS BANK of the late C19. No. 32 has C17 origins but was re-fronted in the 1750s, with a four-bay pediment which steps out in a Baroque manner and a later Greek Doric porch. In the pediment is a Diocletian window. Conversion to a bank, or banks, accounted for the interiors. No. 28, now a shop, has rusticated stuccowork to the front and a nice three-light Gothick window to the rear of c. 1780.

At the N end where the subsidiary triangle opens, on the W side, the Assembly Rooms (see above), followed by minor two- and three-bay houses of 1837 with brick pilasters (Nos. 14–16) and the lower No. 17, whose steep roof still gives it an early C18 appearance despite later sashes and a C20 shop window. In the middle is the WAR MEMORIAL, a plain stone-clad cenotaph type. On the E side N of No. 28 the remains of the EAGLE INN, C17, but rebuilt in the early C19, and with later C19 pub frontages. The N side of this space is graced by No. 20, CANTERBURY HOUSE, on the l., of five plus one red brick bays with a central pedimented doorcase flanked by C20 bowed display windows replacing original sashes. Early C19, as are the remains of the RAILINGS to the front, once forming a generous bow but with the centre section missing. Between this and a three-storey C19 brick house and shop is a long, irregular and greatly altered early C18 range fitted out with eleven bays of C19 and C20 sashes and casements above a variety of shop windows and bay windows. Some bridging beams inside indicate the original date. In front is a cast-iron RAILING, a relic of cattle market stalls. This closing N section gains much from its position facing back down the Market Place.

Tucked away round the corner to the E is HILL HOUSE, Dereham's 'one half-aristocratic mansion'*, which is invisible

---

* George Borrow, Dereham's most famous son, was born in 1803. In *Lavengro* he wrote: 'Pretty, quiet D—, thou pattern of an English town – with thy one half-aristocratic mansion, where resided thy Lady Bountiful ...'. The lady was Lady Eleanor Fenn, wife of the antiquary Sir John Fenn (1739–94) who had bought a job-lot of old papers in a sack only to discover they were the C15 Paston Letters, which he edited and published in 1787.

from the main thoroughfare. Handsome brick w façade of
c. 1740, five bays wide with a projecting pedimented three-bay
centre, windows with stone keyblocks and corners heavily
emphasized by giant rusticated brick pilasters. Hipped roof with
two segmental dormers. Sash windows and a roundel in the
pediment. Central six-panelled door within an eared surround
with a pediment. The interior has an open string staircase with
two turned balusters to each tread; dado panelling. Fragments
of Perp windows set up in the garden, presumably by Sir John
Fenn.

A sortie along THEATRE STREET, NW of Hill House, brings
THEATRE ROYAL SURGERY. By *David Summers*, 1978. Well
done. A dominating pair of pantiled roofs with a low entrance
link. So called because the eminent East Anglian actor-manager
David Fisher built a theatre on the site in 1815. This neighbourhood is a patchy late C18 and C19 development of modest
houses, some (Nos. 35–37) with giant pilasters, a recurrent
Dereham feature (*see* Commercial Road below). Nos. 24–25
have simple early C19 doorcases.

Back at the Canterbury House corner, where Quebec Road
meets Swaffham Road, the GEORGE HOTEL, consisting of an
older s and a later N part. The former (No. 19 Market Place) is
stuccoed and has naive giant pilasters with, instead of capitals,
branches painted on in black. It probably has an early C18
timber frame, now invisible. Two-storey C19 bay window to the
r. The four-bay N part is blandly dressed in mid-C19 brick. In
front is a small square MILESTONE of *c*. 1770, the year the
Turnpike opened. London is 100 m. distant.

QUEBEC ROAD goes off to the N, with comfortable later C19
villas on both sides. 100 yds along on the E side Nos. 12–14
were the only pair built by one *W. Austin* in 1849, who intended
three more pairs. Italianate, in two colours of brick, each three
bays wide with rather mechanical Venetian windows to the first
floor and arched sashes below. Immediately N, EVATON LODGE,
1928 by *Bottle & Olley* of Yarmouth, in a suburban Arts and
Crafts style.

From this point we must retrace our steps s and shadow the
Market Place to the w via QUEBEC STREET. On the l. opposite
the new Post Office are two gables of early C18 houses, that to
the s with English bond brick. Nos. 12–14 further s are surprisingly large late C18 three-storey houses, quite plain, but only on
the w side is there a more homogeneous Georgian character,
despite the succession of late C19 and C20 shopfronts. About
half-way down is Nos. 29–31, the brick three-storey façade
rebuilt in the early C19 but with a couple of bridging beams
remaining from *c*. 1730 and the roof still with curved wind-
braces. Facing the Red Lion behind the Corn Hall stands the
CONSERVATIVE CLUB (Nos. 7 & 7A), another mid-C18 house
of three storeys and five bays, with four giant rusticated
pilasters, two of them hacked away at the ground floor to make
way for a shop window. Sashes, some original, and a good
open-string staircase with three balusters per tread and a steeply

ramped handrail. The rest of the interior obliterated since conversion to a club in 1930; giant single-storey rear extensions added in the 1970s. The RED LION has four C18 sashes to the first floor facing RED LION STREET and one original bridging beam in each floor, competing with the Brewer's Tudor timberwork. Roof of the taper-tenoned purlin type of the mid C18. At the S end of Quebec Street No. 1 is a less elaborate five-bay house of the same date as the Conservative Club, with another decent staircase and an open pediment to the central door. Converted for a shop in the C19.

At the S end of Quebec Street CHURCH STREET links the church and the bottom of the Market Place. The E end of the street has the familiar late C18 or early C19 brick aspect, although a few buildings have C17 origins. In the centre on the S side is THE PRIORY (No. 15), a brick three-storey house of *c.* 1750 with five bays of sashes, entered through a central door within an open pedimented doorcase on a pair of Roman Doric columns. It has a double-pile plan and another good if plain façade to the S. Later stick-baluster staircase, and some rooms with reeded surrounds to doors and windows. Nice simple spear-headed RAILINGS stand guard outside. No. 17 to the W has a C19 connection, and is used by the same firm of solicitors since 1949: early C19 with a later C19 shop display window. No. 27, at the W end on the S side, is of C17 origins, re-faced in the C18, with a five-bay façade. On the N side the large PHOENIX HOTEL, rebuilt in the 1970s with a crude brick front, ignores the scale of the street. Its annex has a gable-end to the street with Victorian bargeboards; altered internally, though three early C18 bridging beams remain to the first floor. Next W is CHURCH HOUSE, overlooking the churchyard. Late C17. It has nine bays to the E side, of which three are two-storeyed, with sashes, the rest of one single storey rising to the same height with windows with two transoms and buttresses between. These are alterations of 1906 when the house was converted to a church hall and offices. The single-storey part has inside a dramatic arch-braced roof of 1906 with a high gallery reached by a C17 closed-string staircase with turned balusters and a heavy moulded handrail. Various patchings to the fabric and the visible part of the roof structure date from 1984.

The area round the church has been well presented in the shake-up of central Dereham which took place over ten years from the mid 1970s. A pleasant GARDEN was created in front of the church tower in 1979, but the handsome late C18 cast-iron GATES leading to the church were removed to store at Gressenhall Museum in 1980, supposedly for restoration and reinstatement. A little to the S, also overlooking the churchyard, in ST WITHBURGA LANE, stands BISHOP BONNER'S COTTAGE MUSEUM, which despite the date 1502 in the S gable-head and another over the plank door to the r. of the E front has not a brick or a timber earlier than *c.* 1620, and certainly the original plan-type was early C17. Until used as a museum from 1962 (S cottage only) and 1968 it was three dwellings (the third door was where the extreme r. window now is), and indeed three winder stairs remain inside. Timber-framed and thatched, but mostly re-cased in flint and brick *c.* 1680. One storey and attic with a partly underbuilt jetty running along the main E front, over which is a broad frieze of painted pargeting – vine, rose, stars, etc. – which looks *c.* 1680 too. The pargeting was discovered during a restoration in 1904 and painted in 1968. The roof – at least the N and S parts – has upper crucks. The house in the earlier C20 was one of a terrace but now stands isolated. Bishop Bonner was Rector of Dereham from 1534 until his elevation to the see of London in 1540 but there is no known connection between him and this house.

The GUILDHALL, further S, has a late C18 three-bay domestic-looking stuccoed front with a porch on two Greek Doric columns *in antis*. It now forms part of the DISTRICT COUNCIL OFFICES, which have been neatly fitted into the space behind (*see* above). The S return, sandwiched between the long late C18 WALL running S down the lane and a late C19 (partly serpentine) wall running parallel to it, has a big two-storey bow with sashes and a single bay of tripartite sashes to its l. A doorway under a nine-vaned fanlight leads into a staircase hall, the stairs with turned balusters with bobbins and a ramped and wreathed handrail. Behind this block is a whole series of C19 extensions. Abutting the house to the N a brick wall, partly C16, of mixed bond to the ground floor and with two segmental-headed windows flanked by a door to the l. and two doors to the r., all with ashlar jambs. This is supposed to remain from the former Guildhall of St Withburga, suppressed and sold in 1548 to Thomas Wodehouse.

Further S at the end of a drive on the W side is the OLD VICARAGE, put up for the Rev. Charles Wollaston when he came to the parish in 1806. Originally three by three bays, with an oddly plain E (entrance) front. Timber porch and a full-height arched recess either side; just one sash to the first floor (recesses filled with ivy). Stick-baluster staircase at the back of Wollaston's house ahead of the front door flanked by one long room r. and l. Wollaston was succeeded by Rev. B.J. Armstrong (the diarist) in 1850 and he at once had the house extended a further two bays W, so the staircase is now roughly in the centre and the extended passageway gives the illusion of a double-pile plan.

From the Guildhall one can cut E through the grounds and car park of the Council Offices, glancing into THE QUEEN MOTHER'S GARDEN on the N opened in 1983 in the space behind the houses on Church Street and St Withburga Lane, to ALDISS COURT set back from the High Street. This is a small shopping mall with flats created in the 1980s out of derelict C19 flint and brick warehouses, but involving only one new range. Small and discreet and set back from the road-line. A similar new mall, NELSON PLACE, opens from the E side of the High Street.

The HIGH STREET is the main shopping street. No. 1 Aldiss Court and the adjacent Nos. 12–14 High Street have curved glass shopfronts of *c.* 1910 with a hint of Art Nouveau in the interlace at the top of the mahogany glazing bars: certainly the best in Dereham. Nos. 18–20 further s have been altered, outwardly early C19 but No. 18 has an intriguingly steeply pitched roof, of a type made in the C17. Then Nos. 26–28A, a once-pleasant seven-bay range with C18 origins, dominated by late C20 shopfronts, followed by a broad three-bay, three-storey house with a central first-floor window in an arched recess, early C19. No. 56 (BEECH HOUSE), further s, is a mid-C18 house, still pleasantly Georgian on the outside, three storeys high and with seven sashes. Pedimented doorcase on Roman Doric columns; panelled door. Subdivided for flats, when the main staircase was removed. A stick-baluster stair remains in the early C19 rear extension. The C18 front area RAILINGS are simple but attractive. The more modest and slightly later C18 four-bay Nos. 58–60 have also been converted, to two houses, and the interiors gutted.

The E side of the High Street maintains the pattern, with an interruption s of Norwich Street for the Baptist Church (*see* above). There are however still three C17 timber-framed buildings, even if they are hard to spot. The first is THE BULL pub, originally one room deep and on the lobby-entrance plan, cased in brick *c.* 1730 and re-roofed. No. 31 also retains its timber frame but appears all brick and has a C20 shopfront. Nos. 53–57, before the road splits, is the same but with C19 shopfronts: C17 with early C18 brick cladding and the s parts derelict at the time of writing; Nos. 53–55 with clasped purlin roofs. The upper floor rendering has partly fallen off to reveal studding behind. The road then splits. The l. fork, LONDON ROAD, has the former Congregational Chapel (*see* above), and then a sharp turn N up COMMERCIAL ROAD. The street was built up from 1838 and starts with a decent brick terrace, Nos. 81–95, two storeys with pilasters. Further on, larger detached villas. No. 21 on the E side is a clay lump house of *c.*1840. In 1890 *George Skipper* (who was born in Dereham and whose father was a builder living in Commercial Road) cased the front and flank walls in brick, adding the bays with tented leaded roofs and stained glass in the upper windows, and the excessively elaborate Cosseyware stacks.

This leads to NORWICH STREET, which by the time of the 1815 enclosure map was built up only as far as Commercial Road. On the s side towards the town the only building of note is No. 31, a three-storey, four-bay house with a centre and side pilasters and a doorcase with an open pediment. In the late C18 it was a flint-built house only two bays wide (the E half), as demonstrated by the remains of the exterior wall with a window inside at the back and also a butt join in the s elevation. Around 1810 the w half was added and the whole re-fronted in brick. Stick-baluster staircase. One first-floor room has a quaint serpentine balustraded mantel-shelf designed for holding a display

of pot plants. Now offices. Typical front RAILINGS of the time
of the re-fronting. An early C19 brick WALL runs up and returns
into Commercial Road. Diagonally opposite this point is the
KING'S HEAD HOTEL. Early C18 brick with burnt headers to
the five-bay r. part, the bay to the l. added later in the C18.
Early C19 extension to the N. No original interiors remain.

A brief detour N up COWPER ROAD to view ST NICHOLAS
WORKS at the junction with Georges Road. The firm of J. W.
Gidney & Son was established in the C18 making agricultural
implements, and in 1846 *W. T. Gidney* had these works built for
iron and brass founding. A narrow two-storeyed E part of six
bays and an equally long single-storey W part, fitted with the
firm's own cast-iron windows, and with the bifurcating strap
hinges to a door on the S side which are found all over East
Anglia after 1846, including the S chancel door of the church.
Back to Norwich Street. E of the King's Head stands the WAR
MEMORIAL HALL, built for James Elvin as a coachmaker's
works in 1818 and converted to its present purpose in 1949
when the interior was drastically altered. It has a broad front of
three storeys, with three low segment-headed windows on the
upper two floors, but on the ground floor a broad doorway (of
1949) with Ionic pilasters and a segmental pediment and blank
arches to its l. and r. Giant rusticated angle quoins. E of this
point is railway territory, though the little STATION has closed.
It is of 1846 (by *Samuel Morton Peto*) and has decorative chimneys. 150 yds behind, i.e. NNE of the Memorial Hall, now surrounded by new housing, the former Whitbread MALTHOUSE,
a huge double rectangle of red brick built in 1881, fallen derelict
and at the time of writing half converted to flats (begun 1994).
E of the derelict railway tracks Norwich Street becomes
NORWICH ROAD. On the r., facing the station, is the premises
of F. & G. SMITH MALTINGS, of 1870. Two big parallel ranges
with the familiar kiln cones at the S end. Remarkably, in operation, and moreover at the time of writing operated by hand in
exactly the same way as in 1870. So the three malting floors N of
the kilns are covered in sprouting grain and all the plant,
including the timber refrigeration ducts, is intact. The brick
inverted cone containing the four gravity-fed furnaces can be
circumambulated inside, and above, under the open pyramid
roofs, men walk back and forth turning roasting grain by hand
at 230 degrees F. The heat can be tolerated because the relative
humidity is zero. It is certainly the last traditional maltings in
Norfolk; is it the last in the country to eschew mechanization?
130 yds S of this stands the CMC FURNITURE WAREHOUSE,
built as Skipper's leather works in 1874: U-shaped, three storeys.
S again a depressing wasteland of derelict maltings and industrial buildings.

Outlying houses

Where the High Street splits, the r. road, Baxter Row, eventually
leads to SOUTH GREEN where once stood prosperous Georgian

houses set in a generous landscape, but post-war industrial development and the huge housing estates of the 1970s and 80s have not been kind. Only MOORGATE HOUSE survives, half claimed by semi-derelict factory units immediately s. Three widely spaced bays with a pediment over the advanced middle bay, a Venetian window below it, and a pedimented portico porch on two pairs of Tuscan columns. This E front was added *c.* 1800 to a house thirty years older; the newer bay contains the too-large stick-baluster staircase.

QUEBEC HALL, Quebec Road, ¾ m. N of the church. Samuel Rash was a prominent local brewer who prospered with the town in the mid C18, and had built his stuccoed brick Gothick house in 1759. The three-storey façade was three bays wide including a full-height canted bay in the middle, fitted with two-light Y-tracery windows. This is practically unrecognizable: crushed in between C19 and C20 extensions is one cant of the bay at the back. The rest is a loose but large group of three- and four-storeyed blocks shooting out in every direction including a three-storey entrance porch to the SW front. Stick-baluster staircase lit through an oval lantern. Since 1960 it has been a residential home, which involved further alterations, but was until 1920 the home of General Bulwer who laid out the gardens to show the disposition of troops at the battle of Quebec. To the N and E is a hamlet of bungalows for the residents.

DILLINGTON HALL, 1¼ m. NW. A solid three-storey, five-bay red brick pile of 1795 for John Daniel. Open-pedimented central doorcase, sashes and hipped roof. Large three-storey rear block linked to the original by a lower double-pile element. Nothing anywhere is elaborate; even the staircase is a simple stick-baluster affair.

HUMBLETOFT, ⅞ m. NW, off Sandy Lane. A large house set in its own grounds representing many periods. In the W end of the long E–W block are two early C16 rooms, that to the W with evidence of a smoke bay, and next to it a good display of ribbon moulding on the fire bressumer and also multiple roll mouldings there and on the spine beam. The fireplaces themselves are all of 1913, when the long N extension was built, polygonal corner windows added and other alterations. The N front is of mid-C18 brick, with a moulded platband and casements dating to 1913.

HEATHFIELD, 400 yds NE of the last, is a five-bay late C18 house with sashes and quite large mid-C19 rear extensions. Facing it to the E HEATHFIELD COTTAGE, dated 1740 in brick on the W gable. Just one storey and attic. Every timber inside seems to be reused apart from the roof of taper-tenoned purlins. Certainly reused are the two pairs of upper crucks.

WINDMILL, 1 m. E of the town on Cherry Lane. A five-storey brick tower mill built in 1836. It ceased working in 1937, fell into disrepair, but was restored as a landscape feature in 1985–7 by the millwright *John Lawn* for the District Council. Boat-shaped cap, four stocks and sails, no shutters. Of the major machinery only the brakewheel and windshaft remain.

OLD JOLLY FARMERS, Yaxham Road in Toftwood, 1⅛ m. SE of
the church. Thatched and with a brick skin, but a late C17 timber-
framed house on the lobby-entrance plan with an old-fashioned
arrangement of two service rooms at the E end.

BORROW HALL, 650 yds W of the last on Dumpling Green. A
pleasant five-bay brick house of *c.* 1740 notable as the birth-
place of the novelist George Borrow (1803–81). Platband and
five bays of sashes, the latter renewed 1990, but a model of how
such work should be done.

WATER TOWER, Cemetery Road. A competent Italian Gothic
three-storeyed affair of 1881.

₆₀₃₀   DERSINGHAM

ST NICHOLAS. A big church. Wide Dec chancel, long Dec
arcades, and simple Dec N doorway. The rest Perp. The chancel has a wide five-light E window with reticulated tracery and
three Dec S windows, two of which have reticulation units. The
W one has a delightful lowside extension. It is a square with
four quatrefoiled circles. Headstops to all chancel windows,
externally and internally. Sedilia and piscina with detached
shafts and cinquefoiled arches and a hoodmould also on headstops. The nave is remarkably wide. The arcades are of six bays.
The piers are octagonal with concave sides and a small trefoiled
blank arch at the top of each side (cf. Narborough and also
Suffolk). The arches have two sunk-quadrant mouldings. Perp
windows of three lights in aisles and clerestory. Depressed,
almost straight-sided arches. Hammerbeam roof from the 1877
–9 restoration (cost £6,000), and aisle roofs of the same date.
Perp W tower with five-light transomed W window. Perp three-
light belfry windows. Battlemented parapet with stone angels of
1911 at the corners. Tall tower arch. Vestry and organ chamber
added N of the chancel in 1911 and fitted with a *Foster & Andrews*
organ made in 1884. – FONT. C14. Octagonal, with two blank
arched panels on each side. – FONT COVER. Turned balusters
support a C15 section with crocketed pinnacles. It was over-
restored in 1914 when the C17 balusters were renewed in replica.
– SCREEN. Late C14. On the N dado only are six painted Saints,
their companions on the S side obliterated. Wide one-light
divisions. The dainty cusping in two tiers renewed in 1877. –
40   CHEST. A remarkable piece with the signs of the four Evangelists
and some reticulated tracery in the front panels, foliage trails
and little animals in the border round them. An inventory of
1360 mentions it and there is no reason to doubt a mid-C14
date. The carved r. half of the lid made in 1984 by *Kenneth
Bowers* (chancel). – STAINED GLASS. S aisle E window by *Kempe
& Co.*, an Annunciation, †1912. Theirs also the Nativity in S
aisle, †1921. Two other S aisle windows by *Chris Powell*, one
†1932. – MONUMENTS. John Pell †1607. Tomb-chest with six
small kneeling figures of his sons carved on two panels, and his
three daughters on the back. These panels separated by pan-

elled marble pilasters. Black top slab with incised figures and
inscription. – Mrs Margaret Hodgson †1743. By *Francis Stafford*
of Norwich. A detached Corinthian column on a bracket in
front of an obelisk. – Mrs Elizabeth Pell †1732. By *Robert Page*.
Two Corinthian columns support a flattened pediment on
which recline two putti. Draperies in front of inscription panel.
– CROSS. In the churchyard, s of chancel. Stone, C14. Just a
socket stone and part of the shaft. – HEADSTONES. Many, the
earliest of 1686 outside the porch commemorating Sarah Fitlin.

DERSINGHAM HALL, Manor Road, NW of the church. The
H-plan house of *c.* 1600 easily recognizable despite the C18 and
C19 alterations. Brick and carstone under the stucco. Two-
storey, three-bay entrance front (E) flanked by cross wings with
stepped gables. Over the central range a triple cluster of chimney flues. The cross wings also with stepped gables at the back.

BARN. Between the Hall and the church is the TITHE BARN.
Dated 31 July 1671. Carstone and clunch with red brick dressings. Quite large, with stepped gables. It is really a pair of threestead barns end-to-end, notable for its date and size. Blocked
opposing doors to the E side.

WEST HALL MANOR COTTAGES. They have declined from a
mid-C17 manor house, with a butt join marking two building
periods within the century. Two storeys and attics. Casements
and a C20 porch. Shaped gable to rear.

MOATED SITE. Large, with a causeway to the N, it lies 200 yds SW
of the church. (AR)

DEVIL'S DITCH *see* GARBOLDISHAM

DICKLEBURGH   *1080*

ALL SAINTS. Quite a big church. Dec the unbuttressed W tower
and its sturdy arch towards the nave. The stair-turret added in
Tudor brick. Dec also the four-bay arcades. Quatrefoil piers
with fillets and in the diagonals thin shafts with fillets. Polygonal
capitals. Double-chamfered arches with an incision along the
middle of each chamfer. The chancel arch of the same design.
Perp aisle windows have stepped embattled transoms under
depressed arches. Long chancel, all Perp and all renewed.
Niches outside l. and r. of the E window. Elaborate S porch with
flushwork panelling. Entrance with fleurons and heads in a
moulding. In the spandrels the emblem of the Trinity and three
crowns. Niches l. and r. and above the entrance. Eight clerestory
windows on each side. Nave E gable is stepped. – FONT. Against
the stem four lions and four Wild Men; against the bowl the signs
of the Evangelists and four demi-figures of angels with shields.
– SCREEN. The base only, very unusual in the design of the
panels. Each has one large quatrefoil with big square leaf cusps
and inside each foil more small cusping. Figure carving in the
spandrels. – PULPIT. Jacobean, with the familiar short broad

blank arches with arabesque-work. – DOOR to the vestry, original, with ironwork. – STAINED GLASS. E window by *Hardman & Co.*, †1871. – MONUMENT. Dame Frances Playters †1659. By *Edward Marshall*. The architectural forms typical of the mid-C17 Artisan Mannerism, e.g. the shanks of a pediment below the two columns. In the middle, above an inordinately tall inscription, a frontal demi-figure. Top with open segmental pediment ending in scrolls.

SCHOOL, to the SW of the church. 1812 and 1842. Each date contributed one bargeboarded gable. Between them is a five-light window, and another either side.

MANOR HOUSE, ½ m. S. Georgian, red brick, five bays, two storeys, hipped roof. C19 central porch.

The VILLAGE straddles the main A140 road and only just achieves an identity round the church. N of the church is the KING'S HEAD INN, a C17 timber-framed building with cross casement windows to the front and rear wings and a stack with four octagonal flues. Various C17 and C18 COTTAGES line the main Norwich Road interspersed with a few early C19 brick cottages.

Two outlying clusters of farms and houses at DICKLEBURGH MOOR (½ m. NNE) and at HIGH COMMON (½ m. SSE). At Dickleburgh Moor the leading house is DICKLEBURGH HALL, a C16 brick house rather altered over the years. Four bays of cross casements and a four-centred entrance with a carved bressumer above, rebuilt diamond-flued stack. MANOR FARMHOUSE is a C17 timber-framed house with clay lump infill and some cross casements; thatched roof. LOWBROOK FARMHOUSE is also thatched, timber-framed and fitted with cross casements, but benefits from a stack with diamond flues; C17. High Common contributes little.

DIDLINGTON

ST MICHAEL. Chancel of the later C13 with a Victorian E window in plate tracery reflecting a C13 original in the N wall. Otherwise the side windows are lancets, and there is a handsome early C14 piscina with a steep pointed trefoiled arch and fine mouldings. Triangular arch to a recess to its E. Dec W tower and four-bay N arcade. The latter has octagonal piers but half-quatrefoil responds and double-chamfered arches. The primitive S arcade is Perp, see the lozenge-shaped piers with chamfered angles (cf. Deopham). The tower has ogee tracery in the small W window and bell-openings. Crenellated parapet. Mainly Perp aisle windows, those to the N (boarded at time of writing) still with Dec overtones. C15 clerestory. The church was restored 1855–73 (all roofs, E window and others, some re-facing to walls). Nearly flat nave roof retains a lot of C15 members including arched braces. The nave is all but redundant and without most fittings and the chancel separated by a glazed partition screen added 1967. – FONT. The bowl octagonal, C13, of Purbeck marble and with the characteristic two shallow arches to each side, unfortunately whitewashed. The stem is Dec or Perp. – COMMUNION RAILS. C18. Of white marble. Kelly reports that they come from the Hall, moved by the Amherst family. It was the Amhersts who came into possession of the Hall in 1852 and funded the church restoration. – BENCHES. Four, pushed to the N aisle wall, three with cut-out backs and all with poppyheads. C15. – STAINED GLASS. E window by *Hardman & Co.*, 1853, a Nativity, Crucifixion and Resurrection, all good. S aisle E window in style of *George Hedgeland*, commemorating William Amherst †1855. Good clear strong colours. N aisle E window similar. – MONUMENTS. Parts of three foliated coffin-lids cemented into nave W wall. – Tablets to Robert Wilson †1701 and Edward Wilson †1708, similar but not identical, both with naive weeper cherubs r. and l. of the inscription (chancel s).

DIDLINGTON HALL was a large house mostly reconstructed in 1879–86 in a kind of Italianate Georgian, surprisingly by *Norman Shaw* for William Amherst (cost £37,000). Demolished 1950 after mortification by army use in the war, but the red brick STABLE RANGE SE of the church remains complete with clock tower carrying a cupola.

DISS   *1080*

The meres of SE Norfolk are a familiar feature. Diss is a town built around a six-acre mere. To the S is a public park. How much could imaginative planning have made of it! The principal streets of the town are to the N and E of the mere, the church and Market Place to the NE. Unlike most market towns Diss did not suffer a major fire in the C16 or C17, so an unusually high proportion of timber-framed buildings remains in the narrow streets round the church. The Market Place is, or was, triangular in the C13, but colonization came early and it received a C15 chapel in the middle, of which fragments survive in buildings on Market Hill. The trade from the C15 was mainly in textiles and dairy produce, but the town in the late C20 is becoming a commuter dormitory for London, thanks to the inter-city rail service.

ST MARY. Tall W tower of *c.* 1300 and later with arches for processions through its ground floor to the N and S. These arches and the W doorway into the church have the continuous chamfered mouldings of that time. Y-tracery in the bell-openings. Niches in the W buttresses. On top a thin Gothic framework for the wind-vane. This dates from 1906, but is a copy of an older one. Perp S aisle lit through windows with stepped embattled transoms; on one set-off of the buttresses an animal lying. One buttress has a niche above the animal and flushwork panelling. The details of the windows are of 1850 (restoration by *Augustine Browne*) and taken over from the N aisle, probably correctly. The tall Perp S porch has flushwork panelling too and animals on one set-off of the buttresses. The N aisle is a little simpler. Two-storeyed N porch with a frieze of quatrefoils and shields.

The N chapel has a five-light N window. The chancel was rebuilt in 1857. Five-bay arcades with octagonal piers and double-hollow-chamfered arches, Dec and not Perp. Perp clerestory of ten windows either side. – DOOR. The W door traceried and now hung so that the tracery is to the inside. – STAINED GLASS. Old bits in the S aisle W window. – In the N and S aisle windows by *Hughes* and *Ward & Hughes*, dated 1866 and 1882; terrible. – Chancel E window by *F. W. Oliphant*, 1858, an important work. It has panels depicting the Nativity, Crucifixion, Entombment and Resurrection. A further S window by him was removed in 1980. Also taken away, tragically, a S window by *Wailes*, †1864, similar scenes, and his fine S chapel window with Sacrifice of Isaac, 1859. E window in same chapel by *Lavers & Barraud* remains. – MONUMENT. Richard Burton †1705. Plain tomb-chest with black lid (N aisle).

BAPTIST CHAPEL, Denmark Street, overlooking the mere and not an asset to it. 1859–60 by *W. Woods*. In the Italianate style, with two blunt short W towers and arched windows.

UNITED REFORMED CHURCH (formerly Congregational Church), Mere Street. Red brick, 1839. In 'the style of the latest and purest Gothic' according to contemporaries. By *Thomas Farrow* of Diss. Castellated porch in the W gable-end facing the street, under a four-light Perp window. Two tiers of cusped two-light windows to the flanks.

UNITARIAN CHAPEL (Masonic Hall). *See* Perambulation, below.

FRIENDS' MEETING HOUSE, Frenze Lane. 1745. Red brick. The S front faces a small graveyard and has two panelled doors, one under a pedimented hood, the other with a flat hood. Three large sashes alternate with them. Hipped roof. Doorway in the W gable also with a pedimented hood; two two-light cross case-ments to each floor of the N front. A later C18 extension to the N, forming an L-shape. Its W front has a door flanked by one sash r. and l. W gallery inside, on a single timber post.

MUSIC CENTRE. 1983 by the *County Architect's Department*, brick and hexagonal, roofed by a polygonal cone. Very much in the style favoured by the County Architect (*J. F. Tucker*) and epit-omized by the Rosemary Musker High School in Thetford.

PERAMBULATION

The natural starting-point is the MARKET PLACE, triangular and falling away from the church to the S so that the C18 and C19 shops on the E side have their access from a raised terrace. No. 10 has a platband, flush-framed sashes and a Doric door-case. The free-standing SHAMBLES (Nos. 4–5) are early C19 with a loggia of seven Doric columns. On the W side the KING'S HEAD HOTEL, a three-storey timber-framed building with irregular wings r. and l. Some of the original C17 cross casements light the centre three bays. Following this some shops with nice details: No. 15 has an iron balustrade, Nos. 16–16A early C19 pilasters to the doorcase, No. 18 a C17 jettied gable-end. The best building is in the NE corner, DOLPHIN HOUSE (formerly

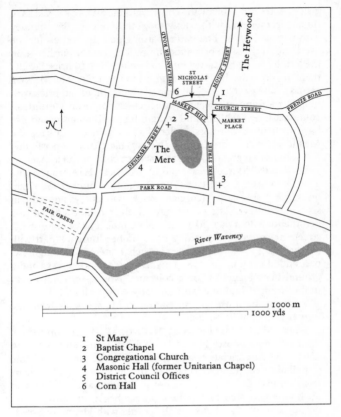

1   St Mary
2   Baptist Chapel
3   Congregational Church
4   Masonic Hall (former Unitarian Chapel)
5   District Council Offices
6   Corn Hall

Diss

an inn), half-timbered with two jetties on moulded bressumers
and a gable towards the church (N). The date *c*. 1520. This
brings us to CHURCH STREET, where No. 23 (DOLPHIN
COTTAGE) is a contemporary extension, also of two storeys and
attic and also with a jetty to the N on a moulded bressumer. On
the N side the partly C16 flint and brick CHURCHYARD WALLS
make a pleasing impact. Then No. 1. It once had the date 1637,
but this is obscured and the timber frame covered by an early
C19 brick façade. No. 7 of 1742, brick, stuccoed to the road, but
with a cross casement at the back.
    To the N from the Market Place MOUNT STREET runs past
the church. Opposite the tower No. 2, gault brick, early C19
(seven bays, the centre projecting, porch on two pairs of slender
Greek Doric columns). No. 3 has a C16 timber frame, apparent
from the first-floor jetty. Nos. 14–19 is an C18 range of timber-
framed houses, still with enough cross casements to be pleasant.
Nos. 30–33 are early C18, timber-framed in two storeys and five
bays, No. 35 has a late C17 stack. Of the early C17 Nos. 49–50,
two storeys in four window bays, the timber frame showing

inside. Across and still by the churchyard the SARACEN'S HEAD,
timber-framed and with a jetty too, but here C17. Big chimney
with panelled sides. The bargeboarding and the corbels for the
overhang in the style of c. 1700 are probably C20. Farther N on
the E side No. 62 has a C17 interior behind the C19 brick façade,
then No. 60, a five-bay house of grey brick, c. 1780. The MANOR
HOUSE follows (No. 59), all refined Georgian, of red brick with
hipped roof and an elegant semicircular porch on Corinthian
columns. Good fanlight and margin lights. Two storeys in five
bays with three dormers under shallow gables. Built for the
Meadows family. THE GROVE (No. 57) has a C16 timber frame,
but subdivision and C19 alterations detract from the impact.

Back to the Market Place and up MARKET HILL to the NW.
The DISTRICT COUNCIL OFFICES are in another Georgian
house, probably early Georgian. Brick, two storeys and attic in
six window bays. The sashes have flush frames. Steps up to a
pedimented doorway. Moulded platband. The N side of the
street substantially C17. No. 2 has a timber-framed E part with
a jetty facing E, but the façade somewhat altered. The higher W
part added early in the C18. This has three window bays and a
ground-floor loggia of Ionic columns. Nos. 4–6 again a C17
timber-framed building with an early C18 cladding. The C20
shopfronts one must ignore. Buried inside are walls from the
former chapel of St Nicholas.

Where Market Hill meets ST NICHOLAS STREET on the l. a
timber-framed house (No. 23) with a handsome angle-post on
which the Annunciation and the Nativity are carved (cf. the
Guildhall, Eye, Suffolk). The date of this is late C15, but apart
from some C16 overhangs the house is rather altered. Many of
the houses here are C17. On the S one can begin with Nos. 17–18,
now at least partly a bank, on the corner with Denmark Street.
Nos. 19–20 have an early C19 shopfront attached and E of
No. 23 are two more. No. 25 has a C19 gault brick façade but a
jetty remains at the back. The N side continues the C17 tradition
with, from the E, No. 3. Jettied first floor and a little pargeting in
panels at the back. No. 6 has a gable facing the street, No. 8
three cross casements from the early C18, but No. 9 is c. 1580.
Two storeys and dormer attic, the timber frame plastered. A
plain brick porch in front entered under a depressed arch.
Mullioned windows. To its W the remarkably civilized façade of
the CORN HALL, 1854 by *George Atkins* of Diss. It has nothing
of the boisterous character of most corn exchanges. The three-
bay front is dominated by the vigorously projecting centre
portico carried on pairs of giant unfluted Ionic columns beneath
a boldly dentilated pediment. The effect is striking. Blind pedimented windows r. and l.; consoles to central door hood under
the portico. The façade is ashlar, the rest is brick, the W flank
rendered and scored in imitation. The interior has a hall articulated with giant Doric pilasters supporting a continuous entablature. The original glass roof supported on iron beams was
unhappily removed in 1970. W of this only No. 13 defends its
C17 origins with any conviction.

From the w end of St Nicholas Street to the N in SHELFANGER ROAD, PINE HOUSE, a red brick house of the early C18 with a hipped roof (now divided into flats, but with a good panelled room inside on the ground floor, with pedimented overmantel and doors; DOE). Opposite stands Lacon's OLD MALTINGS, a two-storeyed L-shaped range of brick with giant recessed arches, dated 1788. s from the end of St Nicholas Street, down DENMARK STREET, the houses are from the C18 and C19 with one or two exceptions such as the thatched C17 cottages at Nos. 23–24, on the E side. First on the l. is the bulk of the Baptist Chapel, and the E side also has Nos. 47–50, late C16 timber-framed houses with jetties towards the street. The fine stack with its clustered flues to Nos. 52–54 tells of the C17 as does the less elaborate stack to Nos. 57–58. A private road off to the l. more than half-way down leads past two C19 semi-detached houses to the MASONIC HALL, built in 1822 as the Unitarian Chapel, a modest but charming Regency building. White with a hipped roof and a porch of two pairs of Doric columns carrying a pediment. Further still is the PARK HOTEL with a semicircular Ionic porch animating the conventional three-bay, two-storey early C19 type. On the other side of the street two C17 buildings (Nos. 100–103) lead on to LINDEN HOUSE, a mid-C19 three-bay house, and to DENMARK STREET HALL (up another private drive almost opposite that to the Masonic Hall), built as the Baptist Chapel in 1789. It is a supremely modest single storey of stud and weatherboarded construction, on a square plan.

At the s end of Denmark Street FAIR GREEN, a spacious green with attractive rows of cottages dating from the early C17, and a MALTHOUSE at one end, renovated in 1974. The medieval market was held here, not in the Market Place. Nos. 33–34 have pargeted panels and mullioned windows. Nos. 35–36 are also an early C17 pair with a gable to the l. higher than the rest. Pargeting and mullioned windows again and a distinguished stack with six star-topped octagonal flues. Back to the Market Place by Park Road and MERE STREET, where at the foot on the E side Nos. 25–35 are a curious early C19 composition of four houses. The two outer ones have pediments across their fronts, the two middle instead a raised octagonal upper floor with a small pediment over each side. C20 shopfronts have a disfiguring effect. PARK HOUSE opposite is a minor if dignified example of the early C19 two-storeyed, three-bay house. No. 42 retains its mid-C18 cross casements to the upper floor, surrendering all below to commerce. The remainder of the C18 houses on the w side have done likewise. On the E side Nos. 13–15 have fluted Greek Doric columns to their early C19 shopfronts, Nos. 9–12 of the mid C17, with cross casements and in the N house some brick nogging between the studs (renewed). At the top No. 1 began as a timber-framed house of the late C15 with a carved angle-post. Much brick used as well, most of it later.

To the N of Diss between Shelfanger and Burston is THE HEYWOOD, a strip of land rather than a settlement. As one proceeds N first CHESTNUT TREE FARMHOUSE, 1 m. N of the church. On the stack with its quadruple shafts the date 1574. Timber-framed, of two storeys and attic in three bays. The façade received a red brick skin in the mid C19. Next HEYWOOD HALL, 3 m. N of the church. An early C17 brick manor house of two storeys and attic in four bays. The S gable is stepped and has a stack with two diamond shafts. Finally, HEYWOOD MANOR, ½ m. further NNW. Same date but less impressive, although the big stack with its moulded brick tries hard.

DITCHINGHAM
3090

ST MARY. Tall, unusually opulent Perp w tower. Galleted flint with ashlar dressings. Doorway with tracery. Hoodmould on headstops. Niches l. and r. In them figures which are – a great exception – original, though much repaired. Base frieze with shields alternating with hearts surrounded by the Crown of Thorns. Four-light window, traceried sound-holes, a row of three shields under a hoodmould. Tall three-light bell-openings and flushwork-panelled battlements. Arch to the nave with engaged shafts and polygonal capitals. The rest of the church also Perp, but much renewed. The N aisle and its arcade is of 1875–6, by *Frederick Preedy* while carrying out a general restoration. His also the nave roof, chancel arch and benches, the seats apparently replacing those *Salvin* put in in 1846. The chancel E window seems in order. Chancel roof C19 but before Preedy, for it was painted in 1862–3 by *Mrs Scudamore*, the rector's wife. S porch with buttresses again decorated with hearts inside the Crown of Thorns. The hoodmould of the entrance has fleurons. A niche above again with fleurons. Rider Haggard paid for its restoration in 1896. That date is right for the roof. – FONT. On a traceried step. Plain, with eight shafts against the stem and shields and roses against the bowl. – PULPIT and READING DESK. By *Salvin*, 1846. – SCREEN. Called C16 by Cautley, but mostly Victorian. – SOUTH DOOR. C15, traceried. – STAINED GLASS. Bits of original glass in a nave S window. – In the chancel interesting glass installed in 1822 for Rev. Newling, commemoration date 1802. Figures of knights. Dark yellow dominates. – N aisle window by *J. Powell & Sons*, as a memorial to Henry Rider Haggard, the novelist, †1925. – MONUMENTS. Brasses to Philip †1490 and Margery Bozard (chancel floor, the figures 19 in. long) and to Roger Bozard †1505 and son. – WAR MEMORIAL, a bronze soldier recumbent, by *Derwent Wood*, 1920.

ALL HALLOWS CONVENT, ⅜ m. E. Group of red brick buildings, opened in 1858 as a House of Mercy, i.e. an institution to reclaim young women. The original buildings are the W and N wings. They are by *Henry Woodyer*. The E and S wings were added in 1864. The four wings are arranged in a cruciform fashion and characterized by two tiers of steep gabled dormers. A separate house for the sisters was built from 1876. To its S the chapel to which *Augustus Frere* added a circular w extension in 1893–5. This has a conical roof. He also built the range between the old building and the chapel. The REREDOS by *Alan Henderson*. Additions of 1955 by *J. P. Chaplin*.

DITCHINGHAM HALL. A very fine, restrained design of – it is said – *c.* 1715 for the Rev. John Bedingfeld. The house is not as its builder left it, but the changes have been wrought in an extraordinarily careful way. The original house faces s, that is looks towards a lake and past a magnificent cedar tree. It was seven by five bays. The original seven-bay façade has two storeys and dormer attic with a three-bay pediment enclosing a shield (with the Bedingfeld arms). The brick is mauve with red dressings. The doorway has Corinthian pilasters carrying a segmental pediment. A little (very typical) decoration round the upper middle window. A platband separates the floors; sash windows (not original) under finely gauged skewback arches. Hipped roof clad in slate since 1910, replacing plaintiles. Stacks with delicate panelling, still following C17 patterns.

In 1715 one entered the hall through the s door and was faced with three round arches defining the staircase hall. Spacious staircase with three turned balusters to each tread and carved tread ends. To the E (i.e. the r.) the dining room and kitchen. This is much the same today. The first additions were the provision of a two-storey wing running N from the E end of the house containing a new kitchen and associated service rooms. A parallel range was added N of the W end of the house, but freestanding from the main house, thus creating an odd open courtyard at the back. All this *c.* 1780–1800. The materials again red brick and slate, the quality not so high. In 1910 a new drawing room was added between the N end of the main house and the free-standing service block, by an unknown architect for William Carr, who bought the house in 1886. At the first floor is a suite of rooms approached by a staircase projecting into the now three-parts enclosed courtyard. The W front thus became nine bays long, with a central three-bay pediment and details to match the s façade, and the new segmentally pedimented door in the W front became the main entrance. The original hall became a library, only to change back again in 1983. Good later C18 fireplaces brought in by William Carr adorn the principal ground-floor rooms. The GROUNDS were landscaped in the C18, and appear much as they do now in an engraving by Butcher of 1778, with an attribution to *Capability Brown*. Drawings by him for a different layout are kept at the house.

THE GATE HOUSE, ¼ m. s of the church, on Norwich Road. Dated 1613 in large iron numerals on the s gable of a cross wing. Red brick concealing a timber frame. The gable-end has transomed windows of six, five and three lights, all with ovolo-moulded mullioned and transomed windows and all with pediments. A second date 1918 and initials RH refer to Rider Haggard's remodelling. Round the corner, in a surprising position, the porch, also with pedimented windows.

HALL FARMHOUSE, ¾ m. NW. Of *c.* 1700. With Dutch gable-ends and panelled chimneyshafts. The front has five bays of sashes in two storeys and a Doric doorcase, part of an early C19 refurbishment.

TINDALL HALL, ⅝ m. N. Colourwashed C18 brick, probably a rebuilding of a C17 house. Three-bay w front fitted with cross casements and augmented with pilasters to the middle bay and engaged columns to the doorcase. The rebuilt quadruple diamond shafts to the stack remain in C17 guise.

DITCHINGHAM HOUSE, ½ m. S. The house was a normal Georgian red brick house of three by four bays in two and a half storeys, but two bay windows were added to the E front and a porch to the N, (entrance) front. The porch on four unfluted columns and glazed. Built for Rev. William Buckle around 1780, it came to Rider Haggard after his marriage into the Margitson family, who had acquired the house in 1817.

DITCHINGHAM LODGE, ¾ m. S, by the meandering River Waveney. Of the mid C18, five bays and three storeys, the floors with stringcourses. Centre three bays advanced, with a porch on unfluted columns and a six-panelled door under a rectangular fretlight. In the rear wing sashes give way to casements, a typical Georgian contrivance. The staircase has three turned balusters to the tread, the tread-ends carved. The house also came to Rider Haggard by the same route as Ditchingham House.

WAVENEY LODGE, 1½ m. SSE. Rambling early Victorian, with Tudor details. Inside are quaint Gothick wall paintings with thin arcading of many shafts and behind it a landscape. Rustic, but very pretty.

ALL HALLOWS FARMHOUSE, Drapers Lane. Dated 1688. Red brick façade but the rest is timber-framed with a clay lump infill. The S windows irregularly spaced and anyway renewed. External stack to E gable.

HOLLYBUSH FARMHOUSE, Thwaite Road. A late C16 timber-framed house on the lobby-entrance plan. The E and W gables have renewed diamond-mullioned windows. Winder to S of stack. Jowled principal studs to the frame with, E of the stack, a queenpost roof. Four-centred brick fireplace at first floor W end.

CUDDONS, Yarmouth Road. c. 1700, only three bays wide, with the door off-set from the centre giving a lop-sided appearance. The reeded doorcase is C20. Moulded cap to the ridge stack.

ALMA HOUSE, Yarmouth Road, to the E, just before Broome. Superior early C18 brick house with blue brick detailing disposed behind forecourt walls with railings to the street. Six-bay W front fitted with cross casements. Doorcase with fluted Doric pilasters. Platband at first floor. Hipped roof with a panelled stack. Other elevations with cross casements too. The staircase has three turned balusters to the treads.

COUNCIL HOUSING. 1947–76, by *Tayler & Green* for the then Loddon Rural District Council (*see* Introduction, p. 165). In the village, 1 m. SE of the church. There are three parts, first WINDMILL GREEN, off Thwaite Road, 1947–8. The three informally sited terraces arranged round a green were claimed by the architects to have been the earliest in England to replace what was seen as the bad habit of pairs which was universal in low-cost pre-war rural housing. This claim has proved justified, for Tayler & Green's work for Loddon remains *the* outstanding rural housing put up in England by a local authority at that time. Essentially very simple blocks with interest in the detailing of porches and trellises, and by the use of vernacular materials such as flint, brick and pantiles. SCUDAMORE PLACE followed in 1958–64, the old people's community. A day room has on one side a two-storeyed warden's house linked by a screen wall, on the other terraced bungalows. Facing bricks here instead of the colourwash used for the earlier houses. A further gently curving terrace lies to the w, of practically the same design, but with contrasting treatment of finishes and brickwork. BEEVOR'S GARDENS was added in 1971–6, but the freshness of the earlier blocks has evaporated.

BROOM HEATH. The Neolithic long barrow on the Heath is some 160 ft long by 83 ft broad and 6 ft at the highest point. It has not been excavated, but Windmill Hill sherds have been found on its surface. Other round barrows nearby.

DOCKING

ST MARY. Wide, not long, nave with a big Perp s window and a N aisle of 1875, added by *Frederick Preedy*. However, the Victorian character of the interior is mainly due to *Ewan Christian*'s extensive alterations in 1838 which included new roofs, seating and gallery (Christian was then only twenty-four years old, working under *John Brown*, the Diocesan Surveyor). C15 s porch, the arch re-cut in the C19. Two ogeed niches above. Low early C14 chancel. E window of five lights with reticulated tracery was redone by *Preedy*; Y-tracery in side windows. The mid-C19 s vestry provides an entry from the Hall. Stately Perp w tower for which money was left in 1415. Four stages. Three-light bell-openings. Inside, the appearance is as Christian and Preedy left it: four-bay N arcade. – FONT. Pretty Perp piece, but much damaged. With eight statuettes of female figures with children against the stem and eight seated figures against the bowl. These might be Saints or representations of the offices of the Church. Buttresses with crocketed niches divide one from another. – STAINED GLASS. In s chancel two windows †1947 from the *John Hardman Studio*. w window by *Clayton & Bell*, *c*. 1870–80. – MONUMENT. Mrs Woolmer Cory †1837. She is shown in long garments with a baby in her arms rising heavenward. Gothic surround.

WESLEYAN CHAPEL. 1821. Small, of brick, with arched windows and doorway.

DOCKING HALL. The early C17 elevation of John Hare's house can be appreciated in *Ewan Christian*'s rebuild of 1858. Principal front to N: seven bays, two storeys and gabled attics, projecting end bays and central porch. Plenty of polygonal stacks. Quite an attractive and disciplined composition, but Christian could not resist polychrome brick for the porch entrance arch.

BURNSTALK, former workhouse, 1½ m. w. Of thirty-six bays. 1836
by *John Brown*. Brick, and late classical in style. Raised six-bay
centre, of which the outer bays project, long lower fifteen-
bay wings each with a three-bay pediment at the centres over
advanced bays. Rendered and colourwashed and converted to
housing.

In the VILLAGE nothing outstanding. In the HIGH STREET one
might notice THE LODGE at the junction with Well Street, an
irregular five-bay late C18 brick house with rusticated pilasters.
In SEDGEFORD ROAD is the CAGE, or LOCK-UP. Early C19,
flint and brick, with a heavy door and locking-bar in the w
gable-end. One might have been flogged for drunkenness in the
STOCKS attached to the public house on Station Road before a
spell in the lock-up. These are early C18. Handily placed is the
HARE PUBLIC HOUSE. Brick and clunch, the front stuccoed.
Two storeys in four bays. C19 sashes. Late C17 lobby-entrance
plan, altered. MANOR FARMHOUSE, Station Road, is C17 too,
but altered. The seven-bay façade has cross casements. C19
alterations and additions, including the porch.

DOWNHAM *see* WYMONDHAM

6000

DOWNHAM MARKET

ST EDMUND. Elevated above Church Road. Of carstone with
ashlar quoins. w tower E.E., and high, and a little odd in its
combination of paler true carstone and the darker, rougher
ferruginous conglomerate. The bell-openings have two lights
with a separating round shaft in front of a screen of quatrefoils.
The lights have pointed trefoiled heads and there is a quatrefoil
pierced through the spandrel. A later polygonal stair-turret, of
brick in its upper parts, cuts into the N bell-opening. Brick parapet and battlements, corner pinnacles and recessed lead spire.
In the N aisle two lancets amid Perp windows, discovered in
1873. Are they re-set? The s aisle also has Perp windows. Those
at the w end of both aisles have stepped transoms with battlements. Perp s porch and Perp N doorway. An odd small doorway in the E wall of the s chapel. The chancel is all renewed
externally. The arcades inside are confusing. The N arcade is an
even five bays with octagonal piers and wave-moulded arches,
the s arcade consists of two wide, tall, then two narrow, low
arches, and then again one wide, tall arch. All piers are octagonal. The first two bays on the s have moulded arches (sunk
quadrants and waves), the others three double-chamfered ones.
It seems likely that the original church had a s transept and
ended to the w, where the narrow bays end, that it was then
linked up with the new tower, and that in the C14 the piers and
arches were renewed. The second pier from the E is made by
attaching responds either side of a piece of solid wall. Nave roof
with tie-beams on arched braces alternating with angel figures

against the principals. Restored 1899. Early c16 roll-moulded purlins and rafters in s chapel. Perp chancel arch with castellated capitals. Wide openings to the s chapel, the arch into the chancel four-centred and stilted. The opening to the N chapel and the chapel itself are of 1873.

FONT. C15. Octagonal, with angels holding shields with emblems. The stem is by *William Lawrie* of Downham, 1855. – SCREEN. Short and all of 1910, with coving. – PULPIT. 1910, traditional. – LECTERN. Brass eagle presented in 1886, also traditional. – STAINED GLASS. Six c15 jumbled scenes in tower w window. E window by *Wailes* †1872, who also made two windows in s chapel, †1860. By *Mayer & Co.* of Munich are six: three in the chancel, an Agony in the Garden and Christ appearing to Mary (both †1875, installed 1882) and a Good Samaritan †1886; in s chapel the Raising of Jairus' daughter, †1860; s aisle w, Suffer Little Children, 1897. s aisle at E end a Raising of Lazarus by *Heaton, Butler & Bayne* †1896, the feet of Christ badly drawn. – SCULPTURE. A Gothic Crucifixus in relief above the chancel s door, outside. – A short spiral-fluted Norman colonnette outside the N transept chapel. – WEST GALLERY. Of wood, c18, handsome, restored 1842: three raised and fielded panels and acanthus carving. – MONUMENTS. Three ordinary wall monuments over s arcade, †1752 to †1775. – ROYAL ARMS. Of Queen Anne (w end).

THE TOWN

From the church one can see across the flat plain of the Fens to the w and s and realize that the town takes advantage of a ridge. In 1845 White reported the town to be 'clean and neat' and to possess 'two long and well-built roads'. One of these, Bridge Street, extends w into Railway Road and to the Relief Channel (cut 1955–60) and the River Great Ouse, ½ m. from the church. Here were quays serving the port of Downham, which dealt in grain and brewing until the arrival of the railway in 1846. There still remain large mills and warehouses round the station and waterways. The market was confirmed before the Conquest and flourished until the rise of those at King's Lynn, Swaffham and Wisbech (Cambs.) smothered business in the mid c19. Of the Benedictine cell granted to Ramsey in 1178 we know little. Although Downham has the same population as Swaffham (5,800 in 1991) its buildings cannot compete.

MOUNT TABOR CHAPEL, Bridge Street, for the Methodists. 1859. Three-bay gault brick front with tapering angle pilasters and central engaged columns, the moulded capitals with a running dentil course hacked off with the cornice that linked them. Big pedimental gable. Carstone slips to returns. Redundant and converted.

WESLEYAN CHAPEL, Lynn Road. The usual three-bay, gault brick gable elevation with panelled pilasters and parapet with pediment. This rebuilt 1876. Converted.

TOWN HALL, Market Place. 1887, by *J. J. Johnson* of London.
The best of the lesser town halls of Norfolk, though the long
and altered w front detracts. But one sees first the gault brick E
front in five bays with cross casements and a Dutch gable. The
N façade overlooks Bridge Street and is too much for it.
Asymmetrical free Renaissance with an indeterminate number
of bays. Over the off-set entrance rises a square tower with
pilasters at the corners. To the l. an elaborate Dutch gable, to
the r. a frieze of small casements and everywhere small panels of
carstone slips. The interior was never plush and there were
alterations in 1936–7. One room to each floor to the E front; large
hall behind the w front, with a cast-iron balcony added 1897.

COURT HOUSE, London Road. 1861. The tall three-bay hipped
block set back is in the Italianate style of these buildings throughout the country, but in plain dress. In front and to the N is a
later three- by three-bay single-storey addition clasping the
main block and rather spoiling it. Disused at the time of writing.

HILLCREST FIRST and MIDDLE SCHOOLS, Hillcrest. The first
phase of this complex was completed in 1979 by *R. W. Haydon*
of the County Architect's office. Low-slung, monochrome
buildings with vertical windows cutting the otherwise horizontal
planes.

Perambulation

We start in the MARKET PLACE, no more than a widening of
Bridge Street, which until 1835 had a row of houses in the middle. The CLOCK TOWER presented in 1878 by James Scott
demands immediate attention, for it is a Gothic cast-iron folly
by *William Cunliffe* of London painted in black and white.
Octagonal plinth and shaft, the latter with two tiers of Gothic
panelling on each facet. Square clock stage, four clock faces
and Gothic gables over each. Cunliffe fixed his name to all four
faces, two gone; other inscriptions. To the w the Town Hall (*see*
above), to the E Nos. 11–12 and No. 13, both late C17 brick
houses seriously altered for shops. No. 11 has a carriageway,
one of fourteen in the centre of the town. Marking the corner of
Market Place and High Street to the N is LLOYDS BANK (No.
26), an C18 brick house altered for a bank in the C19 and given
a prominent segmental pediment over the corner entrance.

HIGH STREET runs N–S at the E end of Market Place, and to the
N on the w side only C18 and C19 houses converted to shops in
the block up to Paradise Road, none memorable. On the E side
more of the same apart from the NATIONAL WESTMINSTER
BANK: mid-C18 classical front comprising nine bays with a
three-bay pediment over advanced bays. Next to it the former
CINEMA (now antiques centre), a great hulk which shouldered
its way on to the street in the 1930s with a once cheery front.
Oriel window at first floor, stuccoed rusticated quoins, steps up
to the vestibule in which are staircases curving up r. and l.
Facing effectively down the High Street, at the corner of Paradise
Road, the CASTLE HOTEL, of the mid C18, five bays and two

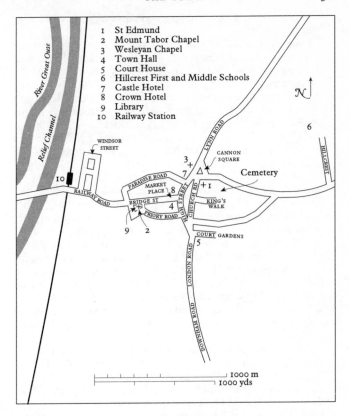

1   St Edmund
2   Mount Tabor Chapel
3   Wesleyan Chapel
4   Town Hall
5   Court House
6   Hillcrest First and Middle Schools
7   Castle Hotel
8   Crown Hotel
9   Library
10 Railway Station

Downham Market

storeys, whitewashed, with a one-bay pediment. In the pediment a Diocletian window, a Venetian window below, and a tripartite doorway below that in which a pedimented wooden doorcase from inside a house has been set. These three features have intermittent rocky rustication in their surrounds and the whole first floor is rusticated. Top parapet with battlements, curving up at the corners. Mansard roof. Handsome arched iron lamp-holder with the words Castle Inn in Egyptian lettering.

Further N the houses become more C19 than C18 and the street scene round CANNON SQUARE more C20 than C19. On the E side of this, properly in Church Road below the church, there were once attractive steps of 1819 but these replaced 1969 by an appalling RETAINING WALL, all massed concrete with lame square flint panels to break it up. LYNN ROAD continues N. On the W side Nos. 19–31 are a typical mid-C19 terrace of carstone slips and further out before the Retreat Estate is reached (ordinary council houses, of which sixty-six were built in Downham before 1939) No. 58 on the E side: red brick façade but brown Wisbech brick the remainder, late C18, five bays of C19 sashes, open pedimented doorcase and unfortunate concrete roof tiles.

Lynn Road and CHURCH ROAD were until the by-pass to the E opened in 1979 the main A10 artery, and Church Road itself has nothing. S of the church KING'S WALK runs E to the CEMETERY, laid out 1856 and given two dull carstone CHAPELS in the lancet style but with exaggerated W bellcotes developed out of buttresses. Between them and slightly W the conventional cemetery-keeper's house. COURT GARDENS lies where Church Road meets London Road, nicely marked by a seven-bay terrace of superior houses at Nos. 19–23, all carstone slips and gault brick dressings, c. 1840. Beyond that first the NATIONAL SCHOOL of 1841, a small oblong carstone box with big simple four-light Gothic windows in both end walls. E of this lay the former Union Workhouse of 1836 (by *Donthorn* for £5,000, catering for 250 inmates and Elizabethan, with the central gate-house motif of other Norfolk workhouses) but demolition left only Donthorn's two small single-storeyed LODGES fronting the site, which now has sheltered housing. LONDON ROAD continues with the Court House (*see* above), becomes DOWNHAM ROAD and ⅜ m. further S lies CROW HALL. Late C18 carstone house with brick dressings of seven bays in two storeys and attic. Pediment over advanced three centre bays and projecting wings to N and S, between which was added c. 1840 a single-storey link.

Back to the Court House and NW to pick up the S end of High Street. On the l. (i.e. W) No. 4 London Road, THE PRIORY, consisting of a rectangular late C16 carstone and brick wing with stepped N and S gable-ends each carrying hexagonal-flued stacks. Good brick mullioned windows, especially to N gable. Late C18 gault brick extension to E and a high, probably C17, wall running W along Priory Road. HIGH STREET continues N; on the W side Nos. 2–4, a short terrace of gault brick houses dated 1753, the ground floors obliterated by C20 shopfronts, which leave the late C19 fascias and canopy boxes in place. Moulded first-floor sill band. Then Nos. 8–12 with two big late C17 Dutch gables projecting to the street and in them windows with pediments on little corbels. The E side up to the Market Place lined with C18 houses, variously altered.

Similar houses in BRIDGE STREET, linking Market Place with the river and railway. Opposite the Town Hall the CROWN HOTEL presents a pinched four-bay brick S front with a two-bay projection and a hipped roof. This looks c. 1700, but the carriageway at the r. leads to the yard of a coaching inn and a long rear range which in the C17 and C18 comprised separate buildings gable-end to each other. The N end starts with a mid-C18 block with an upper storey (the assembly room) raised on cast-iron columns, then to the S a two-bay flint and brick house of c. 1710 with casements and sashes and next a similar-sized C17 carstone and brick three-bay house. Good main staircase within a spacious open well: closed string, heavy turned balusters, moulded handrail and panelled square newels. This is

Jacobean but the timber-framing of the stairwell is Brewer's
Tudor. Further N is a second C17 staircase of similar type but
smaller. Butt-purlin roofs, greatly renovated.

The remainder of Bridge Street with only secondary highlights. Next to the hotel No. 14 is a seven-bay C18 house, No.
16B has the date 1655 but has been altered, Nos. 42–44 once
more C18, three bays, mansard roof (with concrete tiles favoured
by C20 Downham), former shop window to r. On the s side
No. 15 boasts a five-bay rendered and colourwashed late C18
brick front and a vaguely Doric central porch with five-vaned
fanlight. NELSON HOUSE adjacent, also C18 and of four bays
and two storeys and attic, but with a swish early C20 curved
plate-glass display window out front. No. 53 has a bowed early
C19 shopfront, Nos. 59–61 are an early C18 pair, five windows
in all, those to the r. of uPVC. Then the Tabor Chapel (see
above) and so to the LIBRARY. This was the Friends' Meeting
House, of thin brown brick and erected 1701, a perfectly simple
one-storey rectangle given a C20 doorway and two new windows
on conversion in 1956. Nothing of its former use inside.

The extension to Bridge Street is RAILWAY ROAD leading to
the river and relief channel. Right at the W end the STATION.
1846. Of carstone slips, with two shaped gables separated by a
three-bay link along the front. The Tudor timber bridge over
the river replaced by a commendable cast-iron bridge of 1879
by *David Oldfield*, in turn sacrificed for a plain concrete BRIDGE
in the 1960s, and a similar one to the relief channel. Immediately
E of the station are a few terraces of late C19 housing for mill
workers, e.g. Windsor Street of 1898.

ROMANO-BRITISH FIELDS. To the E of the Old Bedford River
and N of the Roman road (see Denver), soilmarks indicate
Romano-British fields and settlements in this important farming region. (DG)

DUNSTON   2000

ST REMIGIUS. Unbuttressed W tower, all renewed. Fake Anglo-
Saxon quoining. Stair turret with C19 pinnacles. The nave has
Perp, the chancel plain E.E. windows except for the E window,
which probably in 1898 received an alabaster inner screen of
tracery, undeniably effective. All windows C19, except perhaps
the NW chancel lancet. The nave has an arch-braced roof which
owes more to the C16 than any other century. The exterior is
rendered and looks awful. – FONT. C15. Octagonal. Four lions
against the stem, symbols of four Evangelists against the bowl.
– SCREEN. Perp. One-light divisions, ogee arches, simple tracery over. – BENCHES. A few original ones, with poppyheads.
Some with early C20 angel ends. – STAINED GLASS. In the
chancel SE window some early glass of *c.* 1300, with a kneeling
donor, a lady, before St Remigius, all re-set into glass by *J. Dixon*,
†1873. St Christopher, late C15, is below. – MONUMENTS.
Elizabeth Long †1757, by *Rysbrack* (over s door). – Israel Long

†1750, by *Rysbrack* too? (N door). – Brass to Clere Talbot
†1647, with his two wives in shrouds. He is 2 ft 3 in. long.

DUNSTON HALL, ¼ m. SW. Neo-Elizabethan, but with High
114 Victorian stamped all over it. Symmetrical, brick, of three to
four storeys, with polygonal angle-shafts and finials. A remarkable number of decorated chimneyshafts. Cross casements for
windows, terracotta in the finials. To NE various STABLES and
OUTBUILDINGS. Begun 1859 by *J. C. Buckler* for Robert Kellett
Long, but finished by *Edward Boardman*, 1878. After a period as
a furniture depository the mansion was thoroughly and well
restored in the early 1990s, with a ballroom added in the same
style and the outbuildings rebuilt. Inside, the entrance hall has
a four-centred stone fireplace with a Renaissance surround and,
opposite, a five-bay screen announcing a hall-and-screens-
passage plan. It has rather lush Elizabethan and Jacobean
carving mixed together. Behind lies the open-well closed-string
staircase with turned and twisted balusters (i.e. late C17 in style).

DUNSTON MANOR, ¼ m. NW. Early C18. A double pile with shaped
end-gables to N and S. The E front of five bays and two storeys,
but to the l. and r. of the doorway two more very narrow
windows. The lower cross casements now replaced with sashes,
though the flush frames remain. Upstairs they remain C18.
Moulded platband between the floors. The converted STABLE
BLOCK adjacent has the W gable still shaped as well.

At the end of the lane is quite a rarity: a surviving open hall in
THE END HOUSE, i.e. it escaped the insertion of a floor.
Timber-framed with a brick E gable, presumably C17 as it is laid
in Flemish bond. The main fabric is early C16, towards the end
of the open hall period, and this feature, at the S end, is tiny as
the latest ones were. The location of the screens passage is just
about apparent. The roof, of butt- and clasping purlins and
cambered collars, goes with the brick gable.

WATERMILL. *See* Stoke Holy Cross, p. 673.

8030

DUNTON

ST PETER. Redundant. In the W tower sound-holes with various
tracery patterns of Dec and Perp origin. Money was left for
building in 1441 and 1444. The tower arch would fit these
dates. Some windows of the church are of *c.* 1300, others Perp.
Blocked N door and two Dec windows. Dec S porch. Intersecting four-light chancel E window. Inside, the reader's desk
and the lectern stand on curious oblong stone bases with tops
changing to elongated octagons by means of angle scallops and
heads. What were they? The S one seems to be of *c.* 1200. C19
roofs. – SCREEN. *c.* 1920. – STAINED GLASS. E window, †1863,
excellent, by *Heaton, Butler & Bayne*. Two large figure groups
of the Feeding of the Hungry and Clothing the Naked. Nave N
window by the same (He is Risen), †1896. Chancel N window
1883, by *Ward & Hughes*. – MONUMENTS. William Case, who
died in 1857 defending Lucknow during the Indian Mutiny, a

pedimented tablet by *Patterson* of Manchester (chancel N). –
SOUTH DOOR. Late C14, with five panels.

MANOR HOUSE, Hempton Road. Late C17 but very much re-
done in the C20. Shaped gables, the W one C20.

SHRUNKEN VILLAGE EARTHWORKS, in pasture fields to the NW,
SW and W of the church. (AR)

EARSHAM

ALL SAINTS. W tower with a shingled spire. Brick crenellations,
Y-tracery in bell-openings. Nave and chancel have Perp windows, but the shafting of the windows inside the chancel and
the piscina show that the real date of the chancel is *c.* 1300. In
the nave also it is patent that the present state is the result of a
lengthening and heightening. The older parts of the walls are
probably Norman. The Perp windows have castellated stepped
horizontals between the lights and the tracery (cf. e.g. Shelton).
The nave roof has arched braces and longitudinal braces. The
chancel roof is of the hammerbeam type, both C15. The N
porch has an entrance with one order of fleurons outside and
one inside and an arch-braced roof. – FONT. C15. Octagonal.
Decorated step. The Seven Sacraments and the Crucifixion
against the bowl. – PULPIT. C19, octagonal on a group of eight
columns. – NORTH DOOR. C15, with a kind of vertical reeding
and a band of cusped panels. – STAINED GLASS. In the E window are foreign C16 and C17 pieces imported by *J.C. Hampp* in
1802 and probably set by *S.C. Yarington c.* 1810 (Hampp was a
Norwich merchant, *see* Introduction, p. 70). Especially good
are four large early C16 panels. The glass was rearranged in
1960s. – MONUMENTS. A number of tablets, the most attractive the one of 1724 with a shield in front of, and drapery
behind, an obelisk. – Also a number with urns in front of
obelisks.

EARSHAM HALL, 1¼ m. NW. Partly C17, partly C18, and partly
Victorian. The C17 part, originally no doubt offices, has a
lantern. The estate came to the amateur architect *John Buxton*
from his mother and he set about rebuilding the house in
1704–8, only to sell it in 1721 to the Windham family. Buxton
moved to Channonz Hall and extensively remodelled that
(demolished 1784), and finally to Shadwell Park, his house
there being engulfed in C19 work. So Earsham is his only surviving building, apart from the stables at Channonz. The house
is plain, seven by five bays, and three storeys high. The E façade
has the three middle bays a little recessed. Later glazed porch.
Parapet and hipped roof behind. To the r. extends the three-bay
DINING ROOM added in 1750, originally of one storey, but now
with the addition of a late C19 billiard room above. The single-
storey hipped LIBRARY of 1785 in the SW corner of the house is
often attributed to Soane because he was working on the Music
Room (*see* below), but there is no evidence according to Ptolemy
Dean: octagonal when built, but altered to a Greek cross plan.

Plaster ceiling and frieze but most original bookcases removed. Staircase with three turned balusters to each step. It is known that the younger *Deval* made some of the good chimneypieces in 1783, very likely the one in the dining room with its pair of marble Tuscan columns supporting a Greek frieze; in the hall the chimneypiece has swags to the jambs and a broken pediment to the overmantel. A further chimneypiece upstairs by *Soane* intended for the Music Room. The broken pediment reappears over several doorways. Most of the upstairs rooms have C18 panelling.

Extending to the N is the two-storeyed SERVICE RANGE to the C17 house, with a shaped gable in the centre bay and a brick C18 skin. Further single-storey offices by *Soane*, 1789: very modest exterior, barrel-vaulted servants' hall (now kitchen), and the original kitchen top-lit from a timber lantern.

In the grounds, ¼ m. N of the house, is the MUSIC ROOM, by *Sir John Soane*, 1784–5, converted from an orangery for William Wyndham.* Grey brick, one-storeyed, with a very elegant stone three-bay centre. It has four attached unfluted Ionic columns carrying a pediment with a medallion and garlands. Between the columns an arched middle doorway and lower straight-headed windows with small square ones over. The shafts of the columns have the fluting below the volutes which is characteristic of the late C18. Shallow domed ceiling inside, and a coffered alcove at each end. RAILINGS. To the front; by *Soane*.

C17 timber-framed HOUSES are everywhere apparent, the earliest perhaps UPPER GREEN FARMHOUSE 1½ m. WNW of the church, rather too altered with C20 dormers and windows. THE CLOSE, Mill Road, is rather exceptionally a brick C17 house, with stepped gables. W door under a four-centred arch and with moulded jambs. N wing has an agreeable gable-end stack with four round shafts. QUEEN'S HEAD public house, The Street, is dated 1683 on a moulded brick fire surround. The timber frame partly bricked over.

EAST BILNEY

ST MARY. The chancel of 1883 was erected to the memory of Henry Collison, the rector; the rest looks Victorian too. Original unbuttressed W tower, with a three-light Perp W window. It received a new bell-stage in the 1880s and the original bell-openings became the twin lancets. Original N and S doorways of *c.* 1300. – STALLS. Of dubious age, much of the ornamental Jacobean carving and knobs on the top being reused. These doubts are regrettable since stalls in the Jacobean style are not something common. – STAINED GLASS. Crucifixion with St Mary and St John in the E window, 1883, by *Holiday* of *J. Powell & Sons*. Other glass in the chancel of same time but less quality.

* Soane's notebook for 8 August 1784: 'settled the alterations of Mr Wyndham's garden room & sent over the workmen from Norwich'. I am grateful to Ptolemy Dean for this and other references.

EAST BILNEY HALL (residential home). By *F. Codd*, *c.* 1866 for the Collison family. Irregular plan with a porch at the back on Ionic columns. Gault brick.

MARTYR'S COTTAGE, Church Road. An early C16 timber frame with brick nogging, all but rebuilt in the 1980s. Roll- and hollow-moulded windows at the back and inside are nice roll-moulded bridging beams in the NW room. Also ashlar jambs to the lower fireplaces.

BILNEY HOUSE, Church Road, is the former Rectory put up in 1836 by *Arthur Browne* for the Rev. Henry Collison. Very much Gothick Elizabethan, of three bays with a gabled porch in the middle, and lit through two- and three-light mullioned windows with ogee tracery heads. The internal fittings remain largely in place, with good Gothick plasterwork and some stained glass.

PEARCE ALMSHOUSES, Fakenham Road. A row of three, 1838, red brick, one-storeyed, Tudor-Gothick style, with three gabled porches to the road. Over the middle one the inscription to Rebecca and William Pearce, who paid for them.

EAST BRADENHAM   9000

ST MARY. Jambs of Norman windows in the chancel. The church was otherwise rebuilt in the C14 and C15. Main restoration 1853. Dec arcades of four bays and clerestory. The piers are octagonal, the arches double-hollow-chamfered. The capitals of the piers differ. They seem earlier on the S side than on the N, in the SE bay and in the chancel arch. The clerestory has quatrefoiled circular windows above the spandrels, not the apexes of the arches. Two three-light Perp windows in nave E gable. The rest Perp, i.e. the W tower (restored 1893 for £1,000), embraced by the aisles and with heavy buttresses. Two-light Perp bell-openings. Battlements of brick. Reduced tower arch. Perp also the aisle windows. N porch formerly two-storeyed, but the floor taken out and the brick-mullioned parvis window blocked. – FONT. Plain and octagonal. – FONT COVER. C17, with scrolls, central shaft and an obelisk with a ball finial. – ORGAN. 1786 by *Samuel Green*. A chamber organ originally for Huntingfield Hall. – STAINED GLASS. E window, *c.* 1855, by *M. & A. O'Connor*. – MONUMENTS. John Green †1684. Two busts in a decorated white marble surround. Open pediment above and two weeping cherubs. – Gibson Lucas †1758 by *T. Rawlins* of Norwich. Pretty, with all the usual paraphernalia: obelisk, cherubs' heads, a Rococo cartouche, and garlands. Apron with Sienna marble.

HUNTINGFIELD HALL, 1 m. NNE. Merely a farmhouse, but a C16 one, at least in the original two-storey block. The W gable-end adorned with a royal arms in a pedimented brick frame with an octagonal shaft above. C19 brick absorbs all the rest.

MANOR FARM, 1 m. E. Late C16 timber-framed house extended and re-faced in the C18 with brick. W front in two storeys and attic. Central two-storeyed porch with a moulded brick pediment under a sundial dated 1671. Main façade has five bays of sashes. C17 brick returns with serrated flues to the chimneystacks.

EAST CARLETON

St Mary. C13, added to and changed each century since, but its appearance owes most to the big restoration of 1881. The tower was rebuilt and given a bell-stage in 1895, but there is C16 brickwork above the three-light w window. Continuous nave and chancel and a N aisle, the aisle C13 in origin. Most of the rest and most of the details look 1881, see the E window. The only unrestored item is the s doorway. This is Dec and it is set within a porch erected as a memorial in 1915. The three-bay arcade has round piers of 1881 supporting C14 double-chamfered arches. – FONT. C15, octagonal; trefoiled panels to plinth.

St Peter, E of St Mary. Of this former parish church in its own churchyard there is no more left than a low piece of the wall of the tower. Bequests for 'making the new tower' begin 1503 and end with the battlements in 1537. It was ruined already in the mid C16.

Curzon Hall, ½m. s on Spring Lane. The manor belonged to the Curzons only until the C14 but the house is late C16. Timber-framed but with stepped brick end-gables and a three-storeyed porch also with a stepped gable. The porch has in addition polygonal angle-shafts and pediments above the windows. Most of the windows are C20 along with various alterations and additions. The rear has a stair-turret.

Walnut Tree Cottage, Rectory Road is, or was, an early C16 open hall floored in the C17 and with stacks inserted. Timber-framed.

East Carleton Manor. By *James Fletcher-Watson* for Colin Chapman, 1964. Like Fletcher-Watson's Watlington Hall essentially Georgian in style, with two storeys and dormer attic in seven bays, but here is a pedimented two-storeyed portico of three bays formed of very thin unfluted columns like a New England house. The first floor has a balcony. The SHOOTING LODGE is a late C17 farmhouse with a shaped gable to the s range. L-plan with the main front to the s entered through a central door under an open pediment. Platband at first floor and a moulded eaves cornice. Windows renewed.

North Farmhouse, Intwood Lane. Mid-C16 timber-framed house of one storey and attic with a C17 brick part added to its l., of two storeys. In front of both is a clay-lump extension of the early C19, encased in brick. The C16 part has a wide chimney bay and queenpost partition timbers in the roof; the C17 roof was altered in the early C19, probably when the front was added.

Majority Cottage, Wymondham Road. This was part of the Boileau estate based on Ketteringham Hall 1 m. w. In 1848 Sir John's eldest son reached majority and to celebrate the fact the thatched mid-C16 timber-framed house was remodelled. Bay windows, chimneystacks and details including the Boileau arms in a roundel all of 1848. The returns are of clay lump. Inside it is apparent that the l. end was floored c. 1600 and a stack inserted. Curved braces in the roof.

EAST DEREHAM see DEREHAM

EAST HARLING

9080

ST PETER AND ST PAUL. The best church in its neighbourhood. The major periods are the early C14, the late C14 and the mid C15. Very spectacular to look at, with its picturesque, short C15 lead spire rising out of a crown of eight flying buttresses over the pierced crenellated tower parapet. The 'steeple' was finished in 1450 according to a churchwardens' account seen by Blomefield. The tower itself is of c. 1300 below – see the w doorway, the w window (cusped intersecting tracery), the tall niches on the w buttresses at the level of the w window, the bell-openings (cusped Y-tracery) and the tower arch. The outer wall of the s aisle must be structurally of c. 1300 too, see the one surviving window head now covered by the porch, but visible from inside. This, with its trefoiled circle, may even be a little earlier than the tower. The chancel seems Dec, in spite of the Perp windows. It has one s window with a reticulation motif and towards the N vestry a seven-foiled circular window. The arcades inside (five bays) are a little later; late C14 probably. The piers are quatrefoil with four thin shafts in the diagonals on the N side, four spurs instead on the s side. Arches with two sunk-quadrant mouldings (N) or two waves (s). The chancel arch of the same type. The capitals are already polygonal. Later Perp s porch and clerestory. This work may belong to the time of Sir William Chamberlain (†1462) and Sir Robert Wingfield (†1480), husbands of Anne Harling, i.e. to c. 1440–80. The spire and the glass of the E window certainly do, but the s porch had to be rebuilt in 1840 a little lower than before: flushwork-panelled exterior. It stands in the w bay of the aisle, a Norwich device. Clerestory of nine closely set three-light windows, shafted inside. There is also an E window above the chancel arch. N aisle windows Perp with two-centred arches (a new window made for the N aisle in 1489), two tall s aisle windows under four-centred arches matching the clerestory. The N chapel windows also with four-centred arches. The interior is made splendid by the roofs and the fitments. The nave roof is of unusually steep pitch. It has ten bays of hammerbeams with finely traceried spandrels, arched braces on them carrying on right up to the ridge, wall-shafts, and longitudinal arched braces. Scissor-braced chancel roof of the restoration in 1878–9.

FURNISHINGS. FONT. C15. Big, octagonal, with panelled stem and quatrefoils against the bowl. – FONT COVER. C17. –

SCREENS. Of the rood screen there is only the early C16 base, relocated to the W end of the nave. Richly traceried and coloured. Along the top are pointed, cusped, diagonally placed quatrefoils. – The screen to the S chapel has three-light divisions and its ribbed coving. – At r. angles to this screen a third and earlier one. Shafts instead of mullions. – Finally a part of a fourth screen has become the front of a bench in the S aisle. The part is the tops of ogee-headed one-light divisions, and some cresting. – WEST GALLERY. Turned balusters and moulded handrail. C17. – STALLS. Six in the chancel, with figures and animals on the arm-rests and misericords with shields. – BENCH ENDS. With poppyheads. – MISCELLANEOUS WOODWORK. Jacobean panels in the S lobby. – A length of a crenellated tie-beam under the tower arch. – WALL PAINTING. Intriguing large fragment, apparently of a Doom, on the N aisle wall. Devils and many other figures, and an elaborate architectural setting; late C14? (DP). – STAINED GLASS. In the E window twenty panels of c. 1480 glass of the Norwich School from the Annunciation to the Pentecost and Sir William Chamberlain and Sir Robert Wingfield kneeling. Periodically removed for safe-keeping and last re-installed in 1947.

MONUMENTS. Two alabaster effigies, Knight and Lady, of the Harling family (unicorns on the jupon). They lie (wrongly) on a tomb-chest with a quatrefoiled front and under the cusped and subcusped canopy of Sir Robert Harling †1435 (inscription records that 'mangled by force of arms he died in Paris'). The cusps are demi-figures of angels, an eagle, a pelican. – Sir William Chamberlain †1462. Big monument between chancel and N chapel. Tomb-chest with shields on its front. Canopy with vaulted ceiling and panelled sides with niches for figures. Broad diagonal buttresses. Top with ogee arches on pendants. Top frieze with shields and fleurs-de-lys. – Sir Francis Lovell †1550 and Sir Thomas Lovell †1567. Identical monuments, very dignified, without any figures and almost without any decoration, either in the Early Renaissance fashion of before 1550 or in the strapwork fashion of after. Curiously shaped inscription plates. Fluted columns l. and r. Top with a semicircular gable in the middle. – Sir Thomas Lovell †1604. Alabaster. Two recumbent effigies on a tomb-chest. In front of this three Corinthian columns. On the top an achievement and two obelisks. Original iron railing in front. Restored 1958.

A substantial VILLAGE with a square. Nice houses, both detached, of grey brick, near the church, and terraced, in the village proper. Of the former, one might select ANNADALE HOUSE, on CHURCH ROAD. The grey brick is a re-facing of 1826 applied to a red brick late C18 house: two storeys, three bays and with giant pilasters separating each bay. EASTFIELD HOUSE, on the other side of Church Road, is a larger construction of the 1840s in a Neo-Jacobean style, all stepped gables and dramatic stacks. The village even has a proper little square, MARKET PLACE, with a selection of C18 and C19 houses and shops, none of which is individually important. Only from the early C19, e.g. Duffus Cottage (N side), Stepp Cottage (E), are they wholly of brick. Before this timber-framing with clay lump or wattle-and-daub infill was the norm, see e.g. Market Stores (S) and Eastern House (N). On Market Street, opposite the square, is the Swan Inn, again early C18; carriage entrance to l., timber studs exposed to rear. To the S is a coved jetty to a pair of C16 cottages, altered in the C19.

Harling was a fair-sized village even at the time of the Domesday Book and its status was helped from the late C15 by the fact that East Harling Hall was the mansion of the Lovells from c. 1490 until its demolition in the early C19. From it comes the bronze medallion by *Pietro Torrigiani* now at Westminster Abbey which represents Sir Thomas Lovell † 1524.

Windmill, I m. ese on the Kenninghall Road. Brick tower mill of the early C19. No machinery except the upright shaft from Topcroft post mill, installed in 1975.

Deserted village earthworks. A campsite 3½ m. sw marks the site of Harling Thorpe; between a stream and an E–W hollow way at least four crofts are evident as ditched enclosures. A small outcrop of masonry next to the stream may be part of a mill rather than a church. (AR)

EAST LEXHAM

8010

St Andrew. Round tower, very probably Anglo-Saxon, see the NW bell-opening of two tiny arches on a turned, sausage-shaped baluster. The SW bell-opening has a very sturdy, short column instead, and the E bell-opening a Maltese cross. The body of the church is rendered but one can see the long and short W quoins. No chancel arch. N and S doorways of c. 1200. E window and angle piscina Perp. Restoration 1837, which provided the roof. – Two misericords made up as parts of a chair, both with heads. – Stained glass. In the E window, of c. 1859, probably by *Clayton & Bell*, and good, if typical, work of the date.

Lexham Hall. A very fine Queen Anne house built for Edmund Wodehouse, replacing a house of the 1630s for John Wright. *Sanderson*, it is known, designed a study in 1770, and *Sir Jeffry Wyatville* made some alterations for Col. Keppel in the early C19, which were destroyed in the fire of 1948. The resulting restorations and external and internal alterations of 1948–50 by *James Fletcher-Watson*, in his usual sympathetic manner. The N front of seven bays with a slight three-bay projection formerly with a pediment, perhaps of later date. Nicely carved medallions. The original central entrance converted to a window during the repairs. The E side has seven bays too and a central entrance behind a porch with an open pediment added by *Fletcher-Watson*. To the S the façade is longer and decidedly odd, owing to the fact that the l. third is recessed a little and remodelled by *Fletcher-Watson*. The r. part is clearly early C18, with its hipped roof and five bays. Then follows a doorway (1948–50) under the Venetian window of the staircase, which must be somewhat later than the early C18 (unless it is recent), and a Dutch gable, added boldly by *Fletcher-Watson*. Then two more of the simple bays of the old house heavily disguised by a bow window to the ground floor (*Fletcher-Watson*). The interior is mostly remodelled but has good fireplaces, brought in from elsewhere after the fire. Staircase with twisted balusters and carved tread-ends. DAIRY to W of house, *c.* 1850. Octagonal.

1010

EASTON

ST PETER. Nave, N aisle and chancel. The NW tower fell in 1778. The exterior is from the restoration of 1883 by *R. M. Phipson*. Two-storey S porch, the floor inside taken out, with a dated sundial: 'Tempus Fugit/E H 1694'. Most of the windows are Perp, but there are interesting earlier remains. The S doorway is late Norman and rich. One order of shafts (one of them polygonal) with decorated waist-bands. The jambs have their own intersecting trail and leaf decoration, harking back to Anglo-Saxon tradition. The roll-moulded arch is decorated too, but has been turned outside in, at the same time no doubt that the arch was made pointed. Also hinting at, but probably not Anglo-Saxon, are the long-and-short quoins to the SW corner of the nave. As one enters the church, one is faced with a wide pointed Norman arch, blocked. This seems to be the S arch of the NW tower. The N side of the nave in that place is indeed all a stark repair-job in brick, noticeable from afar. The short N aisle has tall octagonal piers with round capitals and raw arches. It is poor work, but apparently work of the C13, and that is borne out by the E window, which has bar tracery with a quatre-foiled circle (renewed). The church raised to include a clerestory in the mid C15, work in progress in 1465. This is partly obscured by the late C15 roof which takes scant regard of the windows. – FONT. Octagonal, of Purbeck marble, C13, with the usual two very shallow arches for each side. – PULPIT. C16 linenfold panelling and tracery. – SOUTH DOOR. With ironwork.

EASTON HALL is now the Norfolk College of Agriculture. Seven-bay C18 brick façade with two early C20 bay windows and other details. Stepped gables. The early C18 staircase has twisted balusters.

WEST LODGE, Lower Easton. Early C17 lobby-entrance house given a face-lift in 1743. The façade of this date has five bays, converted to three bays in the early C19 and re-windowed. The C18 windows had raised brick surrounds, of which one remains. The stack had a barrel-vaulted passage bored through in 1743. To the rear are C17 brick window pediments. Good C17 staircase with tapering carved balusters.

BELLEVUE, Lower Easton, is still recognizable as an early C16 open hall house, floored in the C17 and provided with a gable-end stack. Timber-framed but re-worked 1728. Of the old plan particularly see the service doors. The roof survives, with a tie-beam on arched braces and wall-posts.

MILL FARMHOUSE, ¾ m. N of the church. From the late C17 see the rusticated quoins and the pattern of the restored mullioned cross casements. Much C19 reconstruction and extension.

EAST RAYNHAM

ST MARY. 1866–8. By *Clark & Holland*, rather obscure architects from Newmarket. The chancel was paid for by the rector, the Rev. Charles Phayre, and the nave by the fifth Marquess Townshend, the total cost being £7,000. It is largely a copy of the medieval building, to judge by Ladbroke's drawing, and the style is early Perp. An odd thing was a S chancel porch, converted to the organ chamber. Three-bay arcades. In the church a very big and sumptuous EASTER SEPULCHRE. This was made by the will of Sir Roger Townshend's widow to commemorate him and herself. The will was made in November 1499. She left the money for the monument and 'cunningly graven a Sepulchre for Easter Day'. There are no visible restorations, but the statuary is incomplete. Tomb-chest with three panels with shields set in ornate foiling or tracery under a Purbeck marble slab. Broad surround, panelled recess, with a four-centred arch. Big attic, again with foiled or traceried panels (mouchette wheels). Against the back wall five stepped niches of very fine, partly pierced work with fragments of the former statuettes. Above is a carved stone funeral helm, reinstated in the 1950s. Opposite is a recess E of the piscina on three reused spiral-fluted Norman shafts which seem to be upside down, carrying a stilted arch. Nave roof with longitudinal braces on collars but no kingposts. – FONT. C15, octagonal, with traceried stem and roses etc. in the bowl panels. Traces of paint. – CHEST. Dated 1602. Traces of marquetry scenes in perspective, separated by fluted pilasters. – Other timber furnishings of 1868. – STAINED GLASS. Ordinary glass in W window of 1868 by *Lavers, Barraud & Westlake*. – MONUMENTS (*see* also above). Brass to George Townshend, a boy, *c.* 1500, a 9 in. figure (S aisle floor). – Brass to Robert Godfrey †1522, a 15 in. figure in academical dress (N aisle floor). – Lord Charles Vere Ferrars Townshend †1852. Relief of white marble with two big sentimental angels. – ROYAL ARMS. Carved wood, Hanoverian (NW tower arch pier).

RAYNHAM HALL. *See* p. 600.

EAST RUDHAM

ST MARY. Rebuilt after the tower collapsed in 1873 and reopened 1876. But old materials were apparently used quite extensively (newly constructed were the E half of the N nave, chancel N and E walls, tower and S porch). The S doorway e.g. of *c.* 1300 is convincing. In the S porch, with its C19 lierne vault, some original bosses were inserted, but the original upper storey was removed. Also the s transept is essentially as it was and very interesting. To the E two three-light windows with intersecting tracery, to the s a window with four lights under one segmental arch. Trefoiled lights and trefoils, round and pointed, above. All this is early C14. To the w an octofoil as a window; C19. The chancel has renewed lancets N and s and a five-light E window entirely of 1873 in design as well as construction. The new tower is a little disappointing; one might have expected something better. Small arch into the nave. The concrete roof tiles are late C20 and positively bad. The interior is poor work too, with ugly piers and impoverished roofs. – PILLAR PISCINA. With interlace on the top knob masquerading as Norman, but it is surely either re-worked or all C19. – SCULPTURE. Parts of an alabaster reredos, e.g. Annunciation, Coronation of the Virgin, Crucifixion, Martyrdom of St John Evangelist; also a larger Coronation of the Virgin. – Seated stone figure no doubt from some external niche.

PRIMITIVE METHODIST CHAPEL, Broomsthorpe Road. 1862. Brick. Three bays with arch-headed sashes. Unusually tall proportions, with pilasters to the sides and an advanced central bay. Pyramid roof.

The VILLAGE has a central GREEN with brick houses of the late C18 or early C19, with sashes and doorcases of minor design. To the N side THE CROWN public house has a C17 NE wing and C17 details in the main N gable, otherwise all is late C19. On STATION ROAD, Nos. 21–22 are early C17, of flint with brick dressings. Some façade windows in C17 openings, and more in the w gable.

EAST TUDDENHAM

ALL SAINTS. Quite a big church, perfectly approached by an avenue of trees and a lychgate of 1893. One notices at once the happy effect of black-glazed pantiles for church roofs. The w tower of c. 1300 was originally a sw tower with diagonal w buttresses rising to the second stage. But the former s arcade was ripped out to widen the nave at an unknown date. In the w wall of this former nave, under the gable, a cusped recess, presumably a former window, and to its l. and lower a window with Y-tracery. The oldest element of the church is the s doorway. This is E.E., not large and very odd. One order of shafts with stiff-leaf capitals and water-holding bases. The geometrical decoration of the arch is still late Norman, chevron-like, but the hoodmould has close stiff-leaf decoration with all the leaves turning inward. The s porch is Perp and the most ambitious in this neighbourhood. Money was left for its building in 1458, and more money left in 1502 for its 'soleryng', but there is no evidence a second floor was actually built. Instead it has a high domed plaster vault inside. Flushwork-panelled base and buttresses. Entrance with the Annunciation in the spandrels, finely carved and preserved, probably by the same carver as the angels on the s porch at Ringland. Flushwork frieze above forming words: Gloria Tibi T R. A niche above has a nodding ogee top. Cusped blind windows either side. Perp nave and chancel, except for one Dec chancel N window which has an intersecting ogee arrangement in three lights, very much a Lincolnshire motif of the 1330s and 1340s. The windows restored. There was a former N chapel – see the blocked arch – and there is a blocked window E of the double-chamfered N doorway. – FONT. Late C12, circular, with a broad band of stiff-leaf trails. – BENCH ENDS. Many with poppyheads. – SOUTH DOOR. C15, with an iron foliated cross. – STAINED GLASS. E window, 1950, by *Leonard Walker*. Parts of the panels of the old *c.* 1830 E window re-set (by *George King & Son*) in s nave. – MONUMENTS. Brass of a civilian and two wives, *c.* 1500 (19 in. figures; nave, W wall). – Effigy of stone, *c.* 1300, the legs not yet crossed. Head with mail coif on a pillow set diagonally. He is holding his heart in his hands.

OLD HALL, ⅝ m. SE, off Norwich Road. s front of C16 brick, with a two-storey porch. C18 cross casement windows. The N front has three stepped gables, the W one being the gable to a C17 additional range. Fenestration again C18. The W gable has an ovolo-moulded doorway. The C17 W façade has five bays, with ovolo-mullioned windows, some original. The hall has C16 roll-moulded bridging beams.

BERRY HALL. Built as the Rectory in 1754. Three by five bays. Two storeys. Entrance in the narrow E front: advanced and raised centre bay with a porch on unfluted columns. The tall first-floor sashes are part of alterations of 1949.

MOCK BEGGAR HALL, Common Road. Curious name. The C17 brick house has stepped gable-ends and a two-storeyed porch to the N front, with a four-centred entrance arch and a pediment. The W gables have small windows and stacks with twin octagonal flues. Much late C19 rebuilding. DOVECOTE. Late C17, square, two windows under pediments. Roof missing.

HARRISON'S FARMHOUSE, also Common Road. Timber-framed hall house of *c.* 1540 converted to a lobby-entrance plan in C17. Much of the frame replaced with brick and plenty of C18 and C19 alterations. Roll-moulded seven-light mullioned window visible inside. C17 roof of butt-purlins, collars and straight wind-bracing. Around 1800 a brick BARN was abutted to the gable-end and communicating doors knocked through.

EAST WALTON

ST MARY. Round late C12 tower with a W lancet and paired lancets as bell-openings under four-centred hoods. Three-bay nave with very big Perp windows. They have clear C18 glass so that the impression is that of a glass-house, an impression which pleases today. Perp also the chancel. Pretty traceried gable inside above the priest's doorway. E window of five stepped lights under an arch, rere-arch inside. The s porch seems to be

C14. Stone benches inside. The interior is reduced in its effect by the disappearance of the original roof, the fine stone head-corbels of which remain. The chancel arch is c. 1300 and is very tall too and enriched by delicate openwork leaf carving. Now it is cut by the C18 nave ceiling and the upper parts visible only from the roof space. The C18 provides thin wooden fluted pillars to the lower round arch. The ceiling is quite effective. Chancel with a crown-post roof, probably c. 1840. – BOX PEWS. C18, as is the three-decker PULPIT. – FONT. Simple, Perp, octagonal.

CHAPEL OF ST ANDREW, in ruins, in the garden of Abbey Farm, N of the church. It belonged to the Priory at West Acre. w gable wall with a round-headed doorway and a rectangular opening above. The side walls also remain. In the s wall remains of a window which seems to have been a two-light window with a circle over, i.e. later C13. Also a blocked two-bay arcade with an octagonal pier.

On THE GREEN a most curious structure. Gault brick with a bar-rel roof, bound by iron hoops; 7 ft high by 9 ft long. The little chimney and the excessive thickness of the walls reveal it to be a FURNACE for the production of iron tyres for carts, carriages, etc. Of the mid C19.

EAST WINCH

ALL SAINTS. The earliest evidence is the C14 pier and responds of the former N chapel. The pier is quatrefoil with four spurs in the diagonals. E respond semi-octagonal. The s chapel has the same responds, also C14, but the chapel itself was built by *Sir G. G. Scott* during his restoration of 1875–8, on the site of the mortuary chapel of the Howards. The N chapel was longer to the w than it is now. The quatrefoil pier now disappears in the responds of the chancel arch. That indicates that, when the nave was rebuilt Perp, the chancel arch was moved to the E. The late C14 w tower also seems earlier than the nave, see the fillets of the responds to the tower arch. Four-centred w door-way and a three-light panel-tracery window above. Perp the aisles, chancel and clerestory windows. The top parts of the E window seem a crude C19 remodelling and can hardly be Scott's work. Pretty sanctus bellcote with a little tracery. Attractive Perp brick s porch with brick windows, including their tracery. Flushwork to s face. The roof is C19. Bequests for 'building church', i.e. the nave, are recorded in 1388 and 1416, which seems slightly early for the details. The main campaign probably of the 1430s. The Perp arcades have four bays. Piers with two broad wave mouldings and a broad fillet to the nave and finer members to the arches. Double-chamfered arches. A shaft rises to the stone corbels which support the wall-posts of the roof. The roof itself is a hammerbeam type of 1878. Good Perp s aisle roof with tracery spandrels of the arched braces. Chancel roof restored by Scott. Crude arched braces on stone corbels support the ringing-floor of the tower – a rare motif.

FURNISHINGS. PILLAR PISCINA. Norman, the base like a
one-scallop capital, the shaft spiral-fluted, the top a two-scallop
capital. – FONT. Octagonal, Perp, with shields and foliated panels.
One shield is that of the Howards. – FONT COVER. By *Comper*,
1913, copying a C17 original. – PULPIT. 1876. – SCREEN. Part of
the C15 dado, with three ornamental painted panels. – BENCHES.
Re-seated 1861, but several simple, low C15 benches in aisles,
with poppyheads. – CANDELABRA, by the altar, of wrought
iron, *c.* 1915–20. – SOUTH DOOR. C15, still with its wooden
lock. – STAINED GLASS. E window by *Clayton & Bell*, †1876; N
chancel window signed by *T. F. Curtis* of *Ward & Hughes*, 1901.

EAST WINCH HALL. Rebuilt after a fire in 1964. The early C19
house was of three storeys and three bays with an enlargement
of 1908 for Sir William Lancaster.

HALL FARMHOUSE, Lynn Road, E of the church. N front of two
storeys in five bays; unfluted columns to central porch. Sashes,
those to ground floor on consoles with heads. This all Georgian.
W gable of galleted carstone has a platband, and the rear wing
has C17 origins. C17 staircase with splat balusters.

CRANCOURT MANOR, ⅝ m. s. The mansion of the Howards, of
which only a large rectangular moated site remains.

GAS COMPRESSION STATION. An excellent design of 1977 by
the *Architects' Design Group* and *British Gas Architect's Department*.
The three turbines contained in a single-storey building with
square compressor caps in white standing on top.

EAST WRETHAM *see* WRETHAM

ECCLES   *0080*

ST MARY. Round tower, probably Norman and of only two
storeys, restored in 1950. The chancel must be E.E., though the
outside was all renewed in the C15. Restorations of 1885 con-
fuse the issue more and the E window is all of 1870. But inside
is a handsome double piscina with some stiff-leaf decoration
and pointed trefoils in the spandrels. The chancel arch, however, is Perp and has fleurons all up one order of jambs and
arch. Blind tracery panels r. and l. The s aisle was pulled down
in the mid C18. It must have been of *c.* 1300 or slightly before.
Low quatrefoil piers and sunk mouldings. The s doorway, set
back when the aisle was given up, is of the same style. So is the
N doorway, with a pretty chain of cusped reticulation motifs up
jambs and arch. N porch (now vestry) Perp. The entrance has
damaged heads and fleurons up jambs and arch. The masons at
Eccles, of more than one generation, must have liked that
motif. Roofs 1885. – FONT. Octagonal with heads under the
bowl. – PULPIT. Panelled early C17 piece with the top rail
carried on carved brackets. – ROOD. With cross and Saints
(Mary and John), 1959. – MONUMENT. On s wall of chancel, to
Samuel Bircham †1732.

ECCLES HALL. Late C17 or early C18 for the Lamb family. Whitewashed brick. Seven-bay façade of two storeys, the centre three bays recessed behind a C20 conservatory and the outer pairs of bays with big shaped gables ending in semicircles. The garden front also has two shaped gables. Now Eccles Hall School.

EGMERE

9030

1⅞ m. WNW of Little Walsingham

Egmere was a sizeable settlement until the C15, but declined and the church fell into disuse.

ST EDMUND. The church is in ruins, but enough remained in 1602 for Sir Nicholas Bacon to use it as a barn. What stands is the W tower up to the bell-openings, which were early C14 (see also the triple-chamfered tower arch), and fragments of the nave N and S walls. In the N wall is a round-headed doorway, which might be C12.

EGMERE FARMHOUSE, Egmere Road, ⅜ m. NE. The mid-C19 brick house of two storeys and three bays is not of particular interest for its date, but the FARM BUILDINGS are. They form a model farm complex by G. A. Dean for the Holkham Estate, 1851–6, consisting of parallel ranges of cattle sheds with a yard between. A cart shed closes to the N and stables to the S.

COTTAGES. A little group of two-storeyed houses built in 1878–80 of shuttered concrete. They were part of the Holkham estate, but who was the architect?

EARTHWORKS S and E of the ruined church relate to the post-medieval use of the site, but others to the W in grass beyond an arable field include a T-junction of hollow ways and four or five tofts belonging to the village that dwindled away in the late Middle Ages. Other odd earthwork enclosures lie N of the modern road. (AR)

ELLINGHAM

3090

ST MARY. Unbuttressed C14 W tower with two-step battlements decorated with flushwork panelling. These added in the C15. Nave and chancel with divers windows. Perp S porch. Shields in the spandrels on tracery. Hoodmould and frame of the entrance with fleurons. The rest basically a C14 rebuild of a C13 church. There was a S aisle, replaced in the C15 when the chapel also was added to the E. The arcade is of four bays, the W two of which represent the C14. They are simply cut through the wall and have one slight continuous chamfer. The bigger aisle required another two to the E, rebuilt in 1853 by *John Brown*. They probably represent the original state, as the details correspond to those of the S chapel. The C15 arch-braced aisle roof runs through from W to E. To the S of the chapel E window a niche. Aisle windows are of three lights under four-centred arches.

Of the C13 is the blind wall arcading. In the nave N wall part of two bays remain, cut into by two N windows. There is an E.E. wall-shaft with a dragon above, and independent of it, a little higher up, the head of a bishop with the characteristic low mitre. This bit of E.E. design no longer fits in with the rest of the wall. In the chancel the same quandary. The N arcading starts with a C13 capital but continues in a disturbed way. Only the chancel SE window has its full shafting, with fine capitals and a hoodmould on stiff-leaf stops. It is impossible to piece the C13 state together; it is not supported by any exterior evidence. The interior restoration was in 1868 (roofs renewed, new E window and chancel arch taken down). The church had needed a new E wall even in the C18. Further work in chancel 1900 by *Fielden & Horseman* of London. – FONT. Octagonal. C15, alternating shields and roses in the bowl. – BOX PEWS. – PAINTING. Liberation of St Peter, a replica of the altarpiece of St Peter Mancroft at Norwich, by *Charles Catton*. – STAINED GLASS. E window, 1870, by *Lavers, Barraud & Westlake*. By *Kempe & Tower* one chancel N window (†1910), by *Ward & Hughes* another (1887). – MONUMENT. Elizabethan tablet without figures. Worn inscription framed by two fluted Doric colonnettes carrying a pediment.

MILL. A delightful picture of a white weatherboarded C18 mill and the MILLER'S HOUSE. The mill of three storeys, attics and a lucam. The house adjoining to the N of three bays only, with Gothick Y-traceried windows.

ELSING   *0010*

ST MARY. Formerly in the floor of the church and now (since 1979) remounted in the chancel is the most sumptuous of all English church brasses, the memorial to Sir Hugh Hastings †1347. It is unfortunately not complete. Many smaller parts are missing. The figure, in armour, is 5 ft 6 in. long. Two angels hold his pillows (one angel lost). Over his head a cusped ogee arch at the apex of which is a plaque with tiny angels receiving his tiny soul. Steep gable and in it St George on his horse spearing a dragon in an octofoiled circle (cf. the Crouchback and Aymer de Vallance monuments in Westminster Abbey). To the l. and r. a broad band with on either side four tiers of canopies and mourning relatives under them (two of them lost). They represent or represented among others, on the r., Edward III, Thomas Beauchamp Earl of Warwick, Lord Grey of Ruthyn, on the l., Henry Plantagenet Earl of Lancaster, the Earl of Pembroke, Lord Stafford. Diapered grounds or grounds with foliage trails. The figures are delightful studies in manners if not character. Finally at the top two angels (one lost) in the corners, two plaques with the Coronation of the Virgin between. The brass was originally much more colourful, gilded and inlaid

Elsing. Brass to Sir Hugh Hastings †1347

with coloured pastes and glass to give it the appearance of enamelling. In the NW corner of the nave is a reconstructed copy of it.

Sir Hugh Hastings's monument is where it is because he had the church built. Blomefield recorded an inscription in the E window: 'ys churche hath been wrowt by Howe de Hastyng and Margaret hys wyf'. It is a uniform job, evidently done to one plan, which must date from c. 1330, the year in which Margaret inherited. W tower with flushwork panelling in the battlements, reticulated tracery in the bell-openings with two minor reticulation units within the major one. Perp W doorway. In the W nave wall are patches of masonry from the previous church. Large three-light nave windows with somewhat coarse Curvilinear tracery based on the petal motif. Battlemented parapets. Curiously bald N and S porch entrances have boldly cusped ogee arches, the former under a stepped gable. Inner N doorway with an ogee arch, cusped and subcusped. The chancel has less interesting windows, save for the five-light E window with its intricate Curvilinear tracery. N vestry with a Y-tracery E window. Plain sedilia and piscina with ogee arches. Extremely wide nave and no aisles (nearly 40 ft); so wide that the roof construction posed real problems, only solved by the latest version of 1781: kingposts on arched ties; unattractive. Tall but narrow tower arch. Pamment (buff paving-stone) floor, somewhat bare.

FURNISHINGS. FONT. This is also probably Dec. Octagonal, with a wavy frieze, each wave being filled by an ogee trefoil; battlements over. – FONT COVER. Fine Perp canopy with re-cut figures. Original colouring on the W side, the other sides well re-coloured. Flying buttresses with tracery etc., all rather architectural. – SCREEN. Late C15. Dado with nice carving; the paintings (four either side) defaced and faded. – STAINED GLASS. In the chancel SE window a small figure of the Virgin from a Coronation. This dates from the time when the church was built. Also one complete figure of an Apostle of c. 1375, red and brown. The SW chancel window with two further complete 47 Apostles, green and yellow and brown and lilac. The glass was rearranged in 1901 and all windows have canopies above the figures. – MONUMENTS. For the Hastings brass, see above. – Dame Anne Browne †1623. Tomb-chest with black marble lid. Inscription, still in black-letter, against the back wall.

ELSING HALL. Mostly of c. 1460–70 for the Hastings family, but much restored and embellished by *Thomas Jekyll* in 1852 for the Browne family. Again restored after the Second World War. The medieval plan was of a hall with a solar wing at r. angles to the E, from the E wall of which projects a small gabled chapel. The N front is of knapped and squared flint with ashlar and brick, mostly Jekyll's work. The chapel has a three-light E window and two-light side windows. C19 chapel doorway. To its W the hall, with a wide bay window and a porch. The bay window has four lights and a transom. The porch has an arched entrance with tracery in the spandrels and above the porch a room with a three-light window. More rooms to the w with mullioned windows represent the service wing. Handsome c16 chimneys. The hall has an open timber roof with three roll-moulded c15 tie-beams, a large fireplace on the s and a timber gallery. All this is only to a very limited degree medieval. The arch towards the bay window has c15 shafts. Opposite the bay a winder staircase, projecting polygonally from the s wall, is completely by Jekyll. Altogether most of the decorative detail belongs to the c19 or c20. The principal staircase is an c18 dog-leg type with turned balusters and a panelled dado. Also c18 the panelling in several rooms. Those which Jekyll decorated have linenfold panelling to the doors, which are under four-centred arches.

The s front makes a splendid show seen across the water of the widened moat. Not much is not Jekyll's vision. It has two timber-framed gabled projections with jettied upper storeys. Next to the r. one is the polygonal hall stairs.

Remains of a brick and flint GATEHOUSE unearthed in the early 1980s N of the house by the moat.

GUILD HOUSE, School Road. A small, interesting brick building of the mid c17, in two storeys. N front with a doorway and chamfered mullioned windows. A row of arched niches under the eaves might have been for pigeons. w and s windows with pediments, the windows renewed c20. Winder by the stack. The cellar beneath lit through splayed lancets.

OLD RECTORY, School Lane. A c17 timber-framed house with brick gable-ends. The façade re-skinned in brick to present six bays of c19 mullioned casements. c18 dormers. Two good c17 fireplaces under four-centred brick arches.

ELSING MILL. Watermill of 1809, for producing paper, converted to a corn mill in the 1830s, now converted to a house. Brick with weatherboarded upper parts. Three storeys, c20 casements. Lucam. The E side has the wheelhouse, with the undershot iron water wheel intact. No other machinery survives.

EMNETH

ST EDMUND. A sizeable Perp church with an E.E. chancel. The chancel has two-bay arcades to the chapels. These have circular piers and round arches with one step and one chamfer. The SE respond has a waterleaf capital. The date of this c. 1210. One N window looks into the present chapel. The chapels were re-modelled in the c15 with the nave and aisles, so that from the outside the aisles appear to embrace the chancel. The N chapel has been converted into a two-storeyed vestry. The ground floor is tunnel-vaulted and originally c. 1300. The E window has three tall stepped lancets, shafted inside. Perp nave of six tall bays. The piers are lozenge-shaped with broad concave sides continued without capitals into the arches. Thin shafts to the four fronts, that towards the nave running right up to the roof. Those to the arch openings have capitals. Perp also the chancel arch and the tower arch. Both have pretty demi-figures of angels. Specially pretty rood-stair with castellated top. Perp s porch, formerly two-storeyed. Perp clerestory with three-light windows. Sanctus bellcote. The nave roof has tie-beams on arched braces standing on small figures, alternating with smaller arched braces standing on horizontally placed figures of angels. The w tower is much repaired with brick. Big four-light w window. Three-light bell-openings with transoms. Concave-sided lead spirelet probably of the C18. – FONT. Perp, octagonal, with tracery and foliage motifs. Also an angel with a shield. – SCREEN. Tall, with one-light divisions. Cusped ogee arches. Ribbed coving. – STAINED GLASS. In the N aisle original figures in the tracery. E window by *William Wailes* †1866. Scenes from the Life of Christ. w window by *Wailes* too †1869. s chapel windows by *Clayton & Bell*. – MONUMENTS. Richly foliated C13 coffin-lid in the s chapel, where also the two following. – Sir Thomas Hewer and wife, dated 1586. Two strapwork panels, and three columns carrying a pediment. No effigies. – Sir Thomas Hewer and wife. By *Nicholas Stone*, 1617. The fee was £95. Standing marble monument against the N wall of the s chapel, opposite the former. Two recumbent effigies, three columns in front carrying the tester. In the E wall a small rectangular recess with the effigy of a child, asleep, slightly on its side. – The churchyard thick with dozens of respectable if not exceptional C18 HEADSTONES.

Several older brick HOUSES of interest. w of the church is the late C17 CHURCH FARMHOUSE, seven bays with brick quoins, these quoins also to the projecting middle bay. Of the C19 are the sashes and, of course, the slate roof.

HAGBECH HOUSE, ¼ m. E. The pair of late C17 brick and lime-stone GATEPIERS draw one's notice to the HOUSE, which is a C17 stable building converted in the C18. Of that date are two sashes to the s front and the doorcase, though not the door itself nor its pediment. At the back the original loose-box doors are blocked.

OXBURGH HALL, ¾ m. NW, on Meadowgate Lane. Later C17 with substantial alterations since. The s front has two tall bays of 1920 carrying Dutch gables. C17 Dutch gables to the E and w returns, i.e. with pediments on top. The house is of T-plan and from the outside all that is early in the stem of the T is the three-light cross casement to the w side below the large staircase windows. The staircase itself is a fine early C18 piece in an open well. It has an open string and carved tread-ends, three balusters to the tread, each with three ball turns and with fluted columns as newel posts. The stairwell dado has panelling enriched with fluted pilasters.

A mid-C18 octagonal brick DOVECOTE 175 yds E is in a derelict condition at the time of writing. Inside are thirteen tiers of nesting boxes. The five-bay brick STABLES, also of the mid C18, reveals how long a clasped-purlin roof structure could persist in use in outlying areas.

DIAL HOUSE, 1⅞ m. SE on the Outwell–Wisbech Road. A small, pleasant, five-bay brick house with pretensions. Note the giant angle pilasters, the panelled parapet, and lighter-coloured red brick window surrounds. The moulded eaves cornice and the first-floor stringcourse are more common embellishments for its date, which is given on the sundial in the parapet: 1730. The staircase is a demure version of that at Oxburgh Hall: open string with floral carved tread-ends, vase and bobbin mouldings to the three balusters per tread.

BANYER HALL, N of the village on Lady Lane. The H-plan mid-C17 house retains two arched timber doorways inside the S range, elsewhere some ovolo-moulded spine beams, but now looks very C20 after the restorations of 1985.

INGLETHORPE MANOR, ⅜ m. SW and difficult to find. 600 yds W of the church on the main road are white railings on the l., of very thin verticals placed very close together. A long drive S to the house. Of 1857–60 by *John Dobson*, the Newcastle architect, for Charles Metcalfe in the Tudor style. Red brick. Two storeys and through-eaves dormers providing a third storey. SW front of four irregular bays plus a square tower. The outer gable-heads begin with stepping and continue flat. External and partly external stacks, one-, two- and three-light mullioned windows. Apart from a long-demolished house in Hampshire this must be Dobson's most southerly job.

7090

FELTWELL

ST MARY. A Papal indulgence was offered in 1494 for money to repair the tower and bells following a fire. One window in the N side was being glazed in 1508 and there are references to leading the church in 1522 and 1523. Sumptuous Perp W tower with double-stepped openwork parapet and pinnacles. The Dec chancel has a big five-light E window with petal tracery and reticulated side windows. Dec sedilia and piscina of large, somewhat raw forms. The ogee heads have a flat top, i.e. are slightly truncated. Dec S arcade of five bays. The piers have four major and in the diagonals four minor shafts. Arches with double sunk quadrants. The S aisle has big Perp windows with stepped embattled transoms. Five clerestory windows to S only. The N side, including the lush arcade and the even lusher arcade of the N chancel chapel, is all of 1861–3 by *Frederick Preedy*, replacing a narrower original. It cost £1,500. The two-bay chancel arcade has heavily moulded arches on a stumpy compound pier with subsidiary shafts and stiff-leaf capitals with figures. Preedy's windows are lancets, or have reticulated and Geometric patterns. – SCREEN. Only very partially of the late C15. The design, if reliable, is unusual. Tabernacle work and canopies in the head. – BENCHES. A fine set of thirty-six with low backs pierced with different tracery patterns, and poppyheads on the ends. On the arm-rests little animals and also groups of two figures. – STALLS. 1860 but with C15 poppyheads. These and the benches might well be from the 1494 work. – STAINED GLASS. Much by *Adolph Didron* and *Eugene Oudinot* of Paris,

dated 1859–63. In the C13 French style, very rich and very good.
The best are Didron's, especially the E window with figurative
medallions and the N chapel window depicting the Prodigal
Son. They were commissioned by the Rector, E.B. Sharpe, and
constitute the best group of Continental C19 glass in the county.
– MONUMENTS. Brasses to Francis Hetht †1479 (13 in. figure)
and to Margaret Mundford †1520 (18½ in. figure; both chancel,
S wall). – Wall monument in chancel to Francis Moundeford
†1590. Kneeling figure flanked by strapwork pilasters. Another
tablet to Osbert Moundeford †1580 also has strapwork pilasters
and the kneeling figure of Moundeford, his wife and daughter.
– Large brass to the Rev. William Newcombe †1846, in the
Pugin style (chancel, N wall).

ST NICHOLAS, ¼ m. NW and now redundant. The carstone round
   tower has largely collapsed (in 1899 while being repaired, taking
   the nave roof with it). Inside there is a wide Norman semicircular arch into the tower with one order of shafts. The chancel
   of the church has also been pulled down (by *Frederick Preedy*
   in 1861 while he was working at St Mary's). So what remains is
   a short nave with aisles and a tall clerestory which is externally
   of cut flint with flushwork panels between the two-light C15
   windows. The flushwork has crowned letters as decoration.
   Perp S porch of brick entered through a four-centred arch with
   continuous hollow and roll mouldings. Its timber roof is Perp
   too. Three-bay arcades inside. The S arcade is of the C13 with
   quatrefoil piers, the four lobes keeled, the bases so-called water-
   holding. Perp N arcade with piers of the same type but slimmer
   and with the shafts of polygonal section. At the E end of the N
   arcade, built into the NE corner of the church as it is at present,
   a Norman column has been re-set with a shaft decorated with
   chevrons and with a waterleaf capital. It is not necessarily *in
   situ*. – FONT. Octagonal. Re-cut in 1830.

FELTWELL RECTORY. By *Henry Harrison* for Rev. E.P. Sparke.
   1832.

The VILLAGE. Feltwell is a giant parish, stretching W into the flat
   fens, almost without habitation. Until the fens hereabouts were
   drained in 1632 Continental ships could moor at Feltwell. The
   village itself is large too, practically a small town on a prominence just under the fifty-foot contour. Its two churches attracted
   separate congregations until the 1860s but apart from them the
   place is not important architecturally. The principal house was
   the early C19 FELTWELL HALL, next to St Mary. Big, plain,
   red brick house of two and a half storeys with a one-bay pediment and a parapet. It looked like a real town-house but has
   been demolished. GRANGE FARMHOUSE on Old Methwold
   Road is C17 with early C19 additions, two storeys, a gable to the
   r. of the main W front. The C19 stairwell is lit from a glazed
   dome. WHITE FARMHOUSE, Long Acre, is of the same pattern
   but the C17 E wing is timber-framed and the C19 block has
   clunch as well as brick.

DENTON LODGE, 2¼ m. ENE of the church. An unremarkable
   house of *c.* 1770 built for Osbert Denton, a corn merchant of

King's Lynn: two storeys, three bays, mansard roof. It has a central stack and a narrow projecting porch beneath it, and an added bay to the w. What is remarkable is the sundial, taking the place of the first-floor porch window. It is canted back on the r. to get the right inclination to the sun, has its gnomon, and is inscribed with names of trading ports across the globe: Bantam, Surat, Diu, Bagdat, Constantinople, Rome, Amsterdam, Lisbon, Teneril (Tenerife), Corvo, Cape Raz and Barmudus (Bermuda). At noon in Feltwell, one can gauge the time in these other locations, presumably ports where Denton had an interest.

0080   FERSFIELD

ST ANDREW. Of *c.* 1300 the s doorway and the s aisle w window. The rest Perp, except for the odd, small and narrow, unbuttressed w tower, which may be of any date, but certainly has a Perp w window. The chancel externally all Victorian, with lancets. s arcade of two bays. The pier has an elongated polygonal projection without capitals and slender polygonal ones with capitals, the latter towards the arch openings. Double-chamfered, four-centred arches. Squint in the form of a cruciform arrow-slit from the s aisle to the chancel. s porch described as new in 1493. – FONT. Norman, altered. Top rim of rope moulding. – FONT COVER. Simple, C17, with volutes. – PANELLING. In the chancel, with Jacobean and other bits. – MONUMENT. Stone effigy of a priest (chancel), late C13. – Wooden effigy of Sir Robert du Bois, *c.* 1340. Most unusually it retains much of its medieval polychromy, revealed from under C18 repainting in the 1960s. The decoration includes heraldic ermine on the surcoat and helmet, and the belt and other details are said once to have been set with coloured glass imitating enamels (DP). – Ledger-stone to Francis Blomefield †1752, the Norfolk historian, who was rector of Fersfield.

RECTORY, The Street. C17, timber-framed and with a brick skin. Two-storey porch with a modest doorcase. C19 improvements include four bays of sash windows and a canted bay to the s end. C18 cross casements to rear wing.

VALLEY FARM. *See* Bressingham, p. 217.

6000   FINCHAM

ST MARTIN. Flint and carstone and stone dressings. Commanding Perp w tower with panelling along the base and on the battlements. Big w doorway and four-light w window with details from the 1847 restoration. Very tall arch towards the nave on polygonal bases and with richly moulded responds. The buttresses have decorative panels and the plinth course is enriched with trefoil arcading. The E buttresses of the tower stand out into the aisles. There are a few dates known from money left in wills: 1458, £7 6s. 8d. for tower; 1476, 8 marks (£5.33) for 'building tower'. The body of the church is of the same time, nave and aisles and a two-storeyed N vestry (built for Sir Nicholas Fincham, but incomplete at his death in 1503). The S aisle is externally the show-front, facing the street and the village. Here the battlements have flushwork and tall pinnacles. The windows are mostly of three lights with stepped transoms under four-centred heads. Panel tracery. The clerestory windows, including one to the E, are of three lights too. Battlements with flushwork also on the chancel S side. The chancel windows again with stepped transoms, that to the E of five lights. The N aisle has windows like the S but the battlements and buttresses lack the flushwork decoration. The N clerestory is of two-light windows with reticulation units.

Tall arcades of five bays, the piers of transverse lozenge shape with four polygonal projections, long to the nave and aisle, small towards the arches. The long ones have capitals in the S arcade, no capitals in the N arcade. Roof with alternating major and minor hammerbeams. Angel figures, grotesques and secular heads attached to them. Collars also arch-braced, the purlins and ridge piece moulded. W. Blyth, writing in 1863, saw the date 1488 on the roof. There seems to be quite a bit of restoration, especially in 1909, when £11,000 was spent. The aisle roofs have pierced tracery spandrels and must also be later C15. Hammerbeam roof in the chancel also, most likely dating from the chancel restoration of 1870. Nice ancient brick paving. – FONT (from the destroyed St Michael, demolished in 1744). An interesting Norman piece, early C12. Square, with figures under arches. The arches are on little engaged circular columns with cushion capitals and framed above and below by dogtooth. To the E the three Magi, to the S the Nativity, with manger, ox and ass, and a shepherd, to the W the Baptism, to the N – most unusual – Adam and Eve and the (re-worked) tree. The bowl is on five thin columns. – SCREEN. Fine delicate piece of three-light divisions, with tracery a little out of the ordinary in that it has curved transoms. The dado has three trefoiled arches to each bay, those to E side reused. – PULPIT. 1870. The TABLE by the S doorway is the tester of the former pulpit. – BENCH ENDS. The poppyheads alone are old. – STAINED GLASS. Various chancel and nave windows with indifferent C19 glass. By far the best is in the W tower window by *Wilmshurst & Oliphant*, 1852 (the date of restorations to the S porch). Big figures of four Evangelists in strident colours. – BRASS (nave floor). Woman in a shroud, 18 in. long, *c.* 1520. – TEXTS. Dated 1717 and painted on boards hung around the walls: Ten Commandments, The Creed and Psalm 23 among others.

FINCHAM HALL. Partly early C16 for the Fincham family, partly Elizabethan. From 1572 to 1620 the house had four different owners culminating in the Hare family of Stow Bardolph. Of the earlier period chiefly the NE tower of brick, polygonal with an entrance and a few steps to a former entrance into the house. This little lobby room has a rib vault of round ribs with a shield in the centre (cf. Oxborough). The tower has two-step battlements and a machicolated cinquefoil frieze below them. The windows have cusped arched lights to the ground floor and additional hoodmoulds above. The E end wall has a big stepped brick chimney-breast, the diamond flues rebuilt. The S wall also with Tudor brickwork but with C19 sashes. The main façade (N) however is altered, more stone than brick and with a blocked Elizabethan doorway with pilasters. It has a semicircular arch and a pair of fluted Ionic pilasters. The present C19 doorway immediately r. The brick mullioned and transomed windows look all renewed. Three straight gables. Inside there is discernible the remains of the screens passage entered from the blocked doorway and the screens truss itself, the passage now hosting a staircase and the truss with strong arched braces. Other than this nothing survives of the hall and solar plan, the NE tower probably representing private rooms attached to the solar.

The HIGH STREET has a number of decent, if modest, HOUSES from the C18 and early C19, mainly of brick but with carstone and flint used also. On the N side is TALBOT'S MANOR HOUSE, its late C18 three-bay façade applied to a pair of early C18 blocks. NELSON HOUSE, further W, has recently been split into three, but started as an early C17 timber-framed house with a roof of cranked upper crucks. A three-light diamond-mullioned window can be seen in the W wall of the S range, but little else from the C17 survived the C18 brick reconstruction and alterations in 1984. On the S side the most interesting house is the OLD RECTORY, another early C17 building reconstructed in 1827 by *Donthorn*. To Donthorn belongs the front insertion with the porch under a shouldered gable. He remodelled the flanking wings as well. Bay windows all C20. The ridge stack carries the date 1624. A circular DOVECOTE is in the grounds. Bits of tracery and other details from the demolished St Michael's church, probably put up in the early C19.

7020

FLITCHAM

This may be the site of the C7 church founded by St Felix, the Bishop of the East Angles.

ST MARY. Of flint. Partly in ruins, but nevertheless interesting as a Norman cruciform church, certainly nothing to do with anything St Felix might have been up to. Sturdy Norman central tower of carstone as well as flint. On the second of three stages large blank arcading, three arches to each side. Norman window to the S under the former transept roof-line. Deeply splayed lancet to the N. C14 bell-openings with reticulation. Plain unmoulded arch towards the nave. The S chapel dates from the early C14. S window with Y-tracery. The chapel has no roof and the church no chancel. In the nave signs of two Norman windows. The nave and four-bay S arcade otherwise Perp. Piers with various polygonal projections under double-chamfered arches. Clerestory, Y-tracery and intersecting nave windows,

nave w window, nave roof and s porch roof are all from the
restoration of 1881. – FONT. 1881, octagonal, of black marble,
taken from St Mary, Sandringham. – BENCHES. Given by
Edward VII in 1907.

FLITCHAM PRIORY. Augustinian. Founded from Walsingham in
1251 by Sir Robert d'Aiguillon. Small. Some featureless masonry
remains in the house called FLITCHAM ABBEY, ¼ m. E of the
church.

FLORDON

1090

ST MICHAEL. A modest church without a tower (but with a
Victorian brick bellcote), though the brick w wall indicates the
site of a round tower. In the N and S walls of the nave are double-
splayed Anglo-Saxon windows and the remains of quoins marking the E extent of the nave before the C14. Chancel Dec with
three-light E window (cusped intersecting tracery). The chancel
arch shapeless (one slight chamfer) but probably earlier. C15 S
porch. – PULPIT. Jacobean, with two tiers of blank arches;
much stylized leafwork. – STAINED GLASS. In the E window
C14 and C15 canopies and a complete C16 St Peter. Also bits in
a nave S window.

FLORDON HALL. The Kemp family had the manor from the C15,
and it was Robert Kemp who had the timber-framed house we
see today built some time between 1595 and 1612 – see the arms
over the porch door of Kemp impaling Harris. A good E-plan
house with brick gable-ends to the cross wings and the central
full-height porch. Polygonal corner shafts to these parts. Semicircular porch entrance under a pediment. The windows are
now mainly C19 or C20 cross casements, although one five-light
mullioned window remains to the N return, the mullions ovolo-
moulded as one would expect. That the originals had moulded
hoods is evident from the blocked openings in the gable-heads
of the façade. External stacks to the N and S and the rear, with
octagonal flues.

The timber frame shows here and there on the interior, the
bridging beams ovolo-moulded and the principal studs boasting
moulded jowls at their tops – not at all common for Norfolk.
The plan is of a central hall with the porch opening into its
lower end, although now this has been divided into two rooms
and is not easy to appreciate. Parlour to the S with a C19 staircase in the same wing. The opposite wing also has a staircase,
this time c. 1600: plain flight of wooden treads. General restoration 1973.

About 50 yds S is a HOUSE used for some years as a pig-sty,
which was possibly a dower house. Two storeys and attic, brick,
c. 1600, i.e. contemporary with the Hall. Hoodmoulds over the
blocked windows. An upper flight of stairs survives, of solid
treads, very archaic for the early C17. The BARN is a sixteen-bay
timber-framed structure with alternating tie-beam trusses supported on arched braces. c. 1620–30.

FORDHAM

Fordham is a windswept place, without a village.

St Mary. Of carstone with ashlar dressings. Nave and chancel and C19 bellcote. A w tower was demolished in 1730. The s aisle also was pulled down, but the three-bay arcade can still be visualized, now with mid-C14 two-light windows presumably re-located in 1730. The chancel arch has high polygonal bases to the engaged columns and a wave-moulded arch. The nave roof is a classic domestic type of 1730: tie-beams and principal rafters supporting collars on arched braces, two tiers of staggered butt-purlins with curved wind-bracing to one tier only. Another ten years and the wind-bracing would be straight.

Snore Hall. The house of the Skipwiths remains now an extremely puzzling building. The old work is to the s, bounded by diagonal stepped buttresses with blunt pinnacles, all *c.* 1470–5, and a commendably early example of domestic brick for a building of this scale and status. The s side is rather plain, with late C16 windows, all renewed. The centre upper window dates from the 1930s, a period of some alteration. The w gable-end is more complex: the gable-head has a panelled shaft running up its middle, a square projecting embattled two-storey porch added probably in the 1490s and an upper projecting window to its r. Blank friezes of oblong cusped panels at its base and above the first floor. The e gable-end rather mutilated by *H. J. Green* while he was altering the internal arrangements and adding the bays to the n façade and the hipped extension to the e in 1903. Green was extending the n range, which is of the very late C18. The stack is of 1584–5.

Internally, the original block comprises only two rooms on each floor, plus, of course, the porch and its small upper chamber. The porch has a tierceron vault and the upper chamber a metal-clad door: it might have been a strongroom. The w rooms are larger than the e ones, and contain little of interest, the timber fire surround and overmantel to the King's Room (first floor w) having been removed. The two e rooms have some fancy bridging beams, the two to the ground floor ribbon- and roll-moulded respectively. They are not *in situ*, are forty years too late in style, and one at least has mortice holes, indicating that it started life as a tie-beam with a wall-post and arched braces. The C18 additions have been knocked about quite drastically, and nothing in the roof is older than the C18 either, when it was reduced in height. The new stack allowed the creation of two secret chambers, one above the other, each 3 ft by 3 ft by 6 ft.

Before the insertion of the stack there was presumably some sort of internal division of the rooms, which would have looked, as they still do, very like the plan of a C12 upper-hall house, or a variant of the Great Chamber type of the C14. Certainly the first floor was always the more important – it provides the only access to the upper porch chamber and benefits from the elaborate projecting window. It was also open to the roof. Although first-floor halls were still being constructed, especially in special-ized buildings such as Dragon Hall, Norwich, or Abbey Farm-house, Old Buckenham, the date is rather late. And there is no sign of the kitchen or any service provisions at all.

Excavations of the original N wall in 1990 revealed two blocked windows of Elizabethan proportions, evidence of a projecting fire-hood built into the 1585 stack, and a winder stair, which must have projected externally, giving into the King's Room. This certainly looks like a Great Chamber plan, but is still too small and no less unlikely for the 1470s. Foundations exist run-ning N from the house, and these appear to be the footings for a timber-framed structure, leading to the theory that the brick wing was a magnificent solar block attached at r. angles to an existing timber hall-house, the principal room of which was reached via a staircase behind the high end of the hall.

FORNCETT END   *1090*

St EDMUND. Small red brick church of 1904 with a missing chancel marked by a weatherboarded patch at the E end. Three three-light cusped windows to N and S flanks and a small gabled entrance porch with bellcote to W.

METHODIST CHURCH, 300 yds W. Late C19. Red brick with white brick dressings. Three bays of side windows set in recessed arches. N gable with stuccoed pedimented doorcase and a window either side. The windows have all unfortunately been replaced with uPVC.

A scattered VILLAGE, surprisingly heavily built up between and after the two World Wars. C17 and C18 timber-framed cottages are fitted in here and there. On Long Stratton Road CHESTNUT TREE FARMHOUSE, a late C16 lobby-entrance house with bricked gable walls and a thatched roof. Stacks with octagonal and lozenge flues. LIMETREE FARMHOUSE, on the same road, has a C19 brick skin but inside are sunk quadrants to the bridg-ing beams in the early C17 Wymondham manner. Early C19 clay lump outbuildings. CORNER FARMHOUSE, further along, has a stepped gable to the W wing.

FORNCETT ST MARY   *1090*

St MARY. Redundant and forlorn. Thin unbuttressed W tower of the C13, at least in the lower stages; the construction of the upper stage mentioned in a will of 1432. Perp bell-openings replaced in the general restoration of 1869. Battlements with flushwork panelling to W side only. Nave and chancel, the latter built in 1869 with the vestry and roofs. Perp nave windows, Dec-style chancel windows plus one lancet. – PULPIT. Simple; C17, the backboard with fluted Ionic pilasters. – COMMUNION RAIL. Jacobean, used as a font rail. – DOOR. The N door has C16 linenfold panels.

OLD HALL FARMHOUSE, Low Road. Late C16 timber-framed house with an early C17 brick SW wing containing a good staircase with turned balusters and heavy turned newels. Two plaster ceilings, the upper one with plaster vine trails. The W (rear) elevation has fluted pilasters to the doorcase.

YEW TREE FARMHOUSE, Low Road. A complete C15 'Wealden' house with screens passage preserved intact with two arched service doorways. The arrangement quite typical, with jettied end bays, but the open-hall disposition now gone.

THE CROFT, Cheynes Lane. C16, timber-framed and thatched. Mullioned windows crouch under eaves, and in a gable-end is a five-light window with ovolo-moulded mullions.

FORNCETT ST PETER

1090

ST PETER. An Anglo-Saxon round tower complete to the top, i.e.
3 with circular windows half-way up, bell-openings of two lights with a deeply recessed shaft and arched or triangular heads three quarters of the way up, and eight more circular openings just below the crenellated top. Narrow, but not small, arch towards the nave on the simplest imposts. The chancel has herringbone flushwork to three quarters of its length, but the windows, like those of the nave and aisles, are Perp. N porch with flushwork-panelled base and a panel with IHS above the entrance. Arcade of three bays, quatrefoiled piers with fillets and thin shafts with fillets in the diagonals. Polygonal abaci, sunk arch-mouldings, i.e. later C14. Roof with embattled tie-beams and arched braces. – FONT. C15. Octagonal. – PULPIT. Two-sided, with Jacobean blank arches. – BENCHES. Typical of this area, with poppyheads and unusually many figures l. and r. Not Perp; apparently skilful work of 1857. – STAINED GLASS. In S chancel St Peter and St Paul, 1854 by *F. W. Oliphant.* – MONUMENT. Thomas Drake †1485 and wife. Of alabaster. Tomb-chest with shields in cusped lozenge fields. Spiral-fluted angle colonnettes. On top an incised slab with demi-figures.

RECTORY, Church Road. Early C18. Brick, with shaped end-gables and, on the façade, the middle three out of five bays emphasized by rusticated brick pilasters. Rusticated pilasters also to the doorcase, and a second order of reeded pilasters. Stringcourse between floors and sashes with exposed boxes. Interior as good as the exterior: fielded panelling to principal room, staircase with turned balusters and a moulded handrail dropping to column newels.

The VILLAGE. Clay lump can be seen, or not seen, at Nos. 1–2 Aslacton Road, a pair of mid-C18 cottages, and behind the brick of ALBOROUGH, Mill Lane, *c.* 1820. The C17 prosperity of the area is evident in the number of houses and farmhouses from the period, none of which is individually outstanding. Nos. 1–3 The Street (CHURCH COTTAGES) is an early C17 timber-framed house masked by a brick skin; THE HOMESTEAD on The Street is a lobby-entrance C17 house with its BARN. From the late C17 is CHESTNUT TREE FARMHOUSE, Walton Road, unusual in that the attached BARN to the E is roofed with the house.

FOSS DITCH   7090

This extensive earthwork runs for about 7½ m. between the Wissey and Little Ouse rivers along the edge of the Weeting–Cranwich boundary. The ditch lies to the E. A section cut in 1949 at the Wilton–Weeting boundary disclosed Romano-British pottery stratified beneath the rampart; this and documentary evidence would place its construction after A.D. 390 and before 1050. This and the Devil's Dyke, running N from a tributary of the Wissey, probably formed one boundary system. Whether this was a division between a C5 sub-Roman population along the fen edge and incoming Anglo-Saxons to the E, or between rival Anglo-Saxon political groupings in the C6 or C7, is uncertain. It may be a C6–C7 Saxon defence. (AR)

FOULDEN   7090

ALL SAINTS. Quite a big church, but the W tower collapsed in the C18 and the remains were removed after Ladbroke drew the church in the 1820s. Tower arch blocked as a window. Bellcote C20. The church is mostly C14, namely nave, both aisles and also the chancel, although this with its panel-tracery windows appears Perp (see, however, the piscina and the priest's doorway). The S porch has a good reticulated E window, a good entrance with double wave mouldings, and a good S doorway with its hoodmould on headstops. Also on the S side an outer tomb-recess with a cusped ogee arch and a foliated tomb-slab, said to be that of Sir John de Crake who, also supposedly, built the church to replace the church of St Edmund to the SW on the banks of the Wissey. The N porch plain. In 1479 there was to be a burial in the 'new north porch'. Its roof has principals on wall-posts. Unusually tall arcades of four bays with octagonal piers and double-chamfered arches. Tower arch and chancel arch of similar character. The clerestory has a circular E window with a quatrefoil. C15 chancel roof on arched braces, nave roof C19, with kingposts. – FONT. C15, octagonal, plain. – PULPIT. Simple, Perp, polygonal, with blind tracery. The base C19. – SCREEN. The base only, C15, with ten damaged painted figures. – BENCHES. The ends with poppyheads and animals on the arm-rests. – BOX PEWS. C18, in aisles. – PANELLING. C17 chancel dado on E wall. – MONUMENT. Robert Long †1656. Attributed to *Martin Morley* of Norwich on the strength of the similarity of the monument to that to Thomas Windham at Felbrigg.

FOULDEN HALL. Of the late C16 house of the Holdich family only the gable-ends with their external Elizabethan chimneys remain, rising to quadruple octagonal flues. Between them is a

C19 block with a porch and bay windows. Another C16 stack with octagonal flues to the back, now set within a C19 extension. Inside, little bits of the original timber frame remain, and the wind-braced roof. The late C16 staircase with its turned balusters and newels is said to come from Didlington Hall, when that was demolished in 1950.

FRAMINGHAM EARL

2000

ST ANDREW. Norman round tower, not early. Three stages. The windows have a continuous roll moulding, and the arch towards the nave not the very simplest imposts. There is a lancet in the strips of W wall either side of the tower. Norman also the nave, which is remarkable for the huge flints selected to form its W cornerstones. The nave has its original doorways and chancel arch. The S doorway is specially ornate. The odd l. impost of three rolls ought to be noted. The arch has a roll, a scallop motif, and a hoodmould with a star in a roundel. The N doorway is simpler but has decorated capitals and abaci too. Crenellation in the arch, in the hoodmould billet. S porch E.E., with a niche over the entrance and lancets E and W. C19 N porch. Two Norman S nave windows and one N are in fact C19. The chancel arch has been too much restored, but the arch itself remains in a reasonably good condition. It has again zigzag, crenellations etc. The chancel itself, however, is not Norman, but the one surviving part of an Anglo-Saxon church. It was apsed, as 1984 excavations revealed, but given an E.E. straight end. It has the double-splayed circular windows which occur in quite a number of Saxon churches in Norfolk. Otherwise E.E. lancets with hoodmoulds on little stiff-leaf tops. One buttress strip to S side. The C19 restorations were essential if hard, the petal-tracery E window being amazingly discordant. Inside they account for the roofs, font, W gallery, the openings r. and l. of the chancel arch. – PULPIT. C17, panelled with masons' mitre; from Sotterley in Suffolk. – STAINED GLASS. Two very good C15 figures in elongated medallions, St Margaret and St Matthew, both in white and yellow against a dark blue background, but St Margaret's dragon ruby in addition (nave N and tower). E window by *Ward & Hughes, c.* 1860.

OLD HALL. Early C18. S front of five bays, raised up mid C19 when the porch was added. W gable with a stepped early C18 stack.

FRAMINGHAM PIGOT

2000

ST ANDREW. 1859 by *Robert Kerr*. The preceding church had a round tower and Saxon double-splayed circular windows. The new aisleless church has a stone tower at the NW corner, crowned by an octagonal top and spire that look odd in this countryside. The ground stage has spherical triangles, then con-

ventional Dec windows, then lancets. The church is faced with
squared knapped flint and exhibits the Dec style. The w door
flanked by arcading. Big three-light Curvilinear window above.
Nave and chancel windows are an essay in Geometric Dec
forms current *c.* 1280–1315. They all have internal shafts.
Splendid ashlar interior with a very decorated tower gallery
opening to the s into the church. Stone vestry screen N of chancel with polished marble columns. – Norman PILLAR PISCINA.
– STAINED GLASS. Chancel windows by *J. Hardman & Co.*,
1860s. So too the tower window.

MANOR HOUSE. 1862–4 by *J. Norton* for George Henry Christie
(of the auctioneers), with a N wing added 1895. Brick dressed
with stone. Neo-Tudor. s front in seven bays, with a three-
storey porch. Cross casement windows, battlemented parapet,
romantic stacks with multiple flues.

OLD MANOR FARMHOUSE, Fox Road. The C17 house runs E–W,
of two storeys. One ovolo-moulded mullioned window testifies.
Hipped roof with a rebuilt panelled stack. C18 and C19 extensions.

FRENZE   *1080*

1¼ m. E of Diss

ST ANDREW. Small. Nave with bell-turret. The chancel had to be
demolished in 1820 because of its derelict state and there was a
general restoration in 1900. Flint and rubble with some brick
under a pantiled roof. Two-light windows of the early C14, the
three-light reticulated E window re-located from the same place
in the absent chancel. Gabled s porch with Tudor brick and
diagonal buttresses, repaired no doubt in 1521 when Margaret
James left a cow in her will for this purpose. Roof 1900. – FONT.
Octagonal, with elementary, very flat blind tracery of the late
C13 to early C14. – PULPIT. Jacobean. Large and oblong, not
polygonal. With back panel and polygonal tester. The STALL in
front of it has monkeys carved on the arms; probably C15. –
FAMILY PEW. Jacobean, opposite the pulpit and of the same
make: frieze panels and turned balusters below the top rail,
rather good. – BENCH. One with traceried front and poppyheads
on the ends. – BRASSES. An important set, principally to the
Blennerhassett family of the Hall (spelt variously). Ralph
Blenerhaysset †1475 (25 in. long; chancel). – John Blenerhaysset
†1510 (only three quarters of his wife Jane †1521; the effigies
were 28 in. long; chancel). – Thomas Hobson, *c.* 1520, in his
shroud (11 in.; nave N side). – Johanna Braham †1519, dress of
a religious votary (28 in.; nave, near W end). Also Sir Thomas
Blenerhaysette †1531, Anne Blenerhaysett †1551 and Mary
Blenerhaiset †1587, the wife of Francis Bacon.

FRENZE HALL. The manor of the Blennerhassetts and Nixons
forms a group with the church and a handful of farm buildings.
Skinned in brick *c.* 1870. Internally it has a C17 timber frame,
externally a stepped brick stack to the N.

FRING

ALL SAINTS. Of the C14. In the Norwich Cellarers' Rolls is a
reference in 1327 to the building of the church. According to
Kelly there was a thorough restoration in 1897 but it cost only
£350. W tower with a pretty lozenge-shaped W opening. Tracery
of the four-petalled-flower type. Bell-openings with Y-tracery.
Tall double-chamfered arch into the nave. (Cautley reports a
fireplace in the tower with a Norman pillar piscina as its lintel.
Scallop capital to the pillar.) Cusped Y-tracery in nave and
chancel. N and S doorways with sunk-quadrant mouldings. An
ogee-headed niche S of the chancel arch seems to have been a
squint. A cusped ogee-headed piscina in the chancel, with a
shelf. The chancel E window reduced in size. Ladbroke c. 1825
shows it with a casement window. Roofs C19, of lower pitch
than the originals. – FONT. Octagonal, C13, of the Purbeck type,
with two shallow pointed arches on each side. – PAINTINGS.
Superb though much-damaged paintings, contemporary with
the church, and very reminiscent in style and colouring of the
Ante-Reliquary Chapel paintings in Norwich Cathedral (cf.,
e.g., the turquoise foliage on the chancel arch). To the S of the
chancel arch a painted niche, and then the Annunciation with
an elegant swaying figure of the Virgin beneath a canopy. On
the adjoining part of the S wall, St John the Evangelist with
palm and book, and on the adjacent window more painting
including a standing figure on the W splay. Large St Christopher
on the N wall, with delicate scrollwork borders.

WHITE HOUSE, to the SE, on the Bircham Road. Early C19, of
gault brick. Two storeys in three widely spaced bays with giant
pilasters at the angles. Centre bay broken forward under pediment. The ground floor has a porch with unfluted columns
without bases and no pediment; two arched windows set in
blank arches. Hipped roof behind parapet.

FRING HALL. The 1807 house of A. T. Dusgate was burnt and
rebuilt in the C20. Brick, two storeys and dormer attic and a
façade in six bays.

FRITTON

ST CATHERINE. Isolated to the N of the village. C12 round tower
with late C15 octagonal top using much brick. Unmoulded
tower arch on the simplest imposts. The nave N doorway is the
same (leading to the vestry of 1874). Nave and continuous
chancel. Upper parts of nave have brick courses, possibly C17,
though the nave was heightened in the C16 according to a will
of 1502 which left money for the operation. Chancel has been
gone over in the C17 too – see the brick in the gable wall. S
doorway C14. S porch substantially C15, but re-roofed and
gabled in 1853. The fenestration is also from the 1853 restoration, but the pairs of lancets in the nave could well represent the
original state (S nave windows the same as in Ladbroke's day).

Nave roof replaced in 1913, with the minor fittings. – FONT. C15. Against the stem four lions, against the bowl four lions and four demi-figures of angels. – SCREEN. Eight painted panels of the dado are preserved, the most interesting two crowded panels of John Bacon (†1511) kneeling with his family before the four Latin Doctors. Several of the family hold rosaries, while an inscription asks for prayers for Bacon's soul. Tracery and rood figures are C20. – WALL PAINTINGS. On nave N wall a St Christopher, given in 1506, incorporating scenes from the saint's legend, but now much deteriorated. Further E, a large St George and the Dragon, naively over-restored. Over the opening to the rood stair, a small figure of St Edmund of Abingdon (archbishop of Canterbury †1240), a rare saint but here identified by an inscription. This painting is stylistically dateable to the mid C13, so must have been painted not long after Edmund's canonization in 1246. Other small fragments in the nave include a consecration cross. (DP) – STAINED GLASS. Minor. E window by *J. Powell & Sons*, c. 1865. – MONUMENT. S chancel wall, to Elizabeth Holmes †1762, a tablet with cartouche and an obelisk above. – SOUTH DOOR. Early C16, with iron plate and handle, restored 1619 (inscription).

FRITTON HALL. Gable-end with a stepped gable and vitrified headers of dark blue colour used as diapering, which is usual, but also in horizontal zigzags, which is unusual. It is a C17 L-plan house with a timber-framed wing to the NW. C19 and C20 fenestration. To the S two BARNS, one dated 1749.

ISLAND HOUSE, 300 yds S of the last. Said to be 1684, but one would have thought more c. 1650: two-storeyed timber-framed house with a jetty to upper floor; lobby-entrance plan but now with a C19 porch.

A group of C17 timber-framed houses stands around FRITTON COMMON complementing these two houses. FRITTON END FARMHOUSE and THE THREE NAGS pub have C19 brick skins.

FUNDENHALL

½ m. SE of Ashwellthorpe

ST NICHOLAS. Norman central tower with one original N, one original S window. Above that E.E. The bell-openings have two pointed lights, separated by a thin shaft, the two under one round arch. Norman S doorway with one order of shafts with volute capitals. E.E. N doorway with fine arch-mouldings. Inside only the W side of the W arch of the central tower is Norman (nook-shafts). The church had a thorough restoration in 1869 which added the N porch. Plain chancel. – SCREEN. Only the coving remains and the tracery above a wide arch which must have been the whole width of the tower arch. The coving supported the rood loft. But above the wide arch there is a flat loft floor instead. Traces of painting. The whole is a rare survival. – FONT. C15. Octagonal bowl with shields to alternate facets. Angels against the stem hold shields.

Timber-framed HOUSES of minor interest of the C17 abound. The best is THE GRANGE on Whip's Lane, near the church. The C17 part has acquired a brick skin, an C18 extension to N and a *c.* 1850 extension to E, the latter of five bays. At Rattees Corner is RATTEES, an early C19 red brick house of three bays with a Doric doorcase.

FUNDENHALL STREET is a hamlet ¾ m. SW. MANOR FARMHOUSE closes the street to the N. Late C16, timber-framed, two-storeyed, with a full-height porch in front of the ridge stack. C17 BARN immediately N, also timber-framed. Most of the other houses C17 too: see THE ROOKERY, DAIRY FARMHOUSE and LYNDALE.

0080   GARBOLDISHAM

ST JOHN BAPTIST. Early C14 aisle windows and doorways, and chancel arch. The rest Perp. W tower with small chequer pattern of knapped flint and stone. Flushwork emblems on a base frieze. Buttresses with flushwork panelling and emblems. Tall battlements with flushwork panelling. Four pinnacles and four angels instead of subsidiary pinnacles. The tower originally had a W porch (cf. e.g. Lakenheath across the Suffolk border). Tower bequests are gratifyingly specific: in 1463 John Smyth left 20s. 'to new tower for stipend of mason in first year of work'. Further donations 1466–8. N porch with large inscription commemorating William Pece (chaplain 1500) and others invoking Christ, St John Baptist, Zachary, Elizabeth, and Johannes again. Niches l. and r. of the entrance. The chancel was reconstructed in 1862 by *G. E. Street*, the date of general restorations. The interior is earlier than any part of the exterior. Arcades of four bays with octagonal piers, but circular columns to the second bay. The arches have two hollow chamfers and differ slightly. The date is most probably still in the C13. The nave roof is about contemporary with the N porch: ties on arched braces, moulded butt-purlins. – FONT. Octagonal, with square roll-moulded panels to the C13 bowl. The stem is C19. – SCREENS. In the N aisle. Only the base with four painted Saints is original C15 work. The base has carved mouchette wheels. Rood screen, also only the base, but of four bays r. and l. of the centre. – BENCH ENDS. Some are old. – STAINED GLASS. In the chancel, by *Powell*'s, of the 1880s, quite good, approaching the Aesthetic Movement in quality.

ALL SAINTS, ¼ m. N. Ruined in 1734. But the C14 tower stands nearly to the top, its E wall broken off.

GARBOLDISHAM OLD HALL was burnt out in 1955 and then demolished. The C16 E-plan house, owned by the Bacon family in the early C18, was remodelled in the mid C18, to five bays with projecting three-bay wings.

GARBOLDISHAM MANOR, ¾ m. N of St John's Church, on Kenninghall Road. By *George Gilbert Scott Jun.*, 1869–73, it has been pulled down. The stables and service wing survive, the former restored and converted to domestic use in 1983–4. The house was built for Cecil Montgomerie, and was one of the earliest of the Queen Anne style country houses, done at the same time as J.J. Stevenson was designing his Red House in Bayswater, but earlier than Stevenson's Ken Hill in Norfolk (q.v. Snettisham). It had decidedly C17 characteristics, of four bays with two-bay projecting wings topped with large convex Dutch gables, i.e. with pediments. The big E-plan STABLES give the scale, splendid with horizontal bands of yellow and red brick, typical of the style in its shaped gables and, on the court-yard side, timber cross casements and decorative brickwork. Generous hipped dormers flank the carriage entrance, which is accented towards the house by a similar convex gable. A cupola sits above it. A reduced SERVICE WING also remains, less flam-boyant but with the same elements. One should note too the swept entrance to the drive from the road: rusticated PIERS with complex stone obelisks.

The WALLED GARDEN of Scott's house survived, with walls 16 ft high. Against the N wall the interesting WALL HOUSE was created in 1978–81 by *Michael Neylan & William Ungless* (job architect *W. Ungless*). Against is not the right word, for the wall bisects the house, giving a long one-storey range under a gabled pantile roof to the N and a smaller symmetrical mass to the S, hipped, with a row of horizontal windows under rather brooding eaves. The N rooms intended for offices, the S for recreational use. Visually linking the two parts is an observation turret sitting astride the wall and carrying the twin flues of the fireplaces. The split aspect of the house is more obvious externally than intern-ally, for the communicating doorways which had to be knocked through the wall reduce the visual impact of a continuous barrier.

MANOR COTTAGE, 50 yds N of the last. An altered *c.* 1600 timber-framed house, originally of the lobby-entrance type. The S gable wall is outwardly its most attractive feature with its burnt headers in early C18 brick. The roof structure of queen-struts and clasped purlins is a late manifestation of the type found in THE OLD MANOR a further 80 yds NE. Of the two C16 builds the N wing is the earlier, with full-blown queenposts to the roof (only one pair surviving) and again clasped purlins. The S wing has staggered butt-purlins. The whole is timber-framed and plas-tered with herringbone panels.

No. 82 BACK STREET also has herringbone panels to its plaster. Early C18. At the N end of Back Street, on the E side, is JACQUES, with a raised six-light dais window testifying to its 66 origins as a hall house. The stack was inserted in the C17 when the hall was floored, but the late C15 screen is identifiable, and over the hall are the smoke-blackened timbers of a small crown-post roof with four arched braces. A second, simpler, crown-post lies to the N, more smoke-blackened than the hall bay, and S of the stack is the close-studded solar, timber-framed like the rest. When floored (and altered again in the C18) the orientation of the house switched round, with the kitchen moving from the N to the S, a very common event with these minor hall houses,

when the fireplaces were inserted and a new room created out
of the upper parts of the hall.

BRECKLANDS HOUSE, W of St John's Church on Church Street.
Timber-framed, with a group of four brick chimneyshafts to the
W gable, the decoration on two of them of spiral and diaper.
These must be early C16, as is the gabled two-storey stair-turret
to the rear. A downstairs room has the multiple-roll-moulded
cruciform bridging beams of the period; complete close-studded
timber frame.

In the region there are many HOUSES of clay lump as well as of
timber-framing. Two from the mid C18 are EDWARDS
FARMHOUSE 1 m. NE of the church and STUBBINGS
FARMHOUSE 1¼ m. NE, the former still with the lobby-entrance
plan. Both are on Mallows Lane.

WINDMILL, 1 m. S. In 1837 there were three corn mills in
Garboldisham: a post mill of *c.* 1780, a smock mill of *c.* 1788
and a tower mill of 1820, quite a group of types. Only the post
mill, the last in Norfolk, survives, and this has been restored
since 1972 and at the time of writing produces flour from an
electric mill. A late example and of standard form: circular brick
roundhouse, weatherboarded buck, no sails, and the buck
entered from a wide ladder staircase running on a track. Inside
are the usual cross trees, quarter bars and machinery.

COUNCIL HOUSES, Hopton Street, ¼ m. S of the church, by *George
Skipper*, 1919–20. This crescent of clay lump houses was demolished in 1988 and replaced by less interesting buildings. Others
were at Harling, and more remain in Suffolk, at Hopton.

BARROWS. There are a number of unexcavated barrows on the
Heath W of Devil's Ditch; three have a diameter of 40 ft, the
fourth is 90 ft in diameter and 18 ft high. The last is also known
as Boadicea's Grave or Soldier's Hill.

DEVIL'S DITCH. An undated and unexcavated linear earthwork,
with a ditch to W, running N from Waveney to a small tributary
of the Thet, meets a Roman road at a very acute angle. It is best
preserved close to the main Thetford–Diss road on the Heath.
(AR)

GARVESTONE

0000

ST MARGARET. Dec the S arcade (four bays, octagonal piers,
double-chamfered arches), the S doorway, and the chancel arch
(half quatrefoil with thin diagonal shafts). Perp the W tower
with a wave-moulded arch into the nave. It has a fireplace inside.
Three-light W window with panel tracery. Bell-openings of
mixed Dec and Perp forms, probably C15 (mouchettes with
supermullions), and flushwork decoration of the parapet. Nave
and S aisle windows Perp under four-centred heads on the
S. The S aisle has wall arches inside, also one on the W side.
Y-tracery chancel windows with a Perp E window. – FONT.
Stem with fleurons, bowl with shields surrounded by crinkly
seaweed leaves.

GUNTON'S FARMHOUSE, Reymerston Road. Good late C16 timber frame faced with brick in the C18 and given four bays of cross casements. Pedimented doorcase. Brick gable-ends are C16: hollow-chamfered mullioned windows. The staircase has some solid treads and, a surprise, a long gallery with arched braces up to the tie-beams on the first floor. Clasped purlin roof.

VALHALLA, Tanners Green. A low C16 open hall floored internally in the C17, but with the service passage intact, and service doorways. The timber frame skinned with brick and visually of the early C19, with five casement windows.

CHURCH FARMHOUSE, Dereham Road. Same history as Valhalla, the brick facing dated 1871 and of a full two storeys in three bays. The service passage lies towards the E end, the site of service doors only evident from the mortices of their arched heads.

MOATED SITE. In an isolated location 1 m. WSW from the church, large, well preserved and with outer enclosure bounded by a large ditch to S. (AR)

GASTHORPE
1 m. E of Riddlesworth

9080

ST NICHOLAS. In ruins. A large fragment of the W tower remains. The rest all smothered in ivy. The chancel had flushwork battlements with initials. The chancel windows had in 1960 ogee-headed lights which seemed to be of the C14. Otherwise probably C15.

Two HOUSES SW of the Post Office have a jettied N range. C16, timber-framed, with herringbone decoration to some of the infill. External stacks to S and W gables.

GATELEY

9020

ST HELEN. Perp, with a chancel and N vestry added in 1866 by *J. B. & W. Atkinson* of York. W tower of C15. Only the N and S doorways of the church are earlier, say of c. 1300. On the SW buttress of the nave two shields. The nave has an arch-braced roof and four Perp four-centred windows to each side. – SCREEN. With eight painted figures in the dado panels; late C15. Female figures on the N side and male on the S, reflecting the seating arrangement of men and women in the church. The female figures include the locally venerated 'Puella Ridibowne', and the male 'saints' Henry VI and Master John Schorn (DP). Schorn was rector of North Marston, Bucks, c. 1290, and is shown here conjuring the Devil into a boot, his most celebrated miracle (cf. Cawston). – BENCHES. With poppyheads. A few have openwork backs with different tracery patterns. Animals on the arms are all reptilian-based, including a caterpillar. – COMMUNION RAIL. With turned balusters; later C17. – MONUMENT. Robert Sharbrook †1803. The centre a heart-shape of polished white marble, with the inscription. Cherubs and clouds around.

GATELEY HALL. The house has two parallel roof ridges, both ending in big shaped gables with chimney flues to both sides. Pairs of shaped gables were still common enough in Norfolk in the 1720s. On one S gable the date 1726 refers to reconstruction for Elizabeth Seagrave; the rear (E) range indeed retains C17 walling. The W façade of the house, five bays and two storeys with a parapet, looks 1726 and has some chequerwork brick. Doorway with pediment on fluted pilasters. The sashes are C18 too. Inside is a completely unexpected, fabulous display of mid-C18 Rococo decoration in mixed plaster and wood, the best in the entrance hall. Against the rear wall is a large symmetrical surround to a small mirror, all scrolls and vegetation. Opposite, between two façade windows, a classical landscape with three figures, a broken column and obelisk. Much larger is the fireplace overmantel with a more English rustic scene: shepherds, animals, houses, a church spire and trees. This is above a rich fireplace frieze and between domed recesses. Ceiling with floral decoration within hexagonal panels and good, though more common, Rococo ceilings in the adjoining room to S and the stair vestibule (to E). Under the landing a large eagle, almost detached and without any frame. The staircase itself is 1726 with slim turned balusters and carved tread-ends. In addition there are good doorways with broken pediments, that from the hall to the S room on fluted pilasters below a Doric frieze.

EARTHWORKS, NE of the Hall. A sunken way with two appended ditched enclosures probably marks the site of a single farm of medieval or early post-medieval date, deserted through emparking. Such small and intimate relics of the pre-modern landscape are rare in Norfolk. (AR)

7010   GAYTON

ST NICHOLAS. Mostly early C14, but with a Perp chancel and a clerestory later than the tower and the arcades (see the former roof-line against the tower). In the tower are ringing-chamber windows with Y-tracery below the Dec bell-openings. The tower top has flushwork-panelled battlements and the signs of the four Evangelists instead of pinnacles and an odd squashed dome, which has inside a very unusual C15 stone-ribbed brick domical vault. Low diagonal W buttresses. In the aisles windows with Y-tracery, cusped Y-tracery, Y-tracery with a small trefoil in the spandrel (S aisle W), and one most curious oval window with a squashed quatrefoil (N aisle E). Blocked N chancel doorway. Flint S porch with a sundial dated 1604, the inscription eroded and the gnomon missing. Tall arcades of four bays with octagonal piers and double-hollow-chamfered arches. The chancel arch is much lower. Nave roof rebuilt but hammerbeams remain to E and W ends. Sloping boarded aisle roofs. Clerestory, with alternating two-light and circular windows, high enough for a (blocked) E window. Perp chancel with very simple arched and framed sedilia and piscina. Roof from the 1850 restoration, which required some rebuilding of the upper walls. E window 1850 in a bigger, older opening. – FONT. Simple, octagonal, Perp. – STAINED GLASS. E window by *George Hedgeland* †1852. Good.

GAYTON HALL, Back Street, SE of church. Set in a miniature park with a lake. Interesting building sequence. The first house was a small two-storey early C19 shooting-box for Andrew St John, but this was enlarged *c.* 1820 by a wide, shallow bow to the r. and the whole raised into two and a half storeys. The original door re-set in a recessed arch immediately l. of the bow without too much regard for vertical orientation with upper windows. About 1930 a further balancing two bays added r. of the bow, which then became central to the elevation. S return with a three-bay loggia of round brick arches.

HALL FARMHOUSE, Back Street. Flint and brick, colourwashed. A two-storey three-celled house dated on the S gable 1587 with a through-passage plan. C19 sashes. A chimney bay to the l. with ridge stack. Gables on kneelers. The rear has an outshut and a blocked window with a king mullion. Various bridging beams with tongue stops.

WINDMILL. E of the church a tall, eight-storey derelict brick tower mill, of the 1820s. A BAKEHOUSE and GRANARY at the foot, the former of 1867. The two-storey MILLER'S HOUSE is earlier, *c.* 1800. Three bays of sashes.

ORCHARD FARMHOUSE, Orchard Road. C17 farmhouse of flint with some carstone, raised in height and fitted with casements and dormer windows in 1982. To the road is an C18 clunch and brick bay with longer returns.

EASTGATE HOUSE, 1¼ m. NE. Built in 1836 as a workhouse by *William Donthorn*, but not his best. Terrible minimum Tudor, i.e. no longer late Classical, as workhouses of about 1835 usually were. Of carstone with gault brick dressings. Converted 1996–7 by *Jeremy Stacey* to residential use.

EARTHWORKS. Earthworks on the N side of the road at the W end of the village indicate that Gayton has shrunk. A hollow way with ditches butting it at r. angles expresses sites of medieval tofts along the village street. DESERTED VILLAGE EARTH-WORKS N of the road and ¼ m. W of Well Hall include ditched enclosures and a hollow way. They probably represent the medieval settlement of Well. (AR)

GAYTON THORPE

ST MARY. Small, of rough flintwork. Beautiful round tower with big shafted two-light Norman bell-openings. Column to separate the two lights. Zigzag decoration in the arch. W window below of two splayed lancets. Round-arched opening into nave. The lower external courses have carstone from the Sandringham quarries. Chancel with Y- and intersecting tracery, i.e. of *c.* 1300, if it represents the original state. To the l. and r. of the chancel arch heads of a knight and lady of *c.* 1300. Perp nave, but the carstone quoins at the W indicate an earlier build. Roof of hammerbeams (replaced by tie-beams) sending arched braces up to the collars, alternating with arched braces directly up to the collars. Restored 1900. – FONT. Octagonal, Perp. With the Seven Sacraments and a seated Virgin. – REREDOS. Of C18 fielded panelling with a pediment.

GATEHOUSE FARMHOUSE. C18, carstone, flint and brick house of one and a half storeys, at some point raised up to its present height, as the gable-ends show. Casement windows. The BARN to the E is C17 but unremarkable apart from the fact that it is timber-framed, this not being a timber-framed part of the county. Tarred weatherboarding. The roof structure somewhat altered.

ROMANO-BRITISH VILLA. On the common close to a tributary of the Nar is the site of a villa excavated in 1922–3. It consisted of two conjoined winged-corridor-type buildings, with a detached bath-house nearby. Most of the rooms had tessellated floors, and finds include painted wall plaster and marble veneer. The villa was occupied from the late C2 to the C4. (DG)

BARROW. Known as the Hill of Peace, the only barrow remaining from a large group (JW).

6020

GAYWOOD

Technically Gaywood is in King's Lynn. By about 1900 E expansion of King's Lynn along Lynn Road and Gayton Road reached the village and by the 1930s Gaywood had effectively become a suburb.

ST FAITH. Of brick with ashlar dressings. Little now remains of the Perp church which followed the Norman one. The restorations of 1808 by *Francis Goodwin* (rendering the walls), 1898 by *H. J. Green* and 1906–9 by *W. D. Caröe* saw to that. Of Caröe's time is the chancel chapel, chancel roof, the vestry and restorations to the transepts. In 1923–6 the whole nave was rebuilt and given aisles (also by *Caröe*), and in 1989 the SW nave chapel was added. Caröe's nave arcades are wide and four-centred, with spacious crossing arches to go with them, not unsuccessful. Externally however the E window is Dec (three-light, reticulated tracery), but the transepts so re-worked in the C16 as to seem Tudor under the repairs, and the Perp W tower looks C17 Gothic. Norman bits built into the outer N aisle wall and the inner S and W walls of the S aisle. A Norman doorway was reused in the N porch when the porch was rebuilt in 1923. It has one order of colonnettes and zigzag in the arch. – FONT. Octagonal, Perp, but with C17 inscriptions on the bowl alternating with tracery patterns. – PAINTINGS. Two interesting C17 panels, one illustrating the Arrival of Queen Elizabeth at Tilbury in 1558 with the Defeat of the Armada in the background, the other the Discovery of the Gunpowder Plot. –

CHANCEL STALLS and PULPIT. 1909 by *Caröe*. – STAINED
GLASS. E window by *Powell*, 1909; Christ in Glory with rich
Perp architectural canopies. S aisle E by *Rosemary Rutherford*,
1967.

CREMATORIUM, Gayton Road. *See* King's Lynn, p. 478.

QUEEN ELIZABETH HOSPITAL. *See* King's Lynn, p. 478.

KING EDWARD VII HIGH SCHOOL, Gaywood Road. *Basil* 122
Champneys is principally remembered for his schools and colleges
in the Dutch Queen Anne revival style, but this school is neither
as cleanly articulated as his later Bedford College, nor as charming as Newnham College, Cambridge. Begun 1903, opened in
1906 by the king and paid for by a local benefactor, William
Lancaster, who was knighted there and then in the Great Hall.
Cunningly Champneys designed the façade to face the railway
line to Sandringham, probably at his patron's suggestion. The
materials are brick and plaintiles, the leitmotifs Dutch and
shaped gables and, of course, the white-painted windows. The
big main block has Dutch gables staring over the roofs of the
projecting side wings, themselves ending in shaped gables.
Their junctions with the entrance (E) side are marked by an
odd pair of round stair-turrets, projecting further still. Four tall
rounded casements separated by pilasters with Ionic capitals
light the hall, galleried inside on square piers under a ribbed
barrel vault. Two compact blocks N and S bristle with more
gables. Immediately in front a bronze STATUE of Edward VII,
signed by *W. R. Colton* R.A., 1906, Baroque and slightly camp
(can this inscription have been added? Colton was not made up
to R.A. until 1919).

The PORTER'S LODGE, on the road by the present main
entrance, reveals *Champneys* in his domestic mood, and to this
we look to his own house, Hall Oak, Hampstead, of 1881: square,
hipped roof, clustered stacks at the apex, oversized dormers with
segmental tops like Newnham.

ALMSHOUSES, W of Porter's Lodge. Simple quadrangular set of 78
eight, rebuilt in 1649 following a fire, the entrance in the N side
under a gable. Brick, single-storeyed and calm. The windows
are mainly C18 casements, though one (to No. 5) retains its
sunk-quadrant moulded jambs, as does an exterior window on
the N. The arched braces to the roof collars are from the 1904
restoration.

BISHOP'S TERRACE (Nos. 71–77 Lynn Road), ½ m. NW of the
church at the actual village centre. Very late C16 and built as a
single house. Symmetrical façade on the E-plan with straight
gables and pedimented windows, including the central porch.
Only two cross casements survive, lighting the first floor, but
they are renewed. Elsewhere quite a collection of different
types, mostly in reduced openings. The ground floor cruelly
hacked into shopfronts and the interior features removed.

MEMORIAL CLOCK. In front of the last. 1920. Moved from the
centre of the road junction a little E and set on a plinth of engineering bricks. Square. Limestone base, carstone above with limestone dressings and a clock stage tempered with half-timbering.

GAYWOOD HALL, Gaywood Hall Drive, E of the church, well
placed at the S of Gaywood Park on the site of the bishop's
palace. 1851 for Richard Bagge, one of the family of Lynn
merchants. Various uses since the 1930s (it is now the Norfolk
College of Arts and Technology) have altered the interiors save
for minor cornices and main staircase with cast-iron balusters.
Big single-storey extensions to the back (SE) 1985. Knapped
flint with gault brick dressings. Asymmetrical. Central four bays
of sashes in two storeys and a closed and glazed porch on
unfluted columns. Sashes to ground floor tripartite. Three-bay
wings set back r. and l., that to E preceded by a square three-
storey tower carrying the date.

GELDESTON

ST MICHAEL AND ALL ANGELS. C12 round tower, the arch to
the nave rebuilt C14, the top rebuilt C19. The rest of the church
mostly Victorian as well, especially the chancel (1864–6 by
Thomas Penrice) and N transept (1864 by *J. L. Clemence*).
Transept with a conspicuous twin arch from the nave, on a
marble column with stiff-leaf capitals. The nave S wall looks
untampered-with and early even if the two two-light windows
are Perp. The S porch is Perp. In the spandrels of the entrance
the Instruments of the Passion and the emblem of the Trinity.
Above the entrance a niche with a shield. Flushwork in the
buttresses. The nave has a scissor-braced roof with principals
on arched braces dropping to wall-posts. Chancel with paired
lancets and quatrefoils. – FONT. Octagonal, with four lions
against the stem, four roses and four shields (including again
the Instruments of the Passion and the emblem of the Trinity)
against the bowl. On the step an inscription referring to William
Garneys and his wife. – STAINED GLASS. The E window 1957,
by *Leonard Walker*. – In the churchyard a number of attractive
HEADSTONES.

GELDESTON HALL. Thomas Kerrich had his family home built
in 1777 and the last Kerrich sold up in 1930. The architect is
not known. Simple, when built, of five by three bays, two
storeys and a hipped roof with dormers. The main (entrance)
front to the S. Grey brick. During the course of the C19, probably
around *c.* 1880, the parapet was raised in height to form a further
half-storey above a thin cornice engulfing the dormers, the
porch was removed from the S front and a new entrance made
in the E return. At the same time a tripartite window was
inserted in the S front and the interior plan altered. The surprisingly bold staircase is all late Victorian. Renovations of 1990–1
have returned the house to two storeys and dormer attic and
substituted a partly balustraded parapet for the cornice.

At WEST END, ½ m. W, is RUSH FEN COTTAGE and CHILVERTON'S
COTTAGE, an early house, split up and altered. The timber
frame only skinned in brick at the E end, to Rush Fen Cottage,
and here the exterior details all seem C20. However there are

two octagonal jowled posts at the first floor, with trenches for passing braces in the posts and in the tie-beam which links them. The posts have capitals and straight braces to an aisle plate. So we have one bay of an aisled hall, probably C14. Chilverton's Cottage was added in the C17: two ovolo-moulded mullioned windows s of the stack, one with the date 1618.

DANEGELTS, The Street. The house is newer than the name suggests, but still a timber-framed C16 hall house with an inserted C17 floor and a C17 roof of butt-purlins. The C17 stack was inserted in the screens passage, but the exterior passage doors remained where they were, thus creating a lobby-entrance: a text-book progression.

OLD HOUSE, by the crossroads near Kells Acres (*see* below), SW of the church. Red brick, C18. The doorcase has panelled pilasters and consoles behind a trellis porch. Sash windows. The front of five bays divided into a two-bay mid-C18 part to the l. (with a C19 canted bay) and a later r. part. The garden has a long undulating forcing wall to the street, i.e. a CRINKLE-CRANKLE wall. Late C18.

MANOR FARMHOUSE, Dunburgh Road. The façade has various cross casements and a five-light mullioned window to the l. The ovolo mouldings early C17. The s side has a two-storey porch with a four-centred arch below a triangular niche. C17 door and frame inside.

KELLS ACRES and KELLS WALK, ½ m. WSW of the church. Linked closes of council houses by *Tayler & Green*, 1947–54. One of their best. The houses group themselves, apparently casually, into an organic village with terraces set at angles and of different heights. As the land slopes away s towards the Waveney valley, terraces, literally terraces, of single-storey houses pick up the architect's established themes, finishing at the bottom (KELLS WAY) with more two-storey groups. At the w end of Kells Way, set back at an angle to the other houses and to each other, two groups of pairs of old people's cottages. Yellow brick, red brick and colours. The drawback is the UPVC replacement windows. Further houses intended but not built. On the work of Tayler & Green in the Loddon Rural District, *see* Introduction, p. 165.

GILLINGHAM

4090

ST MARY. A Norman church of nave, central tower and chancel. The chancel however was replaced in 1859–69 by a super-Norman aisled nave with chapels and its own apsed chancel. The C19 three-bay nave has piers of the Durham-Norwich type with zigzag and spirals. The architect was *T. Penrice* of Lowestoft, a pupil of G.G. Scott, and one can only marvel at his self-assurance and that of his client the Rev. John Farr, both convinced that they could do Norman better than, at least the local, Normans. One further wonders why the original roof was left as an albeit restored, but substantially C13, scissor-braced type. The carved winged angels at the bottom of the moulded wall-posts are, of course, of 1859. The view from the E is of two apses (centre and S), flat pilaster buttresses, the main apse with single round-headed lancets. Externally, the Norman tower has a S and a N window with continuous zigzag moulding. The bell-openings are twin, with zigzag in the arch and cushion capitals to the dividing column, the whole set under a blank arch. To the l. and r. a blank arch also, each of the three with roll, billet and bobbin decoration.

Penrice's chancel arch is roll-moulded and in the apse are two bays of blank arcading beneath each window. The S aisle W window has so much nailhead ornament encrusting the internal jambs that one feels one could saw wood with it. All this is astounding, and our attitude to it is coloured by whether the old chancel had to come down or could have been saved. The Norman nave was truncated, possibly in the C17, leaving a square space abutting the tower and now used as a porch. The W door was re-set. Inside this fragment of a nave are two bays of a C13 scissor-braced roof, like those over Penrice's new nave. W doorway with one order of shafts and one-scallop capitals. Roll moulding and hoodmould with billets. N doorway also with one order of shafts but with primitive volute capitals. Arch with zigzag. In the S wall of the former nave one Norman window. Lighting the space under the tower are two similar splayed windows, one N and one S. This central space is preserved to perfection. Four plain arches on imposing square piers with simple imposts. A little decoration on the W and E imposts. The presence of four tower arches suggests transepts, but they seem not to have been provided. – FONT. Neo-Norman, square, the stem with spiral decoration. – SCREEN. Two panels of the dado with fragments of an inscription. – STAINED GLASS. W window by *Charles Kempe*, †1895. – In the apse and S chapel glass by *William Warrington*, 1859. – MONUMENT. Wall monument to Sir Nicholas Bacon †1666. An alabaster and marble cartouche with Corinthian columns (nave, S wall, W of tower).

ALL SAINTS. Of the neighbouring church of All Saints, just to the N of the churchyard of St Mary, only the tower remains upright. The rest fell in 1748. Two-light Perp W window. Brick arch to the E indicating the C15, and indeed there are bequests of 1461–77.

OUR LADY OF PERPETUAL SUCCOUR (R.C.). Also a neighbour of the Anglican church – to the S. By *F. E. Banham*, built in 1898 for J. G. Kenyon of the Hall, a convert to Rome, who had lived in Italy and became a Papal Chamberlain. An Italophile, he specified the Italian style, partly to break from the Anglican plan and style then being adopted for new Catholic churches elsewhere in the diocese and partly as a contrast to St Mary. Red brick and large for a private chapel, with a nicely detailed and confident W end consisting of two tall thin towers ending in open lanterns. Between them is a pedimented centrepiece. Two tiers of pilasters to the nave walls, containing blind recesses to the base and oculi to the attic storey. Apsed E end, without windows. Barrel-vaulted interior, simple and effective. The side walls have a continuous moulded entablature on pilasters with recessed arches to the nave; the vault has transverse ribs. Kenyon's daughter removed the applied marble facing originally fitted. Good cast- and wrought-iron W SCREEN.

GILLINGHAM HALL, E of the three churches. A big two-storeyed Jacobean house of red brick, re-windowed and internally remodelled in the C18. It was probably built for Sir Nicholas Bacon †1624. The W front is in the shape of an E, but with one more bay to the l. and r. beyond the projecting three-storey wings. Gables with rounded finials to apexes and to their broad kneelers. Stack with four octagonal shafts. At the back towards the N an excessively tall stair-turret or look-out in six storeys, square below, octagonal above and crowned with an ogee cap. It reaches high above the roof-line of the house. Beautiful new staircase at the back towards the S put in about 1710 or 1720, with three twisted balusters to each tread and carved tread-ends. The windows are segment-headed. At the back also a C17 N wing. On the S side a later Georgian canted bay window of grey brick was added and also a whole new three-bay wing incorporating a drawing room.

GILLINGHAM HOUSE, once the Rectory. Late C18, six bays, two storeys and dormer attic. Doorcase of thin pilasters rising to a canopy. W gable has an external stack. Good chimneypiece inside and ribbed plaster ceilings.

Among other HOUSES of note, BOUNDARY FARMHOUSE, Beccles Road, has two Dutch gables, and a good door and doorcase from the early C18 with an eared surround. On The Street, Nos. 14–16 are a pair of C17 cottages, rather altered. HILL FARMHOUSE, Yarmouth Road (E of the Hall), has a stair-turret against the S front and sash windows. C18, of two builds. Late C18 is its BARN, with intersecting tracery in a blind W gable facing the Hall and no doubt a wholly decorative feature. Decorative too the stepped gables.

FORGE GROVE. Council housing of 1955–8 by *Tayler & Green*, on the old main road (i.e. before the by-pass was built), SW of the church. A simple layout of two long terraces, one two-storeyed, the other single-storeyed, aligned with each other in a row. They used to be in quiet brown, yellow and black brick, with only one colourwashed house, but all that changed quickly. The simplicity of style and the manner in which the terraces sympathize with their surroundings were revolutionary in their day, and, one might say regrettably, still are. For Tayler & Green's council housing for Loddon Rural District Council *see* Introduction, p. 165.

GISSING

ST MARY. Round tower with those characteristic circular windows which are considered a hallmark of Anglo-Saxon construction but which carried on well into the Norman period. Below on the W side a flat Norman two-light window with incised zigzag

surround. Bell-openings also Norman, of two lights with a
dividing shaft with a heavy early scallop capital. Tall tower arch
with plain imposts and zigzag in the arch. Norman s doorway
into the nave. One order of shafts with more advanced scallop
capitals and again zigzag in the arch. The nave quoins on the
other hand may show some traces of long-and-short work, but
there is no certainty about it. s chapel of two bays with a short
octagonal pier and pointed arches of just one slight chamfer, i.e.
of the early C13. The N chapel has now one large round arch
also with a slight chamfer. It may be an alteration from two former
pointed arches, when the chapel became the funeral chapel of
the Kemp family. The chapel has two windows with Y-tracery.
In the nave one Dec N window. The rest Perp. Perp N porch of
two storeys with flushwork panelling. Entrance with fleurons in
the arch. Niches l. and r. Money was left for its construction in
1474. The climax of the church is its nave roof which, in spite of
the building's small size, is a double hammerbeam roof. The
hammerbeams are crenellated and end with angel figures. The
wall-posts have figures under ogee niches, but were apparently
longer, having been cut off to allow insertion of the larger side
windows. – FONT. C15. Octagonal. – SCREEN. To the Kemp
Chapel. Only a high balustrade; Jacobean. BENCH ENDS. A few.
– MONUMENTS. Four Kemp tablets make instructive compar-
isons. Not one of them has any figures. They are Robert †1614
(alabaster), Sir Robert †1710, a copy of Stanton's monument to
Dean Fairfax in the cathedral (GF), Robert †1734 (chancel),
and several members of the family by *Charles Regnart*, before 1815.

GISSING HALL, 200 yds NW. Sir William Kemp remodelled the
former Rectory into the big mid-C19 house we see now. Red
brick. The effect relies on the busy skyline contrived by the
multiplication of gables, porches and towers, loosely based on a
Jacobean E-plan house, though the recesses of the E are filled
in. The SE front has a central gabled porch, a bay either side
and projecting stepped gables at the ends. But it is asymmetrical, as a four-storey clock tower has shouldered its way into
the façade next to the l. stepped gable. Plain interiors save for
the cantilevered stone staircase with its scrolled iron balusters.

OLD HALL, ¼ m. SW. Immediately s of the moated site of the earlier
Gissing Hall (demolished). Early C17 timber-framed house,
decaying rapidly, but still with scraps of pargeting.

A collection of C17 and C18 timber-framed cottages make up the
VILLAGE. Only THE COTTAGE, Upper Street, needs singling
out: s end is late C16, despite the evidence of the C19 and C20
windows, and has a wind-braced roof. To the N is a C17 cross
wing, jettied to side and gable.

9020

GODWICK

ALL SAINTS. Only the tower remains, still with its arch towards
the nave. Flint with brick dressings. Brick bell-openings with
Y-tracery. The church was called in 1602 'wholly ruynated and

decaid long since'; so the tower is no doubt of the C17 (cf. Litcham).

GODWICK HALL. In 1580 the land was acquired from the Drurys by Sir Edward Coke, the Chief Justice, and he had the house built in 1586. The Cokes remained here till their move to Holkham. The house has been demolished, having been long in ruins. It was of red brick with diaper of vitrified blue brick, and had a two-storeyed porch with gable, steep pediment above the entrance and a brick trefoil frieze below the roof. A broad projection was to the l.

There is a WALLED GARDEN and, 300 yds S of the former Hall, a BARN. Brick, laid in English bond. Long, with pedimented doorways and windows. The seven three-light windows of brick are mullioned and transomed like the former house. It was once two-storeyed and with an attic, so it was built as a house, not a barn. Plenty of later openings. The roof is interesting in that it is of the Waxham barn type – alternating hammerbeam and arch-braced trusses, three tiers of butt-purlins, collars and wind-bracing. The date presumably also 1586.

EARTHWORKS of DESERTED VILLAGE. An E–W street runs to the N of the church and is bordered by five or six tofts on the N. Two side roads run off to the S. The site, though well preserved, is made more complex by earthworks of the Hall garden and by numerous post-medieval clay pits. Godwick, never populous, had ceased to be a village by c. 1600. (AR)

GOODERSTONE 7000

ST GEORGE. Unbuttressed C13 W tower with a Dec W window and cusped lancets to the ringing chamber, cusped Y-tracery bell-openings, Dec parapet. Dec also the arch to the nave (three chamfers dying into the imposts). E.E. chancel with three stepped E lancets shafted inside and lancets to the sides. Priest's doorway on the S. Double piscina, arches with pointed trefoils. Low sedilia, 12 ft long, without any superstructure, just one arm l. and one r. Strange arrangement to the W of the sedilia: a window with a lowered sill (former lowside window?) and an aumbry with a shouldered lintel. Dec S aisle and S porch, although the W window is a lancet. The aisle E window fully Curvilinear. The porch has one charming and very unusual motif, circular side-windows, each with three trefoils set in. Dec (or Early Perp) four-bay S arcade with polygonal projections without capitals to nave and aisle, and semicircular ones with polygonal capitals to the arches. The chancel arch may be of the same date. Four good Perp N windows, three with basket arches, and all with transoms and stepped upper transoms. Nave roof is a C15 hammerbeam, re-assembled and partly renewed in the C17. Perp clerestory. – PULPIT. Simple, Jacobean, with fluted frieze. – SCREEN. C15. Tall, of one-light divisions with simple tracery. Painted on the dado the twelve Apostles with Creed texts, and demi-figures of angels above. On the centre doors damaged figures of the four Latin Doctors. (DP) – STALLS. C15. At the back of the screen. – BENCHES. Late C15 or early C16. A fine set with pierced backs with tracery patterns, poppyheads, and arm-rests where figures have been sawn off. Long benches for the nave, short ones for the S aisle. – STAINED GLASS. In the S aisle bits of the C14, also of figures.

GOWTHORPE MANOR see SWARDESTON

7030
GREAT BIRCHAM

ST MARY. A Late Norman doorway with colonnettes with scallop capitals and zigzag in the arch, reused in the E wall of the SW tower, and in the process made pointed. It opens into the S aisle. Of the early C14 the tower itself, the E windows of the aisles, the good N doorway with two orders of colonnettes, the chancel windows (but the E window is of 1850) and also the arcades and the chancel arch. Both have the same mouldings. Arcades of four bays. Piers with four shafts with fillets and four thin hollows in the diagonals. Double-hollow-chamfered arches. Seats round the piers. Perp alterations account for the big, five-light, transomed W window of the nave (renewed), and the big N porch with a little flushwork and three ogeed niches above the entrance. Inside is blank arcading including the two two-light windows on either side. All roofs c. 1850. – FONT. Of c. 1200. Purbeck marble, octagonal, the familiar pattern with two shallow round arches to each side. This is quite early for an octagonal font. – ALTAR TABLE (S aisle). With mighty bulbous legs. Inscribed 'Donum' and '1640'. – PULPIT. C17, with the usual blank arches and panels above them which have cherubs' heads and wings. The steps are C18. – BOX PEWS. 1850, with poppyheads (cf. Bircham Newton). – SCREEN. C15. One-light divisions. In the dado ornamental stencilling of small roses and fleurs-de-lys.

WINDMILL, W of the village. Brick tower mill of 1846 with a new cap of 1979 and steel stocks 1980 and 1983, this restoration by *John Lawn*. All machinery intact, but not necessarily the original pieces.

BARROWS. On the common is a widespread line of Bronze Age barrows running NW–SE, that at the N end being a bell with a diameter of 90 ft. On the other side of the road are two bowls and a bell, all of over 100 ft in diameter. The bell originally contained a central cremation under a cairn of flints, with a bronze awl and several buttons covered with incised gold leaf, all within a handled urn similar to some finds made in Wessex barrows.

8000
GREAT CRESSINGHAM

ST MICHAEL. The lay parts rebuilt in the C15. Various bequests
26   1415–51. Perp W tower by, it seems, *James Woderofe*, who

ceased to be active in 1451. Over the w doorway is a frieze of shields and crowned Ms in foiled circles, and traceried spandrels (cf. Hilborough next door). Big three-light panel-traceried w window. Battlements with shields. Perp s porch also attributed to *Woderofe*, 1439. Base frieze of flushwork with crowned Ms and crowned swords (for St Michael). Niche above the entrance with a defaced figure (St Michael?). Angle-shafts inside for wall arches (cf. Hilborough again). Perp N and s aisle windows, but the N doorway indicates an earlier date. Clerestory windows of Dec mouchette forms, but probably C15 too. Fine chancel of *c.* 1300 with, to the l. and r. of the big Perp E window (with stepped-up and stepped-down transoms), broad flat buttresses carrying massive pinnacles of a section of a spur between two keeled shafts. These are odd; they look *c.* 1200. The N and s windows uncommon in their tracery but also convincingly of *c.* 1300.

Inside, the chancel has very big, massive wall arches on attached semicircular shafts in four bays. The arcades of four bays originally of the same date, but only the w responds are complete in that state, the rest rebuilt in 1885. Of the C13 nave the clustered sw respond remains. Very fine roof of alternating hammerbeams and simply arched braces. Simpler hammer-beam roof in the chancel. – FONT COVER. Jacobean, simple. – BENCHES. Some few with original poppyheads. – PANELLING. Jacobean, at the E end of the s aisle. – STAINED GLASS. Much C15 glass in the heads of the N aisle windows. – SOUTH DOOR. C15, probably 1439. – MONUMENTS. Brasses to Richard Rysle †1497 and wife, 18 in. figures; to William Eyre †1509 and wife, 3 ft figures; to John Aborfeld †1518, 19 in. figure.

MANOR HOUSE. Formerly known as Great Cressingham Priory although there was never a religious house here (but the land was held by the Chapter of Norwich). Fragment of a sumptuous brick house of *c.* 1545, but still without any Renaissance details. John Jenney came to the site in 1542 and of his great courtyard-planned house only the SE block stands, and of this the s front 69 alone gives an impression of what the building was like. This front has three polygonal towers with one window bay between each, now with C19 cross casements, the lower r. window partly formed into a door. The flanking towers seem to have risen higher than the present roof-line, perhaps matching the central one, which develops into a twin-flued stack. The w tower has three lancets to the ground floor. The first floor has the really spectacular decoration. First a frieze of intersecting arches upside down with big leaves all of brick; above this the whole upper floor and the turrets are faced with blind brick tracery in vertical terracotta panels, of the kind one expects in the Hanseatic towns rather than in England. In the panels small emblems, repeating a hand holding a hawk and a wreath with the monogram of John and Elizabeth Jenney.

The E gable has the same frieze as that below the panelling, but right side up, running just below the roof-line. The terracotta details are virtually the last in England of a fashion most popular

in the 1520s, but link the house with a group of halls in Norfolk
(cf. Great Snoring and East Barsham, Vol. 1) which also relate
in their use of terracotta to the series of tombs of this material
(e.g. the Bedingfeld tombs at Oxborough, the Jannys tomb in St
George, Colegate, Norwich, and the Wymondham Abbey tomb,
all of the 1520s). The tombs are generally Renaissance, the halls
less so, Great Cressingham least of all, despite its late date.

The rear also displays the terracotta frieze and a plinth. Half
of the façade is now inside a late C16 two-storey addition of lobby-
entrance plan. Diapered brick to ground floor, some pargeting
under the eaves to E side and a rebuilt gable with the date 1674.
Inside this part are many roll-moulded bridging beams and
joists. The earlier block has two arched fireplaces in the chimney
turret. To the l. of the 1540s wing is a stone four-centred carriage
entrance, purely Perp, which formed a gateway into the central
courtyard. This links to another turret of the same type as those
to the house, but reduced. Further W is the remains of yet
another turret, so all in all a substantial enclosure.

On THE STREET two houses. THE VINES, timber-framed, faced
with brick. Two storeys with, to the E front, an C18 platband
and C18–C20 details. The rear has a C17 mullioned window.
C17 ridge stack. The bridging beams are C17 and inserted, but
of an earlier house nothing has come to light. THE GRANGE,
built in the late C18 as the Rectory. Gault brick. S front of two
storeys in five bays. Entrance front to E of three bays with a C19
Gothic porch. W front with an early C19 iron balcony.

GREAT DUNHAM

ST ANDREW. An Anglo-Saxon church, or rather one which in all
probability belongs to the overlap, that is the later C11 or early
C12, but essentially still in an Anglo-Saxon guise. Built with
much use of Roman tiles for arches. Nave, central tower, chancel
and former apse (foundations discovered in the C19). The
blocked W entrance is triangle-headed, and surrounded at some
distance by an ornamental band. The band, however, is of
Norman billets. The angles of the nave and the tower have
unmistakable long-and-short work and the tower windows are
double-splayed. The bell-openings are of two lights with a deeply
recessed shaft. To the W and E there are two circular holes
above them. Perp crenellated parapet. Inside the nave, starting
only at a height of about 5 ft, blank arcading on the N and S
sides, with imposts decorated in Norman nailhead and zigzag.
The arcading is cut into for the later windows. W arch of the
tower unmoulded and Norman-looking, with dogtooth imposts,
but the E arch surrounded again at some distance by two bands
in a wholly Saxon way. The rope motif of the E imposts is also
within Saxon possibilities. Above the W arch high up was a doorway. In the N nave one splayed round-headed lancet, and an
early C13 angle piscina (SE nave, by the pulpit). Later additions
include the blocked C13 N door and the nave S window with two

lancet lights and a quatrefoiled circle over, i.e. plate tracery. Yet later the early C14 three-light w window with intersecting tracery. Perp chancel and Perp also the s porch with nice entrance, heavily moulded arch within a square surround and later brick diagonal buttresses. C19 crown-post nave roof. – FONT. Octagonal. Stem with eight hung-up shields. Bowl with four defaced shields and the signs of the four Evangelists. – PULPIT. Re-assembled out of four arcaded Jacobean panels. – READER'S DESK. One similar Jacobean panel.

ROOKERY FARM, ⅜ m. s, at junction with Great Fransham Road. In the garden and the buildings, especially a BARN, many fragments, mostly Norman, from the demolished church of ST MARY which stood 50 yds w of St Andrew in the Old Rectory garden. The ruined wall which remains may represent the E wall of the church. ROOKERY FARMHOUSE is early C19, itself reusing masonry, and three bays in two storeys and two later C19 canted bay windows. Porch with unfluted columns.

In the OLD RECTORY garden there are, moreover, odd stones of the C12 and C13. St Mary had a separate incumbent till about 1500.

SHRUNKEN VILLAGE EARTHWORKS including a moated (?) site in a pasture field N of the Rectory. (AR)

GREAT ELLINGHAM

0090

ST JAMES. Essentially an early C14 church. w tower with characteristic doorway and bell-openings. Battlements with chequer flushwork. Recessed lead spire. Aisled nave and chancel in one, also with much chequer flushwork. Dec aisle windows and doorways. The s doorway is shafted inside; in front of the N doorway a porch, again with chequer brickwork. The chancel has tall three-light windows to the s, two-light windows to the N, and a five-light E window with details just going Dec. Here the wall is again chequered. An odd feature is the w window of the clerestory, which is cut in half by the tower. Yet the clerestory can hardly be earlier than the tower. It may be either a calculated oddity or a miscalculation. The clerestory windows are above the spandrels of the arcade arches, not the apexes.

The four-bay arcades are Dec too, earlier on the s than the N side. On the s quatrefoil with very deep continuous hollows in the diagonals and double-chamfered arches, more C13 than C14, on the N side with four shafts and four separate hollows and arch-mouldings with sunk shallow hollows. In the s aisle a large and wide niche with a little tripartite nodding ogee vault inside. Cusps, crockets and finials, so C14. Remains of exquisite C15 painting, including little angels above a cloth of honour on the back wall, originally behind a carved image of the Virgin and Child (DP). Restored 1981–5 by *Anna Hulbert*. In the chancel the sedilia have been destroyed, apart from the two end shafts. Nave roof with tie-beams on arched braces and tracery above the braces. Re-seated, re-floored and given minor furnishings in

1905. – FONT. Octagonal, with shields in barbed quatrefoils, i.e. Kentish tracery. – SCREENS. Bases only of rood screen and S parclose screen. The base of the rood screen has fields traceried all over. A fragment of the N parclose screen has the tracery only painted on. – WEST GALLERY. Early C18, quite a nice composition. – WALL PAINTINGS. Exposed during the restoration of 1924. In the S aisle, the figure of St Michael on the jamb of a window, conserved by *Anna Hulbert* in 1980. By the S door, a small figure of St Christopher next to a wayside cross. This must have formed part of a rare cycle of St Christopher subjects, combined with the more usual single figure of the saint; the plaster is now in dangerous condition. – MONUMENTS. Brass to a Lady, *c.* 1500, 27 in. figure (N of the altar). – Fysher Colman †1758. By *T. Stafford* of Norwich. Tablet with Rococo cartouche against an obelisk.

BAPTIST CHAPEL, Long Street. 1824 but restored in 1887 when the total-immersion font was installed. The gallery was added in 1847. Brick, with a porch using modified Doric columns to support an Ionic architrave. This in the gable-end, which at three bays is wider than the flanks. The datestone 1699 refers to the first Baptist meeting here.

ISLAY HOUSE, Church Street. A very typical timber-framed cottage with lath and plaster infill built in the mid C17 and given a brick skin in the late C18. Lobby-entrance plan in two cells. The frame remains inside and so do the pair of central fireplaces with the winder staircase behind. The type was the most common house-plan in the county from the C17 to the C19.

THE OLDE THATCHE SHOPPE, also Church Street. A C15 manor house redone in the late C16 and altered since. Timber-framed again, various infill materials. Main fireplace bressumer dated 1580, though rebuilt, with the winder immediately behind. Clasped purlin roof of the C16.

OLD HALL. Timber-framed Elizabethan house with two cross gables. Two-storey front, the end-gables of three storeys. N wing now bricked to ground floor leaving the studwork exposed above. The staircase rises to the attics: sturdy turned balusters on square bases between newel-posts with panelling and ball finials. The handrails moulded.

The BARN 25 yds NW is C17, timber-framed, with some clay lump in the infill, weatherboarded outside. The roof has wind-bracing. 150 yds SE of the house is another BARN, of the date of the house, also timber-framed and weatherboarded. No question of clay lump here. Arch-braced tie-beams, curved wind-bracing.

GREAT FRANSHAM

8010

ALL SAINTS. Former S arcade E.E. of four bays, the piers, capitals and abaci circular, the bases and arches remade Perp. Mid-C14 chancel arch partly rebuilt (cf. Beeston chancel arch). The E window with its curious trellis tracery is probably Victorian. The C13 W tower has a W window and bell-openings with cusped

Y-tracery, i.e. early C14, albeit restored. The N side of the nave has C19 three-light Perp windows, the S side rebuilt after the aisle was removed. C14 are the dying mouldings of the N doorway. – FONT. C15, octagonal, shields to bowl, arcading to stem. – BRASSES. Geoffrey de Fransham †1414. Good, large figure (5 ft); thin buttresses support an ogee gable (chancel, N wall). – Cecily Legge, c. 1500, in her shroud, 18½ in. (nave SW).

THE THATCHED HOUSE, Station Road. Mid-C17 lobby-entrance timber-framed house with remains of a queenpost roof.

HYDE HALL, 1 m. E. c. 1750. Brick, with an outshut added to the rear. Two and a half storeys in five bays. The porch has C18 fluted Ionic columns but has been re-assembled under a bowed gable. (DOE reports a fine stair with turned balusters and carved tread-ends.)

GREAT HOCKHAM HALL see HOCKHAM

GREAT MASSINGHAM

7020

ST MARY. Fine substantially E.E. S porch with polygonal angle buttresses and spirelets. It is not in its original condition, Ladbroke showing in his 1825 drawing a second storey and the side windows blocked. The sides now have tall open arcading on a dado, twice three openings, cusped. This work was by *Daniel Penning* of Eye, 1863, when he was undertaking a general restoration costing £2,000. The S doorway with two orders of colonnettes is E.E., but the porch roof Penning's. Late C13 S arcade. Five bays, quatrefoil piers, moulded arches. The N arcade seems to have been the same, but the piers were partly remodelled in the Perp style when both aisles were modernized. The S aisle was given animals on the battlements at the W and E corners. Perp windows, but that at E end of N aisle remained Dec. Finally C13 the chancel arch and perhaps the whole chancel, see e.g. the clasping E buttresses and the piscina (with a later ogee arch). The E window is much renewed, but could be of the original design. Five stepped lancet lights under one arch. A trefoil at the top of each light. Side windows Perp, as is the sedilia, with four-centred arches. Perp four-stage W tower with big transomed four-light W window above the moulded doorway. Angle buttresses have tracery panels at each stage. Flushwork battlements. Very tall tower arch. Perp clerestory of five bays. Pretty Perp N aisle roof (arched braces with traceried spandrels); nave roof seems to be part of Penning's restoration. – FONT. C14, octagonal, with cusped ogee arches under coarsely crocketed gables. – SCREEN. Late C15; with painted leaves and flowers in the dado panels. – BENCHES. C15. Pierced backs in different elementary but charming designs. Panelled buttresses support the arms. One bench panelled and with figures. – STAINED GLASS. Some original C15 bits in the chancel S and N tracery.

ABBEY FARMHOUSE, Abbey Road. Remains of an Augustinian priory, founded before 1260. The S wall of the present house contains a medieval doorway with a smaller medieval doorway set in, and a lancet window over. At the NW corner of the house a buttress. Big stack to the W side. Rough traces of masonry further W, some distance away. The house itself is early C19, of three storeys in five bays, with giant pilasters at the angles. Doric doorcase on brick columns.

KENNEL FARMHOUSE, Castle Acre Road. Nice very late C18 bowed porch on a pair of columns. This towards the N end of the front. The other end has early C17 evidence in the stone quoins and blocked gable window.

On WEASENHAM ROAD two HOUSES from the early C18. SOUTH VIEW survives in better condition, with a platband and casement windows. PRIMROSE COTTAGE and FANTASIA were a little row, converted to two houses in the C20 and re-windowed.

<h1 style="text-align:center">1000   GREAT MELTON</h1>

ALL SAINTS. Unbuttressed W tower for which a donation is recorded in 1430. Flushwork-panelled parapet with shields in cusped fields. The rest rebuilt in 1883 by *J. B. Pearce* and the N transept added. In the lowest courses of the nave and chancel one can recognize perhaps C11 flintwork. – BENCHES. With poppyheads, late C15; in the porch. – STAINED GLASS. E window by *Gibbs & Howard* †1876, a Crucifixion. Also by *Gibbs & Howard* the Light of the World in a S chancel window, †1897. – MONUMENT. C14 coffin-lid with foliated cross; in the porch.

ST MARY. Of this second parish church only the tower stands immediately S of the tower of All Saints. It is also unbuttressed and also C15. Brick tower arch.

MELTON HALL. The E-plan house built for Thomas Anguish in 1611 was of brick, with polygonal angle-shafts. Now demolished after years of ruination. C18 octagonal DOVECOTE to the SW.

HIGH GREEN is the main settlement, $\frac{5}{8}$ m. SW of the church. WHITERAILS FARMHOUSE is $\frac{1}{4}$ m. S of this. It is an early C16 timber-framed hall house with tie-beams on arched braces, and probably a crown-post on top of that. The early C17 added the internal floors and the brick gable-end with the octagonally flued stack. At the same time a whole new wing added, of three bays, with pediments over the windows and a moulded platband. There are now mainly C19 details. Stepped S gable with more pediments. At the back three external stacks. Polygonal newel to the C17 winder inside. Wind-braced roof.

<h1 style="text-align:center">1090   GREAT MOULTON</h1>

ST MICHAEL. Short W tower of flint and red brick, rebuilt in 1887 with the N aisle. The tower arch however is Norman and rests on the simplest imposts. The nave and chancel walling is also

Norman. Perp s porch with flushwork panelling. Entrance with leaf in one, a Green Man in the other spandrel. Niche over. Roof with arched braces. Perp also the chancel arch, prettily decorated, with small heads up a w and fleurons up an e moulding of the jambs, and along the arch on the w as well as the e. Arch-braced nave roof. – FONT. C15. Octagonal, with four flowers and the signs of the Evangelists against the bowl. – SCULPTURE. Outside the s porch a Norman column with volute capital and rosettes in heavily projecting discs half-way up all four sides. – WALL PAINTINGS. Hideous, 1909. – STAINED GLASS. s chancel window by *Clayton & Bell*, †1889, a St Michael and St George. – MONUMENT. In the churchyard 20 yds ssw a tomb-chest has quatrefoils, trefoils and shields in the C15 side panels; lid and base later, so it seems an assembled piece.

OLD RECTORY. A stuccoed Italianate house, as characteristic of anything one might see illustrated in the patternbooks of villas in the 1840s. In fact the building was just completed in 1832 (drawings dated 1831) and is an unusual style for *W. J. Donthorn*, who specialized in the Tudor-Gothic. It was for the Rev. J.S. Wigget. The asymmetrically placed tower on the s front with its low-pitched pyramid roof and the windows of three separate arched lights ought to be sampled. The tower has an upper loggia. The entrance hall rises through two storeys to a square lantern; open-well staircase with cast-iron balusters.

MANOR HOUSE, Aslacton Road. C17, timber-framed, three bays in two storeys. The central porch late C19. Bridging beams with sunk-quadrant mouldings.

LAURELS FARMHOUSE, New Road. An early C17 timber-framed house with two-storeyed porches to back as well as front. But to the w is a C16 wing.

GREAT RYBURGH

9020

ST ANDREW. Norman round tower with a sturdy one-step tower arch towards the nave. C14 octagonal top stage. The base of the tower and the NW corner of the nave have carstone and carstone quoins. Perp w doorway. Nave and chancel and long transepts. The latter have in their end walls Dec windows with reticulated tracery. That in the s window has inside the reticulation much finer small tracery (cf. Great Walsingham). The transept arches seem Perp, and so does the chancel arch, so the earliest date probably *c.* 1370–80. Perp nave windows. s porch is late C19. Dec side-windows to chancel but a Perp (remodelled) e window. The pretty plaster decoration of the chancel roof with a repeating wreath motif is by *Comper* and dates from 1912. – REREDOS. By *Comper*, 1912, alabaster and gilt. – TILES. A number of the C14 near the font. – STAINED GLASS. All, and there is much, by *William Wailes*, †1866–82. The best are the s chancel window with the Annunciation scene, and the s nave window with the medallion of St Luke. – MONUMENT. A jumble of parts of the C16. The main piece could be an Elizabethan tomb-chest (fluted pilasters and three shields between). Above, the plain back wall of another piece, also probably Elizabethan.

On STATION ROAD, Nos. 25–27 have a jettied first floor and one mullioned window each surviving from the C17.

GRESSENHALL

ST MARY. The core is Norman, but the effect of the church is entirely that of a big, prosperous Perp church. Nave and aisles, tall transepts, a crossing tower, and a chancel. Externally the Norman part appears only in the two-light windows of the tower. The most interesting of these, having an arch made of zigzag, faces W and thus is visible inside and outside. Belfry stage rebuilt C19. The W window is Dec and has Curvilinear tracery. All else is Perp. Money left for the new S porch in 1453. It has two animals at the corner. Chancel buttresses decorated with shields and, on the set-offs, with animals (cf. Diss). The chancel windows have stepped transoms. Inside one looks first of all to the crossing arches for Norman evidence. However they have been altered entirely. To the W the arch has two continuous chamfers, to the other sides odd, but certainly post-Norman, capitals. All four arches are pointed. Arcades of three bays with octagonal piers and double-chamfered arches. Clerestory with six C15 two-light windows each side. In the chancel sedilia and piscina Late Perp with very unusual details, including some defaced geometrical ornament on the back wall. Nice N doorway to a former vestry with a crown and a mitre instead of capitals. The C15 ceiling of the S transept has been restored in the 1950s and very prettily decorated. FURNISHINGS. FONT. Octagonal, Perp. Eight shields against the stem; four shields against the bowl; the other four sides defaced. – SCREEN. Only two units survive. – SOUTH DOOR. With big tracery, C15, probably post-1453 with the porch. – DOOR to stair-tower C15, with painting and ironwork. – SCULPTURE. Small stone panel of the Stoning of St Stephen (above the sedilia). – STAINED GLASS. Crucifixion in W window, by *Ward & Hughes*, 1875, copying that in Brisley Church. – MONUMENT. Large incised slab with figures of a Civilian and his wife; *c.* 1360 (S transept; 6 ft 6 in. figures).

ST NICHOLAS, Rougholm. S transept and ruins of N transept and chancel at Union Farm, just S of the Norfolk Rural Life Museum.

VOLUNTARY AIDED SCHOOL, Church Lane. 1842, at the expense of John David Hill of the Hall, as an inscription records. Brick with stone dressings. One storey, with a Gothic window and a window r. and l. with arched lights. The SCHOOL HOUSE abuts to N: two storeys, three bays, an advanced centre bay with a four-centred Gothic window; four-centred doors and five first-floor windows with arched lights.

NORFOLK RURAL LIFE MUSEUM, 1⅜ m. NE of the church. Built in 1776–7 at a cost of £15,000 as the Union Workhouse. The date is early for Norfolk, though not for Suffolk. Red brick. Completely Classical, the design has an H-block presenting itself as a seven-bay range with a three-bay pediment and a wooden cupola. Either side with short projecting one-bay wings. To the E are two L-shaped extensions formerly with an open arcade to the ground floor linking with the main block. Plans for similar W wings came to nothing. Various additions of 1835–6 followed the Poor Law Amendment Act. A house, CHERRY TREE COTTAGE, was added for aged married couples in 1853 and a chapel by *R. M. Phipson* opened in 1868. The buildings became a museum in 1975; it now houses the Norfolk Archaeological Unit.

MILL, Fakenham Road. The mill has gone, apart from one wall, but the MILLER'S HOUSE remains. Early C19, two storeys in three bays, of colourwashed brick.

SPARROW GREEN FARMHOUSE, ¾ m. SW of the church. Some of the C16 timber frame remains, but it mostly received a brick skin *c.* 1680, unusually early for that embellishment. Two storeys. Central two-storey porch has remains of a mullioned window. Projecting wing has a stepped gable, and in its flank more timber-framing in the first floor.

GRIMSTON

ST BOTOLPH. Quite a big church. E.E. S doorway with colonnettes and some half-dogtooth in the arch. C13 S arcade of three bays with piers of four almost detached shafts and double-hollow-chamfered arches. Why such arches also start against the W wall from both the S and the N responds is hard to explain. C13 priest's doorway in the chancel. The N arcade and the fourth bay of the S arcade are later, say of *c.* 1300. This fourth bay is really a transept, though the arch is only a little wider and only a trifle higher than the others. The arches from the aisle into the transept rest on the outside on a figure corbel. The transepts very obviously raised in height using carstone courses. Their main windows C14. The chancel arch corresponds to the transept arches. Sedilia and piscina are ogee-headed and Dec. Tall ogee-headed niches to the l. and r. of the spiky reticulated E window. The window and chancel roof are of 1889. Perp aisle windows and clerestory. The nave was restored in 1895–6 and provided with a queenpost roof. Perp W tower with W doorway and big three-light W window. Tall tower arch towards the nave. Upper stage added later in the C15 and restored in 1977. – FONT. Octagonal, with five E.E. columns. – SCREEN. Of one-light divisions, mostly C19. Dado with ornamental C15 painting; alternating red and green panels, with foliate designs enclosing tiny stencilled beasts. – STALLS. With blank-traceried fronts and fine MISERICORDS. They have heads to support the mercy seats. – BENCHES. At the W end of the nave. With poppyheads and animals and figures on the arms, e.g. a man in the stocks with a hog slung over his back. – WALL PAINTINGS. Consecration cross on the s wall. The c14 paintings recorded in the s transept are no longer visible. – STAINED GLASS. s chancel window shows a scene of Paul appearing before Agrippa, by *M. & A. O'Connor, c.* 1851.

CLOCK TOWER, junction of Congham and Lynn Roads. A jubilee monument of 1897. Hexagonal, of carstone, with buttresses at each corner and a gablet over the clock faces on alternate facets. The N facet has a doorway and two windows above.

SCHOOL and SCHOOL HOUSE, Gayton Road, by the church. The HOUSE 1830, of carstone with carstone slips, two storeys in three bays. Four-centred door and Gothick windows. Attached to the w gable by a linking piece of 1878 is the SCHOOL, 1850, five-bay front with a gabled porch. Windows under four-centred arches, some with intersecting tracery.

VILLAGE. Several minor FARMHOUSES. From the late c16 is WHITEHOUSE FARMHOUSE, Elder Lane. Altered in the c18 to enclose a low timber-framed house in the w parts of the four-bay façade. There is a garderobe chute of flint and brick, but the main material outwardly is clunch. Windows variously case-ments and sashes. Slightly later is ELDER FARMHOUSE, Elder Lane. Front of two storeys in three bays with a doorcase with stone pilasters, c18. The E return with a platband continuing into rear (N) side where there is a wing dated 1644. IVY FARMHOUSE, Congham Road, also c17. Three-bay E front somewhat altered, and with a two-bay extension to the r. dated 1733. The s gable shows that the house was raised up from one storey and attic, probably in 1733. CHURCH FARMHOUSE, Gayton Road, has an E front comprising a gable to the r. with windows inserted into c17 openings and a wide bay to the l. The gable continues as a cross wing. Pair of c18 BARNS to s, of carstone and clunch.

POTT ROW is a hamlet 1 m. w. WHITEHOUSE FARMHOUSE. Small two-celled c17 house with a cross passage altered by being raised in height and given a small r. extension. THE SHAWS, Chequer Road. Two-storey, five-bay façade with pilasters to the corners and a projecting middle bay under pediment. Platband. Doorway l. of centre under pediment. This all *c.* 1800 added to an c18 house, its age showing in the carstone and sandstone masonry at the back.

ROMANO-BRITISH VILLA. ⅝ m. w of the church is the site of a considerable Romano-British villa, probably of courtyard plan, with a bath suite in the E wing. Unfortunately when it was excav-ated in 1906 the evidence for dating was largely ignored. It was one of a group of settlements near Peddar's Way (*see* also Appleton and Gayton Thorpe). (DG)

GRISTON

ST PETER AND ST PAUL. Mainly c14. In the chancel on the N side remains of what seems to have been a small lancet. Also on the s side a single-chamfered priest's doorway. The other chancel windows early c14, that in the end wall of four lights. The tall, four-stage W tower was being rebuilt in 1477. Top storey completed only in 1568. Flushwork decoration of base and battlements, Perp window and bell-openings, the W window glazed in 1484 at a cost of 36s. 8d., although only a small panel of fragments survives. Tall tower arch. Aisleless nave with Perp windows with two-centred arches. The nave roof belongs to the 1884 general restoration by *J. B. Pearce*, but the six carved angels must be C16. – FONT. Plain, octagonal; an inscription in blackletter commemorates the completion of the steeple in 1568. – PULPIT. Elizabethan, with blank arches; rich relief. The tester is plainer and corresponds to the READER'S DESK. – SCREEN. Probably of the late C14. One-light divisions with ogee heads. Simple tracery. Above the entrance close reticulation. – BENCH ENDS. Some from the C16 in chancel with poppyheads; also a C16 BOX PEW; the rest 1884. – COMMUNION RAIL (now under the tower). Jacobean. – SCULPTURE. Odd architectural fragments close to the N doorway. – STAINED GLASS. Small figures in the heads of one and a half S windows.

GRISTON HALL, ⅝ m. SW. Two blocks, the W one with the date 1597 above the four-centred archway of the central porch. The size of the original windows in the porch and on the main elevation can be determined by the brick hoods over the C19 casements. The gable-heads carry diamond stacks, triple to the N, double to the S. The rear range is slightly later.

PARK FARMHOUSE, Caston Road. Also C16, and of through-passage plan: a wooden four-centred arch to this remains inside but so much was reconstructed in the early C18 and the C19 that little else survives. The construction is mixed clay lump and timber-framing.

WAYLAND PRISON, on a redundant RAF base. 1979–84 by *John Harris* at a cost of £16.5 million and on a site of 70 acres. The 448 inmates occupy four parallel two-storey brick cell blocks containing 112 cells, each of seven blank bays under flat roofs. Enormous WORKSHOP block like any conventional factory unit. The brick-lined CHAPEL could double as a gymnasium, lit through slit windows fitted with STAINED GLASS by *Mark Angus*, 1983. Two-storey galleried HOUSE BLOCK added to the W in 1990 by the *Department of Works*.

Such was the popularity of clay lump in the area that virtually all buildings earlier than the C19 are made of it. Even CHURCH FARMHOUSE, Church Road, of 1847, has it on a flint and brick plinth.

HACKFORD

ST MARY. Plain Norman N doorway which has been moved W at some point. Chancel of the early C14 (cusped Y- and intersecting tracery). Perp nave, W tower, and S porch. The tower has bequests for construction from 1471 to 1523, the last to be paid only when workmen were actually building. The porch is faced with knapped flints and has flushwork panelling on the base

and buttresses and traceried spandrels. This is work of 1870 as
we see it now. Scissor-braced roofs of 1886 by *H. J. Green*.
Windows restored, at least externally, for they have original
rere-arches inside. Rough-looking chancel interior. Trefoiled
piscina. Chancel and tower arches of brick, the former with the
rood-beam brackets. – FONT. Octagonal, late C14. Shields in
cusped fields and symbols of the Passion. – STOUP. C15, by the
S door. Decorated like the stem of a font. – STAINED GLASS.
Small angel in a N window. – SOUTH DOOR. C15.

4090   HADDISCOE

ST MARY. An interesting and puzzling church attractively elevated on an escarpment. It has a round tower divided by three
bands, each stage marginally smaller in diameter than the one
below, and with handsome later battlements with flushwork
chequer. The twin bell-openings are clearly Saxon and as clearly
Norman, i.e. must belong to the so-called C11 overlap. Triangular
heads to the two lights, but a coarse billet surround. The shafts
are too restored to be taken as evidence. Doorway into the nave
with simple imposts. Doorway above this. C15 flushwork parapet. C15 S porch but a Norman S doorway, very decorated, with
decorated capitals, a surround with chip carving, zigzag of two
kinds, and scalloping in the arch, and above it in a niche, again
with a decorated frame, a seated figure, like those on seals. The
lower part of the legs is vertically placed, not at an angle.
Considering the rarity of Norman sculpture in Norfolk, this figure
deserves to be better known. The N doorway is also Norman,
much simpler, but also with a scallop motif in the arch. The
resemblance of the billet motif to that in the tower ought to be
noted.

The puzzle of the church is the N arcade. It is clearly cut
through a pre-existing wall, but the imposts of bay four indicate
that this bay at least is Norman, i.e. probably the entry to a
former transept. Bays one, three and five have two or three continuous chamfers. So it looks as if the aisle as such is raw early
C14 work (and the N doorway was re-set). Although restored by
E. H. Sedding in 1908 the aisle windows confirm such a date, as
do the quatrefoil clerestory windows. But bay two has imposts
again, and imposts different from those of bay four. Were they
done for the sake of symmetry, an unlikely idea, or was there an
early C14 N chapel as well as a Norman N transept? Two small
ogee-headed niches in the W pier of this bay might relate to a
chapel. Chancel of *c.* 1300, see the chancel arch, the double
piscina, and also the internal shafting of the (C19) E window.
Nice beading runs below the window. The two head-corbels
were put in to support the lenten rail. Arch-braced nave, aisle
and porch roofs, repaired in the 1908 restoration. Renewed
Perp windows, and in addition in the chancel blocked circular
windows, perhaps a Georgian alteration? – FONT. Perp, with
four lions against the stem and four angels with musical instru-

ments and the signs of the four Evangelists against the bowl. – SOUTH DOOR. With splendid ironwork of *c.* 1100 applied to a renewed door. It is heavily restored as Cotman's drawing of 1814 shows. There is a large central foliated cross, two opposing C-hinges and two sets of scrolls to the hinges. All elements are greatly barbed. The ring plate is twisted. – WALL PAINTING. On the N nave wall a head of St Christopher with the Christ Child, and further E three heads from a Three Living and Three Dead. C14. Surrounded by whitewash, these isolated fragments now give a very odd impression. On the S wall part of a consecration cross and of a post-Reformation text. (DP) – STAINED GLASS. In S aisle, commemorating Mia Arnesby Brown (wife of Sir J. Arnesby Brown), painter of children and flowers †1931, with a view of the church in the background, by *Martin Travers*. – MONUMENT. Inscription slab of Purbeck marble with a Dutch inscription, translated by Leonard Forster: 'Here lies buried Barbele Jans wife of Pier Piers the dike reeve [she] died anno 1525 the second day in December'. Pier Piers was a Dutchman responsible for drainage and dyke maintenance. Several other black slabs.

WHITE HOUSE, ¼ m. SE. A handsome early C18 brick house of five bays and two storeys with a hipped roof. Pilasters to corners. Segment-headed ground-floor windows with segmental hoods, upper windows with wooden mullion-and-transom crosses, renewed C20. Old leading. Doorway with Doric pilasters and a moulded pediment.

MOCKMILE TERRACE, 200 yds E of the church. This is some of the excellent housing work done by *Tayler & Green* in the Loddon Rural District (*see* Introduction, p. 165). A single, colourwashed terrace, built in 1949–50. One gable with decorated bargeboards towards the main road. First-floor windows arranged in a frieze, but now all of uPVC.

HALES   3090

ST MARGARET. A perfect Norman country church, isolated ¾ m. S 17 of the village, the sister of Heckingham to the N. Thatched. Redundant since 1973. *H. J. Green*'s restoration of 1896 was discreet. Round tower, nave, chancel and apse. Apart from the tower the extent of Norman decoration implies a mid-C12 date. The tower has Dec bell-openings and a C15 flushwork parapet but inside the tower are two blocked round, i.e. probably Saxon, windows. In the nave an exceptionally fine N doorway, crisply carved and full of ornamental invention. By the same craftsman surely as the door of Heckingham. Capitals with foliage, and decoration spilling on to an area of the walls close to the capitals. Six orders in the arch with zigzag, chip-carved motifs, bobbins etc. Hoodmould with wheels. Cotman drew ironwork on the door in 1818, since gone, door and all. The S doorway is simpler, but also has interesting decorative mouldings: five orders in the arch with zigzag, on scalloped capitals. In the s nave one small Norman window, yet with sturdy shafts and a roll moulding. The same applies to chancel and apse. The buttresses are flat above but have nook-shafts below, likewise the quoins of the nave. The E windows have square imposts and there are also blank windows forming an arcade, with decorative sills continuing round the buttresses as a sill band. Unfortunately C13 windows (lancets and Y-tracery) interrupt the Norman composition. Double-chamfered chancel arch without responds. Blocked Norman tower arch hidden by the late C18 W gallery. Boarded nave roof, plastered chancel and apse roofs.

FURNISHINGS. FONT. Late C15. Octagonal. With four lions against the stem, four demi-figures of angels and four flowers against the bowl. – FONT COVER. Jacobean, thin and nice. Scrolled openwork type with a central turned baluster. – SCREEN. Six panels of the dado, but only one with tracery; the panels are painted alternately red and green. (– ORGAN CASE. 1815, and quite charming; removed to Bury St Edmunds.) – WALL PAINTING. A considerable amount, much of it recently uncovered. In the spandrels of the chancel arch, C14 paintings of angels blowing the Last Trump, doubtless the remains of a Last Judgement. Also C14, a figure of St James in the jamb of the SE window over the pulpit, with a foliate border above, and part of a St Christopher on the s wall. Other remains in the nave include consecration crosses, and an odd canopy to a recess in the jamb of the NE window. In the chancel, an upper border of scrollwork and chevron pattern, and C14 painting in and around the image niches flanking the altar, including a canopy and cusping on the N, and rosettes and IHC monograms on the s. (DP)

HALES HOSPITAL, E of the village centre. Built in 1764 as a House of Industry, the first amalgamated workhouse in the county, and early even in England. Large, on an H-plan. Red brick, two storeys, with segment-headed windows. Altered in 1836 by *John Brown*. Unfortunate recent additions for out-patients; the main blocks disused.

HALES HALL, ⅛ m. w of the church. The manor was bought by Sir James Hobart in the 1470s, later Attorney-General to Henry VII. In the 1480s he built a triple-moated complex aligned roughly W–E. The W enclosure seems to have been an orchard and pleasure gardens of unknown character (now a dense wood), in the centre was his house, and the E enclosure contained his barn to the s and an ancillary building for further storage and accommodation for his retinue to the N. These last two remain, the N building restored as the present Hales Hall from 1971. The site was defensible. In addition to the moats there were walls enclosing the centre and W courts, and between the barn and the present Hall to the E there remains a brick wall with firing loops. The Hobarts left in 1647. The estate was bought by Lady Williamson who lived in the original house and repaired the accommodation block, but the house was abandoned in the 1730s and the remainder declined into a tenanted farm. Small-scale excavation in 1961 and later chance finds on the site of the house have revealed an octagonal base of a corner tower, another

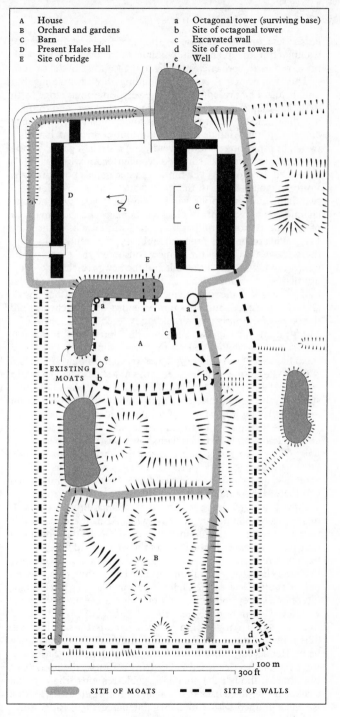

A	House	a	Octagonal tower (surviving base)
B	Orchard and gardens	b	Site of octagonal tower
C	Barn	c	Excavated wall
D	Present Hales Hall	d	Site of corner towers
E	Site of bridge	e	Well

EXISTING
MOATS

100 m
300 ft

SITE OF MOATS   SITE OF WALLS

Hales Hall. Plan

larger octagonal tower base to the S, and several stretches of walling, but the plan is impossible to recover. Other well-preserved earthwork enclosures lie to the E and SE of the E court.

The two principal standing buildings are stimulating but tantalizing. The present Hall is one very long brick range, with dark blue diapering and small mullioned windows, and through it at the W end an archway. This has to the outside (N) polygonal angle-shafts and finials and a wide four-centred arch with a two-light projecting window over it, and a straight gable. To the inside the archway has simply a wooden beam with spandrels decorated with foliage. The timber-framed gable above projects. Four octagonal shafts to the ridge stack. There is one original two-light mullioned brick window on the N side, with hollow-chamfered jambs, plenty of blocked openings and the remainder of the fenestration of timber mullioned windows introduced by Lady Williamson and replaced since 1971 in replica. In 1599 there was a disastrous fire, which consumed the E half of the range, but it was quickly rebuilt and the newer brickwork, without diaper, is obvious. The archway has a late C15 crown-post roof running N–S, the room to the W a queenpost roof (four posts), and a further queenpost structure extends E of the archway until the point of the early C17 rebuilding is reached: the new roof is a butt-purlin type with two tiers of purlins and collars. Inside this part is a brick-vaulted cell, of mysterious purpose. The E end room has a Jacobean chimneypiece salvaged from Bawburgh Hall.

61 Opposite, to the S of the site, is the BARN, also late C15, and at 184 ft the largest in Norfolk. Red brick with blue diapering, stepped gables and thatched. There are three tiers of ventilation loops. It has an imposing roof inside, with ten bays of queen-post trusses rising to collars on braces, and three bays at the E end separated off and roofed with crown-posts above the queen-posts. This area has a four-centred fireplace and an internal floor, so it had domestic purpose. The E gable wall has blocked windows, and on the S side two three-light timber mullioned windows to the ground floor and three above.

From the barn to the Hall is a contemporary brick WALL with diaper decoration and a gateway, widened in the C20. In this wall are similar vertical loops splayed on the inside, which can only be for defence. In the late C15 the wall turned W before the barn was reached, and opposite the gateway was a bridge over the moat into the central enclosure. The bridge disappeared only c. 1900. Close to the Hall is a rectangular C17 brick building of one storey and attic, built outside the defended area but within the E arm of the outer moat.

Three C17 FARMHOUSES. On Church Lane is HALES HOUSE. The lobby-entrance C17 house is to the rear of the 1892 brick wing. Rendered timber frame between brick gables. Sashed in the C19. On Beccles Road is ORCHARD FARM, the house C17 but altered, though the shaped N gable remains. Big external stack to the E gabled back to the main roof. GREEN FARMHOUSE is timber-framed with a brick N gable dated 1759. Ridge stack with little pilaster strips.

GARDENSIDE and THE BOLTONS. Virtually a new village centre, on Haddiscoe Road opposite the pub. By *Tayler & Green*, 1949–54. Stepped up along the road. One colourwashed terrace using quite strong colours and one group of houses in brick, with brown, yellow, black and, in three gables, white. The rainpipes are made use of as a decorative motif, sloping forward from the ground to reach the projecting eaves, just as at Bergh Apton (cf.), though only two houses retain this idiosyncrasy, and almost all houses now have uPVC windows. Good bus SHELTER in front. On the work of Tayler & Green, *see* Introduction, p. 165.

HAPTON

1090

ST MARGARET. W tower built in 1848, the date of a general overhaul. Dec nave and chancel arch. The arch has seaweed capitals on filleted responds, one with a Green Man, *c.* 1310, the two-light nave windows with cusped and squashed reticulation units in the tracery, same date. Two-light Perp chancel windows. – FONT. Octagonal, Perp, plain, with shields. – BENCH ENDS. A few, with poppyheads, C15. – STOUP. In S porch, round, Norman.

Former PRESBYTERIAN CHAPEL. Built in 1749 and still timber-framed, with clay lump infill. Three arched upper windows. Below only a doorway with an original DOOR. Late C20 pantiled roof and internal adaptation to form a house.

HAPTON HOUSE, The Street, next to the last. C18 red brick façade, but the stack with its three octagonal flues suggests the late C16, and so too do the mullioned windows to the rear. Timber-framed.

HAPTON HALL, ¼ m. E of the church. Typical early C19 three-bay gault brick front with hipped roof; sashes. Larger red brick rear parts.

HARDINGHAM

0000

ST GEORGE. A C13 church with a S porch-tower and an aisleless nave – wide and high. The tower has quatrefoil sound-holes and bell-openings of two cusped lights with a circle in bar tracery. The brick parapet no doubt to do with the restoration work recorded in a will of 1523. Bold entrance arch, its mouldings to the inside repeated as the outer mouldings of the much more finely detailed S doorway. In the nave a W lancet, in the chancel a C13 double piscina of the type of Jesus College, Cambridge, i.e. with an arch intersected by two half-arches. The sedilia is of a different composition but the same time. Also of the C13 the chancel arch, the priest's doorway, and a shallow N chapel off the nave. The four-light E window of the church with reticulated tracery is different in Ladbroke's drawing, but supposed to be reliable. The chequered flushwork E wall, though, is downright suspicious. Perp S chancel windows, restored. – FONT. Of the (late) C13 too. Octagonal with trefoiled arches with leaf cusps on colonnettes; not an ordinary piece. – BENCH ENDS. Some original poppyheads. – STAINED GLASS. E window †1899 and most of all others with glass by *Lavers & Westlake*. – MONUMENT. Edward Pawlet Heyhoe †1788, big tablet of various marbles. – TOWER DOOR. C15, with tracery patterns.

HARDINGHAM OLD HALL, ¼ m. SW. Elizabethan or Jacobean. Probably built for the Thwayts who bought the manor in 1580 and resold 1606. Two-storeyed porch, not in the middle, with polygonal angle-shafts cut off at the top when the gable was replaced with the present unsuitable hip. Doorway with pilasters, a round arch and ovolo mouldings. On the ground floor are pedimented windows. The big hipped roof probably of the late C17 when the bay to the r. was added, giving the lopsided appearance. The rear has a pair of external stacks and staircase towers. C18 casements. Late C18 the stick-baluster staircase.

HARDINGHAM HALL, 1¼ m. SE. The original part of the house seems to be of the early C18 but it was all remodelled *c.* 1820. The S front has seven bays of sashes in two storeys, is of red brick, and has a late C19 one-bay projection flanked by giant pilasters and crowned by a pediment. This replaced the C18 porch. To the r. is the return of the E wing added *c.* 1900, one of several Victorian and Edwardian additions, all remarkably tactfully done. The W (entrance) façade retains an C18 platband and four blocked windows with brick surrounds. Nearby a circular C18 DOVECOTE, not in its original position; brick. STABLES. Quadrangular. The five-bay coach-house which forms the entrance dated 1878.

HARDINGHAM GROVE, ⅝ m. NE. Timber-framed early C17 house faced with brick in *c.* 1880 and extended. Two storeys and attics. The C17 part now with a high shaped gable to the porch and a shaped gable-end. The first floor of the new wing has a timbered external passageway supported on brackets.

SCHOOL HOUSE, Station Road. Mid-C19 Gothic school. Gault brick, flint and stone. Diagonal buttresses, various Gothic windows, octagonal chimneyshafts.

3000

HARDLEY

ST MARGARET. Norman round tower with the upper stage repaired and given brick dressings in 1501–4 according to bequests. The body of the church with Perp windows, that to the E end of four lights. The chancel was in fact built in 1456–62, with windows set in wide depressed wall arches inside. N porch however is C14, with an ogeed entrance arch. The lopsided position of the tower suggests that there was a N aisle whose arcade was removed to widen the nave. Roofs are arch-braced. – FONT. C15. On two steps, one of them with cusped quatrefoils. Against the stem four lions, against the bowl the signs of the four Evangelists and four demi-figures of angels. – PULPIT. Jacobean, simple, with flat carving. – SCREEN. Very little is original. Only one C15 panel remains, to the S. – BENCHES. A few C15 ends with poppyheads behind the ends of the C18 benches. Also one complete Perp bench at the W end. – WALL PAINTINGS. On the S side a St Christopher with vine-scroll border and the background decorated with ermine, and to one side a much smaller figure of St Catherine holding the wheel; second half of C14. – Consecration cross on W wall. – BRASS. In chancel, to Drake William Playters †1632, an inscription plate and coat of arms.

HARDLEY CROSS, ⅞ m. ENE. On the River Yare, marking the boundary between the Yarmouth and Norwich river jurisdiction. C16, of limestone. Roll-moulded square tapering shaft rising out of a square plinth. Iron railings of 1899. Plaque records restoration 1834 by *P. Baines*, further restoration 1991 by *Colin Jeffries*.

HARDLEY HALL, 1 m. S of the church. A flint, stone and brick house probably built soon after the manor was acquired in 1554 by William Drake. Two storeys with a flat front and a central porch. With its wave-moulded surround the inner doorway still looks pre-Reformation, as does the original door. The porch entrance with initials W and M (for William Drake and wife) in Roman lettering is probably Elizabethan. Both inner and outer openings have four-centred heads. Two bays l. and three r. of the porch fitted with C19 casements in reduced openings. Octagonal chimneyshafts to the former hall and the kitchen chimneys. The hall has a four-centred fireplace with roll mouldings up the jambs and through the arch. W gable with diaper brickwork. The rear, S side, has a pair of external stacks separated by a stair-turret with a stepped gable.

CHESTNUT FARMHOUSE, 1 m. WNW. Of the mid C17, showing the influence of Artisan Mannerism. The S end of the house, only one window wide, is bewilderingly ornate. Two storeys and a third in the gable. The ground floor has angle pilasters. The windows are framed by bulgy pilasters and the ground-floor window has two pediments side by side, an extraordinary solecism. It is of six lights, with ovolo-moulded mullions and a central king mullion. Upper windows replaced, in reduced openings (cf. Porch House, Brooke).

HARDWICK

ST MARGARET. Round tower, largely collapsed. It fell in 1770 leaving a scrap attached to the nave wall. Nave and chancel in one. Very plain Norman N doorway. The S doorway is Norman too, but seems to have been tampered with in the C13: billet and dogtooth mouldings. A variety of windows, Perp or with Y-tracery. C15 S porch of brick and flint chequer. Roof with arched braces and longitudinal arched braces, probably C15. It runs from W to E without a break. Major restoration in 1882; in 1986 the E wall rebuilt. – FONT. C15. Plain, with panelled stem and quatrefoiled bowl. – SCREEN. Perp. One-light divisions, pointed arches with fine tracery in two layers in depth. Dado with fine tracery. Altered in 1611, and the top rustically renewed in 1661 after damage by Puritans, and with a painted inscription recording the date and the churchwardens' names. – FAMILY PEW. Jacobean, with a tester. Used as a vestry, which has done it no good. – COMMUNION RAIL. Jacobean, with flat balusters. – WALL PAINTING. Fine late C14 St Christopher on N wall, though much of the detail, such as an angler, recorded in the C19 copy hanging below is now lost or hard to decipher. On either side of the saint is a tree, that on the r. with an owl which was shown being scolded by other birds. (DP) – STAINED GLASS. Late C14 fragments in the chancel windows. – MONUMENTS. Thomas Gleane †1660. Alabaster and limestone tomb-chest with shields, the middle one set in a flat cartouche. Its ornament is characteristic of the 1660s. – Sir Peter Gleane †1683. Plain limestone tomb-chest with two shields and an inscription tablet.

HARDWICK HALL, ¼ m. S. C17 timber-framed farmhouse with many additions. The S gable-end is jettied on the first and attic floors, with reused roll-moulded bressumers of c. 1540. Some blocked windows inside, later roof. Immediately NE stands a late C16 BARN with a queen-strut roof.

THE STREET has several C17 timber-framed houses.

0090

HARGHAM

In the Parish of Quidenham

ALL SAINTS. The early C14 W tower now stands alone, as the two w bays of the nave collapsed in the mid C18. Unbuttressed, three stages. The belfry sound-holes are square with ogeed quatrefoils. What remains of the rest is of the same date but with C15 alterations and restorations of 1874. The Perp windows belong to the last date except for the paired trefoil lancet w of the vestry. Roofs and pews 1874, the former scissor-braced, as was the fashion then. Angle piscina C14: double ogee arches and with mouchette tracery.

CROSS, ¼ m. W of the church. c. 1400. Square plinth with chamfered angles and part of a square shaft.

HARGHAM HALL. The five-bay house of Hugh Hare c. 1690 was extended by one bay to the S to provide an entrance to the principal W front in c. 1800 and given a hipped roof at this point. The original part is of colourwashed brick with sash windows. The porch bay projects slightly and has a doorway in the form of a Venetian window. The S return also of c. 1800 and 1815. The house was not long built when the five-bay E front had its moulded brick stringcourse interrupted in the early C18 to allow for a taller central first-floor sash window, which, like the four others at this height, still has its original glazing bars. Central C20 door. Also early C18 is the closed-string staircase rising to the attic with twisted balusters and the characteristically heavy handrail. A SUMMERHOUSE in the walled garden immediately N has a big shaped gable, probably early C18 too.

MOATED SITE. Almost square with a causeway on its N side. Well-preserved although clipped by a road to the SE. (AR)

HARLESTON

Harleston was a new settlement set up in the C13 within the then
more important parish of Redenhall. It was laid out as an elongated triangle round a market place, the market becoming one of
only thirty-one still surviving in C17 Norfolk. The town had by
then become an important local centre, and its market continued
to thrive in the C19, specializing in lambs and cattle. Its slow
decline in the C20 has left an unusual number of good unaltered
C17 and C18 houses, and a celebrated C14 house behind Keeley's
Yard. The C15 church was only a chapel-of-ease, on the site of the
market's clock tower, demolished 1873.

ST JOHN BAPTIST. 1872 by *R. M. Phipson*. Flint with stone trim.
Nave, aisles, transepts, chancel and polygonal apse. No tower.
Clerestory with circular foiled windows. Four-bay arcade of
alternating clustered and round piers, the w bays screened off in
the late C20. Simple but steep arch-braced nave roof. –
STAINED GLASS. E apse window by *M. & A. O'Connor, c.* 1872.
Other glass by *O'Connor*, *W. G. Taylor* and *Wailes & Strang*
from the 1880s, none very good.

PERAMBULATION

A walk through Harleston is easily done. One can start at the
former STATION, Station Road (closed 1960), 1855, grey brick,
Italianate, symmetrical, with pilasters to the side bays rising into
pediments. From here one moves southward into REDENHALL
ROAD. A little to the l. on the E side the finest of the brick
houses of the town, and a fine early Georgian house anywhere,
CANDLER'S HOUSE, of seven bays and two storeys with a
hipped roof. Moulded platband between the floors and sash
windows in flush frames. Doorway flanked by Corinthian
pilasters with an entablature curving up to a point in the middle
and a broken segmental pediment over. The window above the
doorway has a slightly enriched surround and a head as a keystone. The development NE of this point, i.e. out of town on
Redenhall Road, is mainly early and mid-C19, though RICH-
MOND HOUSE has a C17 timber-framed core behind the brick
skin. Then, to the SW and into the town, a good group, chiefly
No. 4 on the E side (C18, two storeys, five bays, partly rebuilt
late C20), and on the W side No. 5, a five-bay house with brick
quoins, the attic storey above the cornice, and a doorway with a
pediment on Composite columns framing a large early fanlight.
C20 shop display window badly intrudes on the r. This C18
brick front is a modernization of a C17 timber-framed house, for
which a rear wing remains. The entrance hall has large-framed
panelling and fluted pilasters. No. 3 much the same, i.e. it also
has a C17 timber frame encased with C18 brick to present a
two-storey, three-bay house, with an attic storey above the
cornice. This last added as a new feature a little later. The bow
windows are C20, the rear wing C17. Of the C17 again No. 1

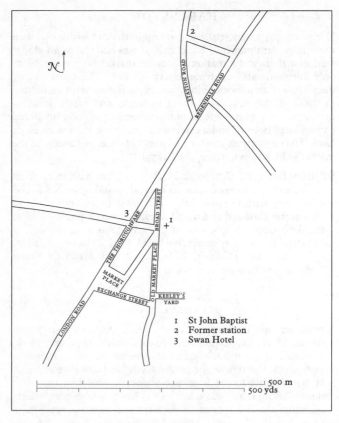

Harleston

(HEYDON HOUSE), modernized in the C18 but not given a
brick skin, so the first-floor jetty remains. Two storeys, five bays
of sashes. Nice tent-shaped porch and a doorcase with a pulvinated frieze. C17 wing at the back and in the garden a GAZEBO,
an octagonal brick structure of *c.* 1830, with a thatched roof,
Gothick windows and some plaster decoration to the roof
inside.

Here the street splits. THE THOROUGHFARE is the continuation and was by-passed in 1981 so is more enjoyable now than
before. One's impression is of nicely scaled C18 and C19 houses
and shops, but many have C16 and C17 nuclei (of the former
Nos. 12, 25, 29 and the CARDINAL'S HAT INN; the latter Nos.
2–4, 9–15, 21, 26, 33, 35, 37). A little way down on the r. finds
No. 27, a small chopped-about timber-framed house of *c.* 1540
with a length of carved jetty bressumer and clustered chimney
flues. Then one arrives at the SWAN HOTEL, with a Georgian
nine-bay front, of three storeys, quite undecorated (ground
floor rendered and painted) except for burnt headers to the

brickwork and a moulded platband and cornice. A carriage arch
cuts through the middle. However a wing at the back has, on
the upper storey, still the low horizontal windows of the C17.
The back of the front range reveals timber-framing as well, but
it is here disguised as C18 demi-columns and pilasters in two
tiers. Good scrolly iron inn-sign. Opposite on a corner No. 14,
early C18, with a Dutch gable and cross casements. It may well
hide an earlier timber frame. After that the small MARKET
PLACE, with nothing in need of recording except the thin but
attractive Victorian CLOCK TOWER of grey brick. This was built
in 1873 by *H. H. Collins* of London, when the old church had
been moved from this site to its new site (i.e. demolished). The
clock tower rises from the corner of the MIDLAND BANK,
which is of the same date. On the s side the MAGPIE HOTEL,
plastered and colourwashed and dating from *c.* 1710. Two storeys
in five bays of (mainly) C19 sashes. LONDON ROAD exits to the
s, with a few altered C17 houses at the beginning, giving way to
C19 villas further on and at Nos. 30–38 a surprisingly large and
townish three-storey terrace.

From the Market Place E along EXCHANGE STREET to the
former CORN EXCHANGE, built in 1849 by *John Bunn*. This has
a windowless front with paired giant Tuscan columns supporting a ponderous and featureless architrave. The ceiling inside of
deep rectangular coffers, those in the middle with roof-lights.
Now partitioned for shops. Exchange Street leads into the OLD
MARKET PLACE, with a number of good houses, of which the
best last. On the w side the former POST OFFICE, a severe
mid-C19 front of three bays and three storeys with a one-bay
pediment, distinguished by the quite unusual articulation of
coupled pilaster strips or lesenes. It is this that gives the façade
its odd restlessness. THE OLD HOUSE has C16 parts inside,
but the six-bay front was added in the C18. Two storeys and
dormer attic. On the s side a six-bay house with a pretty doorcase under an open pediment. On the E side No. 2 is C17 and
timber-framed, Nos. 4–6 early C18, and then No. 8, a late C17
house with a shaped gable and odd segmental hoods for the
windows, like eyebrows. No. 14, C17 and timber-framed again,
which brings us to Nos. 16–18. Through the middle is a carriage
arch to KEELEY'S YARD, facing the top of Exchange Street.
The pair are of two storeys and dormer attic, and have at the
bottom C19 shopfronts inserted into the C18 red brick front.
This however conceals a C16 timber frame. In the yard behind
is a cross wing which is in fact a C14 raised aisle hall house, one
of only two known for certain in Norfolk (the other is at Lodge
Farm, Denton; there are a number in Suffolk. *See* Introduction,
p. 86). Both the beam and the aisle-posts it supports are plain,
and the upper braces from the latter have had to be reconstructed
from the moulding fillets remaining on the posts. Above are
crown-post trusses with solid arched braces going four ways.
The timbers are heavily soot-blackened, proving an open fire.

From here one can turn N into BROAD STREET, where are
many congenial C17 and C18 houses. Most arresting is OLD

BANK HOUSE, on the r. before the church. It is C17, but with the inevitable C18 fronting. Irregularly spaced sashes and two doorways. The r. door much the wider, with a Doric doorcase having fleurons in the metopes, a very slangy Classical. This takes us back to where the main street splits.

HARPLEY

ST LAWRENCE. Of flint. Mainly built when John de Gurney was patron and rector (1294–1332), with Perp additions. The earliest part is the chancel arch. This is no doubt earlier than the late C13. The capitals have stiff-leaf and other leaves. Then, clearly of the late C13, the S aisle. The windows have Y-tracery, and there are fine sedilia and a double piscina inside, too important really for an aisle. The tower was added early in the C14 at the W end of the S aisle. Dec bell-openings and battlemented parapet. The arch towards the nave has three continuous waves. But the main Dec work was the remaking of the chancel, quite a splendid job. The first S window has ogee forms, the second a barbed trefoil above two lights, the third, starting higher, has reticulation. Below this inside are sumptuous sedilia and a double piscina. Fragment of diapering on the back wall. Near to the reticulated window is a small priest's doorway with an elaborately cusped and subcusped ogee arch. In line with this, in the N wall of the chancel, a bigger doorway with an even more elaborately cusped ogee arch and openwork spandrels (restored in 1849) leads into a two-bay vestry, which is rib-vaulted (single-chamfer ribs). The E window of the chancel is an 1878 replacement of a group of earlier windows, leaving the former jambs visible inside.

The Perp additions are considerable. The nave and the S arcade were renewed (five bays, thin octagonal piers, double-hollow-chamfered arches). A clerestory was added c. 1400 with three-light windows and the arch-braced roof without collars was erected (angel figures in the cornice). The N aisle with its Perp windows was built and received an arcade identical with that on the S side. The W front was given a very large five-light window with a transom over ogeed lower lights. The S aisle was enriched by pretty battlements with close panelling (cf. Walpole St Peter) when John Brewe was rector (1389–1421). There are coats of arms of the Knollys family. The S porch is also Perp. It is two bays deep and has side windows and a front with some panelling and three niches. Between the side windows inside some more panelling. In the chancel the plain Easter Sepulchre and the embattled top of the N doorway are Perp too. The restoration came in 1878, at which point the organ chamber and chancel roof were built.

FURNISHINGS. ROOD SCREEN. Of tall one-light divisions with ogee arches and pretty, small tracery above them. Probably late C14. The gaudy flat repainting is of 1865; further restorations 1877. – BENCHES. Perp. With charming pierced, quatre-

foiled backs. The ends have poppyheads or little figures instead
and small animals on the arms. – STAINED GLASS. In the S aisle
E window big Perp canopies. In the W window angels and
Saints. In the side windows glass of the 1930s, The Lord is my
Shepherd. Quite good. Who made it? – MONUMENT. The brass
to John de Gurney has gone but the burial-slab remains in the
chancel. – SOUTH DOOR. A splendid Perp piece with, on the
frame, figures of Saints and the Four Doctors of the Church in
niches. On the wicket signs of St Luke and St John.

WILLIAM HERRING'S ALMSHOUSES, Nethergate Street. 1850,
brick. U-plan arrangement of one-storey houses. Shaped gables
and iron casements.

MANOR FARMHOUSE, ¼ m. NE. Two-storey, three-bay C16 W
parts formerly with a jettied, i.e. timber-framed, W gable. In the
C17 it was redone in flint and brick. In the C18 a brick addition
of four bays attached to the E.

ROUND HOUSE, ½ m. SE. With pointed windows. Dated 1841.
Despite the name it is hexagonal, two storeys and with a little
metal trellis porch.

Further S, a prominently placed WINDMILL, a derelict brick tower
mill, without cap or sails, built in 1832. Mildly famous for
damage caused to it in June 1889 by giant hailstones.

LONG BARROW, on the Heath out to the SE, 270 yds SW of that on
West Rudham Heath (see p. 770). It measures 150 ft long by
90 ft at its wider end, and has a 15-ft wide ditch flanking the
mound. The road has truncated the N end. Although the barrow
has not yet been excavated, Windmill Hill pottery has been
picked up on its surface, as at Ditchingham (see p. 307). ROUND
BARROWS are to be seen from the road further W near the
Peddar's Way.

HEACHAM   6030

ST MARY. Mainly flint but with roofs of graded Cumberland
slate, always memorable in Norfolk. Late C13 crossing tower,
late C13 nave and aisles, and a good C13 S doorway. The doorway has two orders of detached shafts with crocket capitals and
a finely moulded, deeply undercut arch. Double-chamfered N
doorway, now the entrance to a kitchen extension of 1992. The
five-bay nave arcades have alternating circular and octagonal
piers and double-hollow-chamfered arches. Seats round the
piers. The unbuttressed tower still shows the roof-lines of the
transepts. The present nave aisles were continued c. 1820 at a
low level to enclose the tower on both sides, these extensions
deploying carstone. On the N side the removal of the transept
has necessitated the piling up of a huge carstone buttress, partly
galleted, and oddly pierced, as if with little ashlar-dressed
windows near the top. On the S side less colossal but also substantial buttresses, and the blocked arch of the transept E
window. Circular bell-openings, a vigorous motif. Polygonal
stair-turret to SE corner. Rebuilt crenellated parapet and a small

timber lantern. Crossing arches of the same style as the arcades.
N aisle E arch has undercut mouldings and quatrefoil responds.
Perp aisle windows, those to N renewed in the C19, Perp clerestory
with circular windows, those to N side containing quatrefoils.
Perp S porch, formerly graced by a quadripartite vault of which
springers and wall arches remain. A small vaulted niche to the S
gable. W end of nave lit through a good five-light Curvilinear
window with embattled transom and squashed mouchette tracery
devices of c. 1330–40. The chancel to all intents and purposes is
early C19, having been reduced in length and patched with carstone. The C13 priest's door remains. C19 kingpost nave roof.

FURNISHINGS. FONT. On cruciform steps. Square stem with
quatrefoils and plain rather rounded bowl. – SCREEN. Late C15.
One-light divisions and good panel tracery. – WALL PAINTING.
On the SW crossing pier, fine C14 figure of St John the Baptist
holding the *Agnus Dei* in a disc, set against a lozenge background. Part of a canopy below, and scrollwork above. (DP) –
Scrollwork of c. 1300 around the W crossing arch. – SANCTUS
BELL. On top of the tower, C13, one of the oldest in England,
and reported to sing hoarse. – MONUMENTS. Brass to a knight,
c. 1485, a 27 in. figure (W wall). – Robert Redemayne †1625.
Standing monument. No effigy. Tomb-chest, two black Ionic
columns, two hanging arches with round and triangular billet.
Top structure with panelled strapwork pilasters and a painted
coat of arms (N aisle E). – Nicholas Styleman †1830, an old-
fashioned Adamesque wall monument by *J. B. Armer* of
Snettisham (chancel). Various monuments to the Rolfe family
of Heacham Hall. – S. C. E. N. Rolfe †1852. Divers inscriptions
framed in a carpet of glazed tiles. In 1614 John Rolfe married
the Virginian Indian Princess Matoaka Pocahontas (1595–1617),
one of the first New World Indians to have been baptized. Her
alabaster monument (NW crossing pier) of 1933 by *Otilie Wallace*.

THE TOWN

Before the late C19 attempt to develop Heacham as a seaside
resort the village extended only as far as Lynn Road, Station Road
and Hunstanton Road to the S and SW of the church with an
extension running down the present Lodge Road. The Hall was to
the NW and its legacy is a pleasant park N of the developed area.
With a few C17 exceptions the dates of the better buildings fall
into the C18 and C19, but all are of only local interest. Even the
demolished Heacham Hall was modest of its type and rebuilt in
1778. Carstone from the Snettisham quarries is found everywhere,
sometimes coursed with clunch, usually dressed with brick. Of
seaside developments the C20 contributes only six big and intim-
idating CARAVAN PARKS, fortunately well to the W by the sea,
bounded by Jubilee Road and South Beach Road.

Our perambulation begins at the church. Immediately E the
VICARAGE, an ordinary brick house of 1986, and at once SE
Nos. 16–26 CHURCH LANE. Built 1763 as a U-plan set of

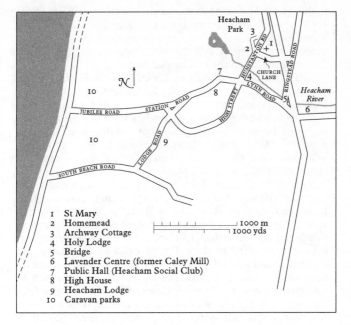

1	St Mary
2	Homemead
3	Archway Cottage
4	Holy Lodge
5	Bridge
6	Lavender Centre (former Caley Mill)
7	Public Hall (Heacham Social Club)
8	High House
9	Heacham Lodge
10	Caravan parks

1000 m
1000 yds

Heacham

almshouses, largely rebuilt 1913. Two storeys. Carstone, clunch and red brick dressings. Central archway in the middle block. Facing the w end of the church on HUNSTANTON ROAD an attractive if minor triangular green formed by two ranges. To the s THE HOMEMEAD, of colourwashed carstone and brick. Late C18. Two storeys in six bays, the outer two being additions. The porch to the l. on plain Greek Doric pilasters must be c. 1830. An early C19 cottage continues to the N (No. 30) linking with ARCHWAY COTTAGE (No. 40) which turns at r. angles to close the green and continues with Nos. 42–46. In the corner Archway Cottage has a round carriage arch and was the former s lodge to the Hall. c. 1740. Carstone dressed with brick. Rest of the range mid-C19, and all of one storey and dormer attic, the windows all C20.

On the E side at the junction with Church Lane stands CHURCH HOUSE, apparently a C17 BARN converted to form a house late in the C18, further altered as the Vicarage in 1857 and fitted out with Gothic details: two-storey porch, bargeboards. Then, moving s, TURRET HOUSE, c. 1830, of red brick, two storeys with a simple porch extending quite far on simple columns. Late C19 addition at N, the most striking feature a two-storey tower incorporating miscellaneous medieval fragments brought in, very Gothic. Immediately behind is No. 27, dated 1907 and done in a provincial Arts and Crafts. Next is CHESTNUT HOUSE, dated 1829, standard two-storey, three-bay house with a brick façade and carstone returns, and then

nothing until Nos. 1–11 at the junction with Lynn Road to the
s. Of coursed carstone with brick dressings, the *c.* 1840 terrace
is curious, for each single-bay, two-storey house has its own big
gable facing the street. Mostly sashes below, casements above.
Clustered stacks on the rear hipped roofs.

Round the corner to the E on LYNN ROAD to HOLY LODGE
(the name promoted from Holly Lodge in 1990s). Large C17
clunch-built house with carstone extended to the W in C18 brick.
The earlier part with a late C19 porch, a time of some remodelling – see the bargeboarded gable-ends and the octagonal chimneyshafts. MILLBRIDGE NURSING HOME further E also began
as a two-storey, five-bay C17 house of which traces remain in
some brick upper-window openings to the garden (E) front and
in the S gable. The tented porch is *c.* 1900, as is the whole of the
NE wing. The nice iron GATES are *c.* 1750 slung between rebuilt
piers. 300 yds E on RINGSTEAD ROAD a curious early C19
BRIDGE over the Heacham River. Very worn carstone, and so
weathered that the polygonal turrets N and S of the parapet on
each side almost stand alone. Parapets raised into gables in the
centres. Double-chamfered arches, with coat of arms above on
both sides. From here one can look E to the big and bald
LAVENDER CENTRE (formerly Caley Mill) on the other side of
the by-pass. Early Victorian Tudor, of carstone, three storeys in
five bays, with a four-storeyed porch open on the ground floor
to N and S under four-centred arches. Polygonal buttresses
rising into finials.

Retracing one's steps to Hunstanton Road, the WHEATSHEAF
INN is an improved public house of the 1930s, here dressed as
Tudor with chequered gable-heads r. and l. and a centre with
half-timbering. Unusually its panelled rooms and plan are
intact (in 1997). STATION ROAD continues W. At the junction
with the narrow High Street a group of sensibly designed new
houses and refurbishments of 1996–7 done in Flemish bond
mellow brick. In keeping, apart from the top-hung casements to
the street elevations. 250 yds W on a corner next to the bowling
green the PUBLIC HALL (Heacham Social Club). 1897 by
Milne & Hall of London, for G.E. Strachan (of the Hall).
Originally one bay wide: central door under projecting pedimented hood on console brackets and with a wide Venetian
window over. An outsized plaque gives details of the enlargement in 1926 by provision of an archway r. and l. and a nine-
bay hall to the rear. A little further on is HIGH HOUSE on the
opposite side, becoming hedged in by 1980s developments. The
most satisfying of Heacham's houses, dated 1726. Coursed and
dressed carstone with brick detailing. Two storeys and four bays
with pilasters to the corners. Sash windows. Platband. Rendered
central porch, of the mid C19. The three dormers alternately
segmental and triangular-headed.

Much further SW LODGE ROAD splits off and runs down
towards South Beach Road. On the way HEACHAM LODGE,
two-storey, five-bay, late C18. Of red brick with a low parapet
and gable-end stacks. Central doorway under a pediment on

engaged columns. Cast-iron RAILINGS in front (square-section verticals and turned standards. Carstone walls either side).

MANOR FARMHOUSE, $\frac{1}{2}$ m. NNW of the church on Hunstanton Road. A two-storey, four-bay C17 house much remodelled. Ground floor with evidence of C17 windows reduced in size. Tall C19 porch. S gable has a stack ending in four octagonal flues. The most obvious C17 part is the two-storeyed rear service block, with two arched openings, themselves re-worked.

HECKINGHAM

ST GREGORY. A Norman church of round tower, nave, chancel and apse, the sister of Hales to the S. Redundant. The body of the church is now thatched. Of the round tower only the lowest parts are Norman. The tall and rather bald polygonal part with its brick quoins looks late C15 and there are indeed bequests from 1486 and 1507 to the 'makyng of the stepille'. Of the windows of the church the only Norman ones which remain are two in the apse, deeply splayed inside, and even they are externally altered. The flat buttresses of the apse are a characteristic Norman motif, here without the shafting of Hales or the decorated sill band. Neither is there a blind arcade. The only outstanding Norman feature is the S doorway, the work evid- 16 ently of the same craftsman who worked at Hales. The workmanship is equally crisp, the ornamental inventiveness equally striking. The date, like Hales, is probably mid C12. Four orders of shafts, with four pairs of nook-shafts and decorated capitals. Decoration even along the edges between the shafts. Arch with chevron, crosses, zigzag, bobbin etc., motifs. Hoodmould with wheels. The N doorway was Norman too, but only a fragment survives, having been moved. Late C12 brick and flint S porch, with brick shafts supporting a hollow-moulded four-centred arch under a square hood with brick shields in the spandrels. The N aisle was built by cutting very roughly through the Norman wall. The three arcade openings have no responds or imposts, just a slight chamfer. The aisle wall is redone in brick with some flint, but the intersecting tracery in the E and W windows indicates an early C14 date which may also be that of the arcade. Arch-braced roofs in the porch, the nave and the aisle. – FONT. Norman, plain square bowl, on an octagonal stumpy central stem and four squat little columns with volute capitals at the corners. – BENCH and STALL. Early C16. Parts are combined to form the reader's desk. – STAINED GLASS. Bits of the C15 in the head of the three-light Perp S window. E window, an Annunciation, c. 1910. One Saint in the Norman lancets r. and l., †1908.

HECKINGHAM HALL. Timber-framed C17 wing with a polite front added to the S forming a T-plan. The new part of the late C18, two storeys, five bays, fluted pilasters and entablature round the door. Older part with three-light casements and a central door.

HEDENHAM

ST PETER. To the N of the village on a pleasing promontory. Thin
W tower, nave and chancel, in their details mostly Victorian.
Surprisingly the nave has a brick stepped E gable. The tower has
a C15 W window and flushwork crenellations. C15 too the S
porch, with flushwork buttresses and fleurons in the arch and a
good roof with moulded arched braces. In the nave one good
Dec window with a segmental head and reticulated tracery.
Reticulated also the chancel E window. A wall monument on
the chancel S exterior wall too weathered to date, but C18. The
chancel was being worked on and leaded in 1372, but the fabric
is early C14, see the restored ogeed piscina and sedilia. Inside it
was redecorated in 1862–3 in the self-confident High Victorian
Gothic style by *E. J. Tarver*. This does it no harm. Tarver's is
the chancel arch. – FONT. Octagonal. Eight shafts against the
stem, shields and flowers in cusped panels against the bowl. –
WEST SCREEN. Apparently one major part of a reredos of *c.* 1700,
with acanthus foliage and a figure of St Peter. – COMMUNION
RAIL. Of the early C18, reused as a low chancel screen. Twisted
balusters and square panelled newels. – STAINED GLASS. Chancel
E by *J. Hardman & Co.*, *c.* 1860, S and N by *Clayton & Bell*,
c. 1865. – MONUMENTS. Chalice brass for Richard Grene †1502.
– Robert Bedingfield, 1594. Brass inscription tablet in stone
surround with two colonnettes and a pediment. – Francis Bacon
†1663. Large tablet with a frightening skull in a roundel at the
foot. – John Richmond †1694. The inscription on a panel curving forward and flanked by Ionic columns under a broken segmental pediment. Attributed to *W. Linton* of Norwich (GF). –
Philip Bedingfeld and others, *c.* 1725, inscription in an architectural surround; good.

HEDENHAM HALL. The park was incorporated with that of
Ditchingham Hall in the C19, so they back on to each other.
The late C16 or early C17 house sits right on the junction of the
main road and Church Road. E-plan, re-fronted *c.* 1710–20.
The house still has brickwork in English bond, stepped gables,
and on the first floor an original stone fireplace. The work of
c. 1710–20 is the adding of broad giant brick pilasters at the
angles of the projecting wings and the change to sash windows.
In the middle of the five-bay front a doorway with fluted Ionic
pilasters carrying a pulvinated frieze and a segmental pediment.
The gable-end stacks terminate in octagonal shafts, that to the S
with six. Entrance hall with doorcases and fireplace of *c.* 1710–20.
Staircase remodelled *c.* 1740. Simple panels with guilloche in
the Kent style. Venetian window with unfluted columns inside
as well as outside. Three turned balusters to the step and simply
carved tread-ends. The house was painted more or less in its
present state as early as 1735 by *Bardwell*, the painting in the
overmantel of the entrance hall chimneypiece.

OUTBUILDINGS generally late C17. STABLES in red brick,
partly rebuilt, especially to S. The l. bay has pilasters and a door
and cross casement under moulded brick hoods. Stepped W

gable fitted with ovolo-moulded mullioned windows. Tie-irons in form of numerals 9 and 7; one assumes prefixes 15 or 16 are missing, and one also assumes this is a re-facing of a timber-framed building, with brick end-gables. Original jowled principal studs inside could be 1597, the re-facing and ties possibly 1697. The GARDEN WALL has a doorway in the N return dated 1908. Against the W wall is a brick HOUSE with stepped gables and a buttress at the NW corner. A date of 1676. PARK BUNGALOW, 200 yds NNE, has a DOVECOTE dated 1769; hexagonal, brick, angle pilasters with little capitals and bases, cupola in centre of roof. Re-roofed 1980.

HEDENHAM LODGE, S of the Hall. Dated 1711, with shaped end-gables. The W front is of five bays and two storeys with wooden mullioned and transomed cross-windows. Slight pediment to the doorcase. Platband between floors. Four square shafts to the ridge stack. The E side boasts a stair-turret, the stairs have turned balusters, square newels and closed strings.

HILL HOUSE, Woodton Road, $\frac{3}{8}$ m. NW of the church. Early C18, with stepped gables and quadruple-flued stack.

OLD RECTORY, 300 yds WNW of the Hall. Georgian, five-bay S front, two storeys, blue brick with red brick trim. Centre door behind a Doric portico. First-floor platband.

HILL FARMHOUSE, $\frac{3}{4}$ m. SW of the church. C16 hall house with a C17 stack inserted in the cross-passage (to create a lobby-entrance plan). Diamond-mullioned E window. The C17 provided the staircase tower with its winder. Queenpost roof replaced with a C17 butt-purlin type with wind-braces.

VALLEY FARMHOUSE, Church Road, S of the church. This has had the same treatment, and also a C19 brick skin. But it still has its pair of service doors off the cross-passage. C17 winder by the stack.

Nos. 56–57 CHURCH ROAD is more difficult to interpret. It may be two small late C16 houses, together only three windows wide. The brickwork all C19, and exterior details C19 or C20, but a heavy timber frame remains inside, and part of one truss of queenposts to the roof.

SMITH'S KNOLL, Church Road, looking towards the church. Two parallel terraces of council houses and four single-storey houses in a contrasting direction. Designed by *Tayler & Green* for the Loddon Rural District Council (*see* Introduction, p. 165) in 1949–50. The houses are colourwashed.

HELHOUGHTON   8020

ALL SAINTS. Of the early C14, but reduced. W tower with a handsome four-centred doorway which has fleurons and ballflower in the arch. Four-centred, blocked, window above. The bell-stage has gone, resulting in the hanging of the bells in the ringing chamber. Chancel with windows with cusped Y-tracery and cusped intersecting tracery. The chancel cut down too, and the E window re-assembled. Nave of 1790, with pointed brick-framed windows, reusing much of the original masonry. Y-tracery. The restoration of 1890 effaced any Georgian character one might have enjoyed. But the high original roof-line against the tower shows a prouder nave, with aisles and clerestory. That the piers were octagonal is evident from their stones reused in the walling. – FONT. Late C12, cut down to size. Square base to the bowl, transition to an octagon by big shapeless spurs or blobs. – BRASS. Hands, heart and inscription scrolls, to William Stapleton and wife, *c.* 1440 (chancel). – PULPIT. 1790, like almost everything else here, cut down.

THE BUCK public house, no longer used as the pub. Flint with brick trim. Two storeys in four bays, the upper windows all casements, the lower ones mixed. Canted bay window C19. Datestone 1786.

HELLINGTON

ST JOHN BAPTIST. On a slight hill with only one house for company. Norman round tower with Dec bell-openings. The tower arch bricked in. Norman s and N doorways. Both are amply decorated. The s doorway has three orders of colonnettes, the N doorway two. The capitals have scallops or upright volutes. In the arches zigzag, bobbins, two orders of scallops at r. angles to the wall, St Andrew's crosses. Billet mouldings in the hoods. Dec nave and chancel. The nave walls have been raised and the roof is early C19. The responds of the chancel arch have bands of foliage. A hoodmould on the E side on two jolly heads. In the chancel and nave a variety of unusual and rather heavy tracery motifs, including in tracery heads elongated double-cusped quatrefoils and trefoils and what is known as Kentish tracery (split cusps). The windows are shafted inside, and there are again hoodmoulds on headstops. C19 E window. N chancel wall rebuilt C18 in brick. C19 scissor-braced chancel roof. The s porch is Dec. It is somewhat battered but must have been quite a spectacular piece, with its big niches set diagonally l. and r. of the entrance. Pointed arch. The W and E sides have three cusped openings either side. Not very well built and the suggestion has been made that it has been moved. – FONT. C19, plain, with a panelled stem and quatrefoiled circles. – STAINED GLASS. Bits of C14 grisaille in a chancel s window. – E window, mixed quality, Crucifixion and other scenes, probably by *J. & J. King*, †1858.

HEMPNALL

ST MARGARET. Some long-and-short work at the NW corner of the nave suggests C11, but the church all rebuilt since. Early C14 W tower, the bell-openings with Y-tracery. The tower base filled in for vestries and a kitchen in 1975 (by *Michael Gooch*). Handsome WEATHERVANE, dated 1727. Two-storeyed s porch

with the upper windows flanked by niches. The nave and aisle
windows all renewed during the 1857 restoration. Chancel only
a short projection without fittings. The previous chancel was
already 'ruinated' in Blomefield's time. The N arcade of two
bays dates from the C13. Round piers with round capitals and
abaci, double-chamfered arches. The S arcade, judging by the
sunk-quadrant mouldings, probably early C14. The piers are
octagonal. The extra E bay is Victorian. Roofs 1857. – FONT.
Octagonal, with four beasts and four seated figures against the
stem, four beasts and four demi-figures of angels with shields
against the bowl. On one shield the emblem of the Trinity, on
another the Instruments of the Passion. 28s. was left for the
new font in 1438.

PARK FARMHOUSE, Barondole Lane. The external stack to the W
with its four octagonal flues shows that the apparently late C19
brick house is in fact early C17. Timber-framed, and with a
more obvious C17 rear wing.

THE HAVEN, Furze Road. Early C16 hall house, still with the
cross-passage. It was floored in the C17. Tie-beams on arched
braces, principals with wind-braces.

HEMPNALL HOUSE, 1¼ m. S of the church at Lundy Green. The
façade is of gault brick, three bays and with a central porch with
a stepped gable, and stepped gables to the return walls. This is
an addition of 1871, and there were alterations to the early C17
rear block at the same time. The timber frame skinned with
brick. The two bays E of the stack have upper crucks in the
roof, a system used in Norfolk in the early C17.

THE STREET is the main thoroughfare. CONNAUGHT HOUSE
on the S side is of painted brick, four bays; mid-C18 sashes are
original. Some C17 houses, e.g. FORGE COTTAGE and LIME
TREE COTTAGE. The PARSONAGE on the N side is also a C17
timber-framed house dressed up with an C18 brick skin and a
Gibbs surround to the door. Small STABLES to the rear are
c. 1730, of red brick.

HEMPNALL GREEN is a little hamlet ⅝ m. SE. VILLA FARMHOUSE
represents the early C18: stuccoed, five bays, two storeys, sash
windows, doorcase with rustication and a segmental arch. Of
the same time THE GRANGE, brick, two storeys, four bays,
doorcase with fluted pilasters.

HEMPTON
⅜ m. S of Fakenham

There were once two churches. Now only HOLY TRINITY.
Chancel 1855 by *J. H. Hakewill*, the architect to the Church
Building Society. Transepts and nave 1952–5 by *J. P. Chaplin*,
with stone from St Michael-at-Thorn in Norwich. – PAINTING.
By *J. P. Chaplin*, 1955, in the Ravilious–Rowntree style.

PRIORY, Abbey Farm, SE of the church. Some few inarticulate
stubs of wall. The priory was Augustinian and founded as a
hospital in 1135 by Roger de St Martin.

WENSUM HOUSE, Dereham Road. Stuccoed flint. Tripartite sashes to the ground floor, ordinary sashes to the first floor. The end quoins and door and window surrounds rusticated. The date *c.* 1760–70.

THE GREEN has THE BELL INN, an C18 house of three bays with the centre projecting. This and the gable-ends with quoins. Platband to first floor. The windows all C19 replacements.

VILLAGE EARTHWORKS, in a field N of Shereford Road. A moated site, with a hollow and tofts. In the SW corner is the site of St Andrew's Church. (AR)

1000   HETHEL

ALL SAINTS. Unbuttressed W tower, perhaps pre-Norman, as it has long-and-short W quoins. Y-tracery bell-openings. Later two-stepped battlements. Minimum N arcade of three bays with octagonal piers and double-chamfered arches. There was a N chapel as well, but that was rebuilt as, or converted into, the Branthwaite family chapel or MAUSOLEUM. It has a brick N façade of rather Vanbrughian character, with rusticated quoins, blank arched windows filled with blue brick, and identically filled in segment-headed windows in the heavy parapet above. Inside, three blank tablets. The date is unrecorded. It seems to be *c.* 1730 and the first interment was in 1740. The Gothick doorway from the E, dated 1819, is clearly later. The S porch of the church is Perp, but has a later stepped gable. The nave and N aisle windows are of an elementary C17 or C18 type with wooden frames. Chancel windows Victorian but of the same design as in Ladbroke's drawing of the 1820s. – MONUMENT. Miles Branthwaite †1612 and wife Mary. Alabaster. He rests on his elbow above and behind her, in legal dress. Columns r. and l. carrying obelisks. Coffered arch and inscription plate framed by fine strapwork and fruit. Against the tomb-chest kneel their children, a boy and two girls.

1000   HETHERSETT

ST REMIGIUS. A Dec church generously provided with aisles and transepts. The transepts and the chancel rebuilt during the big restoration of 1874, the transepts left flush with the aisles. Four-stage W tower with a flushwork chequer base and buttresses. Niches in the W buttresses. Small recessed lead spire. Most of the windows Victorian although the Dec petal tracery of the three-light chancel E window is clearly original and re-set. Clerestory of 1874. Two-storeyed Perp N porch of cut and knapped flint. The arch has salamanders on the capitals. Weathered niches l. and r. of the two-light upper window. Tierceron vault inside with finely carved figured bosses (cf. Wymondham). Dec arcades of five bays, that to the S leaning alarmingly, and braced by C18 brick buttresses against the aisle. Quatrefoil piers with hollow-moulded fillets in the diagonals. Double-hollow-chamfered arches. Oddly the nave has three w bays under a higher roof than its two E bays, because the E part was used as the sanctuary until 1874. Roof of 1874, seating 1857, transept and chancel arches of course are 1874. Also of 1874 the painted texts over the arcade arches and aisle windows. – PISCINA. C14, trefoiled, in s aisle (chancel angle piscina is 1874). – FONT. Octagonal, C14, with quatrefoils of various kinds and a central supporting column with eight hexagonal satellite colonnettes. – SCULPTURE. One angel bracket of stone from the former roof (under tower). – MONUMENTS. In the s transept, hidden behind the organ, decayed effigies of a Knight and Lady of the Berney family, C14, on a tomb-chest with shields in cusped fields alternating with tracery. – Wall monument to Isaac Motham †1704 in s aisle. By *William Stanton*. Corinthian columns carrying a segmental pediment both broken and open. Putto heads at the foot. An odd thing is that the date is carved 170¾, an optional old/new-style form of dating sometimes met with. – Ledger slab in Tournai marble to John Luke Iselin †1816. He was a Swiss merchant based in Norwich. – Other black ledger slabs. – STAINED GLASS. E window, 1913, Crucifixion in C15 style. Similar glass in side windows. The best is in the N aisle, an Adoration in Arts and Crafts style, 1911 by *R. Anning Bell*.

THICKTHORN HALL, off the Old Norwich Road, 1¼ m. E of the church. 1812 according to Kelly. Rendered and colourwashed brick. Three by two widely spaced bays. Two storeys with one-storey extensions to s, w and E. The last must be a slightly later addition. Their style looks *c.* 1820–30. The principal (s) front has giant pilasters partly covered by the extension so that on the ground floor it has five bays. The three-bay first floor also with pilasters. The windows are sashes, of course. The extension here includes a porch with Greek Doric pillars. 50 yds NE is an early C19 KITCHEN GARDEN with a large octagonal building against one wall.

COUNTY FIRE SERVICE HEADQUARTERS, Old Norwich Road, 1976 by the *County Architect's Office* (job architect *B. Johnson*). Two storeys, red engineering brick, with a sloping clerestory, all very James Stirling-looking. It is rather successful in a clean, functional way, until one contemplates the glazed roof addition, which does the building no favours. The site is fronted by an C18 five-bay house under a hipped roof, with a bay added r. and l. in the 1970s to increase office accommodation.

WOODSIDE FIRST SCHOOL. 1972–6 by *B. Johnson* of the *County Architect's Office*. Hexagonal with a central hall under a dome.

HETHERSETT HIGH SCHOOL, Queen's Road. 1979–80 by *County Architect's Office*, County Architect *J. F. Tucker*. In the pavilion style and with the separate blocks arranged round a rectangular covered way, in the same spirit as Terrington St Clement (q.v.). Originally seven blocks, apparently placed without formality, all different sizes, rectangular or square, under contrasting pyramid or gabled roofs. The taller pyramid pavilion is the library and English department, dividing the central court into two. Red brick, concrete tiled roofs, painted blockwork to interiors.

PERAMBULATION. Hethersett is a large village (population 4,600 in 1991, and expanding with new housing estates in every direction except s) with the church set to the E, unusually isolated. A walk can begin at Hethersett High School on Queen's Road (*see* above). To the NW off Great Melton Road is Lynch Green leading to CEDAR ROAD and CEDAR GRANGE. Early C17 brick house with stepped gables and some rebuilding in the C18. Back on LYNCH GREEN, No. 29 has to the E front a lower s part, early C16, rendered timber frame. It has an inserted floor inside and a queenpost roof truss, so one assumes an open hall. The C17 part to the r. has a lobby-entrance plan, and a stepped N gable with the date 1729. Windows mostly replica cross casements of the 1980s. No. 43 (THE THATCHED COTTAGE) is also a C16 open hall house, timber-framed. One storey and dormer attic. First floor inserted in C17. Butt-purlin roof with curved wind-braces.

Retracing one's steps to Queen's Road and into CANN'S LANE, Nos. 5–7, the MANOR HOUSE and MANOR HOUSE COTTAGE, set back on the E side. The N bay is late C16, of brick laid in English bond, with a polygonal buttress at the r.

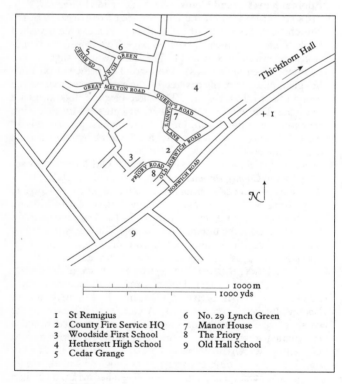

1	St Remigius	6	No. 29 Lynch Green
2	County Fire Service HQ	7	Manor House
3	Woodside First School	8	The Priory
4	Hethersett High School	9	Old Hall School
5	Cedar Grange		

Hethersett

corner. Good octagonal chimneyshaft. This part is of one storey and attic with a basement still with fragments of C16 mullioned windows. To the S is an early C17 addition (No. 7) of two bays and two storeys, the brick still in English bond. Renewed casement windows.

Cann's Lane emerges at OLD NORWICH ROAD and a r. turn brings the County Fire Headquarters (*see* above), followed by the KING'S HEAD public house. C18 in three builds stepping down from the W. Further SW to THE PRIORY, surrounded by walls and a fence. It has its façade to the SE, but at the S end is a brick and flint wing, of two storeys and an attic, which is later C16. It had an external stack to its former E side, now incorporated internally into the additions put on in 1607–8. The gable is stepped and has the date 1608. Also with a stepped gable is the two-storeyed porch with a C19 arch but a re-set door-frame inside with carved spandrels and shields and the date 1607. This C17 front has plenty of varied brickwork of the C17 to the C19. The rear remodelled in the C18, with a further re-set late C16 door-frame.

After that on the S side, HETHERSETT OLD HALL SCHOOL. Red brick, 1774 with additions. The five-bay façade faces the road, with two full-height canted bay windows and three bays between them. Hipped roof. Curved porch on four Ionic columns. The hall inside has a screen to the l. composed of two Corinthian columns *in antis*. Doorways with eared surrounds. Open-well staircase with stick balusters and a ramped and wreathed mahogany handrail, an early manifestation of the type for a house of this size in Norfolk, if it is 1774. Early C20 wing added to the rear, the first floor with false timbering typical of the time and oriel windows. The assembly hall occupies a former BARN to the NE, dated on the SE gable 1754 (initials STB). Brick and pantiles. Five bays with pilaster strips, the l. bay converted to a small dwelling. Inserted windows and a blocked central cart entrance. This leaves us as far SW of the centre as the church is to the E.

CANTLEY HOUSE, Cantley Lane. A brick C17 house in five bays and two storeys with attics. Platband and cross casements (renewed). Stepped E gable. To the W is a timber-framed C16 wing cased in C19 brick. Big central stack containing a fireplace and bread oven. Bridging beams with sunk-quadrant mouldings.

HILBOROUGH   *8000*

ALL SAINTS. First, the chancel, of the early C14, windows with intersecting tracery and sedilia and double piscina with cinque-foiled pointed arches. E window of five lights. Contemporary perhaps the arcades, now of three bays but originally of four. The Perp chancel arch was pushed one bay W when it was built, and so stands inside the earlier arcade. The piers are of quatre-foil section with the foils almost detached. Moulded capitals,

double-hollow-chamfered arches. But essentially the church is
Perp. Tall w tower of knapped flint chequered with stone,
becoming very casual above the ground stage as if carelessly
restored. Sumptuous w front. Doorway with figures in the
spandrels, two tall niches l. and r., and outside them big blank
flushwork tracery. A frieze of foiled circles with shields above,
and then a three-light w window. Pierced battlements with
shields. Pinnacles. The s aisle and s porch are also of knapped
flint and are referred to in a will of 1516, for 'reparacion and
makyng upp'. An earlier will, of 1490, left money for the parvis,
which, as the porch is single-storeyed, refers either to plans not
proceeded with, or to the tower. The aisle windows have panel
tracery with stepped transoms, the arches are of brick (cf.
Fincham). The s porch has a base frieze of crowned Ms in
flushwork very similar to that of nearby Great Cressingham,
and also jamb mouldings of the same design (and of those used
at Wiveton porch). Niche above the entrance. Wall arches on
corner-shafts inside. c15 nave roof consists of hammerbeams
and arched braces to a high collar, much repaired in the restoration of 1859. In the chancel and N aisle also old roofs. – FONT.
Early c14, with Geometrical tracery to its eight facets. –
BENCHES. Some with c15 pierced traceried backs. Poppyheads
and arm-rests, deprived of their figures. – ROYAL ARMS. Of
James I. Painted, with a rose and thistle and plenty of leaves
below. – ALTAR TABLE. By *Pugin*, from West Tofts, *c.* 1850. –
CURIOSUM. Brazier to heat the church. – MONUMENTS. Ralph
Caldwell †1792 (*see* below, Hilborough Hall). Big tablet. Below
a marble door surround are named tablets of other members of
the family. The door probably led into a family chapel.

ST MARGARET. Two ivy-clad crags of flint are all that remain of
the church. They lie opposite the lodge to Hilborough Hall on
the road to Cockley Cley.

HILBOROUGH HALL. A strong, puritanical block in two and a
half storeys. Built of gault brick in 1779 for Ralph Caldwell.
Caldwell was the agent at Holkham and the enriching details
are from there: rusticated ground-floor quoins below a platband,
above the platband a stringcourse and between them balustrading under the first-floor sashes. The broadly spaced five-bay
entrance (S) front has a three-bay projecting centre under a
pediment. Three-bay E and four-bay N fronts, the latter with the
central two bays advanced. Hipped roof. The interiors are a
surprise, with Adamesque decoration possibly executed, it has
been suggested, by *William Ivory*. The principal downstairs
rooms start with the square hall entered from the S front: a
marble fireplace and a frieze of winged lions and bulls' skulls.
The whole E front is the drawing room, distinguished by a
restrained plaster ceiling; a door at the NW corner leads into the
dining room. This has a shallow apse at the S end (behind the
hall), and a good overmantel in which is a painted relief panel of
Minerva and Perseus by *Biagio Rebecca*. The walls have fielded
panels and the ceiling is again in the Adam style.

WATERMILL. The datestone tells us that the brick mill is of 1819.

The initials R.C. presumably refer to a second Ralph Caldwell of the Hall. The w bay is the MILLER'S HOUSE, of flint with brick dressings and decaying at the time of writing. The two-storey mill itself has eleven bays of casements, not all in use, and a weatherboarded lucam above loading doors on two levels. Secondary lucam to the E. The MACHINERY is virtually intact: three sets of stones with their hoppers and skirts on the first floor, the usual pit wheel, wallower, stone nuts and, of course, water wheel below.

The small VILLAGE straddles the main Thetford–Swaffham Road. ELM COTTAGE is an early C17 timber-framed house, partly re-faced in the C19, but with an early C18 N gable. This has diaper brickwork. S front with C19 casements and eyebrow dormers. The roof has the upper crucks popular c. 1600–25. THE NUNNERY, opposite, is more polite. Early C18, of brick, with vertical burnt-brick bands. One and a half storeys, in three bays with the centre slightly advanced and given a C19 gault brick porch. C19 details. Further N, THE SWAN public house. Colourwashed brick. Two storeys and attic in three bays. Platband and cross casements. The date 1718 is half a century too early.

WARREN FARMHOUSE, 2¼ m. NW. Flint and gault brick estate house in the Gothick mode, dated 1845. Part of the Hilborough estate. Octagonal turrets at each corner and to the porch. Door under four-centred arch. Each front of three bays and two storeys.

BARROWS. On the E edge of the parish and Smuggler's Road lie three barrows, two of them of bowl type. This may have formed part of the Little Cressingham group (see p. 520).

HILGAY   6090

ALL SAINTS. An avenue of lime trees leads to the church. This consists of a medieval body severely restored by G. E. Street in 1862 and a gault brick tower of 1794 replacing one which collapsed in 1792. The old tower was of c. 1200 judging from the blocked tower arch (behind the dull W gallery) and a round-headed window discernible to the S. The body of the church, really now only the C14 S aisle, is of carstone with limestone dressings and was low in Ladbroke's time (c. 1823). The Perp windows all renewed, but the three-light reticulated E aisle window looks original Dec. Street gave the nave a steep-pitched roof dwarfing the tower (which perhaps he intended to replace later). At the E end he added a chancel extending as far E as earlier foundations went. There is a four-bay arcade of octagonal piers with double-chamfered arches. The E pair are lower and narrower to fit with the SE chapel, low enough to allow four-light triforium openings above them. All these details are Street's, no doubt reusing some medieval material. The two W arcade bays are excessively high and wide. The nave has a decent C19 queen-post roof but the S aisle retains some of its original roof, a coarse roof with arched braces and some pierced wheels and tracery above the inner brace. – PULPIT. Of marble and stone, circular and polychromatic, probably by *Street*. – FONT. Stone bowl with cinquefoiled arcade and marble columns supporting it; it must be *Street*'s too. – LECTERN. A C17 timber eagle, brought in 1962 from St Mary Beswick in Manchester. – SCREEN. Three bays r. and l. of the opening. Renewed Perp tracery. Now under the W gallery. – Two PARCLOSE SCREENS of similar C15 style and repairs, in the SE chapel. – BENCHES. Some late C15 poppy-heads on C19 benches. – STAINED GLASS. E window, *c.* 1870, looks like *Ward & Hughes*; S aisle E window, a Good Samaritan of 1895, probably by *Clayton & Bell*. – MONUMENT. Wall monument to Henry Hawe †1592, who built the Hall, and his wife Ursula. Two kneeling figures below a coffered arch in a strap-work frame.

WOOD HALL, ½ m. SE. The Abbot of Ramsey held the manor but upon the Dissolution it passed to James Hawe. It was his son Henry Hawe who built the present house, which is dated 1579. Of brick, on the E-plan, the entrance front to the N. The porch projects as far as the wings. Straight gables. The wings have polygonal angle-shafts and pinnacles and early C19 cross case-ments of five and four lights, those to the ground floor under studded friezes, those to the first floor under pediments. The N porch has reeded and fluted clasping Ionic corner pilasters to the ground floor supporting a frieze (with the date), and similar Tuscan pilasters above. The gable has square panelled pinnacles. A drawing of 1806 shows the porch without these embellish-ments, so they may be the work of *Humphry Repton*, who was engaged upon work in the park in that year for William Jones. There was a fire in 1806 which required the reconstruction of the two bays W of the porch, and signalled the replacement of many windows and the extension of the SE wing. In his Red Book Repton proposed Gothic alterations, but only a straight-forward repair was done to this front. The S front is substan-tially a mirror of the N, but with a canted bay to the extended E wing and a big external chimney-breast E of the porch. E and W returns both with two external stacks rising to polygonal flues. Inside, the high, and only, point is the C16 staircase with its closed strings, turned balusters and newel-posts with strapwork. The house is of a type as familiar in Suffolk as it is in Norfolk.

ROMANO-BRITISH SETTLEMENT. Beside the Wissey on the E edge of the island are the earthworks of a farmstead, with pad-docks or small fields and platforms for buildings. (DG)

MOATED SITE. NE of the village and N of Thistle Hill Road, a large rectangular moated site with, to the W, earthworks of two other ditched enclosures, and fishponds. (AR)

HILLINGTON

ST MARY. Perp W tower. £5 was left for it in 1434. Doorway and window openings C19. Perp chancel, described as new in 1439, much restored in 1892. Mostly built of the slate-blue carstone from the Sandringham quarries. The windows all C19, as is the large N chapel. Chancel arch 1892, but the tower arch still C15. The nave was rebuilt in brick with flint trim in 1824, absorbing the old S aisle. The imitation Perp windows have cast-iron tracery. This might be by *Donthorn*. – FONT. C15, octagonal, from St Mary, Islington (in Norfolk). – ORGAN. 1756 by *Snetzler*; with a very pretty Louis XVI case. – STAINED GLASS. One of the ffolkes memorial windows in the N chapel is by *J. Hardman & Co.*, †1860. – W window by *Wilmshurst & Oliphant*, †1840. – MONUMENTS. In the N transeptal chapel are three big table tombs to members of the ffolkes family, †1705–73. One has large quatrefoils holding shields. – Richard Hovel †1611, with a later inscription. Tablet with two pairs of small kneeling figures. – Sir William Browne, President of the Royal College of Physicians, †1774, and Lady Browne †1763. Two big tablets with architectural surrounds, conservative in style, different in all details, yet of much the same character. His tablet has his portrait in profile in a medallion. They are both signed 'Sir W. B. Archit.' and may thus be *Sir William Browne*'s own design, if he had architectural ambitions. They were carved by *Joseph Wilton* of London, probably after the death of Lady Browne. – Lady Browne West †1828 by *Humphrey Hopper*. Standing monument of white marble. She leans over a sarcophagus holding her child (she died in Bombay eleven days after childbirth; the child lived only hours).

UP HALL, Congham Road, opposite the church. The brick changes from English bond to Flemish bond at about 3 ft in height. Late C18, of two storeys in three bays. Two-storey pedimented porch in the middle is C19.

FIELD FARMHOUSE, Fakenham Road. Rather boring C18 house of two storeys in three bays, unusually built entirely of Sandringham carstone.

HILLINGTON HALL. Sir William ffolkes commissioned the house and outbuildings from *Donthorn*, 1824–8. It made much use of carstone, was Gothic, had a large central tower *à la* Wollaton and a monstrous porte cochère. All except some fragments of walling was demolished in 1946, and these remains were attached to a new house of 1953 by *Marshall Sisson*, in turn demolished in 1998. At the time of writing the third house on the site is being built, by *Purcell, Miller & Tritton* (job architect *Michael Morrison*). Two pairs of gateway lodges, the stables and other bits and pieces remain from Donthorn's time.

LODGE on Flitcham Road, *c.* 1828, of blue Sandringham carstone and brown carstone. Irregular Gothick disposition comprising a central arch with a three-storey tower to N and a single-storey lodge to S. Gothick windows. Ruinous. *Donthorn*'s one presumes also is the ROAD BRIDGE immediately N, over the River Babingley. The Lynn Road LODGE is a variation, in that the arch has a two-storey lodge either side stepping down to a single storey and a storey above, with an eight-light Gothick window. The arch is four-centred to the road but ogeed to the park, and is framed by two taller polygonal turrets.

Crenellated parapets. The passage under has rib vaults springing from stiff-leaf corbels. Low curving walls extend E and W
from the lodge, terminating in square piers carrying the remains
of C15 village crosses. The W one has a tall shaft. Facing these
across the road are similar quadrant walls, also with C15 stone
crosses.

STABLES, in the Park, c. 1830, *Donthorn* again. Carstone and
brick. Two storeys in seven bays under a hipped roof, the end
bays projecting; central porch with a four-centred entrance
arch. Gothick three-light casements. Clock tower restored 1983
by *J. Brian Jones*. A GAZEBO in the kitchen garden is also by
Donthorn, and he takes the credit for altering the big square late
C18 DOVECOTE.

On the N side of LYNN ROAD some ESTATE COTTAGES of
the mid C19 immediately W of the pub. Two pairs (Nos. 11–12
and 14–15), each of four bays in one and a half or two storeys,
plaintiled roofs, cast-iron lattice windows, clustered flues to
stacks. The pub (the FFOLKES ARMS) is of chunky carstone
slips, three bays, two storeys and a casement in the central
gable.

MOATED SITE. ⅜ m. N of the church is The Wilderness, where a
large moated site marks the position of the Old Hall which was
replaced in 1624. (AR)

HINGHAM

ST ANDREW. A large church, about 160 ft long, with a tower 120 ft
high. The church is historically specially important because it is
datable. It was built for Remigius de Hethersett, who was rector
from 1319 to 1359, i.e. it is a consistently Dec building. The
restorations of 1870 uncovered an apsidal foundation, but of the
earlier church above ground there is no sign. The six-stage W
tower has a patterned base frieze (quatrefoils, cusped wavy
lines, triangular lines and rosettes) and a patterned vine trail
above the doorway. The doorway has three orders of shafts with
big fleurons in the arch. Set-back buttresses, those to the W
diagonally connected across the angle. Dec windows and bell-
openings. Battlements rebuilt in 1663. The aisles and clerestory
have ballflower friezes below the eaves – not at all common in
Norfolk. S porch rebuilt 1873. The chancel is long and has tall
windows; it was raised in height in 1880. The windows have an
elaborated form of petal design first seen in the S walk of the
Norwich cloisters, with cusping like that in the gallery at Ely.
This would date Hingham chancel to *c.* 1335–40. In this context
it is instructive to note that in the quiet period at Norwich
between the building of the S and W cloister walks, one Simon
de Hethersett maintained a mason there in 1336*. Just such
a mason would have known of the Norwich, and probably

* One may assume that Simon knew or was related to Remigius, being contemporaries, being associated with the same nearby village, and both paying for architectural work at the same time, with strong stylistic links.

the Ely, tracery patterns. The E window of the S aisle is exactly like the Norwich W walk. The chancel E window is very large. It was originally Perp but underwent a drastic alteration to receive the glass mentioned below. A two-storey N vestry is attached, added in 1886. Sedilia and piscina are mutilated beyond recognition.

Tall six-bay arcades with quatrefoil piers and thin additional shafts in the diagonals. Arches with two sunk wave mouldings. The tower arch has the same type of responds, but polygonal capitals. Late Perp only the N and S chancel chapels and probably also the clerestory windows, which are placed over the spandrels, not the apexes of the arches. In 1469 Peter Cooper left money for the building of the Lady Chapel (S chapel). Nave roof with alternating major and minor hammerbeams; renewed in 1872, when the clerestory received attention. *Soane* made alterations to the chancel in 1785 and made a Gothic reredos, now gone. – FONT. Disappointing, of 1858. – STAINED GLASS. The whole E window is filled with German glass of *c.* 1535, bought by Lord Wodehouse of Kimberley in 1813 from J. C. Hampp (who made a business of this, *see* Introduction, p. 70) and installed by *S. C. Yarington* in 1825. In the church at Schleiden near Cologne is a Deposition made from the same cartoon as the panel here and dated 1535. In the middle light St Anne with the Virgin and Child and St Andrew. In the side-lights large scenes of the Crucifixion, Deposition, Ascension and Resurrection. Smaller scenes round the Resurrection. Also, at the top, St Andrew and two kneeling donors.

MONUMENTS. The Morley monument against the chancel N 30 wall is one of the most impressive wall monuments of the C15 in the whole of England. It commemorates Thomas, Lord Morley, †1435, but, according to the heraldry, it must have been made somewhat later. The arms of his son Robert and Robert's wife Elizabeth Roos are carved, but they married only in 1442. The style of sculpture would fit the 1440s better. It is of red stone and reaches up to the full height of the chancel wall. It consists of the tomb-chest with shields and with, on the lid, originally brasses under a double canopy. The recess is very high and has against its back wall tracery of a type more characteristic of the early C14 than of the C15 (three lights intersecting plus three lights intersecting, and a foiled circle at the top), illustrating how such earlier forms were still in favour in the middle of the Perp period even in a prestige example such as this. At the foot of this back wall and at the foot of the jambs are ten kneeling figures of the family; mourners, as it were. The upper part of the jambs and the underside of the arch carry a frieze of shields. To the l. and r. of the recess are polygonal buttresses, again encrusted with small figures. They go up nearly as high as the centre, where above the recess a superstructure rises with a frieze and cresting and then the figure of Christ seated under a canopy flanked by kneeling figures of Lord Morley and his wife. Inclusion of donor figures in this way was unusual. On top of the buttresses an Annunciation. The tomb is like no other in

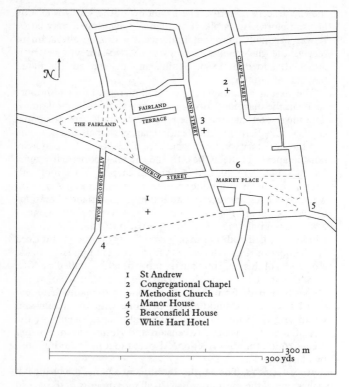

Hingham

England, but it is exactly like a gateway, and is big enough, if
one thinks away the tomb-chest and back wall: the monument
is palpably based on Erpingham Gate at Norwich. – Abraham
Lincoln. Memorial with a bust erected in 1919 because some of
his ancestors came from here (N aisle).

CONGREGATIONAL CHAPEL, Chapel Street. 1836, but with a
façade of 1898 by *A. F. Scott*: Dec windows and a quadrant
entrance bay in front entered through an arched door under a
gable.

METHODIST CHURCH, Bond Street. 1900. A gabled Tudor effort
with polygonal angle turrets, two four-centred doorways into
the integral porch below a five-light window.

THE TOWN. Despite having a medieval market the town never
grew and during the C17 and C18 the population was static at
800–1,000, and even in 1991 was only 1,900. The village however seems bigger than the population suggests. The failure of
Hingham to expand in the C19 was due to the railway not
coming here; the market had ceased by 1839. To the W of the
church three large houses, not individually memorable, on
ATTLEBOROUGH ROAD. The one to the S, the MANOR
HOUSE, has a C17 core and an early C19 N front with a porch

on Ionic columns. To the N a green, THE FAIRLAND. The houses on the N side burnt down in 1688, replaced with C18 and C19 houses and shops including the Boys' and Girls' NATIONAL SCHOOLS, 1841 and 1857. Only THE UNICORN on the E side (No. 12) can boast a C17 timber-framed wing at the back. Behind it FAIRLAND TERRACE is a pleasant row of six early C19 cottages. Following the N side of the church leads E to another, larger green, known as the MARKET PLACE. This has an informal shape and an island has grown up in it, but there are quite a number of unusually townish and stylish Georgian houses. The most remarkable are the following. At the S end of the E side BEACONSFIELD HOUSE (No. 13), early Georgian, of three bays with giant pilasters and a parapet. Red brick, three storeys, with a central porch on two unfluted columns. The return to the S has blind windows. To its N the ADMIRAL'S HOUSE (No. 12) with an embattled wing to the S. The main elevation of two storeys and dormer attic in five bays, that to centre projecting and wider than the rest. Open pediment over the door. The stepped gables are C17. Admiral Sir Philip Wodehouse lived here, hence the name. Then LITTLE LONDON (No. 11), of the mid C18, red brick, two and a half storeys in five bays, doorcase with unfluted attached columns and an open pediment. Next QUORN HOUSE (No. 10), c. 1780, also of five bays but in two storeys, with a one-bay pediment and a porch on unfluted columns in the projecting middle bay. After that at r. angles, i.e. facing S, SOUTHERNWOOD, with shaped end-gables from the early C18. One small oval window to each floor at the r.

The N side of the Market Place has a coherent group of C18 and C19 houses and shops, most prominent being the WHITE HART HOTEL (No. 3), a timber-framed C17 building rebuilt in the 1770s to benefit from the opening of the turnpike in 1770 and given an early C19 façade. Two storeys but an irregular seven-bay elevation of round-headed sashes. Porch on unfluted columns with a white hart standing on top. No. 6 has a C17 rear wing but the stuccoed three-bay façade is c. 1810. The stepped gable to the E of No. 7 dated 1843. Shaped gables feature on one house on the S side of the Market Place (No. 16). No. 21 and Nos. 22–23 both C17 timber-framed houses, re-faced. On the W side, in the alley behind the Post Office, No. 29 has some exposed C17 timber studwork. BOND STREET runs N out of the Market Place and on the l., opposite the Methodist Church (*see* above), No. 12, MANSION HOUSE. A good late C17 house with shaped gables: seven bays and chequer brickwork. Some windows have raised frames. Moulded platband between the floors. No. 18 has a thatched roof and a C17 timber frame, and opposite, Nos. 13–21 are a row of shops and houses also C17 and timber-framed.

GURNEY'S MANOR, ¾ m. SSW. Another house of the Georgian five-bay brick type, with one-bay pediment. Simple doorcase under a minimal open pediment. There is a C17 wing to the rear.

HOCKERING

ST MICHAEL. Chancel and N arcade of about 1300–20. The chancel is badly over-restored, probably during the 1856 restoration. Are the big brick raking buttresses of that date? There were other campaigns in 1895 and 1911. The chancel windows are lancets or have Y- or intersecting tracery. There is a lowside window too. The chancel arch is a remarkable C19 piece in the E.E. mode, complete with marble shafts, stiff-leaf carving and dogtooth decoration. The sedilia and piscina however are substantially original: trefoiled arches with high-relief naturalistic foliage carving in the spandrels. The N arcade is of three bays, with quatrefoil piers and double-chamfered pointed arches, and the aisle has two late Dec two-light windows. This does not look like work of 1500, when money and oak were left for making a new aisle. More probably this refers to the aisle roof, which remains, arch-braced. The nave and chancel roofs also early C16 and arch-braced. Perp W tower with chequer flushwork on the buttresses, panelling in flushwork on the battlements. Two-light W window and bell-openings. Two three-light Perp S nave windows, restored. – FONT. C15 stem with carved figures, but a C19 bowl. – PULPIT. Simple, five-sided, Jacobean, and the usual blank arches. – BENCH ENDS. Two good early C16 ones in the chancel, one with Flamboyant tracery and a pair of hounds on the arm-rests, one looking over its shoulder. The other has a deerhound and a stag. – MONUMENT. Coped coffin-lid with a foliated cross (chancel S).

HOCKERING HOUSE. *Cecil Smith* designed the house in 1968 for John Berney in Neo-Georgian mode. Brick in two storeys. Nine-
128   bay S front, the centre three broken forward under a pediment. Seven-bay N (entrance) front with the three centre bays this time recessed under a single-bay pediment. Cut-back hipped roof. The windows, needless to say, are sashes.

Three HOUSES on THE STREET. MANOR HOUSE, N side, E of the church. C17 brick house of two storeys and six irregular bays, now with C19 mullioned windows with transoms. Three C19 dormers. Stepped gables. Further C17 fragments to rear. Adjacent, and formerly outbuildings, is MANOR FARMHOUSE. Converted timber-framed and brick farm buildings originally of C17, with some early C18 diapered brickwork. On the S side, YEW TREE FARMHOUSE, an early C18 house with chequered brickwork and eight bays. The window openings are C18 but the cross casements replaced in the C20. Platband.

HOCKHAM

HOLY TRINITY. Basically of the first half of the C14. Nave and aisles and a fine tall chancel. The tower collapsed in the early C18, and its depressing replacement of 1854 is a round bell-tower on two buttresses connected high up by an arch. The chancel has a tall four-light E window with reticulated tracery,

shafted inside, and to the S among others a straight-headed
two-light window with shafts attached to the mullions. There is
also a lowside window with a transom at its base. In the S aisle
also reticulated windows and a small W window with a little
mouchette wheel. The N aisle is simpler, but Dec too. Inside,
both arcades are Dec, but they differ considerably. The S arcade
is earlier. Quatrefoil piers with the foils to the nave and aisle
broadly filleted. Moulded bases and capitals and double sunk
quadrants to the arches. The N arcade has thinner quatrefoil
piers with shafts without capitals in the diagonals and double-
chamfered arches. The nave roof replaced in 1953 but the S
aisle has bits of C14 timber overhead. Good S aisle piscina with
an ogee rising to a crocketed finial between buttresses. In the
chancel a double piscina and sedilia of the dropped-sill type
with a plain dividing column. The arches are trefoiled. – FONT.
Octagonal, with flat Geometrical tracery; probably of *c.* 1320
since tracery patterns on fonts lagged twenty or thirty years
behind tracery in windows. – PAINTINGS. Excellent C15 paintings above the chancel arch. Majesty with dove over outline
of the original rood, the whole forming a Trinity (cf. the dedication). Kneeling figures and shields of the Trinity and *Arma
Christi* on either side of the Majesty, and angels above. The
rood itself is flanked by the Annunciation, rather than the usual
figures of the Virgin and St John. The figures have inscribed
scrolls, and are set against a rich diapered background. On the
N aisle wall, important mid-C14 paintings in poor condition,
including the Adoration of the Magi. (DP) – BENCHES. C15 and
a good group. With poppyheads of all kinds including pairs
of men and animals. On the arm-rests other figures, e.g. a
mermaid and a man who prays and at the same time touches
the back of his head with his feet. – STAINED GLASS. A N and a
S aisle window by *E.R. Suffling*, †1901; N aisle E by *Kempe &
Co.*, †1926.

GREAT HOCKHAM HALL. Very handsome five-bay Queen Anne
house of 1702 for Philip Ryley nicely set in a small park by the
church. Red brick. The entrance front faces E, entered through
a later C18 porch with engaged fluted and Tuscan columns.
The sashes replaced mid C19. Hipped roof with a flat and three
pedimented dormers, the centre pediment segmental. S front
also five bays and basically the same, but no porch. At the W
end a single-storey two-bay saloon added *c.* 1880. Long entrance
hall from the porch leads to a staircase hall beyond an archway.

LITTLE HOCKHAM HALL. The brick C19 façade hides an early
C17 rear wing. Timber-framed but with a stepped S stack and a
ridge stack with six octagonal flues. The two principal ground-
floor rooms heated from four-centred brick fireplaces, with
chamfered or sunk-quadrant mouldings.

The GREEN in the centre of the village is dotted with late C17 and
C18 timber-framed COTTAGES. No. 47 VICARAGE ROAD is a
house with a through-passage plan, late C16. Timber frame,
winder stairs by stack. The entrance is in the centre of the
façade with a three-light transomed casement r. BRIARDENE,

Shropham Road. Late C16 timber-framed house on the lobby-entrance plan, somewhat altered. Simple wall paintings on the chimney-breast of a tree and birds.

HOCKWOLD

Hockwold and Wilton to the E are now virtually amalgamated; they form one civil parish, but each has its own church. St Peter in Hockwold is now redundant. Brandon, the centre of the flint industry, is five miles E, and the material is prominent everywhere.

St Peter. The tall sw tower is of the mid C14, including the arch into the aisle. It has octagonal responds, and fluted plinths which might be Anglo-Saxon. The w window and the belfry windows have reticulated tracery and so too does the s aisle (there is no n aisle). Nave w window of three lights and inter-secting tracery. The N side of the nave is supported by three sloping flint buttresses, the two w ones clearly from the restoration of 1857, but the other may be one of the three made in 1535 for £9. There were other repairs at the time – the porch e.g. needed 'mendyng' in 1503. Late Perp clerestory under four-centred arches and an uncommonly fine roof. Alternating tie-beams and false hammerbeams, with queenposts on top of the ties and punched arched braces below them. The hammer-beams have carved angels on arched braces carrying pierced arched braces right up to the ridge piece, which is, naturally, moulded. It must be early C16, possibly as late as 1533 when 40s. was given to 'hallow' the church. Four-bay s arcade with octagonal piers. Bench sedilia and cinquefoiled piscina in the chapel at the E end of the aisle. – MONUMENTS. Wall monu-ment in chancel to Jermyn Wyche and Maria Hungerford, 1719, signed by *Robert Singleton* of Bury St Edmunds. Badly carved, which is unlike Singleton, so is it a studio piece? Two busts on a gadrooned plinth and above them a still-life of musical instru-ments. Columns l. and r. with putti standing outside them. – Cyril Wyche †1780 by *John Ivory* and *J. de Carle* of Norwich. With crying putti by a broken column. Fallen torch.

Hockwold Hall, Station Road. A late Tudor house of red brick, the N front on the E-plan, with far-projecting wings. At the back a polygonal projection, originally probably for the staircase. Built for the Heveningham family, altered by Cyril Wyche in the early C18 and again altered in the early C19. The N front has a two-storey crenellated square porch and in the E wing one can see four early C17 four-light mullioned windows. The internal arrangements are all altered. The owner in the C17 was the regicide William Heveningham, which resulted in confis-cation at the Restoration.

Red House, Station Road. Early C18 four-bay house of brick on a flint plinth. Thatched. Arched two-light casements.

College Farmhouse, South Street. The timber frame of heavy scantling with arched and tension braces points to the late C15. The N door led once into the screens passage of the hall but now serves the cellar under the inserted C18 stairs. The doorway has a four-centred head with punched spandrels and hollow- and wave-moulded jambs. The opposing S doorway survives too, but relocated to the first floor, with similar details. A blocked four-centred doorway from the screens passage to a service room remains as do wave- and hollow-moulded spine beams, upstairs and down. The roof all replaced above the ties. The hall was probably floored in the C17 and the plan altered. The brick W gable wall has a tremendous stepped external stack with a York stone fireplace inside to the ground floor. N front with a first-floor jetty partly concealed by C19 extensions.

No. 42 South Street (GAINSBOROUGH HOUSE). Late C17 timber-framed house on the lobby-entrance plan, re-worked with brick and flint in the later C18. Windows and doors C20. The N gable formerly jettied.

ROMANO-BRITISH SETTLEMENT. Along the N bank of the Ouse, the remains of a dense settlement have been found, including two temple sites. (DG)

HOE 9010

ST ANDREW. Long nave, chancel and tower-stump – all of one height. No chancel arch survives inside either. Unbuttressed tower, for which donations are recorded for bells and windows in 1509. The arch to the nave could be this date too. The nave 1794, chancel 1820, with a four-light intersecting E window. – FONT. Octagonal, Perp. Against the stem pretty vertical bands of quatrefoils. Against the bowl flowers in cusped fields. – COM-MUNION RAIL. C17.

HOE HALL, N of the church. There is a date 1845 inscribed into the brick at the NE corner. Gault brick. Two storeys and five bays, with giant pilasters at the corners and flanking the central porch against the advanced centre bay. The porch on unfluted columns. At the rear a flint and brick wing of the C17, raised a storey in the C19, so that one notices from the C17 only the triple octagonal flues to the N stack.

GORGATE HALL, 1¼ m. W of the church. Large ten-bay, two-storey red brick house of the mid C19 facing S. Rusticated quoins to the centre five bays and to the ends. Sashes and hipped roofs.

HOLKHAM 8040

ST WITHBURGA. The church lies dramatically on a mound in the extensive park of Holkham Hall, not far from the lake. It is a large and interesting building, though severely restored by *James K. Colling* in 1868–71 sweeping away the decoration by *Joseph Rose* from his restoration in 1767. An inscription below the E window confirms: 'restored and partly rebuilt 1869'. It was done at the expense of Juliana Countess of Leicester who died in the following year and whose memorial is inside. The oldest evidence of the church came out at the time of the restoration: the foundations of a tower inside the W bay of the nave. It preceded the present tower and may have been Saxon or Norman. Many Norman stones with decoration were also found. The tower now stands to the S of the church, incorporating a wide porch, a little E of the W end. It is large and sturdy and dates from the early C13, see the lancet windows. Early C14 bell-openings with Y-tracery. However, all this is largely rebuilt. Quite a show made of the balustraded flight of stone steps within the porch storey. Of the same date as the tower the S aisle W lancet, the pair of lancets immediately W of the tower and the strange, wide, irregular arch between nave and S aisle, W of the chancel arch. This must have led into a transept. Foundations of the outer walls of such a transept exist. The arch has nook-shafts with foliage capitals facing the aisle. The same shafts and capitals inside the S doorway. Then, early in the C14, the N chapel arcade and the E bay of the N aisle arcade were built. They have quatrefoil piers and boldly moulded capitals. A little later the chancel arch appears to have been made. It cuts clean through the N arcade arch. The story is complicated, as the responds are an addition to the square imposts (straight joints). Dec S aisle window of two lights E of the tower with a reticulation unit. The other windows of the same design are of 1870, as is the five-light E window. The whole E end was in fact rebuilt. The three W bays of the N and S aisle arcades seem to belong to the later C14: octagonal piers, double-chamfered arches. Two late Perp panel-tracery windows to S chancel chapel, one to N side.

FURNISHINGS. By *Colling* presumably the stone PULPIT, stone FONT, stone REREDOS and the tower staircase. – WOODWORK, e.g. pews, screen, all by *Robinson Cornish* of North Walsham. – STAINED GLASS. In the S chapel an enamel heraldic glass panel of 1769 by *William Peckitt* of York. Bright orange, blue and ochre colours commemorating the repair of church and chancel of 1767–8 for Margaret Countess Dowager of Leicester. Most of the remaining glass is in C14 grisaille style, in the E window and W tower by *Lavers, Barraud & Westlake*, 1870. – MONUMENTS. Four C12 or C13 coffin-lids with foliated crosses, etc. (W end), two more in N chapel. – Two monuments by *Nicholas Stone*, or rather workshop of Stone, i.e. *Robert Pook*, both made in 1639 and both in the S chapel. Miles Armiger †1639, alabaster, with a good kneeling figure facing a prayer desk under an arched architectural niche. – Meriall Coke and husband †1636, and William Wheatley and Anthony Wheately, her father and grandfather, with their wives, all gathered into one standing monument. Alabaster, with three kneeling couples in a row facing each other across three prayer desks. Pediment above and bust in the pediment. Against the base fifteen children. – Juliana Countess of Leicester †1870. By *Sir Joseph Edgar Boehm*. Tomb-chest with recumbent figure of the Countess asleep. – Arthur George Coke †1915 in the Dardanelles. Pedimented

103

marble wall monument by *A. Drury*. For other pre-1870 Coke
monuments, *see* Tittleshall. – BRASS. Jane Osborne †1618. Coat
of arms, inscription and a griffin's head, incomplete (s chapel).
– MAUSOLEUM, to the W of the church. 1870, Gothic, with a
stone roof and cross gables over side lancets. One supposes it is
by *Colling*.

HOLKHAM HALL

Holkham Hall, the seat of the Cokes, Earls of Leicester, lies in a
vast park, close to the sea but not within sight of it. Thomas Coke,
later the first earl, was born in 1697. He went on the Grand Tour
in 1712 and stayed away till 1718. Those were the very years in
which the purity and nobility of Palladio's style began to be preferred by a small group of virtuosi to the more forceful and less
exactingly disciplined Baroque of Wren, Vanbrugh and Hawksmoor.
The leader of the group was Lord Burlington, the first architect
leader Colen Campbell, who was involved in the design of
Houghton, and its most brilliant exponent William Kent. In 1714
Coke fell in with William Kent and they toured northern Italy
together, and from then until the 1730s they communicated frequently. Correspondence passed between Coke and Burlington
also. The site was occupied by Sir Edward Coke's Elizabethan
house, called Hill Hall, and the idea of rebuilding on a splendid
scale seems to have originated in Thomas Coke's mind about
1722, the same year that building had started at Houghton. On
the existing evidence it is likely that *Coke* himself designed the house
in consultation with *Lord Burlington*, employing first *Brettingham*
as a draughtsman and supervisor and later *Kent* in a more responsible role. This was not new: Sir Roger Townshend at Raynham
and Sir Jacob Astley at Melton Constable had done much the
same in the C17, and Sir Andrew Fountaine at Narford in 1716–18
probably was his own architect, each with his own advising professional. Coke did not immediately consult Kent or Burlington
but in 1722 was advised by a *Mr Tallman*, possibly the collector
and antiquary John Talman, and in 1724 paid *Colen Campbell* sixteen guineas for a survey. Nothing is known of these, but in 1726
Matthew Brettingham produced two plans and five elevations.
These show the house with an attic storey but without the side
pavilions. By the late 1720s the general scheme was established
including the four pavilions, and this seems to mark Brettingham's
decline, replaced by *William Kent*, who worked up the design of
the house and was designing buildings for the park. Brettingham,
however, as a local man, remained as site architect and was well
placed, especially after Kent's death in 1748, to influence design,
tempered or led, there is no doubt, by *Coke*'s own ideas.
Brettingham's plans of the 1720s are annotated in Coke's hand,
and it is unlikely that Brettingham, aged twenty-seven in 1726 and
on his first major commission, could have come up with such an
advanced design, especially as he produced nothing else in the
same league and had not studied architecture abroad. Thomas
Coke's Grand Tour was specifically geared to such study and he

even trained under one Signor Giacomo for several months while in Rome. Kent's work was initially confined to the park, later to the interior of the private wing and the Stone Hall, and his own drawings are only for buildings in the park, and for the hall, library and N and S fronts of the house. In other words the plan and elevations of the house were established before Kent's name first appears in 1729 in connection with the Obelisk and Temple.

Already in 1731 John Lord Hervey saw what he called 'a Burlington house with four pavilions on paper' and a 'park in embryo'. Construction was both delayed and slow. The foundation stone was laid in 1734 and work started on the SW wing (the family rooms), which was completed in 1741, and at first linked to the Elizabethan house to the SW by a corridor. This was the only part Kent saw completed and the only part where the interior schemes are wholly his. In 1753 the S front was finished and the N front begun and by 1759 (the year of Thomas Coke's death with debts of £90,000) the exteriors were virtually complete. Coke's widow immediately dismissed Brettingham as site architect in favour of *James Miller*, the woodcarver, whose skills by then were more relevant. The house was finally published as complete in 1761, though finishing touches took three more years.

Brettingham claimed in his book *The Plans, Elevations, and Sections of Holkham in Norfolk*, 1761, that he designed the house, with no mention of Kent, but this was later corrected by Brettingham's son who remarks that the plans were by 'the Earls of Burlington and Leicester, assisted by Mr Kent'.

EXTERIOR. In plan Holkham consists of a central block connected by straight, one-bay links to four oblong blocks to the NW, NE, SW and SE. The windows at rustic level and in the *piano nobile* are carried through at the same levels and only the great height of the *piano nobile* rooms in the centre block and the angle towers make this part higher than the rest. The idea is Palladian and specially reminiscent of such villas as that of the Trissinos at Meledo. The house in fact is a testimony to Whig appreciation of the Antique. The style is Palladian too, even to the choice of locally made brick as a building material, although it is clear from letters discovered in 1996 that in 1734 Coke was intending to build in Bath stone, some of which had earlier been supplied by Ralph Allen for garden buildings. This proved impossible, partly because of difficulties in carriage. The brick is light fawn, chosen, it seems, because the colour was considered similar to that of antique brick (red brick is used instead in the less visible courtyard elevations) and looks from a distance like stone. But neither from far nor from near can it have the beauty of the ashlar surfaces of Houghton (q.v.). The main block consists of a rusticated basement with small windows and a superb *piano nobile*; that is all, except for the four square angle turrets or eminences, each with one small window to each side and a pyramid roof. The rest of the main block has a balustrade in front of the low roof. The GARDEN FRONT, to the S, has a pedimented portico of six Corinthian columns in front of five tall

85

arched windows. The loggia at *piano nobile* level formed by the
portico was not originally accessible from outside. The windows
of the *piano nobile* are either pedimented or, when greater
prominence demands it, of the Venetian type. The latter appear
under the turrets towards the garden. The N front is content
with a central pedimented projection but Venetian windows
recur within it, in the bays l. and r. and under the turrets. These
are set within recessed round relieving arches, a form first used
by Lord Burlington on the N front of Chiswick Villa begun
c. 1725 (imitated from a Palladio villa elevation he owned). It
became a very popular motif to the end of the C18. The corner
eminences at Houghton, in Campbell's design, have pedimented
tops, as at Wilton. At Holkham they have pyramid roofs, as in
several Palladio villas, and as imitated by Burlington *c.* 1721 at
Tottenham Park.

The four wings are of five bays to the S and three to the N.
The ground floor is rusticated. Above them is a Venetian window
in the centre to the N, but otherwise there are only a few pediments to windows. The centre of each wing is raised by a half
storey. The sides as well as the centre are crowned by pediments,
the centre ones open at their base. The way the façades of the
wings step in and out in tune with the stepping up and down of
the roof-line was famously described by Wittkower as 'staccato'
– and is the antithesis of Baroque principles. There are open-
ended E and W courts between the wings. From the Venetian
window in the centre of the W side of the house one looks across
the court towards the S end of the lake. The wings were dedicated
to the chapel (SE), the kitchen (NE), guest rooms (NW), and
rooms for the family (SW).

INTERIOR. The arrangement of wings extending from a central
core was necessary at Holkham, for the interior of the centre
block is more consistently palatial than that of almost any other
house in England, and reserved entirely for state use; the services
and private chambers occupy the wings. Moreover, the interior
is smaller than one expects. The *piano nobile* has no more than
thirteen rooms round two inner courtyards separated by the
Stone Hall, an apartment of surprising grandeur. The decorative details are derived from antique sources via the pages of
Desgodetz's *Edifices Antiques de Rome* of 1682 and from Inigo
Jones, as is spelt out in Brettingham's book. Nevertheless there
was scope in some places for Kent's invention. The principal
craftsmen were *G.* and *W. Atkinson* and *Joseph Pickford* for the
marble, especially in the hall, *Thomas Clark* for the plasterwork
of the ceilings, *Thomas Carter* for the chimneypieces, *Marsden*
and *James Miller* for woodcarving, *Thomas Hall* for ironwork.

The house is entered at ground level through a projecting
single-storey VESTIBULE added in the 1850s. This opens abruptly
into the STONE HALL, through a doorway internally framed by 84
black marble columns carrying a pediment. The inscription
panel erected over the door by Lady Leicester in 1764 reads:
'THIS SEAT, on an open barren Estate, was planned, planted,
built, decorated and inhabited the middle of the XVIIIth Century

1 Stone Hall
2 North Dining Room
3 North Tribune
4 Statue Gallery
5 South Tribune
6 Drawing Room
7 Saloon
8 South Dining Room
9 Landscape Room
10 Green State Bedroom

FAMILY WING

GUEST WING

5

4

3

6

COURT

2

7

1

8

COURT

14

9

10

12

13

11

11 Green State Dressing Room
12 North State Dressing Room
13 North State Bedroom
14 State Sitting Room
15 Library
16 Chapel

15

16

CHAPEL WING

KITCHEN WING

30 m
100 ft

Holkham Hall. Plan of *piano nobile*

by THOS COKE EARL OF LEICESTER'. Above, the internal treatment of the window can be appreciated, with big and bold Corinthian columns. But what dominates the hall is the broad and stately staircase rising straight ahead up to the *piano nobile*, and its monumental architectural setting. It is a superb effect and Kent's, Coke's and Brettingham's handling of it is flawless. Possibly inspired by Burlington's 1730 Assembly Rooms at York, the design is ultimately from Palladio's basilican design after Vitruvius. The ground floor is faced with polished slabs of pink Derbyshire alabaster. It carries a gallery with Ionic columns, also pink alabaster, and an entablature of garlands, bucrania and putti based on those from the Temple of Fortuna Virilis in Rome. The gallery forms a coffered apse at the far end, and a broad straight flight of stairs leads up into this apse. A frieze with a Greek key pattern runs below the ground-floor facing, a frieze with a wave pattern between it and the cast-iron balustrade of the gallery. Splendid, deeply coffered cove, sumptuous plaster ceiling with its fields framed by bands of flowers, leaves, etc. Hardly any of the coffers are regular in shape but rather are differing trapezoids to maintain the perspective. The room was not finished until 1764 and Kent's proposed alterations were themselves changed in 1757: he had intended at first Corinthian columns, not Ionic, the room shaped as a 46 ft cube, and the staircase in two flights. The final arrangement is probably by Thomas Coke himself, assisted by Brettingham. Everything in this hall is grand and dramatic, yet all the motifs are of classical derivation.

On the gallery of the Stone Hall are later relief panels by *Stoldo Lorenzi* (Lorenzo I), *Chantrey* (The Passing of the Reform Bill, 1832), *Westmacott* (The Death of Socrates) and *Banks* (The Death of Germanicus); also *Chantrey*'s *tour-de-force*, the Two Woodcocks (representing birds killed by the sculptor, a frequent visitor, with a single shot in 1829), and some of the famous Coke Collection of antique statuary. Much of the house is indeed a museum of statuary and a temple to the arts generally. The bust of Thomas Coke, the first earl, by *Chantrey* showing him as a Roman senator is after a model by *Roubiliac*. Bust of Coke of Norfolk, the first earl of the second creation (*see* below), to the r., also by *Chantrey*.

The description of the rooms follows the usual route of the public, a route probably followed by more than two centuries of visitors; for already in the C18 visitors were taken round. We know the story of a party arriving, being told that they could not see the house 'for an hour at least, as there was a party going round', being taken to a room to wait, and there finding yet 'another large party awaiting the guide'.*

To the w of the hall, on the entrance side, is the NORTH DINING ROOM, a cube room with a dome and a lower coffered apse with pilasters and a coffered arch in front. On the l. and r. walls are big Roman heads in oval medallions. Drapes held by

* Lady Beauchamp Proctor in 1772.

eagles frame them. Four pedimented doorways. Two chimney-pieces by *Thomas Carter*. The next room is that in the NW corner, the NORTH TRIBUNE, an octagon, with niches for statues in the diagonals. The doorways have broken pediments here.

The whole centre of the W side is the STATUE GALLERY, starting and ending in an apse, the apses introduced without pilasters or coffering of their arches. The design seems to be based on Burlington's Chiswick, and in turn on Palladio. The centre is a Venetian window, from which one can examine the W court, the two W wings and part of the lake. Chimneypieces by *Joseph Pickford* after Inigo Jones. Niches for the SCULPTURE collected by Thomas Coke on his Grand Tour and augmented with the help of the younger Matthew Brettingham up to Coke's death in 1759. In the SW angle the SOUTH TRIBUNE, identical to its companion except that the niches are filled with bookcases topped by swan-necked pediments. There is a date 1753. The S front begins with the DRAWING ROOM in white and gold. The ceiling has heads at the intersection of the frames of the panels. Below it is a beautiful frieze with griffins added in 1757 on Coke's orders.

The SALOON forms the centre of the S façade and windows look out through the S portico to the park beyond. Its ceremonial entrance is direct from the Stone Hall. It has a deep coffered coving, the coffers becoming trapezoid for the same reason as those in the Stone Hall. The oblong centre of the ceiling is again coved and coffered, but with a different pattern. The design comes from Desgodetz. The doorway from the Stone Hall is particularly grand and carries a broken segmental pediment. The doorway is flanked by two fireplaces of white and pink marble by *Thomas Carter*. The SOUTH DINING ROOM again has griffins in the frieze. As so often in Georgian dining rooms, the motif of the vine is prominent. Broken pediments over the doors, chimneypiece with pairs of female caryatid figures. Ceiling based on an Inigo Jones design. The square room in the SE corner is called the LANDSCAPE ROOM, but was made as a dressing room; here the doorways lose their pediments, but the Corinthian columns to the Venetian window make up for the loss. It is followed by the GREEN STATE BEDROOM facing E with a ceiling pattern of an oval centre continued N and S by two semicircles. Fireplace with two young female termini caryatids. Then follow the GREEN and NORTH STATE DRESSING ROOMS finished 1759 for Lady Leicester. The NORTH STATE BEDROOM is in the NE corner, and the ceiling pattern is again different, an oval in a square. Altogether the patterns of the ceilings deserve study. This applies also to the last of the state rooms, the STATE SITTING ROOM, to the E of the Stone Hall. The doorways in this room are the plainest of all because it was designed as another dressing room, and only since 1909 has it changed its purpose.

Two of the WINGS require some description. In the SW WING Kent's LIBRARY, occupying the whole W side, was finished by

1741.* Bookcases with broken pediments line the walls and the ceiling is perhaps Kent's most remarkable, for the diamond fields in the flat ceiling are above coving with triangular pendentives cut back as if for windows. The chimneypiece was executed by *Marsden*, as was the one in the Sitting Room. An unbroken enfilade runs from the Library to the altarpiece of the Chapel in the SE wing, over 300 ft long, indicating that the Palladian plan could accommodate a Baroque vista. The SE WING has the CHAPEL finished in 1760, lined with pink Staffordshire alabaster to half its height below a Greek key frieze. The ceiling by *James Miller* is tightly coffered. The altarpiece (*Guido Reni*'s Madonna) at the E end is framed by a pair of Corinthian marble columns supporting a segmental pediment and flanked by pilasters r. and l., i.e. a tripartite composition. A screen of two Corinthian columns and pilasters at the W end, below the family pew.

STABLES to the E. By *William Burn* for the second Earl of Leicester, who employed him during 1851–5. Two courtyards open to the N, that to the E heralded by two low buildings of one and two storeys, with corner eminences like the Hall itself. The W court has a nine-bay frontage, the outer two bays recessed and the centre three projecting under a pediment. Various uses now (tea rooms, bygones collections, pottery). GAME LARDER, on the S side of stable court and E of the Hall, 1803 by *Samuel Wyatt*. Octagonal with a circular interior lined with alabaster and fitted with a remarkable free-standing cast-iron frame for hanging game.

In front of the N façade Lion and Lioness by *Boehm*, 1871. Facing the garden façade a FOUNTAIN with the group of Perseus and Andromeda (really St George and the Dragon) by *Charles Smith*. This dates from c. 1850. The balustraded TERRACES to the S and W of the Hall were laid out by *W. A. Nesfield* and *William Burn* between 1849 and 1857. To the E of the house is the former ORANGERY, c. 1850, by *William Burn*. It has a pedimented three-bay centre with three-bay wings recessed to either side. The windows under round arches and the parapet balustraded. Further E a small, one-bay TEMPLE, 1859, also by *Burn*, with Roman Doric columns under a pediment to each side.

The PARK. The park and its buildings are the joint creation of the first earl (died 1759) and of the great agricultural reformer Thomas William Coke, the first earl of the second creation, who inherited in 1776 and died in 1842. Thomas William Coke doubled the size of the park. Work on the park and some of the buildings within it began before a brick of the house was laid and at an early date the grand approach was settled. The route was from the S, starting with the Triumphal Arch (not built until later), then the long South Avenue to the Obelisk and the Temple off to one side, then suddenly over the hill to the house below. All these buildings are by *William Kent*. The park was

---

* Neither this nor the chapel wing is normally open to the public.

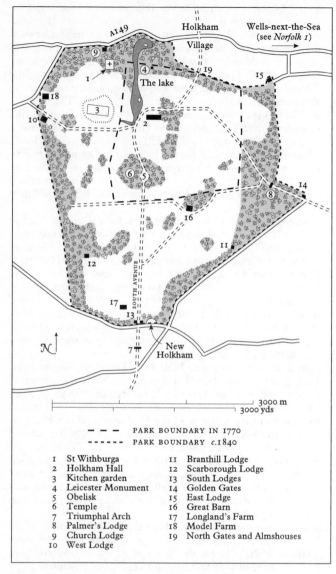

Holkham Park

laid out by *Capability Brown* in 1762 on the basis of a scheme by
Kent, but his work was not extensive and the park after the
completion of the house was not an adequate foil. The first
KITCHEN GARDEN begun in 1728 to the w of the house proved
inadequate, and the lake was an eyesore. After 1780 *Thomas
William Coke* set about fitting improvement, much of it to his
own design, according to *Humphry Repton*, who had himself

made a Red Book for the pleasure gardens by the lake in that year (the gardens were built but demolished in the 1840s). *William Eames* and *John Webb* were called in to work on the new LAKE, the most conspicuous feature. This replaced the kitchen garden. Eames made the N sluices (the first lake was tidal) and in 1801–3 Webb dug out the new lake in its present form. In 1780 a farm was bought on the W side of the lake and the new kitchen garden built. For this Coke employed *Samuel Wyatt*, the beginning of an association lasting until Wyatt's death in 1807. In all Wyatt designed over fifty buildings for Thomas Coke, almost all of interest, not just for their fine Neoclassical detail, and enlightened attitude to housing and agrarian method typical of his patron, but also in the use of new materials, especially cast iron and slate.

The second KITCHEN GARDEN alone cost £10,000, covering six acres within an enclosure of thirty acres defined by a HA-HA. The garden declined after the First World War, but has been progressively restored since the mid 1950s as a garden centre. Twenty-three buildings in all crowd the E end of the walled area. The first in time is the VINERY, 1782–4, by *Wyatt*, outside the walls to the S. It has a N front of two storeys in seven bays, the central entrance with a pair of Ionic unfluted columns *in antis* under a wide, shallow fanlight. Sash windows either side, the upper windows centre-hung. The roof was raised in the C20. Behind is a full-length GLASSHOUSE with cast-iron braces and sash windows. Various other glasshouses, melon pits and subsidiary buildings of the 1780s and later.

The LEICESTER MONUMENT, ½ m. N of the house, com- 102 memorates the first Earl of Leicester of the second creation (i.e. in 1837), Thomas William Coke, more familiar as Coke of Norfolk (1754–1842). The monument rightly celebrates him as a great agricultural reformer. In the forty years between 1776 and 1816 he raised the yield of the land to such an extent that the rent roll went up from £2,200 to £20,000. The monument was duly commissioned by his tenants and cost them £4,000. It was designed by *Donthorn* and erected by the stonemason *James Watson* in 1845–8 on the site of Kent's N lodges. A Corinthian column 120 ft high stands on a plinth decorated on three sides with bas-relief panels (of Granton Pier stone) by *John Henning Jun*. At the corners are a Devon ox, a Southdown sheep, a seed-drill and a plough – the principal symbols of Coke's improvements. The capital has, instead of the Corinthian acanthus leaves, turnip leaves and a mangel-wurzel, and above is a kind of rotunda and a wheatsheaf.

A little farther away from the house to the S but, like the monument, in axis with it, the OBELISK, a sturdy piece, 80 ft high, put up in 1729–30 by *Kent* on the highest point of the estate and said to mark the beginning of the building works. Limestone. On the base spare square panels of vermiculation were finished in 1732. Square tapering shaft capped with a pyramid. To the W of the obelisk the TEMPLE, also of 1729–31, and by *Kent*, the first building on the estate to use the characteristic Holkham brick. This has a portico of two square piers framing two Roman Doric columns *in antis*, triglyph and metope frieze, and pediment. The front of the portico is connected with the body of the building by two arches (a motif used by Palladio e.g. on the Villa Capra). Lower side bays with the Palladian motif of a fragmentary pediment. Equally Palladian the tripartite lunette windows, i.e Diocletian, in the drum of the octagonal dome, another borrowing from Chiswick Villa. Inside are four niches with semicircular heads; the doorway from the portico has a broken pediment.

From the Obelisk the long SOUTH AVENUE leads to the South Gates and Lodges of 1847 (*see* below) and then to *Kent*'s TRIUMPHAL ARCH, designed in 1739 but not complete until 1752: a large tripartite structure of one wide and two narrow arched openings. It is of Holkham gault brick, with a little red brick to the N side, and partly with unusual whole-flint rustication. Flint rustication was used by Kent at the temple at Euston in Suffolk in 1746, but the house there was altered by Matthew Brettingham. The middle bay rises to a Diocletian window and a pediment in an attic storey over a cornice with outsized dentils. All three archways are groin-vaulted inside. Outer arches also pedimented. The Holkham arch was executed by *Brettingham*, quite faithfully following Kent's designs except that Kent originally envisaged tall obelisk-like pyramids over the side-arches, an inscription panel instead of the Diocletian windows and in all the pediments rocky landscapes.

Near the arch, i.e. at NEW HOLKHAM, *Wyatt* constructed a most unusual semicircular arrangement of cottages and school in 1793–5, but these were demolished in 1913 and replaced with five standard semis dated 1913 to 1937.

LODGES. After the expansion of the Park in the late C18, new perimeter lodges were required and *Wyatt* provided five, all of gault brick and all spare and Neoclassical. PALMER'S LODGE, of 1799, is the only monumental one. Tripartite with giant Doric engaged columns and a pediment, but only one wide archway. To its l. and r. niches with rectangular panels over. A Coade-stone plaque in the pediment by *Bernasconi*. Then r. and l. again a short Doric screen linking to the low, hipped-roofed lodges, bare of detail. The render is in fact Parker's Roman cement. CHURCH LODGE, Wells Road, 1784, has a canted end linked by a two-storey wing to a conventional house. Overhanging eaves and sash windows. WEST LODGE followed in 1790, the canted end elaborated here into a taller octagonal structure entered under a pedimented porch so shallow that it is almost just a pediment supported on Doric columns without bases. BRANTHILL LODGE, 1805, repeats the canted bay to the w end, and WELLS LODGE, 1803, was the simplest, based on a cube, but enlarged by *Burn* in 1852 and called East Lodge. Finally four later lodges, first SCARBOROUGH LODGE, isolated within the park ⅝ m. NW of Longlands Farm, *c.* 1820. Plain, two storeys, pyramid roof. Better are the SOUTH LODGES by *S. S. Teulon*, 1847. Two simple square pavilions under pyramid roofs. Rusticated quoins and bay windows to the South Avenue. The

other two by *William Burn*, 1852: GOLDEN GATES, E of Palmer's
Lodge, on the main road from Fakenham to Wells (and the railings); and EAST LODGE already mentioned (continue W down
a track where Mill Road, Wells, suddenly cuts N to the W of the
hospital, having been moved in 1782 to extend the park).

FARMS. Apart from the immediate buildings round the house and
the park there are, or were, numerous estate farms and houses,
mostly by *Wyatt*. The finest of all Wyatt's farm buildings is the
GREAT BARN, 'the handsomest and best proportioned barn in
England', *c.* 1790, a large gault brick barn of traditional layout
in an austere Neoclassical guise, just as were Wyatt's lodges (*see*
above). Fivestead, i.e. of five external bays including two
threshing floors. The threshing areas are reached through two
opposing pedimented transepts with segmental-headed doorways. The main block has pedimented N and S gable-heads,
and clasping the gable-ends are hipped single-storey workshop
outshuts. Semicircular lunettes under the eaves of the main
block. The detailing is very spare.

Thomas Coke enlarged LONGLAND'S FARM to the S of the park,
to *Wyatt*'s design in about 1795. The FARMHOUSE of two
storeys and attic in three bays, gault brick and a hipped roof.
Pedimented narrow wings to the sides. Pedimented doorcase.
Cottages added to the E early in the C19. The main BARN to the
NW is also by *Wyatt*, much simpler and more conventional than
the Great Barn. STABLES to the W, again *Wyatt*'s, 1792. Of one
storey, elaborated into two storeys at the corners and with,
oddly, four small pediments on each main front. In 1859–60
G. A. Dean put up the GRANARY buildings to the N and the estate
WORKSHOPS. Gault brick, with a two-storey office in the centre
graced with a wide porch on posts. The surprise is the CLOCK
TOWER in four storeys, with a pyramid roof on which is an
octagonal bellcote. Dean's design dates from 1853 and was crit-
icized at the time for its over-elaboration.

MODEL FARMHOUSE, on the B1155 to Burnham Overy Town.
Wyatt, 1786. Built as an inn (the New Inn) to cater for visitors
to the annual sheep-shearings. Gault brick, two storeys, pedimented doorway to the S front. Sash windows in recessed arches
on the ground floor, cf. Soane's contemporary Shotesham Park.
In 1852–3 *G. A. Dean* provided the dairy farm buildings to the
W, arranged round a courtyard.

HOLKHAM VILLAGE. The main entrance to the house and park
was changed from the S to the N in the 1840s. One enters from
the village by the NORTH GATES, by *S. S. Teulon*, 1848. Five
four-centred arches set in gault brick walls connect to the
ALMSHOUSES either side. These are by *Burn*, 1851–5, in an
alien Tudor style. Long, projecting, one-storeyed lodges with
cast-iron windows. Stepped gables. On the avenue between the
gates and the main road stand many estate houses, semi-
detached and detached or in groups. They remind one that
Thomas William Coke spent, he claimed, £500,000 on farm
buildings and estate housing. Quite simple ones, dated 1817–21,
and late C19 ones in a vague Tudor style. Ten more built by

Wyatt in 1805–6 have been demolished. The INFANTS' SCHOOL is 1837 with additions of 1882 carrying Tudor chimneyshafts (N wing). The SENIOR SCHOOL is *c.* 1890, with pediments over the windows, a veranda to the first floor of the W wing and a turret. Elaborate chimneyshafts again. VICTORIA HOTEL, of the mid C19, flint with gault brick dressings. Two storeys and attic in six bays. Pilasters between the bays and at the ends. The OCTAGON stands nearest the park. 1801, by *Wyatt.* Two cottages in the form of an octagon under a pyramid roof, fitted with sashes and casements. This at least was intended as a landmark seen from within the park.

On Wells Road, ROSE COTTAGES are by *Wyatt,* 1785–6, the earliest of the Holkham Village houses. Three-bay centre in two storeys with lower side pieces containing four back-to-back cottages. Finally, a survivor from an earlier era, THE ANCIENT HOUSE, Wells Road. Flint with brick dressings. Two-storey porch *c.* 1620 under a stepped gable and lit through a mullioned window. The end-gables also stepped, but these presumably part of a C19 reconstruction by *S. King* of London.

DEFENDED ENCLOSURE. On an island in the salt marshes S of Burrow Gap is the site of an oval fort covering some six acres. The W is naturally protected, but on the NE is a single bank and ditch and on the S and SE there are double banks. The entrance is on the S. Unexcavated but possibly Iron Age. (JW)

HOLLAND'S WALL *see* YAXHAM

HOLLAND'S WALL *see* YAXHAM

8000

HOLME HALE

ST ANDREW. There is evidence for a C12 nave (W wall) to which a N aisle was added in the C13. The W tower was rebuilt in the C15. The church was called 'new' in 1383, and in 1469, and there is indeed much Perp work. In the tower E wall, visible only from the inside, is a round-arched upper doorway, Norman at the latest. It is round-arched all the way through the considerable thickness of the tower wall. Higher up is a cusped light. Norman also a fragment of a colonnette used upside down as part of the C13 angle piscina in the chancel. Of the C13 the N arcade too. Four bays, circular piers, circular capitals, triple-hollow-chamfered arches. Dec N and S doorways (the latter blocked) and the aisle W window. Chancel E window of 1893, general restoration in 1868 (£659). The four-stage W tower was building 1431–62 according to bequests, in 1431 in fact already under way. It has double-chamfered doorways to E (not a real tower arch, the arch mouldings dying into the jambs), N and S. S arch blocked to form the vestry window. Was it a processional way? Three-light Perp bell-openings and crenellated parapet. Aisle, S nave and chancel windows Perp. The clerestory has four panel-tracery windows to the N and a three-light E window. Roof with C15 hammerbeams (angels) alternating with arched braces, and longitudinal wall arches. The carpenter had his measurements wrong and needed a short extra bay to meet the tower. Good C19 stone corbels in the aisle. – FONT. Plain, octagonal and with a splayed stem. – SCREEN. A handsome piece of *c*. 1500 or a little earlier, with two wide ogee-headed one-light divisions either side of the ogeed entrance. Much fine tracery, especially two of rose-window type in the spandrels of the entrance. – PULPIT. With Jacobean panels, the upper tier with basic strapwork. – READER'S DESK. Similar, two panels meeting at an angle. – BENCHES. Of quite an unusual type in N aisle, with ends with a straight top (i.e. no poppyheads) and little figures and animals in relief, set in hollowed-out recesses. C15. The rest are of 1868. – STAINED GLASS. A little insignificant medieval glass in the S windows and a Crucifixion in the E window of 1895.

OLD RECTORY, 1846 by *Donthorn*, immediately NE. Brick painted red and partly rendered. Horrible concrete tiles to the roof. Five bays, the outer ones broken forward slightly. In these bays the cross casements remain, otherwise sashed.

OLD NAG'S HEAD, Church Road. Two storeys and attic, with C19 and C20 details. It was an early C16 timber-framed open hall house given floors, a big chimney bay and brick gable-ends in the C17. Gables redone in the C20. The high end was to the E, with the hall. Service partition still *in situ*, and one four-centred passage doorway.

HOLME HALE HALL. Of the late C16 house of the Bedingfelds (a minor branch) little is to be seen behind the early C19 S façade, remodelled for Robert Farrand, who succeeded in 1819. Rendered brick, five bays, two storeys. Central Doric porch. Gabled roof with three pedimented dormers. The pedimented single-bay side pavilions are a pretentious idea of Farrand's. In the mid C19 a single-storey, three-bay addition was made to the E, set back and containing a billiard room; given a second storey in 1871. STABLES, red brick with gault brick dressings, *c*. 1820, have a seven-bay façade with two carriage entrances. Circular DOVECOTE, contemporary with the stables but derelict at time of writing. 100 yds W is an attractive Regency FOOTBRIDGE, of cast iron, with a segmental arch.

BURY'S HALL, $\frac{7}{8}$ m. S. Late C19 façade of five bays in two storeys. Octagonal Neo-Tudor shafts to the stacks.

ERNEFORD HOUSE, $\frac{5}{8}$ m. WSW. Colourwashed brick. Front of two storeys and attic in seven bays, with two bays covered by an extension. The cross casements are all of *c*. 1700, at least to the ground floor. Platband between floors. The plan is a lobby-entrance, still with the winder by the stack. Roof with staggered butt-purlins and wind-bracing.

HOLME-NEXT-THE-SEA

ST MARY. Perp and 1778. Internally without any character, but quite an impressive exterior, thanks to the big broad SW tower containing the porch. Entrance with quatrefoils in the spandrels.

Tierceron star vault inside. The window above with a curious truncated concave-sided gable as a hoodmould and a cross above it. Above that are sound-holes filled with a grille of panel-tracery units. Three-light Perp bell-openings. Brick battlements, probably of 1778, when the nave was rebuilt (the existing aisled nave demolished 1771). A passage of 1983 is all that links tower to nave. Interestingly the N side of the tower, invisible from the village, is of much cruder flintwork. Grisly concrete pantiles to nave and chancel replaced in about 1977 the rare (for C18 Norfolk) and handsome Westmorland slate. The nave formerly went on N of the tower, see the jambs of a large W window. In the chancel the E window is of 1778 and so is the N wall; the wave-moulded chancel arch and the priest's doorway are Perp. Nave and chancel roofs and the seating are 1884, by *Frederick Preedy*. – FONT. 1885. Green and red marble shafts under the bowl, quite good. – STAINED GLASS. W window by *Jane Nelson*, 1874, as depressing as the rest of the nave. – MONUMENTS. Brass to Henry Nottingham and wife, *c.* 1405, 18 in. figures, and an inscription recording that they lie here 'Yat maden this chirche stepull and quere' and also gave two vestments and bells. – Palimpsest brass, on the obverse an inscription of 1582, on the reverse part of lettering and canopy of two large continental brasses (cf. King's Lynn, St Margaret). Both brasses are in the nave, to the S of the chancel arch. – Richard Stone †1607 and wife. Inscription in Latin and in English. They 'lived in wedlock joyfully for 64 years and 3 months', she apparently outliving him as her date of death is blank. Not in its original state. Flattened against the wall. Alabaster figures and two black obelisks.

Some minor interest on KIRKGATE. Nos. 5–9 were built as a clunch and flint BARN of the early C18; converted to three cottages. Nos. 11–12 have chequered flint and clunch of the C17. Two storeys and attic. C20 details, some windows in original openings. Early C18 is the WHITE HORSE public house on the other side. Two storeys in three bays of whitewashed clunch. C19 sashes intrude. WHITEHALL FARMHOUSE has the dates 1774 on the E gable and 1670 on a bridging beam inside, but the late C20 has seen off the building's character.

HOLVERSTON
⅜ m. W of Hellington

3000

HOLVERSTON HALL. Hidden in a hollow. A brick house of *c.* 1550 with a C17 extension abutting the W end and reducing the façade by one bay to three bays. Three-storey early C17 porch with polygonal angle-shafts and a stepped gable. Four-centred entrance under a pediment. Windows are renewed cross casements. The C17 wing to the l. largely reworked C19, as are the rear elevations. The roof of diminished principals and clasped purlins, curved wind-bracing. Interior otherwise altered.

ORCHARD FARMHOUSE, on the main Loddon Road. Shaped
early C18 gables. Four bays, with rusticated brick quoins round
the (blocked) door.

HONINGHAM

ST ANDREW. E of the village and right on the main A47 road. C15
w tower with a tall parapet and battlements, both with flushwork panelling. On the pinnacles C19 seated Evangelists. The
nave and chancel underwent a restoration in 1897 which was
thorough enough to hide any outwardly medieval material
except for the N and S door jambs (slight continuous mouldings). Ladbroke showed Y-tracery S windows in his drawing
c. 1825, indicating an early C14 date. Nave roof 1926. – FONT.
Early C14, the bowl with quatrefoils on colonnettes. – SCREENS.
To chancel 1928; to tower 1950. – MONUMENT. Thomas
Richardson †1642. The best part of the church. Three-quarter
figure with a baton and sword set in an oval recess. Fat black
columns r. and l. support an arch with a cartouche. – STAINED
GLASS. C17 and C18 foreign glass set in the tower W window,
c. 1860, by M. & A. O'Connor. O'Connor also the N chancel
windows (one signed Taylor & O'Connor), 1850s. E window by
William Warrington, †1866, the Good Shepherd.

HONINGHAM HALL. Built as a mansion for Thomas Richardson,
the Lord Chief Justice, in 1605, of brick, unfortunately demolished in 1967. To the r. of the site, a STABLE BLOCK remains,
with stepped gables as the house had, mullioned and transomed
windows, those to the S under pediments.

Of outlying FARMS little to report. GREENACRES FARMHOUSE,
Colton Road, ¾ m. SW of the church. Late C17, timber-framed,
with a C19 S wing. Parts of the frame exposed to the N.
CHURCH FARMHOUSE, Taverham Road, has a rusticated
doorcase with Doric pilasters set in a three-bay, two-storey S
front. This of the mid C18. Slightly earlier wing behind.

WINDMILL, ¾ m. W of the church. Early C19 but stripped out in
1975 and converted to a house in 1981.

HORNINGTOFT

ST EDMUND. The W tower collapsed in 1796. The bellcote is
from the restoration of 1871. Nave and chancel E.E., with
lancets and also two later two-light windows with Y-tracery.
The line of stone quoins on the S between nave and chancel
suggests that the nave is the earlier. Early C13 also both doorways and the priest's doorway with just one dogtooth at the top
of the chamfers of the jambs. Only the four-light E window is
Perp, with its crenellated transom. The church, according to
Ladbroke's c. 1823 illustration, had a S porch taller than the
nave and with finials, perhaps of the early C17. – FONT. C15. Of
Suffolk type, i.e. octagonal and with four lions against the stem

and four angels with shields and four lions against the bowl. – SCREEN. Pieced together from the C15 original in order to fit the narrower space after the chancel arch was rebuilt in 1871. Painted lower panels seem to be copied from *Pugin*'s Glossary. Two complete original sections were left over and have been put in the chancel. – PULPIT. C17, hexagonal, with guilloche relief carving.

MOATED SITE. To E of the Brisley–Fakenham road manorial earthworks comprise an almost circular dry moated site set within a ditched enclosure. These are in very good condition despite damage from a small gravel pit. (AR)

7020

HOUGHTON

ST MARTIN, in the park ⅜ m. SSE of the house. The flint facing to the walls was renewed in the C19, which makes the whole look of that time. £5 had been left for the 'reparation' of the S aisle in 1502. Dec chancel arch and (renewed) E window. Interior with short piers alternating between octagonal and quatrefoil. The arches have one chamfer and one hollow chamfer on the S side, two hollow chamfers on the N. The N aisle windows could indeed be original Late Perp work. Sir Robert Walpole had the N aisle parapet replaced with a classical cornice, presumably in 1726 when the W tower was rebuilt. The clerestory in its details (Y-tracery) might also be of Walpole's time. – CHANCEL STALLS with C17 backs. – BOX PEWS. – WEST GALLERY on four piers. Probably early C19. – MONUMENT. Effigy under a nodding, trefoiled ogee arch; Perp.

HOUGHTON HALL

The years 1715–20 are the great divide between Wren's classical version of the Baroque and the pure classicism of Lord Burlington's circle, initiated, it seems, in 1710 at Wilbury, Wiltshire, designed in imitation of Inigo Jones by William Benson, and brought to full fruition – now in direct imitation of Palladio – by Colen Campbell at Wanstead in 1715 and Lord Burlington's town house in 1718. Houghton followed in 1722, but, as John Harris has recently pointed out, the traditional ascription of the design solely to *Campbell*, as given in *Vitruvius Britannicus*, is in doubt; *James Gibbs* seems also to have been involved from the beginning.* The sequence is as follows. The old house had been inherited by Sir Robert Walpole, the 'Prime Minister' of George I and II, in 1700 and partly reconstructed in 1707 and 1716, although what this looked like we do not know. The original had gone up only *c.* 1660. In 1720–1 a new house was conceived with *Thomas Ripley* as the supervisor. He was busy in the summer of 1721 selecting timber and the Aislaby sandstone from Yorkshire with which the

* See J. Harris, 'James Gibbs, Eminence Grise at Houghton', *Georgian Group Annual Symposium*, 1988, pp. 5–9, and J. Harris, 'Who designed Houghton?', *Country Life*, 2 March 1989, pp. 92–4.

brick walls of the house are cased. The foundation stone was laid
on 14 May 1722 and the first stone courses above the completed
cellar were reached on 7 December. At the latest then the plan
must have been established by May 1722, but probably a year or
so earlier if Ripley was bringing in materials. Undated elevations
undoubtedly by *James Gibbs* show the w and side fronts complete
with corner domes. Slight differences between these elevations
and the actual façade suggest that they are designs, not measured
elevations of an existing building done to show the impact of
domes, as has been hitherto assumed. The elevations must be of
1721 or early 1722. Gibbs seems soon to have been replaced by
Campbell, whose revised design dated 1723 substituted the domes
with pedimented towers on the plan of Wilton, a Jonesian feature
more in tune with developing Palladian orthodoxy. When in 1725
Campbell published the design of Houghton in the third volume
of *Vitruvius Britannicus* he excluded all mention of Gibbs and
claimed the whole design for himself. His subterfuge has deceived
subsequent generations until now, when John Harris has pieced
together what seems to have been the true story. Walpole, however, preferred to build Gibbs's domes, not Campbell's towers,
and Edward Harley, Gibbs's patron in 1732, stated that the domes
were 'part of the first design'.

The sw dome is dated 1725 and the se 1727. Edmund
Prideaux's view of 1725 shows the house under scaffolding and
the completed sw dome, the other roofs apparently temporary
hipped structures for weather protection. Campbell's elevations
refer to his 'first design 1723 CC', a year after work had in fact
been started and only two years before the first dome was capped.
Campbell died in 1729. Not surprisingly he and Gibbs had
sustained, and continued to nurture, a bitter personal rivalry.

The interiors of Houghton were largely in the hands of *William
Kent*, who made a design for the saloon in about 1725 and for a
chimneypiece for the Stone Hall (dated 1726); he seems to have
finished in 1731. An inscription above the s front doorway confirms 1722 as the date of commencement and 1735 as the date of
completion. But John, Lord Hervey, and Sir Thomas Robinson
could already in letters of 1731 describe the use made of the principal rooms and refer to their furniture. The chimneypiece in the
Marble Parlour was made in 1732.

EXTERIOR. The house is outwardly of Yorkshire stone, of beautiful golden ashlar masonry. It is an oblong, of nine by five bays,
with a rusticated ground floor, a tall *piano nobile*, and a lower
second floor. In addition there are, on the pattern of Palladio's
villas, two service blocks connected with the main block by
quadrant colonnades. The main block has four projecting corner
erections capped with the controversial stone domes. These
domes have no parallels among Georgian mansions. They have
been traced back tentatively to Decker's *Fürstlicher Baumeister*,
which Gibbs owned, or to a drawing of the Wren circle at All
Souls College. In any case they add a continental warmth and
opulence to the cool perfection of the rest.

The entrance (E) side has smooth blocked surrounds to all main windows, a feature not used by Campbell but favoured by Gibbs, e.g. at St Martin-in-the-Fields, at exactly the same time, to the extent that they are generally referred to as 'Gibbs surrounds'. This treatment is also given to the Venetian windows in the angle pavilions (again a motif which goes back to Inigo Jones and beyond him to Italian High Renaissance and Mannerism). The centre windows have alternating open segmental and straight pediments. Above the middle window are reclining statues of Britannia and Neptune by *Rysbrack*. According to Campbell and the Gibbs plan there was to be an outer staircase in two arms leading up to the *piano nobile*. It was indeed built, and was separated from the front by an area, but was removed by Walpole's grandson, the third earl.

87   The garden side (W) is altogether more Palladian in spirit and was intended in Gibbs's plan to have a detached portico reached by outer staircases of two arms, each in three flights. As built, the façade has an attached centre portico of giant Ionic columns and had outer stairs of a different type to those originally conceived on the entrance side. These, however, were also demolished by the third earl, but were replaced in 1973 by a rusticated staircase in two arms. Simpler treatment to the windows of the *piano nobile*, only the centre one pedimented. Rich carving in the portico pediment, and three statues on top of the pediment.

The N and S sides are plainer. An oddity is the surrounds of the upper windows which have tripartite keyblocks with flat scrolls and a rolled scroll to the sill. The design appears on Gibbs's elevations, and is quite alien to the Palladian purity of Campbell.

The CONNECTING LINKS are of quadrant shape only to the garden. To the entrance they are dog-legged or L-shaped. They have coupled Tuscan columns on this side, single ones in the quadrant. The SERVICE RANGES, which on balance are more likely to be by *Campbell*, are of seven by seven bays and have an internal courtyard. To the E they have a three-bay pediment and a cupola behind, to the garden and also the N and S arched ground-floor windows separated by attached Ionic columns with alternating blocking. In the S wing are the kitchens, in the N wing an orangery was projected.

INTERIOR. According to John, Lord Hervey, the 'base or rustic storey' was dedicated 'to hunters, hospitality, noise, dirt and business', and the *piano nobile* to 'taste, expense, state and parade'. The PLAN is an elaboration of the familiar double pile introduced in the mid C17, with Palladian motifs grafted on, and so represents a turning-point, not a completely new direction in taste, i.e. as one might expect of Gibbs but not Campbell. The layout is very similar to that of Ditchley (Oxon.), which Gibbs had just completed. Kent was probably the *spiritus rector* for the decoration of the interior. We know at least that he designed furniture (Lord Hervey) and painted ceilings (Sir Thomas Robinson). The execution is of the highest quality throughout, including mahogany for doors, window shutters and the principal staircase, which is among the earliest instances of its use.

The main room on the ground floor is the vaulted entrance hall, called the ARCADE, which extends from E to W. The STAIRCASE lies to its S, with wood carving probably by *James Richards*. It is oblong, with an open well. The balusters are sturdy, with some acanthus to the panelled newels, and there is much more ornamental carving in addition, e.g. a compact garland all up the pulvinated closed string. At gallery level the balustrade is carried on prominent scrolled brackets to which acanthus has been liberally applied. The walls have decorative grisaille painting by *Kent*, scarcely capable of competing with the full-blooded decoration around. Apart from the story of Meleager and Atalanta there are painted heraldic devices, statues on plinths and busts in oval niches. Sash windows at the upper level make this interior look like an open courtyard, an effect later repeated by Ripley at Wolterton. In the middle of the spacious well stands

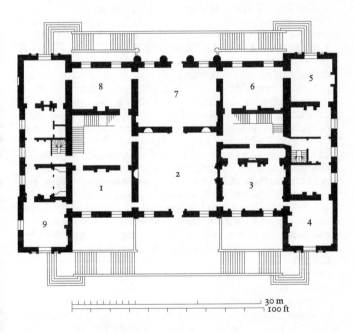

1	Common Parlour (Parlour)
2	Stone Hall (Hall)
3	Marble Parlour
4	Cabinet Room (Cabinet)
5	Green Velvet Bedchamber
6	White Drawing Room (Carlo Maratti Room)
7	Saloon (Salon)
8	Yellow Silk Room (Yellow Drawing Room)
9	Library

Houghton Hall. Plan of *piano nobile* in 1767
(with original room names in brackets)

a bronze statue of a gladiator by *Hubert Le Sueur*, given to Sir
Robert by the eighth Earl of Pembroke. It was put, probably by
Kent, on a substructure the full height of the ground floor, with
four Doric columns and a metope frieze with bucrania.

The remaining ground-floor rooms were fitted up with large-
framed panelling (gun room, supper room in the SE corner) or
tapestry-hung (hunting room, where Sir Matthew Decker dined
in 1728), and with bedchambers. This was the floor where Sir
Robert and his successors spent most of their time.

On the *piano nobile* the axis of the entrance hall below is represented by the Stone Hall and the Saloon, two apartments of
astounding grandeur and lavishness. But first the COMMON
PARLOUR, E of the staircase.* Ceiling with modillion cornice
and a trail of carved foliage, and, above the marble chimneypiece, framing a picture, deeply undercut wooden garlands etc.
They are by *Grinling Gibbons*, and are without doubt the most
masterly piece of woodcarving in the house, either remaining
from the previous house or brought in.

88   The STONE HALL is a cube 40 by 40 by 40 ft, in the early
C18 entered from the E external staircase (the door now a
window). These are the measurements of the hall in Inigo
Jones's Queen's House at Greenwich as well, but how sober is
1620 compared with 1720. The principal difference lies in the
ceiling, but a heightening of effects in all details plays an equally
important part. The sumptuous carving round the pedimented
doors, *Rysbrack*'s classical reliefs in panels, the capitals of the
columns (garlands suspended from the volutes) and the frieze
between them in the doorcase between the hall and the saloon,
the statuary niches r. and l., the powerful brackets to the
balustraded gallery echoing those to the staircase, lions' heads
and garlands below the balcony, and of course *Rysbrack*'s splendid chimneypiece of *c.* 1726 under a pediment both broken and
open with its Roman relief, its youthful caryatids, bust of Walpole,
and its big guilloche – all must be observed. And finally there is
the ceiling on a coving made by *Giuseppe Artari* (a favourite of
the Italophile Gibbs, who was paid £560 10s. for it between
February and May 1728) with merry putti holding on to, and
frolicking around, garlands. Very occasionally a little leg is even
hanging over the elegant Greek key frieze below. In the centres
of the four sides are reliefs of Sir Robert, his wife, son and
daughter-in-law. The coving leads to a flat centre with the arms
of Walpole in relief. The group of Laocoön in bronze opposite
the fireplace (by *Girardon*, copying the Roman original in the
Vatican) was bought by Sir Robert in Paris. All forms in the hall
are big, none dainty or playful. It is the same in the other state
rooms, especially as regards the chimneypieces.

The NE doorway opens to the MARBLE PARLOUR, incomplete in 1731, which was built as the dining room, a new thing
then, for which purpose there is a very interesting arrangement.
To the l. and r. of the fireplace, which is in the back wall, are

* The tour follows the route taken by visitors, i.e. anticlockwise.

alcoves connected behind the fireplace and thus affording a welcome serving space accessible directly from the secondary staircase. The whole of this alcove arrangement is in various marbles, including Carrara marble, and is groin-vaulted, and the arched entrances are framed with engaged Ionic columns. The lavish chimneypiece has a *Rysbrack* relief illustrating the Sacrifice to Bacchus, installed in 1733; the fireplace itself carved by *Abraham Swan*. As was usual for dining rooms, grapes appear frequently in the decoration. The ceiling is gilt and has stucco-framed panels of various shapes and in them decorative paintings by *Kent*, who must be credited with the whole room.

In the NE corner the CABINET ROOM, nothing to do with government but intended for Sir Robert's small pictures (mostly sold to Catherine the Great in 1779 by the bachelor and spend-thrift third earl). The pretty blue Chinese wallpaper was hung in c. 1792. *Kent's* ceiling has a painted Minerva, the chimney-piece decorated with a shell motif. The centre of the N side is concerned with a bedchamber and dressing room, the former with another of *Kent's* coved and painted ceilings, then, at the NW corner, the GREEN VELVET BEDCHAMBER. Elaborate gilt cornice featuring a running scroll of foliage and an oval ceiling panel with Aurora by *Kent*. In the corners the star of the Garter (referring to Sir Robert's knighthood in 1726). The room is dominated by *Kent's* STATE BED of 1732, for which the green velvet trimmed with gold alone cost over £1,200. Splendid double shell against the backboard carried on a broken pediment.

Then the three state rooms behind the W façade, first the WHITE DRAWING ROOM. Another good chimneypiece presenting a large frontal face of Aurora in the middle of the frieze and caryatids in profile to the l. and r. developed out of foliated and scrolled consoles. The ceiling has eleven recessed painted panels by *Kent* separated by a geometric arrangement of elaborate gilded cornices. In the centre octagon a nude Venus. The SALOON with its generous coving is the climax of the house, completed by May 1731. Again all the details ought to be sampled, and especially the aedicule surround of the principal window and the doorway to the hall, the carving attributed to *Richards*. The ceiling begins with a carved gilt frieze depicting the story of Diana, which allows for emblems and scenes from the chase, then a modillion cornice introduces the coving painted with busts and big fleshy foliage in painted lunettes leading up to the centre octagon decorated by *Kent's* Phaeton and Jupiter. Marble chimneypiece with paired Ionic columns and a broken pediment containing a bust. The YELLOW SILK ROOM follows, where the more rigid arrangement of the ceiling panelling confirms that it was copied from the dining room of the preceding house, with Sir Robert's Garter star added as a centrepiece. Until 1792 the room was hung with yellow damask and originally contained Sir Robert's big Van Dycks (bought 1725, sold 1779).

The S front contains a series of rooms mirroring the N front intended for family occupation, with the quite small LIBRARY at the SE corner where plenty of prodigious craftsmanship makes up the full-height mahogany bookcases designed by *Kent c.* 1728 and set back into the wall.

In the library hangs a portrait of George I by *Sir Godfrey Kneller*, a reminder that Walpole was one of the greatest collectors of his day and a patron of living English and continental artists. In 1739 George Vertue called the collection at Houghton 'the most considerable in England', and it was the contents as much as the house itself which impressed visitors. The White Drawing Room was originally called the 'Carlo Maratti' room on account of its pictures. *Maratti*'s portrait of Innocent IX of 1669 now hangs at St Petersburg. Walpole or his various agents began buying in 1718, usually at auction, and his interest was principally paintings by Netherlandish, French and Italian masters. Nevertheless he had seven Knellers in all, five of which hung in the Common Parlour, and in 1728 commissioned a portrait of his son Horace from *Hogarth*. In 1725 came the first of the *Van Dyck*s, and in 1734 *Poussin*'s Holy Family with St Elizabeth and John the Baptist.

On Sir Robert's death in 1745 he had debts of £50,000 and the house was mortgaged, forcing the second earl to order two sales in 1748 (sixty pictures) and another in 1751. By 1777 it was suggested that the collection be purchased for the nation but in the event the bulk of Sir Robert's paintings went to Catherine the Great in 1779. Josiah Wedgwood thought the sale marked the decline of the British Empire.

The STABLES form a big quadrangle added *c.* 1733–5, possibly by *William Kent*. They are faced with carstone outside, with red brick inside. The front is fifteen bays wide, the returns also of fifteen bays. The ground-floor windows are lunette-shaped. The centre has an arched gateway and a top pediment. On the corners are polygonal turrets. The stables and coachboxes are groin-vaulted in brick, the groins being managed by the most curious dovetailing.

PARK AND GARDENS. There was a scheme of planting as early as *c.* 1707, intended, of course, to serve the old house which lay immediately W of Walpole's new mansion. It consisted of a series of geometrical avenues and plantations, which were during the 1720s expanded in a similar manner. To the W lay the main gardens: a broad grassy walk lined with topiary and closed N and S by dense plantations of trees cut through by straight and sometimes curved walks. These are now reduced, but the appearance of the house set in a great plain of lawn remains the same. The PARK beyond was a C17 deer park of about 220 acres, expanded after 1720 to 300 acres, with a broad avenue running off E and W in line with the house and set about with blocks of trees, some of which are indicated on *Thomas Badeslade*'s 1720 map. From the late 1720s probably *Charles Bridgeman* presided over further expansion to the E and S, this time not as a mere enlargement of the existing pattern but as a series of straight and oblique avenues 'a mile or two in length' as a fitting foil for the seat of political power. The old village (*see* below) and the former stables, completed only in 1721, had to be removed, and the park reached 500 acres by 1735. In 1742 *Walpole*, and it was probably his own idea, made a cutting to the E through a shallow hill, allowing a view from the *piano nobile* of the land towards Raynham Hall, and at the same time long and wide avenues were planted to the N and S, again aligned with the house. After Walpole's death in 1745 little more was done. By 1770 the house and estate were in poor condition, and, apart from the partial obliteration of the W gardens in the late C18, the setting of the house remains much the same as in Walpole's day. The S avenue may be appreciated if the visitor walks 100 yds W of the S gates in the village, for the road passes across it. Although the idea was periodically envisaged, the stratum of boulder clay underlying the park was too thin for a lake – just a few ponds.

WATER TOWER, to the NW. The design of *Henry, Lord Herbert*, later ninth Earl of Pembroke. Two of his drawings for it survive. The design seems to be before 1733 but Isaac Ware does not include the building in his plan of the park of 1735. However it stands at a focal point for one of Bridgeman's avenues. Stuccoed and rendered brick with stone trimmings. Three-bay façade with slender unfluted pilasters. Rusticated ground floor with blank arches. Pediments to all four sides. The influence on Lord Pembroke came from Campbell.

WEST LODGE. A little square thing, rendered and whitewashed. Built *c.* 1830. Pedimented gables point out in each direction.

NORTH LODGE. Similar but a little altered.

SOUTH LODGES, at New Houghton. *c.* 1729–30 by *Kent* or *Thomas Ripley*. The pair of lodges are of whitewashed brick with rusticated quoins and gables elaborated into pediments. The wrought-iron GATES between them by *Jean Tijou* of *c.* 1710 were brought from Cholmondeley Castle (Cheshire) in 1798 and are very fine, with carriage and pedestrian gates.

MONUMENT, 270 yds S of the Hall. An octagonal medieval cross base with a filleted shaft.

OLD VILLAGE. The old village was removed and the park enclosed in the 1720s to make way for the house. All that remains are earthworks N of the Hall which include a sunken way flanked by numerous house platforms and a back lane. (AR)

The NEW VILLAGE on the new site at NEW HOUGHTON ¾ m. S of the Hall was begun in July 1729. At the N end of a wide avenue running ¾ m. S towards Harpley are two rows of five detached houses, each comprising two or three dwellings. The houses are of four bays of casements (replaced) and two storeys, whitewashed brick with pyramid roofs, and a six-bay house on the W side. The house on the E side has been extended into five bays. At the S end of the group is one single-storey ALMSHOUSE on each side of the avenue and at r. angles to it, each consisting of four dwellings with a door and window, altered. Also part of the composition are two FARMHOUSES. The one to the W, HOME FARMHOUSE, is similar in style to the stables. It has five bays and two storeys with the centre bay raised by a half storey and given a lunette window and a pediment. Brick quoins to the whole and to the middle bay. The other is VILLAGE FARMHOUSE, smaller, only three bays wide. Both have a range of BARNS, those to Home Farmhouse the grander.

HOUGHTON-ON-THE-HILL

8000

ST MARY. Unbuttressed C14 W tower attached to an early Norman nave with one double-splayed rounded lancet in N and S walls. Long-and-short quoining at the corners and, incidentally, some to the tower quoins as well. Roman brick is also used. The long (27 ft) chancel described by Blomefield replaced in 1760 by a small altar chamber with a typical hipped roof. The round chancel arch of the church of *c.* 1090 remains, without elaboration, and made entirely of Roman brick. That there were two round-arched openings to a mid-C12 S aisle is still apparent, but the aisle was demolished in the C14 and a doorway inserted, and probably at the same time the two niches flanking the chancel arch were cut. The church served a settlement to the N, of which a few mounds may be discerned, but the last buildings disappeared by the C19 and the church fell into disrepair, so that it stood as an ivy-clad ruin until 1994 when a programme of repair was begun by the County Council and English Heritage. It was during this work that extensive remains of WALL PAINTINGS were discovered, which are now undergoing long-term investigation and conservation.*

These paintings are of extraordinary importance. All four walls of the nave have them, partly hidden beneath at least two later schemes, but the original cycle is of the date of the nave, and so among the earliest known in England. On the E wall is an enormous depiction of the Holy Trinity in a lobed mandorla, with the nimbused heads of a number of figures gazing up from bottom l. Below this (i.e. immediately above the chancel arch) is a border of bust-length Saints holding scrolls, each contained in a roundel. To the N of the arch is the Resurrection of the Dead, with an angel blowing the Last Trump and little naked figures clambering out of their graves. The whole E wall composition must have formed a great Last Judgement, with the Trinity in place of the usual Majesty. The quality of the draughtsmanship is quite high, and the colours, mainly red and yellow ochres, still vibrant. On the other walls the remains are much more scanty, and still being investigated, but include a scene of Christ with a cross-nimbus on the N wall to the r. of the original window, which also retains some of its original decoration. The early date of the paintings is evident partly from the style, which includes such Anglo-Saxon reminiscences as the quatrefoil on God's knee in the Trinity. A dating of *c.* 1090 would make this Trinity – showing God enthroned with the crucified Christ – the earliest known representation of the Throne of

---

* At the time of writing hardly any conservation work has been undertaken, so much more remains to be exposed.

Grace or *Gnadenstuhl* type, which became the standard way of representing the Trinity throughout Europe from the C12 onward. (DP)

HOWE

St Mary. An Anglo-Saxon church. The tower is round and has double-splayed windows, both round and round-arched. There was apparently a w doorway as well, of which imposts remain, and the arch towards the nave has a N impost moulded in a typically Saxon undecided way. The tower now carries a pyramid roof. In the nave, on the N side, is also a double-splayed window, and the S doorway has at least imposts which support an C11 date. At the SW corner of the nave are quoins of Roman tiles. In the nave two small windows with Y-tracery, i.e. early C14 in style. They are placed in internal blank arches. In the chancel Dec and Perp windows, mixed. The nave roof is supported by demi-figures of angels, but much was restored in 1895. Pointed chancel arch C19. – BENCHES. Bits of old benches with poppy-heads. – STAINED GLASS. E window by *Heaton, Butler & Bayne*, 1865, and one N chancel window by same firm.

Howe Hall, ⅜ m. SW. An early C17 timber-framed house of the through-passage type with a stair-tower at the back, rather compromised by a late C17 rear wing. The main part bricked over in the C18, and there are C18 casements to the first floor but later ground-floor details. This main, S, front, of two storeys and four bays. The N wing has a more convincing C17 pedigree. Enclosing GARDEN WALLS to S.

Wolferd Green Cottages, ⅞ m. W of the last. A tall, narrow rectangular early C18 range of two storeys with a shaped gable facing the road and chequered brickwork, probably a fragment of a bigger house. A C19 wing has grown up behind.

HUNSTANTON

St Mary. Much restored in 1853 and 1865, by *Frederick Preedy*, who designed St Edmund, New Hunstanton (*see* below), and was Henry Le Strange's cousin. The sequence as follows: 1853 the nave, clerestory; 1865 chancel, chancel screen, pulpit. In consequence all the windows have a new look, and the lead roofs add to the impression of newness. But the church is an old church, although only the interior and the tower show it. One of the most remarkable windows from *c.* 1853 is the five-light E window with a curious pattern of tracery consisting of four unfoiled circles l. and four r., and a larger trefoil in the apex. The other chancel windows of the same date. Preedy's four-light w window is an economy model: a large circle in the tracery containing six plain smaller circles and an encircled quatrefoil in the centre. The arcades are late C13. Five bays, piers circular in the w bays, and then octagonal. The arches are

hollow-chamfered. The w bays are older than the e bays, but
building probably continued without a break. Seats round the
piers. Circular clerestory windows alternating between trefoils
and sexfoils (there was no clerestory before 1853). The church
has a NW, not a W tower, C15, of three stages with angle buttresses. Fine, tall s porch rebuilt 1864, originally with an upper
storey. Entrance with an openwork cinquefoiled arch, as had
the original. Two circular side windows containing mouchette
wheels, which might be reused late C14 work. The nave roof is
a remarkable piece, throwing in every motif – scissor-bracing,
arch-bracing, wind-bracing – how much bracing does one need?
It is by *Thomas Earp*, c. 1853, and a more elaborate version of
the New Hunstanton roof (*see* below).

FURNISHINGS. (PISCINA. A Norman capital reused, in the
vestry.) – FONT. Norman, square, plain, on four short polygonal
columns. Scalloped underside. Angle colonnettes to the bowl
and a circle of zigzag on the s face. – SCREEN. Big, early C16;
eleven painted Apostles on the dado and St Paul. The same
artist painted the screens at St James Norwich, St Mary Magdalen
New Catton (qq.v. Vol. 1), and North Elmham. Upper parts
restored and given new coving by *Bodley*, 1892. – STALLS. 1928
by *Sir Walter Tapper* and very austere. – PULPIT. Absolutely
confident High Victorian display made as a memorial to Henry
Styleman Le Strange (†1862), who paid for all the works. Red and
green marble columns, alabaster figures of the Four Evangelists
and Christ in the round, and angels above these. Presumably by
Preedy. – STAINED GLASS. e window by *Frederick Preedy*, 1867,
also to commemorate Henry Styleman Le Strange. With fifteen
scenes from the Life of Christ. This is the best of all Preedy's
windows. *Sir Henry* helped with his money and his skill in the
restoration of the nave. He designed e.g. the glass of the s aisle
e window, a Tree of Jesse, c. 1862, made by *Preedy*. Le Strange
was recognized as an artist; for he painted also the roof of the w
tower and part of that of the nave of Ely Cathedral. – MONU-
MENTS. Brass to Sir Edmund Grene and wife Agnes c. 1490.
The figures are 25 in. long (at w end near s door). – Sir Henry Le
Strange †1485. Tomb-chest in a broad stone setting, intended
also to serve as an Easter Sepulchre (cf. East Raynham) and to
be modelled on the Morley monument at Hingham, according
to Sir Henry's will: 'to be spent on my sepultur xx li and that it
be made a part aftr the sepultur at hengham churche. . . of the
morleys'. On the front of the stone tomb-chest shields in rather
mechanical tracery crosses. Purbeck marble top. The recess has
panelled sides, four-centred arch with coffering and rosettes on
the underside, panelled back wall, big attic with shields in
cusped quatrefoils and an achievement. All over-restored. No
effigy. e of this monument another much shallower, ogee-headed
recess. – Sir Roger Le Strange †1506. Brass on tomb-chest. The
chest has small brass shields in very elaborately cusped quatrefoils or stars. The effigy brass has a swagger figure under a tripartite canopy. The supports of the canopy have in four tiers
members of the Le Strange family. Sir Roger's figure is 3 ft long

(N aisle E, moved in C20 from chancel). – In the churchyard two
HEADSTONES, both 1784, one to William Webb, the other to
William Green. Inscription to the latter reads:

> Here be the mangled remains of poor William Green
> an honest officer of Government who
> in the faithful discharge of his duty
> was inhumanely murdered
> by a gang of smugglers in this parish.

ST EDMUND'S CHAPEL, S of the lighthouse. A prominent ruin.
Bases of a C13 rectangular nave and chancel consolidated and
raised, especially round the S door. Built in 1272 and further
consolidated in 1989–90.

LIGHTHOUSE, Lighthouse Close. Built in 1830. Rendered and
whitewashed brick, four storeys, circular of course. Connected
by wings with, formerly, two gabled two-storeyed houses, the S
one demolished and the remainder converted in 1964.

HUNSTANTON HALL. The mansion of the L'Estrange family
(the name was changed to Le Strange in 1839 and adopted by
the Stylemans who inherited in 1760) has greatly suffered by
two fires, one in 1853, the other in 1947. Sold and converted to
flats 1948. P. G. Wodehouse was a frequent visitor and the house
is the model for Rudge Hall in *Money for Nothing*, the Octagon
described in e.g. *Very Good, Jeeves*. It is a moated mansion,
partly of the 1480s, partly Jacobean and partly Victorian. It is
approached by an ARCHWAY with columns and a coat of arms
in a strapwork surround. This is by *Thomas Thorpe*, 1623–4,
who was a bricklayer working at the time at Blickling. This
leads to a crenellated walled FORECOURT, and across the moat
to the Perp brick gatehouse, which probably went up in 1487.
The GATEHOUSE is flat to the outside and inside, three windows
wide and embattled. The archway has a four-centred arch and
has to the outside decorated spandrels. The doors are C15. To
the l. and r. of the gatehouse four-bay ranges built in *c.* 1625–40
continue and embrace the INNER COURTYARD. *William Edge*
was busy at Raynham Hall from 1619, but he worked on and off
for Sir Hamon L'Estrange at Hunstanton from *c.* 1625 to the early
1640s, and it is likely these ranges are his. Also with him were
Richard, Thomas and *John Edge*. To the outside the ranges are of
carstone and flint in a chequer pattern, to the inside they are
carstone alone. The windows are mullioned and transomed, the
parapet crenellated. The r. range was gutted in 1947. Each of
the long sides has three round-headed C17 doorways towards the
courtyard. In line with the gatehouse, on the far side, was
the hall. Of this however only the porch survived the fire of
1853. The PORCH is dated 1618. It has two columns like the
outer archway, but they carry obelisks which are set against a
prettily diapered ground. The top is raised in the middle by
little more than a semicircle containing a shell. After the fire of
1853 a new, more self-confident house was built to the NW, lopsided to the former layout. It might be by *Frederick Preedy*. It
incorporates some C14 walling at the back, the oldest remaining

part of the house. The STABLES to the N certainly by *Preedy*,
1873, Gothic.

In the PARK is THE OCTAGON, set on an island in an octagonal pool, 200 yds S of the Hall. *c.* 1640 and attributed to
William Edge, for Sir Hamon L'Estrange (an alternative dating
of 1655 sometimes given, but both Edge and Sir Hamon
†1643). The plan reflects the name; the materials are coursed
carstone with ashlar details and moulded brick. Arched doorway under pediment. Rustication. Remaining facets with alternating blind and open mullioned windows under their own pediments. Temporary C20 roof.

THE OLD TOWN. The main road is OLD HUNSTANTON ROAD,
running E–W to the S of the developed area, with, at its E end,
Church Road to the S towards the Hall and Waterworks Road
to the N. On the main road starting at the W end various pieces
of evidence from the C17. Nos. 1–6 THE BIG YARD are a conversion of a set of BARNS, in carstone giving way to clunch to
the E. Nos. 53–55 are of flint with brick dressings, with two
blocked C17 windows at first floor in gable-ends, now divided
into two houses and given various C20 embellishments. Nos.
69–73 repeat the pattern, each of two bays and two storeys
and attic. Nos. 79–81 similar but late C18. Opposite Sea Lane
THE LODGE HOTEL presents a long seven-bay façade to the

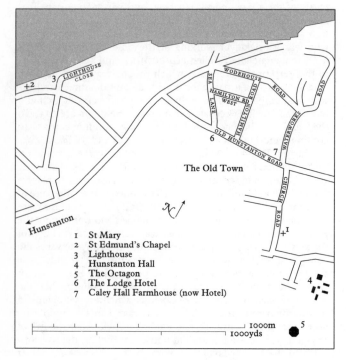

Hunstanton. The Old Town

road, done in brick with a poor but small C20 single-storey extension. The rest is of carstone. Sashes and tripartite sashes. The W, entrance, front has two canted bay windows. Further E on the S side CLIFF FARMHOUSE, late C17, with chequerwork in the E and W gable-ends fashioned from carstone and clunch blocks. The house was extended N and raised in height in the C18. At the junction with Waterworks Road is CALEY HALL FARMHOUSE, now a hotel. Galleted knapped flint, brick and carstone. The E front has four bays, one of which is an offset two-storey porch entered through a four-centred arch. On its S side is a blocked C17 window. The date 1648 appears on the S gable. The service wing to the N bears marks and masonry of the C17 too.

On SEA LANE, No. 18 is a late C17 single-storey house with assorted C19 and C20 inserts and an added first floor. Nos. 36–38 are a row of coastguard cottages dated 1818: coursed

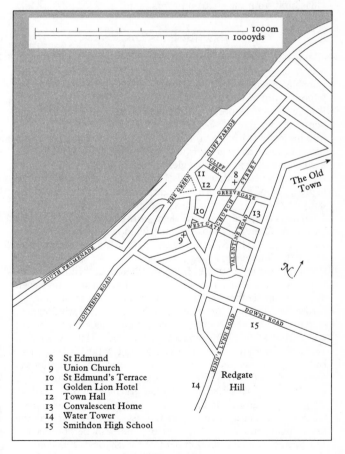

8   St Edmund
9   Union Church
10 St Edmund's Terrace
11 Golden Lion Hotel
12 Town Hall
13 Convalescent Home
14 Water Tower
15 Smithdon High School

New Hunstanton

carstone, casements, hipped roof. Round the corner in WODE-
HOUSE ROAD the range continues in No. 35 and Nos. 37–41.
Oddly, both ranges have their service outshuts to the front not
the back.

No. 8 HAMILTON ROAD WEST is by *Gerald Lacoste*, 1935, a
minor Modern Movement house of three offset rectangular
blocks lit through a glazed frieze to the S side and by fewer
separate casements to the N, but including corner windows.
Flat roof of course. On the opposite side (N) a house of 1971,
like the school (*see* below) a Miesian steel and glass box in one
storey, almost square on plan. Three steel portal frames glazed
to N and S with concrete block walling to returns. By *Spence &
Webster* (job architect *Robin Spence*). Nos. 2–4 HAMILTON
ROAD, near the main road, is dated 1921: two storeys, six bays,
of concrete blockwork under a flat roof with a parapet and
cornice.

The area N of Old Hunstanton Road is filled with holiday
villas built from the 1920s onwards.

NEW HUNSTANTON

ST EDMUND. 1865–9 by *Frederick Preedy* for Henry Le Strange at
a cost of £3,700. Brick and flint with carstone banding and
horrible concrete roof tiles (of 1982). Geometric style. The big
W porch with its two internal chapels was added in 1874 and the
N aisle in 1879. S porch *c.* 1914. Three stepped W lancets, the
centre of two lights, five-light E window, two-light to aisles. The
interior lost its furniture in 1962, and with it its character. Four-
bay arcade of alternating round and octagonal piers. Chancel
arch with a twin and one single shaft each side, with shaft-rings
decorated with ballflower and elaborate seaweed foliage to the
capitals. Roof like a barn: straight braces from corbels to the
collars and on the collars a braced kingpost construction. – FONT.
Plain and octagonal, imported 1893. – STAINED GLASS. E window
by *Charles Kempe*, *c.* 1890. S chancel window by *Preedy*, †1876. S
aisle SE window by *Ninian Comper*, 1912. Minor C20 glass elsewhere, by *William* and *John Lawson*.

UNION CHURCH, Westgate. Built for all Nonconformist denom-
inations in 1870 for £750. This has a polygonal apse, no tower,
and two bands of terracotta, fired with a running scroll motif. A
further band of polychromatic tiles. Y-tracery side windows.

THE TOWN. The idea to develop Hunstanton as a seaside resort
came from Henry Le Strange of Hunstanton Hall. At first, in
1843, building sites were advertised and a few buildings erected,
but Le Strange soon looked for a planned scheme. He
employed his friend *William Butterfield* who laid out the central
areas in 1861 as a series of triangular greens with the buildings
'singly and in groups, in masses of irregular form and size, interspersed with gardens and open spaces'. At least that was the
grand plan, and a lot of it paid off, and can be appreciated
today, but the main development of the 1870s was as conventional squares and terraces, e.g. at Cliff Terrace, 1873, and two

blocks on Cliff Parade. ST EDMUND'S TERRACE is one of Butterfield's own (three storeys on basement, coursed carstone). The railway reached Hunstanton in 1862 (off Southend Road, closed 1969), and the pier was built to the designs of *J. W. Wilson*, originally 50 yds longer. A very effective design, tall and impressive but destroyed in a storm in 1978. The amusement arcade at the landward end is of 1962–3, replacing the pier-head pavilion burnt in 1939. The church as we have seen came in 1865. The population in 1991: 4,700.

The centre is THE GREEN, with the shaft of the VILLAGE CROSS which originally stood in Gipsy Green, Old Hunstanton, and was moved by Henry Le Strange in 1846. Socket stone with shields and part of the shaft of four keeled rolls and subsidiary keeled rolls, C15. BANDSTAND of 1994. On the s side was the Sandringham Hotel of 1875 built for the Great Eastern Railway, demolished 1967 (next to the Princess Theatre), to the w the site of the pier, and to the NE the Golden Lion Hotel (formerly the Royal Hotel) and the Town Hall. The GOLDEN LION when built in 1846 had only the cross for company. *Butterfield* has been suggested as the architect. It is in the Tudor-Gothic style, of coursed carstone, two storeys with attic. Mullioned windows and a pair of gables face The Green. Staircase with twisted balusters and closed string. The Town Hall and Theatre of 1896 adjoin. The TOWN HALL is by *G. J. & F. W. Skipper*. Carstone. Two storeys. The middle has a big gabled ashlar centre with a clock face in the gable-head surrounded by strap-work decoration. First-floor windows grouped with two-four-two mullions, separated by Ionic pilasters. Recessed side bays. Arched cross casement windows. s gable with a canted entrance porch and a two-storey bay window. The eight bays to the rear form the Hall.

The surrounding streets are all of the same style, carstone, gables, and a general prosperous and solid (and not a bit cheerful) Tudor character. VICTORIA BUILDING (Barclay's Bank) in GREEVEGATE has a date 1872. On the opposite corner NATIONAL WESTMINSTER BANK, 1919. The houses following this are in pairs to repeating designs but very much cut about in the C20. Greevegate leads to the main KING'S LYNN ROAD, and to Valentine Road where is the former HUNSTANTON CONVALESCENT HOME, built in 1872–4. This is different. It has carstone and brick and also some half-timbering. Closed in 1979 and converted to flats. The CHILDREN'S CONVALESCENT HOME of 1907 is used as council offices.

The sea-front, i.e. the SOUTH PROMENADE, is filled today with the usual seaside attractions, which began after the sea wall went up in 1928. The Blue Lagoon swimming pool of 1927–8 was demolished 1967 (replaced by Oasis Leisure Centre 1983–4); boating lake 1932 (now under the Sea Life Centre, 1989).

WATER TOWER, Lynn Road at Redgate Hill. 1911, and very prominent. Two were built for the new town, but only the s one remains. It has three storeys and a front in three bays, all tame

Norman in style, with recessed blind panels and a central door. Upper floors with oculi and more blind arched panels. Converted to a house.

Large estates of houses at REDGATE HILL, begun 1969, continue to expand.

SMITHDON HIGH SCHOOL, Downs Road. By *Alison* and *Peter Smithson*, 1950–4, the paramount example among the innumerable interesting post-war schools of England of a rigidly formal, symmetrical layout. Dennis Clark Hall was the single assessor in the 1949 competition, the Education Committee strangely taking little interest in a building which departed so radically from pre-war school design, and which has bequeathed a maintenance headache in a class of its own. In conjunction with the detail, which is evidently inspired by the reduced Classicism of Mies van der Rohe (see e.g. the Illinois Institute of Technology at Chicago, 1939), it is a ruthlessly spare building conceived as a steel frame completely glazed, or nearly so. Of gault brick are panels in the E and W ends, set into the projections of the I-section RSJs. This brick was questioned at the time as being not only non-functional but compromising the purist spirit of the rest. The architects said it was to give an effect of permanence needed by schoolchildren. The stanchions are exposed, and the result has both great crispness and a certain elegance. The steelwork is itself technically advanced, being designed on the so-called plastic theory (engineers *Ove Arup & Partners*, partner in charge *R. S. Jenkins*; steel fabricated by *Boulton & Paul* of Norwich, supplied by *Dorman Long & Co.* of Middlesbrough). Inside, the brick, the steel beams, etc., are all exposed, which is crisp also and of course honest but much too austere for a school. A contemporary review suggested that the 'building seems to ignore the children for which it was built'. The school is the forerunner of the Brutalist movement in British architecture, which the Smithsons went on to develop themselves, perhaps with rather less grip, in so-called 'architecture of the welfare state' compositions.

The plan is easily described: a two-storeyed oblong 290 by 103 ft, with three internal courtyards, the centre one roofed to provide the full-height hall. The E arm separating the open courts contains the stage rooms for plays etc. (now administrative offices); the other is a dining area. This continues to the N of the hall. To the S is a wide circulation area. All of these spaces open directly into the other, so the hall has to be curtained to provide privacy and dining-area smells permeate everywhere. The remainder of the ground floor has cloakrooms, staff rooms, service rooms, and the caretaker's flat at the W end. Ten open-tread staircases rise to the teaching rooms on the first floor. This arrangement was revolutionary at the time, even Mies producing no plan quite like it, but it proved to have so many drawbacks, even while in building, that the experiment, noble and committed though it was, has never been repeated.

The façades are strictly symmetrical, although on the N (entrance) side single-storey kitchens, workshops, a craft room

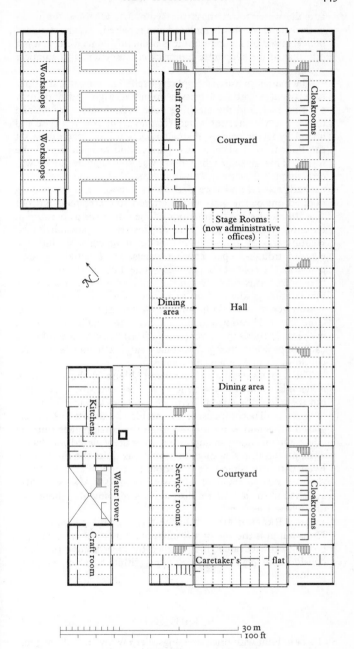

Hunstanton, Smithdon High School.
Ground-floor plan

and the water tower mask the symmetry. Of these the water
cistern alone (endlessly replaced and repaired) with its standard
panels raised on an open frame is brilliantly conceived, so it is a
pity that in the silhouette the brick chimney tends to compete
with it.

The main structure is simplicity itself. The long N and S sides
have twenty-eight steel trusses providing a ground floor only
7 ft 8 in. high and the teaching floor 11 ft. These were welded
together on the site, not bolted, fixed to a 4 in. concrete base and
linked by facing frames of smaller section into which were set
the floor-to-roof glazing, two panes wide to each bay of the
frame. This glazing, when new, was spectacular. But it was
directly glazed, without sub-frames, so that as the steel frame
twisted, moved and corroded on its exposed site the glazing
popped out or the glass just shattered (the architects did not
visit the site for the competition). The frame warps because in
its entire welded length there are just two expansion joints.
Heating was by slow-response under-floor coils, set into the
exposed trough-shaped flooring panels, which could not compete with the cold of the exposed N side, but roasted the green-
house-like S classrooms when the sun shone, even in winter. A
temperature gradient of up to 30 degrees C could exist in any
season across the width, and the frame distorted the more.
Conventional heating and fan systems were installed in 1990–1;
in the early 1980s the lower panes of each window assembly on
each floor were changed to black sandwich panels and the
windows set in wooden sub-frames.

The GYMNASIUM also is a separate block (to the SW), but it
is again in itself strictly symmetrical. The structure is the same,
but there has of course to be more gault brick than glass in the
long walls. To compensate the architects almost completely
glazed the E and W returns, so again the black panels ruin the
effect. One wonders in any case if an entirely glazed wall facing
a main road in a school gymnasium was quite the right thing.
Even with this alteration it is doubly a pity that the *County
Architect's Department* in 1974 set up the SWIMMING POOL
attached to the S, under a distracting swooping glass-fibre roof
of scalloped section.

ROMANO-BRITISH VILLA. On the E side of the parish of New
Hunstanton is the site of a Roman building discovered in 1953
but not yet excavated. It is marked by *terra sigillata*, tiles, and
considerable masonry foundations within a sub-rectangular
enclosure.

ICKBURGH

ST PETER. Flint with brick dressings. Perp W tower, with diagonal
buttresses and many set-offs. Bell-openings with Y-tracery and
a crenellated parapet with flushwork. Tower arch with double-
hollow-chamfered mouldings and corbels of angels with shields.
The church itself rebuilt in 1865–6 at the expense of Francis,

third Lord Ashburton. The architect was *R. M. Phipson*, the Diocesan Surveyor. He was fond of big, unexpected figure and foliage carvings, especially outside, but also inside. The nave, N aisle, chancel and N chapel represent good workmanlike stuff from Phipson, essentially Victorian, but not inspired. Much better are the FURNISHINGS and glass. – WOODWORK. ROOFS, PEWS, ALTAR RAIL, ORGAN CASE all by *Henry Ringham* of Ipswich. His son *William* assisted. The angels in the roof are powerful pieces. – Richly carved stone PULPIT, of marble and with Biblical scenes. – STAINED GLASS. E window by *Clayton & Bell*, *c.* 1865 (Crucifixion above a Last Supper). Remaining windows by *Heaton, Butler & Bayne*, *c.* 1865 (Saints etc.). Phipson was in charge of the work, and the effect is surprisingly fine.

ALMSHOUSES. Built in 1887 for Claire Eugenie Hortense, Lady Ashburton. Single-storeyed with half-timbered gables. Black-letter inscriptions.

NOS. 1–2 BRIDGE STREET seem to be a pair of C19 flint houses with gault brick dressings – and indeed they are – but they are a conversion from a C13 LEPER CHAPEL. One and a half storeys, with six two-light casements. The two doorways are C13 and arched, that to the E with dogtooth.

On THE STREET, MANOR FARMHOUSE and WEST FARMHOUSE are both C17 timber-framed houses with colourwashed brick additions, both with a lobby-entrance plan.

ILLINGTON   9090

ST ANDREW. Redundant. Norman nave, of which one S and one N window and the inner outline of the N doorway are preserved. The windows were discovered during the 1887 restoration, which provided new windows throughout. An earlier restoration in 1847. Of the former S aisle remains of two separate arches survive, separated by a chunk of solid wall (with the Norman window). Perp chancel and Perp W tower. The tower has ogeed niches l. and r. of the doorway, nice sound-holes to S and W, buttresses with chequered flushwork, and battlements with panelling in flushwork. It has an extravagantly tall ground stage. Two Perp S chancel windows with panel tracery, repeated in the E window. Roofs rebuilt in 1887, reusing what could be reused. – FONT. Octagonal, plain, C14. – PEWS and PULPIT. 1847. – BIER. Jacobean, like a converted table. – SCULPTURE. Alabaster fragments.

INGOLDISTHORPE   6030

ST MICHAEL. Redundant and hedged in by houses of the 1980s and 90s. All Dec, except for the Perp chancel and clerestory. However there was a big restoration in 1857–8 by *G. E. Pritchett* for the Rev. William Beckett at the same time as the Vicarage was built (*see* below). W tower with lancets to the ringing chamber

and two-light bell-openings. The Perp side windows of the
chancel have Dec mouchettes and an encircled quatrefoil above
the normal panelling, illustrating C15 masons' indifference to
the C19 and C20 notion of an orderly transition from one style
to the other. E window inserted by *Pritchett*. The clerestory
windows alternate between two lights and quatrefoiled circles.
Four-bay arcades, octagonal piers, double-chamfered arches.
C19 scissor-braced roofs with corbels carved by *W. Brown* of
King's Lynn. – FONT. Octagonal, Norman, with interlace, beaded
interlace, and intersecting arches. The font was square originally.
C19 base and Perp stem. – SCREEN. With ogee-arched, broad,
single-light divisions and much pretty tracery over. – STAINED
GLASS. By *M. & A. O'Connor*, chancel N and S and tower W, all
1859–63. The E window made by *M. & A. O'Connor* to *Pritchett's*
design. S aisle E window by *Preedy*, †1876. – BRASSES. Three
under the tower to the Rogerson family, C17. – CROSS. Base and
a little of the octagonal shaft left (outside the porch).

OLD VICARAGE, to the E. By *G. E. Pritchett* for the Rev. William
Beckett, 1856–8. It cost £2,000. Coursed carstone with stone
dressings. High Victorian. Six-bay entrance front (N) fitted out
with cross casements to the ground floor and sashes in rusticated surrounds above. Arched entrance door behind a timber
porch. Conservatory to the rear.

INGOLDISTHORPE HALL. Built in 1745 for John Davy. Red brick
still laid in English bond. The entrance front to the E of five
bays in two storeys, with a clumsy early C19 central canted bay
forming the entrance. The door with rather Greek motifs in the
stuccoed pilaster strips. Hipped roof. The garden front (W) has
a flight of steps from the basement up to the entrance, which
has a doorcase with Corinthian pilasters. Parapets and water
downpipes dated 1757. Added wings extend N and S. The staircase was moved into the canted bay on the E when that was
built: one fluted and one turned baluster per tread. Ground
floor has two good C18 chimneypieces, as do the two W first-
floor rooms. The STABLE BLOCK to the N is *c.* 1830, of two
ranges forming an L-plan and walls completing a courtyard.
Octagonal angle towers.

OLD HALL FARMHOUSE. This was the principal house until
1745. Approached from the S through a gateway with forecourt
walls. Early C17, rather chopped about; originally an H-plan, but
now an odd-looking L-plan. Carstone and brick. Central porch
to the S. Cross casement windows. Stepped gables, those of the
C17 to the N ends of the E and W wings. Against the N gable of
the W wing is a C17 projection fitted with an ovolo-moulded
casement. Various areas of plank and muntin panelling inside.

1000   INTWOOD

ALL SAINTS. Of flint with some ashlar dressings. C12 round W
tower with a polygonal top added in the C15 and the bell-openings altered 1985. Nave and chancel, the nave of Norman

1. Breckland Heath, Peddar's Way
2. Coastal cliffs at Hunstanton, from the north

3. Forncett St Peter, St Peter, from the north-west, Anglo-Saxon, with later aisles and porch
4. South Lopham, St Andrew, from the south-east, central tower c. 1120
5. Burnham Deepdale, St Mary, font, early twelfth century, with Labours of the Months
6. Fincham, St Martin, font, early twelfth century, south face with Nativity

3 | 5
4 | 6

7. Castle Acre, Priory west front, *c.* 1130, and Prior's House, twelfth century with later additions
8. Castle Rising, St Lawrence, begun *c.* 1140
9. King's Lynn, No. 30 King Street, late twelfth-century hall, subdivided *c.* 1400
10. Thetford Castle, motte, *c.* 1067–9
11. Castle Rising, keep, mid twelfth century, from the south-east

12. Wymondham, Abbey, nave interior, mid twelfth century
13. Wymondham, Abbey, from the south-east, twelfth century, with
    fourteenth and fifteenth-century towers
14. King's Lynn, St Margaret, west front, begun mid twelfth century

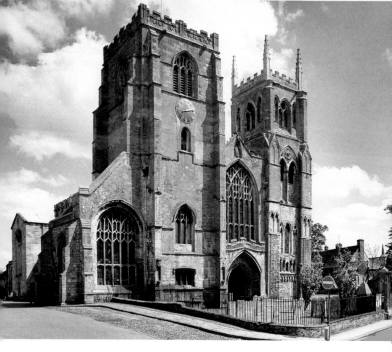

15. Haddiscoe, St Mary, south doorway, *c.*1100
16. Heckingham, St Gregory, south door, mid twelfth century
17. Hales, St Margaret, from the south-east, mid twelfth-century nave and chancel
18. Pulham St Mary, St Mary, double piscina, mid thirteenth century

19. West Walton,
St Mary, tower,
c. 1240
20. West Walton,
St Mary, nave,
c. 1240
21. West Walton,
St Mary, nave,
capitals, *c.* 1240

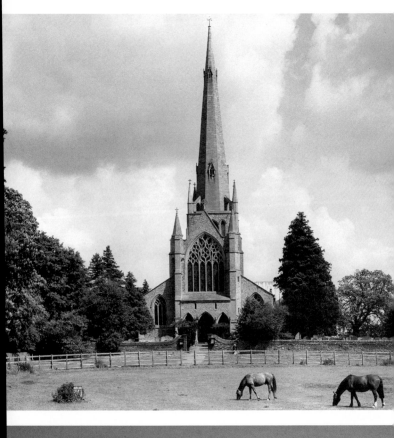

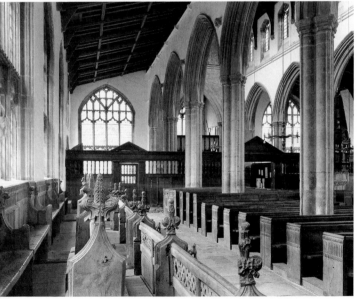

22. Snettisham, St Mary, from the west, fourteenth century
23. East Harling, St Peter and St Paul, from the south-east, fourteenth century with fifteenth-century spire
24. Merton, St Peter, screen, fourteenth century
25. Walpole St Peter, St Peter, south aisle and seating, mid fourteenth century

| 22 | 24 |
| 23 | 25 |

26. Great
    Cressingham,
    St Michael,
    tower by James
    Woderofe, early
    fifteenth century
27. Terrington
    St Clement,
    St Clement,
    from the south,
    fifteenth century
28. King's Lynn,
    St Nicholas,
    nave and south
    aisle, early
    fifteenth century

33. King's Lynn, Red
    Mount Chapel,
    c. 1485, upper part
    1505–6
34. King's Lynn, Red
    Mount Chapel,
    interior, 1505–6
35. Shelton, St Mary,
    from the south-
    west, late fifteenth
    century
36. Shelton, St Mary,
    interior, late
    fifteenth century

33 | 35
34 | 36

37. Swaffham, St Peter and St Paul, nave roof, early sixteenth century
38. Dereham, St Nicholas, south chapel, detail of ceiling, late fifteenth century
39. Dereham, St Nicholas, chest, Flemish, early sixteenth century
40. Dersingham, St Nicholas, chest, mid fourteenth century

37 | 38
   | 39
   | 40

| 41 | 43 44 |
| 42 | 45 |

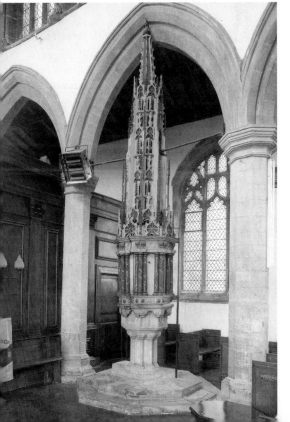

46. Attleborough, St Mary, door to the north porch staircase, early fifteenth century
47. Elsing, St Mary, chancel, stained glass, Apostles, fourteenth century
48. Wiggenhall St Mary the Virgin, benches, early fifteenth century
49. Wiggenhall St Germans, St Germaine, benches, *c.*1500
50. Shelton, St Mary, royal arms, late seventeenth century

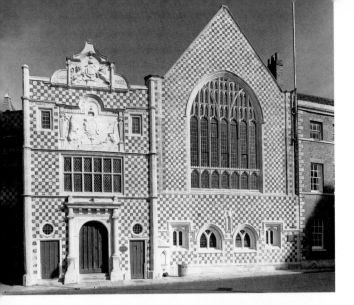

51. King's Lynn, Nos. 28 and 30 King Street, timber-framed exterior, with fourteenth century shop fronts
52. King's Lynn, St George's Guildhall, King Street, 1410–20
53. King's Lynn, Hampton Court, warehouse arcade, mid fifteenth century
54. King's Lynn, Guildhall, 1422–8 by John Turnour; extension to left, 1624
55. King's Lynn, South Gate, 1437 by Robert Hertanger

51	54
52	55
53	

56. Fordham, Snore Hall, late fifteenth century, west front, *c.*1470, porch, *c.*1490
57. Methwold, Old Vicarage, fifteenth century, with early sixteenth-century brick gable
58. Blo Norton, Blo Norton Hall, screens passage *c.*1585, detail
59. Old Buckenham, Abbey Farmhouse, first-floor hall, mid sixteenth century

60. Cringleford, bridge, *c.*1520
61. Hales, Hales Hall Farm Barn, late fifteenth century
62. Newton Flotman, Dairy Farm Barn, late fifteenth century
63. Blo Norton, Church Farmhouse, fifteenth century

64. Ketteringham, Church Cottage, early sixteenth century
65. Wymondham, Green Dragon, No. 6 Church Street, mid fifteenth century
66. Garboldisham, Jacques, Back Street, late fifteenth century
67. New Buckenham, houses between Market Place and Boosey's Walk, *c.* 1520–9

64 | 66
65 | 67

68. Oxborough, Oxburgh Hall, gatehouse, *c.* 1476–87
69. Great Cressingham, Manor House, *c.* 1545, south front
70. Breckles, Breckles Hall, *c.* 1583, east front

71. Wymondham, Market Cross, 1617–18
72. New Buckenham, Market House, 1559, with columns of 1754
73. Swaffham, Market Cross, 1781–3, probably by James Wyatt
74. Thetford, Thetford Warren Lodge, early fifteenth century
75. Denver, Denver Hall, gatehouse, 1570

71 | 73
72 | 74   75

76. King's Lynn, Customs House, by Henry Bell, 1683
77. King's Lynn, Customs House, statue of Charles II
78. Gaywood, almshouses, 1649
79. Scole, White Hart Inn, 1655

76	78
77	79

84. Holkham, Holkham Hall, Stone Hall, completed 1764
85. Holkham, Holkham Hall, south front, by Sir Thomas Coke, Matthew Brettingham and William Kent, 1734–53
86. Holkham, Holkham Hall, Saloon, completed 1753

87. Houghton,
    Houghton Hall,
    west front, by
    Colen
    Campbell and
    James Gibbs,
    1721–35
88. Houghton,
    Houghton Hall,
    Stone Hall,
    1721–35,
    chimneypiece
    by Michael
    Rysbrack
89. Raynham Hall,
    Marble Hall,
    remodelled
    c. 1704; ceiling
    by William
    Kent, 1726–31
90. Langley,
    Langley Park,
    library, detail of
    ceiling, c. 1740

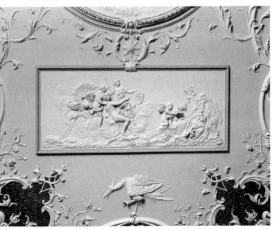

91. Kimberley, Kimberley Hall, south-west front, early eighteenth century, enlarged by Thomas Prowse and John Sanderson, 1755–7
92. Langley, Langley Park, north front, 1730s, altered mid eighteenth century
93. Wymondham, Cavick House, staircase, c. 1720
94. Langley, Langley Park, Lodges to Chedgrave Road, designed 1784 by Sir John Soane
95. Langley, Langley Park, Lodges to Norwich Road, designed 1784 by Sir John Soane

91	93
92	94
	95

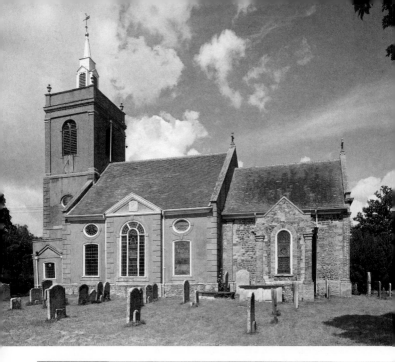

96. North Runcton, All Saints, from the south, by Henry Bell, 1703–13
97. Thetford, United Reform Church, exterior, 1817
98. Stow Bardolph, Holy Trinity, monument to Susanna Hare †1741, by Peter Scheemakers
99. King's Lynn, St Nicholas, monument to Sir Benjamin Keene †1758, probably by Robert Adam

100. West Harling, All Saints, monument to Richard Gipps, 1780, by Joseph Wilton

101. Tittleshall, St Mary, monument to Thomas Coke, first Earl of Leicester, †1759, by Charles Atkinson; busts by L.F. Roubiliac

102. Holkham, Holkham Park, monument to Thomas Coke, first Earl of Leicester, by William Donthorn, 1845–8

103. Holkham, St Withburga, monument to Juliana, Countess of Leicester, †1870, by Sir J.E. Boehm

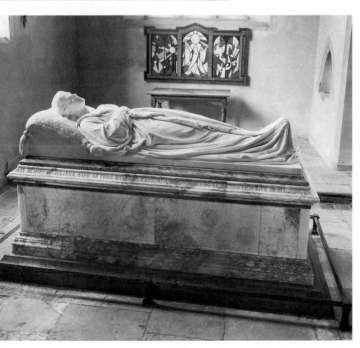

108. Kempstone, Kempstone Lodge, by Samuel Wyatt, 1788–93
109. Marham, Home Farm, 1861
110. Sandringham, Sandringham House, Norwich Gates, by
     Thomas Jekyll, 1862
111. Holkham, Great Barn, by Samuel Wyatt, *c.*1790

112. Shadwell Park, east front and stables, remodelled by S.S. Teulon, 1856–60
113. Shadwell Park, stableyard, by S.S. Teulon, 1856–60
114. Dunston, Dunston Hall, by J.C. Buckler, completed by Edward Boardman, 1859–78
115. Snettisham, Ken Hill, by J.J. Stevenson, 1878–80

116. Gillingham, Our Lady of Perpetual Succour, R.C., by F.E. Banham,
     west front, 1898.
117. Feltwell, St Mary, detail of stained glass by Didron & Oudinot, 1859–63
118. Diss, Corn Hall, by George Atkins, 1854
119. Thetford, Guildhall, by H.J. Green, 1902

120. King's Lynn, Nos 1–11 Guanock Place, London Road, 1825
121. Bressingham, Bressingham Lodge, by S.S. Teulon, 1842
122. Gaywood, King Edward VII High School, by Basil Champneys, 1903–6
123. Hunstanton, Smithdon High School, by Alison and Peter Smithson, 1950–4
124. Thetford, Rosemary Musker High School, Croxton Road, by the County Architect's Department (J.F. Tucker), 1983

120	122
121	123
	124

130. King's Lynn, Bespak factory extension, North Lynn Trading Estate, by Cambridge Design (Julian Bland), 1978–80

131. King's Lynn, Magistrates' Court, by Leonard Manasseh Partnership, 1979, with St Margaret behind

masonry, especially in the quoins. The two-light openings to the nave with their Dec tracery are of 1852, done during *John Brown*'s restoration. The C14 S porch has a plate recording the restoration. The four-centred doorway is Brown's. The rest of the exterior and interior details of 1852 as well, including the three-light Perp E window and the N vestry. – WEST GALLERY of 1853, made by *W. Ollet*, the son of the Cathedral carpenter, who executed all the new woodwork. – FONT. 1852, with a cover. – STAINED GLASS. E window Ascension scene by *Heaton, Butler & Bayne*, 1888. The style is more 1865. Other glass by *Robert Kerr*, 1853. – PEWS. 1852. – MONUMENT. Brass plaque to Clement Unthank †1900, by *P. Orr* of Madras. Unthank fell off a horse at polo in Lucknow (chancel).

INTWOOD HALL. Sir Thomas Gresham built a house here in 1560, but nothing apart from the garden buildings remains. The present house is red brick Tudor, 1807, by *Arthur Browne* for Joseph Salusbury Muskett. Solid, two and three storeys, crenellated, with occasional pinnacles and picturesque clumps of stacks. Wide three-bay main S front with three Wyatt windows to the ground floor, the centre one a doorway. Windows otherwise mullioned cross casements. Crenellated gable above, hardly a pediment. A further three-bay range set back to the W. *J. B. Pearce* is said to have worked on the house later in the C19.

Of the C16 are GARDEN BUILDINGS and a WALLED GARDEN, the latter to the NW, rather altered *c.* 1845 during improvements and restorations. In the NE angle is an octagonal GAZEBO, brick, late C16, with three facets glazed with casements. Octagonal roof. The rear elevation is jettied. Panelled interior. E of the hall itself is another GAZEBO, free-standing. Built *c.* 1550–60 for Sir Thomas Gresham and restored in 1852 with the church (i.e. by *John Brown*) for Joseph Muskett. Square plan, of brick, with polygonal clasping buttresses terminating in stone pinnacles added in 1852. Doorway under a four-centred arch with the Gresham arms and the Gresham grasshopper. The return walls seem earlier, perhaps of C15 brick. Inside is a corbel of a man with a shield. Flint floor dated 1852.

ISLINGTON

ST MARY. Redundant and virtually ruined until tidied up in 1972, when the nave was retained as a roofless space at *Marshall Sisson*'s suggestion. The chancel W wall built then and provided with three lancets. Transepts and Perp W tower. Brick belfry with two-light openings. The rest E.E. The transepts and chancel have pairs of lancet lights. The N transept N window is a stepped group of three lancet lights. Chancel E and S transept S have Perp windows instead. – MONUMENTS. Edward Bagge †1846. Four-centred arch, relief of reclining figure conversing with an angel. – Sons and daughters of Anthony Dixon, 1723. Panel with pediment on fluted pilasters. – FONT and PULPIT removed (the former to Hillington).

ISLINGTON HALL. To the SW. The house built in 1619 burnt out
in the 1970s. It was enlarged to the E in 1780 to form a half-H-
plan and the fronts rebuilt. The 1780 wing in five bays.
Pedimented door and upper windows with alternating pediments. This all reconstructed as a replica in 1991 by *David
Trundley*.

KEMPSTONE
8010

I m. NE of Great Dunham

ST PAUL. Disused and inaccessible. Tower plain C14. Mostly
Perp. Nave and chancel, the chancel arch with polygonal
responds. Roofs missing at time of writing. The following noted
in the first edition (1962), but now removed or decayed: – FONT.
C15, with traceried stem and bowl. – BOX PEWS. C18. – BIER.
C17.

KEMPSTONE LODGE. 1788–93. One of *Samuel Wyatt*'s Holkham
108   estate farmhouses for T. W. Coke. Very simple design of a centre
block of two storeys in three bays. Gault brick, hipped roof.
Pedimented central porch on columns flanked r. and l. by a tripartite sash within recessed segmental arches. Sashes to upper
floor. Slightly projecting to either side are pedimented two-
storey wings presenting only one bay to the façade. They are a
little altered. The chimneypots were originally conceived as little
Roman altars.

KENNINGHALL
0080

ST MARY. Norman S doorway, quite big, with one order of shafts
carrying fluted capitals. In the arches and on the square imposts
are bands of dogtooth decoration. On the E jamb is a carved
dog, on the W a horse, which seem to be *c.* 1300. Of the same
date or a little later are the chancel two-light cusped Y-tracery
windows, although heavily restored in 1874, and the N nave
doorway. The doorway goes with the N arcade. Five bays, or
four if one does not count the transeptal E bay as one. The piers
alternate between quatrefoil with thin shafts in the diagonals
and octagonal. Double-hollow-chamfered arches. The fifth, i.e.
E bay, a little later. The semi-quatrefoil responds have polygonal
capitals and the arch is simply double-chamfered. The chancel
arch of the same time as the arcade arches. Perp W tower datable
to 1485–93 on the basis of bequests. Flushwork base with
emblems. Perp also the N aisle windows and the four-light
chancel S window. The small doorway to the N chancel chapel
is Perp with the letters W. B. The buttresses on the S side are
decorated with shields. The clerestory without a S aisle deserves
notice. C15 nave roof with tie-beams and kingposts. Above the
two E tie-beams lively tracery of 1890–1, the date the nave was
restored. The kingpost chancel roof is all 1874. – FONT COVER.
Tall Perp canopy, i.e. late C14: central drum with eight radiat-

ing buttresses; further buttresses above. The very top is a restoration. – SCREEN. Above the S doorway a length of the top of the screen. – ROYAL ARMS. Of Elizabeth I, on the crenellated tie-beam before the NE chapel, robustly and rustically painted. – BENCHES. Only two fragments of poppyhead benches under the tower and one bench with a pierced traceried back. – STAINED GLASS. E window and two chancel S windows by *Heaton, Butler & Bayne*, the first of 1899, the others 1926 and 1938. – MONUMENTS. Of a brass of *c.* 1500 only the two groups of kneeling children are preserved. – Three-bay tomb-chest of George, Lord Audeley, *c.* 1500 with shields in quatrefoils and traceried panels. The E and W ends have been mutilated.

KENNINGHALL PLACE, 1¼ m. ESE. Fragment of, probably, the service wing of a mansion built for Thomas Howard, third Duke of Norfolk, in 1505–25, which stood immediately S and SW. The main house was demolished *c.* 1650, when the surviving range was most probably first used domestically, as it is today. Of red brick, diapered with blue to the S and W. At the angles, except at the NE, are polygonal shafts. The windows and doors now date from the early 1980s but there are plenty of older scars, particularly on the N side where the upper of the two floors retains five C16 windows, three of which have arched brick heads with elementary intersecting tracery and bowtell and casement mouldings to the brick jambs. The W gable, which has the best of the diapering, has a stepped gable-head, and a three-light brick window to the ground floor converted to a doorway. The interior has a lot of timber partitioning and fine moulded early Tudor bridging beams. Roof of queenpost trusses with arched braces rising to canted collars, where there are butt-purlins, and, below, through-purlins. Arched wind-bracing. The use of queenposts at this date rather than the more usual crown-posts in a building of this importance underlines its original subsidiary function.

At CANDLE YARDS, ⅜ m. E, is a double moated enclosure, the largest in the county. It surrounded East Hall, demolished in 1520, which was the precursor of Kenninghall Place. (AR)

BAPTIST CHAPEL, Church Street. Date unknown but must be late C18, with a rear extension of 1807. Flint and brick, the flint used on the façade. Usual two-storey, three-bay design. Inside, a total-immersion FONT (or pool) and a panelled gallery on three sides. Converted to a pottery.

The VILLAGE. This consists mainly of the Market Place with Church Street rising out of it SE up the hill to the church. Both have buildings of character. On the MARKET PLACE the WHITE HORSE public house (N side) is the only building of the C17, greatly altered by successive generations: timber-framed, the frame visible from inside only, formerly lobby-entrance. W of it is a HOUSE with exactly the same history, only the timber frame behind the early C19 brick is here of the early C18. The S side of the Market has pleasant enough brick C19 shops and houses of which the most interesting is the late C18 clay-lump POST OFFICE with its brick N gable. Like most clay-lump houses of this date it is of one storey with a dormer attic. THE LIMES is set back to the E side: two storeys in three bays, brick, ordinary.

CHURCH STREET has far more to offer the antiquarian. First the Baptist Chapel on the N side (*see* above). CHURCH FARMHOUSE started life in *c.* 1500 as a hall house but has had a C19 staircase inserted into the screens passage. One four-centred service door remains, and, in the roof, there is enough to show that there was the usual crown-post roof structure. The same roof type to the cross wing placed at r. angles to the high end of the hall, i.e. the E. The whole is timber-framed, the hall set to the r. of the main elevation and jettied. The jetty demonstrates that the hall cannot have been open to the roof, but of one storey only, and the screens passage indicates that it was not a first-floor hall. So it stands at the beginning of the modern tradition. C17 stacks emerge through the roof. Beyond the church WOODWELL FURLONG is an early C18 timber-framed lobby-entrance house.

On the S side are two early C19 clay-lump groups, WHITE HOUSE etc. and the houses immediately W of them. Further E CAREY'S COTTAGE is very early C17 – see the sunk-quadrant bridging beams downstairs, the blocked four-light diamond-mullioned window in the first floor and the diminished principals in the roof. Thatched, lobby-entrance plan. The timber frame has tension braces, as has the house to the E of the Red Lion public house. The RED LION itself is another early C19 clay-lump house. Further on and out of the village to GILLS FARMHOUSE and THE NUTTERIES, both C17 timber-framed houses with wattle-and-daub, the latter built as a pair of cottages. GRANGE COTTAGE is an example of a hall house with the C17 stack inserted between the hall and the solar, rather than in the screens passage. Only one storey now. The passage to the S of the hall still exists with two square-headed service doors (one blocked) and the hall itself has a C17 fireplace and chamfered bridging beams. Blocked four-light diamond-mullioned window to the S. The roof disappointingly altered.

KESWICK

2000

ALL SAINTS. The nave and chancel demolished 1597 and rebuilt indifferently in 1893 by *Herbert Green*. Remains of the medieval chancel still visible immediately E. Before Green all that remained was the C12 round tower and the W nave wall. The tower has brick bell-openings and an octagonal top stage, much restored in 1893. Y-tracery. Apsidal chancel. – STAINED GLASS. E window signed *William Morris*, †1922, but very ordinary.

KESWICK HALL, Keswick Hall Road. A large complex of offices and flats developed from the teacher-training college after it closed in 1981 and the facility moved to the university. The college was founded in 1948 out of the mansion erected for Richard Hudson Gurney in 1817–19 by *William Wilkins Jun.*

The house consists of two parts facing S (although the entrance is from the N), both of gault brick. The E part is an imposing but, for Wilkins, an unadventurous seven-bay, three-storey block with a central three-bay pediment. Hipped slate roof. The ground floor was originally an open trabeated loggia on eight Roman Doric piers under a full-length triglyph frieze, in the mid C19 filled in by French windows and the piers reduced to pilasters. In 1837 Wilkins added a new wing for the same client attached to the W and projecting one bay from it. Two-storey single-bay balustraded side pieces frame a giant bow rising through two higher storeys to a low hipped roof; as high as the three storeys of the older wing. Three big sashes to each floor under hoods on scrolled consoles, the ground floor with paired pilasters.

In 1949–57 *Seely & Paget* added various extensions, those to the E enormous, appearing from the S as a letter F: three storeys, casement windows, hipped roofs. These wings are dated 1951. Further extensions to the W of 1960 and 1983–9. The N front of Wilkins's house is very cramped, just a three-bay hipped entrance enlivened by pilasters to the ground floor supporting a triglyph frieze, and a recessed entrance. Sashes to the first floor and an odd square balustraded roof terrace. The doorway leads to an atrium with two Ionic columns on the E side, and then to the staircase hall fitted with a big open-well staircase with turned balusters enriched with acanthus. The S bow room is tripartite with square scagliola pillars. The house has been split up for offices of several commercial concerns; Seely & Paget's E block is now flats.

OLD HALL. An attractive, very mixed building, consisting of a centre block with a stepped gable on the garden side, probably originally the porch. The main (W) front is in four bays and is entered through a late C18 doorcase under a broken pediment on columns. N gable stepped, S gable rebuilt *c.* 1970. In addition there is a separate three-bay building to the l., and this was linked to the core in the alterations of *c.* 1800. These included the building of a big drawing room with a coved ceiling and a spacious bow, almost entirely glazed, and of a doorway. The columns and the window fluting below the capitals are the same in both new pieces. Handsome winder staircase in the former porch, with a cast-iron balustrade. It is Soanian, and traditionally by *Soane*. The main stack evidently once an external stack of *c.* 1600. C17 panelling to ground- and first-floor rooms. To the road, GARDEN WALLS, *c.* 1600 with C18 additions to the E return.

WATERMILL. The mill, the Miller's House and a castellated rounded attachment form a happy group. The mill is a conventional three-storey later C18 timber-framed and weatherboarded structure. Slightly unusual is the sweep of the roof on the N side to form an open access to the interior. The two W bays and the lucam are all C19. Only partial machinery. The MILLER'S HOUSE also C18, now brick. Double pile. Three bays and three storeys. Nice doorcase of Corinthian pilasters and pediment.

Low Farmhouse, Low Road. A three-cell c16 timber-framed
house fitted with casements and a door to the r. Two storeys
and attic. The rear has remains of mullioned windows. Its barn
has brick and flint walls with bits of clay lump, but there is a
timber-framed core which needs some interpretation due to
later alterations and partitions. The aisle-posts and passing-
braces show it to be a five-stead aisled barn with aisle spurs and
straight braces to the tie-beams; none of the trusses is complete
at the time of writing. Probably of the mid c14. Honeysuckle
Cottage, further along Low Road, was the parsonage until
1845. Again there is a brick skin over a c16 timber frame. The
frame complete only to the first floor. Blocked mullioned window.

_1000_   KETTERINGHAM

St Peter. Unbuttressed w tower, rebuilt in 1609 and with upper
parts from 1870. The lower parts of flint with carstone quoins,
unusual in this area. Continuous nave and chancel, under a
hammerbeam roof of 1908. A c17 quadrant-moulded tie-beam
marks off the chancel. Norman masonry and lancets in the
nave, restored or renewed during the main restoration in 1837.
In the chancel E.E. lancets and plain piscina. The piscina has
undercut capitals to the shafts and a trefoiled head. Perp five-
light E window. Brick N vestry of 1845 with a stepped gable, and
w of it a large sloping c18 buttress against the nave. w gallery
with inscription recording donation by Sir John P. Boileau,
1841. – Font. c15. Octagonal, with fleurons in panels on the
stem and a vine trail, and on the bowl the signs of the Evangelists,
a seated figure and two flowers. – Pulpit. Plain three-decker of
1837. – Painting. Wedding Feast at Cana in the reredos;
Flemish, later c16, possibly a copy by _Frans Francken the Elder_
of _Collaert_'s engraving after _Maerten de Vos_. – Stained glass.
In the E window whole early c15 figures and many bits. – North
door. c15.
    Monuments. A surprising number. Brass to a Lady, c. 1470,
the figure 34 in. long (chancel, s wall). – Brass to Thomas
Hevenyngam †1499 and wife. – Brass to John Colvyle, a baby,
c. 1530. – Tomb-chest (chancel s) with three cusped lozenges.
Recess with four-centred arch. Cresting on top. Against the back
wall groups of kneeling brass figures: Sir Henry Gray, Lady
Gray and their children; late c15. – Lady Heveningham, and her
husband Sir William †1678 (chancel s). He was a judge at the
trial of Charles I and was subsequently tried for treason and
deprived of his estates. Tablet with small kneeling figures facing
one another across a prayer-desk, a theme more associated with
the early c17 and earlier. Another unusual thing is that an angel
with a baby flies over the group in front of the inscription tablet,
so that the inscription must leave space for the intruder. In the
predella two napkins full of bones. – Edward Atkyns †1750
(chancel N). Big, with a sarcophagus almost detached on lions'
feet and a fine inscription tablet above in a frame of brown

marble. Arms at the top in a cartouche. The whole set in a plain Gothic arch. By *Robert Page*. – Edward Atkyns †1794 and his son Wright Edward Atkyns †1804, by *Sir Richard Westmacott*, 1807. Mourning young woman below a big broken column with a branch of weeping willow on the top. Military still-life at its foot (the son was a Captain of Dragoons). – Harriet Peach †1825. By *J. Flaxman*. Relief with the young woman carried up by two angels, a favourite motif of Flaxman's. – Mary Atkins †1829, by *E. Gaffin*. Urn and two putti. – Frances Mary Peach †1832. Seated woman by an urn, by *Daniel William Willson*, 1833. – Nathaniel William Peach †1835, by *Edward Physick*. Urn in relief and a wreath. Several brasses in Victorian surrounds to the Boileaus, of 1855–69.

BOILEAU MAUSOLEUM, in the churchyard 15 yds E of the church. The Boileau family (*see* below, Ketteringham Hall) did not get on well with the vicar and in 1853 Sir John Peter Boileau emptied the vaults of the chancel to create a family mausoleum – an illuminating insight into mid-C19 squirearchical attitudes – and had to reinstate them after the resulting row. Instead he constructed the mausoleum in 1854: small, square, of gault brick with ashlar quoins. Iron door in the W wall, within a Doric doorcase. Pediment with a central acroterion.

CHURCH COTTAGE, just N of the church on Church Road. Early C16 timber-framed hall house with an added E–W wing. L-shaped. The C16 N–S wing has a bricked-over ground floor, so it looks half-timbered. Partly jettied on the E side. The upper framing is of heavy scantling with tension braces to the wall-plate. Mid-C19 details everywhere, especially prominent the moulded stacks. The E–W wing is C17, most probably added when the hall was floored over and its stacks first put in.

HALL FARMHOUSE, 200 yds W of the church. With stepped gables. C16, divided into two houses. Two storeys and attic. Façade to E, in five bays. Open pediment to doorcase in l. bay. Various casement windows. Two ridge stacks and a stair-turret, with a C19 staircase inside, but a four-centred doorway at the first floor.

HIGH ASH FARMHOUSE, 2 m. w. Four-bay house with a timber frame. C19 additions. Main C16 front to N fitted with C19 and C20 casements. Returns of C17 brick; stepped gables and indecipherable datestones. E return has pedimented windows. C17 winder staircase with an octagonal newel.

KETTERINGHAM HALL, now a school. Sir John Boileau bought the Tudor house in 1836 and employed *Thomas Allason* on the reconstruction of 1839–40 in an unconvincing Gothic. *Thomas Jekyll* made a few minor alterations in 1852. Red brick. Symmetrical E façade of nine bays with angle-shafts and battlements. Steep gable above the porch. Hipped roof with a flat. The windows are cross casements. The chapel-like hall to the r. of the elevation was a new feature introduced by Allason, its gable-end showing and with a big six-light Perp window under a canopied Saint. In the gable a datestone: 'Victoria 1840'. Also of 1839–40 is the five-bay Gothic conservatory added to the l.

of the asymmetrical five-bay s front. Of the C16 is the rear wing
to the SW, on a half-H-plan, with a gable r. and l. Jekyll filled the
courtyard in 1852. Polygonal C16 stacks appear here and there.

Inside is a spacious imperial staircase with plain cast-iron
balusters supporting a ramped mahogany handrail rising in one
flight to an oriel bay. This bay, added in 1844, has STAINED
GLASS, mostly Flemish panels, including roundels of Daniel
and Moses in the Rushes, 1573. From here the staircase returns
in two flights. The library in Jekyll's wing has a Gothic chimneypiece.

The entrance to the STABLE YARD is under an arch between
two turrets put up in 1899 for Sir Francis Boileau. The l. turret
has a C2 B.C. Greek stele RELIEF and the r. turret has two.
There are inscriptions also. They are Asia Minor pieces. The
C18 KITCHEN GARDEN was altered in 1898 principally by the
addition of a gazebo in the SE internal angle. In the grounds
near the lake fragments of the Perp tracery of the W window of
Norwich Cathedral. They may have been placed here when the
W front of the cathedral was restored c. 1851.

In the HIGH STREET C16 timber-framed houses and later C18
ones with clay lump. Of the best a selection. IVY FARMHOUSE.
C16 and C17, the earlier part to the l. This has moulded cruciform bridging beams. The C17 part with casements. C19 clay-
lump outshut to rear. THE THATCHED HOUSE. C16, rendered
over. One storey and attics in three bays, the l. bay an addition.
The stair-turret to the N façade is C20. WELLGATE COTTAGE
on the N side of the road. Split into two, C16. One storey and
dormer attic. Plenty of additions. N gable wall of clay lump.
APPLETREE COTTAGE and WHITE HOUSE are an C18 pair, of
clay lump. Four bays in two storeys. External stacks and a ridge
stack. C19 casements.

BARROWS. Two round barrows at the Five Ways. (JW)

KILVERSTONE

ST ANDREW. Sturdy round tower of three stages with round-
headed Norman windows to the ringing chamber and two-light
C12 belfry windows with central columns. Later Norman S
doorway. One order of shafts with volute capitals. The arch has
a zigzag moulding at r. angles to the wall surface. The church is
small and aisleless, but must once have had a N aisle. – FONT.
Just the base of a Norman one. – ROYAL ARMS. Of George I,
dated 1716; plaster, handsome. – STAINED GLASS. An attractive
window of 1908 in the Selwyn Image style, possibly by *Leonard
Walker* (nave s). A lancet, also nave s, by *Morris & Co.* depicts
St Andrew, c. 1890. The remainder of the furnishings, roofs,
and not a little of the fabric are of the 1906 restoration by *Boardman*
who was then working at the Hall.

KILVERSTONE HALL. Of c. 1620 (date on waterheads), altered
internally c. 1725, modernized in 1913, additions 1928. The flint
and gault brick exterior appears more Victorian than anything

else. The N front is in five gabled bays of two and three storeys with some C17 flintwork but mostly of 1913. The fanlight behind the porch is of *c.* 1725, and of the same time are the two principal ground-floor rooms, one with an alabaster panel over the fireplace with dancing putti in relief. A whole wing was added to the S too, now replaced by the 1928 block. The first house was built for Thomas Wright, who had acquired the manor in 1587, and it only passed from the family in 1849.

During Josiah Vavasour's brief ownership, 1900–8, *Edward Boardman* was employed on new outbuildings such as the crazy-looking WATER TOWER of *c.* 1905. Octagonal in plan, of flint and decorative brick, it has balconies and a timber bartizan at the tank storey, which is itself set below a copper broach spire. Purposeful STABLES round two sides of a courtyard dated 1901. The central gabled entrance is below a bellcote and inside is a rare genuine piece of reused ship's timber from one of Lord Fisher's commands (he was a Sea Lord), deliberately placed for aesthetic purposes. The Fisher family came to the estate in 1908. At the SW corner is a two- to three-storey house, nicely done and with a first-floor corner loggia. These additions also *Boardman*'s. Part of the grounds is given over to a wildlife park open to the public.

The whitewashed brick LODGE on the main road is dated 1906. Presumably by *Boardman* too. One storey with a steep pyramid roof with dormers.

KIMBERLEY

ST PETER. By the W gates to Kimberley Hall. Dec chancel, some of the windows renewed with improbable tracery in the 1904 restoration paid for by the second Earl of Kimberley. The E window is restored but apparently to the original design, see Ladbroke's 1820s drawing. Perp W tower for which there are bequests to build 1536–60, improbably late for anything other than alterations. Flushwork on the buttresses. The considerable upper part rebuilt in 1631 and an inscription to prove it. Inside, the restoration of 1904 was responsible for the nave roof, reconstruction of the chancel arch, the N chancel wall and a new screen. Seating and pulpit 1875. There had been a previous restoration in 1835 which provided its own chancel roof and fittings, but these obviously were not liked. The nave has an elaborate and compact hammerbeam roof. Nice fleuron decoration to the segmental rood-stair doorway. STAINED GLASS. Much in the E and SE windows, quite a number of English C14 and C15 figures and also larger Flemish figures. Set here *c.* 1825. N chancel by *Clayton & Bell*, †1873, S nave by the same, †1871, a Resurrection and Saints. – MONUMENTS. Brass to John Wodehouse and wife, *c.* 1530. 18 in. figures (chancel floor). – Dame Elizabeth Strutt †1651, attributed to *William Wright* of Charing Cross (GF). Tablet with effigy kneeling in profile (N wall). – SOUTH DOOR. Plain but C14.

KIMBERLEY HALL. The manor came to Sir John Wodehouse in
the 1380s, and it is the ruins of his house, built by 1402, which
survive as fragments no more than 5 ft high ½ m. E of the church
on a moated site. The new house was built after 1700 on top of
the only hill for miles, by *William Talman* for Sir John Wodehouse,
fourth Baronet. Plans survive in the RIBA. The large but plain
mansion of red brick was enlarged in 1755–7 for Sir Armine
Wodehouse by four corner towers of the Houghton and Holkham
type, by the gentleman-architect *Thomas Prowse* assisted by *John
Sanderson*. The immediate precursors are Langley, Norfolk, built
in the late 1730s and remodelled in the 1740s, and Hagley Hall,
Worcestershire, by Sanderson Miller with help from Prowse,
and only just finished in the 1750s. Kimberley is two and a half
storeys high; the towers have four storeys. Lower wings of one
and a half storeys and seven bays flank the NE front and are
linked to the main block by quadrant passages added in 1835–8
by *Anthony Salvin* for the second Baron Wodehouse. The centre three bays of the wings broken forward under pediments.

91   The house itself is eleven by five bays. On the entrance (NE)
and garden (SW) sides two bays are in the towers, and of the
recessed nine the middle three carry pediments. Otherwise there
is no more in the way of accentuation than a pediment over the
middle window of the NE side and of the NW return. Here the
middle bays of the ground floor were originally an open loggia.

Inside, there are three main rooms to each of the long sides,
and while much of the decoration is of 1770 by *John Sanderson*
(who often worked with Prowse and Miller), yet more is by
Fletcher-Watson, 1951. Fletcher-Watson's most dramatic work
is in the creation of the present entrance hall, which had been a
billiard room, turning the then central window of the NE front
into the doorway behind a portico on four Ionic columns. He
had nothing less in mind than a two-storey hall with an imperial
staircase leading up to a pair of Corinthian columns and pilasters.
Not only did the ground-floor and first-floor rooms disappear
but so did the SW first-floor bedroom, i.e. his new space runs
right across the middle of the house at first-floor level, more or
less belatedly creating a triple-pile plan.

The room to the l. of the entrance has a fine frieze with lions,
urns and foliage, and a fine pedimented doorway with a classical
scene depicted in the plaster frieze. The opposite doorway has
a relief panel showing Moses in the Bulrushes. A recess in the
NW has an arch carried on caryatids. This is all by *Sanderson*.
Drawings of 1770 exist by Sanderson for the octagonal cabinet
in the N tower. The main staircase from Prowse's time is in the
SE tower, complete with a wrought-iron balustrade. Its domed
coffered ceiling, though, looks as if we are back with Sanderson.
On the first floor runs a groin-vaulted corridor. This, John Harris
suggests, may go back to William Talman's activity. The extensive
cellars are largely groin-vaulted.

THE PARK. Laid out by *Capability Brown* from 1762. Two of his
plans have come down to us, one of 1763, the other of 1778. His
is the LAKE, ¼ m. SW of the house. Nice open parkland.

WEST LODGES. Early C19, simple square rooms with pyramid roofs and a sash within an arched recess. The s lodge extended in 1960, the N in 1989.

VILLAGE. THE GREEN has the church on the E side. On the s side THE OLD SMITHY, a four-bay C17 timber-framed house remodelled in the C18 and fitted with metal casements. The smithy itself is to the side. To the N GREEN FARMHOUSE in limited mid-C19 Gothic Revival dress: red and blue brick, mullioned windows with arched heads and hoodmoulds, polygonal and circular gable stacks. Built for the Wodehouse family, as was No. 7. This dates from 1866, a pair of estate cottages, brick and thatched, one storey and dormer attic. Many more similar ESTATE HOUSES were built in 1866, e.g. at Station Road.

STATION FARMHOUSE, just s of the site of the former station, is of brick with burnt brick headers. Moulded platband between the floors. It has shaped gables and the date 1716 on the s one. The casements are C19.

MANOR HOUSE, Coston Lane. W wing with blocked or reduced C17 windows. The roof renewed in the C18. Stepped N gable with external stack. GARDEN WALL. Late C17, of brick and flint and with rusticated gatepiers.

BARROWS. There are two, or possibly three, barrows, known as the Forehoe Hills, on the s side of the Barford road ½ m. w of Carleton Forehoe.

KING'S LYNN   6020

INTRODUCTION

The historic core of King's Lynn is delightful. The area fronting the river is predominantly of Georgian brick to the streets but with plenty of evidence of earlier building behind the façades. The sequence of Nelson Street, St Margaret's Place and Queen Street is one of the most satisfying Georgian promenades in England, often used for film sets, so even C20 street furniture is minimal. Defoe attributes to the town 'more gentry and gaiety' than to Norwich and Yarmouth. Of Lynn's medieval greatness the churches are witness, together with the evidence for the friaries, the two guildhalls, several houses and the warehouses. It was one of England's busiest ports, serving the Ouse and its tributaries and exporting wool and cloth. Even in the C18, when Defoe wrote, it could still be said that Lynn supplied six counties wholly and three partly.

The town was first called Bishop's Lynn, having been founded in 1095 by Bishop Herbert de Losinga, who in the previous year had transferred the see from Thetford to Norwich. There was already an existing settlement which appears to have been based round a salt-water lagoon, or series of inlets, with its centre round the present All Saints Street. Losinga's town developed to the N of this, between All Saints Church and the Saturday Market Place where St Margaret's Church and Priory were established from

Norwich *c.* 1100. In 1101 Losinga granted St Margaret's Church, the Priory (both under construction), the market and the land to the monks of Norwich. Rapid expansion in the C12 required a town extension, and it was Bishop William Turbe who laid out the new town N of the Purfleet from *c.* 1145 with its market on Tuesday Market Place and its church of St Nicholas as a chapel of ease to St Margaret. This was all on his own land, not that of the Norwich Benedictines, and in 1204 the grant of 1101 was bought back by the bishops and both settlements were united under the royal charter of that year, the town very aptly named Bishop's Lynn. The name changed to King's Lynn at the Reformation.

In the late C11 not only was the coastline of the southern Wash rather different, but so were the river patterns. Wisbech was at the southern tip of a large bay marking the outflow of both the River Nene and the Great Ouse, while Lynn stood on the E coast of its own narrow-necked lagoon served principally by the River Gay and, to the S, the Nar. It was the diversion of the Great Ouse to Lynn via the Brandon Creek in the middle of the C13 that set the course of the town to prosperity. By the late C17 the coast-line had receded to its present position and Vermuyden's great drainage schemes had accelerated the natural deepening and widening of the Great Ouse. This process had begun after *c.* 1250 and has implications for the street plan, as the E bank of the river began gradually to migrate W, releasing land for reclamation and subsequent development as trade increased at the expense of Wisbech.

Losinga's town round the Saturday Market was protected from the river immediately to its W by the 'great bank', an earthwork running along the present line of Nelson Street, St Margaret's Place and Queen Street. By about 1500 the river had moved *c.* 165 ft W and was consolidated a further 150 ft W at the new South Quay only in 1855. The progress of construction of the buildings in the area between the Millfleet and the Purfleet can therefore be established, as can their plans and type. To the N, on Bishop Turbe's 'newe lande', much the same pattern emerges: originally the W side of Tuesday Market was washed by the river, with King Street forming the line of the bank. As the C13 pro-gressed it became possible to build along the W side of King Street, on narrow plots, these plots elongating in stages until river movement ceased in this area in the C17. The movement of the river in the first town was rather slower, but began earlier when there was less pressure for land next to it. This resulted in more generous-sized plots, reflected today in the surviving buildings dating from the C14 to the C17 around open courtyards.

On the E sides of these modern streets are the earlier sites, of which archaeological evidence remains of C12 buildings, one, at Nos. 28–32 King Street, still standing. They were often the domestic and first trading quarters of the merchant classes who were to dominate the social and economic life of the town until the C19. As land became available opposite, warehouses were built straight on to the river front, to become redundant and be replaced by domestic quarters and shops as the inexorable westward movement of the Great Ouse left them stranded. Warehouse design changed from the later C15 from ranges parallel to the river, as at Hampton Court, to blocks set gable-end to the river, such as the Hanseatic Warehouse of 1477 on St Margaret's Lane, the latter configuration capable of extension as necessary.

The number of houses built by the mendicant friars is, as usual, a sign of importance in the later Middle Ages. Of the Greyfriars uncommonly much survives. Of the Blackfriars (founded 1272), Austin Friars (1293) and Whitefriars (c. 1260) scantier fragments and the names of streets are a record. Unlike other towns, their houses did not lie especially close to the town walls, simply because these lay far away across open fields to the E.

The walls of Lynn remain in several places, especially St Anne's Gate at the N end of St Anne's Street, and on the E side in Kettlewell Lane, Wyatt Street and The Walks. On the S side they are represented by the South Gate. The area of the town was considerable, about ½ m. by ⅞ m., enclosing an area which was not fully built up until the C20. The choice of site for the walls was not however dictated by an estimate of the likely growth of the medieval town, but by the existence of an older sea-bank which provided a natural base for the original ditch and fence fortification. Four timber towers, or bretasks, are recorded in the C13 ringing the town at the most important points of entry. Murage grants for the later flint and brick walls are recorded from 1294 to 1339, and it is fragments of these we see today, mentioned in the Perambulations where they occur. Of the two principal gates the South Gate was rebuilt in 1437 and the East Gate in 1542, the latter demolished in 1800. Henry Bell's 'Groundplat' gives a good indication of the extensions built to the N and S in 1643.

The *Survey of the Newland* of *c.* 1250 and Vanessa Parker's reconstruction of the older town and South Lynn indicates that little had changed by the time of Bell's 'plat' of *c.* 1685. The river development reached as far E as the modern St Anne's Street, Chapel Street, Broad Street, Tower Street, Friars Street and Checker Street. Damgate (now Norfolk Street and Littleport Street) was a ribbon of dwellings and shops linking Tuesday Market with the East Gate just as Friars and Checker Streets defined the entry to the town from South Gate along the E boundaries of the Whitefriars' precinct.

Lynn's prosperity was based entirely on trade. By the C12 merchants from the cloth manufacturing towns of Ghent and Bruges organized huge quantities of wool for export: about 1,500 bales by the 1260s, 2,000 in the early C14. In the other direction came wine, mainly from Gascony, later coal, timber and luxury goods, stimulated by the establishment of the Hansa at Lynn after 1271. For the next sixty years the extent of Lynn's trading interests was exceeded only by London and Southampton. By the late C14 trade was more diversified, and in the C15 a trade war with Baltic merchants reduced commerce until the issue was settled in 1475 and the Hanseatic League began their great warehouse at St Margaret's Place (*see* Perambulation 1a). Cereal export dominated from the C16, especially in the C18 (*see* General Introduction,

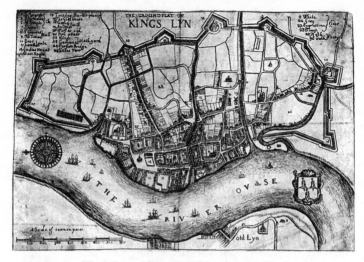

King's Lynn. Henry Bell's 'Groundplat' of 1685

p. 126), and coastal shipping remained important. In 1761 83,000 quarters of grain went to other English ports, especially London, but 125,000 to Europe, and it was Europe, not the expanding world markets of Empire, that interested Lynn merchants.

Coal and wine continued to be imported for distribution inland, and until the railway age Lynn was the chief East Anglian port for both. The prosperity this engendered continued until continental trade was disturbed by the Napoleonic Wars; then came a brief revival; then the railway arrived in 1844, and it was the turn of coastal trade to fall into irrevocable decline. In 1869 the new Alexandra Dock arrested the shrinkage of trade, and the Bentinck Dock of 1883 similarly, but the great trading days of the port were at an end.

The C19 brought major changes to the fabric of the town, beginning with the construction of London Road in 1811–13 and the terraces which line it. The population doubled to 20,000 between 1811 and 1851, but fell to 17,000 in the 1860s, mirroring trade patterns. As the century progressed the spare land reaching to the walls was filled, and it was the availability of building land on virgin sites which prevented wholesale, and probably destruct-ive, redevelopment of the original settlements. Much old building survives, even though most of the houses in the historic core were re-fronted and modernized in the C18; the C19 saw the same process in the High Street, Broad Street and Norfolk Street, albeit with a heavier hand.

By 1900, with the exception of The Walks (*see* Perambulation 1b), the area within the walls was too small to hold the town, which burst out E and N towards Gaywood and South Wootton, where council houses were erected in the 1930s, and the same in South Lynn. Nevertheless in 1960 Lynn, like Thetford, was a fos-silized medieval town with an intimate pattern of streets opening quietly to the river on the W or dramatically into the dominating spaces of the two market places. Just as in Thetford London over-spill arrived in 1962, here responsible for further new housing estates at Gaywood and North and South Wootton, increasing the population to 38,000 in 1975 (1991 population 35,000). This expansion triggered development in the town centre, outside the historic core, and this time it was very destructive indeed. Whole streets were swept away in the space between London Road and the High Street, to be replaced with car parks and shop-ping malls. The pedestrianized shopping streets arrived in the 1970s, with vehicle access to the rear of the shops. As the *Municipal Review* put it in 1971, this work involved 'the removal of a mass of obsolete buildings', something one now regrets, and in the same year it was estimated that one fifth of medieval Lynn had perished in the previous nine years. But a great deal remains. There are still good C19 terraces at the S end of London Road (Buckingham Terrace, Guanock Place, all 1825–*c*. 1840), and more in St John's Terrace and Portland Street of the 1830s and 40s.

One result of the clearances of the 1960s was the series of archae-ological excavations, some of the first really important medieval and post-medieval urban archaeology in England to concentrate on a commercial centre. Similar examination and repair of major standing buildings transformed our understanding of the develop-ment of the town (see, e.g. Vanessa Parker, *The Making of King's Lynn*, 1971, and the work of the King's Lynn Preservation Trust, founded in 1957, whose renovations begin at Hampton Court and Thoresby College).

Early House Plans

The survival of domestic properties in Lynn, or domestic with a shop or warehouse attachment, is too fragmentary before the later C14 to outline a coherent development. The earliest is Nos. 28–30 King Street, a stone-built Norman hall with two pairs of round arches one above the other. It is quite possible that the ground floor was in the form of an open arcade with the living accommo-dation above. Like the 'Jew's House' in Lincoln the date is likely to be late C12, or at any rate after the foundation of the 'newe lande' after 1150.

Whether it had its flank to the street when built, like the examples of C12 dwellings in Lincoln, is not clear, since in the late C12 the E side of King Street must have been very close to the river line. Two documents quoted by Blomefield and by Clarke and Carter may relate to it. The first of 1173: 'in the north part of this town, a hall called Boyland-hall, with a kitchen, cellars, chambers [etc.]; it is mentioned to have a great stone front. . .' The second: 'John of Oxford Bishop of Norwich granted in 1187. . . 3 marks of silver per ann[um] to be paid out of his stone-house which he had built on the sea bank by St Nicholas Chapel. . . one of the cellars that is in front of the house for to put wine in'. These references may not relate to the same building but two things are clear: they refer to a two-storeyed structure with a 'cellar' to the ground floor, and confirm the presence of at least one stone-built house in Lynn in c. 1180. As we have noted, the standard plan for merchants' properties was to have a house on the E side of the street, on a line from Millfleet to St Anne's Fort, and their warehouses on the opposite side of the road. Where sites were large enough, in the area s of the Purfleet, houses with contiguous ranges could also be constructed on the W side, e.g. Clifton House from the C14 and Hampton Court in the C15. The warehouse range at Hampton Court is the W wing of a quadrangular structure with an open brick arcade originally facing directly on to the river.

The courtyard plan, used for the larger houses, was confined to the first medieval town on account of the larger sizes of the plots. Thoresby College is c. 1510, Hampton Court C14, and Clifton House an amalgam of dates commencing in the C14 also. By their nature these buildings are very grand, all using stone and brick in their construction.

More common are houses of an L-shaped plan, with a street front often used for shops, and a range running back at the rear, usually on the s, which contained the hall. The first floor of the street range was generally a private chamber, and the usual means of access to the rear was through a passage opening from the centre of the façade or set to the N. Nearly all the houses on the W sides of Queen and King Streets are of this type, the latter more altered than the former. This plan predominated from the C14, and at No. 29 Queen Street is an example which was completely rebuilt about 1630, removing any provision for a shop. Houses with shops began to disappear after 1560.

Houses with halls lying parallel to the street are occasionally found in towns, where wider street frontages were available. No. 2 St Anne's Street is an example from the early C15, having a single range jettied at the front and rear. Nos. 30–32 Pilot Street started as the same form at the same time, to be subsequently split into two houses. The resulting hall ranges were then too small for practical use, especially as the rear access passageway had to run between them, and hall ranges were added to the rear in conventional L-plan manner. The rear jetty of the original build runs through the houses at the W end of the added halls.

Timber was the main building material until the end of the C16, usually carried on a flint, brick or stone plinth, or a mixture of all three. By the C14 brick was coming into use; an early example is the cellar of Clifton House. By the C15 brick had replaced stone in buildings of prestige or where timber was never appropriate, e.g. at the Marriotts Warehouse, which stood either on a causeway or a peninsula in the river. Stone became popular once more in the 1540s when large amounts of dressed material suddenly swamped the market at the Dissolution. Timber-framing was rare after c. 1620, although in 1806 the Paving Commissioners still had to forbid the construction of any more jettied timber-framed buildings. As far as major timber-framed buildings are concerned the last of them was the Greenland Fishery House of 1605, and this stands on brick cellars and breaks from the L-plan standard by having the living quarters on the street front, not in a rear range. By the time St Nicholas' House, St Nicholas Street, was built in 1645 this development had become a recognizable double-depth plan.

The front range of St Nicholas' House is a remodelling of the C18, a trend that characterized the century, often without altering an older plan, such as Clifton House in 1708 or No. 6 King Street in 1739. The early C19 front at No. 14 King Street conceals a late C17 double-pile plan. Of new town houses the Norwich pattern was followed, beginning with *Henry Bell*'s mansion in Tuesday Market for Sir Charles Turner of 1703, fourteen bays wide and with a segmental pediment. It was demolished in 1768 so its plan is obscure. In an alley opposite, behind and incorporated into National Westminster Bank, stands a good seven-bay elevation with cross casements and originally a double-pile plan. In the same square is the rebuilt mansion of 1768 (now Barclays Bank) for the merchant George Hogge, again a double-pile variant.

None of these C18 houses had warehouses incorporated within them, and of C19 houses there is nothing remarkable in King's Lynn. The important merchant families had long since established their houses, which they sold between them from time to time. The story is rather of terraced houses, all typical and beginning late, in 1807 at Valinger's Road, 1819 at 14–20 Nelson Street and then the s developments round London Road and to the E by the railway station up to the 1840s.

CHURCHES

We begin with the two main churches, as their importance is so much greater than the rest. The alphabetical sequence begins with All Saints.

St Margaret, Saturday Market. Of white limestone, 235 ft long.   14
The earliest parts are the beginning of the two w towers, dating from around the middle of the C12. Such a twin-tower façade seems unusually ambitious, but this was a priory as well as a town church. The sw tower is still largely of the C12–C13. It has a high plinth with broad buttresses which are shafted all over. The front of each buttress has no fewer than eleven shafts alternating thick and thin, an East Anglian motif, found already at Great Paxton, Hunts, in the C11. Between the buttresses, Norman intersecting arcading, followed by a small Transitional arcade with waterleaf capitals and pointed trefoiled arches. Proper E.E. plate tracery above, and then the C13 bell-openings with bar tracery. In both cases the motif is an unfoiled circle, suggesting that the tower was completed *c.* 1260–70.

Then, in the C14, a new bell-stage was added. There was a tall lead spire as well, but this fell in 1741. The other tower, built from 1453 onwards, is externally Perp throughout, with much more bare wall. Only one small window below the clock, with two continuous chamfers, indicates an earlier date. The rest of the exterior looks all Perp, but should only be examined after the interior has been further considered.

Inside, the towers still have their Norman arches to the nave, and in the sw tower the lower arch to the s aisle remains. Above its e side the line of the Norman aisle roof is visible. All these arches have a filleted outer moulding, indicative of a date around 1200. Three internal walls of the sw tower have very impressive wall passages at first-floor level, with the stepped internal arcading familiar from Norman clerestories; the short columns Norman, the tall middle ones E.E., a Transitional mixture comparable to the external wall. Facing the nave, the e tower piers repeat the external buttresses' feature of eleven multiple shafts, but with the subtle difference that the corner shafts are slightly angled, as if to take a vault.

The Norman church was completely rebuilt in the C13. Chancel, crossing and transepts are internally of that rebuild. In the nave only the bases of the piers survive. Today's length of the church is that of the C13. The chancel has four bays with vigorous composite piers. Their diversity reflects the love of variety found e.g. in the E.E. work at Lincoln Cathedral. The piers are of two types, the first and third pair with a circular core with four sturdy attached shafts, the second pair with attached shafts and slender hollows in between. The responds are of the second type, with thin diagonal shafts as well, the e ones keeled. But the abaci vary without system between a form adapted to the piers and an octagonal form. All piers have beautiful, ample stiff-leaf capitals. Richly moulded arches; carved headstops to the hoodmoulds.

The chancel e window is Perp, a remarkable rose under a pointed arch and with quatrefoiled circles in the lower spandrels. It is largely a reconstruction by *Ewan Christian* in 1875, after fragments had been discovered in 1872. Outside, below the rose window, are three tall Perp niches. The clerestory of the chancel is Perp too, with three-light windows of c. 1480. Internally it has a wall passage with detached arcading, and the remarkable thing is that this motif must be taken over from the E.E. clerestory; for the clerestory shafts have E.E. leaf capitals and were only lengthened and provided with new Perp bases. The chancel aisles have Perp windows. The s chancel chapel is five bays long, the n chapel only three. The s chapel was building in 1433, when money was left for the job.

The crossing has tall arches in all four directions, those to e and w being the more ornate ones, the former with stiff-leaf capitals, simpler than those of the chancel, and finely moulded arches. The crossing tower is short and featureless. In the Middle Ages it carried a lead-covered octagonal wooden lantern, modelled probably on that of Ely. The arch from the s transept to the s chapel is also E.E. The stiff-leaf decoration of the capitals is hacked off. The transept exteriors are again Perp, with much plain wall and big end windows of five lights.

The nave is externally more impressive than internally. It has a spectacular w window of seven lights between the towers (blocked in the 1740s, reopened 1866), a statue in a niche above, and a doorway below which is thinly shafted and stands in a shallow porch. The splayed jambs of the porch have dainty four-light blind windows with tracery. Panelled battlements on the porch. Three-light aisle windows and three-light clerestory windows. Attached to the NW tower on the N side is a tall chapel with an entrance from the E side. This is what remains of an outer N aisle. The chapel has tall five-light and four-light windows. The E side now displays a most curiously shaped giant blank arch. The interior of the chapel is characterized by soaring, finely moulded Perp shafts and arches. Otherwise the Perp interior of St Margaret is, alas, disappointing. It is of 1742–6, an attempt by *Matthew Brettingham* (*see* Holkham Hall) to be Gothic in an age when Gothic was not a favoured style, an attempt inadequately rectified by *Scott* in 1875 when it was. Five bays, the piers with four shafts and four hollows on C13 bases; very broad basket arches. The arches towards the transepts are left more Georgian in their details than the others. The reason for the rebuilding was a storm which blew the SW spire of the church on to the nave in 1741. The king as well as Sir Robert Walpole gave £1,000. Scott's restoration of 1875 involved lowering the nave floor, revealing the pier bases, laying encaustic tiles by *William Godwin & Co.*, removing Brettingham's flat plaster nave ceiling and replacing the Georgian fittings. The chancel restoration by *Ewan Christian*, also 1875, but less drastic. Tiles by *Godwin & Co.* and *Henry Minton*.

Francis Goodwin* designed the Trinity Chapel in the N transept in 1809, contractor *William Newham* (of an important C19 family of Lynn builders and architects). The transept had to be reduced in size for road widening.

FURNISHINGS. FONT. 1875, artificial stone. REREDOS. By *Bodley*, 1899, of wood with many gilded figures and foliage, carved by *Robert Bridgeman*. – STALLS. *c.* 1370–80. Panelled fronts, little animals and poppyheads on the ends. MISERICORDS with many good heads, also flowers, a coat of arms, and a Green Man. – SCREENS. Behind the stalls and otherwise between chancel and aisles a number of C14 screens, that is of dates earlier than most surviving screens. Two have circular shafts instead of mullions, and all have ogee forms and crocketed gables. One has two-light divisions, the other three-light. The latter has reticulated tracery with small mouchettes in the reticulation units. The earliest, because the detail is boldest, is the SW one, the only Perp one is the SE. – In the crossing to the N a screen of 1584, but in its inscription also referring to King James. Dado with blank arches, above two tiers of open arcading (cf. St Nicholas). – PULPIT. A splendid early Georgian piece, good enough to be by the carver of the Houghton staircase. Also with marquetry its splendid big tester, restored 1993. – ORGAN CASE. Rococo. By *Snetzler*, 1754. – LECTERN. Late medieval. Big brass lectern with eagle of the same type as those at Redenhall and at Clare in Suffolk. (– SCULPTURE. Four wooden C17 figures in the S chancel chapel. They are from the former altarpiece, which was by *Henry Bell*, 1684.) – PAINTING. In the vestry four monochrome panels of early Georgian date, attributed by Croft Murray to *Pellegrini*. – ROYAL ARMS, 1660s, over chancel arch. – STAINED GLASS. Plenty, but none is arresting. E rose window by *Ward & Hughes*, 1865. NW porch, a large abstract design by *Michael Clarke*, 1967. – BRASSES. Two of the most famous and biggest brasses in England, both of latten plates fitted together, not cut-out figures, i.e. both probably Flemish. In the S chancel chapel. Adam de Walsokne †1349 (mayor 1334 and 1342) and wife. In civil dress, under a rich canopy. At the foot horsemen, a windmill, etc. To the l. and r. bands of pairs of prophets and apostles. – Robert Braunche †1364 (mayor 1349 and 1359), and two wives. At the top three canopies with souls, angels and seated figures. At the foot the Peacock Feast offered by Braunche to Edward III in 1349 when the king visited. To the l. and r. mourners. Other mayors of Lynn had brasses, but in 1787 most were sold for scrap, and in 1804 the sexton stole the rest. – MONUMENT. Sir William Hoste †1828. Putti with trophies.

To the S of the W part of the S chancel aisle remains of a CHAPTER HOUSE have been excavated. It was hexagonal with internal arcading and dated from the C13. The priory buildings lay to the S (*see* Perambulation 2).

ST NICHOLAS, St Anne's Street. A chapel of ease founded in 1146 by Bishop Turbe to serve his New Lands N of the Purfleet; not a parish church. Nothing remains of the first building and, except for the SW tower, all we see today was built at one go in the early C15 and called 'de novo edificato' in 1419. It is perhaps the best example in the county of the influence of the friars' large preaching churches. Moreover it is extremely large – 203 ft long – and in its details very advanced (*see* General Introduction, pp. 57–8). E.E. tower (*c.* 1225), lying lower than the rest. The W doorway has continuous chamfers; to the W, N, and S is a blank giant arch on three orders of thin shafts. On the first floor are windows of two lights with a quatrefoil in plate tracery and a little nailhead decoration (blocked on S side). Bell-openings with a circle in bar tracery suggest a heightening *c.* 1275. The pretty lead spire is by *Sir Gilbert Scott*, 1869, replacing one collapsed in the 1741 gale. The E wall of the tower, inside the church, is different. It has three lancets, the outer two blocked, and probably represents the W wall of the C13 church, before the tower was built.

The Perp church is eleven bays long without any structural division. A remarkable thing is the amount of red brick used – all of the N aisle, the five E bays of the S aisle and the E wall. More at clerestory level. The rest of stone. Externally the only accents are the doorways in the second and seventh bays to the N and the splendid S porch of two storeys in front of the second bay. A further door in the fifth bay, heavily cusped and subcusped under hoodmoulds forming half of an octagon. Above the porch entrance a row of flat niches, above that very delicate panelling between three more niches. Panelled parapet. The whole is carved with copious mouldings and decorative devices (e.g. emblems of Trinity, Instruments of Passion etc.). Inside the porch a lively lierne star vault with figured bosses and head corbels for the springers. The details of St Nicholas are notably wilful, especially the window tracery, in spite of the fact that it follows the same principle throughout. The aisle and chapel windows and the clerestory windows all have segmental arches. In the aisles and chapels they have two-centred arches under, and these are again subdivided. There are every so often unexpected diagonal lines. The same character appears in the N aisle W window, and even in the huge W and E windows, of eleven and nine lights respectively. On the W side the doorway cuts into the window. The doorway itself is double, i.e. two doors separated by a Y-shaped arch, and r. and l. of the W window rise big buttresses containing statuary niches under ogeed panelled canopies with heraldic beasts on top. Two square niches with angels flank the window.

The INTERIOR shows no signs of a change of plan from E to W, and presents a single open space.* At the E end are two vestries flanking the sanctuary, but no indication of this is apparent outside to disturb the uniform rectangle (sanctuary arrangement altered in 1981 by the *Donald Insall Partnership*). The openness was increased in 1853 during *John Brown*'s extensive restoration which swept most of the Georgian fittings away. Piers of lozenge plan, finely subdivided, the mouldings on all four planes made up of two sunk hollows separated by a roll. Capitals only to the thin shafts under the arches, the mouldings of which have double waves. The abaci here are concave-sided. The shaft towards the nave rises to the roof. Before it reaches the wall-posts it is flanked by two niches with little vaults under nodding ogees developing into crocketed pinnacles. The roof has tie-beams on shallow arched braces with traceried spandrels. Above the tie-beams tracery and arched queenposts, also with tracery. Each alternating truss has angels as hammerbeams. The N doorways again very capricious. They have heads of three sides of an octagon and the W one is cusped and subcusped. In the chancel on the N side yet another such doorway. Double concave-sided gable, cusping and subcusping. To its r. a demi-figure of an angel in an oblong niche. It is too small for an Easter Sepulchre. Opposite is a badly mutilated, once very rich sedilia and piscina. Three vaulted ogee canopies with miniature vaults and upper cresting over which peer six winged angels. A big head corbel below.

FURNISHINGS. Other than those enumerated, all are by *John Brown*, 1852–3. – FONT. Given in 1627 by Bishop Harsnett of Norwich. Octagonal. The bowl with strapwork. The stem could be Perp, especially as the two-step base with quatrefoiled circles is Perp.‡ – FONT COVER. The original of 1627 was copied and replaced in 1903 and since removed. – STOUP. In the N aisle a former stoup, in appearance similar to a small font. Perp

28

* The screen with its rood was removed 1559.
‡ St Nicholas had been licensed for baptisms in 1378 but faced opposition from St Margaret. A plaque in the floor at E end of N aisle records the first baptism on 10 March 1627.

with quatrefoiled circles and one figure. – DOORS. S and W doors with Perp tracery. The S door the more exuberant, with four orders of carved panelling and canopies, and a double-leaf wicket door under an ogee head fitted cleverly into the whole tracery scheme; some nice figures. – REREDOS. With painted figures by *Hardman*, *c.* 1880; it has gone. – STALLS. Some misericords are now in the museum, and others in the Victoria and Albert Museum. Little original seating remains, but there are four bench ends, one with the figure of a bishop in a medallion, another with a man riding a horse backwards. – LECTERN. Brass with an eagle, late C15. The same type as at Billingford and also Peterborough Cathedral, St Mark's (Venice), Christ's College (Cambridge), Isleham (Cambridgeshire) and Thorverton (Devon). Stem with lions at the base and a ball at the top, on which is the magnificent eagle with outspread wings. The eagle has been stapled to the floor of the N chancel aisle to prevent flight. – SWORDREST. Dated 1743 and 1760. Of wood. – CHARITY BOARD (at the W end). Inscription and, in the framing band, poor people; 1600. – STAINED GLASS. E window by *Ward & Hughes*, *c.* 1860, thirty-two scenes from the Life of Christ. – S chancel, the Parable of the Talents by *W. Warrington*, 1854. – MONUMENTS. Many; some are noteworthy. One may single out the following: Richard Clarck †1602 and Matthew Clarck †1623, erected for the latter *c.* 1604. Tablet with small kneeling figures: Richard and wife Joan to l., Matthew and his wife Sarah to r., with two sons and five daughters. – Sir Thomas Greene †1675 and wife, Susannah Barker. Two painted and very realistic nearly frontally kneeling figures on cushions, the children (four sons, five daughters) in the predella below facing each other across a prayer-desk with a lowering skull over it. Corinthian columns l. and r. and a segmental pediment. Attributed to *Thomas Cartwright I.* (GF) – Thomas Snelling †1623 and wife Margaret. Two kneeling painted figures face each other across a prayer-desk between Corinthian columns. – Sir Benjamin Keene †1758, the Ambassador to Spain. Noble round bowl on a big square base. Scene of ships in harbour and a portrait medallion. No figures. Probably by *Robert Adam*, 1762. – Elisabeth Hendry †1764 (by the tower), an oval cartouche with two cherubs' heads, a skull and drapery. She was a 'sincere friend and truly valuable woman'. – Rebecca Cooper and son, drowned 1838 in a shipwreck depicted in low relief. By *James Thompson*. – There is also a LEDGER STONE to Robinson Cruso, in the nave, †1773 aged ten years, nothing to do with the fictional character. *Henry Bell* put up a W reredos in 1704, removed in 1985. – CHURCHYARD GATES. *See* pp. 497–8.

ALL SAINTS, Church Lane (off All Saints Street). The first church of the new town, but the date of foundation is unknown. In the S wall of the chancel part of the Norman corbel table and remains of the pier and arch of a former Norman S chapel. The floor was then about 3 ft lower than it is now. Other disturbances in the same wall point to the existence of an anker-hole or anchorite's cell which projects from the E end of the chancel, connecting with the sanctuary by a piscina with no back to it. It is probably C14. Marks of the anchorite's domestic buildings on the S wall further W. Transepts were added to the church in the C13 – see the moulding of the former steep-pitched roof on the S side. Of the same date stones with dogtooth decoration now exhibited in the N transept. The Perp window tracery is C19 (the two general restorations are of 1860 and 1887). The rest is mostly Perp. Nave and aisles and lengthened chancel. Chequer flushwork in the clerestory. The tower collapsed in 1763. Victorian bellcote on the yellow brick W wall. Arcades of four bays. No emphasis in the arcades of the transept openings. Piers with polygonal projections to nave and aisles, wavy, filleted projections with capitals to the arches. Chancel arch similar. Four-centred arches from the aisle to the transepts. C15 nave roof has hollow-chamfered tie-beams on arched braces with pierced tracery spandrels. Hammerbeam roof in chancel is C19. Good boss carved with the figure of Christ in the S aisle roof. – FONT. C15, octagonal, the bowl with tracery and cusping, on a C19 stem. – SCREENS. One with six painted Apostles remains (W end), another is Jacobean, with two tiers of open arches. It was brought from West Lynn. – STAINED GLASS. E window by *Hardman & Co.*, 1874; S transept E window, an Ascension scene looking like *William Wailes*, as does the S window, *c.* 1860.

GREYFRIARS, St James' Street. Founded *c.* 1264 by Thomas Feltham. Enlarged 1364, or at least had a patent to do so in that year. By 1287 the original site probably went as far as Tower Place, London Road, and Greyfriars Road. Suppressed in 1538 and the site sold in 1545 to John Eyre, with the other mendicant precincts. The survival of the tall hexagonal tower is a rarity. The tower stood on the odd cross-passage between nave and chancel which was usual in English friars' houses. It dates from the later C14, perhaps 1364, but was built into the C13 church of which the S archway in the crossing and a little of the adjoining nave wall remain. Beneath the tower the big arches to E and W have C14 shafts with polygonal capitals. The tower is of brick with stone dressings and is hexagonal, with a polygonal stair-turret to one side. Two tiers of Early Perp transomed openings, parapet with deep panels. N and S of the central lantern, a tierceron vault with brick cells. Gargoyles and other carving were revealed during the restoration in 1974 to have traces of orange ochre paint. – Under the vault a CROSS from the Blackfriars Cemetery; C11. In the circular top Crucifixus and, on the other side, seated Christ. Below, a figure on one side, two panels with animals on another and animals and interlace on the edges.

Of the chancel the W jambs of the first windows are recognizable. The chancel was 88 ft long and aisleless. The nave probably had a S aisle, see one base which may have belonged to the N jambs of the doorway to the chapter house. – To the SE in the public garden part of a long line of ARCADING (three arches with continuous mouldings, then some wall and another two arches). This has nothing to do with the Greyfriars. It belonged to a C14 house in Tuesday Market and was transferred to this site.

ST JOHN EVANGELIST, Blackfriars Street. By *Anthony Salvin*, 1844–6 with the aid of the second parliamentary grant at a cost of £6,164. Of stone. It was commissioned by Daniel Gurney, for whom Salvin had rebuilt North Runcton Hall, to provide for Anglicans in the expanding town, with an emphasis on free seats for the poor: at the consecration address it was remarked that 'it is a poor man's church. The subscribers emphatically intended it to be such'. E.E. style, without a tower. Five-bay arcade on circular piers (the W pair rebuilt 1889–90 when two heavy flying buttresses were added to the W end). Trefoils in circular openings as clerestory windows. Plain interior with some black-letter painted inscriptions. The triple E lancets embellished with stone arches in 1873. In 1980 the two W bays, including the aisles, converted to a meeting room and kitchen. – FONT. Plain, octagonal, with pointed arches, raised on red marble columns 1946 and moved to N aisle 1980. – REREDOS. Of carved stone, 1896. – PULPIT. 1882. E.E. style, with a trefoiled arcade laid over an arched arcade and marble trimmings. – STAINED GLASS. E lancets with medallions and ornamental roundels by *William Wailes*, *c.* 1846. The main scenes are Christ in Glory, Ascension and Crucifixion. In the S chancel window is a panel perhaps by *Hardman*.

OUR LADY OF THE ANNUNCIATION, London Road (R.C.). 1896–7 by *W. Lunn* of Great Malvern replacing a church of 1845 by *Pugin*. Humble but quite large, of carstone in crazy-paving patterns, Bath stone dressings and a starved SE (ritually SW) turret, carrying a spirelet. Small single and double windows to the S, larger windows to the N. On the N side a single-storey shrine has a painted barrel-vaulted roof and walls of brick-sized carstone laid in wavy courses. It is a replica of the Holy House at Loreto, and the altar is a copy also. From 1897 to 1934 this was the official shrine of Our Lady of Walsingham. Five-bay S arcade (octagonal piers, polygonal capitals, chamfered arches). – STATUE of Our Lady (in the shrine), 1897, made in Oberammergau. In the only N three-light window STAINED GLASS by *Wailes*, *c.* 1860.

ST JAMES. *See* London Road Methodist Chapel.

ST PETER, West Lynn. *See* p. 766.

ST HELEN, Saddlebow. *See* p. 625.

RED MOUNT CHAPEL, The Walks. A pilgrims' chapel on a mound, and one of the strangest Gothic churches in England. The mound, later incorporated into the Civil War defences, was probably a Norman motte. Licence to build the chapel was given in 1485 to Robert Curraunt, but he in fact completed it that year. It served as a wayside chapel on the pilgrimage to Walsingham. It is an octagon of red brick with stone dressings with a recessed cruciform stone top part. That the two parts are of different dates is obvious from the difference in construc-tion, the severance of the moulded W staircase handrail and the overhang of the cruciform top over the N staircase. The top is

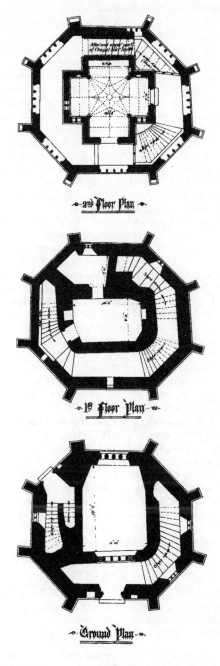

King's Lynn, Red Mount Chapel.
Plans of ground, first and second floors

1505–6 and has been attributed to *John Wastell* on stylistic grounds. The building stands on a tunnel-vaulted basement, oblong in shape. The cruciform core above contains the chapel proper, a small apartment but lavishly vaulted with a fan vault in the middle and with panelled pointed tunnel vaults over the arms. It is reached by two staircases which run round the space between the core and the outer octagon, each doing about a half-turn. From the front entrance on the W side the staircase leads to behind the altar, and one reaches a N entrance into the chapel by a corridor. The other staircase starts from a back door on the NE and leads to a W entrance into the chapel. From the back door another small staircase descends to the basement. The octagon has simple windows of two to four lights. Eight angle buttresses, all pierced by a small arched hole.

STEPNEY BAPTIST CHURCH (now the New Life Christian Fellowship Hall), Blackfriars Street. 1840–1. Gault brick. Five-bay front with a pediment all across. Two doorways. The ground floor is still Classical, but the elongated windows on the upper floor are turning Italianate. Transomed casements to returns.

LONDON ROAD METHODIST CHAPEL, London Road. 1858–9 by *J. A. Hillam*. Gault brick façade, round-arched windows in three bays, centre bay projecting. Rustication much used. On the parapet a shaped gable contains a clock face. The elongated upper windows, an Italianate fashion of the 1840s, are characteristic. Gallery on iron columns with Corinthian capitals.

From the back yard one can see the last remaining bit of the former CHAPEL OF ST JAMES in County Court Road. The chapel was founded before 1146, which indicates the extent of C12 Lynn in this area, and was rebuilt on Mendicant lines, i.e. with an octagonal tower over the passageway between nave and chancel. The nave was demolished in 1548. The crossing and one bay of the chancel converted to a WORKHOUSE in 1580, which itself was rebuilt in 1681, Henry Bell being on the committee. Finally demolished in 1910 leaving only part of one cruciform crossing pier, less of an E pier, and a wall slung between them filled with a C17 mullioned window.

UNION CHAPEL, Market Street. *See* Public Buildings.

JEWISH CEMETERY, Millfleet. A little brick compound of C16 brick in the N and E walls, later brick elsewhere. The N entrance leads into the yard with its HEADSTONES. The original function unknown but used as a cemetery 1811–46.*

WALLS AND GATES

EAST GATE, by the Gaywood River, Gaywood Road. Demolished 1800 having been reconstructed in the 1440s. Of the medieval WALLS fragments of C13 brick and stone extend N along Kettlewell Lane. Stilted arches in front of shallow chambers on

---

* The New Conduit Street MEETING ROOM and the CONGREGATIONAL CHURCH both demolished in the 1960s, as was the WESLEYAN CHAPEL, Tower Street (in 1960). The last was by the Methodist builder and architect of Lynn, *Samuel Newham*, 1812. It cost £4,000 and was described as magnificent and capacious.

w side, ashlar-faced buttresses to E. Much more fragmentary evidence to the S in Wyatt Street.

SOUTH GATE, London Road. The only surviving town gate in 55 any state of preservation. Stone front to the S, brick and stone to the N. Three storeys, with stringcourses. It is solidly rectangular but has polygonal corner turrets to the S corners and square ones to the N. Tall central carriageway, and, since the C19, low pedestrian ways either side. Two three-light mullioned upper windows N and S. Battlements between the taller corner turrets. A gate was first recorded here in the late C13 but the earliest parts are from the rebuilding of 1437 by *Robert Hertanger*. It was again partly rebuilt in 1520 by *Nicholas* and *Thomas Harmer*, although the S side remains largely as left in the C15. Restored 1982–4. The winder staircase in the NW corner was removed in 1841 and replaced in steel in 1984. It leads to the first-floor rooms with a fireplace, privy hole and gunports in the turrets. A single room occupies the whole upper floor, with fireplaces in the E and W walls. This was used more for civic than military purposes.

ST ANNE'S GATE, off North Street. The C15 N gate in the walls; the ruins hardly overwhelming. Brick. The S wall has two depressed arches and there is part of another further E with the springer for the vault of a chamber to the S. Two barrel-vaulted passages to the rear. The arches blocked in the C19. Some of the walling is to do with ST ANNE'S FORT, erected 1626–7.

GUANOCK GATE, The Walks. Picturesque set of ruins owing little to the Middle Ages and in fact described as 'modern' in 1835; the whole area was landscaped from the mid C18, partly at the expense of Charles Turner (*see* below, p. 489). Square turrets with a pointed arch between and a crenellated parapet: C13 in spirit. Arched openings r. and l. and then stretches of crenellated walls extending N and S, with arrow slits.

PUBLIC AND OTHER BUILDINGS

TOWN HALL and GUILDHALL, Queen Street and Saturday Market. A delightful group of three or four buildings developed along the bend from the Market into Queen Street, all quite different, and yet forming a perfect sequence. It starts in the Market with the former GAOL, built in 1784. The design is by the carpenter *William Tuck*. Gault brick, five bays and two and a half storeys. The centre bay has rustication round the doorway and up to the panels with chains, the barred lunette window, and the open pediment. A sundial in a raised section of parapet. The decoration is derived from Dance's Newgate Prison. The CELLS are in the rear yard, mostly rebuilt in 1937, but there are nevertheless four from the C18 hollowed out of the N and W walls: iron-bound doors with shuttered lattice grilles either side. Then follows the gabled front of the GUILDHALL proper. This 54 was built for the Guild of Holy Trinity in 1422–8, after its predecessor burnt out and initial work done in 1421–2 under *John Turnour*. The front is of flint and stone in a chequer pattern.

Low ground-floor windows of two different designs lighting an undercroft, the middle windows formerly the doorways. Tall upper window of seven lights with a low transom and others in the tracery. Polygonal corner turrets truncated at the top. To the l. of the Guildhall a staircase was built in 1624 with its own projecting porch, eminently fanciful. Faced with flint chequer, like the old Guildhall. Thin polygonal angle buttresses. Smashing doorway with short attached Doric columns on tall bases. One small subsidiary doorway r. and l. Transomed six-light window, and a big cartouche above this, thriftily reused from Elizabethan times. Gable of convex and concave curves with an achievement of Charles I, altered in 1664 in memory of the mayor, William Wharton. The porch opens into a hall with fluted Ionic columns and a staircase with fat turned balusters rising to the STONE HALL, which occupies the whole upper floor. In the 1820s a plaster ceiling lined in imitation of ashlar was added, but this removed in 1992 to reveal the original timbers, made by *Nicholas* and *Peter Rollesby* of Bacton. Chamfered wall arches and tie-beams on big shallow arched braces. Traceried spandrels. The upper registers have scissor-braced trusses. E of this room is the former COURTHOUSE, 1767, fitted out in 1895. Behind the Guildhall, the former ASSEMBLY ROOMS by *William Tuck* and the bricklayer *Thomas King*, added in 1766–8. Gault brick, quite plain, of two storeys in five bays. A small card room to the E. Finally in Queen Street the TOWN HALL, 1895 by *Tree & Price* of London, perfectly fitting in its use of chequer flint and a free and easy mixture of Gothic forms with certain Renaissance details. Two storeys. A tall gable closes the composition to the N, with a nine-light Perp window. Splat-baluster staircase in the generously proportioned entrance hall, lined with small-framed panelling.

DISTRICT COUNCIL OFFICES, Chapel Street. Built privately by *Raymond, Spratley, Crapnell Partnership* in 1973–4 but bought in 1980 for council use and extended 1989.

GUILD OF ST GEORGE. *See* Perambulation 4, p. 505.

BRIDGE over the Gaywood River, Gaywood Road, by the site of the East Gate. The two early C16 stone arches have ribs underneath and a concrete C20 superstructure.

COUNTY COURT (former), London Road. 1861 by the obscure *Huddleston* of Lincoln. Gault brick. In the humble palazzo style used for such buildings at that time. Two storeys and attic arranged in five bays. Heavy stringcourse at first floor, and the upper windows linked by a continuous string. The small attic squeezed under the overhanging cornice, which has an achievement with the royal arms. Interior thoroughly spoilt.

MAGISTRATES' COURT. *See* Perambulation 1a.

POLICE STATION, St James' Street. 1953–5 by the County Architect, *C. H. Thurston*. A corner site. One might say plain Neo-Georgian, or plain neo-Norwich-Town-Hall, with its portico of square pillars and a little lead cupola.

SWIMMING POOL, St James' Road. 1975 by the *West Norfolk District Council Architect's Department*. With a bright new viewing area added 1982–3 at the deep end.

FIRE STATION, Kilham's Way, N of the town. The usual tower, here six storeys high. 1972 by the *County Architect's Department*, *George Hayden*, County Architect.

CUSTOMS HOUSE. By *Henry Bell*, an accomplished gentleman- 76 architect and merchant of Lynn (*see* General Introduction, p. 155). Built of stone in 1683 as a Merchants' Exchange for Sir John Turner M.P. and one of the finest late C17 public buildings in provincial England. Turner let the first floor to the Collector of Customs, who bought the entire building in 1718 and embarked on modifications. In 1989 it was sold privately. The building stands on its own by the quay, in a most becoming situation. Five by four bays with two orders of pilasters, Roman Doric below, Ionic above. Hipped roof with dormer windows carrying alternating triangular and segmental pediments. There was a balustrade at the base of the roof, removed after the gale of 1741. Top balustrade and tall lantern, cruciform below, with pedimented, arched little openings, and octagonal above. The ogee cap replaces an obelisk which was also a casualty of 1741. The ground floor is partly arched and was originally open to the street, although the W side was very soon blocked, if ever open at all. The iron windows here are C19. The Collector in 1718 would have wanted the arcades blocked. The first-floor windows have mullioned and transomed cross casements. In a niche on the N side above the door, a STATUE of Charles II. 77 Inside, there were four columns, of which the two W ones survive, one encased. In their place masonry and timber partitions were inserted by the Collector after 1718. Of the same time is the staircase with its dumb-bell balusters and bolection-moulded panelling; it does not really fit its space and was rearranged in its lower flight in the early C20. Panelling and details on the first floor for the comfort of the Collector. The W room was originally two rooms, which is why there are two fireplaces. Large-framed panelling. These modifications probably 1741. The smaller NE room has panelling in a manner more likely for 1718. The style is more influenced by Edward Jerman's London Royal Exchange (1667–71) and the Maastricht Town Hall (1659–64), Holland, than by Wren.

CORN EXCHANGE, Tuesday Market. 1854 by *Cruso & Maberley*. Jolly and vulgar, as so many Corn Exchanges are (cf. e.g. Sudbury or Newark). Four attached giant Ionic columns in front of Ionic pilasters, the capitals of the two orders jostling with each other for space. Three doorways, with a cartouche bearing the King's Lynn arms with a pelican on top. Sheaves of corn r. and l. Big attic above the centre with statue of Ceres. So prestigious was this building that the pretty Market House which had replaced the Angel Inn only twenty-four years previously was demolished to make room. In 1996 the huge interior space with octagonal cast-iron columns supporting a glass roof (replaced in 1877) was remodelled for a concert and community hall by *Levitt Bernstein Associates*, one of the first recipients of Arts Lottery money. The foyer is overlooked from a balcony r. and l., with an unusual and effective balustrade of clapping hands, by *Jon Mills*. The glazed roof has roller blinds with heraldic shields and riverside scenes, by *Sharon Ting*. Steel concert-hall staircase beyond to the r. and then the hall itself.

MUSEUM (since 1904), Market Street. Built as the Union Baptist Chapel in 1859, by *Robert Moffatt Smith*,* but looking very like Street. Italian Gothic in two colours of brick. The first such use of the style in Norfolk for Nonconformist chapels. Canted apse with tall Dec windows, thin tower with a short spire.

LIBRARY, London Road. One of the libraries paid for by the Scots-American Andrew Carnegie. 1904–5 by *H. J. Green*. Fan-shaped plan on a corner site, the corner emphasized by a short square tower with a first-floor oriel above a big Perp archway. Faced in random carstone with lavish terracotta dressings and decoration. Top-lit octagonal entrance lobby complete with librarian's kiosk and three well-lit family rooms fanning out behind.

TECHNICAL COLLEGE, Tennyson Avenue. 1958–60 by *G. W. Oak* (County Education Committee), with the usual long piece of curtain walling. Greatly enlarged; the best part is the LIBRARY BLOCK, 1972–3 by *George Hayden* (County Architect). More average but more dominating is the nine-storey tower, opened 1973, same architect.

KING EDWARD VII HIGH SCHOOL, Gaywood Road. *See* Gaywood, p. 355.

HIGH SCHOOL FOR GIRLS. *See* p. 503.

RAILWAY STATION. The first buildings erected in wood in 1844 by *John Sugars*, but rebuilt using gault brick in 1877 in standard Great Eastern style; vaguely Classical, the end-gables with unclassical Lombard arches. Central entrance with glazed roof, and inside a single-storey timber-framed buffet between brick ends. It has applied panelling to dado and parapet.

GENERAL HOSPITAL, Hospital Walk. 1834 by *Samuel Angell* and the contractor-architect *John Sugars*; additions 1847, 1852 and later. The earlier parts of yellow brick. The oldest building is the one with the pediment and the Ionic pilasters on the first floor. The parts of 1847–52 are adjoining. Closed 1997.

ST JAMES' HOSPITAL, Exton's Road. Built by *Medland & Maberley* in 1856 as the Workhouse. Red and yellow brick. Tudor style, gabled.

DISTRICT HOSPITAL (Queen Elizabeth Hospital), Gayton Road. A new version of the 'best buy' concept which failed to achieve wide acclaim in the 1960s. By *McDonald Hamilton and Montefiore*, 1972 (construction 1975–9). Two storeys, a concrete frame, and planned from a central thoroughfare. The design is closely based on the hospital at Bury St Edmunds, and is repeated again at the James Paget Hospital (*see* Gorleston, Vol. 1).

CREMATORIUM, Gayton Road by Mintlyn Woods, 1 m. E of the District Hospital. An amazing design by the *King's Lynn and West Norfolk District Architect's Department* (job architect *David Grace*), 1979–80. More to one end than the middle is the trape-

---

* I am grateful to Elizabeth James for pointing out the name of the architect. Moffatt Smith, of Manchester, built at least twenty-three Nonconformist chapels, mainly Congregational.

zoid chimney flue, with a gabled roof sloping away on one side, and in the opposite direction another, much longer spike of a roof, almost horizontal, both looking like paper darts. Great glulam ridge pieces run the length of the two roofs. The plan so arranged as to facilitate arrival of mourners at the thin end, departure of the deceased in the middle and exit of the mourners at the thick end into the garden of remembrance.

TAIL SLUICES of the new relief channel of the Ouse, s of the sugar beet factory, $1\frac{7}{8}$ m. up-river from South Quay. They are very big and were completed in 1959 (cf. Denver, p. 281).

DOCKS. Tying up ships on the quayside and loading was a tricky business in Lynn because the Great Ouse is so markedly tidal. Speed was essential, or the operations had to wait for the tides. Bigger steamships were seriously affected, and in the 1840s came the railway, precipitating a slump. ALEXANDRA DOCK, linked to the railway network, was opened in 1869 N of Tuesday Market Place off the present John Kennedy Road. An immediate success, of brick, mostly now faced with concrete, not quite a rectangle 800 ft by 400 ft, linked to the river by a channel with two sets of lock gates. The dock connected with another in 1883, BENTINCK DOCK, similar but larger and set at an angle. The connection also with lock gates and two swing bridges (1883, riveted steel, made by *Cleveland Bridge Engineering Company* of Darlington). Various warehouses line the edges, none notable; neither is the CONTAINER TERMINAL of 1984.

Factories

BESPAK FACTORY, North Lynn Trading Estate. Important extensions 1978–80 by *Cambridge Design* (job architect *Julian Bland*). Tubular steel grid clad with asbestos panels linked to the existing buildings to form a courtyard. The interior very open, with the frame left exposed in a manner between the Sainsbury Centre, Norwich, and the terminal building at Stansted Airport.

DOW-AGRO CHEMICALS. The administrative building on the Great Ouse Channel, 1960, by *Fry Drew & Partners* (job architect *D. R. Preston*) is an elegant two-storeyed block designed round a central courtyard. Recessed bluish brick to the ground floor, weatherboarded above, all very horizontal, like the landscape. The line of windows in the upper storey could hardly be simpler or more effective. Generous entrance hall and circular staircase.

PERAMBULATIONS

Four walks are necessary, and the two Market Places are the obvious starting-points. The principal streets of the historic core (the line of Nelson Street, St Margaret's Place, Queen Street and King Street) are described in the first part of Perambulation 1, and the later parts in Perambulations 2 and 4.

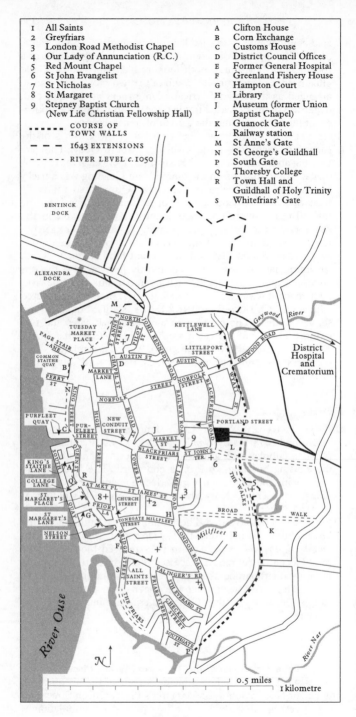

1	All Saints
2	Greyfriars
3	London Road Methodist Chapel
4	Our Lady of Annunciation (R.C.)
5	Red Mount Chapel
6	St John Evangelist
7	St Nicholas
8	St Margaret
9	Stepney Baptist Church (New Life Christian Fellowship Hall)

······· COURSE OF TOWN WALLS

– – – 1643 EXTENSIONS

- - - - - RIVER LEVEL c. 1050

A	Clifton House
B	Corn Exchange
C	Customs House
D	District Council Offices
E	Former General Hospital
F	Greenland Fishery House
G	Hampton Court
H	Library
J	Museum (former Union Baptist Chapel)
K	Guanock Gate
L	Railway station
M	St Anne's Gate
N	St George's Guildhall
P	South Gate
Q	Thoresby College
R	Town Hall and Guildhall of Holy Trinity
S	Whitefriars' Gate

King's Lynn

1a. Saturday Market and the area to its w and n: St Margaret's Place, St Margaret's Lane, South Quay, College Lane, Queen Street, King's Staithe Lane, King's Staithe Square, Purfleet Place, Purfleet Street, New Conduit Street, High Street, Saturday Market

SATURDAY MARKET PLACE, i.e. the area N of St Margaret's Church, is the embodiment of the smaller English market even though on the N side there is little of importance apart from the public buildings. Behind the façades to Nos. 3–4 *c.* 1700 evidence remains. No. 9 is of brick, rendered later, an early two-storey C18 range converted to a hotel and incorporating the mid-C19 corner to the High Street, and a C19 front with Ionic pilasters further w. To the w of the church the street name changes into ST MARGARET'S PLACE, visually an important part of the Market Place, and here the houses are all pleasant. The C17 house at the corner of College Lane presents a gable to the E and N, one of the few Lynn houses still to do so. Brick hoodmoulds from windows predating the sashes. Inside, an upstairs room has good early C17 panelling and a small rear courtyard retains scars of C15 openings. Otherwise the interior, and those to the two solid C18 houses attached to its s, were rather cut about in 1982 to form offices for the new Magistrates' Court (*see* below). The first house, of five mid-C18 bays, has a good Ionic doorcase. No. 2, with its quaint sagging window over the carriage entrance, is a C15 house redone in the C17 and fronted in the early C18. An L-shaped hall plan. The front is in English-bond brick, two storeys and five bays. The ground floor has C17 small-framed panelling but the roof is a late C15 crown-post type with straight braces from the ties to the post, which is a King's Lynn characteristic. Two good doorcases in the passage range, one with Doric details. The hall has a fine early C18 staircase with two turned balusters to each tread. The rear quarters exhibit early C17 bridging beams with sunk-quadrant mouldings. The rear roof also with three crown-posts of the same type. At the back is an early C16 brick WAREHOUSE, somewhat chopped about but still with its own crown-post roof of the same type again. THE VICARAGE comes next, *c.* 1810, three storeys and three bays (the centre one blind) towards the church, three bays and entrance on the s side facing the garden. Remains of an early C16 house to the w.

ST MARGARET'S HOUSE, by the junction with St Margaret's Lane, is a building of enormous interest. Council offices since 1971, a time of considerable restoration and alteration by *Purcell, Miller & Tritton*. The front is a brick range of two storeys and attic in nine bays, with rustication at the corners and to the projecting centre bay built after 1751. Doorcase with open pediment on Doric pilasters. This gives nothing away concerning the earlier fabric, but the building soon shows itself as a quadrangle formed of two parallel warehouse ranges running w towards the river, closed by a shorter w range. In the early C16 the warehouses were extended further w and a new short w wing built between them replacing the earlier one. The material is brick but a significant amount of timber-framing appears also. The buildings were put up for the Hanseatic Steelyard in about 1475, permission being given then under the provisions of the Treaty of Utrecht of the same year. Of the four such warehouses in England these alone remain. The range along the s in St Margaret's Lane has a deep underbuilt jetty on the street side, which might be the earliest build, but is entirely brick to the courtyard, and so is the N wing. Both have been altered and the interiors are like offices everywhere, but their roofs are, or were, of the crown-post type with braces to the ties. The closing W range has two storeys, later W extensions and too much detail of 1971. The roof however is open to view and represents in its mechanics the point of change from the crown-post to the side-purlin roof. Here we have tie-beams, principal rafters, two tiers of purlins, butted below but clasped above, collars and curved wind-bracing. In 1751 the complex was bought by Edward Everard and the E parts converted to St Margaret's House.

HAMPTON COURT opposite is a courtyard house *par excellence*, but each of its four ranges has a different date and may be on the site of earlier buildings, so when precisely the courtyard plan was determined is difficult to say. At any rate the present form was reached by *c.* 1600. Restored 1958–60 and converted to fifteen flats in 1962, setting a standard for such work which is reached depressingly rarely. The restoration by *Pamela Cunnington*, the conversion by the *King's Lynn Preservation Trust* (adviser *Marshall Sisson*). One should start in the courtyard itself. All elevations rendered and colourwashed. The S RANGE is the earliest, as is clear from the early C14 stone ground floor and less clear from the brick and timber-framed upper storey. It was a hall house and evident are remains of three arched doorways – one to the l. to the screens passage, two to the r. (more complete) to two service rooms. Various C20 doors and windows and eleven gabled dormers in the roof. There are three arched stone openings from the screens passage to the kitchen range to the E and the hall has an inserted C16 stack. The roof was fascinating but had to be reconstructed. It was a hybrid combining trusses with passing-braces and cross braces and a more modern crown-post roof. Tie-beam on arched braces and wall-posts. There is nothing to show any communication in the C14 from this range to the street (E) range.

The next in order of construction is the W RANGE and this is of the mid C15. Brick. The side facing the courtyard has renewed details, but the E front has a remarkable arcade of seven four-centred arches carried on columns with moulded capitals. The arches were first blocked probably in the C17, but the two N arches were obscured earlier by the N range. But here we have a WAREHOUSE built parallel to the river, and right on its bank. This is the type impossible to extend as the river migrated W, only really possible on the wide sites available in the S of the town; it was superseded by the narrower gable-end type of warehouse. Back to the street to view the E RANGE. Added *c.* 1480. Brick ground floor and a jettied and timber-framed

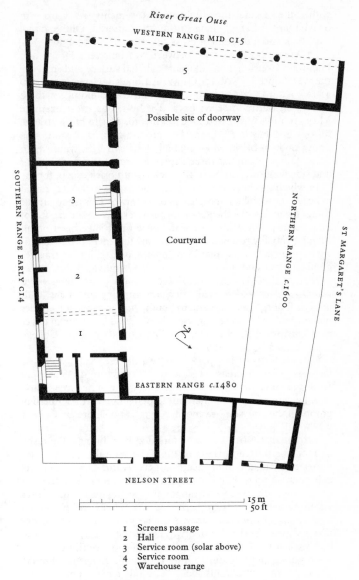

King's Lynn, Hampton Court.
Conjectural plan of ground floor, *c.* 1500

upper floor, with brick nogging, all colourwashed. To the l. of the courtyard entrance is a roll-moulded window which probably served a shop; now with sashes. The archway is segment-headed and has the arms of Richard Amfles, who took possession in 1482. Roll- and hollow-moulded bridging beams under the arch. Finally the N RANGE was built *c.* 1600; of brick and still with some original three-light cross casements. Its N front to St Margaret's Lane is long but a little battered. One external C17 stack and a three-light cross casement.

ST MARGARET'S LANE, between St Margaret's House and Hampton Court, has an enjoyable cobbled surface and shadows the warehouse to SOUTH QUAY. To one's l. SOMMERFIELD AND THOMAS WAREHOUSE is a mid-C18 building of three storeys and attic in seven bays. To the r. one must examine MARRIOTT'S WAREHOUSE carefully, for its site has a strange history. It looks like a barn. The ground floor is of stone, the upper floor of brick, with originally four two-light windows to each. The N return has three depressed arches, formerly a door and side windows, but now all blocked with brick except for the door which has become a window. The date is early C14, raised in height, or rebuilt, in the late C15 or early C16. This is the strange thing, for in the C14 the E bank of the river was about 120 ft E of its present position and the warehouse must have been on an island, probably reached by a causeway. Its function was to provide a quick loading platform for seagoing ships to transfer goods to river craft for the journey inland and vice versa.

131 Next N the MAGISTRATES' COURT, 1979 by the *Leonard Manasseh Partnership*. Red brick, unassuming and neat, with piles 60 ft deep. The elevation to South Quay in three units under hipped roofs of varying heights, and, off-set, the polygonal tower as an historical accent. The building extends E along College Lane towards Queen Street.

QUEEN STREET is a perfect, outwardly Georgian, walk and its pleasures are increased by the necessity to turn off W at every corner in order to reach the river and Quay. The street starts happily with a curve, brought out to perfection by the Guildhall group on the one side (*see* above, p. 475), and Thoresby College on the other.

THORESBY COLLEGE was founded by Thomas Thoresby in 1500 for thirteen priests of the Trinity Guild and was still under construction at his death in 1511. At the Dissolution the college was sold to Robert Houghton and the N range converted to a house, the S and W ranges into warehouses and other accommodation. In 1963 the house was bought and presented to the *King's Lynn Preservation Trust* as one of their first restorations. Three good Perp doorways face the street, the central one with a traceried door and a mutilated inscription commemorating the founder ('Orate pro anima magistri Thomae Thoresby fundator huius loci'). The other two doorways are mainly C19. The rest of the long façade with its sashes and five dormers with Dutch gables is early C18. The big courtyard inside like Hampton Court (*see* above) was possible because of the large square plots that became available in this part of the town as the river bank migrated W. In the NE corner the line of the C13 quay was excavated in 1964.

The W range originally contained the refectory, a fine five-bay hall with a hammerbeam roof, floored during subsequent occupation. Above the modern stairs leading to the N end of the hall is a ceiling with moulded joists. The priests' lodgings would have been in the N and E ranges. The N range has been rendered and externally Georgianized, with sash windows and a Doric doorcase, although half a brick arch remains at the W end. In the centre a good staircase of *c.* 1700, closed string and turned balusters, similar to those in the Customs House and the Duke's Head Hotel. The S range probably housed kitchens, brewhouse and other services. It has GATES by *Louis Osman.*

Opposite the college, the BURKITT HOMES of 1909, red and Tudor. Quadrangular, single-storeyed, with a two-storey

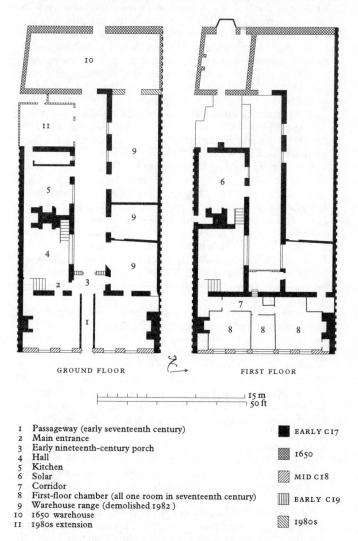

GROUND FLOOR   FIRST FLOOR

```
                                           15 m
                                           50 ft
```

1	Passageway (early seventeenth century)
2	Main entrance
3	Early nineteenth-century porch
4	Hall
5	Kitchen
6	Solar
7	Corridor
8	First-floor chamber (all one room in seventeenth century)
9	Warehouse range (demolished 1982)
10	1650 warehouse
11	1980s extension

- ■ EARLY C17
- ▨ 1650
- ▨ MID C18
- ▥ EARLY C19
- ▨ 1980s

King's Lynn, 29 Queen Street. Plans of ground and first floors

gatehouse, slightly out of place in this street. The unusual cast-
iron RAILINGS and gates to the street were restored in 1989. On
the w side are modest Georgian frontages of brick, with late C18
doorcases. No. 29, next to the College, has a mid-C18 two-storey,
five-bay façade with two dormers, applied to a house of the
early C17, with the central pedimented doorway leading to the
rear, and the actual entrance, via the usual covered passageway.
Façade of English bond brick. The rear aspect shows us a hall
range to the S, with a four-light dais window, the whole arranged
on the L-shaped plan employed from this point N to fit with
the size of the building plots. This plan-form existed from the
later medieval period, but for a new house the provision of a
two-storeyed hall is a remarkably archaic event in c. 1630. The
owner then was a merchant, William Hoo. The hall has a splat-
baluster staircase rising to the solar at the W, now ending pathetically in a cupboard, for the solar, with its fine small-framed
panelling and fluted pilasters, is now a separate flat (carved out
in 1982 when the whole W side of the street was relinquished
by the District Council, who had used the buildings as offices).
At the E end of the hall a similar staircase dog-legs up to the
first-floor corridor in the street range. This corridor has been
partitioned off the W side of what was, when built, a single room
with the stairs opening directly into it. There is more small-
framed panelling and two unassuming chimneypieces. Until
demolished in 1982 an early C17 warehouse range extended W
from the N end of the house, parallel to the hall range and forming a very narrow courtyard. In 1650 a further WAREHOUSE
added at the W end; this remains, incorporated by a 1980s
extension into the rear flat. No. 27 is another L-plan house, C16
but altered when the early C19 brick façade added. Rear warehouse range truncated 1982. The rear wing of No. 19 has the
remains of a transomed hall window, accessible through
THREE CROWNS YARD.

CLIFTON HOUSE, No. 17, on the corner with King's Staithe
Lane, provides the most remarkable catalogue of various building periods from the Middle Ages onwards. What one sees first
from the street is the result of a rationalization in 1708 for the
merchant Samuel Taylor. The brick façade to Queen Street is
of two storeys in seven bays with a modillion cornice, fitted with
small-paned sash windows (twelve plus twelve). It consciously
betrays nothing of the interior. In the second bay is the doorway
behind a pair of barley-sugar columns, a Baroque motif rare in
England. They rise to a segmental pediment. The door does
not lead directly into the house, but to a covered passage to the
garden behind, and one enters through a door in the angle
between the two main wings, a common enough arrangement.
The main rear elevations were kitted out in the early C18 in the
same manner as the front.

The precise building history is as yet unclear but it appears
that there was a medieval house on the L-plan on the N part of
the site, the hall running parallel to King's Staithe Lane. An
undercroft of four bays remains, with octagonal central piers

and quadripartite brick rib vaults, all mid-C14. However a C13
door in the s wall leads into a further room with a tiled C13
floor. This lies parallel to the undercroft and had a central and
a wall fireplace, presumably representing a still earlier hall
house. In the late C16 these two elements were knocked together
and the house was extended by a warehouse range (now converted to a dwelling) running w towards the river and the look-
out tower at the back, overlooking a garden court (accessible
from Three Crowns Yard). There were once other look-out
towers along the river, but this is the only survivor. The TOWER
is five storeys, square on plan but with a taller canted staircase
projecting to the s. Stringcourses between the floors, the mullioned windows pedimented. The stair has a single central
newel-post and remains of delicate late C16 wall paintings in
an upper room. The street range possesses a good staircase of
1708 with three twisted balusters to each tread and carved
tread-ends. Various pieces of C17 and C18 panelling and modest
stucco decoration on the walls of other rooms.

Further on, new FLATS on the e side of Queen Street required
the demolition of a house which contained Norman arches,
now lost. We turn w down KING'S STAITHE LANE, with its
warehouses originally serving Clifton House. It is altogether
characteristic of houses in Queen Street and King Street (and of
others at Lynn) that they developed on narrow sites to a considerable depth in order to reach the migrating river and their
warehouses. As we noted in the Introduction, warehouse design
changed also. The river bank at this point was consolidated in
its present position about 1700, ironing out the numerous
minor inlets that building evidence reveals. The brick WARE-
HOUSES, converted to flats and shops in 1978 by the Borough
Council (job architect *Colin Shewring*), on the s side of the lane
began as a narrow mid-C16 structure, doubled in width by an
early C17 N addition. The rear has reused ashlar, especially
towards the e end.

SOUTH QUAY at this point has, to the s, new developments
of FLATS, either entirely new or conversions of previously derelict
warehouses, all 1989. To the N is a large irregular late C17 or
early C18 three-storey range belonging to BANK HOUSE. John
Wood's 1830 map shows the building, like all on South Quay, to
be hard by the river, the quay being constructed in its present
form and position only in 1855. Round the corner in KING'S
STAITHE SQUARE is the surprisingly small façade of the house,
altered in 1977 for a pub and since converted back. Two storeys
and dormer attic, and, between the attic windows, a statue of
Charles II set in a niche topped by a broken swan-necked
pediment. When was this put up? Henry Bell's 'Groundplat' of
King's Lynn of *c.* 1685 has an open site but William Rastrick's
1725 plan shows the building. The doorway with its Gibbs
surround and the two canted bay windows must be early C19.
Good RAILINGS and GATES. The house became the LYNN
BANK from 1782, founded by Joseph Gurney, among others.
Near the gates is a small grey brick building with arched windows

and Ionic pilasters, built as the bank's new COUNTING HOUSE in 1789. The whole area of this square and Purfleet Quay opposite is riddled with brick cellars of the C17 and later. There are extensive elliptically vaulted ones under Bank House. The E side of the square has some attractive C18 houses in a row. No. 4 was a house of *c*. 1735 converted to a warehouse to serve the adjacent No. 5, which was a mustard mill put up in 1752. Both converted to houses and flats in the 1980s. No. 5 is three-storeyed, with a brick niche.

One leaves the square with its commanding river views by PURFLEET PLACE and immediately has a wonderful view of the Customs House (*see* Public Buildings, p. 477) on the N bank of the Purfleet River. Nos. 1–3 are a short terrace of *c*. 1825; brown brick brought up-river from Wisbech, and a nice stucco band at the first floor with palmette and acanthus leaves (cf. London Road, p. 491). From here l. over the river and r. into PURFLEET STREET. On the corner with King Street Nos. 14–15 are an early C17 pair, probably timber-framed. The C20 has not treated the street well, e.g. the remarkable C14 No. 8 with its internal jetty was demolished in 1966. Neither is its extension well treated, NEW CONDUIT STREET, for we are on the fringes of the new King's Lynn with its emphasis on car parks and shopping developments.

From here one may return to Saturday Market via High Street, or continue with a long loop E to Red Mount.

1b. Beginning at New Conduit Street, by Blackfriars Street to the area near the railway station (St John's Terrace, Waterloo Street, Portland Street, Littleport Street); S to the E town defences, Red Mount and The Walks

To the E of New Conduit Street is BLACKFRIARS STREET. A little way along on the N the Stepney Baptist Church (*see* Churches, p. 474), then St James' Park opens on the S with St John's Church and, facing it, ST JOHN'S TERRACE. This, the Belgrave Hotel at the E end and the streets to the N were built in response to the opening of the railway station in 1844. Brown brick, mixed roofing now. Nos. 1–2 have been demolished, a pity as the whole was a fine twenty-two-bay sequence with a raised centre, and the pruning affects the symmetry. Up to No. 9 built by 1846, the rest *c*. 1850, with tiny changes in detail. Each house of two bays separated from their neighbours by pilasters but unified by a continuous first-floor balcony in wrought iron. Stick-baluster staircases inside. Round the corner to the N and the railway station (*see* Public Buildings), and then off to the l. into WATERLOO STREET and PORTLAND STREET where are some terraces developed after 1849, the best Nos. 3–15 Portland Street.

From here a digression N into LITTLEPORT STREET, to No. 17, on the N side. An early C18 brick house reduced in the late C19 to four bays. C19 porch in the middle behind which is a pair of unfluted Ionic columns to the original C18 doorcase. The saloon in the E side has apsed ends, the staircase stick balusters. At this point the bridge and fragments of walls on Kettlewell Lane and Wyatt Street (*see* above, Walls and Gates) may be viewed.

The line of the wall can be picked up again S of the station by retracing one's steps to St John's Church and proceeding E down a track, St John's Walk. A bank marks the site of the town walls; the Red Mount Chapel lies to the SE (*see* Churches, p. 472). An impression of the exceptionally big area – unnecessarily big – enclosed by the TOWN WALLS can here be appreciated. Little in fact remains of the masonry, but 130 yds S of the Red Mount are fragments of GUANOCK GATE (*see* Walls and Gates, p. 475).

THE WALKS. As early as 1713 the corporation laid out New Walk (the present BROAD WALK), to promote the underused land into a public recreation area. Developments continued into the C20, and until the railway bisected it it extended N to Gaywood Road, the N section finally closing in 1870. The lime-planted promenade was provided with seats in hedged recesses by 1762, removed mid C19, and was extended E of Guanock Gate after common land was purchased in 1813, and planted *c.* 1835. In the early C19 the Town Wall Walk (now THE WALK) was created, shadowing the former walls and extending N to the Red Chapel. E of the chapel ornamental planting had existed by the 1770s, paid for by Charles Turner, and further planted in 1841 after being designated a pleasure ground in 1829. To the N ST JOHN'S WALK was laid out 1887–1929, and to the W ST JAMES' PARK was created in 1902, complete with decorative iron railings.

One returns to Saturday Market along St James' Street (*see* Perambulation 2).

2. E and S of Saturday Market: St James' Street, Tower Street, London Road, County Court Road, Valinger's Road, South Everard Street, Guanock Terrace, South Gate, Southgate Street, Friars Street, Church Lane, All Saints Street, Hillington Square, The Friars, Bridge Street, Stonegate Street, Nelson Street, Priory Lane, Church Street, Saturday Market

One leaves Saturday Market Place by ST JAMES' STREET to the E. Hardly out of the square the WHITE HART, a C17 house almost totally rebuilt in the C19; only one sunk-quadrant bridging beam to the first floor. Then No. 7, a social club but built in 1858–9 as the LYNN SAVINGS BANK by *Medland & Maberley*. Of red brick with ashlar dressings in the Tudor style. The façade only two bays wide, with a four-centred doorway r. and an oriel window l. to the upper floor. The corbelling under with a pelican (for King's Lynn). On the S side Nos. 6–14 show their age in the jettied first floor. They were a row of five mid-C15 shops, now reduced to three. A continuous crown-post roof survives, which has braces down to the ties and up to the crown purlins. Each had a ground-floor shop with an unheated chamber above. The stacks are all insertions. The rest of the street has late C18 and early C19 brick shops, No. 30 with a good early C19 shopfront for a butcher's façade, a door each side of a seven-light transomed display window. Just past Tower Street on the l. the CITROËN GARAGE, Nos. 33–39. Three storeys. A reinforced concrete skeleton with angular curtain walls of 1908.

A detour N up TOWER STREET to the MAJESTIC CINEMA at the N end. 1928 by *John Laurie Carnell* and *William Dymote White* following the precedent for cinemas incorporating a restaurant, café and a ballroom set by the Regent, Brighton, 1921 and the Picture House, Chesterfield, 1923. Brick with stuccoed pilasters and cornices: three-arched loggia below three twin transomed casements and a square tower with offset angles to the SE corner. The loggia has a screen of ovolo-moulded cross casements above the double doors into the balconied foyer. Ballroom converted to a second auditorium. Returning S to No. 21, rather antiseptically restored in the 1980s (new brick under the first-floor jetty and internal partitioning). A late C15 timber-framed house, with a four-light mullioned window with a king mullion to the first floor, lighting the upper chamber. This has three tie-beams carrying three crown-posts, the outer two with straight braces to the ties and arched braces to the purlin. Further S No. 29, WHINCOP HOUSE, is a pleasant later C18 red brick house of two storeys in four bays. Doorcase with fluted Corinthian pilasters rising to an open pediment. So back to St James' Street and on to the Police Station (*see* Public Buildings, p. 476), passing on the S the church of the Greyfriars (*see* Churches, p. 471).

LONDON ROAD, laid out in 1811–13, snakes its way S from this point, and was the focus for suburban expansion from the 1820s. Burnett, writing in 1846, thought London Road a very fine approach to the town with handsome and elegant houses. Today it is choked with traffic but the buildings remain. Opposite Tower Gardens the Methodist Chapel and the remains of St James' Chapel (*see* Churches, p. 474) and the former County Court (*see* Public Buildings, p. 476). Passing Broad Walk, set back on the l. is FRAMINGHAM'S ALMSHOUSES. Henry Framingham was a philanthropist who established a house on Broad Street in 1704, here rebuilt in 1846–8 by *Sharman* of Spalding, in a Tudor style. The U-shaped arrangement familiar for almshouses, and some familiar vocabulary. Three one-storey ranges. The centre has a gable above an arched doorway, arched windows and decorated chimney flues. Side ranges similar but more spare. Modernized internally 1957–9 by *Harold Marsh*.

Now to concentrate on LONDON ROAD. The house numbering is consecutive starting with No. 1 on the E side and returning from the bottom on the W side. The N parts, as far S as Valinger's Road, were already built up by 1830, with spaces and gardens between the houses. On the E side building was less tight. S of Valinger's Road down to Buckingham Terrace on the W side all was open fields until about 1845 but the other side was lined

with houses from c. 1820. On the E side Nos. 23–24 are typical
of the larger houses, a red brick pair with brown brick façades,
three storeys and basement and with steps up to the front doors.
No. 25 is c. 1840, four bays with a square porch and a parapet
hiding the roof. Then Nos. 32–35, a short terrace begun c. 1825
but not complete until c. 1840. Stuccoed stringcourse at the first
floor with the palmette and acanthus decoration popular at that
moment. On the W side building went only as far as No. 95 by
1830 and the Catholic church (see Churches, p. 472) next door
had to wait until 1845 (and 1896).

VALINGER'S ROAD, which goes off to the W, had some building on its N side by 1830 too. A brown brick terrace, Nos. 7–10,
is early C19, the houses with doors under open pediments. No.
14 dated 1807, three bays in two storeys with a dormer attic.
Back on our route, the three houses immediately N of the R.C.
church (Nos. 95–97) begin a rather more consciously up-
market development. Brown brick, three storeys in three bays.
Nice Ionic doorcases and panelled doors, palmette and acanthus
stucco band at first floor. Nos. 89–90 are c. 1840, a variation
on the same theme. Stucco band with a Vitruvian scroll. No. 79
on the corner of South Everard Street (a street of the 1840s)
makes the best of its site. Brown brick with stucco dressings.
The two-bay front to London Road has rustication to the ground
floor but minimal paired pilasters above, where the sashes change
to French windows opening on to an iron balcony. Then a
cornice below a small attic storey. The S front is wider and has
a porch with Doric columns in antis. Opposite and a little way
along is No. 49, CHARFORD HOUSE, 1825, three storeys on a
basement in three bays, with a cast-iron veranda. Nos. 60–77,
BUCKINGHAM TERRACE, make a proper end to the street, on
the W side. Built in 1825 by the Society of Friends, each house
is of two bays and three storeys except No. 77 at the N end (this
is wider and intended for the builder). Brown brick. Unusual
angular tracery in the fanlights. A pediment in the centre over
the carriage arch, stucco band at the first floor and iron railings
in front (renewed 1989 but replicating the originals). Nos. 1–11
GUANOCK PLACE opposite are another row of brown brick 120
terraces of 1825. Three storeys high, each house two bays
wide, doorways with engaged partly fluted columns. The stucco
platband has acanthus and tulip devices over a running scroll.
Then, facing us, the South Gate (see Walls and Gates, p. 475).

From this point W into SOUTHGATE STREET. The street and
Friars Street which follows were established in the late medieval
period on the same lines as now, bordering the precinct of the
White Friars. Nos. 3–5, 7–8 and 9–11 are all early C18 two-
storey houses of red brick, each pair with large square central
chimney stacks. No. 7 has a pleasant doorcase with fluted Doric
columns and an open pediment. FRIARS STREET is still named
after the Whitefriars, and the area is interesting for its post-
Reformation developments, so it is a pity that it became run-
down in the C20 and some of its best buildings disappeared in
the 1960s, e.g. a fine hall house at Nos. 26–28 and Nos. 1–5

with a crown-post roof. Nos. 47–49 is early C17 as one can see from the stack with five diamond-section flues, but it has an early C19 façade. Apart from some large-framed panelling in the entrance passage to No. 49 the interiors are essentially C20. Most houses are modest, apart from No. 33, early C19, gault brick, three storeys and three bays. ELSDEN'S ALMSHOUSES, w side, three single-storey ranges with stepped gables of 1866.

At the N end CHURCH LANE leads to All Saints Church. Nos. 5–6 are a mid-C18 pair, gault brick, with a mansard roof. They were converted to flats in 1978 by *Readhead, Freakley*. The GATES to All Saints churchyard are a surprise: *c.* 1760, wrought iron, with a scrolled overthrow. Continue W into ALL SAINTS STREET. To the N is HILLINGTON SQUARE, four- and five-storey deck-access blocks of flats put up 1968–71, demolishing some pretty Georgian houses in the process. On the S side Nos. 26–36 are a homogeneous row despite their different treatment in recent years. Mostly early C19, though Nos. 27–29 are of the mid C18, the last with a mansard roof. No. 25 is dated 1812. From the W end of All Saints Street S into THE FRIARS, which leads to the modest WHITEFRIARS' GATE. It guarded the N entrance to the precinct. C15, of brick with stone trim. A stilted arch below three niches with wave-moulded arches. The S side just has the archway.

BRIDGE STREET begins with a former public house, altered and restored in 1967 as a Quaker meeting room. Early C18, of rendered and colourwashed brick. The roof is, surprisingly, a late example of the clasped purlin type. No. 37 is a tiny late C18 brown brick house. The row comprising Nos. 30–36 was scheduled for demolition in the 1960s but the houses were bought and converted in 1967 by *Desmond Waite*, a process which altered their appearance as little as possible. Behind their stuccoed fronts they are all of the mid C16, of brick and flint, but little remains inside. Nos. 33–34 have shaped gables to the dormers. Inside, a clasped purlin roof with undiminished principals. Opposite, a nice row of Georgian houses was replaced with maisonettes as part of the Hillington Square development. Then the most spectacular, and latest, of Lynn's timber-framed houses, GREENLAND FISHERY HOUSE. There is plenty of brick: to the gable walls, under the first-floor jetty and as nogging between the studs on the upper floor. It was built in 1605–8 for a merchant, John Atkin, with a hall to the upper floor. It is only one room deep (there were rear cross wings) and runs parallel to the street, a luxury not often available in C17 Lynn. The door marks a passageway to the rear, and in the passage was a door to the domestic front range at the S and another to the shops in the N part. The upper floor has three projecting windows, of which only the r. one can be dated *c.* 1620, the others being late C17 insertions. The original fenestration here seems to have been a row of clerestory-like mullioned windows under the attic jetty. The S room has a big fireplace with a staircase to its l. rising into the first floor. Here the hall ran the entire length of the house and was heated from each end. On the S wall are wall paintings of *c*. 1605 and on the E wall painted wooden panels, with inscriptions of the mid C17. The room now subdivided. In the attic was a room at the S end corresponding to a late medieval solar, also heated and again with wall paintings. Restored in 1945.

STONEGATE STREET lies to the E. No. 9 on the N side is a C17 brick house brought up to date by means of an early C19 brick skin. Doorcase has reeded jambs and a metope frieze. C17 panelling in the rear W room and in two more rooms on the first floor. Back to the Greenland Fishery, across the creek of Millfleet into Nelson Street.

NELSON STREET like Queen Street begins on a curve. It has specially much of interest. First on the l. a former C19 MALTINGS converted to flats in 1978 (Borough Council, job architect *Peter Wharton*); on the r. a good red brick WALL follows the curve of the road; 1818. It marks the garden of No. 30, LADYBRIDGE HOUSE, which has a yellow brick façade of two storeys and dormer attic in four bays. Pedimented doorcase to r., with Roman Doric attached columns. The door leads to a covered passage to the rear, emerging through an open-pedimented doorcase. S front (garden façade) C18, extended in C19. N elevation has an outshut clad in Cumberland slate, a rare thing in Norfolk. Opposite is No. 19, OXLEY HOUSE, late C17 but rebuilt early C18, of five bays and two storeys with a hipped roof. One-bay projection with pediment. Doorway with segmental pediment on demi-columns. Rusticated quoins and a platband at first floor. Bay window to the garden, S, front. The door opens into a staircase hall, the early C18 staircase very fine with its two vase-turned balusters to each tread. The dado rail however is set against C17 panelling and the upper flights of stairs revert to this period, with heavier turned balusters and a closed string. Nos. 22–28 on the other side started as a sequence of early C17 brick lobby-entrance houses but they show late C18 brick fronts now. Then Nos. 14–20, a row of brick houses built in 1819; two and three bays each.

On the W side it must be stressed that the following houses have, just like those in Queen Street and King Street, deep sites with wings and warehouses at the back. The river bank was right on the street line in *c*. 1050, 30–60 ft back by *c*. 1250 and 130 ft further W by *c*. 1350. There was therefore more opportunity earlier for big quadrangular houses in Nelson Street, and more time for their alteration. No. 15 is a fine mid-C18 house rebuilt in 1788. Six bays in two and a half storeys. Brown brick with quoins and a big pedimented doorway on unfluted columns. Spacious staircase with wrought-iron balustrade. Ceiling with the geometrical patterns of e.g. Houghton. S ground-floor room and main first-floor rooms with large-framed panelling. Converted to flats 1989–90. Then Nos. 11–13, BURNHAM HOUSE. The front is all of the mid C17, of English bond brick, two storeys and dormer attic in nine haphazard bays. Two doorways, first-floor stringcourse and six early C18 cross casements to the upper floor. There are two doorways because the late C15 courtyard house was divided quite early. Of the early work only the N jamb of the carriage arch to the l. shows externally. The rear yard elevations have a number of good cross casements of c. 1710 and one or two C16 mullioned windows. The door to No. 11 leads via a covered passage to this yard, and from here into the house. C17 and C18 panelling in several rooms, an early C18 staircase with two turned balusters to each tread. The front roof is early C18 too. The door to No. 13 has an C18 internal passage-way to a winder staircase; large-framed panelling in front room. At the rear are remains of a C15 WAREHOUSE, just some N and S walls. No. 9 follows. This too was a courtyard house of the late C15, but was rather rebuilt early in the C19, and altered since. Only the front range remains, and it is used as offices. Gault brick ground floor and probably an underbuilt jetty to the first floor. The central door is very fine indeed: late C15, under a four-centred arch with a crocketed ogee finial; a pelican in the spandrel. Further arch above and a late C17 classical frieze.

Opposite, Nos. 8–10 have colourwashed early C18 brick façades separated by a carriage arch; No. 6 is of early C19 red brick. Nos. 2–4, on the corner with Priory Lane, was built c. 1540 on a site cleared at the Reformation, and was for a long time a celebrated public house. Moulded dragon post at NW corner in front of a C16 panel with figures, said to be the Annunciation. Deep coved jetties to N and W elevations. A four-light diamond-mullioned window with a central king mullion remains to the first floor. Inside there are three arches in the W wall which were probably made for a shop, as they have rebates for shutters and there was a door immediately r. For Hampton Court opposite, *see* Perambulation 1a.

The area S and E of St Margaret's Church was occupied by the Benedictine priory, with domestic and monastic buildings extending E to Church Street and S beyond Priory Lane. Along PRIORY LANE we see on the S Nos. 5–7, a C17 brick row with a platband and some early C18 cross casements to No. 7; the other two with C20 windows. Opposite and much more inter-esting, Nos. 12–20. These are buildings from St Margaret's Priory which survived the Reformation. They date from the C14, but there is an association with accounts for a new hall in 1445–8. The whole is 173 ft long. Divided into six flats in 1974–5 by *Michael Gooch*. Two storeys. There is a rebuilt stone arch with hollow and wave mouldings leading to the rear from the W end, possibly marking the site of a gateway. The seven blocked doorways relate to C18 alterations, but the blocked timber doorway under the projecting first-floor hall stack is prob-ably C15. Some stone one-light windows. The back looks nicely over St Margaret's churchyard through variously restored stone lancets. The upper floor of No. 17 has two two-light cusped windows lighting the hall. The hall, as is apparent inside, is an early flooring of a C14 open hall, not a proper upper hall. Bits of the crown-post roof remain to E end: arched braces from ties to crown-posts and from posts to purlin; also there are intersecting arched braces from the tie-beams to the rafters.

Round the corner in CHURCH STREET Nos. 17–18 contain further remains of the priory. At the back is C14 masonry but the range – and exactly what kind of a building this was a part of is unknown, probably always domestic – was mainly rebuilt *c.* 1470. The rendered brick façade is C18, with altered fenestration. At the back shadows of doorways with, on the first floor, three stone windows with four-centred heads to the lights. Wave-moulded bridging beams inside. The best part is the very fine crown-post roof: arched braces from posts to tie-beams and from posts to purlins. Further S FRIARSCOT has a late C17 brick façade of two storeys and dormer attic in four bays. The two-light cross casements are repaired C17 work (the house completely restored in 1989). The two main ground-floor rooms have early C16 roll-moulded bridging beams and against the back wall is an inserted C17 stack, interrupting a first-floor mullioned window.

3. Tuesday Market from SE *corner and the area to the* N *and* E*: St Nicholas Street, St Anne's Street, North Street, Pilot Street, Austin Street, Chapel Street, Norfolk Street, High Street, Tuesday Market*

TUESDAY MARKET PLACE. One of the most splendid open spaces in provincial England, not quite rectangular but narrowing towards the N end. Roads open W towards the river, which, in the C12, lapped the W edge of what is now the square. Unfortunately it has lost its most notable feature, the MARKET CROSS, an ambitious domed octagon built by *Henry Bell* in 1707–10. But all four sides have houses and commercial buildings of interest.

First, in the SE corner, LLOYDS BANK, 1928. A Classical design and the little brother of Lloyds Bank in Norwich, by *Munro Cautley*. NATIONAL WESTMINSTER BANK was a mid-C18 shop and domestic building re-fronted in the mid C19. Seven fluted Doric columns to ground floor and a carriageway to the r. originally leading to the rear and a house of *c.* 1700. In 1994 this carriageway was merged with the interior and the rear courtyard roofed with a steel and glass canopy, so that the ground floor of the earlier house is within it, its upper floor above it: a pleasant seven-bay S elevation with two-light cross casements. Then Nos. 5–6, DUKE'S HEAD HOTEL. This is the most prominent house in the square, and if not the most beautiful, certainly one of the most curious in Lynn. It is nine bays wide and two and a half storeys high. Built in 1683–9 for Sir John Turner, who destined it for an inn to accommodate those from outside visiting his Exchange (*see* Customs House, Public Buildings, p. 477), but certain details such as the stuccoing and the decoration above the first-floor windows seem to be early Victorian. Original no doubt the corner quoins, and the quoins to the projecting middle three bays, the surround of the central window with pilasters and a broken segmental pediment, the surround of the window above this with its side volutes, the

surrounds of all the windows of that stage, and also the big
three-bay broken segmental pediment out of which rises a
higher one-bay normal pediment – a pre-Archer conceit, one is
tempted to say. The architect may have been *Henry Bell*. It was
built round a courtyard with galleries opening into rooms, but
so extensive have been the enlargements of 1967 that only one
open inn-gallery is recognizable, and its two round columns are
embedded in later partitioning on the first floor leading off the
grand staircase, i.e. a basically medieval arrangement carrying
on late. The staircase remains, with bulbous turned balusters
and panelled newels. The principal first-floor room to the w
has two bolection-moulded chimneypieces and large-framed
panelling (similar panelling in the room below is of 1967). No. 7,
MAYDEN'S HEAD HOTEL, has a late C18 brick front of two
storeys and dormer attic and six window bays, but in the range
running E along Market Lane is an eleven-light mullioned and
transomed window with two king mullions, of *c.* 1550. No. 8
and No. 10 are now offices. The front rebuilt late C18; the two
together are nine bays wide. Two storeys and dormer attic.
There is however a four-centred C16 carriage arch r. of centre
and a square carriageway to the l., the latter turning into a four-
centred C16 version at the back. In the gardens it is just about
apparent that these carriageways remain from an enormous C16
house built round a courtyard. One five-light mullioned window
to first floor. Both the rear wings rebuilt in the C18. Nos. 11–12
was a C16 range too but the evidence was obliterated during
reconstruction about 1830. Two storeys in seven bays, the centre
bay projecting slightly. Pleasant C19 pub front to the l.

On the N side of the square No. 14 has a double doorway
carrying a broad segmental pediment on four Corinthian
pilasters. Sham timber-framing to first floor. This mid-C18 front
has peeping over it on the r. the roof of a cross wing, the C16
origins of which are visible only in its stone quoins. Nos. 15–16
have a complicated history. There was a range of early C16
houses pulled together with a smart new S front in *c.* 1720, but
it is difficult to determine the plans of the original houses or even
to define their extent because of C20 alterations. The façade has
nine bays and two storeys with a dormer attic too above a parapet. A finely detailed doorway carrying its open segmental pediment on brackets, now blocked; late C18 sashes, those to first
floor with rubbed brick aprons. Moulded platband beneath a
panelled parapet. The back has a hipped block fitted with early
C17 mullioned casements, and a gabled wing parallel to the
front range. This has more mullioned windows, one of which is
six-mullioned and looks into an early C16 open hall. The hall is
partly timber-framed and has roll-moulded bridging beams on
roll-moulded arched braces. The inside of the front range has a
nice early C18 staircase: two round balusters with bobbins to
each tread and a ramped and wreathed handrail ending at
newels formed by miniature unfluted Corinthian columns. Nos.
17–17A is a three-bay mid-C18 house split into offices.

The W side begins at the N corner with a house with a surprise,

No. 18, Bishop's Lynn House. It was a late C14 merchant's house with a warehouse at the back parallel to Page Stair Lane, but the warehouse demolished in 1975 for Social Security Offices. The cellar of the early house remains only under the N part. It has two octagonal brick piers from which spring eight chamfered brick ribs crossing to wall-piers. Between these are four-centred wall arches. In the late C16 the house was divided into two and the s part was bought by the leading Lynn merchant William Bagge in 1725, who re-fronted his part. This is two and a half storeys high in five bays. Pedimented Doric doorcase on unfluted pilasters. The sashes all early C19. Attic storey above a thick cornice. In *c.* 1760 the Bagges bought the rest of the property and Thomas Bagge in 1803–4 employed the building firm of *S. Newham & Son* to rebuild the N part. Brown brick, similar height, endowed with a handsome bow window extending right up to the roof. The best interiors belong to *c.* 1725–30. Large staircase hall, approached from the front door by a passage lined with large-framed panelling. In the hall a good Kentian fireplace. Open-string staircase around three sides with three bobbin-turned balusters per tread. No. 19 converted to offices as well. A late C18 house of five bays and two storeys, with a further two bays to the N rebuilt *c.* 1840 to match. The doorcase central to the original five bays: pediment on engaged fluted Roman Doric columns. The cantilevered staircase in the N extension sits happily in its oval well lighted by a lantern dome. A long wing towards the river. Then the Corn Exchange, *see* Public Buildings, p. 477. Barclays Bank was erected as a mansion for another leading merchant, George Hogge, in 1768. The front was rebuilt in replica 1956–7 by *Ellis Middleton*. It is Georgian, of yellow Stamford brick and Clipsham stone, nine bays with a three-bay pediment. The porch and the Ionic columns on the ground floor to the l. and r. of the porch are not original but do correspond to C19 drawings. The interiors remodelled in 1984 but three good chimneypieces remain: two in the first and second floors (SE rooms of both) are late C18 and Adamesque, but the one in the first-floor banking hall is *c.* 1730 and Kentian in derivation, with birds and vegetation carved in high relief under a gadrooned cornice.

The s side has to the w the Globe Hotel (for which *see* below, p. 505). No. 23 has an early C19 brick and stone façade, five bays wide and three storeys high. This is fitting enough, but the interest is inside. The late C17 house proves to have a double-pile plan and to have been re-fitted *c.* 1740. Nice staircase with two bobbin-turned balusters to each tread, first-floor landing with equally nice pedimented doorcases. The main room at this level with large-framed panelling. Of the C17 the small-framed panelling in the room immediately s, its chimneypiece with fluted pilasters, and the clasped purlin roof. C18 and C19 buildings run to the E end of the square, the last, No. 29, with good plate-glass shop windows.

From Tuesday Market first N towards St Nicholas. In St Nicholas Street on the r. an unusual thing – a bay for dustbins made out of the C15 remains of the NW GATEWAY to the precinct of the Austin Friars. On the l. at the end, Nos. 10–11, the TUDOR ROSE HOTEL, is an amalgamation of two houses (No. 11 formerly St Nicholas' House). Extensive restorations 1972–3. The earlier house is to the W, of the mid C15 and timber-framed, though at the back brick and carstone dominate. Two storeys. At the l. a four-centred stone arch flanked by columns and closed by an excellent traceried DOOR. It has five vertical panels with early Perp tracery patterns. To the r. another four-centred doorway and a three-light window all under one hoodmould. Jettied first floor with brick infill between the upper studs. Two pairs of early C17 cross casements (renewed) to first floor and a fifth set somewhat to the r. of the others. This lights an internal gallery connecting the old building with the newer No. 11 to the E, added in 1645. It is double-piled, parallel to the street. The façade was rebuilt in the mid C18: two storeys and dormer attic in five bays; mid-C19 sashes. The C15 house had a hall range to the rear, i.e. a conventional L-shaped plan; both E and W sides lit through mullioned windows. The hall has an inserted early C16 stack with double-roll-moulded stone jambs to the fireplace. E of it one of the two arched doorways for the screens passage can be examined. Crown-post roof at the front, with arched braces from ties to crown-posts in the Lynn manner. The internal gallery linking the C15 house with the C17 house remains. The back of the mid-C17 range (No. 11) has an upper floor with six two-light cross casements and a Dutch gable to the E.

Now into ST ANNE'S STREET which heads off N shadowed on the E by RAILINGS to the churchyard, 1749, with a secondary gate at the N. On the l. a big house (Nos. 14–18) dating from the C17 but dressed up in a late C18 skin; two and a half storeys, nine bays including the central porch bay with a Venetian window over a Doric doorcase. Two rear wings of the C17, of brick. (Inside, a good fireplace and plaster ceiling. The fireplace has coupled Tuscan columns and a wooden overmantel. Another fireplace with broad pilasters and, in the overmantel, baluster colonnettes. Some C17 panelling.) Two houses of note, both at the top on the l. Nos. 4–6 represents the earliest survival of a parallel hall in Lynn. It is C13 and is of rendered rubblestone, though the two-storey front elevation is unrewarding. The back has a blocked C13 stone doorway and the roof is reported to be a scissor-braced type, the scissors meeting with notched lap-joints, and with a later queenpost attached to the S. No. 2 is divided into flats and an office, again a parallel hall house. The date though is c. 1400 and the material timber. Two-storey front range jettied back and front. At the front the first floor has two big arched braces and two four-light mullioned windows, the back has the same arched braces but in the middle. Inside there are visible the rebates on the front studs for the shutters of the original shop. ST ANNE'S GATE (see Walls and Gates, p. 475) marks the line of town walls N of North Street. For the docks beyond see p. 479.

TRUE'S YARD, at the junction with St Anne's Street and
North Street, is a pair of fishermen's cottages restored 1990–1
by *Robert Freakley* (job architect *Jim Crome*). They are the last
representatives of hundreds crammed into this quarter until
slum clearances of the 1930s. A house and smithy on North
Street and the former Naval Reserve pub on St Anne's Street
have been converted to a museum and research centre. The
house is early C18, brick, two storeys, with a canted E end sliced
back and flat-roofed when the road was widened in the 1960s.
Rebuilt full height with a first-floor balcony. In this part good
large-framed panelling. Former smithy set back to the E, English
bond brick but *c.* 1800. The house and pub are connected by a
low glazed link of 1995–7 by *Jim Crome* (working on his own)
and the late C18 pub converted: two storeys, four bays, late C19
pub front. Behind are the two-storey COTTAGES of 1802, each
with a plank door and one window to each floor, casements
above, later sashes below. One-up, one-down plan with a central
stack off-set to the S to allow the narrowest of winder stairs on
the N side, back-to-back. The 1841 census returned eleven people
living in the W house.

Our route returns to St Nicholas Church, where overlooking
the churchyard from the S will be found the EXORCIST'S
HOUSE (No. 8 Chapel Lane). Brick and flint, dated 1635 but
with a Dutch gable to the N, an early example. PILOT STREET
ambles off to the NE, now a cul-de-sac. On the l. good churchyard RAILINGS of 1749. At the end a row of houses, the
sequence opening with some modest late C18 ones (Nos. 22–24,
No. 26), and an early C19 house. Nos. 30–32 are different
indeed for the house is C15, with a hall parallel to the street.
Two storeys, with a passageway in the middle leading to the
living quarters which are arranged in two cross wings, ripe for
division into two houses, which has happened. The front range
is jettied back and front, so the rear wings would appear to be
additions of the late C15, that to the N itself jettied. The S front
room has a bridging beam on arched braces and in both parts
the redundant rear jetty is apparent. Crown-post roof with
arched braces to the ties as well as the purlins.

Retracing one's steps to the Exorcist's House one turns into
AUSTIN STREET. By the Council Offices to the W are the consolidated remains of the C15 NE PRECINCT GATE of the Austin
Friars. It has a depressed four-centred head to both sides. To
the E, AUSTIN HOUSE, No. 15, set back on the N side, has a
mid-C18 front with C19 details; four widely spaced bays hiding
an early C18 core.

Now W to CHAPEL STREET. At the N end facing St Nicholas
Street a couple of late C18 brown brick houses, Nos. 78–80, of
three and four bays, No. 78 with an open pediment to the doorcase. The site of the Austin Friars is occupied by the DISTRICT
COUNCIL OFFICES of 1973 (*see* Public Buildings, p. 476).
Then, opposite, Nos. 37–39, LATTICE HOUSE. It is known to
have been occupied in 1487 when the house comprised a single
range parallel to the street – an unusual thing then or at any

time before the C17 in Lynn, but *see* also Pilot Street above. It probably had shops to the street and living accommodation above. The timber frame is jettied to both the E and S sides, with a dragon beam and post at the corner. Various casement windows of C17 or earlier derivation. The whole house was restored 1982–3 by the District Council (*R. W. Edwards*, head of design services, job architect *D. C. Pitcher*), and opened as a pub, a use it held also from 1714 to 1919. There are three wings to the rear, the S wing added *c.* 1490, the N wing early C16, centre wing C19. S side with mullioned windows from 1982. There are thus three medieval ranges and all have crown-post roofs, that to the S wing still open (or reopened) to the roof. The truss is suitably decorated: chamfered crown-post, hollow-chamfered purlin braces. The E (front range) roof with arched braces descending to the ties, N roof a combination of the two types. Opposite is No. 42, WESTGATE HOUSE, its early C19 façade irregular because an early C18 house lies behind it.

NORFOLK STREET, at the S end of Chapel Street, was a major medieval thoroughfare linking the East Gate with the Tuesday Market, but its position as a principal shopping street, particularly developed *c.* 1780–1820, has had unfortunate consequences. The shops which line it have all been altered, usually with plate-glass fronts. Highlights are few.* No. 5, S side towards the High Street, is in its core an C18 inn round a courtyard, altered early C19. Three bays and of three storeys with dormer attic. The arched carriageway to the rear set to the l. Into the High Street, and so to Tuesday Market.

4. S and W of Tuesday Market: High Street, Library Court, Purfleet Street, Purfleet Quay, King Street, Aickman's Yard, Ferry Street, Common Staithe Quay, Page Stair Lane, Tuesday Market

Leaving Tuesday Market from the SE corner we go into HIGH STREET, the principal shopping street and hence the most interfered with. It was pedestrianized in 1972. On the l. Nos. 61–62 set the scene. They are a pair of three-storey shops each of two bays put up *c.* 1825 in red brick. On the corner with Norfolk Street No. 56A has its gable-end facing the street and is indeed a C16 timber-framed building, but much altered and the façade rebuilt above the level of the attic jetty in 1969. On the W side LIBRARY COURT runs off, and has the best house. It has a mid-C19 front to High Street (No. 81), of five bays and two and a half storeys, ashlar-faced with alternating triangular and segmental pediments to the first-floor windows. In the alley behind is first a two-storeyed early C17 domestic range and beyond that, i.e. further W, a warehouse. A general remodelling

---

* To the E on the S side No. 26 has a jetty, disguised by the addition of a late C19 shopfront. Probably C16. Nos. 37–38 are similar, Nos. 51–53 are early C17 but only displaying their age by the four diamond-section flues to the ridge stack. The material brick and a little rubblestone. Some masonry will relate to the Hospital of St John Baptist, founded on this site before 1135 and dissolved 1545. On the N side Nos. 99–100 perhaps had its origins in the late C15, but the façade re-done several times since. Hall range to the rear.

c. 1730 inside and out probably for the owner John Exton, mayor in 1735. The domestic part has a pedimented doorway, the warehouse two early C18 sashes. The main front room on the first floor facing the High Street has large-framed panelling to three walls and a chimneypiece with a swan-necked pediment. Three nice panelled doors have egg-and-dart surrounds. The room s of this retains its C17 chimneypiece: fluted pilasters and frieze; in the overmantel three pairs of Roman Doric columns up to the cornice. In two second-floor rooms similar chimney-pieces. Also on the w side but much further down Nos. 102–103 has a seven-bay façade with rusticated quoins and cornice (mostly lost), the middle first-floor sash under a segmental pediment. The house was part of a larger façade built in 1756 for the merchant Edward Everard Jun. Opposite, Nos. 21–23, early C19 but an amalgam of three distinct premises. The artic-ulation of the N section is the best: three storeys, five bays (centre three projecting) and an iron balcony at first floor. The rear was extended in 1833 according to a datestone. Near the s end on the w side, the former LYNN DRAPERY EMPORIUM, 1898, with large first-floor display windows. The ground floor knocked into a pub. Then another shop façade dated 1898 with a Dutch gable, then two more Edwardian fronts: one with a two-bay façade with arched first-floor niches containing bowed casements and a bowed oriel above rising into a cupola; the other of four bays, three storeys, panelled pilasters and pedimented first-floor windows.

High Street is bisected by Purfleet Street (*see* Perambulation 1a) which, turning w towards the river and the Customs House (*see* Public Buildings, p. 477), guards the entrance to PURFLEET QUAY, economically important from the C13. The Quay, with the side elevation of No. 1 King Street, was tidied up in 1988 with old anchor chains and a brick pavement. On the N side a WAREHOUSE, used now as offices. In an engraving of *c.* 1680 it is shown with a look-out tower to the E side. Some stone quoins to the ground floor remain from the early C17 construction, but the three storeys above rather altered. Three blocked openings on the ground floor remain facing E and N for the reception of goods, and three elliptically vaulted cellars, parallel to each other, running E–W.

KING STREET is the street richest in pleasant houses. It is only 240 yds long, but its importance can be guessed from the fact that it was the widest street in the town until London Road was laid out in the early C19. Nearly every house repays attention, but few are entirely as they seem externally. On the w side the L-plan predominates, with long ranges of warehouses at the back continually elongated as the river receded w. The Georgian houses are of red or yellow brick. Starting on the w side, No. 1 has fronts to both King Street and Purfleet Quay. Mid-C18 E façade of three bays, with a nice open-pedimented doorcase on attached Ionic columns. The s return rather earlier C18, with two sashes to each floor and a line of rusticated quoins. No. 3 was a C15 hall house of the L-plan type, but the hall rebuilt in the C18, and the whole converted to flats in 1989. The front of the mid C18, red brick, five bays, with a similar doorcase to No. 1 set to the r. This leads to a passage to the rear, not directly into the house. Sash windows with the addition of a C19 Venetian window over the door. The hall range on the s at the back rebuilt early C18 in four bays. Very fine staircase of *c.* 1710: three twisted balusters to each tread, moulded and ramped handrail ending at a newel composed of four twisted balusters hunched together. No. 3A might once have been part of the house, but was rebuilt in two bays in the early C18, with giant pilasters r. and l.

No. 5, *c.* 1740, four bays, two storeys and a top storey added in the C19. Doric pedimented doorcase to the l. The hallway is at the back and in it another choice staircase, this time with two turned balusters to each tread, carved tread-ends and dado panelling. It is in an open well and is supported at the turns on fluted Ionic engaged columns. Large-framed panelling to front ground-floor room, chimneypiece with a picture mantel with scrolled side consoles. More such panelling and minor if decent plasterwork in other rooms. On the E side, Nos. 4–6 was a big timber-framed house of the late C16, using much brick, and yet more brick since. In the C18 it was divided into two houses, the four bays to No. 6 (i.e. l. of the passageway) receiving a respectable brick front in 1739. The upper sashes may still be of that date. No. 4 has only two bays. The ground floor bricked over in the C19 but the upper floor merely plastered. Both have re-cast rear cross wings reached from the segmental passageway in the middle. In No. 6 a good chimneypiece in the first-floor main room. No. 8, CHANCERY HOUSE, converted to offices. The two first-floor rooms with very early C18 panelling, but the façade is a century later. Four bays, two storeys and dormer attic. The stick-baluster staircase no doubt also early C19. No. 10 (now offices) has a carriage arch just l. of the centre. Brick, early C18, four bays wide, two storeys high. The windows C20 replacements. No. 14, also offices, appears early C19 but is a late C17 double-pile house. The façade is a simple three-bay composition but there is a door to the l. leading to the passage to the back. Nos. 16–18 are timber-framed and late C16, with an early C19 brown brick front providing each house with two bays. Very much altered.

Now back to the w side. Nos. 7–9, a complicated story: a late C14 hall in the wing behind the street front. The façade is *c.* 1830, in yellow brick, two storeys in seven bays. Central panelled door, and, to its l., a passageway to the rear, emerging under a chamfered C15 arch. This is the standard L-plan, so the hall should be to the N side of the rear yard, entered through a doorway in the angle with the front block. And so it is, but the surprise is that the hall is late C14, admittedly altered in the C15, and given an early C18 face-lift. Also curious is the apparent lack of a timber frame, suggesting that from the start the house was built of brick and stone. The hall has been changed to a two-storey, five-bay elevation lit through late C18 sashes within early C18

sash boxes. In the middle is a good panelled door under a split
overlight; *c.* 1710. To the r. are the stone jambs of the first hall
entrance modified in the C15 and to the l. are the stone jambs of
the dais window. On the inside these have bowtell and wave
mouldings, so *c.* 1370 must be the earliest possible date. Next to
this window another one, with an ogee head and a cinquefoiled
light, with wave-moulded jambs. The hall was floored in the
late C16 and divided. The W room has fine early C18 large-
framed panelling, and the room further W, and actually in an
early C18 addition, has the same but slightly later. Running to
the N of the hall is a passageway contrived in the C17 out of part
of the yard of the adjacent house and terminating to the E in a
contemporary staircase with closed strings and turned balusters.
The stair takes one to the room over the hall, attired in early
C18 large-framed panelling. In the gable of the hall range the
hollow-chamfered jambs remain of two late C14 windows. The
roofs were rebuilt in the early C16 and the stacks inserted late
C16. In the yard behind three C16 timber-framed and brick
buildings variously converted. Nos. 11–13 has a stately white
stuccoed early C19 front of two storeys and six bays, the r. three
bays on the ground floor opened into a wide carriage arch.
Stick-baluster staircase and panelling inside.

No. 15 is another L-planned hall house, this time early C16
and of brick. The four-bay façade to the street has its carriage
arch to the l. and an array of mid-C18 flush sashes with their
glazing bars. Three alternating pedimented and segmentally
pedimented dormer windows. More such sashes adorn the
two-storey, five-bay hall range behind to the N of the yard, but
the six-light dais window remains. Cross wing added to the W.
Sunk-quadrant bridging beams in the former hall, from the C17
flooring. Two or three rooms with large-framed panelling. On
the S side of the yard is No. 15A, also early C16 but much more
altered in the early C18 and later. A little Venetian window high
in the courtyard front lights a splendid and unexpected C18
staircase hall. The stairs are cantilevered out from the walls, have
tread-ends carved with sea-dragons and delicate fluted balusters.
The newels reeded and fluted. The balustrade returns gallery-
like at the S and the ceiling has a plaster chandelier rose with
undercut floral swags.

No. 19 has the handsome name-plate of 'John Aickman's
Foundry' with the date 1827 over the carriageway. Brown brick
and sashes. In AICKMAN'S YARD the foundry buildings have
been converted to houses but the C17 brickwork shows that
they had a different original function, probably warehousing.
Next to this the front of the former HIGH SCHOOL FOR
GIRLS, flats since 1982. Five bays with a two-storeyed stone
porch projecting towards the street and opening to the passage
to the rear. Brick, rendered and scored as ashlar, and given
rustication. There is a C17 stack and some C17 walling to the S
return, but the house was basically rebuilt in the C18. At the
back an agreeable ogeed veranda with two octagonal iron piers.
The stairs set to the N of the front range, with turned balusters

and a wreathed handrail, late C18. In front iron RAILINGS of
c. 1825.

On the E side, Nos. 28–32, one of the most interesting of all
Lynn's houses. Externally there are two distinct parts – the two-
51 storeyed timber-framed r. part and the smaller three-storeyed l.
part clad in an early C19 brick skin – but internally they are one.
An excellent restoration completed in 1983 by *Michael and
Sheila Gooch*. The timber-framing has seven bays of studs and a
frieze of window openings under the first floor. The studs themselves prove to have, on close examination, mortice slots for a
pentice hood, i.e. this is a late C14 shopfront. Steep gabled roof.
Of the two doorways to the C19 part the r. one led to a passageway. Two rear wings of C15–C16, and a third demolished. Inside
the material is all limestone and (later) brick. A late C12
9   Norman hall ran from the N end to the middle of the timber-
framed section. It had two round arches to each floor of the N
and S walls, of which those at the N remain, the others quite
obvious. They have chamfered piers. About 1400 a dividing
wall was inserted splitting the hall longitudinally, and c. 1480 a
stack was intruded into the E wall. It would appear that the hall
was parallel to the street, possibly with an open arcade to the
ground and the domestic quarters above. But the Norman plan
was abandoned in the C15 and the S cross wing became the
conventional open hall, with four bays of a crown-post roof
of King's Lynn type (braces from crown-post to ties as well as
to the purlin). Pointed arch to the N doorway, and four-light
mullioned windows N and S. The N cross wing has a similar
roof, only one truss remaining. Still on the E side, No. 40 and
No. 42 provide another opportunity to see a C14 timber-framed
shop, though the C20 shopfront to the one, and the early C19
brick skin to the other, do not immediately imply it. The door
to No. 42 leads to a timber-framed passage running up to an
arched internal doorway. Various bits of timber and an arched
brace possibly to a former jetty.

Now back to the W side. Nos. 23–25 has a solid early C18
façade of three storeys and five bays. In the middle a doorway
with big rusticated blocks, and rustication to the quoins r. and l.
The door leads to a passageway and a tiny rear yard between
two early C17 wings, both of which have stepped W gables.
Converted to flats in 1989.

No. 27 has a fine ashlar front added shortly after 1715. Five
bays, two and a half storeys. Doorway with segmental pediment
on Corinthian half-columns. Upper windows pedimented, the
central one segmentally. Much delicate detailing. The carriageway to the r. has C20 doors, and above it is a Venetian window,
repeated at the back. This little bit rebuilt in 1814. The doors
lead to a former passageway elaborated at the W end into a staircase hall, likely enough in 1814, with eight Corinthian columns
standing about. Stick-baluster staircase. The two-storey rear wing
rebuilt c. 1695 probably for the Rotterdam merchant Hubert
Vinckesteyn. It has sash windows. Small-framed panelling in this
wing, much of the later large-framed version to the front block.

The previous timber-framed house owned by the merchant
John Dynnesdale in 1580.

Then the ST GEORGE'S GUILDHALL. The site was acquired 52
by the guild in 1406 and the hall built 1410–20. The building
was restored for its present theatrical purpose in 1948–51 by
Marshall Sisson and presented to the National Trust. Brick
and stone. It is rectangular, with the gable facing the street
pierced by three doorways, the middle one blocked. Big double-
transomed six-light window above. The window is early C16
rather than early C15. The corners had polygonal turrets, now
partly embedded in adjacent buildings. The side walls have big
stepped buttresses with pedestrian passageways cut through
them, best seen from the N, where the sequence of three-light
transomed windows is more or less intact. Inside is a small foyer,
like a modern cinema if it were not for the heavy wave-moulded
and chamfered beams overhead. Steps lead down to the undercroft to one's r. and up to the hall on the E (these stairs of 1951).
The whole of the s side given over to a passageway. The
UNDERCROFT owes its elliptical brick vault to the early C18
merchants who used the premises as a warehouse, replacing a
former flat wooden ceiling. It is now a restaurant. In the upper
HALL itself one's attention at once goes to the scissor-braced
roof of no fewer than sixty-one trusses, possible over such a
span without tie-beams because of the external buttressing.
Since World War II this is the biggest surviving medieval guildhall in the country.

There is much more to the site than this, for at the back is a
series of WAREHOUSE buildings, now in various uses, which
were attached end-wise to each other as the river migrated w, so
as always to present a gable to the loading quay. The sequence
begins with an early C15 ashlar-faced building with three doorways and C16 and later brick to the first floor. Next w is a building rebuilt in the C18, and then a late C15 brick range, very
much rebuilt, although the N side is more intact. At the river is
a WATERGATE.

Back at the street there is No. 29, SHAKESPEARE HOUSE.
C18 and C19 brick façade, with a carriageway leading to the N
flank of the Guildhall. Here there proves to be a late C15 brick-
built hall wing, of which a six-light mullioned window remains.
The interior cut about and converted but a single octagonal
crown-post has lived on over the hall. Finally the GLOBE HOTEL,
with fronts to the Tuesday Market and King Street. Its early
C18 credentials often used to promote an attribution to Henry
Bell, but this is hard to see. Colourwashed brick. Three storeys
in five bays. Much added to in the C19 and entirely C20 inside.

FERRY STREET runs from here to the river. At the end the
CROWN AND MITRE, a late C16 building heavily rebuilt. It has
a mid-C19 pub front, and two cross wings, one C18, the other
(to the s) with a blocked C16 basket arch. At the entrance to
COMMON STAITHE QUAY stands the PILOT OFFICE, 1864,
red brick, with a little three-bay loggia to the ground floor and
a tower, square below, octagonal above. The office still with

its fittings. The square is a pleasant open space with some residential building to the N of 1989–90, which does no harm.
PAGE STAIR LANE returns to the Tuesday Market.

GAYWOOD. *See* p. 354.

KIRBY BEDON

2000

St ANDREW. Mostly of 1876, the year of the first restoration. The
Perp windows all 1876, so too the chancel arch and roofs. In
1884 *R. M. Phipson* rebuilt the tower (see his spherical triangles
to the ringing chamber) and the S porch; the first S porch originally of 1479. There is however a genuine Norman S doorway.
It has one order of colonnettes rising to a crocket capital (E) and
a cushion capital (W). Square imposts and a roll-moulded round
arch. – FONT. Octagonal, panelled stem with trefoil niches,
bowl with two ogee-headed panels to each side. Early C15. –
SOUTH DOOR. C13 planks, with bold, large iron hinges with
strapwork and a rectangular lock plate with circular ring bars.
The ironwork more mid-C12. – NORTH DOOR. C13 also, but
simple. – COMMUNION RAIL. Later C17, with dumb-bell balusters. – STAINED GLASS. Original bits in the S windows and one
N window. E window has a Good Shepherd, by *Jones & Willis* of
London, 1937. – MONUMENTS. In the chancel a brass with a
heart and inscribed scrolls, but no name or date; C15. – Brass to
William Dussyng †1505 and wife, in nave. Figures depicted
naked under their shrouds. – Robert Sheppard †1600 and wife,
Anne. Alabaster tablet with kneeling figures facing one another
under a strapwork achievement. – Francis Cremer †1730. Good
architectural surround. – Tomb slab of Richard M. Phipson
(1827–84), the architect, responsible for nearly a hundred church
restorations in East Anglia. – HARVEY MAUSOLEUM, in the
churchyard. 1868 for Sir Robert John Harvey of Crown Point
Hall, who shot himself in 1870 after the collapse of the Crown
Bank. Gabled with an arched entrance.

St MARY. Ruins opposite St Andrew. Round tower and parts of
the walls of nave and chancel. The C13 round tower has a C14
belfry stage. Tower arch blocked and a small C15 doorway
inserted.

THE OLD RECTORY, Woods End Road. Early Georgian, five
bays, two and a half storeys, red brick, doorway with pediment
on unfluted columns fitted with Ionic capitals. Open string
staircase with three turned balusters to each tread and a ramped
and wreathed handrail. The WALLED GARDEN made from
materials salvaged from the demolition of Kirby Old Hall in 1841.

A few outlying BARNS. HILL FARM has a late C17 BARN with a
timber frame sandwiched between brick gable-ends, a form widely
used for houses, and an early C18 BARN of flint with brick dressings. MANOR FARM, ½ m. SE of the church, has a BARN dated
1693, with up-market shaped gables. The shaped gable to the N
transept entrance is C20. Two tiers of purlins inside, the upper
tier clasped. Another BARN dated 1887 imitates the gables.

KIRBY CANE

ALL SAINTS. Anglo-Saxon round tower. At the foot remains of
the typical lesenes or pilaster strips. One-light bell-openings and
a later crenellated parapet. Narrow, low, semicircular tower
arch. Late Norman s doorway with one order of colonnettes.
The shafts decorated with chevron and spiral cable designs.
Zigzag arch. Also continuous zigzag along the inner order. This
is set at r. angles to the wall surface. Hoodmould with unusual
flowers, almost a pre-ballflower form. Beast's head in the apex.
Nave and chancel with a number of windows characteristic of
c. 1300–10 (cusped intersecting and cusped Y-tracery). In the
chancel on the s side two windows higher up. They could be
Norman completely altered (the E one not shown in Ladbroke's
drawing of c. 1823). In the N aisle C13 lancet windows, but the
window and hipped roof near the w end belong to a remodelling of 1758, and the eaves have a brick dentil cornice. The
chancel s roof clad with Cumberland slate. Vestry against N
chancel wall added in 1738 for Sir Charles Turner (tablet inside).
The arcade is so rough that it cannot be in any original state.
The slight double chamfers of the arches and the octagonal piers
would match the intersecting etc. tracery, and as the aisle is anyway much too wide for a minor C13 job the lancet windows are
presumably re-set. The arcade has three bays and is followed by
the two-bay N vestry. The E arch of this is blocked, the other
houses the organ. The aisle has a coved ceiling, the chancel a
plaster domed ceiling with diagonal ribs. Both must be of the
C18 or early C19. Apart from this the interior is unrestored. C13
scissor-braced nave roof. The former rood stairs rise from the
sill of a s window, suggesting that the lower part of the stair was
removed with the rood screen at the Reformation, and the window inserted. – FONT. Against the stem eight shafts. Against the
underside of the bowl eight heads (the hairstyle of one is typical
of c. 1360–80). Against the bowl shields in cusped fields. – SOUTH
DOOR. Mid-C12 iron straps to the hinges, with split curls. –
PULPIT. Jacobean and hexagonal. – COMMUNION RAIL. Later
C17, with turned dumb-bell balusters. – STAINED GLASS. In the
N aisle lancet †1869, Christ the Shepherd. The two-light window next E †1895, Christ and the Virgin, very pictorial. Both
good. – MONUMENT. Rough C16 tomb-chest with shields in
the chancel, said to commemorate Jon Copeldike †1593. –
Elizabeth Catelyne †1681, broken segmental pediment on Ionic
columns.

KIRBY CANE HALL. Next to the church. Built for the Catline
family, a late Georgian s front of seven bays and three storeys
with a porch on unfluted columns and Doric pilasters. This
added by Lord Berners after 1800 to a house otherwise of the
C17, to which four-light mullioned and transomed windows to
the E and w gable-heads testify. They have segmental pediments. Moulded platbands to both floors of the returns. Two
further brick mullioned and transomed windows to the E face of
the two-and-a-half-storey rear range. As one enters from the s

the two principal ground-floor rooms are separated by a passage leading to the two-storey staircase hall. Both rooms with good C18 fireplaces. The oak staircase is dated 1642: closed string, heavy turned newels and balusters.

Close by to the E a SUMMERHOUSE of the late C17. Two storeys, also brick, square, with castellation. On the ground floor an arched entrance to the S flanked by arched windows, all with square brick hoods. Above and to the returns is a curious framework of sunk brick panels separated by platbands and pilaster strips, and over the entrance a four-light altered window.

ROW FARMHOUSE, Yarmouth Road. Shaped E and W gables, lobby-entrance plan, renewed casements to three-bay S front. The reeded doorcase with corner paterae of a type hugely popular in the early C19.

WELL TERRACE. By *Tayler & Green*, 1949–50, for the Loddon District Council (*see* Introduction, p. 165). Two straight colour-washed terraces, knitting together the scattered village. Nice screens between the two-storey houses, of metal trellises and brick walls with wooden trellises. The upper windows arranged more closely than below, now almost all of uPVC.

KIRSTEAD

ST MARGARET. S doorway of *c.* 1190. One order of colonnettes, one capital with waterleaf. Pointed arch with two slight chamfers. The fabric of the nave as a whole is of the same date though the windows are Victorian restorations (two-light plate tracery), by *H. W. Hayward*, who built the tower and chancel in 1864, the latter with an apse, both of knapped flint. Nave roof 1864. – MONUMENTS. A number of Kerrison tablets.

KIRSTEAD HALL, opposite the church. A very fine Jacobean front, formerly with a date panel 1614. Probably built for Thomas Spooner who was certainly the owner in 1626. Red brick with blue brick diaper. Very flat E-plan, the S front with three stepped gables, the smaller middle one over the porch. The E projection is slightly later than the rest. The porch has polygonal corner shafts and a four-centred doorway under a pediment. Two stepped gables to the back. Two storeys with attics increasing to two and a half storeys in the wings. Mullioned and transomed windows up to seven lights, mostly with pediments. On the S front the upper window r. of the porch is late C20. Of the chimney-shafts some are still round and decorated as a hundred years before. The chimneypieces inside all brick and four-centred, the staircase has turned balusters and acorns on top of the newels and some C17 panelling remains. The internal planning is of a hall with a passage to the service rooms, but the 'new fashion' in building left this unexpressed on the symmetrical exterior; apart from the pediments this is all of the new order that one can find.

Of satellite buildings the FORECOURT WALLS are contemporary, so too are the STABLES to the E, with stepped gables.

DOVECOTE. At the bottom C17 brick, but rebuilt in the C18, octagonal with an octagonal lantern and ogee cap (of fibreglass).

KIRSTEAD HOUSE FARMHOUSE, ½ m. SW. C17 lobby-entrance house with a timber frame clad with brick. Two storeys in four bays. A small ground-floor room has a plaster ceiling – a surprise that – with a centre rose surrounded by garlands and with angels in the spandrels. It might be of 1654, the date of an upper room overmantel. Roof of clasped purlin type with curved wind-braces.

WALNUT TREE FARMHOUSE, Seething Road. A small C16 timber-framed house of two storeys, with a cross wing added which has the date 1613. Various windows, altered in 1970s, but some mullioned windows remain of diamond or sunk-quadrant section depending on which part they light. The C17 additions included the clasped purlin roof.

Nos. 1–2 and Nos. 3–4 WINDETT FARM COTTAGES, Seething Road, are both early C17 timber-framed houses with clasped purlin roofs and a lobby-entrance plan, altered variously.

GREEN MAN HOUSE, ⅞ m. S, at junction of Kirstead Green and Green Man Lane, formerly a public house. An attractive composition of the early C18 (the date 1716 used to be on the façade) with three low shaped gables along the front and three to the back, the latter enveloped by later building.

COUNCIL HOUSES. A small group of four by *Tayler & Green*, E of the last, Nos. 13–19 Green Man Lane. 1950. Standard Tayler & Green, two storeys, still colourwashed in pale green, fawn, mustard and pink. On these architects' work for the Loddon District Council, *see* Introduction, p. 165.

LANGFORD

In the Stanford Battle Zone (*see* Introduction, p. 14)

The church is surrounded by a chain-link fence and the village demolished.

ST ANDREW. The tower collapsed *c.* 1764. The church now consists of a rendered nave and chancel. It is Norman. There are two original windows, one in the N, one in the S wall of the nave, both blocked and only visible from inside; also the S doorway and the chancel arch. The doorway has two orders of shafts with cushion capitals, but one shaft to the l. with elementary volutes. The arch has a chain of bobbin motifs and two orders of chevron. The chancel arch is remarkably wide. It has three orders to the W, with cushion capitals, and rolls and bobbin motifs in the arch. Three-light intersecting E window. The restoration was in 1888 at the expense of Lord Amherst (both roofs, and general work). The corrugated iron covering the windows removed 1993–4 and the roofs retiled. – FONT. Octagonal, big, with good C14 tracery motifs. – MONUMENT. Sir Jacob Garrard †1666, but only erected *c.* 1730, by *Christopher Horsnaile Sen.* for £400. Semi-reclining effigy and behind, to the l. and r. of a big urn, the two standing figures of Sir Jacob's son and grandson, both in Roman dress. Big architectural background. A fine piece. – Sir Nicholas Garrard †1727, a plain ledger. – SOUTH DOOR. Woodwork and ironwork of C15.

3000

LANGLEY

ST MICHAEL. C14 w tower (see the arch towards the nave) with cusped Y-tracery to the bell-openings, but with a three-light Perp w window. Nave with early C19 three-light windows under brick four-centred arches. Chancel remodelled in 1803. The E window is of brick, arched, with Y-tracery. C14 s priest's door. The interior of the chancel re-Gothicized in the later C19. In the nave s wall a very strange oblong recess with a C14 hoodmould on headstops. It is secured by an iron grille. The nave has a good C15 arch-braced roof, with wall-posts and bosses. – FONT. Big, simple, Perp. Panelled stem, bowl with quatrefoils. – BOX PEWS. Tapered off at the w end to allow for sufficient space round the font. – STAINED GLASS. In the E window four French scenes, C15, bought in 1802 by the Beauchamp Proctor family. Many smaller foreign roundels etc. in other windows. The Norwich merchant J.C. Hampp (*see* Introduction, p. 70) imported the glass, which was installed by *S.C. Yarington*, 1803 and 1820. – In the w window three large early C19 figures, and smaller ones by *Robert Allen*. – BRASS to Robert Berney †1628. – MONUMENTS to the Beauchamp Proctors of Langley Park. Sir William †1773. Graceful female figure by an urn, against an obelisk. – Sir Thomas †1827. White marble, Gothic. Relief with his figure rising out of a Gothic tomb-chest to be received by an angel. Both wear long flowing robes. – Emma and Julia †1827 and 1828. In the tympanum at the top cherubs' heads.

LANGLEY PARK SCHOOL. A country house with which *Matthew Brettingham* may have been involved, although probably not from the start. The house was built for Mr Recorder Berney. It was described as newly built in 1737, and in 1739 as 'lately built in the newest manner'. In 1740, according to his son, Matthew Brettingham did not claim acquaintance with Berney. Berney sold in 1739 to George Proctor (who had previously lived for some time in Venice) in order to clear his debts, and Proctor in turn left the house to his nephew William Beauchamp who had to attach the Proctor name as a condition of inheritance. That was in 1744. A painting of 1742 shows the house without its corner towers, so it has been suggested that Brettingham's involvement went only as far as adding them, the attic storey and the wings for George Proctor. A motive for such a remodelling so soon after construction might be the usual one of a new owner's changed requirements, or as the result of a criticism in 1736 that the new building was so bad that it ought to be pulled down. The walls between the centre and the towers and the stretches on the sides between them are thicker than the others, as they would be if they started as external walls. *John Sanderson*

was involved in the 1750s, probably with internal alterations; his
bill is from December 1757.

The resulting house is a stylistic hybrid. The red brick, the
banded Doric pilasters which carry an entablature complete
only over the pilaster capitals, and the elevation, of two storeys
of equal height and a third treated as an attic above the entablature, are all typical of the turn-of-the-century idiom epitomized by Buckingham House. The central N doorway, of stone, is
also typical of that style: Ionic three-quarter columns set against
a rusticated background carry a broken pediment. What is
unusual is the extension of the central block, of 1:3:1 bays to the
S, but seven evenly spaced bays to the N, by means of square   92
angle projections. A Palladian character, but not Palladian proportions, is imparted by the extra pyramid-roofed storey added
to each projection, so that they read like angle turrets. The plain
parapet and under-emphasized three-bay central pediments
front and back presumably belong to this remodelling.

The short, low quadrant links to the SW and SE pavilions,
originally of seven by three bays, also belong to this remodelling. The four-column Greek Doric S entrance porch was added
in c. 1829–30. The pavilions rebuilt in altered form by *Anthony
Salvin* in the late 1840s. The extension of the garden front has
short screen walls extruding from the corner turrets, with statues in pedimented niches.

INTERIOR. Inside the house the great thrill is the plasterwork.
ENTRANCE HALL with a domed circular centre. Four allegorical
figures. Also four medallions with heads in profile. The STAIR-
CASE to the r. has wall decoration to the first-floor landing,
again with large medallions bearing profile busts. The stair rises
in a single flight, but splits in two near the top: three twisted
balusters to each tread and carved tread-ends; ramped and
wreathed handrail and dado panelling. In the SALOON (staff
room) there are two large stucco high-relief panels of outstanding quality. That above the chimneypiece represents the Lapiths
and the Centaurs, the one opposite the Departure of Helen
(after Guido Reni). Also smaller mythological reliefs above the
doors l. and r. of the large reliefs and two large putti on the sides
of the pediment above the principal entrance in the long wall.
Between the windows oval mirrors with four standing nudes.
Decorative framing and ceiling plasterwork typical of immigrant
continental stuccoists. To the l. and r. of the saloon are the
BREAKFAST ROOM, with two arches towards the serving space,
and the RED ROOM, with yet more Rococo stucco.

The LIBRARY in the E wing has a ceiling with Rococo tendril   90
trails composed round an oval relief of Diana and Actaeon, a
somewhat artless composition compared to those in the Saloon.
Entablature with delicate relief decoration in the frieze. Since
the early C19 it has been attributed to *Charles Stanley*, the Dane
who came to England in 1727 and stayed until 1746. He made
large funeral monuments as well as stucco reliefs, and might
well be responsible for the reliefs in the Saloon at Langley Park
as well. The library has a Venetian window to the E and a

1 Entrance hall
2 Staircase
3 Saloon (staff room)
4 Breakfast room
5 Red Room
6 Library
7 Ballroom
8 Dining room
9 Kitchen

30 m
100 ft

Langley Park. Plan

canted bay to the N. Adjoining it is the BALLROOM, with thick and luscious Victorian decoration in a Baroque style, another of the many instances in which Victorian artists and patrons showed their appreciation of the past by endeavouring to outdo it.

A mystery is the DINING ROOM, w of the Breakfast Room. Externally it is clearly part of the Victorian alterations, but internally it is original Georgian work much more restrained than that of the other rooms. Yet it is in the Holkham-Kent-Brettingham style. Could it be re-erected by *Salvin* and originally have been in the other wing, which is now all kitchens and offices? Centre with domed circle in the ceiling. A big star in the shallow dome. At one end a screen of fluted Ionic columns defining the serving space. White marble fireplace with three heads.

The first floor is divided by a wide corridor leading from the main to the subsidiary staircase. The room above the entrance hall has a delightful ceiling by *Adrien de Clermont*, with his usual frolics, monkeys, an owl, etc. *c*. 1750 for Sir James Dashwood, second baronet.

STABLES. To the SE. Nine bays, the centre a raised archway, the rest blank. Parapet with ball finials. Converted to a teaching block. Built round three sides of a courtyard, very likely by *Brettingham*, *c*. 1746. The big modern windows are regrettable.

The PARK. *Capability Brown* was instructed in 1765 and drew a plan, which remains in the house. Various belts of trees round the boundaries and plantations within; much of it has now reverted to agriculture.

CROSS. The C15 village cross, which must have stood where the village was, was removed to a position SW of the house to mark the meeting of the boundaries of four parishes. It is a fine specimen with a slender square shaft against which, on very long shaft-like pedestals, stand four Saints. The top is missing.

LODGES. One pair, the THURTON LODGES, on the main Norwich road; the others, the CHEDGRAVE LODGES, to the S on the Chedgrave Road. Both are by *Soane*, designed in 1784 for Sir Thomas Beauchamp Proctor. The latter, erected only in 1790, take the form of a triumphal screen of gault brick with Portland stone dressings, a single tall archway flanked by lodge blocks with arched sashes to the front and arched recesses to the sides. To the l. and r. of the archway oval paterae, still an echo of Robert Adam. They were supplied by *Coade & Sealy*, as were the extraordinary chimneypots on the shoulders of the arch. On the lodges stand two handsome stone greyhounds as supporters with the motto '*Toujours Fidele*'. These by the mason *James Nelson*. What is on the other hand entirely Soane is the thinness of the mouldings, especially those on top of the lodge blocks.

The Thurton Lodges are small square single-storey blocks with pedimented gable-ends above a central recess containing two unfluted columns flanking an arched window and supporting a metope frieze, i.e. a more conventional composition. They are severe for their date, with a calculated economy of design and line that was to become a hallmark of Soane's mature style.

They are beautiful things, handled with faultless precision. Cast-iron GATES. Together the two lodges provide a precedent for Soane's Tyringham gateway (Buckinghamshire) of the 1790s. There is a design for a lodge on Avenue Road, commissioned from *George Davey* by Sir Thomas Proctor in 1871, but it seems not to have been built.

LANGLEY ABBEY. The abbey was a house of the Premonstratensian Canons. It was founded in 1195 and on an average consisted of fifteen to twenty canons. The site has been cleaned up by the County Council in stages from 1989.

The most substantial part of the ruins is the C13 CELLARIUM, i.e. the W range of the cloister. This is now a barn. The remaining features have been much altered. The range was divided into an oblong S part and a square N part. The former had quadripartite rib vaults carried on a row of five piers. The latter also had quadripartite rib vaults on one central pier, but the vaulting was reconstructed in brick in the C14 or C15. In the E wall, towards the cloister, the two-bay LAVATORIUM (with a central boss with an eagle grasping a bird) and also, in the thickness of the wall, a straight stairway up to the former upper floor. To the W two doorways. One leads to the former outer court, the other now leads into the C14 GATEHOUSE range, of which only the N wall stands.

Evidence of the CHURCH is scanty. It was an early C13 building with narrow aisles, square transepts, and a chancel with two chapels all ending in one straight line to the E. The S aisle seems the result of a change of mind during building. The space for it was taken off the cloister, which is thus not square. At the W end a tower was added in the C14, and N of transept and chapel an outer chapel. The remains at the W end are confusing, especially as the C13 W portal seems to have been re-erected in the W wall of the C14 W tower.

Of the CHAPTER HOUSE enough is visible to confirm that it was also of the early C13 and was six bays deep and three bays wide. It had quadripartite vaults of single-chamfered ribs. The entrance arch is pointed and cusped, i.e. of the late C13. Towards the E end of the S wall fragments of blank arcading survive. The capitals of the shafts have foliage. The dormitory was above the chapter house and extended to the S as usual. Below here indications of vaulting. Of the refectory little can be seen. To the E of the S part of the dormitory range at some distance Perp remains of the infirmary E wall. The range to the SW of the gatehouse range is probably C16, and formed part of the STABLES. Timber-framed with a jettied upper storey underbuilt in brick. Many patches and repairs. Thatched roof. The first-floor frame is mostly intact, with arched braces to the tie-beams, and a clasped purlin roof with curved wind-bracing.

ABBEY FARMHOUSE. *c.* 1800, red brick, two storeys with a three-bay S front with an open-pedimented doorcase.

STAITHE FARM, S of the Abbey on Langley Street. The HOUSE is early C18 with a four-bay N front, the storeys separated by a platband. The BARN immediately S, C17, brick, has a clasped purlin roof with curved wind-braces.

Near the church 100 yds NE of THE GRANGE is the best BARN. It is a C16 aisled barn of five bays with jowled aisle-posts support-ing the ties on arched braces. Clasped purlin roof with tension braces. Brick skin disguise.

HARDLEY ROAD and MONKS TERRACE. Two groups of council houses by *Tayler & Green*, 1949–50 and 1954–5, the one single-storeyed and colourwashed, the other a two-storeyed terrace on a curve. The latter consists of three semi-detached houses with weatherboarded upper floors.

LARLING

9080

ST ETHELBERT. Perp W tower for which bequests were made in 1473–94, the first 'ad fabrica nova campanilis'. It was restored in 1889 for £230. Four stages, two-light Perp belfry windows. Sumptuous late Norman S doorway protected by a porch rebuilt in 1898. Two orders of shafts, variously patterned. They have foliated rings. Jambs and arch with all kinds of Geometrical decoration. Chancel and S aisle of *c.* 1300, though the E window is from the 1867 restoration. Although restored the N nave wall is the most substantial Norman element. In the aisle hand-somely traceried lozenge windows and a C14 piscina and stepped sedilia divided simply by stone arms. The chancel has more usual tracery and a small double piscina. Its dividing shaft incidentally is Norman. The S arcade has three bays, octagonal piers and double-chamfered arches. Roof of 1867. Another restoration in 1895 provides most of the fittings. – FONT. A square early C13 block with chamfered corners. – STAINED GLASS. Old bits arranged in the W window. – E window, 1901, a Crucifixion, probably by *Clayton & Bell*.

LARLINGFORD FARMHOUSE and MANOR FARMHOUSE seem to be C17 buildings rebuilt in the late C18. The former has its original timber-framed and clay lump range to the rear. SHRUBB FARM COTTAGES are also late C17, timber-framed and with rendered clay lump infill. Privy tower at the back. Clasped purlin roof. If the clay lump is C17, then it must be among the earliest known, but the normal practice was to replace wattle and daub infill with the clay in the early C19.

LAUNDITCH

9010

A linear earthwork consisting of a bank with a ditch on its W once ran for 3¾ m. from the source of the Nar S to a tributary of the Wensum, serving over much of this distance as a parish bound-ary between Beeston, Bittering, Longham and Wendling. It has mostly been destroyed, but one stretch survives in a denuded state immediately N of its intersection with the main E–W Roman road through the county (i.e. 2½ m. W of Gressenhall on the Litcham road). The maximum height from base of ditch to crest of bank is 7½ ft and the maximum width of the monument is *c.* 60 ft. Excavation of the intersection in 1992 showed that the ditch underlay the Roman road and that the monument belongs to the pre-Roman Iron Age. (AR)

1010
LENWADE
1½ m. WSW of Alderford

WATERMILL. Part of a picturesque group by Lenwade Bridge over the River Wensum. C19. Whitewashed brick, three storeys, eight bays of sashes with the lucam set to the right, and a two-storey, two-bay MILLER'S HOUSE attached to the W gable. The actual BRIDGE was a triple-arched brick structure with a ramped parapet by *Matthew Brettingham*, 1741. Demolished 1993 and replaced by a steel bridge.

Brettingham's bridge is illustrated in the pub sign of the BRIDGE PUBLIC HOUSE. A late C18 brick building, colourwashed. Two storeys in seven bays.

LENWADE STREET runs off opposite the pub and has a number of minor buildings. LENWADE MILLS is an early C19 brick-built watermill in three storeys. To the W is a lower MILL HOUSE, same date. WENSUM HOUSE, late C18, two storeys in three bays, Doric doorcase. The WHITE HOUSE has a double pile. The N wing is the early C18 part, two storeys in five bays. Central door under a canopy, rusticated quoins. The S wing early C19. Finally THE GOTHIC HOUSE, an early C19 flint Gothick confection with brick dressings under a hipped roof. Two storeys in three bays. Y-traceried door, Y-tracery windows, in three parts.

9000
LETTON

ALL SAINTS. Scanty foundations, ½ m. SE of Letton Hall.

LETTON HALL. By *Sir John Soane*, 1783–9 for Brampton Dillingham. Soane is responsible for a great many houses in East Anglia in the 1780s, a time when he was consolidating his position after his disappointing period with the Bishop of Derry in Ireland. It is also a period when his mature style evolved: spare, refined Neoclassical, thin details, recessed arches. These appear at Letton, Soane's début with country houses, not yet as fully worked as at Shotesham Park or the Langley Lodges, but present nevertheless. Letton is not a large house, five by five bays, two and a half storeys, with a lower W service court extending a considerable distance. Gault brick, with arched windows on the ground floor and first floors. The entrance (S) façade, including the porch, is a later addition, but the two Tuscan porch columns are original, though re-set. The original porch was elliptical. At the E end of the N front a C19 bay was added to the drawing room. Inside, fine staircase hall, oblong with apsed ends. The stairs are formed of cantilevered stone treads with a wrought-iron baluster of simple but effective design.

Some stucco. Skylight. Some discreet plasterwork also in other rooms, and some fireplaces by *William Lane Sen.* of Norwich.

Soane's OUTBUILDINGS are an early example of the axial arrangement he favoured for other houses, e.g. Shotesham.* Symmetrically arranged in a line W of the house are the service block, stables and walled garden, all of red brick rather than the gault brick of the house, reflecting their lower status. The SERVICES have three ranges round an open court, the S front of ten bays in two storeys, with round-headed windows. The STABLES (altered in the late C19) also comprise three blocks, the W one forming part of the walled garden yet further W. Two-storey centre block divided into three bays by thin pilasters and with a central pediment. Round-headed cast-iron windows and a clock tower. Side wings mainly single-storeyed. The WALLED GARDEN is more recognizably from the time of the house: the two main entrances have pilasters inside segmental arches, typically Soanian.

About 30 yds N of the house is an octagonal GARDEN HOUSE of 1882, with four stained-glass windows depicting the seasons. Further N still, at the end of the garden, a late C19 SUMMER-HOUSE with three three-light Perp windows, no doubt reused from the church, all rather overgrown at the time of writing. Another 220 yds N is a circular brick DOVECOTE with its nesting boxes, late C18.

LEXHAM HALL *see* EAST LEXHAM

LEZIATE   6010

ALL SAINTS. In 1960 the ruins were hardly recognizable, reported to be by the road to Pott Row, about ¼ m. N of the B-road, but in 1994 could not be found.

LITCHAM   8010

ALL SAINTS. Brick W tower of 1669 (its predecessor destroyed by fire 1636), the inscription says by (i.e. paid for by) Matthew Halcott, a rich tanner. The brick is laid in Flemish bond. W window with intersecting tracery. Bell-openings with Y-tracery. The buttresses only go as far as the ringing-chamber floor. The W wall of the church as it was before the fire is still visible inside. It has a small doorway and a three-light window with intersecting tracery, i.e. after *c.* 1310, but just as possible a century later. The other windows are Perp, except for those of the chancel, which seem a renewal of about 1800 in the intersecting pattern then popular. Perp also the arcades, see their typical piers with polygonal projections, bigger to nave and aisles, more delicate

---

* I am grateful to Ptolemy Dean for pointing this out.

to the arches. The multiple-moulded arches are also typically Perp. The piers could be by the same mason who made the piers at Weasenham St Peter. The arcades have bearded heads as stops to the hoodmoulds. They repeat in the angles between the arcades and chancel arch, which was constructed with the arcades. The church was in fact re-dedicated in 1412, the new work associated with this being the nave, aisles and chancel. The one octagonal pier probably relates to an earlier nave arcade. Main restoration 1850. Roofs repaired 1968–78, having been plastered over in 1791 (the chancel roof still is), tower roof 1962, windows partly renewed 1979–80. W gallery partly of cast iron, 1853.

FONT. Octagonal, Perp, with hung-up shields in cusped panels. – SCREEN. With eight paintings of female Saints to N, and eight male Saints S, according to the seating arrangement of men and women in the church. The males include the local figures Walstan and William of Norwich (cf. Loddon); also, three defaced panels on each leaf of the doors (DP). The date is 1436. Big, cusped and subcusped ogee arches and much good panel tracery. Restored and painted 1901–3. – PULPIT. C15, hexagonal, with Perp tracery. It was bought in a London antique shop in 1890 by Rev. Keppel, and a stair was made up for it from salvaged parts. The fluted newels were originally part of a font cover. – STALLS. Two C15 MISERICORDS with defaced heads (sanctuary). – BOX PEWS of 1877. – COMMUNION RAIL. C17. With turned balusters. – CHEST. Pretty front with small blank arches in two tiers containing tracery of spherical triangle type, separated by decorative buttresses. Frame with big rosettes, etc. It must be C14. – STAINED GLASS. S aisle E, †1850 with a St John; S aisle †1851, Christ with St Mary. Both by *Ward & Nixon*. – N aisle E end has fragments of early C15 glass in tracery head. – LEDGER STONES. Thirty-two in all, spread about, mostly C17. A helpful plan of them, with drawings, hangs on the N nave wall, done in 1901.

LITCHAM HALL. The date 1781 appears on a rainwater head, but details inside appear earlier and the hall is not aligned with the main door, suggesting a re-fronting. However the house is not on a map of 1760. Built for Nicholas Raven, who died in 1801. The main front is to the S, set back from the road. Red brick, two storeys in five bays and with a raised middle bay terminating in an open pediment. This is odd. What has happened is that the original three-storey house was cut down in 1854 for Peter Raven, leaving the central pediment the only testament to the original height. Moreover the house was at first much larger and the present block is the remains of a U-plan building, minus its projecting wings. Pretty and unusual modillions of 1854 adorn the central pediment and the main eaves cornice. They look like curved triglyphs. The entrance door, also 1854, has a tripartite surround and a fanlight, just unusual. Platband between the main floors. The returns present gable-ends of the service wings to view. One-storey addition to the l., a greenhouse to the r. Plain interiors and stick-baluster staircase which would be early for 1781, dull for 1854.

PRIORY FARMHOUSE, at the S end of the village at the bottom of Church Street. Matthew Halcott's house (*see* church above). A former chapel and, probably, hermitage, converted into a farmhouse. It seems to be *c.* 1320–30, with C17 alterations. Angle buttresses at the angles. The N side has two shaped gables and brick-framed windows from the C17 work. S side with C19 casements, the centre one with Y-tracery. The main S door is C14, with undercut arch-mouldings. The C14 chapel has two crown-post roof trusses, with one octagonal post remaining. In the C17 part, two of four queenpost trusses remain. To the N also evidence of a jettied timber frame. Good C17 staircase with heavy square balusters.

VILLAGE. To the N of Priory Farmhouse SCHOOL HOUSE, C18, of brick, with pebble quoins. Doorway with pediment on Corinthian columns. Seven bays in two storeys, sashes. The two new ground-floor N windows replace a shop display window. The SCHOOL has a new building, in this context thoroughly odd-looking in its mid-C20 idiom. To the N of School House and opposite it two more Georgian brick houses. Both have pedimented doorways. One, of four bays, is BLENHEIM HOUSE, *c.* 1840. Clasping pilasters. The other, of five bays, is the POST OFFICE, later C18. Rusticated quoins and a platband. At the N end of Church Street, THE BULL INN. C17 timber frame with brick gable-ends carrying the stacks, and C19 windows. The STABLE BLOCK fronts Mileham Road: C18.

LITTLE CRESSINGHAM

8000

ST ANDREW. The church is partly in ruins, and all the more dramatic, especially as one has to pass through the ruined nave to reach the covered parts. The burst tower stood in a SW position and served as a porch, possibly coming down in 1781 when a faculty was issued for the new brick wall dividing ruined from whole bays, although the church was described as ruinous before that. The W bay of the nave is also open to the sky. Perp aisle windows and Perp arcades of four bays. The arcades have finely moulded projections without capitals to nave and aisle looking very like those at Attleborough. The S aisle has wall-arches embracing the windows, which extended also round the W end. The W wall has blank flushwork externally in front of the N aisle and a tall base of chequer flushwork below the large blocked nave window. The flushwork cheats in using plaster instead of freestone. The chancel is Dec, see the chancel arch and the E window, roughly reconstructed in the C19. The N aisle is also mainly a C19 reconstruction. – STALLS. With poppy-heads. – STAINED GLASS. N chancel window by *Powell*, 1855. – MONUMENT. Big tablet to first Viscount Clermont †1806.

CLERMONT HALL, 1 m. S. Long, whitewashed Georgian house, by *Sir Robert Taylor* in 1777–8, but virtually rebuilt in 1812 by *William Pilkington* for T.H. Fortescue, second Viscount Clermont. S front regular; three bays either side of a full-height

canted centre bay. N front not quite regular, with a segmental
portico of heavy unfluted columns in front of a canted bay containing the entrance – a curious motif. A lot of the interior had
to be gutted in the early 1970s because of dry rot, but the rooms
were anyway altered between the wars.

WINDMILL. Tall tower mill combined with a water wheel, a
unique arrangement. Built c. 1821. Two pairs of stones were
driven by water and on the floor above two more powered by
wind. Cap and sails are missing. Restoration began in 1981 and
continues at a snail's pace (*Norfolk Windmills Trust*). Next to it is
a small brick PUMPHOUSE with a pointed door and Y-tracery
windows still with its Bramah three-throw pump driven by
another water wheel. The building is early C19 and was built to
convey water to the gardens of the newly rebuilt Clermont Hall,
1 m. away. This it did until 1934. Restored by the *Norfolk
Windmills Trust* in 1989.

BARROWS. At least four round barrows survive of a once much
larger group. One, now no longer visible, contained a rich burial
of a male crouched skeleton with an amber bead necklace,
gold-covered beads, a bronze knife and a dagger. Bell Hill is one
of the largest bowl barrows in Norfolk (*see* also Hilborough,
p. 401). (JW)

8010   LITTLE DUNHAM

ST MARGARET. Much good C13 work. S doorway with hoodmould on headstops and a good head in a diagonally placed
quatrefoil above. Lancet windows in nave and chancel S. Angle
piscina with a shaft of the C13, with an arm-rest for the combined
sedilia. Of the former three-bay N chancel chapel, really an extension of the nave aisle, only one bay remains, with a late C13 E
window (three stepped lancet lights under one arch), probably
re-set from the original E wall. Quatrefoil piers, depressed two-
centred arches with two hollow chamfers. (A little ornamental
PAINTING in the arches.) The W respond has an excellent head
with horns and big leaves l. and r. N arcade of three taller bays,
also with quatrefoil piers. Circular seats around the piers.
Double-hollow-chamfered arches. Dec the restored N aisle side-
windows. Perp W tower with diagonal buttresses to W, a three-
light W window and nice square quatrefoil sound-holes. A will
of 1431 left money for the building of the 'new' tower and
another in 1449 to 'edify' it. Perp S windows. C19 E window. –
FONT. Octagonal, Perp, with shields in quatrefoils and heads on
the underside. – SCULPTURE. Fragment of an Anglo-Saxon
cross-shaft with interlace. – MONUMENT. Thomas Rogers
†1758. Tablet with cartouche against an obelisk and a cherub's
head at the bottom.

OLD RECTORY. A datestone 1731 announces an enlargement of
the C17 brick house, and in 1783 the rear wing and staircase
added: turned balusters. Four-bay front fitted with C20 sashes.
Pilasters round the door.

DUNHAM LODGE, ¾ m. E of the church. A simple, indeed plain,
red brick house built for Edward Parry in 1784–5. Two storeys
above a basement with the central doorway reached by an outer
staircase curving up in two arms. A parapet conceals the roof.
Five by three bays. N return with a tall bow. Nice minor contemporary interior, including a stone staircase with iron balusters.
Drawing room with pilasters and fluted columns. Contemporary
STABLES with seven bays of arched recesses with Diocletian
windows. Three centre bays advanced under a pediment.

OBELISK, ⅜ m. SE. Erected by John Drostier in 1814 to commemorate peace and Admiral Nelson. Brick with stone dressings. It
belonged with the demolished Curd's Hall in nearby Little
Fransham and was visually linked with it by an avenue of trees.

LITTLE ELLINGHAM   0090

ST PETER. Unbuttressed SW tower with porch and quatrefoiled
sound-holes, C13 or early C14. This is the only part still with
mostly medieval fabric, as a fire in 1867 destroyed the nave and
required repair to the chancel. Reconstructed in 1869 by *T. H.
& F. Healey*, apparently accurately but with the addition of a
vestry W of the tower. The details of the chancel point to *c.* 1310.
A tomb recess in the N wall. In the chancel a SHELF on three
heads and below it a Norman SLAB, reused. – FONT. Octagonal,
of porphyry; 1869. – STAINED GLASS. The E window depicts
the Ascension etc., in the style of *Preedy*, 1869. In a S nave window another Ascension, by *Kempe*, 1893.

LITTLE ELLINGHAM HALL. 1855, which is also the date of the
remarkable CLOCK TOWER with a domed top. It rises out of a
cruciform base developed as two dwellings with entrances in the
diagonals. Gault brick with red brick dressings.

LITTLE FRANSHAM   9010

ST MARY. The W tower fell in 1700, and the domestic, transomed
four-light window was then set in the W wall. In the apex of the
gable the date 1583. What does that refer to? In the nave tall
two-light windows with cusped Y-tracery, i.e. early C14. In the
chancel Dec reticulated tracery, see especially the charming
motif of a reticulation unit within a bigger one in the three-light
E window. But money was left in 1404 to make the two windows on the N side of the chancel (pairs of mouchettes with
daggers), indicating just how long Dec could last if the motive
was to imitate an existing style. In 1438 one William Martenet
left 40s. to make the S porch, which has an upper storey of brick
dated 1743. Nave roof with hammerbeams, longitudinal braces
and varied tracery in the spandrels above the hammerbeams.
The chancel roof is C17, complete with butt-purlins and wind-
bracing. – FONT. Square, early C13, with trefoiled arches to three
sides of the bowl and an oval panel with foliage on the fourth.

Colonnettes with cushion capitals provide support. – BENCHES. Reused traceried backs and ends with arm-rests.

FRANSHAM OLD HALL, ⅜ m. S. Handsome late C16 E gable with six blocked windows under moulded brick pediments. The external stack is suspicious, perhaps an addition, but it has a large panel with the arms of Elizabeth I framed by a broad vine border. A second stack has four octagonal shafts. The N (entrance) front reflects a major C18 remodelling although there is a C17 mullioned and transomed window among the five bays of three-light C18 equivalents. The doorway has a segmental pediment on carved consoles. Rear with an C18 outshut containing a good staircase: fluted newels and turned balusters, moulded handrail. The roof is C18 too, with staggered butt-purlins and collars.

FRANSHAM PLACE, formerly the rectory. Nice Georgian house of
107   c. 1800 of two and a half storeys in three bays under a hipped roof. Red brick with more costly gault brick to the façade. The ground-floor sashes set within arched recesses. Porch has pairs of unfluted columns formerly with Ionic capitals, now supporting an angular bald entablature. Low side bays either side with a sash each.

LITTLE MASSINGHAM

ST ANDREW. Dec the W tower, the aisle arcades (three bays, octagonal piers, double-hollow-chamfered arches), the S aisle E window with Curvilinear tracery, perhaps the S doorway (unless this is older), and the chancel arch. Chancel windows Dec, with a three-light reticulated E window. Most other windows Perp. Perp the S porch with flushwork panelling and angle buttresses. Clerestory walling of red chalk, a seldom-met building stone from the Hunstanton cliffs. Simple hammerbeam nave and chancel roofs; aisle roofs C19. *Thomas Jekyll* added the N vestry in 1857. – PULPIT. 1857. By *Thomas Jekyll*. Of stone, with naturalistic foliage. – MONUMENTS. Sir Robert L'Estrange †1517. Tomb-chest with cusped lozenges enclosing shields. In the top frame holes probably for protective metal hoops (moved to tower). – Also two tablets of c. 1648 and c. 1783.

LITTLE MASSINGHAM HOUSE. Queen Anne-style house, of two storeys and dormer attic in five bays, the centre three projecting under a pediment. 1904–5 by *Wimperis & Best* for Mrs E. W. Birkbeck. Red brick with Ancaster stone dressings. The terribly old-fashioned design was stipulated by Mrs Birkbeck. *The Builder* records that it was to be like Bixley Hall (demolished 1904) which the architects visited. Stone carving by *Jago* of London.

The LODGE on Station Road of the same time by the same architects. This is in the Edwardian Vernacular style. Three bays in one and a half storeys. The entrance is set in a curved recess. Mansard roof with an outsized gabled dormer containing two windows each with their own hipped roof. All very jolly.

LITTLE MELTON *1000*

St Mary and All Saints. All of the early C14, although the
roofs and floors re-done during the restoration of 1896. Flint
with stone trim. w tower with a Perp w window but Y-tracery in
the bell-openings. Y-tracery also in the chancel, though the two-
light E window has reticulated tracery. Again Y-tracery in the s
aisle E window. The other s and the N windows have the same
tracery but with lozenge vesicas under four-centred arches and
look Perp. But the arcades are again of the early C14; four bays
to the s, two to the N. Octagonal piers, double-chamfered arches
with hollows to the outer faces (on the N side one chamfer and
one hollow chamfer). Responds with big bossy leaf brackets. –
FONT. A very large specimen of the octagonal Purbeck type of
the C13, i.e. the type with two very shallow pointed arches on
each side. The stem consists of a central column surrounded by
eight colonnettes. – SCREENS. C15 chancel screen, painted and
with broad one-light ogee-headed divisions and panel tracery
over. – Also remains of the dado of another screen reused in the
pulpit and stall-fronts and partly at the W end of the s aisle. –
WALL PAINTINGS. C14. Warning against Idle Gossip: two
women seated on a bench, their heads close together (N wall; cf.
Colton); fragmentary St Christopher (N wall); more in the N
aisle, including foliate scrollwork. On the chancel E wall an
Annunciation. (DP) – MONUMENTS. Tablets to Richard and
Bridget Scottowe †1655 and †1718 on chancel N wall. Black
and white marble (attributed by Jon Bayliss to *Martin Morley*).
– Four engraved copper plates below to more of the Scottowe
family of silversmiths. – s wall monument to Thomas and Mary
Johnson, 1718.
Windmill, ¼ m. E. A stump of a brick tower mill, probably of the
1830s. The first miller, Thomas Burrows, recorded in 1836.
Manor Farmhouse, ¾ m. E on School Lane. The brick is still
English bond, which for Norfolk means only earlier than *c.* 1700,
but the stepped end-gables and polygonal angle-shafts suggest
c. 1600. So too do the sunk-quadrant mouldings of the ground-
floor tie-beam to the l. room. Early C19 stick-baluster staircase.
Grey Cottage, Green Lane. A C16 timber-framed hall house
floored in the C17 and altered in the C19.

LODDON *3090*

Holy Trinity. Built towards the end of the C15, *see* below. A
large, alas much restored, church whose length is emphasized
by the clerestory windows, following each other almost without
interruption. There are fifteen of them on either side and they
have brick relieving arches. Brick is in fact the material of the
walls, which are flint-faced. The chancel projects by one bay
beyond the chapels and ends in a very tall five-light window
with a four-centred arch. Large three-light Perp aisle windows,
as mechanical as the E window owing to the restorations of

1870–1900. Aisles as well as clerestory are embattled. On the N side embattled square rood stair-turret. The W tower has flush-work panelling on base and battlements, the latter mentioned in wills of 1500–4. The showpiece of the church is the S porch, added slightly later. It is two-storeyed and has a three-stage polygonal stair-turret in the NW corner. The front is panelled in flushwork. Base frieze of stone carved with encircled quatre-foils, etc. Decorated buttresses. Decorated entrance spandrels (with six shields). Decorated frieze above the entrance. Two two-light windows and a niche with a group of the Trinity under an elaborate miniature vaulted canopy. Flushwork-panelled battlements. Inside is a tierceron star vault. In the S doorway one order of mouldings with flat arched panels, the two meeting at the apex distinguished by little crocketed gables. The interior has tall seven-bay arcades and no division between nave and chancel. The piers have a lozenge shape with thin shafts to nave, aisles and arches. Only those towards the arches have capitals. Hammerbeam roof with collar-beams and solid carved spandrels.

FURNISHINGS. – FONT. William Benys left £3 6s. 8d. for the new font in 1487. On three traceried steps, the top step cross-shaped. Animals against the foot; a little higher, but still against the foot, the signs of the four Evangelists. Against the stem defaced (in 1642) figures. Against the bowl, also defaced, the Seven Sacraments in vaulted niches. – PULPIT. Large, of 1603, each panel with two slender blank arches under a detailed strap-work frieze. The stone base is C19. – SCREEN. The dado painted with scenes from the Life of Christ and the Martyrdom of St William of Norwich, an uncommon theme for screens. Also uncommon the fact that the scenes each have several figures against landscape backgrounds. Much defaced and partly redrawn. About 1520–30. The tracery cut away in the early C19. – BENCHES. Some old ones, with poppyheads, at the W end and in the porch. – COMMUNION RAIL. C17, with turned balusters, reused in the chancel stalls. – PAINTING. In the S aisle a very interesting painting showing Sir James Hobart, Attorney General to Henry VII, and his wife, kneeling. In the background the church of Loddon and a fortified bridge. The inscription records that he built the church and she the bridge of St Olave's. Restored 1972. The Hobarts lived at Hales Hall (see p. 376). – DOOR. To the parvis from the porch, late C15, with studs and simple T-shaped strapwork hinges. – STAINED GLASS. 1841–2 by S.C. Yarington in the E window, small figures. – MONU-MENTS. Brass to Denis Willys †1462, a heart held by two hands (N door). – Brass to John Blomevile and Dame Katherine Sampson †1546, in shrouds. – Brass to Henry Hobart †1561 in armour. – Henry Hobart †1541. Tomb-chest with shields in lozenges and brass effigies (N aisle E). – James Hobart †1613 and his wife †1609. Big tomb-chest with pilasters and shields in three-dimensional strapwork surrounds. On the lid still brass effigies (chancel S). – Lady Dionys Williamson †1684 (N aisle E). Semi-reclining matron on sarcophagus with gadrooned edges. White marble. Of excellent quality. Indeed it is attributed to

Grinling Gibbons himself (GF), although other authorities name *Joshua Marshall*. Lady Williamson, who was from the Hobart family, gave £2,000 for the rebuilding of St Paul's after the Fire, £4,000 for the rebuilding of St Dunstan-in-the-East, and £2,000 for St Mary-le-Bow. – Churchyard RAILINGS, Gothic, of cast iron. By *J. S. Benest*.

PERAMBULATION

In front of the church is a square, CHURCH PLAIN, used not very imaginatively as a car park. On its N side the amusing (in the first edition, shocking) BRANCH LIBRARY, which started as a school, built in 1857 by *J. S. Benest* and *A. Newson*, and added to in 1881. Converted 1970. It is of gault brick and flint with three steep gables and a turret at the W end marking the SCHOOL HOUSE, very restless and very demonstrably different from the restrained, well-mannered standard of the Georgian red brick houses, minor and major, of Loddon. Next to it No. 33, a late C17 brick house with stepped gables, and Nos. 35–37 less obviously late C17. The road winds away to the N and confusingly becomes the MARKET PLACE. No. 2 is early C17. On the W side of Church Plain a modest group of late Georgian houses, and then a range (Nos. 15–21) dated 1604, which fits well with the external stack to the N return. The façade Georgianized and raised into three storeys. Then the SWAN INN, five bays and two and a half storeys, the ground floor altered. Late C18 red brick front, C17 timber-framed rear wing.

BRIDGE STREET leads to the N out of the square but there is less of note. First the former TOWN HALL, red brick, Jacobean style, of 1870. The hall has a big shaped gable and in front of it two attachments with shaped gables flank the entrance. Then BUGDON HOUSE, with its irregular mid-C18 front and late C18 metal casements where the windows are not blind. Doorcase under open pediment *c.* 1820. After that Nos. 13–17, set back from the road. Two storeys and six bays of cross casements. Good red brick with burnt headers and a moulded platband. To the S a shaped gable, but at the back two straight gables. All late C17. Bridge Street then offers, on the r., the KING'S HEAD, partly C17, and by the river on the l. LODDON MILL. Weatherboarded C18 water mill with an early C19 HOUSE attached to the S. Back towards the start of Bridge Street and off W into GEORGE LANE where at once the METHODIST CHURCH and school, red brick and red terracotta, of 1887–9 in the Perp manner. The interior plain, galleried only to the W end. Boarded roof. Further along to CROSSWAY TERRACE, HOBART ROAD and DRURY LANE, a *Tayler & Green* estate, with its seventy-eight houses the largest of those built by Loddon RDC after the war (*see* Introduction p. 165). The estate was built in 1951–69. Informal plan, no r. angles, variety of colour in the brickwork, use of patterned brickwork, bargeboards, trellises, etc., big linking walls. Some of the houses and terraces have been irrevocably altered, partly by the council, partly by their new private

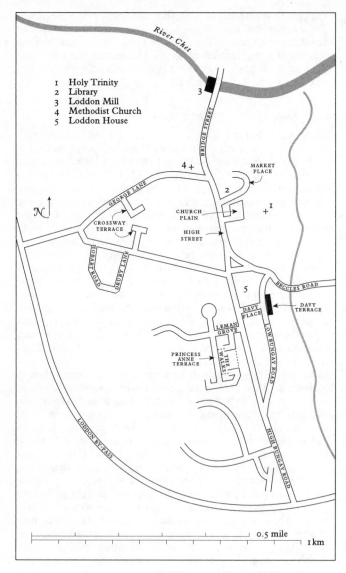

1 Holy Trinity
2 Library
3 Loddon Mill
4 Methodist Church
5 Loddon House

Loddon

owners from the late 1980s. The street pattern creates an impression of a small village within a village, and was an instrumental force behind the philosophy of the *Essex Design Guide*, 1973, leading ultimately to such developments as the Bowthorpe villages from 1975 (*see* Norwich, Vol. 1, p. 343).

To the s of Church Plain is the HIGH STREET. On the E side, No. 1, formerly THE INSTITUTE, now a shop. Early C17,

flint and brick, narrow but high, with renewed wooden mullioned and transomed windows with stone jambs. Stone also to
the quoins. Adjoining to the s Nos. 3–5, same date but brick,
with a mid-C19 shopfront. Good fireplace with carved bressumer spandrels. High Street boasts unassuming C18 and C19
shops and houses; only Nos. 22–24 have an earlier timber frame
behind the C19 red brick façade. Then to the E into BECCLES
ROAD: LODDON HOUSE (No. 2) is the most ambitious house
in the little town. It was built c. 1711 and is of five bays with
later two-bay additions r. and l. The five bays have brick quoins,
the middle three bays are emphasized not only by separate
quoins of even length, but also by an extra storey with an arched
middle window reaching into an open pediment. The same
arrangement at the back. The doorway has fluted Corinthian
pilasters, a frieze curving up to a point, and a broken segmental
pediment with volutes. Opposite, an early C19 house. But this is
only the addition to FARTHING GREEN HOUSE, of five bays
and two and a half storeys with a doorway with a rusticated surround and a segmental pediment. The moulded platband and
flush frames to the sashes indicate c. 1740. Large early C20 additions at the back. More nice Georgian houses follow, especially
No. 9, MALTBY HOUSE (two storeys, five bays, doorcase), and
No. 4, THE CHESTNUTS (same disposition, Doric doorcase).

Retracing to the s end of the High Street one can continue s
into HIGH BUNGAY ROAD and to No. 1, THE BEECHES, a
pleasant late C18 three-bay house with two-bay wings and a
three-bay pediment. Its original iron RAILINGS remain to the
street. Off to the l. DAVY PLACE, 1963, is an old people's community of twenty-two one-storeyed houses, again by *Tayler &
Green*. Closer planning than fifteen years before, terraces
instead of pairs, clever exposure of an C18 retaining wall at the
back. A single long range, DAVY TERRACE at the end, on LOW
BUNGAY ROAD.

Back to High Bungay Road and a little further s off LEMAN
GROVE a council estate, partly of the older, clumsier housing of
between the wars, partly by *Tayler & Green*, who designed a
terrace, PRINCESS ANNE TERRACE, in 1950, and facing it, at r.
angles, THE WALKS, 1947, two terraces of semi-detached
houses of wide frontage with only paved footpaths in front.
Remarkable for their time, but there are now too many uPVC
windows, and in 1969 between the terraces *Tayler & Green* built
single-storeyed sheltered housing. This mitigates the austere
early effect.

LODDON HALL, 1 m. SE. Late Georgian, of gault brick. Five bays,
two storeys, hipped roof, porch on unfluted columns supporting a fluted frieze. One-storey, one-bay attachments. A C17
timber-framed BARN 100 yds N and a range of early C18 FARM
BUILDINGS to its E. The latter is a long two-storey brick range
with a Dutch gable.

THE ELMS, Stubbs Green. 1 m. SW of the church. C17 timber-
framed farmhouse with a stack with five diamond flues. The
BARN to the SE also C17 and timber-framed. Queenpost roof.

LONGHAM

1¼ m. WNW of Gressenhall

St Andrew. Perp tower and nave. The tower reduced. Three-light Perp w window and bell-stage partly rebuilt. Wave-moulded arch to the nave. Three-light Perp nave windows. Chancel rebuilt in brick *c.* 1890 but reusing the s windows. Nice Perp s porch. The entrance arch seems re-set, with shields on the capitals and tracery in the spandrels. – FONT. Octagonal, late C19, with panelled stem. – SCREEN. C15. Dado with foliated spandrels and some original paint still adhering. Nice tracery at the top.

Longham Hall, right by the church, both isolated from the cluster of buildings that make up the village ⅝ m. E. A typical gault-brick house of two storeys in three bays, with sashes and a simple doorcase on columns. *c.* 1840.

LONG STRATTON

St Mary. Round tower of coursed flints, round to the top where are rendered C15 battlements. With a lead spike. Nave, aisles, and chancel. The church was restored 1847–8 by *John Brown*. All windows Perp except for the seven Dec clerestory windows on each side, which have two trefoiled arches supporting a squashed mouchette in the apex. Both these types were used indiscriminately until the end of the C14 and beyond. Big three-light Early Perp E window. Inside, the church is very congenial; both arcades are of four bays and both are of the C14, the N arcade early, the s arcade later. The N arcade has quatrefoil piers with fillets and in the arches one chamfer and one wave moulding. The s arcade has the usual octagonal piers and double-chamfered arches. Arch-braced nave roof. Single-handed clock over the tower arch. – FONT. C15 Perp. Panelled and traceried stem, bowl with quatrefoils. – FONT COVER. Jacobean. Very charming and airy. Balusters, volutes and a finial. On the cornice an inscription from St John 3:5. – PULPIT. Jacobean, with broad blank arches covered in delicate strapwork and rectangular panels above similarly treated. – BENCHES. Many ends, many poppyheads. Some may date from 1420, when money was left for benches. – STAINED GLASS. Much in the E window, of mixed dates and origin, all put together as a pattern. The large panel of the Baptism of Christ is French, late C15. They were installed, possibly by *Yarington* (according to Birkin Haward), for Rev. William Walford in 1805. s chancel window with Christ Walking on Water etc., Norwich School, †1866, possibly by *J. & J. King*. Another s chancel window attributed to *Joseph Grant*, *c.* 1858, Suffer Little Children and Restoring the Blind. – SEXTON'S WHEEL. In a case near N door. Wrought iron. One of only two surviving ones; the other is at Yaxley in Suffolk. They were used to determine the day of the Lady Fast, a voluntary, movable fast-day to be kept for seven years. The wheel consists, as one can see, really of two wheels. The sexton attached bits of

string to six of the fleurs-de-lys of one wheel and then set both
in rapid motion. The day which the string of the one wheel
caught in the other was the day to be observed. Its date is probably just pre-Reformation. A sexton's wheel is illustrated in the
Basel edition of Brant's *Narrenschiff*, published in 1497. –
SCREEN. base only, re-worked. – MONUMENT. Sir Edmund
Reve †1647 and wife (chancel N). Big, rather bald standing
monument attributed to *Thomas Stanton* (GF). Two effigies, she
recumbent, he a little behind and above her, propped up on an
elbow in the usual manner, dressed in his legal robes (he was a
judge of Common Pleas from 1639). Above is an architectural
set-piece with inscription panels below a broken segmental pediment with an achievement. – FOUNDER'S TOMB. So-called.
A wide C14 niche supposed to be for Robert de Swaffham.

SOUTH NORFOLK HOUSE, the District Council Offices by
Lambert, Scott & Innes (job architect *Michael Innes*), 1978–9,
are tucked away round the back in Swan Lane in the manner of
new rural civic offices in the 1970s and 1980s. The building
looks from a distance like a medieval castle behind its walls, and
the impression is one of a jumbled roofscape, an interesting way
of integrating large new offices into an old village. In fact there
is nothing jumbled about it. The masses are composed of two
attached irregular hexagons and there is a tall tower off to one
side, as wide as it is tall. The red brick is strikingly bright under
the grey roof-cladding and the blue engineering bricks to the
quoins are an effective foil. The tower has a pyramid roof, and
so too have the hexagons, though radically treated. The entrance
polygon has a set-back roof truncated at the top. The other is
cut into to provide glazing. There is a multiplicity of levels,
often linked by glazed passages, and inside not only is all open-
plan, but the massive concrete structure is fully expressed.

LEISURE CENTRE, Swan Lane, 1982 by *Norfolk County Council
Architect's Department* (job architect *M. G. Clarke*); competent
handling.

The large VILLAGE has gathered itself into a long strip either side
of the main Norwich–Ipswich road; on the E side only a little
infilling in the late C20, but whole estates have grown up to the
W. The oldest houses right on the road, which, from the S,
changes its name from Ipswich Road to The Street to Norwich
Road. A walk must start at the church at the S end. Just S, at the
junction with Hall Lane, CHURCH STORES and THE OLD
COACH HOUSE, an early C18 timber-framed and, probably,
clay lump range. In the C19 the sashes of the S house were
replaced by mullioned windows, the reverse of the usual practice.
Opposite, CORFE LODGE, a C17 timber-framed house with a
C19 stuccoed front in three bays. Pilasters between bays. The
porch with a pair of fluted half-columns. The lower CORFE
COTTAGE attached represents the unimproved state. Further N,
on the W side, FLINT HOUSE, a rather uninspired former
school of 1850 converted to workshops and of the materials one
would expect from the name. The other side has GRIFFIN
COTTAGE, dated in an oval 1719. This oval now recessed by the

thickness of the early C20 brick skin which was applied directly to the timber frame. Casements and mullioned windows, all renewed.

On THE STREET a little further N the ICEHOUSE, on the l. at the end of a row of shops. Early C19. Its earth covering removed so the domed top sticks out like a bald brick head. It served the demolished Manor House. On the other side of the road a C17 timber-framed block with a gable towards the road.

On the W side the LIBRARY, 1980, by the *County Architect's Department*, County Architect *J. F. Tucker*. Small, square, red brick with a high clerestory to the E which has an exposed ten-sioned timber frame inside. Opposite again two or perhaps three altered C17 HOUSES (now a shop, an estate agent's and a dental surgery). Brick S gable with four blocked rectangular windows and two round attic windows below the truncated stack with its two octagonal flues. The rest timber-framed. Towards the street two modest bowed early C19 shop display windows; N gable faces the street. The rear gable of this wing also has two round attic windows and remains of a mullioned window to the S flank. A small early C18 HOUSE, now a shop, stands free from its neighbours immediately N, again edge-on to the street. Opposite Swan Lane a long C17 RANGE (now an off-licence and a veterinary surgery) has a continuous first-floor plastered jetty. Large roof unfortunately with C20 machine-tiles. Some C20 casements have replaced C18 and C19 ancestors and excite the same sentiment. The CRAFT SHOP on the W side was re-faced in 1897, with a shaped gable. The SWAN INN is C17, timber-framed, of two storeys and dormer attic fitted up with C19 sashes. The interior rather opened-out but with a huge brick fireplace. NETHERTON HOUSE follows: C17 but with a late C18 gault-brick cladding and a narrow frontage to the street having a full-height bay window in the middle. A row of early C18 cottages come after. Opposite these the HALIFAX BUILDING SOCIETY, C17 once more and with two houses attached to the N, all under a continuous roof. The GUILD HOUSE is set back from the street. An early C18 brick house with additions to S and W, so that it appears from the road as a double-roofed structure entered through a two-storeyed brick porch with a pair of unfluted columns. Further N, on the W side again, the meek WESLEYAN CHAPEL. 1830, round-headed sashes and pilaster strips. New interior arrangements and fittings 1989. In NORWICH ROAD the THATCHED COTTAGE, C17, timber-framed, made out of two dwellings. N of this the town fades away.

At WOOD GREEN ⅝ m. E a WINDMILL, crowded by C19 and C20 commercial mill buildings. Early C19 brick tower raised two storeys to its present five in the mid C19, now with only a coni-cal cap.

LOVELL'S HALL *see* TERRINGTON
ST CLEMENT

LYNFORD

1¼ m. ESE of Mundford

CHURCH OF OUR LADY OF CONSOLATION (R.C.). By *Henry Clutton*, 1877–8 for Mrs Lyne-Stephens of the Hall, who was a Catholic and inherited from her husband over £1,000,000 in 1860. Tiring of the long drive to Thetford for services, she commissioned the church (and was a great benefactor of Catholic churches generally, e.g. Our Lady in Cambridge, 1887). Small, a simple oblong with a circular W bell-turret on a big buttress. Knapped flint and stone dressings to the side buttresses and pierced panelled parapets. Single-light Perp side windows, twin two-light W windows and a four-light E window. Over the N doorway a statue of the Virgin and Child under a rich canopy. The quality of the work is very high and inside typically Puginesque: mosaic chancel floor, corbel table and stringcourse over the windows, which rise up in stone into the timber of the barrel-vaulted and ribbed roof. – ALTAR and REREDOS. A *Pugin* design of six traceried bays rising into a detailed cornice flanking a central tabernacle. Also Puginesque of course is the fact that there is an E window behind it, contrary to the needs of Catholic liturgy, but insisted on by Pugin.

Mrs Lyne-Stephens died in 1894 and the new owner, a Protestant, apparently planted the trees which screen it 'to hide the terrible eyesore'.

Attached PRESBYTERY. Originally Home Farmhouse. Two storeys, each of three windows in a flint and brick elevation. C18 evidence inside, but much re-worked. Reverted to a private house in 1894.

LYNFORD HALL, ½ m. N of the church. Built for Mr Lyne-Stephens and his wife, a French ex-ballet-dancer and noted beauty, by *William Burn*, 1856–61. It replaced a house of 1717 (which had been remodelled by *C. R. Cockerell* in 1828) for the Sutton family. Lyne-Stephens, a banker, was reputedly the richest commoner in England, and made his first fortune by inventing opening eyes for dolls. He died in 1860. The house is a kind of Parisian Neo-Jacobean, of red brick with stone trim. Irregular, of two storeys with attics. The N front has a projecting centre elaborated into a porch crowned by a shaped gable with refined Raynham-type volutes. To the r. another such gable without volutes. A three-storey domed corner tower closes the elevation. To the l. of the porch are two smaller bays, also with shaped gables and a balancing tower, this time polygonal. The S front facing the extensive gardens is basically of seven bays with much broader outer bays with canted two-storey windows and shaped gables. Five gabled dormers between. A lower, six-bay wing extends E, terminating under a broad shaped gable in the same manner. The interior was burnt out in 1928 and reinstated two years later, for Sir James Calder. It is now a country club, its setting spoilt by a caravan park to the E. IRON GATES, running N from the NW corner of the house; very sumptuous French Neo-Rococo. GARDENS. Laid out by *Burn* s of the house as a series of balustraded terraces, restored in a simplified way from 1970.

TEMPLE OF MERCURY, 170 yds ESE of the Hall, by *Burn, c.* 1862. Circular, with six Roman Doric columns in front of blind walling with openings. The roof unfortunately fallen in and derelict at the time of writing.

LYNG

ST MARGARET. Perp nave, the large windows with stepped embattled horizontals above the ogee lights in the tracery. s porch, formerly two-storeyed. The entrance has a straight-sided arch, not the usual curved four-centred one, and there is a brick C18 Dutch gable, the pediment too big. Chancel rebuilt 1912, the concrete tiles put on in 1972. The interior somewhat lopsided, because a N aisle arcade was ripped out when the nave was rebuilt in the C15, leaving the (blocked) C14 N doorway intact and an E nave window N of the chancel arch. The church is now aisleless. C14 also the chancel arch. Unbuttressed W tower with bell-openings with Y-tracery but a Perp tower arch. Y-tracery continued popular for belfries until the mid C15. Moreover the tower is not in line with the C14 chancel arch, but instead central to the new width of the nave after the Perp alterations. The whole tower must be Perp, not just the arch. Enormous C19 hammer-beam roof. – FONT. Octagonal, C13, of Purbeck marble, with the familiar two shallow pointed arches on each side. Eight shafts and central column, restored or renewed. – SOUTH DOOR. C15. With a band of quatrefoils and tracery. – STAINED GLASS. A St Margaret in the E window, 1968, by *Farrer Bell*. – ALTAR CLOTH. C15. Made up of parts of three vestments. Of five strips, mostly green and gold, also yellow and brown. Two strips with somewhat stocky figures of Saints at r. angles to the strip, two strips with angels along the strip. One purely ornamental strip. Restored 1983.

ST EDMUND, ¾ m. SE. In ruins. No more than some masonry around an arch, reinforced in brick.

LYNG HOUSE, S at Primrose Green. Rectangular brick house with a lower service wing. Dated 1734 on W gable. Burnt headers form vertical strips between the seven windows. C18 pedimented doorcase. One sash window either side made blind by late C18 alterations inside the entrance hall. Blind window above door, but the others, regrettably, are C20 aluminium. Stick-baluster staircase, i.e. part of the late C18 work. The service block has a mullioned and transomed window.

MILL HOUSE, on the Wensum. Brick, four bays, two storeys, sash windows. All of the mid C18, altered.

OLD SMITHY COTTAGE, The Common. House and smith's workshop to one side. Late C18. Four bays and two storeys. Door flanked by rusticated pilasters. The C18 casements remain. Platband and a moulded eaves cornice.

EARTHWORKS. S of the river and 380 yds NE of the church. Large complex of probably manorial earthworks include three almost square ditched enclosures, one with fragments of flint and mortar walling. (AR)

MANGREEN see SWARDESTON

MARHAM   7000

HOLY TRINITY. Of flint and carstone. Norman N doorway, with one order of single-scallop shafts and a tympanum with a lozenge pattern, an unusual feature in Norfolk (cf. Norwich Cathedral, N transept). The W tower looks like Early Perp, but there are donations for its construction in 1450 and 1520, the year in which the bells were hung, i.e. Late Perp. The W doorway and the five-light Perp W window must owe a lot to the C19. The window has panel tracery and a crenellated transom. The tall wave-moulded tower arch alone looks wholly mature Perp. Perp bell-openings. C14 S porch rather re-worked in one of the three C19 restoration campaigns (1844, 1867 and 1875). The three Perp S aisle windows with stepped transoms are C19, and of 1867 are the N nave windows (no N aisle). Continuous chancel, its windows also renewed or restored, but the four-light E window is nicely balanced between Dec and Perp forms. The E bay of the S aisle is a chancel chapel entered from the chancel through a four-centred opening. The four-bay S arcade is Early Perp again. Octagonal piers. Some capitals have blank merlons. Nave roof of 1844, chancel roof 1846. – FONT. Octagonal, Perp, with a variety of blank tracery motifs on stem and bowl. On the stem it is instructive to see that they include tracery motifs of *c.* 1300 and of *c.* 1330. – BENCHES. A fine set of C15 low benches with traceried openwork backs and poppyheads, but no decoration of the arm-rests. – MONUMENTS. In the SE chapel to John Steward †1604, and wife Anne. Clunch tomb-chest with recumbent effigies under a plain canopy on three octagonal columns. The columns are bulbous and have big leaves up their lower parts. On the top strapwork and coat of arms. The tomb-chest has clasping corner pilasters and painted tracery patterns. – Henry Villebois †1847. Signed by *R. Westmacott Jun.* White marble wall monument in chancel. Two angels kneel from l. and r. over an altar with book and cross.

ST ANDREW. This second parish church of Marham stood to the E, where the Vicarage now is. Only a few carved architectural fragments remain.

ABBEY. In the grounds of Abbey House, on Shouldham Road. A Cistercian nunnery, founded before 1249 by the Countess of Arundel. The S wall of the nave survives, with the unusual motif of two large circular late C13 windows, one quatrefoiled, the other sexfoiled. On the S side corbels originally supporting the cloister walls. Also a substantial fragment of the W range with the outer parlour, a C14 room, rib-vaulted in two bays. The ribs have roll and fillet mouldings.

In a pasture to the S and W of the ruins very substantial EARTH-WORKS mask collapsed remains of the claustral buildings and possibly an infirmary. There is a large fishpond. (AR)

Of MARHAM HOUSE nothing except a little L-shaped house remains. It was quite big, and had a long single-storey extension added by *Donthorn* in the 1820s, but was largely pulled down in 1931. The C19 work, including more additions of 1861, was for the Villebois family.

HOME FARM, Shouldham Road. 1861, for Henry Villebois. A model farm complex principally comprising a house, barn and a pair of pavilions guarding the entrance from the road. Gault brick under slate roofs. The HOUSE has a T-plan and a façade of three bays with pilasters at the corners, including the projecting central bay with its gable. The windows are two-light Y-tracery Gothick casements. The BARN also has three bays and pilasters and a stringcourse dividing the façade horizontally. Central doorway. Honeycomb ventilation panels. The PAVILIONS are two-storeyed, square and have recessed panels and hipped roofs.

GROVE HOUSE, Squire's Hill. Early C19 three-bay house with a nice bowed Greek Revival porch: pair of Roman Doric columns and pilasters. Other than the gault-brick façade the house is of clunch.

To the E of the village is a TOWN six times the size, built to serve the airforce base. Marham had been a World War I base, opened in 1916, closed in 1918, then redeveloped in 1936–7. It is still in use, so no description of military buildings. The houses are mainly in groups of terraces of 2–5 dwellings, some semi-detached, some detached, depending on rank. There is also a school, and leisure facilities. Construction began in the 1950s and continued to the 1980s. There is nothing of note except the abruptness with which one comes across it. It has no place in the landscape, and its unexpectedness is singular indeed.

MARLINGFORD

1000

ST MARY. Norman S doorway with one order of shafts and one outer upright zigzag frieze. Arch with correct and incorrect circles. Unbuttressed W tower Dec, of knapped flint. Y-tracery W window and ogeed belfry tracery. Crenellated parapet. Dec also the two-bay N arcade. This has an octagonal pier and double-chamfered arches. Chancel 1816, N aisle 1881. – FONT. Octagonal, of Purbeck marble, with two shallow blank arches on each side; C13. – COMMANDMENT BOARD. A large hand-coloured early C19 engraving. – HOURGLASS STAND. Nave NE corner. – MONUMENT. Nathaniel Life †1727. Tablet with broken column before a pyramid. – STAINED GLASS. S chancel by *Powell & Sons*, from a *Holiday* cartoon? *c.* 1905, Faith and Charity.

OLD HALL, ⅝ m. NNE. The lobby-entrance house dated 1608 was built for Clement Jermy and given a new S façade in 1679, after being bought by Nathaniel Life (whose monument is in the church). Brick front with two stepped attic gables. Windows of

the cross type (altered) in five bays and two storeys. The doorway with Doric pilasters and a triglyph frieze is a Georgian
alteration. Inside is a staircase with turned balusters and panelled newel-posts, probably part of the 1679 remodelling. Several
panelled rooms, the panelling raised and fielded, and also, above
fireplaces, three painted landscape panels.

MARLINGFORD HALL. S of the church. Built for Major Charles
Ewen in 1868 and altered by *Boardman* after 1881. Three stepped
gables to the N front with two bays between them.

WATERMILL and MILLER'S HOUSE, a very pretty group by the
Yare, E of the church, now light engineering works. The mill is
weatherboarded, late C18.

THE SQUARE, Barford Road. Built as a timber-framed C16 house
with brick and flint gable-ends. The E wing is the earlier, with
blocked windows in the S gable, and one would guess it to be a
floored open hall house. Brick S wing added 1674 according to
a datestone. Divided into separate houses in the late C20.

MARSHLAND ST JAMES   5000

ST JAMES. 1 m. SE of the village, a mission church of 1896–7.
Architect not known. Plain rectangle with apsed chancel built
of Fletton brick. Various PAINTINGS in the apse including the
sun and stars on the vault, by *Lilian Dagless*, 1955. – SCULP-
TURE. Continental C17 painted wooden statue of St James.

METHODIST CHURCH. 1891 by *J. W. Crouch* of nearby Wisbech.
There is nothing of note in this Fenland backwater. It is the only
civil parish in Norfolk where the DCMS has identified no listed
buildings.

MATTISHALL   0010

ALL SAINTS. Quite a big church, almost entirely Early Perp but
alas very drastically restored. Strong W tower with angle buttresses changing to the diagonal at the bell-stage. Bell-openings
with mouchettes and supermullions. On top a short spire with a
cupola and weathervane dated 1640. Flushwork panelling on
the buttresses and the parapet, which might relate to the 'emendation' for which money was given in 1385. In 1445 money was
left for building the body of the church, a porch being specifically mentioned. A porch was being roofed in 1453. The present
S porch is virtually all Victorian and regrettable, but the N porch
is Late Perp, with an Annunciation in the spandrels of the
entrance and three niches above it with ogee arches. Flushwork
in the battlements. The entrance blocked in the C20. The N
porch certainly and perhaps the original S porch would accord
with 1445–53. The church is all of one date, except for the Late
Perp S chapel (donations 1507): galleted flint, Perp windows.
Tall arcades of four bays with long polygonal projections without capitals to nave and aisles and semicircular ones with capitals

to the arches. The arch mouldings still such as were usual in the
Dec period. Similar chancel arch. The S chapel has three-
centred arches into the aisle and chancel. Wall arches in the
aisles and also the S chapel. Nine clerestory windows, shafted
inside. One clerestory window also on the E side. Good roofs,
with old paint. In the nave tie-beams midway down the clerestory.
Hammerbeams carved with angels and Saints, and renewed.
The three E bays are ceiled and painted, with the date 1617.
The N aisle roof is original too. So are, in the S aisle roof, the
little figures on the wall-posts. – FONT. The solid stem with concave sides is Perp. – PULPIT. The tester is of the C18, and so too
is probably the rest, masquerading as Jacobean. – SCREENS. Of
the mid-C15 rood screen the dado also survives, with blind tracery and painted figures of the Apostles holding Creed texts. In
the spandrel above the Apostle with the text referring to Christ's
conception is a tiny carved Annunciation (DP). – S aisle screen
with ogee-headed one-light divisions. The arches are cusped
and subcusped. Close Dec tracery. The whole no doubt C14. –
BENCH ENDS. With poppyheads. – STAINED GLASS. N aisle W
window, by *H. W. Lonsdale*, †1884, the Acts of Mercy. S aisle W
window, by *H. Bryans*, †1908. – MONUMENTS. Brass to a
Civilian, *c.* 1480 (1 ft figure; nave). – Brass to Geoffrey Dane,
c. 1510 (18 in. figure; N aisle). – Brass to a Civilian and wife,
c. 1510 (nave).

VILLAGE. The church stands in the middle of the village on
CHURCH PLAIN. Several nice houses on all sides, none older
than the C18. On the W side, CHURCH COTTAGE and TALBOT
HOUSE are a pair, brick, two storeys, eight bays of three-light
cross casements, doorcases with fluted Doric pilasters. To the
SW SYCAMORE HOUSE. Brick, laid with burnt headers in a
chequer pattern. The S façade of two storeys with mixed fenestration and a platband between the floors. N front with a platband too. All this early C18. Two-storey, three-bay extension of
c. 1850. The PRIMITIVE METHODIST CHAPEL of 1856 converted to a garage: three bays with pilasters. VICTORIA STORES
is *c.* 1840, with a good bowed shopfront with an egg-and-dart
cornice. To the S and E some pleasant early C19 brick houses
generally of two storeys in three bays. SEVERAL HOUSE has a
doorcase with an open pediment, ETHERTON has six bays and
a pedimented doorcase.

DEREHAM ROAD runs to the W. The pattern again is of early C19
brick houses often with shop display windows. The older houses
are further out, i.e. they were less prone to redevelopment. Of
the C19, LONDON HOUSE on the N side: the shop with two rusticated giant pilasters and display windows flanking the doorway. Opposite, MADINGLEY, early C19, brick, spoilt by late
C20 plastic windows. The OLD VICARAGE has five early C19
bays and a porch on unfluted Doric columns attached to an
early C18 house, shown by the platband to the E gable. Also on
the N side MOAT FARMHOUSE: C17 timber-framed house with
an C18 brick skin and given cross casements and plain casements.
The interior is on a lobby-entrance plan. QUAKER HOUSE. An

C18 Quaker chapel with a farmhouse. Three-bay front with a central door and flanking sashes. The inside is groin-vaulted in plaster and there are galleries on square Roman Doric columns.

MATTISHALL HALL. Brick house with an early C18 E front in two storeys with attic and six bays. Three early C18 casements l. of the door; the two r. of the door are late C18 Gothick; those to the first floor are C20. Moulded brick platband between the floors. The N return continues the platband and has a doorcase with Corinthian columns. Two early C19 additional bays. Five-bay W front, early C19.

IVY FARMHOUSE, Thynne's Lane. Early C18, brick, two storeys and attic in seven bays. Sash windows. Doric pilastered doorcase. Hipped roof. The staircase has a mixture of twisted and turned balusters. The STABLES dated 1741 have chequered brickwork.

MATTISHALL BURGH

0010

ST PETER. The walling of the nave looks Norman in its coursed flint. Dec W tower, unbuttressed. Y-tracery in the W window and mixed Y- and ogee tracery in the bell-openings. Double wave-moulded arch into the nave. Early C14 also the oddly long N transept with intersecting tracery in the N window and an arcade of two bays towards the nave, as though it were an aisle. Quatrefoil pier, double-chamfered arches. Ogee-headed piscina in the E wall. Of the same time the S porch entrance, perhaps reused. Perp chancel E and S windows, the E window renewed. Chancel piscina with an octagonal shaft and cusping in the arches. Scissor-braced nave roof with purlins and ridge piece. Chancel roof C16, with clasped purlins and wind-braces. – FONT. C13. Octagonal, of Purbeck marble, i.e. with the usual two shallow blank arches on each side. The shafts beneath are renewed. – SCREEN. With one-light divisions and ogee arches; simple and over-restored. – ORGAN. A barrel-organ.

GROVE FARMHOUSE. C18 three-bay brick façade with a two-storey porch. Casements. Rear pile late C16, timber-framed and with a brick skin. Six octagonal chimneyshafts to the stack go with this.

MAYPOLE GREEN see TOFT MONKS

MERTON

9090

ST PETER. Just inside the grounds to the Hall. Norman round tower. Two-light bell-openings. Plain wide tower arch on the simplest imposts, and long-and-short work. An E window into the church above it. The rest mostly of c. 1300 and unusually fine. The windows are characterized by slender circular shafts in front of the mullions. Tall two-light nave N windows with cusped Y-tracery. Chancel with windows of an impressive sub-stantial design, really simply intersecting and cusped but in such a way that some quite unpierced areas remain, almost as in plate tracery. It adds richness without removing clarity. The sedilia and double piscina again excellent, and the tracery of the piscina of the same type as that of the windows. S aisle perhaps a little later, though still pre-Curvilinear. E window restored: normal cusped intersecting tracery with a sexfoiled top circle. The S aisle windows simpler, but again not quite of a standard pattern. Piscina in the S wall. The S arcade has four bays of octagonal piers and moulded arches. The chancel arch is similar, though taller. The graceless S porch is by *E. B. Lamb*, 1856. The N porch of about the same date. – FONT. C15. On two high steps. Hexagonal with shields. Angels against the underside of the bowl. Their wings reach up and frame the shields most decoratively and unexpectedly. – FONT COVER. Tall Perp canopy, largely a reconstruction and replacement in 1843 by one *Capt. Kitto*. – PULPIT and READER'S DESK, i.e. a two-decker. Jacobean. – SCREEN. C14. Two-light divisions. Excellent, with very fine and dainty, thornily cusped tracery. – COMMUNION RAIL. Three-sided. Sturdy twisted balusters, i.e. *c.* 1690. – Jacobean family PEW. – STAINED GLASS. In the chancel mostly of *c.* 1830–40 and typical of the elementary standards of that moment of relinquishing the pictorial mode of the C18. But in a N window also some original C15 parts of figures set into glass †1844. E window probably by *E. B. Lamb*, probably 1856. S aisle E window by *S. C. Yarington*, 1827, moved from the E window. – MONUMENTS. Brass to William de Grey †1495 and two wives. Slab with kneeling figures (nave, NE wall); five sons and five daughters. – Thomas de Grey †1562, in armour (S chapel). – Robert de Grey, 1632, attributed to *William Wright* (GF). – Arnaldo de Grey †1889. Large stone slab with a curiously foliated cross. – Michael de Grey †1897. Smaller slab, also with a cross but with two kneeling angels as well. The two slabs, looking more like the Eric Gill period than the Arts and Crafts, were designed by *Margaret de Grey*, née Ponsonby, widow of the one and mother of the other.

MERTON HALL. Most of the house was consumed by fire in 1956. What remains is the gatehouse, dated on rainwater heads 1620, and the NE wing, added to the old house by *Edward Blore* in the 1840s. The original house was begun in 1613 for the de Grey family on the E-plan. It was of two storeys, increasing to three in the pair of stepped cross wings on the N, entrance, side.

The surviving GATEHOUSE is separated from the site by a small courtyard. Two storeys in three bays. It has to the outer and the inner side, i.e. N and S, three steep shaped gables which are among the earliest examples in England of the fully formed type (cf. Blickling: there were no shaped gables to the 1613 work). Central door each side within a large arch. The archway is framed, also on both sides, by coupled Tuscan columns. The windows are mullioned and transomed and carry pediments. The end-gables are shaped as well, terminating in chimneys

with replacement C19 star tops. Over the centre is a wooden
clock tower.

The NE WING, now the present house, was added by *Blore* in
1846 for the fifth Lord Walsingham, reputedly for the accommodation of the Baron's illegitimate offspring. In the style of
the old house, i.e. red brick with stone dressings, Jacobean,
stepped gables, angle-shafts and pinnacles, and a galaxy of polygonal star-topped chimneyshafts. The wing is pure Blore: big,
solid, functional, and conventional.

To the SE the STABLE BLOCK by *Milne & Hall*, 1898. Brick
but with a timbered centre, and plenty of brick nogging. More
star tops and stepped gables. Now offices and flats.

GROTTO, about ¼ m. WSW of the Hall. Tudor, red brick, tiled.
Of the 1840s and by *Blore*. It has stepped gables with pinnacles
and the entrance is in a gable-end. In the opposite gable is a
timber oriel. Inside is a mosaic floor and the rest is covered in
seashells, even the roof. For which of the fifth Baron's ladies
could this delight have been built?

THE HASSOCKS, ½ m. NNW of the church S of the lane into the
village, is of two builds. The original rear part is *c.* 1650, clay
lump and brick, all rendered. The entrance has been moved
and the central stack would seem to indicate lobby-entrance
planning. Hipped brick porch of 1994. Three-light cross casements. In 1685 a new brick front was added to the E gable,
forming a T-plan, of three bays in two storeys, the windows all
renewed timber cross casements with gauged brick lintels. The
brick still laid in English bond with some burnt headers. A
moulded brick platband separates the floors.

In the VILLAGE, ⅝ m. NW of the church, are numerous C18 COT-
TAGES of clay lump or minor timber-framing. Lots of them
have moulded brick casements of the 1870s which seem to
correspond to an improving campaign on the part of the Merton
Estate, see e.g. THE THATCHED COTTAGE.

METHWOLD 7090

ST GEORGE. Apart from the Dec E window with Curvilinear petal
tracery and the double-chamfered chancel arch, all is Perp here,
and dominated by a steeple 120 ft high. The tower has three
stages, but its distinguishing feature is the additional uncommonly slender panelled octagonal top stage or corona. This
rises behind the battlements and tall pinnacles of the square
lower parts and ends in its own openwork parapet with pinnacles. Of its four stages the first stage is blank, the second has
a little arcade of cusped arches, the third the same but with an
open louvred window, the top is the parapet. The spire rises
behind this and is crocketed. The tower itself has a W doorway
with traceried spandrels and a hoodmould on lively busts, and
a four-light Perp window; the ringing chamber with lancets;
belfry stage with reticulated openings. The tower arch is tall and
has demi-figures of angels instead of capitals. The same motif

characterizes the capitals of the arcades, though some have impressive heads instead. The arcades have four bays, and the piers are given an odd section with slim polygonal projections to the arches and deep projections with two hollow chamfers to nave and aisles. The roof has alternating tie-beams and hammer-beams, the latter with a whole flight of carved angels. The ties are crenellated and carry their own queenposts. Perp windows all round, those of the clerestory segment-headed and oddly beetle-browed, those of the N aisle with transoms. The N aisle was under construction in 1440. S porch with wave-moulded arch and a sundial dated 1721. Unusual sanctus bellcote on the SE corner of the nave. – COFFER. Iron-bound; C15. – BENCHES. Two pairs with C15 poppyheads. – BIER. Dated 1737, yet in its details still entirely pre-classical. Inscribed 'MAD BY ME WILL AYRES'. – SCREEN. 1909. – STAINED GLASS. In the chancel and one S aisle window big figures of c. 1856 in the style of the early C14. By the *Rev. Frederick Sutton.* – In a N aisle window scenes by *Henry Holiday,* 1866, i.e. when he was young (made by *Powell & Sons*). The glass is very close to the Pre-Raphaelites in the figure style, but lacks Morris's ornamental genius. Even so, a remarkably good piece for its date. – MONUMENTS. Sir Adam de Clifton †1367. A splendid brass figure in armour, 5 ft 9 in. tall. Under a canopy, the details of which – cusping and subcusping – still in the style of early C14 stone monument canopies, without a trace of Perp. It was taken away and bits sold in the C17, but what remained was re-assembled here in 1860. – Henry Partridge †1793. Urn with profile head in black silhouette – a fashionable technique, here applied to memorial sculpture. – Also Henry Partridge †1803 by *John Athow* of Norwich. – CROSS. In the churchyard. Of the C14 the socket stone and octagonal shaft.

METHODIST CHURCH (Wesleyan). Opposite St George. Dignified three-bay brick façade of 1831 with giant pilasters and a central porch. Miniature central pediment with the date in front of a low parapet concealing the hipped roof. Flint at the back, with two-light plate-tracery windows.

OLD VICARAGE (No. 11 Crown Street). Excellent early C16 brick
57   N gable-end attached to a slightly earlier timber-framed range. The gable is stepped at the top on three tiers of moulded kneelers and with a polygonal chimney going up its middle to end in triple octagonal flues. This has decoration in three tiers above a plain section: cusped blank trefoiled arches, then diaper, then a vertical chevron meander. The latter two motifs are familiar from other Tudor chimneyshafts. Of the windows only the attic pair are original. They are straight-headed, of two arched lights. The timber-framed part is, for Norfolk, very high quality. Two storeys, jettied to the W on wall-shafts with carved braces. Below is a six-light mullioned window, in the first floor a five-light example. The E side is close-studded, lit through two upper four-light mullioned windows. Inside, the bridging beams and joists are roll-moulded, the former having spiral ribbon decoration in the lower N room. The N end of this room has a free-

standing chimney-breast associated with the brick gable-end, repeated in the room above. This, and the smaller room to the s, have WALL PAINTINGS of floral motifs perhaps dating from two different periods, in the early and late C16. The wall-posts at this level carry arched and tension braces to the wall-plates. Roof structure of collars on arched braces, through purlins and arched wind-braces, that is, early C17. The rest is clearly earlier, the bridging beam decoration and the close studding indicating *c.* 1490–1510.

NEW HALL (No. 19 Crown Street), to the w of the former Vicarage, a house of *c.* 1700. Two storeys on a basement, seven bays, hipped roof over a hollow eaves cornice. Sashes, but the windows no doubt originally with wooden crosses. The material is flint with red brick dressings.

HALL FARM, ⅜ m. w of the church. Two C18 clunch BARNS. The HOUSE of two storeys in four bays, the façade details C20. External C17 stack to s.

Another BARN on Old Severall's Road dated 1697, also clunch and with brick dressings.

MIDDLETON

ST MARY. Of carstone. E.E. chancel, see the fine band of stiff-leaf along the sill-line of the windows inside, the double piscina with polygonal shaft, and the two-light windows with quatrefoil plate tracery. All this is however heavily restored (in 1862), to the extent that only the lower courses of the exterior walls are C13, and the renewed plate tracery of the windows made to look more like bar tracery. The five trusses of bold arched braces of the chancel roof also 1862, as are the smaller arched braces of the nave, though the moulded purlins and principals are C15. Dec window at the E end of the s aisle (three-light, mouchette tracery), other windows Perp. Perp w tower with tall arch to the nave. w door and three-light window C19. C15 or C16 English bond brick repairs to the base of the tower. Arcade of four bays with octagonal piers, very late C15. The wave-moulded arches die into the piers. Against the tower can be discerned marks from an earlier arcade. The aisles embrace the tower, and there the tower arches also die into their imposts. s porch rebuilt. It has a pointed tunnel vault and chamfered transverse arches. – SCREEN. Two bays of the dado with painted Saints (chancel). – STAINED GLASS. Chancel windows by *Ward & Hughes*, 1850s and 1860s, the E window †1867 with a Crucifixion. *Clayton & Bell* and *J. Powell & Sons* did the glass in nave and tower, various dates. – POOR BOX. Simple baulk of wood set against a poppyhead (SE tower pier). – CROSS in churchyard to N; C15, part of square shaft. – A socket stone for another cross to the s by the gate from the roaring A47, probably C15. – Some good C18 HEADSTONES.

Opposite the church CHURCH FARMHOUSE and a little w THE CROWN pub, both C18 and both illustrating the use of carstone.

MIDDLETON TOWER. Beautifully placed inside a moat, 1 m. NNE

of the church. Largely *c.* 1860 and *c.* 1900, but incorporating a three-storeyed brick gatehouse built for Thomas, seventh Lord Scales, †1460. Rectangular in plan and one room deep, with polygonal corner turrets. From the end of the C17 until 1856 it was a ruin, when Sir Lewis Whincop Jarvis acquired it, completing the restoration by 1864. The C15 four-centred entrance arch is approached from the s over the moat. Above it a fine oriel on a traceried bracket and a second, smaller, oriel to its r. both renewed in Sir Lewis's time. There is now no trace of the third oriel to the l. Two two-light cusped second-floor windows under square hoods; C15, restored in the C19. The turrets project higher. Inside all is Victorian including the hammerbeam roof to the Hall and the C18-style staircase. The extensions to the l. are first the staircase hall, then a lower two-bay section with an oriel to the ground floor. These of 1856–64. The tall, rather severe, four-storeyed block following is of 1876. The final addition to the w is of 1905 and made for the Ramsden family. STABLES, 120 yds w. Carstone with brick. *c.* 1870.

ESTATE COTTAGES. One of 1861 (THE COTTAGE), carstone and brick, two storeys, bay windows, clustered octagonal chimney-shafts. A pair on STATION ROAD, more interesting as an Arts and Crafts derivative of 1906, again carstone. One storey and attic in four bays, the centre two bays recessed, the outer two under low swept roofs. Carstone banding.

MIDDLETON HALL, NW of the church. For the Everard family, early C19. Faced with limestone. Three storeys and attic in six bays. s front has a porch on unfluted columns. Sashes set in recesses, some to the first floor blind. Big bows to the E and w returns. Staircase hall graced by plaster roundels and a staircase with twisted balusters. More plasterwork in the E ballroom. Satellite buildings include an ORANGERY 120 yds NNW, early C19, five by two bays. The now windowless front has five arched openings. A little wrought-iron PERGOLA between orangery and house. LODGE, on the main road, 1837. Coursed carstone dressed with gault brick. Only one storey, with a rear wing and the entrance in the angle with a gable. Ghastly C20 replacement windows.

OLD HALL, ⅜ m. NNW of church. Two storeys. The l. bay early C18; middle two bays dated 1753; r. three bays C17, denoting the original extent of house. Repairs after a fire in *c.* 1970. DOVECOTE 60 yds NW. Square, late C18, of gault brick.

MIDDLETON MOUNT, ⅜ m. NNW of the church. A large motte commanding extensive views. Excavation has recovered the plan of a small and utterly flattened bailey to the SE, now left open for public access. This was occupied in the late C11 and early C12. (AR)

BLACKBOROUGH PRIORY, at Blackborough End, 1¼ m. SE. Founded by Robert Scales for Benedictine monks *c.* 1135, but handed to nuns *c.* 1200. All that remains is a not at all telling E–W wall and, further s, the gable-end of a building with a small lancet window in the gable.

MANOR FARMHOUSE, Setch Road, out to the E of Blackborough End. A T-shaped C17 house remodelled in the C19, with a s

front in five bays. Casement windows. The E and W returns
have platbands and C17 brick trimming.

MILEHAM   *9010*

ST JOHN BAPTIST. The oldest piece is the blocked chancel S
doorway, late C12, i.e. Norman, of two orders and with small
scallop capitals. The pointed arch must have been remodelled
in the C13. Also probably Norman is one high blocked circular
window on the N side of the unusually lofty chancel. The church
to which these belonged received aisles in the early C13. The N
aisle arcade is simply three pointed arches cut through the wall
and given thin keeled shafts at the corners of the rectangular
piers. The arches have one slight hollow chamfer. The S arcade
is a little longer to the E. It has a circular pier and respond and
an octagonal pier and respond. The circular pier has an octagonal abacus too. The piers are short and thick and the arches
have just a slight chamfer. The alarming lean to the arcade was
stabilized in 1981 by steel braces connecting to a concrete raft
under the S wall. Early C14 two-stage NW porch-tower W of the
N aisle with angle buttresses and Y-tracery to the bell-openings.
N doorway, S doorway, S aisle W window, and a chancel S window of the same period. The nave W window is Dec; three
lights, reticulated tracery with further sub-tracery inside the
reticulation units. Perp aisle and clerestory windows, restored in
1882 (roofs replaced also, by *William Curtis*). There are four
clerestory windows either side. Perp chancel arch. Tall C14
niches l. and r. of the E window, made with nodding ogee
arches, the r. one more ruined than the l., and with two-tiered
Late Dec tracery patterns. Nice C15 aisle roofs with arched
braces and traceried spandrels, almost Flamboyant, crowned
by good deep ashlaring with brattished cornices.

FURNISHINGS. FONT. Octagonal, Perp, with traceried stem
and pointed quatrefoils against the bowl. – PULPIT. Polygonal
and late C15, with a stem and tracery panels. – READER'S DESK.
A reused C15 stall front sandwiched between poppyhead ends. –
POOR BOX. Wooden, of the columnar type, dated 1639. –
STAINED GLASS. The W window is almost complete, of *c.* 1350
and *c.* 1450. In the upper half of the tracery lights are whole C14
figures of Saints John Baptist, Catherine and Margaret under
canopies, and foliage etc. In the lower parts is the C15 glass: a
mixture of fragments and three further figures (St Barbara, St
John Baptist and St Margaret). – Also some C14 and C15 glass
in the chancel windows. – MONUMENTS. Two fine later
medieval coffin-lids with foliated crosses, standing by the nave
doors. – Two wall monuments to the Barnwell family of the
demolished Mileham Hall, †1787 and †1802. – BRASS to
Christopher Crowe †1526 and wife (18 in.; S aisle, E end). –
LEDGER to Margaret Goose †1638 on the NW nave pier, with
typical lettering. – CROSS in the churchyard, W of the church
tower. C15. The base with its pointed quatrefoils is a tomb-chest.

The shaft is only partially preserved and has narrow niches with nodding ogee heads.

CHURCH FARMHOUSE, The Street. Lobby-entrance C17 timber-framed house with a five-bay brick skin added to form a polite late C18 façade. Thatched roof, which is less polite. Sashes. Good chimneystack with four shafts. The winder staircase remains to the rear of the stack, which has an C18 passageway running right through it. Good staircase of *c.* 1730: turned balusters, moulded handrail, dado panelling.

HALL FARMHOUSE, The Street. Bits of C16 brickwork are apparent in the N gable, which might represent a brick gable-end of a timber-framed house. But any timber parts were rebuilt in early C18 brick. Six-bay front in two storeys and attic, details rather too much C20. Rear pile added *c.* 1800. Excellent minor domestic C18 interiors, particularly the fielded panelling in many rooms. Closed-string staircase with turned balusters and dado panelling.

THE HALL YARDS, Burwood Hall, 300 yds w of the church, s of Litcham Road. Motte-and-bailey castle of the FitzAlans, established *c.* 1100. The lower part of a small keep sits within a low motte, and to the N is a bailey with wet ditches. Around the outside a near circular bailey or ringwork, and N of the village street next to Burwood Hall a rectangular enclosure surrounded by bank and ditch. The site bisected by the road (B1145). (AR)

BURWOOD HALL. Within the N extension to the castle moat, by the road. Rebuilt in 1793. Brick, seven bays in two storeys and quite plain. The windows are two- and three-light cross casements. Pediments to the gable-ends. A keystone has the date and initials of Thomas Coke of Holkham. Like Kempstone Lodge (2⅞ m. SW) it may be by *Samuel Wyatt*, since both were outlying parts of the Holkham Estate.

MINTLYN

⅞ m. s of Bawsey Church

ST MICHAEL. Ruinous. NE of Mintlyn Farm, by the former railway. The village was depopulated in the late C16 and the chancel probably was demolished then. Carstone with limestone dressings. A fragment of the w wall stands high up with a Perp four-centred window missing much of its tracery; also a smaller fragment farther E. The rest is choked in nettles, and the reported Norman arch and tympanum of the s doorway seen by Claude Messent in 1931 survives only as a couple of pieces in the King's Lynn museum. The FONT is a plain circular C12 bowl in the garden of Whitehouse Farmhouse ½ m. SE.

CREMATORIUM. *See* King's Lynn, p. 478.

MORLEY ST BOTOLPH

ST BOTOLPH. Badly damaged in the late 1950s but restored, and the nave re-roofed *c.* 1962. W tower, nave and chancel, in most of

the details restored Perp. The E window, though, is Y-traceried.
There were bequests for work on the nave in 1435 and 1444. –
FONT. Octagonal, with tracery on the stem and close panel tra-
cery on the bowl. Top battlemented.

MORLEY MANOR, 1 m. SW of St Botolph. Timber-framed. Long
front with two cross gables. Between them eight bays of windows
in an unusual rhythm, three of which are blind. Pedimented
doorcase with Doric engaged columns. Probably early C17, re-
fronted in the early C18. The E wing is a barn. The C18 staircase
has twisted balusters and scrolled tread-ends.

POST OFFICE STORES, ⅜ m. S of the church. The C19 shop front
has two display windows, one either side of the central door,
pilasters r. and l. The house behind is C18, timber-framed.

MORLEY ST PETER   0090

ST PETER. Hugs the ground. Stump of an unbuttressed W tower.
Nave with Perp windows, S porch rebuilt C16 and chancel
rebuilt C19. – FONT. Octagonal, Perp, simple. – STAINED GLASS.
E window by *A. L. Wilkinson* of *G. King & Son*, 1952, Virgin
and Child. – MONUMENTS. Martin Sedley †1609. Tablet with
flat alabaster frame. – John Turner Graver-Browne †1861. By
Gaffin. Still romantic and pre-Victorian, with an urn on a
branch of weeping willow.

MORLEY OLD HALL, ½ m. SW of St Peter. A very fine, not very
large brick house of *c.* 1600 in a secluded position, surrounded
by a moat. Built for the Sedleys, owners of the manor from
1545. The E front consists of two projecting wings one window
deep with stepped gables and mullioned and transomed windows and, recessed between them, just the five-light hall
window and the rather inconspicuous doorway. Above these
the first-floor windows and then two high dormers with a window and a roundel over. All windows and even the roundels are
pedimented, at least in the façade. The house is remembered as
tall rather than broad owing to the fact that four tiers of windows are everywhere squeezed into three floors. At the back the
big hall chimney-breast. In the S wing the parlour to the E, the
staircase to the W. N wing has two service rooms of equal size. In
the roof trusses with upper crucks.

MORLEY HALL. Part of Wymondham College. The house was
built for John Graver-Browne in 1839–41; the architect is
unrecorded, though the contractor was *G. W. Minns.* It is a
simple three- by five-bay gault-brick pile three storeys high. The
ground-floor windows with pediments, the main façade with
giant pilasters. Glazed entrance porch to E return.

WYMONDHAM COLLEGE. The new buildings by *G. W. Oak*, the
County Architect, 1955 etc. Various additions since, of which
the best is the Library, 1980 by the *County Architect's Department*
(job architect *C. Garner*). Square interior with free-standing
piers set away from the walls and supporting a high and wide
light-well tapering up to the top.

WOODLANDS, Attleborough Road. Timber-framed C16 house with brick end-gables and a brick-skinned front. Seven bays with a central C17 porch. Elevation with platband and C19 windows. The side wing has a stepped central pediment – an unusual thing – and a crenellated parapet. Of the timber frame there is visible jowled principal studs, tie-beams with arched braces and a roof with clasped purlins on diminished principals.

2090

MORNINGTHORPE

ST JOHN BAPTIST. Round tower, round to the top but with a battered profile. The lower parts early C12 but the upper stages Late Perp, possibly identifiable with a will of 1504. Two-light Perp w window. The battlemented parapet is C19, and different from Ladbroke's view of c. 1825. The C12 work represented by the unmoulded arch to the nave. Unmoulded square imposts, with two thin incised parallel horizontal lines. Nave and chancel apparently Early Perp, but a blocked round-headed window cut into by the s porch may indicate the C12. Blocked N door. The pretty piscina has an ogee arch, and in the spandrels a flower and a lion's face with its tongue stuck out; it is considered Dec by Cautley. Mid-C14 chancel arch has circular responds, polygonal capitals and wave mouldings in the arch. The roofs, E window and s porch renewed by *Herbert Green* in his restoration of 1889 (cost £1,150). An earlier restoration re-worked the s chancel windows. – FONT. C15. Octagonal. Against the stem four lions, against the bowl four lions and four demi-figures of angels. – FONT COVER. Timber, C19. – STAINED GLASS. E window, †1875, by *J. & J. King*, Life of Christ panels. One N and one s chancel window perhaps by *J. Dixon*, †1851 and †1852. – MONUMENTS. Elizabethan monument without effigy or inscription. Tomb-chest with Doric pilasters and shields. Back wall with Ionic pilasters and a four-centred arch. Oblong panel with coat of arms. The monument probably commemorates Richard Garneys, who bought Boyland Hall in 1571. – Margaret Gostlin †1723, by *Thomas Stayner*. Marble tablet with barley-sugar columns.

BOYLAND HALL. 1571, remodelled C19 and demolished 1947.

MANOR HOUSE, by the church. On the E side are remnants of the late C17 house of the Howes family, but the bulk is of the late C19 in similar style with much use of polygonal corner turrets, prominent stacks and stepped gables.

FRIAR'S FARMHOUSE, Church Street. A two-storeyed early C17 timber-framed house with cross wings r. and l. rising into attic storeys. Central porch is C19. N wing with a good external stack with octagonal flues.

TOWER MILL, ⅝ m. WSW of church. A very charming group of the brick tower mill and the bigger gabled mill buildings. c. 1830.

MORTON-ON-THE-HILL   *1010*

ST MARGARET. In the grounds of the Hall. The round tower
collapsed in 1959. Its unmoulded and splayed tower arch without any imposts remains. The circular window which helped
establish an Anglo-Saxon date has of course disappeared. Early
also the nave NW quoin, of carstone. The C19 S porch and part
of the nave roofless. The S nave has Y-tracery windows and a
Perp window. Chancel of early C14: lancet, Y-tracery, intersecting tracery in the three-light E window. The E wall however was
repaired *c.* 1850 when the N chapel rebuilt. Two-bay N arcade
with octagonal pier and coarse mouldings. – FONT. *c.* 1850.
Octagonal, cusped blank arcade to stem, shields round bowl. –
SCREEN. Parts reused as chancel panelling. – BENCH ENDS.
With poppyheads. – SOUTH DOOR. Shallow traceried panels
carved in relief. – COMMUNION RAIL. Jacobean, with vertically
symmetrical balusters. – MONUMENT. Thomas Southwell
†1609. Tomb-chest with three shields in simple strapwork surrounds. Four-centred arch on pilasters and an achievement on
top.

MORTON HALL. Thomas Southwell (†1609) built an Elizabethan
house here. It came to Thomas Berney in 1819, and *c.* 1830 he
added the present wing. In *c.* 1955 the older part demolished.
Red brick. The E front with a far-projecting central entrance
bay rising through both storeys to end in a pediment. Polygonal
cupola on top of that. Three bays of sashes r. and l. The entrance
bay with its own side sashes. Big stacks to N and S. Some parts
of the GARDEN WALLS to the W are late C16: English bond red
brick.

MOULTON ST MICHAEL *see*
GREAT MOULTON

MULBARTON   *1000*

ST MARY MAGDALEN. Dec W tower with a belfry stage perhaps
corresponding to a bequest in 1393 for a new bell. Dec nave,
Perp chancel, but a broad three-bay N aisle of 1875 added by
Phipson. Also 1875 the vestry, S porch and windows. The S porch
is in fact reduced from two storeys (by Phipson) and still has its
early C14 outer arch mouldings. Inner S doorway with similar
mouldings but of mid century. Inside all seems of 1875 (Phipson's
piers are quatrefoil), though the nave roof is early C19 and the
chancel roof C17. Dec the rather damaged triple-chamfered
chancel arch. – FONT. Octagonal, simple, with quatrefoils, seems
C17. (– SCULPTURE. Small fragment of an alabaster altar in
N aisle, with scenes from Life of St John Baptist.) – BENCHES
and PULPIT. 1872. – STAINED GLASS. Figures etc. of the C15 in
the chancel E and one S window. They came principally from
Martham in 1815 and were re-set possibly by *Dixon*. There is an

Adam and Eve. – MONUMENTS. Sir Edwin Rich †1675 (nave w). Big tablet flanked by coarse foliage scrolls and with an over-sized and damaged hourglass at the top. – Sir Edwin Rich †1651, son of the last, erected by his brother (nave s). Big tablet with a broken pediment and a cartouche rising out of it. – Mrs Sarah Scargill †1680 aged thirty (sw chancel arch pier). A very curious conceit. The wooden back of a Bible as a pedestal carries a copper diptych which, when one approaches it, is closed. It can be opened by a ring-pull and contains a long inscription by Mrs Scargill's husband, the rector. The r. wing reads as follows:

> Dear Love, one Feather'd minute and I come
> To lye down in thy darke Retireing Roome
> And mingle dust with thine, that wee may have,
> As when alive one bed, so dead one Grave;
> And may my Soul teare through the vaulted sky
> To be with thine to all Eternity.
> O how our Bloudless Formes will that Day greet
> With Love Divine when we again shall meet
> Devest of all Contagion of the Flesh
> Fullfill'd with everlasting joys and Fresh
> In Heaven above (and 't may be) cast an eye
> How far Elizium doth beneath us lye.
>   Deare, I disbody and away
>   More Swift than Wind
>   Or Flying Hind
>   I come I come away.
>   David Scargill

– George Gay †1729 (chancel N). Tablet with weeping putti at the top, on a pediment.

VILLAGE. Mulbarton has an uncommonly large triangular green known as THE COMMON. The church stands at the N point. The Common has many houses of indifferent character, and there is pressure as a commuter village so close (5 m.) to Norwich.

Immediately SE of the church is OLD HALL (now an antiques centre), formerly the manor of the Rich family. Timber-framed, with brick gable-ends. The rear is an E-plan: two gabled wings and a stair-turret in the middle. Façade of seven bays, with mullioned and transomed windows, all c. 1700 and a bit old-fashioned. In fact it is a re-facing and some details elsewhere have carried over from the early C17 house, e.g. the diamond-mullioned window in the SE wing. Of c. 1700 the shaped gable to the s. The early C17 roof is of diminished principals with clasped purlins. The very large brick BARN (also in commercial use at time of writing) is of similar dates, the early C18 alter-ations involving two new W bays and a shaped gable. This was extended to form a house, as the mullioned windows etc. indi-cate. It has still some turned balusters to the staircase. Butt-purlin roof with straight wind-braces. On the s side of The Common, MULBARTON HALL. C18, brick, six bays with a two-bay pedi-ment. The façade extended l. and r. in the C19. To the E, THE MALT HOUSE, a C17 lobby-entrance house extended C19. The original timber-framed but re-faced with brick and of only one

storey and attic. C18 cross casements. The staircase by the stack
with C17 turned balusters at the top.

To the E is RECTORY LANE. The OLD RECTORY is a three-
bay timber-framed C17 house extended in C18 and C19. The C18
S front has five bays of sashes. Its BARN was the coach house.
Dated 1731 and with shaped gables. Moulded brick eaves cornice to main elevation. THE LODGE, further E, is early C19. Three
bays and two storeys, porch on two Ionic columns. To the W
front is a nice cast-iron veranda with Greek key decoration and
reeded columns, added c. 1830. Stick-baluster staircase.

To the NW of the church is NORWICH ROAD. THE OLD
FORGE. Brick. Two wings enclose a little courtyard in front of
the main block. c. 1830. WORLD'S END, a pub. Two-storey
timber-framed house with a C17 stepped gable. C18 three-storey
addition, and most details C20. PADDOCK FARMHOUSE is of
two storeys and attic in five bays. The upper windows are two-
light late C17 cross casements. Moulded platband between the
floors. Pedimented doorcase.

KENNINGHAM HALL, ⅞ m. SE of the church. A C17 timber-
framed house to which has been added an early C19 three-bay
front block of colourwashed brick. In the C17 wing is a pargeted
overmantel with geometric designs.

MUNDFORD   8090

ST LEONARD. Nave and chancel and a tower in a SW position,
outside the nave. The chancel is E.E., see the three stepped
lancet windows in the E wall, with fine outer concave quadrant
mouldings and engaged shafts inside, and the piscina (pointed
arch on two shafts). The double wave mouldings and polygonal
capitals of the chancel arch indicate Perp. The church was
restored in 1899, with a new N vestry, at the expense of H.A.
Campbell. The nave is Dec – see the two-light windows with
mouchette designs. The roof is a hammerbeam type much
renewed 1899–1900. Chancel roof also renewed, a false hammerbeam prettily painted by *Comper* in 1912. N door has C14
mouldings. The N porch of flint and brick is probably of the
early C17. Chamfered brick round arch and brick E and W two-
light windows, their mullions of hollow keeled section. Of the
same section are the rendered brick central mullions of the nave
windows, so they have been restored. The tower is of 1854 and
replaces the W tower which fell in 1747. The new design is from
N France, with a saddleback roof with a little flèche and diagonal
S buttresses. This due to the patronage of Mrs Lyne-Stephens
of Lynford Hall (*see* p. 531), formerly a French ballet-dancer. –
FONT. Octagonal, Perp, with a foot opening out towards the
bowl without capitals or interruption and three symbols of
Evangelists sticking out from it. St Mark's bull is missing. There
is no base now. – BENCH ENDS. Some with poppyheads. –
PAINTING. Stencilling to the E window jambs, shafts and
between the lancets. – The remainder of the furnishings by

Sir Ninian Comper, 1911–12. The SCREEN is quite extraordinary: full width, coved and ribbed to both sides, the wider W coving supporting the organ and standing on four richly moulded posts. Under the organ a large sculpted Crucifixion flanked by three Saints r. and l. On the dado are reused late C14 posts finished with crocketed pinnacles. – ORGAN. 1912 by *Harrison & Harrison*. – PULPIT. Linenfold panelling and emblems in top panels. – STALLS. Also with linenfold panelling. The ensemble is all remarkable in design and remarkably out of place in this modest chancel. The sentimental altar RETABLE and the terrible STAINED GLASS in the E window seem to be by *Comper* too. All paid for by Capt F. Montagu of Lynford Hall.

WEST HALL, ⅔ m. NW of the church. A C16 timber-framed house with a masonry S gable-end. Various C17 and C18 additions. Two-storey C16 block with jettied first floor. Entrance front to E. Late C18 sashes and door to ground floor, blocked mullioned windows above. C17 stair outshut to rear and more blocked windows. Bridging beams with roll and hollow mouldings. Good dog-leg C17 staircase with splat balusters. The C17 additional block of flint and brick has a reused C15 bridging beam with leaf trail.

A pleasant VILLAGE with 1960s and 70s housing spreading to the N and W of the church, through which one passes to reach West Hall. ST LEONARD'S STREET linking the church with the village green has on the E side No. 33, THE OLD RECTORY, late C17, with an early C19 façade in three bays of flint with brick dressings and sashes. Clunch appears in the long rear wing. A little N at the junction with West Hall Road stands a C17 thatched five-bay lobby-entrance house of one storey and attic, bricked in the early C19. To the E on the N side are C17 timber-framed cottages at Nos. 24–26A, again faced with brick in the C19 and under a thatched roof. C19 and C20 details to the façade but a C17 stack with serrated bundled flues. To their l. a semi-detached pair for the Lynford Estate dated 1885, flint with brick dressings, and to the r. two more pairs of 1890 without flint. On CROWN ROAD the CROWN HOTEL, facing a tiny triangular village green: a brick and flint building with a later flint and clunch wing to the rear and archaeological evidence of the C17 only to the S of the W front. Two storeys and attic in four wide bays of C19 sashes. No. 17 (BRECKHOLM) to the N is of flint with gault-brick dressings. Quite a singular design. The façade is of five bays but only one storey on a basement, and the three middle bays are set back to form a veranda with a pair of fluted columns and engaged columns *in antis* rising to support the eaves of the hipped roof, which ignores the fact of the recess. Steps up to the door. Early C19.

3090

MUNDHAM

ST PETER. Opulent Norman S doorway. Two orders of colonnettes with decorated shafts, capitals approaching waterleaf in their design. Arch with zigzag, roll, inturned volutes, etc., hood-mould with two orders of scallops at r. angles to the wall surface. Dec chancel, mostly renewed, but the N window and the piscina in order. Sedilia simply the dropped sill of the window. Two little arches in the jambs. Perp W tower with flushwork panelling on the battlements. Perp nave, with three-light windows like those of the N aisle of 1887. Two-bay arcade. Nave roof single-framed with scissor-bracing high up, and with barber's poling and other painting on the cornice. Chancel roof arch-braced and with collars. – FONTS. Under the tower a disused square Purbeck marble font with flat arches. Norman. The other font C19. – SCREEN. C15. Simple, with one-light divisions and flat cut-out tracery, and with some remains of colour. – WALL PAINTING. On the N wall a late St Christopher in poor condition; interlace borders with sprouting leaves. Restored by *Monica Bardswell* in 1948. (DP)

ST ETHELBERT, ½ m. ESE. Ruin of the N chancel wall of the former second parish church.

ABBEY FARMHOUSE, E of the ruin. Timber-framed. Gable-end with two jetties. On the front two window pediments with foliage, also the date 1654. Four mullioned windows to first floor. Octagonal chimneyshafts with star tops, as if they should be of a century or more earlier. There is a rear wing with a brick stair-turret in the angle, and another to the S of the early C18 terminating in a shaped gable.

MUNDHAM HOUSE, to the SE. Early Georgian, five bays, two storeys and dormer attic, hipped roof, early C19 doorway with open pediment.

FARMHOUSES of the C17 are scattered about. On Bergh Apton Road stands WHITE HOUSE FARMHOUSE, a timber-framed lobby-entrance house. In Brooke Road HALL FARMHOUSE: two storeys, three bays, thatched, remains of a shuttered six-light mullioned window in the back wall.

NARBOROUGH 7010

ALL SAINTS. Norman nave, see the blocked N doorway W from where the N aisle starts. Chronologically next the SW tower with a W lancet, bell-openings with Y-tracery (except that to the E, with a pretty Perp design), and a double-hollow-chamfered arch to the aisle which dies into its imposts, i.e. early C14. Tower top with later flushwork panelling. The W bay of the S aisle, including the first of the octagonal piers, belongs to the same build. Then, however, the N aisle appears to have followed. Three bays, piers with four main shafts and four thin, filleted shafts in the diagonals. Arches with two wave mouldings. The other three bays of the S aisle are Dec. Octagonal piers with alternating straight and concave diagonal sides and at their top a shallow blank pointed trefoiled arch (cf. Dersingham). C19 Perp S aisle windows. C19 Perp N windows, but the reticulated E aisle window seems C14. Pretty S doorway with fleurons in the arch.

Chancel Perp, with good five-light E window. In the S aisle two external tomb recesses. Clerestory with eight windows. Vestry of 1906 N of the tower.

FURNISHINGS. BENCH. One in the S aisle with poppyheads and coat of arms. – STAINED GLASS. C16 angels in the tracery of the chancel N window. – SCULPTURE. Two copper reliefs, both C18, one (Descent from the Cross) probably Italian, the other (Adoration of the Shepherds) French. – MONUMENTS. Demi-effigy of a Lady, wearing a wimple (chancel N), probably that of Dame Agatha of Narburgh †1293. – Brasses to Henry Spelman †1496 and wife (27 in. figures, chancel floor), John Eyer †1561 and wife (kneeling figures, chancel S, good), John Spelman †1545 (2 ft figure, chancel floor), Sir John Spelman †1545 and wife (kneeling figures with a panel of the Resurrection above; chancel N), John Spelman †1581, palimpsest of an early C15 brass of two ladies (22 in. figure; chancel floor). – Sir Clement Spelman †1607 and wife. Alabaster. Big standing wall monument. Two semi-reclining effigies resting on an elbow, he above and behind her. Above and behind is the inscription panel and to the l. a kneeling child, to the r. a baby under a tent. The figures quite stiffly carved. – Sir John Spelman †1662. Standing wall monument with inscription framed by bunched hanging garlands. – Clement Spelman †1679, formerly thought to be by Cibber, a confusion partly brought about by a mis-identification of a drawing in the V & A, which has nothing to do with this monument. It is possibly by *Sir William Wilson* (GF). What remains is a standing alabaster figure in the robes of the Recorder of Nottingham. This standing figure is an early example of a type most popular about 1700–10. Originally also the pedestal beneath the statue was 8 ft tall and stood in the chancel with Clement Spelman's coffin inside in an upright position. It is said that he insisted on this upright position in order not to be trodden on. The monument was moved and the pedestal reduced in 1865. – Andrew Fountaine †1706, a cartouche attributed to *William Woodman* the elder (GF).

NARBOROUGH HALL. At the back (E) is reused ashlar as a plinth course. The Spelman family inherited in the C15, built a Tudor T-shaped mansion and added bits and pieces until there was a major remodelling *c.* 1770. Of the C16 work much can be gleaned as the nine bays in the centre of the wide S front are of Tudor brick, although partly taken down and rebuilt. The stepped W gable is visible from the roof space, a roof that also survives: butt-purlins with curved wind-bracing and solid arched braces to the collars. Then the C18 work added the sashes and enlarged the front with two-bay gault-brick extensions either side, very slightly projecting, making thirteen bays in all. The central full-height canted bay window also appeared, again of gault brick, with four Roman Doric columns, since glazed in. Battlements were also appended over the whole length of the elevation. Inside there are various pieces of C16 panelling, some linenfold, and the date 1581. Also a good Gothick chimneypiece with clustered colonnettes.

Two picturesque WATERMILLS, one of brick, the other bigger, stuccoed, and more diversified. NARBOROUGH MILL, on the NE side of the former A47 road, has carstone and weather-boarding too. Late C18. Three storeys and attic, of five bays and an additional bay added 1980 to the r. This bay by *Robert Freakley* had to go up because an earlier C18 block in this position collapsed. The ground floor has recessed arcading. The rear wall weatherboarded.

IRON AGE FORT. In Camphill Plantation are the earthworks of a univallate irregular oval fort, of 3½ acres. There is an entrance to the SE, but the W side was levelled in the C19. A number of Iron Age and Romano-British sherds have been recovered from the central area. (DG)

DEVIL'S DYKE (or Bircham Ditch). A linear earthwork, now mostly destroyed, which ran S from the Iron Age fort at Narborough to a tributary of the Wissey in Beachamwell. It consists of a bank with a ditch on its E side. It is undated, but if contemporary with the Foss Ditch (*see* p. 343) would be post-Roman and of the C5–C7. It is mentioned in a Ramsey Abbey charter of 1053. The best-preserved stretch is to the N and S of the A1122 in Beachamwell parish. (AR)

NARFORD   7010

(ST MARY. The church of a village which has disappeared. The church is redundant and lies now all on its own amid trees near the lake NW of the Hall. Of flint, and short in its proportions. Of the C13 chancel, recognizable only the stone arm between the two-seated sedilia which is otherwise no more than a dropped window-sill. Early C14 the N recess on short shafts. The rest of the chancel of 1902. Early C14 forms in the aisle E windows and the N doorway. C14 also the two-bay arcades. Octagonal piers, double-hollow-chamfered arches. The details simple on the S side. The chancel arch corresponds to the S arcade. The church was much restored in 1857, when the tower was rebuilt in memory of Charlotte, wife of Andrew Fountaine. At the same time the roofs were renewed and the windows restored. – FONT. Octagonal and plain. – FONT COVER. Jacobean, with a spire on four turned posts. – PULPIT. Elizabethan or Jacobean, with the familiar blank arches. Presently in the stables of the Hall. – MONUMENTS. Mrs Price †1740. Grey sarcophagus below a grey obelisk; no effigy. – Sir Andrew Fountaine, 1753 by *John Powley*, but with, in front of the concave-sided grey obelisk, a bust by *Roubiliac*. The model for it is in the hall of Narford Hall.)

(NARFORD HALL.* A large, complex building in which several periods are represented. The long S front consists of a seven-bay house begun in 1702, with a tall domed Victorian entrance

---

* I have not seen Narford Hall or the church. The description which follows is largely taken from the article in the *Georgian Group Journal*, 1987.

tower on its r. Beyond this to the NE are Georgian additions, partly remodelled in the C19, which may be on the site of buildings pre-dating the C18 house. Sir Andrew Fountaine of Salle purchased the estate in 1690, and the first stone of his new house was laid in June 1702. An elevation of the proposed house of *c.* 1700 shows the seven-bay S front with some minor deviations from the actual building: a segmental doorway pediment rather than the broken segmental pediment that was built, carving and a garland in the three-bay main pediment, plain eaves instead of balustraded parapets and a cupola. There appears to be no basement storey and it may be that the older buildings to the NE were retained for services. The façade is of carstone with ashlar dressings, and the centre three bays are all ashlar. Rusticated quoins to centre and outer corners. The doorway has attached columns and in addition to its pediment a radial seven-vaned fanlight. This part of the house was complete by 1704, and an attribution of the design to *Henry Bell* of King's Lynn has been suggested. Sir Andrew died in 1706, succeeded by his son, also Sir Andrew (1676–1753). He took an active interest in architecture and was connected with Burlington's circle of emerging Palladian architects, so his continued additions and improvements to the house display developing Palladian taste from the early C18 into the 1730s.

Behind the centre bays of the original S front is the SALOON, made memorable by its painted decoration made for Sir Andrew II. This is (after the burning of his work at Castle Howard) the finest work of *Giovanni Antonio Pellegrini* in England. This Venetian painter, whose style leads from that of the early Ricci to the Rococo of, say, Pittoni, arrived in 1708 and left in 1713. He painted ten scenes from antique and biblical stories: Minerva and Arachne, Lucretia, the Rape of Europa, Susanna and the Elders, Minerva with Chiron and Achilles, Angelica and Medoro, Nessus and Dejanira, Romulus and Remus, Narcissus, and Sophonisba taking poison. The Norfolk Tour (1772–1808) describes them as a present from Lord Burlington, and it is interesting that Pellegrini also decorated Burlington House. The STAIRCASE belongs to the elder Sir Andrew's time and is in fact dated 1704. It has three dainty twisted balusters to each step. Fine stucco ceiling. The walls have portraits of English kings from James I to George II as Prince of Wales, by an English imitator of Pellegrini.

In 1716 Sir Andrew II returned from the Grand Tour and immediately remodelled the courtyard to the NE and created a library on the *piano nobile*, finished in 1718. A late C18 account by Benjamin Ibbots suggests Roger Harrison as the architect, but he may be confused with *Roger Morris*; in any case the professional may have acted only as the foreman or executive architect, relying on designs by *Fountaine* himself. The LIBRARY WING faces W, is of four bays on a basement, has segmental pediments over the first-floor windows, arched attic windows cutting into the balustrade and relates to Campbell's designs for Wanstead House published in 1715. There is a big coved ceiling with paintings of Morning, Noon and Night, and in the cornice are portraits of notable literary and scientific figures. The parquet floor is *Ketton*'s of 1860. The CLOSET beyond (N) the library has a ceiling by *Adrien de Clermont* c. 1735.

Further additions were made c. 1735. The MUSIC ROOM, to the E of the original house, is a four-bay block with a Kentian fireplace; to the W of the dining room is the octagonal CHINA CLOSET (Fountaine was a noted collector). At the same time the big bow was added to the W front of the 1702–4 block, and a second big bow with a ground-floor Venetian window extends the N façade of the DINING ROOM behind the saloon. *Robert Ketton* raised this fat bow into its full height in c. 1860 and provided the two Corinthian columns inside to separate this addition from the old front line. In the Dining Room is a strange fireplace in grey and white marble with a relief of the story of Cimon, probably Italian. Then *Ketton*'s work, c. 1855–60, pulled the various parts together, and gave the house High Victorian grandeur for the fifth Andrew Fountaine. His forms are individually feeble, a kind of mixed Renaissance with Italian, French and English elements, but he knew how to compose. Apart from the details already noted, to the r. of the old façade he set his principal accent, an entrance with a domed tower. To its r. he remodelled the Queen Anne and the Music Room, which were knocked into one. In the front bay of the former a coved C18 ceiling with busy monkeys and other animals. This is again by *Clermont*, c. 1735.

In the GROUNDS N of the Hall and beyond the lake a TEMPLE. The plan is shown in Campbell's 1725 engraving, so it cannot be much later than the example at Chiswick, c. 1722, an early example of the antique garden fashion. The present irregular lake is from 1860, and the temple has been relocated. Of the formal PLANTATIONS of the 1720s, shown in Prideaux's sketches of c. 1727, only ghosts remain. The CLOCK TOWER, ORANGERY and WALLS probably c. 1860 and by *Ketton*. The orangery has seven bays of casement windows under semi-circular arches. Centre bay with rustication.)

NECTON   8000

ALL SAINTS. The commanding W tower is undoubtedly very impressive, regardless of the fact that it is in all its impressive details – tall bell-windows, pierced parapet, two-tier lantern of the Shipdham type – of 1865. Or should one's evaluation be influenced by the date? Half the cost was met by Col. Mason of the Hall. The S porch was replaced in 1852 by the Mason Chapel, also with chequerwork, Perp windows and crenellated side parapets. At the same time the N porch became a vestry. Nave and aisles with Perp windows and a handsome clerestory with eight closely set three-light windows, also Perp. Perp chancel windows, that to E restored. The two E bays of the N aisle were rebuilt early in the C19 using too much brick. But the N chapel E window (consecrated in 1326) and the S aisle W window are Dec, and so are the arcades inside. Four bays, quatrefoil piers and double-hollow-chamfered arches. Two more bays, a little lower, for the N chapel opening off the chancel. A partition was erected behind them in 1992 and a further vestry built. The clerestory is impressive inside too, and reads together with the splendid hammerbeam roof, both c. 1490. The jambs of the windows with big, almost too big, fleurons, and shafts etc.; the E window blocked and altered. The roof rests on wall-posts with standing figures. There are alternating hammerbeams and simple arched braces rising to collars. Angels along the hammers and, in two tiers with spread wings, along the wall-plate. The angels' wings a little deficient in feathers. In addition many bosses. Much of all this has its original colouring (restored in 1982). Chancel roof plastered. In the S (Trinity) chapel a Dec angle piscina.

FURNISHINGS. FONTS. Octagonal, with tracery panels and shields, made in 1788, an unusual date. Late C14 bowl under the tower, one facet with tracery designs. – PULPIT. A sumptuous octagonal piece of 1636, with back panel and tester and much studding of all uprights. – PAINTING. In the reredos, a copy of *Sebastian del Piombo*'s Raising of Lazarus, signed *Wm. Rimer*, 1851. STAINED GLASS. E window by *De la Roche* of Paris, installed by *T. Wilmshurst*, 1844. Sugary figures. N chapel E window by the same. In the Trinity Chapel a Crucifixion etc. by *Ward & Nixon*, c. 1850. – MONUMENTS. In the churchyard a remarkable C14 TABLE TOMB near the priest's door, with a stone effigy of a woman, the carving in low relief. Traditionally supposed to commemorate the Countess of Warwick. – Also the upper half of a similar effigy under the tower. – In the S chapel porch two monuments by *Pugin* to the Mason family, 1835, both in the Court School Decorated style: central wide ogee arch flanked by narrower ones, plenty of tracery carving and figures of angels in the side bays. – BRASSES. To Ismayne de Wynston †1372, 30 in. figure (nave w). – Philippa de Beauchampe †1384, inscription in Old French, 3 ft 7 in. figure (N chapel). – William Curteys †1499; 19 in. figure; nave. – John Bacon †1527; 12 in.; chancel. – Robert Goodwyn †1532; 18 in.; nave. – Mary Rust †1596, in contemporary costume; N chapel.

NECTON HALL was a big house of Elizabethan origins built for the Mason family, re-worked 1863–5 for Col. Mason, and demolished 1949. The red brick STABLES, c. 1865, remain, converted to farm use. Costessey-ware details. T-plan, two and a half storeys with lower side wings. Five-bay E façade, centre three brought forward under a shaped gable. Stepped gables to other sides.

CHURCH FARMHOUSE, Tuns Road, dated 1859; also built for William Mason of the Hall. Red brick, two storeys in three bays, Costessey-ware roundel to first floor. Triple polygonal chimney flues.

NEEDHAM

2080

St Peter. Nothing special, but of a nice variety of periods. Norman round tower with a polygonal top of Tudor brickwork and C19 crenellations. Brick s porch, pretty, with polygonal angle-shafts and a stepped gable. Friezes of moulded brick with quatrefoil etc. motifs. Arch-braced roof. Three bequests for its building survive, two in 1469, one in 1470, which would seem convincing if the style of the porch was not so clearly early C16. Short chancel of 1735, of red brick picked out with burnt headers; the windows altered in 1884. Perp nave roof with arched braces up to high collar-beams. – FONT. C15, octagonal. Against the stem four lions, against the bowl the signs of the Evangelists and four roses. – BENCH ENDS. Late C15. With a border with fleurons and with poppyheads. One back with a carved trail and an inscription: 'Use wel thy tyme for dethe is comyng M The sentence of God Allmighty is everlastyng E'. – TOWER STAIR DOOR. C15. – STAINED GLASS. N nave and N chancel windows have some C16 and C17 fragments. – The CHURCHYARD WALL to s of late C16 red brick.

Village. Needham is stretched out along the main A143 road. Many of the houses turn out to have C17 and C18 timber frames. The most interesting is perhaps No. 99 HIGH ROAD, a simple late C16 timber-framed house with a central through passage opening into a hall l. and service room r. It only had a single door into the service room, now blocked. Of the roof the tie-beams alone survive, but these have mortices for a queenpost upper structure. The whole cased in brick. The former FISHMONGERS' ARMS has an early C17 timber frame and a thatched roof. On the opposite side, SHINGLE COTTAGE; a C19 lean-to at the back covers the original four-centred main doorway, carved with roses in spandrels. The door also of the same time, c. 1530–40. Various mullioned windows at the back. The front shows the plan has changed to a lobby-entrance.

NEW BUCKENHAM

0090

St Martin. An uncommonly sumptuous Perp church, due perhaps to John Coke, who in 1479 ordered that he should be buried in the new aisle and left money for its leading. In 1509 John Dikke left money 'to the makyng of a newe Ile'. From the arcades one can assume Coke's to be the s and Dikke's the N. Donations for an aisle continued until 1515. Knapped flint with much flushwork. The base frieze of the w tower has an entertaining variety of tracery motifs such as mouchette wheels, which also run round the s aisle and s porch, suggesting they were built at the same time. The tower buttresses have panelling and emblems, the battlements a chequer pattern. The sound-holes are closely traceried. The bell-openings have three lights. The pinnacles are on a square plan. In the spandrels of the w doorway shields. There is flushwork panelling around it

and a frieze above it. The tower seems later C15. The s porch
has a flushwork-panelled front and battlements with panelling
and shields. Arch re-done in 1983. The ten closely set clerestory
windows on either side of the church are not easily forgotten.
The voussoirs are of brick and flint alternately, and there is
more flushwork panelling between them. Good roof with corbels showing the twelve Apostles with their emblems, not very
expertly cleaned and decorated in 1968. Donations for a roof
were made in 1524 and 1528. The N aisle exterior on the other
hand is decidedly behind the scenes. What is not Perp? The s
doorway, which can hardly be later than the early C14, and the
C13 chancel, heavily restored in 1870 and virtually rebuilt in
1895. The 1870 restorations by *W. Fawcett* of Cambridge.

Inside the church, the arcades take us back to the Late Perp
style. Both are of five bays. The s arcade seems earlier than the
N. It has the usual four shafts and four hollows. On the N side
the piers are elongated lozenges and the shafts very thin, with
continuous casement mouldings into the arch. – FONT. On a
quatrefoiled step. Against the stem four lions and four Wild
Men. The bowl is dated 1619, and an interesting example of
how the Jacobean carver re-cut and remodelled motifs of the
Perp style. – DOORS. Both s and w doors are traceried. –
STAINED GLASS. E window by *Charles Kempe*, †1890, and a N
chancel window †1894. – EASTER SEPULCHRE doubling as a
monument (chancel N). C15. Four-centred arch under a square
hood with angle buttress-shafts and cresting. The brass of a
woman in profile against the back wall is missing. The window
above seems to be composed with the tomb. – REREDOS. By
H. B. Walters of London, 1909. – BENCHES. Six C15 poppyheads. – BOARDS. Removed from the Market House (*see* below):
one with two angels and the shield of St James, one with two
angels and three shields, the third with two harts and a walled
town with its gatehouse.

CASTLE. Built in the 1140s by William d'Albini II to replace Old
Buckenham Castle, which he had handed over to the Augustinian Canons for them to erect a priory out of the materials. That
was in 1146, when work on the new castle was sufficiently
advanced. The castle consists of an inner bailey and two outer
baileys, to the w and s and to the E, all with earth walls. The
inner bailey is roughly circular and 141 yds in diameter. The
circular keep stands near the E side of the rampart. Like Castle
Rising and Castle Acre there was a stone gatehouse, set to the
NE of the inner bailey facing the town. Then, in the later C12,
the castle was turned round, the height of the rampart greatly
increased, burying the gatehouse, a bigger gatehouse was built
to the w, and the w–sw–s bailey made. The principal interest of
the KEEP lies in the fact that it is circular, yet apparently not
later than *c.* 1150. It would thus be the earliest circular keep in
England, even if yet earlier ones existed in France (Château-sur-
Epte). Its walls are 11 ft thick at the foot, and the total height of
the keep may have been something like 40 ft. Its diameter is
68 ft. The keep was two-storeyed and internally divided by a

cross wall. What we see now is the featureless basement. The castle was demolished in the 1640s, by the then owner Sir Philip Knyvet, perhaps at the request of Parliament.

Inner and outer (i.e. W–SW–S) baileys are connected by a BRIDGE. This in its present form dates from the C19. In the outer bailey stood the Chapel of St Mary, and this survives, SE of the keep, as a BARN at the bend in the road. It dates from the mid or later C12 and has lost its chancel. Norman still the splayed S doorway. The little doorway in the NW corner is E.E. The jambs of the windows indicate a Perp date.

THE TOWN

The little town was laid out to the E of the castle after 1146, certainly before the 1190s, and has preserved its layout. For this it deserves to be better known. There were ditches round it linking to the outer baileys of the castle, and in the NE angle the ditch remains. The streets cross more or less at r. angles. Alterations to the layout happened after the foundation of the parish church by Robert de Tateshale (i.e. after 1243).

Perambulation

The MARKET PLACE does not look a market place now, with the neat irregular grass in the middle. It was until the 1520s more open to the S, but by 1529 a line of houses had encroached N of 67 Boosey's Walk. Towards the N, on an island site, an early C19 FORGE, complete with fittings. Most striking is the rectangular MARKET HOUSE or CROSS with the upper floor on plain 72 wooden columns. Its present form is an adaptation of before 1718 from the original shops put up in 1559. The columns are of 1754. The middle column was a whipping-post. On the upper floor were three boards from the underside of oriel windows, brought in and subsequently removed to the church. There is a crown-post roof inside.

On the S side the range of houses is C16. The three jettied ones at the E end are of 1529, timber-framed with rendered wattle and daub. They have a common roof of square-section crown-posts with arched braces to the crown purlin. The principal house on the W side is ST MARY'S, with a late C18 brick front attached to a timber-framed core. Of seven bays, but with a gross Victorian-Jacobean porch on four Ionic pilasters. BLAIR HOUSE, really two houses, is early C17 and timber-framed. Timber as well the early C18 KING'S HEAD public house, given a brick front and altered. On the E side is THE ROOKERY; its Tudor brick WALL to the street has an entrance with a four-centred head between two polygonal buttresses. The HOUSE itself is C17, with a stepped gable, and a re-fronting. To the N side PICKWICK COTTAGE, C15, with a mid-C19 brick skin over the incomplete timber frame and a C20 bow window, sashes etc. To the E is the C15 privy tower and stair-turret. CRAWFORD'S and CORNER COTTAGE to the E is an early C16 timber-framed

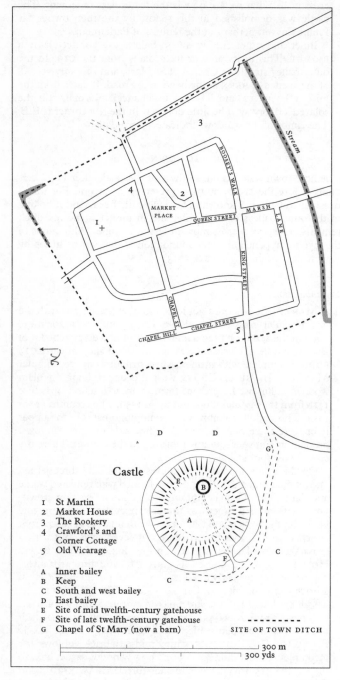

Castle

1   St Martin
2   Market House
3   The Rookery
4   Crawford's and
    Corner Cottage
5   Old Vicarage

A   Inner bailey
B   Keep
C   South and west bailey
D   East bailey
E   Site of mid twelfth-century gatehouse
F   Site of late twelfth-century gatehouse
G   Chapel of St Mary (now a barn)

- - - - - - - - SITE OF TOWN DITCH

300 m
300 yds

New Buckenham

house floored in the C17 when it was probably subdivided into two dwellings, so the former open hall is not at once apparent. Central recess as in hall houses of the Wealden type and jetties r. and l. On the corner opposite (i.e. on the Norwich Road) THE RETREAT, another mid-C19 brick skin over a late C16 timber frame.

Proceeding s from the Market Place into QUEEN STREET, on the w side THE PLEASANCE, c. 1500. The ubiquitous mid-C19 brick facing to a timber-framed house. Two storeys in three bays. Close-studded frame with a middle rail, tension and arched braces. Evidence of an open hall to the N. Roof of queenposts but reconstructed. At the corner of BOOSEY'S WALK and MARSH LANE to the s is LANE'S END, of the same date. Jettied N range, now underbuilt. ALMSHOUSES on Marsh Lane dated 1861, brick with shaped gables. The THATCHED COTTAGE built as three houses in 1606. Usual C19 and C20 exterior details. Good fireplace inside under a roll-moulded bressumer and with its winder staircase hard by.

KING STREET runs w. The story is more of the early C17, with occasional earlier structures. Almost all are timber-framed behind later cladding, and a selection only is necessary. On the N the POST OFFICE and ANTIQUE SHOP is of 1598, but re-faced in the mid C19. Timber frame with rendered wattle and daub. FAIRVIEW is still identifiable as a C16 open hall house, floored in the C17, much altered in 1970s. The OLD WHITE HORSE INN has had the worst luck with its grisly Fletton brick skin of the 1940s. On the s side at the w end TUDOR ROSE COTTAGE, with a date 1738 and the initials IEL (Joseph and Elizabeth Lucas). Rare indeed to find a date plaque later than the true age, for it is c. 1500, merely re-fronted in 1738. Cross passage plan, clasped purlin roof. Some interior alteration. The three HOUSES next w in a little range are C17, again timber-framed. BAKEHOUSE COTTAGE seems late C16, very heavy scantling to the frame; w bay added late C17 and the façade altered. The casements C18.

Cutting N at the w end is CHAPEL STREET. On the w corner the complicated OLD VICARAGE, with a claim to being the C15 guildhall. The s range is the original timber-framed part, with a C19 brick skin and additions to the N (1872) and NE (1894). W wall with a C16 stack embedded in a C17 stepped gable and various window openings. The s part greatly altered inside. Heavy scantling frame, a C17 fireplace in the w room, N wall with a blocked hollow-mullioned six-light window. Another one to the E. Tie-beams on arched braces, presumably indicating an open hall. Crown-posts repaired or replaced. Further N is MCINTYRE HOUSE, 1624, again re-faced in the mid C19. Lobby-entrance house with a winder by the stack, and rather mixed details. First-floor s room with a plastered ceiling in an alcove, with a Tudor rose pendant and floral trails. Opposite No 1, a good example of a medieval town-house with the jettied short end facing the street. Early C16 but altered, so that the site of the hall is difficult to identify. CHAPEL HILL is a cul-de-sac extension to the N, with picturesque timber-framed cottages known to have been built 1615–35.

NEW HOLKHAM see HOLKHAM

NEW HOUGHTON see HOUGHTON

NEW HUNSTANTON see HUNSTANTON

8010

NEWTON
NE of Castle Acre

ALL SAINTS. Flint with dressings of limestone, brick and carstone. Late Saxon, with a central tower of the same width as the chancel. The windows are double-splayed, and there are above the present ceiling two triangular-headed openings, one to the W, one to the E. The tower has a pyramid roof, which, though later, is what such towers originally had been covered by. Bell-openings of two lights with a recessed shaft. The arches are repaired. The E arch of the central space has a small unmoulded arch on the simplest imposts. This also seems Saxon. The W arch was given double wave mouldings, perhaps when the Dec S and W nave windows were set in. A lancet in the S tower wall, where a transept may formerly have projected. In the N chancel wall one blocked window, otherwise C14 windows.

2090

NEWTON FLOTMAN

ST MARY. Perp W tower; bequests were made in 1431–66, plausible enough dates. On the crenellated E parapet an inscription of 1503 to Ralph Blondevile. Big C19 W window. Original brick staircase in the N stair-turret, with a stone newel. Plenty of brick in the tower, visible inside, extending to the triple-chamfered arch towards the nave including the engaged responds. Double-chamfered stone chancel arch. Nave with intersecting tracery and Perp windows, chancel with C20 E window and Perp windows. The details all too renewed in the 1890s to be of value. – FONT. Octagonal, with shields in cusped fields. – BENCHES. With poppy-heads, C15. One arm with an animal (W end S side), another re-cut animal facing it. – STAINED GLASS. E and W windows by *Charles Kempe*, †1898 and †1902, both good, the latter commemorating the Boer War. – MONUMENT. Thomas Blondevile, erected in 1638 by his son-in-law Robert King. A curious tri-partite monument with two outer Tuscan columns and two inner pilasters. Top with semicircular pediment between obelisks. In the three panels from l. to r., four female weepers (Elizabeth and Patience, Blondevile's two wives, and daughters), Blondevile kneeling before a prayer desk, and a brass plate with three generations of Blondeviles, 'grandsyre, father and the sone'. Below is a brass plaque to Patience King †1638, Blondevile's daughter.

OLD RECTORY, Church Road. Kelly provides the date 1835. Gault brick, two storeys, three bays.

BRIDGE. The bridge across the River Tas is partly C15. Of four brick and ashlar arches, widened and repaired at the SE end in 1835, as a datestone on the parapet testifies. The three original stone arches have single-chamfered ribs, and, under the soffits, chamfered transverse ribs.

MAID'S HEAD. Public house on Old Street. The patently fake timber studding conceals a genuine early C16 timber frame to an open hall house. Only one crown-post roof truss remains. Floored probably in the early C18. The other internal details all C20.

DAIRY FARM, part of the Shotesham Estate (q.v.). The HOUSE is C17, timber-framed, extended in the C18, and not very inspiring. The BARN is late C15, also timber-framed and of great 62 interest indeed. The five-bay frame is virtually complete, on a brick plinth. Jowled studs with arched braces to the tie-beams, upon which are double queenpost trusses, one above the other,

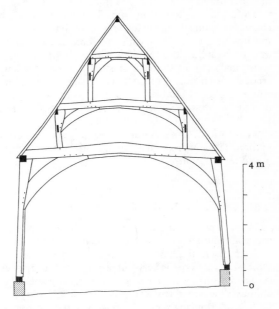

Newton Flotman, Dairy Farm Barn. Section

a great rarity. The queenposts are themselves arch-braced. The triangular-section purlins are clasped. The whole is of great quality of execution, as well as design. Well restored 1993 by *Colin Jeffries*.

LODGE, on Ipswich Road at the entrance to the Shotesham Park drive. *c.* 1790. Gault brick. Two Ionic columns support a pediment. If it is by *Soane*, it is not his best. Iron railings.

NORDELPH

5000

HOLY TRINITY. 1865 by *John Giles* of London. E.E. with a flèche between nave and chancel. Brick, nothing fancy. Scissor-braced nave roof with principals on arched braces. The two trusses marking the internal division of nave and chancel rest on paired wall-shafts. – STAINED GLASS. E window excellent, by *Heaton, Butler & Bayne.*

WESLEYAN CHAPEL. 1861. Still Classical, and not trying to look grand.

NORTH BARSHAM

9030

ALL SAINTS. Nave and chancel and early C19 W bellcote. The church originally continued to the W and probably also to the E, but its present size pre-dates Ladbroke's 1824 drawing. Altogether much restored over a long period, 1865–98, then the nave re-roofed and re-floored in 1911. The nave only two bays, the chancel only one. Original features point to the late C13, notably the three-light windows with the three lancet lights stepped under one arch. Re-set W door with early C14 forms. – FONT. Octagonal, C13, of Purbeck marble, with two shallow pointed arches to each side. – PULPIT. With parts of 1635, but with an equal number of Victorian elements. – STAINED GLASS. In the E window on N side some C14 fragments. – MONUMENT. Philip Russell †1617, minor alabaster tablet.

CHURCH FARMHOUSE. A minor early C19 house of three storeys in three bays. Doorcase has fluted Doric pilasters. Hipped roof, mixed fenestration.

NORTH CREAKE

8030

ST MARY. A note in the church registers reports that in the former glass of the E window William Careltone was seen kneeling with an inscription that he 'construxit hunc cancellum anno Dom MCCCI'. That is very interesting; for the chancel has tracery in its windows which bears out exactly such a date, and although the actual stonework belongs to the 1895 restoration, Ladbroke's drawing shows the tracery of the E window just as it is now. The patterns of the chancel windows are, to the S, cusped Y-tracery with a trefoil in the spandrel, to the E (five lights) a group of four trefoils and a quatrefoil, all unencircled, and to the N a similar type, though with two ogee-headed lights. *Frederick Preedy* was the restorer of 1877, but there is little sign of his hand now beneath the work of *Hicks & Charlewood,*

1895–7, which, apart from the tracery, included the reredos, pulpit and rood screen.

Inside there is a most sumptuous (though alas over-restored) EASTER SEPULCHRE, with buttresses crowned by pinnacles, a cusped and subcusped arch, and a gable with charming open-work tracery and crockets and a big finial. There are no ogees here, though there are in the similarly sumptuous sedilia and piscina opposite. They also have much crocketing and in addition painted diapering against the back wall. Also of *c.* 1300 evidently the S porch and S doorway. The porch has quatrefoil side openings. Dec the (re-set) vestry E window. Perp N tower (doorway with shields in quatrefoils; battlements with flint and stone panelling; three-light bell-openings) and the nave and N aisle windows. Various bequests relate to these parts, for the tower 1435–50; the N aisle was being leaded in 1459. The S side of the nave is specially impressive, with a clerestory though no aisle, and hence with sheer giant buttresses. The clerestory is a Perp addition. Perp arcade of four bays inside. Octagonal piers, double-hollow-chamfered arches. In the S wall a Perp tomb recess. Perp chancel arch. Very good late C15 nave roof with hammerbeams on horizontal figures, long polygonal wall-posts, longitudinal arched braces between them, a wall-plate decorated with angels with spread wings, and also angels against the purlins. N aisle roof simpler, with arched braces. The chancel roof seems all a renewal of 1877, though Cautley calls the figures against the ashlar posts original.

FURNISHINGS. FONT. Circular C12 bowl. – FONT COVER. An enthusiastic piece of 1897. – SCREENS. Of the rood screen three painted panels late C15; the rest is by *Hicks & Charlewood*, 1897. – Of a parclose screen fragments in the N aisle. – ALTAR. In N aisle, 1978 but reusing four C14 painted panels. – WALL PAINTING. Fragmentary Doom above the chancel arch. – STAINED GLASS. E window and two chancel side windows by *Percy Bacon*, 1880s. – BRASS. A civilian under a tripartite canopy holding a church, *c.* 1500. 3 ft 3 in. figure (in the sanctuary floor).

CREAKE ABBEY, 1 m. N. Founded for Augustinian Canons in 1227 by Sir Robert de Nerford. First a priory, but made an abbey in 1231. A chapel associated with a hospital had been built by 1206. Dissolved 1506 after a disastrous outbreak of plague and given to Christ's College, Cambridge. The plan was of an aisled nave, transepts with square E chapels and a chancel, but the parts W of the crossing were lost after a fire of 1484 and remain only as foundations. The remains mostly late C13, namely the crossing W and E piers and beginnings of the arches (polygonal projections and finely moulded arches), the entrance to a chapel or former aisle E of the S transept (responds with two slight hollow chamfers), the arch from the same aisle to the chancel, a small doorway from the S transept towards the former dormitory, and the chancel walls with giant blank arcading above a dado of *c.* 10 ft. There were also shafts articulating the dado. The chancel was of six bays. The N side was altered in the early C14, when a pair of large chapels was built, opening to the S in two bays. Quatrefoil piers with hollows between the lobes, big E window without tracery, pier towards the N transept octagonal. Of the nave the N wall is visible, but no detail. There are doorways into the cloister in the first and last bays. The remains were consolidated by *R. M. Phipson* in 1864.

Immediately S is ABBEY FARMHOUSE, incorporating parts of the DORMITORY, with a walled garden representing the site of the cloisters. The house was formed in the early C19, with a five-bay S front. In the porch is a C15 four-centred arch with an ogeed top and colonnettes. To the N, i.e. facing the cloister, are remains of lancets and two more C15 doorways. A wing at r. angles in a line with the S transept has further lancet windows, and the N two bays must be a complete part of the monastic range.

OLD RECTORY, Church Street. By *S. S. Teulon* for the Rev. Thomas Keppel, who was a wealthy man. Teulon only set up in practice in 1840, and this house, of 1845, is one of his earliest surviving works. Red brick with gault-brick trimmings. Neo-Tudor style. The plan is vaguely cruciform, having a range running E–W, crossed by one running the other way. The entrance is in the W gable of the E–W wing. Plenty of gables. Just to the S of the entrance porch is an external stack, amusingly pierced by a window on each of the two floors. An octagonal lantern on the roof lights the staircase well, but the details are all now of the end of the C19. A kitchen wing extends N linking with a pair of cottages. N again the STABLES and carriage house.

Nos. 24–28 CHURCH STREET is remarkable for its shaped E gable, yet dated 1778.

Nos. 179–181 Church Street (HALL FARM COTTAGES) show the influence of Wyatt's Holkham Estate architecture, but are probably not by him. *c.* 1800. Red brick. The S front has a three-bay centre and lower recessed side attachments. Platband at first floor. Hipped roofs. Sash windows.

WINDMILL, ⅜ m. NNW. The stump of a former brick tower mill, newly erected when offered for sale in 1820. Top two storeys dismantled.

NORTH ELMHAM

RUINS, to the N of the parish church on the summit of a low hill. The bishops of East Anglia resided from *c.* 800 or earlier 'in the village which is called Elmham', according to the First Register of Norwich Cathedral (there is a South Elmham in Suffolk which may have been the bishops' seat before Danish invasions caused the see to collapse). The see lapsed in the mid C9 and was only revived *c.* 955. A church, almost certainly on this site, was the cathedral from the re-establishment of the see until 1071, when the see moved to Thetford. In 1094 finally it was settled at Norwich. Of the appearance of the cathedral all we know is from two late C13 descriptions of it, both (or more probably one copying the other) giving it as a timber chapel.

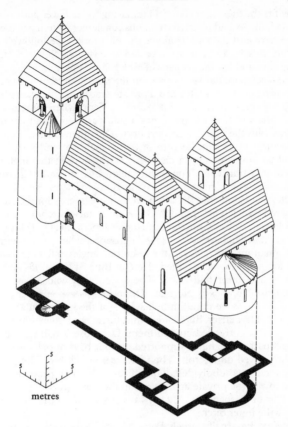

North Elmham, Bishops' Chapel. Reconstruction of *c.* 1091–1119

Interestingly enough, post holes for an earlier timber structure were discovered during the excavations published in 1962–3.

Although commonly referred to as a cathedral, Stephen Heywood's arguments that the visible ruins are those of a private chapel erected by Bishop Herbert de Losinga to serve his manor between 1091 and 1119 are compelling.* The ruins are confusingly mixed up with those of Bishop Despenser's fortified manor house, for which he obtained a licence to crenellate in 1388. They lie in a moated enclosure, itself in the SW corner of a larger moated enclosure, both of Despenser's time. In the NW corner a substantial mound may be the relic of a Norman motte later incorporated into the rectilinear moated layout.

The remaining buildings are only 123 ft long, and are of early Norman construction. The work is characterized by big blocks of dark-brown conglomerate with ashlar dressings to all the openings, mostly now robbed. Two phases are distinguished,

* Stephen Heywood provided valuable information for the following account of the 'cathedral' and the parish church.

the first by the use of coursed flint facing to the lower parts of the E end, the second by the ferruginous conglomerate to the W tower, the nave and the E parts above the flintwork. One followed the other closely. Tall narrow nave and W tower, which is as wide as the nave and has the remains of ashlar-faced tower arch responds and a semicircular stair-turret on the S side, an extremely early occurrence. It may have had a private first-floor chapel, explaining the stair-turret, like that at Brook, Kent (where the tower is also the width of the nave, has a stair-turret and had connections with the prior of Canterbury). The other, earlier, phase is the most interesting feature of the chapel, a N and S transept and an apse (without a chancel), and towers in the angles of nave and transepts. The former feature is an Early Christian tradition going right back to the Emperor Constantine's St Peter's in Rome, but the armpit towers are a rarity for which the nearest parallels are found in Germany, in the churches spawned by Hirsau Abbey Church (e.g. Hamersleben, c. 1115, Talburgel, 1142, and Halberstadt, 1147). The transepts are characterized by quadrant buttresses in the re-entrant angles, a feature also to be found at Norwich Cathedral and at Bury St Edmunds Abbey. The nave never had aisles. The N doorway, whose bases are recognizable, is early Norman. Opposite this was another doorway of the same date, immediately E of the semicircular stair-turret. Despenser duplicated this turret and then erected a defensible entrance between them. Despenser's hall was above the E part of the nave, supported on four bays of piers forming a two-naved undercroft. The pier bases are visible. The rest of the nave was subdivided. The offices were in all probability in the tower, the private apartments in the transept.

Part of Despenser's CURTAIN WALLS stands at the NE corner over the inner ditch.

ST MARY. Externally largely Perp, but this is deceptive. Between 1071 and c. 1100 the parishioners probably occupied the former timber cathedral church, but when that was taken down to be replaced by Herbert's chapel St Mary was founded, S of the episcopal site. Perhaps the most curious fact about the church is the rearrangement of E.E. stiff-leaf capitals above the N doorway. In all probability they come from some chancel arcading, which may have included sedilia and piscina. The chancel is in fact mainly of the C16, though all details are restored out of existence (except perhaps the E window inner shafts). It had been rebuilt before, in 1382–7. S doorway of c. 1300, shafted inside, aisle windows Dec, S chapel Perp (added 1540–2 using stone carried from Walsingham Abbey), clerestory Perp, and W tower Perp. The whole exterior re-faced with flint in 1864. The tower is impressive. It has a W porch vaulted with diagonal, ridge and transverse ribs with a damaged boss showing the Coronation of the Virgin, a big fleuron frieze on the N and S walls of the porch, and fleurons with salamanders also along the arch of the inner portal. Big three-light W window, big straight-headed, largely blocked openings to the ringing chamber, and then the three-light bell-openings. Panelled crenellations and corner pinnacles. The clock face partly blocking the ringing-chamber windows is of the 1950s, made of aluminium designed for flat-bed lorries by the *North American Aluminum Company*. The clerestory has twelve two-light windows and returns into the nave E gable.

The interior has several surprises. For one thing the E responds of both chancel chapels are early Norman, i.e. from Bishop Herbert's foundation. They probably belonged to the Norman nave which was shortened by one bay. There is a Norman window high up to the l. of the s arch. In any case, in the C13 a new, proud nave was built, with six bays, tall altern-ating circular and octagonal piers, and arches with a slight chamfer and a keeled roll. The E respond of this arcade seems either to have gone down quite naively to the level of the Norman responds, or, more likely, the whole arcade was height-ened when the clerestory was decided on, and the arches re-set on raised piers (using larger blocks of masonry). Only the E bay remained the same height, now serving the chancel chapels. Later still the Perp chancel arch was inserted to create a struc-tural division of chancel from nave. Probably from this time the arch-braced nave roof, restored by *John Brown* in 1852. Brown's restoration included a new stone reredos and repair to sedilia and piscina. Chancel re-roofed 1838.

FURNISHINGS. FONT. Plain, C17. – PULPIT. 1626, with thin coupled fluted angle colonnettes. The pulpit was carved by the parish clerk, *Francis Floyd*, who was paid £1 for it in 1614 and £4 3s. 4d. in 1626 for finishing it. The date is on the back board now used as a cupboard door in the vestry. Base of 1882. – SCREENS. On the dado of the rood screen seventeen painted Saints are preserved, all *c.* 1505. The rood was taken down in 1550 having been painted in 1548 by *William Tulney*, the remainder dismantled probably in the C17 and discovered used as flooring in 1852. The pieces re-erected 1882, with the Saints in the present order. Most of the panels are by the same elegant hand as the artist of Hunstanton and St James, Norwich. From the l. the panels 5–10 are by a different artist. Finely carved spandrels, on the N side with figures too. – The W screen is of the early C17 with long column-like balusters in two tiers, pos-sibly by *Floyd*. – Chapel screens, 1882. – BENCHES. With a vari-ety of C15 poppyheads and animals on the arms, also the bust of a man. Three stalls by the font probably C14. – ALTAR TABLE. Dated 1622, by *Francis Floyd*. – STAINED GLASS. C14 glass in N and s windows, including a specially good figure of the Virgin and Child. E window by *Clayton & Bell*, 1874 (Transfiguration). – MONUMENTS. Two good tablets, nice to compare: Richard Warner †1757 and Richard Milles †1820, the latter by *Henry Westmacott*. The former is Rococo, the latter very Grecian (both chancel). – RAILINGS. By the road. Late C18, with plain over-throw. Copies opposite to Elmham Park (*see* Elmham House below).

ELMHAM HOUSE, ¼ m. w. Of *Donthorn*'s solemn house remod-elled in 1830 for G.J. Milles only the KITCHEN WING and

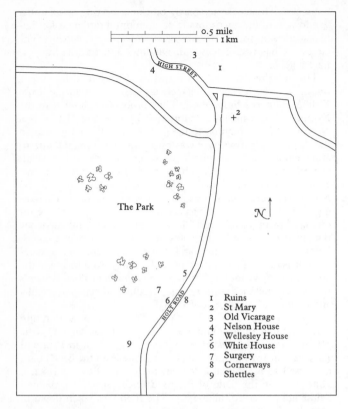

0.5 mile
1 km

3
HIGH STREET
4   1

2

The Park   N

5
7
6   8   1   Ruins
                2   St Mary
                3   Old Vicarage
                4   Nelson House
                5   Wellesley House
                6   White House
9   7   Surgery
                8   Cornerways
                9   Shettles

North Elmham

STABLES were spared demolition in 1924. These were remodelled into the present house in 1928 for Mrs Edward Birkbeck.
In the PARK, THE VINERY, formerly various outbuildings of
the early C18, of brick; GAME LARDER, 150 yds NE, 1840, octagonal, brick, conical roof; DOVECOTE, further NE, also 1840,
circular, brick, conical roof.
VILLAGE. High Street lies NW of the church, Holt Road to the S.
On HIGH STREET, the OLD VICARAGE, an early C19 brick
house of three by four bays. The S front has a veranda on iron
props. NELSON HOUSE, beyond, at the corner. C17 timber
frame, engulfed in an C18 brick reconstruction and given a
face-lift in the early C19. The two-storey façade has four bays of
two- or three-light cross casements, and an early C19 shopfront.
Facing it at an angle is BRIDPORT HOUSE: giant pilasters to its
narrow three-bay brick façade, early C19.
    From the church the long HOLT ROAD drops down the hill,
at the bottom sparsely furnished with attractive minor houses.
Low walls on the r. define Elmham Park. First, THE LODGE,
c. 1830, probably by *Donthorn*. Brick and gault brick. One storey.
Three-bay façade with twin pilasters in the one-bay returns. Rear

wing. Stack with four octagonal flues. A little way down, set in the wall, a cast-iron MILE-PLAQUE of c. 1830, attractively lettered (London 111 miles). On the same side (w), WELLESLEY HOUSE, opposite the school. Early C18 brick house fitted out with C19 cross casements. Also early C18 is THE WHITE HOUSE, colourwashed brick, five bays in two storeys and attics. The cross casements here are substantially original. This used to contain the doctors' surgery, replaced 1986–7 by the surprisingly large brick SURGERY immediately behind, by *Ian Steen*. Red brick, with a huge pantiled roof coming close to the ground. Big circular window in the gable-end facing the street. Open-plan interior. On the other side, CORNERWAYS. A C16 house, timber-framed with a C17 brick gable facing the road. Façade of two storeys, irregular, with C18 and C19 casements. Extensions dated 1640 (date at rear). A C17 painting of a ship in a cupboard. (E and SE of this point an ESTATE of late C20 housing, quite well organized.) Further s, at a bend in the road and hidden behind high walls on the r., stands SHETTLES. C15 timber-framed farmhouse extended to N c. 1600 and later, producing a lengthy range. The C15 house has been given C20 windows and a late C17 stack, which destroyed the open hall plan. One crown-post roof truss remains. In the early C17 block are mullioned and transomed windows with hollow chamfers. The roof here is of clasped purlins with wind-bracing.

The high walls go with an early C19 house set back, used as the vicarage after the one by the church was sold, and before a new vicarage was built, so also called OLD VICARAGE. Attractive three-bay front, simple porch on Doric columns. Then, also on the w side, RACKHAM HOUSE, a standard late C19 red brick villa. S of Eastgate Street on the E a group of five semi-detached COUNCIL HOUSES of 1929 illustrating the typical urban design of rural municipal housing of between the wars. They have cavity walls, a feature then becoming popular.

EASTGATE STREET runs E, partly with late C20 infill. At the far end OLD HALL FARMHOUSE, of flint with brick dressings. The C17 block has the date 1669 facing the road, but has suffered some C19 rebuilding towards the s end. Renewed cross casements. C17 ridge stack, rebuilt in the C20.

NORTH LOPHAM   0080

ST NICHOLAS. Dec and Perp. Dec the chancel (three-light E window with reticulated tracery, restored in 1862), the s aisle (two-light windows with reticulation or petals, the E aisle window a three-light petal-traceried one), and the s porch. Perp the w tower (bequests from 1479 to 1526, and a large commemorative inscription to Johannes Kailli and the initials of other donors), two two-light nave N windows with panel tracery, and the s arcade inside. The three-stage tower is of knapped flint and has flushwork emblems and letters against the base (crowned T for Trinity, crowned MR for Maria Regina and crowned

A for St Andrew, to whom the church was previously dedicated). The arcade piers have semicircular projections with capitals towards the arches, longer chamfered ones without capitals towards nave and aisle. Four bays, arcades with sunk-quadrant mouldings. The roofs are all C19. – FONT. C14, octagonal, with tapering sides and shallow, elegantly cut tracery motifs (cf. South Lopham). The stem has rolls and flutes. The COVER is C17. – BENCH ENDS. With tracery and, instead of poppyheads, animals and a figure. – STAINED GLASS. Of 1868 in the E window, by an unknown artist. Birkin Haward suggests a Norwich workshop.

METHODIST CHURCH (Wesleyan), The Street. 1810, brick, with flint returns. Three bays of sashes and two doors in the usual early style, under an oversized hipped roof. Gallery on cast-iron columns.

VILLAGE. North Lopham is essentially THE STREET. Everything of consequence is on it. Of the C16 are Church House and Church Farmhouse, on opposite sides. CHURCH HOUSE (W side) was a timber-framed hall house of the C16 now with four C20 first-floor casements and two C20 gabled porches. Of the hall arrangement are remains of two arched service doors W of the hall, one blocked. CHURCH FARMHOUSE is later in the C16 and was always floored. Timber-framed again, with a pedimented door and ground-floor C18 casements. The four clustered chimney flues are effective. Stair-turret to rear. Roof of clasped purlins and diminished principals. The BELL public house and the KING'S HEAD public house (W side) are both C18 timber-framed buildings with C19 details. Of c. 1600 is the tiny timber-framed COBBLER'S COTTAGE (W side), clad in plastered wattle and daub, and thatched. What is clear is that it was a single-celled, single-storeyed building without a fireplace, open to the roof inside. In the middle of the C18 it was floored, given a dormer and a fireplace set into a new N gable. Later in the C18 a further room was added against the new gable and a permanent staircase provided, and then it was divided into two houses. This is the smallest kind of permanent house to have survived in the county. Other than this the story is one of early C19 clay lump, or, at THE THATCHED COTTAGE (W), mid-C18 clay lump.

NORTH PICKENHAM

ST ANDREW. Mostly rebuilt by *D. Male*, 1863. A small church. The W tower and N transept remain of the old church. Male's windows favour the Dec style, but the transept has big Perp windows. – REREDOS. Set in the wall behind the altar are glass mosaic panels by *Salviati*, 1863. – STAINED GLASS. In the W window, by *Henry Holiday* of *J. Powell & Sons*, c. 1864. Quite excellent for its date. Already with influence from the Pre-Raphaelites, if not from Morris. Good colours too. Scenes of Baptism, Good Samaritan, Sacrifice of Isaac, Moses and Serpent.

E window and N transept E window by *M. & A. O'Connor,* *c.* 1864–5. These also good.

NORTH RUNCTON

6010

ALL SAINTS. The first of a handful of C18 churches in Norfolk, 96 facing a group of irregular widely spaced cottages across a small green. Built in 1703–13 after the steeple of its predecessor fell in 1701. By *Henry Bell* of King's Lynn, who lived in the parish, contributed £15 to its cost and was a trustee of the rebuilding. Carstone with brick dressings. Rendered rather than stuccoed. W tower in three stages, the lower two with rusticated quoins; the bell-stage has clasping pilasters. Moulded parapet cornice. The graceful little lantern has pedimented openings in each direction and a tiny flèche on top. Rounded W doorway with flanking unfluted columns and a wide pediment over. Vestries attached to N and S with high pedimented parapets, the windows to the W blocked, which makes the pediments on those faces look silly.

The three-bay nave is square with a slight middle projection to N and S distinguished by rusticated quoins; both have pediments. On the N side two prominent swept buttresses. Large chancel with a S extension for the organ added in 1894 and the Gurney vault *c.* 1837 on the N side between chancel and nave. This is a large low stone structure with panelled side walls and a flat patio-like top. The chancel itself has its carstone exposed, and each side decorated with four brick pilasters with moulded capitals and bases, on the S partly obscured by the organ chamber. Windows arched, segment-headed, and oval. Chancel E window with a segmental pediment over a floating cornice. The nave S front has a big arched middle window flanked by segment-headed windows with oval openings over. This corresponds to the internal arrangement, an arrangement derived from Wren or All Saints, Northampton (which itself may be by Bell). Square centre with a domical vault, four giant unfluted Ionic columns on very tall bases, four flat-ceilinged arms, and four flat-ceilinged corner pieces – the plan which reached Wren from Byzantium via Venice and Holland. Festoons slung between the volutes of the column capitals. Tower arch with Ionic pilasters. Tripartite chancel arch composed of Ionic columns in pairs set in depth. Both have the same festoons and coffered soffits.

FURNISHINGS. *H. J. Green* reorganized the interior in 1887, bringing in many pieces. – PANELLING and REREDOS behind the altar, right up to the flat ceiling of the chancel, with fluted giant Corinthian pilasters. It was designed by *Bell* in 1684, and intended for St Margaret, King's Lynn, and is the only one of his altarpieces remaining: that in St Nicholas, Lynn, was destroyed in the C19. Painted panels by *Lamponi*, of the Evangelists, also a depiction of Christ Risen in the centre. These were not part of Bell's design and were added only in 1899 and 1901, the year the whole was installed here. – COMMUNION RAILS. 1713. Turned balusters. – CHANDELIER. Of brass, two tiers, also 1713. – FONT. Marble vase type installed in 1907 from St Margaret, King's Lynn. – PULPIT. 1887, of Jacobean arcaded type. – STAINED GLASS. A St George, signed M.M.W. 1933 (who is that?), N nave w end. At the E end St Katherine (spelt with a K because the glass commemorates Sir Somerville Gurney whose wife was Katherine) and in the s nave a Good Shepherd, early C20 by unidentified artists. – Several nice wall MONUMENTS, cartouches with inscriptions. Dated 1720, 1727 (N), 1718, and *c.* 1720 (S). One of the N monuments to Sir John Cremor †1668, a cartouche erected by Earl Fitzwilliam in 1720; the contract of 1718 for a 'little monument' awarded to *James Fisher* of Camberwell (GF). – ROYAL ARMS. Painted, to George I, 1719, under the tower, with the addition of two angel supporters on side panels.

RUNCTON HALL. Demolished in 1965. The house was by *Anthony Salvin*, 1833–6, for Daniel Gurney, much added to in 1853–4, again by Salvin. Yellow brick, a tower with a turret at one angle of 1853. The staircase came from a house in St Anne's Street, King's Lynn. Three slim balusters to each step. What happened to it after the house was demolished? (Two iron GATES of the late C17 and of 1839.)

OLD RECTORY, Rectory Lane. An early C19 gault-brick pile under a hipped roof. Three-bay s front with angle pilasters and a plat-band, centre bay broken forward under pediment. Recessed sashes.

NORTH RUNCTON LODGE. Early C17, remodelled early C19. Three centre bays with cross wings r. and l. ending in shaped gables: two-storey canted window bays. The middle section of C17 form, with former end-stacks, but now with a central porch on a pair of unfluted wooden columns and pilasters. C17 bridging beams in this part. Stick-baluster early C19 staircase.

NORTH TUDDENHAM

ST MARY. Later C14 w tower, the buttresses with chequered flushwork, the battlements with flushwork panelling and pinnacles. Three-light Perp w window. Y-tracery and Dec windows above. Powerful arch towards the nave on polygonal responds. The rest is Perp, including the two-storeyed N porch, which has Y-traceried side windows, a form which lasted well into the C15. The inner doorway, as so often, shows that the walling is earlier. The unaisled nave has considerable width. Chancel windows Perp, five-light E window C19. The main restoration was in 1868. The chancel walls were stencilled in the 1880s and the walls, including the nave, covered below the windows with rich encaustic tiles. These were painted over in 1978, but happily later uncovered. – FONT. Lions' faces against the foot, shields in cusped fields against the bowl. – SCREEN. Base with eight early C16 painted figures; quite good. From another screen a part with four painted figures under the tower. Money was left between 1499 and 1504 for painting the 'perke', i.e. screen, and the date might fit either fragment. – STAINED GLASS. The w

window has Saints by *Ward & Hughes*, 1868, and three good
panels of the C15, with one pane carrying the date 1467 (salvaged
from a builder's yard in the 1870s; the glass not used here went
to Welborne). Remains of cycle of Life of St Margaret. More
C15 panels in nave N and S windows, which are otherwise again
by *Ward & Hughes*, as are the chancel windows. The new glass
cost £650 in 1868. – MONUMENTS. In chancel. Tomb-chest
with shields separated by broad pilasters. – Katherine Skippe
†1629. Big tablet, black and white, without figures. Still strapwork at the front, but the open scrolly pediment at the top already
post-Jacobean. It is supported on a pair of Doric columns. – A.
Skyppe. No date, but probably late C17. Bust in an oval recess
framed by the backs of books. The inscription runs:

> What stronger circle can art magick find
> Where a schollers spyrit can bee confind
> Than this of bookes! Note how he spent his time
> Scorneinge earths drosse to thinke on things sublime
> So longe thy love to learninge shall be read
> Whilst fame shall last: or statues for the dead.

– CURIOSUM. A collecting shoe, i.e. a square shovel with a handle,
rather like a dustpan.
OLD LANE HOUSE, Low Road. Timber-framed, C17, with
renewed three- and four-light mullioned windows and a stack
with four octagonal moulded flues.

NORTHWOLD

ST ANDREW. The story of the church begins with the beautiful
arcades, which are mid-C13. They have quatrefoil piers looking
almost like a cluster of four independent shafts and capitals
partly of rich stiff-leaf, partly moulded. The W bay is later, as
the arches and responds show, but not later than Dec, which is
clear from the mouldings as well as the aisle W windows. This
needs stressing; for though they were surely added with a view
to the erection of a W tower, the tower itself appears to be Perp
throughout. Money was indeed left for its building in several
bequests, 1465–82. It is an ambitious four-stage tower. Diagonal
buttresses with flushwork devices. Such devices (e.g. mouchette
wheels) appear also on the base frieze and a frieze above the
doorway. Double-stepped battlements with flushwork panelling
and eight pinnacles.
   The aisle and chancel windows are mostly restored Dec. The
chancel was partly rebuilt in 1840 and restored in 1895. Dec the
S porch entrance with its double sunk-quadrant mouldings, but
the S doorway belongs to the arcade. The arch mouldings are
very varied and undercut. Ambitious, somewhat restless clerestory with a commemorative inscription: 'pray for the sole of
John Sterling'. Three-light windows under four-centred heads
with knapped-flint surrounds and between them blind straight-
headed transomed stone windows. Late C15. The nave roof has

hammerbeams alternating with arched braces starting from wall-posts. The latter stand on big figured stone corbels. The NE vestry is medieval and was originally two-storeyed. – FONTS. 1882 with a FONT COVER of 1887. – A big C18 baluster font in the chancel. – EASTER SEPULCHRE. A very lavish composition of the late C15, unfortunately poorly preserved. Against the tomb-chest or base four sleeping soldiers in agitated attitudes and little trees separating them. To the l. and r. badly damaged buttresses. Top cresting. The back wall of the shallow recess has busy vaulting in two tiers, the upper tier with pendant canopies and star and fan vaults of complicated forms. – WALL PAINT-ING. In the N aisle, fragmentary Three Living and Three Dead (DP). – STAINED GLASS. E window by *Heaton, Butler & Bayne* †1873. – MONUMENTS. Robert Burhill †1727 (nave). A wooden tablet, with painted garlands l. and r. – Ann Gordon †1732, swags, putti and achievement around the inscription panel. – Several good stone tablets. – The churchyard has many C18 HEADSTONES, S of the church.

Several nice houses round the church, especially the early C18 MANOR HOUSE, to the S on the High Street. Two storeys and attic in five bays, with a late C18 entrance tower added to the W end, and a further four bays beyond that, with wrought-iron balconies at the first floor. Shaped E gable and the S gable of the rear wing. No. 43 High Street (SYCAMORE HOUSE) to the W represents the mid C18: five bays, three storeys, red brick, porch with renewed Ionic columns, though the capitals are C18. The panelled door itself has a Roman Doric surround. No. 96 is plainly of late C16 origins (see the ridge stack with its octagonal flues) despite the date 1736 in the W gable-head. The other gable has diapered brickwork. A little aloofness is provided by the ramped WALLS enclosing a forecourt and cutting off the street with a set of iron railings and gates.

MANOR FARMHOUSE, ¼ m. W. Gable-end dated 1635. This has brick-pedimented mullioned and transomed windows, ovolo-moulded. The stepped external stack has its inglenook intact inside. Two wings to rear, the S one dated 1807.

CROSS, a little to the WSW of the last. Medieval cross shaft on a C19 base, late C14, tapering square shaft with rolled edges.

POOLY FARMHOUSE on the Thetford Road ½ m. S of the church is of clunch, with brick dressings, late C17.

NORTH WOOTTON

ALL SAINTS. 1850–3 by *Anthony Salvin* for the Hon. Mrs Mary Howard at a cost of £2,200. A simple E.E. essay of nave, chancel and W tower. The tower has a blank E.E.-style arcade to the second stage. The two W arches glazed. Plate tracery in bell-openings and nave windows. The chancel is content with lancets. – STAINED GLASS. E window by *Ward & Hughes* (*Henry Hughes*), †1877. The rest of the stained glass by the same work-shop, c. 1883–c. 1900.

CHURCH COTTAGE, immediately s. A tiny house of one storey
and attic and one room to each floor. The single-bay extension
is later. Carstone with brick. The stack to l. has lozenge flues.
The date *c.* 1640.

THE PRIORY (Church Farmhouse), s of the church. Dated 1718.
Carstone with brick trim. Two storeys in three bays. Doorway
with big brackets and a pair of columns to the canopy, on which
is a wrought-iron balustrade. Various plain and tripartite sashes,
mostly C19. Bridging beams still ovolo-moulded, staircase with
turned balusters. C19 rear range, set parallel.

WOOTTON MARSH stretches bleakly (winter) and shimmeringly
(summer) w and N to Bulldog Sands and The Wash.

NORTON SUBCOURSE   *4090*

ST MARY. Round tower with very elongated late C13 bell-openings.
They have Y-tracery. Nave and chancel are all in one, without
structural division, and are thatched. The windows are all of
one moment and ring the changes very nicely on the possibilities of simple early C14 tracery: cusped Y, Y with ogee top,
two lights with a spherical triangle at the top, two lights with a
reticulation unit. All three doorways of the church are also of
this moment. The chancel E window, of five lights and with
reticulated tracery, is the only more ambitious motif. There
may be some renewal of the windows, but they fit very well
with the contracts for a new chancel roof (carpenters *Roger* and
William Gunton), 1 May 1319, to be of twenty-five couples of
oak, and for the nave roof (*John Gunton*), 4 October 1319.
Cautley says the roofs have since been replaced, but this is
uncertain as the ceilings are plastered. In the w wall, inside,
high up and not centrally placed, a blocked niche (cf. Toft
Monks). In the chancel a low tomb recess with an ogee arch and
the sedilia and double piscina, also ogeed. One tie-beam across
the nave near the chancel. This is an C18 security measure. It
rests on Ionic pilasters. The casing of the beam is later. – SEAT-
ING and REREDOS, both 1898 (Kelly). – FONT. C13, of Purbeck
marble, octagonal, with the usual two flat pointed arches on
each side. – STAINED GLASS. Some original C14 glass – note the
prevalence of green and yellow.

Timber-framed houses of the C17 are common in SE Norfolk,
often with brick gable-ends. Such is WALNUT FARMHOUSE,
Low Road. Thatched. Two storeys. Blocked mullioned window
to first floor.

OLD BUCKENHAM   *0090*

ALL SAINTS. Re-set Norman N doorway with one order of shafts
carrying single-scallop capitals. Arch with cable- and stud-
decorated mouldings. Norman also the w wall, with big blocks
of carstone. Against this is a polygonal w tower, i.e polygonal

from the ground. With pretty shafts up the angles provided with dainty little shaft-rings. Bell-windows with Y-tracery, and in the diagonals flushwork imitation of such windows. All this is Dec but the crenellated parapet is C17. Nave and chancel in one, whitened and thatched. The chancel is of the same date as the tower, apart from the E end added during the restoration of 1858. The N arcade of four bays seems somewhat later, say later C14. Quatrefoil piers with thin hollows in the diagonals. Double-hollow-chamfered arches. The N side of the church was originally the more visually important, see the shields and sacred initials on the buttresses between the Perp windows. – FONT. Octagonal, C15 with shields and encircled quatrefoils alternating round the bowl. Plinth with heads and engaged columns. – SCREEN. The base only. Made up into the partition between N aisle and vestry. – STALL ENDS. With poppyheads flanked by well-preserved little seated figures. Re-seated 1858. – STAINED GLASS. The SE nave window by *Charles Kempe*, 1898, and in the adjoining window the Good Samaritan, which Birkin Haward attributes to *J. & J. King* of Norwich, 1878. In the heads of these two windows original Perp glass. – MONUMENTS. Brass to Thomas Browne, *c.* 1500; a stork with scroll; and a chalice brass of *c.* 1520.

VILLAGE. To the W of the church CHURCH GREEN, an enormous green which makes the cottages and houses bordering on it appear tiny. Among the houses one on the E side, SUNNYSIDE FARMHOUSE, partly C15 but mostly late C16, timber-framed and brick. Wings r. and l. of S front, which has a two-storeyed porch lit through a five-light cross-casement to its first floor. Mullioned windows r. of porch. The ridge stack has four octagonal flues. W wing with jettied attic storey, E wing an C18 addition. W room with wave-moulded fireplace jambs. On the N side of the green the BAPTIST CHAPEL of 1857, replacing one of 1831, with a hipped roof. The façade has clasping pilasters. Also to the N is SUNNYDENE, an early C18 lobby-entrance timber-framed house with an early C19 brick skin. A little S of the Green on CAKE STREET, the MANOR HOUSE, a handsome building of the early C19. It is of gault brick, and has three wide bays with coupled giant pilasters at the angles, and single giant pilasters and a pediment framing the middle bay.

CASTLE. Rectangular earthwork of uncertain date. The shape is more Roman than later, but there is no other reason to assume a Roman date. On the other hand nothing certainly survives that could be connected with a bailey. The castle erected by the Normans inside this fortification was given by William d'Albini II in 1146 to the Augustinian Canons to build a priory out of its materials. William did not really need Old Buckenham as the construction of his new principal castle at Castle Rising, begun in 1138, was well under way, and he had another in neighbouring New Buckenham probably still under construction in 1146. The earthworks are utterly different from Albini's replacement fortification at New Buckenham, and are a larger version of that around Weeting Castle. Of the PRIORY, on Abbey Road, no

more remains than a lump of flint and rubble representing the
NE crossing pier.

ABBEY FARMHOUSE, immediately N of the priory fragment.
Restored in the 1960s and 70s. Two ranges at r. angles of about
equal length, the E–W block being a mid-C16 timber-framed
upper hall with the jetties N and S underbuilt in brick. Punched
through the brick is a four-centred timber arch, opened, or
reopened, during restorations. The windows here are C20. The
first-floor fenestration is more interesting, on the S front anyway,
as it consists of a continuous range of mullioned windows with
taller similar windows at intervals. Before 1971 all that showed
was four C19 Y-tracery Gothick casements, so all this is C20,
but based on surviving evidence in the timber frame. The W
gable is of brick with octagonal corner turrets with pinnacles
and a pair of decorated brick chimney flues at the apex of the
gable, one with spiral, the other with chevron moulded brick
decoration. The SW corner of the gable thickens to contain the
garderobe chute.

Inside this wing, the upper hall is partitioned but once spanned 59
the entire length in five bays. Tie-beams on arched braces with
queen-struts above. The rest of the roof is a replacement. Big
fireplace at W end with a roll-moulded bressumer introduced
from elsewhere. Over the fire surround and on the arches of the
framing are WALL PAINTINGS in the form of C16 distemper floral
and leaf patterns overlaid here and there with early C17 stencil
work.

The other wing runs S from the E end. The two N bays are of
stone, doubtless reused when the priory was dissolved, i.e. the
same date as the N range. The other two bays are early C18 and
of brick. Fireplace bressumer in the N bay is four-centred with
shields, but there was a fire which gutted most of the rest of the
interior.

WINDMILL, Green Lane. John Burlingham had a post mill on the
site of the Methodist Chapel, but went bankrupt in 1805 – a
serious thing then – and it took him eight years to satisfy his
creditors. But he bounced back and had this monster built in
1818. It is the largest diameter tower mill in the country and
drove five pairs of stones. The boat-shaped cap probably dates
from 1879 when *Smithdale & Son* fitted a new windshaft and
other gears. Capped in 1976 but being restored by the *Norfolk
Windmills Trust* at the time of writing.

WAR MEMORIAL, on the Green ¼ m. S of the church. 1919 by *Sir
Reginald Blomfield*. Octagonal stepped stone plinth bearing a
Latin cross with a bronze sword attached; shaft and arms are
elongated octagons in section.

WARREN HOUSE, Sandy Lane. Built in 1768 for Robert Brown.
Seven bays, fitted with three-light casements, mostly still C18.

Of older, and outlying, FARMHOUSES, the only two needing mention are Fen Farmhouse on Fen Lane and Mill Farmhouse on
Fen Street. MILL FARMHOUSE is an early C15 open hall house
floored in the early C17 with a new stack and an extension.
Timber-framed. A four-light mullioned window remains to the

first floor. The main door is at the point where the C15 gives way to the C17 and through it one reaches the former hall l., and the screen r. Little remains of either. The hall had a kingpost roof, one octagonal post surviving with its moulded base and neck mouldings. FEN FARMHOUSE is a later version of the same thing, the first date c. 1500. Two-light first-floor mullioned window. Plenty of C20 details. Inside a C17 fireplace, winder stairs and a queen-strut roof with clasped purlins.

BUNN'S BANK. See Attleborough.

OLD HUNSTANTON see HUNSTANTON

OUTWELL

ST CLEMENT. Of Barnack stone and ragstone, embattled and quite ambitiously detailed, e.g. with decoration along the base. The oldest part is the W tower. This is of the C13 to the lower (former) bell-openings with two lights separated by a round shaft and a circle pierced in the spandrel. The upper bell-stage is Dec; the W doorway, the W window, and the tall tower arch are Perp. The pyramid roof is said to be of the later C18. Dec also one S window, the first from the W. All the rest is Perp. Two-storeyed S porch, the front mutilated, rib-vaulted in two bays inside, S aisle with two wide segment-headed windows with embattled transoms, one of seven, the other of six lights. Arches below the transoms too. This pattern recurs in other windows. Buttresses with shields and pinnacles. Tall three-light clerestory. Chancel projecting one bay, largely rebuilt in 1862–3 by *William Smith* of London. Five-light E, three-light N and S windows, all with embattled transoms. The N chapel has an E window similar to those of the S aisle. Small niches high up to its l. and r. A N chapel in a transeptal position is of brick. It was built for John Fincham, who died in 1527 (arms on the stone roof corbels inside), and was the last part to be built. The N side of the whole is more modestly appointed. Blomefield recorded a date 1420 in a window.

The INTERIOR has five-bay arcades with octagonal piers and arches on the S side with two wave mouldings, on the N side with a chamfer and a hollow chamfer. Both arcades are of the early C14. Tall chancel arch with a window over. One-bay N and S chapels separated by arches from the aisles too. Good roofs. In the nave with alternating tie-beams and hammerbeams and tracery in the spandrels. Angels on tie-beams, hammerbeams, and wall-plates. Against the wall-posts figures under canopies. The ties have queenposts. S aisle roof and N transept roof with hammerbeams. The same type of roof in the chancel S chapel. The N chancel chapel has moulded beams and angels with shields. – FONT. Perp, simple, octagonal, with cusped tracery patterns. – LECTERN. Of latten, the material used for medieval 'brasses', late C15. Lower part of stem renewed. – POOR BOX. Jacobean, of unusual design. A shape like a Venetian lantern placed on a tall baluster. – GATES to the S chapel. Of wrought iron; C18. – STAINED GLASS. Of the early C16 many small figures in the head of the S chapel E window; one large bearded figure in a N chapel N window. – ORGAN. By *Holdich* of London, 1840–50. – MONUMENTS. Brass to Richard Quadryng †1511, a 2 ft 3 in. figure. – In the S chapel a round-arched and cusped and sub-cusped recess of the C14. Also in the S chapel the Purbeck marble tomb-chest and recess of Nicholas de Beaupré †1511. The recess has spiral-fluted colonnettes, a top frieze of quatrefoils and a cresting. – In 1567 Edmund de Beaupré died, and for him an alabaster tablet was put up above the earlier monument. At the same time the inscription recording Nicholas was set into the back wall of the recess. Both tablets have strapwork and good garlands of 1567.

BEAUPRÉ HALL situated ½ m. N was demolished in 1966. The Beaupré family built their manor house in the first years of the C16, with a symmetrical W façade of *c.* 1525, and the remainder on a modified courtyard plan. The gatehouse was enriched with much dressed stone and had polygonal turrets to inside and outside. Then, r. and l., connecting ranges to end pavilions with polygonal angle-shafts. In the N pavilion was the chapel. The gatehouse led to a narrow court, and across it one reached the hall porch. An exit at the back corresponded to the entrance. The hall range was somewhat older than the rest, *c.* 1500, but the porch and bay were of *c.* 1570, put up by Sir Robert Bell, Chief Baron of the Exchequer, whose family had inherited in 1567. The NE wing was also Sir Robert's.

BEAUPRÉ HALL FARM, ⅜ m. N, on the main road. A T-plan Jacobean house with stepped end-gables to the main (S) front, the W gable with a set-off at the first floor continued from the façade and a roll-moulded eaves stringcourse. The three-light attic window has a pediment. The original stepped external stack was against the N wall, now rather difficult to appreciate because of the later C17 addition forming the stem of the T.

VILLAGE. Outwell and Upwell (cf. p. 740) form one long village winding along the Well Stream for four miles. The stream forms the boundary of Norfolk and Cambridgeshire, and so one side of the village is in the one, the other in the other county. In 1882 the Wisbech and Upwell Tramway built a line linking with Wisbech, not quite a tramline, not quite a railway. Various goods offices etc. were built of which the last survivor is the TRAMWAY GOODS OFFICE. Red brick under a hipped slate roof. Just a box with segmental windows and a door to the S. The line closed to passengers in 1929 and to goods in 1966.

DIAL HOUSE. *See* Emneth, p. 333.

OVINGTON 9000

ST JOHN EVANGELIST. A Norman church consisting of a long nave and chancel, re-worked *c.* 1300 and restored in 1867, and a

Perp w tower. The unbuttressed tower has flushwork panels below the w and belfry windows. Money was left for its construction in 1458. One Norman s window and Norman s doorway, badly preserved, with one order of shafts, scalloped capitals and billet in the arch. The chancel and nave have windows of the early C14: lancet, Y-tracery, intersecting tracery. Wave-moulded tower arch. – FONT. Originally at Watton until 1840. C14. Octagonal, with a spreading stem and, growing out of it, four big demi-figures of angels.

The FARMHOUSES are generally early C19, though DAISY FARM-HOUSE seems late C18: three bays, two storeys, central door behind a pedimented porch on columns.

OXBOROUGH

ST JOHN EVANGELIST. The steeple (i.e. with a spire) fell in 1948 and destroyed the nave and s aisle. The nave is roofless and laid to grass, the N aisle remains; a wall was built in 1949 in the former chancel arch. 12 yds of s aisle wall still stand. At 150 ft, the steeple was one of the tallest in Norfolk. The Bedingfeld Chapel at the E end of the s aisle fortunately was spared. What remains of the church still tells that it was Perp throughout, except for the N porch, N doorway, and N aisle w window – the latter on the verge of Perp. The N arcade is Perp (six bays, octagonal piers, double-chamfered arches). Two-light clerestory windows and two-light N aisle windows, three with transoms and panel tracery. Perp also the charming composition of piscina and sedilia in the chancel. The sedilia have traceried backs. A frame with some original colouring and a frieze of demi-figures of angels surrounds sedilia and piscina. Tiny rib vaulting. Big five-light chancel E window and panel-traceried side windows. Among the Perp windows the difference between those of the church and those of the Bedingfeld Chapel is telling. The latter have four-centred arches and no proper tracery. Margaret Bedingfeld, in her will of 1513, ordered her body to be laid to rest in the chapel yet to be built. It is faced with ashlar and had two four-centred arches opening from the chancel, now blocked. Roof with roll-moulded timbers and arched braces with tracery in the spandrels. When the chapel was ready we do not know, nor do we know the exact date of the two identical, extremely lavish MONUMENTS which are the fame of the church. The monuments are of terracotta, a material suddenly made fashionable by the first artists working in England in the Italian early Renaissance style. The nearest relations of the Bedingfeld monuments are those to the first and second Lord Marney at Layer Marney in Essex, who died in 1523 and 1525, the Ferrers monument in Wymondham Abbey, the Berney monument at Bracon Ash and the slightly later Jannys monument in St George, Colegate, Norwich, 1533–4. These three Norfolk examples are very probably by the same craftsmen as the Oxborough monuments.

But the Bedingfeld monuments are far more elegant. They have tomb-chests with ornamented pilasters and ornamented arched panels and a superstructure or canopy with short pendants and little semicircular and triangular cresting motifs. Behind this cresting rise shallow bow-fronted drums again with Renaissance ornament. It is all far from correct, e.g. the pilasters in front of the drums, but insouciant and lively. They were restored in 1966. – Other monuments include the monuments to Sir Henry Bedingfeld †1583, Governor of the Tower under Mary Tudor. This is of alabaster and has an inscription in a broad strapwork frame flanked by Corinthian columns. – Also Sir Henry Bedingfeld †1684. High inscribed base. Above is a further Baroquely shaped cartouche and two putti. Attributed to *Arnold Quellin* (GF). – Anne Bedingfeld †1682, with later inscriptions to Sir Henry †1704 and his second wife, attributed to *William Woodman* the elder (GF). Open scrolly pediment. A skull and two swags at the foot. Garlands l. and r.

OTHER FURNISHINGS. BENCH ENDS. Those saved from the destruction are in the chancel. – LECTERN. Fine brass eagle of the same type as those of St Gregory (Norwich), Holy Trinity (Coventry), Lowestoft, Oundle, Southwell Cathedral, Newcastle Cathedral, St Michael (Southampton), and also Urbino Cathedral. These lecterns were probably made in East Anglia about 1500. It is inscribed: 'Orate pro anima Thomas Kyppyng quondam rectoris de Norburgh'. He died in 1489. – SCREEN. Moved to East Dereham in 1949. – STAINED GLASS. Some original, i.e C15, glass in the heads of chancel windows, restored by *King & Son* of Norwich.

ST MARY MAGDALENE. The E wall and N wall still standing, in the rectory garden, ½ m. SSW. There is a Norman round-arched doorway.

OUR LADY AND ST MARGARET (R.C.), in the grounds of the Hall, 100 yds NW of the gatehouse. Of 1835–9 for Sir Henry Richard Paston-Bedingfeld as a family chapel. The design is usually attributed to A. W. N. Pugin but Rory O'Donnell has pointed out that not only was that attribution first made only in 1909 but that Pugin himself did not claim it. It has a nave, an apse and a chantry chapel to the E (liturgically the S as the apse faces N). Three gables of later vestries, added to the W side in gault brick, contrasting with the studied antiquity of the local red brick (reused from demolished cottages) laid in an indeterminate bond. The chantry chapel is stone-faced and of the 1860s. Lancets everywhere, splayed inside. The chapel is interesting for its fittings. – ALTAR RETABLE. Made up in the C19, incorporating a typical Antwerp altarpiece of *c.* 1530–5, attributed to the studio of *Pieter Coecke van Aelst*. Carved scenes: the Crucifixion in the centre flanked by Carrying the Cross and the Deposition. The scenes in the predella seem English and German. The wings belong to the Antwerp work and have painted scenes of the Life of Christ etc., and on the outside standing Church Fathers. – STALLS. Foreign, C17. – COMMUNION RAILS. Two, both Flemish or French of *c.* 1700, one of them

used as a w gallery railing. – STAINED GLASS. A large number
of fragments, including one French C14 roundel, and one fine
English seated figure (of John the Baptist) of the early C14. Also
a group of pieces in the apse lancets dated 1521, Netherlandish
or German. w window by *Thomas Willement*, 1838, heraldic.
– MONUMENTS. Geraldine Trafford, †1860 in childbirth. She
is led up to heaven by an angel as she holds the baby in her
arms. – Sir Henry Richard Paston-Bedingfeld †1862. Lavish
alabaster tomb-chest and on it a recumbent effigy of white
Carrara marble.

OXBURGH HALL

Licence to crenellate his house was given to Edmund Bedingfeld
in 1482, but he may have begun construction immediately after he
inherited in 1476.* He had built a square mansion, 174 ft by
171 ft, with a courtyard and a moat closely surrounding the mansion. Of the four ranges the hall range (s) opposite the gatehouse
was alas pulled down in 1775, though not before Mackenzie drew
a ground plan. Sir Richard Bedingfeld, who decided to do this,
served his ancestral home badly; Sir Henry Richard Bedingfeld,
the sixth baronet, who about 1835 decided to rebuild, served it
well: for while the early Victorian rebuilding was by no means
archaeologically correct, it gave us the picturesque house that we
see now. The family had held office under Queen Mary; Sir Henry
Bedingfeld was Governor of the Tower when it held Princess
Elizabeth. The family remained Catholics and possibly this
prompted Sir Henry Richard to appoint the young *A. W. N. Pugin*,
with *J. C. Buckler*, to restore the house, a house described by Sir
Henry Richard in 1830 as a ruin. However Pugin's hand cannot
be easily detected. Apart from its romantic appearance the restorations created the suites of rooms that make up the present house.
The kitchen (E wing), servants' hall (N, now tea room), billiard
room (N, now shop), dining room (E), library (W) and west drawing room (W) are all of this time. Buckler raised the mighty SE
tower and erected the four charming towers in the kitchen garden.
Most of the fenestration is also his. Sir Henry Edward Bedingfeld,
seventh baronet, succeeded in 1862 and immediately rebuilt the s
range as a corridor to link the E and W ranges and redecorated some
of the principal rooms. His architect is not known. The house
came to the National Trust in 1952.

EXTERIOR. The chief survival of the late C15 house is the tremend-
68 ous GATEHOUSE, the most prominent of the English brick gatehouses of the C15. By 1487 Sir Edmund was able to entertain
Henry VII and Elizabeth of York within it. The polygonal turrets which flank the entry rise to a height of seven storeys, or
rather tiers, the tiers being separated externally by arched, cusped
brick friezes. There are in fact only three internal storeys. Double-
stepped battlements on top. The entrance has a finely moulded

* The licence, dated 3 July 1482, pardoned Bedingfeld for any works he had earlier
carried out.

four-centred head, and the windows above arched lights. The one on the first floor is of four lights with stepped transoms and arched heads below them as well. This lights the King's Room. Above the upper window an arch connecting the two turrets is provided with machicolation, i.e. holes to pour or throw down on the heads of those ready to attack the entrance whatever might prevent them. Towards the courtyard two projections, also polygonal, but less prominent and not at the angles. On the top at the angles themselves polygonal turrets. Inside, the entrance has a depressed pointed tunnel vault with thin transverse and longitudinal ribs, repeated in the vaults of the side chambers. The wooden double-leaf DOOR is original. In the turret rooms exceedingly pretty ribbed brick vaults and smaller vaults to the window bays facing the courtyard. The staircase in the W tower is also of brick, i.e. ingeniously constructed (cf. Welle Manor Hall, Upwell, p. 741, and the earlier Caister Castle, see Vol. 1). In the E turret towards the outside still cross-shaped slits for defence. They are placed so as to guard the BRIDGE which spans the moat on three arches (early C18, replacing a drawbridge). The MOAT itself is as spectacular as the house it complements: nowhere less than 42 ft wide nor less than 10 ft deep and faced on the sides away from the house by proper brick revetments (renewed in the C19).

In addition to the gatehouse the N, E and W ranges are basically original, though much renewed. All of the oriels, battlements and stepped gables, e.g., are *Buckler*'s. Cusped arched brick friezes appear here also, and double-stepped battlements and stepped gables. A mighty SW tower has entirely gone. It was not like the SE tower, but kept the balance. There are several examples of chimneystacks emerging through the thickness of the walls, often at the apexes of gablets. This was one of the principal constructional methods of dealing with chimneys before the advent of the internal axial stack about the middle of the C16. The decorated flues are, needless to say, also *Buckler*'s.

The first need to rebuild parts of the house was occasioned by the Civil War in which the Bedingfelds declared for the king, resulting in damage to the E wing. To the r. of the SE tower the repairs can be noticed, work here and elsewhere not being complete until 1725.

The COURTYARD is smaller and more intimate than the size of the house would suggest, made more so by the single-storey open arcade added to the E and W and parts of the N range c. 1800, the arcading filled in c. 1840. The eight-bay S range of c. 1862 is one storey, Gothic, and is only a corridor linking Buckler's SE tower with the fourth baronet's saloon at the SW corner, lit through arched windows and with buttresses and a crenellated parapet. Two- and three-light cusped windows serve the remaining ranges also, all of two storeys and dormer attic.

The original hall on the site of this S range (the courtyard had been open on this side since 1775) was much wider and of a conventional screens-passage type, the passage to the W, and beyond it the customary service rooms. A small porch stood at the courtyard entrance to the passage, and at the other end (s) an exit led to a second bridge over the moat. In 1774 the high end of the hall had a dais window to both the court and the moat. Blomefield reports that this hall, which 'may be justly accounted one of the best old Gothick halls in England', was 54 ft long, 34 ft wide and 54 ft high and had a roof 'in the same style and form with that of Westminster' (Hall), i.e. one presumes a hammerbeam roof.

INTERIOR. The visitor enters by the s range doorway and so to the sw corner pavilion, originally the site of the kitchen and closet, but converted for Sir Richard as a picture gallery after 1780, which involved a complete rebuild, apart from the late C15 plinth course on the w side. It is now the SALOON. Buckler's alterations include blocking the two w sashes and Gothicizing the three to the s. The w RANGE was completely reorganized c. 1835–40 for Sir Henry Richard into just two state rooms separated by a staircase. The WEST DRAWING ROOM redecorated by *Crace & Co.*: wallpaper for Sir Henry Edward after 1862; delicate ribbed ceiling of rectangular and star-shaped fields with heraldic painting by Crace & Co. after 1870. The w staircase was given a closed string, twisted balusters and panelled dado in the 1830s, as if it were Queen Anne. Wonderful Spanish leather wall covering. The LIBRARY received its redecoration in the mid C19, including probably the not very accomplished Gothic chimneypiece and the better tripartite canopied overmantel, reused from a church reredos. Bookcases with cresting.

The DINING ROOM at the w end of the N RANGE was until the 1970s a second library, and the only library in 1774. Elaborate 1830s dado panelling incorporating some C17 elements, timber chimneypiece and overmantel of such exuberant carving that it defies description. The NORTH STAIRCASE is a smaller version of the w staircase, again with Spanish leather hangings, and the remainder of the N range (apart from the gatehouse) is devoted to a shop and tea rooms.

On the FIRST FLOOR first the NORTH BEDROOM over the dining room, with a heavily carved overmantel, reached by a passageway, again with Spanish leather wall coverings. The BOUDOIR in the w range, next to this bedroom, has reticulated ceiling ribs. The MARIAN HANGINGS ROOM in the N range adjacent to the gatehouse (renamed 1975) has NEEDLEWORK hangings done by Mary Queen of Scots and Bess of Hardwick c. 1570. They came to Oxburgh from Cowdray Park, Sussex, in 1761. The KING'S ROOM occupies the first floor of the gatehouse. Rere-arches to the window alcoves facing the courtyard and the depressed four-centred fireplace all of the 1480s. The grid of roll-moulded bridging beams and linenfold panelling are C19. The E tower of the gatehouse was formerly a garderobe. The w tower affords the visitor the first opportunity of examining the C15 brick staircase within it, which rises to the QUEEN'S ROOM. Star vault in the garderobe tower and to the courtyard

MOAT

MOAT

30 m
100 ft

1   Gatehouse
2   Porter's lodge (guard room)
3   Porter's lodge (armoury)
4   Laundry (tea room)
5   Wash house (tea room)
6   Drawing rooms (east drawing room)
7   Dining room (morning room)
8   Hall (demolished)
9   China room (demolished)
10 Pantry (demolished)

11 Closet (part of saloon)
12 Kitchen (part of saloon)
13 Servants' hall (part of west drawing room)
14 Storeroom (part of west drawing room)
15 Breakfast room (part of library)
16 Bedchamber (part of library)
17 Library (dining room)
18 Bridge to moat (demolished)

Oxburgh Hall. Mid-eighteenth century plan
(with present use of rooms in brackets)

window alcoves. The tour returns one to the base of the gatehouse. The whole E wing and the first and attic floors of the
remainder, not here described, are still occupied by the Bedingfeld
family and not open to the public.

THE PARK is defined to the main road by a brick boundary WALL,
of late C15 origins but mainly rebuilt early C19. At the NE end,

closest to the parish church, is CHURCH LODGE. About 1835, probably by *J. C. Buckler*. He left a pair of tall polygonal towers flanking a wide four-centred carriage archway, but the plan was completely altered about 1948 when the arch was filled in and converted to domestic use. Further w is CHAPEL LODGE, which has its late C17 stepped brick N gable wall integral with the park walls. The rest remodelled late C19. E and SE of the Hall are GARDEN WALLS, *c.*1830–5, probably by *J. C. Buckler*, of red brick, with four square towers at intervals. One now provides the entrance for visitors. The WILDERNESS, to the NE, was laid out in the C19 and restored in the 1970s by the *National Trust*: charming summer walks.

CHANTRY HOUSE, immediately E of the Bedingfeld Arms pub. The name may refer to a chantry founded in 1483. Much is of that time. The materials are clunch, brick and reused limestone, with some timber-framing in the E side. The centre block is a former open hall house with a screens passage. One and a half storeys. The N front has an inserted doorway in the middle. The blocked screens door to the E still has its corresponding door open to the S front. Various C18 windows and blocked former windows. There is a C15 piscina inside and a fireplace reusing late C12 shafts r. and l. with scallop-type capitals. Clasped purlin roof. The E wing lengthened to the s in C17 brick, parts with timber-framing, fragments of former windows and five C19 casements. Crown-post roof. The w wing is C18, with four doorways in the façade and four segment-headed windows.

OXWICK

1¼ m. SW of Colkirk

ALL SAINTS. In ruins, roofless, inaccessible and overgrown at the time of writing. Continuous nave and chancel, the latter with Y-traceried windows, so the date very early C14. N and S doorways later C14. The tower has disappeared entirely. The church was declared redundant in 1946.

PATTESLEY

1¼ m. SE of East Raynham

PATTESLEY HOUSE. In the flint w wall of the house is a blocked C14 doorway of the former church of St John Baptist, converted to a house in the early C17. The church was already about 1600 'whollye ruinated and decaied', and now forms the main domestic block. Plenty of later extensions to the rear and sides. There is an early C17 staircase outshut and a good dog-leg staircase with square balusters and decorative carving. The main s front appears as a late C18 elevation with transomed C20 casements to the ground floor. Nothing else of particular interest preserved.

PENTNEY

ST MARY MAGDALEN. Norman nave and chancel, lengthened at each end and now a single vessel. The walls are of rendered (partly) carstone, clunch, flint and ashlar; now with a dull, uninterrupted slate roof of *c.* 1850. From the Norman nave a S window with a detached C12 shaft, also the fragmentarily pre-served blank interlaced arcading on the N and S walls: each of two and part of a third roll-moulded arches on shafts with cush-ion capitals. The walls here have stone quoins at the W end of the thicker part (visible inside) indicating the W end of the Norman church. Long, late C13 chancel, on the N side still with four widely spaced small lancets. Good three-light E window with flat Late Geometrical tracery (heads of the lights pointed-trefoil-cusped, above pointed as well as rounded trefoils and daggers). One deeply splayed round-headed lancet on S nave wall W of the doorway. The building was extended to the W to link up with the tower. This is of flint rubble, with diagonal buttresses and chequerwork plinth. Dec bell-openings, and battle-ments with chequer flintwork. Two-light Perp W window. The roof is *c.* 1850, arched braces to nave, scissor-braces to chancel. – FONT. C14, like a short octagonal pier, without carving. – WALL PAINTINGS. During stripping of the internal emulsion in 1996 a consecration cross was revealed on the E wall l. of the window, parts of a second to the r. and dado painting to the N and S chancel walls. – STAINED GLASS. E window with good Crucifixion by *Ward & Hughes*, 1885.

CROSS, ½ m. SW. C14. Unusual cruciform base, the arms in the form of buttresses. Square plinth, octagonal socket stone and much of the octagonal limestone shaft survives.

PENTNEY PRIORY, 1¾ m. SW of the church. Augustinian; founded before 1135 by Robert de Vaux. Quite a big house, usually with fifteen to twenty canons. The imposing GATEHOUSE alone re-mains obvious, of the late C14. Of flint, carstone and some brick dressed with ashlar, and very broad. To the outside (N) are two polygonal turrets whose battlements are, however, lower than those of the flat-pitched gable over the centre. Below this a two-light window and below that the broad archway with its four-centred head and double wave and hollow mouldings. In the spandrels shields in Kentish quatrefoils (i.e. split cusps). The turrets each have two high trefoiled lancets and nook-shafts to the angles. Beyond the turrets the wall still continues at the same height, terminating in stepped buttresses, and here the staircases were housed. The E and W returns have similar windows and partly external brick chimney flues added in the C15. The walls slope back from the N end, so the interior is less wide than the N front. The S front is nearly as ambitious: similar mouldings to the four-centred arch, but no spandrel decoration; four stepped buttresses; one two-light C14 trefoiled window to each floor, those to the ground blocked. The INTERIOR was three-storeyed, with rooms with fireplaces, but one looks up to the sky. Nevertheless there remains a central vessel which was vaulted in two bays, and small doorways r. and l. into narrow rooms along the flanks. It is a shame that the building could not at least have a temporary roof.

ABBEY FARMHOUSE, by the Gatehouse, reusing a lot of the priory stone. In the early C18 a secondary gate stood here, and this was incorporated *c.* 1740 into the house. W front of two storeys and attic in three bays, the pedimented middle bay entirely of stone. Platband between the floors. Altered four-centred arch with a niche either side. Extensions in one storey r. and l. The E face of the arch of the gateway remains inside, with polygonal side turrets terminating in ogeed finials and a stone roof sloping away. Splat-baluster mid-C18 staircase masquerading as C17.

NARBOROUGH HOUSE, Lynn Road. A three- by three-bay gault-brick house of the early C19 with rusticated quoins. Three storeys. E entrance porch added late C19, and each front also with additions of this time. The main interest is the association with *Burne-Jones*, who, it is said, designed some pieces of STAINED GLASS and also the chimneypiece in the SW room.

PETERSTONE PRIORY *see* BURNHAM OVERY TOWN

2000

PORINGLAND

ALL SAINTS. Round tower, probably *c.* 1200 with an octagonal C14 top. The cusped belfry windows alternate with blind windows. Dec chancel, see the side windows with diagonal petal tracery and the handsome three niches in the E wall. The three-light E window was unblocked in 1857, and in the next twenty years intermittent restorations went on. The chancel arch was completely rebuilt. Perp nave with a clerestory with brick windows under four-centred arches, probably added after 1495 when money was left for 'making up of church walls'. At the E end of the S side they are shorter because the nave window is taller. Hammerbeam roof on wall-posts with longitudinal arched braces. They have foliage in the spandrels. The arched braces rising from the hammerbeams carry collar-beams. The roof is also presumably after 1495. The S porch 1861. N porch used as a vestry since the C19, and in 1973 converted to a passageway to a new octagonal vestry. – FONT. Perp. Octagonal. Against the stem four lions, against the bowl the signs of the four Evangelists, two lions, one flower, and an angel. – BENCHES. With poppy-heads on 1861 woodwork. – PAINTING. Small North Italian C16 triptych. St Paul, two angels raising the host, St Peter. – STAINED GLASS. C15 glass in the chancel including three figures in E window.

CHURCH FARMHOUSE, to the SE. *c.* 1600. Timber-framed. The N range has a porch containing some Jacobean details including a window pediment. Moulded door-frame with turned balusters framing it – a rare but not unique feature. The upper floor is jettied. To the r. of the porch early C18 cross casements and a C17 transomed mullioned upper window. SW gable with pedimented windows and octagonal flues to the stack. E range also early C17, rather more altered. Quadrant-moulded bridging beams. Good staircase, with quadrant-moulded closed strings and bulbous turned balusters. Diminished principal roof with clasped purlins in E range.

PORCH FARMHOUSE, to the E. Very slightly earlier than Church Farmhouse, *c.* 1590. Flint and brick with ashlar dressings, rather than timber-framed, but similar elements are disposed. The porch is not centrally placed because there is a through-passage plan. Four-bay façade, the windows originally mullioned, and one remains to the W gable. The gables have staircase outshuts and stacks with twin octagonal flues. The stairs are winders, with octagonal newel-posts. Stone surrounds to fireplaces. Clasped purlin roof on diminished principals.

A few C17 HOUSES. Nos. 8–10 CHURCH LANE is dated 1693. Shaped N gable and a platband to façade. Much altered. MARGIN COTTAGE, The Street, has been reclaimed as a single house from the original four. Late C17. Partly timber-framed, especially to S. Bridging beams with sunk-quadrant mouldings.

POTTHORPE   9020
NW of Brisley

No church. Of note CHESHAM HOUSE, *c.* 1800, three bays, Roman Doric doorcase. Nice contemporary railings in front. WALNUT HOUSE is a C17 building greatly modernized in the early C19. Flint and brick.

POTT ROW *see* GRIMSTON

PUDDING NORTON   9020
1½ m. S of Fakenham

ST MARGARET, S of the farm buildings of Pudding Norton Hall. In ruins. The tower stands almost to the top. It is unbuttressed and has a splayed lancet window, perhaps with a round arch. Also perhaps C12, see the carstone quoins, giving way in the upper stages to C13 limestone quoins. Of the nave parts of the S and N walls survive.

PUDDING NORTON HALL. C17 manor house of the Paris family (here 1576–1698) which has declined into a farmhouse, and been mostly rebuilt in the C18 and early C19. Stuccoed brick front of five bays in two and a half storeys, the centre three bays recessed. Central porch on four unfluted columns. Main elevation with parapets. The projecting end bays fitted with tripartite bay windows. The N stack has C17 chamfered brick. The BARN has a platband and honeycomb ventilation panels.

EARTHWORKS OF DESERTED VILLAGE. The church stands
c. 50 yds W of the line of the deserted medieval village's main
street. Desertion took place in the late C16. Earthworks of the
N–S street, side lanes and tofts are the best preserved in Norfolk,
and cover the whole of a pasture field. Curiously, Pudding
Norton survives administratively as a civil parish. (AR)

PULHAM MARKET

ST MARY MAGDALEN. Quite big, aisled, with a broad four-stage
tower. W doorway with fleurons and crowns in the arch mouldings and flowers in the spandrels. Niches l. and r. of the W window. The window has stepped, embattled transoms. Flushwork
panelling on base, buttresses and battlements. The lavish N porch
is no doubt also of the mid C15; money was left for it in a will of
1456. It is flushwork-panelled and has crowns and fleurons in
the spandrels and three niches. The porch is continued to the E
by the N aisle, suggesting the aisle is a later addition. N and S
aisle windows and clerestory are Perp. In the chancel all the
windows are from the 1873 restoration which also provided the
vestry, pulpit, font and seats (cost £1,800 according to Kelly).
The arcades are five bays long. The S arcade is the earlier. Its
piers are quatrefoil with thin polygonal shafts in the diagonals.
The first bay has a double wave moulding in the arch, the
others and the N arcade have double-chamfered arches. The N
arcade piers have the familiar four-shafts-and-four-hollows
moulding. Nave roof with arched braces and collars, and a panelled E bay. Repaired 1873. The aisle roofs are also original and
also arch-braced. In the S aisle small angel figures above the
apexes of the arcade. – PAINTINGS. Over the chancel arch and
in the last bay of nave roof. Medieval paintings re-done in High
Victorian manner in 1873. – SCREEN. Parts under the tower. –
STALL ENDS. With poppyheads and with poppyheads and figurines l. and r. – STAINED GLASS. Bits in a N aisle window. E
window by *Heaton, Butler & Bayne*, to designs by *Holiday* also
used at St Mary, Paddington, †1838. Three good large panels of
Christ Washing Feet, Crucifixion and Mary Magdalen with
Disciples. – BANNER STAFF LOCKER. In the S aisle W wall.

The VILLAGE. A market was granted in the C12 but by the mid
C17 had disappeared and the village never expanded. THE
GREEN is spacious and pretty, with two pubs squaring up to
each other on the N–S axis. The CROWN INN to the S is the
more attractive: a long plastered range of C17 origins with a
lobby-entrance plan, thatched roof and C18 casement windows.
A respectable amount of the timber frame survives inside. On
the E side a series of C17 thatched houses, all altered quite well
in the C20, DRAYTON HOUSE, WILLOW COTTAGE and
THATCHED COTTAGE. The opposite side has THE LAURELS,
early C18, timber-framed with clay lump, and a stumpy porch
off-set to the l. To the E of the church the OLD RECTORY, a
C19 red brick N façade of two storeys in five bays entered from

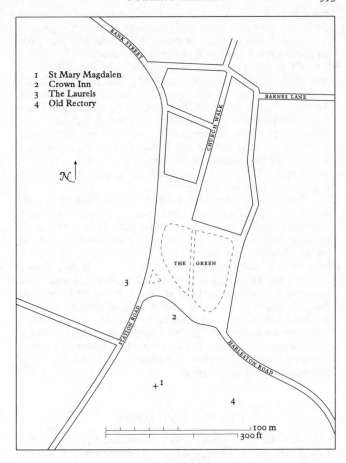

1 St Mary Magdalen
2 Crown Inn
3 The Laurels
4 Old Rectory

BANK STREET

CHURCH WALK

BARNES LANE

N

THE GREEN

STATION ROAD

HARLESTON ROAD

100 m
300 ft

Pulham Market

a plain rendered porch. W elevation of the mid C18, also five
bays. From the N end of The Green BANK STREET runs off to
the NW. Immediately on the N a row of three C17 cottages lit
through C19 casements, GOODWIN HOUSE, ROSE COTTAGE
and JAPONICA COTTAGE. Next door to the W another,
ANDREWS, with a very steeply pitched thatched roof. In the
other direction, i.e. behind the Falcon Inn N of The Green, a
little collection of streets (CHURCH WALK, BARNES LANE)
with many more timber-framed C17 cottages and C18 clay lump
ones, all prettily set in relation to one another. From the W end
of the church one can follow STATION ROAD to the S. At 300 yds
on the r. THE BEECHES, just N of the former railway station.
Of two storeys and three bays, early C19, with Gothick (i.e.
derived from Batty Langley) windows and a curved porch with
giant polygonal Gothic (academically medievalizing) piers. At
the end of its own drive a little further S THE HALL: the front of

three bays is early Victorian, but behind it is a C17 stepped gable with casement windows. Then GOTHIC HOUSE, ½ m. s of The Hall on the l., a C17 timber-framed house but with early C19 alterations including four-centred windows.

MANOR FARMHOUSE, 1⅞ m. NE. Externally just a timber-framed and plastered oblong house, probably with some clay lump infill. Some mullioned windows still show. Internally much of interest survives: the C16 hall screen, plain, with broad chamfered muntins, and traces of painting. There is a plain winder staircase behind the dais end of the small hall, and further fragments of painting, here of two female figures. Plain panelling with chamfered muntins in the upper rooms. One of the fireplaces with a fluted brick arch. The house evidently belonged to a well-to-do yeoman, not a rich man.

HILL HOUSE, now a hotel but formerly the WORKHOUSE, 1¼ m. NW on the main A140 road. Red brick, star-shaped, and with pedimented gables, i.e. just post-classical. There is a central octagon from which the four wings radiate, connected at the ends by lower ranges. Built in 1836 by *William Thorold*.

In the small hamlets surrounding are many C17 timber-framed HOUSES and FARMHOUSES, almost all more picturesque than interesting. The best perhaps is DUCKSFOOT FARMHOUSE, Bush Green, 1¼ m. NE of the church on a crossroads. Timber-framed, of three bays. C17 stack inserted in the middle giving a lobby-entrance, then in the C18 a further bay added to the S. C20 additions at the back. Inside are moulded timbers, a blocked diamond-mullioned window, and a queenpost roof with clasped purlins. The roof must date to *c.* 1550.

PULHAM ST MARY

ST MARY. Quite big, with a strong W tower. The S porch is something phenomenal. Two-storeyed, stone-fronted, with flushwork panelling on the sides. Openwork cresting of reticulation units. Supporters as pinnacles. Small frieze above the base panelling. Doorway with crested capitals, the Annunciation in the spandrels and fleurons up one order of jamb and arch mouldings, inside and out. Two niches l. and r. Above these eight small figures of angels making music. Frieze of shields in cusped fields, including those of Passion and Trinity. Two upper two-light windows and five niches. Ceiling with moulded beams inside. Fleurons also on the inner doorway. There is no reason to connect this porch with William of Wykeham, who held the living from 1357 to 1361; it is evidently C15 work and later than the S aisle. The tall W tower has flushwork-panelled battlements. The chancel is much older. Its splendid double piscina of the type of Jesus College (Cambridge) and Hardingham in Norfolk dates it as mid-C13. Straight top; below it an arch and two half-arches intersect. All three of the fine roll mouldings join in the intersecting. In the N wall two splayed lancet windows. The four-light E window, if correctly reproduced by *G. F. Bodley* in 1886–7

during his general restoration (£5,000), must be some generations later, as it has reticulated tracery. Tall Perp N windows in
the nave. Perp S arcade of four bays. Quatrefoil piers with the
foils polygonal. Double-chamfered arches. When the aisle was
built or rebuilt, the nave was widened on that side. The aisle
roof is original, with arched braces and tracery in the spandrels.
– FONT. C15. On the bowl the four Evangelists and angels with
shields with the Instruments of the Passion. The stem was
replaced by Bodley (eight high-relief figures of Saints), who added
the FONT COVER (small, of the type with vanes and a central
crocketed pinnacle). – SCREEN. Ten mid-C15 painted figures
are preserved, if defaced. They are quite good, and once there
were more in the bays taking up the spare wall S of the chancel
arch created when the nave was widened. The upper part is
Bodley's: moulded stiles support a cornice coved and ribbed on
both sides, with top cresting and a crucifix. He is also responsible for the plain organ case, vestry, the painted decoration of the
chancel roof, work to the roofs and various fittings. – BENCHES.
Many C15 ones with poppyheads; two also with traceried panelling and little buttresses on the back. – LECTERN. Wooden
eagle, probably C16, on renewed stem. – STAINED GLASS. In
the head of the nave NE window Christ from a Coronation of
the Virgin, and two angels, early C14. – In the head of another
N window twelve complete C15 figures. – Late C19 glass elsewhere, some by *Burlison & Grylls*, according to Birkin Haward.
OLD RECTORY, divided into three houses (Nos. 1–3 The Street).
It presents itself as an early C19 brick house with casements
and gabled dormers, but in fact is a C16 timber-framed house.
THE STREET has several other C16 and C17 houses, some faced
with C19 brick. LYMEHURST is such a one, externally of five bays
in two storeys, but a timber frame inside and two four-centred
doorways. WAVENEY COTTAGE and the POST OFFICE are also
C16, the KING'S HEAD public house early C17, lobby-entrance.
STATION ROAD repeats the formula – see THE BEECHES, late
C16, with a S cross wing and stacks with octagonal flues.
HARROLDS and THE LAURELS are both C17, faced with brick.
PENNOYER'S SCHOOL, Norwich Road, in the angle of a junction.
Behind the present red brick C19 village school (closed 1988)
and attached to it is the schoolroom established by William
Pennoyer in 1670. It was built into the chapel of the Guild of St
James, suppressed in 1547. This dated from 1401, and there
remains a small rectangular flint chapel with two arched win-
dows with hoodmoulds either side, each altered by the insertion
of a central mullion probably in 1670, and with C19 plate glass.
On the N side is a priest's door leading into a later outbuilding.
The W end has diagonal buttresses, and a Diocletian window in
the gable-head. Inside is a blocked W doorway, quite big, and
with similar mouldings to the church S porch; to the E, embedded in the Victorian school, is the NE buttress. Only the chapel's
E wall and SE buttress are missing.
To the E of the school, in front of the King's Head, is the VILLAGE
SIGN, 1969, with a relief depiction of the R34 airship. The plaque

records that the R34 was the first airship to cross the Atlantic, a double crossing, landing here in July 1919.

The surrounding area is studded with C16 and C17 FARMHOUSES, some disguised with brick skins, almost all with C19 or C20 windows, dormers or other embellishments. GARLIC FARM-HOUSE, Garlic Street, is C16; UPPER VAUNCE FARMHOUSE, Back Road, dates from the C17; CROSSINGFORD LODGE, Doctor's Lane, has details from both centuries.

PYNKNEY HALL *see* TATTERFORD

8030   QUARLES
                         2 m. ENE of North Creake

CHURCH. Only foundations are preserved.

0080   QUIDENHAM

ST ANDREW. C11 round tower with blocked circular windows, their upper voussoirs roughly done with carstone. Octagonal top stage which accords well with the donation of 10 marks (£6 13s. 4d.) in 1400 for the tower building. Shingled spire. Arch towards the nave quite tall and with the plainest imposts. Is this then Anglo-Saxon, or early C12? It could be either. Relatively early Norman N doorway. One order of shafts with volute cap-itals. Roll-moulded arch with some small delicately carved motifs. The door itself has been replaced but the ironwork of *c.* 1130 apparently transferred. In the chancel N wall, re-set, three shafts with various volute capitals, Norman rather than Saxon. Late C13 S doorway. The W window of the S aisle probably con-temporary. This wall is of knapped flint. The S aisle exterior otherwise and the arcade all Victorian, or at least a Victorian re-facing, as the original responds point to *c.* 1300, and the emblems on the S buttresses to a Perp remodelling. Fine early C14 chan-cel, though the E window does not in its present form appear in Ladbroke's drawing. The other windows however seem to bear out the style. The chancel windows are nicely shafted inside. – SCREEN. A part of a C16 rood screen now under the tower. Straight top and animals and angels in the spandrels. – POOR BOX, on a sturdy turned shaft. Dated 1639. – STAINED GLASS. E window in the style of *Heaton, Butler & Bayne*, *c.* 1880, two N nave windows by *M. & A. O'Connor*, †1849 and †1851. – MONUMENTS. Two tablets on the N chancel wall, Lady Anthea Sandys †1679 and Lord Sandys †1700, are a nice illustration of changes at the end of the C17.

QUIDENHAM HALL, since 1948 a Carmelite nunnery. Of the mansion of the Hollands built in 1606 round a courtyard no more remains than some traces of the mullioned, pedimented fenestration towards the N front. A model at Gressenhall, however, shows it to have been a six-bay house with stepped gables over each bay. The four-bay, four-storey N front with octagonal turrets is now approached from an arcaded brick cloister of 1954–7 by *Dewing & Herriott* which runs right up to it. John Bristow bought the house *c.* 1740 and added the E wing with its simple façade: two storeys, seven bays, the centre two broken forward under a pediment, ground-floor sashes with segmental pediments, triangular pedimented to centre only. The pediments seem to be of 1892. Bristow sold to the third Earl of Albemarle in 1762, who in 1811 remodelled the centre and added the W wing. The W front has a loggia of four giant unfluted Ionic columns carrying a pediment. The S façade is odd for it is of nine bays in two and a half storeys flanked by chunky three-bay bows which are really the returns of the E and W wings. The centre three bays set back. Porch on Tuscan columns and pilasters.

The INTERIOR was redecorated by *C. Heathcote Tatham*, *c.* 1820 for the fourth Earl, but much of that had to be obliterated for the new purpose of the house. His library remains. Apsidal end with two Corinthian columns and at the other end four more Corinthian columns forming a screen. The chimneypiece overmantel with two Corinthian pilasters below an open pediment. Rather heavily moulded plaster ceiling. The main staircase ceiling has a lovely strapwork design with, in the centre roundel, the Hand of God descending as a pendant and holding a model of Noah's ark containing Noah, his wife and animals and the date 1619.

MOUNDS. NW of the church and close to the river a mound may be a small Norman motte, while another $\frac{1}{8}$ m. SSE in the park is probably a prospect mound. It has an ice-house built into one side. (AR)

RAINTHORPE HALL   *2090*

$\frac{7}{8}$ m. N of Tasburgh

A brick mansion, the upper floor partly timber-framed with exposed studs. The building, now with flanking wings, gradually assumed its present form. White tells us it was begun in 1503, i.e. in the time of the Appleyards, and it must indeed be assumed that the house is of the early C16 and was not rebuilt but only very thoroughly remodelled and added to by Thomas Baxter in the late C16. The plan is roughly an E on the N side, but the porch is set to the r. and there is, to its l., a two-storey bay window. The wings have straight gables and two bays of small windows l. and r. of the twin chimney flues which rise out of the gable apexes. The porch is three-storeyed and has sturdy polygonal angle-shafts and an entrance arch still entirely Perp. The spandrels e.g. carry tracery. The windows are all mullioned and transomed. The back of the house has a polygonal stair-turret with its original winder and, on the l., projecting far, a wing of 1885. There is also a bay on this side which carries the date 1615. This can obviously not be the date of the house.

Heraldry inside and outside proves much of the work to be that
of Thomas Baxter, a lawyer who bought the property in 1579.
As his wife's arms also occur, and as she died in 1587, that gives
in addition a *terminus ante quem*. However, the Perp porch
entrance cannot possibly be so late, and that is not the only
indication of an earlier date. The house is entered in the usual
way direct into the hall. The screen has disappeared, and the
wall towards the buttery and pantry also, so that the whole centre
is now on the ground floor one big room. The hall does not
go through two storeys and the hall bay is divided too. On the
ground floor the bay is entered by an arch again entirely Perp.
The stair-turret corresponds to the exit from the hall in line with
the entrance and is thus in a customary position. Above the hall
lies the Great Chamber, and this has a plaster ceiling with thin
ribs arranged in a geometric pattern, probably late C16. The
wings are later than the centre, as is evident from their omission
of the diapering with dark-blue brick and their butt-purlin
roofs, the older part having clasped purlins. The Baxters sold in
1628 and the next major events occurred under that enthusiastic antiquarian Frederick Walpole from 1852 until his death in
1876. His are the hall chimneypiece with its mixed Renaissance
carving, most of the panelling, which was also brought in from
elsewhere and rearranged arbitrarily, and much STAINED GLASS.
The glass is particularly fine, dating from the C13 to the C19.
Walpole renewed the mullioned and transomed windows in
stone leaving some C16 timber. Sir Charles Harvey bought the
house in 1878 and in 1885 added the five-bay w extension to the
s front. The unusual thing about the extension is its sympathy
with the original.

STABLES, 100 yds NW of the house. Added by Harvey in 1879.
Brick.

₃₀₉₀   RAVENINGHAM

ST ANDREW. In the grounds of the Hall. The church is unfortunately all rendered. Round tower with an octagonal E.E. top.
Double-step Perp battlements with flushwork panelling. The
chancel fenestration seems all early C14 (E window 1885), and
such a date would fit the extraordinary recess inside, if it is *in
situ*. It has been so restored that little is actually medieval,
although medieval must have been the model. It looks exactly
like a founder's tomb cum Easter Sepulchre, so it is doubly suspicious to find it on the s side. Perhaps it is re-set from the N
and remade. It has a cusped and subcusped arch, all cusps
covered with foliage, a gable with a frieze of foliage inside and
crockets outside, a cusped pointed trefoil in the gable, and a big
finial. Inside is a memorial slab to Roger Castell †1708. C14
piscina. The nave has a N aisle, of octagonal piers with double-
chamfered arches, ruthlessly cemented over. Of the mid C14.
The windows are mixed. The nave s windows are large and
Perp. C19 clerestory. Nave roof from the 1885 restoration. –

FONT. Perp. Octagonal. With four lions against the stem and four Saints and the signs of the four Evangelists against the bowl. – SOUTH DOOR. Ironwork in the form of three foliated crosses. Strap hinges and split curls. A beautiful piece of simple early C12 craftsmanship. – STAINED GLASS. E window by *Kempe*, 1885. – MONUMENTS. Brass to Margaret Castyll †1483, 2 ft 2 in. figure (chancel W, floor). – The chancel has lavish decoration in imitation of the tomb recess referred to above. It extends over both side walls and was put in to receive commemorative tablets of the Bacon family. The first Bacon so commemorated is Sir Edmund (†1820). The style of this display of Dec decoration is very early Victorian and might well point to a date *c.* 1840. – Major Edward Hodge †1815. Free-standing. Big white marble base and a white marble urn on it.

RAVENINGHAM HALL. A substantial, late C18 house of red brick built for Sir Edmund Bacon (†1820, *see* above). Seven by five bays, two and a half storeys, with a three-bay pediment to the principal, S, front over advanced bays. The four-bay screen walls extending E and W led originally to little side wings, now pulled down. The N front basically similar but with two two-storey canted bays. So the house remained until Capt. Nicholas Bacon (later twelfth and thirteenth baronet) engaged *Somers Clark*. He brought forward the ground floor of the N front to include a porch, added the narrow two-storey extensions to the E and W sides and the three-bay S portico on Tuscan columns. The dormers and the circular S pediment window are also of this time, all dated on the N 1905.

Internally yet more by Somers Clark, notably the plasterwork of the entrance hall behind the S door, with its apsed entry and exit and a shallow groined vault, and the beautiful, not at all usual, plaster ceiling of the staircase, with groin vaulting rising from fan-like corner pieces and big honeysuckle ornament in the centre. The cantilevered staircase itself is, however, Georgian. The STABLES go with the first build, and are arranged round three sides of a yard. Two storeys, arcading to W front. Domed clock tower.

CASTELL FARMHOUSE, ¾ m. SE. The Castell family acquired the manor in 1225 but it passed to the Bacon family in 1735. C16, timber-framed. L-shaped plan. Mostly upright studs show externally. The main (SE) front is quite flat and flanked by polygonal angle-shafts. Jettied first floor lit through restored or renewed casements. Chimneyshafts generally of grouped lozenge type, variously decorated. The N gable has a six-light mullioned ground-floor window. The brick gable above laid in English bond with diapering.

GROVE FARMHOUSE, 1¼ m. SE. Brick stepped gable-ends with polygonal angle-shafts. The E gable has ovolo-moulded and pedimented windows in three storeys, in six-, four- and three-light versions. The W gable improved by a stepped external stack. The house itself is timber-framed and plastered. S front has four bays of C19 cross casements. Jettied upper floor. The two-storeyed porch is directly under the ridge stack (clustered polygonal shafts) indicating the lobby-entrance plan, here used in the late C16. The two rear wings now have a late C17 infill block with a shaped gable and two oval windows. The late C17 staircase has turned balusters.

COLUMN, Beccles Road. 1831 by *J. T. Patience*. Commissioned by Sir Edmund Bacon. Of cast-iron in two octagonal sections on a plinth, and with panels to each facet under crocketed gables. It gave mileages to London, Norwich, etc., now badly weathered.

BARN at Brundish Farm. Five-bay timber-framed barn of the late C16. Clasped purlin roof with curved wind-braces.

8020

RAYNHAM HALL

Raynham Hall is the paramount house of its date in Norfolk. It is also, especially as seen from the w up the avenue, one of the most attractive of the major houses in the county, warm and comfort-able-looking, in spite of its size. Moreover, it is not in a local style, but is a provincial hybrid introducing to the county the Classicism of Inigo Jones, himself still at the start of his career. This is at once apparent from the fact that not only are the main elevations sym-metrical, but so is the plan, the first such combination in Norfolk.

Sir Roger Townshend began to build a new house in 1619 in col-laboration with a local master mason, *William Edge*. The old house stood to the SW, probably unoccupied since his father was killed in 1603 when Sir Roger was eight. In 1622 he changed the plan, remade the foundations, and building proceeded slowly. Sir Roger was in no hurry; he was young and lived from 1622 mainly at Stiffkey after his grandfather Sir Nathaniel Bacon died. Only in 1635 was wainscoting being bought for Raynham, and it is only in this year that there is any evidence of occupation: Sir Roger died suddenly there on 1 January 1637, perhaps explaining why major details of the apartments were not finally completed until Horatio Townshend, the first Viscount, moved from Stiffkey in 1656. He spent over £3,000 on the house in 1659–62, and afterwards con-centrated on the park.

The house was again unoccupied after Horatio's death in 1687 until Charles Townshend, the second Viscount, returned from his Grand Tour in 1697, married in 1698 and put the Hall back in order. He engaged a second master mason named *William Edge* (presumably a relative of the first) to draw a model of the house in 1698, and Edge continued to send plans to Townshend in London for approval. So it may be that *Charles Townshend* and Edge II between them repeated the relationship established by Sir Roger. It was they who, in 1703–6, altered the E and W fronts and the plan of the hall. The carpenter was *Matthew May*, the stonecutter was *Miles Poemerroy* with his assistant *William Lacey*. On 21 June 1703 Townshend wrote that the work 'fills us at present with London workmen and a great deal of dust'. Finishing touches went on until 1709. Plans and elevations recording the house in 1671 indicate the nature of these changes, which make the exterior (and interior) more regular than it had originally been. Finally the interiors were remodelled for Charles Townshend by *William Kent* in the 1720s, with *Thomas Ripley* as executive architect.

The recent remarkable discovery of the first account books and memoranda detailing activities from March 1619 to July 1622 show, as John Harris surmised many years ago, that Sir Roger in 1619 made special efforts to see new buildings by Inigo Jones at Newmarket and in London. In particular in October 1619 he tipped workmen at Whitehall, where Jones's Banqueting House was being built, and in November he tipped the porter at Sir Fulke Greville's house in Holborn, which had just been completed on the basis of a surviving design by Jones. This house is clearly the source of the great pedimented gables which crown the skyline at Raynham. Sir Roger may have seen Jones's drawings too. He was accompanied on this six-week London trip by William Edge, the first time the two names are associated.

Between April and October 1620 Sir Roger and Edge were abroad, but where they went or what they saw we do not know. Sir Roger bought himself drawing instruments and in the following two years Edge was paid for 'drawinge plattes', and in 1622 a model was made of the house (by *John* and *Thomas Moore*), a very early instance of this in England. So it seems fair to envisage the house as a joint creation of them both, inspired above all by Jones's new style, but also perhaps by their experiences abroad. Their activities after 1622 are not documented in detail, but Sir Roger probably maintained a lively interest in new developments, such as the Venetian window motif of Jones's Catholic chapel at St James's Palace, designed in 1623, which finds an echo at Raynham. He came after all from a family deeply interested in architecture: both his great-grandfather Sir Nicholas Bacon and grandfather Sir Nathaniel Bacon were pioneering patron-architects, as too was his remarkable grandmother Lady Jane Berkeley, who assumed responsibility for the boy after 1603. Sir Roger's slow building programme would have provided scope for incorporating new ideas during the course of construction.*

EXTERIOR. The house is in the form of an oblong of eleven by seven bays. The materials are brick and stone, the brick being bonded in the Flemish way on the s front, but the rest all English bond, except where the alterations of 1703–6 were made. In 1621 Ketton stone was supplied from quarries in Rutland by *Arnold Goverson*.

The W FRONT has three storeys raised on a basement, an attic 80 storey above a cornice, and two projecting bays r. and l. The windows have moulded frames, and those on the ground floor of the wings three prominent keystones pushing up through the lintel. The wings have a platband and a sill band below the first-floor windows, with, between the two, scarcely projecting aprons. This is also similar to Jones's design for Sir Fulke Greville's house. Originally the fenestration was of cross casements. The windows of the first floor of the recessed centre are smaller than

---

* Credit for the evidence in these arguments must go to John Harris, 1961, and to the researches of Linda Campbell and James Rosenheim, in 1989.

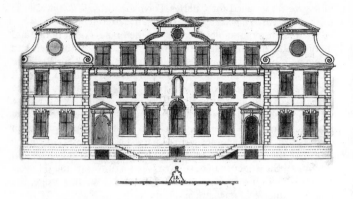

Raynham Hall. West and east elevations

any others, for they light the upper part of the hall lying parallel
to the front. The wings have Dutch gables derived from Jones's
Holborn house, and the centre an odd fancy pediment, similar
to the gables in character. Dutch gables, i.e. shaped gables
crowned by a pediment, were a new thing in the early C17. Here
they have big circular windows and prominent simple volutes
ending in Ionic capitals, a contortionist trick which might have
appeared a pretty conceit to Edge or to Roger Townshend but
would never have been tolerated by Jones. Similarly, the central
gable or pediment with its open segmental sides and its raised
pedimented centre seems too rustic for Jones, even if the oval
cartouche in its centre is an accomplished piece that could almost
surround the bust on a funeral monument in Rome.

Originally the front had two doorways, in the end bays of the
recessed centre, leading to screens passages either side of the
original hall. These were blocked in 1703–6 and fitted with windows, and the arched window formerly in the centre made into
the present door. The niche above, shown in the 1671 elevation,
was just blocked. With its thin Corinthian columns, its scrolly
broken pediment and the foliage in the frieze, the doorcase looks
more 1680s than twenty years later, and is squeezed uncomfort-

ably into the space available: the capitals are crowded by the hoods of the original windows either side.

The GARDEN FAÇADE (E) is no less intriguing. This side as 81 built and as recorded in 1671 was a very restless composition, in spite of its classical portico, and much more Venetian. The two-bay wings hardly project at all and were always the twins of those on the entrance side, complete with Dutch gables. The central motif is an attached Ionic portico of four columns rising on the upper floor and into a half-storey crowned by a pediment. This, the first classical elevation in Norfolk and one of the first in a provincial house, John Harris compares with the drawings connected with the Prince's Lodging, Newmarket, a house known to have been by Jones. The portico stands on a rusticated ground floor. This rustication did not exist at the beginning and may well be of the time of the 1703–6 alterations.

The two bays l. and the two bays r. of this centre were certainly altered then. At first they each had a doorway on the ground floor, two arched windows with a small circular window above them, and above that a big Venetian window. As we have noticed, the Venetian window was in 1622 a total innovation for England, so one would have to see the lost model or Edge's 'plattes' to tell if the Raynham design anticipates or follows Jones. However, given the long construction period and a possible sign of a break in construction on the N front, these windows are very unlikely to have been constructed before the end of the 1620s. Charles Townshend altered these bays to copy exactly the elevation of the wings, even reproducing the aprons, with brick laid in the Flemish bond of the day: the work improves the façade.

Over these bays is a stone balustrade, as there was before 1671, but the attics are set right back so that the raised central portico stands alone (the upper floor is the Belisarius Room, *see* below), and extends back a considerable distance, formerly with four attic-level windows on the S side.

The S FRONT is of seven bays and has what looks like an original doorcase. Unfluted Ionic pilasters on a rusticated ground and segmental pediment. All first-floor windows with aprons. The N FRONT also raises no problem. Owing to a fall in ground level the basement here is much more prominent but still not a full storey in height, with a stubby central doorcase with attached unfluted columns and a triangular pediment. Behind this lies the original basement kitchen with four bulgy Tuscan columns. This also could be before 1635.*

INTERIOR. The principal rooms were remodelled for the second Viscount Townshend in 1724–32; the accounts survive at the house. *Thomas Ripley* was executive architect and responsible for paying the bills: he paid out £10,398 for the interior in 1726–32, and a further £5,000 was expended on the service block and the park. He did not pay *Kent* for his contributions between 1726 and 1731, so Kent's name does not appear in

---

* At least two bricklayers were at work on this front, one who used queen closers up to a point in the middle of the first-floor windows and a later man who did not.

Ripley's accounts. This is awkward, and the suggestion has been made that Kent took only a minor role; but his contribution is significant. The second Viscount, the rightly celebrated Turnip Townshend, was Secretary of State in the Walpole government, having taken to politics after 1709. He provided himself with a *Vitruvius Britannicus* and quite deliberately set about imitating Walpole's power-base mansion at Houghton, apparently even with the same combination of executive and designing architects, and most of the craftsmen, e.g. *Giovanni Bagutti* (working under Artari at Houghton) and *James Richards*. Townshend grumbled in November 1724 that his plumbers were negligent because they found better work at Houghton. The chief structural alterations had been made twenty years before, but the visitor must assimilate work of four distinct periods.

The plan of Raynham before 1671 consisted of the great hall (Marble Hall) of one and a half storeys, taking up the entire recessed section of the w front, although the outer bays formed the screens passages. This was an archaic plan type for vernacular buildings, but was retained in houses of substance for social reasons. Behind it, but with no communication, lay the chapel, set at r. angles, and above this the Belisarius Room, which looked into the hall through two balconies at high level. In the angles of this T-shaped arrangement were the two principal staircases, each with another balcony on the landings. Two smaller rooms flanked the chapel, with external doorways to the E. The s and N fronts had three rooms each; the kitchen rose through two storeys – basement and ground floor – in the NW corner.

89   The MARBLE HALL was modified by *William Edge II* for (or with) *Charles Townshend*, probably by August 1704 when the house was fit for reoccupation. He closed the screens passages and inserted the twisted baluster staircase into what had been the s passage, and it was probably he and not Kent who replaced the central chimneypiece in the E wall with a doorway and blocked the balconies from the Belisarius Room. The present grand appearance, however, is due to *Kent*. Marble was cut in 1726. Unfluted Ionic pilasters support a modillion cornice below the former balconies and the high w windows. Under it a delicate frieze of heads and garlands. The ceiling, presumably made by *Mansfield* (who was paid £743 between 1726 and 1731) to Kent's design, is deeply ribbed, with a central oval containing the Townshend arms and octagonal panels either side filled with floral motifs. Five doorcases, three with simple pediments on scrolled consoles.

Continuing anti-clockwise, out of the SE doorway (the s doorway is blind). The short passage had in the C17 seven steps down to the chapel to the N (*see* below) and off it to the E was the MAIN STAIRCASE. It was probably reduced to its present back-stair dimensions by Edge II or *Matthew May*, and Edge changed much in the basement including the floor levels and altered all the lower staircases in 1703–4. Turned late C18 balusters. To the s into the STONE PARLOUR, which incorporates the

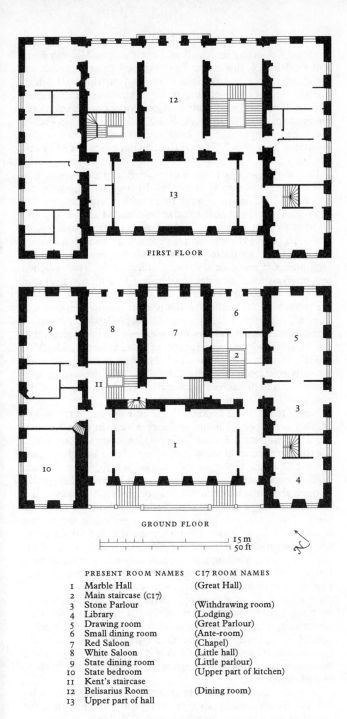

FIRST FLOOR

GROUND FLOOR

|—————|—————| 15 m
|—————|—————| 50 ft

	PRESENT ROOM NAMES	C17 ROOM NAMES
1	Marble Hall	(Great Hall)
2	Main staircase (C17)	
3	Stone Parlour	(Withdrawing room)
4	Library	(Lodging)
5	Drawing room	(Great Parlour)
6	Small dining room	(Ante-room)
7	Red Saloon	(Chapel)
8	White Saloon	(Little hall)
9	State dining room	(Little parlour)
10	State bedroom	(Upper part of kitchen)
11	Kent's staircase	
12	Belisarius Room	(Dining room)
13	Upper part of hall	

Raynham Hall. Plan of ground and first floors in 1671

s entrance doorway (blocked) and one window. Mid-C17 black
and white marble fire insert. To the w the LIBRARY, which has
absorbed a service stair; to the E the DRAWING ROOM, which
has had various uses including those of state bedroom and great
parlour. Black and white marble chimneypiece under open pedimented overmantel, by *Kent*. From here one may appreciate
the *enfilade* right along the E front, introduced by Kent to match
one in the floor above. Typical Kentian doorways gilded by one
Mr Jones.

First the SMALL DINING ROOM, originally an ante-room to
one of the two external entrances. Enlarged to the w at the
expense of the staircase and fitted with a chimneypiece in
1703–4. Then the RED SALOON, built as the chapel and still
referred to as that in 1705, but converted in the Ripley–Kent
phase. Its ceiling is lower than the adjoining rooms, but its floor
was also lower by those seven steps already noticed from the
1671 plan. On that plan is shown a gallery on the s side reached
by a doorway from the s staircase landing, but this was so altered
that even in the cellar evidence cannot be recovered. Originally
the room was not heated, so the present marble fireplace was
inserted, and may be *Ripley*'s: veined marble, with a rectangular
panelled overmantel and a swan-necked pediment. Doorcase into
the Marble Hall has a pediment on Ionic columns. Moulded
plaster cornices with palms and helmets on the walls intended
for dispersed portraits. Very simple but effective ceiling of a
central oval with half-ovals around. Greek key patterns to the
ribs, modillions to the cornice.

Next E is the WHITE SALOON, the little hall in 1671, basically
another ante-room. Chimneypiece removed. In the NE corner
the STATE DINING ROOM (little parlour in 1671). *Kent* added
the tripartite screen at the w end, where a lathe and plaster partition had been, based on the arch of Severus: three round-
headed openings, the centre one higher and with roundels pierced
through above the lower arches. Very restrained decoration. Also
a simple ceiling, a recessed oval. Pedimented marble chimneypiece. The small ante-room beyond converted to the serving
space out of a C17 closet. Finally the STATE BEDROOM in the
NW corner, adapted from the two-storey C17 kitchen, so requiring a new floor. Modillion cornice. A doorway was cut in the s
wall leading to the space formerly taken by the N screens hall
passage, and so to the main STAIRCASE. It had been the second
staircase in the C17, altered by Townshend (and his craftsmen)
in 1703–5 and completely re-worked *c.* 1731 by *Kent*. Fine
wrought-iron lyre-shaped balustrade and painted walls (painted
statues in large arched painted niches, painted busts in circular
painted niches, and painted vases and cartouches). It rises to a
lantern, and on the upper landing Kent had to alter levels to
provide headroom.

Over the chapel is the BELISARIUS ROOM, named after
Salvator Rosa's portrait (sold), and originally no doubt the great
chamber, sited at r. angles to the Marble Hall in a similar manner to that at Ashley Park in Surrey, the house of Sir Roger's

guardian Lady Jane Berkeley.* It is the only state room sited on the first floor and its decoration is of several periods. This large, one-and-a-half-storeyed saloon has a sumptuous ceiling which by comparison with the very similar ceiling at Coleshill must be of the early 1660s, and must form part of the refurbishments undertaken 1659–62 for Horatio Townshend. In 1661 an otherwise unknown craftsman from London called *Mr J. Scott* was engaged to complete the interiors including plasterwork; his bill alone was more than £1,500. Large central oval, very deep, with ribs in four directions to the modillion cornice and, at the E and W ends, similar tripartite ribs. Plasterwork all in bold relief and with vivacious stucco foliage. *Kent* added painted panels (Fame kneeling before a bust of Alexander Pope in the centre, stags and hinds in other panels) and also a frieze of heads linked by festoons under the C17 modillion course, probably made by *Bagutti* who was paid £47 in December 1727. The chimneypiece is pure *Kent* – Kentissime one might say. So is the great triumphal arch of the E wall, mirroring the portico outside, the windows set within Ionic pilasters.

Various minor features of the upper floors deserve notice, e.g. large-framed panelling S of the Belisarius Room in the staircase passage; small-framed C17 panelling in the central S bedroom; an excellent chimneypiece in the SW bedroom (still on the first floor). This is high-quality London work of the 1630s, with a lugged overmantel set with scrolled end pieces and fish-scale patterning. Fireplace itself of black and white marble. Three further excellent timber chimneypieces of the same period in the W attic rooms. There is also on the second floor some panelling with trophies hanging down pilasters.

In the BASEMENT is the PILLARED HALL, already referred to as part of the kitchen offices reached from the N front doorway. W of this little of the original kitchen in the NW corner is decipherable, but to the S is a groin-vaulted undercroft below the Marble Hall. Five square piers with vermiculated blocks run down the centre (the N one embedded in the later wall separating the boiler room). Sir Roger Pratt approved of this basement, but the manner in which the vault is keyed into the outer W wall suggests that Edge II had to strengthen the whole structure. Of the floor level of the C17 chapel, in the middle of the house, nothing may be gleaned following Edge's works.

SERVICE BLOCK. Immediately NW of the house and linked to its basement by a passageway. Traditionally ascribed to *Kent* and built 1729–31. But it has no Kentian features at all, and *Ripley* paid out £1,168; it is much more likely to be his. Rectangular, large and hipped-roofed. Two storeys and dormer attic, the E front in thirteen bays. Doorway with a fanlight, and, towards the S end, three C20 doors for garaging. The upper sashes all with thick C18 glazing bars. Platband. Long internal corridor receiving light from four small open yards. Partly converted to several flats, but intended for occupation from the start.

* I am grateful to Nicholas Cooper for pointing this out, and for other valuable comments.

WATER TOWER. N of the service block. Handsome, square and tall. Late C19. Red brick with gault-brick dressings to top stage, including the stumpy mullions to the upper windows.

The PARK. The first works were concerned with building a bridge across the River Wensum, for which *Edge* had drawn the 'platt' in March 1621. It was of brick, with stone dressings, and formed what appears to be a grand new approach to the proposed house from the SW. The new road crossing it extended ⅝ m. from the green in the village of West Raynham to the house, and is still marked by a later broad avenue of trees. It is this avenue which makes the view of the house so impressive as one approaches from the church. On the N side, by the river, stands the Old Hall, on the other the church. *Edge* was also building walls and fences, e.g. in September 1621 a fence 262 yds long and a brick wall of 1,399 yds.

The actual park, it seems, had to wait for Horatio Townshend, who began buying land in the 1640s and 50s and in 1664 was raising funds 'to make up my parke'. Between 1664 and 1667 further purchases were made and Townshend had walls and fences built to contain his 500 deer in the deer park, but it is not clear if this involved formal landscaping. Nevertheless by 1667 the park spread over 800 acres.

The next activity was in 1699, when Charles Townshend began not with the house but with further landscaping, though what he did is also unclear. Later, in 1724, Townshend ordered a survey of his lands and transformed the gardens round the house from the closed C17 style to the more open landscape then coming into fashion. The lake was excavated 1724–6, flooding Edge's road and bridge, and formal vistas laid out to the N and NW over his father's deer park. The Earl of Orford in 1732 thought the grounds 'the finest in England that I ever saw'. Prideaux's drawings of *c.* 1727 give the view W from the house: topiary r. and l. of the road (so the present avenue of trees is later), iron railings across it, the lake in the middle distance, and a prospect of West Raynham beyond. Further topiary to the open aspect before the E front. *Kent* even advised about grouping of trees in 1735, the only time he is connected with the park.

EAST RAYNHAM OLD HALL. A group of C16 brick buildings. Of the Hall all that remains is a two-storey GATEWAY with one pedestrian and one carriage entrance facing E, both blocked. Four-centred arches with hoodmoulds. The gable above not to its original height, but with three brick shields and panels set vertically, tarred between the diamond tiles like imitation flushwork. The returns each of two bays and each with a blocked doorway. The house attached to the rear has been remodelled, but was part of the original build: remains of two fireplaces. Another HOUSE to the s has been divided up, but in origin clearly late C16. It began as a barn (three blocked ventilation slits to s side) but was extended and received a four-centred doorway in the centre of the N front, where staircase towers project. C19 extensions and stepped gables. E of these two stands a huge brick

STABLE BLOCK. Two storeys in fifteen bays (two windows blocked), with various casement windows, doors and stable entrances below a platband. E side with long coved and plastered eaves cornice. All this *c.* 1680, but the stepped S gable-end of flint remains of a mid-C17 building. A mid-C18 BARN to the NW, at r. angles, also with a stepped gable.

LODGES. The EAST LODGE on Fakenham Road has a red brick frontage of two storeys. A full-height canted bay fitted with sashes either side of the Doric doorcase with an open pediment. Mansard roof carrying three dormers. This all *c.* 1760–70, but at the back some evidence of the C17. The GATES 500 yds N on the same road, dated 1925, which must be a mistake for 1825, consist of two identical lodges edge-end on to the road and with whole white flint rustication. Gault-brick details and corners. Pedimented gables over a single recessed sash. The returns with doorways and more rustication. Cast-iron GATES. Another LODGE by the church, *c.* 1840, ordinary.

CHURCH. *See* East Raynham.

REDENHALL   2080

ST MARY. An imposing church in an elevated position above the road, benefiting from the by-pass opened in 1987. Mighty Perp W tower with big polygonal buttresses covered with flushwork panelling. Base frieze with shields in cusped fields. W doorway with niches l. and r. Angels with shields in the spandrels. Row of shields above. Four-light W window. Three-light bell-openings. Close flushwork panelling of this and other stages on all sides except S. Double-step battlements also with flushwork panelling. The tower carries the date 1616 on the N side, but that refers only to repairs (and the stairs inside). It was begun about 1460 but according to numerous bequests was still in building in 1498. By 1514 the great bell was being made. On the SE pinnacle is the rebus of 'shell-tun', referring to Richard Shelton who became rector in 1518. Two-storeyed N porch with flushwork panelling too, a niche between the small upper windows, and a tierceron star vault with crowned bosses inside. Perp N and S aisle windows, the latter with stepped transoms. Beautiful Perp clerestory, ashlar-faced, with eight closely set windows on each side. Simple hammerbeam roof, the wall-posts on stone heads. Dec chancel, but the S wall and the E end with its five-light window re-done in the C19. S aisle flintwork the same. Dec S doorway with a trefoil window over, and Dec arcades (four bays, octagonal piers, double-chamfered arches).

FURNISHINGS. FONT. C19. Octagonal, with four lions against the stem and four demi-figures of angels and the signs of the Evangelists against the bowl. Presumably a copy of the font for which money was left in 1505. – SCREEN. The dado has twelve heavily over-painted figures. Upper works 1920. – LECTERN. Brass double eagle of *c.* 1500, probably made in East Anglia, the 44 same type as at St Margaret (King's Lynn) and Clare in Suffolk.

– C16 timber eagle lectern in the chancel. – ORGAN CASE. 1897, for the Jubilee, in the High Victorian spirit with its Neo-Gothic forms and enormous Green Men.* One can walk right through and under it into the tower. – Chancel PANELLING. Very ornate High Victorian including a wooden triple-canopied sedilia against a window. – W DOOR. With very late C15 folded panelling, not yet linenfold, and carved modestly on it two horse-shoes, a hammer, and a pair of tongs, as if given by the Guild of Farriers. – S DOOR. Early C16 and with fourteen fully formed linenfold panels. – CHEST. A chest of cypress-wood brought from Gawdy Hall in 1922, said to be Venetian of the C15. The flat carving of the front with three seated figures and much scrollwork with putti is hardly more than raised patterning. Painted inside the lid, very summarily, the Annunciation and a fleet on the high seas. Inside the back panel are painted drag-ons. The work is rustic and appears later; the whole may be a made-up piece (N chapel). – Another CHEST (nave W), Flemish, C17, richly carved with two arcaded panels to the front and pilasters with figures. – STAINED GLASS. In the N chapel heraldic glass by *S. C. Yarington,* 1825 for Rev. John Holmes of Gawdy Hall; other fragments taken from Gawdy Hall itself. – S chancel window by *Thomas Baillie,* †1866, Christ Preaching, with ten subsidiary medallions. – A N aisle window with the Ascension is attributed (by Birkin Haward) to *Ward & Nixon, c.* 1850. – MONUMENTS. Tomb-chest under a four-centred arch between N chapel and chancel, relying on little more than shields as decoration. Possibly to Sir Francis Gawdy †1588. – Tobias Frere †1655 (attributed to *Martin Morley* by Jon Bayliss), by the organ. Black and white marble, the figures partly painted. Ionic pilasters r. and l. of inscription panel, and outside the pilasters peculiar caryatid figures in profile, each with one foot. – Simon Kerrich †1748, by *Thomas Singleton* of Bury (the son of the more accomplished Robert). Pedimented wall monument with Corinthian columns flanking an inscription cataloguing infant deaths of his children by three wives (S aisle). – John Kerrich †1757, next to the last in location and similar in style. – Offley Smith †1777. Oval panel raised above the N arcade and finished with an urn. – The marble reredos of the N chapel is at the same time a memorial to members of the Wogan family. Put up at the request of Elizabeth Wogan †1788. By *J. Francis Moore.* A celestial relief with a lady being received by an angel and Christ in Majesty in the clouds above. The surround in the Louis XVI style. – ROYAL ARMS. Painted, over chancel arch. To Queen Anne, 1707.

GAWDY HALL, 1¼ m. NW. An Elizabethan house Gothicized in the C19 and demolished in 1939.

COLDHAM HALL, 1¾ m. NNW. Simple C18 stuccoed house of three bays in two storeys.

CLINTERGATE FARMHOUSE, 2⅜ m. NNW. C16 timber-framed house of two storeys and five bays. Two-storeyed projecting

* Replacing one of 1842 by *John Brown,* 'a chaste design in Perpendicular Gothic' according to the *Norfolk Chronicle.* The organ itself is of 1845.

r. wing. The stack has six round moulded flues with star tops.

MOATED SITES, adjacent to Gawdyhall Big Wood, ⅞ m. NW of church; a fine medieval wood containing many earthwork ditches and banks. On the S edge is a roughly circular moat, and at the NE corner is ABBEY YARD, a rectangular moat set within an outer ditched enclosure. (AR)

REFFLEY see SOUTH WOOTTON

REYMERSTON   *0000*

ST PETER. The church is an archaeological puzzle. The W tower and both arcades appear of the C13, but in what order did building proceed, and what is the reason for the many irregularities? The W tower is tall and with diagonal and angle buttresses. Its top is dated 1714, the lancets below indicate the C13, and the arch towards the nave has a moulding of two keeled rolls between a normal roll which occurs in the arcades, but not everywhere. The tower E wall has a lower former roof-line indicating perhaps that it pre-dates the arcades, and was itself remodelled in the C13. The arcades are of four bays. The piers are all round with round abaci on the N side, but alternately octagonal and round on the S side. The capitals all have stiff-leaf decoration on the N, but on the S only the first from the W has it. The shape of the third may be due to the leaves having been chopped off. The first arches from the W are double-chamfered, the next two have the same moulding as the tower arch, the fourth finer mouldings. These latter go well with the fine N doorway with two orders and dogtooth decoration in the hoodmould, and also perhaps with the cusped Y-tracery of the N aisle W window, the excellent tracery (with three foiled top circles) in the N aisle E window, and with the S doorway with continuous chamfers. Perp S aisle windows. Small C15 clerestory windows, the central mullion thickened to accommodate the wall-posts of the arch-braced roof inside. – FONT. Octagonal. Stem with fleurons. At the foot were four lions, but only one remains. Bowl with the signs of the four Evangelists and four seated prophets. Remarkably crinkly hair. – PULPIT. A Jacobean three-decker, lunette arcading. – BOX PEWS. With poppyheads. – COMMUNION RAIL. Very luscious and obviously alien. Bought in Belgium. Probably of *c.* 1700. With thick acanthus foliage and small figures in two medallions. – STALLS. Gothick, C18. – STAINED GLASS. In the E window three big Flemish figures of the early C16; very much renewed (by *George King & Son*). – MONUMENT. Robert Long †1688. Big tablet attributable to *W. Linton* of Norwich (GF).

OLD HALL, ½ m. NW. N front with a one-storeyed porch and one bay l., one bay r. The porch has ovolo mouldings to the door jambs and a little carving above. Then heavy chimney-breasts and very heavy hoodmoulds. Octagonal chimney flues. Colour-washed brick. A date 1620 on the gable with a stack further r. probably refers to the details enumerated, which are additions to an older timber-framed house.

REYMERSTON HALL, ¾m. NW. Early C19, of red brick, three widely spaced bays, with four giant pilasters and a porch on paired columns and a Doric frieze. Sashes, tripartite to ground floor. Hipped roof.

CALVELEY HALL, ⅝m. SW. C17 timber-framed house with brick gable-ends, one dated 1726 in tie-irons. One storey and dormer attic. Various C18 (and later) cross casements.

TUDOR COTTAGE. Timber-framed. A through passage can be identified, suggesting the C16, a date confirmed by the clasped purlin roof.

RIDDLESWORTH

ST PETER. Early C14 W tower with a tall doorway from the S, a blocked doorway on the N and a simple doorway (i.e. not an arch) into the nave. In 1855 Thomas Thornhill, whose family owned the Hall for most of the C19, paid £900 to have the chancel taken down, the aisleless nave doubled in size and a new chancel erected. Cusped windows under square heads or two-light trefoiled windows were provided for the nave, a three-light Perp E window for the chancel. The nave has a dentil eaves cornice. Also of 1855 are the S porch and door. Most of the fittings are from Knettishall, Suffolk, which was closed in 1933. – PULPIT. Jacobean, with back-panel and tester, panelled. – COMMUNION RAIL. With twisted balusters; late C17. – FONT. Plain octagonal; C17. – PAINTINGS. Two restored panels from a screen (Saints) in the chancel panelling. – MONUMENT. Sir Drue Drury †1617. Very good tablet with kneeling knight and two splendidly Mannerist angels in long garments holding a curtain open. The type similar to the monument to Mrs Margaret Pope in North Barningham, and so possibly also by *Maximilian Colt* (GF).

RIDDLESWORTH HALL. The third house on the site, now a school. The Elizabethan house of the Drurys was replaced in 1792 by a five- by five-bay block to *Thomas Leverton*'s design for Sylvanus Bevan. The main front had a central three-bay pediment on four giant pilasters and Soanesque Venetian ground-floor windows l.and r., all on a rusticated basement. This burnt down in 1899, to be replaced by a large and restrained Classical house of 1900 by *H. J. Green* of Norwich. Leverton's rustication and pediment were re-created, the latter with Corinthian columns, in the long asymmetrical S front. Twelve bays to N front, also asymmetrical. The interior decoration is in the Adam manner then in vogue, with screens of columns (hall and drawing room), and oval plaster ceilings (drawing room), cf. Somers Clark's work at Raveningham Hall.

RINGLAND   *1010*

ST PETER. Picturesquely raised on a hill at the W end of the village. The C13 W tower has Dec bell-openings (cusped Y-tracery) and later, C15, flushwork-panelled battlements. Flushwork panelling also against the base and gable of the S porch, which is of fine knapped flint. The entrance has angels in the spandrels. Of the early C14 the chancel, with simple dignified tracery consisting of multi-cusped quatrefoils (restored, especially the three-light E window), the arcades of four bays (octagonal piers, double-chamfered arches), and the N doorway with the odd adjoining quatrefoiled lozenge window. Was this a clerestory window once? The present clerestory was made *c.* 1460–70 and is exactly how a Perp clerestory should be: seven closely set two-light windows on each side under four-centred arches with beautifully modulated tracery plus a (blocked) E window. Inside this clerestory spreads the roof, which is what has made Ringland famous among Norfolk churches. It is a roof of the type of St Peter Mancroft (Norwich) and of Framlingham in Suffolk, that is, a hammerbeam roof disguised by ribbed coving like that of a rood loft and by vertical boards standing on the coving. The boards have quatrefoil decoration. The roof rests on long wall-posts and longitudinal arched braces. Angels against the front of the hammerbeams. No collars. Bosses at the intersections of the principals. – FONT. Against the stem four lions, against the bowl the signs of the Evangelists, two demi-figures of angels, and two flowers. – SCREEN. Panels with eight painted figures of Apostles, Creed texts encircling their bodies, stand against the wall of the nave. – BENCH ENDS. Some, with poppyheads. – COMMUNION RAIL. Jacobean, ponderous. Now in the aisles. – DOOR. Into the tower, heavily iron-bound. – STAINED GLASS. An unusual amount is preserved. It is in the clerestory, and dates from the same time as the tracery. Whole figures of the Virgin, the Trinity, the Annunciation, all with small donors, and further larger figures of donors. Also small bits in the heads of the S aisle windows. It was restored and re-set in 1857 by *J. & J. King.*

THE STREET twists away to the E of St Peter's, with big houses of the 1980s at regular intervals, many of them rebuilds of C19 properties. No. 26 on the NE is mid-C17: two storeys, four bays of four-light mullioned windows, but with a two-storey early C18 brick porch finishing in a shaped gable. Rebuilt tapering external stack to the E gable. BARN at Pond Farm, further E, beyond a double bend. The W gable has the date 1671. Its stepped gable and much of the remainder of the building are C19, but the N flank has some decent early C18 chequered brickwork. Another C17 BARN at Low Farm is well preserved and of unusual quality. Timber-framed, weatherboard and wattle and daub, thatched. Jowled principal studs with arched braces to tie-beams and straight braces to wall-plate. Wind-bracing.

RINGSTEAD

St Andrew. Much of the early C14 but over-restored inside and
out, N aisle added in 1865. W tower with Y-tracery in the bell-
openings, *c.* 1300. The S and W faces partly rebuilt 1865 and
given two W buttresses. S doorway also of *c.* 1300, though the
porch is 1865. Chancel with fine two-light windows, intersecting tracery under a flattened arch. It consists of a half-arch l.
and a half-arch r. intersected by a whole arch. The date probably early C14. The chancel arch could match such a date.
Angle piscina good, with ogee arches and bold finials. Scissor-
braced roof. The three-bay nave has Perp windows. – FONT.
Octagonal C15 bowl on a C19 base. – BRASS to Richard Kegell
†1482 (chancel floor). A 3 ft figure. The inscription says that he
'totaliter fieri fecit' the roof of the chancel. – STAINED GLASS. S
chancel window by *Preedy*, †1863, St Andrew and St Peter.

St Peter, in the garden of the former rectory ¼ m. SW. Only the
C12 circular tower survives from the demolition in 1792 after
the parishes of Great and Little Ringstead amalgamated. The E
side shows remodelling as a grotto with rustication and an
architrave round the entrance. Pedimented gable. The house,
Ringstead Bury House, is *c.* 1800, with a brick front, carstone and clunch elsewhere, five bays and two storeys in size.
Porch added to the E gable-end, with reused columns.

St Andrew, 1½ m. SW, near Barrett Ringstead Farm (*see* below).
Ruinous. A plain oblong. On the S a pair of blocked lancet windows, on the W an opening, on the E a large window, but without tracery. Probably C13 with C14 alterations.

In the High Street one should notice Nos. 20–26, a row of
four C18 cottages with a barn and another cottage at r. angles.
The BARN is converted to a house. Some C18 leaded casements
remain. The Gin Trapp Inn is a two-storey early C18 lobby-
entrance house of whitewashed clunch. The details all C19. On
the W side opposite, the Old Rectory. Two storeys. Coursed
carstone. E front fitted with C19 and C20 windows. S gable has a
C19 canted bay window rising through two storeys and, in the
gable-head, a date 1643. Of the same time is the external N gable
stack.

Barrett Ringstead Farmhouse in three builds. Coursed
clunch. Two storeys. The W part has a stack with the date 1754,
the E end with a stack dated 1714. Various blocked and C20
windows. The BARN 25 yds NE dated 1717, also of coursed
clunch, and with brick-dressed quoins.

East End Farmhouse, Burnham Road. A C17 farmhouse
apparently of several builds. To the W is a two-storey porch with
brick quoins, a four-centred archway and a stepped gable. The
main front has chequered flint and carstone and C18 cross casements. Platband between the floors and remains of C17 windows above.

Ringstead Mill, ¾ m. N, on the Peddar's Way Footpath. A six-
storey early C19 affair, of tarred gault brick. Temporary protective cap over the canister which shows it to have been a

six-sailer, one of six in the county. In 1927 a house was built to the E for Professor and Mrs Cornford, by *Henry Hughes* (who also converted the mill at Burnham Overy the previous year).

ROCKLAND ALL SAINTS   9090

ALL SAINTS. Unbuttressed W tower, late C13, with Dec top. Nave and chancel, the nave with long-and-short quoins and herring-bone laying of the flints. This may be Anglo-Saxon but may also be immediately post-Conquest. C13 porch, gabled. Chancel windows mainly reflect the restoration of 1860. – FONTS. A square Norman bowl, damaged, and an octagonal companion of 1880. – BENCH ENDS. Some C15 poppyheads attached to C19 benches. – MONUMENT. Anglo-Saxon coffin-lid with a cross near the top connected by a staff to another cross near the foot. Four interlace panels between. The crosses are of the *alisée patée* type.

ST ANDREW. Remains of another parish church, just SE of All Saints. The tower remains split top to bottom. The two fragments look as if they were stiffly conversing. About enough remains to date to mid C14.

The Wayland Union WORKHOUSE was by *William Thorold*, 1836–7, to the N of the village street. Demolished.

ROCKLAND ST MARY   3000

ST MARY. Slim unbuttressed W tower of the mid C14, the W win-dow an ogee-headed lancet, the ringing-chamber windows with brick jambs. The tower arch also fits a mid-C14 date (double-chamfered). Dec S doorway, with wave and roll mouldings. The rest mostly renewed during the 1892–3 restoration. That was at the expense of John Hotblack of Norwich. His son paid for the S porch, and the N vestry added 1937. – SOUTH DOOR. Plank, late C14, with iron striking-plate. – FONT. C15. Octagonal, with a panelled stem and on the bowl demi-figures of angels holding shields. Thoroughly re-cut. – STAINED GLASS. Sugary E win-dow by *Ward & Hughes*, †1883, Suffer Little Children. Virgin and Child in E window, by *A. L. Wilkinson*, †1945.

ST MARGARET, no more than 10 yds NE of St Mary. Completely ruined. Just one lump of flintwork (the first edition noted 'some lumps').

OLD HALL, The Street. The N front presents two gables; in the W one is an early C17 door. Early C18 range with a shaped gable to the S, lit in the first floor through a four-light mullioned win-dow. Two early C19 agricultural-looking outbuildings NE and NW.

THE NORMANS, Run Lane. An early C18 house with two external stacks to the E front and rusticated quoins to the corners. A C19 crenellated canted bay intrudes, as do a C20 porch and other details. W front with a three-storey C19 porch.

CHANTRY HOUSE, Church Lane. Brick, of two and a half storeys in three bays. C20 door, but mid-C18 cross casements, with leaded glazing. Central first-floor window blind and inscribed: 'God Preserve the Industrious E S S 1756'. Hipped roof. C18 casements also to the rear.

OLD FARMHOUSE, Surlingham Lane. C17, with hoodmoulds of mullioned windows and a good ridge stack. The windows themselves C20. L-plan, the E front with a gable to its l.

9090

ROCKLAND ST PETER

ST PETER. Round tower with a polygonal top. It is probably all C14, i.e. not a Norman base. The upper stage with two-light ogee windows alternating with blind windows. The tower staircase has an entry with a shouldered lintel and a little quatrefoil window into the nave. Nave and chancel; the nave thatched, with shallow transeptal N and S projections, only 3 ft deep. They are lit through cusped spherical triangles on cusped lights. Short chancel rebuilt in 1909. Ladbroke drew it ruined in the 1820s. The N porch has a Dec entrance. The brick repairs to the porch are dated 1624 and amount almost to a rebuilding. The S vestry of 1909 replaces a porch. Most of the windows of the church are Perp. Scissor-braced nave roof of 1950 by *John Burton*, when restorations took place following a fire. – FONT. Octagonal, Dec. Encircled quatrefoils on the stem, tracery on the bowl. – SCREENS. Tall C15 rood screen of ogee-headed one-light divisions. Perp tracery over. Also the parapet of the rood loft in twelve panelled lights. This screen comes from Tottington, in the Battle Zone (*see* p. 14). The rood beam has late C19 Holy Figures, brought here in 1973 from St Sampson, York. – Part of the C15 screen of a ruined Rockland church is under the tower. This also has one-light ogee-headed divisions and Perp panelling. – PULPIT. Front rail dated 1631, which may also be the date of pulpit; the stem and plinth C20. Also from Tottington. – BENCHES. Twenty of the late C14 with traceried ends, poppyheads, and animals on the arm-rests. From Tottington too. – STAINED GLASS. E window by *Jones & Willis*, *c.* 1909.

Of HOUSES only a couple need be mentioned. No. 1 Low Lane (YEOMAN COTTAGE), thatched, built as two cottages *c.* 1650, complete timber frame and C17 brick fireplace. Exterior overmodern in appearance. THE ROOKERY, The Street, is more interesting despite looking all early C19. The SW gable has a five-light mullioned window, the mullions hollow-chamfered. So early C17. Earlier still is the plan-form, for a through-passage is recognizable and a plank and muntin screen exists which presumably divided a hall from the passage. Sunk quadrant-moulded bridging beams to ground-floor room, these (in this area) also early C17. It appears to be an early C16 hall house floored in the early C17 and extended.

WYMONDHAM COLLEGE. *See* Morley St Peter.

PILLAR (The Dial Stone). *See* Wymondham, p. 806.

ROKELES HALL *see* WATTON

ROUDHAM

St Andrew. In ruins and ivy-clad. Dec s tower. Battlements with panelling in flushwork. One big circular sound-hole to the s. All walls stand, though devoid of features, except for the w window, which has its Y-tracery. At the time of writing the c18 wrought-iron tower screen remained.

Lodge, by Harling Road station. In the form of a *cottage orné*. One of the lodges to Shadwell Park (*see* p. 638). It is the same as that at Brettenham (*see* p. 218). Modest Gothic cast-iron windows, thatched roof and a tree-trunk veranda. The most likely date is *c.* 1830. Another lodge, and the most complete of them all, is to the w of Roudham Hall. It has its little outbuilding still attached by a covered passage lit through arched windows. The problem with the 1830 date is that the lodges do not appear on the 1904 O.S. map. Is this simply an omission?

Roudham Hall. Fairly ordinary mid-c18 two-storey, five-bay house. A timber-framed barn, 50 yds se, retains its c17 queen-strut roof with clasped upper purlins.

Deserted village earthworks. Along the n side of the road past the church, earthworks survive for over ⅝ m. Numerous tofts and ditches run from the road towards a low-lying former fen to the n. Immediately n of the Hall are two moated sites. Population decline began in the late medieval period, but was at its strongest between *c.* 1675 and *c.* 1750. (AR)

ROUGHAM

St Mary. Dec and Perp. Dec w tower with later doorway. Excellent c14 Crucifixion panel above, under a nodding ogee arch and with kneeling figure of Mary at the Foot of the Cross and figures r. and l. set in their own nodding ogee niches. Leaf trail in the square head to the panel. Two-light Curvilinear bell-openings. Dec the reused e window of the n aisle (three-light and of the intersecting ogee type, common in Lincolnshire, not in Norfolk), Dec the s doorway. Oddly starved n arcade representing the last phase of lozenge pier design in the early c16. Seven bays, i.e. no structural division between nave and chancel. The capitals have fleurons or ballflower decoration. Arches of just one hollow chamfer. The first n aisle was demolished in 1693, but was rebuilt in 1913 by *Sir Charles Nicholson* when he restored the rest of the church (£13,000), and set up within the aisle an extraordinary arrangement of an internal vestry, just over half the width of the aisle and not projecting externally. Two doorways and two high pierced windows looking out under the aisle roof. Nicholson's also the kingpost roof, much better than most roofs of its date, with a boarded e bay over the altar. Big Perp three-light windows, restored, those in the chancel with embattled transoms. The E window has five lights and the same motif. Four two-light clerestory windows on N side only. Dado panelling right round the interior, including the vestry, renewed 1913. – FONT. Octagonal, plain, ogees to stem. – COMMANDMENT BOARD, under the tower, an engraving, hand-coloured, late Georgian. – ROYAL ARMS. Tower, to George II, dated 1739. – SCULPTURE. Wooden panel with very small frieze of figures of six Saints separated by yet smaller seraphim under ogee arches. C14 and very good. Was it part of a reredos? It looks like part of a miniature tomb-chest (chancel s wall). – SCREEN and CHANCEL STALLS. 1913 by *Nicholson*. – STAINED GLASS. In the nave SE window two small figures in the tracery lights. – MONUMENT. Gibbsian pedimented marble tablet to Roger North †1734 (chancel). The pediment carries an urn. Egg-and-dart border to inscription panel. – Many other monuments to the North family, including that to Charles North †1906 (chancel), a coloured marble wall monument in C17 style. – BRASSES. Sir William Yelverton †1472 and wife, she with a butterfly headdress; 26 in. figures (by the lectern). – (William Yelverton and wife, *c.* 1510.) – John and Roger Yelverton †1505; two babies in swaddling clothes, upright, under an ogee canopy; 9 in. figures. – William Yelverton †1586, with two wives (2 ft figures; chancel s), and two separate groups of children. – Thomas Keppel North †1919. In the churchyard (s of tower by an obelisk), a headstone, with a high-relief carving of a twin-engined biplane and an interesting inscription recording that North, as superintendent of the Vickers works, designed the first aeroplane to cross the Atlantic.

ROUGHAM HALL, N of the church. *Roger North*, lawyer, musician and writer on architecture, bought the estate in 1691. He found an 'ancient mannor house... disposed to 3 pavilions, and a midle', partly timber-framed and partly of brick and stone. This he remodelled into a Classical house with a seven-bay centre fronted by an Ionic portico and with three-bay projecting wings r. and l. One of his intentions was to retain as much of the original walling as possible.* He lived here until his death in 1734. It was demolished in the 1780s, but the marks of it remain in the grass immediately w of the later Hall. A capital and base from the portico survives as a sundial. Of North's PARK (unusually, begun after he had started on the house) there is still visible a wide avenue running due s passing w of the church, with at its N end a radial, or rather fan-shaped, planting of chestnut trees focused on a point 100 yds s of the Hall. w of the Hall are earthworks of a trapezoid-shaped formal garden.

The present house partly of 1878, partly of 1906. Inside, the early C18 staircase from Finborough Hall, Suffolk: turned balusters enriched with leaf decoration, carved tread-ends.

Octagonal DOVECOTE, very late C17 and by *North*, who described it in his treatise. Flint with angle pilasters of brick. Thatched

* For North's own account and description of his works *see* H. Colvin & J. Newman (eds), *Of Building: Roger North's Writings on Architecture*, Oxford, 1981.

roof with a tall lantern in which are nesting boxes. It stands proudly between church and Hall.

HALL LODGE, The Street, immediately NE of the church. Oblong, timber-framed house, with narrowly set studs and tension bracing at the corners. Dated 1907. S of the church a brick cottage dated 1908 but with a timber-framed, jettied and rendered first floor.

EARTHWORKS of SHRUNKEN VILLAGE. A pasture field *c.* 270 yds W of the Hall is traversed by an E–W sunken way with embanked tofts to N and S. At the E end another way joins from the NW. This part of the village was lost to enclosure for sheep in the late C14 and early C15. (AR)

ROUGHOLM *see* GRESSENHALL

ROYDON
Near Diss

0080

ST REMIGIUS. Round tower with C19 polygonal top. Perp bell-openings. Restored 1923. The nave Norman, which must be presumed to have been broken through early in the C13 by a four-bay S arcade. The result is heavy square pillars with only a slight chamfer. It is stopped by spurs at the foot, heads on leaf bits at the top. The arches are pointed and have also only a slight chamfer. The arcade must have been re-worked when the aisle itself was rebuilt in 1864. The S porch built by *Vulliamy* in 1840 was then removed and re-erected at the E end of the aisle to become the organ chamber in 1922. It has diagonal buttresses and pinnacles. Good Perp N porch with flushwork panelling. The entrance arch is decorated with fleurons. There are also niches in the jambs and niches l. and r. of, and over, the entrance. Perp nave roof. Dec chancel, much renewed, though the windows probably represent what was there before. Inside, a low N recess. Perp nave windows. – PULPIT. Jacobean. – STAINED GLASS. E window with C13-style grisaille and roundels, *c.* 1850.

ROYDON HALL, ¼ m. NW. A late C18 red brick house of two and a half storeys in five bays arranged 2–1–2 under a low hipped roof. Lower single-storey projections r. and l. Rather ugly C19 porch in the middle and uglier plate-glass sashes. The Frere family house.

Several C17 HOUSES, notably THE HERMITAGE, Baynard's Lane, though the timber-framed part survives only at the S end. GROVE FARMHOUSE, Diss Road, is timber-framed with a C17 N wing and a four-centred chimneypiece. THE MANOR HOUSE at Bremen's Green, ⅝ m. E of the church, and S of a moat, is split into three houses but with C16 origins and still with an E-plan. THE POPLARS nearby is again C17 and timber-framed, given C19 details but retaining its stack to the rear wing. Some small-framed panelling in the hall.

7020
ROYDON
Near King's Lynn

ALL SAINTS. Rebuilt 1857 by *G. E. Street*, who would have been
reluctant to use the Norman style for a new building. Yet this
was chosen, because there were two original Norman doorways.
They both have an order of colonnettes and zigzag decoration
in the arch. The capitals and hoodmoulds, however, differ, and
the N doorway at least has been completely rebuilt. The early
C14 W tower could also be kept from the old building. Y-tracery
W window by Street; Y-tracery bell-openings. The nave was
given shallow buttresses and round-headed windows. Chevron
in the arch of the S porch on waterleaf capitals, all 1857. Shafts
and waterleaf again to the E end. Internal details carry through
the scheme: dogtooth and roll mouldings in chancel arch;
round arches over piscina and sedilia. Kingpost roofs. Even the
FONT is Neo-Norman, so is the wooden PULPIT. – STAINED
GLASS. W tower in style of *William Wailes*, †1859. Three lancets
of E window by *Clayton & Bell*, †1876.

6000
RUNCTON HOLME

ST JAMES. Late Norman tower, but the nave W window, also
Norman, must be earlier, as it presupposes a W wall and not a W
tower. It is shafted outside and has continuous roll moulding
inside. The tower arch, though it looks early too, must belong
to the tower. The three-stage tower has set-offs at each stage
and pretty bell-openings of two lights with an intermediate shaft
and nook-shafts with two shaft-rings each. The top of the tower
is of brick, rebuilt in the C15. Late Norman also the S doorway.
The shafts have shaft-rings too. The waterleaf capitals support
chevron-decorated imposts, and the arch has dogtooth. The
brick S porch itself is entered through a double-chamfered arch
and has a pointed tunnel vault with transverse ribs. The nave
shows the remains of one blocked window on the S side. The
walls of the nave are of carstone, except for the brick upper
courses rebuilt during the restorations of 1841–2 by *William
Newham* of Lynn. The stilted chancel arch is puzzling. It has a
Norman respond, but this may be reused. The chancel is of
brick, of 1842, and with a vestry added to the N in 1856. The
windows of the church are mostly renewed. C19 chancel roof
with false hammerbeams on head-corbels. Against the hammers
shields. – SCREEN. Early C15. Four one-light divisions with
depressed arches on hollow and wave-moulded muntins. Tracery
over. – PULPIT. A sumptuous mid-C17 piece with the usual
sturdy blank arches, a tester, and a back-panel flanked by
dolphin volutes. – STAINED GLASS. In the S nave a two-light
window with the Annunciation by *Veronica Whall*, 1928, still
Arts and Crafts in derivation. – MONUMENTS. Some C18
tablets.

MANOR FARMHOUSE, Downham Road. A very rare, for Norfolk,

C14 aisled hall house with octagonal aisle-posts on bases and with polygonal roll-moulded capitals (*see* also Rush Fen Cottage, Geldeston). Double braces rise from here to the tie-beam and the arcade plate. Floored over and generally altered. The C14 part is hidden on the r. of the s façade by additions of 1916, although C16 hoodmoulds can be seen over various windows. Outwardly of brick and carstone, though timber-framed when first built.

RUNHALL   *0000*

ALL SAINTS. Norman round tower with lancets, but a belfry stage fitted with two-light windows for which bequests run 1473–1507, the last for a new bell (the bell is by *Richard Brayser II*, of Norwich, i.e. before 1513). Yet still a Y-tracery belfry window. In the nave, N and S doorways of *c.* 1300, the former with roll-moulded jambs. The window next to the N door goes with it, but has as its hoodmould a reused Norman billet-moulding. Perp windows otherwise. The restoration was by *E. J. Tarver*, 1869–70. The chancel was consumed by fire a long time ago, *c.* 1560, and the arch walled up. Inside, a pretty doorway to the rood-loft stair, with a little tracery and the old colour preserved. Roof of 1871, as are the internal posts, creating the illusion of a nave with aisles. – FONT. Late C14, octagonal, with quatrefoils to bowl and trefoiled panels to the stem. – DOOR to the tower. With much original ironwork dating from the mid C12 to the C16. A dragon and a snake are discernible from the earliest work and invite comparison with Staplehurst, Kent. The door itself has been battered about.

No village, only scattered FARMS. Most farmhouses are C17 timber-framed buildings on the lobby-entrance plan, with later alterations. WOOD FARMHOUSE at East Green is cased in brick with some flint and masonry. HALL FARMHOUSE, Welbourne Road, received its brick skin only in the C19, leaving the E gable still with exposed timbering. The earliest probably CHURCH FARMHOUSE, C16 frame with wings added C17, altered C18.

RUSHALL   *1080*

ST MARY. Round tower. One former circular opening to the W. Does that indicate a Saxon date? Polygonal Perp top. E.E. chancel, the E wall with two, not three lancets. In the N wall of the nave a blocked arch to a former chapel. Perp nave windows. C15 S porch. – PRAYER DESK. With four highly Flamboyant panels, perhaps Spanish.

SCOTLAND YARD. Timber-framed hall house of the early C15, surviving almost intact despite flooring, insertion of stacks and extensions E and W in the later C16. The E extension altered most of the parlour end to the E of the hall. Screens passage with two arched service doors opening to the W into, originally, two rooms. To the E, in the centre of the C15 house, is the hall, lit through diamond-mullioned windows in the N and S walls. The crown-post truss remains: cambered tie-beam on heavy arched braces carrying a square crown-post with a base and a decorated capital; arched braces in four directions to crown purlin and collars.

Some C17 HOUSES, the best of which is COLLEGE FARMHOUSE: timber-framed, three-light cross casements to upper floor, two doorways, diamond flues to stack. RUSHALL HALL, also C17 and timber-framed and with cross casements, deserves mention.

RUSHFORD

ST JOHN EVANGELIST. This was the church of the College of priests founded in 1342 by Edmund Gonville, who also founded Gonville and Caius College (Cambridge) in 1348, three years before his death. He became rector in 1326 and may have undertaken some rebuilding straight away, although the chancel arch and the two arches which led into former transepts, and the angle-shafts close to them indicative of former vaults, all seem *c.* 1300. So Gonville may not have done much.

The College was surrendered in 1541 and granted to the Earl of Surrey, who, in 1545, had the lead stripped from the church and college roofs and the chancel and transepts of the church demolished. In 1585 the nave was restored for Robert Buxton of Shadwell Park and in 1904 the apse was added to the E end and a further restoration took place. The 1585 repairs obviously involved lowering the height of the nave and inserting the brick lancets in the C14 window embrasures. So the tower and the walls of the nave are all that really is medieval. The nave has wall arches inside of *c.* 1300. The solid and imposing tower has a stair-turret to the S and two-light Y-traceried windows light the belfry stage. In the late C19 a vestry was added on the site of the S transept. The S porch of knapped flint and brick with some flushwork decoration is Perp, probably of *c.* 1480. It was originally two-storeyed. The 1904 restoration was as drastic as any of the previous events, but the FURNISHINGS are presumably *Teulon*'s work, re-located from Brettenham church when that building was re-furnished in 1903. Wall stencilling also.

COLLEGE. The former College founded by Edmund Gonville in 1342 (*see* above) lies S of the church, close to the banks of the Little Ouse. It was for a Master and five priests. This foundation preceded Gonville's more famous Cambridge college by six years. It is built of flint, enriched with stone, and originally had four ranges round a court. Only two survive, and the N façade was heavily restored, indeed rebuilt, by *S. S. Teulon* for the Buxtons (of Shadwell Park, where Teulon worked 1856–60) in 1855 to provide a vicarage. For C14 details, i.e. cusped, straight-headed windows and doorways with continuous mouldings, one must study the inner (E) side of the W range. The three doorways have had windows inserted.

Teulon's façade has a two-storey porch, and to its r. a cross
gable and beneath it a large window with five stepped lights,
up the centre light a stylized tree in relief, a blank quatrefoil
frieze at the foot, and a blank frieze of reticulation units transom-
wise across. This, and the rest of the façade, is rather playful
Teulon. The window lies relatively high up, and there are
indeed no ground-floor windows to the N. The hall, to the l. of
the porch, receives its light from the court. It is impossible to
say whether the external hall stack was a C14 feature; the present one is C19. Remains of the service doors to the W of the
hall can however be determined. The double ogee-moulded
hall ceiling beams look C14 and also look like relocated roof tie-
beams, suggesting an open hall until the time of the Earl of
Surrey, who acquired the house after the Reformation and
clearly remodelled it. Of the roof nothing is earlier than the mid
C16, and little of that.

RUSHFORD HALL, across the Little Ouse, a long early C18 house,
lies in Suffolk.

RYSTON   6000

ST MICHAEL. Of carstone. The W tower with its saddleback roof
is of 1858, by *W. Lawrie*, but the tower arch is Norman. Oddly
it is four-centred. Early C14 S doorway and porch, the latter
with a cinquefoiled niche with a figure. Straight-headed Perp
nave windows. In the chancel two small lowside windows and a
big three-light Dec E window with Curvilinear tracery using
mouchette patterns. All these details restored but probably
accurately so. The roofs date from 1901 and, for the date, are
exceptionally dull. Angle piscina with a little bit of pretty tracery.
– STAINED GLASS. The chancel and two S nave windows with
Saints by *William Wailes*, *c.* 1860–70. Also more in the S nave. –
MONUMENTS, to the Pratt family, in whose park the church
still stands. Sir Roger Pratt, the architect, †1684 (*see* below). A
black floor slab only. – Lady Anne Trafford, widow of Sir Roger
Pratt, who married Sir Sigismund Trafford in 1692, †1706.
Semi-reclining figure in contemporary dress; no back architecture but a gadrooned cornice to the tomb-chest. The piece is
attributed to *Thomas Stayner* (GF). – Pleasance Pratt †1807, a
wall monument. By *John Bacon Jun.*, with charming groups of
small figures by and below an urn.

RYSTON HALL. Built for himself in 1669–72 by *Sir Roger Pratt*, a
distinguished amateur who was one of the most important post-
Reformation architects in England. Pratt had been the designer
of that domestic classic, Coleshill in Berkshire, and of Clarendon
House in Piccadilly. Clarendon House, though demolished as
early as 1683, was one of the most influential houses of the century. After his marriage, aged forty-eight, to Anne Monins,
Pratt retired to Ryston, which he had inherited in 1664 from his
cousin, and proceeded to rebuild. Of his work here, however,
only the shell remains. So the general disposition is his, a double

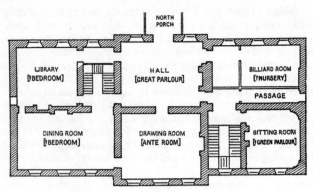

Ryston Hall. Ground-floor plan as built

pile of nine bays with a three-bay centre, consisting of a basement for offices and a raised principal floor. A painting surviving in the house shows that Pratt's house had an upper storey in the centre three bays only. The flanking roofs were high and hipped and had dormer windows. The centre was crowned front and back by big, surprisingly clumsy segmental pediments of brick, derived perhaps from certain of the less pure Parisian buildings (*see* e.g. Le Muet's *Manière de bien bastir*, which Pratt possessed). Clasped between the pediments was a clock turret, above which rose a square bellcote. The windows had mullion-and-transom crosses on the principal floor. All this, though appropriately modest for a country squire, was oddly provincial after his more famous and influential houses. Surviving brick-work is laid in English bond, which shows how late in the century that fashion persisted. Pratt reckoned the total cost of the 'main house, all out walling & making the courts and gardens' at £2,800.

In 1787–8 *Sir John Soane* remodelled the house, and the present fenestration and N porch are his. He raised the outer bays to match the centre and put on a uniform roof. The principal windows have blank tympana, a motif characteristic of Soane's early houses in Norfolk. Nice, simple Soane staircase with typical segmentally capped stone piers. He added the one-bay hipped pavilions to E and W, with thermal windows perversely placed at basement level. More alterations in 1864 by *Salvin* for the Rev. Jermyn Pratt, principally bathrooms and sculleries. More importantly E. R. M. Pratt in 1913 raised the present pinched mansard roof over the centre, reorganized the chimneystacks and added the three-bay colonnade to the S front. Of his time too the links to Soane's pavilions. Early C18 STABLES in the service yard to the W. Of galleted carstone and brick dressings: six bays, round-headed windows, clock tower turning into a cupola on open arches. SUMMERHOUSE 40 yds E of the house with an open loggia in Greek Revival style: Ionic engaged columns. Seven bays, with a pediment over the central three.

SADDLEBOW

2½ m. ssw of King's Lynn

ST HELEN. 1863, of flint, converted to a house in 1983. Three
Perp windows to s, outbuildings to N serving the former school,
E end broken through by double doors.

SEECHE ABBEY FARMHOUSE, I m. S. Red brick laid in English
bond, with a little diaper decoration, c. 1570. Three stepped
gables to s front, that in the middle to a slightly projecting porch.
Attached to it the w gable, but the E gable separated by two
bays of renewed three-light cross casements. Two more such
gables to the N front.

SAHAM TONEY

ST GEORGE. Transitional priest's doorway. Pointed arch with two
slight chamfers and one order of shafts, still with Norman-
looking capitals. In the s aisle two two-light windows with plate
tracery, one with a trefoil, the other a cinquefoil. This and the
five-bay arcades (circular piers, circular abaci, capitals with
slightly different mouldings, double-hollow-chamfered arches,
stiff-leaf headstops) are C13 work. Two N clerestory windows
also have plate tracery (quatrefoil and cinquefoil), but the others
all cusped Dec Y-tracery, so has this been changed? Dec chancel arch and three-light reticulated N aisle windows. Chancel
restored in 1864 by J. C. Buckler. Perp windows. Buckler's is the
elaborate timbering in the roof, but probably not the stocky
boxed arched braces of the nave roof. Perp some more s aisle
windows and the w tower. This has a base with a frieze of
emblems, including G for St George and M for St Mary. w
doorway with St George and the Dragon in the spandrels.
Four-light w window. Patterned sound-holes and three-light
bell-openings. Tall arch towards the nave. Donations suggest
the tower was rebuilt 1491–7, with new bells made 1497–1507.
Tower restored 1938. In the two-storey s porch an ornate niche,
all renewed. Does it represent an original one? Parvis staircase
has a flight of steps inside the aisle. The parvis chamber is used
as a children's playroom. – FONT. 40s. left in 1522 for a new
font, octagonal and quite plain, just shields in cusped fields
and quatrefoils. – FONT COVER. Very handsome; with inscription and date 1632. Unfluted Ionic columns, an ogee cap, and
on top a pelican (under tower). – SCREEN. C15. Nice; with
one-light divisions and ogee arches, cusped and subcusped
to the centre. Tracery in the six dado bays. – PULPIT. With
a memorable, probably early Victorian stair-rail, for the rector
to snake up and down. – BENCH ENDS. Some in nave and
chancel; with poppyheads and engaging lions as arm-rests. –
STAINED GLASS. In the chancel, the E window c. 1845 by
William Wailes, a Last Supper. A Nativity in s aisle E by *Lavers
& Westlake*, †1899, and an Ascension in the adjacent s aisle
window, 1890.

To the E of the church is a big mere with the core of the village grouped to its s and w.

OLD RECTORY, immediately w of the church. A late C18 red brick house of two storeys and attic in eight bays, rather irregular to s front. The entrance in the off-centre canted bay. Above this an C18 inscription in a panel 'MANNERS MAKYTH MAN'. Stacks with moulded bands. E front faces churchyard, and the sash windows give way to casements.

SAHAM HALL, ¾ m. WSW. A Neo-Georgian house of 1910 for Charles Randolph, burnt out 1973 and subsequently repaired. Three by six irregular bays of red brick.

THE LODGE, Chequers Lane, ½ m. NE. Two-storey brick house dated 1724. Six-bay s front with sashes; the two which look original are C20 replicas. Platband between floors. MEADOW FARMHOUSE. Similar date, but with brick patterning of burnt headers. Two storeys in three bays, centre bay advanced. Platband between floors.

On HILLS ROAD two more C18 farmhouses. First HUNT'S FARM-HOUSE, dated 1746, two storeys, three bays, sashes (replaced) and a doorcase with unfluted columns. PARK FARMHOUSE, brick, two storeys, four bays of cross casements, porch with stepped gable. Main gables stepped. c. 1710.

PAGE'S PLACE, ⅜ m. N of church. A range runs N–S with two wings branching to the E. Casement windows, ridge stack with four connected octagonal flues. This points to the late C16. s wing with a similar, but external, stack. Plenty of alterations.

WINDMILL, ⅜ m. SE. A brick tower without cap or sails. Built in 1828 for and by *John Bristow*, converted to a house in 1948 (by *David Potter*). Clutch of one-storeyed rooms at the base added 1980–1.

HIGH BANKS. Part of the ditches of an Iron Age or Romano-British rectangular enclosure of seventeen acres with a single rampart and ditch survives; the rampart was levelled in C19. Nearby, a hoard of C1 enamelled horse-trappings was found in 1838. (DG)

₆₀₂₀

SANDRINGHAM

ST MARY MAGDALENE. A medieval church, but successfully Victorianized first by *S. S. Teulon* in 1857–8 for Lady Harriet Cowper (before the estate passed to the Prince of Wales in 1862), and then by *Arthur Blomfield* in 1890. Of carstone slips dressed with ashlar. The s porch is Perp and has a niche above the entrance flanked by windows, and carstone flushwork to the lower s wall. Two low storeys, but the internal floor gone. The w tower, also Perp, has pretty pierced tracery panels of square and rectangular shape and a three-light w window with panel tracery. s transept and N aisle added by Blomfield. The latter with two small gables and a larger gabled chapel to the w. The interior is mostly 1857, modified by the further works of 1890, 1909 and 1921, sweeping away much of Teulon's work. Teulon's is the three-light E window, but he also provided a chancel screen, font and crane for the font cover, a reredos and, in 1859, the choir STALLS, only the last remaining. Even the chancel arch is 1857. Arch-braced nave roof of 1921. Hammerbeam chancel roof 1890. At first one hardly takes in the various fittings, for as a result of the connections with the royal family the chancel is the most lavish of all Norfolk parish churches. There is in the chancel no part of roof or walls not either painted or encrusted with rich decorative schemes, almost all introduced after 1910 as a memorial to Edward VII, and paid for by the royal family and friends. On the N and S walls are painted angels in niches engraved on to copper grounds. The other areas of wall have repeating stencilled patterns of IHS. Panelled dado with musical angels under elaborate miniature Perp canopies, kings and queens round the E window in equally lavish canopies.

BAPTISTERY. Rich wood panelling and a marble baluster font, made in Florence in 1909 and given by Edward VII. – The total-immersion FONT, brought in 1886 from Rhodes by the Duke of Edinburgh, is outside the tower, cut from a solid block of marble about A.D. 850 and decorated with circled Maltese crosses and Latin crosses. – ALTAR and REREDOS, the former designed by *Barkentin & Krall* (*C.C. Krall* himself) and presented by Rodman Wanamaker, an American, in 1911, the latter designed by *W.E. Tower* in 1920. Both are of solid silver. – PULPIT. Oak and silver, by *Barkentin & Krall* (*Walter Stoye*), 1924–6, also presented by Rodman Wanamaker. – SCULPTURE. Statuette of St George, aluminium and ivory. By *Alfred Gilbert*, 1892. – STAINED GLASS. In the upper porch openings C15 images of St Catherine and St Etheldreda. Some C16 Flemish glass in the tracery of a N aisle window installed by *Reginald Blomfield* in 1909. – E window by *W.E. Tower*, c.1911 (Crucifixion). *Kempe & Tower, Heaton, Butler & Bayne* and *Clayton & Bell* did the rest of the glass, none very good. – MONUMENTS. Queen Victoria †1901. Two angels hold a decorated roundel with relief of the sovereign's head. Sculptor not known (N aisle W). – Edward VII †1910 and Queen Alexandra †1925, on opposite chancel piers. Relief profiles in roundels in rectangular frames. – George V †1936 at Sandringham and Queen Mary †1953, also opposite each other by the pulpit, and similar to the last. Both by *W. Reid Dick*. – George VI †1952 at Sandringham, a bronze profile bust also by *Reid Dick*. All these are private, not public, memorials and there are of course no actual burials. – LAMP STANDARD. W of the church. Quite elaborate shaft with a ribbon of flowers spiralling round. Cast iron by *Barnard, Bishop & Barnard* of Norwich, late C19.

SANDRINGHAM HOUSE. The estate was bought by the Prince of Wales, the future King Edward VII, in 1862 from Charles Cowper. Of the seven-bay house of 1771 the Prince retained only *Teulon*'s mid-C19 conservatory, and rebuilt the rest in a frenetic Jacobean. The new house was begun in 1870 to the designs of the obscure architect *A.J. Humbert* of London. The house as it was is illustrated in R.H. Mason's *Norfolk*

Photographically Illustrated. In 1883 a ballroom was added, projecting E from the S end of the E front. This is by *Colonel R. W.
Edis.* In 1891 a fire damaged the upper parts of the house. A
second storey was subsequently added, also by *Edis,* and various pieces of decoration. The contractor was *John Thompson &
Co.* of Peterborough, holders of the Royal Warrant. The house
is of brick with ample Ketton stone dressings and the style is
Jacobean. Many gables, mostly straight. Two ogee-shaped cupolas, one of them on a turret breaking the symmetry of the E
façade. The two stone bay windows on the entrance side are
after 1891. The ballroom is Jacobean too, but more flamboyant.
It has a coved and stuccoed ceiling. Attached to the garden
front on the S is a projecting piece of different design, connecting the house with the long, originally single-storeyed bowling
alley. The link contains the billiard room which was adapted
out of Teulon's conservatory. The bowling alley, like much else,
received its upper parts in 1892. In the 1960s a proposal to
demolish and replace the whole house by a design of *David
Roberts* was resisted and instead *Sir Hugh Casson* undertook
internal modernizations.

NORWICH GATES. Designed by *Thomas Jekyll.* Very heavy and
sumptuous cast and wrought ironwork. The gates were made
by *Barnard, Bishop & Barnard* of Norwich, shown at the Great
Exhibition of 1862, and given by the City of Norwich to the Prince
of Wales as a wedding present in the following year. The ESTATE
WALLS of carstone slips and brick piers run l. and r.; similar walls
will be noticed everywhere in Sandringham and West Newton.

WATER TOWER, 1 m. SE. By *Martin ffolkes,* built in 1878. Extraordinary Italianate octagonal tower beginning with a battered
carstone plinth with rusticated sandstone quoins, above which
are four storeys of carstone slips dressed with red brick. Two-
light arched windows with little columns between the lights and
a deep stone cornice below the tank stage. The steel tank is
exposed, with pretty iron cresting. Attached an even taller and
slenderer polygonal staircase tower finished by a splayed cornice. Converted by *Michael & Sheila Gooch* to a house in 1977.

THE FOLLY, ¾ m. SW. By *C. S. Beck* of Glasgow, 1874. Small
shooting lodge with a timber-framed upper floor over a raised
veranda and bargeboarded gables. Small polygonal turret at the
NE corner.

GARDENS. Apart from some obviously older trees the arrangement dates from the 1860s. The two LAKES excavated in the
1870s by *W. B. Thomas.* Formal garden added to N of the house
in 1947 by *Geoffrey Jellicoe.* To the N and NW woods now form
Sandringham Country Park.

SANTON

3½ m. NW of Thetford

ALL SAINTS. Isolated by the River Ouse. A medieval chapel stood
here, rebuilt in 1628 for Thomas Bancroft with material from

the former structure. Not much of this shows now, except for some brickwork high in the w nave gable. In 1858 the chancel, tower and N porch were added at the expense of the Rev. William Weller Poley, using parts of the s transept of West Tofts church. The only remarkable parts are the E.E. stiff-leaf corbels on heads. The E.E. windows are all C19. Medieval the two hoodmould stops in the form of balls of leaf which are above a s window in the tower. Octagonal bell-stage. The tower is in a sw position, not unusual in this area of Norfolk. – PULPIT. C17, hexagonal, but re-worked in 1858. – SCREEN. With trefoiled arches, panelled dado and ballflower in the cornice. It is said to have come from West Tofts, and may indeed be by *Pugin*, of 1850.

MOATED SITE. To the w of the church a small square moated site survives in the area of a deserted settlement. (AR)

SAXLINGHAM NETHERGATE 2090

ST MARY THE VIRGIN. The present evidence nearly all Perp, and, naturally, Victorian. The exception is the s doorway, with simple C12 imposts. w tower with brick and flint chequer at the top. The pretty clock on the s side dated 1794. The Perp nave windows (with stepped embattled horizontals between the lights and the tracery) are all renewed or new. Perp chancel E window and priest's doorway. Four-bay N arcade of 1867, when the aisle was built, by *J. S. Benest*. The arcades have a commendably medieval appearance: thin piers, essentially lozenge-shaped with slim shafts in the main directions and a hollow and a wave in the diagonals. Only the shafts to the arcade openings have capitals. Four-centred arches. – FONT. C15. Octagonal. Against the stem four lions, against the bowl also four lions and four demi-figures of angels with shields, on which the emblem of the Trinity, the Instruments of the Passion, and three crowns and three chalices. – SOUTH DOOR. C15, plank, with two quatre-foil iron openings. – REREDOS. C15, assembled from part of a screen. – STAINED GLASS. Unusually much, and including some of the oldest glass in Norfolk, notably the four C13 medallions in one chancel s window. They depict on one St John and St James, on another two St Edmund, on the last a Saint being beheaded. There are also in the next window w two good late C14 Saints: St Philip with loaves and St James the Less. A Virgin and Child in the lowside window, *c.* 1500, and there is much more C15 glass. – s nave, †1910, by *Hugh Arnold*, three good Saints and predella panels. – MONUMENT. John Baron †1734. Two pilasters carrying a pediment. Two cherubs' heads below the pediment.

OLD RECTORY. By *Soane*, 1784–7 for the Rev. J. Gooch. A very simple four-bay house of gault brick with the centre three bays elaborated into a big bow. This is a half-storey higher than the rest of the house. N front of three bays, with a porch on Roman Doric columns, added as a replica only in the 1970s. Inside no special effects, except that Soane even on this scale manages to give the staircase an apsed end. Off to one side additions by *Feilden & Mawson* (job architect *G. C. Barnes*), 1972. There are two hipped pavilions, one single-storeyed, the other in two storeys, much too severe for the house but fortunately small.

OLD HALL, by the church. A fine, timber-framed Elizabethan house on an E-plan with a gabled, full-height central porch. The porch entrance has ovolo-moulded jambs and above is a mullioned and transomed window under a shallow timber pediment. This motif repeated r. and l. in the main wall, although renewed. Projecting wings are gabled too. Internal details are progressively later than the late C16, such as the simple Jacobean staircase with flat balusters in the s wing and the early C18 panelling in a room adjacent. The roof of collars and staggered butt-purlins is also an C18 replacement.

VILLAGE. Many timber-framed HOUSES. First THE STREET, the interest on the w side. No. 25. Early C17 timber frame with brick and flint gables but given an early C19 three-bay façade. Original clasped purlin roof. BEECHVIEW (former post office) has an early C16 queenpost roof and C18–C20 alterations. OLD CARRIER ARMS, former pub. Through-passage plan of the early C17 with just one room either side. C18 casements to façade. Winder by the stack and clasped purlin roof. YEW COTTAGE is a lobby-entrance house, late C17, in four bays extended s into five. SAXLINGHAM HOUSE has an early C16 queenpost truss in the roof with arched braces. The house extended by two bays to the s in the C17. Into BROADEN LANE. On the e HILL COTTAGES, converted into multiple occupation and re-converted back. Thatched, five bays of C20 casements, two storeys and attic. It is, or was, a late C15 open hall house with service doors into the screens passage identifiable, and a queen-post roof just recognizable among the C18 timbers. CHURCH HILL. ADELAIDE HOUSE (former public house) has three early C18 cross casements and a shaped w gable to the otherwise timber frame. CHURCH HILL COTTAGES began as an open hall house in the early C16. Of this the one queen-post truss with arched braces remains N of the central stack. In the late C16 the stack was inserted in the screens passage to create a lobby-entrance and the s part re-roofed with clasped purlins.

Out to the SE THE GREEN. SAXLINGHAM HALL. Brick. The early C18 provides the E block: two storeys and attic with a full-height C19 porch with a shaped gable and a ridge stack with three octagonal flues. The N gable shaped. Turned baluster staircase. The modifications c. 1850 for Edward Steward. His is the block to the s, also with shaped gables and a linking piece with a crenellated parapet. HALL FARMHOUSE was a C16 open hall house with a queenpost roof (only ties and mortice-holes of this survive). To N a stack was added in the C17 and further bays put on. GREEN FARMHOUSE has a similar history.

SAXLINGHAM THORPE 2090

ST MARY. The scanty ruins were buried in trees and ivy until clearance in 1991. Broken w tower. Three walls of the church still stand high. Late C15, of flint, ashlar and dressed in brick. In the chancel two splayed windows suggest C12, as does the archaeological evidence for an apse.

SCARNING 9010

ST PETER AND ST PAUL. Perp, with a two-storeyed s vestry built in 1576 and still entirely Perp. w tower with flushwork panelling along the base, three-light w window, traceried sound-holes and two-stepped battlements. Two Evangelist statues survive as pinnacles. Continuous wave-moulded arch to nave. Robert Kyrby left 13s. 4d. each year for six years 'to the belding of the stepull' in 1521. John Dykman in 1524 made the same arrangement while workmen were actually employed. Numerous similar bequests until the last recorded in 1547 from Thomas Secker: 20s. 'as the new werke goethe forewarde on the tower'. Late Perp indeed. Aisleless nave with three-light Perp windows. The chancel over-restored. It has Y-tracery windows and a C19 Geometric e window. – FONT. C13. Roughly square, on five supports. Bowl with angle columns and, in the fields between, colonnettes carrying stiff-leaf motifs. – FONT COVER. Tall, like a crocketed spire. Largely Jacobean (but not the base). – SCREEN. Good. Perp, with one-light divisions and very dainty panel tracery. Some remains of colour. At the SE corner a wooden frame for the sanctus bell. – STAINED GLASS. e window by *Wailes*, very rich, very High Victorian, *c.* 1862. His too the other chancel windows.

SCARNING DALE, ⅝ m. WNW. A two-storeyed timber-framed house of the C17 on the lobby-entrance plan. C20 casements and bay windows attached. Half-timbered and jettied early C20 addition as a cross wing. The C17 house has a roof of diminished principals and clasped purlins.

Minor C17 HOUSES are RAILWAY FARMHOUSE, Fen Road, timber-framed, lobby-entrance plan, one and a half storeys in four bays, and OLD HALL, Watery Lane, also timber-framed, C17 stacks and, inside, some C17 and C18 panelling and a C17 dog-leg staircase. The common early C19, gault-brick, two-storey, three-bay houses with doorcases or porches on columns are represented by THE GRANGE, Dereham Road, and POPLAR FARMHOUSE, Manor Lane.

SCOLE 1070

ST ANDREW. Mostly of *c.* 1300, but the church was burnt out in 1963 and re-fitted, which explains its antiseptic feel. The biggest casualties were the hammerbeam nave roof and chancel arch.

Unbuttressed W tower with bell-openings with Y-tracery. Battlements with chequer flushwork. The details of the body of the
church nearly all Victorian, from the restoration by *J. K. Colling*
in 1874. Of medieval date the S arcade of four bays (octagonal
piers and double-hollow-chamfered arches). The chancel arch
was of the same design. Contemporary also the S aisle piscina. –
FONT. Perp. Four lions against the stem, eight demi-figures of
angels against the bowl. – LECTERN. Good foot, square, with
big angle leaves. Perp. – WALL PAINTINGS. A little in a niche
on N side. – STAINED GLASS. E window by *Patrick Reyntiens*,
1965. – S aisle E by *Edward Moore*, a Resurrection of 1920.

WHITE HART INN. The sumptuous sign, which once extended
right across the road (and was in a style entirely in the C16 tradition), was dated 1655. The same date is given by Blomefield for
the inn itself. It was built for John Peck, who was a Norwich
wool merchant, and it must be one of the most ambitious buildings in England erected especially for the purpose of offering
hospitality to travellers. It lies half-way between Ipswich and
Norwich on the strategic Roman road, and between Bury and
Yarmouth on the A143, as important a junction in the late C20
as in the mid C17. It is of red brick, still laid in English bond. In
the C19 a post office occupied the N end and a butcher's shop
the S end, but that is the only deviation, and one which reflected
the original plan of one large centre room and two small side
ones. The front consists of five wide parts, each crowned with a
Dutch gable. Giant rusticated angle pilasters. Flat pilasters in
the two orders between. Decoration with raised ovals with lugs
l. and r. Some windows have flat raised frames. At the back three
projections, l., r. and middle, and in one recessed part wooden
pilasters in two orders, really as part of the timber-framing (cf.
The Swan at Harleston). The centre projection houses the staircase. Square chimneystacks with arched panelling. Inside, a
solid staircase going up through both floors and with sturdy
turned balusters of a type some sixty or seventy years older than
the house. String with a simple chain of ovals and lozenges,
also rather an Elizabethan motif. The first and attic floors have
long corridors at the rear serving bedrooms. A meeting room on
first floor with a moulded ceiling, and another in a room adjacent, which also has a chimneypiece with Ionic pilasters.

C17 timber-framed HOUSES may be represented by STREET
FARMHOUSE, Norwich Road, a lobby-entrance house, and THE
MOAT HOUSE at Scole Common ⅝ m. N. Georgian is SCOLE
LODGE, Norwich Road, now a nursing home, three bays in two
and a half storeys with lower side pieces set back. The STABLES
behind (i.e. N) are also late C18: three carriage doors and five
upper casements. The cupola on the roof has six columns over
a clock stage.

ROMANO-BRITISH SETTLEMENT. Around the junction of the
Roman Pye Road (the modern A140) and the River Waveney
was the site of a large village, of which several areas have been
excavated. This may be the site of VILLA FAUSTINI, a posting
station mentioned in the Antonine Itinerary. N of the river,

79

earthworks survive in pasture fields (DG). Further excavations 1993–4, unpublished at the time of writing.

SCOULTON 9000

HOLY TRINITY. Lonely, just N of the Norwich–Watton road. Broad W tower of the C14 (see the Dec W window and the wave-moulded arch towards the nave). The bell-stage is octagonal and connected with the substructure by broaches. Nave and chancel, the former thatched, the latter pantiled (in 1972). Y-traceried windows of the early C14, except for the big, five-light (renewed) Perp E window. The restoration was in 1885. On the S side a two-light window with a transom extends from one of the lights below the transom as a lowside window. C15 S porch with flushwork on the buttresses. Dec arcades inside of three bays with octagonal piers and double-hollow-chamfered arches. In the chancel the Easter Sepulchre on the N side looks earlier than the rest, i.e. still C13. The slab at the foot of the recess has five depressions, perhaps for cresset lights. The trefoiled piscina opposite is fine and more in harmony with the Y-tracery of the windows. – FONT. Plain octagonal C14 type. – PULPIT. C17; with back panel and tester. – SCREEN. Panels of the dado reused in various contexts. Also Jacobean panels reused. – DOORS. C15 S door and one also to tower stairs.

Of HOUSES, little of note. FROGS' ABODE, ¼ m. NE of the church, has a nearly complete timber frame if one ignores the rebuilt brick N gable wall. Two storeys, early C18. The OLD RECTORY has a late C18 two-storey W block added to the C17 house to form a double pile, a common event. TOLLGATE FARMHOUSE: late C18, with a grander three-bay front with a big square porch added in the early C19.

SCULTHORPE 8030

ST MARY AND ALL SAINTS. Externally mostly Victorian. The original chancel was demolished in the C18 but replaced in 1846–7 by *R. & J. A. Brandon*, who provided extravagant Dec windows, the centre one on the S side cut into by the priest's door. Plainer three-light intersecting E window. The S aisle added in 1860–1 by *Thomas Jekyll*, and given three pairs of tre-foiled lancets. Originally the S porch tower could be of the early C14, see the quatrefoil responds to the entrance and Y-tracery bell-openings. The top, of course, is later. Original also the Perp N aisle lit through four two-light flat-headed windows. E and W aisle windows with three lights. Five bays of octagonal piers inside, double-chamfered arches. Jekyll had fun with the W bay of the nave, which he also added, stressed by two demi-columns with stiff-leaf capitals and a band of stiff-leaf all up the jamb moulding. Similar leaf capitals to his three-bay S arcade of cir-cular piers. The chancel seems to be correctly rebuilt and looks

Perp. C19 scissor-braced nave and chancel roofs and a good straight-braced S aisle roof, with carved and pierced spandrels. – FONT. Norman, square, with angle colonnettes and on them heads of lions and rams looking up and biting the cable mould-ing which circumambulates the rim. On one face of the bowl the Adoration of the Magi; figures within intersecting arcading, much re-cut. On the other faces elaborate interlace. The five legs are by *Jekyll*. – ORGAN CASE. By *Snetzler*, 1756. The very charming decoration almost too Classical for that date. One would expect a date about 1770. However, the organ came from the York Assembly Rooms in 1860, so was a prestige piece. – STAINED GLASS. Some excellent early *Morris* glass: two panels of Christ on the Waves in a chancel S window, designed in 1864 by *Ford Madox Brown*; and Spes, Fides and Caritas in the S aisle E window, the latter designed by *Burne-Jones*, 1865 (the same figures at Langham). The chancel E window by *Ward & Hughes* (designed by *Thomas Willement*), 1859, a Baptism, Ascension and Christ with Moses. The SW nave window has the Story of Ruth in six panels, by *Robert Bayne* of *Heaton, Butler & Bayne*, 1862. Two chancel N windows of 1889 by *Powell & Sons* show-ing Holman Hunt's *Light of the World* and *The Good Shepherd*. – MONUMENT. Wall monument in the form of an elaborate ogee Dec tabernacle, to Major-General Sir John Thomas Jones of Cranmer Hall †1843, by *Myers* of Lambeth (chancel). – BRASSES. Henry Unton †1470, 2 ft figure, nave floor at E end; John Humpton †1521, wife and children, 19 in. figures, next to last. Two other inscriptions.

CRANMER HALL, 1 m. NW. Built in 1721 as a three-storey house for Robert Donne, but this was reduced to two storeys in 1955, having been given a neat Roman Doric pedimented doorcase to the main E façade in 1930. The alterations are an improvement. Red brick, seven-bay E front, the three-bay pediment containing a coat of arms added in 1831 when Sir John Jones received the family baronetcy (the arms have grenades and militaria, because Sir John's career was with the Royal Engineers). Rusticated brick quoins. Similar quoins to the r. and l. returns. The door-way round the corner with its swan-necked pediment on fluted Ionic columns is another piece of 1930 vintage. The house was at its largest after *Philip Webb* added the rear wing and made alterations to the interior in *c.* 1880. The Webb wing has three gablets growing out of the parapet containing alternately round and square windows. The main rooms are the hall entered from the E doorway, the dining room to the N and the drawing room to the S, the latter with an added canted bay window against the S front. Fielded panelling and fielded doors throughout. The staircase (W of the hall) is an oddity: closed string, bobbin balus-ters; clearly C19. If it is Webb's work, he was having a bad day. Until the Second World War the home of Sir Lawrence Jones, author of *A Victorian Boyhood*.

The STABLES, of *c.* 1880 too, so likely to be by *Webb*. Red brick, one storey with attic. Two entrances under gables.

THE LODGE. *c.* 1800 and looking like a Wyatt farmhouse of the

Holkham Estate type, even if it is not. Flint and brick. U-plan.
Divided into separate occupation now. Two storeys, with a
four-bay central s front. The porch has lean wooden columns.
Side wings have four bays of sashes.

GROVE FARMHOUSE, 1¼m. s. Georgian (c. 1790), of red brick,
five bays, two storeys. Roman Doric porch.

No. 46 Creake Road (TRAFALGAR COTTAGE). A cruciform two-
storey house, formerly divided into four cottages. 1859. The
gables are stepped and the stack has clustered flues. Casements.

SEDGEFORD   7030

ST MARY. Norman round tower, embraced by later aisles and
given an added flat W front. Also the top storey is octagonal. It
has Y-tracery in the bell-openings, and is probably late not early
C14. The flat aisle ends do not quite meet in the middle so a
strip of convex wall runs vertically up the centre, and in this
strip is a quatrefoiled opening above a triangular-headed window, and at the bottom the C19 W window. Blocked C12 upper
doorway into nave, barely visible. Tall blind arches in the aisle
W bays towards the tower. Of c. 1310 the chancel, with a N lancet
and in addition an extremely odd two-light Y-tracery window
with a circular shaft. Fine seaweed capitals and arches in which
the sub-arches and the super-arch merge. There are in fact two
sets of mouldings, one for the original doorway into a vestry,
and when that was blocked the window tracery was inserted
into the gap, but the door and window are or were virtually
contemporary. The chancel was shortened in 1780. Of c. 1300
or even a little earlier the low six-bay arcades. Circular piers,
except for one octagonal one on the N. Double-chamfered
arches, moulded bases and undercut capitals. The s transept is
a Dec addition, see the filleted s respond and shape and position of the arch connecting it with the s aisle, but is a puzzle, for
it cuts into an obviously Perp clerestory window. So it must
have been raised and the two-light ogee-headed windows re-set
or reused in the C15. A N transept was also projected but not
carried out, though the present bay replacing it is also medieval.
Perp aisle windows. Wide Dec N and s porches with stilted
arches. In the W bay of the s aisle a fireplace employing a coffin-
lid as a bressumer. Perp clerestory with knapped flint and four-
centred windows. Good C15 arch-braced s transept roof moved
from the chancel. The restoration in 1882 by *Frederick Preedy*
confined itself to the nave roof (arch-braced), chancel fittings
and glass (*see* below). – FONT. Square, C13, of the Purbeck type,
with four shallow blank arches and five supporting columns
(centre one C19). Raised on steps. – BENCH. One bench has a
back and arms with C15 pierced quatrefoil panels, the rest C19
(nave W). – WALL PAINTINGS. Foliate designs in the spandrels
of the nave arcades, clearly contemporary with the arcades but
surprisingly archaic for a date of c. 1300. Masonry pattern on
nave W wall, and (repainted) on E wall of N aisle. In the s aisle

defaced remains of a large C14 St Christopher, and to S of chancel arch remains of colouring on a C14 niche. Late C19 painting by the *Rev. J. A. Ogle* in the chancel (DP). – STAINED GLASS. C15 fragments in the chancel N lancet. *Preedy* provided a S chancel window, *c.* 1871, Life of Christ; transept S, Transfiguration, 1870. Tower W window †1863, Mary and Martha.

LYCH GATES, on to Church Lane. Erected of carstone in 1852 to commemorate twenty who died in a typhus outbreak.

SEDGEFORD HALL, ⅝ m. SE. Two storeys and attics. E front of seven bays entered from a segmental porch on fluted columns. The porch is early C19 but the rest is of the mid C18. The sashes have flush frames. The interior remodelled in 1960s and a N wing added at the same time.

WETHERED MANOR, Docking Road. Early C19 remodelling of a C17 house, of carstone with brick dressings. Five bays, two-storeyed porch, the entrance with C19 engaged Ionic columns. C17 window openings filled in on the main front.

MAGAZINE COTTAGE, Docking Road. Very interesting. It is supposed to be, and there is no reason to doubt it, a powder magazine built for Sir Hamon L'Estrange of Hunstanton in *c.* 1643, when he was holding King's Lynn for the Royalists. The present appearance is only partly due to C19 repairs and conversion. Brick-dressed carstone. One storey over a basement. Gothick windows to S and W sides. To the E is a rusticated door, and there is plenty of other rustication and quoining round and about. Gable-ends have three square pedestals supporting ball finials.

WEST HALL. A farmhouse now, built *c.* 1600 of carstone and brick with a five-bay addition of *c.* 1800. Of the earlier time are noticeably the triple octagonal flues to the stack and a three-light brick casement to the W, and other blocked windows and door.

SEETHING

ST MARGARET AND ST REMIGIUS. Norman round tower, the top repaired using brick in the parapet and a little round the bell-openings. The round-arched slit windows are typically Norman. The round arch towards the nave rests on the simplest imposts. Lead spike as a spire. The W nave wall r. and l. of the tower rebuilt in brick. The nave is nicely thatched and may have the faint trace of a Norman window at the W end of the N side. Otherwise the windows are early Dec (cusped Y-tracery) and Perp (two three-light S nave windows). The chancel fenestration seems all of *c.* 1320, or reflects that style. The three-light E window certainly is C19. In the S porch an arch-braced late C15 roof, reused during the C19 rebuilding, the doorway with wave mouldings. Cinquefoiled piscina next to the space only for a drop-sill sedilia. The wooden door frame to the rood stair retains original colour. – FONT. Extremely fine Perp piece of *c.* 1480, almost completely undamaged. At the corners of the foot the signs of the four Evangelists, very small. Against the stem four statuettes. Against the bowl the Seven Sacraments and the Baptism of Christ, well cut and naturalistic, with a developed sense of perspective. – SCREEN. Late C15 dado only, formerly with one surviving painted figure, now only with stencilled floral ornament and a pretty band of raised gilding, and some colour on the back. Upper parts carved by the churchwarden in 1898. – SOUTH DOOR. Perp, with an unusual pattern of panelling. The panels are arched, but so long and slim that the whole looks almost like linenfold. – PAINTINGS of the C14. On the N wall the Three Living and the Three Dead (damaged on the l.) and St Christopher. Then the Life of Christ, with Annunciation, Nativity, Resurrection, Ascension, and the Coronation of the Virgin. This series shows a type of iconoclasm most unusual in wall painting: the heads have been systematically gouged out. At the E end of the wall, a large bearded figure, probably St John the Baptist. On the E wall, slight remains of decoration, with doubtless more to be uncovered. The paintings on the S wall are not easy to decipher, though the easternmost painting shows two women gossiping and three devils around them; one of the women holds a rosary, and the devil at the bottom holds another. To the W further paintings, including a figure playing a harp. (DP) – STAINED GLASS. A C15 angel in the chancel on the N side; also bits in the nave on the S side. E window by *J. H. Gathercole* of Norwich, †1861, St Paul, St Peter and St John; terrible garish colours.

SEETHING HALL. Two-storey, three-bay late C18 house of colourwashed brick under a hipped roof. The upper sashes have Gothick intersections in the glazing bars.

THE STREET has a number of thatched C18 cottages. POND FARMHOUSE has pantiles and is a late C16 timber-framed house with another bay added to the S in the C17. Two storeys and attic in five bays, fitted with C19 and C20 casement windows. Good moulded timbers inside and remains of mullioned windows. MERE HOUSE is of brick with gault-brick dressings. Georgian, two storeys and seven bays, renewed cross casements, pilasters.

MILL LANE, NE of the church. One of the groups of council housing done by *Tayler & Green* for the Loddon Rural District Council (*see* Introduction, p. 165). The group is of only thirteen houses and was built in 1950–1. It was a specially charming composition, essentially a long terrace with old trees and a pond. The pond, in front of the single-storey groups, is stagnant; the trees decayed. Most sold off, and only two still colourwashed; most with dreadful uPVC windows. This does not detract from the subtle projection and recession of the houses.

CONTROL TOWER, Seething Airfield, 1½ m. S of the church. 1942–3 for the 448th Bomb Group, USAF. Two-storey rectangular block of rendered Fletton brick, partially galleried to the N (i.e. facing the runways). Restored as a museum 1985–7; interior rooms substantially intact.

SENGHAM see TATTERSETT

SETCHEY
s of King's Lynn

St Mary. 1844 for Daniel Gurney (architect not known). Just a small three-bay nave and a smaller chancel. A lancet to each nave bay. Plain w doorway below three blocked lancets. Three lancets to e end.

The Gables, Main Road. Formerly an inn a little too near Lynn to have been prosperous, and with too much competition (see below). L-shaped with a mid-c17 Dutch gable facing the road at the end of the n range. The gable wall with platband and a c19 canted bay window. N side of three bays and two storeys, the openings altered. The wing running s to the road has four bays fitted with various sashes under a hipped roof. At the back a stair-turret in the angle. Inside is an early c17 doorway communicating between the two wings and another into the stair-turret, the pair repeated in the floor above. They have moulded jambs. Winder staircase.

Bull Cottage (formerly the Bull Inn, now three houses). A small U-plan c17 building of two storeys and attic. Presumably there was once a central porch. The elevations have too many blocked, reopened and new windows to enumerate.

SHADWELL PARK
¼ m. s of Brettenham

S. S. Teulon's extravagant remodelling of 1856–60 conceals a complicated building history. The house was originally built in 1727–9 by John Buxton, an amateur, who also built Bixley Hall and Earsham Hall. As early as c. 1725 Sir Edward Lovett Pearce, who did most of his work in Ireland, assisted, with a design for the front. Shadwell was intended as a retreat from Channonz Hall at Tibenham. The park with a lake of sixteen acres was made by Buxton's son in the mid c18; planting by 1743, lake by 1754, the latter enlarged in the mid c19. His grandson in 1760 employed Brettingham to produce plans, and also in 1789 Soane, but nothing seems to have come from either. The first of the main alterations were by Edward Blore, 1840–3 for Sir John Jacob Buxton and, after 1841, for the Dowager Lady Buxton. Blore more or less encased the first small three-bay house with additions to the s and new services to the N. When Sir Robert Jacob Buxton came of age in 1850 he with his mother set about rebuilding the church of St Mary in 1852 and the College at Rushford in 1855, employing S. S. Teulon for both, so it was virtually inevitable that Teulon was chosen as the architect of the northern extensions to the house. Teulon's work of 1856–60 is prodigious. No effort was spared to combine heavyweight Gothic structure with the most intricately carved detail. Symmetry was taboo throughout.

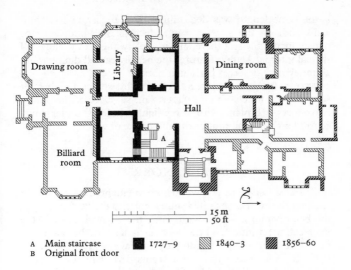

A Main staircase   ■ 1727–9   ▨ 1840–3   ▨ 1856–60
B Original front door

Shadwell Park. Ground-floor plan

The centre of the entrance (E) side e.g. has a tall tower with an oriel on figure corbels and a round stair-turret starting only halfway up, again on a figure corbel. Capitals and friezes abound with naturalistic foliage, inside as well as outside. One goes on discovering little men and little beasts among the leaves, all carved, Mark Girouard suggests, by *Thomas Earp*. The whole E front is amazingly varied. To the r. of the tower a stretch of white brick is followed by one of flint with a shaped gable, and then it goes round the corner to the STABLES with an even more extraordin- 113 ary entrance tower ending in an octagonal E.E. timber lantern. Inside the stable yard also every feature has its own shape and details. To the l. of the porch tower the facing changes to Caen stone and, after Teulon's staircase window, which, though Gothic, has a stepped-up sill to expose the staircase behind, the detail turns noticeably chaster and smoother. This is all Blore's work and the difference is more than the difference between the two architects: it is the difference between the 1840s and the 1860s. Blore's also is the whole S front, and the S half of the W side, until with the big four-light Perp window to the Music Hall Teulon's style returns.

Inside, everything is spacious – there are fifty-two rooms altogether and the effect of the central hall, cruciform and very tall, is indeed startling. It is very ecclesiastical and had when built an organ and plenty of stained glass. High up, Teulon displayed his love of tricky timberwork as he had at the crossing of St Mary's Church. The beams make an arched crossing in the middle and have zigzag edges to add more liveliness. The stiff-leaf and figurative carvings, again presumably Earp's, are amazing. The main W window of the hall carries the date of Teulon's alterations: 1858. The fact that none of the four arms of the hall is the same length was determined by the existing courtyard walls and, on the s, by the outside wall of Buxton's 1720s house, incredibly still there, albeit already altered by Blore. Of special internal Teulon features the heavily carved dining room chimneypiece deserves particular notice.

GROTTO in the gardens ⅜ m. SE. Flint with seats and niches for statues. Also an elaborate BOTHY, ¼ m. SE, c. 1840, clay lump, two storeys, L-plan, with three-light windows under four-centred arches. The roof burnt off at time of writing.

SHELFANGER

ALL SAINTS. Early C14 w tower with battlements decorated with chequer flushwork. Sexfoiled sound-holes to the w. Y-tracery in the bell-openings. Of the same time the chancel, see e.g. the intersecting E window. The N doorway is again of the same time or a little later. One N window of the nave is Dec, the others Perp. Scissor-braced nave roof seems early C14 too (that in chancel is C19). The s side of the church is puzzling. There is no aisle, but the asymmetrical position of the tower seems to presuppose one. On the other hand there is a sexfoiled circular window high up in the w wall on that side, and that is too high for an aisle. It could be a sound-hole re-set, as it matches that to the w face of the tower. The nave windows are mostly Perp. Lovely timber N porch, presumably the one for which money was left in 1506. It has flint between the studs and a four-centred doorway with floral carved spandrels. Four-light mullioned windows E and w are re-done. Arch-braced roof with hollow and wave mouldings to purlins and ridge piece. – FONT. Octagonal, with heads against the underside of the bowl and tracery on the bowl, Perp as well as Dec motifs. The letters A B refer to an Adam Bosville who is mentioned as patron of the church in 1362 and in 1375. – SCREEN. Some of the tracery of the upper part now under the tower arch. It is decidedly Dec, with lush and extensive reticulated and mouchette motifs. – STAINED GLASS. E window †1876, probably by *Clayton & Bell*. By the same firm two other chancel windows and one in s nave. – WALL PAINTINGS. Mid-C13, in recesses on either side of the altar. To the s the Virgin and Child, flanked by the adoring Magi and Shepherds, of superb quality; to the N only foliate scroll-work (DP).

OLD BAPTIST CHAPEL, The Street. 1824. A meeting-house type. Central door and two sashes to each floor.

CHURCH FARMHOUSE, opposite the church. Does the splendid four-centred door come from the church? It has six panels of heavy linenfold carving and parchment-like scrolls in the spandrels and must be early C16. The rest of the house c. 1830: four bays of sashes.

LIMETREE FARMHOUSE, Common Road. C16 timber-framed house to which was added a C17 range to form an L-plan. This last given a C19 brick skin.

SHELFANGER HALL, ½ m. SW. *c.* 1600 on an earlier moated site. Bricked ground floor leaving a hint of a jetty. Five bays of C20 casements and other C20 intrusions. The OLD RECTORY, Rectory Road, much the same, as is STREET FARMHOUSE, Rectory Road. Here though the early C17 plan still displays a lobby-entrance. This plan-form repeated with the added interest of a winder staircase by the stack in GUNN HOUSE, The Street.

SHELTON

2090

ST MARY. Apart from the great Fenland churches W of King's Lynn and St Peter Mancroft in Norwich, Norfolk has hardly more than half a dozen Perp churches of the first order. Shelton 35 is one of them. It was built for Sir Ralph Shelton, who in his will made in March 1497 ordered his executors to 'make up completeley the church of Shelton aforesaid, in masonry, tymber, iron, and leede, accordinge to the form as I have begunne it. . .'. His will was proved in May 1498. The church was indeed clearly completed to the same plan to which it had been started (with one exception, *see* below), and so we can assume that Shelton represents one ideal of a new church of about 1490 or 1500. All that was kept from its predecessor is the W tower of flint and the W window of the S aisle, which is Dec. The rest is of red brick with stone dressings, the brick being diapered with vitrified, i.e. dark blue, headers, and laid predominantly in header bond. The S aisle has a two-storeyed porch and three windows, the N aisle no porch, a N doorway oddly squeezed half under the W window, four windows, and between the third and fourth the rood stair-turret. So the fourth windows of each aisle represent chancel chapels. The church has indeed no projecting chancel, and its shortness at the E end is certainly an aesthetic fault, but chancels were by the 1490s considerably out of fashion (*see* Introduction, p. 58) and it is unlikely that something more ambitious was ever planned. The E end as it is has one very tall, rather narrow three-light double-transomed window and beneath it one of the East Anglian E sacristies, accessible by a small doorway S of the altar. Its only window is a low three-light window with uncusped lights flanked by statuary niches. The windows of the aisles are also of three lights. The tracery pattern includes three stepped embattled horizontals between the ogee-headed lights and the panel tracery above, and the raised middle horizontal sits on two encircled quatrefoils. The arches are four-centred. The S windows have monstrously big gargoyles above their heads. There is a stone-faced clerestory of nine windows on each side, closely set and with triangular buttresses between, as at St Andrew, Norwich. Finials were evidently intended or built on every second of these buttresses and on the aisle buttresses.

The S porch is of two storeys, the upper cutting into the C14 W window of the aisle by means of a projecting passageway linking the blocked first-floor door inside with the tower stairs. The entrance has spandrels with the Shelton arms. Above it a very tall canopied niche with an elongated panelled statue pedestal and small one-light windows l. and r. Inside, a fan vault (no longer a tierceron star vault) was begun or – less likely – built and later taken down. It was intended to have two tiers with four panels to the lower, eight to the upper registers, with ribs running round between them. Only the wall ribs come down to us, but they have brattishing like Henry VII's Chapel at Westminster, so right up to date. In the first floor the blocked doorway already referred to and a blocked window looking into the nave, so apparently the upper floor was intended for the priest.

Now the INTERIOR. The arcades run to the E end without any break. There are five bays, the two E ones narrower. The piers are slender, the windows large. So the impression, white-washed as the interior is, is one of light, spaciousness and even-ness. The piers have a lozenge section with four slender shafts in the principal directions and a hollow and a wave moulding in the diagonals. Only the shafts towards the arches have capitals. In the spandrels are flat canopied niches for images. To their l. and r. Perp panelling extends, the window mullion being car-ried down. Above the canopies demi-figures of angels were to carry the wall-posts of the roof. But, alas, the roof was taken down in the C18 and a plaster ceiling substituted; no doubt it was a hammerbeam roof.

It will have been noticed that we have reason to assume less generosity after than before Sir Ralph's death. The most poignant argument in this direction is the fact that a canopy was begun between the last two N piers to rise above his well-deserved monument, but that there is no monument to his memory now and that the canopy again may have been left unfinished. The E window, only three lights wide, as we have seen, rises right up to the present ceiling, a very exceptional proportion. The aisles have tall and wide blank arcading which is cut into by the upper storey of the porch. So, unless the C14 church had this motif already, it looks as if the second floor of the porch was an after-thought.

FURNISHINGS. FONT. The usual C15 East Anglian font, with four lions against the stem, and, against the bowl, four lions and four demi-figures of angels holding shields with the Instruments of the Passion, the symbol of the Trinity, three crowns and three chalices. – SCREEN. It is unfortunate that only the early C16 dado survives of a screen which ran right across from the N to the S wall. Crocketed ogees in the heads of each bay, crosses at the bases. – LECTERN. This seems an original piece. It con-sists of what look like two very elongated bench ends with the book-rest between, but may be made from a muntin salvaged from a screen and split lengthways. – BENCHES. A chair in the chancel is made up of bench ends, two of them with a flower on the arm-rest. – COMMUNION RAILS. A Jacobean rail has disap-peared since described in the first edition. Used as stall-fronts is

36

another probable communion rail. Later C17, with dumb-bell balusters. – ROYAL ARMS. Of William III, gorgeously carved, over the tower arch. – STAINED GLASS. Much early C16 glass in the aisle windows, mixed with faded C19 patterns and borders. Two big kneeling donors in the S aisle E window. Donors also in the chancel E window. – MONUMENTS. Under the incomplete canopy a rather bald Elizabethan tomb-chest with shields of the Shelton family. An identical tomb-chest in the N aisle NE corner. Between the chancel and the S aisle a later C16 tomb-chest with three shields in lozenge-shaped cusped fields. Against the S aisle S wall a Jacobean monument with kneeling figures, not in its original state. It is to Sir Robert Houghton †1623. There are two sets of kneeling figures, Sir Robert and wife facing each other beneath the coffered round arch of the superstructure and two figures of his children in front, oddly on the top slab of the chest. The superstructure is contained by, not a shallow shaped gable against the wall, but more of a representation of one, with crudely if engagingly painted skull and crossed bones, and texts. 1623 is early for a shaped gable anywhere.

RECTORY. The two-storey, three-bay SE façade of brick with tripartite sashes and a central doorcase with pilasters is late C18, but at the back and to the W is a C17 wing lit through cross casements and more tripartite sashes.

SHELTON HALL, ⅝ m. SE. The house of Sir Ralph Shelton, on a moated site, was a tremendous brick courtyard house with gatehouses etc., but fell into ruins in the C18. The C18 house on the site is of four bays and two storeys with a dormer attic and a hipped roof. Three C19 stacks. To the S in the early C20 a four-bay extension was added. To the E is a C16 timber-framed OUTBUILDING which from the jetty appears to have had domestic purpose. Converted to a garage.

Various C17 timber-framed HOUSES in the countryside around. PRIMROSE FARMHOUSE at Shelton Green ⅞ m. ESE is on the lobby-entrance plan, skinned with C19 brick and with (rebuilt) octagonal flues to the stack and a brick porch.

SHEREFORD

8020

ST NICHOLAS. Some carstone in the otherwise flint and stone-dressed church. Round tower with a small unmoulded round-headed arch towards the nave and traces of a small upper W window. The silly conical roof is C19. One Norman S window in the nave. Late Norman S doorway. Two orders of colonnettes with simple crocket capitals. Two roll mouldings in the arch. Re-set N doorway a little later. Several windows and the priest's doorway of the early C14, with Y-tracery. E window with bold Curvilinear tracery. Three lights, a big cusped and subcusped quatrefoil in a circle at the top. The chancel N wall has inside an Easter Sepulchre recess, quite plain. The N arcade has been pulled down. It had octagonal piers and double-hollow-chamfered arches. Roofs C19. – FONT. Circular, Norman, on a circular stem with four attached demi-shafts. Bowl with scalloped underside.

MOATED SITE. Small but well preserved, SW of the churchyard. (AR)

SHERNBORNE

ST PETER AND ST PAUL. Rebuilt by *H. J. Green* of Norwich, 1898, with *Sir Reginald Blomfield* as a consultant. Green, the Diocesan Surveyor, did not need assistance for a modest village church, but the Prince of Wales paid and Blomfield was a favourite. Basic two-light trefoiled or square-headed windows to N side and S aisle, three-light E and W windows and a W bell-cote. The E.E. water-holding bases and the central octagonal arcade pier are original up to 3½ ft and perhaps some other parts, e.g. of the double-chamfered arches. The arcade has two bays and is followed to the E by a piece of blank wall and a wider arch to the S chapel. Scissor-braced nave roof. – FONT. A bar-baric but mighty Norman piece. Square top and rounded bowl on four short columns. Angle colonnettes, four faces in the centres below, and interlace, etc., including inhabited scrolls, above. The rim has punched or incised ornament and the whole has not an inch of uncarved stone. – STAINED GLASS. E window by *Hardman & Co.*, †1924, poor for the date. – BRASSES. Sir Thomas Shernborne †1458 and wife. Good 3 ft 3 in. figures (removed from chancel to N wall).

SHERNBORNE HALL, ⅜ m. W. Only a wing of a larger mansion of the Shernbornes. Gable-end with a stepped gable and thin polygonal buttress shafts decorated with banding. E return with an external stack. All this is later C16, but the fenestration is C20. Three-bay C18 service wing added to the E, itself altered in the C19.

SHIMPLING

ST GEORGE. Isolated amid fields S of the village and Shimpling Hall. Restoration of 1867–74 by an obscure London architect *Ernest Lee* (he designed St Thomas, Brentwood, and St Mary, Whitechapel). Round C13 tower with an octagonal C15 top stage and recessed lead spire, the spire added by Lee. Four bell-openings and four imitation windows in flushwork. The ghost of, perhaps, a Norman window apparent in the S nave wall. Early C14 chancel (windows with intersecting and Y-tracery). Perp nave windows. Timber porch of 1867 (by Lee) reusing material from the earlier porch shown by Ladbroke. Lovely nave roof of steep pitch with eight arch-braced trusses and an embattled wall-plate. One tier of moulded butt-purlins with foliate bosses. Restored by Lee. Chancel roof with two tie-beams and purlins with sunk-quadrant mouldings. One tie-beam dated 1633, which fits well enough. – FONT. C15 and octagonal. Against the stem four lions; against the bowl the signs of the Evangelists and four demi-figures of angels with shields containing the Instruments of the Passion. – FONT COVER. Just the base, but this seems C15 too. – BENCHES. Late C15. One with pierced traceried back. Others just with poppyheads. – SCREEN. Bits under the tower arch. – STAINED GLASS. Early C14 in the heads of three chancel windows; C15 in a nave s window, from the Norwich School, angels playing musical instruments, repaired 1834 by *William Barnes* and 1874 by *D. Chilvers*.

SHIMPLING PLACE, ¾ m. NW. Elizabethan or Jacobean house of the Shardelow family. Two cross gables to the s front. The l. one still has its polygonal angle-shafts but not its pinnacles. Both have stepped gables. The recessed part of the façade is of three wide bays, timber-framed, close-studded, and with the uprights and some tension braces exposed. The ground floor is faced with C19 red brick, probably an underbuilt jetty. Of windows one three-light mullioned window to the E gable, otherwise cross casements and C19 sashes.

All the excitement in Shimpling is on DICKLEBURGH ROAD. Immediately N of the church SHIMPLING HALL, a two-storey, three-bay early C19 brick house fitted with sashes. To the E is LOW FARMHOUSE, a timber-framed C17 house clad with C19 brick. VALLEY FARMHOUSE is the same, but boasts a stack with four octagonal flues and a date closer to 1600.

SHINGHAM

ST BOTOLPH. Redundant. Nave and chancel in one, no longer dilapidated, as it was when Cautley wrote. Norman s doorway and one Norman window. The doorway had two orders of shafts; still in place are their enriched scallop capitals, and several Geometric motifs of decoration in the arch, chevron, rolls and chip carving. Further E two small arched lancets, one bigger than the other. The rest seems mostly early C14, see the windows and chancel piscina. Three-light reticulated E window. Blocked N door with hollow chamfered arches. – FONT. Octagonal, Perp, with shield, flower and leaf motifs. – PULPIT. Jacobean, two-decker. The reader's desk with knobs on the top. – The COMMUNION RAIL is Jacobean too, with turned balusters. – BENCHES. A C15 set with pierced backs and simple tracery motifs, poppyheads, and arm-rests formerly with figures (only one left – a shepherd and his dog), and another with solid backs and flowers as arm-rests. In the early C20 the nave lay unroofed, so their survival is amazing.

SHIPDHAM

ALL SAINTS. Unbuttressed w tower of the C13 rendered above a later brick base with a Perp doorway and battlements. On top – the hallmark of the church, a little clumsy perhaps, but most endearing – a three-tier lantern, of wood, lead-covered. The three little domes have a broken surface, almost reminiscent of Russia, but there are also Gothic flying buttresses to the lower dome and Gothic pinnacles above. Who would venture to date this? Is it of the C16? It certainly is not of the C19 as it is shown in a drawing of 1815. Its nearest parallel is the lantern of St Peter Mancroft, Norwich. The earliest piece in the church is the priest's doorway, which, with its upright leaves in the capitals and heavy roll mouldings and its pointed arch, can hardly be later than *c.* 1190. Of the same time the chancel pillar piscina, with its little central column supporting the draining bowl set in front of and below the pointed arch. This has a corner pier with a weathered capital. A larger arch as part of the same composition frames a single sedile. Dec s and n doorways and n arcade. The last has five bays, octagonal piers and double-chamfered arches. The clerestory also seems to be Dec. Perp most of the other windows (all restored; the chancel e window and the n aisle windows cannot be trusted) and the two-storeyed s porch. The porch has an ogeed statue niche and a three-light parvis window and also a polygonal stair-turret with pink brick carefully arranged as quoins. Perp also the two-bay arcade to the n chapel. In the n aisle an old roof with terrific arched braces as if to support a barn forty feet wide.

FURNISHINGS. FONTS. One is Norman and square, with two rosettes and two sets of three flat arches. Stem consists of five columns with cushion capitals. The other is Perp and has shields in foiled fields. – FONT COVER. C17 volute type, six of the vanes with carved scrolls. – PULPIT. Jacobean; three tiers of panelling to each facet and a fluted and reeded frieze. – STALLS. One good C15 front with three plus four bays of tracery cusping and poppyhead ends. – COMMUNION RAIL. With dumb-bell balusters, probably of the second half of the C17, in n chapel. – COMMANDMENT BOARDS. Painted; very attractive. Dated 1630. They originally formed part of a painted tympanum above the missing chancel screen. The ROYAL ARMS are those of Charles II, i.e. repainted after the Commonwealth (nave w wall but intended to go above the commandment boards). – PARCLOSE SCREENS. To n chapel. Oak and glass, of 1993. – LECTERN. One of the finest wooden lecterns in England. Probably of *c.* 1500. Stand with buttresses in three directions and three lions at the foot just as in the familiar brass lecterns. Double bookrest with closely traceried circles like rose windows, one with quatrefoils and a Tudor rose in the centre, the other three with different mouchette wheels. The stem is a C19 re-creation, but a good one. – STAINED GLASS. e window, a Crucifixion and Last Supper, †1883. n chapel e window, perhaps by *James Egan*, †1906, Nativity. – SCULPTURE. Mother and Child, by *Jane Quail*, of oak, 1990, by the lectern. – MONUMENT. Gothic tripartite wall monument to members of the Bullock family, last date †1868, with Adoration, Crucifixion and Resurrection scenes (n chapel).

SPINKY DEN, Church Close. A late C15 timber-framed range

facing the street. The C16 addition to the rear forms an L-plan. It seems that there were three houses, one to each of the three rooms, or cells, which make up the street range. Not much externally is earlier than C18. Inside are WALL PAINTINGS from *c.* 1680 depicting a hunting scene, and, among other things, a bit of Hebrew text.

SHIPDHAM PLACE, Church Close. The former rectory. Timber-framed early C17 house with a front range added early in the C19. The front has five bays of sashes and a doorcase on columns. The rear pile with C19 and C20 ground-floor windows and five C18 casements above. One good C17 spine beam. C19 stick-baluster staircase.

SHRUB HOUSE, Church Close. C17 timber-framed house with a C19 brick addition at r. angles. In the angle between them is a stair-turret. C19 shopfront with cross casements.

THATCHED COTTAGE, Market Street. Timber-framed, probably late C16, with brick and flint gables of the C17 and C18. Thatched roof. On the junction with MILL ROAD is an early C16 timber-framed house much restored in the C19; the clay lump infill may also be C19.

OLD HALL FARMHOUSE, $\frac{7}{8}$ m. SW on Dereham Road. Another C17 timber-framed house with a brick skin. Two storeys and attic. Three-bay front with giant pilasters, fitted with five bays of C19 sashes. C18 Doric pilasters to the doorcase. The ridge stack has arches to the plinth.

CROWSHILL, 1 m. SW. C17 timber frame with brick gable-ends. Casement windows. Two rebuilt chimneystacks.

ASH FARMHOUSE, 2 m. SW on Dereham Road. Over-restored *c.* 1990. There is C18 chequer brick and evidence of a timber frame. One smoke-blackened late C15 queenpost truss remains in the roof.

BEECH FARMHOUSE, 1¼ m. NE at Thorpe Row. C16 timber-framed house with a brick skin to the S. The screens passage still evident if obscure, as the service doors are re-set. The hall has finely moulded bridging beams, reused probably in the C17 when the hall was floored. Queenpost roof with arched braces to the cambered ties. Externally it appears as a three-bay C19 house.

SHOTESHAM

2090

There are four churches at Shotesham, reflecting four manors and four parishes. The parishes became one in 1731. Two of the churches were in ruins even then.

ALL SAINTS. In the late C14 the nave was given Perp windows and extended, and the chancel rebuilt. Simple C15 W tower. The S nave windows, the SE chapel and chancel windows date from the restoration of 1898–1901, though they may be accurate reproductions. The NW vestry and the winding cast-iron staircase to the tower were added. – FONT. C15, octagonal, with four lions against the stem, four lions and four demi-figures of angels against the bowl. The angels have shields with the emblem of the Trinity and the Instruments of the Passion and three crowns and three chalices (cf. Saxlingham Nethergate, p. 629). – PULPIT and REREDOS of *c.* 1901. – SCREEN. Bits of the dado are copies by *Howard* of Norwich, 1866. – BANNER STAFF LOCKER in the tower. – WALL PAINTINGS. Striking large figure of a Saint (Lawrence?) on the S wall. He is bound at the ankles and wrists and lapped by flames. Like the vine scroll at the NE angle of the nave, reminiscent in style of the paintings at Weston Longville, and likewise *c.* 1360. Above the Saint, fragmentary small figure of a kneeling woman, and on the N wall opposite a male figure with plumed hat; both early C16 and most delicately painted. At E end of S wall, dimly visible remains of large late medieval figure of St George, with raised sword as at Fritton (DP). – STAINED GLASS. E window 1915, by *Heaton, Butler & Bayne.* – MONUMENTS. Several minor tablets. – ALTAR RAIL. C17, turned balusters.

ST MARY, ⅝ m. WSW. The S doorway must be of about 1200, the chancel of the later C13. It has an E window with three stepped lancet lights under one arch. Perp W tower of knapped flint with brick bell-openings, which presumably are part of the 1535 work mentioned in a bequest for 'building steeple'. The nave also is of brick in its upper parts. The three Dec windows are of 1879. Perp N chapel with a doorway to the N, said to have been built for Bartholomew White † 1495. Single-braced nave roof, arch-braced chancel roof. In the chancel the piscina is surrounded by a number of decorative brick panels, representing a swan, a double eagle and a lion. – FONT. C15. Octagonal. Four lions against the stem, four lions and four angels with shields against the bowl. – LECTERN. Very nicely made up from the balusters of a C17 communion rail. – SOUTH DOOR. With a small plate for the ring decorated with a pair of winged dragons, and a quatre-foiled opening with bars. – STAINED GLASS. Some C15 fragments in the N chapel E window. – BRASS. Edward Whyte †1528 and wife Elizabeth Froxmere †1528. Both died of the sweating sickness. The figures 2 ft 6 in. long (chancel).

ST MARTIN, ⅛ m. SE of St Mary. In ruins and overgrown. Unbuttressed W tower (with, as the indefatigable Cautley noted, a BANNER STAFF LOCKER). The openings of the tower have brick surrounds, the bell-openings with Y-tracery. Low remains of nave.

ST BOTOLPH, ½ m. N of St Mary. A few lumps and bumps in the ground.

SHOTESHAM PARK. One of *Soane*'s early houses, begun in 1784, complete by 1789. His early style is less well known than his very original mature work, but is distinctive in its own right. Built for Robert Fellowes, whose father William bought the estate in 1731. A restrained, very beautiful design. Beige brick of the highest quality with occasional Portland stone dressings. The principal, S, front is only five bays wide and two and a half-storeys high, but of very subtle composition. Soane uses giant Ionic pilasters as his articulation but sets them away from the angles, so that the composition starts and finishes with completely bare wall. He also carries the order up to an entablature on Coade stone Ionic capitals which excludes the upper half-storey. The whole is thus a set piece, set against unadorned brick wall. Within this order his five bays consist of three wide and two narrow ones, the narrow ones left bare on the ground floor except for niches. The wide bays carry on the ground floor the *leitmotif* of the house, a tripartite window of the Venetian type but with the side pieces carried on from the glazed centre arch as a blind arch. The blind arch was to become a trade mark of Soane's elsewhere. Above the half-storey an unenriched three-bay pediment. The E side has a smaller attached portico of four unfluted Ionic columns only one storey high, with a side entrance. The rest is plain, except for the fact that the side windows on the ground floor are set in large blank arches, a very subdued but very effective motif. The seven-bay W side is completely plain save for the recessed centre five bays.

INTERIOR. The fine entrance hall or vestibule occupies the centre of the S front. The doorway leading to the staircase hall beyond has a blind arch echoing the main windows. The staircase winds round three sides of its hall and has a cast-iron balustrade, very discreetly detailed. The staircase window to

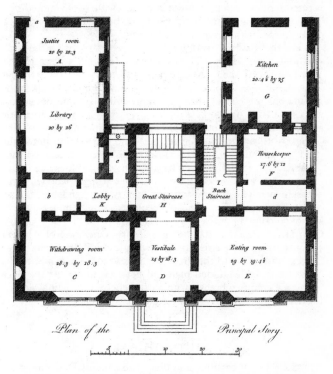

Shotesham Park. Plan of principal floor as completed 1789

the N is of the same type as the façade windows but glazed in the blind arch. To the r. of the hall is the dining room, to the l. the drawing room. The library is to the W side occupying three bays of windows. Beyond that is the justice room with its own separate access, testifying to Fellowes's social and administrative position. On the upper floor a wide corridor from which all rooms are reached, a very sensible, straightforward arrangement.

STABLES with outbuildings by *Soane*, 1784. Red brick. A quadrangular arrangement, each arm of five bays and two storeys, except for the open cart shed to the N. The OFFICES also by *Soane*, and arranged to the rear on an axis with the house and stables, as at Letton.

VILLAGE. The main street through the village is, as so drearily often, called THE STREET. On the S side All Saints Church. The OLD VICARAGE, early C19. Red brick with a gault-brick façade in five bays. The doorcase has an open pediment on unfluted columns. Usual stick-baluster staircase. GROVE FARM-HOUSE was a small timber-framed C16 house to which a taller early C17 addition was made. This part has a lion and a unicorn in brackets supporting a door hood. In the C18 the first house was raised to the same height and given C18 features, such as the vase-turned balusters to the staircase, but the C17 part retains most: a four-centred fireplace with ovolo mouldings, rolled bridging beams, winder staircase beside the stack, clasped purlin roof with diminished principals.

On the N side FORGE COTTAGE, early C18, one storey and attic, C18 casements. Then CHURCH HOUSE, a pleasant C18 pair, also with their C18 casements. TOLLGATE COTTAGE has two C19 canted shop display windows. A floor put inside in the C17, but the early C16 is still represented by one queenpost truss. THE LODGE, *c.* 1830, is notable for its modified Doric porch, the pair of octagonal columns presumably later. Then the DUKE'S HEAD, a former inn. The first edition noted the date 1712, but the 1 and 7 have now disappeared. Shaped end-gables. The front has seven bays plus a narrow blocked end bay on the l. Two storeys, red brick, with two-light wooden cross casements. The doorway altered later. A very handsome house. A roll-moulded four-centred fireplace inside. Timber-framed, though contemporary, rear service wing.

OLD HALL FARMHOUSE, W of St Mary. One wing of a bigger house of *c.* 1700. Two storeys and attic. Five bays, with three cross casements to the first floor (one C20) and sashes to the ground floor. Moulded platband between floors. At the back two big chimney-breasts with partly renewed octagonal shafts.

DAIRY FARM, in the Park. *See* Newton Flotman, p. 563.

6000

SHOULDHAM

ALL SAINTS. Of carstone and flint. The tower is Dec – the wave mouldings to the W doorway, the reticulated W window with its cusped ogee lights, the Y-traceried bell-openings, and the double-chamfered arch towards the nave suggest *c.* 1330–40. Of the same time the nave doorways (that to the N blocked) and the tomb recess in the nave N wall. The recess has a wave-moulded arch. Most of the windows are C15 Perp, especially the two N and S three-light nave windows with rising super-mullions and transoms. The nave restoration of 1870 seems to have been considerate to them but less so to the S porch. A S transeptal chapel is interesting in that the E window has two trefoiled lights and a split cusp, *c.* 1330. The chancel was rebuilt in 1871 by *R. J. Withers*, who provided a generous Curvilinear E window. The cost was borne by Sir Thomas Hare of Stow Bardolph Hall. The late C15 nave roof is something special. It has a fine steep pitch and rests on alternating big and smaller hammerbeams. The hammerposts have carved angels. On the wall-plate boarded coving with a decorated cornice, and on this prominent ashlar struts to the beams. The roof would be single-framed if it were not for the arched braces rising from the big hammerbeams to a collar high up in a similar manner to that at Barney, near Fakenham (q.v., Vol. 1). The S chapel also with a C15 roof, this time a principal-and-purlin type with arched braces to wall-posts, and bosses. – BENCHES. Three with traceried ends and poppyheads and a further five ends stuck on to C19 benches. – FONT. Dull C14 octagonal model. – MONUMENTS. Coffin-lid with foliated cross (outside the S transept), said to come from Shouldham Priory. – Thomas Allen †1841. Signed by *W. Groves.* Standing frontal figure of Faith, rather phlegmatic and soulfully looking up. She holds a wreath. An urn on a base on the l. – STAINED GLASS. Good glass in the E window of 1877 and in the N nave of 1871, both unsigned but looking like *Bell & Almond,* according to Birkin Haward. The chancel window with the Ascension and eleven Disciples, and the nave with a Crucifixion.

Of the PRIORY nothing remains apart from a few earthworks S of Abbey Farm, but the dry summer of 1986 produced clear crop marks showing the Gilbertine house to have had three E chapels and a plan like that of Watton, Yorkshire. Founded *c.* 1190 by Geoffrey Fitzpiers, dissolved 1538 and sold to Thomas Mildmay in 1553. The last of the walling was removed in 1831. The present FARMHOUSE sits over the nave and makes much use of robbed ashlar.

SHOULDHAM HALL. Built *c.* 1830 for the same Thomas Allen whose memorial is in the church. Not very thrilling.

The VILLAGE has a scattering of C18 and C19 houses of little merit. The best are COLTS HALL on EASTGATE STREET, an early C19 gault-brick front to a clunch and carstone house. Its BARN is older, mid-C18, but reusing material from the Priory – see the diagonal corner buttresses and the stepped W and E buttresses. The material is coursed clunch. Roof raised in the C20. On THE GREEN is the five-bay VILLAGE SHOP, mid-C18 with delicate fluted pilasters to the doorcase. The plate-glass shopfront does not help. Next to it is another mid-C18 five-bay HOUSE with a central carriage arch and sash windows. On

WESTGATE STREET is ALEXANDRA COTTAGES, a pleasant semi-detached pair of 1862 in four bays with brick pilasters and casements under hoodmoulds on label stops. Whole flint walls.

EARTHWORKS. In pasture land to the W of All Saints earthworks include large ditched and scarped enclosures of probable medieval date. (AR)

SHOULDHAM THORPE

6000

ST MARY. Of carstone. Nave and chancel, almost entirely rebuilt in 1857–8 by *Salvin* for Sir Thomas Hare. The medieval W tower fell in 1732. The Norman W doorway was originally on the N side. Two orders of octagonal shafts decorated with chevron and herringbone motifs below scalloped cushion capitals. Arch with much zigzag. The chancel has two C13 lancets in the S side with stilted rere-arches inside. – FONT. Perp, octagonal, with a variety of tracery patterns. – MONUMENTS. In the wall one to Jane, Anne and John Stouarde, 1602: three small kneeling figures set within Tuscan engaged columns. Strapwork overthrow to the cornice. – Also a curious tablet in the chancel to Thomas Buttes †1600. In a grey slab an inscription plate, a coat of arms, and an incised alabaster panel with the deceased kneeling.

FOREMAN'S HOUSE, Church Lane. Carstone and brick, split into two dwellings. The exterior details mainly C20 but there are C17 bridging beams with sunk-quadrant mouldings.

SHROPHAM

9090

ST PETER AND ST PAUL. E.E. N doorway with stiff-leaf capitals and a hoodmould with two orders of dogtooth. E.E. also the N arcade of four bays with octagonal piers and double-chamfered arches. Clerestory of circular windows with cusped quatrefoils, aisle and chancel windows Perp but renewed during the restoration of 1867. The chancel windows look accurate, particularly the five-light E window. Perp W tower with chequerwork up the buttresses. Perp chancel with shields at the foot of the buttresses and extremely attractive sedilia and piscina. Three crocketed ogee arches to the sedilia. Shields inside the little vaults. Close panel tracery above the arches. The church contains a few puzzling details. The slab with four-petalled-flower tracery in the nave on the N side is probably a re-set sound-hole. It came from a cottage demolished in 1910, but how did it get there? The two-light window from the E end of the N aisle to the nave can hardly be anything but a squint. Nave roof with kingposts on moulded tie-beams with arched braces and an embattled wall-plate, chancel roof of principals on wall-posts. Aisle roof 1867. – FONT. Late C14, octagonal, with small heads supporting the embattled bowl. – FONT COVER. Elementary Jacobean. –

SCREEN. Moved to its position under the tower when Thomas Beny provided new furnishings in 1528. C14. With shafts instead of mullions, carrying intersecting arches. Simple Curvilinear tracery. – STAINED GLASS. S chancel has a Nativity in a wooded landscape, 1898, by *Mary Lowndes*.

SHROPHAM HOUSE, Watton Road. Of *c.* 1800 for Sarah Leathes. Simple gault-brick house of two storeys in five bays. Hipped roof. Later wing added 1856.

SHROPHAM HALL. An imposing if not beautiful brick house begun in 1685 but not complete until 1739. The façade is of five bays with giant pilasters framing the advanced centre three bays. Parapet, raised in the centre and pierced with sashes on top of which is a gable, with another sash lighting an attic. The parapets to the side bays have blind windows. Early C19 porch with a balustrade, door with a broken segmental pediment. Kitchens and office wing to W added in 1894.

SILFIELD *see* WYMONDHAM

SISLAND 3090

ST MARY. Built in 1761 on the S side of a preceding church which was struck by lightning. Of the old church one pointed arch remains in the new, and rather more masonry in the flint N wall than one first notices. This wall in fact may be early, perhaps C12. Imposts for the old round-headed N door. The new church is an engaging little building. Nave and chancel of brick, once whitewashed, and thatched. Over the W end a weatherboarded bell-turret with pinnacles and a spike. The wooden windows of Y-tracery, a favourite C18 motif. Inside, a W gallery on iron rods. Tripartite chancel arch with unfluted columns carrying pointed arches separating the two parts. – FONT. Octagonal, C15. Against the stem four lions, against the bowl two lions, four demi-figures of angels, and two flowers. – FONT COVER. Simple, C17. – STAINED GLASS. In the chancel various parts of the 1761 glazing; figured roundels and some enamel panels, and very yellow borders.

SNAREHILL 8080
½ m. S of Kilverstone Hall

SNAREHILL HALL. A five-bay brick house of the later C18 whose claim to prominence rests with the cast-iron veranda which extends the full width of the façade, put up in the first years of the C19 with other alterations. The former STABLES and tack room have timber-framed parts from the early C18, but most is C19, incorporating the remains of a CHURCH with long-and-short quoins, a C13 pointed arch and possibly a central tower.

SNETTERTON

ALL SAINTS. Redundant. The chancel seems to be of the late
C13 with early C14 alterations, but is too much restored (in
1852) for this to be certain. Ladbroke's drawing shows the chancel to have been higher in the 1820s, and the then E window
blocked. The double piscina looks decidedly older than the Dec
N window and is probably late C13: two trefoiled arches on
shafts with little capitals. Dec w tower, see the bell-openings of
two different designs. Perp N arcade (elongated piers with thin
shafts and long hollow chamfers) and N aisle windows. Perp
also the s windows. s porch in building in 1501, according to a
bequest; two storeys, wave-moulded arch. 1852 the nave and
chancel roofs. – FONT. C14 bowl with encircled quatrefoils and
tracery patterns. – SCREEN. 1852. One-light divisions without
tracery but with dainty cusping and subcusping. Ribbed coving
to E and W. – STAINED GLASS. E window and W tower by *M. &
A. O'Connor*, c. 1860.

OLD RECTORY. Of the mid-C14 timber-framed hall house we
have only the screen doorways to the service rooms, but they
are worth seeing. Two trefoiled arches with punched decoration
in the spandrels. The frame here is of heavy timbers with the
principal posts rising into the first floor where there are as many
as three tiers of tension braces. The next details are C17 when
the house was evidently remodelled: stacks inserted, of which
one fireplace remains. Diamond-mullioned window upstairs to
the rear. Two-storey, five-bay façade of rendered clay lump and
brick, C18 and later.

SNETTISHAM

ST MARY. Set on a hill E of the village and perhaps the most exciting C14 Dec parish church in Norfolk; and how much more
exciting it would be if its chancel – 40 ft long – had not been
demolished by Sir Wymond Carye in the late C16! Only a few
fragments of its walls remain but these give its length and width.
The commanding crossing tower with its fine spire, 175 ft high
(spire rebuilt in 1895), and dainty flying buttresses that connect
it with the pinnacles of the tower, stands now at the E end.
Below the spire a tall tower with slender blank panelling, open
only in two correspondingly small bell-openings. Two chancel
roof-lines to the E. The two transepts are not of even length.
That on the N side seems earlier than the rest of the church and
is the shorter of the two, having been reduced in 1597. It has
Y-tracery and intersecting tracery. The s transept is three bays
long, the nave five. *Frederick Preedy* reorganized the base of the
tower as a chancel in 1855–6 and made general restorations.
The glory of the church is the W front, with its fabulous six-light
window, the best Dec example in Norfolk. It repays close study,
especially of the use made of the reticulation and the mouchette
motifs. Big buttresses flank the front and develop above, by

means of squinches, into polygonal turrets. Below the w window is a shallow tripartite porch vaulted in three bays. Thin buttresses and openings with continuous chamfers. The aisle (alternating petal tracery and mouchettes) and transept windows are less daring. The s transept s window has five lights; it is not specially large but has good mouchette tracery. In the clerestory alternation of two-light windows and circular windows with three spherical triangles (on the s side the tracery is c19), set within arches of the same shape inside.

The INTERIOR is remembered by its very tall five-bay arcades with piers of composite section, basically four shafts and four thin filleted shafts in the diagonals with hollows between. Polygonal capitals to the cardinal points but the mouldings of the diagonals continue uninterrupted into the arches which have in addition double chamfers and sunk quadrants. Seats round the piers. Nave roof with sweeping arched braces up to the collar and two tiers of moulded purlins, much repaired in 1899 when the transept roofs were replaced. The sawn-off bases to the wall-posts once had winged angels. Homespun bracing to the aisle roofs, no doubt 1899 too. The crossing arches of the same type as the arcade. Handsome if curious half-arches at the E end of the aisles. They are in fact strainer arches bracing the tower and seem to be a slightly later addition. The aisle windows gathered under a continuous stringcourse which also takes in the w wall.

FURNISHINGS. FONT. The bowl is c14 or c15. Octagonal with moulded capitals and abaci to connect with the c19 marble supports. *Preedy* restored it. – PULPIT. Perp, but mostly of 1856, when it was restored and repainted on the original pattern, remains of medieval paint then being seen by Preedy. The painting is startlingly bright. – LECTERN. Latten, a material superseded by brass *c.* 1500. With an eagle. Early Tudor. Of the same group as East Dereham, Walpole St Peter, and also Exeter Cathedral. – SANCTUS BELL. Displayed in nave. c13, which is very rare, and of a slender waisted shape similar to a bell at Chaldon in Surrey (according to an attached note). – STAINED GLASS. The w window †1846 by *William Warrington*. With big shaped medallions of Old Testament subjects. – s aisle w by *M. & A. O'Connor*, 1861. – s and N aisle E by *Preedy* †1858 and †1861. – MONUMENTS. Brass in the s aisle, w end, with figures on both sides: a Lady †1570. Palimpsest with a Lady of *c.* 1500 (mounted on wall). – Brass in the N aisle, w end: John Cremer †1610, wife and seven children, each figure separate. – Sir Wymond Carye †1612. Standing alabaster monument with recumbent effigy on a pillow or a half-rolled-up mat. Coffered arch on two columns. Good strapwork cartouche. Original iron railings (N transept). – Two Styleman monuments with urns in front of an obelisk, †1768 and 1803 (s transept). The signs of the change of style are most informative. – Two more Stylemans opposite: Mary †1807 and Henry †1819, husband and wife. The wife by *Richard Cooke* of London. They are identical, with an urn on a tall pedestal in front of an obelisk.

OLD HALL, W of the church, on the main Lynn Road. Carstone with brick dressings. Complicated building history. In the Middle Ages the manor had been held by the Duchy of Lancaster, and after 1485 became crown property. In the early C17 Sir Wymond Carye held the manor from the crown, and in 1614 Sir Henry Carye bought it from James I. How the house appeared at that time is difficult to say, but it seems to have been an H-plan with a central hall, E solar and W service range, and was presumably C16. These components are still recognizable in the interior. The date 1632 appears on the otherwise C18 W service range projecting S from the principal front.

The Styleman family acquired the house in 1710 and the building we see now took form. S front of nine bays with shallow two-bay wings and a five-bay centre. The wings have Dutch gables and the two-storey central porch an open pediment. It is evident from the fabric that these details were grafted on to an earlier house, probably for Nicholas and Armine Styleman in 1737, the date and initials recorded on two S rainwater hoppers. Another, dated 1734 and also with initials NAS, appears N of the E bow window. The sash windows are not earlier than this. Before his death in 1819 their grandson Henry Styleman engaged a builder, *Richard Egmore*, to remodel the E part internally, including a new entrance hall occupying the E bay of the former hall, entered through a pedimented porch attached to the r. of the five-bay centre, where a window had been. A N staircase beyond this entrance hall with iron balusters and the plaster ceiling above it are likely to be associated with accounts of 1817 which refer to 'new building'. The full-height bow window to the E return also of this time. After the Hunstanton Estate passed to the Stylemans in 1839, they adopted the name Le Strange (*see* p. 439) and eventually sold the Old Hall in 1871. Sir Edward Green bought the estate in 1877 and began the New Hall (*see* below). Restored 1978–80 and now a Sue Ryder Home.

STABLES. Coursed carstone. Of the mid C18. Two storeys and five bays. The S front has tripartite sashes to the ground floor and slatted windows above, with a dovecote in the middle. Platband between the floors. The rest rather rebuilt.

NEW HALL or KEN HILL. By *J. J. Stevenson*, 1878–80. One of the earliest provincial examples of the 'Queen Anne' style which Stevenson, with others, had pioneered in London a few years earlier. The concept is 'Gothic', based on the solar-hall-service disposition of the post-medieval house, but with details of, loosely, Queen Anne's time, and the execution of thoroughly Victorian opulence. The freedom from imitation of anything in particular and yet the character of period allegiance are indeed remarkable. Stevenson's patron was Sir Edward Green, the son of the Wakefield inventor who patented the 'Green's Economizer'. This recirculated previously wasted heat from steam boilers, and made the family fortune. Green took over the firm in 1865 and later consolidated his social rise by purchasing the Old Hall estate in 1877, ignored the Old Hall, and built Ken Hill as a retreat rather than a permanent home. This explains its only moderate size. The first thing unusual about the principal, s, FRONT is the use of a *piano nobile* for the main rooms, the second thing is its irregularity. The raised principal floor allows for better views towards the sea and certainly adds interest and character; the irregularity is the result of the plan. The balustraded STAIRCASE rises to the doorcase beneath an open pediment (and, rather unhappily, directly under a small balcony to the window above). One then enters via a passage similar to a screens passage with, on the r., the DINING ROOM in the projecting gabled wing with its timber oriel. To the l. is the four-bay SALOON, exactly comparable to the great hall familiar from late medieval houses. At the time Stevenson was writing his *House Architecture* from which we learn that 'the place of great reception rooms might in many cases be supplied by a Hall of the old type'. The W bay is emphasized into something of a dais bay and projects in a suitable manner. Behind the hall, at the W end, is the DRAWING ROOM, sited as usual to catch the evening sun. Its position is that of a medieval solar wing. The kitchens are on the ground floor, bedrooms on the first floor.

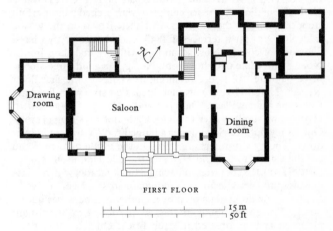

FIRST FLOOR

15 m
50 ft

Snettisham, Ken Hill. First-floor plan

The principal windows have Gibbsian surrounds under segmental arches blocked with keystones. Inside, the plasterwork between the heavy ceiling beams of the saloon is Neo-Adam, as is the rather more elaborate plasterwork of the drawing room. The 'Queen Anne' fireplaces repay study, particularly in the BEDROOMS and more particularly for the lustre-painted tiles by *William De Morgan* in his pre-Fulham style, and here doing for tiles what Morris was doing for wallpaper.

STABLES. Also by *Stevenson*, with a cottage, arranged round a courtyard. Coursed carstone. Arches to the SE screen wall run into the cottage and the return of the stable block at either end. *Stevenson* also provided forecourt WALLS to the SW of the

house, with vermiculated entrance piers to the E side. The
estate incorporates LODGE HILL FARMHOUSE, ⅝ m. SW of the
house. Late C17 carstone house on the lobby-entrance plan.
Two storeys in three bays. Rustication round the central door.
Derelict at time of writing.

SNETTISHAM HOUSE, ⅝ m. S of the church. C18 but remodelled
in 1863 and 1883. Stuccoed brick. N front of two storeys in five
bays, the outer two gabled. Central porch in Gothic style. The
STABLES to the E have more original mid-C18 work. Three-bay
pedimented centre pierced by the carriage arch with extensions
r. and l. The GARDEN WALL to the w of the house dated 1702,
but the SUMMERHOUSE in its Gothick guise must be late C18.
Two storeys in three bays, with a central arched entrance with
an arched window r. and l. A further piece of WALL, this time
serpentine, runs off from the summerhouse.

MANOR FARMHOUSE, Bircham Road. Carstone and brick, two
storeys in three bays. The façade has remains of early C17 windows, at least in their shape. The doorway with a chamfered
surround.

VILLAGE. Plenty of agreeable houses in the village. At the junction of HALL ROAD and Lynn Road is IVY COTTAGE, a
Gothick building of c. 1840, complete with arched windows and
stepped gables to the outshuts. In LYNN ROAD on the w side
first Nos. 37–43, a terrace of 1838, each house of two bays.
Carstone of course. Nos. 37 and 39 with original shop fronts,
No. 43 with a late C19 shop front. No. 45 is a good three-storey,
three-bay late C18 house retaining its sashes to the first floor.
No. 47 (HOPE HOUSE) also late C18, two storeys in five bays
facing the Market Place. Pilasters r. and l. No. 131 (THE ROUND
HOUSE) was built as a tea room for Catherine Styleman (†1793).
One storey but five-sided under a hipped roof. Y-tracery in win-
dows. The attic dormers are C20. On the E side of Lynn Road
are the stables to the Old Hall and the Old Hall itself. No. 12
(THE HOLLIES) deviates in having a brick façade, which is late
C18 despite the datestones announcing 1757. Two storeys in
five bays, the floors separated by a platband. There was once a
porch. No. 44 was built in 1867 as the lodge to Snettisham
House. Carstone dressed in gault brick. One storey in three
Gothick bays. Rustication round the openings. Bow window
faces the road.

OLD CHURCH STREET. ROSE AND CROWN pub. Whitewashed carstone. Two storeys in four bays. Early C17 but the
details C19. To its w is a later range. OLD VICARAGE. Early
C19. Coursed carstone. End pilasters to entrance side. Four
bays, two storeys. Outer bays set back slightly giving a depth to
the front. The porch added late C19.

Nos. 1–2 SCHOOL ROAD are a pair of two-storeyed houses
of the early C18, but one looks above the C19 and C20 ground-
floor alterations to see this, apart from the doorway to No. 2.
First is the moulded platband and then the four cross casements in rusticated surrounds. To the s is a workshop range
with no less than five datestones, all declaring 1793.

WATER MILL, Station Road. Carstone. S part dated 1800, with a granary extended to N in the later C19. Both parts under independent hipped roofs. The undershot wheel and machinery are to the S.

SNORE HALL see FORDHAM

SOUTH ACRE

8010

ST GEORGE. The N chancel chapel and N nave arcade were established by the early C14 (see stained glass, below). The arch from the chapel into the chancel has polygonal moulded capitals to the semicircular responds, a thick fillet running down the respond, and an arch with a sunk-quadrant moulding. These details repeated in the W bay of the N arcade. The rest of the N arcade is later (two bays, octagonal pier, arches with one chamfer and one hollow chamfer), and its replacement left a narrow (15 in.) piece of wall in the middle of the W pier: early C14 on the W side, mid-C14 to the E. A larger area of blank wall between the chapel arch and the E arcade respond probably always existed. The Early Perp tower has a four-centred W doorway with tracery in the spandrels and shields with the Harsyck arms. Panel-tracery three-light W window with a castellated sill. Crenellated parapet. Dec one S window in the chancel, with reticulated tracery. Another, probably re-set, in the nave on the S side over the door. The other two S windows are three-light and Perp. There is no S aisle. The nave N doorway is mid-C14, with double wave-moulded arches. Perp N porch with niches and wave mouldings in the arch too. In the chancel a low tomb recess, a piscina with shelf, and a window with bars towards the N chapel replacing a larger window. Handsome nave roof with hammerbeams and arched braces nearly up to the ridge, and linked to the ridge-piece by square posts. These trusses alternate with smaller arched braces from the principals to the ridge posts. Arch-braced aisle roof. – FONT. Plain, Norman, on five supports. – FONT COVER. Perp canopy, rather crude. The inscription refers to Geoffrey Baker, rector, who died in 1534. Restoration in 1966 by *J. L. Royal* amounted almost to a replacement. Paint on the upper parts conserved by *Pauline Plummer*. – SCREEN. Under the tower arch. Poorly preserved, but very fine. C14 and not too late. With shafts with a ring instead of mullions, and ogee arches very richly crocketed with leaves. These, although already knobbly, still show different species in the style of the early C14. Behind the leaves a delicate reticulation net. In the middle a quatrefoil, perhaps a wrongly placed Perp piece. – BENCHES. Six low Perp benches with poppyheads and a few small animals, e.g. lions, on the arms. – CHEST. With carved front, little blank cusped arches, and large rosettes. – RAILING. Of c. 1620–5; to the N chapel (see monuments, below). – STAINED GLASS. In the N chapel E window grisaille fragments of the early C14, not figurative, restored by *George King & Son*. – In the N window later C15 canopies, more in the one Dec s nave window.

MONUMENTS. Wooden effigy C14(?), lying in the chancel tomb recess but not made for it. The body chopped down to a featureless chunk; only the head better preserved. – Beautiful brass to Sir John Harsyck †1384 and wife Katherine (N chancel chapel). The figures are over 5 ft long. They hold hands. A helmet and shield above their heads. – Brass to Sir Roger Harsyck †1454. In pieces and not exhibited. – Brass to Thomas Leman †1534. Kneeling figure dressed as a priest, 15 in. long (between chancel stalls). A missing scroll led up to a plaque with the Virgin Crowned. – Sir Edward Barkham †1634 and wife, in the N chapel. Big standing alabaster monument. Against the tomb-chest three kneeling daughters and two kneeling sons separated by a gruesome charnel-house panel. Recumbent effigies, old-fashioned by this time. Sir Edward, who was Lord Mayor of London in 1621, wears his mayoral robes over armour. A skull at their head and a skull at their feet. Back wall with arms and two figures, a young woman holding a wreath, and a skeleton in a shroud. Attributed by Adam White to *John* and *Matthias Christmas*. – In the churchyard a headstone with a putto, about 3 ft tall and holding a Rococo cartouche.

THE HALL, immediately w, really a farmhouse. Late C16 timber-framed house faced with flint and brick, and in its details C20. The ridge stack has four octagonal flues.

OLD RECTORY, opposite the church. Brick with stone dressings and flint. Late C18. Two-storey s front in three bays with two full-height bow windows separated by a door and doorcase of Roman Doric columns under a broken pediment. E bay and return added 1841. Stick-baluster staircase.

SOUTHBURGH

ST ANDREW. Largely rebuilt in 1878–82, at the expense of Henrietta Susannah Gurdon, but enough evidence of the old survives. A restoration was at first contemplated by *J. A. Reeve*, the Diocesan Surveyor, but a rebuilding proved necessary. The Y-tracery windows were reused, as was the chancel arch of *c.* 1300. The nave windows are Dec, except for one large Perp window on the s side, a usual improvement. E window with inter-secting tracery. The tower with a recessed spire dates from 1881. – SCREEN. The base of the C15 screen is preserved. – STAINED GLASS. One window (s nave) with somewhat Expressionist figures by *Leonard Walker*, 1935.

WILLOW FARMHOUSE, River Lane. Early C17 timber-framed house with an C18 rear extension which in fact blocks some original windows. Brick returns. The façade windows are C20. The lobby-entrance partly blocked off.

MANOR FARMHOUSE, ⅝ m. SE. Brick. The C17 block doubled in size in the C18. From the first date two cross casements to the first floor.

RED HALL, 1¼ m. w. C18, brick, with rusticated pilasters. Three
bays in three storeys, with a lower service wing at the back.

SOUTH CREAKE

8030

ST MARY. A big church. The chancel is 52 ft long and dates from
the late C13 (see the intersecting and Y-tracery, the chancel
arch, the fine shafting of the five-light E window, still with stiff-
leaf capitals, and the angle piscina, also still with a stiff-leaf
capital). The sturdy W tower is Dec (see the arch towards the
nave and the large four-light W window with its reticulated tracery and the Dec bell-openings), Dec also the aisle E windows,
and the S porch with its nice entrance and the top frieze of stone
and flint with crowned Ms (for St Mary). Late Perp aisle and
clerestory windows, including a tall clerestory E window,
and predominantly Perp the wide interior, made the better by
the pamments and floor tiles. Most of the pamments inserted in
1932. Arcades of five bays. The piers have big polygonal projections to nave and aisle, smaller demi-shafts with capitals to
the arches. Double-hollow-chamfered arches. Seats round the
piers. Perp sedilia and piscina, damaged. Top frieze below the
window-sill with demi-figures of angels. Also Perp the pretty
small window at the E end of the N arcade, looking into the N
chapel or sacristy added c. 1410–20. It is a two-light window,
and its purpose is obscure, probably no more than to allow the
sacrist to view the congregation; it has no liturgical function.
The arch is four-centred and has fleuron decoration. The spandrels have foliage. The aisles were restored 1927–33 and chapels
made at the ends. The late C15 or early C16 nave roof has
hammerbeams on long wall-posts connected by longitudinal
arched braces. On the hammerbeams arched braces up to the
ridge. Most of the angels' wings are of 1958. The aisle roofs are
also Perp. They have arched braces on wall-posts and bosses
etc. Against the solid spandrels of the braces on the S side only
are relief carvings of animals. Chancel roof C19.
    FURNISHINGS. FONT. Perp, octagonal, on two steps, the
upper with blank tracery. Against the stem defaced figures,
against the bowl defaced representations of the Seven Sacraments
and the Crucifixion. Remains of colour. The stanchion for the
font cover remains fastened to the roof ridge. – SCREEN. Early
C15. With one-light ogee-headed divisions separated by compound stiles, with wave mouldings. Much panel tracery above.
Fine, quick rhythm. On the dado blank two-light tracery. The
paintings on the dado are thoroughly defaced. Central doors. –
ROOD. Installed in 1982 from St Mary-at-the-Walls, Colchester
(1872 by *Sir Arthur Blomfield*), and restored by *Pauline Plummer*.
– PULPIT. C15, hexagonal, with tracery panels and some painting, most of the colour stripped off by a bad restorer in 1927. –
BENCH ENDS. Some C15 ends against the chancel walls by
the screen (and a great number of late medieval ones stacked in
the tower ringing chamber). – LECTERN. 1838, an unusual date.

– WALL PAINTING. Over the window at the E end of the N arcade (DP). – STAINED GLASS. Much C14 and C15 glass preserved in the S aisle E (plus a Swiss C16 Betrothal), N aisle E (C14 canopies and head and arms of Christ in the Crucifixion) and four N aisle windows. In 1454, 5 marks were left to glaze a N window. – BIER. 1688, made by *Goodman Foster* for £1 6s. 6d. – CHEST. Early C19 Italian, and a fine panelled piece with egg-and-dart to the bottom rail. – ROYAL ARMS. George II, made in 1740. – BRASSES. Priest of c. 1400, an 18 in. demi-figure (nave W end). – John Norton †1509, with his parents, 3 ft figures (nave floor). The mother has been completely rubbed away.

Former CONGREGATIONAL CHURCH. 1783. The present front is an addition of 1896, of three bays, with intersecting tracery. Behind it lies the old building. Pointed windows with casements imitating three-light intersecting tracery. Brick quoins. Hipped roof.

LEICESTER SQUARE FARM, off the Fakenham Road 1⅝ m. SSE. A model farm of 1791–3 and 1798–9 by *Samuel Wyatt* for the Holkham Estate, and one of the finest in the county. The complex is arranged axially with the house at the W, the barn and two stable ranges E of it forming a yard (now with C19 buildings inside it), then an area of grass before convex brick and flint walls giving on to a beech-lined avenue to the far E.

The FARMHOUSE is of three by two bays, and has rare mathematical tiles imitating gault brick. Entrance to W (garden) side approached by a short flight of steps to the doorway with Doric pilasters and pediment. The centre bay is advanced with its own crowning pediment. The E side has a pair of single-storeyed quadrants reaching towards the stable blocks and terminating in little square hipped blocks, that to the N rebuilt C20. The house itself is of 1801. The BARN is 1793. Red brick with gault-brick dressings. Very Neoclassical for a farm building. Two storeys. The E side has honeycomb ventilation panels below six Diocletian honeycomb panels. There are three projecting cart entrances opposing each other to N and S, all with pediments. The gable-ends and the W side rather mutilated and rebuilt. Of the two STABLE RANGES extending from the S and N ends of the barn W towards the house, the S one is a little sorry-looking now. The original elevation seen in the N range comprises a two-storey granary tower to the E and W ends with a seven-bay lower stable range between. Like the barn their brickwork is laid in English bond, in Wyatt's case a revival rather than a survival.

Also on the Fakenham Road, COMPTON HALL FARM, which may be by *Wyatt* too. Rendered brick two-storeyed HOUSE in five bays, the centre three broken forward very much like those of Wyatt's model farmhouses elsewhere on the Holkham Estate. Much of the S front is of the late C19, but of c. 1800 certainly the plan and concept. The returns to the house are developed as separate three-bay houses: arched central doorways. Screen walls to E and W with two-storey towers. N of the house, on an axis like Leicester Square Farm, is the BARN. Flint and gault brick. Two storeys, organized in elevation as three separate three-

bay structures end-to-end. Each has an opposing cart entrance
with a round-arched window either side, all with plenty of rustication, repeated at the corners. The first floor has honeycomb
ventilation panels. Between the barn and the house a pair of
STABLE RANGES closed the courtyard, although the E range is
now gone. The W stables with two-storey granary towers at
either end and lower stables between, just like Leicester Square.

BURNHAM FARMHOUSE, Burnham Road. A C17 house of
knapped flint with an early C19 N front. The S front of five bays,
the windows C20. Gable-ends with rusticated C17 window surrounds. The BARN is also C17, of coursed clunch blocks dressed
with brick. It is in fact three barns built edge-on to each other.

DEFENDED ENCLOSURE. On Bloodgate Hill ¾ m. SW lies a single
ramparted Iron Age camp. It was originally circular and measured some 800 ft across, but is now much denuded as a result of
C19 levelling.

SHRUNKEN VILLAGE EARTHWORKS, SE of the church, include
three tofts and a hollow way. (AR)

SOUTHERY   6090

ST MARY (old). 300 yds E of the present church is the ruin of the
old one. Carstone, ashlar and brick. Nave and chancel. The
walls stand up, but there are no details, except of various brick
repairs and an ogeed N door. When Ladbroke drew it about
1823, the church was still complete. It had a wooden bell-turret.

ST MARY (new). The new church is of 1858 and was designed by
Higham & Robinson. It is a neat building of carstone slips – thin
tiles of carstone – and Bath stone dressings. Square W tower
with a plate-tracery W window. Broached spire. Two-light plate
tracery designs also to the N windows but otherwise the windows are lancets. N porch added in 1904. Circular piers to the
four-bay arcade. – SCREEN. With Curvilinear tracery. – CROSS.
In the churchyard, a C15 stone cross base with shields and the
letters L.A.

SOUTH LOPHAM   0080

ST ANDREW. South Lopham has the most powerful Norman 4
tower of any Norfolk parish church. It is a central tower, and it
is, to judge by its detail, no later than 1120, and perhaps earlier.
It was restored in 1963. It stands on a W and an E arch with
strong shafts and low, broad block (not scallop) capitals and has
one strong roll moulding in the arch. There are shallow N and S
wall arches too, and they may or may not indicate the existence
or the intention of transepts. The former is unlikely considering
the small S doorway set in the wall here no later than *c.* 1200
and the lancet in the N wall. Externally the tower of South
Lopham has four arched and decorated stages, but all the
decoration is elementary. On the N side an oblong stair-turret

runs up, completely undecorated. The arching is on the first
stage simply two large arches with a pillar between, and they
occur only on the N and S. There follows an arcade of three plus
three smaller arches with single-scallop capitals and a middle
pillar, then a two-light window, and above that the two-light
bell-openings. The details can all be compared with the work of
Losinga's time at Norwich Cathedral, i.e. before 1120. The top
has Perp flushwork-panelled battlements (bequests for 'makyng
of the stepyll' in 1526). Rising up the corners of the tower are
diminishing clasped buttresses.

The nave has Norman evidence too, the chancel has not. In
the nave, N doorway with one order of shafts and zigzag in the
arch, i.e. later than the central tower. It appears to have been
moved in the C14 from the S side and cuts into Norman external render. But the final surprise of South Lopham is that to
the W of that doorway there is, in the usual position fairly high
up, a circular, unmistakably Anglo-Saxon window. So the central tower was added to a Saxon church of some size.

The chancel is Dec, whether one can trust the renewed E
window or not. It was restored in 1866, the rest of the church in
1874. The S aisle also must be Dec; see its windows and the
four-bay arcade of roughly quatrefoiled piers with the lobes to
nave and aisles having broad fillets, left without capitals (though
the abaci take them in) and carrying arches with one hollow
chamfer and one sunk wave. For the dating of the Dec parts
Cox points to the record that Nicolas de Horton, rector from
1361 to 1380, was responsible for the chancel. That demonstrates
how late purely Dec forms were being used in the county, and
there is no reason to doubt it. Big Perp W window, and prominent Perp clerestory of knapped flint with brick in the arches of
the windows and lettered flushwork panels between the windows.
This is c. 1470, about the same date as the simple hammerbeam
roof in the nave. In fact it is a false hammerbeam roof. In the
chancel, roof of very low pitch with tie-beams on arched braces.
– FONT. C14. Octagonal, with very delicately cut, shallow tracery
(cf. North Lopham). C17 crown cover. – BENCHES. C15. The ends
carry blank tracery. In one end a small standing female figure.
Figures of animals and also a young man on the top instead of
poppyheads. – CHEST. A dug-out, 8 ft long, upstairs in the tower.

Nos. 1–2 and Nos. 4–5 THE STREET are timber-framed cottages
typical of the area, of one storey and attic. The better outlying
FARMHOUSES include OAK TREE FARMHOUSE on Low
Common: early C17, timber-framed on the lobby-entrance
plan. The main ground-floor rooms both have sunk-quadrant
bridging beams – an early C17 feature. OXFOOTSTONE FARM-
HOUSE on Brick Kiln Lane has a brick E gable to the S wing
with burnt headers arranged in a diamond pattern; blocked
windows and twin hexagonal flues to the stack. Jettied cross wing
to W. The rest is timber-framed and C16. PRIMROSE FARM-
HOUSE, Primrose Lane, ½ m. SE of the church, has a C19 brick
skin over a C16 timber frame, extended C17. The W gable-end is
jettied over a two-bay C16 shop window.

SOUTH PICKENHAM

8000

ALL SAINTS. Just inside the park to the Hall (*see* below). Round tower with originally a round Norman arch to the nave (remains of PAINTING on it), later reduced in size, at the same time that the top stage was done as a C14 octagon with mouldings up the edge and bell-openings with cusped Y-tracery. The same tracery in the nave on the N side, and in the chancel on the S side. The chancel E window is of four lights and has reticulated tracery. Angle piscina with trefoiled head. The treatment of the mouldings is unusual. There is an odd circular chimney on the N side. From the restoration of 1907 (£1,300) a peculiar roof with arched braces, arched the wrong way structurally, i.e. like looped-up curtains. The roof was raised to take in the reticulated window in the E nave gable. Nave roof collapsed 1604 and rebuilt, rebuilt again in 1907. – FONT. C14. Octagonal. The stem curves out into the bowl. Rolls at the angles. Pointed quatrefoils on the bowl. – PULPIT. Polygonal, early C18. – ORGAN CASE. High Victorian. Gothic. By *Pugin* and made for Augustus Sutton, Rector of West Tofts from 1849. – WALL PAINTINGS. St Christopher, S wall, originally *c.* 10 ft high; C14. Several post-Reformation texts. – MONUMENTS. Two identical tablets l. and r. of the altar, both signed by *John Ivory* of Norwich, the one 1759, the other 1790. – Thomas Lennard Chute †1722, attributed to *Edward Stanton* and *Christopher Horsnaile* (GF).

PICKENHAM HALL. 1902–5 by *Robert Weir Schultz* for the banker G. W. Taylor. Red brick. Five-bay E front, with three cross casement windows. Neo-Georgian, but featuring big shaped gables, in an Arts and Crafts spirit. Entrance in W front under a bold semicircular broken pediment with figures of big boys, the sculpture attributed to *Laurence Turner* (also over the E front doors). Rustication r. and l. S front with two-bay loggia on an Ionic pier. Bays either side with shaped gables.

Neo-Georgian also the STABLES. KEEPER'S LODGE is early C20 and attributed to *Schultz*. Flint dressed with brick. Two storeys and lower wings. S front with a bow window. In the garden two panels from the PARTHENON frieze. These were against a tall parapet to the l. and r. of the pediment of the preceding mansion, which had been built by *Donthorn* in 1829 for W. L. Wiggett Chute.

HOME FARMHOUSE, ⅛ m. N. Early C17 house rebuilt in 1773. W front with a projecting centre bay incorporating C17 flintwork. Door under segmental head. Wing to E.

SOUTH RAYNHAM

8020

ST MARTIN. Unbuttressed W tower of pebble and stone dressings. Two-light Dec W window and belfry windows. Nave with straight-headed Perp windows. A mixture of Dec and Perp windows in chancel. Roofs from the restoration of 1861. – ALTAR. The step, according to Cautley's convincing suggestion, is a former mensa-top (or stone slab). The edge decorated with a close band of square quadripartite motifs. Is it C13?

UPHOUSE FARMHOUSE, $\frac{7}{8}$ m. s. C17 flint house remodelled early in the C19. Of the latter date the tripartite sashes. To the N are blocked mullioned windows from the C17.

SOUTH RUNCTON

ST ANDREW. 1839 by *John Brown* of Norwich, the County and Diocesan Surveyor. Neo-Norman, but replacing a Norman church, drawn by Cotman. The chancel arch, though pitilessly renewed, is in fact original. It has two orders of shafts on drum bases, the capitals midway between cushion and scalloped. Above this surely completely renewed: zigzag in the arch, billet in the hoodmould. Brown's chancel is apsed; the N vestry, also apsed, is of 1856. Big pilasters to W front and pilasters too between the nave windows. – STAINED GLASS. St Andrew, very elementary. In the E window. – MONUMENT. Robert Peel, of Wallington Hall, by *W.J. Donthorn*, carved by *F. Mace* in 1843.

At COLLEGE FARM is a C16 aisled BARN. Timber-framed with brick added as infill, but otherwise weatherboarded. Five bays, plain aisle-posts with the usual tie-beam and arcade plate braces. Roof with diminished principals and arched wind-bracing.

SOUTH WOOTTON

ST MARY. The nave W side and the NW buttress have quoins which look like the long-and-short quoins of an Anglo-Saxon nave. Early C14 chancel, see the Dec tracery of the four-light E window, the Y-tracery on the s side, and the simple sedilia and piscina. NW tower of galleted carstone and brick rebuilt *c.* 1890. Arched W window and bell-openings. To the s is a one-storey extension of 1985 forming the present entrance, through which one goes under a 1985 gallery fitted up with a C19 balustrade from St Matthew, Norwich. The odd shape of the transepts and their canted W walls look C18 rather than late C14, as they are supposed to be. Attached to the N side of the chancel in 1896 a mausoleum, now the vestry. Hammerbeam roof in nave *c.* 1880. – FONT. Late Norman. Square, on nine supports. Monster faces at the corners. – HEARSE, in the new gallery. With long inscriptions; dated 1611. – MONUMENT. Sir Thomas Winde †1603. Altar-tomb sarcophagus with shallow bracket-like pilasters. No effigy (N chancel). – Edmund Hammond †1643 and wife Maria †1660, in the churchyard, just s of porch. Brick tomb-chest, faced with stone.

OLD HALL, Hall Lane. Carstone house with brick dressings and a W façade of two storeys and only two bays. The bays separated by quoins and each gabled. Casements, to the r. with transoms. In the r. gable head the date N H 1665 (Nicholas Hammond).*

SPOONER ROW

0090

2½ m. s of Wymondham

CHAPEL. Built as a school at the junction of Station Road and Chapel Road. Red brick, with straight-headed lancets under hoodmoulds, each separated by stepped buttresses. A low sanctuary to the E. By *John Buckler*, 1843.

PILGRIM'S FARMHOUSE, Chapel Road, to the E of the chapel. Long two-storeyed timber-framed house of the mid C16, modernized in the early C17, fitted with C19 casements and given a brick s gable. A three-celled house, with traces of mullioned windows and a good C17 stair-turret to the rear (E). In it a fine dog-leg staircase with acorn finials and dado panelling. The off-centre stack serves an arched fireplace to the s room, but was extended to the N, heating the principal room. There was once a winder staircase to its w. The N end of this room has two blocked doorways with flattened arched heads, indicative of a C16 through-passage plan. The roof has ties on arched braces and wind-braces; the frame jowled principal studs.

SPORLE

8010

ST MARY. Norman evidence in the chancel, namely remains of blank arcading in the NE and SE corners, clasping buttresses outside, and a blocked N window. Then a complex, not at all clear, C13 and C14 history. The responds and piers and their capitals are all round or quatrefoil, but they differ to a slight degree, and it looks as if the chancel N chapel (of one bay) comes first, the N transept second, the s transept third, and then nave s and nave N. But from the restoration of 1897–8 by *H. J. Green* one should acknowledge the roofs of the nave and N chancel aisle, the s nave arcade and the clerestory above, part of the chancel N wall and the complete reconstruction of the N chapel and sacristy. The sequence therefore depends on how faithful was Green's work. If it was accurate the distance in time for the whole sequence cannot be large. Also there is the break w of the transept arches, if such they can be called. Does it represent a former wall? Externally the evidence of this important E.E. and Dec phase in the history of the church is the blocked N doorway, the excellent chancel E window (three lancets and a big octofoil in plate tracery under one large shafted arch, and flanking niches inside), and the w tower, evidently of the C13. Big w doorway with three orders of colonnettes and a finely

* REFFLEY TEMPLE. Where Temple Road now is was a plain brick building, erected 'by a Friendly Society' in 1789 and enlarged in 1831. Next to it, in a small circular pond, was a tall, needle-like OBELISK, re-erected in 1756. Engulfed by a housing estate and demolished in the 1980s.

moulded arch, tower arch dying into the imposts, bell-openings
with cusped Y-tracery and a cinquefoiled circle in the spandrel.
Top stage Perp with flint and stone panelling. It ought to be
noted how the base course cuts the colonnettes of the w doorway about their bases. On the s side of the nave all, on the N
side most windows Perp (one here has reticulated tracery). The
Perp tracery is typical of the neighbourhood with its stress on
straight shanks of arches. Money was left to make them in 1474,
and in 1496 for the 'reparation' of the s aisle. Perp chancel arch
with double wave mouldings on older semicircular responds. –
FONT. C13. Octagonal, of Purbeck marble, originally with the
familiar two shallow blank arches on each side. – SCREEN.
Remains only of a C15 parclose screen. – WALL PAINTINGS.
On the s wall of the s aisle, many small scenes of the Martyrdom
of St Catherine, contained in some twenty-five compartments
set out in four rows. There is a clear stylistic break between the
first eleven compartments and the remainder; both costume
and style suggest that the former are late C14 while, curiously,
the others may date from several decades later. (DP)

OLD VICARAGE, The Street. C17 timber-framed house with brick
gable-ends, given a fashionable, but irregular, brick front in the
C18. This is of two storeys and an attic. Mixed C18 casements
and early C19 sashes. A C19 wing to the rear matched a C17
wing opposite, altered and joined with the main front block, so
creating a U-plan of dubious pedigree.

WOLFERTON HOUSE, ¾ m. s of the church. Late C18 brick house
with a three-storey block framed by one-storey pavilions r. and
l. The pavilions have arched casement windows, the centre-piece
has two Venetian windows to the ground floor. Pedimented
doorcase.

EARTHWORKS of the DESERTED VILLAGE of Great Palgrave survive in pasture s of Great Palgrave Farm. Six or seven tofts are
strung out along the w side of a former street. Further earthworks
including a small rectangular moat lie to the w and NW of the
farm. This was a satellite of Sporle (as was Little Palgrave,
another deserted site) and never large. It probably disappeared
in the C15. (AR)

9020   STANFIELD

ST MARGARET. Good later C13 chancel, though the (convincing)
E window dates from 1864. The unusual motif is the strong
shafts and well-moulded rere-arches inside. The windows are
lancets or have two lights with Y-tracery. Double piscina with
pointed trefoiled arches. Of the same or a slightly later date the
w tower. Y-tracery w and belfry windows. Trefoil openings below
the bell-stage. Fully C14 the s porch and the N and s doorways.
The N and s windows of the church are Perp, of three lights and
with panel tracery. Good headstops to the straight hoods. –
FONT. Plain octagonal. – FONT COVER. Simple, Jacobean, with
turned balusters and a ball finial on top. – PULPIT. Made into a

rustic two-decker, but originally Jacobean with blank basket arches and arabesques. The tester added C18. – SCREEN. Simple, C15, tracery with carving in the spandrels. – BENCHES. With poppyheads and animals on the arms. – COMMUNION RAIL. Jacobean, with flat balusters.

STANFIELD HALL. *See* Wymondham.

STANFORD   8090
In the Battle Zone (*see* p. 14).

There was only a small village.

ALL SAINTS. Norman round tower with an arch to the nave which has one order of shafts, single-scallop capitals and a roll moulding. C15 polygonal top with four belfry windows and four blank windows of the same design imitated in flush-work. Nave and aisles, chancel, and remains of the W arches of N and S chapels. The S aisle demolished in 1772 and rebuilt during the restoration of 1851–5. The N aisle and chancel were before then in a ruinous state, so the degree of restoration is pronounced. Arcades of three bays. Slender quatrefoil piers with thin shafts in the diagonals. The chancel arch of the same type, and the chancel E window with reticulated tracery (renewed), i.e. all in the style of the early C14. Nave roof C19. – At the E end of the S aisle built-in small architectural fragments, including a little Norman zigzag. The foundations of an C11 apse were discovered beneath the chancel floor in 1851. In 1993–4 the corrugated iron covering the windows was removed and the roofs clad with steel, but resembling pantiles. – STAINED GLASS. In N aisle, parts of a figure by *Rev. F. H. Sutton*, 1853.

STANHOE   8030

ALL SAINTS. The exterior has a crisp look for which the 1853 restoration may be responsible. Of about 1300 the SW tower, used as a porch, unbuttressed, with Y-tracery in the bell-openings. There were 'reparations' in 1470 and a restoration in 1910. The S doorway inside the porch looks, if anything, yet somewhat earlier. Of about 1300 also the W window (three lights, intersecting tracery), the N aisle wall with doorway and windows, the arcades of four bays with octagonal piers and double-hollow-chamfered arches, the chancel arch, and the chancel doorway and windows (Y-tracery). The windows are shafted inside. Dec S aisle windows, Dec sedilia and piscina with ogee arches; good. C19 kingpost nave roof. – FONT. 1853, as are the PULPIT, READING DESK and COMMUNION RAILS. – STAINED GLASS. By *Charles Kempe*, and very early, the E window. It is of 1879 and better than most later Kempe glass, including even the S aisle E window of 1885. A S chancel window apparently a *Holiday* design, †1873, and another †1869 by *Ward & Hughes*, six figurative medallions. Further good s and n aisle windows, †1878–98. – MONUMENT. Small model for a Grecian tablet to Mrs Everard †1841. With two mourning female figures (vestry).

STANHOE HALL, NW of the church on Docking Road. A good, simple house of 1703 built for Jane Turner when she married Thomas Archdale M.P. Her father Sir Thomas Turner, one of the influential King's Lynn family of merchants, lawyers and politicians, paid. Sir John Turner had commissioned the King's Lynn Customs House from Henry Bell in 1683, and perhaps the Duke's Head Inn, also in Lynn, *c.*1684. This association and certain similarities to *Bell*'s style support the attribution to him. The stonemason was *Thomas Kempe*. Brick, seven bays, two storeys, hipped roof. s (entrance) front with slight three-bay projection at the centre. Ashlar dressings and quoins. Doorway with broken segmental pediment on consoles, the pediment above a bolection-moulded frieze. The back has a one-bay projection and doorway with a triangular pediment. Double-pile plan with the usual central corridor, here running E–W on both floors. Many of the chimneypieces have bolection mouldings. Pretty staircase with three twisted balusters to the tread and a panelled dado. The house is advanced for Norfolk, especially the plan, the bolection mouldings and the Classical style. There is nothing vernacular about it. At the E a small ORANGERY, added mid C19.

BARWICK HOUSE. *See* Barwick, p. 195.

STARSTON

ST MARGARET. The battlements of the w tower and the s side of the church have flushwork diapering. s porch with fleurons up the jambs and arch and on the abaci of the entrance. The arch is C15 but the rest of the porch rebuilt during *Phipson*'s 1870 restorations. He added a n aisle as well, and seems to have completely rebuilt the chancel. C15 arch-braced nave roof. – FONT. Octagonal, Perp. Four lions against the stem, four shields and four flowers against the bowl. WALL PAINTING. During the 1870s restoration a superlative deathbed scene was discovered in a tomb recess in the nave n wall, but unfortunately destroyed. It was very close in style to the mid-C13 paintings at Horsham St Faith Priory (q.v., Vol. I). – MONUMENTS. Bartholomew Cotton †1613. Tablet with kneeling effigy. – Robert Ferrier †1767. Pretty tablet with putto heads at the foot.

HOME FARM, immediately N, built as Starston Place Farm. Model farm of *c.*1840, illustrated in the 1846 edition of Loudon's *Encyclopaedia*. The architect was *Samuel Taylor* of Stoke Ferry working for his uncle Meadows Taylor. The materials are flint with red brick dressings and the arrangement is of various stock sheds round a cattle yard. Lodges were included as well, notably PHEASANTRY COTTAGE, perhaps better described as a garden house: single-storey, of clay lump and with a four-centred door-way to the N and generous bargeboards. HOME FARM LODGE reverts to flint and brick, one storey and attic. The HOUSE, also by *Taylor*, was a stark five-bay, three-storey building demolished in 1962.

RECTORY, Harleston Road. Outwardly of 1871 but the remodelling conceals an early C17 timber-framed house. Five bays of sashes in two and a half storeys.

STARSTON HALL, 1¼ m. N. Of *c*. 1600, but cased with mid-C19 brick and given stepped gables.

WHITEHOUSE FARMHOUSE, Cross Roads. C16 timber-framed hall house subjected to the usual insertion of a floor in the C17. The conversion resulted in a lobby-entrance plan. Traces of pargeting cling to the five-bay façade. YEW TREE FARMHOUSE nearby has a late C19 brick skin but is an early C17 timber-framed house with mullioned windows and a fireplace bressumer reportedly from Rushall Priory. The pattern of C17 houses encased in C19 brick is seen everywhere, e.g. THE WILLOWS, Rushall Road, and LAURELS FARMHOUSE, Skinner's Lane.

STOCKTON

3090

ST MICHAEL. Rendered round tower with a pretty, recessed lead spire and round bell-openings with wooden inserts. Brick two-light W window, C16. Nave and chancel in one, thatched. The windows Dec and Perp, except for one late C13 lancet W of the S porch. Perp three-light E window. The porch is of brick and dates from the C16. In the C17 the gable was refashioned to be one of the shaped gables then in use. At the SW corner of the nave a reused corbel with roll mouldings, apparently C17. Arch-braced roof on wall-posts inside. – FONT. Original C14. A heavy piece with the four signs of the Evangelists in figures nearly in the round. – FONT COVER. Jacobean, with crocketed edges. – COMMUNION RAILS. C17, turned balusters and newels. – BENCH ENDS. Some C15 poppy-heads. – STAINED GLASS. C15 and C16 bits in S and N windows. Chancel S has two figures. – The E window by *E. Suffling* of London, *c*. 1890, over-coloured.

CHURCH FARMHOUSE, no longer used as a house. C17 red brick but a timber frame apparent to the S end. Irregular spacing of the E front windows suggests an earlier house too, although the sunk-quadrant mouldings on the tie-beams are fine for early to mid C17. More mid to late C17 is the shaped N gable with the circular window. External stack to W front. Brick C17 BARN, knocked about.

STOKE FERRY

7000

ALL SAINTS. Nave and chancel and bellcote. The chancel was taken down in the C17, the tower fell in 1578 and additions were made to the E and W ends by *William Newham* of Lynn in 1822–3. Rebuilt in 1848 by *Donthorn*. The chancel arch could be Perp. Flamboyant tracery in the windows. – FONT. Octagonal, Perp, with Flamboyant tracery patterns. – STAINED GLASS. E window by *William Culyer* of Norwich, four lights. The rest by *Heaton, Butler & Bayne*: S chancel, Saints, *c.* 1862; N chancel, Saints, *c.* 1880; W window, Suffer Little Children, 1866.

The village centre is known as THE HILL. On it, opposite the W side of the church, STOKE FERRY HALL. Built probably for the Bradfield family in 1792; plain, but imposing. Double-pile plan. Red brick, five bays and two and a half storeys. The centre bay projects a little. The wide doorway with an open pediment on thin Tuscan columns is the only moment of excitement. The ground-floor windows have blank tympana (cf. Soane at Ryston Hall). Considering the house has been offices since 1959 the interior has survived well, see the three-bay hall with pilasters and a groined plaster vault.

CROWN HOUSE, now offices and looking C19 in its rendered carstone façade. Two early C16 bridging beams with double wave mouldings to the S room.

ALL SAINTS LODGE, also opposite the church, on the main road. The W half demolished in 1977 leaving a façade with four C18 sashes and other, blocked, windows. The ridge stack with its eight lozenge flues is late C17, as are the two Dutch gables to the rear.

The VILLAGE has several pleasant houses. On LYNN ROAD is BAYFIELDS, formerly a house and shop, now offices. *c.* 1700. Various blocked openings. The bay window to the r. was for shop display. COBBLES is another early C18 house converted to offices. Door to r. under an open pediment; door to l. now a sash window. A barrel-vaulted entrance passage leads to a closed-string staircase with a moulded handrail and panelled newels. To the W on WRETTON ROAD is CANTERBURY HOUSE. The E front has three bays to the S end all of *c.* 1700: moulded brick platband and eaves cornice, though C19 sashes. N part also three bays, and with flintwork. Stack with triple octagonal flues suggests late C16. In the kitchen a wave-moulded bridging beam, also C16; central room with C18 large-framed panelling. The HIGH STREET runs SE from the church. There are few highlights. No. 1 (PARK HOUSE) is *c.* 1770, of clunch and carstone, with a rendered brick façade. Rather forbidding. Two and a half storeys, four bays. The entrance in the W return. The OLD GRANARY is a converted (1982) mid-C18 maltings with additions of 1910. Two storeys and an attic in the mansard roof. STABLES and the MALTSTER'S HOUSE go with it, the latter the village surgery, with a mansard roof to the rear and a doorcase on fluted columns to the front. The sashes late C19. On the S side of the street THE OLD CHEMIST'S SHOP, with its return backing on to the churchyard. The shop range dated 1824. Rear wing late C18.

STOKE HOLY CROSS   2000

HOLY CROSS. Simple W tower fitted with lancets to all but the belfry stage, where Perp windows are found. Crenellated parapet. Most of the windows renewed during the 1879 restoration. The chancel seems to be of the late C13, although the chancel arch is C19. In the E wall three separate stepped lancets. In the side windows also lancets. The nave windows all altered. There were originally here also divers lancets. Four-centred brick S doorway protected by a porch erected in 1501. Brick entrance arch. Nave roof with scissor-bracing at the top, mostly C13, ash-laring and a wall-plate. C16 chancel roof with arched braces on wall-posts. – FONT. C15, propped against the tower outside. Symbols of the four Evangelists against bowl panels, C15. – MONUMENTS. S wall of nave, outside, Thomas Havers †1719. Segmental pediment over inscription panel, emblems in apron panel. – Dorothy Burnn, †1653. A headstone against the chancel outside wall, and an early example for Norfolk. – STAINED GLASS. E window by *Ward & Hughes*, †1873, but the best is by *J. & J. King* in S and N chancel, †1847–1909. – BANNER STAFF LOCKER, with pointed head, in the tower.

The VILLAGE is disposed along Norwich Road, with spurs leading off. The church is at the S end. RUMMER INN, *c.* 1700, T-plan. Four-bay façade in two storeys with a platband at first floor. No longer a public house. To the S in SHOTESHAM ROAD stands GOSTLEYNS. It has received too much attention since built *c.* 1550, especially in 1948, so one scratches for details. Timber-framed. SE front still with some C18 casements. N gable has a C17 mullioned window, the mullions ovolo-moulded. NW front jettied to S end. Under the jetty a six-light mullioned window, the mullions hollow-chamfered, i.e. C16. Bressumers remain to fireplaces, otherwise rebuilt. C17 bridging beams and C18 roof. Notable is BOSCARNE, a house of 1976 by *James Cornish* for himself. From the road it is an austere two-storeyed building, but there is a three-sided courtyard behind, reduced to a single storey, but with lively massing. That it is untainted by the prevailing 'cottage vernacular' is welcome indeed; rather the style is vaguely Hispanic, but so well done that it fits.

MILL ROAD is ¾ m. N of the church. The gigantic MILL was built over the river in 1776 as a flour mill, but was enlarged from 1814 by Colman's as a mustard mill, their first. Converted to a restaurant in 1962. Timber and weatherboarded, painted dazzling white. Four storeys. The MILL HOUSE also 1776. Two storeys in three bays, altered. First-floor sashes with pediments.

STOKE HALL. Only the quadrangular STABLE BLOCK and its tower survive, isolated on a rise of ground and derelict. By *Salvin* for Henry Birkbeck, 1852–3 at a cost of £8,300. The rest demolished *c.* 1936.

ABBOT'S FARMHOUSE, 1¼ m. E of the church. Also by *Salvin* for Henry Birkbeck, 1860: red brick, three storeys and big enough to cost £3,000.

BLACKFORD HALL. *See* p. 208.

STOW BARDOLPH

HOLY TRINITY. Of carstone. W tower with renewed Norman windows and a wide Norman arch towards the nave. The rest of the tower Perp, with big brick buttresses. The church was restored by *Raphael Brandon*, 1848–9, but in the process he practically rebuilt the nave and chancel and added the chancel aisle. W of the porch on the N side one window in the Norman style, probably based on the existence of one here in the old church. Also of the old church the early C14 arch of the N doorway and the E.E. sedilia and piscina, these however completely renewed. – ROYAL ARMS. Of Charles II, well carved. – STALLS. In the chancel. Two with MISERICORDS referring to the Hare family: one has a hare gripping the Hare arms and on the other a hind holds the arms of Bishop Hind. How they loved that kind of conceit in the C15! – Hare Chapel to the N, 1624, of brick. It abuts the N chancel and has two three-light Perp tracery windows, with a transomed version to the E. This is a Gothic survival rather than revival. In it the Hare MONUMENTS; the Hares held the manor since 1557. Sir Ralph †1623. Alabaster. Tomb-chest and upper structure with two columns and obelisks at the top. Much strapwork – a lively design. – Sir Thomas †1693. White marble. Semi-reclining figure in Roman armour and a wig. No back architecture. Thickly fluted cornice at the top of the base. The attribution is to *Grinling Gibbons* (GF). – Susanna †1741. By *Peter Scheemakers*. Semi-reclining in loose draperies. Classical reredos background with two cherubs' heads in clouds. White and grey marble. – Mary †1801. White marble against a grey obelisk. Standing figure of Hope leaning against an urn with the usual extinguished torch etc. Signed by *McDaniell*. – Sir Thomas †1834. Tablet of white marble. Charity and probably Faith and Hope, and between them two inscriptions. By *William Theed Jun.* – Also tablets †1597 and †1619. – Perhaps the most remarkable monument is the wax effigy of Sarah Hare who died aged eighteen in 1744, of blood poisoning after pricking her finger while busy on some needlework. Her face and hands were cast from the life in accordance with her will and the resulting half-figure placed in a mahogany cabinet with a glass front. Restored 1985–6 by *Jean Fraser* and *Judith Doré*.

STOW BARDOLPH HALL. 1873 by *David Brandon*, demolished in 1994.*

The local public house is, not surprisingly, THE HARE ARMS, an C18 brick house with an attached barn, the barn converted to a restaurant. Pleasant. On the same corner but opposite are the ALMSHOUSES, first of 1603 but rebuilt *c.* 1870 in carstone with three gabled porches and Y-tracery in the windows.

---

* For Sir Thomas Hare, replacing a house of 1796 which in turn superseded the original of 1589. Large, Tudor, of brick, with an asymmetrical tower with steep roof, but not an accomplished building.

STOW BEDON

9090

ST BOTOLPH. Nave and chancel; the W tower fell in the C18. W
porch of 1887 protects an early C14 doorway. Hexagonal bellcote from the thorough restorations of 1852–3 by *John Brown*.
In the chancel a small N lancet, with a round arch inside; perhaps Norman. The piscina also round-arched, and with dogtooth. E window with Curvilinear tracery of the stem-and-leaf
variety, widely popularized in the 1330s by the Lincoln Bishop's
Eye. In the nave a Dec N window and Perp S windows with
embattled stepped transoms. – FONT. Big, octagonal, Perp, but
so re-worked in 1852 as to appear all of that date.
STOW BEDON HALL, ⅞ m. SSE in Lower Stow Bedon. To the W
three bays of an early C18 house. Early C19 extension to the E.
Many details C20.
BRECCLES HALL. *See* Breccles.

STRADSETT

6000

ST MARY, in the grounds of Stradsett Hall. Unbuttressed W tower
of the C13. The unusual twisted shafts of the C13 bell-openings
reused in the Perp top stage. Nave and chancel in one. Most of
the cusped intersecting windows date from the 1891 restoration
funded by Sir Alfred Thomas Bagge of the Hall. The E window,
though, is C15, of three lights and with a row of upper sub-
panels. The S doorway is C13 again, with a hoodmould on two
good heads, but its porch was added in 1891. Priest's door also
C13. C19 hammerbeam roof. – STAINED GLASS. Quite a spectacular E window of glass made in Augsburg, Germany, dated
1540 and bought by Thomas Bagge in 1820. It represents the
Adoration of the Magi and contains many large figures. The
beautiful small Crucifixion with angels above a roundel with
the Holy Lamb in the W window probably also belongs to it. –
Five windows of 1891 commemorating the Rev. Philip Bagge
(rector of Walpole St Peter, †1890). – MONUMENTS. Under
the chancel seats a brass to Thomas Lathe †1418, military dress.
– Wall monument, N chancel, to Thomas Philip Bagge †1823.
Signed by *Sir Richard Westmacott*. Seated mourning woman. –
Mrs Grace Bagge †1834, on the opposite wall. Two embracing
angels in flowing robes. Unsigned, but by *Westmacott* as well. It
is virtually identical to Westmacott's memorial to Elizabeth
Wilmot at Berkswell, Warwickshire, of 1818, and cf. the Maitland
monument, Trinity College, Cambridge.
STRADSETT HALL. Elizabethan house of E-shaped plan with
wings projecting only a little. The length of the S front is
altogether eleven bays. The façade was plastered in 1819 when
a good deal of work was done for Thomas Philip Bagge who
inherited in 1807. Of this date are the sash windows, giving a
late Georgian appearance to the exterior (the original intention
was to demolish the house and to rebuild elsewhere in a new
landscaped park). Two storeys and dormer attic under a wide

hipped roof. The N front is slightly irregular, of three storeys cramped under a low roof. The house was built for the Picot family but came to the Bagges in the mid C18. In front of the façade are fine mid-C18 GATEPIERS and wrought-iron gates with elaborate scrolled overthrows.

PARK. Thomas Bagge first approached Repton in 1808, then John Haverfield and finally *J. C. Loudon*, who remodelled the park between November 1810 and February 1813; the resident foreman was *Alexander McLeish*. Between the house and the large lake behind it Loudon provided a curiosity, a BRIDGE over the ha-ha incorporating a cattle gate, all of cast iron.

PARADISE FARMHOUSE, ¼ m. E. Fragment of a major Elizabethan house reduced in the C18. Carstone with brick dressings. What survives is the E gable wall with two set-offs and big polygonal angle-shafts on bell-based plinths rising to circular finials. In the wall between, probably re-set, an inscription tablet, below a pediment. It reads:

> Condidit has aedes Franciscus nomine Parlet
> Lustra decem atque duos cum pl. . . vixerat annos
> Annum si domini queris si tempora regni
> Ecce notae subsunt hic quae tibi singula monstrant.
> 1600 R. Eli 42*

Both this gable-head and that to the W have C18 brick tumbling. In the W gable two C19 windows in C16 ovolo-moulded brick architraves. The S front is of three bays, fitted up with sashes and a mid-C19 door. Two ovolo-moulded window surrounds again. Plenty of moulded bridging beams inside, of the ovolo and hollow type.

STRATTON ST MICHAEL

ST MICHAEL. Short unbuttressed W tower with a recessed wooden turret carrying a spirelet. Chancel early C14 with reticulation in the E window, but also Y-tracery and a piscina still without an ogee. Blomefield records that the Rector, John Cowall (1479–1509), had a brass of 1487 mentioning that he 'made this chancel new'. It must refer to embellishments only. Perp nave. – FONT. C15. With four lions and four demi-figures of angels. – SCREEN. Only the plain dado. – BENCHES. Perp. Some ends with poppyheads, two with figures in relief below the poppyheads. Some of the benches have castellated tops like little turret platforms instead of poppyheads. – COMMUNION RAIL. Later C17, with dumb-bell balusters. It was apparently originally three-sided. – STAINED GLASS. C15 fragments in nave window heads. E window and a chancel N and S window, *c.* 1850 by *Joseph Grant*. W window of similar date and again by *Grant*.

* 'Francis Parlet founded (built) this house when he had lived for more than 52 years. If you ask what was the year of Our Lord or the regnal date, look, here below are the indications which show each of them to you: 1600, the 42nd year of Elizabeth's reign'.

OLD RECTORY, SE of the church. Late C16 and picturesque. Timber-framed with a jettied upper floor on carved brackets and shafts; one four-light and one five-light mullioned window. Four-centred doorway set to l. Inside is a good staircase with carved newels and a moulded handrail.

SURLINGHAM   3000

ST MARY. Norman round tower with an octagonal top tallying with bequests of 1458–66. This has cusped windows to alternate facets. N arcade of three bays with circular piers, circular abaci and double-chamfered arches, later C13. The W and N walls have lancet windows. The N doorway of brick seems to be C18, the same date probably as the brick chancel with its intersecting windows. Chancel arch C18 too. Y-tracery S nave windows, also C18. The restoration came in 1840. S porch rebuilt 1859. An odd detail is the vestry N wall, which is faced with stone blocks. – FONT. Octagonal, C15. Against the stem four lions, against the bowl four lions and four angels holding shields with the symbol of the Trinity and the Instruments of the Passion and three crowns and three chalices. – STAINED GLASS. Original bits in the N aisle E window. – BRASSES. John Alnwick †1460, a 25 in. figure in academic dress (between chancel stalls). – Richard Louhawkys †1513, a chalice brass (below the altar rails and step).

ST SAVIOUR, ⅜ m. NE. In ruins. Hard to decipher. C12 with a nave, a central space and a chancel. The central space has a brick W arch and a flat buttress to the N. Doubtless it carried a central tower. Parts of both the W and E walls are preserved.

OLD METHODIST CHAPEL, The Green. Odd in that it was a barn converted to a chapel in 1803, closed in 1979 and converted to a house. Each phase recognizable.

MANOR HOUSE, Bramerton Road. Of red and blue brick, originally probably in a chequer pattern. It was a one-storey house raised to two storeys in the C18. C19 sashes and casements. A cross wing added in 1736 has Dutch gables N and S, i.e. shaped gables finishing in pediments. Further C19 alterations.

THE CROFT, The Street. A farmhouse dated 1615. Flint and brick. One storey and dormer attic, now with C19 and C20 details, but with a nice date plaque: Robert Gillyans XXII Mayie 1615. C18 extension to S. BARN 25 yds E. Flint and brick, stepped S gable, suspicious datestone, 1664, re-set. Real date c. 1720.

COLDHAM HALL INN, 1¼ m. ENE of the church, by the River Yare. A pleasant two-storey, three-bay house dated 1802.

SWAFFHAM   8000

ST PETER AND ST PAUL. Open to the N behind old trees, but hidden from the Market Place and approached from it by a narrow passage, Church Lane. Very big grassed churchyard with ranks

of simple monuments. A large church, the size and character of,
say, Lavenham in Suffolk. Of flint and Barnack stone and, with
few exceptions, Perp. The exceptions are the s aisle w window
with reticulated tracery (squeezed in by the tower), the e window of the s transept with Curvilinear tracery, and the blocked
n doorway, which may be even a little earlier still. A second
blocked door at the end of the aisle is later c14, probably for a
chapel. But the grandeur of the exterior of the church is all Perp
of the c15 and the early c16. A rector, John Botewright (rector
1435–74), undertook the rebuilding of the chancel, and compiled the *Swaffham Black Book* from 1454. Mainly an inventory,
it does however state that 'Swaffham church built' in that year,
presumably meaning his chancel finished. The n aisle added,
or rather the wall rebuilt, in 1462 at the expense of John
Chapman. The tower was the subject of bequests from *c.* 1485
but was not complete in 1507 when *Master Gyles* was called in.
The tower roofed in 1510 and the bell-frame installed in 1515,
although the battlements had to wait till 1533. That seems to
mark the completion of the church. It was a little restored in
1848–51, a lot restored in 1876 and 1888–95 by *William Milne*.

Spectacular n side of seven bays with big windows and
clerestory of thirteen windows under basket arches, repeated
on the s side. Crenellated brick parapet to the n only. n transept
(much renewed), vestry of two storeys, the upper floor of which
contains the parochial LIBRARY. Chancel with tall renewed
windows, the e window with its wild Curvilinear forms entirely
of 1853. On the s side, in addition to the transept, the small
projecting chapel of the Guild of Corpus Christi added by a
benefactor †1501. Surprisingly large four-light window.

Less than lavish s porch with a cusped lozenge frieze above
the entrance, a niche, pinnacles, but – and this is lavish – a
pretty little hammerbeam roof inside donated by William Coo
(†1518). It has three bays, with angels against the hammerbeams and tiny angels back-to-back as bosses on the ridge.
Finally the tower. Set-back buttresses. Base course with shields,
mouchette-wheels and panels with crossed keys and crossed
swords (St Peter and St Paul). w doorway with niches for
images. w window of five lights with diagonally placed,
canopied niches in the jambs. Three-light bell-openings.
Openwork battlements, pinnacles, and angels instead of intermediate pinnacles. Also inscribed PETVR and PAWLE. Sweet
little Gothick lantern and spike, lead-covered, erected in 1778
to *John Frost*'s design but rebuilt in 1897.*

The INTERIOR, after this exterior, is a little disappointing in
its uniformity and reasonableness. Seven arcade bays, with thin
piers of four almost detached shafts. There seems to be a change
of plan in the two w bays, for here the piers are on polygonal
bases and have polygonal capitals, but the rest have rounded
bases and capitals of an early c14 type. It would appear that an
early c14 church was extended two bays w and given a high

---

* The original was of 1511 by, probably, *John Patryck*; the plumber *Richard English*.

clerestory in the C15. The arcade has double-hollow-chamfered arches. The chancel arch indeed corresponds to the E piers. The tower cuts into the last arcade bay. Under the tower the springers for a low fan vault, though the tower arch is very lofty, so there must have been a change in plan and the vault never built. The aisle windows are placed in tall blank arches. A big squint, big enough to walk through, connects the N transept with the chancel and at the same time gives access to the vestry. Over the nave a wonderful early C16 double hammerbeam roof 37 with angels with spread-out wings against the end of the hammers; angels also in front of the ridge struts which stand on the collars. Traceried spandrels, decorated wall-plate, long wall-posts. It ought to be remembered that the upper hammerbeams are in fact false (cf. Tilney All Saints) and that the roof was restored in 1888–95 by Milne. – FONT. 1851, of Caen stone. – STALLS. Two engaging early C16 pieces in the chancel. The N one has a scene of a woman holding counting beads at the stall of a shop, and then again looking out of the door. The other has two travellers with backpacks, beneath them a chained and muzzled dog. – STAINED GLASS. In the E window, 1853 by *Wailes* (signed with his monogram). Resurrection and two tiers of Saints either side, very colourful. Chancel side windows by *Heaton, Butler & Bayne* c. 1878 look dull by comparison, S transept E window by the same firm, but better, †1875. In the S chapel rather wooden figures of saintly warriors by *William Morris & Co.*, †1918; World War I battle and other scenes below. C15 fragments in N aisle and transepts. – BRASS to Sir John Audley; c. 1530, a 2 ft 2 in. figure (S transept facing S, mounted on the wall). – MONUMENTS. John Botewright †1474 (chancel N). He was Chaplain to Henry VI and Master of Corpus Christi College. His tomb, in its founder's position, is a low recess with a Tudor arch, coarse cusping, and battlements. Tomb-chest with four shields with the symbols of the Passion, Trinity and Botewright's rebus – three boats and three augers, i.e. a boat-wright. The monument has been moved twice – in 1745 and in the late C19, when the canopy was lowered, leaving room for the priest's effigy but not for the original angel supporters. – Katherine Steward †1590, Oliver Cromwell's grandmother. Kneeling figure within a surround consisting of a pair of true Roman Doric columns (i.e. unfluted) under a strapwork achievement. To the l. of her head 'Resuscitabor et vivam' (S transept).

THE TOWN

Swaffham's importance in the Middle Ages stemmed from its position as a crossroads on main E–W and N–S routes, not for its position on a river. The market and two fairs were established by the mid C13 on the triangular Market Place bounded on the N by the present Lynn Street. It was probably open to the church on the E side, but C17 development has closed this off and The Shambles have grown up within the middle, further reducing the size of the open space. The Market Cross, erected in 1575, stood N of the present Shambles, but by 1783 was invisible from the surviving open part, and was demolished. The late C18 was a period of some social importance for the town, when it became at least locally fashionable. There had been a racecourse since the C17 and the Earl of Orford founded the Coursing Club in 1786. The Assembly Rooms came in 1817. Only the cars spoil Swaffham, clogging the Market Place, but fortunately no new roads have been made for them in the centre, so one can navigate as easily with *Faden*'s 1797 plan as with that printed here. The existing impression of the centre is mid to late Georgian, but there is evidence for C16–C17 work behind many frontages.

Perambulation

The MARKET PLACE has a nice irregular shape, the main part funnel-like, widening to the N and continuing round an island,

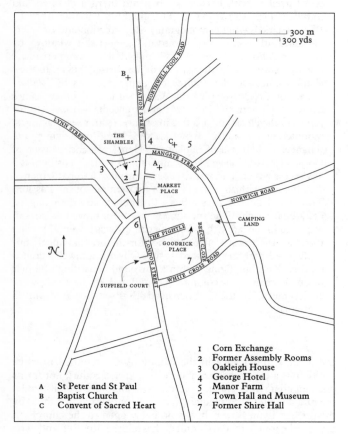

1	Corn Exchange
2	Former Assembly Rooms
3	Oakleigh House
4	George Hotel
5	Manor Farm
6	Town Hall and Museum
7	Former Shire Hall

A	St Peter and St Paul
B	Baptist Church
C	Convent of Sacred Heart

Swaffham

The Shambles. The main funnel-shaped part has in the middle the MARKET CROSS, erected for the Earl of Orford in 1781–3. 73 The *Norwich Chronicle* for 21 July 1781 tells us that the design was 'by that eminent architect Mr Wyatt'. Probably *James Wyatt*. Very elegant, spacious rotunda of unfluted Doric columns, with a lead-covered dome and a figure of Ceres on the top. Apropos Ceres, the town erected the CORN EXCHANGE (now the Job Centre) N of the Market Cross, on a separate small island E of The Shambles, a depressing round-arched structure of red and gault brick like a Methodist church in four by two bays. It is dated 1858, built and probably designed by *Mathias Goggs*, a local builder, a year after J. & M.W. Goggs finished the Dereham Corn Hall. The ground floor had a reading room, library and billiard room. The other principal building is at the W end of the central island, the former ASSEMBLY ROOMS, built in 1776–8 and at first facing W: five bays, the centre three broken forward and rebuilt in the 1950s. In 1827 *William Newham* of King's Lynn added the four-bay stuccoed S front. One storey and fitted with sashes. Hipped roofs. The main room has only partially pilastered walls and a suspended C20 ceiling. Between these two buildings runs the S side of THE SHAMBLES, like the rest of the buildings in the island of C17 origins but progressively altered and added to in subsequent centuries. The Shambles are picturesque but have nothing of importance.

Our tour of the Market Place begins at the NE corner and proceeds clockwise. Opposite the Corn Hall lies No. 63. A double shopfront of *c.* 1965 and two C19 sashes forlornly above, but there are roll-moulded bridging beams inside from *c.* 1540, and it was probably always floored. The early C18 RED LION (No. 87) has been greatly altered in the C20. In the middle of the E side is the dominating mid-C18 MONTPELLIER HOUSE (Nos. 89–91), of flint with gault-brick trim, seven bays and two and a half storeys. Curved porch on Roman Doric columns. Inside very plain, only the first-floor front room with any pretension: chimneypiece overmantel with broken pediment containing a bust; large-framed wall panelling and modillion cornices. The main staircase has disappeared. The GREYHOUND INN (No. 97) follows. This retains bridging beams and wall-plates in the ground-floor N room carved with wave and hollow mouldings of *c.* 1520. Late C18 groin-vaulted cellar on two central piers, a diminutive version of that in Grady's Hotel (*see* below). The exterior, however, was re-done in the C18 and given C19 sashes.

On the opposite side various altered C18 houses mixed with new building. No. 38 (CERES CHEMIST) mid-C18, five bays, three storeys, and a passageway door to the r. The interior has ghosts of its former genteel status in the form of a doorway with a pulvinated frieze and some moulded cornices. Good late C18 staircase added at the back of the rear passageway. Then the PLOWRIGHT SHOPPING CENTRE, contrived in 1982 from the large premises of Plowright engineers. Ugly mid-C19 yellow-brick front with an ungainly shaped gable in the middle. The long C19 buildings of the works and foundry extend to the rear, converted to shops. FITZROY HOUSE follows (No. 32), mid-Georgian, of brown brick, two and a half storeys in five bays. It heralds the best series of houses, to the W of The Shambles, a row of Georgian date, including Nos. 26–30, late C18, of seven bays and three storeys. Open-string staircase with two turned balusters to the tread. Then SWAFFHAM SIXTH FORM CENTRE, converted from two houses, first SCHOOL HOUSE (No. 20), of five bays and two storeys, with a central doorway in a rusticated surround, and the whole ground floor itself dressed with shallow rustication. Giant pilasters at the corners. It can be dated probably by the tablet on the adjoining late C18 HEADMASTER'S HOUSE (also No. 20), which says 1736 and commemorates the foundation of Hamond's School. Conventional two-storey, three-bay design. Minor plasterwork inside. Rear wing of the School House has curved wind-braces in the roof, a late use. Entry to the yard has good vases on rebuilt gatepiers. Finally OAKLEIGH HOUSE (Nos. 16–18), also 1730s, at least the façade. Seven bays and two storeys, with a three-bay pediment. The three middle bays and the corners have rusticated quoins. The doorway has Doric pilasters with alternated blocking and similar treatment of the rustication of the segment-headed middle window and the lunette window in the pediment. Restless keyblocks to all windows, which are early C18 sashes. This, the most imposing Georgian façade in Swaffham, is a re-fronting of an early C17 house, witness the blocked windows to the flint N gable and the two banks of triple octagonal chimney flues. Two C17 wings at the rear, the narrow space between them filled in the C20. The hall and the two ground-floor rooms have lugged doorcases and minor plaster cornices, and fake C20 chimneypieces. The chimneypiece in the hall is flanked by such doors, the left one being false, such was the desire for symmetry in the Georgian decades. The other leads to an early C17 staircase in the N rear wing. It has splat balusters and two tremendous lower newel-posts, each with a high square shaft liberally carved with strapwork and a tall baluster finial with further carving and an open crown cap. The other newels are plain square posts.

The shorter N side of the Market Place has been noted already as invisible from the Market Cross because of The Shambles. The KING'S ARMS (Nos. 21–23) is a longish flint and red brick pub from the C17, with the remains of a platband and renewed casement windows at upper level still of horizontal type. C18 buildings follow, all minor. The POST OFFICE (No. 35) in a mid-C18 house has been raised into three storeys in the C19. No. 39, of the same date, has an irregular seven-bay front in two storeys; r. part rebuilt C20, l. part with four nice C19 Roman Doric columns to the display window and door, under a projecting entablature. The rear passageway has a display of early C16 roll-and-hollow-moulded joists and wall-plates marking the site of a grand hall. Then, at the corner of Station Street, lies No. 59 (CRANGLEGATE), of nine bays (l. bay blind) with an open segmental pediment over the doorway on unfluted pilasters.

Wide platband, dormer windows and, at the back, two large wall stacks. Pretty turned-baluster staircase. *c.* 1740.

Now a foray into STATION STREET. The GEORGE HOTEL (Nos. 1–3) hits one in the face. It has a rusticated ground floor and segmental dormers rising through the eaves; five bays. This façade of *c.* 1860 was added to a range of early C18 brick buildings of which fragments may be determined at the rear. Further extensions in 1979 and 1988–9. No. 8, EVERSLEY HOUSE, opposite, early C19, red brick, two storeys in five bays, doorway with open pediment. A little further N another of the same type, No. 22 (ORWELL HOUSE). Then ASTON HOUSE and DALTON HOUSE (Nos. 24–26), plain, also red brick, of six bays and two and a half storeys. This early C19 façade added to a house of the mid C17, of which only the N gable-end remains. Further N the terrible BAPTIST CHURCH, built in 1858, yellow brick, all round-arched, and with two tall corner towers with Italianate roofs. The interior is more pleasant. A gallery on two sides, sweeping round at the E (entrance) side on twisted cast-iron pillars. Fittings all intact including a marble total-immersion font. On the E side of Station Street less of interest. No. 25, POINT HOUSE, is dated 1788: red brick, three bays, three storeys.

NORTHWELL POOL ROAD hives off to the NE. On it BEECH HOUSE. The mid-C18 two-storey, three-bay house received in the C19 two bay windows, and in *c.* 1910 a larger N wing in a vague Queen Anne style added for Sir Arthur Knyvet Wilson, Admiral of the Fleet. Bobbin-turned balusters to the C18 staircase. The upper staircase landing occupies a barrel-vaulted hall extending right through the house from E to W, lit at both ends, contrived when the house was enlarged. From the S end of Station Street, E along MANGATE STREET, one notices at once the CONVENT OF THE SACRED HEART, consisting of two early C18 flint and red brick houses attached at an obtuse angle and converted to a convent school in 1914. Platband at first floor, C20 casement windows. Both ranges have unfortunately received a third storey in 1942, of wire-faced wartime brick. Opposite, and turning its back on the road in favour of the church, No. 6, CHURCH HOUSE. Very early C18, of flint with brick dressings, two storeys and six bays. The windows two-light cross casements. Fine W gable with diamond patterns, brick tumbling and a panel to the stack with crossed keys like the base of the church tower. And so to MANOR FARM, which shows how near the country is to the little town. The FARMHOUSE has a two-storey, three-bay front added in *c.* 1800 to a rambling series of early C18 structures extending N, with two-light casements on the E side and an external stack to the W. A large BARN to the NW is dated 1797.

A little further E and an avenue to the l. leads off NORWICH ROAD to the MANOR HOUSE, Swaffham's cardinal house, of *c.* 1730–40. A two-storey red brick house facing W in seven bays closed at the ends by rusticated rendered brick quoins. Pedimented doorcase. Hipped roof with one small dormer. Various extensions to S (early C19) and E (1930s). Central staircase hall

has a screen of Roman Doric columns and pilasters; the staircase itself late C19 and of cast iron. The two principal ground-
floor rooms fitted out with large-framed panelling, as are the
two bedrooms above, complete with their dressing rooms. To
the S, at the road junction, GRADY'S HOTEL (a hotel only since
1990), c. 1760. Red brick, three storeys, three bays, porch on
unfluted Greek Doric columns. Late C19 ballroom extension to
the S. The most interesting part is the five- by two-bay cellar,
with a row of square brick piers carrying groin vaults of squared
clunch blocks. The date July 16 1765 is scratched on one of
them.

Back to the Market Place and a sally S on LONDON STREET. On
the W side the WHITE HART, of C17 origin but re-fronted early
C19, with giant angle pilasters. Next the TOWN HALL and
MUSEUM, built as a house in c. 1820, three bays wide, two
storeys, Greek Doric porch. Each wide bay is a slight projection.
The ground-floor windows are arched. Two more Greek Doric
columns in the former dining room N of the porch. Opposite,
the METHODIST CHURCH, 1813, brownish-yellow brick, three
bays, arched openings at the first floor. Recessed centre with
four thin Roman Doric columns. Disappointingly dull interior
with a simple gallery on the W side only. Then follows a respectable sequence. Nos. 5–7 have a symmetrical seven-bay front
added in c. 1760 to an early C18 range of a storey lower. No. 9,
an early C18 flint and brick pair three bays wide, has a late C18
doorcase l. of centre, the other doorway blocked by a window
next to it. No. 11 is another early C18 house raised up to two
storeys and attic in c. 1780; four bays. Then three townish five-
bay blocks of the third quarter of the C18: Nos. 13–15 of two
and a half storeys, No. 17, only two storeys, and No. 23
(CONSERVATIVE CLUB), two and a half storeys and a three-
bay pediment also. The façade unfortunately rebuilt in the
mid C20 and looking very flat. On the W side opposite the
129   Conservative Club, SUFFIELD COURT of 1985–6 has a bald
façade, but the courtyard elevations show that the deck-access
system for sheltered housing can be agreeable on a small scale.
Feilden & Mawson provided two two-storey ranges, with at the
N end a free-standing common room, all three elements linked
only at the first floor by the external access gallery. The materials
red brick and pantiles. The mid-C19 No. 62 (HOLLY HOUSE)
faces White Cross Road. Twelve bays including a narrow
advanced three-bay centre under a pediment. The brickwork is,
unusually, laid entirely in header bond. Split into numerous
bed-sits and flats. Into WHITE CROSS ROAD for the former
SHIRE HALL, not large but of monumental intentions, though
oddly facing nowhere. Stuccoed brick façade, tall, of three bays,
with giant pilasters and a great deep pediment. Recessed entrance
flanked by semicircular niches. Low one-bay wings. Built in
1839 to the design of *John Brown*, the County Surveyor, it was
converted to flats in 1989–90. Continue 250 yds E to HOLMWOOD
HOUSE, difficult to see behind high brick walls. A superior
three- by four-bay block of two storeys built of yellow brick in

about 1840. Double pilaster strips to the corners, small pediments over the centre bays.

Back to the Shire Hall and N along Beech Close brings us to an open space, the CAMPING LAND, given to the town in 1463 for archery and military drill. Here one finds the CHURCH ROOMS, built by *Donthorn* in 1838 as the National School. Clumsy two-part façade, each part of one bay. The l. part has projecting stepped buttresses framing a four-light window one might call Perp. It occupies a corner with THE PIGHTLE (a street) where is GOODRICK PLACE, a pleasant development of closely packed two-storey houses in traditional clothes. 1989, by *Sidney Bernstein Architects Ltd*. Past the Camping Land the churchyard can be reached through a C19 wrought-iron GATE. On the l. the WHITE HOUSE, facing the church. L-shaped, mid-C18, of flint and limewashed brick. North front of two storeys and attic, seven bays of windows, most of which are blind (the façade is mostly only one room deep, lit from the S side), and a pedimented doorcase. From the churchyard back to the Market Place via Church Lane through another pair of wrought-iron churchyard GATES: *c.* 1830, compound piers.

Of outlying FARMHOUSES only two need mention. WOOD FARMHOUSE, ½ m. SE of the church on North Pickenham Road, began as a two-storey early C17 timber-framed range running N–S, with a roof of upper crucks with spurs to the wall-plates. This had an external brick stack to the S gable with triple octagonal flues, which was taken into the early C18 brick S front and so appears now as one approaches the house as a central ridge stack. One storey and dormer attic S front, three bays wide. C18 gabled additions to the E of the timber-framed part. North gable is of flint with some reused ashlar and two dates: 1623 and 1632.

CAROL HOUSE, Watton Road, 1½ m. SSE. Dated 1730 on the W gable. English-bond red brick, two storeys and attic, three bays. Windows all changed.

SWAINSTHORPE   2000

St PETER. C12 round tower with an octagonal late C14 top fitted with Perp two-light windows to alternate facets. The tall wave-moulded arch towards the nave is late C14. S doorway with hoodmould decorated by fleurons and placed on headstops. Perp nave windows possibly relating to a bequest to work on the S side in 1443. The S porch was originally two-storeyed, but rebuilt in 1885 during the general restoration. Chancel with C19 Perp windows. The nave has an arch-braced roof on wooden head brackets and decorated with angels. C14 N arcade of two low bays with an octagonal pier and double-chamfered arches. The narrower arch at the E end goes with the C19 chancel arch. – FONT. C13. Octagonal bowl with the usual two blind arches to each face, re-cut. Eight columns orbit a central shaft below. – BENCHES. Some C15 poppyheads. – Also bits of the dado of the

screen reused in the front stalls. – BRASS to Gilbert Havers
†1628, only an inscription recording that he was a Captain of
Infantry to Elizabeth I. – MONUMENT. John Dearsley †1765.
Handsome tablet of mauve and white marble.

ST MARY. Swainsthorpe originally had two churches, but nothing
survives of St Mary.

SWAINSTHORPE HALL, ¾ m. E by the river. On the S side is a
block from the C17, the brick laid in English bond. Stepped
gable. To the N, mirror-like, is a C19 replica. Apart from a few
details such as the chimneypiece, dated 1654 and with the arms
of the Merchant Adventurers, the rest is C19 and C20.

THE ROOKERY, Ipswich Road, off to the W, in trees. A mid-C16
timber-framed house arranged as a half-H. S façade with two
gables and an external stack. W gable with a mullioned window,
ovolo-moulded, and an external stack at the junction with the
N wing. The ground-floor E room has small-framed panelling
and bridging beams with sunk-quadrant mouldings, so re-
furnished early in the C17. The overmantel of same time. It has
three arcaded bays divided by caryatid pilasters. Roof with
diminished principals and two tiers of purlins, the upper tier
clasped.

DUN COW INN, Ipswich road. Two storeys, four bays, platband
and C19 cross casements, no doubt reflecting the originals.
Shaped gables removed to N, and halved to S, a great pity. Early
C18.

THE VALE HOSPITAL, former workhouse, ½ m. WNW, and
unhappily derelict at the time of writing. Built in 1836–8 and
still Classical. Red brick. Symmetrical composition. Three-
storeyed centre with short projecting wings. Lower outer wings.
The architect was *John Brown*.

SWANTON MORLEY

ALL SAINTS. Big and proud, and historically outstandingly interesting, because it is a dated document of the first order of the
Early – but already completely mature – Perp style in East Anglia.
Work was in progress in 1379, when Sir William de Morley
bequeathed 10 marks and a gold cup to it. There was a bequest
to lead a roof in 1440, but one must not necessarily assume this
marked the completion. The W tower deserves special attention. What will be chiefly remembered is the excessively tall
bell-openings of four lights with a transom. The arches are two-
centred, as are all arches at Swanton, and the lights are ogee-
headed, as are all lights at Swanton. Below the bell-openings
sound-holes with a grid of Perp panel units. The W doorway has
many fine mouldings but only one order of thin shafts. Panelled
battlements at the top. The aisles embrace the tower, and the W
buttresses of the tower are splayed inward as well as outward to
the aisles. All along the W side a base frieze of panelling, and
above it a frieze of quatrefoils. Tall aisle W windows with transoms and charming tracery below them, namely ogee-heads

with little quatrefoiled circles in the spandrels. The same motif
in the tall, straight-headed aisle N and S windows of three lights,
which inside have depressed two-centred rere-arches. The E
aisle windows like those of the Norwich Cathedral choir, *c.* 1370.
The aisle windows restored 1878–91. The two-light side-
windows of the S porch also have the same frieze of quatrefoils
in the tracery heads. N and S doorways with fleurons in one
order of the arch and in the hoodmould. Clerestory includes an
E window, because the chancel is considerably lower. The chancel is humbler too, though the E window has five lights. N vestry
1878.

The arcades inside the church are of four bays. Piers with
polygonal projections to nave and aisle connected to demi-shafts
towards the arch openings by deep hollows. Capitals only to the
demi-shafts. The capitals are round (or half-round), the abaci
polygonal. Complicated and rich mouldings of the three tower
arches. Rather thin chancel arch. Rib-vaulted crypt below the
chancel. The nave roof is a little disappointing. It has arched
braces up to the ridge and alternate wall-posts. In the chancel
hammerbeams with tracery over, owing a lot to 1878. – STALLS.
Two, with lions on the arms. – SOUTH DOOR. Traceried, but
much restored. It has a very narrow wicket. – STAINED GLASS.
Powell & Sons, †1925 to S chancel, †1944 to E window. – ROYAL
ARMS. Painted, over the S door, to Queen Anne, dated 1711.
Between the Act of Union of 1707 and 1714 the royal arms had
the Scottish lion quartered with the English lion, the fleur-de-
lys and the Irish harp. Misspelt motto.

MILL STREET curves and rises round the church to the N out of
the village. NW of the church is HILL FARMHOUSE, Georgian,
red brick, five bays. ½ m. further on is the WHITE HOUSE, Mill
Street. Early C19, gault brick, with giant pilasters and in a handsome and appropriately romantic setting. Two storeys in three
bays. The rear wing of red brick is C18. 35 yds NE is a WELL
HOUSE, flint and brick. Circular under a domed roof and with
an entrance under a reused tympanum with a carved angel. At
GREENGATE, to the S of the village, the ANGEL INN. Timber-
framed C17 building re-faced with brick and altered early
C19. Two storeys. Very big ridge stack with (rebuilt) octagonal
shafts. Very rich end-stops to the bridging beams. THE GABLES,
C17, timber-framed with its ration of later brick. An C18 addition encloses the original gable-head inside, which retains
its pargeted decoration. Also blocked diamond-mullioned windows. The exterior with C19 and C20 windows. Nos. 1–2
ELSING ROAD is an early C18 timber-framed house with a brick
gable-end with two oval windows. The framing bricked over as
usual.

SWARDESTON   2000

ST MARY. Norman nave, see one N and one altered S window.
The other windows here and in the chancel of various dates,

but the style of the early C14 prevailing. One larger three-light
Perp window on the S side as usual. Three-light reticulated E
window. The nave and chancel are in one. The porch is mid-
C15, of flint with brick dressings and a C17 inscription in the
gable: 'Let these Instances of Mortalitie remind thee of thy
own.' S doorway of Tudor brick, quite elaborately moulded
(damaged wave and hollow mouldings). W tower recorded in
donations during the 1470s; it has flushwork panelling in the
battlements. Inside, along the nave walls a series of low round-
arched recesses. Domestic crown-post nave roof on four big tie-
beams, the posts octagonal with moulded capitals, arched
braces to crown purlin and collars. In the chancel a fragmentary
pillar piscina with a single sedile and an ogee-arched piscina to
the E. – FONT. Plain, octagonal. – FONT COVER. C17 and very
pretty. Quite open, with eight turned columns and volutes to the
top. – SOUTH DOOR. C15, oak, with lattice bracing on the back.
– SCREEN. Of one-light divisions with ogee arches and a little
good painted tracery. The dado is not original, but otherwise
C15. – COMMUNION RAIL. C17, turned balusters. – BENCHES.
Twelve C15 bench ends in the chancel with poppyheads and a
charming band of foliage running along close to the edge. –
STAINED GLASS. Some C14 fragments in S nave and chancel
windows. – E window, 1917, commemorating Edith Cavell †1915,
by *E. Heasman.*

VICARAGE, by the church. Built in 1865 for the Rev. Frederick
Cavell, vicar 1864–1910 and father of Edith Cavell, the nurse
shot by the Germans in 1915. Brick with stone dressings. Two
storeys, three bays. The fronts each with a gable to the l. bay.
The entrance (E) front with a Gothick doorway. Transomed
windows.

OLD RECTORY. C16 range to the S, of two storeys and attics. C18
projection to l. with a doorway and sashes. The older main wall
has casements and a timber frame. An early C19 wing added to
N, with the date 1801 and initials of John and Elizabeth Kemp.
Three bays and two storeys, centre bay broken forward. Sashes.
Stick-baluster staircase, with a window fitted with C16 glass of
the Norwich School. The figures are the Kings of England up
to Henry VII.

Three houses. THE CROFT, on THE COMMON. C16 timber-
framed cottage of one storey and attic. Windows C20. The floor
inside seems inserted, and the tie-beams have arched braces.
Clasped purlin roof. The GARDEN HOUSE is C17, also timber-
framed but with the l. part of the S front bricked in. Mixed
fenestration. Winder stair next to the stack. THE DOG public
house, Norwich Road. *c.* 1700, brick. Rusticated brick quoins.
Two storeys and attic in five bays of sashes. Shaped gables N
and S.

GOWTHORPE MANOR, ⅝ m. E. Neither of the dates found tells the
whole story. 1574 is given on the E and W porches and 1669 on
one of the stepped gable-heads. The Styward family held the
manor and built a timber-framed house *c.* 1520 running N–S.
Later in the C16 – possibly 1574, although this seems slightly

early – it was enclosed in brick and altered. Short three-bay W front with two-light mullioned and transomed windows (one of four lights) renewed in 1908, when many alterations took place. Ashlar-faced central porch, single-storeyed and gabled, with ball finials on the shoulders of the gable and to the apex, and the date 1574. Stepped end-gables, that to the N with twin C19 chimney flues, to S with a five-light mullioned window to the ground floor, a pedimented four-light version to the first floor and a two-light attic cross casement. The rear of this wing has a three-storey stair-turret entered through a roll-moulded doorway under a four-centred arch with, in the spandrels, the Styward arms.

In the early C17, presumably before Thomas Berney bought the house c. 1630 because the Styward arms appear over the S chimneypiece, the T-shaped E range was built with the head of the T facing the older part and joined with it by a two-storey connection. This connection has a doorway in its S side under a segmental pediment and unfluted pilasters. All three gables to the E addition are stepped, and all parts have mullioned and transomed cross casements, some under pediments. In the gable-end of the stem of the T, facing E, a second porch very similar to the W porch and also dated 1574, but not ashlar-faced. The date given is difficult to explain. The NE additions are entirely 1908. The main ground-floor rooms converted in the C18 into a single space. The roof is a C16 clasped purlin type with curved wind-braces, while the C17 E wing has a roof of butt-purlins and curved bracing.

The early C17 GAZEBO 10 yds S of the house has one storey, four pilasters round the N doorway and shaped gables. 40 yds W of the house is a splendid BARN, also C17. Brick changing from Flemish to English bond and back again which would suggest c. 1650, but this is getting late for the stepped gables, later even than those to Wilby Hall (q.v.). Good moulded platband. Some windows still mullioned.

MANGREEN HALL, 1¼ m. ENE. Probably built for Henry Davy c. 1700. Five-bay N front crowned by a pair of shaped gables (two big shaped gables to the rear as well). Doorway with fluted pilasters and segmental pediment. Sashes set flush to the wall plane and with exposed boxes, so certainly early C18, though not perhaps c. 1700. Platbands. Set back to the l. is a further bay mimicking the façade under another shaped gable. The main W return shows the house to have a double-pile plan. Beyond this are early C20 two-storeyed extensions. Inside, the staircase is a beauty: twisted balusters with acanthus vase decoration at the bases; carved tread-ends; dado panelling; half-landing with pilastered recess. Overhead is an oval lantern.

WATTLE COTTAGE, Mangreen. Early C16 timber-framed hall house recognizably having had a smoke bay, which is not at all common. This is at about the middle of the present house, which seems to have been extended one bay E in the early C18 and finally by a further bay E and W in the C19. The stack to the l. of the hall is C17 and the hall itself is floored.

8030

SYDERSTONE

St Mary. Round tower with a w doorway and bell-openings of the late C13. The doorway has one order of colonnettes with capitals decorated by small upright stiff-leaf. Y-tracery in the head of the arched door inserted in 1784. Statuary niche over the doorway, with an ogee arch. The bell-openings are round-arched, but have Y-tracery. The E one is rather more delicately cut, with a central column graced by a base and a capital. Double-hollow-chamfered arch into nave. The chancel has a splendid four-light window with Curvilinear tracery, one of the county's best. The side windows are Perp. The nave in its present form is of c. 1784. But its walls half conceal and half display what the church in its original form was like. It was a cruciform Norman building with a s aisle built at the same time, or added shortly after. This was removed, leaving four re-set Y-tracery windows between the former arcade piers. The transept arches are round-headed, on the plainest imposts and have only a slight chamfer. The s aisle has short, strong, round piers with very simple, low, far-projecting undecorated capitals and square abaci. The arches are like the transept arches. In the C14 a N aisle was added. Octagonal piers, double-chamfered arches. This aisle removed too. – MONUMENT. George Hall, 1605. A strange design. In all probability the centre part is the reused front of a tomb-chest of the early C16. Three panels with a cusped quatrefoil and cusped lozenges. This piece was then surmounted by a pediment which, however, also looks Elizabethan rather than Jacobean. The Rev. G. Hall was perhaps a conservative character. Inscription in black-letter below and right at the foot: 'The grave is readye for me. Jobe. 17.1.'

White Hall, I m. E. Early C19 red brick house of two storeys and a five-bay s front. Doorcase with unfluted Doric columns.

1090

TACOLNESTON

All Saints. Architecturally little to report. w tower. Long nave and chancel, no chancel arch. Long s aisle with Perp four-centred windows, that immediately E of the porch of brick. A variety of windows elsewhere. In 1507 money was left in wills for the 'bildyng of the church'. To what can this refer? It could date the arch-braced nave and chancel roof with hollow and wave mouldings. s arcade of five bays with octagonal piers and four-centred arches with multiple hollow mouldings. – FONT. Octagonal, with elementary motifs, perhaps C17. – SCREEN. Parts of the dado stacked in the s aisle. Money was left in 1500 but construction probably c. 1510–20. In two panels paintings of the Annunciation and the Temptation of St Anthony (copied from a Lucas van Leyden engraving of 1509), rudely defaced. Charming small leaf decoration around. The panels are relatively short. Below them a frieze of cusped lozenges. – PULPIT.

Jacobean, with coupled colonnettes at the angles and arches in feigned perspective. Strapwork consoles support the cornice. C19 stone plinth.

TACOLNESTON HALL, ⅝ m. w. Handsome Queen Anne house with additions, originally put up for Edmund Knipe *c.* 1700. Red brick. Low, of eleven bays, the outer two projecting, the centre three with a pediment. Hipped roof. Door hood on very big carved brackets. The window above with a raised, moulded frame. The sashes generally have the thick glazing bars one associates with the early C18. Octagonal stacks with star tops, presumably C19. Inside is a surprise, for an early C16 timber frame presents itself, and the hall has C17 panelling. C18 open-well staircase. The moat was dug only after 1863, at the same moment that the WATER-TOWER was built.

OLD HALL, S of the church. Another house apparently of *c.* 1700, this time built for Sir Robert Baldock. The w front of seven bays, two storeys, hipped roof, and a three-bay pediment. The parallel E wing however is earlier, probably late C16 and timber-framed but remodelled when the new range was added. The tall polygonal chimneys belong to this part. A little exposed timber framing inside. Two ground-floor rooms have respectively C18 and C17 panelling. The new work provided the fine staircase with its turned and twisted balusters.

MANOR FARMHOUSE (formerly Dairy Farmhouse), 1¼ m. S of the church. A delightful piece of late C16 vernacular architecture glimpsed as one turns a bend in Norwich Road. Brick stepped end-gables. The rest timber-framed. Thatched. The odd three-storeyed stair-turret in the centre of the N side has each stage of diminishing area so that it steps up to the gabled roof. Bits of pargeting survive. Ovolo-moulded mullioned and transomed windows. The S side has a full-height porch just as remarkable as its companion, also in three diminishing stages looking like three gables on top of each other. Internal gable-end stacks to the main block.

In addition to these examples Tacolneston is rich in C17 houses. On CHENEY'S LANE see MARY'S FARMHOUSE with the date 1628 on the chimney. There is a C17 BARN to the NW. NORWICH ROAD provides several, e.g. No. 59, and the more ancient Nos. 60–60A. It is in two parts, the w end a late C15 open hall house with two arched service doorways and studs and bridging beams roll-moulded. Blocked mullioned windows. THE DOWER HOUSE is early C17 as is MANOR FARMHOUSE. The latter has brick end-gables, that to the S stepped. The mullioned windows are hollow-chamfered. OLD FARMHOUSE has a brick w gable carrying a stack with twin octagonal flues, and there is another serving the SE wing. Here are C17 ovolo-moulded mullioned windows, but the rest mainly C18 cross casements. Finally OLD HALL FARMHOUSE brings us to the early C18 and red brick. Two storeys in four bays. Cross casements. Its BARN to the E of the same date and type.

TASBURGH

ST MARY. Round tower, round to the top. Half-way up traces of large blind arcading, and on the apexes of the arches a second tier. It is likely that this is a sign of Anglo-Saxon date. Lancets to the top stage C13. Nave and chancel, windows mostly Perp, all renewed. C19 also the hammerbeam roofs to nave and chancel. N porch is C15. S porch with a flint meeting room attached, 1978. – FONT. Perp. Octagonal. The stem has panels with two fleurons in each, one on top of the other. Bowl with a big flower in each panel. – FONT COVER. Small, Jacobean, just with an openwork obelisk. – SCREEN. Dado only, and largely C19. But what remains seems to indicate a C14 date. Blank intersecting ogee tracery on shafts instead of mullions. – BENCH ENDS. Some with C15 poppyheads. – STAINED GLASS. A N chancel window with a panel depicting William Newce †1610 and his two wives and an inscription. – MONUMENTS. In the chancel S wall, set in the sedilia, an Elizabethan tomb-chest with three shields in cusped fields. Back wall with two columns still carrying an ogee arch. – Thomas Newce and wife †1629 and †1632. Alabaster tablet.

TASBURGH HALL. A big Neo-Jacobean brick house with stepped gables, etc., built mainly in 1885 for the Ficklin family. Restless seven-bay front stepping back and forward between the wall plane and the projecting porch and flanking bay windows.

RECTORY, Church Lane. Early C19, two storeys in three bays. Paired pilasters at corners and single ones between the bays. Pedimented doorcase.

OLD HALL FARMHOUSE, Church Road. C15 timber-framed hall house with a cross wing at the W end. There was the usual flooring in the C17. On the S side are three gables.

Former FRIENDS' MEETING HOUSE, ⅞ m. SE. Early C18, red brick; a simple rectangular box under a hipped roof. Cross casements. The two doorways changed to French windows during conversion to a house.

TASBURGH MILL, Lower Street. The early C19 mill has three storeys, brick below, weatherboarded above. Converted to a house. The five-bay MILLER'S HOUSE stands to the SE.

WHITE HORSE FARMHOUSE, Lower Street. Early C17, timber-framed and thatched. Two storeys. The ridge stack has four octagonal flues. Three mullioned windows, the centre one under a gable.

EARTHWORK ENCLOSURE. A univallate and roughly oval enclosure, with the parish church within its rampart on the S side, encloses *c.* 6 hectares (15 acres). It has been badly mutilated by ploughing and quarrying. Excavation has shown that, despite the presence of some pre-Roman Iron Age occupation, the rampart may have been built or strengthened as late as the early C9 A.D. If so this must be of Danish Viking or late Saxon construction. (AR)

TATTERFORD
8020

In the parish of Tattersett

ST MARGARET. 1862 by *W. Lightly*. E.E.; of nave and chancel only. Plans for a tower-porch at the NW corner came to nothing. Flint, stone dressings, angle buttresses. w rose window in plate tracery. Domestic-inspired kingpost roof. – FONT. Ordinary, circular bowl on a column. – STAINED GLASS. E window by *Moira Forsyth*, †1947. S and N chancel windows by *Mayer & Co.*, c. 1862.

PYNKNEY HALL, ⅝ m. WSW. The N front is late C18, its essentially dull character imparted by the 1888 re-facing. Brick. Seven bays, two and a half storeys. Three-bay pediment with a stone plaque dated 1587, the only feature of that date, but there are two first-floor rooms with late C17 panelling and another with early C18 panelling. These may be importations of 1888. Probably built for the Chad family who had inherited in 1781. The S front with three big shaped gables is dated 1880 and was designed by *Ewan Christian* for J.S. Scott-Chad. The middle gable has a segmental pediment. The interior also remodelled, see the Neo-Jacobean staircase.

TATTERSETT
8020

ALL SAINTS. One of the most isolated Norfolk churches. C13 the unbuttressed w tower with lancets to S and W. Two-light bell-openings and brick battlements. Altered but still splayed window into the nave. S doorway and S porch late C13, though the porch acquired Perp side windows and remodelling round the entrance arch. Blocked C13 N door, and the responds of the chancel arch also C13, though the arch itself Perp. Perp nave windows, Perp chancel E window. Brick sedilia and piscina in the chancel S wall. Is it Tudor? C19 nave and chancel roofs, the latter plastered over. General restoration in 1909. – FONT. C15, octagonal. – WALL PAINTING. A late medieval scene of the Martyrdom of St Erasmus on the S wall.

ST ANDREW, Sengham. Of the church, close to Broomsthorpe, nothing remains apart from tuft-covered mounds. In 1947 there were still reported visible foundations.

COXFORD PRIORY, off the road to Broomsthorpe, ¼ m. SE of the church, easily visible. Augustinian. Founded at East Rudham in the mid C12 and moved to Coxford about 1215. The priory had about ten to twelve canons. One tall arch stands to its full height. It was filled in later and a Perp window was set in it. The arch must represent the opening into a N transept. To its r. a keeled arch into a chancel chapel and a window above it. The extent of the straight-ended chancel is visible in lumps of masonry, the extent of the nave in bumps in the grass. More masonry SW of the N arch. Sir Henry Spelman in his *History of Sacrilege*, 1698, tells us that Sir Roger Townshend carried off stone for his new house at Raynham, which involved demolition, the steeple then still standing. This would be in 1619. The act of irreverence caused misfortunes that amazed Sir Roger, who in consequence (Spelman supposes) moved the foundations of his new house elsewhere. The account is colourful and weaves its way between fact and fiction.

EARTHWORKS of DESERTED VILLAGE, in a pasture field overlooking a stream NE of Broomsthorpe Hall. A hollow way and tofts lie s of the remains of St Andrew's Church (*see* above). A good group of four fishponds lies 325 yds w of the earthworks. (AR)

MOATED SITE. Between Coxford Priory and All Saints Church a well-preserved moated site lies in low-lying and very wet ground. (AR)

5020   TERRINGTON ST CLEMENT

ST CLEMENT. Although not over-ornate the church is big in scale
27   and imposing in its masses, one of the grandest in this area round the Wash rich in grand churches. The present building is C15 Perp, but there was a substantial church here already in the late C12. Of Barnack stone. The SW crossing pier stands on a base in which the E aisle respond of a late C12 arcade is recognizable. Similar bases to the w door jamb. The chancel NE window has bar tracery, i.e. belongs to the late C13. Of the same date the sedilia and piscina in the chancel (pointed-trefoiled arches; dog-tooth decoration, stiff-leaf capitals). So the width and length of the C12 and C13 church was the same as that of the present church. Restoration in 1829. Chancel repaired in 1879 for and probably under the direction of *Prof. J. B. Lightfoot* of Cambridge, cost £2,200.

Detached late Perp NW tower, as close as 8 ft to the w façade of the church. Not yet begun, it seems, in 1499, for then Walter Cooper left 40 marks (£26) on condition that 'the said newe stepull be in hand and onwards with workemen within ij yere'. Further bequests recorded until 1527. The tower is ashlar-faced and has diagonal buttresses, a quatrefoil frieze along the base, and panelled and decorated battlements. The N and s sides are very bare. The w front of the church also has ashlar slabs. Five-light window with two transoms over cusping. Canopied niches to its l. and r. Angle turrets. Angle turrets to the aisles as well, the latter with oddly tall spirelets. The SW one rebuilt during another restoration of 1887–1902. Panelled battlements. s porch with quatrefoil base frieze and panelled buttresses and two tiers of panelled arcading below the gable. Clerestory with doubled windows (fourteen on each side): four-centred arches and panelled battlements. The clerestory is supported by a pair of flying buttresses after the first bay from the w. Then they are given up, though the buttresses on the N side make provision for them. s transept parapet with quatrefoils in circles. N transept parapet panelled like the other parapets. Curiously the clerestory continues into the transepts. Rood stair-turret with spirelet.

Inside, the arcades are a little disappointing. Seven bays with plain octagonal piers and double-chamfered arches. Between the clerestory windows shafts on little figures and canopied little niches on top of the shafts. The transepts were intended to be given a much grander appearance than they have now. In the w walls the beginning of slender compound Perp piers (lozenge-shape and finely moulded details) are exposed which were to separate the transept from a w aisle. The plan was not carried out, and now the transepts are short. The window composition on the s side, however, is very effective. Three tiers, the windows in threes, twos, then ones. All of them have segmental heads. Inside there is a real crossing, meant to carry a tower. The present tower is perhaps the result of a decision not to risk a crossing tower. Tall arches, those on the N and s sides in their details corresponding to the future transepts, those on the w and e plainer. Above the e arch a broad five-light window. The seven handsomely stepped niches above the w arch rebuilt in 1968, including the arch itself. The chancel has a five-light e window and a clerestory of brick. Nave roof on arched braces, now mostly of 1829. So are the aisle roofs.

FURNISHINGS. FONT. C15. Octagonal, tracery and cusping 45 in the bowl. – FONT COVER. Probably Laudian Gothic of the early C17, and of unusual interest. The lower part (opening with doors) is Jacobean with clusters of three marbled Tuscan columns, the upper part a tall Gothic canopy. Paintings inside of landscape with scenes, including the Baptism of Christ. – SCREEN. e of the entrance bay, across nave and aisles. Made for £13 in 1788. Solid, with eight composite cast-iron piers. – CREED and LORD'S PRAYER. Painted boards with strapwork decoration in N and s transepts. Dated 1635. – SCULPTURE. Two good stone figures (s vestry), especially a St Christopher, supposedly from the w front niches. In fragmentary condition. – STAINED GLASS. e window by *J. Powell & Co.* Not good, †1918. s and N chancel windows by *William Wailes*, †1860 and †1858, much better. – MONUMENTS. Dorothy Edwards †1721. Alabaster, with weeping cherubs and iron grilles below (chancel N). – John and Mary Ascham (Mary †1704), also alabaster, drapery in the cartouche and cherubs again (chancel N).

LOVELL'S HALL, ⅝ m. s. The hall of the Lovell family. Early Tudor, of brick, above a stone ground floor, half-H-shaped, satisfyingly compact. The two-storeyed stone e porch has a date 1543, which is not contemporary but could be correct. It is flanked by big straight gables. Windows all mullioned, the lower ones with transoms. Rather altered 1940–5 during military occupation.

HIGH SCHOOL. 1979–80 by the *County Architect's Department* (job architect *C. Garner*). The county's pavilion concept (*see* Introduction, pp. 166–7) here applied in a linear form, so that the school is spread out more or less symmetrically round a central covered way with classrooms and departments opening off it as self-contained pavilions.

The VILLAGE is sizeable. On CHURCH GATEWAY, Nos. 35–37.

Formerly a shop – see the C19 display window – but dated 1730 on the s rear cross wing. The front has late C18 upper sashes and a stringcourse between the floors. No. 45 (OLD BEAMS), formerly the public house and c. 1700. Lobby-entrance, rough-cast brick. Stringcourse between the floors. Sashed in the C19. N gable with an external stack. No. 101 (HIGH HOUSE), the most well-mannered in the place. Two storeys and dormer attic in three bays, with a Doric pedimented doorcase. Still the plat-band between the floors, and a parapet with the date 1753. Good chimneypiece in the entrance hall has a carved over-mantel with arms of the Bertie family and a segmental arch over the lot. The stairs with bobbin balusters and carved tread-ends.

At the s of Church Gateway, l. into LYNN ROAD and to TERRINGTON LODGE. Two storeys and three bays to s. Sashes, those to the ground floor tripartite. c. 1740. STABLES to the N, same date. Brick and understated. To the N in NORTHGATE WAY, TOWER HOUSE gets its name from the tall C17 tower at the rear, fitted with cross casements. It presumably goes with the date 1657 on the s gable of the house proper. Façade re-faced 1839, five bays of sashes.

EMORSGATE FARMHOUSE, ¾ m. w, on Pope's Lane. Half-H-plan, with a three-bay recessed centre fitted with C19 cross casements reflecting if not representing the c. 1700 origins of the house. Gabled cross wings r. and l. TERRINGTON COURT, in a Jacobean style of 1810, has in its E façade five gables with five-light mul-lioned and transomed casements. There may be a C16 core.

TERRINGTON ST JOHN

ST JOHN. A church extremely puzzling in one respect. The tower is connected with the nave by a multi-storeyed link containing rooms, a staircase and a covered, gabled passage from the tower on to the roof of the clerestory. When was it built? The answer depends partly on the date of the tower. This stands to the w of the church, more or less in line with the s aisle, about 10 ft away. It is ashlar-faced and has polygonal buttresses developed out of set-back buttresses below, which are connected by a diagonal. The lower lancet windows make a late C13 date likely. Above this it is Perp. It was restored in 1843, the year that the church finally lost its status as a chapel of ease to St Clement.

The CHURCH itself is more easily dated. It is partly early C14, partly Perp. Early C14 the very wide nave with its aisle arcades. Octagonal piers, double-chamfered arches. Also early C14 the w doorway, the N aisle w and NW windows, and the s aisle sw window. Perp w front with a big transomed five-light window, Perp most N aisle and s aisle windows, the chancel, and the s porch. Chancel E window from an 1870 restoration. There had been another in 1853. The porch has a tunnel vault with trans-verse ribs. Charming clerestory with alternating circular win-dows with the motifs of the four-petalled flower and two-light windows under basket arches. Nave roof with the date 1668:

ties on arched braces and moulded butt-purlins. C20 chancel roof. – FONT. Octagonal. Dated 1632. Strapwork in the bowl, tracery in the stem. – PEWS. Five C18 box pews in nave.

LINK BUILDING. This is of brick, faced with ashlar. It consists of a stone-faced brick chamber with a brick barrel vault giving access to the base of the tower through the tower's former E door. There is a small room above this. This room has plain oblong N and S windows and may have been the priest's room. It is barrel-vaulted as well, and is reached by a winder staircase starting from doorways in the lower chamber and also the W end of the S aisle. The stair rises to the nave roof and the roof of the priest's room. On top of the latter are two passages, one on top of the other. The upper of them has a vault of brick and stone. The lower leads to the ringing chamber, the upper to a winder stair up the tower. It seems that the tower was begun late in the C13 but is in its present form mid-C15. If the present church is C14, one can assume that the tower was originally detached like that of the other Terrington and only later linked to the church. The tower has no traces of a lower stair (only from the second stage up), which seems an argument against its original independent existence. On the other hand the tower's NE buttress is encased by the linking piece, so must have come first, but not by much. The link's N wall is quite sheer, studded with lancet lights. – HEADSTONES, in churchyard; C18.

CHURCH FARMHOUSE, Church Road. A lobby-entrance brick house of three bays, with a porch under a stepped gable dated 1663. Casements renewed C20. Winder still by the stack.

THE ELMS, Church Road. With the politeness of c. 1720. Two and a half storeys, three bays, Doric columns support the door hood. Sash windows (not original).

TESTERTON

9020

1¼ m. ENE of Colkirk

ST REMIGIUS. In ruins. What stands is a part of the tower with a buttress and a gaping former W window, which has a four-centred arch, so one may presume C15.

TESTERTON HOUSE, immediately S. Philip Mallet Case had it built in 1802, but its sash windows with their thick glazing bars and the platband between the floors hark back to c. 1750. Two storeys in seven bays.

THARSTON

1090

ST MARY. Perp W tower faced with knapped flint. Wave-moulded doorway with fleurons in the spandrels. Flushwork-panelled battlements. Polygonal stair-turret to S. N porch with vertical flushwork panelling in two tiers to N face, restored 1886, five years after the nave as a whole was restored and re-seated. Similar flushwork to plinth courses on E and W sides. Two-light Perp windows and a minimal three-light chancel E window consisting of trefoiled lights under a square head. The same pattern distinguishes the two-light chancel S window, but the N window closed for the organ. – FONT. C15, and probably by the same carver as nearby Morningthorpe. Against the stem four lions, against the bowl four flowers, two angels and two lions. – BENCHES. Several with poppyheads and a few also with reliefs below them, e.g. the Archangel Michael Weighing Souls. They were restored in 1928. – STAINED GLASS. S chancel window by *J. & J. King*, †1874. – MONUMENTS. Robert Woode †1643 and wife †1646. Alabaster tablet attributed to *William Wright* (GF). Inscription between two black obelisks and, below, the deceased as a skeleton on a half-rolled-up mat. – Sir Robert Harvey †1860, by *T. Gaffin*. White marble. An inscription, set between two standing soldiers, lists his actions during the Peninsular War.* – MAUSOLEUM erected for General Sir Robert Harvey and his family, in the churchyard to the S. 1855. Red brick with stone rustication to the corners, to the pediment at each end and as roofing slabs.

THARSTON HALL. Right on the road, 200 yds S. Jacobean. Brick with blue brick diapering. Two-storeyed porch with shaped gable. Doorway still with shafts and a four-centred head. Stepped gable on the r. The façade has six bays of mullioned and transomed windows. Octagonal shafts to chimneys. In 1664 Robert Gipping was assessed for ten hearths for the Hearth Tax. Roll-moulded bridging beams in the hall. Nice C18 panelling in a ground-floor room.

PICTON FARMHOUSE, Picton Road, ⅜ m. S of the church. A late C16 timber-framed house with brick gable-ends. The stack has four octagonal flues. Windows C19 as are various extensions.

VITTORIA, Low Tharston. Two-storey, three-bay house with an inscription above the doorway recording construction in 1847 for Sir Robert Harvey. Also the BRICK KILN in which two million bricks were burnt for the railway.

THELVETON

ST ANDREW. Nave and chancel. The W tower fell in 1757 and was replaced by a bellcote in 1761. Blocked Norman N doorway. Interior C19 in spirit from the 1864 restoration paid for by Thomas Mann. – FONT. C15. Eight small figures against the stem, two flowers, two lions and four demi-figures of angels with shields against the bowl. – MONUMENT. Thomas Mann †1886. By *C. Stoatt*. Portrait medallion in a wreath. – REREDOS. 1879.

THELVETON HALL. Beautifully regular Elizabethan or Jacobean brick façade on the E-plan. The wings project one bay. Seven bays in all and of two storeys, three in the wings and porch. Stepped gables, pedimented brick mullioned and transomed

---

* Several farmhouses in the area are named after battles and skirmishes in which Sir Robert was involved, e.g. Ciudad Rodrigo and Vittoria.

windows (renewed 1911), polygonal angle-shafts and pinnacles. Built probably after it was acquired by Thomas Havers in 1592. He was a recusant, which explains the chapel which existed until the house passed from the Havers family to Thomas Mann in 1863 (the room on the first floor still exists, subdivided). Above the ceiling of the porch entrance is a secret chamber, also a recusant feature. Little of the interior arrangement remains, although part of the SW staircase survived alteration in 1911–12. There was never a long gallery, as has been suggested. Plenty of small-framed panelling, some brought in, some in replica. The NW bedroom has a C17 chimneypiece introduced in the early C20. In the dining room a chimneypiece of 1849 in the Elizabethan manner by the C19 owner *Thomas Havers*. Thomas Mann made his money in brewing and his acquisition of the house was part of his transition from commerce to the landed gentry. Not only did he have the church restored and the school built but employed *J. T. Musker* of Diss on alterations to the hall. The low flanking wings e.g. are his, as is the S conservatory, billiard room and the entrance LODGE. Edward Mann brought in *Robert Spence* in 1891–2 for further works (wing to S), and in 1911 the billiard room and west drawing room were altered by *Barker & Kirk*.

MANOR FARM. Former C16 timber-framed house converted to stables, probably with a jetty and certainly with a row of three-light blocked mullioned windows to first floor.

THETFORD

INTRODUCTION

The earliest settlements formed here probably about 2000 B.C., at the point where the Rivers Thet and Little Ouse join. The great trading route, the Icknield Way, also arrives here from the Cotswolds, continuing N to Hunstanton and NE towards Norwich. The main crossing developed at the site of the present Nun's Bridges, and by *c.* 500 B.C. was important enough to justify a hill-fort set immediately N, possibly built by the Iceni, who dominated the region until the Roman Conquest. By the mid-Saxon period (mid C7–late C9) a substantial settlement had appeared on the S bank of the Ouse, and in the second half of the C8 a Saxon earthwork was thrown up at Red Castle, acquiring probably in the C9 a timber church dedicated to St Lawrence. It was replaced in stone *c.* 1030. In the two centuries before the Conquest agricultural activity in the surrounding areas steadily increased, and with it the population. The economic and military importance of Thetford was recognized by the Dane Lothbroksson who set up his base here after defeating King Edmund at Hoxne in 870. By about 900 Anglo-Scandinavian defences were probably started and by the time of their greatest extent consisted of a ditch and bank constructed in two semicircles centred on the ford where the present Bridge Street crosses the Ouse. The S enclosure had a radius of *c.* ½ m. and ran from the Red Castle to Nun's Bridges. The part from the Red Castle to London Road can still be recognized. The 150-acre area it contained has been shown to have had sporadic areas of building and streets (four wooden Saxon houses were excavated in 1964), but it must also have had large areas of open land like C14 King's Lynn and C12 Norwich. In the later C11 it did contain the cathedral of St Mary the Greater, St Ethelreda, four other churches, pottery kilns to the SW and the Red Castle. As early as the late C10 or early C11 there seem to have been extramural churches: St Margaret to the SW and to the SE St George (which later became the Nunnery), All Saints and St Benedict's. The area N of the river is hardly better known. St Peter and St Cuthbert were there, if not in their present form; the radial streets of Minstergate, St Nicholas Street, White Hart Street and King Street may all testify to a medieval plan. Defensive ditches were strengthened in the 980s but failed to prevent the sacking by

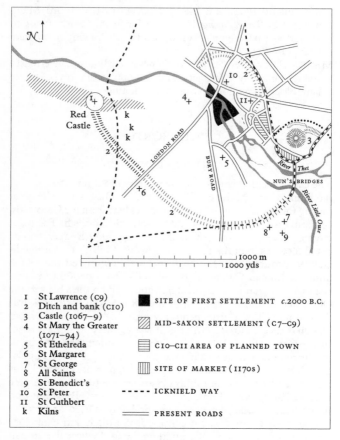

1	St Lawrence (c9)	■	SITE OF FIRST SETTLEMENT *c.*2000 B.C.
2	Ditch and bank (c10)		
3	Castle (1067–9)	▨	MID-SAXON SETTLEMENT (c7–c9)
4	St Mary the Greater		
	(1071–94)	▤	c10–c11 AREA OF PLANNED TOWN
5	St Ethelreda		
6	St Margaret	▥	SITE OF MARKET (1170s)
7	St George		
8	All Saints	-----	ICKNIELD WAY
9	St Benedict's		
10	St Peter	═	PRESENT ROADS
11	St Cuthbert		
k	Kilns		

Thetford. Plan of early settlements

Swein of Denmark in 1004 and 1010, when Thetford was the object of his landings on both occasions. After this Thetford became the centre of Danish occupation of East Anglia and in the next half-century was one of the five biggest towns outside London with a population approaching 5,000. Before 1066 there were 943 burgesses compared with Norwich's 1,320 and population of 5,500.

The Normans at first decided to build a castle and transfer the see of East Anglia from, probably, North Elmham (q.v.). The castle came first, in 1067–9, on an earlier site, and the Red Castle to the w was strengthened by a further ditch cutting across the Saxon defences. The see was transferred in 1071, Bishop Herfast taking over the church of St Mary the Greater and beginning a campaign to take control of the abbey at Bury St Edmunds. This he did not manage and it was left to Bishop Losinga to move finally to Norwich in 1094. After this the town could not compete with the economic rise of King's Lynn and Norwich and the increasing domination of the local markets by the abbot of Bury St Edmunds, and after less than a century of prominence, Thetford began a long decline. As the town shrank the monastic precincts expanded to fill the gap until in the early c15 the civil population was about 1,500, but there were five monastic houses and yet more hospitals. Parish church building remained a flourishing enterprise until the end of the c14 when there were twenty, several with ridiculously small parishes, but these too fell into decline to the extent that a mid-c16 worshipper had the choice of three.

The medieval town was by the c13 mainly on the N bank. The market immediately s of the castle and within the limits of the outer bailey was probably laid out when the castle itself was demolished, c. 1173. The present Old Market Street and Ford Street define it. To its N the block between Nether Row and Pike Lane was heavily built up, and there was a core further NE round the White Hart Street, King Street and Minstergate junction. Surrounding these areas were the various monastic precincts, whose dissolution was to cause the collapse of the already precarious local economy. In the mid c16, houses stood empty or in ruins; the monastic buildings decayed and their stone was carried for reuse elsewhere. The population remained at about 1,500, the level of a century and a half before.

Until the early 1960s this is about the sum of the story. The town became a celebrated rotten borough, with two Members of Parliament until 1867, deeply impoverished throughout most of the c18 and c19 and with one of the worst sewage systems in the country until 1950. However it was set on the main road from London to Norwich, which until 1968 passed up Bridge Street and White Hart Street, and here were to be found, close together, the three full-scale coaching inns – the Anchor, the Bell and the White Hart. The first two survived the arrival of the railway. The major industrial concern was Burrell's Engineering Works on Minstergate, from 1770 to 1930 a significant producer of agricultural machinery and traction engines. In the late c18 and early c19 Thetford saw some revival, and, as elsewhere, a great deal of rebuilding or re-fronting of existing houses. Gault-brick skins were sometimes added over timber frames or flint in an effort to present newer styles to the street, a practice which means that outwardly late Georgian buildings can conceal medieval cores. There are, however, fewer of these in Thetford than one might expect and evidence of older structures is often confined to a few internal timbers (e.g. Nos. 2–6 White Hart Street).

Building materials varied little from the Middle Ages to the C20. Brandon, a few miles NW, was the centre of the East Anglian flint-mining industry, and flint forms the basis of construction. Walls generally are made of whole flints with either cut flint or gault-brick facings, or, if a side or rear wall of a house, often without any finishing at all. It was not a heavily timbered area until the afforestation of the 1950s, and timber-framing is less important than elsewhere in Norfolk or Suffolk. The grey brick was produced locally from gault-clay beds. Red brick, where found, is generally from the railway era, and the C20. An illustration is the flint and gault-brick old railway building of 1845 and its red brick extension of 1889. Another common sight is squared blocks of chalk or clunch which appear everywhere in boundary walls and walls of houses (e.g. for boundary walls see the gardens of Nos. 18–20 White Hart Street, for houses see the gable of No. 46 Earls Street). These come from the ruined monastic buildings, as does some dressed stone. The gable wall of the Central Hotel, Market Place, has plenty.

The rise in population in the first half of the C19 required further accommodation, achieved by in-filling and division of larger houses rather than new works (*see* The Ancient House Museum below). In 1786 the Market Place was moved to its present position, allowing residential development of the area immediately s of Castle Hill, and in 1799 the Guildhall was reconstructed (and again in 1901). A spa was born in 1818 when a pump room was provided over a spring which emerged on the s bank of the River Ouse, but it closed in 1838 and was converted to a house, Spring House. Apart from some Victorian terraces and the railway station of 1845, the next activity was the provision of fifty council houses in Bury Road in 1912–14 on what was a greenfield site, by *S. J. Wearing*. Next was the Newtown Estate of 1920–3 (seventy-two houses) which were provided in the interests of slum clearance, not a population increase, as in 1911 the town mustered a meagre 4,778 inhabitants. St Mary's Estate added a further forty dwellings in 1938–9, the architect again *Wearing*.

In 1958 Thetford was described as 'sleepy today, in an attractive, modest, leisurely way': just the place for an overspill town for London. The development between 1958 and 1971 was enormous, involving a quadrupling of the population, four industrial estates and housing, schools, shops, sewerage and waterworks to go with them. The population was in 1991 19,900, and Thetford is the fourth largest town in Norfolk. The new work was designed by the *LCC Architect's Department* and built by their own contractors in two main phases. The first estate was to the SW straddling the London Road and contained 1,500 houses associated with adjacent industrial estates. The second phase involved the Abbey Estate, 1967–8, 1,000 houses between the railway station and Brandon Road. By the time it was finished 200 acres were given over to industrial use. All this was situated on virgin ground, or sparsely built-up land, but the old centre had to provide the services. The initial proposals fell little short of complete demolition, but instead the ritual of partial demolition for shopping centres, pedestrianization and one-way streets was adopted piecemeal throughout the 1960s and 70s. Thetford has fared well in this, for despite the development the boundaries and road pattern of Norman, if not Saxon, Thetford survive virtually intact. The Thetford by-pass of 1990 relieves some of the road traffic and so there is again a sense of tranquillity in the very centre, at least on Sundays.

CHURCHES AND MONASTIC REMAINS

St Cuthbert, King Street. Marooned in a pedestrianized shopping street since 1976, looking like an ornament. Simple early C13 s doorway with shafts, and in the chancel a C13 double-arched piscina. w tower rebuilt for £1,300 by *T. Farrow* of Diss after a collapse in 1852. It has a flushwork parapet, a stage lower than its predecessor but according to Ladbroke's drawing otherwise similar. Perp s aisle; N aisle of 1902 by *A. J. Lacey*. s chancel chapel converted to a vestry in 1820 and extended 1899. General restoration 1862, nave re-roofed 1902, chancel 1882. – FONT. Moved from St Mary-the-Less in 1976. Square, with tapering sides. This looks Norman, but could be C17. Primitive volutes at the corners. Incised band of scallops between. – STAINED GLASS. N chancel, a Presentation by *Ward & Hughes*, †1873. In the s aisle Saints Christopher and Francis, by *Harcourt Doyle*, †1926.

St Mary-the-Less, Bury Road. Rather forlorn, and redundant since 1975. C11 and C12 origins, but now apparently Perp, with the chancel rebuilt in white brick during the restoration of 1850. The three-stage tower has C19 Perp windows but otherwise is C15, there being bequests 1427–51. It had a fourth stage until the restoration of 1968. Wave-moulded arch inside. Two-bay arcade to the N aisle added 1850. The polygonal pier has capitals only towards the stilted arches. Y-tracery windows, again C19. There is a re-set C12 N door: one order of shafts, cushion capitals and a roll-moulded round arch. – FONT. Moved to St Cuthbert and replaced with a dull C19 font. – SCREEN. 1891, a middle bay and three bays either side. – STAINED GLASS. E window by *Ward & Hughes*, 1866, a Crucifixion. Three Maries in the s chancel, also *Ward & Hughes*, 1865. – MONUMENT. Sir Richard Fulmerston †1567. This was originally a tomb-chest. The large tablet with coats of arms in extremely simple framing is the former front, the lower part is the former ends. The inscription is a copy.

St Peter, King Street, at the junction with White Hart Street. The w tower has buttresses with handsome chequered flint and stone. Its w door opens straight on to the street. Blomefield in

1739 noted that the tower was 'so cracked that it seems very weak'. The upper storey certainly rebuilt in 1789, and the pretty Gothick ogeed doorway dates from that time, but the rest is C15, admittedly with C18 detailing. N aisle with original roof and arcade of four bays towards the nave. Octagonal piers, double-chamfered arches. The same design for the N chapel arcade of three bays. The date late C15. The N chancel chapel now a coffee lounge, the kitchen to its E. A S chancel chapel was demolished before 1820, requiring the insertion of the three-light Perp windows mimicking those to the nave. N nave windows simpler. – Two wrought-iron SWORD RESTS, C18. – SCREEN. Moved from St Cuthbert 1976. – STAINED GLASS. The four S nave windows by *G. B. Burrell*, heraldic, and the date 1791. N aisle W window signed by *Wm. Peckitt*, a coat of arms, dated 1771. – MONUMENT. Peirson cartouche †1721 attributed to *Edward Stanton* and *Christopher Horsnaile*. (GF)

In addition to these three remaining parish churches, scanty fragments of ST GILES in St Giles Lane, off King Street, could be seen until the 1970s. Of ST LAURENCE, a small vaulted crypt below No. 4 Market Place, and of ST NICHOLAS fragments in the garden of St Nicholas House, Minstergate.

ST MARY (R.C.), Newtown, formerly London Road. 1826, with a priest's house (The Presbytery) attached dating from 1829. Flint with gault-brick dressings. Externally very plain. The church has arched windows. The interior however is remarkably fine. Wall panelling painted white and the chancel end with a screen of paired monumental Corinthian columns supporting two entablatures and an arch. The altar painting is a copy of *Pittoni*'s altarpiece at Sidney Sussex Chapel in Cambridge, done in 1835 by *James Barry*, installed when the E window was blocked, probably in the 1840s. The W gallery on two timber piers was added only after the overspill expansion of Thetford increased the congregation, and the W end absorbed a part of the presbytery. The PRESBYTERY built as two houses, converted to one in the C20. Three bays, sashes. Doors in W front and N gable-end lead to staircase halls, both with stick-baluster staircases and ramped and wreathed handrails.

UNITED REFORM CHURCH, formerly Congregational Church, Earls Street. A simple, extremely domestic-looking building with the date 1817. Three widely spaced bays and a low-pitched pyramid roof clad with black-glazed pantiles. Grey brick, sash windows. The Church Book for 1816 has: 'it was deemed expedient that a plain, substantial, and respectable Meeting House should be erected... the expense amounted to upwards of a thousand pounds'. This is what they got. Less domestic inside after the gallery was built in 1843, but reverting again when the same gallery was boarded up to form an upstairs meeting room and kitchen in 1968. Overshadowed by the big, clumsy red ODDFELLOWS HALL of 1891 with its outrageous shaped gable.

BAPTIST CHAPEL, King Street. 1859. Gault brick. Central arched recess under a pedimented gable-end. Round-headed sashes. Two four-panelled doors.

METHODIST CHURCH, Riverside Walk. More of the same, here built as the Wesleyan Chapel in 1830. Gault brick, the façade with four giant pilasters forming three bays. Sashes.

CHURCH OF JESUS CHRIST OF LATTER DAY SAINTS, Station Road, 1972–3 by *D. O. Hendon* (of Lichfield). Strong and confident stuff, as if meant for business and looking twenty years younger. The entrance is set back under a projection and looks like a corridor in a municipal office building. Bold square detached steeple of very slender proportions with four slots at the top reminding one that this is a church. The body of the church like a rectangular warehouse but with dark raised and patterned brickwork to the W end.

Monastic Remains

PRIORY OF OUR LADY. The extensive ruins stand to the W of the town, but of the buildings only low flint rubble mounds remain with the exception of the tall SE pier of the former chancel apse. Around it other walls are a little better preserved than those of the nave or monastic quarters to the S, some (i.e. at the entrance to the N transept) with areas of limestone ashlar still attached to the flint core. Enough however remains for the plan of the various parts to be deciphered, particularly the cellar of the W monastic range and of course the two-storey range in the prior's lodging converted after the Dissolution. The site is in the care of English Heritage.

In 1536 the third Howard Duke of Norfolk petitioned the king to allow conversion of the priory to a college of secular canons, pointing out that Henry's own illegitimate son Henry Fitzroy had just been buried there, but eventual surrender came in 1540. The duke immediately acquired the site, Sir Richard Fulmerston taking most of Thetford's other monastic foundations. After the duke was sentenced to death in 1546 the crown seized his estates and in 1548 the priory buildings were sold to Sir Richard, who began disposing of the materials for building, only to hand the ruins back to the Howard family in 1558 after their lands were restored. The next three centuries saw a continual disintegration of the remains, to the extent that the Eastern Counties Railway in 1845 thought the priory site the best place for their railway station. Fortunately the chosen site allowed a shorter access road to the town centre.

The priory was founded for Cluniac monks from Lewes (the earliest Cluniac settlement in England) by Roger Bigod in 1103–4. It was a house of some importance. The original twelve monks first occupied the cathedral (*see* Blackfriars below), as the bishop had moved to Norwich in 1094. They began building on a new site, the present one, in 1107, and in 1114 the church was consecrated. At that time probably only the E end was built. The nave must have followed quickly, and the W front was reached, it seems, about 1130–40. Meanwhile the monastic quarters were also built and indeed, except for later additions and alterations, completed.

The oldest parts are the w half of the chancel and the transepts. The chancel has aisles, and chancel as well as aisles ended in apses. As the transepts also had an apse each, the scheme of the plan is that of the C10 abbey of Cluny, or, closer to home, of Castle Acre (q.v.), founded in the 1090s. The piers between the chancel and the chancel aisles had shafts towards the chancel but segmental projections towards aisle and arch openings (cf. Norwich and Ely Cathedrals). The aisles were vaulted. The transept apses were provided with blank arcading inside and demi-columnar buttresses outside. In the w wall of the s transept are tall shallow recesses. Of the upper part the pier at the junction of the main apse and s aisle apse stands up highest. It has double shafts towards the high and monumental apse arch, with decorated capitals and roll mouldings in the arch. Remains are also recognizable of the gallery and a shafted clerestory win-

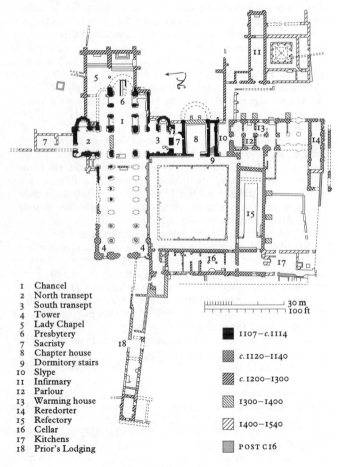

1	Chancel
2	North transept
3	South transept
4	Tower
5	Lady Chapel
6	Presbytery
7	Sacristy
8	Chapter house
9	Dormitory stairs
10	Slype
11	Infirmary
12	Parlour
13	Warming house
14	Reredorter
15	Refectory
16	Cellar
17	Kitchens
18	Prior's Lodging

⌐⌐⌐⌐⌐⌐⌐⌐⌐⌐ 30 m
⌐⌐⌐⌐⌐⌐⌐⌐ 100 ft

■ 1107–c.1114

▨ c.1120–1140

▨ c.1200–1300

▨ 1300–1400

▨ 1400–1540

▨ POST C16

Thetford Priory. Plan

dow. Of the crossing, the nave and aisles, and the w front much less can be distinguished. The w front had two towers and the bay below the N tower still has some internal details (odd w respond of the arcade between N aisle and nave). To the outside there was blank arcading, probably somewhat like Castle Acre. The w portal had four orders of shafts. The aisled nave itself is of eight bays, one more than Castle Acre, and the four w ones are 2 ft wider than the others, indicating perhaps a break in the work.

Of later additions to the church the most important are the Lady Chapel and the lengthening of the chancel by provision of a presbytery, the former of the earlier, the latter of the later C13. The Lady Chapel was built slightly off-set to the N of the chancel, absorbing its apse and that of the N chancel aisle but leaving the s aisle apse intact, at the same time as a cult of the Miraculous Image developed round some relics discovered in a hollow statue. This helped with the monks' funds for the rest of the century. Of details belonging to the Lady Chapel the shafts of the E window are still *in situ*, of details belonging to the presbytery the arcade towards the Lady Chapel remains. This cliff-like E end was a common feature of major churches in the C13, Thetford in this case beating Castle Acre to it by thirty years or so. In the N transept a wall towards the crossing was inserted in the C14, and in the angle between the N nave aisle and the transept a chapel was provided for the monument of the first Howard Duke of Norfolk (†1485). N of the N transept a sacristy was erected in the late C15 complete with fireplace, intended for a mausoleum for the dukes of Norfolk. A number of carved stones in the early Renaissance style were excavated, connected with the monuments to the second duke (†1524) and Henry Fitzroy, but in the end Fitzroy's body was transferred to Framlingham in Suffolk, where the third Howard duke was also buried (†1554). The pulpitum stood between the w crossing piers, the rood screen one bay farther w.

The MONASTIC BUILDINGS are early C12 along the E range of the cloister, a little later along the s and w ranges, although hardly anywhere later than *c.* 1150. They are, therefore, just earlier than the similar layout at Castle Acre, so it is all the more a pity that only bubbles and lumps of flint remain. In the E range, as usual, a SACRISTY lay s of the transept. It was originally apsed and later lengthened. It was followed by the CHAPTER HOUSE, which also had an apse originally, with arcading. In the C14 the apse was taken down and the knapped flint wall was built to square the building. This is early for knapped flint. The arcading seems to have been reused also. After that the stairs to the DORMITORY, which was placed above this range. The SLYPE, i.e. the corridor towards the buildings further E, is the next apartment. This had wall responds and was vaulted in three bays. The buildings further E were connected with the infirmary and arranged in an unusual and very attractive way round their own little cobbled cloister with a well in the middle. The INFIRMARY was of the customary monastic type, resembling a church in plan, with the 'nave' forming the infirmary hall, attached to an E chapel. This range dates from the very early C13, but few of the details survive all along here. The other ranges round the little cloister belong to the C15.

To the S of the slype we jump in date to the second quarter of the C12. First the UNDERCROFT of the remaining part of the dormitory, resting on seven bays of round middle columns. This part was altered shortly after to house the parlour and warming house, the latter with its fireplace in the E wall. Two doors subsequently opened in the W wall. At the S end of the range the REREDORTER or lavatory with its flushing channel along the S side.

The S range of the cloister group contained the REFECTORY, or frater. Its big S buttresses are a C14 precaution, probably of the same time as larger windows were inserted. There is a room at the E end which became an extension to the warming house, but probably started as a corridor. The refectory itself had its access from the SW corner of the cloister.

The W range is not easy to read. The CELLAR lies well below the level of the cloister. It also had columns along its middle axis and was much changed about by cross walls later. A circular scalloped capital from one of the columns can still be seen. The whole W wall is of c. 1200. Presumably the upper floor accommodated the prior. The N end has an outer parlour, created in the early C14 out of a passageway. At the S end were the KITCHENS, at first free-standing but demolished in the C15 and their function moved into the former buttery at the W end of the refectory.

The range running W from the W front of the church almost certainly was for domestic use, either for the prior or his guests or both. It goes by the name of the PRIOR'S LODGING. It started as a small free-standing building on an undercroft at the W end of the two-storey range we see today. This is of c. 1300. The undercroft seems to have had a barrel vault with transverse arches either side of the centre wall, the S half of which has now disappeared. After that two C14 builds extended it to the outer parlour at the N end of the W cloister range. The most striking thing are the two C12 arches in the middle of its S wall. Both are re-located and the smaller of them, with a hoodmould on headstops, leads directly to a staircase to the upper floor, apparent still in the side walls. The larger arch spanned a road. The three-light transomed brick windows in chamfered surrounds are a consequence of full domestic use after the Dissolution. They were themselves blocked and changed again in the C17. In the walls re-set stones from the priory.

To the NW of the church is the C14 GATEHOUSE, reached now by a path which takes one past the big, dull C19 Abbey House. The gatehouse is of cut flint and stone dressings. The wide arches are segment-headed, and there are a three-light and a two-light window above, all cusped. Polygonal turrets at the inner, not the outer angles. Three floors with a winder access in the SE turret, and fireplaces in the W wall of the two upper

storeys. That the first floor was, as usual, the principal accommodation is proven by the existence in the SW turret of a vaulted
garderobe.

To the W are a group of BARNS arranged round the yard of ABBEY
FARM, now a council depot. The S pair are of interest as they
originally belonged to the priory. First is the E one, a conversion
to a house, with dormers, sashes and a thatched roof contrasting with double barn doors and other utility entrances, all very
ugly and all apparently C18, altered C19. The three big stacks
from the later date. However, the roof of the W third is a C16
queenpost structure and the centre third is confusing. It is
certainly a queenpost, but it also has arcade posts and an arcade
plate. Arched braces run to the ties and the plates, and the
queenposts also boast braces to collars and purlins. It looks like
a later C13 aisled timber hall, somewhat altered. The barn to its
W is again outwardly a clunch, flint and brick construction of
the C19, but in reality is a three-bay early C15 first-floor hall
with a crown-post roof. Timber-framed and weatherboarded.
Attached E are four later C15 crown-post bays. The three W
bays have moulded bases and capitals to the square posts,
braces to both the crown purlin and the collars and, amazingly,
big arched braces from the ties to the smaller collar-braces.
There are plenty of tie-beam braces in and around King's Lynn,
but none is known running into the collar-brace. These three
trusses are closer together than the remainder and of higher
quality: most of the rest are reused bridging beams. The first
building must have had a particular use, perhaps a consistory
court.

CHURCH OF THE CANONS OF THE HOLY SEPULCHRE, Brandon
Road, 150 yds from London Road, shoulder-to-shoulder with
new housing and a petrol station. The Canons of the Holy
Sepulchre were a small order with only six houses in England,
all of which followed the rule of St Augustine, leading to virtual
incorporation into that order by the C14. The remains here were
used as a barn for Canons Farm in the C18 – see the blocked
barn doors in the N and S walls, and the entire E wall. We see
now the aisleless nave up to a considerable height and can make
out the W door, the NW door into the former cloisters and a
moulded stringcourse round the interior. The ashlar jambs of
four clerestory windows remain to the N side. All this seems
C14, although the original foundation was by William de
Warenne, third Earl of Surrey, about 1145. At the Dissolution
the buildings were bought by Sir Richard Fulmerston.

NUNNERY, off the road to Euston, $\frac{1}{4}$ m. from the centre. The
remains belong to the Benedictine Nunnery of St George,
founded C11, re-founded c. 1160. At the Dissolution it became a
house and then a barn serving Place Farm and stayed so until
1990 when *Derek Rogers* converted it to offices for the British
Trust for Ornithology. He also converted other buildings on
the site. The nunnery was quite a large establishment. At present
it is set in well-mannered lawns stretching S and W to the Ouse.
The CHURCH, with a S transept and part of the chancel, is

aisleless and stands to the N of the other buildings. Clunch, flint and ashlar dressings. To the S flank are three C16 three-light cross casements, hidden behind lean-tos, but not much else from its C16 domestic life remains. The E and W walls were entirely glazed in 1990, a bold if not entirely satisfactory solution. Otherwise the only feature of special interest is the grand arch towards the transept. This has Norman responds, the E one with a capital with decorated scallops and a depressed two-centred and double-chamfered arch. Within the transept is a computer room, separated by a glass screen. There is nothing unsatisfactory about the blend of old and new here.

Immediately S of the transept and in line with its E wall a blank arch remains embedded in the W wall of the former CHAPTER HOUSE. The arch led to a quadripartite vault. c. 1160, converted to offices in 1990 by *Derek Rogers*. New windows in the S wall. Plain inside.

To the S again is the actual NUNNERY, the former farmhouse, now offices. Squarish in plan, reusing ashlar blocks from the demolished ecclesiastical buildings. Early C17, restored 1990–1 by *Derek Rogers*. S front has three bays, two storeys and attics. In the centre a door behind a Jacobean pediment supported on a pair of panelled Ionic pilasters. Windows are sashes. A good timber mid-C18 chimneypiece has relief carving of eagles, rabbits and foxes, with a watermill in the centre. The SW room and the one immediately above both with small-framed early C17 panelling. C20 staircase.

Much farther S (75 yds S of the church) but also in line, a large oblong building running N–S. Roofless and ruinous. It has a S doorway with a three-light window over. Plenty of reused ashlar. There is a narrower N extension with two blocked four-light mullioned windows. E side also with blocked openings. The date late medieval, altered in the C17. Its purpose is mysterious.

NUNNERY COTTAGES, 35 yds W of the church. The N one, No. 3, is of early C16 origins and formed part of the inner gateway to the precinct. Flint, brick and clunch. Two storeys, remodelled 1857 and given window surrounds with hoodmoulds. The windows themselves late C20. Nos. 1 and 2 were added in 1857. No clues inside. In a direct line 75 yds W is the outer GATEWAY, alone S of Nun's Bridges Road. Rebuilt c. 1600 of brick. The outer, i.e. W, face with a round arch with square spandrels. One tapering pilaster r. and l. rising to the frieze.

AUSTIN FRIARS. *See* Ford Place, p. 716.

BLACKFRIARS. Founded in 1335 by Henry, Duke of Lancaster, and endowed with the Domus Dei, the Church of Holy Trinity, and the remains of the Church of St Mary the Greater (briefly the cathedral). Expansion in 1370 S towards Bridge Street involved demolition of derelict houses. The remains are built into the Grammar School, Bridge Street, notably the W wall of the aisled church with tall wall-arches, the N wall of the N aisle, also with wall-arches, and the narrow tall arch out of the towered central space to the S. This is now within the school library first built in 1575 (*see* Grammar School, below).

PUBLIC BUILDINGS

CASTLE. Motte-and-bailey type, the motte 40–45 ft high from the 10
level, making it the second highest Norman motte in England.
The diameter on the top is 80–90 ft. It was thrown up very
shortly after the Conquest c. 1067–9 on the site of an Iron Age
hill-fort which might be c. 500 B.C. The Norman work very
probably had a timber palisade on the top as a stop-gap until a
stone keep could be built, but plans must have changed in light
of the spectacular decline in importance of the town in the years
following the Conquest. Norwich was favoured instead as the
seat of local government, and for the cathedral. Of the bailey
only traces remain, to the NE. Motte and bailey are separated by
a deep ditch. The castle was demolished in 1173 and the site
was planted in 1820 at the expense of Leonard Shelford. In
1908 it opened as a public park.

GUILDHALL, Market Place. Rebuilt by *H.J. Green* in 1902 at a 119
cost of £10,000 on exactly the same T-plan as its predecessor. A
lively corner to the Market Place; the back towards Guildhall
Street and Cage Lane with a display of arched windows and of
Venetian windows enriched by columns. The N end has a projecting room with a Venetian window under a gable on three
sides. The groin-vaulted room is now used as an art gallery. At
the junction of the gables is a clock tower developing into an
open octagonal lantern under a domed roof; a smaller lantern
to the s over the crossing of the stem and head of the T. These
elements existed in only slightly different form in the guildhall
reconstructed in 1799–1800 when the cost was £4,000, the
biggest change being the raising of the porch in the entrant
angle to two storeys. The STATUE of Justice balancing on the N
gable dates from the additions of c. 1690 made to the flint-built
medieval guildhall, and the Justice inside the large courtroom is
from the 1799 work, the latter of Coade stone.

CARNEGIE ROOM. A public hall replacing the one erected at the
expense of the American tycoon. Behind the Guildhall in Cage
Lane and linked to it by an aerial walk: 1967 by *Hubert Bennett*
of the *GLC Architect's Department*. Brick-skinned, only one or
two storeys, sharp angles and strongly defined blocks. The
complex is both surprisingly large and self-effacing, neatly
tucked away from the Market Place and exposed boldly only to
Raymond Street.

DISTRICT COUNCIL OFFICES, St Nicholas Street. 1991 by *Feilden
& Mawson*. Steel-framed with yellow curtain walls picked out
with red brick details. Several linked blocks of two to four storeys
set at slightly contrived angles, two of which finish with green-
house-like lanterns atop steep pyramid or gabled roofs. The
timber casement windows are a refreshing revival.

ANCIENT HOUSE MUSEUM. *See* Perambulation, pp. 718–19.

BRANCH LIBRARY. On the site of an Elizabethan manor house
pulled down in 1966. The library opened in 1970, by the *County
Architect's Department*, County Architect *G.C. Hayden*.

COURT HOUSE, Old Bury Road, and the BUS STATION are on

the site of C19 maltings, cleared in the late 1960s. The Court opened in 1974: two storeys, brick, vertical panels of flint and glass. By the *Norfolk County Architect's Department*.

RAILWAY STATION, Station Road. The first building of 1845 is to the W side of the complex: cut flint and gault-brick dressings and four extravagant pointed shaped gables, one to each face. The two-bay projection to the r. was added in 1889 along with the platform canopies. The material then was red brick. Restored 1994.

GRAMMAR SCHOOL, Bridge Street (formerly London Road). The story is mixed up with the church of the Blackfriars. Bede records the foundation of a school in A.D. 631, and Herbert de Losinga settled a quarrel in 1114 over its control. In 1335 the Blackfriars were established immediately N of Bridge Street (*see* above), taking over some of the functions of the school. After the Dissolution the site passed to Sir Richard Fulmerston, who in his will of 1566 ensured the continuation of the school. The new school hall went up in 1575 (now the LIBRARY). One storey and attic. Cut flint with brick and stone detailing. C19 machine-tile roof. There were alterations in the early C19 and a virtual reconstruction in 1877. Of the latter year is the entire W wing, the flèche on the roof and the four-light transomed S window. Symmetrical three-bay E front. In the gable of the porch, not *in situ*, a blank early C13 arch, with stiff-leaf decoration framed by a band of interlace. This must belong to the late C12, i.e. a period earlier than the arrival of the Blackfriars (*see* above). It probably comes from another monastic house at Thetford. A second similar fragment in a gable-end to the r., nearby and high up. Further r., two gables to the N block are late C19. Inside, there remains quite unexpectedly the S crossing arch of the Blackfriars' church, dividing the library in two: mid-C14, wave-moulded jambs, polygonal capitals, steep pointed arch.

In 1880 the school was expanded by the SCHOOL HOUSE opposite, on the E side of the road: flint with brick dressings, plaintile roofs; a projecting bay r. and l.; everywhere cross casement windows. Further S the GIRLS' GRAMMAR SCHOOL by *J. Osborne Smith*, opened in 1888: red brick, now with half-timbering in the gable heads, especially to the rear. The cost £2,880.

ROSEMARY MUSKER HIGH SCHOOL, Croxton Road. By the *County Architect's Department*, County Architect *J. F. Tucker*, 124 1983. Conventional block cavity walls clad with brick under pyramid or hipped concrete-tiled roofs. Seven small separate blocks connected by wide covered ways, all of one storey except the Social Studies block, with two storeys, and the one-and-a-half-storey library.

SECONDARY MODERN SCHOOL, Fulmerston Road, serving the first overspill estate. *LCC Architect's Department* under *Hubert Bennett*. Opened January 1961. Mostly conventional brick, but the assembly hall is steel-framed and has reinforced concrete ribs to the ceiling.

NUN'S BRIDGES, Nun's Bridges Road. A group of three brick

bridges over three rivers, the Thet, the Thet Stream and the Ouse. N and s bridges late C18 with two elliptical arches, the centre one early C19 with one semicircular arch. Their interest is in the antiquity of the site, which has carried the Icknield Way since *c.* 3000 B.C.

RED CASTLE, ½ m. W, s of Brandon Road, marked by a clump of trees. The surrounding earthworks were shown in 1958 to be in part the Saxon town ditch. The first earthworks were late C8 with a timber and later a stone church of St Lawrence. The rebuild was of *c.* 1030. In *c.* 900 the Anglo-Scandinavian defences extended as a ditch from Red Castle to Nun's Bridges enclosing a s compound. In the early C12 the Normans dug a circular ditch round the castle as a cover during the construction of the main earthworks. Of any actual palisade or fortification on top of the rise we know nothing.

PERAMBULATION

We start in the MARKET PLACE, not spacious, with trees. To the N Nos. 3–4, on the site of the church of St Laurence. The C16 timber-framed house was partly rebuilt in the early C18, reworked in the late C18 and rebuilt again in 1991 following a fire. The six-bay s front has a gault-brick skin. Inside only fragments from the C16 (a fireplace bressumer and a cranked tie-beam to the front range) but the early C14 UNDERCROFT belonging to St Laurence is more complete. A barrel-vaulted passage leads to a chamber under a sexpartite vault, the ribs chamfered. An E chamber opens from it under a stilted arch, but here the quadripartite vault is cut away. To the W a second formerly quadripartite-vaulted chamber, reduced in size. The material throughout is brick.

On the E side the CENTRAL HOTEL, a three-storey, three-bay hotel of flint, clunch and reused ecclesiastical masonry. The early C19 N gable wall facing Castle Street displays a C12 colonnette, bits of C12 chevron ornament, capitals, bases and C14 cusped tracery. Converted to offices in 1991. The W and s sides of the Market Place are composed of four very different buildings: the RED LION INN, 1837, restored 1960; the MARKET SHAMBLES with cast-iron columns, now shops, *c.* 1900 replacing the original 1837 building; the GUILDHALL in the corner (*see* above, p. 711); abutting the Guildhall the THETFORD MECHANICS INSTITUTE, 1887 by *Edward Boardman*, now a wine bar. From here Guildhall Street runs s, and off it, behind the Guildhall in CAGE LANE, the former LOCK-UP. Rebuilt in 1578, again in the C17 and finally dismantled in 1968 and re-erected on the other side of the street and set in a wall. Not mentioned in T. Martin's *History of Thetford* of 1779. A sad sight now: one of two arched bays survived the move and is fitted with a big wrought-iron grille. The doorway to its l. has gone and so has the gable above. It was an unusual type of lock-up. It was moved to make way for the Carnegie Room (*see* above).

GUILDHALL STREET has been badly used. Of note only No. 19

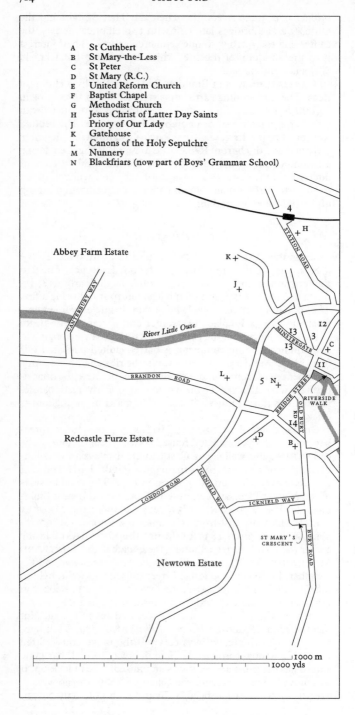

A   St Cuthbert
B   St Mary-the-Less
C   St Peter
D   St Mary (R.C.)
E   United Reform Church
F   Baptist Chapel
G   Methodist Church
H   Jesus Christ of Latter Day Saints
J   Priory of Our Lady
K   Gatehouse
L   Canons of the Holy Sepulchre
M   Nunnery
N   Blackfriars (now part of Boys' Grammar School)

Abbey Farm Estate

River Little Ouse

CANTERBURY WAY

STATION ROAD

Redcastle Furze Estate

BRANDON ROAD

MINSTERGATE

BRIDGE STREET

OLD BURY RD

RIVERSIDE WALK

LONDON ROAD

ICKNIELD WAY

ICKNIELD WAY

BURY ROAD

ST MARY'S CRESCENT

Newtown Estate

1000 m
1000 yds

1 Castle
2 Guildhall (and Carnegie Room)
3 District Council Offices
4 Railway station
5 Grammar School
6 Rosemary Musker High School
7 Nun's Bridges
8 Ford Place
9 Melford Bridge
10 King's House
11 Bell Hotel
12 Ancient House Museum
13 Former Burrell Engineering Works
14 Fulmerston Almshouses

Thetford

(MYHILLS PETS) on the E side, a late C15 timber-framed hall house with a brick W front. Both the front and the rear wing have cruciform bridging beams. To the rear and possibly to the front simple crown-post roofs. Then to the r. in RAYMOND STREET, COUNCIL OFFICES, converted in 1989 from a warehouse and maltings of the late C18, rebuilt 1861. Opposite some minor houses, the grandest No. 38.

OLD MARKET STREET continues SE. This, with Ford Street, was the site of the market re-located here probably in the 1170s. The medieval Market Cross was destroyed in 1807 after the market had been moved back to the present Market Place in 1786. By 1830 only one trader operated from Old Market Street. Here first the former GAOL, rebuilt in 1796 after the market moved, enlarged in 1816 (sold to County Council 1891). Three storeys in four bays. Two entrances in rounded recesses; in panels above them are carved chains. The top windows with their cell bars are original. Converted to two houses and the SE wall rebuilt. There were six cells on the top floor, two to the ground floor and two more off an upper corridor.

Opposite is the former BIDWELL'S BREWERY AND WAREHOUSE, now a general warehouse, five bays with arcades rising through both storeys. Of the mid C19. The BREWERY also of five bays, again with recessed arcading. Beyond at No. 21 is the former MALTSTER'S HOUSE, converted to offices. Big, seven bays, the middle five broken forward under a pediment. The doorcase has a pair of columns with reeded and fluted necks supporting an open pediment. No. 23 has a rendered C20 brick front, but elements of a late C16 timber frame remain, under a clasped purlin roof. Many fragments of C12 carvings incorporated in the walls*. After that the DOLPHIN INN, flint and stone in an irregular chequer arrangement. Brick trim. Moulded plinth course, and the date 1694 in large brick figures. The fenestration, in accordance with the date, already regular, the original type represented by a two-light mullioned window to the first floor. The rest C20. Also in accordance with the date, a moulded brick platband separating ground floor from upper floor. Inside is a sunk-quadrant moulded bridging beam, the ubiquitous C17 type. Other timbers in Brewer's Tudor style. Nos. 51–53 further E on the same side was from the C16 to 1910 a public house. Timber-framed, jettied first floor, horizontally sliding sashes.

Directly opposite is part of the early C19 flint and brick garden wall to FORD PLACE, now a home for the elderly. Built for the Fison family. The house is a big double pile, late Georgian with additions of c. 1860. Gault brick. The N front rather confused; the S front has a hipped wing projecting r. and l. A GROTTO, early C19, is attached to the l.: whole flints, central pointed door and a Y-tracery window either side. The grounds of the house once extended to include the site of the Church of the Augustinians (Austin Friars), 100 yds E, founded in 1387 by John of

* Lower down, No. 27 with shaped gables is demolished.

Gaunt, Duke of Lancaster. Friar's Close occupies the site. In an adjoining field on the bank of the river 75 yds SE of Ford Place a MONUMENT of 1807 to commemorate Lady Tuddenham †1412, whose burial vault was exposed when the foundations of the Friary were removed. Urn with a gadrooned neck on a pedestal with inscription: 'In veneration of this consecrated place and of these illustrious persons this altar tomb was erected by George Beauchamp Esq A.D. 1807'.

Returning NW along FORD STREET, first on the l. Nos. 2–4, a pair of mid-C18 flint and brick houses, then half-way down on the r. a C15 stone pointed doorway ARCH in a garden wall. It has a finial, tall polygonal bases and continuous casement and roll mouldings. At the end on the l., i.e. behind the Old Gaol, is THE PADDOCK, an early C19 house, enlarged to the garden side late C19, and with lawns rolling down to the river.

Back to the Market Place and first to the E along Castle Street towards Melford Bridge. CASTLE STREET is uneventful and pleasant. The most interesting houses are right at the start: No. 1 is a C16 timber-framed house with a coved jetty, Nos. 3–5 are an early C16 pair with an exposed frame and a crown-post roof inside. Nos. 4–6 and No. 14 have their origins in the C17, but nothing of that remains; the latter was the Three Hoops pub until 1930 when the pilasters marked sensible window and door openings. E from here the C19 is the dominant century with three or four flint-faced terraces dating from c. 1830–40, some showing pretty doorcases, e.g. to Nos. 47–51. Unusual shell pediments over two doors inside No. 49. Opposite, Nos. 32–34, three storeys and another couple of good mid-century doorcases. Just after this a new road branches r. to loop back to Old Market Street, and Castle Street widens and has trees along the middle (planted in 1902). At the E end CASTLE HOUSE of c. 1810 looks out across Castle Meadow to Castle Hill: red brick skin at the front, otherwise flint over a core of coursed clunch. Three bays with four giant pilasters defining them and a platband interrupting the rhythm. The stick-baluster staircase typical of its date. Further still MELFORD BRIDGE, over the Thet. Dated 1697. Inscription to record that it was built for John Wodehouse of the distinguished Norfolk family, with his coat of arms. Brick with two semicircular stone arches and a subsidiary brick one. Modest and now looking silly, for the re-aligned road misses it by a few yards.

Back again and now to the W. In KING STREET the best is at the W end. This was from c. 1830 the principal shopping street of Thetford, but was drastically affected by the reconstruction necessary to take the enormous increase in population experienced after 1959. Towards the W end is RIVERSIDE WALK, an entirely new street created in 1968 leading down to the river and an extensive SHOPPING CENTRE with the same name. It is built over former maltings, tanneries and modest housing. These low-rise arcades of pedestrianized shopping streets are more familiar now than in the 1960s, and this example has been an unqualified success: yellow brick facing, uniform shopping

units, flat roofs. The architects were the firms of *Berry, Crane &*
Noble and *Dawber, Fox & Robinson*. The new building does not
detract from the centre of the town because it is tucked away
from immediate view; always corners have to be turned to appreciate the amount that has gone.

On the N side KING'S HOUSE has a stately mid-C18 front of
five bays and two storeys. Gault brick with red brick dressings
to the front, flint and stone the remainder. Parapet curved up at
the corners. Doorway with reeded and fluted Ionic columns
carrying a pediment. Sash windows. The house was rebuilt in
1763 and became Council offices in 1950–1, which involved some
internal rearranging by *S. J. Wearing*. Staircase with wrought-
iron balusters and a ramped and wreathed handrail. The
GARDEN WALLS behind have reused clunch banded with flint
and brick, a common Thetford type. Late C18. In front is a
STATUE of Thomas Paine (1737–1809) who was born here.
Erected for the Thomas Paine Foundation of America. 1964 by
Sir Charles Wheeler. Bronze and gold leaf, the latter replaced in
1973 and later. Opposite, No. 51 has a gault-brick early C19
façade of two storeys and attic in three bays. C20 plate-glass
display windows, sashes above. The late C15 hall house is difficult to identify, most of the timber frame having disappeared
under later alterations. Sunk-quadrant bridging beams with
keeled fillets and bar stops.

On the corner with Bridge Street THE BELL HOTEL, one of
the more celebrated coaching inns. First mentioned in 1493.
The mid-C15 block faces King Street with a long jettied front.
Timber-framed, the ground floor close-studded and with an
angle-post to the dragon beam at the W. The decoration nothing like comparable Suffolk or Essex examples. The carriage
entrance to the l. now glazed to provide an entrance hall. Gabled
roof with C19 ridge stacks. To the rear is a block at r. angles,
C17, with cross casements, and with a ground-floor corridor
added in 1966 by *Feilden & Mawson*: by the same architects are
the two- and three-storey blocks on concrete stilts extending
down Bridge Street (job architect *Bernard Feilden*). At the back
of the main block a C19 extension encloses the former timber-
framed external gallery, making it an internal one. It has a jetty
on arched braces. The studs in the main bar to the N have pronounced heavy scantling; a four-centred arch in the S wall. A
first-floor room has a perspective WALL PAINTING of a series of
arches and in the gallery is an exposed piece of wattle and daub,
the wattles tied with grass string. The roof unfortunately C20.

Round the corner of the church and N up WHITE HART STREET.
On the E side Nos. 2–6, at the moment Council offices and
shops, originally built as the C17 White Hart Inn, one of
Thetford's three coaching inns. This one declined sharply when
the railway came in the 1840s and finally closed in the C20. Big
carriage entrance to the rear yard. The S rooms show the former
timber frame and there is even a dragon beam, though whether
this was intended for a jetty is difficult to tell.

On the W side No. 21, THE ANCIENT HOUSE MUSEUM, which

was exposed as a building of interest in 1867 when the plaster was stripped from the close-studded timber frame. Prince Duleep Singh bought the house in 1921 and presented it to the town for a museum, and while the restoration which followed in the next three years was excellent for the date it is a pity the roof was lost. The house has a plan essentially modern, that is, there is no open hall. Houses in towns were the first to reject the hall house plan, in Norfolk towards the end of the C15 or a little later. Here it is interesting that the screens passage with its two service rooms to the S was not immediately done away with, so the date must be *c.* 1490. The mouldings inside preclude anything earlier still. The generous bow front of *c.* 1800 to the r. and the added sashes date to the moment it was divided into two. The blocked four-centred door l. of the entrance is a mystery. It must be contemporary and may represent a quick change of mind for the use of one of the S rooms, from service to shop – it is certainly in an unconvincing place. First-floor overhang and a wide door canopy – one cannot call it a hood. Inside, the main hall, or here principal room, to the r. boasting an exceptionally fine ceiling with moulded and decorated beams carried on wave-moulded principal studs and a pair of carved braces. The mouldings have fleur-de-lys, punched studs and lascivious double tongue-stops enriching the otherwise common multiple rolls. Wide brick fireplace with a fragment of decorated bressumer. The stairs added to the rear in their own gabled tower: very plain, *c.* 1600. The rear wing always bore the major service rooms, now all very much rebuilt.

Next door the KING'S HEAD INN. Early C18, with a rebuilt brick façade of 1878 over a flint core. The wide frontage has a square-headed carriage arch to the r., assorted C19 and C20 windows (one C18 casement over the carriageway), and four doorways. Chamfered bridging beams inside. Opposite, No. 14 was managed as a theatre by the Fisher family from the early C19 until it closed in 1833. The tall brick façade probably dates from this time as does the deeply coved ceiling to the main first-floor room. It is likely that this was open through both storeys in the theatre's day, the upper parts served by the modest stick-baluster staircase still *in situ*. Pretty late C18 shopfront to the l. Further on No. 22, THE CHANTRY, plastered, long, of seven bays to the street, the centre three recessed. Over the outer pairs of bays are shouldered C17 gables and the whole is linked by a parapet. Nice doorcase in the centre under a segmental hood on reeded columns. The door opens directly into the early C17 hall which has, at the back, a late C17 staircase of two twisted balusters to each tread rising from r. to l. This must be very late C17. It used to have its own ceiling, decorated with painted arabesques. A rear room with small-framed panelling and a deep well. The rear has been rebuilt in the C19. Crossing the main Norwich Road leads us to CROXTON ROAD; almost immediately on the r. a set of four single-storey ALMSHOUSES erected for George and Sarah Tyrrell in 1885. Good decorative red brick, especially the four prominent decorated chimneystacks.

Three projecting bays with gables and, between the bays, two-light cross casements. The boundary wall returns to the rear and throws out little gabled outbuildings.

To the W of the corner of the Bell Hotel and St Peter's Church is MINSTERGATE. First MINSTERGATE HOUSE in the junction with St Nicholas Street, three mid-C18 bays and two mansarded additions of the early C19 tacked on to the S end. It is on the site of the church of St Nicholas, of which only a few loose stones remain. Minstergate is better known for the former BURRELL ENGINEERING WORKS. The brick and flint early C19 block is 80 yds further on the r., extended by two and then another two bays to the SE. It has been partly converted to shops. The original is of six bays in two storeys, with an all-brick façade. On the other side the BURRELL MUSEUM, attractive, built as the paint and finishing shop in 1846–7. Seven bays of double timber doors hung on cast-iron piers and tensioned by steel rods. There is a continuous clerestory on three sides. The segmental roof supported by Belfast trusses. Became a museum in 1987.

To the S of the Bell Hotel BRIDGE STREET leads to the cast-iron BRIDGE of 1829 by *Francis Stone*, the County Surveyor: single-span arch with railings strung between compound lattice muntins. Over this bridge and up White Hart Street went all the Norwich–London traffic until 1968. Overlooking the bridge, BRIDGE HOUSE, early C18, of red brick, with a good pedimented doorcase but disappointing inside – only the early C19 stick-baluster staircase arrests one's attention. Across the bridge and l. into OLD BURY ROAD. No. 1 and Nos. 3–5, put up in 1840 and 1838 respectively according to their datestones. They present respectable flint and brick façades and pretty doorcases and at the back overlook the void of the Court House car park. At the junction with Bury Road FULMERSTON ALMSHOUSES, founded in 1610 under the terms of the will of Sir Richard Fulmerston who died in 1566 after having made a fortune out of the Dissolution. The date 1612 used to be visible on the S gable and on the sundial, and the date 1610 still remains on the plaque on the E face. Flint alternating with ashlar blocks and with red brick trimmings and stone quoins. Symmetrical, one storey, four doors with Gothic panels and eight three-light trefoiled windows. This is much more *c.* 1860 than 1610, so the front must have been Gothicized in the C19. There was a restoration in 1968. From here into BURY ROAD. Quite a number of nice simple flint and yellow brick terraces, all from the years 1840–60. Unfortunately hardly one now has the same fenestration as its neighbour. Also some nice doorcases. ST MARY'S ESTATE is off to the r. up Icknield Way and just a little further, on the r. again, *S. J. Wearing*'s Corporation housing of 1912–14 arranged around a wide curving street, ST MARY'S CRESCENT. ST BARNABAS CLOSE, further S, on the l. Built as the Union Workhouse in 1836 to the design of *William Thorold*, still Classical and with the usual arrangement of wings. Demolished 1978 and now a housing estate consisting of tedious

dwellings arranged spaciously within the confines of the flint
and brick WALL which enclosed the workhouse buildings.

Returning as far as Mill Lane and so to BRIDGE'S WALK and the
disused WATERMILL. A gault-brick, early C19 mill of three
storeys in five bays. The windows replaced. A big gabled lucam
over the loading doors. The tail races emerge as round arches
under the bridge over the river. On Spring Walk 250 yds SSE is
the former PUMP ROOM which belongs to the short-lived saga
of Thetford as a fashionable spa. John Burrell Faux laid out
SPRING WALK as a promenade in 1818 and had the house built
over the spring itself, but the venture was unsuccessful and
closed in 1838. The house is of gault brick, two storeys in three
bays, two French windows and sashes. From here one must
return to the Market Place.

THETFORD WARREN LODGE. 1⅞ m. NW on the Brandon Road   74
and ¼ m. W into a clearing in a deciduous, mainly oak, wood is a
sturdy early C15 tower house, built perhaps for the prior's
gamekeeper (suggestion of S. E. Rigold). The Prior of Thetford
had the rights of free warren over this part of Breckland Heath.
It was burnt out in 1935 and has been preserved by a modern
flat roof. Flint, some brick and stone dressings. Small windows,
mostly with shouldered lintels. The house was two-storeyed
and had one room on each floor, the ground floor with the
narrower window slits. Both storeys with a fireplace in the N
wall served by an external stepped stack. Staircase in the SW
corner reaching up into a polygonal turret above the parapet,
the turret known from Martin's C18 drawing. The S, and only,
entrance is arched, and has a *meurtrière* or hole for dropping
objects on to unwelcome visitors. The NW corner of the first
floor had a garderobe, the chute of which remains. In the care
of English Heritage and open to the public.

Overspill Estates

The adoption of Thetford as an overspill town for London from
1958 resulted in large areas of new houses. Almost everything
was designed by the *LCC* (later *GLC*) *Architect's Department*
under *Hubert Bennett*. In Thetford housing came before factories. The first estate was the NEWTOWN ESTATE to the W of
the town between London and Bury Roads. Expanded 1958–9.
The second estate was the REDCASTLE FURZE ESTATE
between Brandon and London Roads. 170 houses went up in
1965–7 based on the Radburn principle, i.e. that cars and people
are separated. Access to the entrances is by footpath only, these
paths meeting up and converging on a central shopping area.
Cars park at the back. The houses conventional and two-storey;
brick with gabled roofs. The third and final estate is at ABBEY
FARM between the railway station and the River Ouse, which
has a new bridge carrying the principal road, Canterbury Way.
In all 978 houses were built in 1967–72 in long low terraces of
up to eighteen each. Again a conventional building technique
was used.

Factories by 1968 took up 200 acres of land; some were standard units by the Council, others purpose-built. Williams Engineering, 1958, was the first, by the *LCC*: steel frame and curtain cladding. Jeyes, 1968; Thermos and Danepak followed.

SNAREHILL HALL. Near Brettenham, p. 217.

9090   THOMPSON

ST MARTIN. Mostly of *c.* 1300–40 and of flint with ashlar trim. W tower with flushwork base (chequer) and battlements (panelling). The W doorway clearly Dec, and the window over with a small reticulation motif set prettily into each unit of reticulated tracery. The style of the tower begs comparison with nearby Ashill and Caston, as if the same mason did all three. Aisleless nave. S porch with a triple niche above the entrance. The S doorway has three continuous sunk-quadrant mouldings. Windows with intersecting tracery. The chancel is properly Dec. Five-light E and three-light N and S windows with good mouchette tracery curiously blocked off but still visible. Fine piscina and sedilia with broad, low, cusped ogee arches. They have spacious interiors with foliage and carvings of Green Men. Scissor-braced nave roof of forty trusses restored in 1974, as good as that in St George's Guildhall, King's Lynn. The chancel roof was given by Robert Futter and carries the date 1648: principals and collars with braces. The S chapel is an addition built in 1450 for Sir Thomas de Shardelow and lit through a five-light panel-traceried window. General restorations 1910–13. – FONT. Octagonal, with tracery motifs; probably Dec too. – FONT COVER. Perp; miniature size. Thompson is famous for its WOODWORK. – PULPIT and READER'S DESK, panelled and with strapwork panels below the top rails, Jacobean, likely to have been a two-decker originally. The pulpit retains its tester. – SCREENS. The rood screen is of the period of the church. Slim shafts instead of mullions. Ogee-headed lights. Circles with mouchette wheels or three spherical triangles above. Remains of stencilled floral decoration in red and black which one must suppose is C15. Pair of central gates. – Of the screen to the S chapel only the base survives, *c.* 1450. – STALLS. With four misericords, two heads and two shields. – BENCHES. A whole set with poppyheads dated 1625 and 1632. Marvellous. – FAMILY PEW of the Futter family with panelling and strapwork; *c.* 1630. – COMMUNION RAIL. About 1630, with turned balusters. – SOUTH DOOR. C14, with a band of thin foliage trails round the edge and the original ring-plate, and a key 13 in. long. – WALL PAINTINGS. Large painted shield on either side of chancel E window, and other painting showing through losses in the limewash below, so evidently more painting to be uncovered here. Two consecration crosses below the window, and another at the W end of the nave N wall; all probably C14. Painting on the chancel arch, including a small shield on the S side, and further colouring on the arch to the S chapel, which retains a post-Reformation text on the S wall. Fragment of another text on the nave N wall, behind the pulpit. (DP) – ORGAN CASE. Said to be by *Pugin*. This is unlikely – *see* South Pickenham church. – PAINTING. Joseph's Coat, *c.* 1790, by *Giacomo Berger*, who lived in Rome and Naples, was a protégé of the Earl of Bristol, Bishop of Derry, and died in 1822. – LEATHER BOX for a paten.

COLLEGE FARMHOUSE, College Road, ¼ m. SSE of the church. In 1349 Sir Thomas and John de Shardelow founded and built a college on the same lines as Edmund Gonville's at Rushford (cf.), both making use of an existing, but only just completed, church nearby. The material is flint, brick and stone. It was rebuilt *c.* 1400, when the Master was Alexander de Horstead. The main college building was rectangular, disposed N–S with its front to the E, and had a conventional hall, passage and services plan. Fragments, but only fragments, of the passage are visible, and the picture is confused because in the late C17 the arrangement was altered so that the façade became the rear and received a short projecting wing, and the hall was floored. In the early C18 a new W front was created, so today the house faces away from the road. The hall was to the S (now the drawing room), reduced in size when the S gable was rebuilt. The truncated dais window can be seen at the back above one of the many doors and windows inserted in 1975. The N gable wall has two lancets, one trefoiled. The rear wing has C17 details. The present W façade is early C18, remodelled for Richard Cator who purchased in 1700, of two storeys in five bays with the entrance door r. of centre leading into what had been the screens passage; replaced casements, pilastered doorcase, panelled ridge stack. Inside, the principal room is the present dining room, N of the passage: late C16 panelling with Ionic pilasters and a palmette console. The overmantel carries the arms of Futter impaling Bacon, so is post-1534 (Dissolution) and ante-1553 (marriage). The triple and double roll-moulded bridging beams and joists are more early C16 than late. When the college was surrendered in August 1534 there was a Master, Robert Audeley, and four Fellows.

The vernacular HOUSES and COTTAGES are mainly C18, and usually timber-framed with clay lump infill, e.g. HALLFIELD FARMHOUSE, a lobby-entrance building under a thatched roof, and OLD PASTURES, College Road. CHEQUERS INN on Griston Road is from the same mould: a long range with details now C20, though the brick N gable with tumbling is mid-C18. C17 spine beams to N ground-floor rooms. Butt-purlin roof structure.

BARROWS. There are four S of Merton Park and E of Peddar's Way.

THORNHAM   *7040*

ALL SAINTS. Very wide and high nave, partly C13, partly Perp. The arcades of five bays have E.E. alternating circular and octagonal piers and double-hollow-chamfered arches, but the

Perp bases show that they were reused when the nave was heightened. This was done by the use of higher octagonal bases and then by the addition of a clerestory. Fine roof, restored in 1898, with wall-posts on stone head-corbels, longitudinal arched braces to connect them, and hammerbeams, and also subsidiary hammerbeams from the apexes of the longitudinal braces. Perp w tower with quatrefoil sound-holes below the bell-openings and simple flushwork on base and buttresses. The bell-stage fell in the C17 and was replaced in 1935 rather lower than originally. Arched doorway into the nave at a high level. Three-light Perp aisle windows shafted inside and two-storeyed s porch. The flat panelled porch ceiling is C15. The s doorway, however, is again E.E. (two detached orders of shafts). Polygonal parvis stair-tower to the NE served by a plain four-centred door in the aisle. Perp N doorway has colonnettes inside and a four-centred arch. The chancel was practically rebuilt in 1876–7, when *Frederick Preedy* was busy rebuilding the chancel arch and the E end of the nave and aisles at a cost of £2,800. It looks new and townish. Very elaborate double braced roof and a moulded arch to the organ chamber with twin colonnettes on corbels. Five stepped lancets at the E end, with shafts with shaft-rings. – FONT. C15. Octagonal, panelled stem with ogee arches and prominent polygonal bases to each dividing moulding and, on the bowl, shields in elaborately cusped quatrefoils, painted with the Instruments of the Passion and heraldic devices. The base is 1905. – PULPIT. Supposedly dated 1631 but on a C19 stem. Plain, only with some arabesque panels below the top.* – SCREEN. Bears inscription stating that it was given by John Miller and his wife; he died *c.* 1488. Only the dado survives but it has sixteen painted figures of prophets and Saints, the painting of superb quality. Foliage carving in the spandrels of the one-light divisions with ogee arches; tracery below the paintings. The centre with further dado bays missing and the truncated stiles re-set. – WALL PAINTING. Part of a post-Reformation black-letter English text on the w wall (from I Peter 5:6). – BENCHES. With poppyheads and lively animals etc. on the arms (e.g. a unicorn, a post windmill, a ship, a chalice, and three representations of the Deadly Sins – Anger, Sloth and Gluttony). – SOUTH DOOR. C15, with tracery and an ogee-headed wicket. Lock dated 1757.

METHODIST CHURCH. 1870. Red brick with the three-bay front enriched with gault brick. Hipped roof. Rather ordinary.

SCHOOL. 1858. H-plan. The tracery is Second Pointed (i.e. Geometric Dec) and the whole is a not unattractive display of High Victorian Gothic. Coursed knapped flint and stone. The centre between the wings has a porch in an angle.

THORNHAM HALL, ¼ m. SE on Hall Lane. Georgian, Neoclassical, of five bays and two and a half storeys. Built for George Hogge who died in 1811. The centre of the w façade has a big fanlight over the door and a modest later porch, above this an arched

---

* I could not find the date.

window in an arched recess, and above that a Diocletian one. One bay, two-storey wings lit through arched windows in arched recesses to the ground floor and Diocletian windows above. Awkward low hipped roofs. In the middle of the main, gabled, roof is a polygonal observatory, not an aesthetically successful feature. The two principal downstairs rooms have mechanical Adamesque plasterwork, executed flawlessly, as is all at the house. Two-bay groin-vaulted entrance lobby leads from the w door to an apsed staircase well.

RED HOUSE, w of the church, on the N side of the High Street, behind a lawn defined r. and l. by brick and flint walls. *c.* 1770, of three bays and two and a half storeys, with additional lean-to bays set back at the sides. Red brick under a hipped pantiled (black-glazed) roof. On the façade the flanking bays have two-storeyed canted window bays fitted with sashes, leaving the gap between them and the moulded brick eaves filled with a Diocletian window either side. 1770 is early for canted bays, but there seems to be no break in the brickwork. The middle bay has first an open pedimented doorcase on demi-columns and one three-light window to each floor above, both under round-arched heads and both with Gothick Y-tracery. The whole composition seems like the result of a random flick through a builder's pattern-book, which it may well be, but it has charm. The interior not so good.

Some attractive minor HOUSES also on the HIGH STREET. CHESTNUT COTTAGE is dated 1756 and was clearly built as two houses, one door being blocked. CHEQUERS, the pub. Clunch and carstone. *c.* 1680, altered internally in the C20, but the lobby-entrance plan can be identified. On the s side THORNHAM COTTAGE. Galleted knapped flint with brick and some carstone. Two storeys and attics in three bays with additions. Two-storey porch with a brick three-light window above the entrance and a datestone announcing 1624.

ROMAN ENCLOSURE. SW of the village on a slope overlooking the Wash is a rectangular earthwork measuring 133 ft by 175 ft, with a chalk cut ditch, a 20-ft-wide berm, and a footing of chalk blocks to the bank. It was built in the mid C1 A.D. The site was later occupied by an Anglo-Saxon cemetery. (DG)

THORPE ABBOTS 1070

ALL SAINTS. C13 round tower with an octagonal Perp top with brick mixed with the flint. Four bell-openings and four windows feigned in flushwork. Nave and chancel windows all over-renewed, except for one blocked N lancet in the chancel – i.e., E.E. chancel. Also of the early C13 the simple N doorway into the nave. The s doorway is early C14. Perp s windows in the nave. Tudor s porch of brick with a moulded double-chamfered arch, brick two-light side windows and diagonal buttresses. – FONT. Octagonal, Perp. Four lions against the stem, the signs of the Evangelists and four demi-figures of angels against the bowl. – SCREEN. C15. Tall, with much tracery. – PANELLING. In the chancel. Queen Anne style, altered. – STAINED GLASS. E window by *Ward & Hughes*, †1868, a Good Shepherd, Crucifixion and Sower.

THORPE ABBOTS PLACE. Demolished 1963. It was an Italianate mansion of white brick with an asymmetrically placed tower, by *E. M. Barry*, 1869–71.

THORPE-NEXT-HADDISCOE

4090

ST MATTHIAS. A small church with an extremely interesting round tower. Its lower parts are Saxon, its heightened bell-stage is Norman. The Saxon work is characterized by small windows, curiously set in alternating positions, by thin arches carved out of one stone, by a round double-splayed window now looking into the churchyard, and by tall blank arcading, now very much worn. The sharp angle with the nave W wall has flint shafts. The twin bell-openings have an intermediate shaft adorned with a fat shaft-ring. Crenellated parapet with flushwork is C15.

There is a blocked circular window high in the nave W wall, indicating that this wall at least pre-dates the tower. Otherwise the nave is of the time of the bell-openings, see the plain S and N doorways, the former seemingly rebuilt. On the N side in addition a wide, late C13 lancet and a small late C13 window with Y-tracery, on the S side Perp fenestration. C14 S porch, the arch with double wave mouldings. The chancel was rebuilt in brick in 1838, and the windows were clearly re-Gothicized later. Inside there is a very curious double recess in the W wall S of the tower arch. One half has a shelf. Was it an alms cupboard? In the S wall of the nave a blocked triple-chamfered arch, probably to a former chapel. Roofs C19. – FONT. Square, Norman, of Purbeck marble, with, on each side, four shallow blank arches. The stem has corner shafts. – BENCH. Just one old bench is left. – MONUMENT. Thomas London †1661, aged twenty-one. Pediment on consoles. The inscription starts with the hexameter: Longa ars, vita brevis, quam vere dircent (*sic*) olim. Very classical.

THORPE HALL. An attractive C17 to C18 house in a good position. H-plan. Two parts, the higher (W) with a hipped roof and clasping pilasters. Very big chimneystack of six polygonal shafts. The N front has a three-light ovolo-moulded casement but the fenestration is mainly C20. The porch is C16: two storeys, rusticated outer arch, wave-moulded jambs to inner doorway. W wing has a C17 staircase with a roll-moulded handrail.

THORPE PARVA

1070

¾ m. NE of Scole

ST MARY. What remains is the burst round tower, its upper part standing up in three erect shapes as if made by a modern sculptor.

THREXTON

8000

ALL SAINTS. Evidence of a Saxon nave 21 ft wide was found during the restoration of 1865. The round tower is probably early C13 rather than Norman, fitted with late C13 Y-tracery windows and bell-openings. C20 brick parapet. Fine N arcade of the C13 too. One octagonal and two round piers, the latter with round abaci. The piers differ slightly in capitals and bases. Double-chamfered arches. Much original red painting of trails etc. preserved. The W respond has a primitive, perhaps unfinished, leaf corbel. Dec s windows. S porch of 1865, reusing the early C14 S doorway as the outer arch: plain chamfers, semicircular arch. Chancel much restored, including the triple E lancets. C19 vestry attached to N of tower. – FONT. Octagonal, with blank window tracery motifs, pointing to a pre-Perp date. One reticulated, one three-light intersecting design. – PULPIT and READER'S DESK, the latter dated 1613 as the gift of Edward Cofe. Simple. Fluted frieze in pulpit. – STAINED GLASS. Some C15 glass in the N aisle. E window is a good example by *J. Powell & Sons*, †1868, a Nativity, Crucifixion and Ascension.

THREXTON HOUSE. Late C18. Whitewashed. Two storeys in five bays, with giant pilasters to the pedimented centre bay. The porch is no more than a bold pediment on unfluted columns, looking as if it was plucked straight from a copy-book.

THURLTON

4090

ALL SAINTS. Norman s doorway. Two orders of shafts with cushion capitals. Arch with zigzag, a motif of volutes, and billets in the hoodmould. Some of the volutes have been left unfinished. Late C13 chancel has a blocked lancet to the N, otherwise early C14 windows with cusped Y-tracery. Perp replacements to E and S. Perp nave windows, Perp N porch and Perp W tower. The porch has a flushwork gable with brick detailing, shields in the spandrels of the entrance arch and a statuary niche above it. The elaborate inner doorway has a continuous moulding of crowns (mostly broken off) with the group of the Trinity at the apex. Square hoodmould on demi-figures of angels. In the spandrels elongated angel-figures swinging censers, the folds of the garments almost with a C13 look. The W tower is quite big. It has chequer diapering of flushwork on the base, followed by a base frieze of flushwork panelling and a parapet with the same. Four-centred bell-openings. Tall tower arch of reduced form: only the lower 7 ft of circular responds remain. Boarded nave roof of 1859. – FONT. Octagonal. Against the stem four lions, against the bowl four plain shields and four plain roses. – SCREEN. C15. One-light divisions with concave-sided crocketed gables and panel tracery above them. Nice ornamental painting on the posts. – NORTH DOOR. Traceried, C16. – HOURGLASS STAND of iron by the pulpit, C17. – PAINTING. Very large figure of St Christopher (N wall), probably late C15. – MONUMENTS. Ann Denny †1665, broken pediment (its installation required the blocking of the chancel lancet and is attributed by Jon Bayliss to *Martin Morley*). – Margaret Denny †1717, nice cartouche with drapery, attributed to *Edward Stanton* (GF). – STAINED GLASS. E window. Soppy piece depicting the Virtues, †1867, probably by *J. & J. King*.

WHITEHOUSE FARMHOUSE, Low Road. One's attention is arrested by the Dutch gable on the W range and the external brick stack at the NE corner, both C17.

WINDMILL, on the main road. Brick tower mill of *c.* 1800, truncated to three storeys; converted to a house.

COLLEGE ROAD, ½ m. S of the church. One of the *Tayler & Green* groups of cottages built in the Loddon Rural District. This one is a close of semi-detached houses linked by single-storey utility ranges containing the entrance doorways (*see* Introduction, p. 165). It dates from 1946, i.e. before the architects turned to terraces, crescents etc., and apart from the colourwashing and the frieze of first-floor casements is quite conventional. A group of 1938 council houses nearby provides a useful comparison.

LOWER THURLTON, ⅝ m. NE, is another *Tayler & Green* estate, only six houses, built in 1952–3. Three different house types were required, but the architects have made the most of it.

THURTON

ST ETHELBERT. A sumptuous Norman S doorway and a simpler Norman N doorway. The S doorway has three orders of colonnettes with decorated scallop capitals (one on the W side just turning waterleaf), and in the arch zigzag and roll mouldings and on the hoodmould two orders of scallops at r. angles to the wall. Blocked N doorway with two orders, the inner chamfered, the outer roll-moulded. Nave and chancel are under one thatched roof. The windows are of *c.* 1300–30, mostly wide lancets, trefoil-cusped, but there is also intersecting and reticulated tracery. The former W tower is now a bell-turret, i.e. seems to stand on the roof of the nave because the nave overlaps it N and S, creating rooms entered from the nave under four-centred arches. It has a two-light Dec W window, but the upper part is Late Perp of squared knapped flint and brick. – FONT. Octagonal. It could be C17 Gothic. – COMMUNION RAILS. C17, turned balusters and square newels. – STAINED GLASS. Many collected pieces, including an English C15 Trinity and much foreign glass of the C16 to C18. They were installed by *S. C. Yarington* in 1826 for the Beauchamp-Proctors of Langley Hall, with additional glass by *Robert Allen*. Seven of the thirteen windows remain. – WALL PAINTINGS. Discovered in 1988, conserved 1991 by *Andrea Kirkham*. N nave has a very elaborate St Christopher of *c.* 1500, with a crab and lobster etc. beneath the Saint's feet. To the E an indecipherable smaller early C14 subject, with arcading below. Fragments on S nave wall.

THURTON HALL, Hall Road. Brick and some timber-framing, though the front looks like ashlar. The C17 details are the

moulded mullioned and transomed windows and the early C17
doorway in the W gable wall. Façade of two storeys in five bays,
with a two-storeyed central porch and stepped end-gables. The
windows are in segmental recesses ornamented by brick dentils.
The porch is framed by giant pilasters. Six hearths were assessed
in the 1664 Hearth Tax.

BEECH FARMHOUSE, W of the Hall (in Bergh Apton parish). C17
lobby-entrance type much modernized. The E stepped gable is
C20, although the W is original. Two storeys in five bays. BARN,
30 yds N, dated 1681 in the W gable and 1698 in the E gable, yet
the gable-heads are still stepped.

HIGH HOUSE, Hall Road. The E part is a remnant of a larger C17
house. It has a stepped E gable. The rear has a blocked first-
floor window. Two C17 fireplaces and a winder still by the
stack, where it should be. Lower four-bay additions to W.

ST ETHELBERT'S CLOSE, NE of the church, off Vale Road. By
Tayler & Green (*see* Introduction, p. 165), 1949. The layout
includes two small greens. The one-storey houses are, very
nicely, at first invisible. As with most, they have been sold and
given uPVC windows which spoils them utterly.

THURTON LODGES. *See* Langley, p. 513.

THUXTON   0000

ST PAUL. Short unbuttressed W tower with an octagonal top connected to the square parts below by broaches. Very tall C15
tower arch. The tower seems to be a replacement of a Norman
tower, the masonry of which is still evident in the lower courses.
More C11 masonry in the bottom of the N nave wall. A will of
1416 left money towards the tower, a date which would fit the
top and the tower arch at least. A S arcade of the C14 and its
quatrefoil piers have been demolished and the capitals hacked
off. In the chancel, on the S side, a former tomb recess (or small
chapel), also pulled down, which extended beyond the S wall.
Only the front of the tomb-chest with shields remains. In the
nave NE corner a caryatid built to support a former image.
Victorian chancel arch doubtless put in during the restoration
of 1896–8. Kelly reports that apart from the tower the church
was thoroughly restored, and so it is, but the Ladbroke drawing
of *c.* 1823 shows it as now, so perhaps the details can be trusted.
Triple-lancet E window. – FONT. Norman, of tub shape. At the
four corners thick spurs with leaves and one head as decoration.
– PULPIT. Jacobean, re-assembled, with the familiar short,
broad, blank arches. – STAINED GLASS. Enamelled figure of St
Paul in S chancel, *c.* 1830. Crucifixion in E window, †1896.

THWAITE ST MARY   3090

ST MARY. The nave has a mature Norman S doorway of *c.* 1140
with two orders of colonnettes. Decorated shafts and decoration

even in the angles between the colonnettes. One motif is of
small sunk scallop shells. In the arch twisted rope, roll, and a
kind of ornament that looks like beakhead left in the block and
never carved. Hoodmould of two orders of scallops set at r.
angles to the wall surface. A beast at the apex. It seems to go
with the Haddiscoe and Hales work. Unbuttressed w tower of
the C15 with much use of brick including a stair-turret completely of brick. On the w side a row of three shields. From the
position of the s doorway the nave has presumably been lengthened to the w when the tower was added. Low thatched nave
with Perp windows (as shown by Ladbroke) and tiled brick
chancel. The chancel is of 1738, but was remodelled in 1861,
including the three-light E window of Bath stone. Inside all
seems C19. – FONT. Early C14 stem made up of eight shafts, but
later bowl. – SCREEN. Early C14, see the trefoiled arches and
the lack of tracery. The dado has been panelled over, but what
lies behind? – TOWER STAIR DOOR. C15 with its iron ring-plate.
– STAINED GLASS. E window has four roundels with symbols of
Evangelists, 1848 by *Lucy Gower*, re-set after war damage in 1944.

THWAITE HALL, to the N. C17 timber-framed house with a s
front composed of three gables, the middle one a porch. Pair of
wall-stacks to the rear with octagonal or plain shafts. The
nearby BARN early C17 and quite large, timber-framed with a
roof of clasped purlins and queen-struts.

TIBENHAM

ALL SAINTS. In the nave one blocked Norman N window. The
chancel E window, if correctly renewed, of the late C13 (three
stepped lancet lights under one arch). Dec s aisle, complete
with doorway and arcade (four bays, quatrefoil piers with thin
shafts in the diagonals, round capitals, polygonal abaci, arches
with one hollow chamfer and one wave). The nave roof with
arched braces is probably late C14. Tall Perp w tower. Diaper
flushwork on the base and lower part of the buttresses. Chequer
flushwork higher up the buttresses. Panel flushwork on the
battlements. The four Evangelists instead of pinnacles. Tall stair-
turret to SE. The E wall of the tower is sheer, without openings
below the bell-stage. Late Perp, three- and four-light straight-
headed windows in the s aisle and in the clerestory above, but
one good Dec two-light window immediately E of the Perp s
porch (fleurons in jambs). – FONT. Octagonal, with flat-curved
motifs of Dec windows. The stem has shafts. – SCREEN. Bits of
the rood screen reused in connection with the enclosure of the
BUXTON CHAPEL. This chapel, situated at the E end of the s
aisle, is the chief interest of the church. It was licensed in 1635
by Archbishop Laud in order to 'promote the importance of the
said John' (Buxton) and contained brasses, of which the figures
have disappeared, and the balustraded Jacobean FAMILY PEW
raised half-way up. It is reached by a staircase from the E, which
gives a good opportunity to examine the late C14 pierced span-

drels of the aisle roof. There is also part of the Jacobean SCREEN. – The READING DESK no doubt is of the 1630s (NW nave). It is four-sided and four-legged like a table, the legs sloping inwards. – Sumptuous Jacobean PULPIT. Octagonal, with back panel and big tester, the latter with strapwork on top, little openwork obelisks, pendants and a coffered under-surface. The pulpit with arcaded panels. – BOX PEWS. – PAINTINGS. In an altar niche behind the pulpit a painted figure of a man, part of a scene which has gone. – Also, a very different effect from anything else in the church, large aggressive Victorian inscriptions of verses from the Bible on zigzag scrolls.

CHANNONZ HALL, 1½ m. SE. The great Elizabethan house of Robert Buxton was built c. 1569 round three sides of a courtyard but all but the (E) kitchen wing was demolished in 1784. This is now a farmhouse. Of red brick. The date 1569 appears over a doorway, but not in original figures. It is, however, probably correct. Stepped N gable. The front, now back, has three- and four-light mullioned and transomed windows with pediments. 1569 is early for pediments. Moulded brick stringcourses. The doorway on the E side remains, under a pediment. The l. end-gable with polygonal angle-shafts, decorated pinnacles, and small pedimented windows. Also one angle-shaft preserved of the r. gable-end. The opposite side, now the entrance side, has cross casements and a stack with octagonal shafts. Inside, there are panelled doors and some panelled walls dating from 1721 when the amateur architect *John Buxton* undertook repairs for his own occupation. Buxton built the COACH HOUSE to the NE, 1721–4. Red brick with a stepped gable to one end but the roof hipped at the other end. Two storeys in three bays. The STABLES stand to the NE also, c. 1721, presumably by *Buxton* too. Stepped gables. There is a projecting central bay under a stepped gable dated 1860 and three projections to the N side leading into the stockyard.

ALMSHOUSES, Church Street. 1846. One storey, lit through six three-light metal casements (plus two intruding late C20 windows). These and the four doors have hoodmoulds on label stops.

Tibenham has examples of FARMHOUSES from several periods. HASTINGS HALL, N of the church, has a mid-C16 timber-framed house with a cross passage served by opposing arched doors. Two storeys, the upper jettied, and close-studded framing. Inside is just one large room, with appropriate partitioning. CHURCH FARMHOUSE, Church Lane, is late C16, timber-framed, and with a two-storeyed porch at the front and a similar stair-turret at the back. Fine chimneystack with a moulded base and four circular flues. YEWTREE FARMHOUSE, Low Road, is also C16, with a C17 rear wing. Good bridging beams with sunk-quadrant mouldings and a brick fireplace under a depressed arch. TIBENHAM FARMHOUSE and DYSON'S FARMHOUSE, both on Long Row, are C17 and timber-framed. Both have some details of interest: the first with octagonal and lozenge chimney flues, the second with jettied W and N gables and a lobby-entrance plan. SHRUBBERY FARMHOUSE ($1\frac{7}{8}$ m. WNW). Very early C18 red brick house of two storeys in four bays. Stepped gables and a platband between the floors. The windows and the rear wing are C19.

TILNEY ALL SAINTS

ALL SAINTS. The church belongs to the group of C12–C13 Fenland churches with very long naves, built when the land was reclaimed from the sea. The interior shows that the church to the extent of almost its whole length already existed in the C12. Nave and aisles and chancel chapels of altogether seven bays. No structural division between nave and chancel except a drop in the exterior roof level. Round, single-step arches. The capitals in the chapel arcades earlier than in the aisle arcades. In the latter their details, waterleaf and small stiff-leaf, approach 1190. Also the NW respond shows keeling. The piers are circular except for the curious irregularity of one pier on the N side which repeats (and doubles) the section of the NW respond. Yet it does not seem to have been a respond. The chancel projected beyond the E end of the arcades. Traces of Norman lower as well as upper windows. The stringcourse for the upper windows continues along the clerestory of the nave and suggests that the nave had a Norman clerestory. The flat Norman clasping E buttresses of the chancel also survive. In the C13 a W tower was added and connected with the Norman nave by a wide arcade bay. Trefoiled responds and double-chamfered arches. Very tall tower arch (there existed, as we have seen, a clerestory) allowing the view of the upper lancets in the W wall. The tower is ashlar-faced and has big polygonal buttresses. On the first stage three tall lancets in arcading as at Walsoken and West Walton. Inside they have a wall-passage (West Walton has a corresponding external wall-passage). Upper parts and short recessed stone spire referred to in bequests for construction of 1428. Dec the W doorway, with its pretty flanking buttresses. Dec the N doorway and the windows of the N chapel. The N aisle windows and the chancel E window Perp, the latter of five lights with a transom. S aisle and S chapel windows Late Perp and later. S doorway late C13 with shafts and naturalistic foliage in capitals. Perp clerestory. Dec the hammerbeam roof, in two registers of hammerbeams, the upper false, as at Swaffham. Every second hammerbeam on a wall-post with a small figure, the others with a horizontal angel figure. Chancel hammerbeam roof restored 1965–6, so now with only parts C15. – FONTS. One with an octagonal Perp bowl. The other also octagonal and at first Perp-looking, but with four inscriptions on the bowl which show that at least the bowl is of the C17. – STALLS. Simple, with some misericords, one with a head, one with a leaf motif. – SCREENS. Perp parclose screens have tracery. Rood screen of 1618, with a plain dado, five big open arches with late C17 foliage, and a top tier of vertically symmetrical balusters and obelisks. – COMMUNION

RAILS. C17, with muntins dividing open arched panels. – CROSS. In churchyard, S of the S porch. C14 cross base. Square shaft with rolled edges.

Of HOUSES, nothing major. The best is TILNEY OLD HALL. Two-storey S front with a gabled wing to the r. Brick. Divers mullioned windows and casements and a square porch. The stack with quadruple flues. The date late C16 but very much modernized in the C18, though the winder stairs still by the stack. ALL SAINTS HOUSE, Church Road, would be better without the C20 casements. Early C18, two storeys and four bays. Platband between the floors.

TILNEY-CUM-ISLINGTON
see ISLINGTON

TILNEY ST LAWRENCE   5010

ST LAWRENCE. Short Dec W tower formerly with a lead spire. It is of carstone and ashlar. Two orders of shafts to the W door and an undercut arch. Double-chamfered arch into nave. Wave mouldings to the S porch. The square-headed nave windows correspond to Ladbroke's 1820 drawing, so presumably restored accurately. N chancel chapel with two bays of Perp arcades to the chancel. The chancel and transepts of 1846 at which time the ruthless restoration of the rest occurred, inflicted by *Buckler*. The new work E.E. and impoverished in spirit; lancets and plate tracery. – ROYAL ARMS. Of James I, dated 1620; painted.

GRAY'S HALL, Lynn Road. Of the mid C18. Seven bays, two storeys, with a blank half-storey and a parapet. The stone door-case has a pediment. The sash windows have brick aprons. Dentils on platband. Five of the first-floor sashes are original.

DUNCAN'S FARMHOUSE, next to the last. Later C18 three-bay house with a thin porch and a pretty Regency balcony over: thin iron supports carry a concave roof.

TITCHWELL   7040

ST MARY. Small, with a C12 round tower carrying a dear little twisted lead spike. The bell-openings are of two round-arched lights with a polygonal shaft between and cushion capitals, i.e. probably early C13. The E openings blocked when the nave was raised. C19 W window below a triangular-headed one. Arch to nave without responds or mouldings. Norman chancel, see the blocked S window. The E wall also had formerly a different fenestration, but the traces point to a group of lancets rather than to Norman windows. The surviving jambs of these and the Norman window show ashlar PAINTING. In the chancel also half of a C14 ogee-headed piscina has been discovered. Low tomb recess in the chancel N wall, again only a fragment (these relics uncovered in 1902). C13 S doorway with one order of detached colonnettes and a deeply undercut moulded arch. Perp nave windows. Nave roof from the 1890 restoration. – FONTS. Octagonal C12 bowl on a C19 spiral-fluted base, the bowl so worn that it appears circular. Also a stone baluster font of 1798, used as a flower vase (in chancel, originally from Burnham Deepdale). – SCREEN. Late C15 but restored in 1902. Some painting to dado. – STAINED GLASS. In the w window The Sower in a landscape, †1889, good, in the Arts and Crafts style. It might be by *Frampton*. NW nave window is signed by *Frampton*, †1907, but not as good. The other N window by *Heaton, Butler & Bayne*, †1908.

VILLAGE CROSS, S of the church by the coast road. The whole octagonal shaft and the knob at the top are preserved. Square socket stone and some C15 brick in the base.*

8020   TITTLESHALL

ST MARY. Dec w tower and chancel. The tower has a big deep niche above the w window and, corresponding to it, on the N and s, openings with the four-petal motif in a circle. Ogee-headed niches in the NW and SW buttresses. Very elaborately moulded tower arch, mostly in continuous mouldings. The chancel E window is of five lights with glorious reticulated tracery. On the chancel s side Curvilinear tracery including the four-petal motif, and a blocked window and door. On the N side a MAUSOLEUM erected for the Coke interments *c.* 1720. It is of red brick laid in English bond, with raking buttresses and honeycomb ventilation panels, and in 1897 was partitioned for the organ chamber and the burial chamber sealed (it contains various coffins). Aisleless Perp nave lit through three three-light transomed windows N and s. – FONT. Octagonal, C15, tracery on the stem, quatrefoils on the bowl. – STAINED GLASS. E window, †1866 by *Clayton & Bell*. Nice rich figures in very clear colours, one to each of five lights; Christ and Saints. – s nave, two windows by *Heaton, Butler & Bayne*. Especially fine the depictions of the Healing of the Sick, Martha and Mary, and Mary and Jesus, †1877. The other window has a Good Shepherd of 1891.

MONUMENTS. The Coke monuments are all in the chancel, not the mausoleum, and are at Tittleshall because in 1533 Robert Coke bought the manor as the first part of the great Holkham Estate. After the Holkham mausoleum was built in 1870, burials were made there. Bridget Coke, née Paston, †1598. An excellent alabaster monument. Kneeling figure set within a recessed arch, and kneeling children against the base. Beautiful crumpled ribbonwork against the pilasters. Cartouche on top. – Sir Edward

---

* *Donthorn* built a Tudor rectory in 1824 with a two-storey porch, demolished in 1933.

Coke, Lord Chief Justice, the great champion of parliamentary
rights, 'oraculum non dubium... scientiae oceanus', †1634,
husband of the former. Attributed to *Nicholas Stone*, 1639, but
probably by his assistant *John Hargrave*. It cost £400. Black
and white marble. Simple sarcophagus, white recumbent effigy.
Noble Tuscan columns l. and r. carrying a broken segmental
pediment on which recline not two but four Virtues. – Robert
Coke †1679. Black and white marble. Tomb-chest. The cartouches have weird faces contrived out of the folds still in the
mid-C17 manner. Back wall with an open segmental pediment
on elongated black corbels. Volutes l. and r. beautifully engraved.
No effigy. The piece is attributed to *Abraham Storey* (GF). –
Thomas Coke, first Earl of Leicester, †1759. Big Corinthian 101
columns carrying a pediment. Outside to the l. and r. busts of
the Earl and the Countess. The monument is signed by *Charles
Atkinson* (who made most of the chimneypieces at Holkham
Hall), but the busts are by *Roubiliac*. – Mrs Jane Coke †1800 at
Bath. By *Joseph Nollekens*, 1805. White marble. Fine flowing
group in relief of the lady, a putto at the bottom to her r., an
angel also to her r., but higher up, receiving her. Jane Coke was
the wife of Thomas William, the great agriculturalist, and her
monument cost 3,000 guineas. – ROYAL ARMS. To George III,
painted by *L. Cobbe* of King's Lynn before 1801.

WOODFORD LODGE, at the S end of the village, on Fakenham
Road. Outwardly Georgian, brick, of five bays and two storeys.
Two porches, the E one enriched by coupled giant pilasters.
Timber-framed C17 interior.

MOATED SITE, 380 yds N of the church, of a former manor house,
which a map shows had gone by 1596. (AR)

GODWICK. *See* p. 360.

TIVETSHALL ST MARGARET   *1080*

ST MARGARET. The chancel is of *c.* 1300. A plain Easter
Sepulchre inside. Unbuttressed Dec W tower of knapped flint.
Money was left in 1456 for a new tower but only the flushwork-
panelled top stage can be of that date. Perp nave windows and
S doorway with shields in the spandrels, on which the emblem
of the Trinity and the Instruments of the Passion. C15 panelled
nave roof with arched braces and bosses, re-boarded by *H. J.
Green* in the late C19. The interior of the church – left happily
alone – is dominated by the prodigiously large ROYAL ARMS of
Elizabeth I, filling the tympanum above the chancel arch – a
most remarkable survival. Apart from 'God Save our Queene
Elizabeth', the Commandments, and another inscription in
black-letter, the names of those are recorded who 'caused this
for to be done', and the date 1587. It was restored in 1952 by
Maurice Keevil, and again in 1990 by the *Canterbury Cathedral
Wallpaintings Workshop*. – SCREEN. Only the base is in order,
with painting including a shield with four magpies. Of the upper
parts the bare bones alone remain. – BENCHES. With poppyheads

and mutilated figures on the arm-rests; C15. – STAINED GLASS.
In the E window some tiny C14 fragments.

FRIENDS' MEETING HOUSE, Lodge Road, ⅞ m. NE. Nice four-
square red brick house with a hipped roof. Five-bay front with
three windows and two pilastered doorways. The old burial
ground in front. 1812 according to Kelly.

CHESTNUT FARMHOUSE, Station Road. On the first floor are
arched panels of pargeting, not complete. The three-light casements all C19 but one blocked mullioned window remains from
the C17.

AYLMER'S HALL, Carpenter's Walk. Early C17 timber-framed
house extended to the N in the later C17 to form a rather long
range. The earlier bit has a lobby-entrance.

1080

TIVETSHALL ST MARY

ST MARY. Ruinous. The long chancel of c. 1310–20 had Y-tracery
and cusped and uncusped intersecting tracery. Still roofed in
1960 but not at the time of writing, the tiles carried off to
Tivetshall St Margaret. Nave windows Perp, but the S doorway
again of the early C14, and one N window with Y-tracery. The W
tower was also of c. 1320. Today it is a shapeless crag.

RAM INN, Norwich Road. Two storeys and attic. Mullioned and
transomed casements remain to the upper floor from the early
C17, but the building has had considerable C20 attention.

MEADOW COTTAGE, Rectory Road. A late C16 timber-framed
house with internal bridging beams carried on carved studs.
The position of the C20 porch indicates a lobby-entrance.

4090

TOFT MONKS

ST MARGARET. Fine octagonal tower, i.e. octagonal from the
foot. Lancet windows, also circular windows. The bell-openings
also are tall lancets, flanked by blank lancets. C15 battlements
with flushwork panelling. The two nave doorways must have
been Norman originally; see their internal shape. In the W wall
of the nave two puzzling Norman windows l. and r. of the
tower. The tower arch also has imposts which must be Norman,
though the arch is pointed. Above, a round-headed doorway
(with an unexplained niche to its r.; cf. Norton Subcourse). Yet
another round-headed doorway higher up. All this looks as if
the tower may be Norman and only encased polygonally in the
C13. Late C13 chancel re-done in the C19 with two lancets N
and S and a four-light E window. Undercut chancel arch of original build. Nave with various Perp windows. Perp S porch with
a little flushwork panelling in a band of panels with ogee heads.
Arch-braced roof inside both porch and nave, the latter with a
castellated wall-plate. – FONT. C15. Against the stem four lions;
against the bowl four angels in crinkly clouds and the signs of
the four Evangelists. – FONT COVER. C17, probably not the one

which required the elaborate beam above. – STAINED GLASS. E
window designed by *Thomas Derrick*, made by *Gilbert Sheedy*,
1952; Christ Enthroned. – MONUMENT. John Bayspoole †1653.
Alabaster tablet consisting of different pieces. At the bottom an
open book on a base. At the top shields in roundels.

POUND COTTAGE, near the church, on Pound Lane. Of interest
for the lozenge stack, the lobby-entrance plan, the winder *in situ*
next to the chimney and the black-letter script over the E room
fireplace carrying the date 1663.

TOFT MONKS HOUSE, ⅝ m. NE on Yarmouth Road. A datestone
records it was built in 1819 for Wm. Grimmer Sen. Gault brick,
quite substantial in three by five bays. The entrance (S) side
with a one-bay pediment. Door with fanlight and stone rustication. Two stone platbands. Wall to SE links with the COACH-
HOUSE. It has a stable and hay-loft besides.

TOFT MONKS HALL, off the Yarmouth Road. Colourwashed C17
timber-framed house in four bays. N front with the fluted
pilasters and corner paterae to the doorcase typical of the early
C19. Casements. S front with a door as well, up some steps.
Two brick fireplaces under four-centred arches. The frame has
jowled studs.

THE ELMS, I m. SE. With stepped gables, that to N with an external stack. The five-bay front has two-storey canted bay
windows to the end bays and a later Georgian doorway with
Doric columns and an open pediment, but the brickwork is
consistently early C17. The stair-turret at the back also with
stepped gables and with mullioned and transomed casements.
OUTBUILDINGS with stepped gables including the BARN
attached to the W by a crenellated wall. Cart entrance to E with
pilasters r. and l. Wind-braces in the roof.

BULL'S GREEN is a small hamlet ¼ m. SW. BULL'S GREEN
FARMHOUSE has hideous render over the early C17 timber
frame and mixed C19 and C20 casements to the three-bay S
front. Four octagonal shafts to the ridge stack. Lobby-entrance
plan.

MAYPOLE GREEN, a more significant hamlet ⅝ m. W of the church.
The PRIORY has a stair-turret dated 1546 attached to the S
front. Various windows including ovolo-moulded casements.
To the l. sash windows and a door, to the r. a big external stack.
Another at the back. A N wing re-skinned in C18 brick and with
C19 windows predominating.

TOFTREES   *8020*

ALL SAINTS. N and S doorways apparently early C13. Lancets and
cusped lancets to nave mixed with Perp windows on N side.
Short W tower with pointed-quatrefoiled openings. Four
chalders of lime (about 200 bushels) were left for its building in
1523, but this might refer to the missing top storey. Perp chancel
arch on two heads and abaci with fleurons. Statue niches l. and
r. The three-light E window installed in 1506. Lancet to N side,

and a lancet and a Perp window to s, with a priest's door *c.* 1300. Nave roof seems C18, with butt-purlins and wind-braces. The chancel roof has crown-posts, early C16. – FONT. A first-class Norman piece, square, on five short columns with bases of reversed capital type. Angle colonnettes, rams' heads above them, and knot patterns in the four panels. – COMMUNION RAIL. C17, with sparse vertically symmetrical balusters. – SCREEN. 1917. – CROSS. In churchyard. C15, octagonal shaft without its cross.

TOFTREES HALL. Demolished 1958. It was built apparently about 1600, E-shaped, three-storeyed porch with pedimented windows. Mullioned and transomed windows throughout, that of the hall (to the r. of the porch) and those at the gable-ends of the wings of six lights.

2090   TOPCROFT

ST MARGARET. Round tower may be late C11 in the base course but much repaired in the three stages above, and hence mostly octagonal. Four bell-openings and four flushwork panels repeating the details of the bell-openings. The ringing chamber lit through a louvred lancet in each facet. Brick chancel of 1712 with angle and side pilasters, the windows unfortunately re-medievalized in 1876. S arcade of four bays. Octagonal piers, double-chamfered arches. However the pier bases look *c.* 1200, indicating an earlier arcade. The Perp windows all renewed during the 1861 restoration which also provided the hammer-beam nave roof and the biblical TEXTS painted over the arcade and chancel arches. C14 S porch, the entrance with polygonal shafting. – FONT. Perp, octagonal. Four lions against the stem, four lions and four demi-figures of angels against the bowl. Money was left for a font in 1435. – STAINED GLASS. E window has a Last Supper extending over all three lights, *c.* 1885–90. – MONUMENTS. Richard Wilton †1637 (angle between chancel and arcade). An oval flanked by pilasters with a coat of arms on top. – Several to the Smyth family of the Hall, dating from †1743 to †1854, the last signed by *W. Hardy* of Norwich.

TOPCROFT HALL, ⅜ m. SE. In one gable-end two medieval window heads of one light, perhaps not *in situ*. In an attachment to the house outside a Tudor stone fireplace, obviously not *in situ*. The front of the early C16 house re-done *c.* 1900 by *Boardman*, and subsequently Georgianized *c.* 1960. Inside, the timber frame is at once apparent, with roll mouldings to bridging beams. The main first-floor room now partitioned but it still has arched braces to the ties so wide as almost to form arches, suggesting an upper hall chamber like Abbey Farm, Old Buckenham, but here of three bays instead of five.

STREET FARMHOUSE, The Street, SW of the Hall. Timber-framed house of *c.* 1600 on the lobby-entrance plan, the two-storey, three-bay front given casements in the C18. In addition two three-light mullioned windows have been reopened. The house has a central chimney (rebuilt) with fine diamond shafts with moulded tops and a decorated plinth. Clasped purlin roof with arched wind-braces.

LITTLE MANOR HOUSE, also on The Street. Also *c.* 1600, timber-framed and with a lobby-entrance, but only one storey and dormer attic. Blocked diamond-mullioned windows visible in interior.

CHIMNEYS FARMHOUSE, demolished. It stood ⅝ m. SE of the Hall and had truly spectacular chimneys: round shafts with decoration and star tops.

TOTTENHILL

ST BOTOLPH. Technically the church is in the parish of Wormegay, situated on its own. Small, with a small C14 W tower. Of the mid C12, i.e. Norman, the nave, see the one N lancet, splayed inside, the blocked N doorway, and the S doorway. This has one order of colonnettes, incised capitals, herringbone decoration to the imposts, zigzag in the arch, and tympanum with a cross surrounded by a rope moulding which is continued along the bottom of the tympanum. Norman also the chancel arch, again with colonnettes, scalloped capitals and zigzag in the arch. Billet hoodmould with roundels and lions' heads. All of this arch was renewed in 1877 to the designs of *William Lawrie* of Downham, according to Kelly's Directory, but can this be right? The hoodmould certainly is C19 but the rest is surely no more than re-mortared. To the l. and r. of the chancel arch are recesses, shapeless owing to remodelling. E window with intersecting tracery, but this and the whole E wall is of 1864 when *Ewan Christian* was called in to restore. Presumably the choice of intersecting tracery reflected the original. The rest of the windows of C13 and C14 appearance. Roofs raised and renewed: kingpost to nave, scissor-braced to chancel. – FONT. Plain and octagonal, C17.

TOTTINGTON

In the Battle Zone (see p. 14)

ST ANDREW. Forlorn inside a chain-link fence, but the corrugated iron covering the windows removed in 1993–4 and the roofs re-clad in steel, resembling pantiles, like Stanford. Tower, nave and aisles, and chancel. The four-stage tower with angle and diagonal buttresses is probably mid-C15, when money was left for it (1445, and 1459 for the bells). The rest dates from the period of transition between Dec and Perp, but as that period lasted well into the C15 the usual date proposed, *c.* 1360, might be far wrong. The arcades of four bays especially are of a type transitional between the two. They have quatrefoil piers with continuous hollows and fillets N and S. The windows are a real mixture, first panel tracery, then ogeed with reticulation units, next with embattled transoms, then of mouchette patterns, and so on. The restorations were in 1885–6 by *E. P. Willins*: clerestory is all of 1886 and so are the nave and S aisle roofs, the former scissor-braced. The moulded purlins of the N aisle roof look more early C16. – FONT. Plain, octagonal.

UPWELL

ST PETER. Of Barnack stone and ragstone, mostly Perp and embattled. E.E. NW tower. Two-light bell-openings with a dividing round shaft and pierced trefoils in the spandrels, i.e. plate tracery. The top storey is octagonal and Perp; there was a bequest for it in 1452, and for bells from 1468. Until 1842 there was a 40 ft spire. The tower arch to the E is a powerful piece and shows that the C13 church lay where the N aisle now is. It has semicircular responds and double-chamfered arches visible from the tower but blocked to the aisle. However, by about 1310 the present nave had been begun. Its W doorway and W window (cusped intersecting tracery; renewed) show that. Perp aisles, with battlements added in 1842. The windows are three-light with panel tracery. Perp also the tall arch from the tower (S side) into the nave, also blocked but with Perp double wave mouldings continuing into the arch, and polygonal responds. A bequest in 1461 'to building nave' may relate to this or to the Perp clerestory, which has at its SE end a very pretty brick turret with a top for the sanctus bell. The nave restored 1836–8. Two-storeyed Perp N porch butted against the N tower buttresses and with a tierceron vault inside. It opens directly into the tower, not the aisle. The centre is a figure of four ogee leaves. The upper porch window is straight-headed. Long chancel with a C19 E window from the 1887 restoration. Perp six-bay arcades. The slender piers have the same mouldings as the S tower arch, without any capitals except for the thin shafts towards the arches. Colonnettes rise to the roof corbels. The chancel arch, nearly straight-sided, has the same type of mouldings. The church still has its early C19 W and N galleries supported on thin cast-iron octagonal posts, a rare survival. Nave roof with alternating tie-beams and false hammerbeams, the latter with angels with spread wings and angels again as ridge bosses. The aisle roofs also with false hammerbeams and also with angels; quite splendid, and all heavily carved. – FONT. Octagonal, Perp, with demi-figures of angels holding shields. – LECTERN. C15, of latten, East Anglian, of the same type as the lecterns at Woolpit and Cavendish (Suffolk), Chipping Campden (Gloucestershire), Corpus Christi College (Oxford) and Crofts (Lincolnshire). – ROYAL ARMS. Splendidly carved, W end of nave. – MONU-MENTS. Two early C15 brasses to priests, one with a 3 ft 10 in. figure under a tripartite canopy, the other a 2 ft 6 in. figure. They commemorate William Mowbray †1428 (chancel S) and Henry Martyn †1435 (chancel N). – In the churchyard many carved C18 HEADSTONES. One commemorating Martha Southwold †1738, 10 ft N of the chancel, has a relief figure of a long-haired naked woman in a boat, which seems to be sinking. Is that how she died, or is the scene allegorical? The churchyard GATES have fine large ashlar gatepiers with C20 pineapple finials replacing urns, and iron gates; C18.

BAPTIST CHAPEL, I m. S. 1844, grey brick and, with its front of three bays and two storeys and its low-pitched pyramid roof, decidedly domestic-looking. SCHOOL added 1911 by *W. H. H. Davis.*

WELLE MANOR HALL (former Rectory), immediately S of the church. Mainly brick, and important for that reason alone. C19 extensions but basically a late C14 hall house with C15 additions. The main range faces N. It has a late C15 porch with a stepped gable set to the l. To its r. two bays with stepped gables, buttresses and brick trefoil friezes between the floors. To the r. again is a polygonal stair-tower with an arched door. At the back another spacious late C15 stair-turret containing a brick winder staircase (cf. Oxburgh Hall, Oxborough). To its l. a square two-storey stair-turret of the early C15. Both have C19 roofs. Several brick windows and a brick doorway, all probably C15 not C14. In the doorway inside the N porch a C15 door with blank arches and tracery. It leads to the screens passage, the two service doorways *in situ* even if blocked. They have wave-moulded jambs and continuous arches, early C15. A first-floor room with two blocked lancets. Crown-post roof, partly renewed.

Two late C15 brick TOWERS 30 yds N formed part of the courtyard entrance but are now free-standing. Octagonal, with a brick winder staircase entered through a segmental doorway. Three of the sides have moulded brick decoration in three tiers of trefoiled panels.

WACTON   *1090*

ALL SAINTS. C12 round tower, the later upper half recessed and as thin and tapering as a windmill. C18 brick parapet. Nave and chancel in one, without a chancel arch, internally tall and generous in space. Also tall, indeed elongated in appearance, are the five windows N and S, of two lights with ogee tops. Wave-moulded rere-arches inside. The doorways have ogee tops too. The window tracery alternates between a reticulation unit and twin mouchette motifs. Ogee-headed sedilia and piscina, each cusped bay with fine shafts with big fillets N and S. The whole is clearly Dec. – FONT. Octagonal, Perp. Against the foot four lions; against the bowl four lions and four demi-figures of angels. – SCREEN. Tall, of the same date as the architecture, see the shafts with shaft-rings instead of mullions and the few tracery motifs. – NORTH DOOR. With good ironwork comprising two strap hinges, and once a third; *c.* 1350–70. – SOUTH DOOR. Exceedingly large. The ironwork is almost all a C19 replica in the style of the N door, with an elaborate rosette. – COMMUNION RAIL. Early C18, with slender twisted balusters.

WACTON HOUSE, just SE of the church. The front is plain late

Georgian with very large windows, four bays, two storeys; the back is C17 with a stepped gable-end and twin octagonal flues to the stack. One five-light mullioned window.

WACTON HALL, ¾ m. s on Swallow Lane. The six-bay plastered E front hides a timber frame, as so often in Norfolk. The brick N gable and its chimneystack with triple octagonal flues point to the C16. So too does the rear external stack. There were eighteen hearths assessed in the 1664 Hearth Tax. E side with a three-storeyed porch. The porch has polygonal angle-shafts, a round-arched doorway with pilasters, and fat pinnacles in relief over the pilasters. Ovolo-moulded bridging beams to the first-floor rooms and, to the N, some C17 and later panelling.

WHITE COTTAGE, Wacton Common. One of the four timber-framed houses of the 'Wealden' type to be found in Norfolk (see p. 88), and a particularly good one as the hall has not been floored. The date must be in the second half of the C14. The hall in the middle has a six-light mullioned window (renewed), flanked either side by two-storey bays, also with renewed mullioned windows. The entrance to the screens passage to the r. of the hall unfortunately no longer leads to a screen, but an arched door leads to the service rooms and another to the staircase serving the room above. The roof is a queenpost type, with arched braces in three directions. The posts are so tall above the tie-beam that it could almost be mistaken for a raised-aisle structure. One must try not to look at the C20 flat-roofed rear extension.

GRANGE FARMHOUSE, Common Road. Late C16 timber frame with a brick gable-end and a thatched roof. Good stack with four octagonal flues. One five-light mullioned window to first floor, the rest C19 three-light casements.

WALLINGTON

ST MARGARET. The ruins are in a field next to Wallington Hall. The church served the village before it was depopulated by Sir Francis Gawdy (†1605). Three-stage C14 carstone tower with cusped bell-openings. Four archangels above the brick parapet.

WALLINGTON HALL. The original hall house was probably built in the late C15 for Thomas Gawsell, of carstone and rubble-stone. It passed to his son in 1507 and to his grandson Thomas, who sold it in 1525 to the lawyer Sir William Coningsby. Coningsby seems immediately to have demolished the parlour wing at the E end, leaving the external dais staircase intact (on the S side), floored the open hall and enormously enlarged the house to the E. As part of this modification he cased the original part in brick and constructed the most important feature: the brick N porch with its terracotta detailing. Elizabethan and C18 alterations; the restoration in 1918 introduced many of the interior details.

The plan of the former hall house remains identifiable, especially from the N. At the W end is Coningsby's porch. It has polygonal angle-shafts decorated with six tiers of trefoiled terra-cotta panels up to the first-floor level, then continuing undecorated until the thick crocketed pinnacles are reached, rising above a crenellated parapet. A third smaller pinnacle in the centre of the parapet. Four-centred head to the entrance arch under a square surround with carved spandrels. Above this are four zones of terracotta decoration: a frieze of cusped and crocketed blind tracery panels, a stringcourse of modified egg-and-dart motifs, a frieze of simple lozenges, and a single diamond with terracotta emblems below a trefoiled corbel course. Three-light upper window with four-centred heads to the lights. The side walls of the porch have brick diaper. It is all very lively and engaging. The porch gives access in the customary way to the screens passage. To the l. of the porch, the external hall chimney-breast will at once be noticed, and the blocked arch with its four-centred head of the former hall dais window. On the s side the staircase projection at the dais end of the hall, already noted, also follows customary arrangements. It has one original window. The stepped end-gable of the hall towards the w rises above the later w additions replacing a former service range.

Still on the N side, there is E of the hall where the solar wing must have been a full-height projection one bay wide ending in a stepped gable and lit from five-light mullioned and transomed windows in the two principal floors and a three-light equivalent in the attic. This is clearly Elizabethan and could be a little later. E of this is a seven-bay rectangular block fitted with sashes but including a further piece of early Tudor evidence: two shallow narrow projections two storeys high like oriels, with battlements and arched and cusped friezes below. Then the stepped E gable is reached, with a big external stack of brick chequered with carstone and two friezes of terracotta arches and two tiers of little battlements below the triple polygonal flues. So the early Tudor house ran the whole length of the present house.

In the mid C18 the principal entrance to the house was changed from N to S and the façade E of the old hall Georgianized. Four bays of sashes in three storeys under a crenellated parapet. Central door under a shallow pediment. In additional outer bays timber mullioned casements reinstated in 1918.

Internally the house is one room deep, and much altered in 1790 and 1918. The former hall (dining room) is fitted with a good early Elizabethan stone fireplace with a four-centred arch, a later Elizabethan overmantel, and small-framed panelling, all brought in in 1918. Splendid cruciform bridging beams and joists of c. 1525: multiple rolls, ribbon mouldings and double wave mouldings. Of the dais staircase at the SE corner only the upper parts have original treads. E of this on the S side is the main staircase inserted in 1790. It looks earlier. Open well, turned balusters, square newels and a moulded handrail. From this staircase hall a doorway opens N into the Elizabethan projection (sitting room), decorated in 1790 in Rococo style with a marble chimneypiece and low-relief plasterwork forming panels separated by foliate tresses. At the E end of the house reached by a passage along the S façade (passing two further rooms) is a room with early C16 multiple roll-moulded bridging beams and inserted small-framed panelling.

5010

WALPOLE HIGHWAY

ST EDMUND. In its own way a remarkable church. 1844 by *J. C. Buckler* as a chapel of ease to Walpole St Peter. Yellow brick, in the Norman style, with bellcote and polygonal apse. A rectangular plan without aisles, the bays divided by pilaster strips. It is a serious attempt at Norman. Arch-braced roof. – FURNISH-INGS. The then Rector, the *Rev. Arthur Moore* (rector 1839–53), instigated the building and took an interest to the extent of making most of the furnishings himself, and designing some glass. He carved and painted the screen and carved the poppy-heads of the benches, 1846. – STAINED GLASS. By *William Wailes*, 1845, which is early for C19 glass. In the apse figures of Saints. In the nave and W window medallions in C13 style by *Arthur Moore*.

WINDMILL, N of the church. Derelict brick tower mill. The sails fragmentary. C18, twice raised up. To the N a contemporary GRANARY.

5010

WALPOLE ST ANDREW

ST ANDREW. Perp. W tower of brick with stone dressings. In the SW buttress a small doorway and small windows serving a lean-to chamber, perhaps an anker-hole, or anchorite's cell. The belfry windows still with reticulated tracery. There is a bequest of 1443 for building the nave and one of 1463 for a porch. Nothing wrong with these dates, except that the present S porch looks as if it was made in the restoration of 1909. Other work 1862 and 1897. Arcade of four bays. The piers have the familiar lozenge section with four thin shafts with hollows between them. The shafts towards the nave run up to the roof, and more shafts rise awkwardly on the apexes of the arcade arches and continue to support the corbels of the C19 roof. Eight clerestory windows between them with pilaster strips outside and four-centred heads. Pair of rood stair-turrets with spirelets at the E end of the nave. Inside, the S turret is nicely combined with the fanning-out corbel of a former pulpit. The chancel arch corresponds to the arcade piers; the tower arch is simpler and probably later. All windows Perp and restored, those of the aisles with embattled transoms. Embattled also an ornate piscina in the S aisle. – FONT. Perp, octagonal, with quatrefoils and shields. – BENCH. One original one in the N aisle. – PULPIT. C17, with the usual blank arches. The pulpit stands on a Perp stone base. – WEST GALLERY. C17, simple. The balustrade on arched braces. Cast-iron rail. – STAINED GLASS. E window †1897 by *A. L.*

Moore. Crucifixion. S aisle W, the Three Maries, by *Heaton, Butler & Bayne,* †1918.

DAYCOTT'S END (formerly Vicarage), Wisbech Road. Brick. Two storeys in three bays, the centre one projecting. Doorcase with Roman Doric columns. *c.* 1770. The canted returns r. and l. are mid-C19.

PRINCESS VICTORIA public house, ¼ m. E of the church. It carries the date 1651. Brick. Three-bay W front now with C20 door and windows. Platband separates floors. External stack to S gable. Sunk-quadrant bridging beams inside.

WALPOLE ST PETER   5010

ST PETER. The enormous fertility of the silts and muds of the drained Fens transformed the marshlands of W Norfolk and SE Lincolnshire into the richest agricultural land in England. This created wealth, and as a consequence Walpole possesses one of the most impressive churches of its date in the country, the date being Late Dec to Early Perp, i.e. mid C14 to mid C15. Blomefield recorded dates in the chancel windows of 1423 and 1425. The church replaces one swept away in the flood of 1337. Restoration was in 1898. The total length is 161 ft. Ashlar-faced over brick and rubble, and in places, especially the chancel, rendered over brick. The W tower comes first. It is plainer than the rest and has three stages. The base is early C14, so must have survived the flood, but the rest is *c.* 1360. W door with undercut mouldings. Two-light W window, ringing chamber with lancets, belfry with small two-light openings. The arch towards the nave is clearly Late Dec too. It stands on shafts with fillets separated in continuous mouldings by deep hollows. The capitals are round and have many fine mouldings. The arch is triple-chamfered. The nave arcades continue immediately. In fact the W responds were started to carry on the same details. In the event the seven-bay arcade, though with piers on the same system as the tower shafts (i.e. quatrefoil piers with continuous hollows between the lobes and fillets to cardinal points), has finer polygonal bases and capitals and many-moulded arches. The large aisle windows (of three lights to N and S, four lights to W and E, all with embattled transoms) and the closely set clerestory windows (double in number) are entirely Perp. The clerestory windows are under stilted arches. The junction of tower and aisle W walls is externally as telling as the junction internally where the E buttresses are caught high up on corbels in the form of horizontally placed figures. The outside is extremely ornate and very pretty, with its battlements all decorated with small-scale motifs, especially panelling. This is said to have been added in 1634. Rood stair-turrets with spirelets. The turrets have tiny windows, and that on the N side is externally supported by a little man. On the apex of the nave E gable a bellcote with a telescoped pinnacle. One-storey N porch and two-storey S porch, the most ambitious piece of the church. It has a front with panelling and niches and small coats of arms, including that of Sir John Goddard †1435. The parvis has a three-light window with canopied niches r. and l. The interior of the porch has two square bays with tierceron vaulting and very good bosses with religious scenes (Assumption, Last Judgement, Pietà) as well as animals (a dog gnawing bones, a muzzled bear). In the four corners the vault rests on tiny niches with seated figurines. Two open windows to E and W sides, but with rebates for glazing. The N porch has much in common with the porch at Wiveton, which is probably of the early 1440s.

Nothing has yet been said of the chancel apart from the window dates. It has five bays and carries on in date and style from the nave. There are only minute variations in tracery design. It is distinguished by the unusual motif of a passage below the E bay. This was no doubt part of the processional way and was required by lack of consecrated space E of the church (though this explanation is a lot more cogent in a crowded city like Norwich). The passage is also tierceron-vaulted with bosses and is entered under a four-centred arch. It has the felicitous effect inside of making it necessary to raise the altar space by nine steps, and the E flanking windows to match. The interior of the chancel is altogether delightful. It has a chancel arch which goes with the arcade arches, and blank arcading to the N and S which acts in the W parts as a backing of the chancel stalls, and near the E end of the S side is deepened into shallow niches to form sedilia and piscina. These arches have pretty token rib vaults with tiny bosses. In the W bay the bosses were left in the raw, i.e. uncarved. The windows are separated by strips of wall with big niches which still have the Dec motif of nodding ogee arches. To the l. and r. of the tall, seven-light E window there are instead very tall shallow recesses, also ending in token rib vaults. A dog sits on either of them. Of the roofs the best is that of the nave, with tie-beams on arched braces alternating with bigger arched braces supporting the principals direct. Both rest on stone heads. Stone heads also in the aisles. N aisle roof with alternating large and small arched braces, S aisle and chancel roofs of 1812.

FURNISHINGS. FONT. Octagonal, with nodding ogee arches against the bowl. Inscription with the name of the parson, John Whetholme, and the date 1532 on the base. – FONT COVER. Splendid Jacobean piece with an octagonal spire. The octagonal walls below open to give access to the font. Decoration with tapering facing pilasters in pairs, the usual blank arches and
25 openwork arabesques. – STALLS. C15. With some minor MISERICORDS, including the motif of the pelican pecking its
25 own breast. – SCREENS. The grandest is the early C17 W screen extending E of the doorways across nave and aisles. It has three pedimented entrances with fluted pilasters and above the dado open balustrading of bobbin-turned balusters. The rails above and below this with small incised vertical panels. – Of the same time the W tower balcony with its turned balusters. – Perp the

rood screen, of which only the dado remains, with badly painted figures of Apostles and other Saints in six bays r. and l. of the central opening. – A charming C15 parclose screen separates the S chapel from the S aisle. Five one-light divisions, becoming two-light in the tracery. Ogee arches with fine tracery in the dado panels. In the entrance an iron GATE dated 1708. – DOORS. Original, i.e. c. 1435, S and N doors with much tracery. The S door is double-leaf. – PULPIT. Dated 1620. Good, hexagonal, with tester. Arcaded bottom rail and the usual arcaded upper panels. Curving staircase entry. – SEATING. A large variety, much of it now mixed up. Early Perp the openwork frieze in the backs of one row of the rising benches in the S aisle. Simple, broad tracery forms (broad daggers in triangular panels). – Otherwise mostly Jacobean, probably of the time of the pulpit, and all good. The ends have a single blank arch below a panel of fluting and an acanthus top rail. The top rails of the backs with similar acanthus. Near the W end also C18 BOX PEWS. – POOR BOX. Dated 1639, and inscribed 'Remember the Poore'. On a sturdy baluster. – LECTERN. Latten (i.e. a coppery alloy used before brass), Perp, early Tudor. With a specially realistic eagle and an unusually slender stem. Of the same group as Dereham and Snettisham, and also Exeter Cathedral. – CHANDELIERS. A large two-tier one in the nave, bought in 1701, and six small C20 ones in the chancel. – STAINED GLASS. Jumble of fragments in a N aisle window, assembled in 1922. Chancel windows by *Hardman & Co.*, c. 1900. – MONUMENT. Robert Butler, 1632, attributed to *Maximilian Colt* (GF). He is shown in relief kneeling before an altar. Predella below, Composite columns supporting entablature (chancel S). – CURIOSA. SHELTER for the parson to speak from at rainy funerals. It looks like a sedan chair and is a typical C18 idea. – In the S porch INSCRIPTION of the early C19 admonishing people to take off their pattens in church.

The VILLAGE has trees in the middle, always a surprise in the Fens, and prosperous-looking modern houses and bungalows, indicating the strength of market gardening here. The new RECTORY, 1985, is perversely sited so as to block the best view of the church. Some good recent houses hedge the church on other sides, but the oldest by far is Dovecote Farmhouse, immediately NW of the church tower (*see* below).

OLD MANOR FARMHOUSE, The Chase. A ruin until restored in 1985–6 by and for *Bernard Crowson*. L-plan, of brick. Of c. 1500 the wave-moulded plinth and the similar platband. Above this the elevation is set back. The window jambs are chamfered, so probably C16 although their hoodmoulds are early C17, when the house was re-windowed and remodelled. There is a N–S range and an added single bay projecting to the E. There is evidence that the earlier wing began as a timber-framed house jettied to the S. The W front has a big external stack with an arched recess in its base, and set-offs above. Four diamond flues. The S gable has the date 1638 and initials of Bernadas Frencham and wife, rector 1628–61. The E wing with various

blocked (and reopened) windows and doors. Very likely it once
extended further E. The S ground-floor room has two four-
centred fireplaces, and there was another in the N room and
another two above. The bridging beams here with jewel stops.
The E wing has two multiple roll-moulded bridging beams with
running ribbon decoration, which are again *c.* 1500, but reused,
as the whole bay was butted on to the existing house in the C17.
There is a single-flight staircase but of the original there is no
trace, nor even of its site. It is clear that the rooms all had first-
floor ceilings, so at this date (*c.* 1500) it is a very early example
of a storeyed house, i.e. breaking with the open hall tradition.

DOVECOTE FARMHOUSE, Church Road. F-plan late C16 house
with infill between the wings. Restored 1930. S front with three
bays of casements and a set-off between the floors. Moulded
octagonal flues to the stack. Gabled wing to l. with leaded cross
casements. The E and W fronts with four-centred doorways, the
latter with two orders of shafts. Two more octagonal flues to the
external N stack. The E chimneypiece with reeded and fluted
Ionic pilasters, repeated between the windows. Turned balusters
to the staircase. Late C16, but rebuilt, forecourt walls.

TOWNSEND HOUSE, Church Road. 1735 double-pile brick house.
The W front has a porch on unfluted columns. Mixed fenestration. The N gable has four C18 sashes under segmental arches.

TRINITY HOUSE, Trinity Road. A brick early C16 house with a
half-H-plan, altered 1950. The W front has three bays with
flanking cross-wing gables. Roll-moulded set-off at first floor.
There was a through-passage plan and the solar staircase site
can be identified, so the house is an earlier type than Old Manor
Farmhouse, though not earlier in date.

FAULKNER HOUSE, West Drove, 1⅞ m. S of the church. Early C18
with a nice Roman Doric porch with a pediment to the five-bay
S front.

ST PETER'S LODGE, 1½ m. SE of the church. A T-shaped house of
1705 has to the N a gabled wing with a re-set Norman door
with shafts and scalloped capitals. More Norman lancet fragments in the attic. The W end has an external stack terminating
in six diamond flues. Added to the E in 1813 a Tudor block
complete with a two-storey battlemented porch with a four-
centred doorway. Mullioned windows. WALLED GARDEN, 1813
with a gabled DOVECOTE.

WALSOKEN

ALL SAINTS. One of the group of C12–C13 Fenland churches
with very long naves built after the area had been reclaimed
from the sea, like Tilney All Saints. Walsoken is now more or
less a suburb of Wisbech in Cambridgeshire. The church lies a
few yards from the county boundary. It is the grandest Norman
parish church of Norfolk, late Norman, with important E.E.
parts and interesting transitions between the two styles. The
restoration was in 1860. The building is stone-faced. The prin-

cipal remaining late Norman contribution is the arcades, of seven bays between nave and aisles, of a further two between chancel and chancel chapels. The former have alternating circular and octagonal piers. On the nave s side the octagonal piers are angled so their corners face the cardinal directions. This feature, and other similarities, relate Walsoken closely to the infirmary at Ely Cathedral, datable to *c.* 1175. All the piers have varieties of multi-scalloped capitals, except for the E responds of the nave, which are of a scrolly waterleaf type, and the W respond of the N chancel chapel, which has the fully developed crocket form. So here we move into the C13. The arches are round and moulded with zigzag at r. angles to the wall surface. In the chancel upper windows survive, the easternmost longer than the others, because they represented the projecting part of the Norman chancel. In addition there is a nutmeg frieze and, included by it, a simple former doorway to the N. The E window, now Perp of five lights, was originally a C13 group, see the shafting inside and outside, with stiff-leaf capitals. The chancel arch also must be of the C13, though very early, considering its close affinity to the arcades. The arch is now pointed, but its decoration with several kinds of zigzags, e.g. the motif of battlements with triangular merlons, and the shafts with eight shaft-rings, is still more late C12 than early C13.

With the splendid W tower we are in full E.E. The tower has big polygonal buttresses, a sumptuous round-arched W doorway with fine mouldings on three orders of colonnettes with (restored) stiff-leaf capitals, and blank arcading up the buttresses. The lowest stage has an arcade of pointed arches with columns on waterholding bases, the next has a trefoil-headed arcade with a single chamfer, and above that there is a system of long polygonal shafts with tall blank single-chamfered lancets between. The belfry stage and spire added in the C14 – see the ogeed two-light belfry windows. Polygonal pinnacles. The tower arch has keeled shafts and good crocket capitals and the arch itself is tall, pointed and moulded. The first-stage windows are shafted inside. C15 the s priest's doorway. The corbel table of the N aisle is C13, reused when the aisle was remodelled. C15 also the N chapel (see the piscina) and the blocked features in the chancel s wall. The s aisle was in building, or at least being worked on, in 1536 'from the west end of ower Lades quer...'. Of this time the roomy s porch. Perp first (and Early) the W window of the N aisle, later, i.e. C15, the other N aisle windows, the five-light E window of the chancel, the replacement of the s chapel, which has barred windows in two storeys, the roofs, and the embattled clerestory. The last has seven three-light panel-traceried windows. The roofs of nave, s aisle and both chancel chapels have small figures against the wall-posts. The nave roof is a false hammerbeam type, with arched braces to wall-posts. Moulded cambered tie-beams.

FURNISHINGS. FONT. Perp, octagonal. The Seven Sacra- 42 ments and the Crucifixion in small figures against the bowl supported on crocketed ogee arches; Saints against the stem; on the foot an inscription recording S. Honiter, his wife, and John Bedford, Chaplain. The date 1544 is also recorded and shields with the Instruments of the Passion. – STALLS. With faces on the arms and small signs of the Evangelists etc. against the buttresses of the ends. Heavily restored. – SCREENS. Parclose to the chancel chapels from the aisles with very close and dainty tracery in two storeys, a very unusual arrangement. To the N chapel simpler, both early C16. Parclose from chancel to chapels C19. – BENCHES. Eight in the nave, with very solid ends. On these a figure in a niche. To the l. and r. of the poppyhead small seated figures. – SCULPTURE. In the S aisle a small Netherlandish (?) group of St Anne, the Virgin and (formerly) the Child; C16. – Above the tower arch a coarse wooden figure of Solomon and to his l. and r. painted scene of his Judgement; C17. – Above the chancel arch King David with his harp, probably also C17. – STAINED GLASS. E window looks *Ward & Hughes*, c. 1880. S and N aisles more by the same and by *Jones & Willis* and *William Glasby*, all early C20. – MONUMENTS. Funeral recess with a crocketed ogee arch in the N chapel. – Heart burial in the N aisle (two hands holding a heart), c. 1350. – Unusually many handsomely or entertainingly carved HEADSTONES in the churchyard, starting with Robert Pettit †1687 (near E end of S aisle) and going on to †1717, †1731, †1756, etc. – To the S is a CROSS base with part of a square chamfered stone shaft. Obviously medieval, probably C15.

4010
WALTON HIGHWAY
Near West Walton

The converted CORNMILL on Fen Road is uninteresting except for its date. A three-storey brick tower seems to have been built c. 1740, with a strong batter to the top floor. Two further storeys were added in 1815. The earliest of this type elsewhere in the county are the mill in the ruins of St Benet's Abbey, probably built by 1735 (*see* Horning, Vol. 1), and Ludham High Mill (*see* Vol. 1) of 1742.

8030
WATERDEN

ALL SAINTS. Of the W tower only a lump is preserved. There is now a primitive wooden bell-turret. A S aisle has also disappeared and the S porch has been rebuilt in the C17 reusing the C14 arch. In nave and chancel several E.E. lancets. The N nave has in addition a C15 window blocked by a mullioned and transomed window of the early C17. Two more of these to the S side and yet more in the chancel including the E window. But the special interest of the church belongs to an earlier date. There are Norman N and S doorways with the plainest imposts and arches with only a slight chamfer. Moreover the church has upper windows with tapering sides and double splays which look decidedly Anglo-Saxon. One (restored) faces w, the others (damaged) N. Round chancel arch. – FONT. Octagonal; C14. – BOX PEWS.

EARTHWORKS of DESERTED VILLAGE, in a valley to NE of the church. This was never a large village, and only parts of the earthworks survive. A N–S main street, part of which lies beneath a farm track, passes between tofts, those at the NE end being the best preserved. (AR)

WATLINGTON   6010

ST PETER AND ST PAUL. The w tower is buttressed only to the lower half of the first stage. Could this be part of the 1902 restoration, a year when the tower was struck by lightning? The upper windows of two lights separated by a polygonal shaft, i.e. probably of the late C13. Lower brick stair-turret on the s side. The aisles embrace the tower, their w bays blocked by masonry on one side and by a stud partition on the other. s doorway E.E. with one order of colonnettes and undercut mouldings. Dec N doorway, plain; Dec E bay of the N aisle and Dec chancel. The windows are of two lights with the motif of the four-petalled flower in the tracery. The E window, however, is much more sumptuous: of five lights with lavish Curvilinear tracery based on intersecting arches with mouchettes. Sedilia and piscina ogee-headed. A NE chapel has disappeared. Arcade of four bays with octagonal piers and double-hollow-chamfered arches also Dec. Roof with big arched braces reaching up to collar-beams, re-clad in 1902. – FONT. Octagonal, Perp, with eight large standing figures against the stem and sixteen small figures against the bowl; early C16. – FONT COVER. Dated 1671, with columns, a spire, and a pelican at the top, in a similar vein to the one at Wiggenhall St Mary the Virgin. Conical top on eight columns and an arcade. – PULPIT. Dated 1661, with the blank arches more familiar in Jacobean work. – SCREEN. Dec, but very extensively restored. With two-light divisions, shafts instead of mullions, and reticulated tracery in the spandrels. Money was bequeathed from 1435 for its painting. – BENCHES. Backs with pierced tracery, small figures on the arms. – STAINED GLASS. E window by *Percy Bacon*, c. 1900. – MONUMENTS. Wall monument in chancel to John Cake †1628: Ionic fluted columns below a curved entablature and coat of arms. Effigy kneels before a praying desk. – Wall monument to Thomas Cawsel and wife, †1600, in the nave chapel, this time with two headless figures kneeling within a frame of fluted and reeded pilasters.

WATLINGTON HALL. The E front of *Donthorn*'s c. 1830 house had a giant four-bay portico which is reflected in the new house built for the Pope family in 1965 by *James Fletcher-Watson*. Like Watson's other Norfolk houses it is the ubiquitous Neo-Georgian, here of seven bays, two storeys, hipped roof. The portico of the house burnt in 1943 is replaced by a three-bay pediment on giant pilasters. Pilasters at the corners separate the low side loggias. The imperceptibly wider ground-floor windows and the entasis to the chimneystacks are Lutyensesque in nature and, if designed to warm the restraint of the design, are entirely successful.

MANOR FARMHOUSE, Church Road. The only other house of importance. *c.* 1650, brick with ashlar quoins, three bays with, r. and l., a gabled bay. The details are C19 and C20. To the s contemporary WALLS and gatepiers.

WATTLEFIELD *see* WYMONDHAM

WATTON

ST MARY. Norman round tower with a later top which has a frieze with shields in quatrefoils. The spire came down in 1890. The aisle fronts and aisle exteriors all rebuilt in 1840 by *Fuller Coker* when the church was thoroughly gone over. Further restorations 1886–7. It all looks depressing, especially the spread-out W side, where the aisles show their pitched roofs. E.E. chancel with three stepped lancets at the E end and a smaller pair in the S wall. E.E. also the S arcade. Three bays, quatrefoil piers, the shafts almost detached. Double-hollow-chamfered arches. Mushroom capitals and bases. Perp N arcade. Piers with a section of four shafts and four fine hollows. The arches as on the S side, and probably reused. Scissor-braced nave roof is C19. – FONT. Caen stone. C19. The C14 font sold to Ovington to pay for the 1840 restorations. – SCREENS. S aisle parclose screen and chancel screen both 1852. – STALL. Made up of bits of domestic Jacobean woodwork. – POOR BOX. Dated 1639. A strangely endearing, stiffly standing wooden parson with the legend 'Remember the Poore'. – MONUMENTS. Various tablets. – STAINED GLASS. E window is a 1914–18 memorial, signed *Wm. Morris.* A mid-C19 S chancel window with St Peter and St Paul is much better. – Iron GATES of 1902 at the W and E ends of Church Walk.

The TOWN. Watton is a market town extending along the Norwich Road with a central thickening at the junction of the Dereham–Thetford road. It is not immediately attractive. The entry from the Norwich (E) side is dominated by the hangars and workshops of the RAF base and rows of post-war service housing to the S of the road. The difference between officers' accommodation and that of other ranks is one of size and detachment, not of quality. The runways themselves are more easily seen from Griston. The station closed and the houses were sold in the early 1990s.

In the Middle Ages the town was reasonably prosperous and had three manors, the lord of one being in the C17 the architect William Samwell. As with many market towns a fire caused

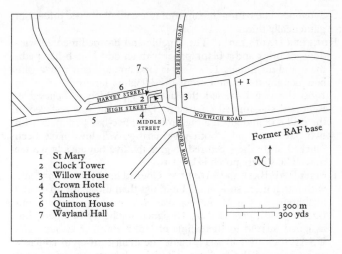

1 St Mary
2 Clock Tower
3 Willow House
4 Crown Hotel
5 Almshouses
6 Quinton House
7 Wayland Hall

300 m
300 yds

Watton

great destruction, here in 1674, and little if anything is earlier than that in the centre. An immediate consequence of the fire is the CLOCK TOWER, paid for by Christopher Hey, the Mercer, to give warning of a similar conflagration. It is an odd building, in the High Street, not in a detached position. Two doors to lock-ups, with hoodmoulds; the original arched openings were altered in the early C19. Above is a blank pedimented field with a small date 1679 carved in. The clock is of 1825. The hare and barrel design is the rebus for Watton (hare = Wat, barrel = Tun). The battlemented parapet has a frieze of brick panels with diaper and fleur-de-lys. The cupola with its pretty weathervane was put up here when the Market Cross was demolished in 1820.

Also dated 1679 is the N gable of the rear wing of No. 30 HIGH STREET, with a late C19 front. The WILLOW HOUSE beyond the crossroads towards Norwich is another C17 building: long, thatched and with exposed timber-framing, rather altered internally in the C18 and again in the 1980s. On the S side of the High Street the late Georgian CROWN HOTEL still has its carriage entrance leading to stables which are at the time of writing rapidly being turned into mews-like cottages. To the W Nos. 77–83 are rendered clay lump ALMSHOUSES of 1831 with an arched door at each end and two in the middle. Gothic intersecting windows. In HARVEY STREET, parallel and N of the High Street, are two little ranges of C17 cottages, No. 8 and Nos. 4–6. Both are timber-framed, both extensively altered. Further W is QUINTON HOUSE, essentially a seven-bay town house of two and a half storeys, and rather a surprise. Of brick, with sash windows and a doorcase with unfluted columns. c. 1750.

WAYLAND HALL, originally the Corn Hall, just N of the High Street in Middle Street. 1853 by *E. B. Lamb*, for him disappointingly staid. It has its gable-end to the street, but not dynamic. The hammerbeam roof is a symbol of civic pride, but pathetically thin.

ROKELES HALL, I m. E. The N gable-end has pedimented windows of brick and a blank panel with an odd Dutch-like pediment and the initials T. S. This is for Thomas Scott †1672 who had bought the manor from the Heighoe family in 1642. In 1960 the panel carried the date 1653, which is believable. Renewed star-topped chimneys. The W front was re-faced in the mid C18 and given a big projecting five-bay pediment with two bays each side, both very narrow. Windows have been blocked and others centred to give the five-bay façade we see now. The square porch is late C19.

Former RAF BASE and MUSEUM. Opened in February 1939 and with much more substantial buildings than those put up during hostilities. By the *Ministry of War Architect's Department*, contractor *John Laing & Son*. Designed for heavy bombers, but assigned instead to Blenheims of No. 2 Bomber Group. The USAF took over in 1943, made the main runway of concrete and expanded the facilities. The later domestic quarters have already been mentioned. Fine OFFICERS' MESS, pale brick, single-storeyed, four bays of sashes r. and l. of a triple-arched entrance, and two-bay projections at the end. Plain interiors. The ANTE-ROOM on the E side converted to Watton R.C. Chapel (St Francis Xavier).

WEASENHAM ALL SAINTS

8020

ALL SAINTS. Nave, aisles and chancel. The W tower collapsed in 1653. The rest is almost entirely of 1905–6, presumably at the expense of the second Earl of Leicester. C15 the S porch, with a C20 parapet and pinnacles, but nice original details: panelling, niches l. and r. of the entrance with miniature rib-vaults, and an entrance enriched by fleurons. Traceried spandrels, flushwork arcade at the base. Before the restoration there was a brick upper storey. The S windows in the Perp style, the N Perp but restored. C14 the S doorway, the N wall (except for the slightly Voyseyish corner chimney), the Dec N aisle arcade (octagonal piers, double-chamfered arches), and the chancel arch. Former N clerestory windows blocked. S arcade 1905. – PULPIT. Jacobean, with arcaded panels. – SCREEN. With eight very damaged figures of Saints. – MONUMENT. In the churchyard W of the church a monument to Richard Jackson †1768, a tomb-chest with a handsome Adam-type urn at the top.

WEASENHAM HALL, SW of the church, right by the lane behind prominent brick garden walls. A big and not very exciting red brick Neo-Jacobean house for the second Earl of Leicester begun in 1904. The architect is not known. Brick with an un-Jacobean hipped roof. Seven-bay S front in two storeys. Two shallow canted bays in centre framing a square bay with a shaped gable. Cross casements throughout. Reluctant polygonal stacks, much too flimsy for the style. Additional wing to r., with three

shaped gables. The library on the s side has bookcases and panelling. Drawing room, also facing s, has two Corinthian columns
and pilasters. Four angle towers and the upper storey of the
porch demolished in *c.* 1960.

BARROWS. In the area of the Weasenham Plantation is a scattered
barrow country of some dozen mounds, including bell, bowl,
disc and saucer barrows. To the NW are a saucer and bell of 150
ft diameter, and to the SE a fine bell 140 ft in diameter and 7 ft
high. These are some of the finest preserved barrows in Norfolk.

WEASENHAM ST PETER

ST PETER. Slightly elevated above the Fakenham–Swaffham road.
Unbuttressed E.E. w tower lit through a lancet w window.
Quatrefoil sound-hole above, twin bell-openings. The parapet
and all other embattled parapets from the comprehensive 1870
restoration. Low tower arch with embattled capitals which must
be later. Perp the remarkably ornate N side with flushwork
arcading in the plinth, three large three-light nave windows with
a pointed quatrefoil frieze below the sills, and embattled transoms including stepped upper transoms. Flushwork also on the
N porch, which interrupts the plinth course. Inner N doorway
with tracery in the spandrels and two good C15 strap hinges on
the door. The s side is simpler, also with three-light Perp windows and a Dec petal-tracery w window. The four-bay s arcade
is, in contrast to the first external impact, oddly starved. Thin
flat lozenge piers without elaboration save for the flattened
responds towards the arches, designed by a mason not happy
with Perp. The chancel and its s vestry essentially all 1870,
having been 'exeedinglie decaied by the Necligence of the
Proprietane' in 1602. – FONT. Perp with quatrefoils to the bowl,
tracery to the stem and the date R. K. M. 1607 carved in later. –
STAINED GLASS. On the N side, in the tracery of two windows,
single complete little C15 figures under canopies. There was
money left in 1437 to make two glass windows. – The E window
signed by *W. Warrington*, †1849; high-coloured.

The VILLAGE on the other side of the road has a pretty irregular
GREEN with a duckpond and C19 houses of just the right scale
dotted about.

WEETING

ALL SAINTS with ST MARY. Round tower, entirely rebuilt during
the rigorous restoration of 1868. Dec chancel and Dec N arcade.
The former has a fine five-light E window with reticulated tracery
broken into at the top by an octofoiled circle, which is an invention from the restoration; cusped ogee-canopied niches inside
to its l. and r. A similar, simpler, blocked N window broken into
to form the priest's door. Money was left for work already
begun in the chancel in 1469, but what was this? Some coursed

masonry *c.* 1200 in N chancel wall. The low N arcade is of four bays with slender piers with four main and four subsidiary shafts. Round moulded capitals and bases look Early Dec. In the nave three Perp three-light S windows with stepped embattled transoms. 1868 crown-post roof to nave and an open barrel structure to chancel. Hardly a stone is earlier than the C19, and hardly a stick of wood, so the dating partly relies on an assumption of faithful restoration which can be assumed from Ladbroke's drawing. – BENCH ENDS. A number of old ones with poppyheads. – STAINED GLASS. E window, a Transfiguration by *George Parlby*, 1905, soft rich colours.

ALL SAINTS, to the SW. In ruins. The tower fell after 1700 and only a few cliffs of the rest remain as a feature behind the gardens of a housing estate.

WEETING HALL was demolished in 1952, and in its grounds W of the church lies the housing estate just mentioned. The early C19 LODGE remains on All Saints (a road name), colourwashed brick, with a rustic veranda under a thatched roof in *cottage orné* style. An altered LODGE on Methwold Road.

HOME FARMHOUSE, N of the church. Early C17 timber-framed house on the lobby-entrance plan, faced with brick and with later C17 additions to the W, and to the E *c.* 1700, resulting in a U-shaped plan. There is nothing externally visible of the C17 work. The four-bay S front has flanking gables r. and l.

WEETING CASTLE, immediately SSE of the church. Maintained as a controlled ruin with eloquent crags of masonry reaching high. It seems to be an example of a Norman country house like Castle Acre a century before. Built for Sir Ralph de Plais. There was no curtain wall, so defence – apart from small windows and thick flint walls on ashlar plinths – relied on the rectangular moat. The main range, probably of *c.* 1180, consisted of an aisled hall with two flanking additions. One of them is a substantial three-storeyed keep-like tower with an important first-floor chamber carried on three round arches to the long sides and two to the others. Other details obliterated.

BROMEHILL PRIORY, Bromehill Farm, 1¼ m. SE. Of the Augustinian priory founded *c.* 1200 by Sir Hugh de Plais nothing is visible, except some worked stones in the farmhouse. The church lay to the NE of the farmhouse and seems to have been aisleless. It was suppressed in 1528 by Pope Clement VII.

GRIMES GRAVES, 2⅛ m. ENE. In the Neolithic period, about 2100 B.C., some 370 shafts were sunk up to 40 ft into the chalk of the Breckland Heath. The surface diameter of the bell-shaped excavations varies from 13 to 26 ft, and the more complex have radiating galleries at the bottom extending waist-high into the chalk and linking with other shafts. The miners' goal was the high-quality flint that lay in the third band of flint from the surface, and the period of greatest production lasted for 500 years. As each gallery was excavated the waste was dumped into exhausted galleries, and then into exhausted shafts, so the surface today is a green cratered landscape, each crater practically touching its neighbour.

Following his work at the smaller Cissbury flint mines in
Sussex Canon Greenwell excavated one shaft in 1868–70, but less
than twenty have been examined since. One is open to the public,
Pit 1, explored in 1914 by A. E. Peake. At its base are seven radi-
ating galleries linking to, as far as one may judge, five other shafts.
BARROW. Large bowl barrow ⅝ m. N of Brandon Station, known
as Pepper Hill. (JW)
FOSS DITCH. *See* p. 343.

WELBORNE   0000

ALL SAINTS. C12 round tower with a C19 brick corbel course and
a shallow conical roof pierced oddly by four lucarnes. They are
there to act as sound-holes, for the tower has only two external
openings – a tiny S lancet and a double-splayed W lancet. The
upper doorway towards the nave altered. The thickness of the
nave W wall indicates that the tower is an addition. C15 S porch
with buttresses embellished by two tall thin recesses and spandrels with tracery round the entrance arch. Chancel of 1874–6
and the nave windows of the same time, all in the Geometric
style, paid for by the Rev. Barnham Johnson. The chancel
replaces one of 1671. The E four-light window has marble shafting inside; more marble shafting to the twin-arched sedilia.
Boarded and panelled chancel roof; thin contemporary scissor-
braced nave roof. – FONT. Plain, octagonal, embattled. –
SCREEN. 1875 by *John Parley*, gaily painted in 1912. – STAINED
GLASS. In the porch E window a jumble of C15 fragments
salvaged in the 1870s from the same builder's yard as the glass
at North Tuddenham. Indifferent glass of *c.* 1880 elsewhere.
SCHOOL. Immediately W of the church and looking like a church.
1847. Two four-light cusped windows under hoodmoulds and a
church-like porch. In the porch a clock face without hands,
which now serve the clock inside the church.

WELLINGHAM   8020

ST ANDREW. Unbuttressed W tower, nave and chancel. Several
lancet windows testify to the late C13, in the chancel particularly. Three cusped lights to chancel E window. The tower is
broader N–S than E–W. Two stages, the upper part crenellated in
1892. In the S wall of the nave Perp windows set inside in blank
arcading (cf. Swaffham). This wall, though, was rebuilt during
the 1896 restoration, seemingly accurately. Blocked N doorway.
Nave roof 1896. – SCREEN. Dated 1532, and inscribed for
the donors 'who had it painted'. The paintings are real scenes,
not just Saints against a patterned ground. The miscellaneous
subject-matter, including scenes of St George and the Dragon
and the Weighing of Souls, as well as the Image of Pity and
standing Saints, reflects the multiple patronage. Partially
restored by *Pauline Plummer* in 1970.

WELNEY

ST MARY. 1847–8 by *J. C. Buckler*. Coursed carstone and some ashlar. Nave and chancel in one. The windows are lancets with plate tracery, generally of two lights, the E window of three. Bellcote at the E end of the nave with a trefoiled opening, like the windows. There is a W gallery on six posts. Reredos of 1887. – STAINED GLASS. 1848, by *Thomas Wilmshurst* in the E window. Faith, Hope and Charity. The centre light has the Charity after Joshua Reynolds's Faith, Hope, and Charity from his New College windows at Oxford, but interpreted in strong colours. The technique is enamel painting, with heraldic motifs around (cf. St George Colegate, Norwich).

WENDLING

ST PETER AND ST PAUL. Above the S doorway an impressive Norman head, re-set, attached to a length of roll moulding. To the W of the porch is the jamb of an original Norman door. The rest Perp, including the transeptal S chapel with its big four-light window. Chancel completely rebuilt, leaving the chancel arch, probably during the harsh restoration of 1858. The chapel at least worked on then, if not rebuilt as well. Flushwork decoration in the battlements of the W tower. – FONT. A badly preserved and probably never well-carved example of the type with the Seven Sacraments. – SCREEN. Removed. Parts of the base were original. – STALLS. With some poppyheads and some Jacobean bits.

ABBEY. A Premonstratensian house, founded before 1267 from Langley, close to Abbey Farm, ⅝ m. ESE. Nothing now stands, but the general plan is discernible amidst low earthworks. There are some fine fishponds.

THE GRANGE, ⅝ m. NE of the church. C17 brick house with diaper to the gable-ends and an early C19 façade. Three bays of tripartite sashes.

MANOR HOUSE. Early C19 gault-brick house of two storeys in three bays with some flint. Hipped roof. Typical of its type, but with an above-average Doric porch.

WEREHAM

ST MARGARET. Right in the middle of the village, overlooking the duckpond. In the W wall of the nave remains of a wide Norman arch, later narrowed. The narrowing seems to have been done *c.* 1300, but the tower must have been built *c.* 1200 – see the deep splays to the three lancets. The upper parts are of brick and early Tudor. The chancel was much renewed during the fierce 1866 restoration, but may have been E.E. although the lancets are a C19 invention. The chancel arch, though of unusual mouldings, makes an E.E. date possible. Equally unusual the details of the s arcade. The bases and capitals have been badly re-tooled following a fire of unknown date. The quatrefoil piers with deep continuous hollows between the foils could be of the c13. The arches are nearly round and thus also baffling. The N arcade is a copy of 1866 when the aisle was added. – FONT. Octagonal, Perp. – PULPIT. Stone, 1866. – MONUMENTS. John Heaton, †1779. With a bust at the top of a tablet. – Several minor tablets in s aisle, mainly to the Adamson family. One †1765 signed *J. Fellowes*, Lynn. It has a broken pediment. – Christopher Adamson †1786. Ionic pilasters to a broken pediment.

A nice stone VILLAGE. The best house is THE MANOR HOUSE on The Green, s of the pond. Flint and carstone and dated on the rear wing 1722; the front re-faced in brick and dated 1729. The façade now is of two storeys in four bays with a recessed three-bay element to the l., both blocks with clasping pilasters. The entrance is in the recessed bays. Parapets. Two gabled wings to the rear. Opposite the pond and s of the church is CHURCH ROAD. Minor mid-c18 houses on the left face three unimaginative semi-detached infills (Nos. 1–6) of 1994. At the junction at the SE end, on Cavenham Road, facing Church Road, is THE WHITE HOUSE. Double-pile plan and an irregular seven-bay mid-c18 façade, suggesting an early c18 interior. Portico porch on unfluted columns. Sashes of various times.

WINNOLD HOUSE. *See* p. 784.

WEST ACRE   *7010*

ALL SAINTS. Next door to the gatehouse of the priory. W tower and arch between nave and chancel probably c14. Otherwise Perp, all embattled. But most of the windows, the N porch entrance, the s doorway, and the priest's doorway were restored *c.* 1638 for Sir Edward Barkham. This is just early enough to be classed as Gothic Survival rather than a revival. The tower Y-tracery window is c17, as are the bell-openings (no tracery). On the ringing chamber a cartouche and the Barkham arms. The clock face is 1907. The N and s nave windows again in a c17 version of Perp. N porch with a Classically inspired entrance with keystones in the arch. s door similar but simpler. Chancel s with Y-tracery windows and the date 1638. E window c19. – COMMUNION RAIL. c17, very pretty, with pierced fretwork oblongs. – SCULPTURE. An extremely interesting small stone panel in the N porch: a seated figure of the c13, apparently from the voussoirs of an arch. Such an arrangement is usual in France, but very rare in c13 England (but cf. Westminster Abbey, Glastonbury etc.). Very probably the piece comes from West Acre Priory. – In the reredos small wooden panels with religious scenes or single figures. Mannerist pieces, no doubt from the Netherlands. – STAINED GLASS. E window, †1907, good. Birkin Haward suggests *Burlison & Grylls*. The portraits of the kneeling family are a period document. – MONUMENTS. Miss F.A. Hamond †1820, aged sixteen. Tablet with mourning woman by a sarcophagus. – Anthony Hamond †1822. Large standing white marble monument. Life-size angel above the sarcophagus, against a back wall with tapering sides and a pediment. The figure of the angel is nearly detached from the ground. By *Joseph Theakston*. – Many minor tablets.

PRIORY. Augustinian. Founded c. 1100 or a little later by Ralph de Toeni. The priory was on the same scale as Castle Acre, and fragments extend on both sides of the River Nar. Dissolved in 1538. The entrance was from the N by the GATEHOUSE, which still stands, although open to the sky. This dates from the C14 and is built of flint with stone dressings. It is wide and flat and has a two-centred, double-hollow-chamfered entrance arch with a lancet window over. Inside is an oblong quadripartite rib vault. A second, inner bay followed. The gatehouse led into the outer courtyard. Of the CHURCH the most prominent fragment is part of the SW TOWER. This is partly Norman (E), partly E.E.(W). The adjoining W façade was E.E., the adjoining aisle wall and the partly preserved W range of the cloistral precinct is Norman. The church, as excavations published in 1929 have proved, had a nave and aisles, a W front projecting to the N and S beyond the aisle walls, arcades partly rebuilt in the C14, transepts of which the N one was also rebuilt in the C14, a chancel lengthened and made straight-ended in the C13, and a N chapel of the C15. The second highest fragment standing belongs to the CHAPTER HOUSE, an apsed Norman structure, re-cast in the C13 after a fire of 1286, and vaulted c. 1300. Only a corner remains. S of the chapter house followed, as shown by excavations and as was usual, the dormitory undercroft and the reredorter. S of the cloister walk was the refectory. Of the infirmary a little was traced to the S of the chapter house and dormitory. SW of the present house (*see* below), running towards the river, are the remains of some more major buildings. They are late medieval and will have been stables and offices. The oblong range on the other side of the river is of c. 1400. It was 110 by 36 ft and was divided into several rooms. Two storeys. Its function is unknown.

Two BARNS 100 yds S of the priory tower. The N one is in fact two barns built edge-to-edge, but their N gable has become detached. The date is difficult to judge, probably early C16, with C19 rebuilding (roof) and alterations. S barn much more discreet, but similar date.

ABBEY FARMHOUSE. An C18 two-storey house of various dates, and with an early C20 face-lift providing canted bay windows and other details. Some reused masonry from the priory.

THE WOODEN HOUSE. NW of the priory gate a picturesque timber-framed and weatherboarded house with the Post Office on the N. The restoration of 1982 was so thorough that the house is now C16 in spirit, not in fact. The plan is of a Wealden house, rare in Norfolk (but *see* New Buckenham, p. 559, and Wacton, p. 742). The central open hall can now be appreciated, however, as the restoration reinstated it. The arch-braced tie-beams originally carried crown-posts. Outside are all the proper jetties and the off-set door leading to the screens passage.

HIGH HOUSE, 2 m. NNE. Built before 1756 for Edward Spelman and re-fronted in 1829 by *Donthorn* for Anthony Hamond. Large, and of unusual composition. Gault-brick façade, castellated. This and the Doric pilasters and pillars date from 1829; the window surrounds of rustication in alternating sizes belong to the early Georgian work. The S front has a deeply recessed five-bay centre and two projecting wings plus, lying farther back, three-bay wings projecting E and W. The back completely flat, of thirteen bays in a tripartite arrangement, the three outer bays r. and l. being entirely of 1829, the inner seven merely a re-facing of the C18 house. The centre three bays are raised and contain on the upper floor the principal room of the house. This is now the dining room, and has a cartouche in the middle of the ceiling which could be of 1829. It contains the head of Medusa and the inscription ΣΟΛΩΝΟΣ (Solonos). The room is reached from the front of the house up a straight, just once interrupted, flight of stairs under a shallow, coffered segmental vault. Ionic pilasters and, at the end, a screen of two Ionic columns. Behind this a broad cross corridor through the central part of the house, and from here the entrance to the dining room. The staircase as well as the corridor already existed in 1756, when they were described by Mrs Lybbe Powys, but Donthorn remodelled them. She calls the corridor a gallery and gives its size as 90 ft by 18 ft. It has two fireplaces.

STABLES by *Donthorn*, c. 1829 for Anthony Hamond. A small courtyard with single-storey ranges and higher corner towers. E range has a barrel-vaulted carriage arch under a pediment. Greek details in the S porch.

WEST BARSHAM

ASSUMPTION. A church without any buttresses. In the N nave wall two circular windows of Saxon date with deep external splays (cf. Witton, Coltishall, and St Julian Norwich, Vol. I). Inside the nave, in the E wall above the chancel arch, another Saxon window or doorway. This is triangle-headed and must have connected with a Saxon central or sanctuary tower. A fragment of this appears in the Ladbroke print of 1824. The vertical joint in the chancel wall may mark the E end of the tower. In the S wall of the nave an interesting plain Norman doorway, interesting because it was framed in the early C13 by a more decorative pointed surround. The Norman part has one order of shafts with shaft-rings carrying worn leaf capitals and a rounded arch. The pointed arch combines a keeled roll and zigzag on the wall surface and at r. angles to it. Norman also a splayed round-headed lancet high in the S wall next to the porch. The simple N doorway late Norman. Chancel of c. 1310, see the three-light intersecting E window and the Y-tracery on the S side. The same also in the nave w window. One Dec nave window N and s (mouchettes). The chancel arch, pointed and completely unmoulded, is a successful piece from the restoration by *W. D. Caröe*, 1935–8, reminiscent of Gill's work at Gorleston. Chancel roof by the same has five braces to each tie-beam. – FONT. C18. Marble bowl on a baluster stem. – BENCHES. 1954 by *Margaret Tarrant*, and very good poppyhead types, with animals as arm-rests. (– SCULPTURE. Adoration of the Shepherds. Small alabaster relief in a contemporary frame, probably Italian, *c.* 1600. The heads are mutilated, and the date 1407 added later. Removed.) – STAINED GLASS. C14 fragments in a s nave window and more in the N nave, moved from the E window when the *Ward & Hughes* glass was put in there in 1893. s chancel window, Jonathan and David, probably by *Clayton & Bell*, †1867. N chancel by *Margaret Tarrant*, †1953.

WEST BARSHAM HALL, immediately NW in a small park. A C20 house of two storeys in seven bays. In the middle of the principal façades is a projecting tower, that to the W with a porch. Red brick and hipped roofs. Begun 1913, abandoned during the war and finished only after 1921.

OLD HALL, Grove Road. Only the N wing remains of an early C17 house. Sash windows.

WEST BILNEY

ST CECILIA. Redundant. Small. Norman nave, see one blocked window on the N side. Plenty of rebuilding including the mid-C20 queenpost roof (reusing some old timber). The chancel has disappeared. Perp W tower with flushwork battlements and two-light bell-openings. The N parapet chewed away by a gale in 1976. A proposal to demolish the tower in 1983 was fortunately resisted and instead it was restored in 1990 by *Neil Birdsall*. There was a general restoration in 1881. Two big altar recesses with pointed heads in the nave N and s walls. A reference to a new window to the altar of the Virgin on the s side 1464. – FONT. Simple, octagonal, Perp, with encircled quatrefoils. – PULPIT. *c.* 1870 but stands over a stall in the Georgian manner.

WEST BRADENHAM

Middle-sized village, with the young River Wissey flowing as a stream E–W through it.

ST ANDREW. Much of the late C13 and early C14: the tower; N doorway with rolls; chancel with Y-windows to N and s and a triple sedilia and piscina (with proper niches); arcades of four bays with quatrefoil piers with spurs in the diagonals and double-hollow-chamfered arches. Dec aumbry in the chancel with a crocketed ogee arch. Cusped clerestory windows. Nave and

aisle roofs substantially C15. SW tower with the ground floor
treated as a porch; C14. The entrance arch big and plain. The
inner doorway has two orders of shafts and a cusped niche
above, much renewed. Chequerboard flushwork along the parapet probably rebuilt at the time of bequests in 1484–6 for bells.
The bell-openings still with Y-tracery. Perp aisle windows. In
the chancel an odd oblong lowside window. – FONT. Probably
C14, with pronounced mouldings on foot and stem. – STAINED
GLASS. E window by *William Wailes*, *c.* 1860. Also by him the
three W windows, †1847–56, that to the nave particularly good,
in C13 mode. The faculty for installation 1858.

WEST BRADENHAM HALL, ½m. NNE. Built some time before
1753, when the Thomsons sold to James Smythe. Red brick. A
handsome five-bay S front, with bays one and five flanked by
giant pilasters and a three-bay pediment in the middle also with
giant pilasters. Hipped roof with side stacks. The entrance was
moved from the N to the S end in 1819 and probably the stick-
baluster staircase as well. In that year the Haggard family
arrived and H. Rider Haggard spent his early life here. The
doorway has an open pediment. The doorway to the added E
side (1930s) comes from a house in Tombland, Norwich. Three-
bay W wing 1936. More additions E and N 1956.

WEST DEREHAM   6000

ST ANDREW. Round tower of big carstone blocks. The tower is of
exceptional diameter (inside 17 ft 6 in.) and 4 ft thick. Remains
of the wide Norman arch towards the nave. Very pretty octagonal
brick top with brick bell-openings and a frieze of little round
arches. This *c.* 1500. The S doorway to the nave is of *c.* 1200 or
a little later. Pointed arch with many mouldings and one order
of shafts. The rest mostly Perp. The nave roof collapsed in 1901
and had to be replaced; the chancel got its roof in 1895, this
after a restoration of 1855. The nave windows with stepped
transoms, the chancel windows with two-centred arches. C17
S porch gable. – FONT. Octagonal, Perp, with quatrefoils. –
PULPIT. Elizabethan or Jacobean, with the usual stubby blank
arches and fluted pilasters. – COMMUNION RAIL. Early C18,
three-sided, with twisted balusters. – BIER. Dated 1683, but still
in pre-Classical forms (under tower). – STAINED GLASS. Original
C14 fragments in the E and one nave S window. – MONU-
MENTS. Robert Dereham †1612 and his father. Tablet without
figures. – Sir Thomas Dereham †1722. Tablet of variously
coloured stone with a coat of arms against a leaf background.
Very decorative, though somewhat conservative, and probably
Italian. – Col. Edmund Soame †1706. Signed by *Robert Singleton*
of Bury St Edmunds. Standing white figure in armour against
a Classical architectural background of white, grey and pink
marble. Billowing cloak, and his helmet on the ground. Rupert
Gunnis rightly called it 'an exciting and remarkable work'. –
Plenty of decent C18 HEADSTONES.

A second church, ST PETER'S, once stood in the same churchyard.

ABBEY. A Premonstratensian house founded in 1188, S of Abbey Farm, 1 m. S of the church. The precinct is huge, roughly rectangular, remote and evocative. The remains show a ruined house with an ambitious ruined outbuilding all of 1697. There are fine gateposts with niches. But apart from the fact that the back wall of the house is of carstone and that the outbuilding (stables) has a diagonal buttress, no evidence of the abbey seems visible save for mounds and depressions in the ground.

The ruined HOUSE was of some interest, as drawings of 1756 in the RIBA library show it was modelled on the type of Italian palazzo popular in the late C16. Its owner, Sir Thomas Dereham (†1697), had been attached to the court of Tuscany and on his return in 1689 built here two three-storey five-bay wings r. and l. of a three-storey gatehouse belonging to the abbey. It had a *piano nobile* with tall round-headed windows, rusticated elevations, an overhanging pitched roof and a courtyard behind with buildings adapted from existing ones. One storey of one five-bay unit remains, plastered, windows with raised surrounds and a central turret with an arched recess. The STABLE BLOCK with the buttress mentioned above is entered through a four-centred carriage arch. Four bays r. and three l. The GATEPIERS at the NE corner of the precinct are associated with the elliptical brick bridge over the ditch, before 1697.

COLLEGE FARMHOUSE, Basil Road. Timber-framed early C17 house sandwiched between carstone and flint gable walls added in 1626. Only one storey and dormer attic, the dormers and other windows being C20 casements. The stepped gables are dated to the N. The N is the least disturbed, with mullioned brick windows and hoodmoulds. Gault-brick two-storey extension dated 1900.

WESTFIELD

ST ANDREW. Early C14 unbuttressed W tower with cusped Y-tracery in the bell-openings. Plain arch towards nave. In the nave, windows with Curvilinear tracery, much restored. C15 S porch with some flushwork: chequer and panelling in the spandrels. The chancel was demolished about 1700 and the present E window with Y-tracery re-set. – FONT. C14, octagonal. With moulded stem. – PULPIT. Simple, Jacobean. – COMMUNION RAIL. Simple, with thin balusters; C17, probably post-Jacobean. Originally the arrangement was three-sided.

WEST HARLING

ALL SAINTS. In a lonely position. The S aisle was demolished in 1733. Late C13 chancel with a hollow-chamfered chancel arch.

Also late C13 is the plate tracery s nave window with a quatrefoil vesica, re-located when the aisle was demolished. It has roll-moulded internal jambs and a depressed rere-arch, and an angle piscina in the E jamb, which has had to be reduced to accommodate it. The piscina has a trefoiled ogee head, so must be *c.* 1300 at the earliest. The three-light chancel E window with cusped intersecting tracery also tallies. It was opened in 1844, having been bricked up. C14 W tower with flushwork in a chequer lozenge pattern on the base, a normal chequer pattern on the battlements. The two-light W window is from the restoration of 1902 and the twin lancets to the bell-stage date from 1756 when the parapet was rebuilt following the demolition of a spire. Two N nave windows and one to the s have Early Perp tracery.

Inside, the nave has a double hammerbeam roof of 1902 (chancel roof also 1902). – FONT. Octagonal, with ogee tracery on the stem and roll-moulded panels to the bowl containing shields and flowers. – PAINTING. A lozenge pattern with fleurs-de-lys against the back wall of the chancel sedilia niche, probably original late C13 work. – MONUMENTS. Brasses to Ralph Fuloflove, a priest, †1479 in his mass vestments (2 ft figure); another to William Berdewell *c.* 1490 and wife; and to a second William Berdewell †1508 and his wife (18 in. figures). These are all in the nave and all are good. – Bust and tablet to Richard Gipps by *Joseph Wilton*, 1780, the bust uncommonly good. White marble. – REREDOS. 1902 but with five C16 Flemish carved panels.

There was another parish associated with West Harling (apart from East Harling), based round Thorpe Farm 1½ m. WSW, which was apparently demolished in 1543. Of HARLING THORPE CHURCH, only bits of walling remain. The West Harling estate of the Gawdy family was sold in 1725 to Joshua Draper who built WEST HARLING HALL, itself demolished in 1931. The architect of this minor example of English Baroque is unknown. All that remains is the GARDEN HOUSE, a flint and stone, two-storey house of *c.* 1780.

BARROWS. The barrows scattered throughout the West Harling heathland area are probably an extension of those in Garboldisham parish (*see* p. 350). Only one, s of Middleton House Farm, has been opened (1932), but without recorded result.

WEST LEXHAM

St NICHOLAS. Short round tower, renewed, with four cusped bell-openings. The rest of 1881, though the chancel masonry looks old and the s porch entrance is certainly C14, but probably re-assembled. The chancel arch seems to date from the early C14. Y-tracery windows favoured for the chancel. – STAINED GLASS. E window 1882 by *L. Lobin* of Tours, figure of Christ.

WEST LYNN

6020

St Peter. Of a Norman predecessor of the church fragments, mainly of arches, built into the E wall of the chancel. The chancel was rebuilt in 1934–5 under the direction of *W. D. Caröe* after a general restoration in 1905. The stone-faced w tower is Dec, see the pretty sound-holes below the bell-openings, with their cusped pointed quatrefoils. Small lead spirelet. The church is aisleless and has transepts lower than the nave. Squint from the N transept to the chancel with a tiny quatrefoil window in the corner. Big Perp end windows of four and five lights. Brick N porch and a vestry opposite on the S side of 1922. The chancel odd under its mansard roof. Nice nave roof with tie-beams on arched braces alternating with arched braces supporting the principals direct, like hammerbeams. Traceried spandrels and traceried queenposts. Figures against the wall-posts. – FONT. With the Seven Sacraments. Simple straightforward carving. The eighth scene is of Christ Enthroned. – PULPIT. Simple, Jacobean. – STALLS. Two; with damaged MISERICORDS. – STAINED GLASS. E window, †1849 by *W. J. Bolton*, a four-lighter and Bolton's only large window in England. Scenes of the Crucifixion and at the Tomb, in C16 style. A small angel in a N nave window also by *Bolton*. – BRASS. Adam Outlawe †1503, 31 in. figure (E nave).

Ferry Square. A picturesque corner by the River Ouse, with a fine view across to King's Lynn. On the w side Nos. 2–4, a C17 brick house much altered and with two cross wings.

Nos. 114–116 St Peter's Road are very modest early C19 houses deserving notice for the plasterwork on the front. A clasped hand above three roundels with sheaves of corn, an anchor and a plough.

WEST NEWTON

6020

St Peter and St Paul. Of carstone. Unbuttressed w tower. The Y-tracery bell-openings might indicate a date early in the C14. The tower arch has one demi-shaft and two continuous chamfers. That also may well be of the early C14. In the w wall a big ogee-headed niche. Simple early C14 S doorway with a continuous wave moulding. The church was so extensively restored by *Arthur Blomfield* in 1881 that it seems now externally almost entirely Victorian. The N aisle e.g. was rebuilt using carstone slips, the roofs new (elaborate arched braces to nave, plain boarded to chancel), window tracery all replaced, the vestry added. The Prince of Wales met the cost. Four-bay arcades with octagonal piers and arches with the untypical sunk-quadrant moulding. Only the E arch has two plain chamfers; it is wider too and indicates the existence of original transepts. – FONT. Perp, octagonal, with shields to bowl and trefoils to stem. – FONT COVER. Said to be Jacobean, but could as easily be early C16; tall and of the type with crocketed fins. –

STAINED GLASS. *Heaton, Butler & Bayne* did everything between *c.* 1880 and *c.* 1910 except for a N aisle window, which is by *Karl Parsons*, †1915, a nice St George.

The VILLAGE of West Newton is part of the Sandringham Estate and is therefore full of buildings due to Edward VII when he was Prince of Wales and to later members of the royal family. The arrangement of buildings all very organized in a highly picturesque manner, but none is individually important and they are too scattered to provide a coherent effect.

CLUB, immediately SE of the church, replacing the Three Tuns pub. 1873. Carstone in slate-like pieces, i.e. carstone slips (such as Blomfield used in the church), brick and half-timbering, casements and clustered stacks. Picturesque, irregular, and of course gabled.

SCHOOL, 200 yds NE of the church. 1881. Picturesque and a little silly. Gabled in all directions and with two little cupolas.

ALEXANDRA COTTAGES, round the corner from the school. 1864. Semi-detached and of carstone slips. Quite conventional, each pair of two bays with small porches and central stacks.

WESTON LONGVILLE

ALL SAINTS. Famous as the living of James Woodforde, diarist and rector here 1776–1803. Unbuttressed low W tower, over-restored, but from the tower arch and the bell-openings it is to be assigned to the C13, from its beginning to its end. The main restoration was in 1880, and of this date are the N aisle windows and probably the chancel windows, although accurately done. Dec chancel, the windows with Curvilinear tracery, the sedilia and piscina delightfully decorated. Ogee arches with crockets. At their springing a tiny Green Man, a little man among foliage, and a face with its tongue stuck out. Frame with fleurons. Perp S aisle windows. S porch with a frieze of nine flushwork panels and a gable niche. Arms of the Merchant Adventurers, incorporated by Edward IV, i.e. after 1461. In 1481 money was left for 'making porch'. Clerestory with five quatrefoil windows in squares, the spandrels filled with knapped flint. Six-bay arcades inside. Octagonal piers, double-chamfered arches. Both sides probably C14, but the details (i.e. a hollow in the arch) on the S side earlier. The crown-post nave roof C19, probably 1880; boarded chancel roof with rafters on arched braces, same date. – FONT. Ordinary octagonal bowl supported on five columns of Purbeck marble. In the base a reused Crucifix of, possibly, Saxon origins. – SCREEN. Late C15, with inscription to the donor Richard Lyon. Tall, of one-light divisions, the arches concave-sided. Much good panel tracery above them. The twelve dado paintings of the Apostles holding scrolls with parts of the Creed are over-restored. – BENCHES. Some; with poppy-heads. – SOUTH DOOR. C14; with long iron strap hinges and an iron ring. – WALL PAINTINGS. Considerable remains of a superb scheme of *c.* 1360 attributable to the same workshop as nearby Little Witchingham (q.v., Vol. 1). On the N aisle wall a fragmentary St Christopher, and a large composition of the Tree of Jesse, with varied and dynamic figures set in bold vine-scroll with bunches of grapes. To the N of the chancel arch a most elegant figure of St John the Baptist beneath a complex perspectival canopy, and to the S an unusual depiction of St John the Evangelist, shown bald and bearded and with a dragon emerging from his chalice. Also remains of post-Reformation texts. (DP) – STAINED GLASS. In the heads of the S aisle windows small C15 figures, much restored c. 1850 probably by *John Dixon*. – MONUMENTS. Minor wall tablets, including that to James Woodforde †1803 in the N chancel. – BRASS. Elizabeth Rokewoode †1533. The figure is 2 ft 3 in. long. On the ends of the inscription plate kneel two children.

OLD HALL, 1½ m. NNW of the church. Moated, the moat in places developed into large ponds and linking directly with the River Wensum running immediately NW. An E-plan house was built for Firmin Rookwood in the mid C16 facing S, altered in the early C17. In the C18 the hall range was demolished, i.e. the parts to the E of the porch and the parts W remodelled and extended. Further alterations C19 and C20. The C20 plan resembles a T with the porch incongruously attached to the E end of the stem of the T, facing S. The porch is a worthwhile piece dated 1606. The doorway has a segmental gable framed by sturdy Doric brick pilasters. On the floor above elongated Doric brick pilasters and a three-light mullioned and transomed window. A pediment on it. In the gable also a pedimented window. These details hard to see through luxuriant ivy. Timber inner doorway with sunk-quadrant mouldings. Strapwork decoration on the large coat of arms (Rookwood), moved to the S gable of the head of the T. A fragment of a window pediment at the back of the house as well. Extensive conservatories added to the W front in 1988–94. One tie-beam on arched braces in the roof, with tracery in the spandrel. When Parson Woodforde dined here on 9 September 1778 he first heard a 'sticcardo pastorale' (*sic*), played by Mrs Custance. The sticcado is a glass xylophone.

SUMMERHOUSE, 130 yds NW overlooking the river. Of c. 1830, of gault brick, hexagonal, with a pyramid roof carrying a lantern.

WESTON HOUSE, 1 m. NNW of the church. The Weston Estate of the Custance family broke up in 1926 and the five- by five-bay house of 1756 was demolished (a club house serving Weston Park Golf Course is on the site; the grounds are a dinosaur theme park). However there remain a pair of LODGES on the Norwich Road. Early C19, gault brick, oblong. Each has a Venetian window to the short side facing the road. Facing the drive is a Doric portico of two columns *in antis* framing the entrance door and rising to a Doric metope frieze which continues right round. Gables with pediments. The chimneystacks have four attached shafts. Rusticated gatepiers linked to the lodges by cast-iron railings.

WEST RAYNHAM   *8020*

ST MARGARET. In ruins and thickly clothed with ivy and elder.
The plan can be made out at least: W tower, nave, N aisle and
chancel. A chapel off the chancel to N. Enough of the chancel
arch lies about to see it was Perp, and enough of the piers to see
they were octagonal. The tower had a N doorway. The living
consolidated with East Raynham in 1721.

THE STREET. POST OFFICE. Early C18 (the re-set datestone at
the back declaring 1719 might agree). Two storeys in five bays
of cross casements, though on the ground floor the N part converted to a shop front in the late C19. Platband. Two rows of
COTTAGES either side are pleasant enough, Nos. 11–13 late
C19, Nos. 24–28 *c.* 1850. Flint with brick dressings.

WEST RUDHAM   *8020*

ST PETER. Redundant. In the W wall of the S aisle is a lancet
uncomfortably close to the tower and above it is a line of a former roof, which suggests that the aisle was originally narrower.
However all the rest of the evidence disproves it unless the lapse
of time between construction and widening was very short. The
S doorway and the three windows E of it are all mid to late C13
and presuppose the present width of the aisle. The doorway
has two orders of colonnettes; the windows, shafted inside, have
different typical late C13 forms. Moreover, the arcade seems to
be C13 too, and this consists of four bays, plus a very narrow W
bay which cannot, however, be an afterthought, because the W
respond has a little stiff-leaf decoration. The S doorway is not in
line with the corresponding arcade arch. Octagonal piers, arches
with two hollow chamfers. Short but heavy W tower, without
parapet or battlements, opening towards the nave with three
continuous chamfers (early C14?). There was once a W doorway
(Ladbroke's drawing *c.* 1823 shows the S door blocked) but it is
now blocked and Y-tracery fills the arch. Perp N side without an
aisle. The nave roof has tall arched braces but no collar, and has
a narrow W bay mirroring the arcade. C14 chancel fitted with
(renewed) Perp windows, though the E window is entirely C19,
as is the S wall and roof. – FONT. Perp, octagonal, simple. –
BENCHES. In the S aisle. C17 Gothic, with poppyheads. –
STAINED GLASS. Some C15 bits were removed to storage in the
1970s and replaced *c.* 1984; in the tracery of the N windows.

THE GROVE, NE of the church, on Lynn Road. Brick and flint,
the E gable and one of the two N wings C17, but the red brick
façade rebuilt *c.* 1962, increasing from six to seven bays.

Also on Lynn Road the former DUKE'S HEAD public house, with
the date 1663. Of this date the ground-floor window surrounds,
but the windows themselves replaced C19.

HALL FARMHOUSE, School Road. The early C17 flint house
increased from two to three storeys in the early C19, the addition
obvious in its red brick. Two-storey porch has a four-centred

brick archway with pilasters rising to a pediment. External C17 stack to S gable, blocked C17 windows to N gable. Two-bay extension *c.* 1810–20.

LONG BARROW. This, the only long barrow to have been excavated (1937–8) in the county, lies on Harpley Common and now stands to a height of about 2–3 ft. A further excavation in 1963. It is 216 ft long and 60 ft wide. A cremation or funerary pyre on a gravel platform recalls contemporary barrows in Wessex, as does a ditch-encircled enclosure on the S apparently used for libations. The only finds were a few flints and a secondary Neolithic flint fabricator in the primary ditch silt, with some bell beaker fragments above.

BARROW. Towards the old East Rudham Station a bell barrow is set beside the disused railway cutting. (JW)

8090
WEST TOFTS
In the Battle Zone (*see* p. 14)

ST MARY. Perp W tower with flushwork base frieze and an inscription recording 'All the begyners of the werk', i.e. those who gave money for the building of the church: Andrew Hewke, John Rolff, John Oliver and his wife, Wylyam Olyver, Wylyam Rolff, John Rolff (again), John Hewke, Robert Rolff, and Sir John Vyse, Parson. (At Santon Downham, a few miles away in Suffolk, is an inscription of names in the same position.) Early C14 N arcade, four bays, quatrefoil piers, double-hollow-chamfered arches. Transeptal S chapel, created, together with the rebuilding of the chancel and N aisle, by *A. W. N. Pugin* for the Rev. Augustus Sutton, rector from 1849, and a member of the Sutton family of nearby Lynford Hall (they sold up in 1856). Chapel and chancel are on a remarkably ambitious scale, the former serving the purpose of a memorial chapel to Jane Mary Sutton †1842. This chapel was the first part built, in 1845–6. Mrs Sutton's MONUMENT is in the chapel, a shrine with two gables and a canopy in the E.E. style supported on six marble shafts. The next work was the reconstruction of the N aisle, 1849, then the S porch, 1850. From this year is the earliest drawing of the chancel. After Pugin's death in 1852 his son *E. W. Pugin* was in charge. Pugin's chancel is taller than the nave and has a W bellcote and an eminently picturesque N extension with a turret – timber-framed at the top – to allow for a staircase to the organ balcony. The windows are in the Dec style, and at the angle to the Sutton Chapel a window is deliberately squeezed in with a raking reveal. There is also outside the chapel a low recess as if made in the C13 for a tomb. The chancel roof is prettily painted.

Of *Pugin's* FURNISHINGS the organ case is now at South Pickenham. He produced designs for organs and organ cases in 1847 with the Rev. Sutton, and the rest of the decoration is derived partly from Pugin's work at Jesus College, Cambridge, 1846–9. The BALCONY with a balustrade painted with angels remains, the carving (and indeed the main contracting) by *George Myers*. The PAINTING in the chancel was done by *John Hardman*'s Corps of Painters, probably *Thomas Early* to Pugin's design. The STAINED GLASS was mainly made by *Hardman & Co.* from Pugin's design, but some of it, formerly in the S transept S and E windows, is by the *Rev. Frederick Sutton*. Most of the glass is stored, but the Sutton pieces are intended for St Mary, Walsingham. – The Sutton Chapel has Minton TILES. – The FONT is decorated by demi-figures of angels against the under-side of the bowl. – The SCREENS (again by *Pugin*, carved by *Myers*) were paid for in 1850.

WEST WALTON   *4010*

ST MARY. One of the most sumptuous E.E. parish churches – not only of Norfolk – complemented by the remarkable free-standing E.E. tower. Free-standing towers were a Fenland speciality. The date of nearly everything that remains is *c.* 1240; the source of the style is Lincoln, both parish churches and cathedral. The building, or rather buildings, are faced in Barnack rag. The TOWER stands completely detached at a distance to 19 the S. Restored 1907 and 1985–6. Until 1985 the interior floors had vanished. The tower is pierced on the ground floor on all four sides. The angles are strengthened by big polygonal but-tresses. The arched entrances have much dogtooth to the N and S: to the W and E they are simpler. Inside there are doorways in all four buttresses but a stair in the SE buttress only. Other doors lead to small rooms with conical vaults. The buttresses have, on the ground stage only, an arched gabled niche with shafts, towards the N and S also with a small head in a foiled circle and with dogtooth in the gables. Above that there is tall arcading in three tiers, each side of the first stage with three central lights open to reveal an internal wall-passage. It looks like an external triforium, unusual and successful. The bell-stage has big shafted two-light windows with dogtooth and a circle in plate tracery in the spandrel. Perp parapet and pinnacles.

The church has a W façade marred by two big later buttresses where there were originally again polygonal turret-like C13 buttresses. Some blind arcading still visible r. and l. W doorway with two pointed arches set into one round one. The trumeau is a shaft. The stiff-leaf capitals were all renewed in the restoration of 1907. Much dogtooth and fleurons. The W window originally also had dogtooth, but the original was replaced with a five-light Perp window, leaving the dogtooth inside and E.E. shafting. Of the C13 and in the same style the S porch and the S and N door-ways. The porch has a rich façade, again with polygonal buttresses carrying two-storeyed arcading and here rising high up, and with an entrance with tall shafts and dogtooth. Stepped brick gable of Tudor date. Inside the porch blank arcading. This is now of only one and a half bays – a sign that the doorway was re-erected when the aisle was given its present width. The doorway has four orders of shafts (two on each side humbly renewed in wood) with mature, windswept stiff-leaf capitals and a complexly moulded arch. The N doorway is similar, but a little simpler. What is more surprising than the re-erection of the S doorway – a comparatively frequent thing to happen in the late Middle Ages – is the existence of a priest's doorway and an ambitious two-light window next to it at the E end of the aisle. They are in line with the S doorway and must either also be re-erected or represent a former transeptal projection for which there is no evidence. The window has a quatrefoiled circle in bar tracery. Inside this there are shafts and delightful mouldings with dogtooth, leaves and fleurons; with the bar tracery an interesting overlap of styles. If c. 1240 the window is contemporary with Binham (cf., Vol. 1), perhaps earlier than Westminster Abbey. Two C14 mouchette windows W of the S porch, others mainly C15.

This view must be seen in conjunction with the whole interior, which is distinguished by the uncommon width of the aisles and by their arcades on circular piers with detached Purbeck shafts and gorgeous stiff-leaf capitals. The nave has six bays and there were in addition two-bay chancel chapels on both sides (blocked). The piers had eight shafts in the chancel and have four shafts in the nave, and all have shaft-rings. The arches have many mouldings. In the chapels they have hoodmoulds on big leaf paterae. The clerestory is original too. The windows are of a single light, set outside under an arcade of small arches so that only every third contains a window, but inside in larger blank arcading so that every other arch contains a window. This is a specially happy conceit. All N clerestory windows blocked when the aisle roof was raised. Nave roof late C15, of false hammerbeams, in the form of figures with shields, supporting ties. Contemporary S aisle roof. Both restored 1965 –73. N aisle roof C18. The chancel arch goes with the arcades, but is of course taller, which leads to some awkward junctions. Above the arch blocked E windows also formerly shafted and decorated with fleurons with crockets. The E bay of the chancel has blank arcading to the N and S. The E window itself has thin intersecting tracery, installed when the chancel was shortened in 1807. Early in the C14 the N arcade needed some support. On its N side are two buttressing piers.

FURNISHINGS. FONT. Perp, octagonal, with arched panels to the stem and quatrefoils to the bowl. – BENCH ENDS. C15, with poppyheads and animals close to them, made into chancel stalls. – WALL PAINTINGS. Between the S clerestory windows painted decoration in the form of wall hangings with patterns of griffins, fleurs-de-lys, etc. They date from the time when the church was just completed, say c. 1240–50. They formed part of a much larger fictive ensemble of masonry pattern and large imitation pierced oculi in the spandrels of the main arcade, the latter similar to real examples in early Gothic architecture in Normandy (DP). In the arcade spandrels C18 roundels with the Twelve Tribes of Israel. – MONUMENT. Priest, mid-C13. Good effigy of Purbeck marble, similar to the contemporary ones at Ely. Head under a flat trefoiled canopy. Thin shafts l. and r. (N aisle E end). – BOARD. On the S wall a board erected in 1677 recording the great Marshland floods of 1613, 1614 and 1671. – Some C18 HEADSTONES S of the church and one dated 1682.

INGLEBOROUGH MILL, 1¼ m. N on Mill Road. Disused seven-storey brick tower mill, without sails, c. 1820. It was built with five of them but acquired a sixth in the mid 1850s.

WEST WINCH   6010

ST MARY. Of carstone with ashlar dressings. Mostly of c. 1300 and Perp. Of the former period the chancel with an E window of three stepped lancet lights and a single splayed N lancet, the two W bays of the S arcade, and the W window of the S aisle (show-ing that the aisle was at that time narrower than now; the ghost of the original roof-line visible outside). There is no N aisle. The two W bays of the three-bay S arcade have polygonal responds, that to the W with ballflower in the capital, to the E with a little dogtooth. The pier between has four keeled main and four keeled subsidiary shafts. The other pier has been rebuilt so that it takes the form of a narrow piece of wall run-ning N–S, with chamfered ends, against which are the responds of the arches. Dec S porch rising above the low aisle, with chequered flint front and a plain quadripartite rib vault inside. Gables to N and S parapets. Two-light reticulated side windows. Sundial in the S gable inscribed Hora Moner 1706. The rest Perp. W tower with flushwork decoration and two canopied niches round the W doorway and a big W window with transoms. Square-headed two-light S aisle windows; three-light N nave windows; three-light renewed clerestory windows. E bay of S aisle also Perp. The chancel arch has a squint to both sides large enough to clamber through. C15 tunnel-vaulted sacristy N of the chancel, with transverse ribs, partly rebuilt and re-fitted in the C19 as a vestry. – FONT. C15, plain, octagonal. – BENCHES. Some C15 poppyheads. – SCREEN. Under the tower. Partly Perp. – COM-MUNION RAIL. C17. Dumb-bell balusters and four figures with attributes (loaf, wine glass, purse and cross) on the posts. – STAINED GLASS. E window †1887, in style of *Clayton & Bell.*

WINDMILL, ⅝ m. N of the church. A brick tower mill of c. 1821. The 1977 restoration provided the new ogee cap, frame, gallery, fantail and stocks. The HOUSE crouching at the foot likewise restored, for Walter Price, interestingly with a piece cut out of the roof for the swing of the sails.

OLD DAIRY FARMHOUSE, ⅜ m. NW of the church. Derelict. A little two-cell, lobby-entrance house of carstone and brick dated 1623 on the stack. Square hoodmoulds over window openings.

WEST WRETHAM *see* WRETHAM

4090

WHEATACRE

ALL SAINTS. Extraordinary early C16 W tower of red brick and flint in big handsome chequerboard patterns. Heavy diagonal buttresses. The bell-openings seem to be C16 or C17 domestic hollow-chamfered three-light mullioned and transomed types. The (blocked) W doorway with its multi-stepped brick arch, the brick arch into the nave, and the Perp brick W window ought to be looked at with special care. The latter is of three lights with six lights at the top in a frieze. Bequest for bells in 1506 and for 'edifying steeple' 1522. Parapet 1880. The exterior of the nave and chancel are completely Victorian (re-faced with flint 1880–5 and given new windows), but the interior is old, if badly treated and in some points obscure. The chancel has a N chapel and had a S chapel. The details are cemented over in the crudest manner, possibly when 'restored' in 1879, but enough remains to show two bays with double-chamfered arches on polygonal piers. The windows, if accurately remade, would also indicate the early C14. With this date the S nave doorway would harmonize. It has a nice crocketed ogee hoodmould on stops with the heads of a king and a queen. The N doorway on the other hand goes with the tower, and the wide nave must indeed have been rebuilt at that time. At any rate one can say that it must have been rebuilt and the tower given its present position after the decision had been taken to do without the S aisle, or after it had been demolished. The chancel arch has the curious feature of being a wide blank arch embracing the entrance arches into chancel and N chapel. The entrance arches C19. – FONT. C15. Octagonal, with four lions against the stem, four flowers and four shields (Instruments of the Passion, emblem of the Trinity, Cross, three crowns) against the bowl. The font has been painted in the C20. – FONT COVER. In an exuberant Arts and Crafts mood. It must be by *Edmund Sedding c.* 1905. – SCREENS. Of the rood screen the tracery seems to be old, restored by *Sedding* in 1908. The screen to the N chapel is of 1904 and has subdued Arts and Crafts motifs, also by *Sedding*. – MONUMENT. Tomb-chest between N chapel and chancel.

WHEATACRE HOUSE, former rectory. Late C18, gault brick, five bays of sashes, central door behind a doorcase with an open pediment.

WHITEWAYS, E of the church. Partly 1948, partly 1957. By *Tayler & Green*. One two-storeyed terrace, but including one single-storeyed house. For the council housing by Tayler & Green, *see* Introduction, p. 165. The later part of Whiteways is more finely detailed. Some Crittall windows remain but mainly uPVC replacements.

0000

WHINBURGH

ST MARY. Redundant. All of *c.* 1300 to the later C14. SW tower with the porch in it. The entrance suggests a date after 1350 (although much restored). There is a cusped statue niche over the entrance. Y-tracery and two-light plate-traceried bell-openings. N windows (plate tracery, Y-tracery cusped) of *c.* 1300, N and inner S doorways of *c.* 1350–60, with wave mouldings. The w window of five lights is Victorian, but its rere-arch remains, with roll mouldings. Chancel rebuilt during the 1886–9 restoration. Good scissor-braced nave roof, of thirty-two trusses, early C14, unfortunately cut off above collar level. It was restored by *Neil Birdsall* 1990–1. – FONT. C14. Plain, with moulded stem and circular bowl. – STAINED GLASS. Chancel s windows, by *Clayton & Bell, c.* 1889.

OLD HALL, 1 m. SE, on Dereham Road. A moated timber-framed early C16 house with brick stepped gables and porch with pedimented doorway. The front was given a brick skin only in the 1920s, and only up to the level of the former first-floor jetty. The moulded bridging beams to the entrance hall suggest that they are original and that therefore the house had an upper chamber, in the manner of Abbey Farm, Old Buckenham. The seven-bay crown-post roof extends the whole length of the house.

WHISSONSETT

St Mary. w tower with bell-openings with cusped Y-tracery. Perp panelled battlements with shields in cusped fields and an inserted Perp w window. The rest Perp too but over-restored in the repairs of 1873. C14 perhaps the N and inner s doorways, the latter with some C14 metalwork to the door. s porch itself is C15 and at the moment miserable under a corrugated iron roof. Otherwise the chancel heavily restored, including the sedilia and piscina with detached shafts, the roofs all renewed and the windows remade. Niches l. and r. of the E window. – FONT. C15, octagonal, panel tracery to the stem, quatrefoils to the bowl. PULPIT. 1870, stone. – SCREEN. 1870. – SCULPTURE. Anglo-Saxon cross with the head in a circle and part of the shaft decorated with interlace. Kelly tells us it was dug up outside in 1902. – STAINED GLASS. E window by *Ward & Hughes, c.* 1860. More by them in s chancel windows, 1889 and †1901. C15 roundels in w tower window. – MONUMENTS. Brass to Thomas Gybon †1484 and brass to another knight, William Bozon, *c.* 1485, both 18 in. figures (nave w). – The churchyard is entered through four mid-C19 cast-iron TURNSTILES.

CHURCH FARMHOUSE. Of the mid C18, of brick in six bays and two storeys. Burnt headers decorate the first-floor windows.

WHITLINGHAM

1⅜ m. ENE of Trowse Newton

St Andrew. On a ridge above the river, on Whitlingham Lane. Became ruinous in the C17 after the belfry stage was added in 1620. Tower collapsed 1940, and all that now stands is part of the sw nave wall and some of the chancel. Perp three-light E window.

TROWSE NEWTON HALL, also on Whitlingham Lane, also difficult to find, on the s side. Mid-C15 house of the priors, later deans, of Norwich. What survived the mid-C19 demolition is the ruinous rectangular N range with fragments of Perp tracery in a four-centred window. Farther s is a four-centred doorway with wave mouldings, standing on its own.

WHITTINGTON
¼ m. SE of Stoke Ferry

CHRIST CHURCH. 1874–5 by *R. M. Phipson*. Phipson contented himself with a plain rectangular box without external or internal division, fitted out in Curvilinear style. The unimaginative four-light E window has a spherical triangle. Bellcote at w end. Continuous arch-braced roof.

Opposite, a BREWERY, later a grain store, the doorway dated 1821. The taller part to the l. is later.

WICKLEWOOD

ST ANDREW AND ALL SAINTS. s tower porch with flushwork chequer pattern on the buttresses. There is a flat ceiling in the porch, but it was probably intended to be vaulted. The outer doorway jambs seem C13, but this is all. The room above with a fireplace and an oven, and the room above that with another fireplace. The chancel was remodelled in 1412, and given two-light Perp windows. The rather Flamboyant E window is from the restoration of 1895. The rest Perp. The three-light nave windows have much brick in the voussoirs. These were renewed in 1865. But is the banding of brick and flint on the w side of the nave medieval? Arch-braced nave and chancel roofs, still mostly C15. Wave-moulded chancel arch. Cusped C15 piscina in nave and another in chancel, the latter with pierced spandrels. – FONT. C15, octagonal, with shields in barbed quatrefoils. – BENCH ENDS. A few, with poppyheads. – STAINED GLASS. In NE nave window some C15 fragments. – MONUMENT. Bartholomew Day †1780, by *Stafford & Athow* of Norwich. – DOORS. N and s are C15.

FORMER WORKHOUSE, ¾ m. SE. Built in 1777 at a cost of £11,000 and altered in 1836 by *John Brown*. Front of twenty-one bays with short wings and a five-bay centre with a three-bay pediment. The open loggia has been glazed. Long used as a school, converted 1994–5 to houses and flats, by *Robert Lord*.

WICKLEWOOD HALL, Low Road. The late C16 timber-framed house partly re-faced with brick in C17 and given a brick cross wing and a two-storeyed porch, both these additions with stepped gables. The windows generally C19, even if in the ori-

ginal openings. Octagonal shafts to the various stacks. There is
C17 and C18 panelling inside.

THE OLD HALL, Low Road. The same story. *c.* 1600, timber-
framed with a rendered timber frame built up under the jetty.
Brick extensions, here of the early C18, with good shaped
gables. The windows C20, the stack with diamond flues. The
timber frame has jowled principal studs. One fireplace bressumer
four-centred.

GREENSLEEVES, Morley Lane. This time the timber frame had
brick end-gables, and the façade was bricked in the C18. Some
of the casements are C18. Lobby-entrance, with the winder
staircase by the stack. Roof with diminished principals and
clasped purlins, and ties on arched braces.

WINDMILL. A fine sight following the restoration by *John Lawn*
for the Norfolk Windmills Trust, 1980–2. It was built in 1846.
Five tarred storeys, boat-shaped cap, fan stage and stocks and
sails. Restorations of mills in Norfolk usually stop short of
providing shutters. Machinery mostly renewed.

WIGGENHALL ST GERMANS ₅₀₁₀

ST GERMAINE. Immediately by the wide, placid River Ouse.
Carstone, brick and ashlar. E.E. w tower with Perp top. The
lower part has a long lancet window to the w and a tower arch
with a hoodmould carrying dogtooth decoration. The responds
are octagonal, however. Perp windows, those of the ashlar-faced
clerestory with basket arches. C16 brick s porch with polygonal
turrets standing on the shoulders of the gable. The s aisle is
propped up by a pair of generous C18 buttresses. The Y-traceried
windows of the N chapel seem to be medieval in origin but re-
assembled, perhaps in the early C19. Perp arcades of four bays.
Piers with four shafts and four thin strips in the diagonals.
Double-hollow-chamfered arches. The chancel chapels of two
bays have the same arches, but octagonal piers of differing details.
The nave has a queenpost roof, the posts, principals and purlins
all moulded, probably C15, but the chancel roof C19. – FONT.
C14 tracery panels to the bowl and stem. – PULPIT. 1631. No
longer blank arches; panels with geometrical patterns instead.
Attached iron HOURGLASS STAND. – READING DESK. Arched
panel with brackets below the desk; turned balusters at the sides;
early C17. – BENCHES. A good set, almost as complete, and of 49
the same design, as Wiggenhall St Mary. Saints in niches, poppyheads at the top, figures on the arms depicting the Seven
Deadly Sins, including a couple of lovers (Lust), a group of
four people, a priest blessing a kneeling person, and also
grotesques. The N aisle arm-rests with scenes from the Life of
St Germanus. They must be *c.* 1500. – MONUMENT. Martha
Appleton †1653, attributed to *Edward* and *Joshua Marshall*
(GF).

ST GERMAINE'S HALL. Facing the river. Late C17 w front with
three-bay Georgianized centre and two slightly projecting wings

with stepped gables. Brick lintel stones, alternately projecting, brick platband between the floors with a dripmould. The rear is rather more altered. Entrance hall with moulded and ribbed bridging beams, a bit old-fashioned.

In the garden 20 yds sw is a contemporary GAZEBO, square, brick, single-storeyed, with rusticated brick quoins and a pyramid roof.

FITTON OAKE, ½m. sw on Fitton Road. Brick. The date 1570 appears on a bridging beam and 1577 is in a terracotta plaque in the gable of the w cross wing. Roughly cruciform. Straight gables. Two-storeyed porch and at the back of the same (later lengthened) arm of the cross two polygonal buttress shafts. Polygonal buttress shafts also at the angles of the adjoining arm of the cross. Traces of mullioned windows. Right in the middle a triple-flued stack. If the restorations of 1976–80 nearly obliterated the exterior's Elizabethan appearance, they did so completely for the interior.

5010   WIGGENHALL ST MARY MAGDALEN

ST MARY MAGDALEN. A big Perp church with an earlier carstone and ashlar tower and some stonework in the chancel, but of brick otherwise. Two turrets at the e end of the nave and a sanctus bellcote on the apex of the gable (cf. Walpole St Peter). The tower may be of the C13 in its two lower stages; it is Dec above. Very low tower arch, no more than a doorway. Both the aisle w windows are blocked, though they were not when Brandon drew the church c. 1845. The side windows are threelight Perp of c. 1430: two crenellated transoms, cusped ogee arches and mouchette devices in the spandrels. Clerestory with three-light windows under depressed arches of the same date, and a two-light version in the tall nave e gable. Money was left in 1432 towards rebuilding, which fits nicely with what we see. Tall arcades between the wide five-bay nave and the aisles. Octagonal piers, double-chamfered arches. They look Dec in a nave otherwise Perp. Perp too the nave roof with tie-beams and queenposts alternating with short beams carrying figures. Solid braces to the ties and plenty of moulding. The chancel roof is a C19 kingpost. Two-storeyed s porch c. 1430, with an inner doorway of wave mouldings and shields in the spandrels relating to the Ingoldisthorpe and Howard families. – SCREENS. Painted panels of the rood screen at the w end. – Parts of the C15 parclose screens at the e ends of the aisles. – Many simple Perp BENCHES. – Jacobean PANELLING against the e wall, of eight painted bays with reeded and fluted Doric columns between them. – STAINED GLASS. Many C14 and C15 figures in the n aisle tracery lights.

THE PRIORY, e of the church on Church Road. It looks like a brick early C17 house, but is a T-plan timber-framed hall house of c. 1500 subsequently remodelled, the hall floored, and cased in brick. The restoration of the 1970s saved it. Stepped s gable with a blocked doorway and a little window to its r. with hollow jambs. Scars of windows to the E side. The N service wing now reduced but the C16 porch remains, and inside is a tierceron rib vault, the ribs of terracotta. From here to the screens passage; the hall on the l., the service rooms to the r. The hall bridging beams are particularly fine: ribbon-moulded with a vine trail. The hall was originally open, as is demonstrated by the two crown-post trusses in the roof, with four arched braces to the collars and purlins. The arched braces from the square-section crown-posts to the tie-beams are a King's Lynn feature. The roof is just right for *c.* 1500, but the ribbon-moulded beams of the inserted floor and the terracotta work (also found in the two-bay cellar vault) must be of about 1525–40 at the latest. The open hall plan, approaching the end of its life by the turn of the C16, was here quickly modified. The house is so-called because it is on the site of Crabhouse Priory, a house of Austin nuns. The register for 1556 describes a house being acquired by Sir Edward Gage, and the dimensions of the principal rooms are given. They correspond almost exactly with those of The Priory.

WIGGENHALL ST MARY THE VIRGIN 5010

ST MARY. Redundant. E.E. S and N doorways with undercut mouldings and two orders of shafts. All the rest Perp. The lower part of the W tower is of rubble, the upper of brick. Angle buttresses to the W are as fat as they are because the stairs are within them. Fine embattled top. Brick also nave, aisles and chancel. The S porch has a tunnel vault with transverse ribs and a sundial dated 1742. The arcade has five bays, with piers of four shafts and thin strips in the diagonals. Double-chamfered arches. Perp S clerestory windows but a rather rigid intersecting design to the N, the latter doubtless the work of *G. E. Street*, who restored in 1862 and again in 1870. His is the nave roof with its octagonal crown-posts as if this were a hall house. Chancel roof is Street's too. Graded Westmorland slate to the roofs of 1862, replacing thatch. In the chancel a plain angle piscina. – FONT COVER. Pretty, dated 1625. With four turned columns and four pendants, an octagonal pyramid roof, and a pelican on top. – PULPIT. Early C17. Cable moulding to the arcades and a reading desk on scrolled brackets. – SCREENS. Dado only of the rood screen; with seven painted Saints and the donor Humphrey Kervile who died in 1526. Parclose screen in the S aisle; also early C16. – BENCHES. One of the most complete sets in Norfolk. Early C16 to the N but early C15 to the S, even if partly restored. Backs with divers pierced tracery motifs. Ends with standing Saints in a niche and occasionally another motif (the Annunciation Lily, a coat of arms). Poppyheads. On the l. and r. buttresses standing or sitting figures, human as well as animal. – POOR BOX. With Jacobean panels. – LECTERN. Brass. With a large eagle and an inscription and the date 1518.

Of the same type as St Martin (Salisbury), Croydon, Bovey Tracey (Devon), St Nicholas (Bristol) and Cropredy (Oxon). – STAINED GLASS. Original C15 bits in tracery lights, mostly in the s aisle. – PANELLING. In the sanctuary, by *W. D. Caröe*, 1930. – MONUMENTS. Brass to Sir Robert Kervile †1450. A heart and four semicircular inscription bands. – Sir Henry Kervile †1624. Of alabaster. Tomb-chest with shields in strap-work cartouches. Also in one panel two standing children, the boy in baptismal robes for he had already died. Recumbent effigies of Sir Henry and wife, both straight-legged. Back wall with coupled Corinthian columns (unfluted) and an inscription in a strapwork surround. No arch.*

ST MARY'S HALL, Church Road. The house, of brick, with polygonal angle buttresses and finials, is of 1864, except for the entrance (s side), which forms part of a mid-C16 gatehouse. Two polygonal towers and a two-bay centre, both crenellated, and at the back the four-centred arch of the main entrance. Nothing corresponding to this remains inside. When Sir Henry, the last of the Kerviles, died in 1624 the house deteriorated and the gatehouse alone survived by 1740. The 1864 work was for Gustavus Helsham. The detached STABLE BLOCK 40 yds NW has stepped gables and brick windows with mullions and uncusped arched lights, i.e. probably of *c.* 1540–50 like the gate-house. Apart from its date the interest lies in the conversion of the upper floor to a ballroom in the late C19. A central octagonal chandelier descends from a timber recess in the roof.

6010

WIGGENHALL ST PETER

ST PETER. An excellent ruin immediately on the brink of the River Ouse (or the Eau Brink – to use the name of a hamlet nearby). The church now stands below the level of the raised banks. Only a few cottages are around. The church makes such an excellent ruin because the walls stand all the way up and only the roofs are gone. Perp nave and chancel with large win-dows. The chancel was under construction in 1421, and the rest may be of the same time, which is interesting because the dominant building material is brick. The s aisle was demolished in 1840 so the three-light windows have been re-set into the reduced arcade arches on this side. The arcade piers have four lobes separated by keels.

FITTON OAKE. *See* Wiggenhall St Germans, p. 778.

0080

WILBY

ALL SAINTS. The architecture mostly Dec, the furnishings mostly of the years after a fire which occurred in 1633. The restoration

---

* Jon Bayliss kindly tells me that the monument is from the same Nottingham workshop that made the monument to Sir Henry Pierrepont at Holme Pierrepont, Nottinghamshire.

was in 1902. Proud chancel with a very tall three-light E window displaying an intersecting design of petals and mouchettes, probably based on the Attleborough aisle-window designs (cf.). Tall two-light N and S windows with Y-tracery. The chancel arch belongs to the same build. Dec nave N doorway under an ogee arch and two orders of double wave mouldings. One Dec and one Perp S nave window and two three-light C15 panel-tracery windows to N. Dec W tower with Curvilinear tracery in the W window and circular quatrefoiled ringing-chamber windows. The entrance to the C15 S porch has fleurons up one order of jambs and arch. – Of the FURNISHINGS the following are of after 1633: the PULPIT, which is a three-decker, panelled under a tester; four FAMILY PEWS with their H-hinges; the base of the SCREEN with a gate with two tiers of turned balusters; the WEST GALLERY, dated 1637, also with two tiers of balusters; the COMMUNION RAIL, whose gate again has two tiers of balusters; the ten BENCHES, which are heavy and clumsy and have fleurs-de-lys instead of poppyheads; and the POOR BOX. Square, on a column, dated 1638. To this we might add the nave roof, with roll-moulded tie-beams and moulded principals. – FONT. Big octagonal bowl. Up its lower half traceried gables. Top battlements. – WALL PAINTING. St Christopher, on the N nave wall. Ample traces of the upper half of the figure.

WILBY HALL, $\frac{3}{8}$ m. N. On an attic window the scratched-in name Elizabeth Windham and the date 1649. That is of course only a *terminus ante quem*. The porch has the arms of John Wilton and his two wives and is therefore after 1635, he having acquired the manor from the Green family in 1622. However, the house is decidedly late C16 in appearance, i.e. red brick, pedimented mullioned and transomed windows, stepped gables, here even for every bay and the slightly projecting wing and the porch. The surround to the porch entrance has the only Renaissance flavour with its Roman Doric pilasters, entablature and corner obelisks. This is to the N front, the porch set to the l. and the wider projecting wing to the r. Two stepped gables to the S front. Three bays of the E wing were demolished c. 1700. The dog-leg staircase carries a moulded handrail on sturdy turned balusters, which, at attic level, forms a balcony.

WILTON

7080

Almost part of Hockwold

ST JAMES. Early C14 and Perp. Of the former period the three-stage W tower with its recessed stone spire – a rare thing in Norfolk. The timbers of the spire renewed in 1439 according to a donation of 53s. 4d. The spire has two tiers of lucarnes. Tower arch with three continuous chamfers and an inner order on three-eighth responds. The chancel arch of the same style, only double-chamfered. Dec also the rest of the chancel. Splendid four-light E window with reticulated tracery. Similar N and S windows of two lights and a priest's doorway. Odd little blocked lowside windows. Inside, a large ogee-headed recess for a monument and a small ogee-headed piscina. The nave must have been of the same period too, see the first window from the w on the N as well as the s side (Y-tracery). The other windows are panel-traceried and C15. C15 also the s porch with pretty two-light side windows with quatrefoils. Interior with wide nave covered by a scissor-braced roof, repaired, but not much, in the C19. Chancel roof similar. – SCREEN. C15 and much renewed. Big three-light divisions, reduced to one and a half bays on the l. and the r. All heads of the lights are ogee-arched. – BENCHES. A good set of twenty-five with low pierced backs decorated with different patterns of tracery. Poppyheads and, on the arm-rests, animals, and also a shepherd with his flock, a group of the Visitation, and other groups of two figures. – CHEST. With richly traceried front, probably C15. – PAINTING. A large area of the N wall with C14 masonry pattern with roses on stalks was reported by Tristram, but it is no longer to be seen. – STAINED GLASS. In the head of one s window in the chancel some early C14 glass. E window by *Burlison & Grylls*, 1874, with four large Old Testament figures. – MONUMENT. Mrs Colborne †1683. Tablet of stone and marble, quite impressive. Skull and crossed bones in the predella, moulded broken pediment with coat of arms above.

CROSS, on the Green, N of the church. Early C14. The shaft a tapering cluster of four slender shafts or lobes. The base of the top is also preserved. The pedestal is brick and the socket stone is an octagon chamfered out of a square. A good example.

6000

WIMBOTSHAM

ST MARY. Of carstone with limestone dressings. Norman doorways and chancel arch and Neo-Norman chancel and apse. The apse, however, is said to tally with foundations traced. In Ladbroke's (*c.* 1825) drawing the apse, if it existed, cannot be seen, but a Norman chancel can be, and is of the same dimensions as the present one. There was no apse in Johnson's 1838 drawing, but a three-light E window instead. The former chancel was taken down and replaced during the restorations of 1853–4, instigated by the Rev. G. E. Dashwood. The s doorway has two orders of cable- and chevron-decorated shafts with scalloped capitals, the former shafts circular, the latter octagonal. Decorated arches and small heads in the apexes of two orders of the arch. The N doorway is a little simpler. Hoodmould with billet frieze and roll- and cable-moulded arch; one order of shafts with cushion capitals. The chancel arch is less ornate. The capitals have simple scallops, the arch roll mouldings only. Short broad w tower of three stages quite closely documented by donations beginning in 1500 and ending in 1525 with a donation to the 'great bell'. Its arch to the nave has two continuous chamfers. In the s wall of the nave one E.E. plate-tracery window of two lights with a quatrefoil in the spandrel and very

833

pretty little stops to the hoodmoulds of both lights. Below it inside is an angle piscina with very big stiff-leaf motifs, much renewed, if not C19. The panelled nave roof is boarded and has leaf bosses. It is original, but very much repaired and raised 2 ft at the restoration. – BENCHES. The ends with poppyheads and arm-rests with animals and also a figure with a rosary. They are by *James Rattee*, 1854. – PULPIT and FONT by *William Lawrie*, 1854. – STAINED GLASS. Apse with a Virgin and Child and other emblems, c. 1853.

WINFARTHING 1080

ST MARY. Virtually Dec throughout. The chancel comes first (Y- and intersecting tracery; the lowside window with an ogee motif perhaps an addition), the extraordinary single-light concoction next to it (with the stained glass – *see* below) must be made up. The nave and s aisle come second, the tower last – see the way the nave NW buttress is interfered with by the tower. Slim two-light N nave windows with a reticulation motif, the aisle E window of three lights and perhaps not correct. Circular quatrefoiled clerestory windows (Victorian on the s side, one only to the N side). The three-light aisle s windows a Perp change. The three-bay s arcade also must be altered. The octagonal piers are Perp. Double-chamfered arches. Shallow scissor-braced nave roof, arched brackets to the s aisle roof, with double brattishing to the wall-plate. W tower with reticulation motifs in the two-light bell-openings but a Perp W window. Double wave-moulded tower arch. C15 N porch has flushwork. – FONT. Norman, round with four short attached columns in the corners. Two of them have heads instead of capitals. One of the columns is spiral-fluted. Barely matching C19 top half curiously like another font placed on top. – STAINED GLASS. A N chancel window of 1957 by *G. King & Son*, emblems of a plough, tree and sword etc.

The VILLAGE has some C17 timber-framed cottages rather altered in the C19, e.g. THE CLERK'S COTTAGE and CHURCH PLACE on Church Lane. CHURCH FARMHOUSE on The Street, again C17 and timber-framed, with gables r. and l., that to N having a jettied first floor, that to s with a five-light mullioned window. On the opposite side Nos. 1–2 started as an early C17 timber-framed house with a N wing terminating in a shaped gable of the late C17. The E part (No. 2) added in brick at the same time. In outlying areas are farmhouses of similar date often cased in C19 brick – ROOKERY FARMHOUSE at Goose Green, 1 m. NNE, is representative. HEATH FARMHOUSE, Heath Road, 1¼ m. NNW, has a C17 timber-framed rear wing with an C18 red brick front of two storeys and attic in four window bays. Finally WALNUT TREE FARMHOUSE, Wash Road, late C16, timber-framed but with a brick SE stepped gable-end crowned by triple polygonal chimneyshafts.

HEYWOOD HALL and HEYWOOD MANOR. *See* Diss, p. 304.

WINNOLD HOUSE
1½ m. N of Wereham

The house is built into a Norman part of the Benedictine priory founded before 1199. The E and N walls incorporate wide shafted buttresses and a frieze above the ground floor and another above the first floor. A C12 lancet to the E also. The S wall has Perp windows with hoodmoulds on heads. The priory was dissolved in the C14 and demolished in 1539, these fragments becoming incorporated into a C17 house, in turn rebuilt in the C19. C19 extension to W.

WOLFERD GREEN *see* HOWE

WOLFERTON

ST PETER. Of the late C13 and early C14, restored by *Arthur Blomfield* in 1885–6 for the Prince of Wales. W tower with sound-holes in the form of cinquefoiled circles. Dec bell-openings have reticulated tracery. A fireplace on the ground floor. Chancel with (renewed) reticulated E window and sedilia and piscina with ogee heads. Priest's doorway with pretty traceried gable inside. Vestry and organ bay to N are Blomfield's. Arcades of five bays with octagonal piers with seats around and arches with one chamfer and one hollow chamfer. The piers etc. are reddened from a fire in 1486. Rebuilding from this date culminated in a new chancel roof of 1490, replaced alas in the C19. Windows with ogee-headed lights under segmental arches, also with cusped Y-tracery, and cusped Y-tracery with a small trefoil in the spandrel. The doorways in their continuous wave mouldings of the mid C14 or a little later. S porch with niches l. and r. of the entrance and Dec windows. The arch of five orders of wave mouldings. In the N aisle W wall a curious blank niche of two ogee arches. What can its purpose have been? Perp clerestory. Nave roof by Blomfield, 1886: with tie-beams and arched braces up to the collars. This arrangement alternates with hammer-beams with horizontal figures and then again arched braces to the collars. – FONT. Octagonal, big, with two blank arched panels to each side. – SCREENS. Of the rood screen only the dado with remains of paintings is original late C15 work. The groined coving is Blomfield's. – Of the parclose screens that on the S, though much renovated, is a very fine C14 piece with ogee arches and very fragile, delicate tracery inside circles and spherical triangles. The other parclose screen is C15. – Tower screen, C15, renewed. – BENCHES. A few with C15 poppyheads. – BOOKCASE. By the entrance. Of an outrageous ultra-Gothic design, said to be German. It comes from Windsor Castle and has a date 1866. – LECTERN. Near the W end. Triangular base and baluster shafts, probably Italian and early C17. – PAINT-ING. Over chancel arch a Christ in Glory, C19; a medieval

Doom was discovered here *c.* 1886. – The altar painting is a copy after Titian signed by *Corsi*, who adds his address in Florence. – LYCHGATE. By *Arthur Blomfield*, 1895. Carstone dressed with limestone.

WOLFERTON STATION. Disused and converted to a museum. Here in 1876 was built a suite of royal waiting rooms for the convenience of the Prince of Wales and guests on their way to and from Sandringham House. The station was on the up-line. Carstone and brick, with a porte-cochère to the front. Gothic windows. Hammerbeam roof, plain but functional fireplace, panelling now *c.* 1930, when the toilets were redecorated. In 1898 *W. N. Ashbee*, the architect for the Great Eastern Railway, built another suite of rooms on the down-line, with a public waiting room as well. Carstone with brick dressings and some half-timbering. The royal waiting rooms to the r. now have a passage (of 1969) connecting with the public rooms. Three bays, the centre projecting, mullioned and transomed windows. The interior is as Ashbee left it: gold-plated fittings to the doors, plaster ceilings, panelling etc. A central reception room with the Prince's room to one side, Princess Alexandra's to the other. The public waiting rooms converted to a house. The STATION HOUSE, GOODS OFFICE, CLOCK HOUSE, GATEPIERS and RAILINGS etc., all of the same time, and most by *Ashbee*. The most interesting thing of all is perhaps the SIGNAL BOX, a very rare survival from 1862, moved a few yards to its present position in 1898 when the track was widened. Carstone with the usual upper glazed box. A pair of ESTATE COTTAGES of *c.* 1870 crowd it.

WOODRISING

ST NICHOLAS. Remains of the tower, half-collapsed. The bell is kept in a low, thatched wooden structure to the NW, and is dated 1861. Bell-frame from the ruined tower. Nave and chancel are the same length and both have Perp windows, but the double piscina in the chancel, the N and S doorways, the (renewed) E window, the charming circular S aisle W window with an inscribed cusped trefoil, and the S arcade of three bays are Dec. The piers are quatrefoiled. The E impost is a head-corbel. Bequest 1463 for the S porch. Hammerbeam nave roof, mostly now C19. – PULPIT. Simple, Jacobean, with its back panel but not its tester. – ORGAN. On the W gallery. A barrel organ. – MONUMENTS. One coped coffin-lid with a foliated cross. – Late medieval tomb-chest with shields in cusped lozenge fields. – Excellent monument to Sir Robert Southwell †1563 (N chancel). He was an admiral. Recumbent alabaster effigy on a slab with fluted edge. Low six-poster over with Roman Doric columns. Flat top, and the arms in a panel against the back wall. Very subdued in its decoration. Two helms above. – Black ledger-stone to Sir Francis Crane †1636 in Paris. The stone has a brass oval with engraved arms. Crane was the founder of the Mortlake Tapestry Works, and Inigo Jones built Stoke Park in Northamptonshire for him. – Weyland family. By *T. Marsh*, after 1822. In a big simple Gothic surround, in the style of the s arcade. – Also Elizabeth Weyland †1845. By the same. – SOUTH DOOR. Probably 1463.

HALL FARMHOUSE. Of *c.* 1600. Brick. Two storeys and attic, much rebuilt. Three bays of C20 windows with two reused C18 cross casements.

WOOD FARMHOUSE. Also C17 in its timber-framed early parts, with an early C19 brick wing added.

ROMANO-BRITISH VILLA. *See* Cranworth, p. 274.

2090   WOODTON

ALL SAINTS. Standing alone beyond a farmyard NW of the village with a pleasantly walled churchyard. Round C12 tower which once had round-headed windows, but the top third is octagonal. Battlements with flushwork panelling. Nave and chancel in one, unfortunately rendered; restored in 1878–9. Dec chancel and s aisle. The chancel E window has (renewed) reticulated tracery and inside a band of dogtooth ornament flanked by thin colonnettes with capitals. s porch from the restoration, N porch medieval but altered and enlarged to form a vestry. The C13 piscina is odd; it has a corbel at the bottom and two similar inverted corbels on the shelf either side of the trefoiled recess. The s aisle has various details of charm: the E window e.g. has at the top of its reticulated tracery a fleur-de-lys outside, a bearded head inside. Inside, the window is moreover framed by a moulding with fleurons. The tracery is moulded in some depth. The s arcade is of the same date, i.e. *c.* 1310, except for the later w bay. The remaining three bays have unmistakable mouldings of the late C13 to early C14. The Perp aisle roof (restored 1966) has arched braces with fine tracery in the spandrels, other roofs (apart from N porch) of 1878. – FONT. C13, of marble, square, with the familiar shallow blank arches, but completely re-cut. – PULPIT. Jacobean, with arches in perspective. – BENCHES. Two with poppyheads. – STAINED GLASS. In the s aisle E window original glass in the head including St Catherine and another Saint. In another aisle window more fragments of C14 style installed *c.* 1860. E window by *Lavers & Barraud*, 1863, moved from Tenterden, Kent, in 1934. – MONUMENTS. Small brass to Christian Bacon †1532 (s aisle). – Ann Suckling †1653. Kneeling figure in an architectural surround with Ionic columns attributed to *William Wright* of Charing Cross (GF). The inscription starts: 'This is ye portraicture of. . .'. Many other Suckling monuments.

OAKS FARMHOUSE, Shotesham Road. Late C16 and later. L-shaped because a C17 wing was added at r. angles to the C16 timber-framed house. Polygonal angle-shafts on the w side, where the gable wall has blocked windows with pediments. The later wing advancing s from the E end with plenty of C18 brick.

HILL HOUSE FARMHOUSE, also on Shotesham Road. This seems to be a C16 hall house with wings at both high and low ends. The hall has a roll-moulded bridging beam, the l. wing a similar beam fortified with leaf-trail carving. This wing jettied outside, the main façade re-fenestrated and bricked. Two stacks both with a pair of octagonal flues. At the back a C17 brick stair-turret and a six-light mullioned and transomed window. The stairs have turned balusters.

NORWICH ROAD has its share too. BEULAH HOUSE is a straight-forward early C19 house of three bays and a Doric doorcase, but its BARN is early C17. Weatherboarded exterior chopped about, the interior framing with jowled principal studs and a clasped purlin roof with diminished principals.

WOODTON LODGE. Late C18 house of two storeys in five bays but with two C17 timber-framed rear wings.

THE WOODYARD SQUARE, ½ m. SE of the church. Not a square but two ranges. Nicely grouped and detailed council housing by *Tayler & Green*, 1950–1 (*see* Introduction, p. 165). The estate fills a gap in the village. The sensitive composition of two-storeyed (W) and one-storeyed (N) houses in relation to contours deserves special praise. The lower terrace has trellises by the doors. Some houses retain the original windows.

HILLARY TERRACE, etc., close to Woodyard Square, on Hempnall Road. Also by *Tayler & Green*, 1954–5 and 1959–60. Nice playing with bricks of various colours. The single-storey range at r. angles facing Tensing Street is the earlier. Replacement windows generally detract. The estate was intended ultimately to link up with Woodyard Square, but this has not happened.

WORMEGAY

ST MICHAEL. W of the village, on its own. Carstone with a little sandstone and ashlar quoins. C13 chancel with two-light Perp windows. The nave was rebuilt in 1893 by *C. H. Lohr* and the chancel restored, leaving the C15 three-light E window intact, or at least as Ladbroke drew it in the early C19. Inside, to the l. and r. of the E window, big ogee-headed niches with naive painting, including lierne rib vaults, in them. The three-stage W tower is late C14 (see the double-chamfered arch to the nave) and was restored in 1896, when the stair-turret was added. Perp two-light W window under a relief carving of the Crucifixion, also Perp in date. The roof is of 1893: moulded arched braces emphasized at the junction of the nave and continuous chancel by a trefoiled truss. – FONT. Octagonal, Perp, with shields in pointed quatrefoils.

ST BOTOLPH. *See* Tottenhill, p. 739.

CROSS. Base and shaft of the C14 village cross on The Green at the E end of the village. The shaft is octagonal.

CASTLE. Motte-and-bailey castle of unusual size, overlooking the approach across a narrow neck of marsh to the W. It consists of a wide but low motte and a large bailey. The Wormegay family built it but it passed to the Warennes in 1167. The whole village occupies virtually an island.

CASTLE MEADOW, Castle Road. A brick farmhouse dated 1754 with an added W bay of carstone making five bays in all. Pedimented central door and a set of mid-C18 sashes within flush frames. Platband between the floors. The rear still has a stepped external stack with a window lighting the inglenook, rather old-fashioned.

On LYNN ROAD two other C18 HOUSES worth seeing; they present different facets of C18 domestic architecture. BRIDGE HOUSE is mid-century, or just earlier, brick, six bays, again with a brick platband and sash windows. Dutch gables to N and S, with dentils in the crowning pediments. The GRANGE is late C18, brick, three bays entered through a central door under an eight-vaned fanlight. Open pedimented doorcase on fluted columns. Sashes with gauged skewback arches and scalloped hoods. Very polite.

WORTHING
1⅝ m. SE of North Elmham

ST MARGARET. ½ m. S of the village, on its own. Round tower, reduced in height to nave level in the C18 and capped with a red brick parapet. Square C16 brick bell-openings filled with wooden slats. Norman S doorway to the nave, with one order of colonnettes, one-scallop capitals, and zigzag in the arch. Rebuilt blocked N doorway, the arch just turning pointed, but the voussoirs and jambs without decoration. C15 S porch. The nave has one three-light Perp window on each side. The chancel disappeared between Armstrong's description of it as thatched in 1781 and Ladbroke's drawing of the 1820s, and the present E wall is built up with the flint and ashlar debris. Good brick tumbling in the gable-head. There is a very wide blocked chancel arch inside, without detail, and re-set in the present E wall a very charming Perp niche with a little rib vault and a canopy on two birds as brackets. C19 kingpost roof. – FONT. A piece made up of a plastered brick plinth, the base of an E.E. font which had four detached shafts, and on top two stones perhaps from a C15 cross which stood N of the chancel, hollowed for the bowl.

WORTWELL
1 m. E of Redenhall

CHAPEL (R.C.), formerly Baptist Chapel, Low Street. Built in 1822. A red brick box with pyramid roof and two sashes, and a C20 central porch. The PEWING etc. all original. Stairs up to two side galleries.

UNITED REFORMED CHURCH (built as Congregational Chapel), High Road. A meeting-house type of 1773, also with a pyramid roof. Brick. One storey in three bays. The tall side windows extended downwards to replace the original pair of doors in the C19 and a central door substituted.

WORTWELL HALL. Late C16 or early C17. Timber-framed, with one asymmetrically placed porch to the r. of the five-bay W front. The whole range is jettied at the first floor, interrupted by the porch. Over the porch is the main stack. Casements replaced in C19. It has a pretty position close to a mill on the River Waveney.

CHAPEL COTTAGE, High Road. A little C17 timber-framed house with external brick stacks at either end.

BRIDGE. Over the River Waveney ¾ m. NE, immediately s of the bridge of 1971 which replaces it (B1062) and leading into Homersfield (Suffolk). An early precast concrete and iron bridge, narrow, single-arched, with an ornate cast-iron balustrade consisting of cross braces between the uprights and the rails. By *Henry Medgett Eyton* (Suffolk County Surveyor), 1869–70, for Sir Robert Shafto Adair of the demolished Flixton Hall. The concrete sides carried on iron rails have ribbed cast panels to the spandrels. Restored in 1995 with new ironwork by *East Coast Castings* of Carbrooke. A plaque tells us it is the earliest surviving concrete and iron bridge in Britain. If not, it must be close.

WRAMPLINGHAM   *1000*

ST PETER AND ST PAUL. Round tower with a polygonal top, the upper parts with two-light bell-openings relating to a bequest of 1439. Beautiful chancel of *c.* 1280. Single lancets with pointed-trefoiled lights and a pointed trefoil over. There are six on the N side and five on the S, because above the former sedilia a two-light window with Y-tracery was preferred. Inside, the lancets form a continuous range with slender shafts between. Sedilia and piscina are, alas, ruined. The E window with C19 plate tracery. The N aisle is of 1872 and by *A. E. Browne* of London, but has a re-set, completely plain, slightly chamfered Norman doorway and some re-set minor Dec windows. There is probably C12 masonry in the nave. The arcade has three bays. Nave roof 1470: roll-moulded wall-plates, principals with collars. – STAINED GLASS. Some C14 glass in chancel windows and a s nave window. Minor C19 glass elsewhere.

WRAMPLINGHAM HALL, ½ m. wsw. Mid-C19 gault-brick house of two storeys in five bays. Late C19 canted bay window.

QUAKER FARMHOUSE, to the NNE of the church, at the N entry to the village from Barford. Timber frame sandwiched between brick gable-ends. Three bays. The central doorway has ovolo jamb mouldings and a three-light overlight. Mullioned and transomed casements, also ovolo-moulded. The gables are stepped, with diaper brickwork and twin octagonal flues to the stacks. The N gable carries the date 1643 in brick, which suits perfectly (two gabled dormers are later additions). Inside, the winder staircase remains, and bridging beams with sunk-quadrant mouldings. Clasped purlin roof.

MILL FARMHOUSE, Wymondham Road, in the centre of the village opposite a pretty millpond. C17, also timber-framed with stepped brick gable-ends, but with a complete later brick skin. An C18 high crenellated brick garden WALL extends along the road.

CROW HALL, Wymondham Road. C17, timber-framed with a flint and brick gable-end. C18 casements. The frame survives complete inside, as do the winders next to the gable-end stacks.

WRENINGHAM

ALL SAINTS. Unbuttressed three-stage W tower, the lowest stage C13. Over the tower W window a brick niche containing a weathered griffin. The collapse of the upper stages in 1852 precipitated a major restoration in 1853. Remainder of church all Perp, but mostly renewed in 1853. The surprisingly large N transept was added at that time. Two Perp S nave windows, one cut into by the 1853 enlargement of the porch, and two more re-set in the transept. The ivy on the walls is an asset – even if it may also be a liability. The roofs substantially C15, if restored. Principal rafters on arched braces and in the chancel angel corbels. – STAINED GLASS. E window probably by *Heaton, Butler & Bayne*, †1896. – PEWS. 1853. Other FITTINGS 1887.

THE POPLARS, ½ m. SW, on Ashwellthorpe Road. With stepped gables at both ends and five rendered timber-framed bays between, with a central two-storeyed porch. The gables have internal stacks with three rebuilt octagonal shafts. The plinths have renewed datestones: 1586. C18 mullioned and transomed casements and some without the transoms. The original diamond-mullioned windows represented by two to the N. Good staircase rising in a dog-leg. Roof with clasped purlins and wind-bracing.

HIGH HOUSE FARMHOUSE, 1 m. W of the church, Wymondham Road. With stepped gables at both ends. Flat front with six-light and five-light transomed windows, the mullions ovolo-moulded. The early C19 door hood has Chinese-looking concave sides.

HIGH COMMON COTTAGE, Wymondham Road. An early C16 open hall house. Timber-framed. Renewed diamond-mullioned windows. The screens passage has its service doors to the W, but of the hall the most recognizable part now is the three queenpost trusses in the roof.

CORPORATION FARMHOUSE, Wymondham Road. C17 brick with a C19 gault-brick façade. French window in a canted bay. At the back a staircase turret with an early C18 shaped gable.

WRETHAM

ST ETHELBERT, East Wretham. 1865 by *G. E. Street* for Wyrley Birch. W tower with saddleback roof, nave, N aisle and chancel.

In the nave reused Norman s doorway with one order of shafts
and zigzag both on the wall and at r. angles to it. Roll mould-
ings and nailhead decoration also. Waterleaf capitals. The
similar capitals to the round arcade piers are however C19.
Windows in Dec style. – FONT. 1883, in C14 style, with cover. –
STAINED GLASS. St Margaret by *Henry Wooldridge*, made by
Powell & Sons, 1874 (N chancel). E window Crucifixion by
Clayton & Bell, 1890; rich.

ST LAWRENCE, West Wretham. In ruins and overgrown. C14
unbuttressed w tower with a w lancet and a later octagonal top.
In the diagonals blank flushwork windows. Flushwork-panelled
battlements. The outer walls of the church also stand. C14 s
doorway.

WRETHAM HALL by *Sir Reginald Blomfield* has been demolished.
It was a big eleven-bay house in early C18 style rebuilt in 1912
after a fire of 1900 for W. A. Noble. It had the misfortune to fall
within the Battle Zone during World War II.

The principal house is now the early C19 three-bay WRETHAM
LODGE, once a rectory. Flint with gault-brick dressings and a
brick stringcourse under the parapet. On the road to Great
Hockham the DOG AND PARTRIDGE INN forms part of a
pretty group comprising two cottages and a former post office
under a long pantiled roof. Flint with brick, the date later C18.

WRETTON   6090

ALL SAINTS. A small church with a carstone chancel. The two
nave doorways might be Norman, though not in an original
state. The w tower perhaps of the late C13. It has a token
cusped lancet as a w window, Y-tracery in the belfry and slits as
sound-holes. C17 parapet. The s arcade of four bays formed of
octagonal piers with triple-chamfered arches of *c.* 1300. In the
chancel one Dec window. The other windows Perp with four-
centred or straight heads. The restoration was in 1863, providing the scissor-braced nave roof and the crown-post chancel
roof. – FONT. Plain, octagonal, C14. – SCREEN. With four one-
light divisions r. and l. of centre and pretty, minor tracery. It
seems late C14. – PULPIT. Early C18, with a carved top cornice.
– BENCHES. Dated 1627; with plain, minimal poppyheads.

WYMONDHAM   1000

There is some evidence of Anglo-Saxon activity in Wymondham,
but the manors belonging to Bishop Stigand were granted by the
Conqueror to William d'Albini. A market was granted by Henry I,
but it is unlikely that the town was in any way planned round it; its
growth was much more organic. The economy was agricultural,
but by the C15 spinning and manufacture of wooden domestic
implements such as spoons was important. The crossed spoons
and spigot were adopted as the town's arms, and appear carved on

the market cross of 1617–18. Some C17 spooners left substantial properties in their wills: Henry Colman in 1624 and Robert Blome in 1644. In the mid C18 Blomefield recorded that Wymondham is famous for making 'tops, spindles, spoons, and such like wooden ware, in abundance: men, women and children are continually employed in this work'. By the end of the C18 woodturning was overtaken by the textile trade as the chief occupation of towns-people, weaving rather than spinning, and by 1836 there were 600 looms in the town.

The population in the early C16 was about 1,000, living in tightly packed timber-framed houses and shops to the N and E of the Abbey precinct. This proved disastrous in the fire of 11 June 1615, which made 327 people homeless and accounted for nearly £15,000 of damage, a figure exaggerated by the inhabitants. The general reconstruction which followed was of great importance, and echoes of moulding patterns and construction techniques are found in the surrounding parishes, providing an excellent oppor-tunity to examine vernacular building techniques current in the years immediately following the fire. Chief of these are roofs with undiminished principals and clasped purlins. The fire was arson and began at two sites, consuming substantial parts of Vicar Street and Middleton Street to the W, and to the E the N side of Market Place, almost all of Bridewell Street and most of the property between there and Fairland Street. The three perpetrators were hanged in December. Until the C18 building material was almost always timber, the framing filled by wattle and daub, and the roofs thatched. Pantiles replaced thatch from the mid C18 and brick became important from the same moment, kilns being established at Norwich Road and Pople Street. Inevitably this led to brick skins being applied over earlier timber-framed structures. Trade was improved by the Turnpike Acts which in 1695 provided the earliest such link in the county, to Attleborough and Norwich. Population in 1991: 10,900, the eighth largest in Norfolk.

THE ABBEY

Wymondham Priory became Wymondham Abbey on the eleva-tion of Prior Stephen London in 1448. It was founded by William d'Albini in 1107. It was for Benedictines, and was a daughter foundation of St Albans, where William's uncle Richard was abbot. The establishment had between ten and twenty monks.

The Abbey, or what is left of it, lies in a churchyard with plenty of informally planted pine trees whose erect or twisted shapes set
13 off the building to perfection. The existing church, dedicated to St Mary and St Thomas of Canterbury, consists of the nave and most of the aisles of the medieval church, dominated by two tall towers standing in axis, one at the W end, the other over the cross-ing. They appear against the sky strikingly and dramatically from whatever side one approaches Wymondham. Their competing heights express a story of centuries of quarrel between the priory and the population of the town, for whose parochial needs William d'Albini had intended part of the church. The arrangement was

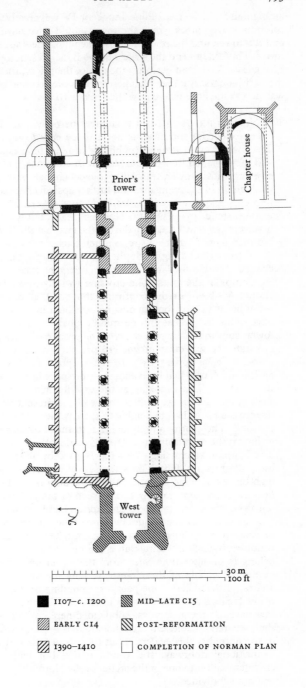

Wymondham Abbey. Plan

ambiguous, and in 1249 Pope Innocent IV was involved and a solution arrived at by which the town should have nave, N aisle and NW tower, and the priory the rest, including the S aisle and SW tower. This did not end the strife, and both the present towers can be regarded as defiant gestures, the one of the priory, the other of the parishioners. Another such gesture was the erection of a solid wall across the nave where now the reredos is.

The Norman PRIORY CHURCH survives partially, and the evidence, except for the nave, is not at once easy to understand.
The church, as excavations (published in 1836) have established,
had the so-called Benedictine plan, with an E apse, a chancel, a
crossing with a tower, transepts, chancel chapels with apses to
the l. and r. of the main apse and further apsidal chapels E of the
transepts, a long nave with aisles, and two W towers. The present
W tower stands to the W of the Norman façade, but two Norman
W towers can only be assumed from the fact that the first pair of
Norman piers from the W are so much thicker than the rest. Of
the E parts (including a lengthening and straightening of the
chancel E end in the late C12) nothing remains except inarticulate lumps in the grass. The crossing with its tower is clearly
enough visible, but the confusing thing is that the crossing
tower lies W of the Norman one, i.e. was built into the Norman
nave. This is because by the middle of the C14 the existing
tower, conventionally over the crossing proper, was in a dangerous state and was taken down. The present tower is sited in the
parochial nave apparently with the purpose of annoying the
parishioners, who had been allocated the space in 1249 by Pope
Innocent IV. Thus, looking at the exterior first, the Norman
shaft embedded in the walling just E of the present NE pier of
the crossing is a shaft belonging to the NW pier of the Norman
crossing. The Norman arch facing E to the N of that piece of
walling is the arch from the Norman N aisle into the N transept.
The Norman SE crossing pier is represented by no more than a
lump of grass and flint. The N transept N wall stands up quite
high but exhibits no features. Above the arch from the N aisle
into the N transept nothing can be seen of the gallery, at least
not from the E, but the clerestory appears and the thinning of
the wall at this level, no doubt because of the wall-passage usual
in English Norman and C13 major churches. The clerestory
window of which traces remain is pointed, and must therefore
belong to an alteration. Seen from the W, on the other hand,
nothing is visible of the clerestory, only the arch, or rather
arches, of the gallery. One pair corresponding to the one arch
below facing E and also the start of one pair facing into the former nave. So the gallery was subdivided here – which is, as we
shall see, remarkable. On the S side there is nothing to bear out
or to contradict this evidence, but there is, a little further W, a
Transitional doorway, still round-arched but with a slight
chamfer, built into one of the arches of the Norman gallery, this
one not subdivided.

Before looking at the Norman evidence inside, the rest of the

EXTERIOR should be examined. The crossing tower was built about 1390–1409 (5s. had been left for its 'reparation' in 1376) and the solid W wall made about the same time, which apart from buttressing it had the further benefits, from the Benedictines' point of view, of providing privacy and of irritating the town. The prior moved the bells to the NW tower while the work was done, in defiance of the 1249 Papal Bull which gave this tower to the town, and as a consequence of the ensuing bitter dispute Henry IV sent the Archbishop of Canterbury to adjudicate in 1411. The prior's tower has a very tall E arch with castellated capitals, small doorways to N and S, and an octagonal upper structure of two tall storeys with thin diagonal buttresses and two-light windows and bell-openings. The tower, like the W tower, lacks a parapet. The bluntness of this ending seems forever to express the discord to which the existence of the towers is due. Of the same time as the crossing tower is the E arch of the chapter house, replacing a Norman apse, and now the only surviving part of the monastic quarters.

The N aisle represents a parochial widening of the Norman aisle. Seven of the nine windows are Perp, but the two immediately E of the porch have cusped Y-tracery and seem original, and suggest an early C14 date for the aisle. They have splayed inner jambs under pointed rere-arches on shafts. In 1509 the Perp windows were inserted into the existing openings, requiring the straightening of the splay to accommodate their greater width, and the rere-arches rebuilt as four-centred. That there was alteration contemplated in 1440–5 is proved by the third window from the E, narrow enough to retain the internal splay and C14 jambs and of different Perp tracery from the rest. The clerestory has flushwork panelling and buttresses with niches between the windows; a length of parapet with shields and initials is near the W end. Fine two-storeyed N porch with a pierced quatrefoil parapet. The entrance has the Annunciation in the spandrels, a frieze with shields in quatrefoils over, and the upper windows flanked by niches. Inside, a tierceron star vault with figured bosses. Stair-turret on the W side higher than the porch.

Then the W TOWER. Land was granted for it in 1445 by the abbot and in 1447 Sir John de Clifton left £20 towards its building; it was completed about 1498. The design has been assigned to *James Woderofe*. Numerous legacies exist, the majority of 1460–80. It is a mighty piece, 142 ft high, with very substantial ashlar-faced and shafted polygonal buttresses, and bell-openings in pairs of two-light windows under one depressed ogee arch. Very large W doorway, shafted, with niches l. and r., shields on trees in the spandrels, and again a frieze with shields over. Five-light W window, clumsily repaired. Against the S side of the tower the monastic buildings abutted, as one can still see. The S aisle however is a post-Reformation rebuilding of 1544–60, using materials from the monastic quarters. The original aisle had been raised a storey in the 1390s for monastic use, with squints into the nave, which was another irritation to the parishioners. The new aisle does not take the former cloister into consideration. It has renewed Y-tracery windows. In the floor of the aisle the stepped contour of the SE support of the SW tower is marked. It gives the width of the original S aisle. S aisle roof of 1903. The clerestory on this side has thin buttress strips between the windows, which were renewed in the C19. Beyond the E end of the S aisle the Norman arcade arches and gallery arches appear blocked. It is evident in this place that the crossing tower was built into the Norman nave. The nave originally had one bay between the W towers and eleven more extending to the crossing. Of these the first three from the E on the S side appear outside in the place just referred to, the others inside the remaining church, though the next two on the S side are blocked.

INTERIOR. It is now time to enter the church and look at the Norman nave, faced with Caen stone. It has arcades and big gallery openings, not subdivided. If the interpretation of the double gallery arches at the E end of the nave (*see above*) is correct, then there must have been a change of plan. In this connection it will be advisable to study the details of the arcades. They are unfortunately much interfered with. Nearly all piers were changed into an amorphous shape in the 1580s. Originally they had coupled shafts, mostly with varieties of scalloped capitals to the arch openings, as can still be seen at the W end. The capitals anyway emerge oddly out of the piers. Whether there were also single and coupled shafts towards the nave reaching right up to the roof it is no longer possible to say. They may have been an innovation in the parts further W, where they survive at least from gallery level. They are, of course, a Norwich Cathedral motif. The arches start on the N side with unadorned and unchamfered single steps which one would be inclined to consider part of the early plan with the subdivided gallery. The arches are then continued with unenriched roll mouldings. On the S side however they have from the beginning zigzag and crenellation, and indeed other motifs (cable and meander) which do not allow for a date before the middle of the C12. Altogether, the development is not simple; for the N side gradually takes up that rich decoration too and yet continues with roll mouldings in the gallery. The gallery openings have the same coupled shafts as the arcade openings.

That is all that can be said of the Norman work. The C15 W tower has one extremely tall and wide arch towards the nave and a small shafted doorway to the tower staircase. The organ (*see below*) stands on a stone gallery added in 1903. Late C15 hammerbeam roof in the nave. Angels against the hammerbeams bearing shields and musical instruments. Long wallposts and longitudinal arched braces with intermediate short supports above the clerestory windows. Big foliate stars as bosses. Alterations at E end in 1694. Specially fine hammerbeam roof in the N aisle begun after the Norman NW tower was demolished about 1445, boarded, and with much tracery in the spandrels, also with a ceilure at the E end. Restored 1845 and 1868. The main restoration of the church by *Hicks & Charlewood* came in 1901–3 (£20,249).

FURNISHINGS. FONTS. Fragments of a beautiful C13 font of
Purbeck marble with stiff-leaf capitals lie in the room over the
porch. – The other font is of the East Anglian standard type,
elevated on three high steps. Against the stem four lions and
four Wild Men, against the bowl the signs of the Evangelists
and angels (whole figures) holding shields. – FONT COVER.
1962 by *Cecil Upcher*, an accomplished piece with two stages of
balusters, the upper stage with volutes, and a soaring spire. –
REREDOS. Big, richly gilt Gothic-imitation piece by *Sir Ninian
Comper*, complete with a tester. Designed in 1913 but constructed only in 1919–27, and not fully gilded until 1934. Three
tiers, the lowest never completed, so the space for the retable is
covered by drapes. Then two tiers of Saints etc. under incredibly elaborate crocketed canopies, in the centre of the upper tier
a mandorla with Christ in Majesty. Cornice at the top and a
deeply projecting and equally dizzy tester. ROOD BEAM with
figures in front, also by *Comper*. – WEST DOOR. Traceried; Perp.
– CHANDELIER (Lady Chapel). Of brass, very large and two-
tiered, dated 1712. – ORGAN. Given in 1793 and moved to the W
gallery in 1903. It is by *James Davis* and cost £680. Enlarged
1953. – CHAMBER ORGAN. N aisle, also by *Davis*. – CORPORAS
CASE, late C13, of canvas with ornamental embroidery. Corporas
cases were to hold the cloth on which the bread and wine were
consecrated. They are very rare: the only other known in England
is at Hessett in Suffolk. – STATUE. Virgin and Child, in Lady
Chapel, 1947 by *Sir Ninian Comper*. – STAINED GLASS. In a S
aisle window some C15 fragments. In N aisle a window of 1840
by *Joseph Grant* is enamelled, not stained. A Virgin and Child
with panels below depicting Nativity, Crucifixion and Ascension.
– MONUMENTS. So-called monument to Abbot Elisha Ferrers, 32
whom it does not in fact commemorate (he ruled from 1532,
†1548). The monument, which in any case is no more than a
façade, is so similar to the Bedingfeld monuments at Oxborough
and the monument at Bracon Ash that it must be of *c*. 1525. It is
clearly the work of the same craftsmen, and made from the
same moulds as the Oxborough monument. It is of terracotta,
in the early Renaissance style, and has pretty quattrocento
decoration in all panels and on all friezes and pilasters. At the
top the same turret-like structures as at Oxborough (with a
pilaster up the middle) and the same semicircular and triangular
cresting motifs. – John Drake †1759 (S aisle E), by *Thomas
Rawlins*. Nice tablet of various marbles with two putto heads at
the foot and an obelisk at the top. – Jeremiah Burroughes
†1767 (S aisle W). Big tablet of white and brown marble with, at
the top, a sarcophagus and a crying cherub. – Sarah Drake
†1793 (S aisle E). With an urn before an obelisk. – Many more
tablets.
To the S of the churchyard in ABBEY MEADOW some stumps of
walls are visible above ground and much of the ground plan of
the conventual buildings has been recorded from the air as
parch marks in grass. In 1834 the larger part of the surviving
monastic evidence was cleared. (AR)

OTHER CHURCHES AND PUBLIC BUILDINGS

METHODIST CHURCH, Town Green. 1870, of gault brick
  dressed with red brick. Odd façade consisting of a gabled projection with quadrants cutting back to a second gable. Gallery
  on cast-iron columns.

UNITED REFORMED CHURCH, The Fairland. The front is of
  1877. Brick, three bays under a pediment. Abundant mechanical
  decoration. Returns have four bays of sashes in two tiers and
  reveal two building stages: the s half 1715, the N half 1815.
  Gallery on fluted columns.

MARKET CROSS. A pretty octagonal structure erected in 1617–18
71 after its predecessor burnt in the fire. The cost was £25 7s., paid
  by Philip Cullyer. The ground floor is open, the upper floors
  supported on eight buttress-like posts, a middle post and arched
  braces. There is a little minor carved decoration of spoons,
  spindles, skewers and foliage, and a little pargeting on the upper
  floor. Pyramid roof. An outer stair leads to the upper floor from
  the back. This staircase completely replaced during the restoration of 1989 by *Feilden & Mawson*. The three-light cross casements lighting the upper room were renewed in the 1863
  restoration, when the plaster was removed from the exposed
  upper studs. The room has a central post supporting cross-trees
  in two tiers reminiscent of a post-mill, and jowled corner studs.

CHAPEL OF ST THOMAS BECKET, now COUNTY LIBRARY,
  Church Street. Founded in 1174 by William, Earl of Arundel,
  shortly after the murder of St Thomas and rebuilt in the C14.
  After a restoration in 1873 it opened as a public hall. 84 ft long,
  quite substantial therefore, though now aisleless, and with one
  blocked Norman window still appearing in the N wall, partly
  covered by the fine arch across. This arch marked the E side of
  a bell-turret. It is as wide as the chapel, has wave mouldings and
  fleurons up two orders of jambs and arches, one to the W, the
  other to the E. On the S side also two small doorways and the
  blocked openings to a former two-bay chapel or aisle. The
  octagonal pier with its double-hollow-chamfered arches indicates a C15 date. The chapel has a hammerbeam roof with the
  collars low down. Perp windows. The s doorway arch dies into
  the chamfered jambs.

TOWN HALL, Middleton Street. Red brick, early C19, five bays
  and two and a half storeys. Tripartite doorway with segmental
  arch. Stick-baluster staircase typical of *c.* 1820.

PERAMBULATION

MARKET PLACE. A walk should start by the Market Cross in the
  Market Place, which is an attractive funnel-shaped space sloping gently downhill to the W into Market Street, with Bridewell
  Street and Fairland Street opening into it from the E. On the E
  side of Market Place, between these two streets, are immediately replacements from the 1615 fire. On the corner with
  Bridewell Street No. 8 has a mid-C19 plate-glass shopfront and

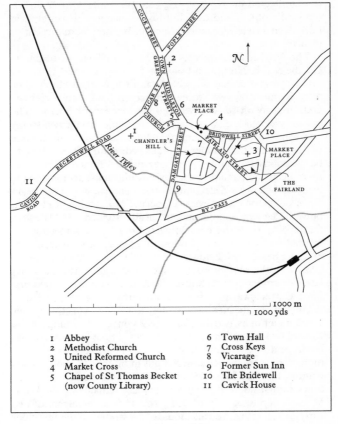

Wymondham

1	Abbey	6	Town Hall
2	Methodist Church	7	Cross Keys
3	United Reformed Church	8	Vicarage
4	Market Cross	9	Former Sun Inn
5	Chapel of St Thomas Becket	10	The Bridewell
	(now County Library)	11	Cavick House

in the N return an underbuilt jetty. Internal timbers with sunk-quadrant mouldings. Nos. 9–10 are the same but the evidence even more submerged behind C20 alterations. The N side a little disappointing, although No. 1 is a late C18 two-and-a-half-storey five-bay red brick house with a doorcase on Doric columns and a metope frieze. The wing to the rear C17. The KING'S HEAD has been demolished. On the S side first No. 12, late C16 but so rebuilt in brick in the C19 as to qualify for that date: five bays, two storeys, with an elaborate doorcase and heavy brackets to the hood. Stick-baluster staircase. Next the CROSS KEYS, half-timbered with a jetty. A jetty also to the rear, now engulfed by later building and visible only inside. The E room has a fireplace under a bressumer with multiple roll mouldings, and the same mouldings to bridging and spine beam. These are c. 1530, but probably brought in – or survived – after the fire. The next four, Nos. 14–18, also c. 1616 and timber-framed, No. 15 with some good internal timbers and a clasped purlin roof, No. 16 with an early C16 rear wing which escaped the conflagration. Nos. 17–18, returning into Queen Street, outwardly of C19 and C20, but inside an upper tier of clasped purlins, in a style very much typical of Wymondham carpenters in 1616–20.

The Market Place merges into MARKET STREET to the W. On the N side No. 49 and No. 47 have brick fronts to earlier buildings, and so too does No. 29, THE WHITE HART. The front is mid-C18, two storeys and seven bays with a carriage arch and an off-set doorway under an open pediment. The sashes have thick glazing bars. At the same time a two-storey rear wing added as a saloon, internally one large room through both storeys with wall niches under pediments. These prove to be additions to another early C17 timber-framed house, one room deep and parallel to the street, with sunk-quadrants to the bridging beams, and detailing at the E end similar to the beam stops of the Market Cross. Opposite, No. 30 has a pleasant bowed Regency shopfront and façade applied to a late C17 frame. Nos. 18–20 have an early C19 brick façade with a double-fronted mid-C19 display window. Two storeys. Fine cruciform bridging beams inside, jowled principal studs to first floor and a clasped purlin roof indicate c. 1580. Next W (No. 16) is another late C16 timber-framed house, converted to offices. Jettied first floor. Carriageway to W leads to a C16 rear wing, also jettied.

On the N side Nos. 19–21 are, unusually, exactly as they seem, a pair of early C18 brick houses converted to shops in the C20, of two storeys and attic in six bays. Three three-light casements and three blind windows to first floor. Nos. 15–17 once more early C17, the jetty underbuilt in brick. C18 shop display window l. of the doorway, two- and three-light mullioned windows to first floor. The winder staircase remains by the stack. Directly opposite, on the S side, No. 12 is an amalgam of two early C16 shops with a roll-moulded bressumer to the first-floor jetty. Some pargeting in roundels between upper exposed studs. The ground floor has a very nice butcher's shop façade of c. 1900–10. Splendid multiple-roll-moulded spine beam and wall-plate to ground floor; clasped purlin roof with tie-beams on arched braces. At the back a late C17 brick cross wing with a platband and two blocked oval windows. The roof here has trenched upper purlins and collars. Nos. 8, 10 and 10A: three late C16 timber-framed shops, very much altered, though the jetty to No. 10 is evident. Roll- and hollow-moulded bridging beams and arched braces to the roofs. The S side of the street finishes with two early C17 buildings, variously converted. Nos. 4–6 have jetties, but serious alterations in early C18 and late C20. No. 2 has inside wave-moulded bridging beams, which must be reused, but C17 sunk-quadrant mouldings to the upper tie-beams. The roof had clasped purlins; only the W part survives.

To finish on the N side. Nos. 11–13 are timber-framed, jettied and altered. At the back a late C16 hall range, its jetty under-built like the early C17 front. The hall range at the back of the mid-C16 No. 7 also has an underbuilt jetty. C20 shopfronts face the street, with two three-light late C18 casements above. No. 3

is the best of all. A two-storey early C16 hall at the back, with jetties and ovolo-moulded mullions to the windows (some C18 sashes as well), including two projecting upper windows of the sub-oriel type introduced to E Norfolk about 1470. The street façade in two storeys, with a late C19 butcher's shopfront entered in the middle through a late C17 double-leaf door under an extraordinary fret light. Jettied first floor lit through three late C18 casements.

MIDDLETON STREET leads NW from the W end of Market Street. It has the stateliest Georgian houses of central Wymondham, although we begin on the E side with three mid-C17 timber-framed shops, altered in C19 and C20, Nos. 2–4 and Nos. 6–8. Opposite is the LIBRARY, for which *see* Public Buildings above. A little further N, on the W side CAIUS HOUSE (Nos. 3–7). Early Georgian, of red brick, seven bays and two storeys with an additional half-storey in a high attic, as high as the three-bay pediment. This stands on giant pilasters, and there are giant angle pilasters. Doorway with unfluted columns carrying a pediment over a metope frieze, i.e. a true Roman Doric order. This lordly façade has been ruined by the most unsympathetic intrusion of shopfronts after 1930, a debasement carried on ruthlessly inside. Only the staircase with its three twisted balusters to each tread and fluted newel columns remains.

Opposite is the TOWN HALL, *see* Public Buildings above. Further on PRIORY HOUSE (Nos. 13–17) on the W side. Another brick house of five bays. This is whitewashed. It has a pedimented doorway with attached margin lights, all within a Gibbs surround. The doorway, the sashes and upper cross casements represent an early C18 remodelling of a late C17 house, of which half the E shaped gable remains externally. There is an imposing staircase hall of *c.* 1710, the stairs with three twisted balusters per tread. A panelled door with a shouldered surround leads off E to a room with large-framed panelling. Principal drawing room at first floor. Opposite again, No. 20, BEECH HOUSE. Quite complicated. There is an early C17 timber-framed range in the middle, to which has been added the street elevation in 1873, itself extended N in 1926. The C17 part has an C18 brick skin, and there are further C18 additions to the E of this. The C17 roof is unusual in that the clasped purlins are not accompanied by diminished principals. Nos. 24–28, a little further N, is an eight-bay rendered brick house in two storeys and attic; late C17 but altered.

TOWN GREEN opens up to the N of Middleton Street, narrows in the middle and opens again at the end, like an hourglass. On the E side Nos. 2–4 are a timber-framed pair from the late C16, altered to form shops and flats in the late C19. Opposite, Nos. 3–5 have the same pedigree, and here the internal studwork indicates that, as normal, the late C16 houses were only one room deep. Like Beech House on Middleton Street, the upper clasped purlins are not set in diminished principals, but instead the rafters have been cut back to accommodate them, only to resume full scantling immediately above. No. 9 was built as an early C16 timber-framed house one room deep, with a jettied first floor. Alterations for shops. The original four-centred back door remains inside, now internal. The N ground-floor partition has three wall paintings. C17 rear wing. No. 17 facing the N expansion of the street is a C17 timber-framed house, re-done in brick. Handsome late C19 butcher's shopfront unaltered.

Facing S down Town Green, and visually part of it, Nos. 1–3 POPLE STREET, a brick range under plaintiled roofs forming a curved façade. Built in 1684 according to the date on a beam in No. 5, somewhat altered in details to front. Two storeys and dormer attics. The W gable has a shaped head. The back has a two-storey tower and plenty of C19 extensions. Interior timbers all in late C17 vocabulary, chamfered and with jewelled tongue-stops. Butt-purlin roof with curved wind-braces.

To the l. up COCK STREET. On the E side first three pairs of brick houses from the late C17 to early C19 (Nos. 4–14). On the W side further along Nos. 19–21, OAK HOUSE and WINCAR HOUSE, a pair of C16 timber-framed houses with a jettied first floor, underbuilt to the N. Mixed fenestration.

Now from the bottom of Town Green S into VICAR STREET which runs towards the Abbey and has a number of nice houses of red or grey brick. At once on the W No. 6, CANTERBURY HOUSE, early C19, rendered and colourwashed. No. 8, ROOK HOUSE, from the early C17, jettied front and rear, though the façade has been underbuilt. C18 sashes and casements, but one four-light diamond-mullioned window at the back. The lobby-entrance plan compromised inside by means of a passage cut through the stack. No. 10, CONON HOUSE. Same date, front jetty underbuilt, winder staircase by stack. No. 12, ABBOTSFORD, set back. A big house of c. 1830 divided into flats. Gabled porch with doorcase of reeded columns and a metope frieze. The internal arrangement unusual in that the single-storey hall imitates a medieval hall parallel to the façade with a staircase at one end pretending to be a solar stair. Opposite is the VICARAGE (No. 5), set edge-on to the road. Flint and brick. The three-bay S front has a central door and bowed windows r. and l. Extensions to NE c. 1910. Inside are some early C18 panelled doors, and large-framed panelling in the SE room. Early C19 stick-baluster stairs. A little STABLE BLOCK to NE, early C19. No. 9, VICAR STREET HOUSE, pleasant, mid-C18, brick, two storeys and attic in five bays. Open pediment over door carried on fluted Doric columns. Early C19 stick-baluster staircase. Of 1793 is No. 16 opposite, gault-brick façade in three bays. Attachment to N added in 1880.

Turn l. into CHURCH STREET. On the r. the ABBEY SCHOOL-ROOM, a small brick building of 1812 under a hipped roof. Two storeys in three bays with entrance attachments to E and W. The ABBEY WALLS run along the S side of the street, in which one can identify C16 brick and flint amid the later work. Nos. 12–14 are three houses knocked into one annexe to the ABBEY HOTEL, two storeys, re-faced with C18 brick. The r. part with a platband between floors, the l. part with a ridge stack with diamond flues. The ground-floor W room has early C16 roll-moulded bridging beams and wall-plate, pointing to the real date. The interior timber-framed, but disguised. The road turns after this to the N, and on the l. No. 8, CHURCHGATE HOUSE. Brick façade of three bays and two storeys. Early C19 casements. The back begins to reveal a different story, first by a two-light ovolo-moulded mullioned window, and more forcefully by an eight-light mullioned window in the upper floor of the cross wing running NW. Inside there are two rooms to the front, the S with an early C17 fireplace, the bressumer carved with roses of Lancaster and York. Where the cross wing meets the front a staircase of *c.* 1560 has been inserted, with turned balusters, albeit renewed. Two first-floor rooms with four-centred brick fireplaces. The timber frame here has jowled principal studs and arched braces, probably early C16.

Then No. 6, THE GREEN DRAGON. This is a classic mid-C15 65 hall house of the usual town plan, i.e. a shop range at the front with the hall and other domestic quarters extending back on a narrow site. The hall jettied on both sides and the rear (now underbuilt to S and enclosed by later extensions to the W). The front jettied too. There is an arched door to the l. and an arcade of three arches r., with a fourth in the N return, all originally open to the street. The jetty at the r. corner on a wall-post. Two four-light mullioned windows to upper floor. The hall range has on the N side a ten-light mullioned window and a similar six-light window above, jammed under the eaves. The hall entrance is in the S side, with a formerly six-light projecting window to its l., which may be the dais window. The door leads to a short passage with a four-centred doorway opening to the l. and another at the N end. The door on the r. of the passage is a later insertion. The hall itself has a replica C20 chimneypiece with a cupboard to its l., which is most probably the site of the winder staircase to the solar. On the r. of the fireplace a stone arch led to the exterior as it was in the C15. Opposite, Nos. 5–7, a late C17 brick house with a shaped S gable. Panelled stack. Converted to offices. The Library is on the N, *see* Public Buildings above.

DAMGATE STREET runs off to the S from the junction of Church Street and Market Street. On the r. No. 2, another timber-framed house. Early C16, the first floor jettied on a bressumer decorated with roll mouldings and staggered bars. The usual alterations and re-fenestration to form a shop. Multiple-roll-moulded bridging beams and a wave-moulded one too to the ground floor. The first part of the E side of the street largely uneventful, but on the W one can mention Nos. 10–12, a C17 brick house, now a shop; Nos. 13–15, early C18 brick house also converted to a shop; No. 14, C17 timber frame with brick front; No. 16, the same but with an early C17 lobby-entrance plan and an early C20 butcher's shopfront. These houses have carriage entrances to rear. No. 18, OAKHOUSE, is a late C15 hall house, on the conventional plan. The façade to the street of two storeys and three bays. C16 plank door in centre, jettied first floor. Hall range to rear is two-storeyed and jettied, but alterations include partial underbuilding of the overhang. Nos. 20–22, HARVEY HOUSE, has a late C18 brick façade with a late C19 shopfront at the N end. At the back is a late C15 hall, with a stepped W gable and various C18 additions. One of two four-centred service doors remains to the E of the hall inside.

On the E side Nos. 29–31. Timber-framed house of early C16 rebuilt a century later. Two storeys and attic. Two central C18 doors. Unusually deep first-floor jetty. Mullioned windows apparent inside. Clasped purlin roof. Carriage arch to r. is later. No. 47, COMMUNITY HALL, an ugly building of 1879 like a Nonconformist chapel. Nos. 49–51 are a C17 range cased in brick, and probably timber-framed. Interest tends to wane until one reaches the extreme S. No. 58 on the W side has an early C19 bowed shop display window, and No. 59 and Nos. 61–63 opposite have more, with renewed glazing. No. 65 was formerly the SUN INN, famous in the early C18. C17 N range with a shaped gable added c. 1720 when the roof was raised. In the 1790s the building was extended S. Brick and flint, the N roof thatched. The N gable has platbands and cross casements. Opposite, Nos. 68–70, early C16, timber-framed with an under-built jetty to the front. C17 stack. Stepped S gable rebuilt in 1979. All greatly altered.

CHANDLER'S HILL goes off to the E by the Sun Inn, and by way of Queen Street one returns to the Market Place, where FAIRLAND STREET passes out from the SE corner. No. 2 on the S side contributes to the Market Place. C17, with a first-floor jetty, but the façade reorganized in 1778, and given C19 doors and windows. The street is a mixture of brick-skinned C17 houses, all converted in one way or another, and wholly C19 buildings of marginal interest.

Back to the Market Place and to BRIDEWELL STREET, which runs off to the NE. The QUEEN'S HEAD INN on the S side is a rebuilding after the fire, timber-framed and one room deep, parallel to the street. The façade is of two storeys, kitted out with C19 casements in four bays. The frame has jowled principal studs and straight braces to tie-beams; tension braces at corners of the walls. Details altered during a 1989 restoration. Next No. 4, THE MANOR HOUSE. Richard Lyncolne's house burnt down in 1615 and this is the replacement. He was a dealer in wool. Timber-framed, with a jettied first floor on which has been nailed a Latin inscription (it reads: 'My servant is not a dormouse nor is the host a leech'). The central door is of 1616 but many of the details of the front, including probably the inscription, are from a modernization of 1864. First floor has close-studded timbers. Sunk-quadrant and chamfered bridging beams, timber frame with jowled principal studs, the roof purlins with tongue-stops, rather an unnecessary elaboration. The ground-floor E room with a wall-plate inscribed: 'Richard Lyncolne A.D. 1616. Live well and die never, die well and live ever'.

No. 3 opposite is also a rebuilding after 1615, seemingly on the same plan as an earlier house, for a hall range is situated at

the back. The front is interesting for its early C17 door frame
with a mullioned overlight and the contemporary shopfront
to the l. The door led to a passage to the hall with access into
the shop. The hall with sunk-quadrant bridging beams. Jettied
first floor. Brick stepped E gable. The hall jetty underbuilt. The
roof has the peculiar clasped purlins set into a notch in the
undiminished principals found elsewhere in Wymondham. No.
5 and No. 7 also early C17, the former with a jetty. Nos. 11–21
have C18 and C19 windows, the range partly jettied and all of
c. 1620.

At the end, standing across, THE BRIDEWELL (now a
museum). A nice, low, Georgian five-bay house with a three-
bay pediment, to which is attached the gaol with its eight barred
windows on the upper floor. The house was built in 1787, but
altered in 1849 by *John Brown*: red brick, with the roof clad
with Cumberland slate and pantiles. The S range was the
MAGISTRATES' COURT – see the tall round-headed sashes.
Cellars with holding cells, one of which still has its door and
lock bar.

OUTLYING AREAS

A few small hamlets, Browick, Downham, Silfield and Wattlefield,
and a few houses which fall into none of them. The hamlet of
Spooner Row has a separate entry (*see* p. 667). The isolated
houses first.

CAVICK HOUSE, ⅛ m. SW of the Abbey. The second-best house
outside the built-up area of Wymondham, constructed for John
Drake about 1720. A beautifully simple and comfortable-
looking Queen Anne-style front of red brick: nine bays and two
storeys under a hipped roof. Fine carved modillion cornice. The
doorway has unfluted Ionic columns and a pediment. Quadrant
walls extend to the l. and r. of the front. The surrounds of the
archways in them and the end-posts are of yellow brick and
Georgian. The drawing room has rich and elegant Rococo
decoration, carved of wood on the walls, moulded in papier
mâché on the ceiling. The chimneypiece frieze has a wolf with a
lamb being chased by a shepherd and his dog. The rest is floral.
In another room is late Georgian, less lavish decoration. Central
staircase hall has large-framed panelling and an open-well stair-   93
case with two twisted balusters to each tread, shaped tread-
ends, open strings and flat moulded handrails.

GONVILLE HALL. In the same direction, i.e. towards the SW,
further out, to the S of the London Road, ⅞ m. from the Abbey.
A large and irregular house of the C16, a fragment of an even
bigger house, modernized and, it must be admitted, sanitized in
1966 by *David Mawson*. It had been owned by Sir Edward
Clere, who sold to a rich lawyer, Thomas Talbot, in 1599. A
C16 three-storey gable projects to the S, still with some brick
mullioned windows and a large stepped stack. The E front
identifiable also as C16, of brick, with a W gable fitted with

five- and six-light brick mullioned windows. The range to the N, running parallel, is C20.

BURFIELD HALL. Yet further out, off the London Road (1½ m. SW of the Abbey), for which Kelly provides the date 1709 but which looks 1720 or 1730. Built for the Blackbourn family out of the proceeds of the cloth trade. Five bays, two storeys, hipped roof, three-bay pediment over projecting centre bays. Immediately behind and centrally placed is a mid-C18 extension, with a further, apparently early C19, block added to the SW. This latter stands on a plinth of C17 brick laid in English bond, probably the relic of an earlier block utilized as a convenient foundation. Inside is an entrance hall with minor mid-Georgian panelling and, to the N, a staircase lit by a tripartite arched sash. Its three turned-and-column balusters to each tread speak of a slightly later date than that in Cavick House. The NE room to the first floor has reused mid-C17 small-framed panelling, half carpenters' mitre and half masons', as if done by a father and son at the moment of transition.

THE DIAL STONE is a square stone pillar 1¼ m. further SW on the main London road. Erected in 1675 to record the bequest of £200 by Sir Edwin Rich for repairing the road. Moved 1985 to the NW side when the Attleborough by-pass was being built. Stone, square-section with two panels to each face. Inscription on S side. Called the Dial Stone on account of a sundial which stood on top until 1730.

STANFIELD HALL. To the E, 2⅜ m. E of the Abbey, the most unexpected and best of the houses. By *William Wilkins* the elder, 1792, but externally Tudorized, probably *c.* 1830–5 for the Rev. George Preston. *William Saul* had made alterations in 1815. This is the same family as the Prestons of Beeston Hall, a more outwardly Gothic building probably also by Wilkins. Stanfield was engraved by Neale in 1819; he shows an essay in the Elizabethan style, enlarging a C16 house of which one wall to the NW remains of coursed ashlar construction. Brick with stone dressings, symmetrical, with polygonal angle-shafts and, in the E entrance front, a porch. Three attic gables to the main façades with apex and kneeler pinnacles matching the angle-shafts. Clustered stacks. Windows all cross casements with four-centred lights. The interior is quite a surprise in sumptuous, if not strictly accurate, Gothic. The porch leads to a lierne-vaulted chamber, the vault carried on triple shafts of C13 style. From here one reaches the staircase hall rising through two storeys to a rich fan vault with an exaggerated drop pendant. In the spandrels to E and W are clerestory windows. Gallery at first-floor level with ribbed groin vaults to the N and S passages. Traceried four-centred wall arches also at this level, and, gilding the lily, a traceried and pierced canopy over a statuary niche in the W wall. The staircase itself of stone, like all these details, cantilevered out, with cast-iron balusters. In the tread-ends seaweed foliage. All this must be Wilkins. In the N ground-floor room are reused roll-moulded bridging beams of the early C16 fitted into the two-storey, three-bay extension apparent from the exterior.

The house is moated and approached over a brick BRIDGE in front of the entrance porch: C16 in its earliest parts, though rebuilt at intervals. Two arches separated by thin buttress piers. A little court N of the house formed by attractive and complete STABLES. Cast-iron round-headed windows. Probably of *Wilkins*'s time.

HART'S FARMHOUSE, closer in, $\frac{7}{8}$ m. E of the Abbey to the S of Norwich Road. An early C17 timber-framed house with various later alterations including an C18 brick wing to SE. That the interior was once quite grand can be made out from the fine early C18 large-framed panelling in the W ground-floor room. There is a shouldered chimneypiece with a panelled overmantel. Closed-string staircase with turned balusters. Roof with arched wind-bracing and clasped purlins.

Finally, to the NW, $1\frac{1}{4}$ m. from the Abbey at Chapel Bell, the OLD MEETING HOUSE, with an attached cottage on its l. It is very modest, of red brick, with a front of two windows and a doorway. The brick is in fact a skin to a timber-framed house of 1687, of which a few timbers remain.

Browick, $1\frac{1}{2}$ m. E of the Abbey

BROWICK HALL. A mid-C18 brick façade to SE, of two storeys and attic in six bays, with three giant pilasters. Rusticated pilasters round the door.

BANHAM'S FARMHOUSE, 250 yds SW of the last, at the road junction. About 1570, the timber frame masked by an C18 brick skin. A surprisingly early lobby-entrance house, with – another surprise – a yellow brick chimneystack with vertical serrations. Two good ribbon-moulded bridging beams and a handsome carved chimney bressumer in the ground-floor N room. It has the arms of Elizabeth I and initials referring to Valentyne Kett, and his wife Alice †1573. A more modest chimneypiece in the room above is a mid-C18 replica.

Downham, $1\frac{7}{8}$ m. NE of the Abbey

OAKLAND FARMHOUSE, on the E side of Melton Road. It began as a late C16 timber-framed house, partly cased in brick *c.* 1690 and given a rear outshut extension early in the C18. SW front of two storeys with a platband separating them, but the rebuilding has left it inarticulate. The rear outshut contains a staircase with two turned balusters to each tread and a moulded handrail.

MANOR FARMHOUSE, Wramplingham Road. A good early C17 brick house on the lobby-entrance plan, though this now altered. The main façade to the E: two storeys and attic in five irregular bays. Mullioned windows under brick hoods, some replaced, and brick hoods to one of the two doors. Triple flues to the ridge stack. Good internal bridging beams have sunk-quadrant mouldings and roll-moulded joists. The S room brick fireplace has a segmental arch and sunk-quadrant mouldings in two orders.

Silfield, 1½ m. SE *of the Abbey*

COLL'S FARMHOUSE. Altered early C18 timber-framed house.

OLD HALL, by the crossroads on W side of the road. Two houses since 1940. *c.* 1650 with two late C17 wings. Brick to ground floor, timber-framed above. Closed-string staircase with bulbous turned balusters and moulded handrail.

SILFIELD LODGE, opposite the last. There is an early C19 block to the s of three bays, with late C19 canted windows added, but at the back, forming a T-shaped plan, is a wing, also of brick, which has a shaped gable dated 1709. Interior from the late C19.

Wattlefield, 2⅞ m. S *of the Abbey*

WATTLEFIELD HALL. A late C18 house when it was bought by John Mitchell, a Wymondham solicitor, in 1856. He brought in *J. C. & G. Buckler,* who added the SE front, two storeys in three bays, the outer bays canted. Cross casements, stepped gables and clustered stacks in the Neo-Elizabethan vocabulary. Linenfold panels to the doors into principal rooms, staircase with turned balusters, four-centred chimneypieces. A rather monumental STABLE COURT to the rear, early C19 and Classical.

MANOR FARMHOUSE, ⅞ m. s of this. The house is early C17, but has an extraordinary early C19 screen façade attached, of brick, in four generous bays. Greek Doric doorcase, sash windows, crenellated parapet. The stick-baluster staircase inserted at the same time, but a bridging beam with sunk-quadrant mouldings of the early C17 remains on view.

WYMONDHAM COLLEGE. *See* Morley St Peter, p. 545.

RINGWORK at Moot Hill 1 m. NE of the town. A tree-covered circular bank within a ditch is probably a minor Norman castle. Dating is unproven because no excavation has taken place. (AR)

0010

YAXHAM

ST PETER. Flint with carstone. Round tower with quadrant pilasters and an unmoulded arch towards the nave on the simplest imposts. Round-headed doorway over. Perp top probably from 1523–8, when money was left for work and bells. Two-light bell-openings. Four-bay s arcade of the C14. Quatrefoil piers with thin shafts in the diagonals alternate with octagonal piers. Double-hollow-chamfered arches. The rest Perp; there was a bequest in 1435 for 'building nave'. Large windows to the N, smaller windows in the aisle, clerestory to the s. s porch C15. Wave-moulded chancel arch. Chancel Dec windows mainly C19. Arch-braced nave roof. – FONT. C15. Octagonal, on a quatrefoiled step. Fleurons on the stem. The stem curves out towards the bowl in extremely pretty vaulted niches. Thin canopies reach up to the bowl and stand there against a panelled background. – SCREEN. In the s aisle, probably a parclose screen of *c.* 1460. One-light divisions with ogee arches. The upper tracery varies. – STALLS. With Jacobean bits. – MONUMENT. A coffin-lid with a foliated cross. – STAINED GLASS. A whole sequence by *J. Powell & Sons, c.* 1845–50. The E window †1836 is the best.

YAXHAM HOUSE. Built as the rectory by *Robert Lugar,* 1820–2 for the Rev. John Johnson. Colourwashed brick. Two storeys in three bays, the outer bays advanced and under pediments. Porch on pairs of Greek Doric columns. Wide eaves in Italianate style. Hipped roof. The chimneypiece inside has both jambs painted by *William Blake,* illustrating the winter and evening scenes from Cowper's *The Task.* The frieze was painted with a view of Olney Bridge, but has gone. Johnson and Cowper were cousins.

HOLLAND'S HALL, 1½ m. SE. Elizabethan house of diapered brickwork. Two storeys and attics. Stepped end-gables. Central porch with stepped gables, polygonal angle-shafts, and a brick doorway with a four-centred arch. First-floor C18 cross casement. Windows r. of porch the same, but one C16 mullioned window remains to l. at first floor.

WILLOW FARMHOUSE, Norwich Road. Two ranges, the rear a timber-framed C15 house much altered in C16 and C17, including insertion of floors and chimneys into the open hall. Early C19 front pile.

WINDMILL, ½ m. ESE. Tower mill without cap or sails built by and for *William Critoph,* 1860. Used as storage for a C20 mill.

YELVERTON   2000

ST MARY. In the chancel one Norman N window. Dec S aisle, see the windows and the two-bay arcade with an octagonal pier and double-chamfered arches. The aisle roof is arch-braced and has tracery in the spandrels. Three Y-traceried clerestory windows, of brick, probably early C16. Dec chancel S window and piscina and sedilia. Perp E window. Early C16 priest's doorway of brick, in the E bay of the S aisle – an unusual date and an unusual place. The W tower is also Perp and also has brick dressings, including the bell-openings, and has been repaired in 1674 according to a plaque: '1674, Thomas Thetford, workeman'. C19 W window. – FONT. Square, with arched panels. C13. – SCREEN. Inscription to Thomas Hotte †1505 and wife Beatrice. On the dado twelve panels painted with demi-figures of angels, illustrating the heavenly hierarchy. Upper parts over-restored. – BENCHES. Some old ones with poppyheads. – STAINED GLASS. E and W porch windows by *S. C. Yarington c.* 1820–30. E window by *William Aikman,* 1928. – MONUMENTS. Brass to Margaret Aldriche †1525 'in her floryching youthe'. A small figure with her hair let down (6½ in.; nave E). – Humphrey Rant †1661. Tablet with convex-curved front. Good; the ornament already Baroque as if made considerably later than the date of death. It is indeed attributed by Geoffrey Fisher to *Thomas Cartwright I* on the strength of its similarity to his signed monument to Charles

Thorold †1691 in St Andrew Undershaft, City of London. – In the chancel s wall, outside, an early c18 brick surround for two inscription plates to W. Hood †1717 and Elizabeth Hood †1705. – Peter Nichols †1840, a draped urn. By *Thomas Denman*.

HILL HOUSE, on the road to Framingham Earl. Early c17 house embellished with a three-bay s front in c18. Timber frame of older N wing intact: arch-braced tie-beams and butt-purlin roof. Hollow mullions to the three-light E gable window.

YELVERTON HALL is not of great moment, but the little OUT-BUILDING to the NE has rusticated brick pilasters and stepped gables. s gable with two upper windows with ovolo-moulded mullions and transoms. A four-light version also on the E front. The roof is of tie-beams on arched braces with clasped purlins, butt-purlins and wind-braces. *c.* 1630.

GLOSSARY

Numbers and letters refer to the illustrations (by John Sambrook)
on pp. 820–7.

ABACUS: flat slab forming the top of a capital (3a).

ACANTHUS: classical formalized leaf ornament (4b).

ACCUMULATOR TOWER: *see* Hydraulic power.

ACHIEVEMENT: a complete display of armorial bearings.

ACROTERION: plinth for a statue or ornament on the apex or ends of a pediment; more usually, both the plinth and what stands on it (4a).

AEDICULE (*lit.* little building): architectural surround, consisting usually of two columns or pilasters supporting a pediment.

AGGREGATE: *see* Concrete.

AISLE: subsidiary space alongside the body of a building, separated from it by columns, piers, or posts.

ALMONRY: a building from which alms are dispensed to the poor.

AMBULATORY (*lit.* walkway): aisle around the sanctuary (q.v.).

ANGLE ROLL: roll moulding in the angle between two planes (1a).

ANSE DE PANIER: *see* Arch.

ANTAE: simplified pilasters (4a), usually applied to the ends of the enclosing walls of a portico *in antis* (q.v.).

ANTEFIXAE: ornaments projecting at regular intervals above a Greek cornice, originally to conceal the ends of roof tiles (4a).

ANTHEMION: classical ornament like a honeysuckle flower (4b).

APRON: raised panel below a window or wall monument or tablet.

APSE: semicircular or polygonal end of an apartment, especially of a chancel or chapel. In classical architecture sometimes called an *exedra*.

ARABESQUE: non-figurative surface decoration consisting of flowing lines, foliage scrolls etc., based on geometrical patterns. Cf. Grotesque.

ARCADE: series of arches supported by piers or columns. *Blind arcade* or *arcading*: the same applied to the wall surface. *Wall arcade*: in medieval churches, a blind arcade forming a dado below windows. Also a covered shopping street.

ARCH: Shapes *see* 5c. *Basket arch* or *anse de panier* (basket handle): three-centred and depressed, or with a flat centre. *Nodding*: ogee arch curving forward from the wall face. *Parabolic*: shaped like a chain suspended from two level points, but inverted. Special purposes. *Chancel*: dividing chancel from nave or crossing. *Crossing*: spanning piers at a crossing (q.v.). *Relieving or discharging*: incorporated in a wall to relieve superimposed weight (5c). *Skew*: spanning responds not diametrically opposed. *Strainer*: inserted in an opening to resist inward pressure. *Transverse*: spanning a main axis (e.g. of a vaulted space). *See also* Jack arch, Triumphal arch.

ARCHITRAVE: formalized lintel, the lowest member of the classical entablature (3a). Also the moulded frame of a door or window (often borrowing the profile of a classical architrave). For *lugged* and *shouldered* architraves *see* 4b.

ARCUATED: dependent structurally on the arch principle. Cf. Trabeated.

ARK: chest or cupboard housing the

tables of Jewish law in a syn-
agogue.

ARRIS: sharp edge where two
surfaces meet at an angle (3a).

ASHLAR: masonry of large blocks
wrought to even faces and square
edges (6d).

ASTRAGAL: classical moulding of
semicircular section (3f).

ASTYLAR: with no columns or
similar vertical features.

ATLANTES: see Caryatids.

ATRIUM (plural: atria): inner court
of a Roman or C20 house; in a
multi-storey building, a toplit
covered court rising through all
storeys. Also an open court in
front of a church.

ATTACHED COLUMN: see Engaged
column.

ATTIC: small top storey within
a roof. Also the storey above the
main entablature of a classical
façade.

AUMBRY: recess or cupboard to
hold sacred vessels for the Mass.

BAILEY: see Motte-and-bailey.

BALANCE BEAM: see Canals.

BALDACCHINO: free-standing canopy, originally fabric, over an
altar. Cf. Ciborium.

BALLFLOWER: globular flower of
three petals enclosing a ball (1a).
Typical of the Decorated style.

BALUSTER: pillar or pedestal of
bellied form. Balusters: vertical
supports of this or any other form,
for a handrail or coping, the whole
being called a balustrade (6c).
Blind balustrade: the same applied
to the wall surface.

BARBICAN: outwork defending the
entrance to a castle.

BARGEBOARDS (corruption of
'vergeboards'): boards, often
carved or fretted, fixed beneath
the eaves of a gable to cover and
protect the rafters.

BAROQUE: style originating in Rome
c.1600 and current in England
c.1680–1720, characterized by
dramatic massing and silhouette
and the use of the giant order.

BARROW: burial mound.

BARTIZAN: corbelled turret, square
or round, frequently at an angle.

BASCULE: hinged part of a lifting (or
bascule) bridge.

BASE: moulded foot of a column or
pilaster. For Attic base see 3b.

BASEMENT: lowest, subordinate
storey; hence the lowest part of a
classical elevation, below the piano
nobile (q.v.).

BASILICA: a Roman public hall;
hence an aisled building with a
clerestory.

BASTION: one of a series of defensive semicircular or polygonal projections from the main wall of a
fortress or city.

BATTER: intentional inward inclination of a wall face.

BATTLEMENT: defensive parapet,
composed of merlons (solid) and
crenels (embrasures) through
which archers could shoot; sometimes called crenellation. Also used
decoratively.

BAY: division of an elevation or
interior space as defined by regular
vertical features such as arches,
columns, windows etc.

BAY LEAF: classical ornament of
overlapping bay leaves (3f).

BAY WINDOW: window of one or
more storeys projecting from the
face of a building. Canted: with
a straight front and angled sides.
Bow window: curved. Oriel: rests
on corbels or brackets and starts
above ground level; also the bay
window at the dais end of a medieval great hall.

BEAD-AND-REEL: see Enrichments.

BEAKHEAD: Norman ornament
with a row of beaked bird or beast
heads usually biting into a roll
moulding (1a).

BELFRY: chamber or stage in a
tower where bells are hung.

BELL CAPITAL: see 1b.

BELLCOTE: small gabled or roofed
housing for the bell(s).

BERM: level area separating a ditch
from a bank on a hill-fort or
barrow.

BILLET: Norman ornament of small
half-cylindrical or rectangular
blocks (1a).

BLIND: see Arcade, Baluster, Portico.

BLOCK CAPITAL: see 1a.

BLOCKED: columns, etc. interrupted by regular projecting

blocks (*blocking*), as on a Gibbs surround (4b).

BLOCKING COURSE: course of stones, or equivalent, on top of a cornice and crowning the wall.

BOLECTION MOULDING: covering the joint between two different planes (6b).

BOND: the pattern of long sides (*stretchers*) and short ends (*headers*) produced on the face of a wall by laying bricks in a particular way (6e).

BOSS: knob or projection, e.g. at the intersection of ribs in a vault (2c).

BOWTELL: a term in use by the C15 for a form of roll moulding, usually three-quarters of a circle in section (also called *edge roll*).

BOW WINDOW: *see* Bay window.

BOX FRAME: timber-framed construction in which vertical and horizontal wall members support the roof (7). Also concrete construction where the loads are taken on cross walls; also called *cross-wall construction*.

BRACE: subsidiary member of a structural frame, curved or straight. *Bracing* is often arranged decoratively e.g. quatrefoil, herringbone (7). *See also* Roofs.

BRATTISHING: ornamental crest, usually formed of leaves, Tudor flowers or miniature battlements.

BRESSUMER (*lit.* breast-beam): big horizontal beam supporting the wall above, especially in a jettied building (7).

BRICK: *see* Bond, Cogging, Engineering, Gauged, Tumbling.

BRIDGE: *Bowstring*: with arches rising above the roadway which is suspended from them. *Clapper*: one long stone forms the roadway. *Roving*: see Canal. *Suspension*: roadway suspended from cables or chains slung between towers or pylons. *Stay-suspension* or *stay-cantilever*: supported by diagonal stays from towers or pylons. *See also* Bascule.

BRISES-SOLEIL: projecting fins or canopies which deflect direct sunlight from windows.

BROACH: *see* Spire and 1C.

BUCRANIUM: ox skull used decoratively in classical friezes.

BULL-NOSED SILL: sill displaying a pronounced convex upper moulding.

BULLSEYE WINDOW: small oval window, set horizontally (cf. Oculus). Also called *œil de bœuf*.

BUTTRESS: vertical member projecting from a wall to stabilize it or to resist the lateral thrust of an arch, roof, or vault (1c, 2c). A *flying buttress* transmits the thrust to a heavy abutment by means of an arch or half-arch (1c).

CABLE OR ROPE MOULDING: originally Norman, like twisted strands of a rope.

CAMES: *see* Quarries.

CAMPANILE: free-standing bell-tower.

CANALS: *Flash lock*: removable weir or similar device through which boats pass on a flush of water. Predecessor of the *pound lock*: chamber with gates at each end allowing boats to float from one level to another. *Tidal gates*: single pair of lock gates allowing vessels to pass when the tide makes a level. *Balance beam*: beam projecting horizontally for opening and closing lock gates. *Roving bridge*: carrying a towing path from one bank to the other.

CANTILEVER: horizontal projection (e.g. step, canopy) supported by a downward force behind the fulcrum.

CAPITAL: head or crowning feature of a column or pilaster; for classical types *see* 3; for medieval types *see* 1b.

CARREL: compartment designed for individual work or study.

CARTOUCHE: classical tablet with ornate frame (4b).

CARYATIDS: female figures supporting an entablature; their male counterparts are *Atlantes* (*lit.* Atlas figures).

CASEMATE: vaulted chamber, with embrasures for defence, within a castle wall or projecting from it.

CASEMENT: side-hinged window.

CASTELLATED: with battlements (q.v.).

CAST IRON: hard and brittle, cast in a mould to the required shape.

Wrought iron is ductile, strong in tension, forged into decorative patterns or forged and rolled into e.g. bars, joists, boiler plates; *mild steel* is its modern equivalent, similar but stronger.

CATSLIDE: *See* 8a.

CAVETTO: concave classical moulding of quarter-round section (3f).

CELURE OR CEILURE: enriched area of roof above rood or altar.

CEMENT: *see* Concrete.

CENOTAPH (*lit.* empty tomb): funerary monument which is not a burying place.

CENTRING: wooden support for the building of an arch or vault, removed after completion.

CHAMFER (*lit.* corner-break): surface formed by cutting off a square edge or corner. For types of chamfers and *chamfer stops see* 6a. *See also* Double chamfer.

CHANCEL: part of the E end of a church set apart for the use of the officiating clergy.

CHANTRY CHAPEL: often attached to or within a church, endowed for the celebration of Masses principally for the soul of the founder.

CHEVET (*lit.* head): French term for chancel with ambulatory and radiating chapels.

CHEVRON: V-shape used in series or double series (later) on a Norman moulding (1a). Also (especially when on a single plane) called *zigzag*.

CHOIR: the part of a cathedral, monastic or collegiate church where services are sung.

CIBORIUM: a fixed canopy over an altar, usually vaulted and supported on four columns; cf. Baldacchino. Also a canopied shrine for the reserved sacrament.

CINQUEFOIL: *see* Foil.

CIST: stone-lined or slab-built grave.

CLADDING: external covering or skin applied to a structure, especially a framed one.

CLERESTORY: uppermost storey of the nave of a church, pierced by windows. Also high-level windows in secular buildings.

CLOSER: a brick cut to complete a bond (6e).

CLUSTER BLOCK: *see* Multi-storey.

COADE STONE: ceramic artificial stone made in Lambeth 1769–c.1840 by Eleanor Coade (†1821) and her associates.

COB: walling material of clay mixed with straw. Also called *pisé*.

COFFERING: arrangement of sunken panels (coffers), square or polygonal, decorating a ceiling, vault, or arch.

COGGING: a decorative course of bricks laid diagonally (6e). Cf. Dentilation.

COLLAR: *see* Roofs and 7.

COLLEGIATE CHURCH: endowed for the support of a college of priests.

COLONNADE: range of columns supporting an entablature. Cf. Arcade.

COLONNETTE: small medieval column or shaft.

COLOSSAL ORDER: *see* Giant order.

COLUMBARIUM: shelved, niched structure to house multiple burials.

COLUMN: a classical, upright structural member of round section with a shaft, a capital, and usually a base (3a, 4a).

COLUMN FIGURE: carved figure attached to a medieval column or shaft, usually flanking a doorway.

COMMUNION TABLE: unconsecrated table used in Protestant churches for the celebration of Holy Communion.

COMPOSITE: *see* Orders.

COMPOUND PIER: grouped shafts (q.v.), or a solid core surrounded by shafts.

CONCRETE: composition of *cement* (calcined lime and clay), *aggregate* (small stones or rock chippings), sand and water. It can be poured into *formwork* or *shuttering* (temporary frame of timber or metal) on site (*in-situ* concrete), or *pre-cast* as components before construction. *Reinforced*: incorporating steel rods to take the tensile force. *Pre-stressed*: with tensioned steel rods. Finishes include the impression of boards left by formwork (*board-marked* or *shuttered*), and texturing with steel brushes (*brushed*) or hammers (*hammer-dressed*). *See also* Shell.

CONSOLE: bracket of curved outline (4b).

COPING: protective course of masonry or brickwork capping a wall (6d).

CORBEL: projecting block supporting something above. *Corbel course*: continuous course of projecting stones or bricks fulfilling the same function. *Corbel table*: series of corbels to carry a parapet or a wall-plate or wall-post (7). *Corbelling*: brick or masonry courses built out beyond one another to support a chimney-stack, window, etc.

CORINTHIAN: *see* Orders and 3d.

CORNICE: flat-topped ledge with moulded underside, projecting along the top of a building or feature, especially as the highest member of the classical entablature (3a). Also the decorative moulding in the angle between wall and ceiling.

CORPS-DE-LOGIS: the main building(s) as distinct from the wings or pavilions.

COTTAGE ORNÉ: an artfully rustic small house associated with the Picturesque movement.

COUNTERCHANGING: of joists on a ceiling divided by beams into compartments, when placed in opposite directions in alternate squares.

COUR D'HONNEUR: formal entrance court before a house in the French manner, usually with flanking wings and a screen wall or gates.

COURSE: continuous layer of stones, etc. in a wall (6e).

COVE: a broad concave moulding, e.g. to mask the eaves of a roof. *Coved ceiling*: with a pronounced cove joining the walls to a flat central panel smaller than the whole area of the ceiling.

CRADLE ROOF: *see* Wagon roof.

CREDENCE: a shelf within or beside a piscina (q.v.), or a table for the sacramental elements and vessels.

CRENELLATION: parapet with crenels (*see* Battlement).

CRINKLE-CRANKLE WALL: garden wall undulating in a series of serpentine curves.

CROCKETS: leafy hooks. *Crocketing* decorates the edges of Gothic features, such as pinnacles, canopies, etc. *Crocket capital*: see 1b.

CROSSING: central space at the junction of the nave, chancel, and transepts. *Crossing tower*: above a crossing.

CROSS-WINDOW: with one mullion and one transom (qq.v.).

CROWN-POST: *see* Roofs and 7.

CROWSTEPS: squared stones set like steps, e.g. on a gable (8a).

CRUCKS (*lit.* crooked): pairs of inclined timbers (*blades*), usually curved, set at bay-lengths; they support the roof timbers and, in timber buildings, also support the walls (8b). *Base*: blades rise from ground level to a tie- or collar-beam which supports the roof timbers. *Full*: blades rise from ground level to the apex of the roof, serving as the main members of a roof truss. *Jointed*: blades formed from more than one timber; the lower member may act as a wall-post; it is usually elbowed at wall-plate level and jointed just above. *Middle*: blades rise from half-way up the walls to a tie- or collar-beam. *Raised*: blades rise from half-way up the walls to the apex. *Upper*: blades supported on a tie-beam and rising to the apex.

CRYPT: underground or half-underground area, usually below the E end of a church. *Ring crypt*: corridor crypt surrounding the apse of an early medieval church, often associated with chambers for relics. Cf. Undercroft.

CUPOLA (*lit.* dome): especially a small dome on a circular or polygonal base crowning a larger dome, roof, or turret.

CURSUS: a long avenue defined by two parallel earthen banks with ditches outside.

CURTAIN WALL: a connecting wall between the towers of a castle. Also a non-load-bearing external wall applied to a C20 framed structure.

CUSP: *see* Tracery and 2b.

CYCLOPEAN MASONRY: large irregular polygonal stones, smooth and finely jointed.

CYMA RECTA and CYMA REVERSA: classical mouldings with double curves (3f). Cf. Ogee.

DADO: the finishing (often with panelling) of the lower part of a wall in a classical interior; in origin a formalized continuous pedestal. *Dado rail*: the moulding along the top of the dado.

DAGGER: *see* Tracery and 2b.

DALLE-DE-VERRE (*lit.* glass-slab): a late C20 stained-glass technique, setting large, thick pieces of cast glass into a frame of reinforced concrete or epoxy resin.

DEC (DECORATED): English Gothic architecture *c.* 1290 to *c.* 1350. The name is derived from the type of window tracery (q.v.) used during the period.

DEMI- or HALF-COLUMNS: engaged columns (q.v.) half of whose circumference projects from the wall.

DENTIL: small square block used in series in classical cornices (3c). *Dentilation* is produced by the projection of alternating headers along cornices or stringcourses.

DIAPER: repetitive surface decoration of lozenges or squares flat or in relief. Achieved in brickwork with bricks of two colours.

DIOCLETIAN OR THERMAL WINDOW: semicircular with two mullions, as used in the Baths of Diocletian, Rome (4b).

DISTYLE: having two columns (4a).

DOGTOOTH: E.E. ornament, consisting of a series of small pyramids formed by four stylized canine teeth meeting at a point (1a).

DORIC: *see* Orders and 3a, 3b.

DORMER: window projecting from the slope of a roof (8a).

DOUBLE CHAMFER: a chamfer applied to each of two recessed arches (1a).

DOUBLE PILE: *see* Pile.

DRAGON BEAM: *see* Jetty.

DRESSINGS: the stone or brickwork worked to a finished face about an angle, opening, or other feature.

DRIPSTONE: moulded stone projecting from a wall to protect the lower parts from water. Cf. Hoodmould, Weathering.

DRUM: circular or polygonal stage supporting a dome or cupola. Also one of the stones forming the shaft of a column (3a).

DUTCH or FLEMISH GABLE: *see* 8a.

EASTER SEPULCHRE: tomb-chest used for Easter ceremonial, within or against the N wall of a chancel.

EAVES: overhanging edge of a roof; hence *eaves cornice* in this position.

ECHINUS: ovolo moulding (q.v.) below the abacus of a Greek Doric capital (3a).

EDGE RAIL: *see* Railways.

E.E. (EARLY ENGLISH): English Gothic architecture *c.* 1190–1250.

EGG-AND-DART: *see* Enrichments and 3f.

ELEVATION: any face of a building or side of a room. In a drawing, the same or any part of it, represented in two dimensions.

EMBATTLED: with battlements.

EMBRASURE: small splayed opening in a wall or battlement (q.v.).

ENCAUSTIC TILES: earthenware tiles fired with a pattern and glaze.

EN DELIT: stone cut against the bed.

ENFILADE: reception rooms in a formal series, usually with all doorways on axis.

ENGAGED or ATTACHED COLUMN: one that partly merges into a wall or pier.

ENGINEERING BRICKS: dense bricks, originally used mostly for railway viaducts etc.

ENRICHMENTS: the carved decoration of certain classical mouldings, e.g. the ovolo (qq.v.) with *egg-and-dart*, the cyma reversa with *waterleaf*, the astragal with *bead-and-reel* (3f).

ENTABLATURE: in classical architecture, collective name for the three horizontal members (architrave, frieze, and cornice) carried by a wall or a column (3a).

ENTASIS: very slight convex deviation from a straight line, used to prevent an optical illusion of concavity.

EPITAPH: inscription on a tomb.

EXEDRA: *see* Apse.

EXTRADOS: outer curved face of an arch or vault.

EYECATCHER: decorative building terminating a vista.

FASCIA: plain horizontal band, e.g. in an architrave (3c, 3d) or on a shopfront.

FENESTRATION: the arrangement of windows in a façade.

FERETORY: site of the chief shrine of a church, behind the high altar.

FESTOON: ornamental garland, suspended from both ends. Cf. Swag.

FIBREGLASS, or glass-reinforced polyester (GRP): synthetic resin reinforced with glass fibre. GRC: glass-reinforced concrete.

FIELD: see Panelling and 6b.

FILLET: a narrow flat band running down a medieval shaft or along a roll moulding (1a). It separates larger curved mouldings in classical cornices, fluting or bases (3c).

FLAMBOYANT: the latest phase of French Gothic architecture, with flowing tracery.

FLASH LOCK: see Canals.

FLÈCHE or SPIRELET (*lit.* arrow): slender spire on the centre of a roof.

FLEURON: medieval carved flower or leaf, often rectilinear (1a).

FLUSHWORK: knapped flint used with dressed stone to form patterns.

FLUTING: series of concave grooves (flutes), their common edges sharp (arris) or blunt (fillet) (3).

FOIL (*lit.* leaf): lobe formed by the cusping of a circular or other shape in tracery (2b). *Trefoil* (three), *quatrefoil* (four), *cinquefoil* (five), and *multifoil* express the number of lobes in a shape.

FOLIATE: decorated with leaves.

FORMWORK: see Concrete.

FRAMED BUILDING: where the structure is carried by a framework – e.g. of steel, reinforced concrete, timber – instead of by load-bearing walls.

FREESTONE: stone that is cut, or can be cut, in all directions.

FRESCO: *al fresco*: painting on wet plaster. *Fresco secco*: painting on dry plaster.

FRIEZE: the middle member of the classical entablature, sometimes ornamented (3a). *Pulvinated frieze* (*lit.* cushioned): of bold convex profile (3c). Also a horizontal band of ornament.

FRONTISPIECE: in C16 and C17 buildings the central feature of doorway and windows above linked in one composition.

GABLE: For types *see* 8a. *Gablet*: small gable. *Pedimental gable*: treated like a pediment.

GADROONING: classical ribbed ornament like inverted fluting that flows into a lobed edge.

GALILEE: chapel or vestibule usually at the W end of a church enclosing the main portal(s).

GALLERY: a long room or passage; an upper storey above the aisle of a church, looking through arches to the nave; a balcony or mezzanine overlooking the main interior space of a building; or an external walkway.

GALLETING: small stones set in a mortar course.

GAMBREL ROOF: see 8a.

GARDEROBE: medieval privy.

GARGOYLE: projecting water spout often carved into human or animal shape.

GAUGED or RUBBED BRICKWORK: soft brick sawn roughly, then rubbed to a precise (gauged) surface. Mostly used for door or window openings (5c).

GAZEBO (jocular Latin, 'I shall gaze'): ornamental lookout tower or raised summer house.

GEOMETRIC: English Gothic architecture *c.* 1250–1310. *See also* Tracery. For another meaning, *see* Stairs.

GIANT or COLOSSAL ORDER: classical order (q.v.) whose height is that of two or more storeys of the building to which it is applied.

GIBBS SURROUND: C18 treatment of an opening (4b), seen particularly in the work of James Gibbs (1682–1754).

GIRDER: a large beam. *Box*: of hollow-box section. *Bowed*: with its top rising in a curve. *Plate*: of I-section, made from iron or steel plates. *Lattice*: with braced framework.

GLAZING BARS: wooden or sometimes metal bars separating and supporting window panes.

GRAFFITI: *see* Sgraffito.

GRANGE: farm owned and run by a religious order.

GRC: *see* Fibreglass.

GRISAILLE: monochrome painting on walls or glass.

GROIN: sharp edge at the meeting of two cells of a cross-vault; *see* Vault and 2c.

GROTESQUE (*lit.* grotto-esque): wall decoration adopted from Roman examples in the Renaissance. Its foliage scrolls incorporate figurative elements. Cf. Arabesque.

GROTTO: artificial cavern.

GRP: *see* Fibreglass.

GUILLOCHE: classical ornament of interlaced bands (4b).

GUNLOOP: opening for a firearm.

GUTTAE: stylized drops (3b).

HALF-TIMBERING: archaic term for timber-framing (q.v.). Sometimes used for non-structural decorative timberwork.

HALL CHURCH: medieval church with nave and aisles of approximately equal height.

HAMMERBEAM: *see* Roofs and 7.

HAMPER: in c20 architecture, a visually distinct topmost storey or storeys.

HEADER: *see* Bond and 6e.

HEADSTOP: stop (q.v.) carved with a head (5b).

HELM ROOF: *see* IC.

HENGE: ritual earthwork.

HERM (*lit.* the god Hermes): male head or bust on a pedestal.

HERRINGBONE WORK: *see* 7ii. Cf. Pitched masonry.

HEXASTYLE: *see* Portico.

HILL-FORT: Iron Age earthwork enclosed by a ditch and bank system.

HIPPED ROOF: *see* 8a.

HOODMOULD: projecting moulding above an arch or lintel to throw off water (2b, 5b). When horizontal often called a *label*. For label stop *see* Stop.

HUSK GARLAND: festoon of stylized nutshells (4b).

HYDRAULIC POWER: use of water under high pressure to work machinery. *Accumulator tower*: houses a hydraulic accumulator which accommodates fluctuations in the flow through hydraulic mains.

HYPOCAUST (*lit.* underburning): Roman underfloor heating system.

IMPOST: horizontal moulding at the springing of an arch (5c).

IMPOST BLOCK: block between abacus and capital (1b).

IN ANTIS: *see* Antae, Portico and 4a.

INDENT: shape chiselled out of a stone to receive a brass.

INDUSTRIALIZED or SYSTEM BUILDING: system of manufactured units assembled on site.

INGLENOOK (*lit.* fire-corner): recess for a hearth with provision for seating.

INTERCOLUMNATION: interval between columns.

INTERLACE: decoration in relief simulating woven or entwined stems or bands.

INTRADOS: *see* Soffit.

IONIC: *see* Orders and 3c.

JACK ARCH: shallow segmental vault springing from beams, used for fireproof floors, bridge decks, etc.

JAMB (*lit.* leg): one of the vertical sides of an opening.

JETTY: in a timber-framed building, the projection of an upper storey beyond the storey below, made by the beams and joists of the lower storey oversailing the wall; on their outer ends is placed the sill of the walling for the storey above (7). Buildings can be jettied on several sides, in which case a *dragon beam* is set diagonally at the corner to carry the joists to either side.

JOGGLE: the joining of two stones to prevent them slipping by a notch in one and a projection in the other.

KEEL MOULDING: moulding used from the late c12, in section like the keel of a ship (1a).

KEEP: principal tower of a castle.

KENTISH CUSP: *see* Tracery and 2b.

KEY PATTERN: *see* 4b.

KEYSTONE: central stone in an arch or vault (4b, 5c).

KINGPOST: *see* Roofs and 7.

KNEELER: horizontal projecting stone at the base of each side of a gable to support the inclined coping stones (8a).

LABEL: *see* Hoodmould and 5b.

LABEL STOP: *see* Stop and 5b.

LACED BRICKWORK: vertical strips of brickwork, often in a contrasting colour, linking openings on different floors.

LACING COURSE: horizontal reinforcement in timber or brick to walls of flint, cobble, etc.

LADY CHAPEL: dedicated to the Virgin Mary (Our Lady).

LANCET: slender single-light, pointed-arched window (2a).

LANTERN: circular or polygonal windowed turret crowning a roof or a dome. Also the windowed stage of a crossing tower lighting the church interior.

LANTERN CROSS: churchyard cross with lantern-shaped top.

LAVATORIUM: in a religious house, a washing place adjacent to the refectory.

LEAN-TO: *see* Roofs.

LESENE (*lit.* a mean thing): pilaster without base or capital. Also called *pilaster strip*.

LIERNE: *see* Vault and 2c.

LIGHT: compartment of a window defined by the mullions.

LINENFOLD: Tudor panelling carved with simulations of folded linen. *See also* Parchemin.

LINTEL: horizontal beam or stone bridging an opening.

LOGGIA: gallery, usually arcaded or colonnaded; sometimes freestanding.

LONG-AND-SHORT WORK: quoins consisting of stones placed with the long side alternately upright and horizontal, especially in Saxon building.

LONGHOUSE: house and byre in the same range with internal access between them.

LOUVRE: roof opening, often protected by a raised timber structure, to allow the smoke from a central hearth to escape.

LOWSIDE WINDOW: set lower than the others in a chancel side wall, usually towards its W end.

LUCAM: projecting housing for hoist pulley on upper storey of warehouses, mills, etc., for raising goods to loading doors.

LUCARNE (*lit.* dormer): small gabled opening in a roof or spire.

LUGGED ARCHITRAVE: *see* 4b.

LUNETTE: semicircular window or blind panel.

LYCHGATE (*lit.* corpse-gate): roofed gateway entrance to a churchyard for the reception of a coffin.

LYNCHET: long terraced strip of soil on the downward side of prehistoric and medieval fields, accumulated because of continual ploughing along the contours.

MACHICOLATIONS (*lit.* mashing devices): series of openings between the corbels that support a projecting parapet through which missiles can be dropped. Used decoratively in post-medieval buildings.

MANOMETER or STANDPIPE TOWER: containing a column of water to regulate pressure in water mains.

MANSARD: *see* 8a.

MATHEMATICAL TILES: facing tiles with the appearance of brick, most often applied to timber-framed walls.

MAUSOLEUM: monumental building or chamber usually intended for the burial of members of one family.

MEGALITHIC TOMB: massive stone-built Neolithic burial chamber covered by an earth or stone mound.

MERLON: *see* Battlement.

METOPES: spaces between the triglyphs in a Doric frieze (3b).

MEZZANINE: low storey between two higher ones.

MILD STEEL: *see* Cast iron.

MISERICORD (*lit.* mercy): shelf on a carved bracket placed on the underside of a hinged choir stall seat to support an occupant when standing.

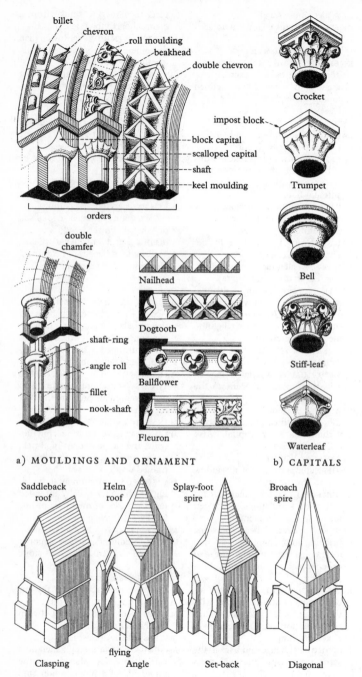

billet
chevron
roll moulding
beakhead
double chevron
block capital
scalloped capital
shaft
keel moulding
orders

double chamfer
shaft-ring
angle roll
fillet
nook-shaft

Nailhead
Dogtooth
Ballflower
Fleuron

a) MOULDINGS AND ORNAMENT

Crocket
impost block
Trumpet
Bell
Stiff-leaf
Waterleaf

b) CAPITALS

Saddleback roof
Helm roof
Splay-foot spire
Broach spire

flying
Clasping
Angle
Set-back
Diagonal

c) BUTTRESSES, ROOFS AND SPIRES

FIGURE I: MEDIEVAL

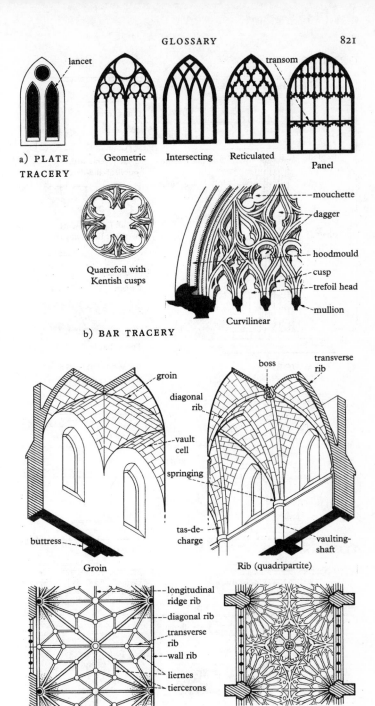

a) PLATE TRACERY — lancet

Geometric   Intersecting   Reticulated   Panel — transom

Quatrefoil with Kentish cusps

Curvilinear — mouchette, dagger, hoodmould, cusp, trefoil head, mullion

b) BAR TRACERY

Groin — groin, diagonal rib, vault cell, buttress

Rib (quadripartite) — boss, transverse rib, springing, tas-de-charge, vaulting-shaft

Lierne — longitudinal ridge rib, diagonal rib, transverse rib, wall rib, liernes, tiercerons

Fan

c) VAULTS

FIGURE 2: MEDIEVAL

ORDERS

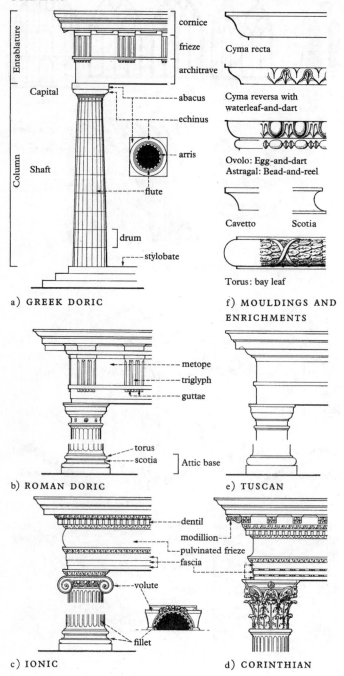

a) GREEK DORIC

f) MOULDINGS AND ENRICHMENTS

Cyma recta

Cyma reversa with waterleaf-and-dart

Ovolo: Egg-and-dart
Astragal: Bead-and-reel

Cavetto   Scotia

Torus: bay leaf

Entablature
cornice
frieze
architrave

Capital
Column
Shaft

abacus
echinus
arris
flute
drum
stylobate

b) ROMAN DORIC

metope
triglyph
guttae
torus
scotia   Attic base

c) IONIC

dentil
modillion
pulvinated frieze
fascia
volute
fillet

e) TUSCAN

d) CORINTHIAN

FIGURE 3: CLASSICAL

a) PORTICO

acroterion · · tympanum · · antefixa

column

anta

naos naos

pronaos

Distyle in antis · · · Prostyle

Anthemion & Palmette · · Guilloche · · Key pattern

Rinceau · · Husk garland · · Vitruvian scroll

Console · · Diocletian window · · Acanthus

Broken pediment · · Lugged architrave

Segmental pediment · · Shouldered architrave

Venetian window

Open pediment · · console · · cartouche · · keystone · · blocking · · Swan-neck pediment · · Gibbs surround

b) ORNAMENTS AND FEATURES

FIGURE 4: CLASSICAL

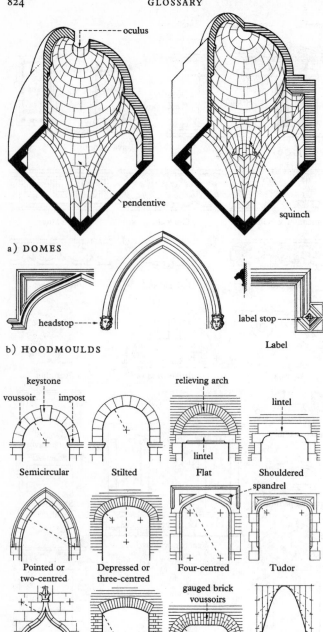

a) DOMES

b) HOODMOULDS

Label

c) ARCHES

FIGURE 5: CONSTRUCTION

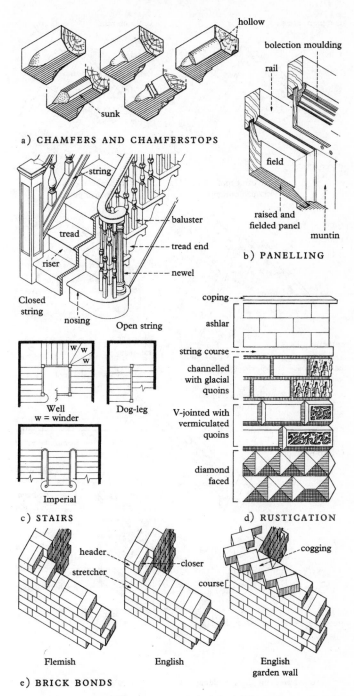

a) CHAMFERS AND CHAMFERSTOPS

hollow

bolection moulding

rail

field

raised and fielded panel

muntin

b) PANELLING

string

baluster

tread

tread end

riser

newel

Closed string

nosing

Open string

Well
w = winder

Dog-leg

Imperial

c) STAIRS

coping

ashlar

string course

channelled with glacial quoins

V-jointed with vermiculated quoins

diamond faced

d) RUSTICATION

header

stretcher

closer

course

cogging

Flemish

English

English garden wall

e) BRICK BONDS

FIGURE 6: CONSTRUCTION

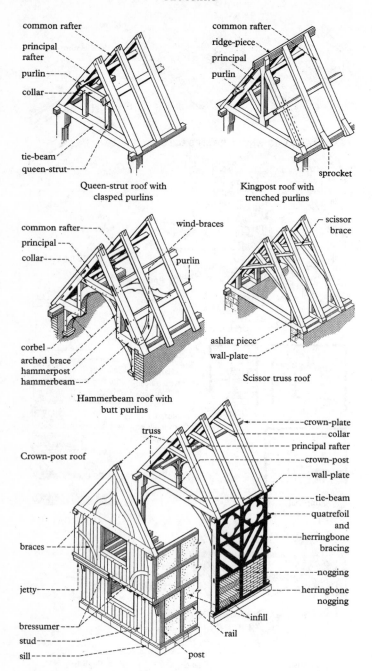

common rafter
principal rafter
purlin
collar
tie-beam
queen-strut

Queen-strut roof with
clasped purlins

common rafter
ridge-piece
principal
purlin

sprocket

Kingpost roof with
trenched purlins

common rafter
principal
collar

wind-braces

purlin

corbel
arched brace
hammerpost
hammerbeam

Hammerbeam roof with
butt purlins

scissor brace

ashlar piece
wall-plate

Scissor truss roof

truss

Crown-post roof

crown-plate
collar
principal rafter
crown-post
wall-plate
tie-beam
quatrefoil and herringbone bracing
nogging
herringbone nogging

braces

jetty

bressumer
stud
sill

post

infill
rail

Box frame: i) Close studding   ii) Square panel

FIGURE 7: ROOFS AND TIMBER-FRAMING

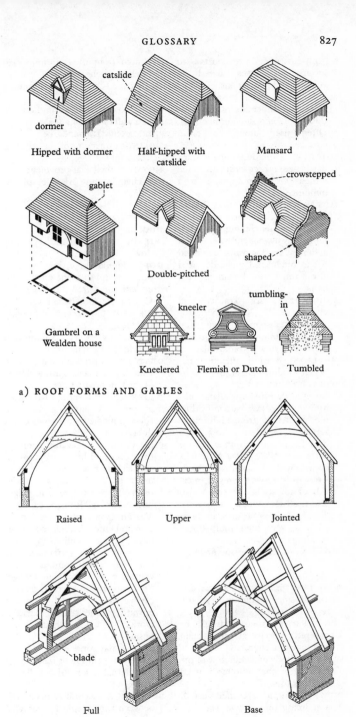

a) ROOF FORMS AND GABLES

b) CRUCK FRAMES

FIGURE 8: ROOFS AND TIMBER-FRAMING

MIXER-COURTS: forecourts to groups of houses shared by vehicles and pedestrians.

MODILLIONS: small consoles (q.v.) along the underside of a Corinthian or Composite cornice (3d). Often used along an eaves cornice.

MODULE: a predetermined standard size for co-ordinating the dimensions of components of a building.

MOTTE-AND-BAILEY: post-Roman and Norman defence consisting of an earthen mound (motte) topped by a wooden tower within a bailey, an enclosure defended by a ditch and palisade, and also, sometimes, by an internal bank.

MOUCHETTE: see Tracery and 2b.

MOULDING: shaped ornamental strip of continuous section; see e.g. Cavetto, Cyma, Ovolo, Roll.

MULLION: vertical member between window lights (2b).

MULTI-STOREY: five or more storeys. Multi-storey flats may form a *cluster block*, with individual blocks of flats grouped round a service core; a *point block*, with flats fanning out from a service core; or a *slab block*, with flats approached by corridors or galleries from service cores at intervals or towers at the ends (plan also used for offices, hotels etc.). *Tower block* is a generic term for any very high multi-storey building.

MUNTIN: see Panelling and 6b.

NAILHEAD: E.E. ornament consisting of small pyramids regularly repeated (1a).

NARTHEX: enclosed vestibule or covered porch at the main entrance to a church.

NAVE: the body of a church w of the crossing or chancel often flanked by aisles (q.v.).

NEWEL: central or corner post of a staircase (6c). Newel stair: see Stairs.

NIGHT STAIR: stair by which religious entered the transept of their church from their dormitory to celebrate night services.

NOGGING: see Timber-framing (7).

NOOK-SHAFT: shaft set in the angle of a wall or opening (1a).

NORMAN: see Romanesque.

NOSING: projection of the tread of a step (6c).

NUTMEG: medieval ornament with a chain of tiny triangles placed obliquely.

OCULUS: circular opening.

ŒIL DE BŒUF: see Bullseye window.

OGEE: double curve, bending first one way and then the other, as in an *ogee* or *ogival arch* (5c). Cf. Cyma recta and Cyma reversa.

OPUS SECTILE: decorative mosaiclike facing.

OPUS SIGNINUM: composition flooring of Roman origin.

ORATORY: a private chapel in a church or a house. Also a church of the Oratorian Order.

ORDER: one of a series of recessed arches and jambs forming a splayed medieval opening, e.g. a doorway or arcade arch (1a).

ORDERS: the formalized versions of the post-and-lintel system in classical architecture. The main orders are *Doric, Ionic*, and *Corinthian*. They are Greek in origin but occur in Roman versions. Tuscan is a simple version of Roman Doric. Though each order has its own conventions (3), there are many minor variations. The *Composite* capital combines Ionic volutes with Corinthian foliage. *Superimposed orders*: orders on successive levels, usually in the upward sequence of Tuscan, Doric, Ionic, Corinthian, Composite.

ORIEL: see Bay window.

OVERDOOR: painting or relief above an internal door. Also called a *sopraporta*.

OVERTHROW: decorative fixed arch between two gatepiers or above a wrought-iron gate.

OVOLO: wide convex moulding (3f).

PALIMPSEST: of a brass: where a metal plate has been reused by turning over the engraving on the back; of a wall painting: where one overlaps and partly obscures an earlier one.

PALLADIAN: following the examples and principles of Andrea Palladio (1508–80).

PALMETTE: classical ornament like a palm shoot (4b).

PANELLING: wooden lining to interior walls, made up of vertical members (*muntins*) and horizontals (*rails*) framing panels: also called *wainscot*. *Raised and fielded*: with the central area of the panel (*field*) raised up (6b).

PANTILE: roof tile of S section.

PARAPET: wall for protection at any sudden drop, e.g. at the wall-head of a castle where it protects the *parapet walk* or wall-walk. Also used to conceal a roof.

PARCLOSE: *see* Screen.

PARGETTING (*lit.* plastering): exterior plaster decoration, either in relief or incised.

PARLOUR: in a religious house, a room where the religious could talk to visitors; in a medieval house, the semi-private living room below the solar (q.v.).

PARTERRE: level space in a garden laid out with low, formal beds.

PATERA (*lit.* plate): round or oval ornament in shallow relief.

PAVILION: ornamental building for occasional use; or projecting subdivision of a larger building, often at an angle or terminating a wing.

PEBBLEDASHING: *see* Rendering.

PEDESTAL: a tall block carrying a classical order, statue, vase, etc.

PEDIMENT: a formalized gable derived from that of a classical temple; also used over doors, windows, etc. For variations *see* 4b.

PENDENTIVE: spandrel between adjacent arches, supporting a drum, dome or vault and consequently formed as part of a hemisphere (5a).

PENTHOUSE: subsidiary structure with a lean-to roof. Also a separately roofed structure on top of a C20 multi-storey block.

PERIPTERAL: *see* Peristyle.

PERISTYLE: a colonnade all round the exterior of a classical building, as in a temple which is then said to be *peripteral*.

PERP (PERPENDICULAR): English Gothic architecture *c.* 1335–50 to *c.* 1530. The name is derived from the upright tracery panels then used (*see* Tracery and 2a).

PERRON: external stair to a doorway, usually of double-curved plan.

PEW: loosely, seating for the laity outside the chancel; strictly, an enclosed seat. *Box pew*: with equal high sides and a door.

PIANO NOBILE: principal floor of a classical building above a ground floor or basement and with a lesser storey overhead.

PIAZZA: formal urban open space surrounded by buildings.

PIER: large masonry or brick support, often for an arch. *See also* Compound pier.

PILASTER: flat representation of a classical column in shallow relief. *Pilaster strip*: *see* Lesene.

PILE: row of rooms. *Double pile*: two rows thick.

PILLAR: free-standing upright member of any section, not conforming to one of the orders (q.v.).

PILLAR PISCINA: *see* Piscina.

PILOTIS: C20 French term for pillars or stilts that support a building above an open ground floor.

PISCINA: basin for washing Mass vessels, provided with a drain; set in or against the wall to the S of an altar or free-standing (*pillar piscina*).

PISÉ: *see* Cob.

PITCHED MASONRY: laid on the diagonal, often alternately with opposing courses (*pitched and counterpitched* or *herringbone*).

PLATBAND: flat horizontal moulding between storeys. Cf. stringcourse.

PLATE RAIL: *see* Railways.

PLATEWAY: *see* Railways.

PLINTH: projecting courses at the

foot of a wall or column, generally chamfered or moulded at the top.

PODIUM: a continuous raised platform supporting a building; or a large block of two or three storeys beneath a multi-storey block of smaller area.

POINT BLOCK: *see* Multi-storey.

POINTING: exposed mortar jointing of masonry or brickwork. Types include *flush*, *recessed* and *tuck* (with a narrow channel filled with finer, whiter mortar).

POPPYHEAD: carved ornament of leaves and flowers as a finial for a bench end or stall.

PORTAL FRAME: C20 frame comprising two uprights rigidly connected to a beam or pair of rafters.

PORTCULLIS: gate constructed to rise and fall in vertical grooves at the entry to a castle.

PORTICO: a porch with the roof and frequently a pediment supported by a row of columns (4a). A portico *in antis* has columns on the same plane as the front of the building. A *prostyle* porch has columns standing free. Porticoes are described by the number of front columns, e.g. tetrastyle (four), hexastyle (six). The space within the temple is the *naos*, that within the portico the *pronaos*. *Blind portico*: the front features of a portico applied to a wall.

PORTICUS (plural: porticūs): subsidiary cell opening from the main body of a pre-Conquest church.

POST: upright support in a structure (7).

POSTERN: small gateway at the back of a building or to the side of a larger entrance door or gate.

POUND LOCK: *see* Canals.

PRESBYTERY: the part of a church lying E of the choir where the main altar is placed; or a priest's residence.

PRINCIPAL: *see* Roofs and 7.

PRONAOS: *see* Portico and 4a.

PROSTYLE: *see* Portico and 4a.

PULPIT: raised and enclosed platform for the preaching of sermons. *Three-decker*: with reading desk below and clerk's desk below that. *Two-decker*: as above, minus the clerk's desk.

PULPITUM: stone screen in a major church dividing choir from nave.

PULVINATED: *see* Frieze and 3c.

PURLIN: *see* Roofs and 7.

PUTHOLES or PUTLOG HOLES: in the wall to receive putlogs, the horizontal timbers which support scaffolding boards; sometimes not filled after construction is complete.

PUTTO (plural: putti): small naked boy.

QUARRIES: square (or diamond) panes of glass supported by lead strips (*cames*); square floor slabs or tiles.

QUATREFOIL: *see* Foil and 2b.

QUEEN-STRUT: *see* Roofs and 7.

QUIRK: sharp groove to one side of a convex medieval moulding.

QUOINS: dressed stones at the angles of a building (6d).

RADBURN SYSTEM: vehicle and pedestrian segregation in residential developments, based on that used at Radburn, New Jersey, USA, by Wright and Stein, 1928–30.

RADIATING CHAPELS: projecting radially from an ambulatory or an apse (*see* Chevet).

RAFTER: *see* Roofs and 7.

RAGGLE: groove cut in masonry, especially to receive the edge of a roof-covering.

RAGULY: ragged (in heraldry). Also applied to funerary sculpture, e.g. *cross raguly*: with a notched outline.

RAIL: *see* Panelling and 6b; also 7.

RAILWAYS: *Edge rail*: on which flanged wheels can run. *Plate rail*: L-section rail for plain unflanged wheels. *Plateway*: early railway using plate rails.

RAISED AND FIELDED: *see* Panelling and 6b.

RAKE: slope or pitch.

RAMPART: defensive outer wall of stone or earth. *Rampart walk*: path along the inner face.

REBATE: rectangular section cut out of a masonry edge to receive a shutter, door, window, etc.

REBUS: a heraldic pun, e.g. a fiery cock for Cockburn.

REEDING: series of convex mouldings, the reverse of fluting (q.v.). Cf. Gadrooning.

RENDERING: the covering of outside walls with a uniform surface or skin for protection from the weather. *Limewashing*: thin layer of lime plaster. *Pebbledashing*: where aggregate is thrown at the wet plastered wall for a textured effect. *Roughcast*: plaster mixed with a coarse aggregate such as gravel. *Stucco*: fine lime plaster worked to a smooth surface. *Cement rendering*: a cheaper substitute for stucco, usually with a grainy texture.

REPOUSSÉ: relief designs in metalwork, formed by beating it from the back.

REREDORTER (*lit.* behind the dormitory): latrines in a medieval religious house.

REREDOS: painted and/or sculptured screen behind and above an altar. Cf. Retable.

RESPOND: half-pier or half-column bonded into a wall and carrying one end of an arch. It usually terminates an arcade.

RETABLE: painted or carved panel standing on or at the back of an altar, usually attached to it.

RETROCHOIR: in a major church, the area between the high altar and E chapel.

REVEAL: the plane of a jamb, between the wall and the frame of a door or window.

RIB-VAULT: *see* Vault and 2c.

RINCEAU: classical ornament of leafy scrolls (4b).

RISER: vertical face of a step (6c).

ROACH: a rough-textured form of Portland stone, with small cavities and fossil shells.

ROCK-FACED: masonry cleft to produce a rugged appearance.

ROCOCO: style current *c.* 1720 and *c.* 1760, characterized by a serpentine line and playful, scrolled decoration.

ROLL MOULDING: medieval moulding of part-circular section (1a).

ROMANESQUE: style current in the CII and CI2. In England often called Norman. *See also* Saxo-Norman.

ROOD: crucifix flanked by the Virgin and St John, usually over the entry into the chancel, on a beam (*rood beam*) or painted on the wall. The *rood screen* below often had a walkway (*rood loft*) along the top, reached by a *rood stair* in the side wall.

ROOFS: Shape. For the main external shapes (hipped, mansard, etc.) *see* 8a. *Helm* and *Saddleback*: *see* 1c. *Lean-to*: single sloping roof built against a vertical wall; lean-to is also applied to the part of the building beneath.

Construction. *See* 7.

Single-framed roof: with no main trusses. The rafters may be fixed to the wall-plate or ridge, or longitudinal timber may be absent altogether.

Double-framed roof: with longitudinal members, such as purlins, and usually divided into bays by principals and principal rafters.

Other types are named after their main structural components, e.g. *hammerbeam*, *crown-post* (*see* Elements below and 7).

Elements. *See* 7.

Ashlar piece: a short vertical timber connecting inner wall-plate or timber pad to a rafter.

Braces: subsidiary timbers set diagonally to strengthen the frame. *Arched braces*: curved pair forming an arch, connecting wall or post below with tie- or collar-beam above. *Passing braces*: long straight braces passing across other members of the truss. *Scissor braces*: pair crossing diagonally between pairs of rafters or principals. *Wind-braces*: short, usually curved braces connecting side purlins with principals; sometimes decorated with cusping.

Collar or *collar-beam*: horizontal transverse timber connecting a pair of rafter or cruck blades (q.v.), set between apex and the wall-plate.

Crown-post: a vertical timber set centrally on a tie-beam and supporting a collar purlin braced to it longitudinally. In an open truss lateral braces may rise to the collar-beam; in a closed truss they may descend to the tie-beam.

Hammerbeams: horizontal brackets projecting at wall-plate level like an interrupted tie-beam; the inner ends carry *hammerposts*, vertical timbers which support a purlin and are braced to a collar-beam above.

Kingpost: vertical timber set centrally on a tie- or collar-beam, rising to the apex of the roof to support a ridge-piece (cf. Strut).

Plate: longitudinal timber set square to the ground. *Wall-plate*: plate along the top of a wall which receives the ends of the rafters; cf. Purlin.

Principals: pair of inclined lateral timbers of a truss. Usually they support side purlins and mark the main bay divisions.

Purlin: horizontal longitudinal timber. *Collar purlin* or *crown plate*: central timber which carries collar-beams and is supported by crown-posts. *Side purlins*: pairs of timbers placed some way up the slope of the roof, which carry common rafters. *Butt* or *tenoned purlins* are tenoned into either side of the principals. *Through purlins* pass through or past the principal; they include *clasped purlins*, which rest on queenposts or are carried in the angle between principals and collar, and *trenched purlins* trenched into the backs of principals.

Queen-strut: paired vertical, or near-vertical, timbers placed symmetrically on a tie-beam to support side purlins.

Rafters: inclined lateral timbers supporting the roof covering. *Common rafters*: regularly spaced uniform rafters placed along the length of a roof or between principals. *Principal rafters*: rafters which also act as principals.

Ridge, *ridge-piece*: horizontal longitudinal timber at the apex supporting the ends of the rafters.

Sprocket: short timber placed on the back and at the foot of a rafter to form projecting eaves.

Strut: vertical or oblique timber between two members of a truss,

not directly supporting longitudinal timbers.

Tie-beam: main horizontal transverse timber which carries the feet of the principals at wall level.

Truss: rigid framework of timbers at bay intervals, carrying the longitudinal roof timbers which support the common rafters. *Closed truss*: with the spaces between the timbers filled, to form an internal partition.

See also Cruck, Wagon roof.

ROPE MOULDING: *see* Cable moulding.

ROSE WINDOW: circular window with tracery radiating from the centre. Cf. Wheel window.

ROTUNDA: building or room circular in plan.

ROUGHCAST: *see* Rendering.

ROVING BRIDGE: *see* Canals.

RUBBED BRICKWORK: *see* Gauged brickwork.

RUBBLE: masonry whose stones are wholly or partly in a rough state. *Coursed*: coursed stones with rough faces. *Random*: uncoursed stones in a random pattern. *Snecked*: with courses broken by smaller stones (snecks).

RUSTICATION: *see* 6d. Exaggerated treatment of masonry to give an effect of strength. The joints are usually recessed by V-section chamfering or square-section channelling (*channelled rustication*). *Banded rustication* has only the horizontal joints emphasized. The faces may be flat, but can be *diamond-faced*, like shallow pyramids, *vermiculated*, with a stylized texture like worm-casts, and *glacial* (frost-work), like icicles or stalactites.

SACRISTY: room in a church for sacred vessels and vestments.

SADDLEBACK ROOF: *see* IC.

SALTIRE CROSS: with diagonal limbs.

SANCTUARY: area around the main altar of a church. Cf. Presbytery.

SANGHA: residence of Buddhist monks or nuns.

SARCOPHAGUS: coffin of stone or other durable material.

SAXO-NORMAN: transitional Romanesque style combining Anglo-Saxon and Norman features, current *c.* 1060–1100.

SCAGLIOLA: composition imitating marble.

SCALLOPED CAPITAL: *see* 1a.

SCOTIA: a hollow classical moulding, especially between tori (q.v.) on a column base (3b, 3f).

SCREEN: in a medieval church, usually at the entry to the chancel; *see* Rood (screen) and Pulpitum. A *parclose screen* separates a chapel from the rest of the church.

SCREENS or SCREENS PASSAGE: screened-off entrance passage between great hall and service rooms.

SECTION: two-dimensional representation of a building, moulding, etc., revealed by cutting across it.

SEDILIA (singular: sedile): seats for the priests (usually three) on the S side of the chancel.

SET-OFF: *see* Weathering.

SETTS: squared stones, usually of granite, used for paving or flooring.

SGRAFFITO: decoration scratched, often in plaster, to reveal a pattern in another colour beneath. *Graffiti*: scratched drawing or writing.

SHAFT: vertical member of round or polygonal section (1a, 3a). *Shaft-ring*: at the junction of shafts set *en delit* (q.v.) or attached to a pier or wall (1a).

SHEILA-NA-GIG: female fertility figure, usually with legs apart.

SHELL: thin, self-supporting roofing membrane of timber or concrete.

SHOULDERED ARCHITRAVE: *see* 4b.

SHUTTERING: *see* Concrete.

SILL: horizontal member at the bottom of a window or door frame; or at the base of a timber-framed wall into which posts and studs are tenoned (7).

SLAB BLOCK: *see* Multi-storey.

SLATE-HANGING: covering of overlapping slates on a wall. *Tile-hanging* is similar.

SLYPE: covered way or passage leading E from the cloisters between transept and chapter house.

SNECKED: *see* Rubble.

SOFFIT (*lit.* ceiling): underside of an arch (also called *intrados*), lintel, etc. *Soffit roll*: medieval roll moulding on a soffit.

SOLAR: private upper chamber in a medieval house, accessible from the high end of the great hall.

SOPRAPORTA: *see* Overdoor.

SOUNDING-BOARD: *see* Tester.

SPANDRELS: roughly triangular spaces between an arch and its containing rectangle, or between adjacent arches (5c). Also non-structural panels under the windows in a curtain-walled building.

SPERE: a fixed structure screening the lower end of the great hall from the screens passage. *Spere-truss*: roof truss incorporated in the spere.

SPIRE: tall pyramidal or conical feature crowning a tower or turret. *Broach*: starting from a square base, then carried into an octagonal section by means of triangular faces; and *splayed-foot*: variation of the broach form, found principally in the south-east, in which the four cardinal faces are splayed out near their base, to cover the corners, while oblique (or intermediate) faces taper away to a point (1c). *Needle spire*: thin spire rising from the centre of a tower roof, well inside the parapet: when of timber and lead often called a *spike*.

SPIRELET: *see* Flèche.

SPLAY: of an opening when it is wider on one face of a wall than the other.

SPRING or SPRINGING: level at which an arch or vault rises from its supports. *Springers*: the first stones of an arch or vaulting rib above the spring (2c).

SQUINCH: arch or series of arches thrown across an interior angle of a square or rectangular structure to support a circular or polygonal superstructure, especially a dome or spire (5a).

SQUINT: an aperture in a wall or through a pier usually to allow a view of an altar.

STAIRS: *see* 6c. *Dog-leg stair*: parallel flights rising alternately in opposite directions, without an open well. *Flying stair*: cantilevered from the walls of a stairwell, without newels; sometimes called a *Geometric* stair when the inner edge describes a curve. *Newel stair*: ascending round a central supporting newel (q.v.); called a *spiral stair* or *vice* when in a circular shaft, a *winder* when in a rectangular compartment. (*Winder* also applies to the steps on the turn.) *Well stair*: with flights round a square open well framed by newel posts. *See also* Perron.

STALL: fixed seat in the choir or chancel for the clergy or choir (cf. Pew). Usually with arm rests, and often framed together.

STANCHION: upright structural member, of iron, steel or reinforced concrete.

STANDPIPE TOWER: *see* Manometer.

STEAM ENGINES: *Atmospheric*: worked by the vacuum created when low-pressure steam is condensed in the cylinder, as developed by Thomas Newcomen. *Beam engine*: with a large pivoted beam moved in an oscillating fashion by the piston. It may drive a flywheel or be *non-rotative*. *Watt* and *Cornish*: single-cylinder; *compound*: two cylinders; *triple expansion*: three cylinders.

STEEPLE: tower together with a spire, lantern, or belfry.

STIFF-LEAF: type of E.E. foliage decoration. *Stiff-leaf capital see* 1b.

STOP: plain or decorated terminal to mouldings or chamfers, or at the end of hoodmoulds and labels (*label stop*), or stringcourses (5b, 6a); *see also* Headstop.

STOUP: vessel for holy water, usually near a door.

STRAINER: *see* Arch.

STRAPWORK: late C16 and C17 decoration, like interlaced leather straps.

STRETCHER: *see* Bond and 6e.

STRING: *see* 6c. Sloping member holding the ends of the treads and risers of a staircase. *Closed string*: a broad string covering the ends of the treads and risers. *Open string*: cut into the shape of the treads and risers.

STRINGCOURSE: horizontal course or moulding projecting from the surface of a wall (6d).

STUCCO: *see* Rendering.

STUDS: subsidiary vertical timbers of a timber-framed wall or partition (7).

STUPA: Buddhist shrine, circular in plan.

STYLOBATE: top of the solid platform on which a colonnade stands (3a).

SUSPENSION BRIDGE: *see* Bridge.

SWAG: like a festoon (q.v.), but representing cloth.

SYSTEM BUILDING: *see* Industrialized building.

TABERNACLE: canopied structure to contain the reserved sacrament or a relic; or architectural frame for an image or statue.

TABLE TOMB: memorial slab raised on free-standing legs.

TAS-DE-CHARGE: the lower courses of a vault or arch which are laid horizontally (2c).

TERM: pedestal or pilaster tapering downward, usually with the upper part of a human figure growing out of it.

TERRACOTTA: moulded and fired clay ornament or cladding.

TESSELLATED PAVEMENT: mosaic flooring, particularly Roman, made of *tesserae*, i.e. cubes of glass, stone, or brick.

TESTER: flat canopy over a tomb or pulpit, where it is also called a *sounding-board*.

TESTER TOMB: tomb-chest with effigies beneath a tester, either free-standing (tester with four or more columns), or attached to a wall (*half-tester*) with columns on one side only.

TETRASTYLE: *see* Portico.

THERMAL WINDOW: *see* Diocletian window.

THREE-DECKER PULPIT: *see* Pulpit.

TIDAL GATES: *see* Canals.

TIE-BEAM: *see* Roofs and 7.

TIERCERON: *see* Vault and 2c.

TILE-HANGING: *see* Slate-hanging.

TIMBER-FRAMING: *see* 7. Method of construction where the structural frame is built of interlocking timbers. The spaces are filled with non-structural material, e.g. *infill* of wattle and daub, lath and plaster, brickwork (known as *nogging*), etc. and may be covered by plaster, weatherboarding (q.v.), or tiles.

TOMB-CHEST: chest-shaped tomb, usually of stone. Cf. Table tomb, Tester tomb.

TORUS (plural: tori): large convex moulding usually used on a column base (3b, 3f).

TOUCH: soft black marble quarried near Tournai.

TOURELLE: turret corbelled out from the wall.

TOWER BLOCK: *see* Multi-storey.

TRABEATED: depends structurally on the use of the post and lintel. Cf. Arcuated.

TRACERY: openwork pattern of masonry or timber in the upper part of an opening. *Blind tracery* is tracery applied to a solid wall.
Plate tracery, introduced *c.* 1200, is the earliest form, in which shapes are cut through solid masonry (2a).
Bar tracery was introduced into England *c.* 1250. The pattern is formed by intersecting moulded ribwork continued from the mullions. It was especially elaborate during the Decorated period (q.v.). Tracery shapes can include circles, *daggers* (elongated ogee-ended lozenges), *mouchettes* (like daggers but with curved sides) and upright rectangular *panels*. They often have *cusps*, projecting points defining lobes or *foils* (q.v.) within the main shape: *Kentish* or *split-cusps* are forked (2b).
Types of bar tracery (*see* 2b) include *geometric(al)*: *c.* 1250–1310, chiefly circles, often foiled; *Y-tracery*: *c.* 1300, with mullions branching into a Y-shape; *intersecting*: *c.* 1300, formed by interlocking mullions; *reticulated*: early C14, net-like pattern of ogee-ended lozenges; *curvilinear*: C14, with uninterrupted flowing curves; *panel*: Perp, with straight-sided panels, often cusped at the top and bottom.

TRANSEPT: transverse portion of a church.

TRANSITIONAL: generally used for the phase between Romanesque and Early English (*c.* 1175– *c.* 1200).

TRANSOM: horizontal member separating window lights (2b).

TREAD: horizontal part of a step. The *tread end* may be carved on a staircase (6c).

TREFOIL: *see* Foil.

TRIFORIUM: middle storey of a church treated as an arcaded wall passage or blind arcade, its height corresponding to that of the aisle roof.

TRIGLYPHS (*lit.* three-grooved tablets): stylized beam-ends in the Doric frieze, with metopes between (3b).

TRIUMPHAL ARCH: influential type of Imperial Roman monument.

TROPHY: sculptured or painted group of arms or armour.

TRUMEAU: central stone mullion supporting the tympanum of a wide doorway. *Trumeau figure*: carved figure attached to it (cf. Column figure).

TRUMPET CAPITAL: *see* 1b.

TRUSS: braced framework, spanning between supports. *See also* Roofs and 7.

TUMBLING or TUMBLING-IN: courses of brickwork laid at right-angles to a slope, e.g. of a gable, forming triangles by tapering into horizontal courses (8a).

TUSCAN: *see* Orders and 3e.

TWO-DECKER PULPIT: *see* Pulpit.

TYMPANUM: the surface between a lintel and the arch above it or within a pediment (4a).

UNDERCROFT: usually describes the vaulted room(s), beneath the main room(s) of a medieval house. Cf. Crypt.

VAULT: arched stone roof (sometimes imitated in timber or plaster). For types see 2c.
Tunnel or *barrel vault*: continuous semicircular or pointed arch, often of rubble masonry.

Groin-vault: tunnel vaults intersecting at right angles. *Groins* are the curved lines of the intersections.

Rib-vault: masonry framework of intersecting arches (ribs) supporting *vault cells*, used in Gothic architecture. *Wall rib* or *wall arch*: between wall and vault cell. *Transverse rib*: spans between two walls to divide a vault into bays. *Quadripartite* rib-vault: each bay has two pairs of diagonal ribs dividing the vault into four triangular cells. *Sexpartite* rib-vault: most often used over paired bays, has an extra pair of ribs springing from between the bays. More elaborate vaults may include *ridge ribs* along the crown of a vault or bisecting the bays; *tiercerons*: extra decorative ribs springing from the corners of a bay; and *liernes*: short decorative ribs in the crown of a vault, not linked to any springing point. A *stellar* or *star* vault has liernes in star formation.

Fan-vault: form of barrel vault used in the Perp period, made up of halved concave masonry cones decorated with blind tracery.

VAULTING SHAFT: shaft leading up to the spring or springing (q.v.) of a vault (2c).

VENETIAN or SERLIAN WINDOW: derived from Serlio (4b). The motif is used for other openings.

VERMICULATION: *see* Rustication and 6d.

VESICA: oval with pointed ends.

VICE: *see* Stair.

VILLA: originally a Roman country house or farm. The term was revived in England in the C18 under the influence of Palladio and used especially for smaller, compact country houses. In the later C19 it was debased to describe any suburban house.

VITRIFIED: bricks or tiles fired to a darkened glassy surface.

VITRUVIAN SCROLL: classical running ornament of curly waves (4b).

VOLUTES: spiral scrolls. They occur on Ionic capitals (3c). *Angle volute*: pair of volutes, turned outwards to meet at the corner of a capital.

VOUSSOIRS: wedge-shaped stones forming an arch (5c).

WAGON ROOF: with the appearance of the inside of a wagon tilt; often ceiled. Also called *cradle roof*.

WAINSCOT: *see* Panelling.

WALL MONUMENT: attached to the wall and often standing on the floor. *Wall tablets* are smaller with the inscription as the major element.

WALL-PLATE: *see* Roofs and 7.

WALL-WALK: *see* Parapet.

WARMING ROOM: room in a religious house where a fire burned for comfort.

WATERHOLDING BASE: early Gothic base with upper and lower mouldings separated by a deep hollow.

WATERLEAF: *see* Enrichments and 3f.

WATERLEAF CAPITAL: Late Romanesque and Transitional type of capital (1b).

WATER WHEELS: described by the way water is fed on to the wheel. *Breastshot*: mid-height, falling and passing beneath. *Overshot*: over the top. *Pitchback*: on the top but falling backwards. *Undershot*: turned by the momentum of the water passing beneath. In a *water turbine*, water is fed under pressure through a vaned wheel within a casing.

WEALDEN HOUSE: type of medieval timber-framed house with a central open hall flanked by bays of two storeys, roofed in line; the end bays are jettied to the front, but the eaves are continuous (8a).

WEATHERBOARDING: wall cladding of overlapping horizontal boards.

WEATHERING or SET-OFF: inclined, projecting surface to keep water away from the wall below.

WEEPERS: figures in niches along the sides of some medieval tombs. Also called mourners.

WHEEL WINDOW: circular, with radiating shafts like spokes. Cf. Rose window.

WROUGHT IRON: *see* Cast iron.

INDEX OF ARTISTS

This index covers artists, architects, masons etc. mentioned as having worked in the places covered by this volume; references to Volume 1 are not included.

INDEX OF PATRONS AND RESIDENTS

Indexed here are families and individuals (not bodies or commercial firms) recorded in the text as having owned or lived in property and/or commissioned architectural work in the area covered by this volume; references to Volume 1 are not included. The index includes monuments to members of such families, but not those to other individuals unless they are of particular interest.

INDEX OF PLACES

Principal references are in **bold** type; demolished buildings are shown in *italic*.

Morley St Peter 98, **545–6**
Morningthorpe 36, **546**, 698
Morton-on-the-Hill **547**
Moulton St Michael *see* Great
  Moulton
Mulbarton **547–9**
Mundford 50, 107, **549–50**
Mundham 48, **550–1**
Narborough 23, 33, 34, 35, 106,
  551–3
  church 55, 114, 116, **551–2**
  Devil's Dyke 37, **553**
Narford 120, 123, 124, 125, 136,
  160, **553–5**
Necton 62, 71, 116, 144, **555–6**
Needham 32, 61, 103, **557**
New Buckenham 85, 88, 101, 105,
  557–62
  Castle 74, **558–9**, 578
  church 62, 116, **557–8**
  McIntyre House 105, 108, **561**
  Market House 112, **559**, Pl. 72
  Market Place 95, **559–61**, Pl. 67
New Holkham *see* Holkham
New Houghton *see* Houghton
New Hunstanton *see* Hunstanton
Newton **562**
Newton Flotman 102, 112, **562–4**
  Dairy Farm Barn 91, 178, **563**,
  Pl. 62
Nordelph **564**
North Barsham **564**
North Creake 55, 56, 146, **564–6**
  Creake Abbey 42n., 49, **565–6**
North Elmham 36, **566–71**
  church 48, 67, 69, 117, 119, 137,
  568–9
  Elmham House *123*, **569–70**
  ruins 39, 78, **566–8**
North Lopham 127, **571–2**
North Pickenham **572–3**
North Runcton 135, 155, **573–4**,
  Pl. 96
North Tuddenham 70, 114, **574–5**
Northwold 48, 59, 62, 116, 127,
  575–6
North Wootton 23, 140, 463, **576–7**
Norton Subcourse 54, **577**
Old Buckenham 50, 94, **577–80**
  Abbey Farmhouse 88, 103, 341,
  579, Pl. 59
  Castle 74, 558, **578–9**
Old Hunstanton *see* Hunstanton
Outwell 69, **580–1**
Ovington **581–2**
Oxborough 24, **582–8**
  Oxburgh Hall 25, 82, 83, 145,
  584–8, Pl. 68

R.C. chapel 67, 69, 141, 143,
  144, **583–4**
St John Evangelist *59n.*, 62, 69,
  72, 113, 285, 364, **582–3**, 797,
  Pl. 31
Oxburgh Hall *see* Emneth;
  Oxborough
Oxwick 266, **588**
Panworth 182
Pattesley **588**
Pentney 35, **589–90**
  Pentney Priory 23, 41, 77, 81,
  589–90
Peterstone Priory *see* Burnham
  Overy Town
Poringland 50, 58, 60, 62, 103,
  590–1
Potthorpe **591**
Pott Row *see* Grimston
Pudding Norton 38, **591–2**
Pulham Market 97, 127, 133, **592–4**
Pulham St Mary 52, 60, 69, 85,
  127, **594–6**, Pl. 18
Pynkney (Pykney) Hall *see*
  Tatterford
Quarles **596**
Quidenham 46, 59n., 100, 108,
  596–7
Rainthorpe Hall 83, **597–8**
Raveningham 56, 62, 69, 110, 161,
  598–600
Raynham Hall 98, 99–100, 123,
  124, 439, **600–9**, Pls. 80, 81,
  89
  church 62, **323**
Redenhall 60, 69, 467, **609–11**,
  Pl. 44
Reffley *see* South Wootton
Reymerston 48, 50, 117, **611–12**
Riddlesworth 54, 114, **612**
Ringland 58, 62, 70, 325, **613**
Ringstead 24, **614–15**
Rockland All Saints 45, 71, **615**
Rockland St Mary **615–16**
Rockland St Peter 65, **616**
Rokeles Hall *see* Watton
Roudham 38, 218, **617**
Rougham *100*, **617–19**
Rougholm *see* Gressenhall
Roydon (nr Diss) **619**
Roydon (nr King's Lynn) 140, **620**
Runcton Hall see North Runcton
Runcton Holme 47, 48, 86, **620–1**
Runhall 47, 69, **621**
Rushall 87, **621–2**, 671
Rushford 218, **622–3**
  College 81, 95, **622–3**, 638
Ryston 137, **623–4**

COMPLETE LIST OF TITLES
2001

Volumes in the new, larger hardback format are marked (NF). Corrected reprints are not listed.

Bedfordshire and the County of Huntingdon and Peterborough *1st ed. 1968 Nikolaus Pevsner*

Berkshire *1st ed. 1966 Nikolaus Pevsner*

Buckinghamshire *1st ed. 1960 Nikolaus Pevsner, 2nd ed. 1994 revised Elizabeth Williamson* (NF)

Cambridgeshire *1st ed. 1954. 2nd ed. 1970, Nikolaus Pevsner*

Cheshire *1st ed. 1971 Nikolaus Pevsner and Edward Hubbard*

Cornwall *1st ed. 1951 Nikolaus Pevsner, 2nd ed. 1970 revised Enid Radcliffe*

Cumberland and Westmorland *1st ed. 1967 Nikolaus Pevsner*

Derbyshire *1st ed. 1953 Nikolaus Pevsner, 2nd ed. 1978 revised Elizabeth Williamson*

Devon *1st ed. in 2 vols. 1952 Nikolaus Pevsner, 2nd ed. 1989 revised Bridget Cherry* (NF)

Dorset *1st ed. 1972 John Newman and Nikolaus Pevsner*

Durham, County *1st ed. 1953 Nikolaus Pevsner, 2nd ed. 1983 revised Elizabeth Williamson*

Essex *1st ed. 1954 Nikolaus Pevsner, 2nd ed. 1965 revised Enid Radcliffe*

Gloucestershire 1: The Cotswolds *1st ed. 1970, 2nd ed. 1979, David Verey, 3rd ed. 1999 revised Alan Brooks* (NF)

Gloucestershire 2: The Vale and the Forest of Dean *1st ed. 1970, 2nd ed. 1976, David Verey, revision in progress*

Hampshire and the Isle of Wight *1st ed. 1967 Nikolaus Pevsner and David Lloyd (being revised and reissued as two volumes)*

Herefordshire *1st ed. 1963 Nikolaus Pevsner*

Hertfordshire *1st ed. 1953 Nikolaus Pevsner, 2nd ed. 1977 revised Bridget Cherry*

Kent, North East and East *1st ed. 1969, 2nd ed. 1976, 3rd ed. 1983, John Newman*

Kent, West, and the Weald *1st ed. 1969, 2nd ed. 1976, John Newman*

Lancashire, North *1st ed. 1969 Nikolaus Pevsner*

Lancashire, South *1st ed. 1969 Nikolaus Pevsner*

Leicestershire and Rutland *1st ed. 1960 Nikolaus Pevsner, 2nd ed. 1984 revised Elizabeth Williamson* (NF)

Lincolnshire *1st ed. 1964 Nikolaus Pevsner and John Harris, 2nd ed. 1989 revised Nicholas Antram* (NF)

London 1: The City of London *1st ed. 1997 Simon Bradley and Nikolaus Pevsner* (NF)

London 2: South *1st ed. 1983 Bridget Cherry and Nikolaus Pevsner* (NF)

London 3: North West *1st ed. 1991 Bridget Cherry and Nikolaus Pevsner* (NF)

London 4: North *1st ed. 1998 Bridget Cherry and Nikolaus Pevsner* (NF)

London 5: East and Docklands *1st ed. in progress*

London 6: Westminster *1st ed. in progress*

London 1: The Cities of London and Westminster *1st ed. 1957, 2nd ed. 1962, Nikolaus Pevsner, 3rd ed. 1973 revised Bridget Cherry, being revised and reissued as vols. 1 and 6 above*

London 2: Except the Cities of London and Westminster *1st ed. 1952 Nikolaus Pevsner, being revised and reissued as vols. 2–5 above*

Middlesex *1st ed. 1951 Nikolaus Pevsner, revised and reissued as vols. 3 and 4 above*

Norfolk 1: Norwich and North-East *1st ed. 1962 Nikolaus Pevsner, 2nd ed. 1997 revised Bill Wilson* (NF)

Norfolk 2: North-West and South *1st ed. 1962 Nikolaus Pevsner, 2nd ed. 1999 revised Bill Wilson* (NF)

Northamptonshire *1st ed. 1961 Nikolaus Pevsner, 2nd ed. 1973 revised Bridget Cherry*

Northumberland *1st ed. 1957 Nikolaus Pevsner with Ian A. Richmond, 2nd ed. 1992 revised John Grundy, Grace McCombie, Peter Ryder and Humphrey Welfare* (NF)

Nottinghamshire *1st ed. 1951 Nikolaus Pevsner, 2nd ed. 1979 revised Elizabeth Williamson*

Oxfordshire *1st ed. 1974 Jennifer Sherwood and Nikolaus Pevsner*

Shropshire *1st ed. 1958 Nikolaus Pevsner*

Somerset, North, and Bristol *1st ed. 1958 Nikolaus Pevsner*

Somerset, South and West *1st ed. 1958 Nikolaus Pevsner*

Staffordshire *1st ed. 1974 Nikolaus Pevsner*

Suffolk *1st ed. 1961 Nikolaus Pevsner, 2nd ed. 1974 revised Enid Radcliffe*

Surrey *1st ed. 1962 Ian Nairn and Nikolaus Pevsner, 2nd ed. 1971 revised Bridget Cherry*

Sussex *1st ed. 1965 Ian Nairn and Nikolaus Pevsner*

Warwickshire *1st ed. 1966 Nikolaus Pevsner and Alexandra Wedgwood*

Wiltshire *1st ed. 1963 Nikolaus Pevsner, 2nd ed. 1975 revised Bridget Cherry*

Worcestershire *1st ed. 1968 Nikolaus Pevsner*

Yorkshire: The North Riding *1st ed. 1966 Nikolaus Pevsner*

Yorkshire: The West Riding *1st ed. 1959 Nikolaus Pevsner, 2nd ed. 1967 revised Enid Radcliffe (being revised and reissued as two volumes)*

Yorkshire: York and the East Riding *1st ed. 1972 Nikolaus Pevsner, 2nd ed. 1995 revised David Neave* (NF)

SPECIAL PAPERBACK PUBLICATIONS

London: Docklands *1st ed. 1998, Elizabeth Williamson and Nikolaus Pevsner*

London: The City Churches *1st ed. 1998, Simon Bradley and Nikolaus Pevsner*

Manchester *1st ed. 2001, Clare Hartwell*

Looking at Buildings: the East Riding *1st ed. 1995 (with English Heritage), Hazel Moffat and David Neave*